★ ★ ★

The Pulitzer Prize for editorial cartooning in 2000 was awarded to Joel Pett of the *Herald-Leader* in Lexington, Kentucky. Unlike most previous winners of Pulitzer Prizes, Pett is as likely to draw cartoons about state or local issues as about national issues. Here is a pair of cartoons from the twenty he entered for the Pulitzer competition.

Cartoonists can criticize politicians for sources of campaign contributions more safely if they don't mention any names. Here, Joel Pett criticizes his own state's Republican Senator, Jim Bunning, for accepting a large sum from the gun lobby—over $1.5 million from the National Rifle Association during his 1998 campaign. (See Chapter 11, "Congress," for financing of congressional election campaigns.)

People lend themselves to caricature; issues don't. Nevertheless, Joel Pett often took on political issues that are difficult to draw, such as racial inequalities. Often, such a cartoon requires a set of panels to develop the point. (See Chapter 16, "Equality and Civil Rights," for a discussion of issues of social and racial inequalities.)

The Challenge of Democracy

Seventh Edition

★
★ **Government in America**
★

Kenneth Janda
Northwestern University

Jeffrey M. Berry
Tufts University

Jerry Goldman
Northwestern University

HOUGHTON MIFFLIN COMPANY
Boston   New York

To our wives: **Ann Janda**
Lori Berry
Susan Kennedy

Editor-in-Chief: Jean L. Woy
Sponsoring Editor: Mary Dougherty
Development Editor: Katherine Meisenheimer
Editorial Assistant: Tonya Lobato
Senior Production/Design Coordinator: Carol Merrigan
Senior Cover Design Coordinator: Deborah Azerrad Savona
Senior Manufacturing Coordinator: Marie Barnes
Associate Internet Producer: Scott R. Diggins

Cover images: © Steven W. Jones/FPG International LLC, © Photodisc, © Photodisc, © Eyewire, © William J. Herbert/Tony Stone Images, © Zigy Kaluzny/Tony Stone Images

Printed in the U.S.A.

Library of Congress Control Number: 2001131511

ISBN: 0-618-14431-5

123456789-VH-05 04 03 02 01

brief contents

iv

contents

A lot has happened since the last edition of *The Challenge of Democracy*. Most obviously, we went through a presidential election that ended up with a disputed outcome. A month after the election, our modern, affluent democracy found itself not knowing the identity of the next president. Citizens were at the same time taken aback by the arguments about what constituted a legitimate vote and bemused by the sight of Florida election officials holding ballots up to a light searching for evidence of a puncture. Angry protesters screamed at each other outside South Florida election offices while lawyers for Bush and Gore went at each other in courtrooms across the state and, eventually, before the Supreme Court in Washington.

Some still dispute that George W. Bush won the election. Yet the country has moved on. Given the enormity of the stakes, the country's stability during this period is a welcome reminder of Americans' faith in our system of government, warts and all. At the same time, the election illustrated some of the enduring conflicts in American democracy. And more to the point, it illustrated the enduring value of the original framework of *The Challenge of Democracy*. As with the previous six editions of this book, we build our text around two themes that remain as relevant today as they were when we first conceived of this project. The first is the clash among the values of freedom, order, and equality; the second focuses on the tensions between pluralist and majoritarian visions of democracy. Knowledge of these conflicts enables citizens to recognize and analyze the difficult choices they face in politics.

But as well as these two themes endure, our lives are being directly affected by a third force shaping American politics. Globalization is changing American politics in fundamental ways. More than ever before, Americans are becoming citizens of the world. We cannot escape the deepening interrelationships with the rest of the world, even if it were desirable to do so. Each day trade, travel, immigration, and the Internet make the world a more interdependent place. In this edition of *The Challenge of Democracy*, we begin to explore some of the ramifications of a smaller world on the large landscape of American politics.

The concept of globalization is introduced in Chapter 1 and is discussed throughout the text. The traditional notion of national sovereignty holds that each government is free to govern in the manner it feels is best. As the world becomes a smaller place, however, national sovereignty is tested in many ways. When a country is committing human rights violations—putting people in jail for merely disagreeing with the government in power—should other countries try to pressure it to comply with common norms of justice? Do the democracies of the world have a responsibility to use their influence to try to limit the abuses of the powerless in societies where they are abused? Another facet of globalization is the growth of international trade. In many ways the world has become a single marketplace and industries in one country often face competitors from many other countries around the world. Must a country just stand by and let jobs "emigrate" from within its borders to other countries where companies can produce the same quality goods at cheaper prices? These are just some of the issues that the Seventh Edition explores.

THEMATIC FRAMEWORK

Through all seven editions, we have striven to write a book that students will actually read, so we have sought to discuss politics—a complex subject—in a captivating and understandable way. American politics isn't dull, and its textbooks needn't be either. Equally important, we have sought to produce a book that students would credit for stimulating their thinking about politics. While offering all the essential information about American government and politics, we feel that it is important to give students a framework for analyzing politics that they can use long after their studies have ended. Based on the reactions to our first six editions, we believe we succeeded in developing a lively book built on a framework that fulfills our goal of helping students analyze and interpret the political process in the United States.

As noted above, two themes run through our book. One deals with the conflict among values and the other with alternative models of democracy. In Chapter 1, we suggest that American politics often reflects conflicts between the values of freedom and order and between the values of freedom and equality. These value conflicts are prominent in contemporary American society, and they help to explain political controversy and consensus in earlier eras. For instance, in Chapter 3 we argue that the Constitution was designed to promote order, and it virtually ignored issues of political and social equality. Equality was later served, however, by several amendments to the Constitution. In Chapter 15, "Order and Civil Liberties," and Chapter 16, "Equality and Civil Rights," we demonstrate that many of this nation's most controversial issues represent conflicts among individuals or groups who hold differing views on the values of freedom, order, and equality. Views on issues such as abortion are not just isolated opinions; they also reflect choices about the philosophy citizens want government to follow. Yet choosing among these values is difficult, sometimes excruciatingly so.

The second theme, introduced in Chapter 2, asks students to consider two competing models of democratic government. One way that government can make decisions is by means of majoritarian principles; that is, by taking the actions desired by a majority of citizens. A contrasting model of government, pluralist democracy, is built around the interaction of decision makers in government with groups concerned about issues that affect them.

These models are not mere abstractions; we use them to illustrate the dynamics of the American political system. In Chapter 12, "The Presidency," we discuss the problem of divided government. More often than not over the past forty years, the party that controlled the White House didn't control both houses of Congress. When these two branches of government are divided between the two parties, majoritarian government is difficult. Even when the same party controls both branches, the majoritarian model is not always realized—as President Clinton found out during 1993 and 1994.

In Chapter 10, "Interest Groups," we see the forces of pluralism at work. Interest groups of all types populate Washington, and these organizations represent the diverse array of interests that define our society. At the same time, the chapter explores ways in which pluralism favors wealthier, better-organized interests. Political action committees, which donate money to political candidates, are a particularly troublesome issue because they give those with money an advantage. Throughout the book we stress that students must make their own choices among the competing values and models of government. Although the three of us hold diverse and strong opinions about which choices are best, we do not believe it is our role to tell students our own answers to the broad questions we pose. Instead, we want our readers to learn first hand that a democracy requires thoughtful choices. That is why we titled our book *The Challenge of Democracy.*

Our framework travels well over time. The civil rights struggles of the 1960s exemplified the utility of our theme emphasizing equality, as do more contemporary controversies surrounding gay rights, the rights of the disabled, and affirmative action. We're just beginning to understand the privacy and personal freedom issues involving the Internet. Our theme of pluralism versus majoritarianism remains compelling as well. Pluralist images of America predate the adoption of the Constitution. In his defense of the proposed Constitution, James Madison defended the pursuit of self-interested goals by various groups in society, each looking out for its own good. A contrary view of democracy—majoritarian government—emphasizes control of government by majorities of voters through our party system. But the party system sometimes has a hard time channeling a majority of voters into majority rule. Prior to the Civil War, fissures in the party system made it difficult to understand exactly where the majority stood. More recently, in the 2000 election, we again saw that the party system doesn't always produce clear majorities. Which majority should the government follow: the majority of the voters, who cast their ballots for Al Gore, or the majority of the Electoral College, which voted for George W. Bush? And exactly what majority is there in a Senate that started the term evenly split between fifty Republicans and fifty Democrats?

Our framework also travels well over space—to other countries with a very different political heritage. One of the most important aspects of globalization is the number of countries that have recently made a transition to democracy or are currently trying to make that change. One of our greatest satisfactions as authors of a book on American democracy is that it has been used in a number of countries overseas where democracy has at least a foothold, if it hasn't yet fully flowered. Houghton Mifflin has donated copies of earlier editions of our book to English-speaking faculty and students in Bulgaria, Croatia, the Czech Republic, Georgia, Hungary, Poland, Romania, Russia, Slovakia, and South Africa. Moreover, the brief edition of our text has been translated into Hungarian, Georgian, Czech, and Korean. We are pleased that *The Challenge of Democracy* is now available to many more students in these countries—students who have been confronting the challenge of democracy in times of political transition.

SUBSTANTIVE FEATURES OF THE SEVENTH EDITION

The Seventh Edition maintains the basic structure of previous editions of *The Challenge of Democracy* while updating the political events of the past few years. We have also drawn on the latest research in political science to make sure that *The Challenge of Democracy* continues to represent the state of knowledge in our discipline.

To accommodate the major changes and new issues in politics that have occurred since the last edition, every chapter in the text has been thoroughly revised. We cannot inventory all the many changes in this edition, but we can illustrate the thoroughness of our revision with selected examples. For example, Chapter 3 ("The Constitution") examines constitutional designs in newly emerging democracies that have been modeled after the United States' Constitution. Chapter 4 ("Federalism") includes a new section on federalism and globalization, focusing on the factors that are binding nations together in an increasingly global political environment. Chapter 8 ("Political Parties") compares both major political party platforms in 2000 in terms of values and campaign themes. Chapter 9 ("Nominations, Elections, and Campaigns") describes the striking differences between the complex American ballot and the short and simple Canadian ballot used in the two countries' most recent elections. In Chapter 11 ("Congress"), the impeachment proceedings against President Clinton and the outcome of the 2000 congressional election are discussed. Chapter 12 ("The Presidency") looks at what lies ahead for President Bush. Chapter 14 ("The Courts") offers a first view of the team directing the new Bush administration's judicial selections. Chapter 16 ("Equality and Civil Rights") includes a new section on gay and lesbian rights. Chapter 17 ("Policymaking") contains extensive new material on the role of nonprofits in civil society and in the governmental process. Chapter 19 ("Domestic Policy") adds sections on both health-care reform and education. Chapter 20 ("Global Policy") analyzes the "Powell Doctrine," our new secretary of state's view on the involvement of the United States in overseas conflicts.

As in previous editions, each chapter begins with a vignette. The purpose of each vignette is to draw students into the substance of that chapter, while suggesting one of the themes of the book. Chapters with new or revised vignettes include Chapter 1 ("Freedom, Order, or Equality?"), which recounts the case of the "Love Bug," a devastating computer virus launched in the Philippines that caused millions of dollars of damage to computers in the United States. The United States, however, had no legal recourse against the man who created and disseminated the virus. Chapter 2 ("Majoritarian or Pluralist Democracy?") begins with a description of the tragedy at Columbine High School in Littleton, Colorado, and analyzes the push for gun control that followed in its aftermath. Chapters 4 ("Federalism") and 14 ("The Courts") recount the involvement of the Supreme Court in the 2000 presidential election. We start the story with Al Gore's initial concession call to George Bush on election night and follow it through to the Supreme Court's decision thirty-six days later. Chapter 10 ("Interest Groups") opens with an account of the violent protests against the World Trade Organization in Seattle. Chapter 12 ("The Presidency") describes George W. Bush's inaugural speech and discusses his challenge in uniting the country in the wake of the election's bitter aftermath. We start the last chapter ("Global Policy") with the story of how private citizen Ted Turner gave $34 million to the United States government so it could pay off part of the vast debt owed by this country to the United Nations.

In light of our new focus on globalization, the Seventh Edition expands the reach of our series of features on "Politics in a Changing America." These boxed features have focused on the participation and status of various groups in American society, including women, African Americans,

Hispanics, youth, and religious fundamentalists. We have now mixed these features with a parallel series on "Politics in a Changing World." In these boxes we examine some of the consequences of globalization, for both the United States and other areas of the world. In Chapter 1, the "Politics in a Changing World" feature details a ranking of twenty countries around the world in terms of the degree to which they are "globalized." (The United States ranks somewhere in the middle.) Chapter 9 includes a feature on the Americanization of elections overseas. Chapter 11 looks at the European Parliament, the legislative arm of the European Union. Chapter 17 discusses offshore gambling through the Internet.

For the series on "Politics in a Changing America," some of the features from the Sixth Edition have been retained or updated, and new ones have been added. Among the new or updated features for this series is an analysis of Latino admissions at the UCLA School of Law in Chapter 2; an analysis of population shifts and the electoral college between 1960 and 2004 in Chapter 9; and a discussion of the conflict between freedom and order in cyberspace in Chapter 15.

We firmly believe that students can better evaluate how our political system works when they compare it with politics in other countries. Once again, each chapter has at least one boxed feature called "Compared with What?" that treats its topic in a comparative perspective. How much importance do citizens in other parts of the world place on freedom, order, and equality? Which countries have the highest percentages of women in their national legislatures? How does the United States compare to other democracies in terms of the size of its government? How do crime rates differ around the world? Some of these features focus on a single country. How does the electoral system work in Israel, and what are the parallels between its recent election and the one in the United States?

The Seventh Edition incorporates a new learning tool into the text. Periodically in the margins of each chapter, we pose a question to students. Each begins "Can you explain why..." and then completes the sentence with a query that highlights some feature of our system of government that may seem counterintuitive. For example, we ask students, "Can you explain why the United States might oppose an International Criminal Court?" Or "Can you explain why Americans generally believe that government should be close to the people, yet so few citizens vote in local elections?" In addition, "Can you explain why government programs aren't always administered by the government?" And "Can you explain why too much free speech could actually destroy the freedom of speech?" In each case, the accompanying text offers material that should help the reader formulate an answer to the question. We hope students will find these questions in the margins provocative and interesting.

We have streamlined and enriched the close connection that we initiated in previous editions between the words in our text and external technology resources. Every chapter now includes marginal icons at places in the text where a particular Real Deal UpGrade CD-ROM resource will deepen students' understanding of the text material. Chapters also include marginal notations to the award-winning IDEAlog and Crosstabs programs that accompany the book as part of our teaching/learning package. A new section at the end of each chapter titled "Internet Exercises" provides activities of particular relevance to the main topics of the chapter.

Each chapter concludes with a brief summary, a short list of recommended readings, and the Internet Exercises described above. At the end of the book, we have included the Declaration of Independence, the Articles of Confederation, an annotated copy of the Constitution, *Federalist* Nos. 10 and 51, a glossary of key terms, and some other valuable appendices.

THE TEACHING/ LEARNING PACKAGE

Our job as authors did not end with writing this text. From the beginning, we have been centrally involved with producing a tightly integrated set of instructional materials to accompany the text. With help from other political scientists and educational specialists at Houghton Mifflin, these ancillary materials have grown and improved over time.

For The Instructor: Innovative Teaching Tools

The *Instructor's Resource Manual*, originally written by the authors and thoroughly revised and updated for this edition by Mary Beth Melchior of Florida International University, provides teachers with material that relates directly to the thematic framework and organization of the book. It includes learning objectives; chapter synopses; detailed full-length lectures (including a lecture format that encourages class participation); ideas for class, small group, and individual projects and activities; Internet exercises; and World Wide Web resources.

A printed *Test Items* bank, also revised by Mary Beth Melchior of Florida International University, provides over 1,500 test items in identification, multiple-choice, and essay formats. A CD-ROM test generation program for Windows and Macintosh is also available that contains all the items in the printed *Test Items* bank.

New to this edition is the *HMClassPrep Instructor's CD-ROM*. This innovative teaching tool includes electronic versions of the material found in the *Instructor's Resource Manual*, PowerPoint slides, videos with accompanying discussion questions and answers, and audio files.

The *companion Web site* for this text, accessible at <college.hmco.com>, offers a variety of teaching aids to instructors, including presentation-quality images of data-oriented figures from every chapter, downloadable PowerPoint slides, suggested answers to the text's "Can You Explain Why?" questions and end-of-chapter Internet Exercises, and additional resources. Instructors using this site will also have easy access to the IDEAlog 7.0 program (described below) and Political SourceNet, a teaching and learning resource. Political SourceNet contains the Crosstabs program (described below), "You Decide..." simulations, primary source documents, Web links, and Internet assignments that require students to think critically about a document, political Web site, or data-oriented map or figure.

The Seventh Edition continues to be supported by <uspolitics.org>, Kenneth Janda's personal web site for *The Challenge of Democracy*. His site offers a variety of teaching aids to instructors who adopt any version of *The Challenge of Democracy* as a textbook for courses in American politics. It is divided into two sides: the student side is open to all users, but the instructor side is limited to teachers who register online at

<uspolitics.org> as *Challenge* adopters. His site offers some material not contained in Houghton Mifflin's own Web site, described above, yet also provides convenient links to the publisher's site.

The Challenge of Democracy, Seventh Edition, *WebCT Webcourselet* and *Blackboard Course Cartridge* provide text-specific student study aids in customizable, Internet-based education platforms. Both platforms provide a full array of course management features for instructors who wish to incorporate educational technology in their traditional classrooms or for those who are teaching distance learning courses.

A *transparency package,* containing full-color overhead transparencies of some of the important graphs and charts from the text, is available to adopters. For information about a variety of additional visual media products available to adopters of *The Challenge of Democracy,* please contact your Houghton Mifflin sales representative.

Finally, instructors who wish to include a unit on state and local politics in their course may package a chapter-length *State and Local Government Supplement* with the text.

For The Student: Effective Learning Aids

The *Study Guide,* written by Haroon Khan of Henderson State University, is designed to help students master the text's content. The *Study Guide* provides chapter summaries, research topics and resources (both print and on-line), exercises in reading tables and graphs, sample multiple-choice exam questions, and advice on improving study skills, finding internships, and participating in American politics.

The *Real Deal UpGrade CD-ROM* is also available for students; it contains chapter outlines, ACE Practice Tests, video clips of famous campaign ads, audio excerpts from notable Supreme Court cases, and other valuable resources.

The *companion Web site,* accessible at <college.hmco.com>, offers a wide array of resources for students. Included are ACE Practice Tests, chapter outlines, on-line versions of the text's end-of-chapter Internet Exercises, and links to Political SourceNet and the award-winning IDEAlog program.

Political SourceNet contains interactive "You Decide . . ." simulations that allow students to play the role of a political leader, make policy decisions, and see the results of their actions; primary source documents; Web links; and Internet assignments. Also included is the Crosstabs program, the floppy disk version of which won a Distinguished Software Award from EDUCOM. *Crosstabs* allows students to crosstabulate survey data on a recent presidential election and on voting records of members of a recent session of Congress.

The *Crosstabs Student Workbook,* which is available separately, describes how to construct and interpret basic crosstabulations, suggests topics that students might study using the "voters" and "congress" datasets, and explains how to write an empirical research paper. An *Instructor's Answer Book* is also available.

IDEAlog 7.0, an earlier version of which won the 1992 Instructional Software Award from the American Political Science Association, is available on the companion Web site and is closely tied to the text's "value conflicts" theme. IDEAlog 7.0 first asks students to rate themselves on the two-dimensional tradeoff of freedom versus order and freedom versus equality. It then presents them with twenty questions, ten dealing with the conflict of freedom versus order and ten pertaining to freedom versus equality. Students' responses to these questions are classified according to libertarian, conservative, liberal, or communitarian ideological tendencies. Marginal notes in the Seventh Edition of *The Challenge of Democracy* refer students to IDEAlog 7.0 at appropriate points in the text.

We invite your questions, suggestions, and criticisms of the teaching/learning package and *The Challenge of Democracy*. You may contact us at our respective institutions or through our collective e-mail address <cod@northwestern.edu>.

ACKNOWLEDGMENTS

All authors are indebted to others for inspiration and assistance in various forms; textbook authors are notoriously so. In producing this edition, we especially want to thank David Bishop, Northwestern University Librarian; Stu Baker, the library's able webmaster; Claire Dougherty, head of Marjorie Mitchell Digital Media Services; Bob Taylor of Northwestern's Academic Technologies; Dennis Glenn, manager of the Advanced Multimedia Production Studio; Tony Becker, database architect and president of Fort Pedro Informatics; and Deborah A. Brauer and Diana Snyder of Northwestern's Political Science Department. At Tufts, thanks go to Sarah Krichels and Louis Tavares for their helpful work as research assistants.

We would like to single out Paul Manna for special acknowledgment.

Paul was a distinguished undergraduate at Northwestern and is now well along the path to his Ph.D. in our profession at the University of Wisconsin at Madison. His creativity helped to make the Seventh Edition of *The Challenge of Democracy* that much better.

For this edition, we were fortunate to have Kevin W. Hula of Loyola College in Maryland and Jeffrey L. Sedgwick of the University of Massachusetts—Amherst assist us with the preparation of the manuscript. They contributed significantly to our efforts to keep *The Challenge of Democracy* current and accurate. Their excellent work is greatly appreciated.

We again owe special thanks to Ted and Cora Ginsberg, whose research endowment helped launch several small investigations by our students that eventually found their way into this edition. We have been fortunate to obtain the help of many outstanding political scientists across the country who provided us with critical reviews of our work as it has progressed through seven separate editions. We found their comments enormously helpful, and we thank them for taking valuable time away from their own teaching and research to write their detailed reports. More specifically, our thanks go to:

David Ahern
University of Dayton

Philip C. Aka
University of Arkansas at Pine Bluff

James Anderson
Texas A&M University

Greg Andranovich
California State University, Los Angeles

Theodore Arrington
University of North Carolina, Charlotte

Denise Baer
Northeastern University

Richard Barke
Georgia Institute of Technology

Linda L. M. Bennett
Wittenberg University

Stephen Earl Bennett
University of Cincinnati

Thad Beyle
University of North Carolina, Chapel Hill

Bruce Bimber
University of California—Santa Barbara

Michael Binford
Georgia State University

Bonnie Browne
Texas A&M University

Jeffrey L. Brudney
University of Georgia

J. Vincent Buck
California State University, Fullerton

Gregory A. Caldeira
University of Iowa

David E. Camacho
Northern Arizona University

Robert Casier
Santa Barbara City College

James Chalmers
Wayne State University

John Chubb
Stanford University

Allan Cigler
University of Kansas

Stanley Clark
California State University, Bakersfield

Ronald Claunch
Stephen F. Austin State University

Guy C. Clifford
Bridgewater State College

Gary Copeland
University of Oklahoma

Ruth A Corbett
Chabot Chollege

W. Douglas Costain
University of Colorado at Boulder

Cornelius P. Cotter
University of Wisconsin, Milwaukee

Christine L. Day
University of New Orleans

David A. Deese
Boston College

Victor D'Lugin
University of Florida

Art English
University of Arkansas

Dennis Falcon
Cerritos Community College

Henry Fearnley
College of Marin

Elizabeth Flores
Del Mar College

Patricia S. Florestano
University of Maryland

Richard Foglesong
Rollins College

Steve Frank
St. Cloud State University

Mitchel Gerber
Hofstra University

Dana K. Glencross
Oklahoma City Community College

Dorith Grant-Wisdom
Howard University

Paul Gronke
Duke University

Sara A. Grove
Shippensburg University

David J. Hadley
Wabash College

Kenneth Hayes
University of Maine

Ronald Hedlund
University of Wisconsin, Milwaukee

Richard Heil
Fort Hays State University

Beth Henschen
The Institute for Community and Regional Development, Eastern Michigan University

Marjorie Randon Hershey
Indiana University

Roberta Herzberg
Indiana University

Jack E. Holmes
Hope College

Peter Howse
American River College

Ronald J. Hrebenar
University of Utah

James B. Johnson
University of Nebraska at Omaha

William R. Keech
Carnegie Mellon University

Scott Keeter
Virginia Commonwealth University

Sarah W. Keidan
Oakland Community College (Michigan)

Linda Camp Keith
Collin County Community College

Beat Kernen
Southwest Missouri State University

Haroon Khan
Henderson State University

Dwight Kiel
Central Florida University

Vance Krites
Indiana University of Pennsylvania

Clyde Kuhn
California State University, Sacramento

Jack Lampe
Southwest Texas Junior College

Brad Lockerbie
University of Georgia

Joseph Losco
Ball State University

Philip Loy
Taylor University

Stan Luger
University of Northern Colorado

Wayne McIntosh
University of Maryland

David Madlock
University of Memphis

Michael Maggiotto
University of South Carolina

Edward S. Malecki
*California State University,
Los Angeles*

Michael Margolis
*University of Cincinnati—
McMicken College of Arts and
Sciences*

Thomas R. Marshall
University of Texas at Arlington

Janet Martin
Bowdoin College

Steve J. Mazurana
University of Northern Colorado

Jim Morrow
Tulsa Junior College

David Moskowitz
*The University of North Carolina,
Charlotte*

William Mugleston
Mountain View College

David A. Nordquest
Pennsylvania State University, Erie

Bruce Odom
Trinity Valley Community College

Laura Katz Olson
Lehigh University

Bruce Oppenheimer
University of Houston

Richard Pacelle
Indiana University

William J. Parente
University of Scranton

Robert Pecorella
St. John's University

James Perkins
San Antonio College

Denny E. Pilant
*Southwest Missouri State
University*

Curtis Reithel
*University of Wisconsin,
La Crosse*

Russell Renka
*Southeast Missouri State
University*

Chester D. Rhoan
Chabot College

Michael J. Rich
Emory University

Richard S. Rich
Virginia Tech

Ronald I. Rubin
*Borough of Manhattan Community
College, CUNY*

Gilbert K. St. Clair
University of New Mexico

Barbara Salmore
Drew University

Todd M. Schaefer
Central Washington University

Denise Scheberle
*University of Wisconsin,
Green Bay*

Paul R. Schulman
Mills College

William A. Schultze
San Diego State University

Thomas Sevener
Santa Rosa Junior College

Kenneth S. Sherrill
Hunter College

Sanford R. Silverburg
Catawba College

Mark Silverstein
Boston University

Robert J. Spitzer
SUNY Cortland

Terry Spurlock
Trinity Valley Community College

Candy Stevens Smith
Texarkana College

Charles Sohner
El Camino College

Dale Story
University of Texas, Arlington

Nicholas Strinkowski
Clark College

Neal Tate
University of North Texas

James A. Thurber
The American University

Eric M. Uslaner
University of Maryland

Charles E. Walcott
Virginia Tech

Thomas G. Walker
Emory University

Benjamin Walter
Vanderbilt University

Shirley Ann Warshaw
Gettysburg College

Gary D. Wekkin
University of Central Arkansas

Jonathan West
University of Miami

John Winkle
University of Mississippi

Clifford Wirth
University of New Hampshire

Ann Wynia
*North Hennepin Community
College*

Jerry L. Yeric
University of North Texas

Finally, we want to thank the many people at Houghton Mifflin who helped make this edition a reality. There's not enough room here to list all the individuals who helped us with the previous six editions, so we say a collective thank you for the superb work you did on *The Challenge of Democracy*. Several individuals, however, bear special responsibility for the results of this edition, and must be named. Peggy J. Flanagan was our Project Editor on the previous two editions, and we were fortunate to have her play that role again. Working on the "output" side of the project, she pulled together text, photos, captions, tables, and graphics, and she oversaw the actual physical production of the book. The proof of her effectiveness is in the beauty of the pages that follow.

Although she's not new to Houghton Mifflin, our Sponsoring Editor, Mary Dougherty, was new to *The Challenge of Democracy*. She quickly won our confidence and directed the Seventh Edition with the greatest of ease. We hope she is around for many more editions of our book. Katherine Meisenheimer did an outstanding job as our Development Editor. She had day-to-day responsibility for the book and repeatedly went beyond the call of duty to keep the project on track. As with Mary, we look forward to working with Katherine again on the next edition. Jean Woy, now Vice President and Editor-in-Chief of History, Political Science, and Economics, signed us to do the book close to twenty years ago. Through all those years, she has had to put up with more shenanigans than any editor should have to endure, but she kept us anyway. Others who made important contributions to the Seventh Edition are Scott R. Diggins, Associate Internet Producer; Tonya Lobato, Editorial Assistant; Carol Merrigan, Senior Production/Design Coordinator; Marie Barnes, Senior Manufacturing Coordinator; Martha Shethar, photo researcher; Janet Theurer, designer and art editor; and Marianne L'Abbate, copyeditor.

Our experience proves that authors—even experienced authors working on their seventh edition—can benefit from the suggestions and criticisms of a gifted staff of publishing experts. No publisher has a more capable group of dedicated professionals than Houghton Mifflin, and we have been fortunate to have their guidance over the seven editions of our text.

K.J.
J.B.
J.G.

Freedom, Order, or Equality?

"ILOVEYOU," said the e-mail message. "Kindly check the attached LOVELETTER coming from me." Thousands of intrigued men and women around the globe eagerly clicked the attachment—only to have the malicious love-bug virus destroy their computer files.

ILOVEYOU messages popped up on e-mail systems around the world on May 3, 2000. The virus proved especially devastating in the United States, wiping out files of private citizens, shutting down e-mail systems across the country, and costing untold millions of dollars in damage. On May 5, the Federal Bureau of Investigation acted under the U.S. Computer Abuse Act. By May 8, FBI agents were in Manila when Philippine investigators raided an apartment to which they traced the virus.

The police eventually identified a twenty-three-year-old computer school dropout as the love-bug's creator. They couldn't charge him, however, because the Philippines had no law against computer hacking. Two months later, the police charged him under a 1998 law regulating the use of "access devices" such as credit cards and passwords.[1] Frustrated FBI agents left the Philippines knowing that they had helped find the culprit but could not bring him to justice.

globalization
The increasing interdependence of citizens and nations across the world.

This vignette illustrates a facet of **globalization**—the increasing interdependence of citizens and nations across the world—and the challenges that globalization presents to American government. Someone in a country halfway around the world caused damage to U.S. companies and distress to American citizens, and our government could do little about it. In this book, we will deal with the many effects of globalization on U.S. government, but we will also point out important effects of U.S. politics on government elsewhere.

The love-bug virus incident also raises the issue of the purpose and value of government at home, which is our main interest in this text. We have strong laws against computer hackers and—with a judge-issued warrant—the FBI can use its surveillance system to search the e-mail of a suspected criminal or terrorist. The FBI's software, originally called Carnivore, is installed at an Internet provider to record to-and-from communications traffic, but it can also capture and archive all messages sent via the Internet provider.[2] Although the British government exercises even more sweeping powers over e-mail communications, some say that the FBI's wiretapping power over the Internet is too great.[3] They see the Internet as embodying personal freedom and would keep it virtually free of government regulation. Others see a different technological threat; they fear the consequences of the "digital divide"—the greater use of Internet technology by wealthy, white, urban, and highly educated segments of society—that will leave other segments of society far behind.[4] How much in the form of government subsidies, if any, should government provide to close the digital divide?

Which is better: to live under a government that allows individuals complete freedom to do whatever they please or to live under one that enforces strict law and order? *Which is better:* to let all citizens keep the same share of their income or to tax wealthier people at a higher rate to fund programs for poorer people? These questions pose dilemmas tied to opposing political philosophies that place different values on freedom, order, and equality.

This book explains American government and politics in light of these dilemmas. It does more than explain the workings of our government; it encourages you to think about what government should—and should not—do. And it judges the American government against democratic ideals, encouraging you to think about how government should make its decisions. As its title implies, *The Challenge of Democracy* argues that good government often involves difficult choices.

College students frequently say that American government and politics are hard to understand. In fact, many people voice the same complaint. More than 60 percent of a national sample interviewed after the 2000 presidential election agreed with the statement "Politics and government seem so complicated that a person like me can't understand what's going on."[5] With this book, we hope to improve your understanding of "what's going on" by analyzing the norms, or values, that people use to judge political events. Our purpose is not to preach what people ought to favor in making policy decisions; it is to teach what values are at stake.

Teaching without preaching is not easy; no one can completely exclude personal values from political analysis. But our approach minimizes the problem by concentrating on the dilemmas that confront governments when they are forced to choose between important policies that threaten equally cherished values, such as freedom of speech and personal security.

Every government policy reflects a choice between conflicting values. We want you to understand this idea, to understand that all government policies reinforce certain values (norms) at the expense of others. We want you to interpret policy issues (for example, should assisted suicide go unpunished?) with an understanding of the fundamental values in question (freedom of action versus order and protection of life) and the broader political context (liberal or conservative politics).

By looking beyond the specifics to the underlying normative principles, you should be able to make more sense out of politics. Our framework for analysis does not encompass all the complexities of American government, but it should help your knowledge grow by improving your comprehension of political information. We begin by considering the basic purposes of government. In short, why do we need it?

THE GLOBALIZATION OF AMERICAN GOVERNMENT

Most people do not like being told what to do. Fewer still like being coerced into acting a certain way. Yet, billions of people in countries across the world willingly submit to the coercive power of government. They accept laws that state on which side of the road to drive, how many wives (or husbands) they can have, what constitutes a contract, how to dispose of human waste—and how much they must pay to support the government that makes these coercive laws.

government
The legitimate use of force to control human behavior; also, the organization or agency authorized to exercise that force.

national sovereignty
"A political entity's externally recognized right to exercise final authority over its affairs."

In the first half of the twentieth century, people thought of government mainly in territorial terms. Indeed, a standard definition of **government** was the legitimate use of force—including firearms, imprisonment, and execution—within specified geographical boundaries to control human behavior. For over three centuries, since the Peace of Westphalia in 1648 ended the Thirty Years War in Europe, international relations and diplomacy have been based on the principle of **national sovereignty,** defined as "a political entity's externally recognized right to exercise final authority over its affairs."[6] Simply put, national sovereignty means that each national government has the right to govern its people as it wishes, without interference from other nations.

Some scholars argued strongly early in the twentieth century that a body of international law controlled the actions of supposedly sovereign nations, but their argument was essentially theoretical.[7] In the practice of international relations, there was *no* sovereign power over nations. Each enjoyed complete independence to govern its territory without interference from other nations. Although the League of Nations and later the United Nations were supposed to introduce supranational order into the world, even these international organizations explicitly respected national sovereignty as the guiding principle of international relations. The U.N. Charter, Article 2.1, states: "The Organization is based on the principle of the sovereign equality of all its Members."

As we enter into a world of increasing globalization in the twenty-first century, human rights weigh more heavily in international politics. Consider what Kofi-Annan, secretary general of the United Nations, said in support of NATO airstrikes against Serbian forces to stop the ethnic cleansing in Kosovo. Speaking before the United Nations Commission on Human Rights on April 7, 1999, the secretary general warned rogue nations that they could no longer "hide" behind the U.N. Charter. He said that the protection of human rights must "take precedence over concerns of state sovereignty."[8]

The world's new concern with human rights is not limited to rogue nations; all nations are grappling with international law. In late 2000, the Japanese government admitted violating a 1907 Hague Convention on prisoners' rights in wartime and gave a cash settlement to survivors of 1,000 Chinese prisoners forced to work under harsh conditions in World War II—the first time that Japan awarded compensation for a violation of international law.[9] National laws in Europe are increasingly being brought into line with laws of the European Union. For example, rulings of the European Court of Human Rights in 1999 led Britain to end its ban on gay men and women in the military.[10]

Our government, you might be surprised to learn, is worried about this trend of holding nations accountable to international law. In fact, the United States failed to sign the 1998 treaty to create an International Criminal Court that would define and try crimes against humanity until the last month of Clinton's presidency, when he signed it over advisors' objections and sent it to a likely death under the Bush presidency.[11]

Why would the United States oppose such an international court? One reason is its concern that U.S. soldiers stationed abroad might be arrested and tried in that court.[12] Another reason is the death penalty, which has been abolished by more than half the countries in the world and all countries in the European Union. Indeed, in 1996, the International

Can You Explain Why...
the United States might oppose an international criminal court?

Commission of Jurists condemned our death penalty as "arbitrarily and racially discriminatory," and there is a concerted campaign across Europe to force the sovereign United States of America to terminate capital punishment.[13]

While the United States is the world's most powerful nation, it is not immune to globalization (see Politics in a Changing World 1.1) and to the erosion of national sovereignty. Ironically, our military strength qualifies the United States to be the world's enforcer of international decisions. As the world's cop, should the United States be above international law if it finds its *own* sovereignty threatened by nations that don't share *our* values? What course of action should we follow if this situation occurs?

Although our text is about American national government, it recognizes the growing impact of international politics and world opinion on U.S. politics. The Cold War era, of course, had a profound effect on domestic politics because the nation spent heavily on the military and restricted trading with communist countries. Now, we are closely tied through trade to former enemies (we now import more goods from communist China than from France and Britain combined) and thoroughly embedded in a worldwide economic, social, and political network. (See Chapter 20, "Global Policy," for an extended treatment of the economic and social dimensions of globalization.) More than ever, we must discuss American politics while casting an eye abroad to see how foreign affairs affect our government and how American politics affects government in other nations.

THE PURPOSES OF GOVERNMENT

Governments at any level require citizens to surrender some freedom as part of being governed. Although some governments minimize their infringements on personal freedom, no government has as a goal the maximization of personal freedom. Governments exist to control; *to govern* means "to control." Why do people surrender their freedom to this

1.1   The "Globalization" of Nations

The text presents a working definition of globalization as "the increasing interdependence of citizens and nations across the world." But citizens and nations differ in their degree of global interdependence. Scholars measure the extent of globalization in different nations by combining various indicators of personal contact across national borders, international financial transactions, and use of international communication through technology. Here is a ranking of the "global top twenty" according to a recent study. Nations were scored on the basis of four sets of indicators: (1) *Goods and services:* convergence of domestic prices with international prices, and international trade as a share of gross domestic product (see Ch. 18). (2) *Finance:* Inward- and outward-directed foreign investment, portfolio capital flows, and income payments and receipts as shares of GDP. (3) *Personal contacts:* Cross-border remittances and other transfers as a share of GDP, minutes of international phone calls per capita, and number of international travelers per capita.

(4) *Technology:* Percentage of population on-line, number of Internet hosts per capita, and number of secure servers per capita.

Although the United States has been catching up in the globalization process, it does not rank among the most globalized nations. First place goes to Singapore, an international city-state in southeast Asia located astride a confluence of cultures. The next eight countries are core countries in Western Europe, but even Canada edges out the United States. Relative to other globalized nations, Americans have little personal contact with people in other countries. Of course, the large population of the United States helps its domestic self-sufficiency, but the process of globalization seems inexorable.

Source: A.T. Kearney/*Foreign Policy Magazine* Globalization Index. "The Global Top Twenty," *Foreign Policy,* January–February 2001, p. 58. Copyright 2001, A.T. Kearney, Inc. and the Carnegie Endowment for International Peace. All rights reserved. A.T. Kearney is a registered service mark of A.T. Kearney, Inc. *Foreign Policy* is a trademark of the Carnegie Endowment for International Peace.

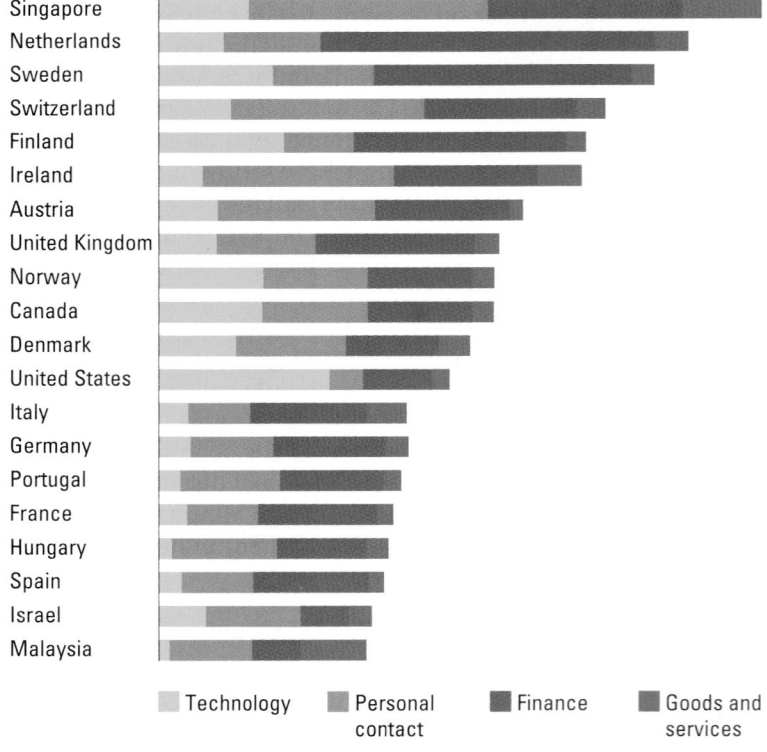

Singapore
Netherlands
Sweden
Switzerland
Finland
Ireland
Austria
United Kingdom
Norway
Canada
Denmark
United States
Italy
Germany
Portugal
France
Hungary
Spain
Israel
Malaysia

Technology | Personal contact | Finance | Goods and services

Leviathan, Hobbes's All-Powerful Sovereign

This engraving is from the 1651 edition of Leviathan, *by Thomas Hobbes. It shows Hobbes's sovereign brandishing a sword in one hand and the scepter of justice in the other. He watches over an orderly town, made peaceful by his absolute authority. But note that the sovereign's body is composed of tiny images of his subjects. He exists only through them. Hobbes explains that such government power can be created only if people "confer all their power and strength upon one man, or upon one assembly of men, that may reduce all their wills, by plurality of voices, unto one will."*

control? To obtain the benefits of government. Throughout history, government has served two major purposes: maintaining order (preserving life and protecting property) and providing public goods. More recently, some governments have pursued a third purpose: promoting equality, which is more controversial.

Maintaining Order

order
The rule of law to preserve life and protect property. Maintaining order is the oldest purpose of government.

Maintaining order is the oldest objective of government. **Order** in this context is rich with meaning. Let's start with "law and order." Maintaining order in this sense means establishing the rule of law to preserve life and protect property. To the seventeenth-century English philosopher Thomas Hobbes (1588–1679), preserving life was the most important function of government. In his classic philosophical treatise, *Leviathan* (1651), Hobbes described life without government as life in a "state of nature." Without rules, people would live as predators do, stealing and killing for their personal benefit. In Hobbes's classic phrase, life in a state of nature would be "solitary, poor, nasty, brutish, and short." He believed that a single ruler, or sovereign, must possess unquestioned authority to guarantee the safety of the weak, to protect them from the attacks of the strong. Hobbes named his all-powerful government Leviathan, after a biblical sea monster. He believed that complete obedience to Leviathan's strict laws was a small price to pay for the security of living in a civil society.

Most of us can only imagine what a state of nature would be like. But in some parts of the world, whole nations have experienced lawlessness. It occurred in Somalia in 1992 after the central government collapsed; in Haiti in 1994 after the elected president had to flee; and in Bosnia in 1995 after the former Yugoslavia collapsed and Croats, Serbs, and Muslims engaged in ethnic war. In each case, U.S. forces intervened to prevent starvation and restore a semblance of order. Throughout history, authoritarian rulers have used people's fear of civil disorder to justify taking power. Ironically, the ruling group itself—whether monarchy, aristocracy, or political party—then became known as the *established order.*

Hobbes's conception of life in the cruel state of nature led him to view government primarily as a means of guaranteeing people's survival. Other theorists, taking survival for granted, believed that government protected order by preserving private property (goods and land owned by individuals). Foremost among them was John Locke (1632–1704), an English philosopher. In *Two Treatises on Government* (1690), he wrote that the protection of life, liberty, and property was the basic objective of government. His thinking strongly influenced the Declaration of Independence; it is reflected in the Declaration's famous phrase identifying "Life, Liberty, and the Pursuit of Happiness" as "unalienable Rights" of citizens under government.

Not everyone believes that the protection of private property is a valid objective of government. The German philosopher Karl Marx (1818–1883) rejected the private ownership of property used in the production of goods or services. Marx's ideas form the basis of **communism,** a complex theory that gives ownership of all land and productive facilities to the people—in effect, to the government. In line with communist theory, the 1977 constitution of the former Soviet Union declared that the nation's land, minerals, waters, and forests "are the exclusive property of the state." In addition, "The state owns the basic means of production in industry, construction, and agriculture; means of transport and communication; the banks, the property of state-run trade organizations and public utilities, and other state-run undertakings."[14]

Years after the Soviet Union collapsed, the Russian public remains deeply split over changing the old communist-era constitution to permit the private ownership of land. Even outside the formerly communist societies, the extent to which government protects private property is a political issue that forms the basis of much ideological debate.

communism
A political system in which, in theory, ownership of all land and productive facilities is in the hands of the people, and all goods are equally shared. The production and distribution of goods are controlled by an authoritarian government.

Providing Public Goods

After governments have established basic order, they can pursue other ends. Using their coercive powers, they can tax citizens to raise money to spend on **public goods,** which are benefits and services that are available to everyone—such as education, sanitation, and parks. Public goods benefit all citizens but are not likely to be produced by the voluntary acts of individuals. The government of ancient Rome, for example, built aqueducts to carry fresh water from the mountains to the city. Road building was another public good provided by the Roman government, which also used the roads to move its legions and to protect the established order.

Government action to provide public goods can be controversial. During President James Monroe's administration (1817–1825), many people thought that building the Cumberland Road (between Cumberland, Maryland, and Wheeling, West Virginia) was not a proper function of the national government, the Romans notwithstanding. Over time, the scope

public goods
Benefits and services, such as parks and sanitation, that benefit all citizens but are not likely to be produced voluntarily by individuals.

Rosa Parks had just finished a day's work as a seamstress and was sitting in the front of a bus in Montgomery, Alabama, going home. A white man claimed her seat, which he could do according to the law in December 1955. When she refused to move and was arrested, angry blacks, led by Dr. Martin Luther King, Jr., began a boycott of the Montgomery bus company.

of government functions in the United States has expanded. During President Dwight Eisenhower's administration in the 1950s, the federal government outdid the Romans' noble road building. Despite his basic conservatism, Eisenhower launched the massive Interstate Highway System, at a cost of $27 billion (in 1950s dollars). Yet some government enterprises that have been common in other countries—running railroads, operating coal mines, generating electric power—are politically controversial or even unacceptable in the United States. People disagree about how far the government ought to go in using its power to tax to provide public goods and services and how much of that realm should be handled by private business for profit.

Promoting Equality

The promotion of equality has not always been a major objective of government. It has gained prominence only in this century, in the aftermath of industrialization and urbanization. Confronted by the paradox of poverty amid plenty, some political leaders in European nations pioneered extensive government programs to improve life for the poor. Under the emerging concept of the welfare state, government's role expanded to provide individuals with medical care, education, and a guaranteed income, "from cradle to grave." Sweden, Britain, and other nations adopted welfare programs aimed at reducing social inequalities. This relatively new purpose of government has been by far the most controversial. People often oppose taxation for public goods (building roads and schools, for example) because of its cost alone. They oppose more strongly taxation for government programs to promote economic and social equality on principle.

The key issue here is government's role in redistributing income, taking from the wealthy to give to the poor. Charity (voluntary giving to the poor) has a strong basis in Western religious traditions; using the power of the state to support the poor does not. (In his nineteenth-century novels, Charles Dickens dramatized how government power was used to imprison the poor, not to support them.) Using the state to redistribute income was originally a radical idea, set forth by Marx as the ultimate principle of developed communism: "from each according to his ability, to each according to his needs."[15] This extreme has never been realized in any government, not even in communist states. But over time, taking from the rich to help the needy has become a legitimate function of most governments.

That function is not without controversy, however. Especially since the Great Depression of the 1930s, the government's role in redistributing income to promote economic equality has been a major source of policy debate in the United States. For example, after the Republicans won control of Congress in 1994, a fierce partisan battle was waged over the Aid to Families with Dependent Children (AFDC) program, created by the Democrats in 1935. The nation's main cash welfare program, AFDC issued government checks to low-income mothers to help them care for their children. The Republicans had long argued that the program was inappropriate and ineffective, and in 1996 they ended it over the strenuous objections of Democrats.

Government can also promote social equality through policies that do not redistribute income. For example, it can regulate social behavior to enforce equality, as it did when the Texas Supreme Court cleared the way for homosexuals to serve in the Dallas police department in 1993. Policies that regulate social behavior, like those that redistribute income, inevitably clash with the value of personal freedom.

A CONCEPTUAL FRAMEWORK FOR ANALYZING GOVERNMENT

Citizens have very different views of how vigorously they want government to maintain order, provide public goods, and promote equality. Of the three objectives, providing for public goods usually is less controversial than maintaining order or promoting equality. After all, government spending for highways, schools, and parks carries benefits for nearly every citizen. Moreover, services merely cost money. The cost of maintaining order and promoting equality is greater than money; it usually means a tradeoff in basic values.

To understand government and the political process, you must be able to recognize these tradeoffs and identify the basic values they entail. Just as people sit back from a wide-screen motion picture to gain perspective, to understand American government you need to take a broad view, a view much broader than that offered by examining specific political events. You need to use political concepts.

A concept is a generalized idea of a set of items or thoughts. It groups various events, objects, or qualities under a common classification or label. The framework that guides this book consists of five concepts that figure prominently in political analysis. We regard the five concepts as especially important to a broad understanding of American politics, and we use them repeatedly throughout the book. This framework will help you evaluate political events long after you have read this text.

The five concepts that we emphasize deal with the fundamental issues of what government tries to do and how it decides to do it. The concepts that relate to what government tries to do are *order, freedom*, and *equality*. All governments by definition value order; maintaining order is part of the meaning of government. Most governments at least claim to preserve individual freedom while they maintain order, although they vary widely in the extent to which they succeed. Few governments even profess to guarantee equality, and governments differ greatly in policies that pit equality against freedom. Our conceptual framework should help you evaluate the extent to which the United States pursues all three values through its government.

How government chooses the proper mix of order, freedom, and equality in its policymaking has to do with the process of choice. We evaluate the American governmental process using two models of democratic government: *majoritarian* and *pluralist*. Many governments profess to be democracies. Whether they are or are not depends on their (and our) meaning of the term. Even countries that Americans agree are democracies—for example, the United States and Britain—differ substantially in the type of democracy they practice. We can use our conceptual models of democratic government both to classify the type of democracy practiced in the United States and to evaluate the government's success in fulfilling that model.

The five concepts can be organized into two groups.

- Concepts that identify the values pursued by government:

Freedom

Order

Equality

- Concepts that describe models of democratic government:

Majoritarian democracy

Pluralist democracy

The rest of this chapter examines freedom, order, and equality as conflicting values pursued by government. Chapter 2 discusses majoritarian democracy and pluralist democracy as alternative institutional models for implementing democratic government.

THE CONCEPTS OF FREEDOM, ORDER, AND EQUALITY

These three terms—*freedom, order,* and *equality*—have a range of connotations in American politics. Both *freedom* and *equality* are positive terms that politicians have learned to use to their own advantage. Consequently, freedom and equality mean different things to different people at different times, depending on the political context in which they are used. Order, on the other hand, has negative connotations for many people because it symbolizes government intrusion into private lives. Except during periods of social strife, few politicians in Western democracies call openly for more order. Because all governments infringe on freedom, we examine that concept first.

feature 1.1

The Four Freedoms

Norman Rockwell became famous in the 1940s for the humorous, homespun covers he painted for the *Saturday Evening Post*, a weekly magazine. Inspired by an address to Congress in which President Roosevelt outlined his goals for world civilization, Rockwell painted *The Four Freedoms*, which were reproduced in the *Post*. Their immense popularity led the government to print posters of the illustrations for the Treasury Department's war bond drive. The Office of War Information also reproduced *The Four Freedoms* and circulated the posters in schools, clubhouses, railroad stations, post offices, and other public buildings. Officials even had copies circulated on the European front to remind soldiers of the liberties for which they were fighting. It is said that no other paintings in the world have ever been reproduced or circulated in such vast numbers as *The Four Freedoms*.

Freedom of Speech

Freedom of Worship

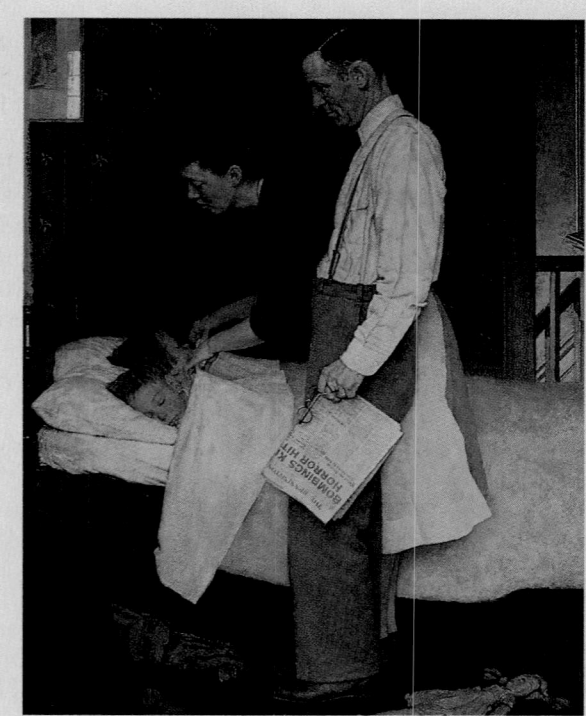

Freedom from Fear   **Freedom from Want**

Roosevelt's "Four Freedoms" Speech

freedom of
An absence of constraints on behavior, as in *freedom of speech* or *freedom of religion*.

freedom from
Immunity, as in *freedom from want*.

Freedom

Freedom can be used in two major senses: freedom of and freedom from. President Franklin Delano Roosevelt used the word in both senses in a speech he made shortly before the United States entered World War II. He described four freedoms—freedom of religion, freedom of speech, freedom from fear, and freedom from want. The noted illustrator Norman Rockwell gave Americans a vision of these freedoms in a classic set of paintings published in the *Saturday Evening Post* (see Feature 1.1).

Freedom of is the absence of constraints on behavior; it means freedom *to* do something. In this sense, *freedom* is synonymous with *liberty*. Two of Rockwell's paintings—*Freedom of Worship* and *Freedom of Speech*—exemplify this type of freedom.

Freedom from is the message of the other paintings, *Freedom from Fear* and *Freedom from Want*. Here freedom suggests immunity from fear and want. In the modern political context, *freedom from* often symbolizes the fight against exploitation and oppression. The cry of the civil rights movement in the 1960s—"Freedom Now!"—conveyed this meaning. If you recognize that freedom in this sense means immunity from discrimination, you can see that it comes close to the concept of equality.[16] In this book, we avoid using *freedom of* to mean "freedom from"; for this sense, we simply use *equality*. When we use *freedom*, we mean "freedom of."

Order

When *order* is viewed in the narrow sense of preserving life and protecting property, most citizens would concede the importance of maintaining order and thereby grant the need for government. For example, "domestic Tranquility" (order) is cited in the preamble to the Constitution. However, when *order* is viewed in the broader sense of preserving the social order, people are more likely to argue that maintaining order is not a legitimate function of government (see Compared with What? 1.1). *Social order* refers to established patterns of authority in society and to traditional modes of behavior. It is the accepted way of doing things. The prevailing social order prescribes behavior in many different areas: how students should dress in school (neatly, no purple hair) and behave toward their teachers (respectfully); under what conditions people should have sexual relations (married, different sexes); what the press should not publish (sexually explicit photographs); and what the proper attitude toward religion and country should be (reverential). It is important to remember that the social order can change. Today, perfectly respectable men and women wear bathing suits that would have caused a scandal at the turn of the century.

A government can protect the established order by using its **police power**—its authority to safeguard residents' safety, health, welfare, and morals. The extent to which government should use this authority is a topic of ongoing debate in the United States and is constantly being redefined by the courts. In the 1980s, many states used their police powers to pass legislation that banned smoking in public places. In the 1990s, a hot issue was whether government should control the dissemination of pornography on the Internet. There are those who fear the evolution of a police state—a government that uses its power to regulate nearly all aspects of behavior. For example, South Africa under the former apartheid regime had laws governing intermarriage between blacks and whites and prescribing where an interracial married couple could live. It is no accident that the chief law enforcement officer in South Africa was called the minister of law and *order*.

Most governments are inherently conservative; they tend to resist social change. But some governments have as a primary objective the restructuring of the social order. Social change is most dramatic when a government is overthrown through force and replaced by a revolutionary government. Societies can also work to change social patterns more gradually through the legal process. Our use of the term *order* in this book includes all three aspects: preserving life, protecting property, and maintaining traditional patterns of social relationships.

Equality

As with *freedom* and *order, equality* is used in different senses, to support different causes. **Political equality** in elections is easy to define: each citizen has one and only one vote. This basic concept is central to democratic theory—a subject explored at length in Chapter 2. But when some people advocate political equality, they mean more than one person, one vote. These people contend that an urban ghetto dweller and the chairman of the board of Microsoft are not politically equal, despite the fact that each

police power
The authority of a government to maintain order and safeguard citizens' health, morals, safety, and welfare.

political equality
Equality in political decision making: one vote per person, with all votes counted equally.

Video: The Status of Women

★ compared with what?

1.1   The Importance of Order as a Political Value

Compared with citizens in other nations, Americans do not value order very much. Surveys in the United States and in twenty-eight other countries asked respondents to select which of the following four national goals was "very important."

● Maintaining order in the nation

● Giving people more say in important government decisions

● Fighting rising prices

● Protecting freedom of speech

Just 33 percent of U.S. respondents thought that "maintaining order" was very important. Compared with citizens in other countries, Americans do not value government control of social behavior.

Source: World Values Survey, 1995–1997.

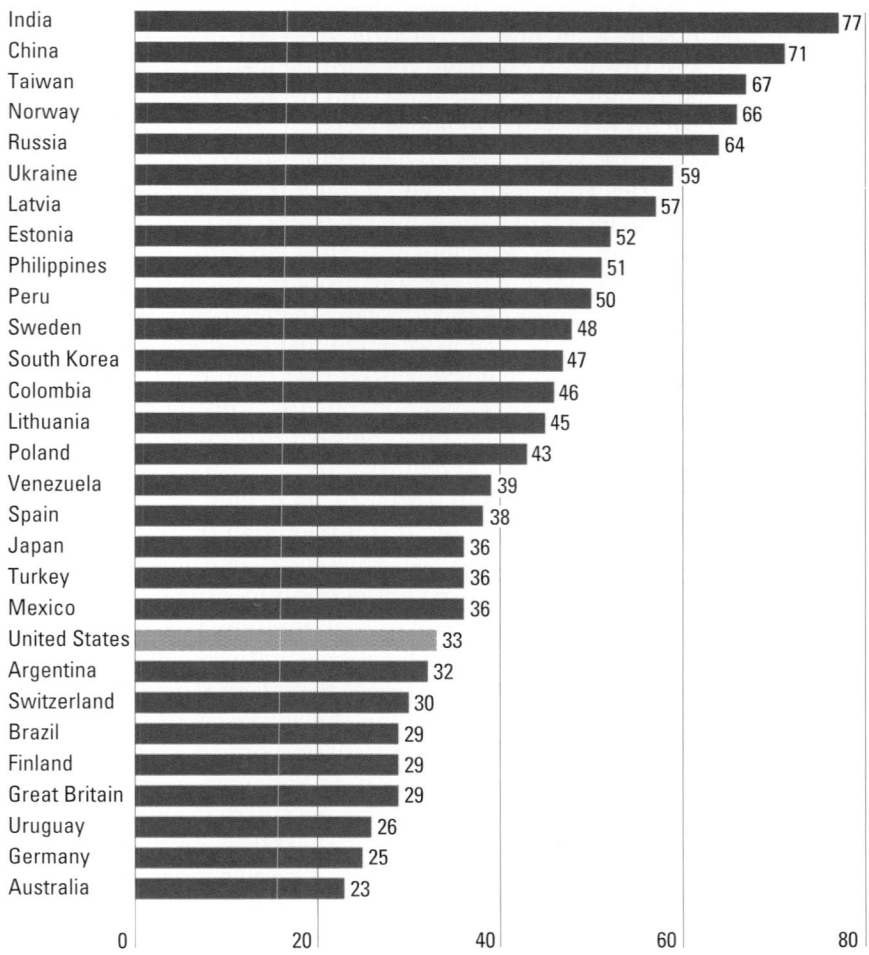

Percentage of respondents who value "order"

India	77
China	71
Taiwan	67
Norway	66
Russia	64
Ukraine	59
Latvia	57
Estonia	52
Philippines	51
Peru	50
Sweden	48
South Korea	47
Colombia	46
Lithuania	45
Poland	43
Venezuela	39
Spain	38
Japan	36
Turkey	36
Mexico	36
United States	33
Argentina	32
Switzerland	30
Brazil	29
Finland	29
Great Britain	29
Uruguay	26
Germany	25
Australia	23

★
A Woman's Place Is in the Sky

*During World War II, women
served in the military in "auxiliary" corps. The U.S. Army
had the Women's Army
Auxiliary Corps (shortened to
WAC), and the Navy had the
Women Appointed for
Voluntary Emergency Service
(WAVES). Women in these
corps usually served in clerical and support units and
were not trained for "men's
work." In today's military,
women often occupy tradi-
tionally male roles—such as
helicopter pilot.*

social equality
Equality in wealth, education, and
status.

equality of opportunity
The idea that each person is
guaranteed the same chance to
succeed in life.

equality of outcome
The concept that society must
ensure that people are equal, and
governments must design policies
to redistribute wealth and status
so that economic and social
equality is actually achieved.

rights
The benefits of government to
which every citizen is entitled.

has one vote. Through occupation or wealth, some citizens are more able
than others to influence political decisions. For example, wealthy citizens
can exert influence by advertising in the mass media or by contacting
friends in high places. Lacking great wealth and political connections,
most citizens do not have such influence. Thus, some analysts argue that
equality in wealth, education, and status—that is, **social equality**—is necessary for true political equality.

There are two routes to achieving social equality: providing equal opportunities and ensuring equal outcomes. **Equality of opportunity** means
that each person has the same chance to succeed in life. This idea is deeply
ingrained in American culture. The Constitution prohibits titles of nobility and does not make owning property a requirement for holding public
office. Public schools and libraries are free to all. For many people, the concept of social equality is satisfied just by offering equal opportunities for
advancement—it is not essential that people actually end up being equal.
For others, true social equality means nothing less than **equality of outcome**.[17] President Johnson expressed this view in 1965: "it is not enough
just to open the gates of opportunity. . . . We seek . . . not just equality as a
right and a theory but equality as a fact and equality as a result."[18]
According to this outlook, it is not enough that governments provide people with equal opportunities; they must also design policies that redistribute wealth and status so that economic and social equality are actually
achieved. In education, equality of outcome has led to federal laws that require comparable funding for men's and women's college sports. In business, equality of outcome has led to certain affirmative action programs to
increase minority hiring and to the active recruitment of women, blacks,
and Latinos to fill jobs. Equality of outcome has also produced federal laws
that require employers to pay men and women equally for equal work. In
recent years, the very concept of affirmative action has come under
scrutiny. In 1996, for example, the University of California's Board of
Regents ended its policy of using race and gender criteria in admitting students and hiring professors.

Some link equality of outcome with the concept of government-
supported **rights**—the idea that every citizen is entitled to certain benefits of government, that government should guarantee its citizens
adequate (if not equal) housing, employment, medical care, and income
as a matter of right. If citizens are entitled to government benefits as a

matter of right, government efforts to promote equality of outcome become legitimized.

Clearly, the concept of equality of outcome is quite different from that of equality of opportunity, and it requires a much greater degree of government activity. It also clashes more directly with the concept of freedom. By taking from one to give to another—which is necessary for the redistribution of income and status—the government clearly creates winners and losers. The winners may believe that justice has been served by the redistribution. The losers often feel strongly that their freedom to enjoy their income and status has suffered.

TWO DILEMMAS OF GOVERNMENT

The two major dilemmas facing American government at the end of the twentieth century stem from the oldest and the newest objectives of government—maintaining order and promoting equality. Both order and equality are important social values, but government cannot pursue either without sacrificing a third important value: individual freedom. The clash between freedom and order forms the original dilemma of government; the clash between freedom and equality forms the modern dilemma of government. Although the dilemmas are different, each involves trading some amount of freedom for another value.

The Original Dilemma: Freedom Versus Order

The conflict between freedom and order originates in the very meaning of government as the legitimate use of force to control human behavior. How much freedom must a citizen surrender to government? The dilemma has occupied philosophers for hundreds of years. In the eighteenth century, the French philosopher Jean Jacques Rousseau (1712–1778) wrote that the problem of devising a proper government "is to find a form of association which will defend and protect with the whole common force the person and goods of each associate, and in which each, while uniting himself with all, may still obey himself alone, and remain free as before."[19]

The original purpose of government was to protect life and property, to make citizens safe from violence. How well is the American government doing today in providing law and order to its citizens? More than 40 percent of the respondents in a 1997 national survey said that there were areas within a mile of their home where they were "afraid to walk alone at night." Only 7 percent felt "more safe" in their community compared to the year before, and 33 percent felt "less safe."[20] Simply put, Americans view crime (which has actually decreased in recent years) as a critical issue and do not believe that their government adequately protects them.

When the old communist governments still ruled in Eastern Europe, the climate of fear in urban America stood in stark contrast to the pervasive sense of personal safety in cities such as Moscow, Warsaw, and Prague. Then it was common to see old and young strolling late at night along the streets and in the parks of these communist cities. The formerly communist regimes gave their police great powers to control guns, monitor citizens' movements, and arrest and imprison suspicious people, which enabled them to do a better job of maintaining order. Communist governments deliberately chose order over freedom. But with the collapse of

Can You Explain Why...
crime rates rose in communist countries after they abandoned communism?

communism came the end of strict social order in all communist countries. Even in China, which still claims to be communist but where the majority of people now work in the private economy, there has been an increase in crime, notably violent crime. As relaxed state controls have created more motives and opportunities for crime, a Chinese professor said, "It's become difficult to control people."[21]

The crisis over acquired immune deficiency syndrome (AIDS) adds a new twist to the dilemma of freedom versus order. Some health officials believe that AIDS, for which there is no known cure, is the greatest medical threat in the history of the United States. At the end of 1999, more than 733,000 cases of AIDS had been reported to the Centers for Disease Control, and some 430,000 of these patients (59 percent) had died.[22]

To combat the spread of the disease in the military, the Department of Defense began testing all applicants for the AIDS virus. Other government agencies have begun testing current employees. And some officials are calling for widespread mandatory testing within the private sector as well. Such programs are strongly opposed by those who believe they violate individual freedom. But those who are more afraid of the spread of AIDS than of an infringement on individual rights support aggressive government action to combat the disease.

The conflict between the values of freedom and order represents the original dilemma of government. In the abstract, people value both freedom and order; in real life, the two values inherently conflict. By definition, any policy that strengthens one value takes away from the other. The balance of freedom and order is an issue in enduring debates (whether to allow capital punishment) and contemporary challenges (how to deal with urban gang members who spray-paint walls; whether to allow art galleries to display sexually explicit photographs). And in a democracy, policy choices hinge on how much citizens value freedom and how much they value order.

The Modern Dilemma: Freedom Versus Equality

Popular opinion has it that freedom and equality go hand in hand. In reality, the two values usually clash when governments enact policies to promote social equality. Because social equality is a relatively recent government objective, deciding between policies that promote equality at the expense of freedom, and vice versa, is the modern dilemma of politics. Consider these examples:

● During the 1960s, Congress (through the Equal Pay Act) required employers to pay women and men the same rate for equal work. This legislation means that some employers are forced to pay women more than they would if their compensation policies were based on their free choice.

● During the 1970s, the courts ordered the busing of schoolchildren to achieve a fair distribution of blacks and whites in public schools. This action was motivated by concern for educational equality, but it also impaired freedom of choice.

● During the 1980s, some states passed legislation that went beyond the idea of equal pay for equal work to the more radical notion of pay equity—equal pay for comparable work. Women had to be paid at a rate equal to men's even if they had different jobs, providing the women's jobs were of "comparable worth." For example, if the skills and responsibilities of a female nurse were found to be comparable to those of a male laboratory technician in the same hospital, the woman's salary and the man's salary would have to be the same.

- In the 1990s, Congress prohibited discrimination in employment, public services, and public accommodations on the basis of physical or mental disabilities. Under the 1990 Americans with Disabilities Act, businesses with twenty-five or more employees cannot pass over an otherwise qualified disabled person in employment or promotion, and new buses and trains have to be made accessible to them.

These examples illustrate the problem of using government power to promote equality. The clash between freedom and order is obvious, but the clash between freedom and equality is more subtle. Americans, who think of freedom and equality as complementary rather than conflicting values, often do not notice the clash. When forced to choose between the two, however, Americans are far more likely to choose freedom over equality than are people in other countries (see Compared with What? 1.2). The emphasis on equality over freedom was especially strong in the former Soviet Union, which guaranteed its citizens medical care, inexpensive housing, and other social services. Although the quality of the benefits was not much by Western standards, Soviet citizens experienced a sense of equality in shared deprivation. Indeed, there was such aversion to economic inequality that citizens' attitudes hindered economic development in a free market after the fall of the Soviet Union. As the director of the Moscow Arts Theater explained, "People are longing for the lost paradise—the lost Communist paradise."[23]

The conflicts among freedom, order, and equality explain a great deal of the political conflict in the United States. The conflicts also underlie the ideologies that people use to structure their understanding of politics.

IDEOLOGY AND THE SCOPE OF GOVERNMENT

People hold different opinions about the merits of government policies. Sometimes their views are based on self-interest. For example, most senior citizens vociferously oppose increasing their personal contributions to Medicare, the government program that defrays medical costs for the elderly, preferring to have all citizens pay for their coverage. Policies also are judged according to individual values and beliefs. Some people hold an assortment of values and beliefs that produce contradictory opinions on government policies. Others organize their opinions into a **political ideology**—a consistent set of values and beliefs about the proper purpose and scope of government.

political ideology
A consistent set of values and beliefs about the proper purpose and scope of government.

How far should government go to maintain order, provide public goods, and promote equality? In the United States (as in every other nation), citizens, scholars, and politicians have different answers. We can analyze their positions by referring to philosophies about the proper scope of government—the range of its permissible activities. Imagine a continuum. At one end is the belief that government should do everything; at the other is the belief that government should not exist. These extreme ideologies—

compared with what?

1.2 The Importance of Freedom and Equality as Political Values

Compared with citizens' views of freedom and equality in fifteen other nations, Americans value freedom more than others do. Respondents in each country were asked which of the following statements came closer to their own opinion:

- "I find that both freedom and equality are important. But if I were to make up my mind for one or the other, I would consider personal freedom more important, that is, everyone can live in freedom and develop without hindrance."

- "Certainly both freedom and equality are important. But if I were to make up my mind for one of the two, I would consider equality more important, that is, that nobody is underprivileged and that social class differences are not so strong."

Americans chose freedom by a ratio of nearly 3 to 1. No other nation showed such a strong preference for freedom, and citizens in four countries favored equality instead. When we look at this finding together with Americans' disdain for order (see Compared with What? 1.1), the importance of freedom as a political concept in the United States is clear.

Source: World Values Survey, 1990–1991. The tabulation was provided by Professor Ronald F. Inglehart, University of Michigan.

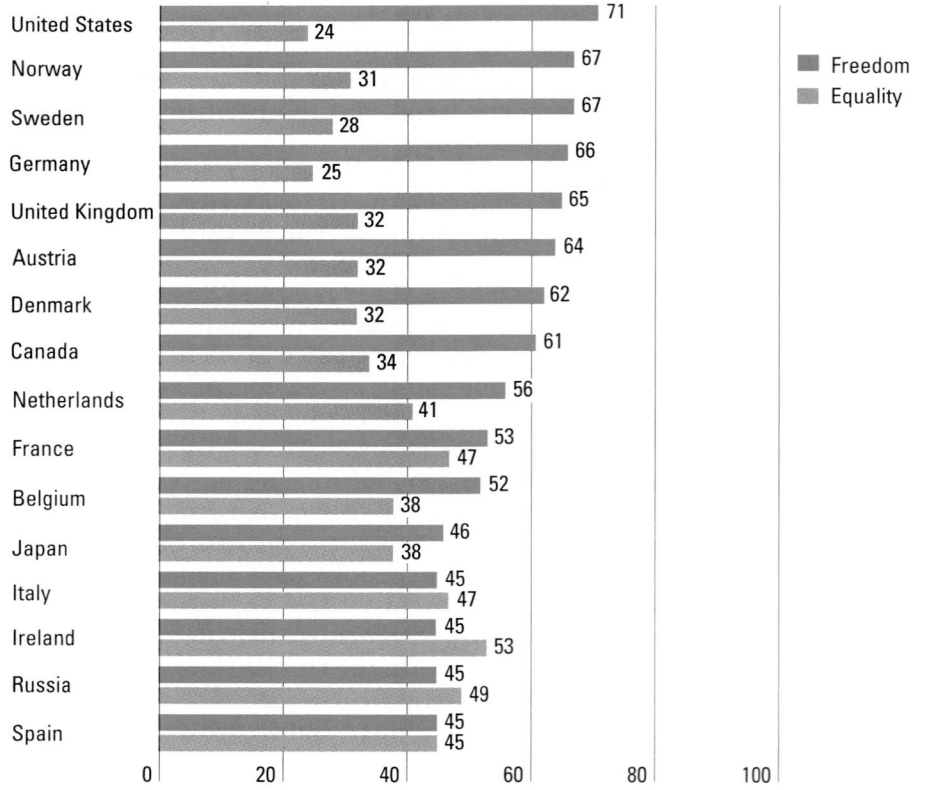

Percentage of respondents who chose freedom and equality

Country	Freedom	Equality
United States	71	24
Norway	67	31
Sweden	67	28
Germany	66	25
United Kingdom	65	32
Austria	64	32
Denmark	62	32
Canada	61	34
Netherlands	56	41
France	53	47
Belgium	52	38
Japan	46	38
Italy	45	47
Ireland	45	53
Russia	45	49
Spain	45	45

figure **1.1**

Ideology and the Scope of Government

We can classify political ideologies according to the scope of action that people are willing to allow government in dealing with social and economic problems. In this chart, the three rows map out various philosophical positions along an underlying continuum ranging from "most" to "least" government. Notice that conventional politics in the United States spans only a narrow portion of the theoretical possibilities for government action.

In popular usage, liberals favor a greater scope of government; conservatives want a narrower scope. But over time, the traditional distinction has eroded and now oversimplifies the differences between liberals and conservatives. See Figure 1.2 for a more discriminating classification of liberals and conservatives.

MOST GOVERNMENT   LEAST GOVERNMENT

POLITICAL THEORIES
Totalitarianism   Libertarianism   Anarchism

ECONOMIC THEORIES
Socialism   Capitalism   Laissez Faire

POPULAR POLITICAL LABELS IN AMERICA
Liberal   Conservative

totalitarianism
A political philosophy that advocates unlimited power for the government to enable it to control all sectors of society.

socialism
A form of rule in which the central government plays a strong role in regulating existing private industry and directing the economy, although it does allow some private ownership of productive capacity.

from the most government to the least government—and those that fall in between are shown in Figure 1.1.

Totalitarianism

Totalitarianism is the belief that government should have unlimited power. A totalitarian government controls all sectors of society: business, labor, education, religion, sports, the arts. A true totalitarian favors a network of laws, rules, and regulations that guides every aspect of individual behavior. The object is to produce a perfect society serving some master plan for "the common good." Totalitarianism has reached its terrifying full potential only in literature and films (for example, George Orwell's *1984*), but several real societies have come perilously close to "perfection." One thinks of Germany under Hitler and the Soviet Union under Stalin. Not many people openly profess totalitarianism today, but the concept is useful because it anchors one side of our continuum.

Socialism

Whereas totalitarianism refers to government in general, **socialism** pertains to government's role in the economy. Like communism, socialism is an economic system based on Marxist theory. Under socialism (and communism), the scope of government extends to ownership or control of the basic industries that produce goods and services. These include communications, mining, heavy industry, transportation, and power. Although socialism favors a strong role for government in regulating private industry and directing the economy, it allows more room than communism does for private ownership of productive capacity.

Many Americans equate socialism with the communism practiced in the old closed societies of the Soviet Union and Eastern Europe. But there is a difference. Although communism in theory was supposed to result in a "withering away" of the state, communist governments in practice

democratic socialism
A socialist form of government that guarantees civil liberties such as freedom of speech and religion. Citizens determine the extent of government activity through free elections and competitive political parties.

tended toward totalitarianism, controlling not just economic life but both political and social life through a dominant party organization. Some socialist governments, however, practice **democratic socialism.** They guarantee civil liberties (such as freedom of speech and freedom of religion) and allow their citizens to determine the extent of the government's activity through free elections and competitive political parties. Outside the United States, socialism is not universally viewed as inherently bad. In fact, the governments of Britain, Sweden, Germany, and France, among other democracies, have at times since World War II been avowedly socialist. More recently, the formerly communist regimes of Eastern Europe have abandoned the controlling role of government in their economies in favor of elements of capitalism.

Capitalism

capitalism
The system of government that favors free enterprise (privately owned businesses operating without government regulation).

Capitalism also relates to the government's role in the economy. In contrast to both socialism and communism, **capitalism** supports free enterprise—private businesses operating without government regulation. Some theorists, most notably economist Milton Friedman, argue that free enterprise is necessary for free politics.[24] This argument, that the economic system of capitalism is essential to democracy, contradicts the tenets of democratic socialism. Whether it is valid depends in part on our understanding of democracy, a subject discussed in Chapter 2.

The United States is decidedly a capitalist country, more so than Britain or most other Western nations. Despite the U.S. government's enormous budget, it owns or operates relatively few public enterprises. For example, railroads, airlines, and television stations are privately owned in the United States; these businesses are frequently owned by the government in other countries. But our government does extend its authority into the economic sphere, regulating private businesses and directing the overall economy. American liberals and conservatives both embrace capitalism, but they differ on the nature and amount of government intervention in the economy that is necessary or desirable.

Libertarianism

libertarianism
A political ideology that is opposed to all government action except as necessary to protect life and property.

libertarians
Those who are opposed to using government to promote either order or equality.

laissez faire
An economic doctrine that opposes any form of government intervention in business.

Libertarianism opposes all government action except what is necessary to protect life and property. **Libertarians** grudgingly recognize the necessity of government but believe that it should be as limited as possible. For example, libertarians grant the need for traffic laws to ensure safe and efficient automobile travel. But they oppose as a restriction on individual actions laws that set a minimum drinking age, and they even oppose laws outlawing marijuana and other drugs. Libertarians believe that social programs that provide food, clothing, and shelter are outside the proper scope of government. Helping the needy, they insist, should be a matter of individual choice. Libertarians also oppose government ownership of basic industries; in fact, they oppose any government interven-tion in the economy. This kind of economic policy is called **laissez faire,** a French phrase that means "let (people) do (as they please)." Such an extreme policy extends beyond the free enterprise advocated by most capitalists.

Libertarians are vocal advocates of hands-off government, in both the social and the economic sphere. Whereas those Americans who favor a broad scope of government action shun the description *socialist*, libertarians make no secret of their identity. The Libertarian Party ran candidates in every presidential election from 1972 through 2000. However, not one of these candidates won more than 1 million votes.

Do not confuse libertarians with liberals. The words are similar, but their meanings are quite different. *Libertarianism* draws on *liberty* as its root and means "absence of governmental constraint." In American political usage, *liberalism* evolved from the root word *liberal*. **Liberals** see a positive role for government in helping the disadvantaged. Over time, *liberal* has come to mean something closer to *generous*, in the sense that liberals (but not libertarians) support government spending on social programs. Libertarians find little benefit in any government social program.

liberals
Those who are willing to use government to promote freedom but not order.

Anarchism

Anarchism stands opposite totalitarianism on the political continuum. Anarchists oppose all government, in any form. As a political philosophy, **anarchism** values freedom above all else. Because all government involves some restriction on personal freedom (for example, forcing people to drive on one side of the road), a pure anarchist would object even to traffic laws. Like totalitarianism, anarchism is not a popular philosophy, but it does have adherents on the political fringes.

anarchism
A political philosophy that opposes government in any form.

Anarchists sparked the violence that disrupted the December 1999 meeting of the World Trade Organization (WTO) in Seattle (see Chapter 10). Labor unions protested the WTO meeting for failing to include labor rights on its agenda; environmental groups protested it for promoting economic development at the expense of the environment. But anarchists were against the WTO on *principle*—for concentrating the power of multinational corporations in a shadowy "world government." Discussing old and new forms of anarchy, Joseph Kahn said, "Nothing has revived anarchism like globalization."[25] When the World Bank held its August 2000 meeting in Prague, an anarchists' Web site promised to "Turn Prague into Seattle."[26] While anarchists were battling Czech police in Prague, anarchists back in Oregon were planning protests at the Democratic party convention in Los Angeles.[27] Although anarchism is not a popular philosophy, it is not merely a theoretical category.

★

"A" Is for Anarchism

Anarchism as a philosophy views government as an unnecessary evil used by the wealthy to exploit the poor. Scores of young anarchists gathered in Seattle in 1999, seeking to disrupt the meeting of the World Trade Organization.

Liberals and Conservatives: The Narrow Middle

As shown in Figure 1.1, practical politics in the United States ranges over only the central portion of the continuum. The extreme positions—totalitarianism and anarchism—are rarely argued in public debates. And in this era of distrust of "big government," few American politicians would openly advocate socialism (although one did in 1990 and won election to Congress as an independent candidate). On the other hand, almost 300 people ran for Congress in 2000 as candidates of the Libertarian Party. Although none won, American libertarians are sufficiently vocal to be heard in the debate over the role of government.

Still, most of that debate is limited to a narrow range of political thought. On one side are people commonly called *liberals*; on the other are *conservatives*. In popular usage, liberals favor more government, conserv-

conservatives
Those who are willing to use government to promote order but not equality.

atives less. This distinction is clear when the issue is government spending to provide public goods. Liberals favor generous government support for education, wildlife protection, public transportation, and a whole range of social programs. **Conservatives** want smaller government budgets and fewer government programs. They support free enterprise and argue against government job programs, regulation of business, and legislation of working conditions and wage rates.

But in other areas, liberal and conservative ideologies are less consistent. In theory, liberals favor government activism, yet they oppose government regulation of abortion. In theory, conservatives oppose government activism, yet they support government control of the publication of sexually explicit material. What's going on? Are American political attitudes hopelessly contradictory, or is something missing in our analysis of these ideologies today? Actually, something is missing. To understand the liberal and conservative stances on political issues, we have to look not only at the scope of government action but also at the purpose of government action. That is, to understand a political ideology, it is necessary to understand how it incorporates the values of freedom, order, and equality.

AMERICAN POLITICAL IDEOLOGIES AND THE PURPOSE OF GOVERNMENT

Much of American politics revolves around the two dilemmas just described: freedom versus order and freedom versus equality. The two dilemmas do not account for all political conflict, but they help us gain insight into the workings of politics and organize the seemingly chaotic world of political events, actors, and issues.

Can You Explain Why...
conservatives might favor *more* government than liberals?

Liberals Versus Conservatives: The New Differences

Liberals and conservatives are different, but their differences no longer hinge on the narrow question of the government's role in providing public goods. Liberals still favor more government and conservatives less, but this is no longer the critical difference between them. Today, that difference stems from their attitudes toward the purpose of government. Conservatives support the original purpose of government—maintaining social order. They are willing to use the coercive power of the state to force citizens to be orderly. They favor firm police action, swift and severe punishment for criminals, and more laws regulating behavior. Conservatives would not stop with defining, preventing, and punishing crime, however. They tend to want to preserve traditional patterns of social relations—the domestic role of women and the importance of religion in school and family life, for example.

Liberals are less likely than conservatives to want to use government power to maintain order. In general, liberals are more tolerant of alternative lifestyles—for example, homosexual behavior. Liberals do not shy away from using government coercion, but they use it for a different purpose—to promote equality. They support laws that ensure equal treatment of homosexuals in employment, housing, and education; laws that require the busing of schoolchildren to achieve racial equality; laws that force private businesses to hire and promote women and members of minority groups; laws that require public transportation to provide equal access to the disabled; and laws that order cities and states to reapportion election districts so that minority voters can elect minority candidates to public office.

Conservatives do not oppose equality, but they do not value it to the extent of using the government's power to enforce equality. For liberals, the use of that power to promote equality is both valid and necessary.

A Two-Dimensional Classification of Ideologies

To classify liberal and conservative ideologies more accurately, we have to incorporate the values of freedom, order, and equality into the classification. We can do this using the model in Figure 1.2. It depicts the conflicting values along two separate dimensions, each anchored in maximum freedom at the lower left. One dimension extends horizontally from maximum freedom on the left to maximum order on the right. The other extends vertically from maximum freedom at the bottom to maximum equality at the top. Each box represents a different ideological type: libertarians, liberals, conservatives, and communitarians.[28]

Libertarians value freedom more than order or equality. (We will use this term for people who have libertarian tendencies but may not accept the whole philosophy.) In practical terms, libertarians want minimal government intervention in both the economic and the social sphere. For example, they oppose affirmative action and laws that restrict transmission of sexually explicit material.

Liberals value freedom more than order but not more than equality. Liberals oppose laws that ban sexually explicit publications but support affirmative action. Conservatives value freedom more than equality but would restrict freedom to preserve social order. Conservatives oppose affirmative action but favor laws that restrict pornography.

Finally, we arrive at the ideological type positioned at the upper right in Figure 1.2. This group values both equality and order more than freedom. Its members support both affirmative action and laws that restrict pornography. We will call this new group *communitarians*. The *Oxford English Dictionary* (1989) defines a communitarian as "a member of a community formed to put into practice communistic or socialistic theories." The term is used more narrowly in contemporary politics to reflect the philosophy of the Communitarian Network, a political movement founded by sociologist Amitai Etzioni.[29] This movement rejects both the liberal-conservative classification and the libertarian argument that "individuals should be left on their own to pursue their choices, rights, and self-interests."[30] Like liberals, Etzioni's communitarians believe that there is a role for government in helping the disadvantaged. Like conservatives, they believe that government should be used to promote moral values—preserving the family through more stringent divorce laws, protecting against AIDS through testing programs, and limiting the dissemination of pornography, for example.[31] Indeed, some observers have labeled President George W. Bush as a communitarian (see Chapter 12 on the presidency).

The Communitarian Network is not dedicated to big government, however. According to its platform, "The government should step in only to the extent that other social subsystems fail, rather than seek to replace them."[32] Nevertheless, in recognizing the collective nature of society, the Network's platform clearly distinguishes its philosophy from that of libertarianism:

IDEAlog aks you to classify yourself in one of the four categories in Figure 1.2 and then asks twenty opinion questions to test your self-classification.

1.2   Ideologies: A Two-Dimensional Framework

The four ideological types are defined by the values they favor in resolving the two major dilemmas of government: How much freedom should be sacrificed in pursuit of order and equality, respectively? Test yourself by thinking about the values that are most important to you. Which box in the figure best represents your combination of values?

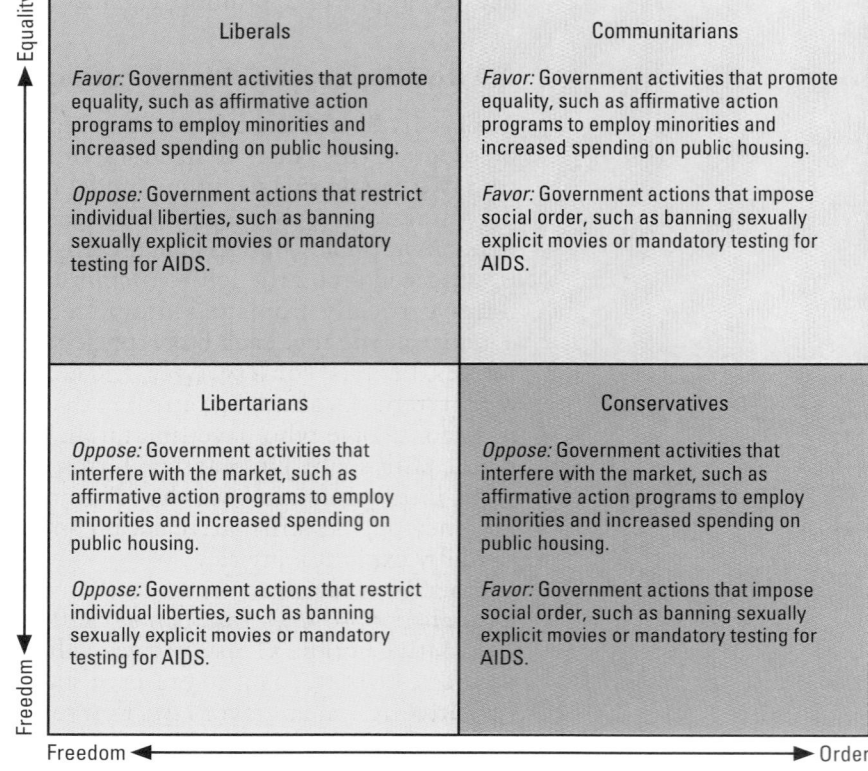

THE ORIGINAL DILEMMA

It has been argued by libertarians that responsibilities are a personal matter, that individuals are to judge which responsibilities they accept as theirs. As we see it, responsibilities are anchored in community. Reflecting the diverse moral voices of their citizens, responsive communities define what is expected of people; they educate their members to accept these values; and they praise them when they do and frown upon them when they do not.[33]

Although it clearly embraces the Communitarian Network's philosophy, our definition of communitarian (small *c*) is broader and more in keeping with the dictionary definition. Thus, **communitarians** favor government programs that promote both order and equality, in keeping with socialist theory.[34]

By analyzing political ideologies on two dimensions rather than one, we can explain why people can seem to be liberal on one issue (favoring a broader scope of government action) and conservative on another (favoring less government action). The answer hinges on the purpose of a given gov-

communitarians
Those who are willing to use government to promote both order and equality.

ernment action: which value does it promote, order or equality? According to our typology, only libertarians and communitarians are consistent in their attitude toward the scope of government activity, whatever its purpose. Libertarians value freedom so highly that they oppose most government efforts to enforce either order or equality. Communitarians (in our usage) are inclined to trade freedom for both order and equality. Liberals and conservatives, on the other hand, favor or oppose government activity depending on its purpose. As you will learn in Chapter 5, large groups of Americans fall into each of the four ideological categories. Because Americans increasingly choose four different resolutions to the original and modern dilemmas of government, the simple labels of *liberal* and *conservative* no longer describe contemporary political ideologies as well as they did in the 1930s, 1940s, and 1950s.

SUMMARY

The challenge of democracy lies in making difficult choices—choices that inevitably bring important values into conflict. This chapter has outlined a normative framework for analyzing the policy choices that arise in the pursuit of the purposes of government.

The three major purposes of government are maintaining order, providing public goods, and promoting equality. In pursuing these objectives, every government infringes on individual freedom. But the degree of that infringement depends on the government's (and, by extension, its citizens') commitment to order and equality. What we have, then, are two dilemmas. The first—the original dilemma—centers on the conflict between freedom and order. The second—the modern dilemma—focuses on the conflict between freedom and equality.

Some people use political ideologies to help them resolve the conflicts that arise in political decision making. These ideologies define the scope and purpose of government. At opposite extremes of the continuum are totalitarianism, which supports government intervention in every aspect of society, and anarchism, which rejects government entirely. An important step back from totalitarianism is socialism. Democratic socialism, an economic system, favors government ownership of basic industries but preserves civil liberties. Capitalism, another economic system, promotes free enterprise. A significant step short of anarchism is libertarianism, which allows government to protect life and property but little else.

In the United States, the terms *liberal* and *conservative* are used to describe a narrow range toward the center of the political continuum. The usage is probably accurate when the scope of government action is being discussed. That is, liberals support a broader role for government than do conservatives. But when both the scope and the purpose of government are considered, a different, sharper distinction emerges. Conservatives may want less government, but not at the price of maintaining order. In other words, they are willing to use the coercive power of government to impose social order. Liberals, too, are willing to use the coercive powers of government, but for a different purpose—promoting equality.

It is easier to understand the differences among libertarians, liberals, conservatives, and communitarians and their views on the scope of government if the values of freedom, order, and equality are incorporated into the description of their political ideologies. Libertarians choose freedom over both order and equality. Communitarians are willing to sacrifice freedom for both order and equality. Liberals value freedom more than order and equality more than freedom. Conservatives value order more than freedom and freedom more than equality.

The concepts of government objectives, values, and political ideologies appear repeatedly in this book as we determine who favors what government action and why. So far, we have said little about how government should make its decisions. In Chapter 2, we complete our normative framework for evaluating American politics by examining the nature of democratic theory. There, we introduce two key concepts for analyzing how democratic governments make decisions.

★ Selected Readings

Ebenstein, William, and Edwin Fogelman. *Today's Isms: Socialism, Capitalism, Fascism, Communism, and Libertarianism.* 11th ed. Englewood Cliffs, N.J.: Prentice-Hall, 1999. This standard source describes the history of the five major "isms" and relates each to developments in contemporary politics. It is concise, informative, and readable.

Etzioni, Amitai. *The New Golden Rule: Community and Morality in a Democratic Society.* New York: Basic Books, 1996. Etzioni examines the balance between liberty and morality in government. He argues for basing order on moral commitments rather than law.

Murray, Charles. *What It Means to Be a Libertarian: A Personal Interpretation.* New York: Broadway Books, 1997. This brief book makes the case for limiting government and promoting personal freedom. Among the government functions that Murray would limit are the regulation of products and services, the development and regulation of energy, housing and urban development, and social security and Medicare programs.

Van Creveld, Martin. *The Rise and Decline of the State.* New York: Cambridge University Press, 1999. A thoughtful survey of the rise of the modern state in the mid–seventh century through what Van Creveld sees as its decline, beginning in 1975. He concludes that the international system is becoming more hierarchical, with more power accumulated in supranational institutions.

 ## Internet Exercises

1. *Freedom versus order: The case of racial profiling*

Justice Talking is a public radio program, created by the Annenberg Public Policy Center at the University of Pennsylvania, designed to examine cases and controversies that appear before the nation's courts. Recently, Justice Talking addressed the issue of racial profiling and considered whether it constituted overt discrimination or a legitimate tool to stop crime.

• Go to the Justice Talking Web site at <**http://www.justicetalking.org/**>, and follow the site's link to an index of its past shows. There you will find the program entitled "Driving While Black: Racial Profiling on America's Highways."

• Listen to these two portions of the broadcast: Time 0:00–2:35 and 20:00–26:15. How is the controversy of racial profiling a modern-day illustration of the nation's original dilemma of freedom versus order?

2. *Freedom versus equality: The case of school vouchers*

Public school vouchers are one of the most controversial school reform issues on the political agenda today. Two groups that have opposing views on this issue are the National Education Association (NEA), and the Milton and Rose D. Friedman Foundation for School Choice.

• Go to the NEA's Web site at **http://www.nea.org/** and use the site's search function to locate a January 1999 issue paper entitled "Private School Vouchers." Read this short piece. Then go to the Friedman Foundation's page at <**http://www. friedmanfoundation.org/**>. Follow the link to "understanding school choice" to locate a series of frequently asked questions about school vouchers.

• How could a citizen who is against vouchers argue that vouchers sacrifice equality in an ill-fated attempt to promote individual freedom? How could a citizen who is for vouchers argue that opposing vouchers sacrifices freedom and is an ill-fated attempt to guarantee equality?

Majoritarian or Pluralist Democracy?

THEY LAUGHED WHILE THEY SHOT THEIR CLASSMATES. Eric Harris and Dylan Klebold, students at Columbine High School in Littleton, Colorado, murdered twelve students and a teacher during a shocking rampage at the school in April 1999. Two dozen other students were wounded. When they were done, the two committed suicide in the school library. Harris and Klebold, described as social misfits by classmates, had in common their lack of popularity, a love of violent computer games, and a hatred of jocks at their school.

The nation was stunned by the violence, and debate immediately ensued about the desirability of tighter gun control laws. Robyn Anderson, an eighteen-year-old friend of Harris and Klebold, bought a semiautomatic rifle and two sawed-off shotguns for them at a gun show.[1] No background check was required, so there was no way of determining if she was a convicted felon or a drug dealer. It's possible, of course, that Harris and Klebold would have gotten guns from other sources if their friend hadn't purchased them at the gun show. What is clear, however, is that it's easy to obtain a gun in America.

Critics charge that it's too easy to get a gun and that the country's weak gun control laws are at the root of the high levels of violence in the United States. When polled, Americans show a decided preference for gun control. Three-quarters of the public favor the registration of all handguns. Four out of five voice support for a requirement that all guns sold be equipped with trigger locks. Sixty-nine percent favor a law that would require all handgun owners to obtain a special license to own a handgun.[2]

In the wake of the Columbine tragedy, gun control supporters saw an opportunity for new legislation, especially for a new requirement that gun shows run a background check on those purchasing a weapon. This requirement would close a loophole in existing law that requires a background check of buyers at a retail gun store. Despite the overwhelming support of the American people for gun control laws, the proposed legislation stalled in Congress, where gun control laws usually flounder. Even though the public has a decided preference for stronger gun control laws, the National Rifle Association and other pro-gun groups have been able to stop most proposals for restricting the sale and licensing of pistols, rifles, and other related weapons. Even though the National Rifle Association represents a minority of the population, this interest group speaks for people who have very intense views and regard gun control as an intolerable abridgement of their Second Amendment right of "the people to keep and bear arms."

The tragedy at Columbine High School prompted efforts by gun control advocates to put some new restrictions into place. Congress rejected such efforts, sensitive to the intense passions of those who believe that gun ownership is a fundamental right and should not be subject to regulation by government. In Colorado and Oregon, where gun control referenda appeared on the 2000 ballot, voters overwhelmingly approved them.

This ability of a small minority to prevail over a less organized majority is a common feature of American democracy. While Congress could not act, gun control advocates in Colorado mobilized a campaign to overcome the interest group politics that stalled the effort to close the gun show loophole. The gun control supporters got an initiative placed on the 2000 Colorado ballot, and 70 percent of the state's voters approved the measure. Clearly, the Columbine tragedy affected voters, and the majority easily turned away efforts by the National Rifle Association to defeat the statewide initiative.

In Chapter 1 we discussed three basic values that underlie what government should do. In this chapter we examine how government should decide what to do. In particular, we set forth criteria for judging whether a government's decision-making process is democratic. This discussion leads us to two contrasting conceptions of democracy, one emphasizing majority rule and the other acknowledging the role of interest groups in influencing the decisions of government.

THE THEORY OF DEMOCRATIC GOVERNMENT

autocracy
A system of government in which the power to govern is concentrated in the hands of one individual.

The origins of democratic theory lie in ancient Greek political thought. Greek philosophers classified governments according to the number of citizens involved in the process. Imagine a continuum running from rule by one person, through rule by a few, to rule by many.

At one extreme is an **autocracy,** in which one individual has the power to make all important decisions. The concentration of power in the hands of one person (usually a monarch) was a more common form of government in earlier historical periods. Some countries are still ruled autocratically, such as Iraq under Saddam Hussein.

Oligarchy puts government power in the hands of an elite. At one time, the nobility or the major landowners commonly ruled as an aristocracy.

Smooth Road, Rocky Road

After the collapse of communism in Eastern Europe, elections in the Slovak Republic went relatively smoothly as democracy easily took hold in the new country. In Zimbabwe, however, the road to democracy has been much more difficult. The 2000 election there was tainted by pre-election violence and was not considered honest by international observers.

oligarchy
A system of government in which power is concentrated in the hands of a few people.

democracy
A system of government in which, in theory, the people rule, either directly or indirectly.

Today, military leaders are often the rulers in countries governed by an oligarchy.

At the other extreme of the continuum is **democracy,** which means rule by the people. Most scholars believe that the United States, Britain, France, and other countries in Western Europe are genuine democracies. Others contend that these countries only appear to be democracies because they hold free elections, but that they are actually run by wealthy business elites, out for their own benefit. Nevertheless, most people today agree that governments should be democratic.

The Meaning and Symbolism of Democracy

Americans have a simple answer to the question, "Who should govern?" It is, "The people." Unfortunately, this answer is too simple. It fails to define who *the people* are. Should we include young children? Recent immigrants? Illegal aliens? This answer also fails to tell us how the people should do the governing. Should they be assembled in a stadium? Vote by mail? Choose others to govern for them? We need to take a closer look at what "government by the people" really means.

The word *democracy* originated in Greek writings around the fifth century B.C. *Demos* referred to the common people, the masses; *kratos* meant "power." The ancient Greeks were afraid of democracy—rule by rank-and-file citizens. That fear is evident in the term *demagogue*. We use the term today to refer to a politician who appeals to and often deceives the masses by manipulating their emotions and prejudices.

Many centuries after the Greeks first defined democracy, the idea still carried the connotation of mob rule. When George Washington was president, opponents of a new political party disparagingly called it a *democratic* party. No one would do that in politics today. In fact, the term has become so popular that the names of more than 20 percent of the world's political parties contain some variation of the word *democracy.*[3]

There are two major schools of thought about what constitutes democracy. The first believes democracy is a form of government. It emphasizes the procedures that enable the people to govern—meeting to discuss issues, voting in elections, running for public office. The second sees democracy in the substance of government policies, in freedom of religion and the provision for human needs. The procedural approach focuses on how decisions are made; the substantive approach is concerned with what government does.

The Procedural View of Democracy

procedural democratic theory
A view of democracy as being embodied in a decision-making process that involves universal participation, political equality, majority rule, and responsiveness.

Procedural democratic theory sets forth principles that describe how government should make decisions. The principles address three distinct questions:

1. *Who* should participate in decision making?

2. *How much* should each participant's vote count?

3. *How many* votes are needed to reach a decision?

According to procedural democratic theory, all adults should participate in government decision making; everyone within the boundaries of the political community should be allowed to vote. If some people, such as recent immigrants, are prohibited from participating, they are excluded only for practical or political reasons. The theory of democracy itself does not exclude any adults from participation. We refer to this principle as **universal participation.**

universal participation
The concept that everyone in a democracy should participate in governmental decision making.

How much should each participant's vote count? According to procedural theory, all votes should be counted *equally.* This is the principle of **political equality.**

political equality
Equality in political decision making: one vote per person, with all votes counted equally.

Note that universal participation and political equality are two distinct principles. It is not enough for everyone to participate in a decision; all votes must carry equal weight. President Abraham Lincoln reportedly once took a vote among his cabinet members and found that they all opposed his position on an issue. He summarized the vote and the decision this way: "Seven noes, one aye—the ayes have it."[4] Everyone participated, but Lincoln's vote counted more than all the others combined. (No one ever said that presidents have to run their cabinets democratically.)

majority rule
The principle—basic to procedural democratic theory—that the decision of a group must reflect the preference of more than half of those participating; a simple majority.

Finally, how many votes are needed to reach a decision? Procedural theory prescribes that a group should decide to do what the majority of its participants (50 percent plus one person) wants to do. This principle is called **majority rule.** (If participants divide over more than two alternatives and none receives a simple majority, the principle usually defaults to *plurality rule,* under which the group does what most participants want.)

A Complication: Direct Versus Indirect Democracy

participatory democracy
A system of government where rank-and-file citizens rule themselves rather than electing representatives to govern on their behalf.

The three principles—universal participation, political equality, and majority rule—are widely recognized as necessary for democratic decision making. Small, simple societies can meet these principles with a direct or **participatory democracy,** in which all members of the group meet to make decisions, observing political equality and majority rule. The origins of participatory democracy go back to the Greek city-state, where the important decisions of government were made by the adult citizens meeting in an assembly. The people ruled themselves rather than having a small number of notables rule on their behalf. (In Athens, the people who were permitted to attend the assemblies did not include women, slaves, and those whose families had not lived there for generations. Thus, participation was not universal. Still, the Greek city-state represented a dramatic transformation in the theory of government.)[5]

Something close to participatory democracy is practiced in some New England villages, where rank-and-file citizens gather in a town meeting, often just once a year, to make key community decisions together. A town meeting is impractical in large cities, although there are some cities that have incorporated participatory democracy in their decision-making processes by instituting forms of neighborhood government. For example, in Birmingham, Alabama; Dayton, Ohio; Portland, Oregon; and St. Paul, Minnesota, each area of the city is governed by a neighborhood council. The neighborhood councils have authority over zoning and land use questions, and they usually control some funds for the development of projects within their boundaries. All adult residents of a neighborhood may participate in the neighborhood council meetings, and the larger city government respects their decisions.[6] In Chicago, the school system uses participatory democracy. Each school is primarily governed by a parents' council and not by the citywide school board.[7]

Philosopher Jean Jacques Rousseau contended that true democracy is impossible unless all citizens gather to make decisions and supervise the government. Rousseau said that decisions of government should embody the general will, and "will cannot be represented."[8] Yet in the United States and virtually all other democracies, participatory democracy is rare. Few cities have decentralized their governments and turned power over to their neighborhoods.

Participatory democracy is commonly rejected on the grounds that in large, complex societies we need professional, full-time government officials to study problems, formulate solutions, and administer programs. Also, the assumption is that relatively few people will take part in participatory government. This, in fact, turns out to be the case. In a study of neighborhood councils in the cities mentioned above, only 16.6 percent of residents took part in at least one meeting during a two-year period.[9] In other respects, participatory democracy works rather well on the neighborhood level. Yet even if participatory democracy is appropriate for neighborhoods or small villages, how could it work for the national government? We cannot all gather at the Capitol in Washington to decide defense policy.

The framers of the Constitution were convinced that participatory democracy on the national level was undesirable and instead instituted **representative democracy.** In such a system, citizens participate in government by electing public officials to make decisions on their behalf. Elected officials are expected to represent the voters' views and interests—that is, to serve as the agents of the citizenry and to act for them.

Within the context of representative democracy, we adhere to the principles of universal participation, political equality, and majority rule to guarantee that elections are democratic. But what happens after the election? The elected representatives might not make the decisions the people would have made had they gathered for the same purpose. To account for this possibility in representative government, procedural theory provides

representative democracy
A system of government where citizens elect public officials to govern on their behalf.

responsiveness
A decision-making principle, necessitated by representative government, that implies that elected representatives should do what the majority of people wants.

a fourth decision-making principle: **responsiveness.** Elected representatives should respond to public opinion. This does not mean that legislators simply cast their ballots on the basis of whether the people back home want alternative A or alternative B. Issues are not usually so straightforward. Rather, responsiveness means following the general contours of public opinion in formulating complex pieces of legislation.[10]

By adding responsiveness to deal with the case of indirect democracy, we have four principles of procedural democracy:

- Universal participation
- Political equality
- Majority rule
- Government responsiveness to public opinion

The Substantive View of Democracy

According to procedural theory, the principle of responsiveness is absolute. The government should do what the majority wants, regardless of what that is. At first this seems a reasonable way to protect the rights of citizens in a representative democracy. But think for a minute. Christians are the vast majority of the U.S. population. Suppose that the Christian majority backs a constitutional amendment to require Bible reading in public schools, that the amendment is passed by Congress, and that it is ratified by the states. From a strictly procedural view, the action would be democratic. But what about freedom of religion? What about the rights of minorities? To limit the government's responsiveness to public opinion, we must look outside procedural democratic theory, to substantive democratic theory.

substantive democratic theory
The view that democracy is embodied in the substance of government policies rather than in the policymaking procedure.

Substantive democratic theory focuses on the substance of government policies, not on the procedures followed in making those policies. It argues that in a democratic government, certain principles must be incorporated into government policies. Substantive theorists would reject a law that requires Bible reading in schools because it would violate a substantive principle, freedom of religion. The core of our substantive principles of democracy is embedded in the Bill of Rights and other amendments to the Constitution.

In defining the principles that underlie democratic government—and the policies of that government—most substantive theorists agree on a basic criterion: government policies should guarantee civil liberties (freedom of behavior, such as freedom of religion and freedom of expression) and civil rights (powers or privileges that government may not arbitrarily deny to individuals, such as protection against discrimination in employment and housing). According to this standard, the claim that the United States is a democracy rests on its record of ensuring its citizens these liberties and rights. (We look at how good this record is in Chapters 15 and 16.)

Agreement among substantive theorists breaks down when the discussion moves from civil rights to social rights (adequate health care, quality education, decent housing) and economic rights (private property, steady employment). They disagree most sharply on whether a government must

Seeking Shelter

Some argue that a democratic government is one that promotes social and economic rights. There is little agreement in this country, however, concerning what qualifies as rights requiring substantive policy measures. This homeless man in Washington, D.C., has firm beliefs on one such issue.

Can You Explain Why...
basic human needs are not rights?

promote social equality to qualify as a democracy. For example, must a state guarantee unemployment benefits and adequate public housing to be called democratic? Some insist that policies that promote social equality are essential to democratic government.[11] Others restrict the requirements of substantive democracy to those policies that safeguard civil liberties and civil rights. Americans differ considerably from the citizens of most other western democracies in their view of the government's responsibility to provide social policies (see Compared with What? 2.1).

A theorist's political ideology tends to explain his or her position on what democracy really requires in substantive policies. Conservative theorists have a narrow view of the scope of democratic government and a narrow view of the social and economic rights guaranteed by that government. Liberal theorists believe that a democratic government should guarantee its citizens a much broader spectrum of social and economic rights. In later chapters, we review important social and economic policies that our government has actually followed over time. Keep in mind, however, that what the government has done in the past is not necessarily a correct guide to what a democratic government should do.

Procedural Democracy Versus Substantive Democracy

The problem with the substantive view of democracy is that it does not provide clear, precise criteria that allow us to determine whether a government is democratic. It is, in fact, open to unending arguments over which government policies are truly democratic. Substantive theorists are free to promote their pet values—separation of church and state, guaranteed employment, equal rights for women, whatever—under the guise of substantive democracy.

2.1 Is Government Responsible?

One of the basic ideological divisions in American society is between those who believe that it is the government's responsibility to provide jobs and incomes to those who are unemployed and those who believe that the government should provide only minimal, transitional assistance while people hunt for a job. In most other western democracies, there is much more support for the view that jobs and incomes for the unemployed are a right. Indeed, as demonstrated in this chart, there are some countries where there is a consensus that it is the government's responsibility to provide such progress.

Source: "Americans Remain Less Inclined to Look to Government Than Citizens of Other Industrial Democracies," *Public Perspective* 9 (February/March 1998), p. 32.

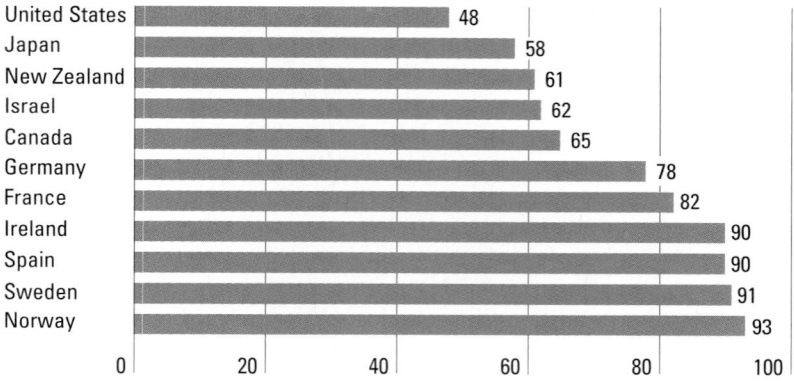

Percentage agreeing that government is responsible for providing a decent standard of living for the unemployed

---

minority rights
The benefits of government that cannot be denied to any citizens by majority decisions.

The procedural viewpoint also has a problem. Although it presents specific criteria for democratic government, those criteria can produce undesirable social policies, such as those that prey on minorities. This clashes with **minority rights**—the idea that all citizens are entitled to certain things that cannot be denied by the majority. Opinions proliferate on what those "certain things" are, but all would agree, for example, on freedom of religion. One way to protect minority rights is to limit the principle of majority rule—by requiring a two-thirds majority or some other extraordinary majority for decisions on certain subjects, for example. Another way is to put the issue in the Constitution, beyond the reach of majority rule.

The issue of prayer in school is a good example of the limits on majority rule. No matter how large, majorities in Congress cannot pass a law to permit organized prayer in public schools because the Supreme Court has determined that the Constitution forbids such a law. The Constitution could be changed so that it would no longer protect religious minorities, but amending the Constitution is a cumbersome process that involves extra-ordinary majorities. When limits such as these are put on the principle of majority rule, the minority often rules instead.

Clearly, then, procedural democracy and substantive democracy are not always compatible. In choosing one instead of the other, we are also choosing to focus on either procedures or policies. As authors of this text, we favor a compromise. On the whole, we favor the procedural conception of democracy because it more closely approaches the classical definition of democracy—"government by the people." And procedural democracy is founded on clear, well-established rules for decision making. But the theory has a serious drawback: it allows a democratic government to enact policies that can violate the substantive principles of democracy. Thus, pure procedural democracy should be diluted so that minority rights and civil liberties are guaranteed as part of the structure of government. If the compromise seems familiar, it is: the approach has been used in the course of American history to balance legitimate minority and majority interests.

INSTITUTIONAL MODELS OF DEMOCRACY

A small group can agree to make democratic decisions directly by using the principles of universal participation, political equality, and majority rule. But even the smallest nations have too many citizens to permit participatory democracy at the national level. If nations want democracy, they must achieve it through some form of representative government, electing officials to make decisions. Even then, democratic government is not guaranteed. Governments must have a way to determine what the people want, as well as some way to translate those wants into decisions. In other words, democratic government requires institutional mechanisms—established procedures and organizations—to translate public opinion into government policy (and thus be responsive). Elections, political parties, legislatures, and interest groups (which we discuss in later chapters) are all examples of institutional mechanisms in politics.

Some democratic theorists favor institutions that closely tie government decisions to the desires of the majority of citizens. If most citizens want laws banning the sale of pornography, the government should outlaw pornography. If citizens want more money spent on defense and less on social welfare (or vice versa), the government should act accordingly. For these theorists, the essence of democratic government is majority rule and responsiveness.

Other theorists place less importance on the principles of majority rule and responsiveness. They do not believe in relying heavily on mass opinion; instead, they favor institutions that allow groups of citizens to defend their interests in the public policymaking process. Health care is a good example. Everyone cares about it, but it is a complex problem with many competing issues at stake. What is critical here is to allow differing interests to participate so that all sides have the opportunity to influence policies as they are developed.

Both schools hold a procedural view of democracy, but they differ in how they interpret "government by the people." We can summarize the theoretical positions by using two alternative models of democracy. As a model, each is a hypothetical plan, a blueprint for achieving democratic government through institutional mechanisms. The majoritarian model values participation by the people in general; the pluralist model values participation by the people in groups.

The Majoritarian Model of Democracy

majoritarian model of democracy
The classical theory of democracy in which government by the people is interpreted as government by the majority of the people.

The **majoritarian model of democracy** relies on our intuitive, elemental notion of what is fair. It interprets "government by the people" to mean government by the *majority* of the people. The majoritarian model tries to approximate the people's role in a direct democracy within the limitations of representative government. To force the government to respond to public opinion, the majoritarian model depends on several mechanisms that allow the people to participate directly.

The popular election of government officials is the primary mechanism for democratic government in the majoritarian model. Citizens are expected to control their representatives' behavior by choosing wisely in the first place and by reelecting or voting out public officials according to their performance. Elections fulfill the first three principles of procedural democratic theory: universal participation, political equality, and majority rule. The prospect of reelection and the threat of defeat at the polls are expected to motivate public officials to meet the fourth criterion: responsiveness.

Usually, we think of elections only as mechanisms for choosing among candidates for public office. Majoritarian theorists also see them as a means for deciding government policies. An election on a policy issue is called a *referendum.* When a policy question is put on the ballot by citizens circulating petitions and gathering a required minimum number of signatures, it is called an *initiative.* Twenty-one states allow their legislatures to put referenda before the voters and give their citizens the right to place initiatives on the ballot. Five other states provide for one mechanism or the other.[12]

Statewide initiatives and referenda have been used to decide a wide variety of important questions, many of which have national implications. Even though they are instruments of majoritarian democracy, initiatives are often sponsored by interest groups who speak for a minority sector of the population and are trying to mobilize broad-based support for a particular policy.[13] In the 2000 election, Death with Dignity and the Hemlock Society worked to get an initiative on the Maine ballot to legalize doctor-assisted suicide for those who are terminally ill and wish to end their lives. Oregon is currently the only state with physician-assisted suicide. Voters in Maine narrowly defeated the initiative.[14] Another example is Proposition 209 in California. Voters there passed an initiative in 1996 that put an end to affirmative action in admissions to the state's university system (see Politics in a Changing America 2.1).

In the United States, no provisions exist for referenda at the federal level. Some other countries do allow policy questions to be put before the public. For example, in Great Britain, Scottish and Welsh voters decided in 1997 to set up regional parliaments to handle local services and to administer programs dealing with education, health, and transportation. The measure barely passed in Wales, but in Scotland, where it gained overwhelming support, the voters even granted the new legislature the power to raise taxes. Tony Blair, Great Britain's prime minister, calls this process devolution and contends that these assemblies will bring government closer to the people.[15]

★ **politics in a changing america**

2.1 Coping with the End of Affirmative Action at the University of California

Affirmative action is one of the most controversial and emotional issues in American politics. Corporations, government, and nonprofits commonly use policies designed to increase the numbers of employees, contractors, or students who come from traditionally underrepresented populations. For minorities, such as African Americans and Hispanic Americans, affirmative action is seen as an appropriate response to long-term patterns of discrimination that made it difficult for members of those groups to advance in society. For some whites, affirmative action is seen as "affirmative discrimination." That is, some in the majority view the policy as a means of disregarding merit so that more minorities can get better jobs or admission to an elite school.

Nowhere has this debate been more divisive than in California where, in the year 2000, the state became a majority-minority state. In terms of population all minority groups combined are now a slightly larger segment of the entire state than whites. Nevertheless, whites are still a majority of voters because a significant portion of the state's minorities are lower in socioeconomic status (and thus are less likely to participate in politics) or are recent immigrants. (It's important to note that not all minorities support affirmative action, and many Asian Americans in California—a large minority there—are critical of it.)

When an initiative to end affirmative action was put on the ballot in 1996, it passed by a 54 to 46 margin. The University of California's Board of Regents had already voted to end af-

firmative action at the eight campuses of the state system, but Proposition 209 made the change a matter of law and made it much more difficult for the university to reinstate such policies.

Admission to the University of California is no small prize. The entire system is highly respected, and the two flagship campuses at Berkeley and Los Angeles are among the most highly respected research universities in the world. For the class entering in the fall of 2000, Berkeley received 32,696 applicants for approximately 4,000 slots. UCLA received a total of 37,460 applications—more than any other college in the United States—for its incoming freshman class of 4,200. Members of a recent freshman class admitted to Berkeley had an average combined SAT score of 1390 out of 1600.

The University of California, like so many other schools, was willing to take minorities with modestly lower test scores because it believed that merit is relative. Those growing up in poorer neighborhoods with fewer opportunities but who succeed in school are to be admired for their determination. In the University of California admissions process, those who take advanced placement (AP) courses get additional points in the calculation that is made for each candidate. But more than half of California's high schools offer no AP courses and most of those are in minority neighborhoods. That's just one of the reasons why admissions officers feel that more than scores and grades need to be considered.

Americans strongly favor instituting a system of national referenda. In a survey, 65 percent of those queried indicated that voters should have a direct say on some national issues. Only 25 percent felt that we should leave all policymaking decisions to our elected representatives.[16] The most fervent advocates of majoritarian democracy would like to see modern technology used to maximize the government's responsiveness to the

Opponents argue that whites or Asians who have excelled in high school and have higher scores and grades than some minorities should not be placed below minorities who have lower scores. If objective standards applied equally to all groups are not used and minorities are favored, then the system should be viewed as discriminatory.

The end of affirmative action had a devastating impact on the enrollment of blacks, Hispanics, and Native Americans. At Berkeley the combined number of those three minorities in the freshman class fell from 1,778 in 1997 to just 717 in 1998, and they totaled 990 in 1999. (It is not just that more minorities were being rejected, but minority applications dropped because students of color felt that their chances of admission were slim or they felt unwanted.) Outreach efforts have succeeded in pushing the number of minority admissions up to 1,169 for 2000, but given California's large minority population, blacks and Hispanics remain underrepresented at the school. As the accompanying figure illustrates, the prestigious graduate programs at Berkeley and UCLA also saw their minority admissions plummet in the wake of the demise of affirmative action.

From the viewpoint of the minorities who saw their chances of admission to top schools damaged by Proposition 209, majoritarian democracy may seem singularly unfair because it allows the majority to use their greater numbers to take advantage of their superior position. For others, the initiative process may be seen as the embodiment of democracy—as an instrument by which the majority can work its will.

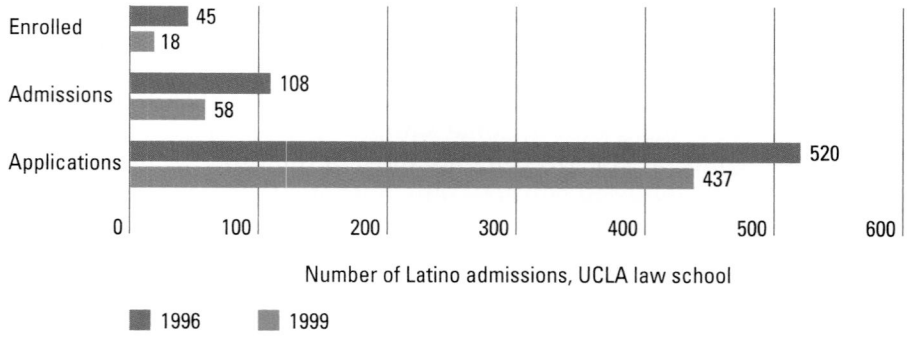

Number of Latino admissions, UCLA law school

■ 1996   ■ 1999

Source: Matt A. Barreto, "Will the University of California Prepare the Next Generation of Minority Doctors, Lawyers, and Professionals?" *Policy Brief*, Thomas Rivera Institute (September 2000), p. 9.

majority. Some have proposed incorporating public opinion polls, first used regularly in the 1930s, in government decision making. More recently, some have suggested using computers for referenda. For instance, citizens could vote on an issue by inserting plastic identification cards in computer terminals installed in all homes. Americans are decidedly cool toward electronic democracy. Roughly two-thirds of the public don't

──────────── ★

Death with Dignity

Maine resident John Speh became an outspoken advocate for the Death with Dignity Act on his state's 2000 ballot. At the time, Speh was dying of stomach cancer and he strongly supported physician-assisted suicide, saying that "it should be up to the individual who's going through it to make that decision." Maine voters rejected the proposal.

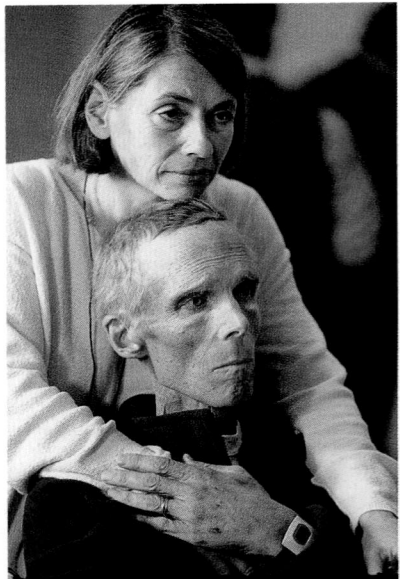

deliberative democracy
That model of democracy in which citizens and their elected representatives exercise reasoned and full debate on questions of public policy.

believe that instant computer voting on referendums would improve our democratic process.[17]

The majoritarian model contends that citizens can control their government if they have adequate mechanisms for popular participation. It also assumes that citizens are knowledgeable about government and politics, that they want to participate in the political process, and that they make rational decisions in voting for their elected representatives.

Critics contend that Americans are not knowledgeable enough for majoritarian democracy to work. They point to research that shows that only 22 percent of a national sample of voters said that they "follow what's going on" in government "most of the time." More (38 percent) said that they followed politics "only now and then" or "hardly at all."[18] Calls for enhancing majoritarian democracy through interactive electronic technology raises other concerns. Some believe that instead of quick and easy mass voting on public policy, what we need is more deliberation by citizens and their elected representatives. **Deliberative democracy** emphasizes reasoned and full debate by those who immerse themselves in the substance of public policy problems.[19]

Defenders of majoritarian democracy respond that, although individual Americans may have only limited knowledge of or interest in government, the American public as a whole still has coherent and stable opinions on major policy questions. One study concluded that people "do not need large amounts of information to make rational voting choices."[20]

An Alternative Model: Pluralist Democracy

For years, political scientists struggled valiantly to reconcile the majoritarian model of democracy with polls that showed widespread ignorance

Federalist #10

interest group
An organized group of individuals that seeks to influence public policy. Also called a *lobby*.

pluralist model of democracy
An interpretation of democracy in which government by the people is taken to mean government by people operating through competing interest groups.

of politics among the American people. When only half of the adult population bothers to vote in presidential elections, our form of democracy seems to be "government by *some* of the people."

The 1950s saw the evolution of an alternative interpretation of democracy, one tailored to the limited knowledge and participation of the real electorate, not an ideal one. It was based on the concept of *pluralism*—that modern society consists of innumerable groups that share economic, religious, ethnic, or cultural interests. Often, people with similar interests organize formal groups: the Future Farmers of America, chambers of commerce, and the Rotary Club, for example. Many social groups have little contact with government, but occasionally they find themselves backing or opposing government policies. When an organized group seeks to influence government policy, it is called an **interest group.** Many interest groups regularly spend much time and money trying to influence government policy (see Chapter 10). Among them are the International Electrical Workers Union, the American Hospital Association, the Associated Milk Producers, the National Education Association (NEA), the National Association of Manufacturers, the National Organization for Women (NOW), and, of course, the NRA.

The **pluralist model of democracy** interprets "government by the people" to mean government by people operating through competing interest groups. According to this model, democracy exists when many (plural) organizations operate separately from the government, press their interests on the government, and even challenge the government.[21] Compared with majoritarian thinking, pluralist theory shifts the focus of democratic government from the mass electorate to organized groups. The criterion for democratic government changes from responsiveness to mass public opinion to responsiveness to organized groups of citizens.

The two major mechanisms in a pluralist democracy are interest groups and a decentralized structure of government that provides ready access to public officials and that is open to hearing the groups' arguments for or against government policies. In a centralized structure, decisions are made at one point, the top of the hierarchy. The few decision makers at the top are too busy to hear the claims of competing interest groups or to consider those claims in making their decisions. But a decentralized, complex government structure offers the access and openness necessary for pluralist democracy. For pluralists, the ideal system is one that divides government authority among numerous institutions with overlapping authority. Under such a system, competing interest groups have alternative points of access for presenting and arguing their claims.

Our Constitution approaches the pluralist ideal in the way it divides authority among the branches of government. When the National Association for the Advancement of Colored People (NAACP) could not get Congress to outlaw segregated schools in the South, it turned to the federal court system, which did what Congress would not. According to the ideal of pluralist democracy, if all opposing interests are allowed to organize, and if the system can be kept open so that all substantial claims are heard, the decision will serve the diverse needs of a pluralist society.

Although many scholars have contributed to the model, pluralist democracy is most closely identified with political scientist Robert Dahl.

Why They Are Called *Lobbyists*

At the national level, interest groups are usually represented by paid lobbyists. These people are called lobbyists because they often gather in the lobby outside congressional meeting rooms, positioned to contact senators and representatives coming and going. Here, lobbyists are waiting to help members of the House Ways and Means Committee understand the importance of their pet tax loopholes.

According to Dahl, the fundamental axiom of pluralist democracy is that "instead of a single center of sovereign power there must be multiple centers of power, none of which is or can be wholly sovereign."[22] Some watchwords of pluralist democracy, therefore, are *divided authority, decentralization,* and *open access.*

On one level, pluralism is alive and well. As will be demonstrated in Chapter 10, interest groups in Washington are thriving and the rise of many citizen groups has broadened representation beyond traditional business, labor, and professional groups.[23] But on another level, the involvement of Americans in their groups is a cause for concern. Political scientist Robert Putnam has documented declining participation in a wide variety of organizations (see Figure 2.1). Americans are less inclined to be active members of civic groups like parent-teacher associations, the League of Woman Voters, and the Lions Club. Civic participation is a fundamental part of American democracy because it generates the social "glue" that helps to generate trust and cooperation in the political system.[24] In short, pluralism is working well in terms of promoting representative democracy because Americans are happy to have their interest groups act on their behalf in Washington or at the state level. At the same time, declining civic participation makes it difficult to enhance instruments of direct democracy at the local level.

The Majoritarian Model Versus the Pluralist Model

In majoritarian democracy, the mass public—not interest groups—controls government actions. The citizenry must therefore have some

figure

2.1   America the Disengaged

Membership across a wide range of civic organizations has fallen in recent decades. Although some newer organizations that didn't exist in 1900 have taken some of this "missing" membership, other indices show the same trend: Americans belong to fewer organizations and participate in civic activities at lower rates than earlier generations. This trend is unfortunate, but the good news is that plenty of civic organizations still exist, enriching their communities and helping to keep our democracy healthy.

Source: Robert D. Putnam, *Bowling Alone* (New York: Simon and Schuster, 2000), p. 54. Reprinted with permission.

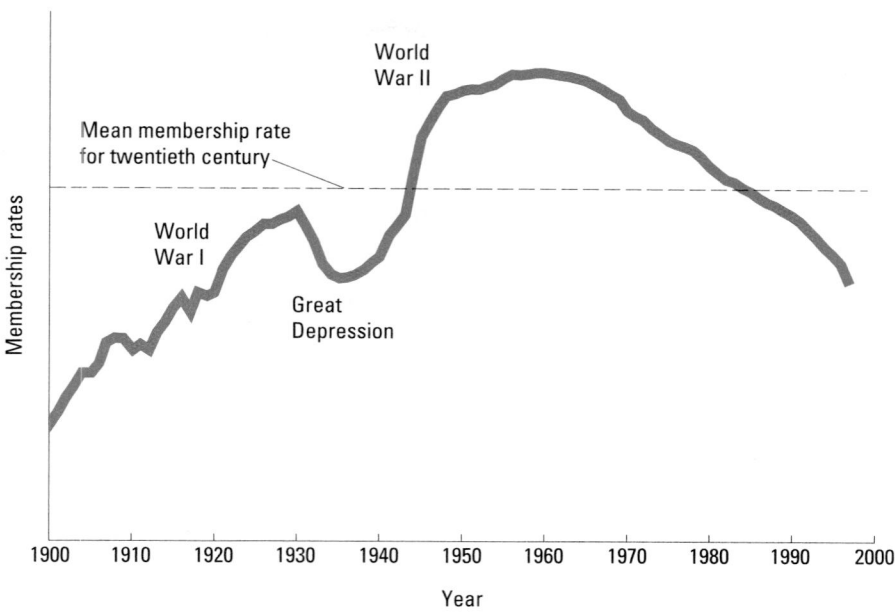

knowledge of government and be willing to participate in the electoral process. Majoritarian democracy relies on electoral mechanisms that harness the power of the majority to make decisions. Conclusive elections and a centralized structure of government are mechanisms that aid majority rule. Cohesive political parties with well-defined programs also contribute to majoritarian democracy because they offer voters a clear way to distinguish alternative sets of policies.

Pluralism does not demand much knowledge from citizens in general. It requires specialized knowledge only from groups of citizens, in particular their leaders. In contrast to majoritarian democracy, pluralist democracy seeks to limit majority action so that interest groups can be heard. It relies on strong interest groups and a decentralized government structure—mechanisms that interfere with majority rule, thereby protecting minority interests. We could even say that pluralism allows minorities to rule.

An Undemocratic Model: Elite Theory

elite theory
The view that a small group of people actually makes most of the important government decisions.

If pluralist democracy allows minorities to rule, how does it differ from **elite theory**—the view that a small group (a minority) makes most important government decisions? According to elite theory, important government decisions are made by an identifiable and stable minority that shares certain characteristics, usually vast wealth and business connections.[25]

Elite theory argues that these few individuals wield power in America because they control its key financial, communications, industrial, and government institutions. Their power derives from the vast wealth of America's largest corporations and the perceived importance of the continuing success of those corporations to the growth of the economy. An inner circle of top corporate leaders not only provides effective advocates for individual companies and for the interests of capitalism in general but also supplies people for top government jobs—from which they can further promote their interests.[26]

According to elite theory, the United States is not a democracy but an oligarchy. Although the voters appear to control the government through elections, elite theorists argue that the powerful few in society manage to define the issues and to constrain the outcomes of government decision making to suit their own interests. Clearly, elite theory describes a government that operates in an undemocratic fashion.

Elite theory appeals to many people, especially those who believe that wealth dominates politics. The theory also provides plausible explanations for specific political decisions. Why, over the years, has the tax code included so many loopholes that favor the wealthy? The answer, claim adherents of elite theory, is that the policymakers never really change—they are all cut from the same cloth. Even when a liberal Democrat is in the White House, many of the president's top economic policy-makers will likely be people drawn from Wall Street or other financial institutions.

Political scientists have conducted numerous studies designed to test the validity of elite theory. Many of these studies look at individual cities to see whether a clearly identified elite rules across different issue areas. One influential study of New Haven, Connecticut, demonstrated that different groups won on different issues. No power elite could be found in that city.[27] Yet other studies, such as one on Atlanta, Georgia, have shown the dominance of a downtown business elite. This group may not be a power elite that controls a broad range of important decisions across policy areas, but it nevertheless is consistently the most influential group affecting the key economic development decisions that are crucial to the future of the city.[28]

It is surely easier for an elite to exist on the local level than on the national level, where far more well-organized interest groups compete directly against one another on different policies. A recent study of national politics examined four broad issue areas and tried to assess whether an elite coordinated and influenced government decision making. By tracking the interaction of representatives of hundreds of groups, the authors determined that there was no elite that coordinated lobbying across the four issue areas. Their evidence supports a critical part of the pluralist argument: each issue area has a separate set of organizations that influence government.[29]

Although not all studies come to the same conclusion, the preponderance of available evidence documenting government decisions on many different issues does not generally support elite theory—at least in the sense that an identifiable ruling elite usually gets its way. Not surpris-

★

The Power Elite?

This picture symbolizes the underlying notion of elite theory—that government is driven by wealth. In truth, wealthy people usually do have more influence in the government than do people of ordinary means. Critics of elite theory point out, however, that it is difficult to demonstrate that an identifiable ruling elite usually sticks together and gets its way in government policy.

Can You Explain Why...
America can be considered democratic when a small group of people has much more in the way of resources and influence than the rest of us?

ingly, elite theorists reject this view. They argue that studies of decisions made on individual issues do not adequately test the influence of the power elite. Rather, they contend that much of the elite's power comes from its ability to keep things off the political agenda. That is, its power derives from its ability to keep people from questioning fundamental assumptions about American capitalism.[30]

Consequently, elite theory remains part of the debate about the nature of American government and is forcefully argued by some severe critics of our political system.[31] Although we do not believe that the scholarly evidence supports elite theory, we do recognize that contemporary American pluralism favors some segments of society over others. On one hand, the poor are chronically unorganized and are not well represented by interest groups. On the other hand, business is very well represented in the political system. As many interest group scholars who reject elite theory have documented, business is better represented than any other sector of the public.[32] Thus, one can endorse pluralist democracy as a more accurate description than elitism in American politics without believing that all groups are equally well represented.

Elite Theory Versus Pluralist Theory

The key difference between elite and pluralist theory lies in the durability of the ruling minority. In contrast to elite theory, pluralist theory does not define government conflict in terms of a minority versus the majority;

instead, it sees many different interests vying with one another in each policy area. In the management of national forests, for example, many interest groups—logging companies, recreational campers, environmentalists—have joined the political competition. They press their various viewpoints on government through representatives who are well informed about how relevant issues affect group members. According to elite theory, the financial resources of big logging companies ought to win out over the arguments of campers and environmentalists, but this does not always happen.

Pluralist democracy makes a virtue of the struggle between competing interests. It argues for government that accommodates the struggle and channels the result into government action. According to pluralist democracy, the public is best served if the government structure provides access for different groups to press their claims in competition with one another. Note that pluralist democracy does not insist that all groups have equal influence on government decisions. In the political struggle, wealthy, well-organized groups have an inherent advantage over poorer, inadequately organized groups. In fact, unorganized segments of the population may not even get their concerns placed on the agenda for government consideration, which means that what government does not discuss (its "nondecisions") may be as significant as what it does discuss and decide. This is a critical weakness of pluralism, and critics relentlessly attack the theory because it appears to justify great disparities in levels of political organization and resources among different segments of society. Pluralists contend that as long as all groups are able to participate vigorously in the decision-making process, the process is democratic.

DEMOCRACY AND GLOBALIZATION

We have proposed two models of democratic government. The majoritarian model conforms with classical democratic theory for a representative government. According to this model, democracy should be a form of government that features responsiveness to majority opinion. According to the pluralist model, a government is democratic if it allows minority interests to organize and press their claims on government freely.

No government actually achieves the high degree of responsiveness demanded by the majoritarian model. No government offers complete and equal access to the claims of all competing groups, as is required by an optimally democratic pluralist model. Still, some nations approach these ideals closely enough to be considered practicing democracies.

Establishing Democracies

Most countries are neither majoritarian nor pluralist; rather, most are governed in an authoritarian manner or are struggling to move out of an authoritarian tradition but are not yet true democracies. By a true democracy we mean countries that meet the criteria for a procedural democracy (universal participation, political equality, majority rule, and government responsiveness to public opinion) and have established substantive policies supporting such civil liberties as freedom of speech and freedom of association, which create the necessary conditions for the practice of democracy. Until recently, fewer than twenty countries fully met all the

In Praise of Nigeria

For years Nigeria was ruled by a corrupt and ruthless dictatorship. Nigeria is an important country in West Africa because of its size and its oil resources, and its recent turn toward democracy was hailed by western leaders. Shortly before he left office, former President Clinton visited Nigeria to demonstrate the United States' support for President Olesugun Obasanjo's push for democracy.

democratization
A process of transition as a country attempts to move from an authoritarian form of government to a democratic one.

Can You Explain Why...
countries on the road to democratization often revert back to authoritarianism?

criteria necessary to be judged a true democracy.[33] What is encouraging, however, is that today the world is awash in countries that are trying to make a transition to democracy. In Africa alone, perhaps twenty countries are moving in some fashion toward a democratic form of government.[34] But **democratization** is a difficult process, and many countries fail completely or succeed only in the short run and lapse into a form of authoritarianism.

One reason why democratization can be so difficult is that ethnic and religious conflict is epidemic. Such conflict complicates efforts to democratize because antagonisms can run so deep that opposing groups do not want to grant political legitimacy to each other. As a result, ethnic and religious rivals are often more interested in achieving a form of government that oppresses their opponents (or, in their minds, maintains order) than in establishing a real democracy. Nowhere is this more apparent than in the new countries of the former Soviet Union and in parts of Eastern Europe. Once freedom came to the former Yugoslavia, the country split into a number of new nations. Their boundaries did not conform exactly with where various ethnic and religious groups live, and in Bosnia war soon broke out among Croats, Serbs, and Muslims. Later, war broke out in another part of the former Yugoslavia. Kosovo, a largely Albanian province of Serbia, began fighting for its independence. The brutal repression of the Muslim Albanian Kosovars by the Eastern Orthodox Serbians brought the United States and the NATO alliance into the conflict. The Serbians eventually conceded defeat.

The political and economic instability that typically accompanies transitions to democracy makes new democratic governments vulnerable to attack by their opponents. The military will often revolt and take over the government on the ground that progress cannot occur until order is restored. As we noted in Chapter 1, all societies wrestle with the dilemma of choosing between freedom and order. The open political conflict that emerges in a new democracy may not be easily harnessed into a well-functioning government that tolerates opposition.[35]

Despite such difficulties, strong forces are pushing authoritarian governments toward democratization. Nations find it difficult to succeed economically in today's world without establishing a market economy, and market economies (that is, capitalism) give people substantial freedoms. Thus, authoritarian rulers may see economic reforms as a threat to their regime. Yet, the electronic and communications revolution has made it more difficult for authoritarian countries to keep information about democracy and capitalism from their citizens. One scholar calls the global tendency toward a uniform type of government (democracy) and a uniform type of economy (capitalism) a movement toward a "McWorld." Nations are being pressed "into one commercially homogeneous global network: one McWorld tied together by technology, ecology, communications, and commerce."[36]

The United States has long regarded helping countries to democratize as a major responsibility.[37] It is common for the United States to apply subtle and even not-so-subtle pressure on countries to move toward a democratic form of government. Student-led protests against an autocratic regime in South Korea had yielded halting steps toward democracy followed by brutal repression to stop the incipient democratic movement. But when student demonstrations broke out once again in 1987, the United States openly criticized the military regime and subsequently called its ambassador back to Washington, a sharp rebuke to an ally with whom we had fought a war. With student unrest growing and the reformers emboldened by the United States' stance, the Korean military leaders announced that free elections would be held.[38]

Established democracies are also not free of the destabilizing effects of religious and ethnic conflict. French-speaking Canadians have pushed for autonomy for Quebec, and India's democracy has been sorely tested by violence inspired by ethnic and religious rivalries. Democracies usually try to cope with such pressures with some form of pluralism so that different groups feel they are being treated fairly by their government. Indeed, majoritarian democracy can be risky where ethnic and religious rivalries endure because a majority faction can use its votes to suppress minorities. Even in stable democracies where ethnic conflict is muted, disillusionment can grow and undermine confidence in the actions of government.[39]

More common than democracies coping with the problem of minority rights, however, are situations in which ethnic and racial minorities are subject to authoritarian rule and are excluded from or discriminated against in the governmental process. One study found 230 minority groups at risk around the globe in the early 1990s. The countries that are home to these groups have failed to establish ways to protect them from the majority or from rival minorities.[40]

American Democracy: More Pluralist Than Majoritarian

It is not idle speculation to ask what kind of democracy is practiced in the United States. The answer can help us understand why our government can be called democratic despite a low level of citizen participation in politics and despite government actions that sometimes run contrary to public opinion.

Throughout this book, we probe more deeply to determine how well the United States fits the two alternative models of democracy, majoritarian and pluralist. If our answer is not already apparent, it soon will be. We argue that the political system in the United States rates relatively low according to the majoritarian model of democracy but that it fulfills the pluralist model quite well. Yet the pluralist model is far from a perfect representation of democracy. Its principal drawback is that it favors the well organized, and the poor are the least likely to be members of interest groups. As one advocate of majoritarian democracy once wrote, "The flaw in the pluralist heaven is that the heavenly chorus sings with a strong upper-class accent."[41]

Given the survey data that show that the people's trust in American government has fallen over the years, it may seem that pluralist democracy is not serving us very well. Indeed, many Americans describe government and politicians in only the harshest terms. Radio talk show hosts like Rush Limbaugh and politicians themselves pile invective on top of insult when they talk about what's wrong with Washington. Yet in comparison to most other countries, people in the United States are actually more satisfied with their form of democracy.[42] It's not at all clear that Americans would be more satisfied with another type of democracy. Surveys show that respondents in states that have instruments of majoritarian democracy such as initiatives or referenda are no more trusting than those who live in states lacking such devices.[43]

This evaluation of the pluralist nature of American democracy may not mean much to you now. But you will learn that the pluralist model makes the United States look far more democratic than the majoritarian model would. Eventually you will have to decide the answers to three questions: Is the pluralist model truly an adequate expression of democracy, or is it a perversion of classical ideals, designed to portray America as democratic when it is not? Does the majoritarian model result in a "better" type of democracy? If so, could new mechanisms of government be devised to produce a desirable mix of majority rule and minority rights? These questions should play in the back of your mind as you read more about the workings of American government in meeting the challenge of democracy.

SUMMARY

Is the United States a democracy? Most scholars believe that it is. But what kind of democracy is it? The answer depends on the definition of *democracy*. Some believe democracy is procedural; they define democracy as a form of government in which the people govern through certain institutional mechanisms. Others hold to substantive theory, claiming that a government is democratic if its policies promote civil liberties and rights.

In this book, we emphasize the procedural concept of democracy, distinguishing between direct (participatory) and indirect (representative) democracy. In a participatory democracy, all citizens gather to govern themselves according to the principles of universal participation, political equality, and majority rule. In an indirect democracy, the citizens elect representatives to govern for them. If a representative government is elected mostly in accordance with the three principles just listed and also is usually responsive to public opinion, it qualifies as a democracy.

Procedural democratic theory has produced rival institutional models of democratic government. The classical majoritarian model—which depends on majority votes in elections—assumes that people are knowledgeable about government, that they want to participate in the political process, and that they carefully and rationally choose among candidates. But surveys of public opinion and behavior, and voter turnout, show that this is not the case for most Americans. The pluralist model of democracy—which depends on interest group interaction with government—was devised to accommodate these findings. It argues that democracy in a complex society requires only that government allow private interests to organize and to press their competing claims openly in the political arena. It differs from elite theory—the belief that America is run by a small group of powerful individuals—by arguing that different minorities win on different issues.

In Chapter 1 we talked about three political values—freedom, order, and equality. Here we have described two models of democracy—majoritarian and pluralist. The five concepts are critical to an understanding of American government. The values discussed in this chapter underlie the two questions with which the text began:

- Which is better: to live under a government that allows individuals complete freedom to do whatever they please, or to live under one that enforces strict law and order?

- Which is better: to let all citizens keep the same share of their income or to tax wealthier people at a higher rate to fund programs for poorer people?

The models of democracy described in this chapter lead to another question:

- Which is better: a government that is highly responsive to public opinion on all matters, or one that responds deliberately to organized groups that argue their cases effectively?

These are enduring questions, and the framers of the Constitution dealt with them too. Their struggle is the appropriate place to begin our analysis of how these competing models of democracy have animated the debate about the nature of our political process.

★ Selected Readings

Berry, Jeffrey M., Kent E. Portney, and Ken Thomson. *The Rebirth of Urban Democracy*. Washington, D.C.: Brookings Institution, 1993. An examination of neighborhood government in five American cities. The authors conclude that participatory democracy on the local level is a feasible and desirable alternative.

Dahl, Robert A. *On Democracy*. New Haven: Yale University Press, 1998. A highly readable overview of the nature of democracy.

Gerber, Elisabeth R. *The Populist Paradox*. Princeton: Princeton University Press, 1999. Based on a survey in eight states, Gerber finds that citizen groups have a high success rate when they use initiatives.

Grossman, Lawrence K. *The Electronic Republic*. New York: Viking, 1995. The author argues that whether we like it or not, high tech is pushing us toward electronic democracy.

Huntington, Samuel P. *The Clash of Civilizations*

and the Remaking of World Order. New York: Simon & Schuster, 1996. Huntington's theme is the growing importance of cultural and ethnic groups in post–Cold War politics.

Pharr, Susan J., and Robert D. Putnam. *Disaffected Democracies* (Princeton: Princeton University Press, 2000). A collection of essays examining why people in the advanced industrialized democracies are so unhappy with their governments.

Putnam, Robert D. *Bowling Alone* (New York: Simon and Schuster, 2000). Putnam argues that declining involvement in civic associations is eroding our social capital.

Internet Exercises

1. *Direct Democracy in the United States!*

The Direct Democracy Center describes itself as "an unfunded, unaffiliated nonprofit group of independent nonpartisan citizens promoting direct democracy in America."

- Go to the Center's home page, located at <**www.realdemocracy.com/**>, and read its proposal to amend the U.S. Constitution.

- What would you say is the overall goal of the proposal? How would an advocate of pluralist democracy react to the proposal? How would an advocate of majoritarian democracy react? How would an advocate of elite theory react?

2. *League of Women Voters "Charting the Health of American Democracy"*

The League of Women Voters, founded in 1920 as an outgrowth of the suffragist movement, is one of the nation's premier political education and advocacy groups. The League is nonpartisan and neither supports nor opposes candidates for office at any level of government.

- Recently, the League's concern with the state of democracy in the United States led it to publish a report entitled *Charting the Health of American Democracy.* Go to the League's home page, located at <**www.lwv.org/**>, and find the on-line version of this report. Read the sections entitled "Introduction—The Diagnosis" and "Summary."

- Does the League appear to be focusing its attention and efforts on concerns about the state of majoritarian or pluralist democracy in the United States? List a few examples from the introduction and/or the summary to illustrate your answer.

The Constitution

Computer Enhanced Image

This image of the Bill of Rights has been electronically enhanced by a special digital computer system. The process used is similar to the ones developed by NASA scientists for satellite image enhancement.

The purpose of this "false color" technique is to bring out details that are hard to see or are invisible to the unaided eye. The same approach that enables scientists to view satellite pictures to evaluate the effects of pollution on our natural resources can allow conservators to assess the condition of the document.

The recent introduction of very powerful computers has allowed electronic image processing to gain inroads in the fields of medicine, aerospace, television and publishing. The image you see here is believed to be among the first to use these techniques to observe and monitor the condition of a historic document on tour.

THE MIDNIGHT BURGLARS made a small mistake. They left a piece of tape over the latch they had tripped to enter the Watergate office and apartment complex in Washington, D.C. But a security guard found their tampering and called the police, who surprised the burglars in the offices of the Democratic National Committee at 2:30 A.M. The arrests of the five men—four Cuban exiles and a former CIA agent—in the early hours of June 17, 1972, triggered a constitutional struggle that eventually involved the president of the United States, the Congress, and the Supreme Court.

The arrests took place a month before the 1972 Democratic National Convention. Investigative reporting by Carl Bernstein and Bob Woodward of the *Washington Post,* and a simultaneous criminal investigation by Assistant U.S. Attorney Earl J. Silbert and his staff, uncovered a link between the Watergate burglary and the forthcoming election.[1] The burglars were carrying the telephone number of another former CIA agent, who was working in the White House. At a news conference on June 22, President Richard Nixon said, "The White House has had no involvement whatsoever in this particular incident."[2]

At its convention in July, the Democratic party nominated Senator George McGovern of South Dakota to oppose Nixon in the presidential election. McGovern tried to make the break-in at the Democratic head-quarters a campaign issue, but the voters either did not understand or did not care. In November 1972, Richard Nixon was reelected president of the United States, winning forty-nine of fifty states in one of the largest electoral landslides in American history. Only then did the Watergate story unfold completely.

Two months later, seven men answered in court for the break-in. They included the five burglars and two men closely connected with the president: E. Howard Hunt (a former CIA agent and White House consultant) and G. Gordon Liddy (counsel to the Committee to Re-Elect the President, or CREEP). Five, including Hunt, entered guilty pleas. Liddy and James McCord (one of the burglars) were convicted by a jury. The Senate launched its own investigation of the matter. It set up the Select Committee on Presidential Campaign Activities, chaired by a self-styled constitutional authority, Democratic senator Sam Ervin of North Carolina.

A stunned nation watched the televised proceedings and learned that the president had secretly tape-recorded all of his conversations in the White House. The Ervin committee asked for the tapes. Nixon refused to produce them, citing the separation of powers between the legislative and the executive branches and claiming that "executive privilege" allowed him to withhold information from Congress.

Nixon also resisted subpoenas demanding the White House tapes. Ordered by a federal court to deliver specific tapes, Nixon proposed a compromise: he would release written summaries of the taped conversations. Archibald Cox, the special prosecutor appointed by the attorney general to investigate Watergate and offenses arising from the 1972 presidential election, rejected the compromise. Nixon retaliated with the "Saturday night massacre," in which Attorney General Elliot L. Richardson and his deputy resigned, Cox was fired, and the special prosecutor's office was abolished.

The ensuing furor forced Nixon to appoint another special prosecutor, Leon Jaworski, who eventually brought indictments against Nixon's closest aides. Nixon himself was named as an unindicted co-conspirator. Both the special prosecutor and the defendants wanted the White House tapes, but Nixon continued to resist. Finally, on July 24, 1974, the Supreme Court ruled that the president had to hand over the tapes. At almost the same time, the House Judiciary Committee voted to recommend to the full House that Nixon be impeached for, or charged with, three offenses: violating his oath of office to faithfully uphold the laws, misusing and abusing executive authority and the resources of executive agencies, and defying congressional subpoenas.

The Judiciary Committee vote was decisive but far from unanimous. On August 5, however, the committee and the country finally learned the contents of the tapes released under the Supreme Court order. They revealed that Nixon had been aware of a cover-up on June 23, 1972, just six days after the break-in. He ordered the FBI, "Don't go any further in this case, period!"[3] Now even the eleven Republican members of the House Judiciary Committee, who had opposed impeachment on the first vote, were ready to vote against Nixon.

Faced with the collapse of his support and likely impeachment by the full House, Nixon resigned the presidency on August 9, 1974. Vice President Gerald Ford, the only unelected vice president, became the first unelected president of the United States. A month later, acting within his constitutional powers, Ford granted private citizen Richard Nixon an unconditional pardon for all crimes that he may have committed. Others were not so fortunate. Three members of the Nixon cabinet (two attorneys general and a secretary of commerce) were convicted and sentenced for their crimes in the Watergate affair. Nixon's White House chief of staff, H. R. Haldeman, and domestic affairs adviser, John Ehrlichman, were convicted of conspiracy, obstruction of justice, and perjury. Other officials were tried, and most were convicted, on related charges.[4]

The Watergate affair posed one of the most serious challenges to the constitutional order of modern American government. The incident ultimately developed into a struggle over the rule of law, between the president on the one hand and Congress and the courts on the other. In the end, the constitutional principle separating power among the executive, legislative, and judicial branches prevented the president from controlling the Watergate investigation. The principle of checks and balances allowed Congress to threaten Nixon with impeachment. The belief that Nixon had violated the Constitution finally prompted members of his own party to

Starr-gazing

Independent Counsel Kenneth W. Starr referred grounds for the impeachment of President Clinton to the House of Representatives in September 1998. Starr presented the House with abundant evidence of Clinton's sexual affair with intern Monica S. Lewinsky and the ensuing cover-up. Clinton's defense focused largely on the methods employed by Starr's office to obtain that evidence. In 1999 Congress decided to let the independent counsel law lapse, after more than two decades and twenty-one investigations of high-level officials. Critics argued that the law, born in Watergate's wake, lacked accountability, allowed unchecked prosecutorial power, and undermined integrity in government.

support impeachment, leading the president to resign. The House of Representatives revisited these constitutional issues in 1998 when it voted to impeach President Bill Clinton.

In early 1999, the Senate, voting mainly along party lines, declined to convict the president and remove him from office. The Republican senators who voted against impeachment may have believed that Clinton's cover-up of a sexual affair with a White House intern, although disgraceful, did not constitute an offense for which the legislative branch should—or could—remove the chief executive from office. In the words of one analyst, impeachment is a mechanism intended "to shield the nation against rogue Presidents, not to punish Presidents who are rogues."[5]

In contrast, Nixon was forced to resign the presidency a little more than a year and a half into his second term. In 1992, 70 percent of Americans still viewed Nixon's actions as having warranted his resignation.[6] In some countries, an irregular change in government leadership provides an opportunity for a palace coup, an armed revolution, or a military dictatorship. But here, significantly, no political violence erupted after Nixon's resignation; in fact, none was expected. Constitutional order in the United States had been put to a test, and it passed with high honors.

This chapter poses questions about the Constitution. How did it evolve? What form did it take? What values does it reflect? How can it be altered? Which model of democracy—majoritarian or pluralist—does it fit best?

THE REVOLUTIONARY ROOTS OF THE CONSTITUTION

The Constitution is just 4,300 words long. But those 4,300 words define the basic structure of our national government. A comprehensive document, the Constitution divides the government into three branches and describes the powers of those branches, their relationships, and the interaction between the government and the governed. The Constitution makes itself the supreme law of the land and binds every government official to support it.

Most Americans revere the Constitution as political scripture. To charge that a political action is unconstitutional is akin to claiming that it is unholy. So the Constitution has taken on symbolic value that strengthens its authority as the basis of American government. Strong belief in the Constitution has led many politicians to abandon party for principle when constitutional issues are at stake. The power and symbolic value of the Constitution were forcefully demonstrated in the Watergate affair.

The U.S. Constitution, written in 1787 for an agricultural society huddled along the coast of a wild new land, now guides the political life of a massive urban society in the postnuclear age. The stability of the Constitution—and of the political system it created—is all the more remarkable because the Constitution itself was rooted in revolution.

The U.S. Constitution was designed to prevent anarchy by forging a union of states. To understand the values embedded in the Constitution, we must understand its historical roots. They lie in colonial America, in the revolt against British rule, and in the failure of the Articles of Confederation that governed the new nation after the Revolution.

Freedom in Colonial America

Although they were British subjects, American colonists in the eighteenth century enjoyed a degree of freedom denied most people in the world. In Europe, ancient customs and the relics of feudalism restricted private property, compelled support for established religions, and limited access to trades and professions. In America, landowners could control and transfer their property at will. In America, there were no compulsory payments to support an established church. In America, there was no ceiling on wages, as there was in most European countries, and no guilds of exclusive professional associations. In America, colonists enjoyed almost complete freedom of speech, press, and assembly.[7]

By 1763, Britain and the colonies had reached a compromise between imperial control and colonial self-government. America's foreign affairs and overseas trade were controlled by the king and Parliament, the British legislature; the rest was left to colonial rule. But the cost of administering the colonies was substantial. The colonists needed protection from the French and their American Indian allies during the Seven Years' War (1756–1763), which was an expensive undertaking. Because Americans benefited the most from that protection, their English countrymen argued, Americans should bear the cost.

The Road to Revolution

The British believed that taxing the colonies was the obvious way to meet the costs of administering the colonies. The colonists did not agree. They especially did not want to be taxed by a distant government in which they had no representation. Nevertheless, a series of taxes (including a tax on all printed matter) was imposed on the colonies by the Crown. In each instance, public opposition was widespread and immediate.

A group of citizens—merchants, lawyers, prosperous traders—created an intercolonial association called the Sons of Liberty. This group destroyed taxed items (identified by special stamps) and forced the official

Uniquely American Protest

Americans protested the Tea Act (1773) by holding the Boston Tea Party (see background, left) and by using a unique form of painful punishment—tarring and feathering—on the tax collector (see Stamp Act upside-down on the Liberty Tree). An early treatise on the subject offered the following instructions: "First, strip a person naked, then heat the tar until it is thin, and pour upon the naked flesh, or rub it over with a tar brush. After which, sprinkle decently upon the tar, whilst it is yet warm, as many feathers as will stick to it."

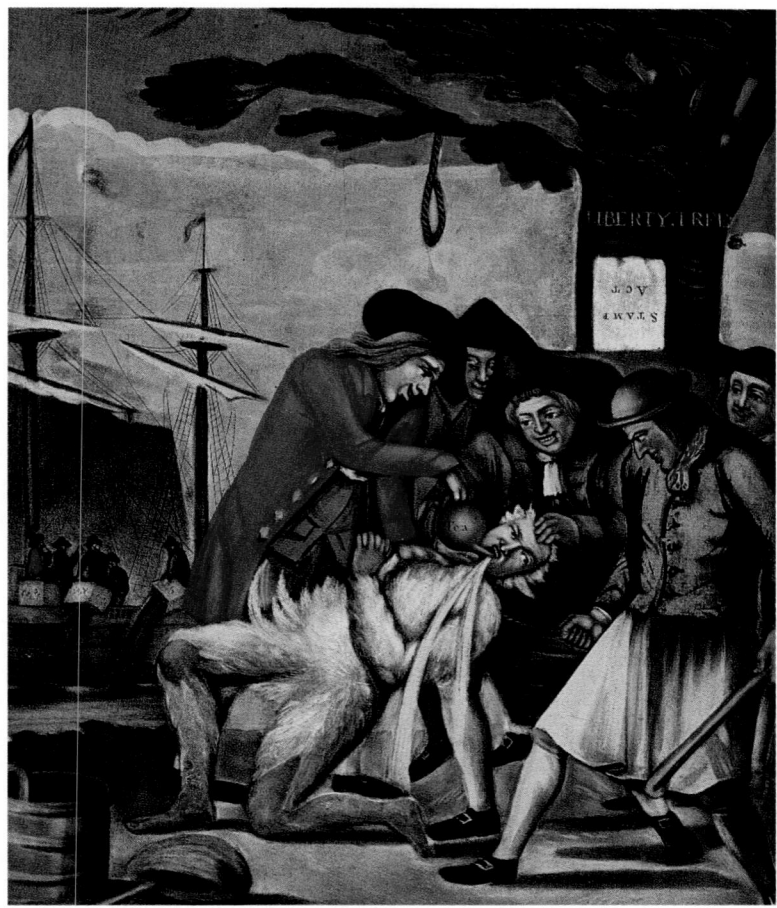

stamp distributors to resign. In October 1765, residents of Charleston, South Carolina, celebrated the forced resignation of the colony's stamp distributor by displaying a British flag with the word *Liberty* sewn across it. (They were horrified when a few months later local slaves paraded through the streets calling for "Liberty!"[8])

Women resisted the hated taxes by joining together in symbolic and practical displays of patriotism. A group of young women calling themselves the Daughters of Liberty met in public to spin homespun cloth and encourage the elimination of British cloth from colonial markets. They consumed American food and drank local herbal tea as symbols of their opposition.[9]

On the night of December 16, 1773, a group of colonists reacted to a British duty on tea by organizing the Boston Tea Party. A mob boarded three ships and emptied 342 chests of that valuable substance into Boston Harbor. The act of defiance and destruction could not be ignored. "The die is now cast," wrote George III. "The Colonies must either submit or triumph."[10] In an attempt to reassert British control over its recalcitrant colonists, Parliament passed the Coercive (or "Intolerable") Acts (1774). One act imposed a blockade on Boston until the tea was paid for; another gave royal governors the power to quarter British soldiers in private American homes. The taxation issue became secondary; more important was the conflict between British demands for order and American demands for liberty. The Virginia and Massachusetts assemblies summoned a continental congress, an assembly that would speak and act for the people of all the colonies.

All the colonies except Georgia sent representatives to the First Continental Congress, which met in Philadelphia in September 1774. The objective was to restore harmony between Great Britain and the American colonies. In an effort at unity, all colonies were given the same voting power—one vote each. A leader, called the president, was elected. (The terms *president* and *congress* in American government trace their origins to the First Continental Congress.) In October, the delegates adopted a statement of rights and principles; many of these later found their way into the Declaration of Independence and the Constitution. For example, the congress claimed a right "to life, liberty, and property" and a right "peaceably to assemble, consider of their grievances, and petition the king." Then the congress adjourned, planning to reconvene in May 1775.

Declaration and Resolves of the First Continental Congress

Revolutionary Action

By early 1775, however, a movement that the colonists themselves were calling a revolution had already begun. Colonists in Massachusetts were fighting the British at Concord and Lexington. Delegates to the Second Continental Congress, meeting in May, faced a dilemma: should they prepare for war or should they try to reconcile with Britain? As conditions deteriorated, the Second Continental Congress remained in session to serve as the government of the colony-states.

On June 7, 1776, the Virginia delegation called on the Continental Congress to resolve "that these United Colonies are, and of right ought to be, free and Independent States, that they are absolved from all allegiance to the British Crown, and that all political connection between them and the State of Great Britain is, and ought to be, totally dissolved." This was a difficult decision. Independence meant disloyalty to Britain and war, death, and devastation. The congress debated but did not immediately adopt the resolution. A committee of five men was appointed to prepare a proclamation expressing the colonies' reasons for declaring independence.

The Declaration of Independence

Thomas Jefferson, a young farmer and lawyer from Virginia, was a member of the committee. Because Jefferson had a way with words, he drafted the proclamation. Jefferson's document—the **Declaration of Independence**—was modestly revised by the committee and then further edited by the congress. It remains a cherished statement of our heritage, expressing simply, clearly, and rationally the many arguments for separation from Great Britain.

Declaration of Independence
Drafted by Thomas Jefferson, the document that proclaimed the right of the colonies to separate from Great Britain.

The principles underlying the declaration were rooted in the writings of the English philosopher John Locke and had been expressed many times by speakers in the congress and the colonial assemblies. Locke argued that people have God-given, or natural, rights that are inalienable—that is, they cannot be taken away by any government. According to Locke, all legitimate political authority exists to preserve these natural rights and is

★

Toppling Tyrants: Then and Now

A gilded equestrian statue of George III (left) once stood at the tip of Manhattan. On July 9, 1776, citizens responded to the news of the Declaration of Independence by toppling the statue. It was melted down and converted into musket balls. A statue of V. I. Lenin, (right) leader of the Russian Revolution and first head of the Soviet Union, stood for years in Valmiera, Latvia. When the Soviet Union started to unravel in 1990, delighted citizens removed the statue. It was melted down and perhaps converted into refrigerator parts.

social contract theory
The belief that the people agree to set up rulers for certain purposes and thus have the right to resist or remove rulers who act against those purposes.

based on the consent of those who are governed. The idea of consent is derived from **social contract theory,** which states that the people agree to establish rulers for certain purposes, but they have the right to resist or remove rulers who violate those purposes.[11]

Jefferson used similar arguments in the Declaration of Independence. Taking his cue from a draft of the Virginia Declaration of Rights,[12] Jefferson wrote,

We hold these truths to be self-evident, that all men are created equal, that they are endowed by their Creator with certain unalienable rights, that among these are life, liberty, and the pursuit of happiness. That to secure these rights, governments are instituted among men, deriving their just powers from the consent of the governed. That whenever any form of government becomes destructive of these ends, it is the right of the people to alter or to abolish it, and to institute new government, laying its foundation on such principles, and organizing its power in such form, as to them shall seem most likely to effect their safety and happiness.

He went on to list the many deliberate acts of the king that had exceeded the legitimate role of government. The last item on Jefferson's original draft of the Declaration was the king's support of the slave trade. Although Jefferson did not condemn slavery, he denounced the king for enslaving a people, engaging in the slave trade, and proposing that the slaves be freed to be able to attack their masters. When South Carolina and Georgia—two states with an interest in continuing the wretched practice—objected, Jefferson and the committee dropped the offending paragraph. Finally, Jefferson declared that the colonies were "Free and Independent States," with no political connection to Great Britain.

The major premise of the Declaration of Independence is that the people have a right to revolt if they determine that their government is denying them their legitimate rights. The long list of the king's actions was evidence of such denial. So the people had the right to rebel, to form a new government. On July 2, 1776, the Second Continental Congress finally voted for independence. The vote was by state, and the motion carried, 11 to 0. (Rhode Island was not present, and the New York delegation, lacking instructions, did not cast its yea vote until July 15.) Two days later, on

July 4, the Declaration of Independence was approved, with few changes. Several representatives insisted on removing language they thought would incite the colonists. But in the end, Jefferson's compelling words were left almost exactly as he had written them.

By August, fifty-five revolutionaries had signed the Declaration of Independence, pledging "our lives, our fortunes and our sacred honor" in support of their rebellion against the world's most powerful nation. This was no empty pledge: an act of rebellion was treason. Had they lost the Revolutionary War, the signers would have faced a gruesome fate. The punishment for treason was hanging and drawing and quartering—the victim was first hanged until half-dead from strangulation, then disemboweled, and finally cut into four pieces while still alive. We celebrate the Fourth of July with fireworks and flag waving, parades and picnics. We sometimes forget that the Revolution was a matter of life and death.

The war imposed an agonizing choice on colonial Catholics, who were treated with intolerance by the overwhelmingly Protestant population. No other religious group found the choice so difficult. Catholics could either join the revolutionaries, who were opposed to Catholicism, or remain loyal to England and risk new hostility and persecution. But Catholics were few in number, perhaps 25,000 at the time of independence (or 1 percent of the population). Anti-Catholic revolutionaries recognized that if Catholics opposed independence in Maryland and Pennsylvania, where their numbers were greatest, victory might be jeopardized. Furthermore, enlisting the support of Catholic France for the cause of independence would be difficult in the face of strong opposition from colonial Catholics. So the revolutionaries wooed Catholics to their cause.[13]

The War of Independence lasted far longer than anyone expected. It began in a moment of confusion, when a shot rang out as British soldiers approached the town of Lexington, Massachusetts, on April 19, 1775. The end came six and a half years later with Lord Cornwallis's surrender of his six-thousand-man army at Yorktown, Virginia, on October 19, 1781. It was a costly war: a greater percentage of the population died or was wounded during the Revolution than in any other U.S. conflict except the Civil War.[14]

Can You Explain Why...
the War of Independence was one of the gravest conflicts?

With hindsight, of course, we can see that the British were engaged in an arduous and perhaps hopeless conflict. America was simply too vast to subdue without imposing total military rule. Britain also had to transport men and supplies over the enormous distance of the Atlantic Ocean. Finally, although the Americans had neither paid troops nor professional soldiers, they were fighting for a cause—the defense of their liberty. The British never understood the power of this fighting faith.

FROM REVOLUTION TO CONFEDERATION

republic
A government without a monarch; a government rooted in the consent of the governed, whose power is exercised by elected representatives responsible to the governed.

By declaring their independence from England, the colonists left themselves without any real central government. So the revolutionaries proclaimed the creation of a **republic.** Strictly speaking, a republic is a government without a monarch, but the term had come to mean a government based on the consent of the governed, whose power is exercised by representatives who are responsible to them. A republic need not be a democracy, and this was fine with the founders; at that time, democracy was associated with mob rule and instability (see Chapter 2).

The revolutionaries were less concerned with determining who would control their new government than with limiting its powers. They had revolted in the name of liberty, and now they wanted a government with strictly defined powers. To make sure they got one, they meant to define its structure and powers in writing.

The Articles of Confederation

Barely a week after the Declaration of Independence was signed, the Second Continental Congress received a committee report entitled "Articles of Confederation and Perpetual Union." A **confederation** is a loose association of independent states that agree to cooperate on specified matters. In a confederation, the states retain their sovereignty, which means that each has supreme power within its borders. The central government is weak; it can only coordinate, not control, the actions of its sovereign states. Consequently, the individual states are strong.

The congress debated the **Articles of Confederation,** the compact among the thirteen original colonies that established the first government of the United States, for more than a year. The Articles were adopted by the Continental Congress on November 15, 1777. They finally took effect on March 1, 1781, following approval by all thirteen states. For more than three years, then, Americans had fought a revolution without an effective government. Raising money, troops, and supplies for the war had daunted and exhausted the leadership.

The Articles jealously guarded state sovereignty; their provisions clearly reflected the delegates' fears that a strong central government would resemble British rule. Article II, for example, stated, "Each state retains its sovereignty, freedom, and independence, and every power, jurisdiction, and right, which is not by this Confederation expressly delegated to the United States, in Congress assembled."

Can You Explain Why...
the Articles of Confederation made the states strong and the nation weak?

confederation
A loose association of independent states that agree to cooperate on specified matters.

Articles of Confederation
The compact among the thirteen original states that established the first government of the United States.

Under the Articles, each state, regardless of its size, had one vote in the congress. Votes on financing the war and other important issues required the consent of at least nine of the thirteen states. The common danger—Britain—had forced the young republic to function under the Articles, but this first effort at government was inadequate to the task. The delegates had succeeded in crafting a national government that was largely powerless.

The Articles failed for at least four reasons. First, they did not give the national government the power to tax. As a result, the congress had to plead for money from the states to pay for the war and to carry on the affairs of the new nation. A government that cannot reliably raise revenue cannot expect to govern effectively. Second, the Articles made no provision for an independent leadership position to direct the government (the president was merely the presiding officer of the congress). The omission was deliberate—the colonists feared the reestablishment of a monarchy—but it left the nation without a leader. Third, the Articles did not allow the national government to regulate interstate and foreign commerce. (When John Adams proposed that the confederation enter into a commercial treaty with Britain after the war, he was asked, "Would you like one treaty or thirteen, Mr. Adams?")[15] Finally, the Articles could not be amended without the unanimous agreement of the congress and the assent of all the state legislatures; thus, each state had the power to veto any changes to the confederation.

The goal of the delegates who drew up the Articles of Confederation was to retain power in the states. This was consistent with republicanism, which viewed the remote power of a national government as a danger to liberty. In this sense alone, the Articles were a grand success. They completely hobbled the infant government.

Disorder Under the Confederation

Once the Revolution had ended and independence was a reality, it became clear that the national government had neither the economic nor the military power to function. Freed from wartime austerity, Americans rushed to purchase goods from abroad. The national government's efforts to restrict foreign imports were blocked by exporting states, which feared retaliation from their foreign customers. Debt mounted and, for many, bankruptcy followed.

The problem was particularly severe in Massachusetts, where high interest rates and high state taxes were forcing farmers into bankruptcy. In 1786, Daniel Shays, a Revolutionary War veteran, marched on a western Massachusetts courthouse with 1,500 supporters armed with barrel staves and pitchforks. They wanted to close the courthouse to prevent the foreclosure of farms by creditors. Later, they attacked an arsenal. Called Shays's Rebellion, the revolt against the established order continued into 1787. Massachusetts appealed to the confederation for help. Horrified by the threat of domestic upheaval, the congress approved a $530,000 requisition for the establishment of a national army. But the plan failed: every state except Virginia rejected the request for money. Finally, the governor of Massachusetts called out the militia and restored order.[16]

The rebellion demonstrated the impotence of the confederation and the urgent need to suppress insurrections and maintain domestic order. Proof to skeptics that Americans could not govern themselves, the rebellion alarmed all American leaders, with the exception of Jefferson. From Paris, where he was serving as American ambassador, he remarked, "A little rebellion now and then is a good thing; the tree of liberty must be refreshed from time to time with the blood of patriots and tyrants."[17]

FROM CONFEDERATION TO CONSTITUTION

Order, the original purpose of government, was breaking down under the Articles of Confederation. The "league of friendship" envisioned in the Articles was not enough to hold the nation together in peacetime.

Some states had taken halting steps toward encouraging a change in the national government. In 1785, Massachusetts asked the congress to revise the Articles of Confederation, but the congress took no action. In 1786, Virginia invited the states to attend a convention at Annapolis to explore revisions aimed at improving commercial regulation. The meeting was both a failure and a success. Only five states sent delegates, but they seized the opportunity to call for another meeting—with a far broader mission—in Philadelphia the next year. That convention would be charged with devising "such further provisions as shall appear . . . necessary to render the constitution of the Federal Government adequate to the exigencies of the Union." The congress later agreed to the convention but limited its mission to "the sole and express purpose of revising the Articles of Confederation."[18]

Shays's Rebellion lent a sense of urgency to the task before the Philadelphia convention. The congress's inability to confront the rebellion was evidence that a stronger national government was necessary to preserve order and property—to protect the states from internal as well as external dangers. "While the Declaration was directed against an excess of authority," observed Supreme Court Justice Robert H. Jackson some 150 years later, "the Constitution [that followed the Articles of Confederation] was directed against anarchy."[19]

Twelve of the thirteen states named a total of seventy-four delegates to convene in Philadelphia, the most important city in America, in May 1787. (Rhode Island, derisively renamed "Rogue Island" by a Boston newspaper, was the one exception. The state legislature sulkily rejected participating because it feared a strong national government.) Fifty-five delegates eventually showed up at the statehouse in Philadelphia, but no more than thirty were present at any one time during that sweltering spring and summer. The framers were not demigods, but many historians believe that a like assembly will not be seen again. Highly educated, they typically were fluent in Latin and Greek. Products of the Enlightenment, they relied on classical liberalism for the Constitution's philosophical underpinnings.

They were also veterans of the political intrigues of their states, and as such they were highly practical politicians who knew how to maneuver. Although well versed in ideas, they subscribed to the view expressed by one delegate that "experience must be our only guide, reason may mislead us."[20] Fearing for their fragile union, the delegates resolved to keep their proceedings secret.

The Constitutional Convention—at the time called the Federal Convention—officially opened on May 25. Within the first week, Edmund Randolph of Virginia had presented a long list of changes, suggested by fellow Virginian James Madison, that would replace the weak confederation of states with a powerful national government rather than revise it within its original framework. The delegates unanimously agreed to debate Randolph's proposal, called the **Virginia Plan**. Almost immediately, then, they rejected the idea of amending the Articles of Confederation, working instead to create an entirely new constitution.

Virginia Plan
A set of proposals for a new government, submitted to the Constitutional Convention of 1787; included separation of the government into three branches, division of the legislature into two houses, and proportional representation in the legislature.

The Virginia Plan

The Virginia Plan dominated the convention's deliberations for the rest of the summer, making several important proposals for a strong central government:

- That the powers of the government be divided among three separate branches: a **legislative branch,** for making laws; an **executive branch,** for enforcing laws; and a **judicial branch,** for interpreting laws.

- That the legislature consist of two houses. The first would be chosen by the people, the second by the members of the first house from among candidates nominated by the state legislatures.

- That each state's representation in the legislature be in proportion to the taxes it paid to the national government or in proportion to its free population.

- That an executive, consisting of an unspecified number of people, be selected by the legislature and serve for a single term.

- That the national judiciary include one or more supreme courts and other, lower courts, with judges appointed for life by the legislature.

- That the executive and a number of national judges serve as a council of revision, to approve or veto (disapprove) legislative acts. Their veto could be overridden by a vote of both houses of the legislature.

- That the scope of powers of all three branches be far greater than that assigned the national government by the Articles of Confederation, and that the legislature be empowered to override state laws.

legislative branch
The lawmaking branch of government.

executive branch
The law-enforcing branch of government.

judicial branch
The branch of government that interprets laws.

By proposing a powerful national legislature that could override state laws, the Virginia Plan clearly advocated a new form of government. It was to have a mixed structure, with more authority over the states and new authority over the people.

Madison was a monumental force in the ensuing debate on the proposals. He kept records of the proceedings that reveal his frequent and brilliant participation and give us insight into his thinking about freedom, order, and equality.

For example, his proposal that senators serve a nine-year term reveals his thinking about equality. Madison foresaw an increase "of those who will labor under all the hardships of life, and secretly sigh for a more equal distribution of its blessings. These may in time outnumber those who are

James Madison, Father of the Constitution

Although he dismissed the accolade, Madison deserved it more than anyone else. As do most fathers, he exercised a powerful influence in debates (and was on the losing side of more than half of them).

New Jersey Plan
Submitted by the head of the New Jersey delegation to the Constitutional Convention of 1787, a set of nine resolutions that would have, in effect, preserved the Articles of Confederation by amending rather than replacing them.

placed above the feelings of indigence."[21] Power, then, could flow into the hands of the numerous poor. The stability of the senate, however, with its nine-year terms and election by the state legislatures, would provide a barrier against the "sighs of the poor" for more equality. Although most delegates shared Madison's apprehension about equality, the nine-year term was voted down.

The Constitution that emerged from the convention bore only partial resemblance to the document Madison wanted to create. He endorsed seventy-one specific proposals, but he ended up on the losing side on forty of them.[22] And the parts of the Virginia Plan that were ultimately included in the Constitution were not adopted without challenge. Conflicts revolved primarily around the basis for representation in the legislature, the method of choosing legislators, and the structure of the executive branch.

The New Jersey Plan

When in 1787 it appeared that much of the Virginia Plan would be approved by the big states, the small states united in opposition. They feared that if each state's representation in the new legislature was based only on the size of its population, the states with large populations would be able to dominate the new government and the needs and wishes of the small states would be ignored. William Paterson of New Jersey introduced an alternative set of resolutions, written to preserve the spirit of the Articles of Confederation by amending rather than replacing them. The **New Jersey Plan** included the following proposals:

- That a single-chamber legislature have the power to raise revenue and regulate commerce.

- That the states have equal representation in the legislature and choose its members.

- That a multiperson executive be elected by the legislature, with powers similar to those proposed under the Virginia Plan but without the right to veto legislation.

- That a supreme tribunal be created, with a limited jurisdiction. (There was no provision for a system of national courts.)

- That the acts of the legislature be binding on the states—that is, that they be regarded as "the supreme law of the respective states," with the option of force to compel obedience.

The New Jersey Plan was defeated in the first major convention vote, 7–3. However, the small states had enough support to force a compromise on the issue of representation in the legislature. Table 3.1 compares the New Jersey Plan with the Virginia Plan.

The Great Compromise

The Virginia Plan provided for a two-chamber legislature, with representation in both chambers based on population. The idea of two chambers was never seriously challenged, but the idea of representation according to

| table 3.1 | Major Differences Between the Virginia Plan and the New Jersey Plan |

Characteristic	Virginia Plan	New Jersey Plan
Legislature	Two chambers	One chamber
Legislative power	Derived from the people	Derived from the states
Executive	Unspecified size	More than one person
Decision rule	Majority	Extraordinary majority
State laws	Legislature can override	National law is supreme
Executive removal	By Congress	By a majority of the states
Courts	National judiciary	No provision for national judiciary
Ratification	By the people	By the states

population stirred up heated and prolonged debate. The small states demanded equal representation for all states, but another vote rejected that concept for the House of Representatives. The debate continued. Finally, the Connecticut delegation moved that each state have an equal vote in the Senate. Still another poll showed that the delegations were equally divided on this proposal.

A committee was created to resolve the deadlock. It consisted of one delegate from each state, chosen by secret ballot. After working straight through the Independence Day recess, the committee reported reaching the **Great Compromise** (sometimes called the Connecticut Compromise). Representation in the House of Representatives would be apportioned according to the population of each state. Initially, there would be fifty-six members. Revenue-raising acts would originate in the House. Most important, the states would be represented equally in the Senate, with two senators each. Senators would be selected by their state legislatures, not directly by the people.

The delegates accepted the Great Compromise. The small states got their equal representation, the big states their proportional representation. The small states might dominate the Senate and the big states might control the House, but because all legislation had to be approved by both chambers, neither group would be able to dominate the other.

Great Compromise
Submitted by the Connecticut delegation to the Constitutional Convention of 1787, and thus also known as the *Connecticut Compromise*, a plan calling for a bicameral legislature in which the House of Representatives would be apportioned according to population and the states would be represented equally in the Senate.

Compromise on the Presidency

Conflict replaced compromise when the delegates turned to the executive branch. They did agree on a one-person executive—a president—but they disagreed on how the executive would be selected and what the term of office would be. The delegates distrusted the people's judgment; some feared that popular election of the president would arouse public passions. Consequently, the delegates rejected the idea. At the same time, representatives of the small states feared that election by the legislature would allow the big states to control the executive.

electoral college
A body of electors chosen by voters to cast ballots for president and vice president.

Once again, a committee composed of one member from each participating state was chosen to find a compromise. That committee fashioned the cumbersome presidential election system we still use today, the **electoral college.** (The Constitution does not use the expression *electoral college.*) Under this system a group of electors would be chosen for the sole purpose of selecting the president and vice president. Each state legislature would choose a number of electors equal to the number of its representatives in Congress. Each elector would then vote for two people. The candidate with the most votes would become president, provided that the number of votes constituted a majority; the person with the next-greatest number of votes would become vice president. (The procedure was changed in 1804 by the Twelfth Amendment, which mandates separate votes for each office.) If no candidate won a majority, the House of Representatives would choose a president, with each state casting one vote.

The electoral college compromise eliminated the fear of a popular vote for president. At the same time, it satisfied the small states. If the electoral college failed to elect a president—which the delegates expected would happen—election by the House would give every state the same voice in the selection process. Finally, the delegates agreed that the president's term of office should be four years and that the president should be eligible for reelection.

The delegates also realized that removing a president from office would be a serious political matter. For that reason, they involved both of the other two branches of government in the process. The House alone was empowered to charge a president with "Treason, Bribery, or other high Crimes and Misdemeanors" (Article II, Section 4), by a majority vote. The Senate was given the sole power to try the president on the House's charges. It could convict, and thus remove, a president only by a two-thirds vote (an extraordinary majority). And the chief justice of the United States was required to preside over the Senate trial. In 1998, the Congress considered whether President Clinton's denial, under oath, of a sexual relationship with a White House intern, who later admitted their affair, fit the constitutional standard of impeachment for "high Crimes and Misdemeanors." Although the House of Representatives voted to impeach President Clinton, the Senate, in a trial presided over by Chief Justice William H. Rehnquist, did not convict him.

THE FINAL PRODUCT

Once the delegates had resolved their major disagreements, they dispatched the remaining issues relatively quickly. A committee was then appointed to organize and write up the results of the proceedings. Twenty-three resolutions had been debated and approved by the convention; these were reorganized under seven articles in the draft constitution. The preamble, which was the last section to be drafted, begins with a phrase that would have been impossible to write when the convention opened. This single sentence contains four elements that form the foundation of the American political tradition.[23]

- *It creates a people:* "We the people of the United States" was a dramatic departure from a loose confederation of states.

- *It explains the reason for the Constitution:* "in order to form a more perfect Union" was an indirect way of saying that the first effort, the Articles of Confederation, had been inadequate.

- *It articulates goals:* "[to] establish Justice, insure domestic Tranquility, provide for the common defence, promote the general Welfare, and secure the Blessings of Liberty to ourselves and our Posterity"—in other words, the government exists to promote order and freedom.

- *It fashions a government:* "do ordain and establish this Constitution for the United States of America."

The Basic Principles

In creating the Constitution, the founders relied on four political principles—republicanism, federalism, separation of powers, and checks and balances—that together established a revolutionary new political order.

republicanism
A form of government in which power resides in the people and is exercised by their elected representatives.

Republicanism.   Republicanism is a form of government in which power resides in the people and is exercised by their elected representatives. The idea of republicanism may be traced to the Greek philosopher Aristotle (384–322 B.C.), who advocated a constitution that combined principles of both democratic and oligarchic government. The framers were determined to avoid aristocracy (rule by a hereditary class), monarchy (rule by one person), and direct democracy (rule by the people). A republic was both new and daring: no people had ever been governed by a republic on so vast a scale.

The framers themselves were far from sure that their government could be sustained. They had no model of republican government to follow; moreover, republican government was thought to be suitable only for small territories, where the interests of the public would be obvious and where the government would be within the reach of every citizen. After the convention ended, Benjamin Franklin was asked what sort of government the new nation would have. "A republic," the old man replied, "if you can keep it."

federalism
The division of power between a central government and regional governments.

Federalism.   Federalism is the division of power between a central government and regional units. Citizens are thus subject to two different bodies of law. It stands between two competing government schemes. On the one side is unitary government, in which all power is vested in a central authority. On the other side stands confederation, a loose union of powerful states. In a confederation, the states surrender some power to a central government but retain the rest. The Articles of Confederation, as we have seen, divided power between loosely knit states and a weak central government. The Constitution also divides power between the states and a central government, but it confers substantial powers on a national government at the expense of the states.

According to the Constitution, the powers vested in the national and state governments are derived from the people, who remain the ultimate sovereigns. National and state governments can exercise their power over people and property within their spheres of authority. But at the same time, by participating in the electoral process or by amending their governing charters, the people can restrain both the national and the state governments if necessary to preserve liberty.

The Constitution lists the powers of the national government and the powers denied to the states. All other powers remain with the states. Generally speaking, the states are required to give up only the powers necessary to create an effective national government; the national government is limited in turn to the powers specified in the Constitution. Despite the specific lists, the Constitution does not clearly describe the spheres of authority within which the powers can be exercised. As we will discuss in Chapter 4, limits on the exercise of power by the national government and the states have evolved as a result of political and military conflicts; moreover, the limits have proved changeable.

Separation of Powers and Checks and Balances. Separation of powers and checks and balances are two distinct principles, but both are necessary to ensure that one branch does not dominate the government. **Separation of powers** is the assignment of the lawmaking, law-enforcing, and law-interpreting functions of government to independent legislative, executive, and judicial branches, respectively. Separation of powers safeguards liberty by ensuring that all government power does not fall into the hands of a single person or group of people. However, the Constitution constrained majority rule by limiting the people's direct influence on the electoral process (see Figure 3.1). In theory, separation of powers means that one branch cannot exercise the powers of the other branches. In practice, however, the separation is far from complete. One scholar has suggested that what we have instead is "separate institutions sharing powers."[24]

separation of powers
The assignment of lawmaking, law-enforcing, and law-interpreting functions to separate branches of government.

Checks and balances is a means of giving each branch of government some scrutiny of and control over the other branches. The aim is to prevent the exclusive exercise of certain powers by any one of the three branches. For example, only Congress can enact laws. But the president (through the veto power) can cancel them, and the courts (by finding that a law violates the Constitution) can strike them down. The process goes on as Congress and the president sometimes begin the legislative process anew, attempting to reformulate laws to address the flaws identified by the Supreme Court in its decisions. In a "check on a check," Congress can override a president's veto by an extraordinary (two-thirds) majority in each chamber. Congress is also empowered to propose amendments to the Constitution, counteracting the courts' power to invalidate. Figure 3.2 depicts the relationship between separation of powers and checks and balances.

checks and balances
A government structure that gives each branch some scrutiny of and control over the other branches.

The Articles of the Constitution

In addition to the preamble, the Constitution includes seven articles. The first three establish the separate branches of government and specify their internal operations and powers. The remaining four define the relationships among the states, explain the process of amendment, declare the supremacy of national law, and explain the procedure for ratifying the Constitution.

3.1   The Constitution and the Electoral Process

The framers were afraid of majority rule, and that fear is reflected in the electoral process for national office described in the Constitution. The people, speaking through the voters, participated directly only in the choice of their representatives in the House. The president and senators were elected indirectly, through the electoral college and state legislatures. (Direct election of senators did not become law until 1913, when the Seventeenth Amendment was ratified.) Judicial appointments are, and always have been, far removed from representative links to the people. Judges are nominated by the president and approved by the Senate.

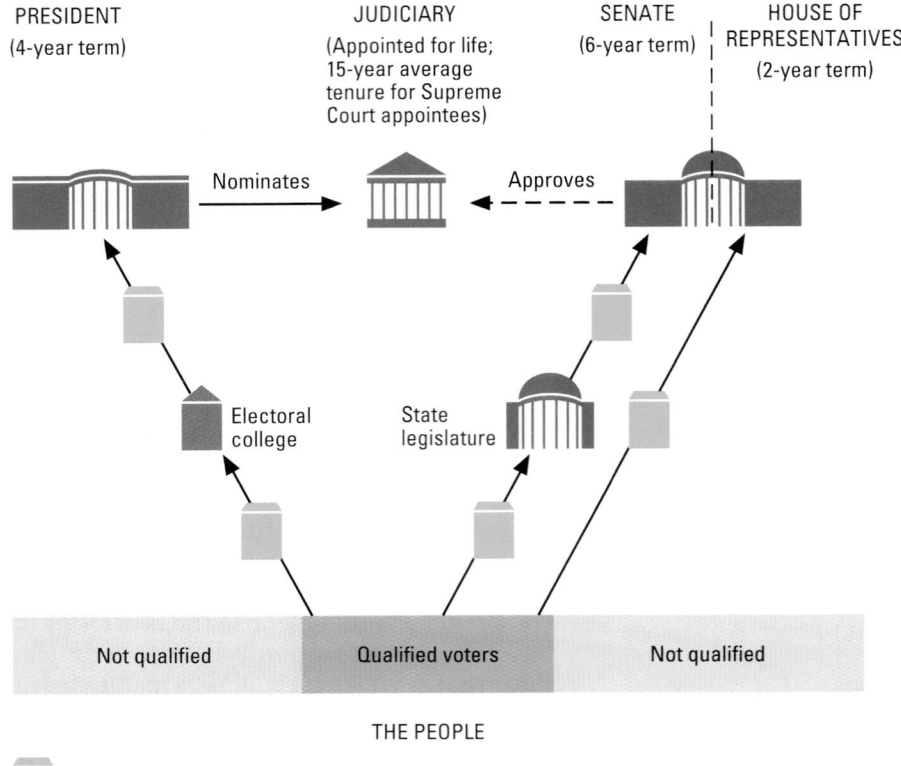

PRESIDENT (4-year term)

JUDICIARY (Appointed for life; 15-year average tenure for Supreme Court appointees)

SENATE (6-year term)

HOUSE OF REPRESENTATIVES (2-year term)

Nominates   Approves

Electoral college   State legislature

Not qualified   Qualified voters   Not qualified

THE PEOPLE

Ballot box

Article I: The Legislative Article.   In structuring their new government, the framers began with the legislative branch because they considered lawmaking the most important function of a republican government. Article I is the most detailed and therefore the longest of all the articles. It defines the bicameral (two-chamber) character of Congress and describes the internal operating procedures of the House of Representatives and the Senate. Section 8 of Article I articulates the principle of **enumerated powers,** which means that Congress can exercise only the powers that the Constitution assigns to it. Eighteen powers are enumerated; the first seventeen are specific powers. For example, the third clause of Section 8 gives Congress the power to regulate interstate commerce. (One of the chief shortcomings of the Articles of Confederation was the lack of a means to cope with trade wars between the states. The solution was to vest control of interstate commerce in the national government.)

The last clause in Section 8, known as the **necessary and proper clause** (or the elastic clause), gives Congress the means to execute the enumerated powers (see the appendix). This clause is the basis of Congress's

enumerated powers
The powers explicitly granted to Congress by the Constitution.

necessary and proper clause
The last clause in Section 8 of Article I of the Constitution, which gives Congress the means to execute its enumerated powers. This clause is the basis for Congress's implied powers. Also called the *elastic clause*.

implied powers
Those powers that Congress needs to execute its enumerated powers.

implied powers—those powers that Congress needs to execute its enumerated powers. For example, the power to levy and collect taxes (clause 1) and the power to coin money and regulate its value (clause 5), when joined with the necessary and proper clause (clause 18), imply that Congress has the power to charter a bank. Otherwise, the national government would have no means of managing the money it collects through its power to tax. Implied powers clearly expand the enumerated powers conferred on Congress by the Constitution.

Article II: The Executive Article. Article II establishes the president's term of office, the procedure for electing the president through the electoral college, the qualifications for becoming president, and the president's duties and powers. The last include acting as commander in chief of the military; making treaties (which must be ratified by a two-thirds vote in the Senate); and appointing government officers, diplomats, and judges (again, with the advice and consent of the Senate).

The president also has legislative powers—part of the constitutional system of checks and balances. For example, the Constitution requires that the president periodically inform Congress of "the State of the Union" and of the policies and programs that the executive branch intends to advocate in the coming year. Today, this is done annually, in the president's State of the Union address. Under special circumstances, the president can also convene or adjourn Congress.

The duty to "take Care that the Laws be faithfully executed" in Section 3 has provided presidents with a reservoir of power. President Nixon tried to use this power when he refused to turn over the Watergate tapes despite a judicial subpoena in a criminal trial. He claimed broad executive privilege, an extension of the executive power implied in Article II. But the Supreme Court rejected his claim, arguing that it violated the separation

figure 3.2 Separation of Powers and Checks and Balances

Separation of powers is the assignment of lawmaking, law-enforcing, and law-interpreting functions to the legislative, executive, and judicial branches, respectively. The phenomenon is illustrated by the diagonal from upper left to lower right in the figure. Checks and balances give each branch some power over the other branches. For example, the executive branch possesses some legislative power, and the legislative branch possesses some executive power. These checks and balances are listed outside the diagonal.

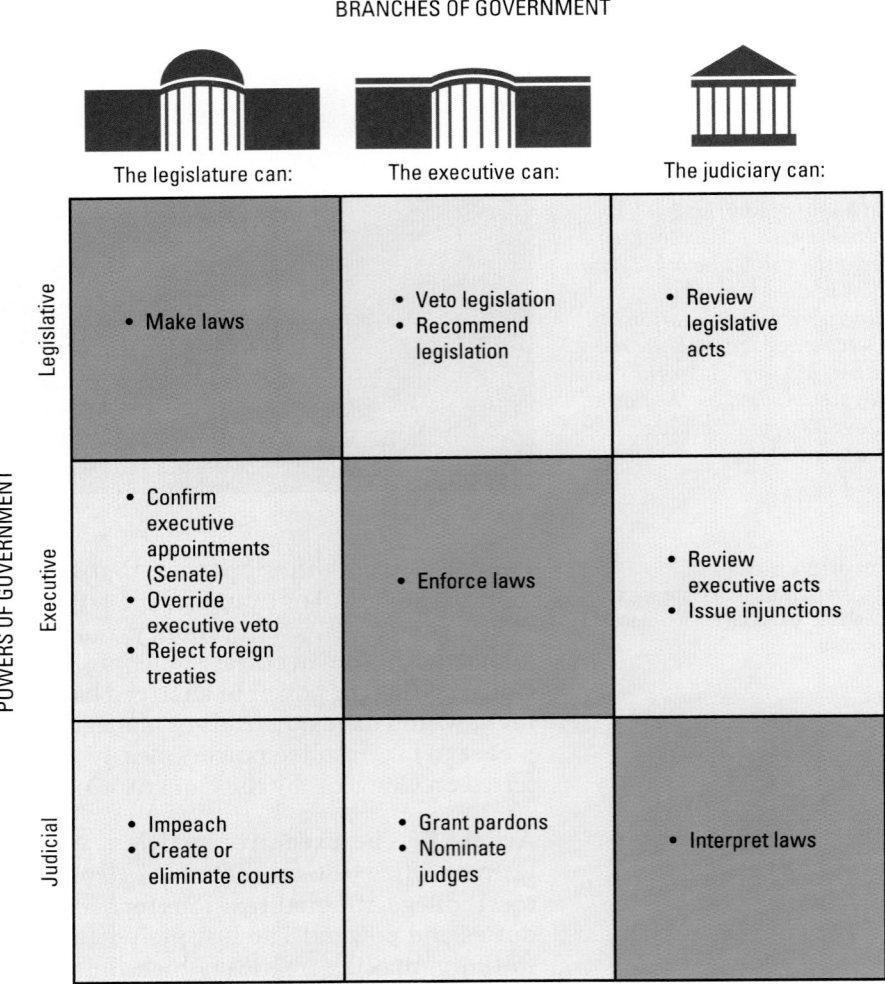

BRANCHES OF GOVERNMENT

POWERS OF GOVERNMENT

	The legislature can:	The executive can:	The judiciary can:
Legislative	• Make laws	• Veto legislation • Recommend legislation	• Review legislative acts
Executive	• Confirm executive appointments (Senate) • Override executive veto • Reject foreign treaties	• Enforce laws	• Review executive acts • Issue injunctions
Judicial	• Impeach • Create or eliminate courts	• Grant pardons • Nominate judges	• Interpret laws

of powers, because the decision to release or withhold information in a criminal trial is a judicial, not an executive, function.

Article III: The Judicial Article. The third article was left purposely vague. The Constitution established the Supreme Court as the highest court in the land. But beyond that, the framers were unable to agree on the need for a national judiciary or on its size, its composition, or the procedures it should follow. They left these issues to Congress, which resolved them by creating a system of federal (that is, national) courts, separate from the state courts.

Unless they are impeached, federal judges serve for life. They are appointed to indefinite terms "during good Behaviour," and their salaries cannot be reduced while they hold office. These stipulations reinforce the separation of powers; they see to it that judges are independent of the other branches and that they do not have to fear retribution for their exercise of judicial power.

Congress exercises a potential check on the judicial branch through its power to create (and eliminate) lower federal courts. Congress can also restrict the power of the federal courts to decide cases. And, as we have noted, the president appoints—with the advice and consent of the Senate—the justices of the Supreme Court and the judges of the lower federal courts.

Article III does not explicitly give the courts the power of **judicial review,** that is, the authority to invalidate congressional or presidential actions. That power has been inferred from the logic, structure, and theory of the Constitution.

judicial review
The power to declare congressional (and presidential) acts invalid because they violate the Constitution.

The Remaining Articles.   The remaining four articles of the Constitution cover a lot of ground. Article IV requires that the judicial acts and criminal warrants of each state be honored in all other states, and it forbids discrimination against citizens of one state by another state. This provision promotes equality; it keeps the states from treating outsiders differently than their own citizens. For example, suppose Smith and Jones both reside in Illinois, and an Illinois court awards Smith a judgment of $100,000 against Jones. Jones moves to Alaska, hoping to avoid payment. Rather than force Smith to bring a new lawsuit against Jones in Alaska, the Alaska courts give full faith and credit to the Illinois judgment, enforcing it as their own. The origin of Article IV can be traced to the Articles of Confederation.

Article IV also allows the addition of new states and stipulates that the national government will protect the states against foreign invasion and domestic violence.

Article V specifies the methods for amending (changing) the Constitution. We will have more to say about this amendment process shortly.

An important component of Article VI is the **supremacy clause,** which asserts that when they conflict with state or local laws, the Constitution, national laws, and treaties take precedence. The stipulation is vital to the operation of federalism. In keeping with the supremacy clause, Article VI also requires that all national and state officials, elected or appointed, take an oath to support the Constitution. The article also mandates that religious affiliation or belief cannot be a prerequisite for holding government office.

supremacy clause
The clause in Article VI of the Constitution that asserts that national laws take precedence over state and local laws when they conflict.

Finally, Article VII describes the ratification process, stipulating that approval by conventions in nine states would be necessary for the Constitution to take effect.

The idea of a written constitution seems entirely natural to Americans today. Lacking a written constitution, Great Britain has started to provide written guarantees for human rights (see Compared with What? 3.1).

The Framers' Motives

Some argue that the Constitution is essentially a conservative document written by wealthy men to advance their own interests. One distinguished historian who wrote in the early 1900s, Charles A. Beard, maintained that the delegates had much to gain from a strong national government.[25] Many held government securities dating from the Revolutionary War that had become practically worthless under the Articles of Confederation. A strong national government would protect their property and pay off the nation's debts.

★ **compared with what?**

3.1   Britain's Bill of Rights

Britain does not have a written constitution, a deliberate scheme of government formally adopted by the people and specifying special processes for its amendment. In Britain, no single document or law is known as "the constitution." Instead, Britain has an "unwritten constitution," an amalgam of important documents and laws passed by Parliament (the British legislature), court decisions, customs, and conventions. Britain's "constitution" has no existence apart from ordinary law. In contrast to the American system of government, in Britain the Parliament may change, amend, or abolish its fundamental laws and conventions at will. No special procedures or barriers must be overcome to enact such changes.

According to government leaders, Britain has done very well without a written constitution, thank you very much. Or at least that

was the position of then prime minister Margaret Thatcher when she was presented with a proposal for a written constitution in 1989. Mrs. Thatcher observed that, despite Britain's lack of a bill of rights and an independent judiciary, "our present constitutional arrangements continue to serve us well. . . . Furthermore, the government does not feel that a written constitution in itself changes or guarantees anything."

In 1995, a nationwide poll revealed that the British people held a different view. Three-fourths of British adults thought that it was time for a written constitution, and even more maintained that the country needed a written bill of rights. These high levels of public support and the election of a new government in 1997 helped to build momentum for important changes in Britain's long history of rule by unwritten law. In October

Beard's argument, that the Constitution was crafted to protect the economic interests of this small group of creditors, provoked a generation of historians to examine the existing financial records of the convention delegates. Their scholarship has largely discredited his once-popular view.[26] For example, it turns out that seven of the delegates who left the convention or refused to sign the Constitution held public securities worth more than twice the total of the holdings of the thirty-nine delegates who did sign. Moreover, the most influential delegates owned no securities. And only a few delegates appear to have directly benefited economically from the new government.[27] Still, there is little doubt about the general homogeneity of the delegates or about their concern for producing a stable economic order that would preserve and promote the interests of some more than others.

What did motivate the framers? Surely economic considerations were important, but they were not the major issues. The single most important factor leading to the Constitutional Convention was the inability of the national or state governments to maintain order under the loose structure of the Articles of Confederation. Certainly, order involved the protection of property, but the framers had a broader view of property than their portfolios of government securities. They wanted to protect their homes, their families, and their means of livelihood from impending anarchy.

Although they disagreed bitterly on the structure and mechanics of the national government, the framers agreed on the most vital issues. For ex-

2000, England formally began enforcing the Human Rights Act, a key component of the government's political program, which incorporated into British law sixteen guarantees of the European Convention on Human Rights drafted by the Council of Europe, a group founded to protect individual freedoms. (The charter was enacted earlier in Scotland, which, along with England, Wales, and Northern Ireland, makes up Great Britain.) Thus, the nation that has been the source of some of the world's most significant ideas concerning liberty and individual freedom finally put into writing guarantees to ensure these fundamental rights for its own citizens. Legal experts hailed the edict as the largest change to British law in three centuries.

It remains to be seen whether the Human Rights Act will, in the words of one former minister in the Thatcher government, "rob us of freedoms we have had for centuries," or as British human rights lawyer Geoffrey Robertson sees it, "help produce a better culture of liberty." Perhaps the track record of the United States and its 210-year experience with the Bill of Rights will prove useful to our British "cousins," who appear ready to alter their system of unwritten rules.

Sources: Andrew Marr, *Ruling Britannia: The Failure and Future of British Democracy* (London: Michael Joseph, 1995); Will Hutton, *The State We're In* (London: Cape, 1995); Fred Barbash, "The Movement to Rule Britannia Differently," *The Washington Post*, 23 September 1995, p. A27; Sarah Lyall, "209 Years Later, the English Get American-Style Bill of Rights," *New York Times*, 2 October 2000, p. A3; Suzanne Kapner, "Britain's Legal Barriers Start to Fall," *New York Times*, 4 October 2000, p. W1.

ample, three of the most crucial features of the Constitution—the power to tax, the necessary and proper clause, and the supremacy clause—were approved unanimously without debate; experience had taught the delegates that a strong national government was essential if the United States were to survive. The motivation to create order was so strong, in fact, that the framers were willing to draft clauses that protected the most undemocratic of all institutions—slavery.

The Slavery Issue

The institution of slavery was well ingrained in American life at the time of the Constitutional Convention, and slavery helped shape the Constitution, although it is mentioned nowhere by name in it. (According to the first national census in 1790, nearly 18 percent of the population—697,000 people—lived in slavery.) It is doubtful, in fact, that there would have been a Constitution if the delegates had had to resolve the slavery issue, for the southern states would have opposed a constitution that prohibited slavery. Opponents of slavery were in the minority, and they were willing to tolerate its continuation in the interest of forging a union, perhaps believing that the issue could be resolved another day.

The question of representation in the House of Representatives brought the slavery issue close to the surface of the debate at the Constitutional

Convention, and it led to the Great Compromise. Representation in the House was to be based on population. But who counted in the population? States with large slave populations wanted all their inhabitants, slave and free, counted equally; states with few slaves wanted only the free population counted. The delegates agreed unanimously that in apportioning representation in the House and in assessing direct taxes, the population of each state was to be determined by adding "the whole Number of free Persons" and "three fifths of all other Persons" (Article I, Section 2). The phrase "all other Persons" is, of course, a substitute for "slaves."

The three-fifths formula had been used by the 1783 congress under the Articles of Confederation to allocate government costs among the states. The rule reflected the view that slaves were less efficient producers of wealth than free people, not that slaves were three-fifths human and two-fifths personal property.[28]

The three-fifths clause gave states with large slave populations (the South) greater representation in Congress than states with small slave populations (the North). If all slaves had been included in the count, the slave states would have had 50 percent of the seats in the House. This outcome would have been unacceptable to the North. Had none of the slaves been counted, the slave states would have had 41 percent of House seats, which would have been unacceptable to the South. The three-fifths compromise left the South with 47 percent of the House seats, a sizable minority, but in all likelihood a losing one on slavery issues.[29] The overrepresentation resulting from the South's large slave populations translated into greater influence in selecting the president as well, because the electoral college was based on the size of the states' congressional delegations. The three-fifths clause also undertaxed states with large slave populations.

Another issue centered around the slave trade. Several southern delegates were uncompromising in their defense of the slave trade; other delegates favored prohibition. The delegates compromised, agreeing that the slave trade would not be ended before twenty years had elapsed (Article I, Section 9). Finally, the delegates agreed, without serious challenge, that fugitive slaves would be returned to their masters (Article IV, Section 2).

In addressing these points, the framers in essence condoned slavery. Tens of thousands of Africans were forcibly taken from their homes and sold into bondage. Many died on the journey to this distant land, and those who survived were brutalized and treated as less than human. Clearly, slavery existed in stark opposition to the idea that all men are created equal. Although many slaveholders, including Jefferson and Madison, agonized over it, few made serious efforts to free their own slaves. Most Americans seemed indifferent to slavery and felt no embarrassment at the apparent contradiction between the Declaration of Independence and slavery. Do the framers deserve contempt for their toleration and perpetuation of slavery? The most prominent founders—George Washington, John Adams, and Thomas Jefferson—expected slavery to wither away. A leading scholar of colonial history has offered a defense of their inaction: the framers were simply unable to transcend altogether the limitations of the age in which they lived.[30]

Nonetheless, the eradication of slavery proceeded gradually in certain states. Opposition to slavery on moral or religious grounds was one reason. Economic forces—such as a shift in the North to agricultural production that was less labor-intensive—were a contributing factor, too. By 1787, Connecticut, Massachusetts, New Jersey, New York, Pennsylvania, Rhode Island, and Vermont had abolished slavery or provided for gradual emancipation. No southern states followed suit, although several enacted laws making it easier for masters to free their slaves. The slow but perceptible shift on the slavery issue in many states masked a volcanic force capable of destroying the Constitutional Convention and the Union.

SELLING THE CONSTITUTION

Nearly four months after the Constitutional Convention opened, the delegates convened for the last time, on September 17, 1787, to sign the final version of their handiwork. Because several delegates were unwilling to sign the document, the last paragraph was craftily worded to give the impression of unanimity: "Done in Convention by the Unanimous Consent of the States present."

Before it could take effect, the Constitution had to be ratified by a minimum of nine state conventions. The support of key states was crucial. In Pennsylvania, however, the legislature was slow to convene a ratifying convention. Pro-Constitution forces became so frustrated at this dawdling that they broke into a local boardinghouse and hauled two errant legislators through the streets to the statehouse so the assembly could schedule the convention.

The proponents of the new charter, who wanted a strong national government, called themselves Federalists. The opponents of the Constitution were quickly dubbed Antifederalists. They claimed, however, to be the true federalists because they wanted to protect the states from the tyranny of a strong national government. Elbridge Gerry, a vocal Antifederalist, called his opponents "rats" (because they favored ratification) and maintained that he was an "antirat."[31] Such is the Alice-in-Wonderland character of political discourse. Whatever they were called, the viewpoints of these two groups formed the bases of the first American political parties.

The *Federalist* Papers

Federalist Nos. 10, 51, 65, 66, 78, and 84

The press of the day became a battlefield of words, filled with extravagant praise or vituperative condemnation of the proposed constitution. Beginning in October 1787, an exceptional series of eighty-five newspaper articles defending the Constitution appeared under the title *The Federalist: A Commentary on the Constitution of the United States.* The essays bore the pen name Publius (for a Roman emperor and defender of the Republic, Publius Valerius, who was later known as Publicola); they were written primarily by James Madison and Alexander Hamilton, with some assistance from John Jay. Reprinted extensively during the ratification battle, the *Federalist* papers remain the best single commentary we have on the meaning of the Constitution and the political theory it embodies.

Not to be outdone, the Antifederalists offered their own intellectual basis for rejecting the Constitution. In several essays, the most influential published under the pseudonyms Brutus and Federal Farmer, the Antifederalists attacked the centralization of power in a strong national government, claiming it would obliterate the states, violate the social contract of the Declaration of Independence, and destroy liberty in the process. They defended the status quo, maintaining that the Articles of Confederation established true federal principles.[32]

Of all the *Federalist* papers, the most magnificent and most frequently cited is *Federalist* No. 10, written by James Madison (see the appendix). He argued that the proposed constitution was designed "to break and control the violence of faction." "By a faction," Madison wrote, "I understand a number of citizens, whether amounting to a majority or minority of the whole, who are united and actuated by some common impulse of passion, or of interest, adverse to the rights of other citizens, or to the permanent and aggregate interests of the community."

What Madison called factions are today called interest groups or even political parties. According to Madison, "The most common and durable source of factions has been the various and unequal distribution of property." Madison was concerned not with reducing inequalities of wealth (which he took for granted) but with controlling the seemingly inevitable conflict that stems from them. The Constitution, he argued, was well constructed for this purpose.

Through the mechanism of representation, wrote Madison, the Constitution would prevent a "tyranny of the majority" (mob rule). The government would not be controlled by the people directly but indirectly by their elected representatives. And those representatives would have the intelligence and the understanding to serve the larger interests of the nation. Moreover, the federal system would require that majorities form first within each state and then organize for effective action at the national level. This and the vastness of the country would make it unlikely that a majority would form that would "invade the rights of other citizens."

The purpose of *Federalist* No. 10 was to demonstrate that the proposed government was not likely to be dominated by any faction. Contrary to conventional wisdom, Madison argued, the key to mending the evils of factions is to have a large republic—the larger, the better. The more diverse the society, the less likely it is that an unjust majority can form. Madison certainly had no intention of creating a majoritarian democracy; his view of popular government was much more consistent with the model of pluralist democracy discussed in Chapter 2.

Can You Explain Why...
having many factions reduces the danger of factions?

Madison pressed his argument from a different angle in *Federalist* No. 51 (see the appendix). Asserting that "ambition must be made to counteract ambition," he argued that the separation of powers and checks and balances would control efforts at tyranny from any source. If power is distributed equally among the three branches, he argued, each branch will have the capacity to counteract the others. In Madison's words, "usurpations are guarded against by a division of the government into distinct and separate departments." Because legislative power tends to predominate in republican governments, legislative authority is divided between the Senate and the House of Representatives, which have different methods of election and terms of office. Additional protection arises from federalism, which divides power "between two distinct governments"—national and state—and subdivides "the portion allotted to each . . . among distinct and separate departments."

The Antifederalists wanted additional separation of powers and additional checks and balances, which they maintained would eliminate the threat of tyranny entirely. The Federalists believed that such protections would make decisive national action virtually impossible. But to ensure ratification, they agreed to a compromise.

A Concession: The Bill of Rights

Despite the eloquence of the *Federalist* papers, many prominent citizens, including Thomas Jefferson, were unhappy that the Constitution did not list basic civil liberties—the individual freedoms guaranteed to citizens. The omission of a bill of rights was the chief obstacle to the adoption of the Constitution by the states. (Seven of the eleven state constitutions that were written in the first five years of independence included such a list.) The colonists had just rebelled against the British government to preserve their basic freedoms; why did the proposed Constitution not spell out those freedoms?

The answer was rooted in logic, not politics. Because the national government was limited to those powers that were granted to it and because no power was granted to abridge the people's liberties, a list of guaranteed freedoms was not necessary. In *Federalist* No. 84, Hamilton went even further, arguing that the addition of a bill of rights would be dangerous. To deny the exercise of a nonexistent power might lead to the exercise of a power that is not specifically denied. For example, to declare that the national government shall make no law abridging free speech might suggest that the national government could prohibit activities in unspecified areas (such as divorce), which are the states' domain. Because it is not possible to list all prohibited powers, wrote Hamilton, any attempt to provide a partial list would make the unlisted areas vulnerable to government abuse.

But logic was no match for fear. Many states agreed to ratify the Constitution only after George Washington suggested adding a list of guarantees through the amendment process. Well in excess of one hundred amendments were proposed by the states. These were eventually narrowed to twelve, which were approved by Congress and sent to the states. Ten became part of the Constitution in 1791, after securing the approval of the required three-fourths of the states. Collectively, the ten amendments are known as the **Bill of Rights.** They restrain the national government from tampering with fundamental rights and civil liberties and emphasize the limited character of the national government's power (see Table 3.2).

Ratification

The Constitution officially took effect upon its ratification by the ninth state, New Hampshire, on June 21, 1788. However, the success of the new government was not ensured until July 1788, by which time the Constitution was ratified by the key states of Virginia and New York after lengthy debate.

The reflection and deliberation that attended the creation and ratification of the Constitution signaled to the world that a new government could be launched peacefully. The French observer Alexis de Tocqueville (1805–1859) later wrote

> That which is new in the history of societies is to see a great people, warned by its lawgivers that the wheels of government are stopping, turn its attention on itself without haste or fear, sound the depth of the ill, and

Can You Explain Why...
some of the nation's founders thought that adding a bill of rights to the Constitution might actually limit individual rights?

Bill of Rights
The first ten amendments to the Constitution. They prevent the national government from tampering with fundamental rights and civil liberties, and emphasize the limited character of national power.

The Struggle over Ratification

table **3.2**   **The Bill of Rights**

The first ten amendments to the Constitution are known as the Bill of Rights. The following is a list of those amendments, grouped conceptually. For the actual order and wording of the Bill of Rights, see the appendix.

Guarantees	Amendment
Guarantees for Participation in the Political Process	
No government abridgment of speech or press; no government abridgment of peaceable assembly; no government abridgment of petitioning government for redress.	1
Guarantees Respecting Personal Beliefs	
No government establishment of religion; no government prohibition of free religious exercise.	1
Guarantees of Personal Privacy	
Owners' consent necessary to quarter troops in private homes in peacetime; quartering during war must be lawful.	3
Government cannot engage in unreasonable searches and seizures; warrants to search and seize require probable cause.	4
No compulsion to testify against oneself in criminal cases.	5
Guarantees Against Government's Overreaching	
Serious crimes require a grand jury indictment; no repeated prosecution for the same offense; no loss of life, liberty, or property without due process; no taking of property for public use without just compensation.	5
Criminal defendants will have a speedy public trial by impartial local jury; defendants are informed of accusation; defendants may confront witnesses against them; defendants may use judicial process to obtain favorable witnesses; defendants may have legal assistance for their defense.	6
Civil lawsuits can be tried by juries if controversy exceeds $20; in jury trials, fact-finding is a jury function.	7
No excessive bail; no excessive fines; no cruel and unusual punishment.	8
Other Guarantees	
The people have the right to bear arms.	2
No government trespass on unspecified fundamental rights.	9
The states or the people retain all powers not delegated to the national government or denied to the states.	10

then wait for two years to find the remedy at leisure, and then finally, when the remedy has been indicated, submit to it voluntarily without its costing humanity a single tear or drop of blood.[33]

CONSTITUTIONAL CHANGE

The founders realized that the Constitution would have to be changed from time to time. To this end, they specified a formal amendment process—a process that was used almost immediately to add the Bill of Rights. With the passage of time, the Constitution has also been altered through judicial interpretation and changes in political practice.

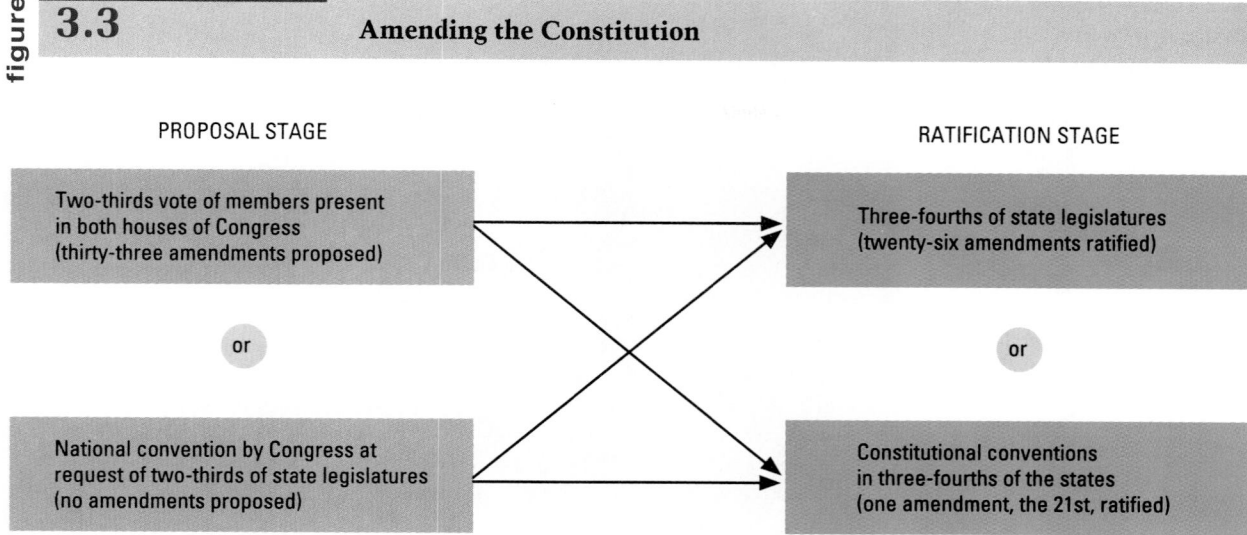

figure 3.3   Amending the Constitution

PROPOSAL STAGE

Two-thirds vote of members present in both houses of Congress (thirty-three amendments proposed)

or

National convention by Congress at request of two-thirds of state legislatures (no amendments proposed)

RATIFICATION STAGE

Three-fourths of state legislatures (twenty-six amendments ratified)

or

Constitutional conventions in three-fourths of the states (one amendment, the 21st, ratified)

Amending the Constitution requires two stages: proposal and ratification. Both Congress and the states can play a role in the proposal stage, but ratification is a process that must be fought in the states themselves. Once a state has ratified an amendment, it cannot retract its action. However, a state may reject an amendment and then reconsider its decision.

The Formal Amendment Process

The amendment process has two stages, proposal and ratification; both are necessary for an amendment to become part of the Constitution. The Constitution provides two alternatives for completing each stage (see Figure 3.3). Amendments can be proposed by a two-thirds vote in both the House of Representatives and the Senate or by a national convention, summoned by Congress at the request of two-thirds of the state legislatures. All constitutional amendments to date have been proposed by the first method; the second has never been used.

A proposed amendment can be ratified by a vote of the legislatures of three-fourths of the states or by a vote of constitutional conventions held in three-fourths of the states. Congress chooses the method of ratification. It has used the state convention method only once, for the Twenty-first Amendment, which repealed the Eighteenth (prohibition of intoxicating liquors). Congress may, in proposing an amendment, set a time limit for its ratification. Beginning with the Eighteenth Amendment, but skipping the Nineteenth, Congress has set seven years as the limit for ratification.

extraordinary majorities
Majorities greater than that required by majority rule, that is, greater than 50 percent plus one.

Note that the amendment process requires the exercise of **extraordinary majorities** (two-thirds and three-fourths). The framers purposely made it difficult to propose and ratify amendments (although nowhere near as difficult as under the Articles of Confederation). They wanted only the most significant issues to lead to constitutional change. Note, too, that the president plays no formal role in the process. Presidential approval is not required to amend the Constitution, although the president's political influence affects the success or failure of any amendment effort.

★

Designated Pourer

The Eighteenth Amendment, which was ratified by the states in 1919, banned the manufacture, sale, and transportation of alcoholic beverages. Banned beverages were destroyed, as pictured here. The amendment was spurred by moral and social reform groups, such as the Women's Christian Temperance Union, founded by Evanston, Illinois, resident Frances Willard in 1874. The amendment proved to be an utter failure. People continued to drink, but their alcohol came from illegal sources.

Calling a national convention to propose an amendment has never been tried, and the method raises several thorny questions. For example, the Constitution does not specify the number of delegates who should attend, the method by which they should be chosen, or the rules for debating and voting on a proposed amendment. Confusion surrounding the convention process has precluded its use, leaving the amendment process in congressional hands.[34] The major issue is the limits, if any, on the business of the convention. Remember that the convention in Philadelphia in 1787, charged with revising the Articles of Confederation, drafted an entirely new charter. Would a national convention called to consider a particular amendment be within its bounds to rewrite the Constitution? No one really knows.

Most of the Constitution's twenty-seven amendments were adopted to reflect changes in political thinking. The first ten amendments (the Bill of Rights) were the price of ratification, but they have been fundamental to our system of government. The last seventeen amendments fall into three main categories: they make public policy, they correct deficiencies in the government's structure, or they promote equality (see Table 3.3). One attempt to make public policy through a constitutional amendment was disastrous. The Eighteenth Amendment (1919) prohibited the manufacture or sale of intoxicating beverages. Prohibition lasted fourteen years and was an utter failure. Gangsters began bootlegging liquor, people died from drinking homemade booze, and millions regularly broke the law by drinking anyway. Congress had to propose another amendment in 1933 to repeal the Eighteenth. The states ratified this amendment, the Twenty-first, in less than ten months, less time than it took to ratify the Fourteenth Amendment, guaranteeing citizenship, due process, and equal protection of the laws.

table **3.3**

Constitutional Amendments: 11 Through 27

No.	Proposed	Ratified	Intent*	Subject
11	1794	1795	G	Prohibits an individual from suing a state in federal court without the state's consent.
12	1803	1804	G	Requires the electoral college to vote separately for president and vice president.
13	1865	1865	E	Prohibits slavery.
14	1866	1868	E	Gives citizenship to all persons born or naturalized in the United States (including former slaves); prevents states from depriving any person of "life, liberty, or property, without due process of law," and declares that no state shall deprive any person of "the equal protection of the laws."
15	1869	1870	E	Guarantees that citizens' right to vote cannot be denied "on account of race, color, or previous condition of servitude."
16	1909	1913	E	Gives Congress the power to collect an income tax.
17	1912	1913	E	Provides for popular election of senators, who were formerly elected by state legislatures.
18	1917	1919	P	Prohibits the making and selling of intoxicating liquors.
19	1919	1920	E	Guarantees that citizens' right to vote cannot be denied "on account of sex."
20	1932	1933	G	Changes the presidential inauguration from March 4 to January 20 and sets January 3 for the opening date of Congress.
21	1933	1933	P	Repeals the Eighteenth Amendment.
22	1947	1951	G	Limits a president to two terms.
23	1960	1961	E	Gives citizens of Washington, D.C., the right to vote for president.
24	1962	1964	E	Prohibits charging citizens a poll tax to vote in presidential or congressional elections.
25	1965	1967	G	Provides for succession in event of death, removal from office, incapacity, or resignation of the president or vice president.
26	1971	1971	E	Lowers the voting age to eighteen.
27	1789	1992	G	Bars immediate pay increases to members of Congress.

*P: amendments legislating public policy; G: amendments correcting perceived deficiencies in government structure; E: amendments advancing equality.

Since 1787, about 10,000 constitutional amendments have been introduced; only a fraction have survived the proposal stage. Once an amendment has been approved by Congress, its chances for ratification are high. The Twenty-seventh Amendment, which prevents members of Congress from voting themselves immediate pay increases, was ratified in 1992. It had been submitted to the states in 1789 without a time limit for ratification but it languished in a political netherworld until 1982, when a University of Texas student, Gregory D. Watson, stumbled upon the proposed amendment while researching a paper. At that time, only eight states had ratified the amendment. Watson took up the cause, prompting renewed interest in the idea. In May 1992, ratification by the Michigan legislature provided the decisive vote, 203 years after congressional approval of the proposed amendment.[35] Only six amendments submitted to the states have failed to be ratified.

Interpretation by the Courts

In *Marbury* v. *Madison* (1803), the Supreme Court declared that the courts have the power to nullify government acts that conflict with the Constitution. (We will elaborate on judicial review in Chapter 14.) The exercise of judicial review forces the courts to interpret the Constitution. In a way, this makes a lot of sense. The judiciary is the law-interpreting branch of the government; as the supreme law of the land, the Constitution is fair game for judicial interpretation. Judicial review is the courts' main check on the other branches of government. But in interpreting the Constitution, the courts cannot help but give new meaning to its provisions. This is why judicial interpretation is a principal form of constitutional change.

What guidelines should judges use in interpreting the Constitution? For one thing, they must realize that the usage and meaning of many words have changed during the past two hundred years. Judges must be careful to think about what the words meant at the time the Constitution was written. Some insist that they must also consider the original intent of the framers—not an easy task. Of course, there are records of the Constitutional Convention and of the debates surrounding ratification. But there are also many questions about the completeness and accuracy of those records, even Madison's detailed notes. And, at times, the framers were deliberately vague in writing the document. This may reflect lack of agreement on, or universal understanding of, certain provisions in the Constitution. Some scholars and judges maintain that the search for original meaning is hopeless and that contemporary notions of constitutional provisions must hold sway. Critics say that this approach comes perilously close to amending the Constitution as judges see fit, transforming law interpreters into lawmakers. Still other scholars and judges maintain that judges face the unavoidable challenge of balancing two-hundred-year-old constitutional principles against the demands of modern society.[36] Whatever the approach, judges run the risk of usurping policies established by the people's representatives.

Political Practice

The Constitution is silent on many issues. It says nothing about political parties or the president's cabinet, for example, yet both have exercised considerable influence in American politics. Some constitutional provisions have fallen out of use. The electors in the electoral college, for example, were supposed to exercise their own judgment in voting for the president and vice president. Today, the electors function simply as a rubber stamp, validating the outcome of election contests in their states.

Meanwhile, political practice has altered the distribution of power without changes in the Constitution. The framers intended Congress to be the strongest branch of government. But the president has come to overshadow Congress. Presidents such as Abraham Lincoln and Franklin Roosevelt used their powers imaginatively to respond to national crises. And their actions paved the way for future presidents to enlarge further the powers of the office.

The framers could scarcely have imagined an urbanized nation approaching 300 million people stretching across a landmass some 3,000 miles wide, reaching halfway over the Pacific Ocean, and stretching past the Arctic Circle. Never in their wildest nightmares could they have foreseen the destructiveness of nuclear weaponry or envisioned its effect on the power to declare war. The Constitution empowers Congress to consider and debate this momentous step. But with nuclear annihilation perhaps only minutes away, the legislative power to declare war must give way to the president's power to wage war as the nation's commander in chief. Strict adherence to the Constitution in such circumstances could destroy the nation's ability to protect itself.

AN EVALUATION OF THE CONSTITUTION

The U.S. Constitution is one of the world's most praised political documents. It is the oldest written national constitution and one of the most widely copied, sometimes word for word. It is also one of the shortest, consisting of about 4,300 words (not counting the amendments, which add 3,100 words). The brevity of the Constitution may be one of its greatest strengths. As we noted earlier, the framers simply laid out a structural framework for government; they did not describe relationships and powers in detail. For example, the Constitution gives Congress the power to regulate "Commerce . . . among the several States" but does not define interstate commerce. Such general wording allows interpretation in keeping with contemporary political, social, and technological developments. Air travel, for instance, unknown in 1787, now falls easily within Congress's power to regulate interstate commerce.

The generality of the U.S. Constitution stands in stark contrast to the specificity of most state constitutions and the constitutions of many emerging democracies. The constitution of California, for example, provides that "fruit and nut-bearing trees under the age of four years from the time of planting in orchard form and grapevines under the age of three years from the time of planting in vineyard form . . . shall be exempt from taxation" (Article XIII, Section 12). Because they are so specific, most state constitutions are much longer than the U.S. Constitution.

The constitution of the Republic of Slovenia, adopted in December 1991, prevents citizens from being "compelled to undergo medical treatment except in such cases as are determined by statute." In the Republic of Lithuania, the national constitution, adopted in October 1992, spells out in significant detail some of the free-speech rights of its citizens, including the protection that "Citizens who belong to ethnic communities shall have the right to foster their language, culture, and customs."[37] The U.S. Constitution remains a beacon for others to follow (see Politics in a Changing World 3.1).

★ politics in a changing world

3.1   A New Birth of Freedom: Exporting American Constitutionalism

When the founders drafted the U.S. Constitution in 1787, they hardly started from scratch. Leaders like James Madison and John Adams drew on the failed experiences of the Articles of Confederation to chart a new course for our national government. They also leaned heavily on the ideas of great democratic thinkers of the past. Today, given the more than 200-year track record of the United States, it is no wonder that many nations have looked to the American experience as they embark on their own democratic experiments.

In the last ten years especially, democratizing countries on nearly every continent have developed new governing institutions by drawing at least in part on important principles from the U.S. Constitution and Bill of Rights. This is certainly the case in the former communist countries of Eastern Europe, most of whom are just completing their first decade of newly established democratic rule. Enshrining democratic ideals in a written constitution corresponds to the ascendancy of freedom worldwide (see the accompanying figure).

Echoing the U.S. Declaration of Independence and the Constitution's preamble, for example, Article 2 of the Lithuanian constitution declares unequivocally, "Sov-

ereignty shall be vested in the people." To protect the rights of citizens and to prevent power from becoming too concentrated, many Eastern European nations have designed government institutions to allocate and share power among different branches paralleling the legislative, executive, and judicial arrangement of the American experience.

Specific guarantees protecting individual rights and liberties are also written in great detail in the constitutions of these new democracies. The Romanian constitution, for example, takes a strong stand on the defense of personal ideas, stating that "Freedom of expression of thoughts, opinions, or beliefs, and freedom of any creation by words, in writing, in pictures, by sounds or other means of communication in public are inviolable." Similarly, the constitution of Bulgaria details important restrictions on government action against the nation's citizens. Protections regarding cruel and unusual punishment, unreasonable detention or search, and privacy within one's home and personal correspondence are just a few of the Bulgarian constitution's guarantees.

Because there is no ready-made formula for building a successful democracy, only time will tell whether these young constitutions will perform well in practice. Just a decade

Freedom, Order, and Equality in the Constitution

The revolutionaries' first try at government was embodied in the Articles of Confederation. The result was a weak national government that leaned too much toward freedom at the expense of order. Deciding that the confederation was beyond correcting, the revolutionaries chose a new form of government—a *federal* government—that was strong enough to maintain order but not so strong that it could dominate the states or infringe on individual freedoms. In short, the Constitution provided a judicious balance between order and freedom. It paid virtually no attention to equality.

ago, humorists asked: "What is the difference between the Soviet constitution and the U.S. Constitution?" The answer: "Under the Soviet constitution, there is freedom of speech and freedom of thought. But under the U.S. Constitution there is freedom *after* speech and freedom *after* thought!" The point is that putting democracy into practice is much harder than theorizing about democracy. Undoubtedly, success will be the product of many factors, including the courage to resist past totalitarian practices, the willingness to make important adjustments to national institutions when the need arises, and, perhaps most important, a measure of good luck.

Sources: The International Institute for Democracy. *The Rebirth of Democracy: 12 Constitutions of Central and Eastern Europe*, 2nd ed. (The Netherlands: Council of Europe, 1996); A. E. Dick Howard, "Liberty's Text: 10 Amendments That Changed the World," *Washington Post*, 15 December 1991, p. C3; Freedom House, Annual Survey of Freedom Country Scores, 1972–1973 to 1999–2000 <www.freedomhouse.org/ratings/>.

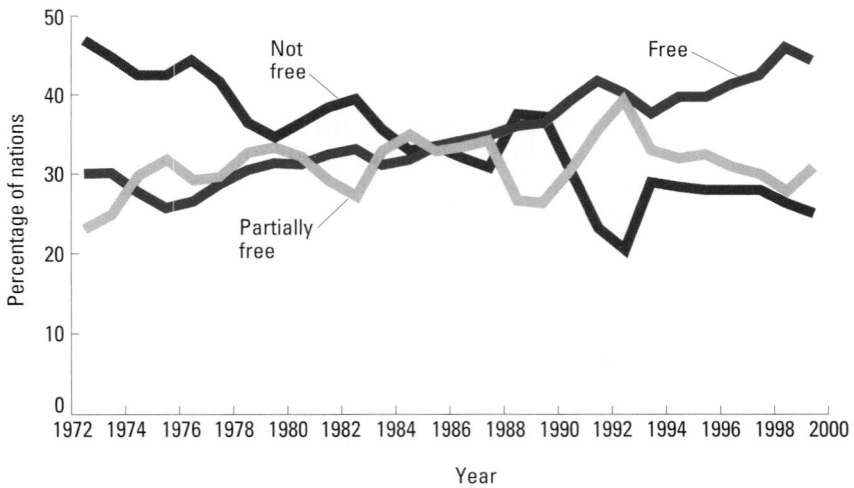

Consider social equality. The Constitution never mentioned the word *slavery*—a controversial issue even then. In fact, as we have seen, the Constitution implicitly condones slavery in the wording of several articles. Not until the ratification of the Thirteenth Amendment in 1865 was slavery prohibited.

The Constitution was designed long before social equality was ever even thought of as an objective of government. In fact, in *Federalist* No. 10, Madison held that protection of the "diversities in the faculties of men from which the rights of property originate" is "the first object of government." More than a century later, the Constitution was changed to incorporate a key device for the promotion of social equality—the income tax. The Sixteenth Amendment (1913) gave Congress the power to collect an income tax; it was proposed and ratified to replace a law that had been declared unconstitutional in an 1895 Supreme Court case. The income tax had long been seen as a means of putting into effect the concept of *progressive taxation*, in which the tax rate increases with income. The Sixteenth Amendment gave progressive taxation a constitutional basis.[38] Progressive taxation later helped promote social equality through the redistribution of income—that is, higher-income people are taxed at higher rates to help fund social programs that benefit low-income people.

Social equality itself has never been, and is not now, a prime *constitutional* value. The Constitution has been much more effective in securing order and freedom. Nor did the Constitution take a stand on political equality. It left voting qualifications to the states, specifying only that people who could vote for "the most numerous Branch of the State Legislature" could also vote for representatives to Congress (Article I, Section 2). Most states at that time allowed only taxpaying or property-owning white males to vote. With few exceptions, blacks and women were universally excluded from voting. These inequalities have been rectified by several amendments (see Table 3.3).

Political equality expanded after the Civil War. The Fourteenth Amendment (adopted in 1868) guaranteed all persons, including blacks, citizenship. The Fifteenth Amendment (ratified in 1870) declared that "race, color, or previous condition of servitude" could not be used to deny citizens the right to vote. This did not automatically give blacks the vote; some states used other mechanisms to limit black enfranchisement. The Nineteenth Amendment (adopted in 1920) opened the way for women to vote by declaring that sex could not be used to deny citizens the right to vote. The Twenty-fourth Amendment (adopted in 1964) prohibited the poll tax (a tax that people had to pay to vote and that tended to disenfranchise poor blacks) in presidential and congressional elections. The Twenty-sixth Amendment (adopted in 1971) declared that age could not be used to deny citizens eighteen years or older the right to vote. One other amendment expanded the Constitution's grant of political equality. The Twenty-third Amendment (adopted in 1961) allowed residents of Washington, D.C., who are not citizens of any state, to vote for president.

The Constitution and Models of Democracy

Think back to our discussion of the models of democracy in Chapter 2. Which model does the Constitution fit: pluralist or majoritarian? Actually, it is hard to imagine a government framework better suited to the pluralist model of democracy than the Constitution of the United States. It is also hard to imagine a document more at odds with the majoritarian model. Consider Madison's claim, in *Federalist* No. 10, that government inevitably involves conflicting factions. This concept coincides perfectly with pluralist theory (see Chapter 2). Then recall his description in *Federalist* No. 51 of the Constitution's ability to guard against concentration of power in the majority through separation of powers and checks and balances. This concept—avoiding a single center of government power that might fall under majority control—also fits perfectly with pluralist democracy.

The delegates to the Constitutional Convention intended to create a republic, a government based on majority consent; they did not intend to create a democracy, which rests on majority rule. They succeeded admirably in creating that republic. In doing so, they also produced a government that developed into a democracy—but a particular type of democracy. The framers neither wanted nor got a democracy that fit the majoritarian model. They may have wanted, and they certainly did create, a government that conforms to the pluralist model.

SUMMARY

The U.S. Constitution is more than an antique curiosity. Although more than 200 years old, it governs the politics of a strong modern nation. It still has the power to force from office a president who won reelection by a landslide. It still has the power to see the country through government crises.

The Constitution was the end product of a revolutionary movement aimed at preserving existing liberties. That movement began with the Declaration of Independence, which proclaimed that everyone is entitled to certain rights (among them, life, liberty, and the pursuit of happiness) and that government exists for the good of its citizens. When government denies those rights, the people have the right to rebel.

War with Britain was only part of the process of independence. A government was needed to replace the British monarchy. The Americans chose a republic and defined the structure of that republic in the Articles of Confederation. The Articles were a failure, however. Although they guaranteed the states the independence they coveted, they left the central government too weak to deal with disorder and insurrection.

The Constitution was the second attempt at limited government. It replaced a loose union of powerful states with a strong but still limited national government, incorporating four political principles: republicanism, federalism, separation of powers, and checks and balances. Republicanism is a form of government in which power resides in the people and is exercised by their elected representatives. Federalism is a division of power between the national government and the states. The federalism of the Constitution conferred substantial powers on the national government at the expense of the states. Separation of powers is a further division of the power of the national government into legislative (lawmaking), executive (law-enforcing), and judicial (law-interpreting) branches. Finally, the Constitution established a system of checks and balances, giving each branch some scrutiny of and control over the others.

When work began on ratification, a major stumbling block proved to be the failure of the Constitution to list the individual liberties the Americans had fought to protect. With the promise to add a bill of rights, the Constitution was ratified. The ten amendments that make up the Bill of Rights guaranteed participation in the political process, respect for personal beliefs, and personal privacy. They also contained guarantees against government overreaching in criminal prosecutions. Over the years, the Constitution has evolved through the formal amendment process, through the exercise of judicial review, and through political practice.

The Constitution was designed to strike a balance between order and freedom. It was not designed to promote social equality; in fact, it had to be amended to redress inequality. The framers compromised on many issues, including slavery, to ensure the creation of a new and workable government. The framers did not set out to create a democracy. Faith in government by the people was virtually nonexistent two centuries ago. Nevertheless, they produced a democratic form of government. That government, with its separation of powers and checks and balances, is remarkably well suited to the pluralist model of democracy. Simple majority rule, which lies at the heart of the majoritarian model, was precisely what the framers wanted to avoid.

The framers also wanted a balance between the powers of the national government and those of the states. The exact balance was a touchy issue, skirted by the delegates at the Constitutional Convention. Some seventy years later, a civil war was fought over that balance of power. That war and countless political battles before and since have demonstrated that the national government dominates the state governments in our political system. In Chapter 4, we will look at how a loose confederation of states has evolved into a "more perfect Union."

★ Selected Readings

Bowen, Catherine Drinker. *Miracle at Philadelphia.* Boston: Atlantic–Little, Brown, 1966. An absorbing, well-written account of the events surrounding the Constitutional Convention.

Brinkley, Alan, Nelson W. Polsby, and Kathleen M. Sullivan. *The New Federalist Papers: Essays in Defense of the Constitution.* New York: Twentieth Century Fund, 1997. An historian, a political scientist, and a law professor respond to critics who claim that the American system of government is broken beyond repair.

Emery, Fred. *Watergate: The Corruption of American Politics and the Fall of Richard Nixon.* New York: Times Books, 1994. A compelling narrative of the greatest political scandal in our times.

Maier, Pauline. *American Scripture: Making the Declaration of Independence.* New York: Alfred A. Knopf, 1997. An exhilarating piece of historical detec-

tive work that tracks the origin of key phrases and ideas in America's most revered document.

Posner, Richard A. *An Affair of State: The Investigation, Impeachment, and Trial of President Clinton.* Cambridge, Mass.: Harvard University Press, 1999. One of the nation's top legal minds tackles the most significant presidential crisis since Watergate.

Rakove, Jack N. *Original Meanings: Politics and Ideas in the Making of the Constitution.* New York: Alfred A. Knopf, 1996. The meaning, intention, and understanding of the U.S. Constitution from a historian's perspective.

Zinn, Howard. *Declarations of Independence: Cross-Examining American Ideology.* New York: Harper and Row, 1990. This famous radical scholar challenges mainstream American political and economic thought, urging readers to declare independence from "all rigid dogmas" that serve to undermine democracy.

Internet Exercises

1. *World Constitutions*

The Texas A&M University library maintains an extensive on-line compilation of constitutions of the nations of the world. The site is located at **<library.tamu.edu/ govdocs/workshop/const.html>**.

- Use this site to link to an English version of the German constitution. Review Article 7, which concerns the topic of education. Then review the Bill of Rights to the U.S. Constitution (either in the appendix of this textbook or on-line).

- How does the way the U.S. Bill of Rights addresses the issue of education differ from the way it is addressed in the German constitution?

2. *UN Declaration of Human Rights*

One of the most important activities of the United Nations is to monitor and attempt to protect individual human rights around the world. To that end, in 1948, the UN General Assembly adopted the Universal Declaration of Human Rights and proclaimed it "a common standard of achievement for all peoples and all nations" toward which "every individual and every organ of society . . . shall strive."

• Go to the UN's home page at **<www.un.org/>** and read the Universal Declaration of Human Rights.

• The Bill of Rights to the U.S. Constitution is sometimes called a "negative rights document" because it protects individuals' civil liberties by prohibiting certain government actions. Do you think it would be fair to say that the UN Declaration of Human Rights is a "positive rights document"? Why or why not?

Federalism

IN THE 2000 ELECTION ON NOVEMBER 7, Democratic candidate Al Gore won more votes for president than his opponent, Republican candidate George W. Bush. Nevertheless, on January 20, 2001, Bush was inaugurated as president of the United States. How can the candidate who *loses* the popular vote *win* the presidency? The simple answer is that the presidency is not decided by a national election but by a federal election in which the states determine the outcome.

The U.S. Constitution sets out the basic ground rules. The selection of a president is determined by electoral votes allocated to each state, not by individual votes accorded to each person. Each state possesses as many electoral votes as it has senators and representatives. There are also three electoral votes for the District of Columbia. Thus, there are 538 electoral votes in total, and a presidential candidate needs at least 270 electoral votes to win the election. State legislatures determine the rules for selecting electors and the manner in which they shall cast their votes. Most state legislatures have chosen a winner-take-all approach that binds all electors to cast their ballots for the winner of the popular vote within the state.

The drawn-out battle for the 2000 election illustrates federalism in action. Our federal system of government allocates responsibility between the central government (the nation) and regional governments (the states). The Twelfth Amendment and Article II, Section 1, of the U.S. Constitution establish the *general* rules governing the selection of the president and vice president for the nation. But the states maintain and supervise their own *precise* rules governing the act of voting and of counting the votes for president and vice president.

The 2000 election put Florida and its twenty-five electoral votes in the spotlight. After the ballots were tallied in all the other states, neither candidate had achieved the 270 electoral votes required by the Constitution to win. Thus, whoever won in Florida would win the election. George Bush's margin of victory in Florida's popular vote was paper thin and grew slimmer as recounts and numerous legal challenges unearthed uncounted votes in Gore's favor. In the meantime, the nation had to wait to find out who the next president would be. On December 12, 2000, following thirty-six days of legal and political wrangling, the Supreme Court of the United States ended the contest.

The Court's 5–4 decision was controversial. The majority, made up of the more conservative members of the Court, declared that time had run out on the recounting of disputed votes because Florida law mandated the selection of its electors by December 12. The minority, the more moderate and liberal justices, maintained that the recounts should have continued.[1]

Two important elements of federalism were at work here: the respective sovereignty of national and state governments and the power of the nation's highest court to oversee and reverse decisions of the state courts. (*Sovereignty* is the quality of being supreme in power or authority.) State legislatures have the power to set the voting rules. Congress may not challenge the votes, provided the states certify their results on time. State courts may interpret and revise the legislature's voting rules. However, the U.S. Supreme Court may be the ultimate decision maker in determining who wins the game.

Sovereignty also affects political leadership. A governor may not be the political equal to a president, but governors have their own sovereignty, apart from the national government. Thus, President Clinton had no power to order the Florida governor to recount the votes according to nationally determined voting procedures. In fact, there was no basis for the president's involvement in Florida's vote-counting controversy. Sometimes, however, presidents may negotiate, even plead, with governors. For example, President John F. Kennedy negotiated repeatedly (and, it turned out, hopelessly) with Mississippi governor Ross Barnett to admit James Meredith as the first black student at the University of Mississippi. Kennedy lacked the power to order Barnett to admit Meredith. In the end, the U.S. Justice Department enforced a federal court order to secure Meredith's admission. Kennedy had to call out the National Guard to quell the rioting that followed.[2]

In this chapter, we examine American federalism in theory and in practice. Is the division of power between the nation and states a matter of constitutional principle or practical politics? How does the balance of power between the nation and states relate to the conflicts between freedom and order and between freedom and equality? Does the growth of federalism abroad affect us here at home? Does federalism reflect the pluralist or the majoritarian model of democracy?

THEORIES OF FEDERALISM

The delegates who met in Philadelphia in 1787 were supposed to repair weaknesses in the Articles of Confederation. Instead, they tackled the problem of making one nation out of thirteen independent states, by doing something much more radical. They wrote a new constitution and invented a new political form—federal government—that combined features of a confederacy with features of unitary government (see Chapter 3). Under the principle of **federalism,** two or more governments exercise power and authority over the same people and the same territory. For example, the governments of the United States and Pennsylvania share certain powers (the power to tax, for instance), but other powers belong exclusively to one or the other. As James Madison wrote in *Federalist* No. 10, "The federal Constitution forms a happy combination . . . the great and aggregate interests being referred to the national, and the local and particular to state governments." So the power to coin money belongs to the national government, but the power to grant divorces remains a state

federalism
The division of power between a central government and regional governments.

prerogative. By contrast, authority over state militias may sometimes belong to the national government and sometimes to the states. The history of American federalism reveals that it has not always been easy to draw a line between what is "great and aggregate" and what is "local and particular."*

Nevertheless, federalism offered a solution to the problem of diversity in America. Citizens feared that, without a federal system of government, they would be ruled by majorities from different regions with different interests and values. Federalism also provided a new political model. A leading scholar of federalism estimated in 1990 that 40 percent of the world's population live under a formal federal constitution, while another 30 percent live in polities that apply federal principles or practices without formal constitutional acknowledgment of their federalism.[3] Although federalism offers an approach that can unify diverse people into a single nation, it also retains elements that can lead to national disunity. Canada is an example of a federal system coping with the possibility of the dissolution of its constituent parts (see Compared with What? 4.1).

REPRESENTATIONS OF AMERICAN FEDERALISM

The history of American federalism is full of attempts to capture its true meaning in an adjective or metaphor. By one reckoning, scholars have generated nearly 500 ways to describe federalism.[4] Let us focus on two such representations: dual federalism and cooperative federalism.

Dual Federalism

dual federalism
A view that holds the Constitution is a compact among sovereign states, so that the powers of the national government are fixed and limited.

The term **dual federalism** sums up a theory about the proper relationship between the national government and the states. The theory has four essential parts. First, the national government rules by enumerated powers only. Second, the national government has a limited set of constitutional purposes. Third, each government unit—nation and state—is sovereign within its sphere. And fourth, the relationship between nation and states is best characterized by tension rather than cooperation.[5]

Dual federalism portrays the states as powerful components of the federal system—in some ways, the equals of the national government. Under dual federalism, the functions and responsibilities of the national and state governments are theoretically different and practically separate from each other. Of primary importance in dual federalism are **states' rights,** a concept that reserves to the states all rights not specifically conferred on the national government by the Constitution. According to the theory of dual federalism, a rigid wall separates the nation and the states. After all, if the states created the nation, by implication they can set limits on the activities of the national government. Proponents of states' rights believe that the powers of the national government should be interpreted narrowly. Claims of states' rights often come from opponents of a given national government policy. Their argument is that the Constitution has not

states' rights
The idea that all rights not specifically conferred on the national government by the Constitution are reserved to the states.

---

* *The phrase Americans commonly use to refer to their central government—federal government—muddies the waters even more. Technically speaking, we have a federal system of government, which includes both the national and state governments. To avoid confusion from here on, we use the term national government rather than federal government when we are talking about the central government.*

★ compared with what?

4.1   O Canada! Veering Between Fragmentation and Unity

Federalism tolerates the centrifugal forces (such as different languages and different religions) that can sunder a nation and provides the centripetal forces that bind it (such as the powers to raise an army and control a national economy). But federalism is no guarantee that the forces of unity will always overcome those of disunity. Consider the example of Canada.

Canada is a federation of ten provinces. But the Canadian province of Quebec is considerably different. Eighty percent of its population is French speaking; almost half speak little or no English. (The vast majority of Canadians outside Quebec speak only English.) Quebec has its own holidays, its own music videos, and its own literature. By law, all signs must be in French. English is scarcely tolerated.

For decades, Canadians have struggled with the challenge of assimilating yet differentiating Quebec. When Canada drafted a new constitution in 1982, Quebec refused to sign it. Quebecers conditioned their union with the other provinces on a constitutional amendment that would recognize Quebec as a "distinct society" within the country. The amendment had to be approved by all ten provinces. It failed when two provinces refused to ratify the Quebec agreement by the June 1990 deadline.

In October 1992, Canadians rejected another constitutional solution to the Quebec question. The reforms were aimed at recognizing Quebec's special status, electing the national senate,

and providing self-government for native peoples. Quebec rejected the reforms because they did not go far enough; other provinces rejected the reforms because they went too far.

Repeated threats of secession reached a crescendo in October 1995 when Quebec's voters confronted the latest referendum on independence. The vote was the closest ever: 50.6 percent voted against independence and 49.4 percent voted in favor of it. Despite that narrow margin, which amounted to roughly 50,000 votes, present support for secession among Quebecers rarely rises above 45 percent. In public opinion polls, even smaller numbers indicate that they would support another vote on the secession issue, but it may only be wishful thinking for now.

Advocates for Quebec's independence, such as the province's premier and leader of the Parti Québécois, Lucien Bouchard, signaled defeat in early 2001. Bouchard quit politics because he was unable to revive public passion for the separatist cause. Perhaps lower unemployment and a stronger economy sapped the cause of its need for independence. In May 2000, Bouchard had argued at his party's convention, "our objective and our obsession is the sovereignty of Quebec as soon as possible." Still, the centrifugal forces of language and culture assure that the separatist issue will not die. While many would say that Canada would not be Canada without Quebec, many might also say that Canada would not be Canada without this conflict over Quebec's status.

implied powers
Those powers that Congress requires in order to execute its enumerated powers.

delegated to the national government the power to make such policy and that the power thus remains with the states or the people. They insist that despite the elastic clause, which gives Congress the **implied powers** needed to execute its enumerated powers (see Chapter 3), the activities of Congress should be confined to the enumerated powers only. And they support their view by quoting the Tenth Amendment: "The powers not delegated to the United States by the Constitution, nor prohibited by it to the States, are reserved to the States respectively, or to the people."

Quebec Demonstration

Sources: Robert C. Vipond, "Seeing Canada Through the Referendum: Still a House Divided," *Publius* 23 (Summer 1993), p. 39; Clyde H. Farnsworth, "For Quebec, the Neverendum," *New York Times*, 5 November 1995, sect. 4, p. 3; "Quebec Bores on Regardless, " *The Economist*, 13 May 2000, p. 39; Christopher J. Chipello, "Quebec's Separatism Effort Is Dealt a Blow," *Wall Street Journal*, 12 January 2001, p. A16.

Political scientists use a metaphor to describe dual federalism. They call it *layer-cake federalism* (see Figure 4.1); the powers and functions of the national and state governments are as separate as the layers of a cake. Each government is supreme in its own layer, its own sphere of action; the two layers are distinct, and the dimensions of each layer are fixed by the Constitution.

Dual federalism has been challenged on historical and other grounds. Some critics argue that if the national government is really a creation of

figure   **4.1**   **Metaphors for Federalism**

The two views of federalism can be represented graphically.

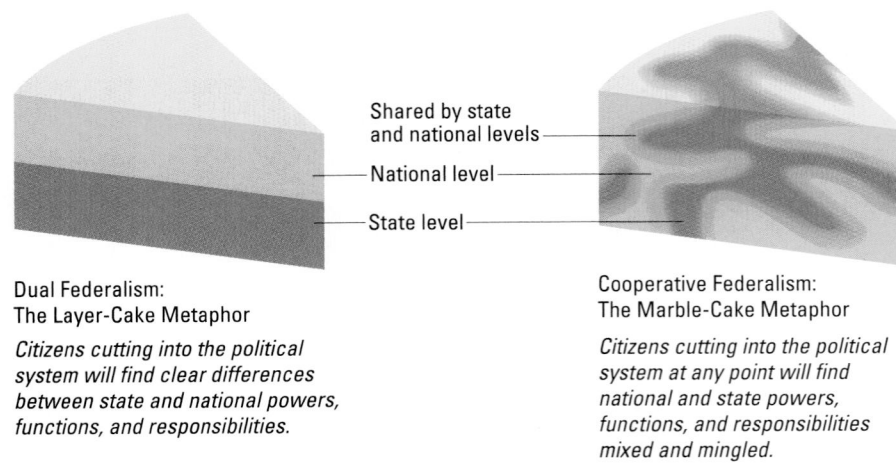

Dual Federalism:
The Layer-Cake Metaphor

Citizens cutting into the political system will find clear differences between state and national powers, functions, and responsibilities.

Cooperative Federalism:
The Marble-Cake Metaphor

Citizens cutting into the political system at any point will find national and state powers, functions, and responsibilities mixed and mingled.

the states, it is a creation of only thirteen states, those that ratified the Constitution. The other thirty-seven states were admitted after the national government came into being and were created by that government out of land it had acquired. Another challenge has to do with the ratification process. Remember, special conventions in the original thirteen states, not the states' legislatures, ratified the Constitution. Ratification, then, was an act of the people, not the states. Moreover, the preamble to the Constitution begins "We the People of the United States," not "We the States." The question of just where the people fit into the federal system is not handled well by dual federalism.

The concept of dual federalism, two levels of government operating on different tracks, each in control of its own activities, suited the American experience from 1789 to 1933. But the demands of the Great Depression gave birth to a new federal concept: cooperative federalism.

Cooperative Federalism

cooperative federalism
A view that holds that the Constitution is an agreement among people who are citizens of both state and nation, so there is little distinction between state powers and national powers.

Cooperative federalism, a phrase coined in the 1930s, is a different theory of the relationship between the national and state governments. It acknowledges the increasing overlap between state and national functions and rejects the idea of separate spheres, or layers, for the states and the national government. Cooperative federalism includes three elements. First, national and state agencies typically undertake government functions jointly rather than exclusively. Second, nation and states routinely share power. And third, power is not concentrated at any government level or in any agency; the fragmentation of responsibilities gives people and groups access to many centers of influence.

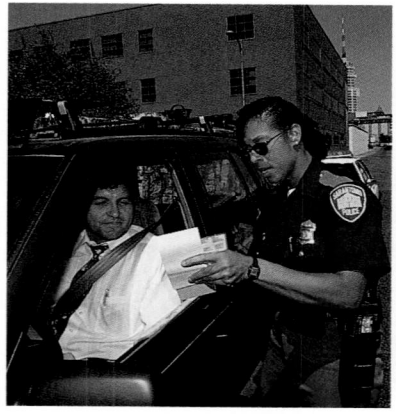  

Local Cops, National Cops, International Cops

Local and national government and international organizations may exercise similar powers, such as maintaining order. A San Antonio, Texas, police officer issues a traffic citation (left). A SWAT team from the Federal Bureau of Investigation stands at the ready during a World Cup soccer match in Secaucus, New Jersey (center). United Nations soldiers stand guard at the Macedonian border with Kosovo (right).

elastic clause
The last clause in Section 8 of Article I of the Constitution, which gives Congress the means to execute its enumerated powers. This clause is the basis for Congress's implied powers. Also called the *necessary and proper clause*.

Can You Explain Why...
the Tenth Amendment and the necessary and proper clause of Article I might contradict one another?

The bakery metaphor used to describe this type of federalism is a marble cake. The national and state governments do not act in separate spheres; they are intermingled in vertical and diagonal strands and swirls. Their functions are mixed in the American federal system. Critical to cooperative federalism is an expansive view of the Constitution's supremacy clause (Article VI), which specifically subordinates state law to national law and charges every government official with disregarding state laws that are inconsistent with the Constitution, national laws, or treaties.

Some scholars argue that the layer-cake metaphor has never accurately described the American political structure.[6] The national and state governments have many common objectives and have often cooperated to achieve them. In the nineteenth century, for example, cooperation, not separation, made it possible to develop transportation systems, such as canals, and to establish state land-grant colleges. The layer cake might be a good model of what dual federalists think the relationship between national and state governments *should* be, but it does not square with recent American history.

A critical difference between the theories of dual and cooperative federalism is the way they interpret two sections of the Constitution that set out the terms of the relationship between the national and state governments. Article I, Section 8, lists the enumerated powers of Congress, then concludes with the **elastic clause,** which gives Congress the power to "make all Laws which shall be necessary and proper for carrying into Execution the foregoing Powers" (see Chapter 3). The Tenth Amendment reserves for the states or the people powers not assigned to the national government or denied to the states by the Constitution. Dual federalism postulates an inflexible elastic clause and a capacious Tenth Amendment. Cooperative federalism postulates suppleness in the elastic clause and confines the Tenth Amendment to a self-evident, obvious truth. The widespread acceptance of cooperative federalism in the twentieth century contributed to an increasing centralization of power in the national government, often at the expense of the states. Today, the flow of power is drifting back to the states.

In their efforts to limit the scope of the national government, conservatives have given much credence to the layer-cake metaphor. In contrast, liberals,

★

All Eyes Are On Florida

This French cartoon from the Paris newspaper, Le Monde, *captures the significance of a single state—Florida—in the 2000 U.S. presidential election.*

believing that one function of the national government is to bring about equality, have argued that the marble-cake metaphor is more desirable.

Conservatives continue to argue that different states have different problems and resources and that returning control to state governments would thus actually promote diversity. States would be free to experiment with alternative ways to meet their problems. States would compete with one another. And people would be free to choose the state government they preferred by simply voting with their feet and moving to another state. This argument for flexibility may encourage behavior that conservatives lament, however; for example, poor people may gain marginally better welfare benefits by moving from one state to another.[7]

Conservatives also continue to maintain that the national government is too remote, too tied to special interests, and not responsive to the public at large. The national government overregulates, they add, and tries to promote too much uniformity. Moreover, the size and complexity of the federal system lead to waste and inefficiency. States, on the other hand, are closer to the people and better able to respond to specific local needs. If state governments were revitalized, individuals might believe that they could have a greater influence on decision making. The quality of political participation would improve. Furthermore, conservatives believe that shifting power to the states would help them achieve other parts of their political agenda. States would work harder to keep taxes down, they would not be willing to spend a lot of money on social welfare programs, and they would be less likely to pass stiff laws regulating businesses. The 1994 "Republican Revolution" brought a chorus of new conservative voices to Congress. It started a legislative wave that called explicitly for a return of power to the states.

What conservatives hope for, liberals fear. They remember that the states' rights model allowed extreme political and social inequalities and that it supported racism. Blacks and city dwellers were often left virtually unrepresented by white state legislators who disproportionately served rural interests. Liberals believe the states remain unwilling or unable to protect the rights or provide for the needs of their citizens, whether those citizens are consumers seeking protection from business interests, defendants requiring guarantees of due process of law, or poor people seeking a minimum standard of living.

These ideological conceptions of federalism reveal a simple truth. Federalism is not something written or implied in the Constitution; the Constitution is only the starting point in the debate. As one scholar observed, "To understand the condition of federalism, one needs to comprehend the functioning of the whole polity."[8]

THE DYNAMICS OF FEDERALISM

Although the Constitution establishes a kind of federalism, the actual balance of power between the nation and states has always been more a matter of politics than of formal theory. A discussion of federalism, then, must do more than simply list the powers that the Constitution assigns the different levels of government. The balance of power has shifted substantially since President Madison agonized over the proper role the national government should play in funding roads. Today, that government has assumed functions never dreamed of in the nineteenth century.

Why has power shifted so dramatically from the states to the national government? The answer lies in historical circumstances, not debates over constitutional theory. By far the greatest test of states' rights arose when several southern states attempted to secede from the union. The threat of secession challenged the supremacy of the national government, a supremacy that northern armies reestablished militarily in the nation's greatest bloodbath, the Civil War. But the Civil War by no means settled all the questions about relations between governments in the United States. Many more remained to be answered, and new issues keep cropping up.

Some changes in the balance of power were the product of constitutional amendments. Several amendments have had an enormous effect, either direct or indirect, on the shape of the federal system. For example, the due process and equal protection clauses of the Fourteenth Amendment (1868) and the Seventeenth Amendment's provision for the direct election of senators (1913) limited states' rights. The income tax mandated by the Sixteenth Amendment (1913) fueled the growth and strength of the national government in relation to the states.

Most of the national government's power has come to it through legislation and judicial interpretation. Let us examine these tools of political change.

Legislation and the Elastic Clause

The elastic clause of the Constitution gives Congress the power to make all laws that are "necessary and proper" to carry out its responsibilities. By using this power in combination with its enumerated powers, Congress has been able to increase the scope of the national government tremendously during the previous two centuries. The greatest change has come about in times of crisis and national emergency—the Civil War, the Great Depression, the world wars. The role of the national government has also grown as it has responded to needs and demands that state and local governments were unwilling or unable to meet.

Legislation is one prod the national government has used to achieve goals at the state level. The Voting Rights Act of 1965 is a good example. Section 2 of Article I of the Constitution gives the states the power to specify qualifications for voting. But the Fifteenth Amendment (1870) provides that no person shall be denied the right to vote "on account of race, color, or previous condition of servitude." Before the Voting Rights Act, states could not specifically deny blacks the right to vote, but they could require that voters pass literacy tests or pay poll taxes, requirements that virtually disenfranchised blacks in many states. The Voting Rights Act was designed to correct this political inequality (see Chapter 7).

The act gives the national government the power to decide whether individuals are qualified to vote and requires that qualified individuals be allowed to vote in all elections, including primaries and national, state, and local elections. If denial of voting rights seems to be widespread, the act authorizes the appointment of national voting examiners to examine and register voters for *all* elections. By replacing state election officials with national examiners, the act clearly intrudes upon the political sovereignty of the states. The constitutional authority for the act rests on the second section of the Fifteenth Amendment, which gives Congress the power to enforce the amendment through "appropriate legislation."

Judicial Interpretation

The Voting Rights Act was not a unanimous hit. Its critics used the language of dual federalism to insist that the Constitution gives the states the power to determine voter qualifications. Its supporters claimed that the Fifteenth Amendment guarantee of voting rights takes precedence over states' rights and gives the national government new responsibilities.

The conflict was ultimately resolved by the Supreme Court, the umpire of the federal system. It upheld the act as an appropriate congressional enforcement of the Fifteenth Amendment.[9] The Court settles disputes over the powers of the national and state governments by deciding whether the actions of either are unconstitutional (see Chapter 14). In the nineteenth and early twentieth centuries, the Supreme Court often decided in favor of the states. Then for nearly sixty years, from 1937 to 1995, the Court almost always supported the national government in contests involving the balance of power between nation and states. With the exception of the 2000 election controversy, a conservative majority on the Court has tipped the balance back to the states.

The Commerce Clause: Engine of National Power.   The growth of national power has been advanced by the Supreme Court's interpretation of the Constitution's **commerce clause**. The third clause of Article I, Section 8, states that "Congress shall have Power . . . To regulate Commerce . . . among the several States." In early Court decisions, Chief Justice John Marshall (1801–1835) interpreted the word *commerce* broadly, to include virtually every form of commercial activity. The clause's grant of the power to regulate commerce to the national government substantially withdrew that power from the states. Later decisions by the Court attempted to restrict national power over commerce, but events such as the Great Depression necessitated its enlargement. One scholar has gone so far as to charge that the justices have toyed with the commerce clause, treating it like a shuttlecock volleyed back and forth by changing majorities.[10] A surprising volley in 1995 signaled a shift back to the states.

Though no longer in office, Republican presidents from Nixon to Bush can claim a role in the transfer of power from nation to states through the

commerce clause
The third clause of Article I, Section 8, of the Constitution, which gives Congress the power to regulate commerce among the states.

appointment of Supreme Court justices with a commitment to limits on national power. The shift toward the states became plain in 1995, when the Supreme Court rediscovered constitutional limits on Congress that had been dead and buried for nearly sixty years.

The Court's 5–4 ruling in *United States* v. *Lopez* held that Congress exceeded its authority under the commerce clause when it enacted a law in 1990 banning the possession of a gun in or near a school. Since the middle of the Great Depression, the Court had given Congress wide latitude to exercise legislative power by regulating interstate commerce. But a conservative majority, headed by Chief Justice William H. Rehnquist, concluded that having a gun in a school zone "has nothing to do with 'commerce' or any sort of economic enterprise, however broadly one might define those terms." Justices Sandra Day O'Connor, Antonin Scalia, Anthony Kennedy, and Clarence Thomas—all appointed by Republicans—joined in Rehnquist's opinion putting the brakes on congressional power.[11]

In yet another reallocation of authority from the nation to the states, in 2000 the Court struck down congressional legislation that had allowed federal court lawsuits for money damages for victims of crimes "motivated by gender." The Violence Against Women Act violated both the commerce clause and Section 5 of the Fourteenth Amendment. Chief Justice Rehnquist, speaking for the five-person majority, declared that "the Constitution requires a distinction between what is truly national and what is truly local."[12]

The Eleventh Amendment: The Umpire Strikes Back.   In 1996, the umpire made another dramatic call curtailing congressional power in favor of the states. In a bitterly fought 5–4 ruling, the same five-justice majority bolstered state power by sharply curtailing the authority of Congress to subject states to lawsuits in federal courts. The ruling came in an obscure suit arising from a Seminole Indian tribe's dispute with Florida officials.[13] A 1988 federal law allowed Indian tribes to sue a state in federal court if the state failed to negotiate in good faith over allowing gambling operations on tribal lands. Many federal laws have provisions that allow people alleging state violations of federal laws to sue states in the federal courts. However, the Supreme Court struck down the 1988 law and breathed new life into the Eleventh Amendment by sharply limiting the power of Congress to abrogate the states' sovereign immunity, or immunity from suit. Now, with the single exception of enforcing Fourteenth Amendment rights, Congress has no authority to deny the states immunity from lawsuits in the federal courts.

The decision extends far beyond the particular facts; it affects whether individuals or groups can use the federal courts to force states to abide by various national laws. The majority opinion asserted that "the states, although a union, maintain certain attributes of sovereignty," including immunity from lawsuits. The decision means that the states will be less accountable to people who believe they have been wronged by a state government in connection with such matters as water pollution or copyright infringement. Though the Indian tribes were losers in this lawsuit, they are big winners today thanks to certain federalism principles that are sewn into the Constitution giving Native American tribes limited sovereignty. Many tribes have exercised this sovereignty to set up casinos on reservation property. Tribal casino profits are tax-free.

★

Indians' Deal

Native Americans have discovered a powerful source of revenue: casino gambling. Gambling activities on Indian land have thrived, thanks to the Indians' special status embodied in treaties, laws, and the Constitution. Americans spend well in excess of $50 billion a year on gambling (lotteries, casinos, bingo, parimutuals). Although gambling brings enormous economic activity for some, it may also exact a high social cost on others—in ruined lives and organized crime that seem to follow in its wake.

Brady Handgun Control Act

The Brady Bill and the Limits of National Government Authority. Congress enacted a modest gun-control measure (known as the Brady bill) in 1993. The bill mandated the creation by November 1998 of a national system to check the background of prospective gun buyers, to weed out, among others, convicted felons and the mentally ill. In the meantime, it created a temporary system that called for local law enforcement officials to perform background checks and report their findings to gun dealers in their community. Several sheriffs challenged the law.

The Supreme Court agreed with the sheriffs, delivering a double-barreled blow to the local-enforcement provision in June 1997. In *Printz* v. *United States*, the Court concluded that Congress could not require local officials to implement a regulatory scheme imposed by the national government. In language that seemingly invoked layer-cake federalism, Justice Antonin Scalia, writing for the five-member conservative majority, argued that locally enforced background checks violated the principle of dual sovereignty, by allowing the national government "to impress into its service—and at no cost to itself—the police officers of the 50 States." In addition, the scheme violated the principle of separation of powers, by congressional transfer of the president's responsibility to faithfully execute national laws to local law enforcement officials.

The *Printz* decision generated only muted congressional protest because the local-enforcement provision was merely temporary. The decision demonstrates, however, that federalism sets real limits on the power of the national government. Nevertheless, Congress retains ample power to secure the cooperation of state governments. Money is its tool.

Grants-in-Aid

Since the 1960s, the national government's use of financial incentives has rivaled its use of legislation and judicial interpretation as a means of shaping relations with state governments. And state and local governments have increasingly looked to Washington for money. The principal method the national government uses to make money available to the states is grants-in-aid.

A **grant-in-aid** is money paid by one level of government to another level of government, to be spent for a given purpose. Most grants-in-aid come with standards or requirements prescribed by Congress. Many are awarded on a matching basis; that is, a recipient must make some contribution of its own, which is then matched by the national government. Grants-in-aid take two general forms: categorical grants and block grants.

Categorical grants target specific purposes, and restrictions on their use typically leave the recipient government relatively little discretion. Recipients today include state governments, local governments, and public and private nonprofit organizations. There are two kinds of categorical grants: formula grants and project grants. As their name implies, **formula grants** are distributed according to a particular formula, which specifies who is eligible for the grant and how much each eligible applicant will receive. The formulas may weigh factors such as state per capita income, number of school-age children, urban population, and number of families below the poverty line. Most grants, however, are **project grants,** grants awarded on the basis of competitive applications. Recent project grants have focused on health (substance abuse and HIV-AIDS programs); natural resources and the environment (radon, asbestos, and toxic pollution); and education, training, and employment (for the disabled, the homeless, and the aged).

In contrast to categorical grants, Congress awards **block grants** for broad, general purposes. They allow recipient governments considerable freedom to decide how to allocate the money to individual programs. Whereas a categorical grant promotes a specific activity—say, ethnic heritage studies—a block grant might be earmarked only for elementary, secondary, and vocational education. The state or local government receiving the block grant would then choose the specific educational programs to fund with it. The recipient might use some money to support ethnic heritage studies and some to fund consumer education programs. Or the recipient might choose to put all the money into consumer education programs and spend nothing on ethnic heritage studies.

Grants-in-aid are a method of redistributing income. Money is collected by the national government from the taxpayers of all fifty states, then allocated to other citizens, supposedly for worthwhile social purposes. Many grants have worked to reduce gross inequalities among states and their residents. But the formulas used to redistribute income are not impartial; they are highly political, established through a process of congressional horse trading.

Although grants-in-aid have been part of the national government arsenal since the early twentieth century, they grew at an astonishing pace in the 1960s, when grant spending doubled every five years. Presidents Nixon and Reagan were strong advocates for redistributing money back to the states, and political support for such redistribution has remained strong. Controlling for inflation, in 1985 over $135 billion was returned to the states. By 1997, over $207 billion was returned to the states.[14] Significant shifts in the purposes of such grants occurred in the same period.[15] Figure 4.2 illustrates the distribution of grants to state and local government by policy area. Health was far more dominant in 1990 than it was in

grant-in-aid
Money provided by one level of government to another, to be spent for a given purpose.

categorical grant
A grant-in-aid targeted for a specific purpose either by formula or by project.

formula grant
A categorical grant distributed according to a particular formula, which specifies who is eligible for the grants and how much each eligible applicant will receive.

project grant
A categorical grant awarded on the basis of competitive applications submitted by prospective recipients.

block grant
A grant-in-aid awarded for general purposes, allowing the recipient great discretion in spending the grant money.

figure **4.2**   **Trends in National Government Grants to States and Localities, FY 1980, 1990, and 2000**

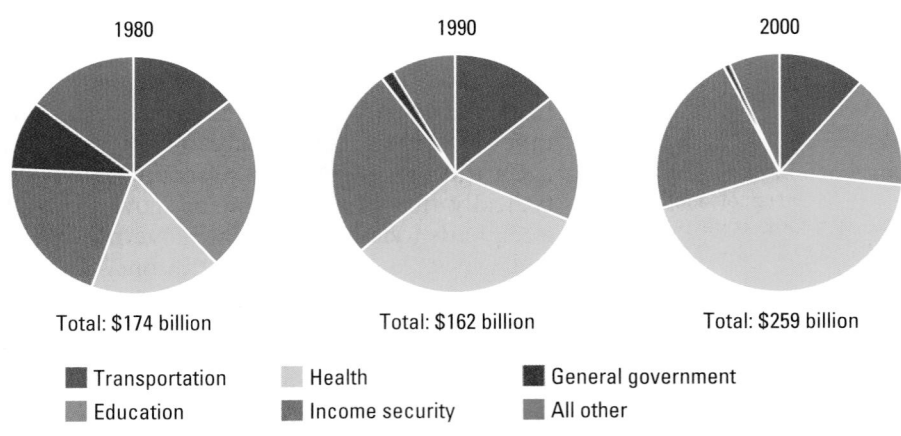

National government grants to states and localities vary substantially. In 1980, education programs accounted for the biggest slice of the national government grant pie. In 1990, grants for health programs took the biggest slice, reaching more than 30 percent of all national government grants to state and local governments. By 2000, health grants exceeded 43 percent of all such national government spending. (By 2005, health grants are estimated to reach half of national government grants to the states.)

Source: Historical tables, Budget of the United States Government FY2001, Table 12.1. Dollar amounts reported here are in billions of constant (FY 1996) dollars.

South Dakota v. *Dole*

Can You Explain Why... you have to be twenty-one to drink in all fifty states, even though Congress has never passed a law declaring a national drinking age?

1980; the opposite is true for transportation policy. The 2000 budget only accentuates this trend.

Whatever its form or purpose, grant money comes with strings attached. Some strings are there to ensure that the money is used for the purpose for which it was given; other regulations are designed to evaluate how well the grant is working. To this end, the national government may stipulate that recipients follow certain procedures. The national government may also attach restrictions designed to achieve some broad national goal not always closely related to the specific purpose of the grant. The use of highway construction funds has proved an effective means to induce states to accept national standards. Congress threatened to reduce millions of dollars in these funds if states did not agree to prohibit the purchase or consumption of alcoholic beverages by persons under the age of twenty-one. Some states objected, claiming that the Tenth and Twenty-first amendments assigned them responsibility for matters such as alcoholic beverage consumption. In *South Dakota* v. *Dole,* the Supreme Court conceded that direct congressional control of the drinking age in the states would be unconstitutional. Nevertheless, the Constitution does not bar the indirect achievement of such objectives. The seven-member majority argued that, far from being an infringement on states' rights, the law was a "relatively mild encouragement to the States to enact higher minimum drinking ages than they would otherwise choose." After all, Chief Justice William H. Rehnquist wrote, the goal of reducing drunk driving was "directly related to one of the main purposes for which highway funds are expended—safe interstate travel."[16] By 1988, every state in the nation had approved legislation setting twenty-one as the minimum drinking age.

In October 2000, following a three-year battle in Congress, President Bill Clinton signed new legislation establishing a tough national standard of .08 percent blood-alcohol level for drunk driving. Thirty-one states define drunk driving at the .10 percent standard or do not set a specific standard. States that refuse to impose the lower standard by 2004 stand to lose millions in government highway construction money.[17] The restaurant industry was not cheering the result. It characterized the law as an attack on social drinkers who are not the source of the drunk-driving problem. The lure of financial aid has proved a powerful incentive for states to relinquish the freedom to set their own standards and to accept those set by the national government. In short, categorical grants clearly increase national power and decrease state power, and block grants increase state power and decrease national power.

THE DEVELOPING CONCEPT OF FEDERALISM

Federalism scholars have noted that each generation, faced with new problems, has had to work out its own version of federalism. Succeeding generations have used judicial and congressional power in varying degrees to shift the balance of power back and forth between the national and state governments.

McCulloch v. *Maryland*

McCulloch v. Maryland

Early in the nineteenth century, the nationalist interpretation of federalism prevailed over states' rights. In 1819, under Chief Justice John Marshall, the Supreme Court expanded the role of the national government in *McCulloch* v. *Maryland*. The Court was asked to decide whether Congress had the power to establish a national bank and, if so, whether states had the power to tax that bank. In a unanimous opinion written by Marshall, the Court conceded that Congress had only the powers conferred on it by the Constitution, which nowhere mentioned banks. However, Article I granted Congress the authority to enact all laws "necessary and proper" to the execution of Congress's enumerated powers. Marshall adopted a broad interpretation of this elastic clause: "Let the end be legitimate, let it be within the scope of the constitution, and all means which are appropriate, which are plainly adapted to that end, which are not prohibited, but consist with the letter and spirit of the constitution, are constitutional."

The Court clearly agreed that Congress had the power to charter a bank. But did the states (in this case, Maryland) have the power to tax the bank? Arguing that "the power to tax involves the power to destroy," Marshall insisted that states could not tax the national government because the powers of the national government came not from the states but from the people. Marshall was embracing cooperative federalism, which sees a direct relationship between the people and the national government, with no need for the states to act as intermediaries. To assume that the states had the power to tax the national government would be to give them supremacy over the national government. In that case, Marshall wrote, "the declaration that the constitution, and the laws made in pursuance thereof, shall be the supreme law of the land is empty and unmeaning declamation."[18] The framers of the Constitution did not intend to create a meaningless document, he reasoned. Therefore, they must have meant to give the national government all the powers necessary to carry out its assigned functions, even if those powers are only implied.

States' Rights and Dual Federalism

Roger B. Taney became chief justice in 1836, and during his tenure (1836–1864) the balance of power began to shift back toward the states. The Taney Court imposed firm limits on the powers of the national government. As Taney saw it, the Constitution spoke "not only in the same words, but with the same meaning and intent with which it spoke when it came from the hands of its framers and was voted on and adopted by the people of the United States."[19] In the infamous *Dred Scott* decision (1857), for example, the Court decided that Congress had no power to prohibit slavery in the territories.

Dred Scott v. *Sandford*

Many people assume that the Civil War was fought over slavery. It was not. The real issue was the character of the federal union, of federalism itself. At the time of the Civil War, economic and cultural differences between the northern and southern states were considerable. The southern economy was based on labor-intensive agriculture, while mechanized manufacturing was developing in the North. Southerners' desire for cheap manufactured goods and cheap plantation labor led them to support both slavery and low tariffs on imports. Northerners, to protect their own economy, wanted high tariffs. When they sought national legislation that threatened southern interests, southerners invoked states' rights. They even introduced the theory of **nullification,** the idea that a state could declare a particular action of the national government null and void. The Civil War rendered the idea of nullification null and void, but it did not eliminate the tension between national and state power.

nullification
The declaration by a state that a particular action of the national government is not applicable to that state.

The New Deal and Its Consequences

The Great Depression placed dual federalism in repose. The problems of the Depression proved too extensive for either state governments or private businesses to handle. So the national government assumed a heavy share of responsibility for providing relief and pursuing economic recovery. Under the New Deal—President Franklin D. Roosevelt's response to the Depression—Congress enacted various emergency relief programs to stimulate economic activity and help the unemployed. Many measures required the cooperation of the national and state governments. For example, the national government offered money to support state relief efforts. However, to receive these funds, states were usually required to provide administrative supervision or to contribute some money of their own. Relief efforts were thus wrested from the hands of local bodies and centralized. Through the regulations it attached to funds, the national government extended its power and control over the states.[20]

At first, the Supreme Court's view of the Depression was different from that of the other branches of the national government. The justices believed the Depression was an accumulation of local problems, not a national problem demanding national action. In the Court's opinion, the

Made in the USA. Sold in the USA.

Pictured on the left, young girls working at thread-winder machines in a factory in London, Tennessee (1910). In 1918, the U.S. Supreme Court held that Congress lacked power to limit the excesses of child labor. The Court reversed itself twenty-three years later. Pictured on the right, nine-year-old Prekash makes a carpet in Pakistan (2000). The worldwide market for handmade carpets is yet another example of globalization. Demand in developed countries like the United States encourages production and reliance on cheap child labor. In 1999, the United States signed a treaty banning abusive child labor.

whole structure of federalism was threatened when collections of local troubles were treated as one national problem.

In 1937, however, with no change in personnel, the Court began to alter its course. The Court upheld major New Deal measures. Perhaps the Court was responding to the 1936 election returns (Roosevelt had been reelected in a landslide, and the Democrats commanded a substantial majority in Congress), which signified the voters' endorsement of the use of national policies to address national problems. Or perhaps the Court sought to defuse the president's threat to enlarge the Court with justices sympathetic to his views. ("The switch in time that saved nine," rhymed one observer.) In any event, the Court abandoned its effort to maintain a rigid boundary between national and state power. Only a few years earlier, the Supreme Court had based its thinking about federalism on a state-centered interpretation of the Tenth Amendment. But in 1941, Chief Justice Harlan Fiske Stone referred to the Tenth Amendment as "a truism that all is retained which has not been surrendered."[21] In short, the Court agreed that the layer cake had become stale and unpalatable.

Some call the New Deal era revolutionary. There is no doubt that the period was critical in reshaping federalism in the United States. The national and state governments had cooperated before, but the extent of nation–state interaction during Franklin Roosevelt's administration clearly made the marble-cake metaphor the most accurate description of American federalism. In addition, the size of the national government and its budget increased tremendously. But perhaps the most significant change was in the way Americans thought about their problems and the role of the national government in solving them. Difficulties that at one time had been seen as personal or local were now national problems, requiring national solutions. The general welfare, broadly defined, became a legitimate concern of the national government.

In other respects, however, the New Deal was not so revolutionary. For example, Congress did not claim any new powers to address the nation's economic problems. Congress simply used its constitutional powers to suit the circumstances.

THE REVIVAL OF FEDERALISM

Like Jason Voorhies in *Friday the Thirteenth*, debates over federalism keep coming back. In the past thirty years or so, federalism has been dusted off and given some new uses. In 1969, Richard Nixon advocated giving more power to state and local governments. Nixon wanted to decentralize national policies. He called this the New Federalism. More recently, Bill Clinton proposed that the national government act as guru, guiding and encouraging states to experiment with vexing problems.

An Evolving Federalism

Nixon's New Federalism called for combining and reformulating categorical grants into block grants. The shift had dramatic implications for federalism. Block grants were seen as a way to redress the imbalance of power between Washington and the states and localities. Conservatives in Washington wanted to return freedom to the states. New Federalism was nothing more than dual federalism in modern dress.

The perception that the federal system was bloated and out of control began to take hold. In 1976, Jimmy Carter campaigned for president as an outsider who promised to reduce the size and cost of the national government. And he did have some success. As Figure 4.3 shows, after 1978 national government aid to states and localities actually did begin to drop and then level off.

Ronald Reagan took office in 1981, charging that the federal system had been bent out of shape. Reagan promised a "new New Federalism" that would restore a proper constitutional relationship among the national, state, and local governments. The national government, he said, treated "elected state and local officials as if they were nothing more than administrative agents for federal authority."[22]

Reagan's commitment to reducing federal taxes and spending meant that the states would have to foot an increasing share of the bill for government services (see Figure 4.3). In the mid-1970s, the national government funded 25 percent of all state and local government spending. By 1990, its contribution had declined to 20 percent. With the Democrats in control of both the presidency and Congress, that figure inched up to 22 percent by 1994, but Republican congressional victories in 1994 made increased spending a hard sell.

In June 1999, the Supreme Court weighed in with its view of federalism. In identical 5–4 votes in three separate cases, the Court again embraced the idea of dual federalism, adjusting the balance of power in favor of the states. The Court in effect immunized state governments from lawsuits brought by individuals claiming state violations of national laws. "Congress has vast power but not all power," declared Justice Anthony Kennedy, author of one of the majority opinions. "When Congress legislates in matters affecting the states," continued Kennedy, "it may not treat these sovereign entities as mere prefectures or corporations. Congress must accord states the esteem due to them as joint participants in a Federal system."[23]

This shift in the balance of power is not secure, however. The 2000 election should have a profound impact on the Court's view of federalism. A conservative appointment would likely shore up the narrow majority. In the meantime, Congress still retains substantial power to yoke the states.

figure

4.3

The National Government's Contribution to States and Local Governments

In 1960, the national government contributed 12 percent of total state and local spending. By 1978, the national government had reached its high point, contributing 34 percent to state and local spending. By 1988, the national government's contribution had declined to about 19 percent. It has now inched back up to the point where such spending represents about 25 percent of the total.

Source: Historical tables, Budget of the United States Government FY2001, Table 15.2.

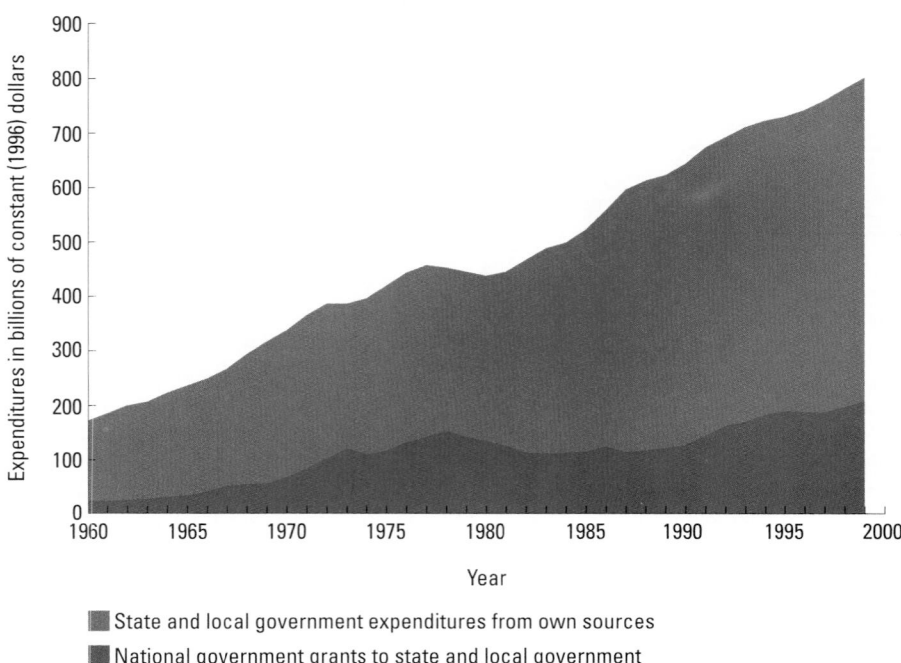

State and local government expenditures from own sources

National government grants to state and local government

Preemption: The Instrument of Federalism

Before 1965, increased national power and diminished state power followed from the growth in categorical grant-in-aid programs—with their attached conditions—emanating from Washington, D.C. Since 1965, Congress has used its centralizing power in new fields and in novel ways.[24]

preemption
The power of Congress to enact laws by which the national government assumes total or partial responsibility for a state government function.

Preemption is the power of Congress to enact laws that have the national government assume total or partial responsibility for a state government function. When the national government shoulders a new government function, it restricts the discretionary power of the states.

Preemption is a modern power. Congress passed only fourteen preemptive acts before 1900. By 1988, Congress had preempted the power of states to legislate in certain areas 350 times, and 186 of these acts were passed after 1970.[25] For example, under the Nutritional Labeling and Education Act of 1990, the national government established food labeling standards and simultaneously stripped the states of their power to impose food labeling requirements. The act therefore prevents the states from providing added protections for health-conscious consumers. Industry groups, such

100% ORANGE JUICE
FROM CONCENTRATE K

Nutrition Facts
Serving Size 8 fl. oz. (240mL)
Servings Per Container 4

Amount Per Serving

Calories 110

	% Daily Value*
Total Fat 0g	0%
Sodium 25mg	1%
Potassium 480mg	14%
Total Carbohydrate 27g	9%
Sugars 23g	
Protein 0g	
Vitamin C 130%	

Not a significant source of calories from fat, saturated fat, cholesterol, dietary fiber, vitamin A, calcium and iron.
*Percent Daily Values are based on a 2,000 calorie diet.

★

Label Me

Food labeling follows a single national standard today thanks to the Nutritional Labeling and Education Act of 1990. The act preempted the states from imposing different labeling requirements.

mandate
A requirement that a state undertake an activity or provide a service, in keeping with minimum national standards.

restraint
A requirement laid down by act of Congress, prohibiting a state or local government from exercising a certain power.

as the Grocery Manufacturers of America, favored preemption because uniform labeling would be cheaper than following fifty different state labeling guidelines.[26]

States will occasionally act in ways that conflict with national objectives. The umpiring function between states and nation falls to the Supreme Court. In 2000, the justices faced such a conflict arising from a Massachusetts state law that withheld state business from companies that did business with the nation of Myanmar (formerly Burma) because it is controlled by a repressive military regime. But a unanimous Court struck down the Massachusetts state law on the basis of the Constitution's supremacy clause, holding that a federal law placing sanctions on Myanmar preempted the state law.[27]

Mandates and Restraints.   Congressional preemption statutes infringe on state powers in two ways, through mandates and restraints. A **mandate** is a requirement that a state undertake an activity or provide a service, in keeping with minimum national standards. For example, through the Medicaid program, the national government requires states to provide their low-income citizens with access to some minimal level of health care. Even though Medicaid is a program funded jointly by the national government and the states—in 1998, it cost $184 billion—it has grown to become the second largest item in state budgets. In 1998, states contributed $80 billion to the program, a burden that has made it difficult to increase funding for state initiatives in health, education, and other areas.[28]

In contrast, a **restraint** forbids state government from exercising a certain power. Consider bus regulation, for example. To ensure bus service to small and remote communities, in the past some states would condition the issuance of bus franchises on bus operators' agreeing to serve such communities, even if the routes lost money. But in 1982, Congress passed the Bus Regulatory Reform Act, which forbade the states from imposing such conditions. Many states now provide subsidies to bus operators to ensure service to out-of-the-way areas.

Whether preemption takes the form of mandates or restraints, the result is additional costs for state and local government and interference with a fundamental government task: setting priorities. Furthermore, the national government is not obliged to pay for the costs it imposes. As preemption grew in the 1980s, the national government reduced spending in the form of grants to the states. For example, the 1988 Family Support Act required states to continue Medicaid coverage for a year to families who left welfare for jobs, but the states had to pick up the tab.

Despite a lack of resources, the national government seems no less determined to tell the states and local governments what to do. The national government has turned increasingly to mandates to control state and local activity without having to pay for it. Even presidential candidate Clinton commented from the stump in 1992 that the national government was "sticking it to all the states in the country and especially the poor states."[29]

Constraining Unfunded Mandates.   State and local government officials have long voiced strong objections to the national government's practice of imposing requirements on the states without providing the financial support needed to satisfy them. By 1992, more than 170 congressional acts had established partially or wholly unfunded mandates.[30]

The question of unfunded mandates rankles governors and mayors. For example, the Americans With Disabilities Act (1990) required all municipal golf courses to provide a spot for disabled golfers to get in and out of bunkers (sand traps). The regulations set precise gradations for all bunkers. The act also required reservation offices at golf courses to install telecommunications devices for the deaf. The legislation aimed to end discrimination and eliminate barriers that cordoned off the disabled from mainstream America. Although these may be entirely laudable objectives, the national government did not foot the bill for the changes it mandated.[31] Municipalities already constrained by tight budgets were forced to fund these well-intentioned but expensive renovations.

One of the early results of the Republican-led 104th Congress was the Unfunded Mandates Relief Act of 1995. The legislation—adopted in the flurry of the first 100 days—requires the Congressional Budget Office to prepare cost estimates of any proposed national legislation that would impose more than $50 million a year in costs on state and local governments or more than $100 million a year in costs on private business. It also requires a cost analysis of the impact of agency regulations on governments and private businesses. Congress can still pass along to the states the costs of the programs it mandates, but only after holding a separate vote specifically imposing a requirement on other governments without providing the money to carry it out. (The law does not apply to legislation protecting constitutional rights and civil rights or to anti-discrimination laws.)

To many state and local officials, the law seemed cosmetic because it applied only to future mandates, not to unfunded mandates already in place. Republican governor John Engler of Michigan put the matter in perspective: "It's like a patient coming into an emergency room. The first step is you stop the hemorrhaging."[32]

The national government continues to support state and local governments. Yet spending pressures on state and local governments are enormous. The public demands better schools, harsher sentences for criminals (and more prisons to hold them), more and better day care for children and the elderly. The proportion of national government aid to states and local communities—either in the form of grants or in direct payments for the poor (such as Medicaid)—was at essentially the same level in 1999 as it was in 1982, but its composition had changed substantially. Payments for the poor made up an increasing share of the national government's contribution to the states. That trend is likely to continue. For the first time in decades, many state and local governments are raising taxes or adopting new ones to pay for public services that were once the shared responsibility of cooperative federalism.

OTHER GOVERNMENTS IN THE FEDERAL SYSTEM

We have concentrated in this chapter on the changing roles of the national and state governments in the federal system. Although the Constitution explicitly recognizes only national and state governments, the American federal system has spawned a multitude of local governments as well. A 1992 census counted nearly 87,000.[33]

★

Her Honor, the Mayor.
Hizzoner, the Mayor.

A mayor is the elected chief executive and ceremonial officer of a city. In some modest-sized cities, mayors serve part-time. Many big-city mayors rise to national prominence, though no mayor has yet made the leap from city hall to the White House. These mayors are (clockwise, from top left): Sandy Janes of Bowling Green, Kentucky; Elizabeth Flores of Laredo, Texas; Willie Brown of San Francisco; and Richard M. Daley of Chicago.

Types of Local Governments

Americans are citizens of both a nation and a state, and they also come under the jurisdiction of various local government units. These units include **municipal governments,** the governments of cities and towns. Municipalities, in turn, are located in (or may contain or share boundaries with) counties, which are administered by **county governments.** (Sixteen states further subdivide counties into *townships* as units of government.) Most Americans also live in a **school district,** which is responsible for administering local elementary and secondary educational programs. They may also be served by one or more **special districts,** government units created to perform particular functions, typically when those functions—such as fire protection and water purification and distribution—spill across ordinary jurisdictional boundaries. Examples of special districts include the Port Authority of New York and New Jersey, the Chicago Sanitation District, and the Southeast Pennsylvania Transit Authority.

Local governments are created by state governments, either in their constitutions or through legislation. This means that their organization, powers, responsibilities, and effectiveness vary considerably from state to

municipal government
The government unit that administers a city or town.

county government
The government unit that administers a county.

school district
An area for which a local government unit administers elementary and secondary school programs.

special district
A government unit created to perform particular functions, especially when those functions are best performed across jurisdictional boundaries.

home rule
The right to enact and enforce legislation locally.

state. About forty states endow their cities with various forms of **home rule**—the right to enact and enforce legislation in certain administrative areas. Home rule gives cities a measure of self-government and freedom of action. In contrast, county governments, which are the main units of local government in rural areas, tend to have little or no legislative power. Instead, county governments ordinarily serve as administrative units, performing the specific duties assigned to them under state law.

How can the ordinary citizen be expected to make sense of the maze of governments? And does the ordinary citizen really benefit from all the governments?

So Many Governments: Advantages and Disadvantages

In theory at least, one benefit of localizing government is that it brings government closer to the people; it gives them an opportunity to participate in the political process, to have a direct influence on policy. Localized government conjures visions of informed citizens deciding their own political fate—the traditional New England town meeting, repeated across the nation. From this perspective, overlapping governments appear compatible with a majoritarian view of democracy.

The reality is somewhat different, however. Studies have shown that people are much less likely to vote in local elections than national elections. In fact, voter turnout in local contests tends to be quite low (although the influence of individual votes is thus much greater). Furthermore, the fragmentation of powers, functions, and responsibilities among national, state, and local governments makes government as a whole seem complicated and hence incomprehensible and inaccessible to ordinary people. In addition, most people have little time to devote to public affairs, which can be very time consuming. These factors tend to discourage individual citizens from pursuing politics and, in turn, enhance the influence of organized groups, which have the resources—time, money, and know-how—to sway policymaking (see Chapter 10). Instead of bringing government closer to the people and reinforcing majoritarian democracy, then, the system's enormous complexity tends to encourage pluralism.

Can You Explain Why...
Americans generally believe that government should be close to the people, yet so few citizens vote in local elections?

One potential benefit of having many governments is that they enable the country to experiment with new policies on a small scale. New programs or solutions to problems can be tested in one city or state or in a few cities or states. Successful programs can then be adopted by other cities or states or by the nation as a whole. This fit President Clinton's brand of federalism. He viewed the states as "the laboratories of democracy." These laboratories received a boost from Republican-led congressional welfare reforms. By 1997, the national government had abolished its largest welfare program, Aid to Families with Dependent Children (AFDC), and replaced it with a block grant program. States are eligible for these funds—to be spent as they think fit—provided they follow national job creation guidelines. Most states have completely halted financial assistance to able-bodied persons who are not working, not training for a job, or not seeking a job. Moreover, the national government has imposed a lifetime assistance limit of five years, and many states have imposed shorter periods for the able-bodied to receive assistance.

The large number of governments also makes it possible for government to respond to the diversity of conditions in different parts of the country. States and cities differ enormously in population, size, economic resources, climate, and other characteristics—the diverse elements that French political philosopher Montesquieu argued should be taken into account in formulating laws for a society. Smaller political units are better able to respond to particular local conditions and can generally do so more quickly than larger units. On the other hand, smaller units may not be able to muster the economic resources to meet some challenges.

The question of how much diversity the nation should tolerate in the way different states treat their citizens is important. Regarding welfare reform, for example, some critics of the recent elimination of AFDC argue that a strong national welfare standard is needed to address poverty. Without one, some observers worry, states will engage in a "race to the bottom," cutting their public assistance budgets too drastically, which will result in fewer and fewer services going to the nation's neediest citizens.[34] Also important is the question of whether the national government (and, indirectly, the citizens of other states) should be called on to foot the bill for problems specific to a particular region. States turn to the national government for assistance to meet national disasters such as earthquakes and floods. States expect similar assistance when confronted with social disasters such as urban riots, crime, and poverty.

Throughout American history, the national government has used its funds for regional development, to equalize disparities in wealth and development among the states. The development of the Sunbelt (the southern and southwestern regions of the country), for example, has been and continues to be helped considerably by national policies and programs: the national government funded the Tennessee Valley Authority (TVA) electrification projects and western irrigation projects; national funding formulas designed to aid poorer areas of the country helped the Sunbelt enormously, particularly in the South; and national largesse in the form of huge defense contracts benefited California. Overall, the national government has poured more money into the Sunbelt states than they have paid in taxes.

FEDERALISM AND GLOBALIZATION

Supreme Court Associate Justice Anthony Kennedy observed that "federalism was our Nation's own discovery. The Framers split the atom of sovereignty. It was the genius of their idea that our citizens would have two political capacities, one state and one federal, each protected from incursion by the other."[35] Federalism is not an obsolete nineteenth-century form of government inappropriate in the contemporary world. In fact, the concept of the nation-state, developed in the seventeenth century, may be heading for the dust bin. (A *nation-state* is a country with defined and recognized boundaries whose citizens have common characteristics, such as race, religion, customs, and language.)

Some scholars have noted that we may be moving from a world of sovereign nation-states to a world of diminished state sovereignty and increased interstate linkages of a constitutionally federal character. According to one leading scholar, "There are, at present among the 180 politically sovereign states in the world, 24 federations containing about

2 billion people or 40 percent of the world population; they encompass about 480 constituent or federated states. In addition to these federations, there have emerged new variants of the application of the federal idea. Just one of many examples is the European Union where individual federations, unions and unitary states have 'pooled their sovereignty' (as they express it) in a hybrid structure which has come to involve elements of confederation and federation."[36]

The creation of a European superstate—either in a loose confederation or in a binding federation—demonstrates the potential for federalism to overcome long-held religious, ethnic, linguistic, and cultural divisions. The economic integration of such a superstate would create an alternative to the dominant currency, the U.S. dollar. And the creation of a single and expanding European market would serve as a magnet for buyers and sellers. But lingering doubts among some nations regarding a common currency (the euro) and power sharing (reductions in veto power for any member) may generate strains similar to the ones America endured more than 200 years ago when it sought to govern itself. For the latest state of the European Union, see Politics in a Changing World 4.1.

CONTEMPORARY FEDERALISM AND THE DILEMMAS OF DEMOCRACY

To what extent were conservative hopes and liberal fears realized as federalism developed from the 1980s to the 1990s? Neither were fully realized under the various renditions of federalism. Federalism of the Reagan-Bush variety was used as a tool for cutting the national budget by offering less money to the states. Contrary to the expectations of conservatives and liberals alike, however, states approved tax increases to pay for social services and education. In 1990 and 1991, thirty-seven states raised one or more major taxes (on income, sales, and motor fuels). Fewer states followed suit in 1992 and 1993, due in part to voter resistance and economic recovery.[37] To be sure, this was risky business for politicians. Raising taxes stirs voter ire; reducing vital services (such as education) also stirs voter ire. In an era when Washington has been less willing to enforce antitrust legislation, civil rights laws, and affirmative action plans, state governments have been more likely to do so. At a time when a conservative national government put little emphasis on the value of equality, state governments did more to embrace it.[38]

Conservatives thought that the value of freedom would be emphasized if more matters were left to the states. Traditionally, state governments were relatively small and lacked the wherewithal to limit large corporate interests, for example. But since the 1970s, state governments have changed. Their legislatures have become more professional. They meet regularly, and they maintain larger permanent staffs. Governors have proved willing to support major programs to enhance the skills of their state's work force, to promote research and development, and to subsidize new industries. State governments have become big governments themselves. They are better able to tackle problems, and they are not afraid to use their power to promote equality.

To the surprise of liberals, who had originally looked to the national government to protect individuals by setting reasonable minimum standards for product safety, welfare payments, and employee benefits, states are now willing to set higher standards than the national government.

4.1 A United States of Europe or a United Europe of States?

The European Union (EU) is one of the great political and economic success stories of the twentieth century. It was born in the 1950s, when six nations (which only a decade earlier had fought against each other in World War II) agreed to create a European Economic Community to achieve limited economic integration. By 2001, the EEC had expanded from six to fifteen members and had been transformed into the European Union, a continent-wide political institution with a unified economy that rivals the U.S. economy and a system of treaties and rules that binds its members into a hybrid federal/confederal political system. But exactly how close the political ties between the members should be remains a subject of hot debate.

Today, the EU is an organization of states, but is not a state itself, whose powers are established by, and limited by, international treaties. Political scientists call such arrange-

ments *international organizations*. (Other examples of international organizations are the United Nations and the World Health Organization.) The EU is different from all other international organizations, however, because it has powers beyond merely administering policies that its member nations delegate to it. Just as the U.S. national government can make laws that apply to all the states and supercede state laws, so the EU is able to make—and enforce—some laws that significantly limit the sovereignty of all its members. For example, in 2000 the EU adopted measures that for the first time will provide a uniform legal basis to combat discrimination based on race, sex, religion, age, or disability. In cases like this, the EU is acting as a *federation*.

Many EU initiatives remain voluntary, however, with member states opting in and out as they choose. In these areas the EU acts as a

When Clinton came to the White House, liberals were delighted. His conservative predecessors Reagan and Bush had sought to reinstate layer-cake federalism and to dismantle the national government's welfare-state efforts to promote social and political equality. But Clinton's experience as a governor created a strange brew when joined with the Democrats' liberal social welfare policies. The Clinton administration was silent on its brand of federalism; no coherent theory of federalism emerged.[39] President Clinton was sympathetic to states burdened by new and costly mandates and restraints. On a few basic themes, liberals and conservatives are singing the same tune: smaller, more efficient government; less micromanagement by the national government; greater flexibility for state and local governments. But trying to pin down these concepts remains as challenging as nailing Jell-O to the wall.

FEDERALISM AND PLURALISM

Our federal system of government was designed to allay citizens' fears that they might be ruled by a majority in a distant region with whom they did not necessarily agree or share interests. By recognizing the legitimacy of the states as political divisions, the federal system also recognizes the importance of diversity. The existence and cultivation of diverse interests are hallmarks of pluralism.

Each of the two competing theories of federalism supports pluralism, but in somewhat different ways. Dual federalism aims to decentralize gov-

confederation, which we learned about in Chapter 3. The best-known example is the euro, which has become the official currency of twelve of the fifteen countries. Three countries—Britain, Denmark, and Sweden—have chosen to retain their own currencies.

Not coincidentally, these are the countries that are also the most reluctant to see any further political integration. They are most comfortable with a loose *confederal* system that allows them plenty of opportunity to veto, or opt out of, policies they disagree with—in other words, a united Europe of sovereign states. Other members, especially France and Germany, favor closer ties. These countries would like a stronger *federal* system, with more power resting in the EU and each member state having less freedom to choose its own course. They favor something closer to a United States of Europe, a European super-

state that could rival the United States for global political power.

These debates are not likely to be solved anytime soon and in fact will only be complicated as the membership of the European Union continues to expand. Currently twelve countries—mostly former communist nations in central and Eastern Europe—are negotiating to join the EU. Before they can do so, they must prove that they can satisfy the "economic and political conditions required," including "adherence to the aims of political, economic and monetary union." What *kind* of political union remains to be seen.

Sources: Suzanne Daly, "A United Europe of States or a United States of Europe?" *New York Times,* 17 December 2000, p. 6; Kesslerman et al., *European Politics in Transition,* 4th Edition, (Boston, Mass.: Houghton Mifflin Company, 2002); European Union Web site <http://www.europa.eu.int/index-en.htm>.

ernment, to shift power to the states. It recognizes the importance of local rather than national standards and applauds the diversity of those standards. The variety allows the people, if not a direct voice in policymaking, at least a choice of policies under which to live.

In contrast, cooperative federalism is perfectly willing to override local standards for a national standard in the interests of promoting equality. Yet this view of federalism also supports pluralist democracy. It is highly responsive to all manner of group pressures, including pressure at one level from groups unsuccessful at other levels. By blurring the lines of national and state responsibility, this type of federalism encourages petitioners to try their luck at whichever level of government offers them the best chance of success.

SUMMARY

The government framework outlined in the Constitution is the product of political compromise, an acknowledgment of the original thirteen states' fear of a powerful central government. The division of powers sketched in the Constitution was supposed to turn over "great and aggregate" matters to the national government, leaving "local and particular" concerns to the states. The Constitution does not explain, however, what is "great and aggregate" or "what is local and particular."

Federalism comes in many varieties, two of which stand out because they capture valuable differences between the original and modern vision

★

Between a Rock and a Hard Place

"I hope I don't have to clean it up," commented David Arroya, a janitor at Fenix Underground, as he assessed the earthquake damage in Historic Pioneer Square in Seattle, Washington, on February 28, 2001. Though there was no loss of life, the quake did cause $2 billion in property damage. The national government provides substantial assistance for disaster areas in the form of grants, loans, and credits.

of a national government. Dual, or layer-cake, federalism wants to retain power in the states and keep the levels of government separate. Cooperative, or marble-cake, federalism emphasizes the power of the national government and sees national and state government working together to solve national problems. In its own way, each view supports the pluralist model of democracy.

Over the years, the national government has used both its enumerated and its implied powers to become involved in almost every area of human activity. The tools of political change include direct legislation, judicial interpretation, and grants-in-aid to states and localities. In the absence of financial incentives, the national government may use its preemption power, imposing mandates or restraints on the states without necessarily footing the cost.

As its influence grew, so did the national government. Major events, such as the Civil War and the Great Depression, mark major shifts in its growth in size and power. To alter its course, conservatives offered New Federalism and argued for cutting back on the size of the national government, reducing federal spending, and turning programs over to the states to solve the problem of unwieldy government. Liberals worried that in their haste to decentralize and cut back, conservatives would turn over important responsibilities to states that were unwilling or unable to assume them. Rather than being too responsive, government would become unresponsive. But neither happened in the 1980s. Congressional preemption forced states to meet national standards, with or without financial inducements. The states proved ready to tackle some major problems. In addition, they were prepared to fund many programs that promoted equality.

The debate over federalism shifted in the conservative direction as a result of successive Republican congressional victories starting in 1994, the formation of a slender but solid conservative majority on the Supreme Court, and the election of President George W. Bush. One truth emerges from this overview of federalism: the balance of power between the national and state governments will be settled by political means, not by theory.

★ Selected Readings

Beer, Samuel H. *To Make a Nation: The Rediscovery of American Federalism.* Cambridge, Mass.: Harvard University Press, 1993. A historical examination of federalism and nationalism in American political philosophy.

Berger, Raoul. *Federalism: The Founder's Design.* Norman: University of Oklahoma Press, 1987. Berger, a constitutional historian, argues that the states preceded the nation and that the states and the national government were meant to have mutually exclusive spheres of sovereignty.

Greve, Michael S. *Real Federalism: Why It Matters, How It Could Happen.* Washington, D.C.: AEI Press, 1999. This short book examines the question: What will it take to reestablish serious federalism constraints on government?

Peterson, Paul E. *The Price of Federalism.* Washington, D.C.: Brookings/A Twentieth Century Fund Book, 1995. Peterson argues that development projects such as roads and buildings are best left to state and local government and that redistributive policies such as welfare and social security are best left to the national government.

Rivlin, Alice. *Reviving the American Dream: The Economy, the States, and the Federal Government.* Washington, D.C.: Brookings Institution, 1992. A lucid examination of economic performance and government performance, resting on a reexamination of the division of responsibilities between the nation and the states.

Zimmerman, Joseph F. *Contemporary American Federalism: The Growth of National Power.* New York: Praeger, 1992. Argues that the expansion of preemption power has altered the allocation of power between nation and states.

Internet Exercises

1. U.S. Term Limits, Inc. *v.* Thornton (1995)
In some U.S. states, governors, state legislators, and other elected officials can serve only a limited number of terms. These same states, however, have been unable to limit the terms of their representatives to the U.S. House and Senate, which seems somewhat odd given that large numbers of Americans favor term limits. Why is that? As you might have suspected, the U.S. Supreme Court has provided guidance on this issue. Even though the Court does not post its opinions on the Web, you can find full-text opinions at FindLaw <**www.findlaw.com/**>, one of the most comprehensive sites on the Internet designed to serve policymakers, lawyers and legal analysts, and law students.

• Go to the FindLaw Web site, and locate the Supreme Court's decision in *U.S. Term Limits, Inc.* v. *Thornton* (1995). Read the summary of the Court's opinion in this case. (The summary precedes the opinion; in other words, read until you get to the line "JUSTICE STEVENS delivered the opinion of the Court.")

• Based on what you find, why can states impose term limits on state officials but not on the individuals who represent them in the U.S. House and Senate?

2. *Statistical Abstract of the United States, State Rankings*
The U.S. Census Bureau maintains one of the largest collections of data about social and economic conditions in the United States as a whole, and all of the nation's fifty states individually. Each year the bureau publishes a summary of this information in the *Statistical Abstract of the United States.* You can link to an electronic version of this publication at the bureau's web site, <**www.census.gov**>.

• Go the U.S. Census Bureau's web site and locate the *Statistical Abstract.* From there, identify the collection of what the bureau calls "State Rankings," and study in particular the following three measures: (1) infant mortality rate, (2) violent crime rate, and (3) persons below the poverty level.

• How might a conservative use this information to argue for a system of "dual federalism"? How might a liberal use this information to argue for a system of "cooperative federalism"?

chapter 5

Public Opinion and Political Socialization

IT TOOK JUST NINETY MINUTES for the jury to recommend that Earl Washington, Jr., receive the death sentence for raping and murdering a Virginia woman named Rebecca Williams. It took seventeen years for Washington's attorneys to obtain the advanced DNA test demonstrating that the evidence at the crime scene did not come from him.[1] Washington's case was a controversial one in Virginia, garnering attention long before the sophisticated DNA tests were developed that would eventually gain him a pardon. Earl Washington is retarded, with an IQ of 69 and a mentality that has been described as that of a ten-year-old.[2] After he was arrested on an unrelated charge a year after the murder, Washington was questioned by detectives about a wide range of crime committed in the region. He confessed to every case that detectives suggested, including the rape and murder of Rebecca Williams. Although he soon recanted, Washington was sentenced to death. After his conviction, a mental health expert who examined Washington questioned the validity of his confession, concluding that his diminished intellectual capacity made him "extremely suggestible."[3] After DNA tests conducted in 2000 proved decisively that the semen found on a bloody blanket at the crime scene and on the victim's body did not come from Washington, he received a pardon from the governor of Virginia.[4]

A Gallup survey in 2000 shows overwhelming support for access to the kind of DNA testing that Earl Washington received. Ninety-two percent of the respondents said that prisoners convicted before the tests were developed should be allowed to get DNA tests now.[5] However, this concern with correcting potential mistakes in the judicial process is not indicative of widespread opposition to the death penalty itself. The Gallup Organization has polled the nation on this issue for more than fifty years. Except in 1966, most respondents have consistently supported the death penalty for murder. In 2000, 66 percent of all respondents were in favor of the death penalty for murder, while only 26 percent opposed it.[6] (The same survey, however, showed that barely half of the American public—51 percent—believe the death penalty is applied fairly.) Other research has shown that a substantial segment of the public favors the death penalty for attempting to assassinate the president (63 percent), for rape (51 percent), and for hijacking an airplane (49 percent).[7] In contrast to the United States, *all* Western European countries have eliminated capital punishment.

Government has been defined as the legitimate use of force to control human behavior. We can learn much about the role of public opinion in America by reviewing how we have punished violent criminals. During

125

The Death Chamber

This uncomfortable apparatus is the electric chair in an Alabama state prison. It dramatizes the ultimate power that government has to control behavior. Capital crimes may draw capital punishment.

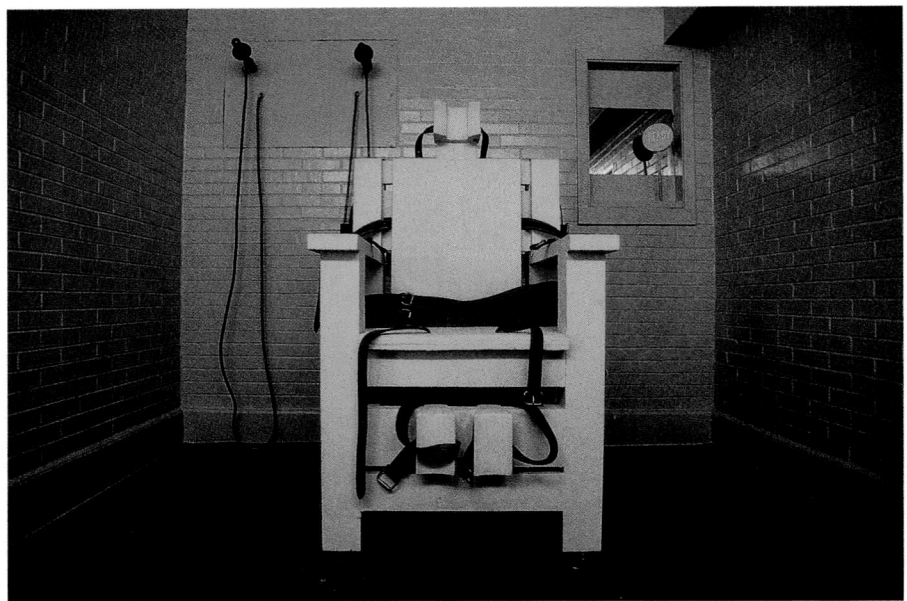

most of American history, government execution of people who threatened the social order was legal. In colonial times, capital punishment was imposed not just for murder but also for antisocial behavior—denying the "true" God, cursing one's parents, committing adultery, practicing witchcraft, or being a rebellious child, for example.[8] In the late 1700s, some writers, editors, and clergy argued for abolishing the death sentence. The campaign intensified in the 1840s, and a few states responded by eliminating capital punishment. Interest in the cause waned until 1890, when New York State adopted a new, "scientific" technique, electrocution, as the instrument of death. By 1917, twelve states had passed laws against capital punishment. But the outbreak of World War I fed the public's fear of foreigners and radicals, leading to renewed support for the death penalty. Reacting to this shift in public opinion, four states restored it.

The security needs of World War II and the postwar fears of Soviet communism fueled continued support for capital punishment. After anticommunist hysteria subsided in the late 1950s, public opposition to the death penalty increased. But public opinion was neither strong enough nor stable enough to force state legislatures to outlaw the death penalty. In keeping with the pluralist model of democracy, efforts to abolish the death penalty shifted from the legislative arena to the courts.

The opponents argued that the death penalty is cruel and unusual punishment and is therefore unconstitutional. Certainly, the public in the 1780s did not consider capital punishment either cruel or unusual. But nearly 200 years later, opponents contended that execution by the state was cruel and unusual by contemporary standards. Their argument apparently had some effect on public opinion; in 1966, a plurality of respondents opposed the death penalty for the first (and only) time since the Gallup Organization began polling the public on the question of capital punishment.

The states responded to this shift in public opinion by reducing the number of executions, until they stopped completely in 1968 in anticipation of a Supreme Court decision. By then, however, public opinion had again reversed in favor of capital punishment. Nevertheless, in 1972, the Court ruled in a 5–4 decision that the death penalty as imposed by existing state laws was unconstitutional.[9] The decision was not well received in many states, and thirty-five state legislatures passed new laws to get around the ruling. Meanwhile, as the nation's homicide rate increased, public approval of the death penalty jumped almost ten points and continued climbing.

In 1976, the Supreme Court changed its position and upheld three new state laws that let judges consider the defendant's record and the nature of the crime in deciding whether to impose a sentence of death.[10] The Court also rejected the argument that punishment by death in itself violates the Constitution, and it noted that public opinion favors the death penalty. Through the end of the 1970s, however, only three criminals were executed. Eventually, the states began to heed public concern about the crime rate. In 1999 alone, ninety-eight murderers were executed, the highest number since 1951.[11]

Does the death penalty deter people from killing? A majority of the public thinks it does.[12] What do people think is the most humane method of execution? Opinion polls tell us that most people favor lethal injection (66 percent) over electrocution (10 percent). The gas chamber has more support (6 percent) than the old-fashioned firing squad or hanging (both 3 percent).[13]

The history of public thinking on the death penalty reveals several characteristics of public opinion:

1. *The public's attitudes toward a given government policy can vary over time, often dramatically.* Opinions about capital punishment tend to fluctuate with threats to the social order. The public is more likely to favor capital punishment in times of war and when fear of foreign subversion and crime rates are high.

2. *Public opinion places boundaries on allowable types of public policy.* Flogging criminals is not acceptable to the modern American public (and surely not to courts interpreting the Constitution), but electrocuting a murderer is.

3. *If asked by pollsters, citizens are willing to register opinions on matters outside their expertise.* People clearly believe execution by lethal injection is more humane than electrocution, asphyxiation in a gas chamber, or hanging. But how can the public know enough about execution to make these judgments?

4. *Governments tend to respond to public opinion.* State laws for and against capital punishment have reflected swings in the public mood. The Supreme Court's 1972 decision against capital punishment came when public opinion on the death penalty was sharply divided; the Court's approval of capital punishment in 1976 coincided with a rise in public approval of the death penalty.

5. *The government sometimes does not do what the people want.* Although public opinion overwhelmingly favors the death penalty for murder, there were only ninety-eight executions in 1999 (but over 15,000 murders).

Make It Quick, the Bag's Heavy

Pollsters sometimes catch respondents wherever they can, but such "parking lot polls" often yield unreliable results. To draw valid inferences from samples with known estimates of error, every person in the population must have an equal chance of selection. True random sampling cannot be done by catching people in parking lots. It requires other methods (e.g., random-digit dialing).

The last two conclusions bear on our understanding of the majoritarian and pluralist models of democracy discussed in Chapter 2. Here, we probe more deeply into the nature, shape, depth, and formation of public opinion in a democratic government. What is the place of public opinion in a democracy? How do people acquire their opinions? What are the major lines of division in public opinion? How do individuals' ideology and knowledge affect their opinions? What is the relationship between public opinion and ideology?

PUBLIC OPINION AND THE MODELS OF DEMOCRACY

public opinion
The collected attitudes of citizens concerning a given issue or question.

Public opinion is simply the collective attitude of the citizens on a given issue or question. Opinion polling, which involves interviewing a sample of citizens to estimate public opinion as a whole (see Feature 5.1), is such a common feature of contemporary life that we often forget it is a modern invention, dating only from the 1930s (see Figure 5.1). In fact, survey methodology did not become a powerful research tool until the advent of computers in the 1950s.

Before polling became an accepted part of the American scene, politicians, journalists, and everyone else could argue about what the people wanted, but no one really knew. Before the 1930s, observers of America had to guess at national opinion by analyzing newspaper stories, politicians' speeches, voting returns, and travelers' diaries. What if pollsters had been around when the colonists declared their independence from Britain in July 1776? We might have learned (as some historians estimate) that "40 percent of Americans supported the Revolution, 20 percent opposed it, and 40 percent tried to remain neutral."[14] When no one really knows what

5.1

Sampling a Few, Predicting to Everyone

How can a pollster tell what the nation thinks by talking to only a few hundred people? The answer lies in the statistical theory of sampling. Briefly, the theory holds that a sample of individuals selected by chance from any population is "representative" of that population. This means that the traits of the individuals in the sample—their attitudes, beliefs, sociological characteristics, and physical features—reflect the traits of the whole population. Sampling theory does not claim that a sample exactly matches the population, only that it reflects the population with some predictable degree of accuracy.

Three factors determine the accuracy of a sample. The most important is how the sample is selected. For maximum accuracy, the individuals in the sample must be chosen randomly. Randomly does not mean "at whim," however; it means that every individual in the population has the same chance of being selected.

For a population as large and widespread as that of the United States, pollsters first divide the country into geographic regions. Then they randomly choose areas and sample individuals who live within those areas. This departure from strict random sampling does decrease the accuracy of polls, but only by a relatively small amount. Today, most polls conducted by the mass media are done by telephone, with computers randomly dialing numbers within predetermined calling areas. (Random dialing ensures that even people with unlisted numbers are called.)

The second factor that affects accuracy is the size of the sample. The larger the sample, the more accurately it represents the population. For example, a sample of 400 randomly selected individuals is accurate to within six percentage points (plus or minus) 95 percent of the time. A sample of 600 is accurate to within five percentage points. (Surprisingly, the proportion of the sample to the overall population has essentially no effect on the accuracy of most samples. A sample of, say, 600 individuals will reflect the traits of a city, a state, or even an entire nation

with equal accuracy. Why this statement is true is better discussed in a course on statistics.)

The final factor that affects the accuracy of sampling is the amount of variation in the population. If there were no variation, every sample would reflect the population's characteristics with perfect accuracy. The greater the variation within the population, the greater is the chance that one random sample will be different from another.

The Gallup Poll and most other national opinion polls usually survey about 1,500 individuals and are accurate to within three percentage points 95 percent of the time. As shown in Figure 5.1, the predictions of the Gallup Poll for seventeen presidential elections since 1936 have deviated from the voting results by an average of only −1.0 percentage points. Even this small margin of error can mean an incorrect prediction in a close election. But for the purpose of estimating public opinion on political issues, a sampling error of three percentage points is acceptable.

Poll results can be wrong because of problems that have nothing to do with sampling theory. For example, question wording can bias the results. In surveys during the 1980s concerning aid to the Nicaraguan Contras fighting the Sandinista government, questions that mentioned President Reagan's name produced more support for increased aid by almost five percentage points.[*] Survey questions are also prone to random error because interviewers are likely to obtain superficial responses from busy respondents who say anything, quickly, to get rid of them. Recently, some newspaper columnists have even urged readers to lie to pollsters outside voting booths, to confound election-night television predictions. But despite the potential for abuses or distortions, modern polling has told us a great deal about public opinion in America.

---

[*] Brad Lockerbie and Stephen A. Borrelli, "Question Wording and Public Support for Contra Aid, 1983–1986," *Public Opinion Quarterly 54* (Summer 1990), p. 200.

figure

5.1   Gallup Poll Accuracy

One of the nation's oldest polls was started by George Gallup in the 1930s. The accuracy of the Gallup Poll in predicting presidential elections over sixty years is charted here. Although not always on the mark, its predictions have been fairly close. Gallup's final prediction for the 2000 election declared the race "too close to call." Indeed, the race in the electoral college remained too close to call for weeks after the election. The poll was most notably wrong in 1948, when it predicted that Thomas Dewey, the Republican candidate, would defeat the Democratic incumbent, Harry Truman, underestimating Truman's vote by 5.4 percentage points. In 1992, the Gallup Poll was off by a larger margin, but this time it identified the winner, Bill Clinton. Although third-party candidate Ross Perot was included in the presidential debates and spent vast sums on his campaign, Gallup kept with historical precedent and allocated none of the undecided vote to Perot. As a result, they overestimated Clinton's share.

Source: The Gallup Organization Web site at <www.gallup.com/poll/trends/ptaccuracy.asp>.

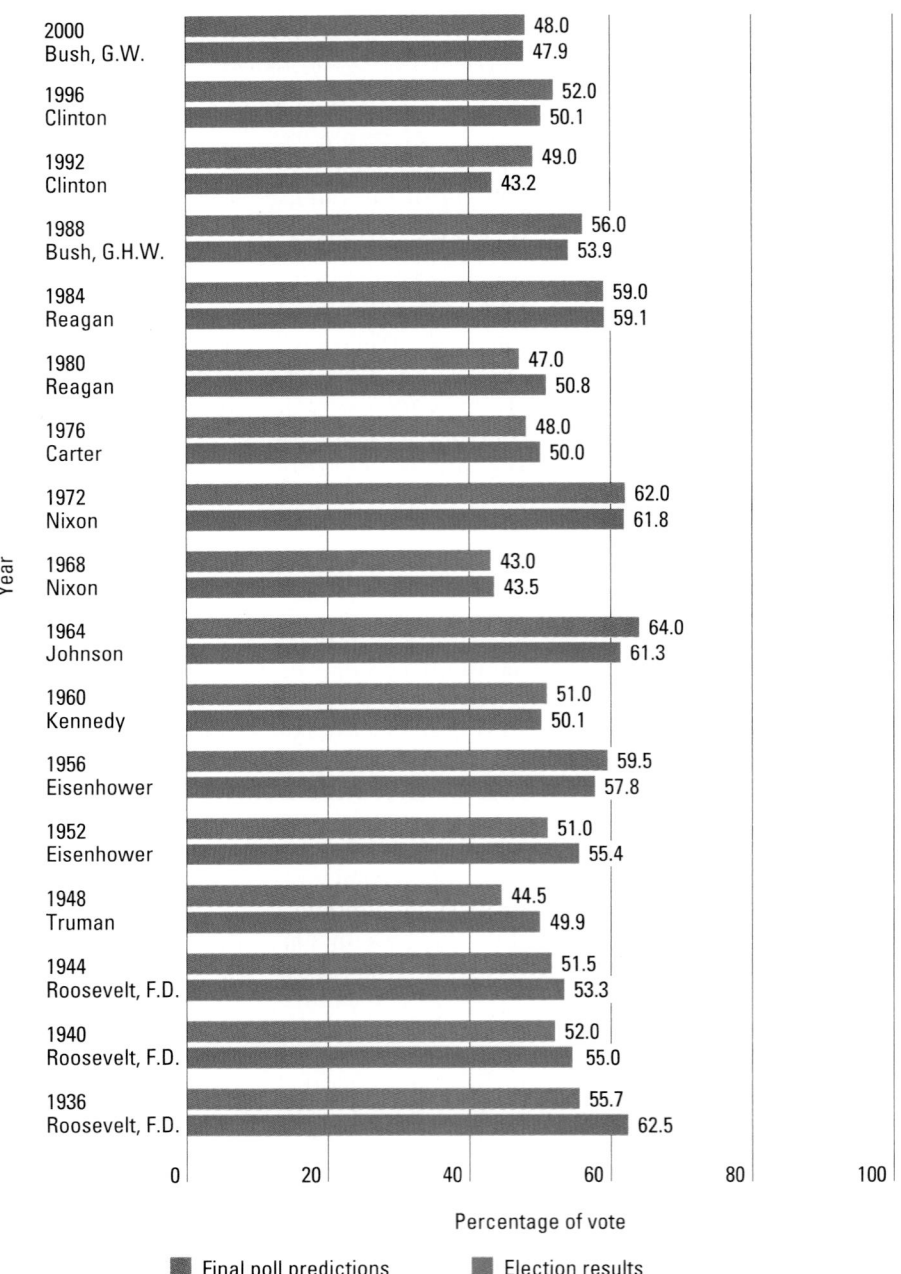

the people want, how can the national government be responsive to public opinion? As we discussed in Chapter 3, the founders wanted to build public opinion into our government structure by allowing the direct election of representatives to the House and apportioning representation there

Stop the Presses! Oops, Too Late . . .

As the 1948 election drew near, few people gave President Harry Truman a chance to defeat his Republican opponent, Thomas E. Dewey. Polling was still new, and almost all the early polls showed Dewey far ahead. Most organizations simply stopped polling weeks before the election. The Chicago Daily Tribune believed the polls and proclaimed Dewey's victory before the votes were counted. Here, the victorious Truman triumphantly displays the most embarrassing headline in American politics. Later, it was revealed that the few polls taken closer to election day showed Truman catching up to Dewey. Clearly, polls estimate the vote only at the time they are taken.

according to population. The attitudes and actions of the House of Representatives, the framers thought, would reflect public opinion, especially on the crucial issues of taxes and government spending.

In practice, bills passed by a majority of elected representatives do not necessarily reflect the opinion of a majority of citizens. This would not have bothered the framers because they never intended to create a full democracy, a government completely responsive to majority opinion. Although they wanted to provide for some consideration of public opinion, they had little faith in the ability of the masses to make public policy.

The majoritarian and pluralist models of democracy differ greatly in their assumptions about the role of public opinion in democratic government. According to the classic majoritarian model, the government should do what a majority of the public wants. In contrast, pluralists argue that the public as a whole seldom demonstrates clear, consistent opinions on the day-to-day issues of government. At the same time, pluralists recognize that subgroups within the public do express opinions on specific matters—often and vigorously. The pluralist model requires that government institutions allow the free expression of opinions by these "minority publics." Democracy is at work when the opinions of many different publics clash openly and fairly over government policy.

Sampling methods and opinion polling have altered the debate about the majoritarian and pluralist models of democracy. One expert said, "Surveys produce just what democracy is supposed to produce—equal representation of all citizens."[15] Now that we know how often government policy runs against majority opinion, it becomes harder to defend the U.S. government as democratic under the majoritarian model. Even at a time when Americans overwhelmingly favored the death penalty for murderers, the Supreme Court decided that existing state laws applying capital punishment were unconstitutional. Even after the Court approved new state laws as constitutional, relatively few murderers were actually executed. Consider, too, the case of prayer in public schools. The Supreme Court has ruled that no state or local government can require the reading of the Lord's Prayer or Bible verses in public schools. Yet surveys continually show that a clear majority of Americans (over 60 percent) do not agree with that ruling.[16] Because government policy sometimes runs against settled majority opinion, the majoritarian model is easily attacked as an inaccurate description of reality.

The two models of democracy make different assumptions about public opinion. The majoritarian model assumes that a majority of the people hold clear, consistent opinions on government policy. The pluralist model assumes that the public is often uninformed and ambivalent about specific issues, and opinion polls frequently support that claim. What are the bases of public opinion? What principles, if any, do people use to organize their beliefs and attitudes about politics? Exactly how do individuals form their political opinions? We will look for answers to these questions in this chapter. In later chapters, we assess the effect of public opinion on government policies. The results should help you make up your own mind about the viability of the majoritarian and pluralist models in a functioning democracy.

THE DISTRIBUTION OF PUBLIC OPINION

A government that tries to respond to public opinion soon learns that people seldom think alike. To understand and then act on the public's many attitudes and beliefs, government must pay attention to the way public opinion is distributed among the choices on a given issue. In particular, government must analyze the shape and the stability of that distribution.

Shape of the Distribution

The results of public opinion polls are often displayed in graphs such as those in Figure 5.2. The height of the columns indicates the percentage of those polled who gave each response, identified along the baseline. The shape of the opinion distribution depicts the pattern of all the responses when counted and plotted. The figure depicts three patterns of distribution—skewed, bimodal, and normal.

Figure 5.2a plots the percentages of respondents surveyed in 2000 who favored or opposed imposing the death penalty for a person convicted of murder. The most frequent response ("favor") is called the *mode*. The mode produces a prominent "hump" in this distribution. The relatively few respondents who didn't know or were opposed to the death penalty lie to one side, in its "tail." Such an asymmetrical distribution is called a **skewed distribution.**

skewed distribution
An asymmetrical but generally bell-shaped distribution (of opinions); its mode, or most frequent response, lies off to one side.

bimodal distribution
A distribution (of opinions) that shows two responses being chosen about as frequently as each other.

Figure 5.2b plots responses to the question of whether homosexuality is a matter of choice.[17] These responses fall into a **bimodal distribution:** respondents chose two categories with nearly equal frequency, dividing almost evenly over whether being homosexual is a matter of choice or something that a person cannot change.

Figure 5.2c shows how respondents to a national survey in 1996 were distributed along a liberal–conservative continuum. Its shape resembles

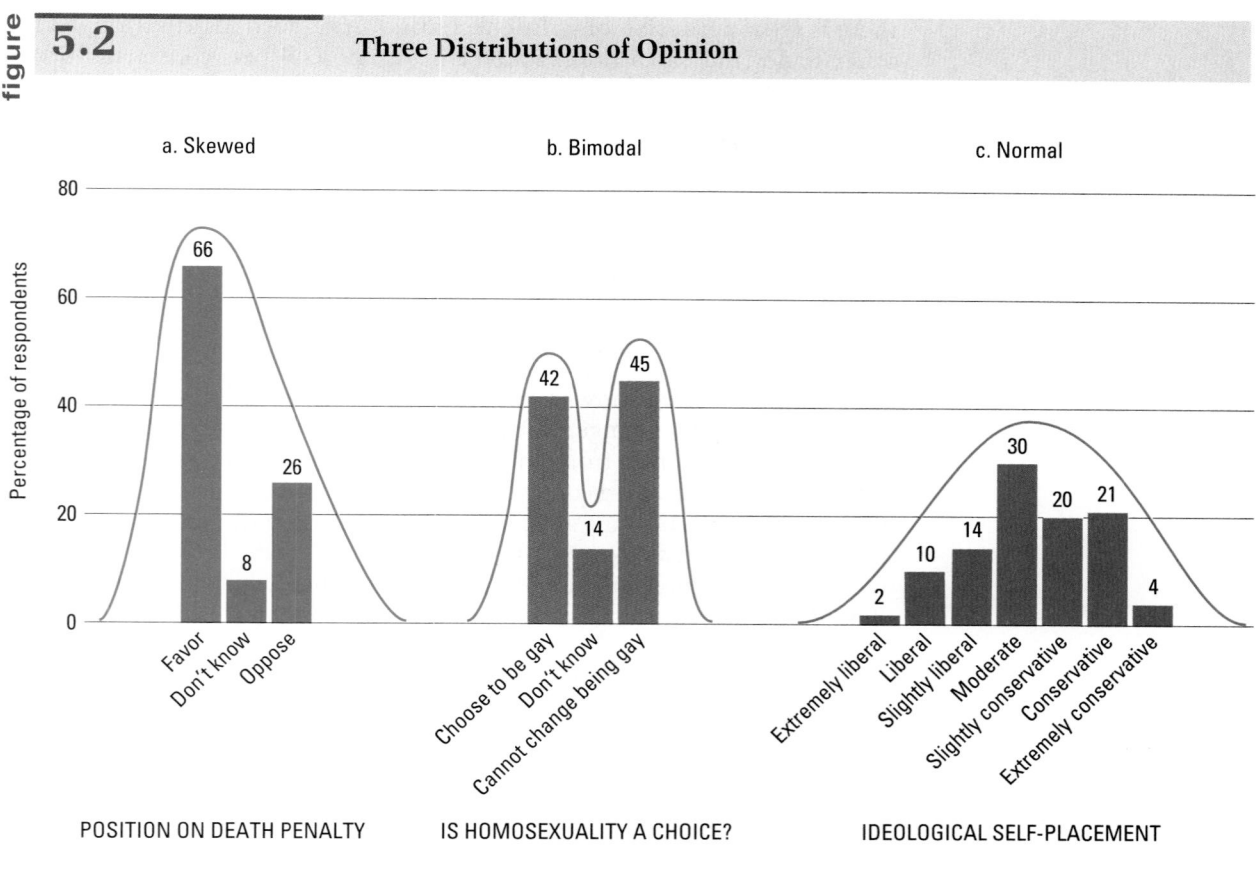

figure 5.2 Three Distributions of Opinion

Here we have superimposed three idealized patterns of distribution—skewed, bimodal, and normal—on three actual distributions of responses to survey questions. Although the actual responses do not match the ideal shapes exactly, the match is close enough that we can describe the distribution of (a) thoughts on the death penalty as skewed, (b) opinions on the causes of homosexuality as bimodal, and (c) ideological attitudes as approximately normal.

Sources: (a) Jeffrey M. Jones, "Slim Majority of Americans Think Death Penalty Applied Fairly in This Country," *Gallup Poll Monthly*, June 2000, p. 65. (b) GSS-NORC Poll conducted May 1994, reported in Alan S. Yang, "The Polls—Trends: Attitudes Towards Homosexuality," *Public Opinion Quarterly* 61 (1997), p. 489. (c) 1996 National Election Study, Center for Political Studies, University of Michigan.

normal distribution
A symmetrical bell-shaped distribution (of opinions) centered on a single mode, or most frequent response.

what statisticians call a **normal distribution**—a symmetrical, bell-shaped spread around a single mode. Here, the mode ("moderate") lies in the center. Progressively fewer people classified themselves in each category toward the liberal and conservative extremes.

When public opinion is normally distributed on an issue, the public tends to support a moderate government policy on that issue. It will also tolerate policies that fall slightly to the left or to the right as long as they do not stray too far from the moderate center. In contrast, when opinion is sharply divided in a bimodal distribution—as it is over homosexuality—

there is great potential for political conflict. A skewed distribution, on the other hand, indicates homogeneity of opinion. When consensus on an issue is overwhelming, those with the minority opinion risk social ostracism and even persecution if they persist in voicing their view. If the public does not feel intensely about the issue, however, politicians can sometimes discount a skewed distribution of opinion. This is what has happened with the death penalty. Although most people favor capital punishment, it is not a burning issue for them. Thus, politicians can skirt the issue without serious consequences.

Stability of the Distribution

stable distribution
A distribution (of opinions) that shows little change over time.

A **stable distribution** shows little change over time. Public opinion on important issues can change, but it is sometimes difficult to distinguish a true change in opinion from a difference in the way a question is worded. When different questions on the same issue produce similar distributions of opinion, the underlying attitudes are stable. When the same question (or virtually the same question) produces significantly different responses over time, an actual shift in public opinion probably has occurred.

We have already discussed Americans' long-standing support of the death penalty. People's descriptions of themselves in ideological terms is another distribution that has remained surprisingly stable. Chapter 1 argued for using a two-dimensional ideological typology based on the trade-offs of freedom for equality and freedom for order. However, most opinion polls ask respondents to place themselves along only a single liberal–conservative dimension, which tends to force libertarians and communitarians into the middle category. Nevertheless, we find relatively little change in respondents' self-placement on the liberal–conservative continuum over time. Even in 1964, when liberal Lyndon Johnson won a landslide victory over conservative Barry Goldwater in the presidential election, more voters described themselves as conservative than liberal. Indeed, the ideological distribution of the public has been skewed toward conservatism in every presidential election year since 1964.[18] Despite all the talk about the nation's becoming conservative in recent years, the fact is that most people did not describe themselves as liberal at any time during the past thirty years. People's self-descriptions have shifted about five percentage points toward the right since 1964, but more people considered themselves conservative than liberal to begin with.

Sometimes changes occur within subgroups that are not reflected in overall public opinion. College students, for example, were far more liberal in the 1970s than they are today (see Politics in a Changing America 5.1). Moreover, public opinion in America is capable of massive change over time—even on issues that were once highly controversial. A good example is racially integrated schools. A national survey in 1942 asked whether "white and Negro students should go to the same schools or separate schools."[19] Only 30 percent of white respondents said that the students should attend schools together. When virtually the same question was asked in 1984 (substituting *black* for *Negro*), 90 percent of the white respondents endorsed integrated schools. Nevertheless, only 23 percent of the whites surveyed in 1984 were in favor of busing to achieve racial balance. And whites were more willing to bus their children to a school with

★ **politics in a changing** **a m e r i c a**

5.1   Are Students More Conservative Than Their Parents?

Do you remember filling out a questionnaire when you enrolled in college? If it asked about your political orientation, you may be represented in this graph. For about three decades, researchers at the University of California at Los Angeles have collected various data on entering freshmen, including asking them to characterize their political views as far left, liberal, middle-of-the-road, conservative, or far right. In contrast to Americans in general, who have shown little ideological change over time, college students described themselves as markedly more liberal in the early 1970s than they do now.

Source: Alexander W. Astin et al., *The American Freshman: Thirty-Year Trends, 1966–1995.* (Los Angeles: Higher Education Research Institute, Graduate School of Education, University of California, 1997); Alexander W. Astin et al., *The American Freshman: Norms for 2000* (Los Angeles: Higher Education Research Institute, Graduate School of Education, University of California, 2001). Used by permission.

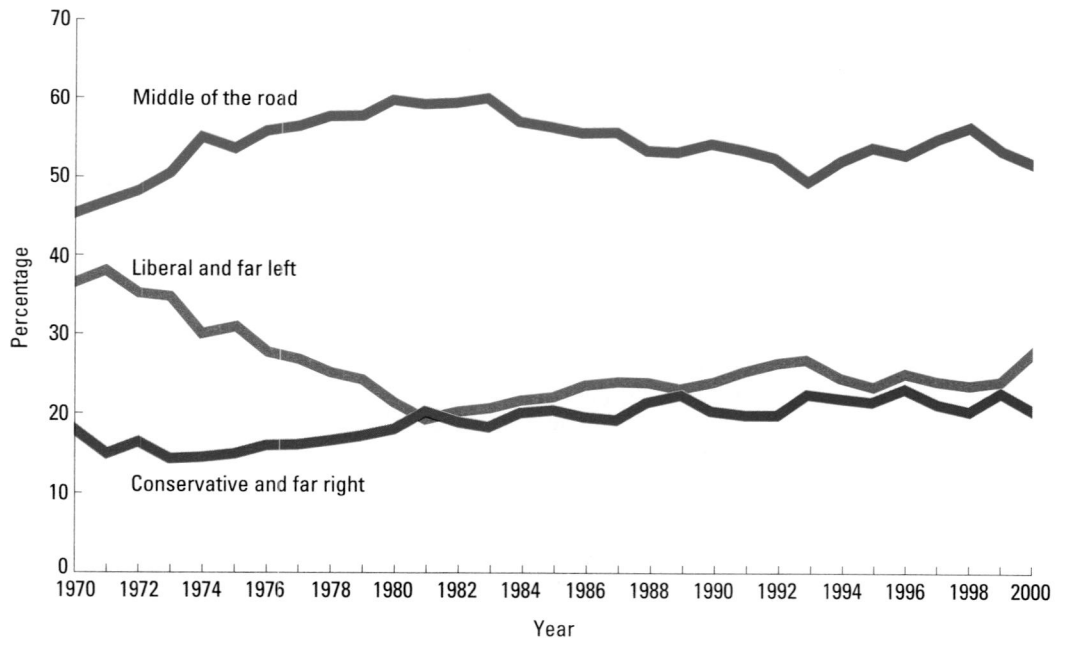

a few blacks than to one that was mostly black.[20] So white opinion changed dramatically with regard to the *principle* of desegregated schools, but whites seemed divided on how that principle should be implemented.

In trying to explain how political opinions are formed and how they change, political scientists cite the process of political socialization, the influence of cultural factors, and the interplay of ideology and knowledge. In the next several sections, we examine how these elements combine to create and influence public opinion.

POLITICAL SOCIALIZATION

political socialization
The complex process by which people acquire their political values.

Public opinion is grounded in political values. People acquire their values through **political socialization,** a complex process through which individuals become aware of politics, learn political facts, and form political values. Think for a moment about your political socialization. What is your earliest memory of a president? When did you first learn about political parties? If you identify with a party, how did you decide to do so? If you do not, why don't you? Who was the first liberal you ever met? The first conservative? How did you first learn about nuclear bombs? About capitalism and communism?

Obviously, the paths to political awareness, knowledge, and values vary among individuals, but most people are exposed to the same sources of influence, or agents of socialization—especially from childhood through young adulthood. These influences are family, school, community, peers, and—of course—television.

The Agents of Early Socialization

Like psychologists, scholars of political socialization place great emphasis on early learning. Both groups point to two fundamental principles that characterize early learning:[21]

- *The primacy principle.* What is learned first is learned best.

- *The structuring principle.* What is learned first structures later learning.

The extent of the influence of any socializing agent depends on the extent of our exposure to it, our communication with it, and our receptivity to it.[22] Because most people learn first from their family, the family tends to be an important agent of early socialization.

Family.   In most cases, exposure, communication, and receptivity are highest in parent-child relationships, although parental influence has declined with the rise of single-parent families. Especially in two-parent homes, children learn a wide range of values—social, moral, religious, economic, and political—that help shape their opinions. It is not surprising, then, that most people link their earliest memories of politics with their family. Moreover, when parents are interested in politics and maintain a favorable home environment for studying public affairs, they influence their children to become more politically interested and informed.[23]

One of the most politically important things that many children learn from their parents is party identification. Party identification is learned in much the same way as religion. Children (very young children, anyway) imitate their parents. When parents share the same religion, children are almost always raised in that faith. When parents are of different religions, their children are more likely to follow one or the other than to adopt a third. Similarly, parental influence on party identification is greater when both parents strongly identify with the same party.[24] Overall, more than half of young American voters identify with the political party of their parents. Moreover, those who change their partisanship are more likely to shift from being partisan to independent or from independent to partisan than to convert from one party to the other.[25]

Two crucial differences between party identification and religion may explain why youngsters are socialized into a religion much more reliably than into a political party. The first is that most parents care a great deal more about their religion than about their politics. So they are more deliberate about exposing their children to religion. The second is that religious institutions recognize the value of socialization; they offer Sunday schools and other activities that reinforce parental guidance. American political parties, in contrast, sponsor few activities to win the hearts of little Democrats and Republicans, which leaves children open to counterinfluences in their school and community.

School.   According to some researchers, schools have an influence on political learning that is equal to or greater than that of parents.[26] Here, however, we have to distinguish between elementary and secondary schools on the one hand and institutions of higher education on the other. Elementary schools prepare children in a number of ways to accept the social order. They introduce authority figures outside the family—the teacher, the principal, the police officer. They also teach the nation's slogans and symbols—the Pledge of Allegiance, the national anthem, national heroes and holidays. And they stress the norms of group behavior and democratic decision making (respecting the opinions of others, voting for class officers). In the process, they teach youngsters about the value of political equality.

Children do not always understand the meaning of the patriotic rituals and behaviors they learn in elementary school. In fact, much of this early learning—in the United States and elsewhere—is more indoctrination than education. By the end of the eighth grade, however, children begin to distinguish between political leaders and government institutions. They become more aware of collective institutions, such as Congress and elections, than do younger children, who tend to focus on the president and other single figures of government authority.[27] In sum, most children emerge from elementary school with a sense of national pride and an idealized notion of American government.[28]

Although newer curricula in many secondary schools emphasize citizens' rights in addition to their responsibilities, high schools also attempt to build "good citizens." Field trips to the state legislature or the city council impress students with the majesty and power of government institutions. But secondary schools also offer more explicit political content in their curricula, including courses in recent U.S. history, civics, and American government. Better teachers challenge students to think critically about American government and politics; others limit themselves to teaching civic responsibilities. The end product is a greater awareness of the political process and of the most prominent participants in that process.[29] Despite teachers' efforts to build children's trust in the political process, outside events can erode that trust as children grow up. For example, urban adolescents have been found to have a more cynical view of both the police and the president than nonurban youth have.[30]

In general, people know far more about the politics of the era in which they grew up than they know about the politics of other generations' formative years. A 1996 study of a group of people who graduated from high school in 1965 and their parents revealed that over 90 percent of the parents knew that President Franklin D. Roosevelt had been a Democrat, but only about 70 percent of their children did. However, two-thirds of the younger generation could name a country bordering Vietnam, compared with less than half of their parents. The author explained that for the parents, "the FDR years formed a core part of their autobiographies," whereas "the class of 1965 was inevitably affected by the [Vietnam] war and the controversy surrounding it."[31]

Political learning at the college level can be much like that in high school, or it can be quite different. The degree of difference is greater if professors (or the texts they use) encourage their students to question authority. Questioning dominant political values does not necessarily mean rejecting them. For example, this text encourages you to recognize that freedom and equality—two values idealized in our culture—often conflict. It also invites you to think of democracy in terms of competing institutional models, one of which challenges the idealized notion of democracy. These alternative perspectives are meant to teach you about American political values, not to subvert those values. College courses that are intended to stimulate critical thinking have the potential to introduce students to political ideas that are radically different from those they bring to class. Most high school courses do not. Still, specialists in socialization contend that taking particular courses in college has little effect on attitude change, which is more likely to come from sustained interactions with classmates who hold different views.[32]

Community and Peers.   Your community and your peers are different but usually overlapping groups. Your community is the people of all ages with whom you come in contact because they live or work near you. Peers are your friends, classmates, and coworkers. Usually they are your age and live or work within your community.

The makeup of a community has a lot to do with how the political opinions of its members are formed. Homogeneous communities—those whose members are similar in ethnicity, race, religion, or occupation—can exert strong pressures on both children and adults to conform to the dominant attitude. For example, if all your neighbors praise the candidates of one party and criticize the candidates of the other, it is difficult to voice or even hold a dissenting opinion.[33] Communities made up of one ethnic group or religion may also voice negative attitudes about other groups. Although community socialization is usually reinforced in the schools, schools sometimes introduce students to ideas that run counter to community values. (One example is sex education.)

For both children and adults, peer groups sometimes provide a defense against community pressures. Adolescent peer groups are particularly effective protection against parental pressures. In adolescence, children rely on their peers to defend their dress and their lifestyle, not their politics. At the college level, however, peer group influence on political attitudes often grows substantially, sometimes fed by new information that clashes with parental beliefs. A classic study, of students at Bennington College in the 1930s, found that many became substantially more liberal than their affluent and conservative parents. Two follow-up studies twenty-five and fifty years later showed that most retained their liberal attitudes, in part because their spouses and friends (peers) supported their views.[34] Other ev-

Morally Straight

These highly decorated Boy Scouts took this oath: "On my honor I will do my best: To do my duty to God and my country and to obey the Scout Law; To help other people at all times; To keep myself physically strong, mentally awake and morally straight." The Boy Scouts of America was founded in 1910 and incorporated by Congress in 1916 "to provide an educational program for boys and young adults to build character, to train in the responsibilities of participating citizenship, and to develop personal fitness." It is one of countless organizations that affect political socialization in America. See the Boy Scouts' Web site at <http://www.bsa.scouting.org/nav/about.html>.

idence shows that the baby boomers who went to college during the late 1960s and became the affluent yuppies of the 1980s (perhaps your parents) became more liberal on social issues than their high school classmates who did not go to college. However, yuppies were about as conservative as nonyuppies on economic matters.[35]

Continuing Socialization

Political socialization continues throughout life. As parental and school influences wane in adulthood, peer groups (neighbors, coworkers, club members) assume a greater importance in promoting political awareness and developing political opinions.[36] Because adults usually learn about political events from the mass media—newspapers, magazines, television, and radio—the media emerge as socialization agents. The role of television is especially important: over 70 percent of adult Americans report regularly watching news on television.[37] Children watch a lot of television too, but not necessarily the news (see Figure 5.3). The mass media are so important in the political socialization of both children and adults that we devote a whole chapter—Chapter 6—to a discussion of their role.

Regardless of how people learn about politics, they gain perspective on government as they grow older. They are apt to measure new candidates (and new ideas) against those they remember. Their values also change, increasingly reflecting their own self-interest. As voters age, for example, they begin to see more merit in government spending for social security than they did when they were younger. Finally, political education comes simply through exposure and familiarity. One example is voting, which people do with increasing regularity as they grow older—it becomes a habit.

figure

5.3   Political Socialization, Age, and Public Opinion

The historical context in which a person grows up often affects her or his political outlook for life. Consider this survey of American opinion toward Russia taken a decade after the end of the Cold War. One's likelihood to view Russia favorably decreases dramatically with age. Respondents who were old enough to remember events like the Berlin Blockade or the Cuban Missile Crisis tended to have much more unfavorable views toward Russia than the generation born at the end of the Cold War, whose views of Russia are shaped much less by memories of the old USSR.

Source: Jeffrey M. Jones, "Majority of Americans Continue to View Russia Unfavorably," *Gallup Poll Monthly,* March 2000, pp. 50–52.

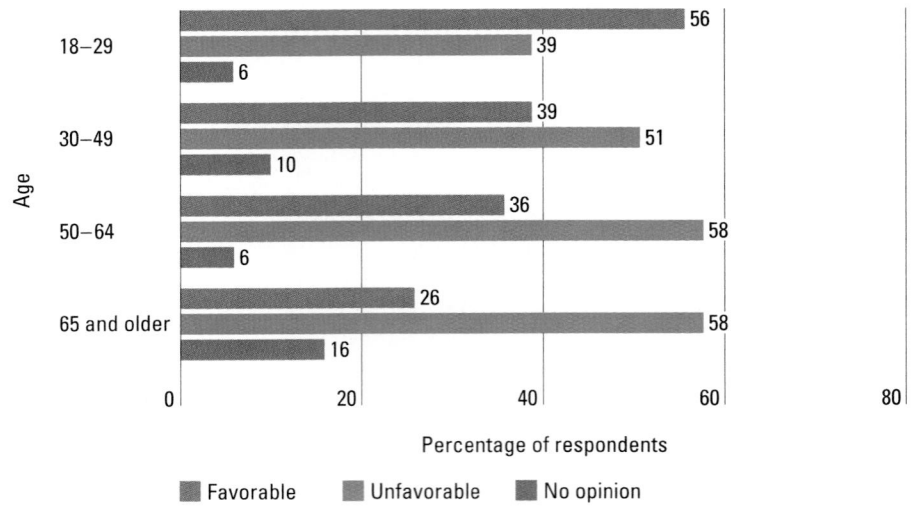

SOCIAL GROUPS AND POLITICAL VALUES

A Statistical Profile of the United States, 1970–1995

No two people are influenced by precisely the same socialization agents or in precisely the same way. Each individual experiences a unique process of political socialization and forms a unique set of political values. Still, people with similar backgrounds do share similar experiences, which means they tend to develop similar political opinions. In this section, we examine the ties between people's social background and their political values. In the process, we will examine the ties between background and values by looking at responses to two questions posed by the 2000 National Election Study, administered by the University of Michigan's Center for Political Studies. Many questions in the survey tap the freedom-versus-order or freedom-versus-equality dimensions. The two we chose serve to illustrate the analysis of ideological types.

The first question dealt with abortion. The interviewer said, "There has been some discussion about abortion during recent years. Which opinion on this page best agrees with your view? You can just tell me the number of the opinion you choose":

1. By law, abortion should never be permitted [13 percent agreed].
2. The law should permit abortion only in cases of rape, incest, or when the woman's life is in danger [32 percent].
3. The law should permit abortion for reasons other than rape, incest, or danger to the woman's life, but only after the need for the abortion has been clearly established [15 percent].
4. By law, a woman should be able to obtain an abortion as a matter of personal choice [40 percent].[38]

The White House Is Not Public Housing

Yes, this regular-looking guy is homeless. Everyone feels uneasy at the sight of poverty, but what should be done about it? Should the government step in to reduce income differences between the rich and the poor, perhaps by taxing the wealthy at higher rates and supplementing the income of the poor? Or should the government take no more from the wealthy than it does from the middle class (or even from the lower class)?

Those who chose the last category most clearly valued individual freedom over order imposed by government. Moreover, the pro-choice respondents did not view the issue as being restricted to freedom of choice in reproduction. Evidence shows that they also had concerns about broader issues of social order, such as the role of women and the legitimacy of alternative lifestyles.[39]

The second question posed by the 2000 National Election Study pertained to the role of government in guaranteeing employment:

> Some people feel the government in Washington should see to it that every person has a job and a good standard of living. Suppose that these people are at one end of the scale....Others think the government should just let each person get ahead on his own. Suppose these people were at the other end....Where would you put yourself on this scale, or haven't you thought much about this?

Excluding those respondents who "hadn't thought much" about this question, 22 percent wanted the government to provide every person with a living, and 29 percent were undecided. That left 50 percent who wanted the government to leave people alone to "get ahead" on their own. These respondents, who opposed government efforts to promote equality, apparently valued freedom over equality.

Overall, the responses to each of these questions were divided approximately equally. Somewhat less than half the respondents (40 percent) felt that the government should not set restrictions on abortion, and just short of a majority (50 percent) thought the government should not guarantee people a job and a good standard of living. (To learn about public opinion in other countries on government guarantees of jobs, see

Compared with What? 5.1.) However, sharp differences in attitudes emerged for both issues when the respondents were grouped by socioeconomic factors—education, income, region, race, religion, and sex. The differences are shown in Figure 5.4 as positive and negative deviations from the national average for each question. Bars that extend to the right identify groups that are more likely than most Americans to sacrifice freedom for order (on the left-hand side of the figure) or equality (on the right-hand side). Next, we examine the opinion patterns more closely for each socioeconomic group.

Education

Education increases people's awareness and understanding of political issues. Higher education also promotes tolerance of unpopular opinions and behavior and invites citizens to see issues in terms of civil rights and liberties. This result is clearly shown in the left-hand column of Figure 5.4, which shows that people with more education are more likely to view abortion as a matter of a woman's choice.[40] When confronted with a choice between personal freedom and social order, college-educated individuals tend to choose freedom.

Education Levels, 1870–1990

With regard to the role of government in reducing income inequality, the right-hand column in Figure 5.4 shows that people with more education also tend to favor freedom over equality. The higher their level of education, the less likely respondents were to support government-guaranteed jobs and living standards. You might expect better-educated people to be humanitarian and to support government programs to help the needy. However, because educated people tend to be wealthier, they would be taxed more heavily for such government programs. Moreover, they may believe that it is unrealistic to expect government to make such economic guarantees.

Income

In many countries, differences in social class—based on social background and occupation—divide people in their politics.[41] In the United States, we have avoided the uglier aspects of class conflict, but here wealth sometimes substitutes for class. As Figure 5.4 shows, wealth is consistently linked to opinions favoring a limited government role in promoting order and equality. Those with a higher income are more likely to favor personal choice in abortion and to oppose government guarantees of employment and living conditions. For both issues, wealth and education have a similar effect on opinion: the groups with more education and higher income opt for freedom.

Region

Early in our country's history, regional differences were politically important—important enough to spark a civil war between the North and South. For nearly a hundred years after the Civil War, regional differences continued to affect American politics. The moneyed Northeast was thought to control the purse strings of capitalism. The Midwest was long regarded as the stronghold of isolationism in foreign affairs. The South was virtually a

★ **compared with what?**

5.1   Opinions on Government Provision of a Job

Compared with citizens of other industrial countries, Americans are much less likely to demand that the government guarantee employment. Respondents from twelve countries (including the former East Germany) were asked in 1991 whether they agreed or disagreed with this statement: "The government should provide a job for everyone who wants one." Not surprising, respondents in formerly communist countries still overwhelmingly considered this an appropriate role for government, but more than two-thirds of the respondents in Japan, West Germany, and the United Kingdom also felt that government should guarantee employment. Only in the United States were citizens equally divided on this issue.

Source: International Social Justice Project, a collaborative international research effort. The data for this chart, kindly provided by Antal Örkény at Eötvös Loránd University in Budapest, came from national surveys conducted in 1991 that were supported in whole or in part by the Institute for Social Research, University of Michigan; the Economic and Social Research Council (United Kingdom); the Deutsche Forschungsgemeinschaft; the Institute of Social Science, Chuo University (Japan); and the Dutch Ministry of Social Affairs.

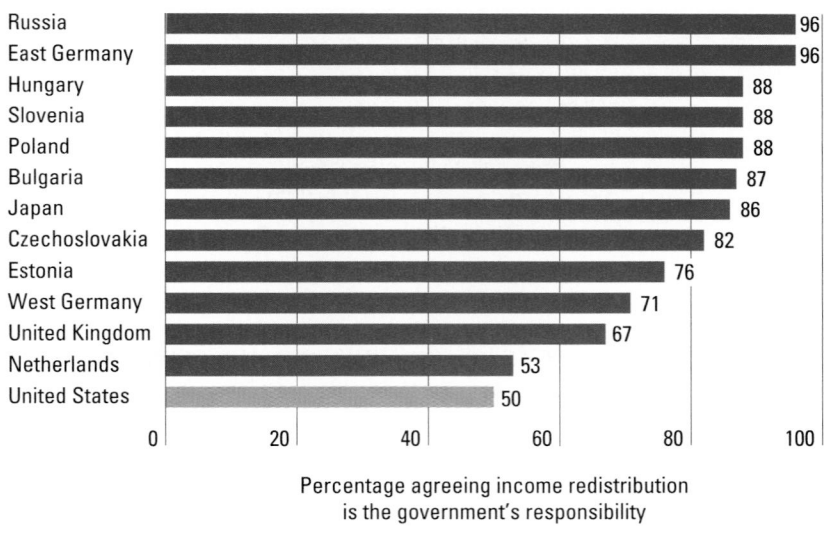

Percentage agreeing income redistribution is the government's responsibility

one-party region, almost completely Democratic. And the individualistic West pioneered its own mixture of progressive politics.

In the past, differences in wealth fed cultural differences between these regions. In recent decades, however, the movement of people and wealth away from the Northeast and Midwest to the Sunbelt states in the South and Southwest has equalized the per capita income of the various regions. One result of this equalization is that the formerly "solid South" is no longer solidly Democratic. In fact, the South has tended to vote for Republican presidential candidates since 1968.

Can You Explain Why...
region has declined in importance in American politics?

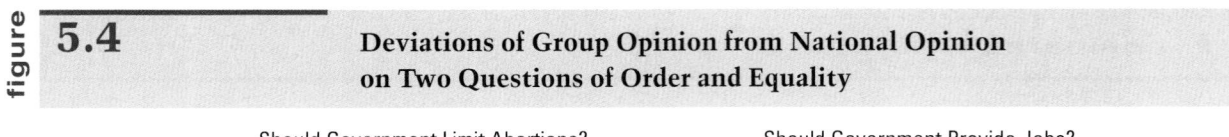

figure 5.4   Deviations of Group Opinion from National Opinion on Two Questions of Order and Equality

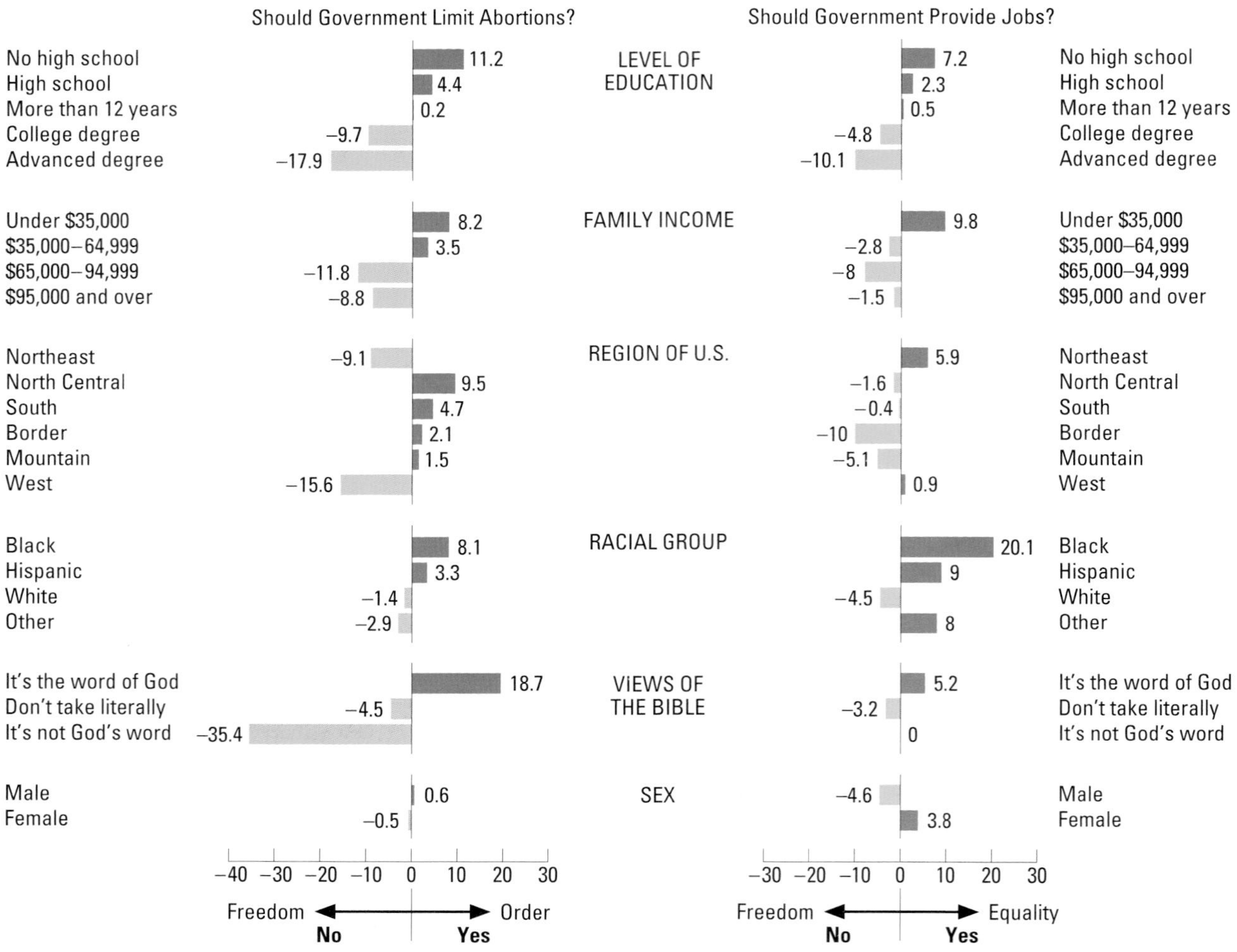

Should Government Limit Abortions?

LEVEL OF EDUCATION
- No high school: 11.2
- High school: 4.4
- More than 12 years: 0.2
- College degree: −9.7
- Advanced degree: −17.9

FAMILY INCOME
- Under $35,000: 8.2
- $35,000–64,999: 3.5
- $65,000–94,999: −11.8
- $95,000 and over: −8.8

REGION OF U.S.
- Northeast: −9.1
- North Central: 9.5
- South: 4.7
- Border: 2.1
- Mountain: 1.5
- West: −15.6

RACIAL GROUP
- Black: 8.1
- Hispanic: 3.3
- White: −1.4
- Other: −2.9

VIEWS OF THE BIBLE
- It's the word of God: 18.7
- Don't take literally: −4.5
- It's not God's word: −35.4

SEX
- Male: 0.6
- Female: −0.5

Scale: −40 −30 −20 −10 0 10 20 30
Freedom ← → Order
No   Yes

Should Government Provide Jobs?

LEVEL OF EDUCATION
- No high school: 7.2
- High school: 2.3
- More than 12 years: 0.5
- College degree: −4.8
- Advanced degree: −10.1

FAMILY INCOME
- Under $35,000: 9.8
- $35,000–64,999: −2.8
- $65,000–94,999: −8
- $95,000 and over: −1.5

REGION OF U.S.
- Northeast: 5.9
- North Central: −1.6
- South: −0.4
- Border: −10
- Mountain: −5.1
- West: 0.9

RACIAL GROUP
- Black: 20.1
- Hispanic: 9
- White: −4.5
- Other: 8

VIEWS OF THE BIBLE
- It's the word of God: 5.2
- Don't take literally: −3.2
- It's not God's word: 0

SEX
- Male: −4.6
- Female: 3.8

Scale: −30 −20 −10 0 10 20 30
Freedom ← → Equality
No   Yes

You can use CROSSTABS to conduct your own research on public opinion. CROSSTABS accesses responses to over fifty questions from a recent election survey, including questions on abortion and government guarantees of employment. See how other social or political groups divide on these issues.

Two questions—one posing the dilemma of freedom versus order (regarding government limits on abortion) and the other the dilemma of freedom versus equality (regarding government guarantees of employment)—were asked of a national sample in 2000. Public opinion across the nation as a whole was sharply divided on each question. These two graphs show how respondents in several social groups deviated from the national mean for each question. The longer the bars next to a group, the more its respondents deviated from the overall sample's view. Bars that extend to the left show opinions that deviate toward freedom. Bars that extend to the right show deviations away from freedom, toward order (in the left-hand graph) or equality (in the right-hand graph).

Source: Data from 2000 National Election Study, Center for Political Studies, University of Michigan. Used by permission of Center for Political Studies.

Figure 5.4 shows greater differences in public opinion on social issues than on economic issues in the four major regions of the United States. Respondents in the Northeast and West were more likely to support personal choice than were residents of the South and Midwest, where they were more likely to favor restricting abortion. People in the Northeast were somewhat more supportive of government efforts to equalize income than were people elsewhere. Despite these differences, regional effects on public opinion are weaker than the effects of most other socioeconomic factors.

The "Old" and "New" Ethnicity: European Origin and Race

Major Sources of Immigrants by Country or Region

In the early twentieth century, the major ethnic minorities in America were composed of immigrants from Ireland, Italy, Germany, Poland, and other European countries who came to the United States in waves during the late 1800s and early 1900s. These immigrants entered a nation that had been founded by British settlers more than a hundred years earlier. They found themselves in a strange land, usually without money and unable to speak the language. Moreover, their religious backgrounds—mainly Catholic and Jewish—differed from that of the predominantly Protestant earlier settlers. Local politicians saw the newcomers, who were concentrated in low-status jobs in urban areas of the Northeast and Midwest, as a new source of votes and soon mobilized them politically. These urban ethnics and their descendants became part of the great coalition of Democratic voters that President Franklin Roosevelt forged in the 1930s. And for years after, the European ethnics supported liberal candidates and causes more strongly than the original Anglo-Saxon immigrants did.[42] More recent studies of public opinion show the differences are disappearing.[43] But if this **"old" ethnicity,** based on European origin, is giving way to assimilation, a **"new" ethnicity,** based on race, is taking its place.

"old" ethnicity
An older outlook on the people comprising America's "melting pot," with focus on religion and country of origin.

"new" ethnicity
A newer outlook on the people comprising America's "melting pot," with focus on race.

For many years after the Civil War, the issue of race in American politics was defined as "how the South should treat the Negro." The debate between North and South over this issue became a conflict between civil rights and states' rights—a conflict in which blacks were primarily objects, not participants. But with the rise of black consciousness and the grassroots civil rights movement in the late 1950s and 1960s, blacks secured genuine voting rights in the South and exercised those rights more vigorously in the North. Although they represented only about 12 percent of the total population, blacks made up sizable voting blocs in southern states and northern cities. Like the European ethnics before them, American blacks were courted for their votes; at long last, their opinions were politically important.

Blacks constitute the biggest racial minority in American society but not the only significant one. Asians, American Indians (Native Americans), and other nonwhites account for another 5 percent of the population. People of Latin American origin are often called Latinos. If they speak Spanish (Haitians and Brazilians usually do not), they are also known as Hispanics. Hispanics are commonly but inaccurately regarded as a racial group, for they consist of both whites and nonwhites. Hispanics make up about 10 percent of the nation's population, but they constitute as much as 28 percent of the population in California and Texas and 40 percent in New Mexico.[44] Although they are politically strong in some communities, Hispanics (comprising groups as different as Cubans, Mexicans, Peruvians,

Irish Americans, Italian Americans, Polish Americans, and members of other ethnic groups have gained political power through elections. Here, Korean Americans in the New York area prepare to participate in government the traditional American way.

socioeconomic status
Position in society, based on a combination of education, occupational status, and income.

and Puerto Ricans) have lagged behind blacks in mobilizing across the nation. However, Hispanics are being wooed by non-Hispanic candidates and are increasingly running for public office themselves.

Blacks and members of other minorities display somewhat similar political attitudes on questions pertaining to equality. The reasons are twofold.[45] First, racial minorities (excepting second-generation Asians) tend to have low **socioeconomic status,** a measure of social condition that includes education, occupation, status, and income. Second, minorities have been targets of prejudice and discrimination and have benefited from government actions in support of equality. The right-hand column in Figure 5.4 clearly shows the effects of race on the freedom-equality issue. Blacks strongly favored government action to improve economic opportunity; other minorities also favored government action but to a lesser degree. The abortion issue produces less difference, although minority groups do favor government restrictions on abortion slightly more than whites do.

Religion

Since the last major wave of European immigration in the 1930s and 1940s, the religious makeup of the United States has remained fairly stable. Today, almost 60 percent of the population are Protestant, about 25 percent are Catholic, only about 2 percent are Jewish, and about 15 percent deny any religious affiliation or choose some other faith.[46] For many years, analysts found strong and consistent differences in the political opinions of Protestants, Catholics, and Jews.[47] Protestants were more conservative than Catholics, and Catholics tended to be more conservative than Jews.

Some such differences have remained, especially on questions of freedom versus order (such as the abortion question), but differences between Protestants and Catholics are so weak that we did not display them in Figure 5.4. (Protestants oppose personal choice on abortion slightly more than Catholics do, despite the Pope's strong opposition to abortion.) There were too few in the Jewish group to include in this analysis.

In recent years, a person's denominational identification is less important politically than his or her "religiosity." One measure of people's religiosity in a Christian-Judaic society is their opinion about the Bible. When asked about the nature of the Bible in 2000, about 35 percent of respondents said it was the actual word of God. About 50 percent regarded it as inspired by God but believed it should not be taken literally. The remaining 13 percent viewed it as an ancient book of history, legends, fables, and moral precepts recorded by humans. As Figure 5.4 indicates, religiosity has little effect on attitudes about economic equality but a powerful influence on attitudes about social order. Those who believed that the Bible is the literal word of God strongly favored government action to limit abortion. Those who thought the Bible was pieced together over time overwhelmingly favored a woman's right to decide.

Classifying respondents by their religiosity reveals that political opinions in the United States do differ sharply according to religious beliefs. A 2000 survey found that white Protestants divided almost equally between those who described themselves as "born-again" or "evangelical" Christians and those who did not. Moreover, 67 percent of these evangelical Protestants agreed that the Bible was the word of God, compared with less than a quarter of white mainstream Protestants. The study concluded that "the conservatism of white evangelical Protestants is clearly the most powerful religious force in politics today."[48]

Gender

Differences in sex, which has become known as *gender* in discussions of American politics, are often related to political opinions, primarily on the issue of freedom versus equality. As shown in the right-hand column of Figure 5.4, women are much more likely than men to favor government actions to promote equality. However, men and women usually differ less on issues of freedom versus order, including on the abortion issue (see the column on the left in Figure 5.4). Still, on many issues of government policy, the "gender gap" in American politics is wide, with women more supportive than men of government spending for social programs.

FROM VALUES TO IDEOLOGY

We have just seen that differences in groups' responses to two survey questions reflect those groups' value choices between freedom and order and between freedom and equality. But to what degree do people's opinions on specific issues reflect their explicit political ideology (the set of values and beliefs they hold about the purpose and scope of government)? Political scientists generally agree that ideology influences public opinion on specific issues; they have much less consensus on the extent to which people think explicitly in ideological terms.[49] They also agree that the public's ideological thinking cannot be categorized adequately in conventional liberal-conservative terms.[50]

The Degree of Ideological Thinking in Public Opinion

Although today's media frequently use the terms *liberal* and *conservative*, some people think these terms are no longer relevant to American politics. Even President Clinton said, "The old labels of liberal and conservative are not what matter most anymore."[51] But when did they ever matter "most"? When asked to describe the parties and candidates in the 1956 election, only about 12 percent of respondents volunteered responses that contained ideological terms (such as *liberal, conservative,* and *capitalism*).[52] Most respondents (42 percent) evaluated the parties and candidates in terms of "benefits to groups" (farmers, workers, or businesspeople, for example). Others (24 percent) spoke more generally about "the nature of the times" (for example, inflation, unemployment, and the threat of war). Finally, a good portion of the sample (22 percent) gave answers that contained no classifiable issue content. Even more than four decades ago, most voters did not use ideological labels when discussing politics.

So perhaps we should not make too much of recent findings about the electorate's unfamiliarity with ideology. In a 1996 poll, voters were asked what they thought when someone was described as "liberal" or "conservative."[53] Few responded in explicitly political terms. Rather, most people gave dictionary definitions: " 'liberals' are generous (a *liberal* portion). And 'conservatives' are moderate or cautious (a *conservative* estimate)."[54] The two most frequent responses for *conservative* were "fiscally responsible or tight" (17 percent) and "closed-minded" (10 percent). For *liberal* the top two were "open-minded" (14 percent) and "free-spending" (8 percent). Only about 6 percent of the sample mentioned "degree of government involvement" in describing liberals and conservatives.

Ideological labels are technical terms used in analyzing politics, and most citizens don't play that sport. But if you want to play, you need suitable headgear. Scales and typologies, despite their faults, are essential for classification. No analysis, including the study of politics, can occur without classifying the objects being studied. The tendency to use ideological terms in discussing politics grows with increased education, which helps people understand political issues and relate them to one another. People's personal political socialization experiences can also lead them to think ideologically. For example, children raised in strong union households may be taught to distrust private enterprise and to value collective action through government.

True ideologues hold a consistent set of values and beliefs about the purpose and scope of government, and they tend to evaluate candidates in ideological terms.[55] Some people respond to questions in ways that seem ideological but are not because they do not understand the underlying principles. For example, most respondents dutifully comply when asked to place themselves somewhere on a liberal–conservative continuum. The result, as shown earlier in Figure 5.2, is an approximately normal distribution centering on "moderate," the modal category. But many people settle on moderate when they do not clearly understand the alternatives, because moderate is a safe choice. A study in 1996 gave respondents another

Can You Explain Why...
the "moderate" ideological category may be overstated?

choice—the statement "I haven't thought much about it"—which allowed them to avoid placing themselves on the liberal–conservative continuum. In this study, 20 percent of the respondents acknowledged that they had not thought much about ideology.[56] The extent of ideological thinking in America, then, is even less than it might seem from responses to questions asking people to describe themselves as liberals or conservatives.[57]

The Quality of Ideological Thinking in Public Opinion

What people's ideological self-placement means in the 1990s also is not clear. At one time, the liberal-conservative continuum represented a single dimension: attitudes toward the scope of government activity. Liberals were in favor of more government action to provide public goods, and conservatives were in favor of less. This simple distinction is not as useful today. Many people who call themselves liberal no longer favor government activism in general, and many self-styled conservatives no longer oppose it in principle. As a result, many people have difficulty deciding whether they are liberal or conservative, whereas others confidently choose identical points on the continuum for entirely different reasons. People describe themselves as liberal or conservative because of the symbolic value of the terms as much as for reasons of ideology.[58]

Studies of the public's ideological thinking find that two themes run through people's minds when they are asked to describe liberals and conservatives. People associate liberals with change and conservatives with tradition. The theme corresponds to the distinction between liberals and conservatives on the exercise of freedom and the maintenance of order.[59]

The other theme has to do with equality. The conflict between freedom and equality was at the heart of President Roosevelt's New Deal economic policies (social security, minimum wage legislation, farm price supports) in the 1930s. The policies expanded the interventionist role of the national government to promote greater economic equality, and attitudes toward government intervention in the economy served to distinguish liberals from conservatives for decades afterward.[60] Attitudes toward government interventionism still underlie opinions about domestic economic policies.[61] Liberals support intervention to promote economic equality; conservatives favor less government intervention and more individual freedom in economic activities.

In Chapter 1, we proposed an alternative system of ideological classification based on people's relative evaluations of freedom, order, and equality. We described liberals as people who believe that government should promote equality, even if some freedom is lost in the process, but who oppose surrendering freedom to government-imposed order. Conservatives do not oppose equality in and of itself but put a higher value on freedom than on equality when the two conflict. Yet conservatives are not above restricting freedom when threatened with the loss of order. So both groups value freedom, but one is more willing to trade freedom for equality, and the other is more inclined to trade freedom for order. If you have trouble thinking about these tradeoffs on a single dimension, you are in good company. The liberal–conservative continuum presented to survey respondents takes a two-dimensional concept and squeezes it into a one-dimensional format.[62]

Ideological Types in the United States

Our ideological typology in Chapter 1 (see Figure 1.2) classifies people as liberals if they favor freedom over order and equality over freedom. Conversely, conservatives favor freedom over equality and order over freedom. Libertarians favor freedom over both equality and order—the opposite of communitarians. By cross-tabulating people's answers to the two questions from the 2000 National Election Study about freedom versus order (abortion) and freedom versus equality (government job guarantees), we can classify respondents according to their ideological tendencies. As shown in Figure 5.5, people's responses to the two questions are virtually unrelated to each other—that is, the responses fall about equally within each of the quadrants. This finding indicates that people do not decide about government activity according to a one-dimensional ideological standard. Figure 5.5 also classifies the sample according to the two dimensions in our ideological typology. Using only two issues to classify people in an ideological framework leaves substantial room for error. Still, if the typology is worthwhile, the results should be meaningful, and they are.

It is striking that the ideological tendencies of the respondents in the 2000 sample depicted in Figure 5.5 are divided almost equally among the four categories of the typology. (Remember, however, that these categories—like the letter grades A, B, C, and D for courses—are rigid. The respondents' answers to both questions varied in intensity but were reduced to a simple yes or no to simplify this analysis. Many respondents would cluster toward the center of Figure 5.5 if their attitudes were represented more sensitively.) The conservative response pattern was the most common, followed by the communitarian pattern. The figure suggests that about four-fifths of the electorate favor government action to promote order, increase equality, or both. The results resemble earlier findings by other researchers who conducted more exhaustive analysis involving more survey questions.[63]

Respondents who readily locate themselves on a single dimension running from liberal to conservative often go on to contradict their self-placement when answering questions that trade freedom for either order or equality.[64] A two-dimensional typology such as that in Figure 5.5 allows us to analyze responses more meaningfully.[65] Although a slight majority of respondents in the 2000 survey (52 percent) expressed opinions that were either liberal (22 percent) or conservative (32 percent), almost as many expressed opinions that deviated from these familiar ideological types.

The ideological tendencies illustrate important differences between different social groups. Communitarians are prominent among minorities and among people with little education and low income, groups that tend to look favorably on the benefits of government in general. Libertarians are concentrated among people with more education and higher income, who tend to be suspicious of government interference in their lives. People in the southern states tend to be communitarians, those in the Midwest tend to be conservatives, and those in the Northeast are inclined to be liberals. Men are more likely to be conservative or libertarian than women, who tend to be liberal or communitarian.[66]

This more refined analysis of political ideology explains why even Americans who pay close attention to politics find it difficult to locate

Use the "Ideology" variable in the CROSSTABS program to learn which groups fall into which types, based on their answers to the questions in Figure 5.5.

How did you answer the questions about abortion and government-guaranteed employment on the self-test?

figure

5.5   Respondents Classified by Ideological Tendencies

In the 2000 election survey, respondents were asked whether abortion should be a matter of personal choice or regulated by the government, and whether government should guarantee people a job and a good standard of living or people should get ahead on their own. (The questions are given verbatim on pages 140–141.) These two questions presented choices between freedom and order and between freedom and equality. People's responses to the two questions showed no correlation, demonstrating that these value choices cannot be explained by a simple liberal–conservative continuum. Instead, their responses can be analyzed more usefully according to four different ideological types.

Source: 2000 National Election Study, Copyright © 2000 Center for Political Studies, University of Michigan. Used by permission of Center for Political Studies.

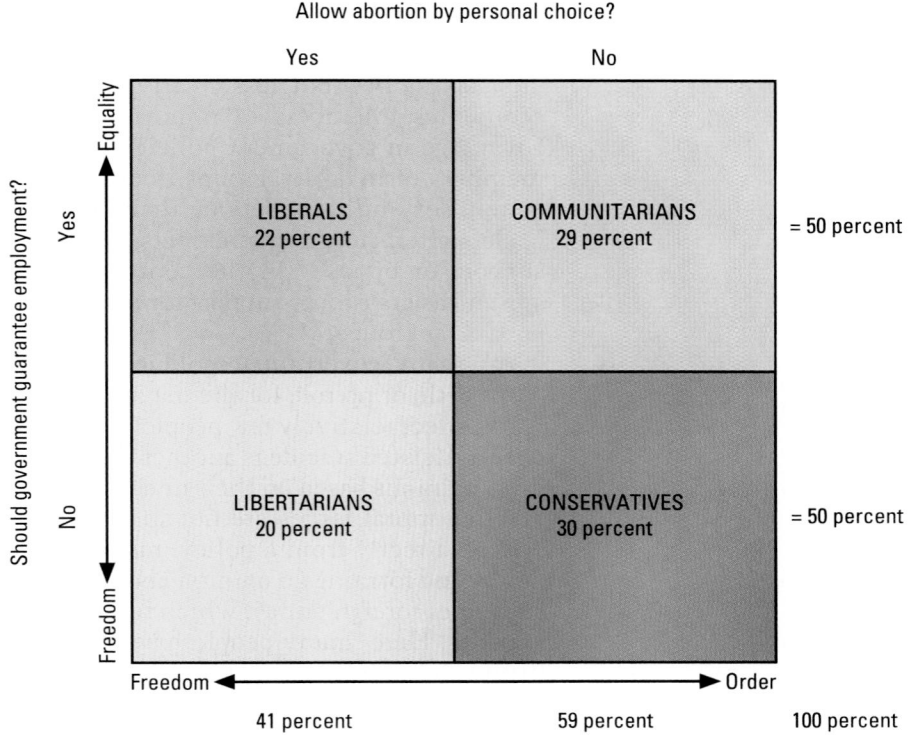

themselves on the liberal–conservative continuum. Their problem is that they are liberal on some issues and conservative on others. Forced to choose along just one dimension, they opt for the middle category, moderate. However, our analysis also indicates that many people who classify themselves as liberal or conservative do fit these two categories in our typology. There is value, then, in the liberal-conservative distinction as long as we understand its limitations.

THE PROCESS OF FORMING POLITICAL OPINIONS

We have seen that people acquire their political values through socialization and that different social groups develop different sets of political values. We have also learned that some people, but only a minority, think about politics ideologically, holding a consistent set of political attitudes and beliefs. Now let us look at how people form opinions on a particular issue. In particular, how do those who are not ideologues—in other words, most citizens—form political opinions? Four factors—self-interest, political information, opinion schemas, and political leadership—play a part in the process.

Self-Interest

The **self-interest principle** states that people choose what benefits them personally.[67] The principle plays an obvious role in how people form opinions on government economic policies. Taxpayers tend to prefer low taxes to high taxes; farmers tend to favor candidates who promise them more support over those who promise them less. The self-interest principle also applies, but less clearly, to some government policies outside economics. Members of minority groups tend to see more personal advantage in government policies that promote social equality than do members of majority groups; teenage males are more likely to oppose compulsory military service than are older people of either sex. Group leaders often cue group members, telling them what policies they should support or oppose. (In the context of pluralist democracy, this often appears as grassroots support for or opposition to policies that affect only particular groups.[68])

For many government policies, however, the self-interest principle plays little or no role for the majority of citizens because many issues directly affect relatively few people. Outlawing prostitution is one example; doctor-assisted suicide is another. When moral issues are involved, people form opinions based on their underlying values.[69]

When moral issues are not in question and when individuals do not benefit directly from a policy, many people have trouble relating to the policy and forming an opinion about it. This tends to be true of the whole subject of foreign policy, which few people interpret in terms of personal benefits. Here, many people have no opinion, or their opinions are not firmly held and are apt to change quite easily, given almost any new information.

Political Information

In the United States today, education is compulsory (usually to age sixteen), and the literacy rate is relatively high. The country boasts an unparalleled network of colleges and universities, entered by two-thirds of all high school graduates. American citizens can obtain information from a variety of daily and weekly news publications. They can keep abreast of national and international affairs through nightly television news, which brings live coverage of world events via satellite from virtually everywhere in the world. Yet the average American displays an astonishing lack of political knowledge.[70]

A Gallup Poll taken in 1997, for example, indicated that only 69 percent of the American public could identify the sitting vice president of the United States, Al Gore. This figure rose to 90 percent after he became the Democratic frontrunner in the 2000 presidential election, but other political figures did not fare so well. Less recognizable was the secretary of state, correctly identified as Madeline Albright by only 33 percent of the public in 2000. Although the speaker of the House of Representatives stands third in line to the presidency, only 6 percent of the public could link Dennis Hastert to that office. As for the Senate, a majority of Americans could not guess the names of either of their senators, but a full

HI & LOIS   **BY GREG & BRIAN WALKER**

66 percent named Regis Philbin as host of the popular television program *Who Wants to Be a Millionaire?*[71]

But Americans do not let lack of knowledge stop them from expressing their opinions. They readily offer opinions on issues ranging from capital punishment to nuclear power to the government's handling of the economy. When opinions are based on little knowledge, however, they change easily in the face of new information. The result is a high degree of instability in public opinion poll findings, depending on how questions are worded and on recent events that bear on the issue at hand. Nevertheless, some researchers hold that the *collective* opinion of the public—which balances off advocates' ignorance on both sides of an issue—can be interpreted as rational. Page and Shapiro analyzed the public's responses to 1,128 questions that were repeated in one or more surveys between 1935 and 1990.[72] They found that responses to more than half of the repeated policy questions "showed no significant change at all"—that is, they changed no more than six percentage points.[73] Moreover, Page and Shapiro concluded that when the public's collective opinion on public policy changes, it changes in "understandable, predictable ways."[74] Other scholars have contended that even collective public opinion may be misleading when the issues involve core beliefs (especially opposing beliefs) or when there is a sharp division in the quality of respondents' information (e.g., the opinions of upper-income respondents, who are usually more knowledgeable, can bias the survey results).[75]

The most thorough recent study of political knowledge was undertaken by Delli Carpini and Keeter.[76] In addition to conducting their own specialized surveys, they collected from existing surveys approximately 3,700 individual items that measured some type of factual knowledge about public affairs, and they focused on over 2,000 items that clearly dealt with political facts, such as knowledge of political institutions and processes, contemporary public figures, political groups, and policy issues. Despite evidence of citizens' ignorance of political facts, as discussed above, Delli Carpini and Keeter concluded that enough of the public is "reasonably well informed about politics . . . to meet high standards of good citizenship." They found, "Many of the basic institutions and procedures of government are known to half or more of the public, as are the relative positions of the parties on many major issues."[77]

Their analysis also found, however, that political knowledge is not randomly distributed within our society. "In particular, women, African Americans, the poor, and the young tend to be substantially less knowledgeable about politics than are men, whites, the affluent, and older citizens."[78] Education is the strongest single predictor of political knowledge, but other cultural or structural factors prevent women and blacks, for example, from developing the same levels of general political knowledge as white males.[79]

Researchers have not found any meaningful relationship between political sophistication and self-placement on the liberal–conservative continuum. That is, people with equivalent knowledge of public affairs and levels of conceptualization are equally likely to call themselves liberals or conservatives.[80] Equal levels of political understanding, then, may produce quite different political views, as a result of individuals' unique patterns of political socialization.

Opinion Schemas

Even people who do not approach politics from the perspective of a full-blown ideology interpret political issues in terms of some preexisting mental structure. Psychologists refer to the packet of preexisting beliefs that people apply to a specific issue as an **opinion schema**—a network of organized knowledge and beliefs that guides the processing of information on a particular subject.[81] Our opinion schemas change as we acquire new information.

The schema concept gives us a more flexible tool for analyzing public opinion than the more rigid concept of ideology. The main value of schemas for understanding how opinions are formed is that they remind us that opinion questions trigger many different images, connections, and values in the mind of each respondent. Given the complexity of the factors in individual opinion schemas, it is surprising that researchers find as many strong correlations as they do among individuals' social background, general values, and specific opinions. Opinion schemas can pertain to any political figure and to any subject—race, economics, or international relations, for example.[82] Often, people who have shared socializing experiences also share schema patterns. For instance, one study found that African Americans' views on the importance of race in determining one's chances in life could be analyzed according to five different schemas.[83]

Still, the more encompassing concept of ideology is hard to escape. Researchers have found that people's personal schemas tend to be organized in ways that parallel broader ideological categories. In other words, a conservative's opinion schema about a politician may not differ factually from a liberal's, but it will differ considerably in its evaluation of those

opinion schema
A network of organized knowledge and beliefs that guides a person's processing of information regarding a particular subject.

facts.[84] For example, George W. Bush's adoption of the traditionally Democratic theme of compassion in the 2000 presidential election might evoke anger in a person with a liberal schema but might be interpreted as an astute move by a person with a conservative schema.

Some scholars argue that most citizens, in their efforts to make sense of politics, pay less attention to government policies than to their leaders' "style" in approaching political problems—for instance, whether they are seen as tough, compassionate, honest, or hard working.[85] When a leader behaves in a manner that style-oriented citizens approve of, they will view his or her policies favorably. In this way, citizens can relate the complexities of politics to their personal experiences. If many citizens view politics in terms of governing style, the role of political leadership becomes a more important determinant of public opinion than the leader's actual policies.

Political Leadership

Public opinion on specific issues is molded by political leaders, journalists, and policy experts. Because of the attention given to the presidency by the media, presidents are uniquely positioned to shape popular attitudes. Consider Ronald Reagan and the issue of nuclear disarmament. In 1987, President Reagan and Mikhail Gorbachev signed a treaty banning intermediate-range nuclear force missiles (INFs) from Europe and the Soviet Union. Soon afterward, a national survey found that 82 percent of the sample approved of the treaty, and 18 percent opposed it. As might be expected, those who viewed the Soviet Union as highly threatening ("hard-liners") were least enthusiastic about the INF treaty. Respondents were then asked to agree or disagree with this statement: "President Reagan is well known for his anticommunism, so if he thinks this is a good deal, it must be." Analysis of the responses showed that hard-liners who agreed with the statement were nearly twice as likely to approve of the treaty as those who were unmoved by Reagan's involvement. The researcher concluded that "a highly conciliatory move by a president known for long-standing opposition to just such an action" can override expected sources of opposition among the public.[86] The implication is that another president, such as Jimmy Carter or even George Bush—much less Bill Clinton, the former antiwar protester—could not have won over the hard-liners.

The ability of political leaders to influence public opinion has been enhanced enormously by the growth of the broadcast media, especially television.[87] The majoritarian model of democracy assumes that government officials respond to public opinion; but the evidence is substantial that this causal sequence is reversed, that public opinion responds to the actions of government officials.[88] If this is true, how much potential is there for public opinion to be manipulated by political leaders through the mass media? We examine the manipulative potential of the mass media in the next chapter.

SUMMARY   Public opinion does not rule in America. On most issues, it merely sets general boundaries for government policy. The shape of the distribution of opinion (skewed, bimodal, or normal) indicates how sharply the public is divided. Bimodal distributions harbor the greatest potential for political conflict. The stability of a distribution over time indicates how settled people are in their opinions. Because most Americans' ideological opinions are normally distributed around the moderate category and have been for decades, government policies can vary from left to right over time without provoking severe political conflict.

People form their values through the process of political socialization. The most important socialization agents in childhood and young adulthood are family, school, community, and peers. Members of the same social group tend to experience similar socialization processes and thus to adopt similar values. People in different social groups that hold different values often express vastly different opinions. Differences in education, race, and religion tend to produce sharper divisions of opinion today on questions of order and equality than do differences in income, region, or ethnicity.

Most people do not think about politics in ideological terms. When asked to do so by pollsters, however, they readily classify themselves along a liberal–conservative continuum. Many respondents choose the middle category, moderate, because the choice is safe. Many others choose it because they have liberal views on some issues and conservative views on others. Their political orientation is better captured by a two-dimensional framework that analyzes ideology according to the values of freedom, order, and equality. Responses to the survey questions we used to establish our ideological typology divide the American electorate almost equally among liberals, conservatives, libertarians, and communitarians. The one-fifth of the public that gave liberal responses—favoring government action to promote equality but not to impose order—was exceeded by the one-third of the public that favored more government to promote order. At almost one-quarter of the public, the communitarians, who wanted government to impose both order and equality, just exceeded the libertarians, who wanted government to do neither.

In addition to ideological orientation, many other factors affect the process of forming political opinions. When individuals stand to benefit or suffer from proposed government policies, they usually base their opinions of these policies on their own self-interest. When citizens lack information on which to base their opinions, they usually respond anyway, which leads to substantial fluctuations in poll results, depending on how questions are worded and intervening events. The various factors that coalesce in the process of forming political opinions can be mapped out on an opinion schema, a network of beliefs and attitudes about a particular topic. The schema image helps us visualize the complex process of forming opinions. This process is not completely idiosyncratic, however; people tend to organize their schemas according to broader ideological thinking. In the absence of information, respondents are particularly susceptible to cues of support or opposition from political leaders, communicated through the mass media.

Which model of democracy, the majoritarian or the pluralist, is correct in its assumptions about public opinion? Sometimes, the public shows clear and settled opinions on government policy, conforming to the majoritarian model. However, public opinion is often not firmly grounded in knowledge and may be unstable on given issues. Moreover, powerful groups often divide on what they want government to do. The lack of consensus leaves politicians with a great deal of latitude in enacting specific policies, a finding that conforms to the pluralist model. Of course, politicians' actions are closely scrutinized by journalists reporting in the mass media. We turn to the effect on politics of this scrutiny in Chapter 6.

★ Selected Readings

Craig, Stephen C., and Stephen Earl Bennett, eds. *After the Boom: The Politics of Generation X.* Lanham, Md.: Rowman & Littlefield, 1997. People born in the early 1960s (and now in their late thirties) constitute "Generation X." Unlike those born during the Depression and World War II, no comparable historical events occurred when they were growing up in the 1970s and 1980s. This book asks whether Generation X exhibits a distinctive profile and finds little evidence for it.

Delli Carpini, Michael X., and Scott Keeter. *What Americans Know About Politics and Why It Matters.* New Haven, Conn.: Yale University Press, 1996. A comprehensive review and analysis of the public's responses to thousands of factual questions about political processes and institutions, public figures, political parties and groups, and public policies.

Herbst, Susan. *Reading Public Opinion: How Political Actors View the Democratic Process.* Chicago, Ill.: University of Chicago Press, 1998. Herbst explores the reactions of legislative staffers, political activists, and journalists to public opinion and argues that many pay less attention to the polls than the public believes.

Kull, Steven, and I. M. Destler. *Misreading the Public: The Myth of a New Isolationism.* Washington, D.C.: Brookings Institution Press, 1999. The authors use public opinion data and focus groups to challenge a belief pervasive among policymakers that the American public is moving toward isolationism.

Reeher, Grant, and Joseph Cammarano, eds. *Education for Citizenship: Ideas and Innovations in Political Learning.* Lanham, Md.: Rowman & Littlefield, 1997. This collection of essays proposes innovative ways to learn about, and teach, politics.

Stimson, James A. *Public Opinion in America: Mood, Cycles, & Swings,* 2nd ed. Boulder, Colo.: Westview, 1998. The results of a massive study of more than 1000 survey questions from 1956 to 1996, this book charts the drift of public opinion from liberal in the 1950s to conservative at the end of the 1970s and back toward liberal in the 1990s.

Traugott, Michael W., and Paul J. Lavrakas. *The Voter's Guide to Election Polls,* 2nd ed. Chatham, N.J.: Chatham House, 2000. A guide for evaluating election polls, including sampling, interviewing, questionnaires, and data analysis. Done in a question-and-answer format.

Internet Exercises

1. *Where Do You Fit?*

The Pew Research Center for the People and the Press is an independent research group that studies public attitudes toward the press, politics, and public policy issues. The center's "Where do you fit?" feature allows citizens to provide information about their personal values and attitudes, partisan leanings, and involvement in politics in order to place themselves among one of ten groups of American citizens.

• Go to the center's Web site at **<www.people-press.org/>** and follow the link to the "Where do you fit?" feature.

• Read over the descriptions of the ten groups that the center has identified. Based on your reading, which group do you identify with most? Least? Why?

• Next, follow the link to the "Where do you fit?" questionnaire and fill it out. Do you obtain the same result that you predicted for yourself? If not, was the result close to what you predicted? If the result of the quiz did not match your prediction, identify at least one question that you would add to the questionnaire in order to improve its accuracy.

2. *Is the Nation Awash in Libertarians?*

The Libertarian Party is one of the most established and active minor political parties in the United States. In the 2000 elections, for example, it appeared on ballots in all fifty states and ran nearly two thousand candidates for public office at various levels, including president.

• Go to the Libertarian Party's web site located at **<www.lp.org>**. From this page follow the link to a feature called the World's Smallest Political Quiz. Once you get to the quiz, you can leave the default settings in place—you do not have to fill it out, unless you're interested—and hit the "submit" button. Pay close attention to the overall results of the quiz that the Libertarian Party reports.

• Notice that the overall number of libertarian identifiers is almost 40 percent, a figure that is nearly double the number reported in the *Challenge of Democracy* (see Figure 5.5). What do you think is the best possible explanation for this large discrepancy?

Would you be more likely to trust the numbers reported by the Libertarian Party or the textbook as being representative of the nation as a whole? Why? (You may have noted a similarity between the World's Smallest Political Quiz and our IDEAlog program. The original computer program for the Libertarian quiz appeared in the mid-1980s. Libertarians kindly supplied their code to help us develop our IDEAlog version, which was first distributed with the 1989 edition of our text.)

The Media

★ ★ ★ ★ ★ ★ ★ ★ ★

AMERICAN INTERNET PROVIDERS DISTRIBUTE NAZI PROPAGANDA to German citizens electronically, although the Nazi Party is illegal in Germany and its publications are banned. Germany is a modern industrial democracy with strong protection of free speech and the press, but these freedoms do not extend to the advocacy of the radical right and fascist parties. Germany's history in the twentieth century was inextricably linked to the rise of Adolph Hitler, and since World War II the country has banned the use of Nazi symbols and made it a crime to deny the Holocaust. The German government is willing to sacrifice some freedom for an increased measure of social order.

Regulating speech and the press becomes a much more difficult task with the globalizing force of the Internet, however. In recent years, German neo-Nazis have joined their American counterparts and turned to the Internet to distribute their message. By putting their Web pages on Web sites hosted in the United States, where they are shielded by the First Amendment protections of free speech and the press, far-right groups have been able to escape the reach of German law.[1] Although the electronic files may be stored on computers in the United States, the materials can still be viewed from Germany or elsewhere over the Web. The role of the Internet has captured the attention of the highest authorities in Germany. In 2000 the German supreme court suggested that German anti-Nazi laws could apply to individuals who put Nazi material on Internet servers outside Germany if it is accessible in Germany.[2]

One effect of the Internet's growth is that it is much easier for like-minded people to find each other. Indeed, this trend challenges some of the arguments that James Madison made in *Federalist* No. 10 about the difficulty of forming a faction in a large republic. Information technology may render moot some of the practical constraints geography offers against the organization of any group.[3] The same technology that can help someone track down old friends for a class reunion can help neo-Nazis discover each other. Finding publications espousing racial hatred and Aryan supremacy—or any other political viewpoint, for that matter—is just a search engine and a mouse click away.

As access to the Internet has grown around the world, its benefits and social costs have multiplied hand in hand. The development of the World Wide Web has allowed millions of individuals to create and publish their own Web pages, giving Web masters the opportunity to shout from their own soapboxes. Unlike the high start-up costs inherent in traditional

Free Speech on the Internet

media like newspapers and television, anyone with a PC can post pages on the Web for a nominal monthly fee.[4] While only 5 million Americans were connected to the Internet in 1995, by 1999 that number had increased to over 50 million and the number continues to rise weekly.[5]

The Internet has also given rise to a new venue for traditional media outlets to offer their wares. On the Web, local publications like the *Topeka Capital Journal* are no more difficult to access than national newspapers like the *New York Times.* What television networks like ABC and CNN offer in national and international news exists alongside the local coverage of individual stations like Baltimore's WJZ, and Americans are logging in for news from all these outlets. Although news Web sites lag far behind their more traditional counterparts in the number of people relying on them as a primary source of information, the numbers are increasing. The day after the 2000 presidential election, WashingtonPost.com recorded an astounding 10.3 million page views, while the *New York Times* Web site recorded 9.6 million page views. In the case of the *New York Times,* those page views came from more than 1 million different visitors. If you consider the fact that the daily print circulation of the newspaper is only 1.2 million,[6] you can see that the face of the media is changing in the United States, driven by the Internet.

Freedom of the press is essential to democratic government, but the news media also complicate the governing process. What is the nature of the media in America? Who uses the media, and what do they learn? Do the media promote or frustrate democratic ideals? Does freedom of the press conflict with the values of order and equality? What, if anything, should or can be done domestically about limiting the use of the Internet by hate groups? In this chapter, we describe the origin and growth of the media, assess their objectivity, and examine their influence on politics.

PEOPLE, GOVERNMENT, AND COMMUNICATIONS

mass media
The means employed in mass communication, often divided into print media and broadcast media.

"We never talk anymore" is a common lament of couples who are not getting along very well. In politics, too, citizens and their government need to communicate to get along well. *Communication* is the process of transmitting information from one individual or group to another. *Mass communication* is the process by which information is transmitted to large, heterogeneous, widely dispersed audiences. The term **mass media** refers to the means for communicating to these audiences. The mass media are commonly divided into two types:

- *Print media* communicate information through the publication of words and pictures on paper. Prime examples of print media are daily newspapers and popular magazines. Because books seldom have a large circulation relative to the general population, they are not typically classified as a mass medium.

- *Broadcast media* communicate information electronically, through sounds and images. Prime examples of broadcast media are radio and television.

Although telephones also transmit sounds and computer networks can transmit words, sounds, and images, both are usually used for more targeted communications and so are not typically included in the term *mass media.* Modern politics also utilize the *fax* (facsimile images sent by telephone) and computers linked over the *Internet,* however. We refer to these as *group media*, instead of mass media, and we consider them separately below.

Our focus here is on the role of the media in promoting communication from government to its citizens and from citizens to their government. In totalitarian governments, information flows more freely in one direction (from government to the people) than the other. In democratic governments, information must flow freely in both directions; a democratic government can respond to public opinion only if its citizens can make their opinions known. Moreover, the electorate can hold government officials accountable for their actions only if voters know what the government has done, is doing, and plans to do. Because the mass media (and increasingly the group media) provide the major channels for this two-way flow of information, they have the dual capability of reflecting and shaping our political views.

The media are not the only means of communication between citizens and government. As we discussed in Chapter 5, various agents of socialization (especially schools) function as "linkage mechanisms" that promote such communication. In the next four chapters we will discuss other mechanisms for communication: voting, political parties, campaigning in elections, and interest groups. Certain linkage mechanisms communicate better in one direction than in the other. Primary and secondary schools, for example, commonly instruct young citizens about government rules and symbols, whereas voting sends messages from citizens to government. Parties, campaigns, and interest groups foster communication in both directions. The media, however, are the only linkage mechanisms that *specialize* in communication.

Although this chapter concentrates on political uses of the four most prominent mass media—newspapers, magazines, radio, and television—

political content can also be transmitted through other mass media, such as recordings and motion pictures. Rock acts such as Peter Gabriel and U2 often express political ideas in their music, as do rappers such as the late Tupac Shakur and Gangsta N.I.P.[7] Motion pictures often convey particularly intense political messages. The 1976 film *All the President's Men*, about the two *Washington Post* reporters who doggedly exposed the Watergate scandal, dramatized a seamy side of political life that contrasted sharply with an idealized view of the presidency. The 1998 political comedy *Wag the Dog* was about media advisers publicizing a phony war to detract from a sex scandal besieging the president. Ironically, the movie hit U.S. theaters just as President Clinton's sex scandal was unfolding; the White House didn't find it so funny.

THE DEVELOPMENT OF THE MASS MEDIA IN THE UNITED STATES

Although the record and film industries sometimes convey political messages, they are primarily in the business of entertainment. Our focus here is on mass media in the news industry—on print and broadcast journalism. The growth of the country, technological inventions, and shifting political attitudes about the scope of government—as well as trends in entertainment—have shaped the development of the news media in the United States.

Newspapers

When the Revolutionary War broke out in 1775, thirty-seven newspapers (all weeklies) were publishing in the colonies.[8] They had small circulations—they were not mass media but group media. The first newspapers were mainly political organs, financed by parties and advocating party causes. Newspapers did not move toward independent ownership and large circulations until the 1830s.

According to the 1880 census, 971 daily newspapers and 8,633 weekly newspapers and periodicals were then published in the United States. Most larger cities had many newspapers—New York had twenty-nine papers; Philadelphia, twenty-four; San Francisco, twenty-one; and Chicago, eighteen. Competition for readers grew fierce among the big-city dailies. Toward the latter part of the nineteenth century, imaginative publishers sought to win readers by entertaining them with photographs, comic strips, sports sections, advice to the lovelorn, and stories of sex and crime.

By the 1960s, under pressure from both radio and television, intense competition among big-city dailies had nearly disappeared. New York had only three papers left by 1969, and this pattern was repeated in every large city in the country. By 1997, only fifty-eight U.S. towns or cities had two or more competing dailies under separate ownership.[9] The net result is that the number of newspapers per person has dropped about thirty-three percent since 1950.[10]

The daily paper with the biggest circulation in 2000 (about 1.8 million copies) was the *Wall Street Journal*, which appeals to a national audience because of its extensive coverage of business news and close analysis of political news. *USA Today*, the only paper designed for national distribution, was second (1.7 million). The *New York Times*, which many journalists consider the best newspaper in the country, sells about 1 million copies, placing it third in circulation (see Figure 6.1).[11] In comparison, the weekly *National Enquirer,* which carries stories about people who return from the dead or marry aliens from outer space, sells about 2.5 million copies. Neither the *Times* nor the *Wall Street Journal* carries comic strips, which no doubt limits their mass appeal. They also print more political news and news analyses than most readers want to confront.

Magazines

Magazines differ from newspapers not only in the frequency of their publication but also in the nature of their coverage. Even news-oriented magazines cover the news in a more specialized manner than do daily newspapers. Many magazines are forums for opinions, not strictly for news. Moreover, magazines dealing with public affairs have had relatively small circulations and select readerships, making them more group media than mass media. The earliest public affairs magazines were founded in the mid-1800s, and two—*The Nation* and *Harper's*—are still publishing today. Such magazines were often politically influential, especially in framing arguments against slavery and later in publishing exposés of political corruption and business exploitation. Because these exposés were lengthy critiques of the existing political and economic order, they found a more hospitable outlet in magazines of opinion than in newspapers with big circulations. Yet magazines with limited readerships can wield political power. Magazines may influence **attentive policy elites**—group leaders who follow news in specific areas—and thus influence mass opinion indirectly through a **two-step flow of communication.**

As scholars originally viewed the two-step flow, it conformed ideally to the pluralist model of democracy. Once group leaders (for instance, union or industry leaders) became informed of political developments, they informed their more numerous followers, mobilizing them to apply pressure on government. Today, according to a revised interpretation of the two-step flow concept, policy elites are more likely to influence public opinion (not just their "followers") and other leaders by airing their views in the media. In this view, public deliberation on issues is highly mediated by these professional communicators.[12]

Three weekly news magazines—*Time* (founded in 1923), *Newsweek* (1933), and *U.S. News & World Report* (1933)—enjoy big circulations in the United States (2.2 million to 4.1 million copies in 1997) and can be considered mass media. Their audience is tiny, however, compared with the 15 million readers of *Reader's Digest.* In contrast to these mainstream, "capitalist" publications, a newer, "alternative" press is more critical of the prevailing power structure. Such periodicals as *Mother Jones* have spearheaded investigations into possible government malfeasance, such as the arms-for-hostages deal in the 1985 Iran-Contra affair.[13]

Radio

Regularly scheduled, continuous radio broadcasting began in 1920 on stations KDKA in Pittsburgh and WWJ in Detroit. Both stations claim to be the first commercial station, and both broadcast returns of the 1920 elec-

attentive policy elites
Leaders who follow news in specific policy areas.

two-step flow of communication
The process in which a few policy elites gather information and then inform their more numerous followers, mobilizing them to apply pressure to government.

figure

6.1   Audiences of Selected Media Sources

Television, newspapers, and magazines differ sharply in their appeal to mass audiences as news sources. The difference shows clearly when the figures for the average number of homes that are tuned nightly to one of the five major television news programs are compared with the circulation figures for the three top news magazines, the seven top newspapers, and the six biggest opinion magazines. Clearly, network television news enters many more homes than does news from the other media. All three news magazines (which are published weekly) have more readers than any daily newspaper, and opinion magazines reach only a small fraction of the usual television news audience.

Sources: Average television news audiences are from *Nielsen Media Research* (1998); magazine circulations are from the *Standard Periodical Directory* (New York: Oxbridge Publishing, 1997); newspaper circulations are from Mark Fitzgerald, "Latest FAS-FAX Report: It Sinks!" *Editor & Publisher,* 6 November 2000, p. 14; *NewsHour* audience was obtained by telephone from the Public Broadcasting Service.

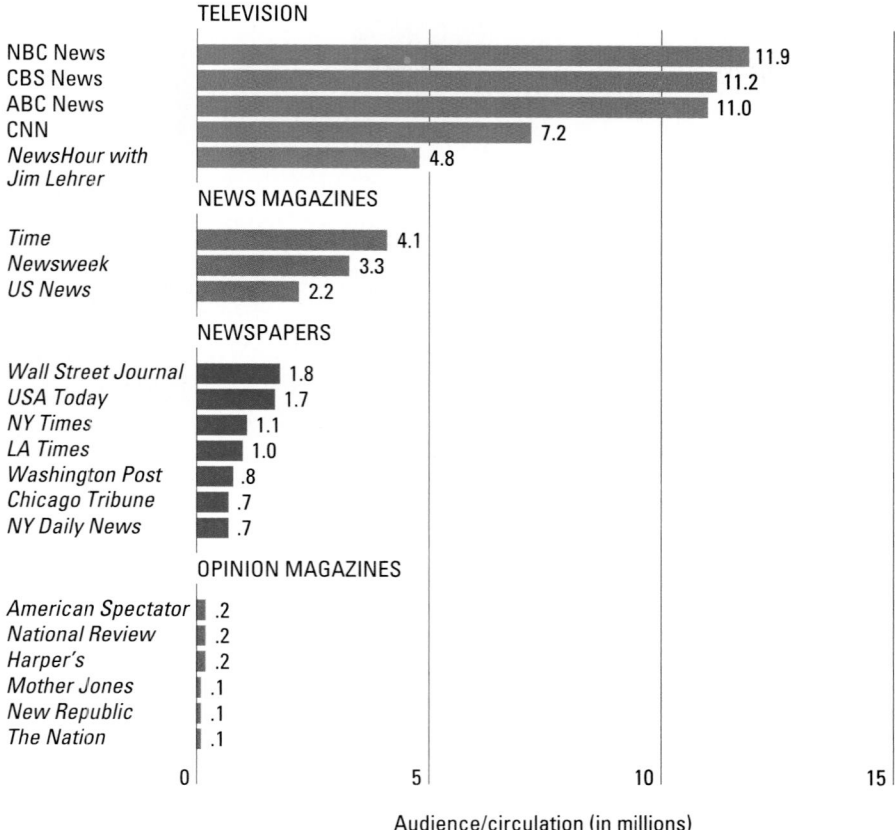

tion of President Warren G. Harding. The first radio network, the National Broadcasting Company (NBC), was formed in 1926. Soon four networks were on the air, transforming radio into a national medium by linking thousands of local stations. Millions of Americans were able to hear President Franklin D. Roosevelt deliver his first "fireside chat" in 1933. However, the first coast-to-coast broadcast did not occur until 1937, when listeners were shocked by an eyewitness report of the explosion of the dirigible *Hindenburg* in New Jersey.

Because the public could sense reporters' personalities over radio in a way they could not in print, broadcast journalists quickly became household names. Edward R. Murrow, one of the most famous radio news personalities, broadcast news of the merger of Germany and Austria by short-wave radio from Vienna in 1938 and later gave stirring reports of German air raids on London during World War II. Today, radio is less salient for live coverage of events than for "talk radio," often criticized for polarizing politics by publicizing extreme views.[14]

Television

Experiments with television began in France in the early 1900s. By 1940, twenty-three television stations were operating in the United States, and—repeating radio's feat of twenty years earlier—two stations broadcast the returns of a presidential election, Roosevelt's 1940 reelection.[15] The onset of World War II paralyzed the development of television technology, but growth in the medium exploded after the war. By 1950, ninety-eight stations were covering the major population centers of the country, although only 9 percent of American households had televisions.

The first commercial color broadcast came in 1951, as did the first coast-to-coast broadcast—President Harry Truman's address to delegates at the Japanese peace treaty conference in San Francisco. That same year, Democratic senator Estes Kefauver of Tennessee called for public television coverage of his committee's investigation into organized crime. For weeks, people with televisions invited their neighbors to watch underworld crime figures answering questions before the camera. And Kefauver became one of the first politicians to benefit from television coverage. Previously unknown and representing a small state, he nevertheless won many of the 1952 Democratic presidential primaries and became the Democrats' vice-presidential candidate in 1956.

By 1960, 87 percent of U.S. households had televisions. By 1990, the United States had more than 1,000 commercial and 300 public television stations, and virtually every household (98 percent) had television. Today, television claims by far the biggest news audience of all the mass media (see Figure 6.1). From television's beginnings, most stations were linked into networks founded by three of the four major radio networks. Many early anchormen of television network news programs came to the medium with names already made famous during their years of experience as radio broadcast journalists. But now that the news audience could actu-

ally see the broadcasters as well as hear them, news personalities (like Dan Rather and Peter Jennings) became instantly recognizable celebrities.

MODERN FORMS OF GROUP MEDIA

group media
Communications technologies, such as the fax and the Internet, used primarily within groups of people of common interests.

The revolution in electronics during the last quarter of the twentieth century produced two new technologies—the fax and the Internet—that have been readily adapted to politics. Neither are "mass" media that communicate with the general public, however. They are called **group media**—communications technologies used primarily within groups of people with common interests.

Facsimile Transmissions

Believe it or not, a technique for scanning an image to generate signals that could reproduce a facsimile (copy) of the image on electrochemical recording paper was invented in 1843. Eventually, the idea was adapted to the telephone, and by the early twentieth century it was used commercially by newspapers to transmit photographs, called Wirephotos. After World War II, the Japanese seized on the technology to transmit their complex written characters. They developed the modern "fax" machine in the 1970s and have maintained a virtual monopoly on its manufacture.

The fax machine quickly became standard communications equipment in practical politics. Campaign managers routinely communicate with campaign workers and media representatives via fax, and it is a major medium for communication among political officeholders in Washington.[16] Interest groups frequently rely on automated fax messages concerning issues before Congress—as many as 10,000 a night—sent automatically by computers to sympathizers across the country.[17] Increasingly, recipients of these faxes respond by faxing fervent messages of opposition or support to their congressional representatives, simulating a groundswell of public opinion—despite the fact that fewer than 10 percent of U.S. homes had fax machines in the mid-1990s (see High-Tech Lobbying, Chapter 10).[18]

The Internet

What we today call the Internet began in 1969 when, with support from the U.S. Defense Department's Advanced Research Projects Agency, computers at four universities were linked to form ARPANET. By 1972, thirty-seven universities were connected over ARPANET. Following the growth of other distinct computer networks (such as BITNET, designed for IBM mainframes), new communications standards worked out in 1983 allowed these networks to be linked, creating the Internet.[19]

In its early years, the Internet was used mainly to transmit *e-mail* among researchers. In 1991, a group of European physicists devised a standardized system for encoding and transmitting a wide range of materials, including graphics and photographs, over the Internet, and the World Wide Web (WWW) was born. Now anyone on the Internet with a computer program called a "browser" can access Web "pages" from around the world. In January 1993 there were only fifty Web sites in existence.[20] Today there are many thousands of sites and millions of Web users.

Like the fax, the Internet was soon incorporated into politics, and by 1998 virtually every government agency and political organization in the nation had its own Web site. The Internet can even break important stories. Matt Drudge, an Internet "gossip reporter," learned that *Newsweek* had gathered information in early January on a possible sexual relationship between President Clinton and Monica Lewinsky, a White House intern, but was sitting on the story, reluctant to report hearsay about the president's sex life. Drudge, who publishes virtually everything sent to him, posted a report of the story on his Web site, the *Drudge Report*, the day Clinton gave his legal deposition in the sexual harassment lawsuit brought against him by Paula Corbin Jones, a former Arkansas state employee. From there the story slithered into Internet newsgroups and then into the mass media with a discussion on ABC's *This Week* the next morning.[21] On September 11, the day after receiving Independent Counsel Kenneth Starr's report on the Lewinsky affair, Congress published it on the Internet. Within hours, millions read the tawdry details on their computers, as the Web momentarily became a mass medium.[22]

Can You Explain Why...
the Internet is not regarded as one of the mass media?

PRIVATE OWNERSHIP OF THE MEDIA

In the United States, people take private ownership of the media for granted. Indeed, most Americans would regard government ownership of the media as an unacceptable threat to freedom that would interfere with the "marketplace of ideas" and result in one-way communication, from government to citizens. When the government controls the news flow, the people may have little chance to learn what the government is doing or to pressure it to behave differently. Certainly that was true in the former Soviet Union. China offers another illustration of how arbitrary government control of the media can be. The Chinese government permitted televised coverage of protests for democracy in Beijing's Tiananmen Square in 1989 and then harshly reimposed censorship overnight to smother the democracy movement. (Many dissidents used fax machines to send news of the government massacre to the outside world.) Private ownership of the media offers a more stable, continuing forum for government criticism.

In other Western democracies, the print media (both newspapers and magazines) are privately owned, but the broadcast media often are not. Before the 1980s, the government owned and operated the major broadcast media in most of these countries. Now, in Western Europe, government radio and television stations compete with private stations.[23] In the United States, except for about 350 public television stations (out of about 1,500 total) and 400 public radio stations (out of about 10,000), the broadcast media are privately owned.[24]

The Consequences of Private Ownership

Just as the appearance of the newscaster became important for television viewers, so did the appearance of the news itself. Television's great advantage over radio—that it shows people and events—accounts for the influence of television news coverage. It also determines, to some extent, the news that television chooses to cover. In fact, private ownership of the mass media ensures that news is selected for its audience appeal.

Private ownership of both the print and broadcast media gives the news industry in America more political freedom than any other in the world, but it also makes the media more dependent on advertising revenues to cover their costs and make a profit. Because advertising rates are tied to audience size, the news operations of the mass media in America must appeal to the audiences they serve.

The average American spends four hours watching television every day, but only about half watch any kind of news for as much as half an hour.[25] About 60 million newspapers circulate daily, but more than 60 percent of their content is advertising. After fashion reports, sports, comics, and so on, only a relatively small portion of any newspaper is devoted to news of any sort, and only a fraction of that news—excluding stories about fires, robberies, murder trials, and the like—can be classified as political. In terms of sheer volume, the entertainment content offered by the mass media in the United States vastly overshadows the news content. In other words, the media function to entertain more than to provide news. Entertainment increases the audience, which increases advertising revenues. Thus, the profit motive creates constant pressure to increase the ratio of entertainment to news or to make the news itself more "entertaining."

You might think that a story's political significance, educational value, or broad social importance determines whether the media cover it. The sad truth is that most potential news stories are not judged by such grand criteria. The primary criterion of a story's **newsworthiness** is usually its audience appeal, which is judged according to its potential impact on readers or listeners, its degree of sensationalism (exemplified by violence, conflict, disaster, or scandal), its treatment of familiar people or life situations, its close-to-home character, and its timeliness.[26]

newsworthiness
The degree to which a news story is important enough to be covered in the mass media.

The importance of audience appeal has led the news industry to calculate its audience carefully. (The bigger the audience, the higher the advertising rates.) The print media can easily determine the size of their circulations through sales figures, but the broadcast media must estimate their audience through various sampling techniques. Because both print and broadcast media might be tempted to inflate their estimated audience (to tell advertisers that they reach more people than they actually do), a separate industry has developed to rate audience size impartially. These ratings reports have resulted in a "ratings game," in which the media try to increase their ratings by adjusting the delivery or content of their news.

figure
6.2   **Local Television News: No News Is Happy News**

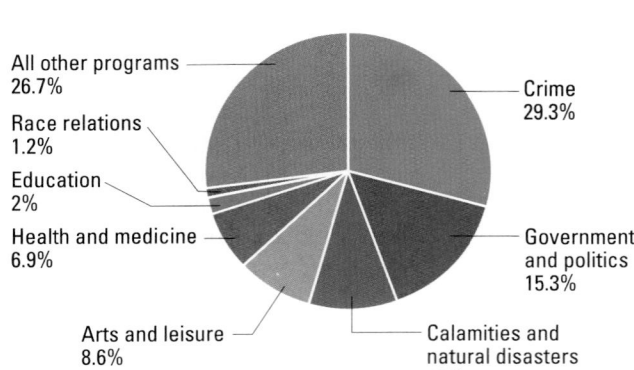

AVERAGE TIME DEVOTED TO EIGHT NEWS CATEGORIES

All other programs 26.7%

Race relations 1.2%

Education 2%

Health and medicine 6.9%

Arts and leisure 8.6%

Crime 29.3%

Government and politics 15.3%

Calamities and natural disasters 10%

From 1996 to 1997, journalism schools at eight universities across the country participated in the first nationwide study of local television news programs. For four months, research teams systematically analyzed the content of early evening local news broadcasts in eight cities: Austin, Texas; Chicago; Eugene, Oregon; Indianapolis; Los Angeles; Miami; New York; and Syracuse, New York. On average, viewers in these cities saw nearly twice as much coverage of crime as news about government and politics. Fortunately, network television news programs broadcast a much higher percentage of political news. Unfortunately, far more people regularly watch local news programs (65 percent) than network news (42 percent). A study of local television news in fifty-eight media markets found that most stations aired an average of only forty-five seconds of candidate discourse during the 2000 elections.

Source: Mark Fitzgerald, "Local TV News Lacks Substance," *Editor & Publisher*, 24 May 1997, pp. 8–9; Tim Jones, "Inside Media," *Chicago Tribune*, 8 February 2001, Section 3, p. 2.

infotainment
The practice of mixing journalism with theater, employed by some news programs.

Some local television stations favor "happy talk" on their news broadcasts—breezy on-the-air exchanges among announcers, reporters, sportscasters, and meteorologists. Other stations use the "eyewitness" approach, showing a preponderance of film footage with human interest, humorous, or violent content. Many stations combine the two, entertaining viewers (most of whom watch local news more regularly than national news) but perhaps not informing them properly, as illustrated in Figure 6.2. Even the three mighty television networks have departed from their traditionally high journalistic standards, following their acquisition since 1986 by other corporations: The Walt Disney Company acquired ABC, General Electric bought NBC, and Viacom absorbed CBS. All three major television networks are now cogs in mighty conglomerates with economic interests far broader than the news.

From 1980 to 1990, ABC, CBS, and NBC suffered severe losses in their prime-time audience, dropping from nearly 90 to only 63 percent of all television viewers.[27] Increasingly, viewers have been watching cable stations or videotapes instead of network programs. Audience declines have brought declining profits and cutbacks in network news budgets. As their parent corporations demanded that news programs "pay their way," the networks succumbed to **infotainment**—mixing journalism with theater—in programs such as "Hard Copy" and "Inside Edition." Sometimes these programs play fast and loose with the truth, as "Dateline NBC" did in a 1992 broadcast on vehicle gas tanks that allegedly exploded in collisions. The program's staff rigged a General Motors pickup truck with an incendiary device to ensure that the truck would ignite in a filmed collision. An investigation by General Motors uncovered the fraud and forced NBC to apologize on the air. Instances of poor journalism and outright fraud have increased as network executives have demanded that television news become more profitable.

The Concentration of Private Ownership

Media owners can make more money either by increasing their audience or by acquiring additional publications or stations. There is a decided trend toward concentrated ownership of the media, increasing the risk that a few owners could control the news flow to promote their own political interests—much as political parties influenced the content of the earliest American newspapers. In fact, the number of *independent newspapers* has declined as newspaper chains (owners of two or more newspapers in different cities) have acquired more newspapers. Most of the more than 100 newspaper chains in the United States today are small, owning fewer than ten papers.[28] Some are very big, however. The Gannett chain, which owns *USA Today*, with the second biggest daily circulation in the nation, also owns more than seventy newspapers throughout the United States. Only about 400 dailies are still independent; many of these papers are too small and unprofitable to invite acquisition.

At first glance, concentration of ownership does not seem to be a problem in the television industry. Although there are only three major networks, the networks usually do not own their affiliates. About half of all the communities in the United States have a choice of ten or more stations.[29] This figure suggests that the electronic media offer diverse viewpoints and are not characterized by ownership concentration. As with newspapers, however, chains sometimes own television stations in different cities, and ownership sometimes extends across different media. As mentioned earlier, none of the three original television networks remains an independent corporation: NBC was purchased by General Electric, ABC was purchased by the Walt Disney Company, and CBS was recently purchased by Viacom, Inc. Although the Viacom name may not be well known to many college students, its other holdings are. In addition to CBS, Viacom brands include MTV, VH1, Paramount Pictures, Showtime, UPN, Nickelodeon, TNN, CMT, Infinity Broadcasting, Blockbuster, and Simon & Schuster.[30]

GOVERNMENT REGULATION OF THE MEDIA

Although most of the mass media in the United States are privately owned, they do not operate free of government regulation. The broadcast media operate under more stringent regulations than the print media, initially because of technical aspects of broadcasting. In general, government regulation of the mass media addresses three aspects of their operation: technical considerations, ownership, and content.[31]

Technical and Ownership Regulations

In the early days of radio, stations that operated on similar frequencies in the same area often jammed each other's signals, and no one could broadcast clearly. At the broadcasters' insistence, Congress passed the Federal Radio Act (1927), which declared that the public owned the airwaves and private broadcasters could use them only by obtaining a license from the Federal Radio Commission. So, government regulation of broadcasting was not forced on the industry by socialist politicians; capitalist owners sought it to impose order on the use of the airwaves (thereby restricting others' freedom to enter broadcasting).

Federal Communications Commission (FCC)
An independent federal agency that regulates interstate and international communication by radio, television, telephone, telegraph, cable, and satellite.

Seven years later, Congress passed the Federal Communications Act of 1934, a more sweeping law that regulated the broadcast and telephone industries for more than sixty years. It created the **Federal Communications Commission (FCC),** which has five members (no more than three from the same political party) nominated by the president for terms of five years. The commissioners can be removed from office only through impeachment and conviction. Consequently, the FCC is considered an independent regulatory commission: it is insulated from political control by either the president or Congress. (We discuss independent regulatory commissions in Chapter 13.) Today, the FCC is charged with regulating interstate and international communications by radio, television, telephone, telegraph, cable, and satellite.

For six decades—as technological change made television commonplace and brought the invention of computers, fax machines, and satellite transmissions—the communications industry was regulated under the basic framework of the 1934 law that created the FCC. Pressured by businesses that wanted to exploit new electronic technologies, Congress, in a bipartisan effort, swept away most existing regulations in the Telecommunications Act of 1996.

The new law relaxed or scrapped limitations on media ownership. For example, broadcasters were previously limited to owning only twelve television stations and forty radio stations. Now there are no limits on the number of television stations one company may own, just so long as their coverage doesn't extend beyond 35 percent of the market nationwide. The law set no national limits for radio ownership, and it relaxed local limits. In addition, it lifted rate regulations for cable systems, allowed cross-ownership of cable and telephone companies, and allowed local and long-distance telephone companies to compete with one another and to sell television services.

Although the law's authors intended to loosen media monopolies, they could not predict its long-range effects. One result of the act has in fact been even greater concentration of media ownership. Media groups entered the third millennium in a flurry of megamergers. The Federal Trade Commission approved the largest of these, the $183 billion purchase of Time-Warner by America Online, in 2000. The AOL/Time-Warner deal merges the nation's largest Internet service provider with the second largest cable system (which had already merged with one of the biggest publishers in the United States). The resulting conglomerate starts with 24 million Internet customers (nearly half of the U.S. market), 12.6 million cable subscribers, and "breathtaking reach in films, music, and publishing."[32] Critics might view this as the vindication of a prediction made over a decade before: a special issue of the opinion magazine *The Nation* warned of the dangers of an impending "National Entertainment State," in which the media would be controlled by a few conglomerates.[33]

The industry countered with the argument that diversity among news sources in America is great enough to provide citizens with a wide range of political ideas. Some outsiders, however, worried that the same owners would increasingly control "competing" media. In 1999, the FCC voted to allow a single company or network to own two television stations in the same major market. The vote overturned regulations put in place in the

1930s and 1940s to ensure diversity of ownership. Prior to this decision, a company could own up to eight radio stations and one television station in a given market.[34]

Regulation of Content

The First Amendment to the Constitution prohibits Congress from abridging the freedom of the press. Over time, *the press* has come to mean all the media, and the courts have decided many cases that define how far freedom of the press extends under the law. Chapter 15 discusses the most important of these cases, which are often quite complex. Although the courts have had difficulty defining obscenity, they have not permitted obscene expression under freedom of the press. In 1996, however, a federal court overturned an attempt to limit transmission of "indecent" (not obscene) material on the Internet, calling the attempt "profoundly repugnant to First Amendment principles."[35]

Near v. *Minnesota*

New York Times v. *United States*

Usually the courts strike down government attempts to restrain the press from publishing or broadcasting the information, reports, or opinions it finds newsworthy. One notable exception concerns strategic information during wartime; the courts have supported censorship of information such as the sailing schedules of troop ships or the planned movements of troops in battle. Otherwise, they have recognized a strong constitutional case against press censorship. This stand has given the United States some of the freest, most vigorous news media in the world (see Compared with What? 6.1).

Because the broadcast media are licensed to use the public airwaves, they have been subject to some additional regulation, beyond what is applied to the print media, of the content of their news coverage. The basis for the FCC's regulation of content lies in its charge to ensure that radio (and, later, television) stations would "serve the public interest, convenience, and necessity." The FCC formulated two rules to promote the public interest concerning political matters. With its **equal opportunities rule,** the FCC required any broadcast station that gave or sold time to a candidate for a public office to make an equal amount of time available under the same conditions to all other candidates for that office. The **reasonable access rule** required that stations make their facilities available for the expression of conflicting views on issues by all responsible elements in the community. Both of these rules were struck down by a U.S. court of appeals in 2000.[36]

equal opportunities rule
Under the Federal Communications Act of 1934, the requirement that if a broadcast station gives or sells time to a candidate for any public office, it must make available an equal amount of time under the same conditions to all other candidates for that office.

reasonable access rule
An FCC rule that requires broadcast stations to make their facilities available for the expression of conflicting views or issues by all responsible elements in the community.

The regulations seemed unobjectionable to most people, but they were at the heart of a controversy about the deregulation of the broadcast media. Note that neither of these regulations was imposed on the print media, which have no responsibility to give equal treatment to political candidates or to express conflicting views from all responsible elements of the community. In fact, one aspect of a free press is its ability to champion causes that it favors without having to argue the case for the other side. The broadcast media have traditionally been treated differently because they were licensed by the FCC to operate as semimonopolies.[37] With the rise of one-newspaper cities and towns, however, competition among television stations is greater than among newspapers in virtually every

★ **compared with what?**

6.1   Reporting Conflicts After the Cold War

Compared with the dramatic change in the way Russian newspapers report on international conflicts since the end of the Cold War, reporting in the United States seems to have changed very little. A 2000 study compared reporting on the invasion of Afghanistan by the Soviet Union in 1979 with the invasion of the breakaway republic of Chechnya by Russia in 1994. The researchers examined the content of 240 articles in the *New York Times* and *Izvestia* (a national newspaper in Russia) written during these conflicts and assigned a quantitative index indicating whether the articles portrayed the events and the parties involved in a positive, negative, or neutral manner. Although the relationship between the United States and Russia has improved dramatically since the collapse of the Soviet Union in 1991, journalists writing for the *New York Times* were no more sympathetic toward the Russian activities in Chechnya than they were of the Soviet activities in Afghanistan. In both cases, American journalists described the events with a decidedly negative slant. In Russia, however, the change in reporting was stunning. During the invasion of Afghanistan, the Soviet media was completely owned and controlled by the government. Not surprisingly, news articles published in *Izvestia* portrayed the invasion of Afghanistan in very positive terms. Since the collapse of the Soviet Union, the Russian media has been partially privatized and has greater freedom to criticize government policy. Reports in *Izvestia* on the Russian army's involvement in Chechnya was predominatly negative. As the emphasis on order has been replaced by an emphasis on freedom, Russian newspapers are beginning to resemble their American counterparts.

Source: Olga V. Malinkina and Douglas M. McLeod, "From Afghanistan to Chechnya: News Coverage by *Izvestia* and the *New York Times*," *Journalism and Mass Communication Quarterly,* 77, 1 (Spring 2000), pp. 37–49.

market area. Advocates of dropping all FCC content regulations argued that the broadcast media should be just as free as the print media to decide which candidates they endorse and which issues they support.

In 1987, under President Reagan, the FCC itself moved toward this view of unfettered freedom for broadcasters by repealing a third rule, the *fairness doctrine*, which had obligated broadcasters to provide fair coverage of all views on public issues. One media analyst noted that the FCC acted in the belief that competition among broadcasters, cable, radio, newspapers, and magazines would provide a vibrant marketplace of ideas. He feared, however, that the FCC had overestimated the public's demand for high-quality news and public affairs broadcasts. Without that demand, the media are unlikely to supply the news and public affairs coverage needed to sustain a genuine marketplace.[38]

In the United States, the mass media are in business to make money, which they do mainly by selling advertising. To sell advertising, they provide entertainment on a mass basis, which is their general function. We are more interested here in the five specific functions the mass media serve for the political system: *reporting* the news, *interpreting* the news, *influencing* citizens' opinions, *setting the agenda* for government action, and *socializing* citizens about politics.

**REPORTING AND
FOLLOWING THE
NEWS**

"News," for most journalists, is an important event that has happened within the past twenty-four hours. A presidential news conference or an explosion in the Capitol qualifies as news. And a national political convention certainly qualifies as news, although it may not justify the thousands of media representatives present at the 2000 party conventions. Who decides what is important? The media, of course. In this section, we discuss how the media cover political affairs, what they choose to report (what becomes "news"), who follows the news, and what they remember and learn from it.

Covering National Politics

All the major news media seek to cover political events with firsthand reports from journalists on the scene. Because so many significant political events occur in the nation's capital, Washington has by far the biggest press corps of any city in the world—over 6,000 accredited reporters: 2,100 from newspapers, 2,000 from periodicals, and 2,200 from radio and television.[39] Only a small portion of these reporters cover the presidency—only about seventy-five "regular" journalists are in the White House press corps.[40] Since 1902, when President Theodore Roosevelt first provided a special room in the White House for reporters, the press has had special access to the president. As recently as the Truman administration, reporters enjoyed informal personal relationships with the president. Today, the media's relationship with the president is mediated primarily through the Office of the Press Secretary.

To meet their daily deadlines, White House correspondents rely heavily on information they receive from the president's staff, each piece carefully crafted in an attempt to control the news report. The most frequent form is the news release—a prepared text distributed to reporters in the hope that they will use it verbatim. A daily news briefing at 11:30 A.M. enables reporters to question the press secretary about news releases and allows television correspondents time to prepare their stories and film for the evening newscast. A news conference involves questioning high-level officials in the executive branch—including the president, on occasion. News conferences appear to be freewheeling, but officials tend to carefully rehearse precise answers to anticipated questions.

Occasionally, information is given "on background," meaning the information can be quoted, but reporters cannot identify the source. A vague reference—"a senior official says"—is all right. (When he was secretary of state, Henry Kissinger himself was often the "senior official" quoted on foreign policy developments.) Information disclosed "off the record" cannot even be printed. Journalists who violate these well-known rules risk losing their welcome at the White House. In a sense, the press corps is captive to the White House, which feeds reporters the information they need to meet their deadlines and frames events so that they are covered on the evening news.[41] Beginning with the Nixon White House, press secretaries have obliged photographers with "photo opportunities," a few minutes to take pictures or shoot film, often of the president with a visiting dignitary or a winning sports team. The photographers can keep their editors supplied with visuals, and the press secretary ensures that the coverage is favorable by controlling the environment.

Most reporters in the Washington press corps are accredited to sit in the House and Senate press galleries, but only about 400 cover Congress exclusively.[42] Most news about Congress comes from innumerable press releases issued by its 535 members and from an unending supply of congressional reports. A journalist, then, can report on Congress without inhabiting its press galleries.

Not so long ago, individual congressional committees allowed radio and television coverage of their proceedings only on special occasions—such as the Kefauver committee's investigation of organized crime in the 1950s and the Watergate investigation in the 1970s. Congress banned microphones and cameras from its chambers until 1979, when the House permitted live coverage (though it insisted on controlling the shots being televised). Nevertheless, televised broadcasts of the House were surprisingly successful, thanks to C-SPAN (the Cable Satellite Public Affairs Network), which feeds to 90 percent of the cable systems across the country and has a cultlike following among hundreds of thousands of regular viewers.[43] To share in the exposure, the Senate began television coverage in 1986. C-SPAN coverage of Congress has become important to professionals in government and politics in Washington—perhaps more so than to its small, devoted audience across the country. Even members of the Washington press corps watch C-SPAN.

In addition to these recognized sources of news, selected reporters occasionally benefit from leaks of information released by officials who are guaranteed anonymity. Officials may leak news to interfere with others' political plans or to float ideas ("trial balloons") past the public and other political leaders to gauge their reactions. At times, one carefully placed leak can turn into a gusher of media coverage through "pack journalism"—the tendency of journalists to adopt similar viewpoints toward the news simply because they hang around together, exchanging information and defining the day's news with one another.

Presenting the News

gatekeepers
Media executives, news editors, and prominent reporters who direct the flow of news.

Media executives, news editors, and prominent reporters function as **gatekeepers** in directing the news flow: they decide which events to report and how to handle the elements in those stories. Only a few individuals—no more than twenty-five at the average newspaper or news magazine and fifty at each of the major television networks—qualify as gatekeepers, defining the news for public consumption.[44] They not only select what topics go through the gate but also are expected to uphold standards of careful reporting and principled journalism. So where were the gatekeepers during the media's feeding frenzy over the presidential sex scandal in 1998? The president of an editors' association lamented, "We spout off all these high ideals and goals of journalism, and then you get a story where the principal characters are of questionable character, and the details have a salacious aspect, and the whole blasted thing is based on anonymous sources."[45] Some journalists attributed the "collapse of all balance and judgment" in the mainstream media to lowered standards "in the face of the information free-for-all that has resulted from the rise of the Internet, talk radio, and 24-hour cable news."[46] Many people expected that these

Can You Explain Why...
the traditional role for "gatekeepers" has declined in the media?

new media would raise the level of public discourse by increasing the amount and variety of news available, but it has become apparent that they also spread "news" of dubious quality. The Internet, in particular, has no gatekeepers and thus no constraints on its content.

The established media cannot communicate everything about public affairs. There is neither space in newspapers or magazines nor time on television or radio to do so. Time limitations impose especially severe constraints on television news broadcasting. Each half-hour network news program devotes only about twenty minutes to the news (the rest of the time is taken up by commercials), and there is even less news on local television (see Figure 6.2). The average story lasts about one minute, and few stories run longer than two minutes. The typical script for an entire television news broadcast would fill less than two columns of one page of the *New York Times*.[47]

A parade of unconnected one-minute news stories, flashing across the television screen every night, would boggle the eyes and minds of viewers. To make the news understandable and to hold viewers' attention, television editors and producers carefully choose their lead story and group stories together by theme. The stories themselves concentrate on individuals because individuals have personalities (political institutions do not—except for the presidency). A careful content analysis of a year's network news coverage of the president, Congress, and the Supreme Court found that the average television news program devotes seven and a half minutes to the president, compared with one minute for Congress and only half a minute for the Court.[48] Moreover, when television does cover Congress, it tries to personify the institution by focusing on prominent, quotable leaders, such as the Speaker of the House or the Senate majority leader. Such personification for the purpose of gaining audience appeal tends to distort the character of Congress, which harbors competing views among different powerfully placed members.

horse race journalism
Election coverage by the mass media that focuses on which candidate is ahead, rather than on national issues.

During elections, personification encourages **horse race journalism,** in which media coverage becomes a matter of "who's ahead in the polls, who's raising the most money, who's got TV ads and who's getting endorsed." A study of network news coverage of the 1996 presidential campaign attributed 53 percent of the stories to the horse race and only 37 percent to policy issues.[49] Other countries give more attention to issues in their election coverage. U.S. television presents elections as contests between individuals rather than as confrontations between representatives of opposing parties and platforms.

media event
A situation that is so "newsworthy" that the mass media are compelled to cover it; candidates in elections often create such situations to garner media attention.

Political campaigns lend themselves particularly well to media coverage, especially if the candidates create a **media event**—a situation that is too "newsworthy" to pass up. One tried-and-true method is to conduct a statewide walking campaign. Newspapers and television can take pictures of the candidate on the highway and conduct interviews with local folks who just spoke with the political hiker. (See Chapter 9 for further discussion of the media in political campaigns.) Television is particularly partial to events that have visual impact. Organized protests and fires, for example, "show well" on television, so television tends to cover them. Violent conflict of any kind, especially unfolding dramas that involve weapons, rate especially high in visual impact.

So, What's in the News Today? ★

Well, it depends on when you bought the newspaper. On Wednesday morning, November 8, 2000 (the day after the presidential election), different copies of the Chicago Sun-Times *(like newspapers across the country) ran conflicting headlines about the election. The only certainty in the headlines that morning was Hillary Rodham Clinton's win in her contest for U.S. Senator in New York.*

Where the Public Gets Its News

Until the early 1960s, most people reported getting more of their news from newspapers than from any other source. Television nudged out newspapers as the public's major source of news in the early 1960s. By the mid-1990s, nearly three-fourths of the public cited television as their main news source, compared with about two-fifths who named newspapers (some named both). Not only was television the public's most important source of news, but those polled rated television news as more trustworthy than newspaper news by a margin of 2 to 1.[50] But studies have found that fewer adults are regularly watching television news, particularly nightly network news (only 42 percent in 1996 versus 60 percent in 1993).[51] As found in the surveys described in Figures 6.3 and 6.4, people are far more interested in local news than in national news. The survey also found that believability of both the networks and their news anchors eroded during the 1990s. Meanwhile, public readership of newspapers and evaluation of their credibility have not declined, and there has been no change in the radio news audience. So television may not be as dominant a news medium as it might seem, and we should inquire into the public's specific sources of news.

In a recent survey of news media usage, 84 percent of respondents said that they had read or heard the prior day's news through print or broadcast media: newspapers, television, or radio.[52] However, a comparable survey found that only 17 percent of citizens claimed they "follow news of public affairs and government" daily, and almost as many said they did so hardly at all.[53] The 50 percent who said they followed the news either "daily" or "most of the time" were more likely to have some college education. They were also far more likely to be over fifty years old than under thirty (51 versus 11 percent) and much more likely to be men than women (41 versus 28

figure

6.3　Regular Use of News Media by the Public

Here are the answers respondents gave in 2000 when asked whether they "regularly" read, watched, or listened to any of these news sources. Over three-fifths said they read a daily newspaper regularly—but perhaps only for sports, comics, or television listings. To a separate question, about 70 percent said they got "most" of their news about the presidential campaign from television. As for television news, many more people watch local than national news. The Public Broadcasting System's NewsHour with Jim Lehrer— arguably the best news program on television—ranks at the bottom of the entire list of twelve sources.

Source: Pew Research Center for The People & The Press, "Internet Sapping Broadcast News Audience," press release, 11 June 2000. National survey of 3,142 adults during April 20–May 13, 2000. The entries show the percentage that "regularly" read, watch, or listen to each medium.

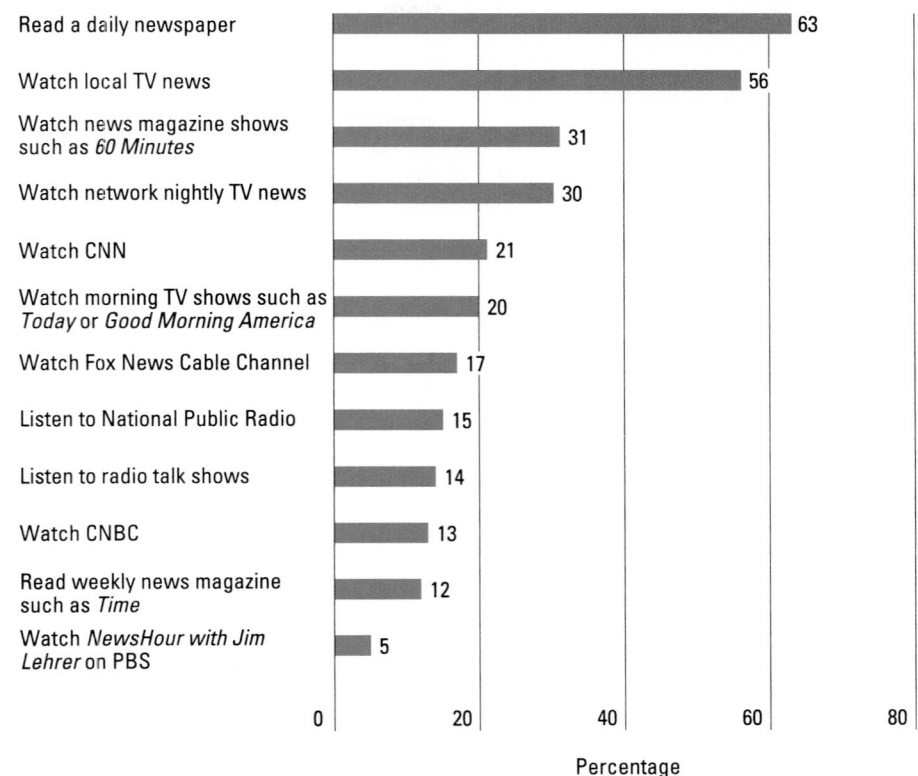

Read a daily newspaper — 63
Watch local TV news — 56
Watch news magazine shows such as *60 Minutes* — 31
Watch network nightly TV news — 30
Watch CNN — 21
Watch morning TV shows such as *Today* or *Good Morning America* — 20
Watch Fox News Cable Channel — 17
Listen to National Public Radio — 15
Listen to radio talk shows — 14
Watch CNBC — 13
Read weekly news magazine such as *Time* — 12
Watch *NewsHour with Jim Lehrer* on PBS — 5

Percentage

percent). Researchers have attributed women's relatively low interest in political news to what was taught to them at home and in school, saying that changes in girls' early learning experiences must occur before such gender differences evaporate.[54] Race bears little relationship to news attentiveness, once controls for level of education are introduced.[55]

What People Remember and Know

If, as surveys indicate, 84 percent of the public read or hear the news each day, and if nearly 75 percent regularly watch the news on television, how much political information do they absorb? By all accounts, not much. A 1997 national survey asked respondents to identify a list of names "in the news." Many more identified Tiger Woods, the young African-American golfer (82 percent); Dennis Rodman, the Bulls basketball rowdy (80 percent); and Ellen DeGeneres, the television comedian who came out as a lesbian (62 percent), than identified Alan Greenspan, chairman of the Federal Reserve Board (20 percent); and Trent Lott, majority leader of the Senate (15 percent).[56]

6.4

Interest in the News

Americans are more interested in domestic news than in foreign news, and their primary concern is being informed about what is happening in their own community. This long-term trend coincides with a favorite political maxim of the late Tip O'Neill, a former speaker of the U.S. House of Representatives: "All politics is local."

Source: John E. Rielly, ed., *American Public Opinion and U.S. Foreign Policy 1999* (Chicago, Ill.: Chicago Council on Foreign Relations, 1999).

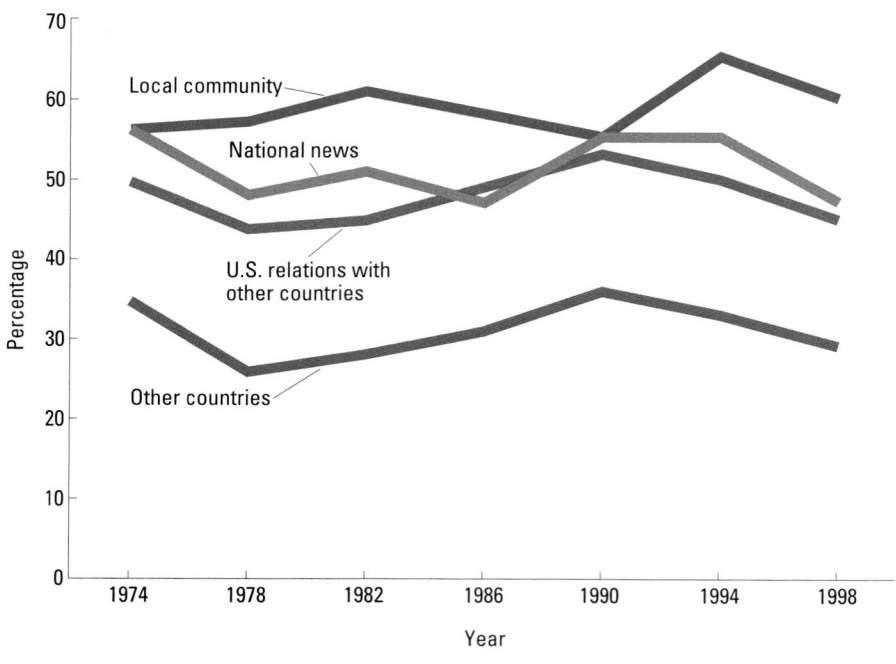

As one would expect, those who are more attentive to the news answer more political knowledge questions correctly than those who are less attentive. Given the enormous improvements in television news coverage and the increasing reliance of the public on television for news, we might also expect the public to know more than it did twenty years ago.[57] Unfortunately, that is not so. Similar surveys conducted in 1967 and 1987 asked respondents to name their state governor, their representative in the House, and the head of their local school district. Only 9 percent failed to name a single official in 1967, compared with 17 percent in 1987. The author of this study attributed the lower performance in 1987 to greater reliance on television for news.[58]

Numerous studies have found that those who rely on television for their news score lower on tests of knowledge about public affairs than those who rely on print media. Among media researchers, this finding has led to the **television hypothesis**—the belief that television is to blame for the low level of citizens' knowledge about public affairs.[59] This belief has a reasonable basis. We know that television tends to squeeze public policy issues into one-minute or, at most, two-minute fragments, which makes it difficult to explain candidates' positions. Television also tends to cast abstract issues in personal terms to generate the visual content that the medium needs.[60] Thus, viewers may become more adept at visually identifying the candidates and describing their personal habits than at outlining their positions on issues. Finally, because they are regulated by the

television hypothesis
The belief that television is to blame for the low level of citizens' knowledge about public affairs.

FCC, the television networks are particularly concerned about being fair and equal in covering the candidates, and this concern may result in their failing to critique the candidates' positions. Newspapers, which are not regulated, enjoy more latitude in choosing which candidates to cover and how. Whatever the explanation, the technological wonders of television may have contributed little to citizens' knowledge of public affairs. Indeed, electronic journalism may work against providing the informed citizenry that democratic government requires.

Recent research has questioned the hypothesis that television is a poor medium for disseminating information on public affairs. One group of researchers studied how citizens constructed political meaning from news gained from television, newspapers, and news magazines about five different issues prominent in 1987 and 1988: the 1987 stock market crash, AIDS, drugs, the Strategic Defense Initiative (SDI), and political change in South Africa.[61] Conceding that people who rely on television for news score lower on political knowledge tests than people who rely on print media, they argued that this was because those who knew more tended to select the print media in the first place. In a series of experiments that presented the same information via all three media, the researchers found that television was actually *more* successful in communicating abstract and distant political issues (SDI and South Africa), whereas the print media did better on the stock market crash, drugs, and AIDS.[62] The researchers also found that respondents learned differently from the media according to their cognitive skills, or ability to learn. People with high cognitive skills learned equally well from all three media, but those with average or low skills learned the most from television and the least from newspapers.[63] The authors' key finding was that "television was more successful in communicating information about topics that were of low salience [significance] to the audience, while print media were superior in conveying information about topics that had high salience."[64] Despite their finding that television news has value for topics of low salience and for people with limited cognitive skills, the point remains that people with high cognitive skills prefer newspapers. Perhaps they are searching for something that other people aren't.

THE POLITICAL
EFFECTS OF
THE MEDIA

Virtually all citizens must rely on the mass media for their political news. This fact endows the media with enormous potential to affect politics. To what extent do the media live up to this potential? In this section, we probe the media's effects on public opinion, the nation's political agenda, and political socialization.

Influencing Public Opinion

Americans overwhelmingly believe that the media exert a strong influence on their political institutions, and nearly nine out of ten Americans believe that the media strongly influence public opinion.[65] However, measuring the extent of media influence on public opinion is difficult.[66] Because few of us learn about political events except through the media, it could be argued that the media create public opinion simply by reporting events. Consider the dismantling of the Berlin Wall in 1989. Surely the photographs of joyous Berliners demolishing that symbol of oppression affected American public opinion about the reunification of Germany.

The media can have dramatic effects on particular events. Soon after the Lewinsky scandal broke in January 1998, President Clinton had to give his State of the Union Speech before Congress and a television audience of 50 million. He disappointed any viewers looking for dirt because he focused on his accomplishments (a robust economy, record low unemployment and inflation, and a virtually balanced budget) and on his proposals for child care, education, and health care. To counter his image as a philandering male, Clinton posed himself as an able president. And his strategy paid off, according to a poll of viewers. Only 33 percent had been "very confident" in his ability to carry out his duties prior to watching, but 48 percent were very confident afterward.[67] The February Gallup Poll found that 70 percent of the public approved of Clinton's job performance—the highest rating of his presidency.

Documenting general effects of the media on opinions about more general issues in the news is difficult. One study analyzed polls on eighty issues in foreign and domestic affairs at two points in time. For nearly half of these issues, public opinion changed over time by about six percentage points. The researchers compared these changes with policy positions taken by ten different sources of information, composed of commentators on television network news, including the president, members of the president's party, members of the opposition party, and members of interest groups. News commentators had the most dramatic effect. The authors of the study could link single television news commentaries to significant changes in public opinion (more than four percentage points).[68] A parallel study of the effects of newspapers on public opinion on fifty-one foreign and domestic issues found that a single story in a leading paper (the study used the *New York Times*) accounted for only two percentage points of opinion change toward the story's position, which fits with the public's lesser reliance on newspapers as a source of information.[69]

Television network coverage of the returns on the night of the 2000 presidential election may have profoundly affected public opinion toward both major candidates. In a report commissioned by cable news network CNN, three journalism experts concluded that the networks' unanimous declarations of George W. Bush's victory that night "created a premature impression" that he had defeated Al Gore before the Florida outcome had been decided. The impression carried through the postelection challenge: "Gore was perceived as the challenger and labeled a 'sore loser' for trying to steal the election."[70] All the networks studied their coverage and vowed to be more careful the next time.

Setting the Political Agenda

political agenda
A list of issues that need government attention.

Despite the media's potential for influencing public opinion, most scholars believe that the media's greatest influence on politics is found in their power to set the **political agenda**—a list of issues that people identify as needing government attention. Those who set the political agenda define which issues government decision makers should discuss and debate. Like a tree that falls in the forest without anyone around to hear it, an issue that does not get on the political agenda will not get any political attention.

The contrast between the media's coverage of the Kennedy and Clinton presidencies clearly demonstrates the media's agenda-setting power. Like that fallen tree, Kennedy's infidelities went unreported and unheard during his term, so they did not concern the public. Because the media trumpeted talk of Clinton's infidelities, the subject became a prime topic of popular discussion.

Apart from scandals, the media can manufacture concern about more commonplace issues. Crime is a good example. Figure 6.2 showed that in 1996 local television news covered crime twice as much as any other topic, continuing a long-standing pattern.[71] Given that fear of crime today is about the same as it was in the mid-1960s, are the media simply reflecting a constantly high crime rate?[72] Actually, crime rates have fallen in every major category (rape, burglary, robbery, assault, and murder) since the 1980s.[73] As one journalist said, "Crime coverage is not editorially driven; it's economically driven. It's the easiest, cheapest, laziest news to cover."[74] Moreover, crime provides good visuals. ("If it bleeds, it leads.") So despite the falling crime rate, the public encounters a continuing gusher of crime news and believes that crime has increased over time.[75]

One study found varying correlations between media coverage and what the public sees as "the most important problem facing this country today," depending on the type of event. Crises such as the Vietnam War, racial unrest, and energy shortages drew extensive media coverage, and each additional news magazine story per month generated an almost one percentage point increase in citations of the event as an important problem. But public opinion was even more responsive to media coverage of recurring problems such as inflation and unemployment. Although these events received less extensive coverage, each magazine story was linked with an increase in public concern of almost three percentage points.[76] What's more, evidence shows that television networks, at least, tend to give greater coverage to bad economic news (which is more dramatic) than to good economic news.[77] This tendency can have serious consequences for an incumbent president, whose popularity may fall with bad economic news.

The media's ability to influence public opinion by defining "the news" makes politicians eager to influence media coverage. Politicians attempt to affect not only public opinion but also the opinions of other political leaders.[78] The president receives a daily digest of news and opinion from many sources, and other top government leaders closely monitor the major national news sources. Even journalists work hard at following the news coverage in alternative sources. In a curious sense, the mass media have become a network for communicating among attentive elites, all trying to influence one another or to assess others' weaknesses and strengths. If the White House is under pressure on some policy matter, for example, it might supply a cabinet member or other high official for a fifteen-minute interview on the *NewsHour with Jim Lehrer*. Its goal in doing so would be to influence the thinking of other insiders, who faithfully watch the program, as much as to influence the opinions of the relatively small number of ordinary citizens who watch that particular newscast. Similarly, criticism of the administration's policies in one medium, especially from members of the president's own party, embolden others to be critical in their comments to other media. In this way, opposition spreads and may eventually be reflected in public opinion.[79]

Socialization

The mass media act as important agents of political socialization, at least as influential as those described in Chapter 5.[80] Young people who rarely follow the news by choice nevertheless acquire political values through the entertainment function of the broadcast media. Years ago, children learned from radio programs; now they learn from television. The average American child has watched about 19,000 hours of television by the end of high school.[81] What children learned from radio was quite different from what they are learning now, however. In the golden days of radio, youngsters listening to the popular radio drama *The Shadow* heard repeatedly that "crime does not pay . . . the *Shadow* knows!" In program after program—*Dragnet, Junior G-Men, Gangbusters*—the message never varied: criminals are bad; the police are good; criminals get caught and are severely punished for their crimes.

Needless to say, television today does not portray the criminal justice system in the same way, even in police dramas. Consider programs such as *Homicide* and *The X-Files,* which have portrayed police and FBI agents as killers. Other series, such as *Law and Order* and even *NYPD Blue,* sometimes portray a tainted criminal justice system and institutional corruption.[82] Perhaps years of television messages conveying distrust of law enforcement, disrespect for the criminal justice system, and violence shape impressionable youngsters. Certainly, one cannot easily argue that television's entertainment programs help prepare law-abiding citizens.

Some scholars argue that the most important effect of the mass media, particularly television, is to reinforce the hegemony, or dominance, of the existing culture and order. According to this argument, social control functions not through institutions of force (police, military, and prisons) but through social institutions, such as the media, that cause people to accept "the way things are."[83] By displaying the lifestyles of the rich and famous, for example, the media induce the public to accept the unlimited accumulation of private wealth. Similarly, the media socialize citizens to value "the American way," to be patriotic, to back their country, "right or wrong."

So the media play contradictory roles in the process of political socialization. On one hand, they promote popular support for government by joining in the celebration of national holidays, heroes' birthdays, political anniversaries, and civic accomplishments. On the other hand, the media erode public confidence by detailing politicians' extramarital affairs, airing investigative reports of possible malfeasance in office, and even showing television dramas about crooked cops.[84] Some critics contend that the media also give too much coverage to government opponents, especially to those who engage in unconventional opposition (see Chapter 7). However, strikes, sit-ins, violent confrontations, and hijackings draw large audiences and thus are newsworthy by the mass media's standards.

EVALUATING THE MEDIA IN GOVERNMENT

Are the media fair or biased in reporting the news? What contributions do the media make to democratic government? What effects do they have on the pursuit of freedom, order, and equality?

Is Reporting Biased?

News reports are presented as objective reality, yet critics of modern journalism contend that the news is filtered through the ideological biases of the media owners and editors (the gatekeepers) and of the reporters themselves.

The argument that news reports are politically biased has two sides. On one hand, news reporters are criticized for tilting their stories in a liberal direction, promoting social equality and undercutting social order. On the other hand, wealthy and conservative media owners are suspected of preserving inequalities and reinforcing the existing order by serving a relentless round of entertainment that numbs the public's capacity for critical analysis. Let's evaluate these arguments, looking first at reporters.

Although the picture is far from clear, available evidence seems to confirm the charge of liberal leanings among reporters in the major news media. In a 1996 survey of over 1000 journalists, 61 percent considered themselves "Democrat or liberal" or leaned that way, compared with only 15 percent who said they were or leaned toward the "Republican or conservative" side.[85] Television coverage in both 1992 and 1996 favored the Democrat Clinton over his Republican opponents, Bush and Dole. In both campaigns, Clinton received more balanced coverage (about 50 percent positive evaluations) than either Republican (only about 30 percent) on the major network news programs.[86]

To some extent, working journalists in the national and local media are at odds with their own editors, who tend to be more conservative. This was demonstrated in a recent study of news executives in national and local media.[87] The editors, in their function as gatekeepers, tend to tone down reporters' liberal leanings by editing their stories or not placing them well in the medium. Newspaper publishers are also free to endorse candidates, and almost all daily newspapers once openly endorsed one of the two major party candidates for president (usually the Republican candidate). The likelihood of a newspaper making an endorsement in the 2000 presidentential election was closely linked to the size of the newspaper's circulation. A survey of newspaper publishers revealed that over 95 percent of the newspapers with a circulation over 100,000 endorsed a candidate in the presidential race. Among newspapers with a circulation under 50,000, less than 65 percent made an endorsement. Newspapers that did endorse a candidate favored Republican George W. Bush more than two to one, although Democrat Al Gore was backed almost as often as Bush in newspapers with the largest circulations (see Figure 6.5).[88]

If media owners and their editors are indeed conservative supporters of the status quo, we might expect them to favor officeholders over challengers in elections, regardless of party. However, the evidence tends in the other direction. Let's compare 1980 (when Jimmy Carter, a liberal Democrat, was president and Ronald Reagan, a conservative Republican, was his challenger) with 1984 (when President Reagan faced Walter Mondale, a liberal Democrat). A comparison of television news in 1980 and 1984 found more negative coverage of the incumbent president both times.[89] The researcher concluded that virtually no *continuing* ideological or partisan bias exists on the evening news. Instead, what was seen as ideological or partisan bias in 1980 and 1984 was actually a bias against presidential *incumbents* and *front-runners* for the presidency.[90]

Can You Explain Why...
newspaper reporters and their editors may balance out ideological bias in the news?

figure

6.5

Newspaper Endorsements of Presidential Candidates in the 2000 Election

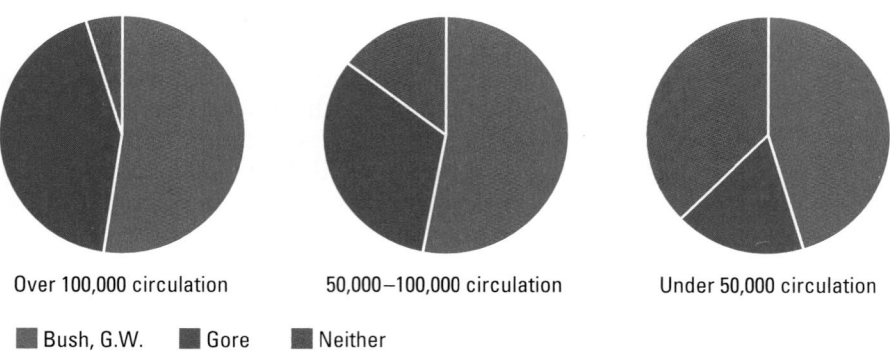

Over 100,000 circulation   50,000–100,000 circulation   Under 50,000 circulation

■ Bush, G.W.   ■ Gore   ■ Neither

In an E&P/TIPP survey of newspaper editors and publishers across the United States, Editor & Publisher *magazine asked, "Which candidate has your newspaper endorsed in the upcoming 2000 presidential election?" Large newspapers were much more likely to endorse a candidate in the national election than were small newspapers and, as in past years, the Republican candidate received the lion's share of the endorsements (3–1 in smaller papers, 5–1 in medium-size papers, and 5–4 in larger papers).*

Source: Greg Mitchell, "Bird in the Hand for Bush?" *Editor and Publisher,* 6 November 2000, pp. 24–27.

According to this reasoning, if journalists have any pronounced bias, it is against officeholding politicians. When an incumbent runs for reelection, journalists may feel a special responsibility to counteract his or her advantage by putting the opposite partisan spin on the news.[91] Thus, whether the media coverage of campaigns is seen as pro-Democratic (and therefore liberal) or pro-Republican (and therefore conservative) depends on which party is in office at the time.

A study of newspaper stories written in the last weeks of the 2000 presidential campaign showed that both major party candidates received negative coverage. Fifty-six percent of the stories written about the Democratic heir apparent, Al Gore, were negative. George W. Bush received negative coverage in 51 percent of the stories.[92]

Of course, the media affect voting behavior simply by reporting the daily news, which publicizes officeholders throughout the year. Noncampaign news coverage leads to greater incumbent name recognition at election time, particularly for members of Congress (see Chapter 11). This coverage effect is independent of any bias in reporting on campaigns. Moreover, bias in reporting is not limited to election campaigns, and different media may reflect different biases on political issues. A study of stories on nuclear energy over a period of ten years found that reports in the *New York Times* were well balanced between pronuclear and antinuclear sources. In contrast, the major news magazines and television news programs tended to favor antinuclear sources and to slant their stories against nuclear energy.[93]

Contributions to Democracy

As noted earlier, in a democracy communication must move in two directions: from government to citizens and from citizens to government. In fact, political communication in the United States seldom goes directly from government to citizens without passing through the media. The point is important because, as just discussed, news reporters tend to be highly critical of politicians; they consider it their job to search for inaccuracies in fact and weaknesses in argument. Some observers have characterized the news media and the government as adversaries—each mistrusting the other, locked in competition for popular favor while trying to get the record straight. To the extent that this is true, the media serve both the majoritarian and the pluralist models of democracy well by improving the quality of information transmitted to the people about their government.

The mass media transmit information in the opposite direction by reporting citizens' reactions to political events and government actions. The press has traditionally reflected public opinion (and often created it) in the process of defining the news and suggesting courses of government action. But the media's role in reflecting public opinion has become much more refined in the information age. Since the 1820s, newspapers conducted "straw polls" of dubious quality that matched their own partisan inclinations.[94] After commercial polls (such as the Gallup and Roper polls) were established in the 1930s, newspapers began to report more reliable readings of public opinion. By the 1960s, the media (both national and local) began to conduct their own surveys. In the 1970s, some news organizations acquired their own survey research divisions. Occasionally, print and electronic media have joined forces to conduct major national surveys.

The media now have the tools to do a better job of reporting mass opinion than ever before, and they use those tools extensively, practicing "precision journalism" with sophisticated data-collection and analysis techniques. The well-respected *New York Times*/CBS News Poll conducts surveys that are first aired on the *CBS Evening News* and then analyzed at length in the *Times*. Citizens and journalists alike complain that heavy reliance on polls during election campaigns causes the media to emphasize the horse race and slights the discussion of issues.[95] But the media also use their polling expertise for other purposes, such as gauging support for going to war and for balancing the budget. Although polls sometimes create opinions just by asking questions, their net effect has been to generate more accurate knowledge of public opinion and to report that knowledge back to the public. Although widespread knowledge of public opinion does not guarantee government responsiveness to popular demands, such knowledge is necessary if government is to function according to the majoritarian model of democracy.

Effects on Freedom, Order, and Equality

The media in the United States have played an important role in advancing equality, especially racial equality. Throughout the civil rights movement of the 1950s and 1960s, the media gave national coverage to conflict in the South as black children tried to attend white schools or civil rights workers were beaten and even killed in the effort to register black voters. Partly because of this media coverage, civil rights moved up on the political agenda, and coalitions formed in Congress to pass new laws promoting racial equality. Women's rights have also been advanced by the media, which have reported instances of blatant sexual discrimination exposed by groups working for sexual equality, such as the National Organization for Women (NOW). In general, the mass media offer spokespersons for any disadvantaged group an opportunity to state their case before a national audience and to work for a place on the political agenda. Increasingly, members of minority groups have entered the media business to serve the special interests and needs of their group (see Politics in a Changing America 6.1).

6.1   ¡Se habla Español!

Hispanics constitute the fastest growing segment of the major minority groups in the United States. Although they accounted for just under 12 percent of the population in 2000, the number of Hispanics is projected to rise over 20 percent by 2035.[1] At present, nearly half of all Hispanics do not speak English, and another 40 percent understand English but prefer to communicate in Spanish.[2] In an effort to tap this expected market of over 32 million, advertisers have increased their spending significantly in Hispanic markets. In 1997 alone, advertising spending in this market increased 17 percent, to $1.4 billion.[3] This increase in advertising revenues has sparked a growth in Spanish-language mass media in areas of the United States with heavy concentrations of Hispanics. This growth can be seen mainly in television and radio; Spanish-language newspapers have had problems.

Television: One major network dominates Hispanic television: Univision. The Univision Network is comprised of nineteen network-owned stations, thirty-three broadcast affiliates, and almost 1,100 cable affiliates. Univision also owns Galavision, a Spanish language cable network with 10 million subscribers.[4] The corporation announced plans in 2000 to purchase the thirteen stations owned by USA Networks, which will give it two stations in each of the top seven Hispanic markets in the United States.[5] The distant runner-up is the Telemundo Network, with eighteen stations, thirty-two affiliates, and 651 cable affiliates. Given the prospect for an expanding market, media entrepreneurs announced the formation of a third major Hispanic network, Azteca America, in 2000.[6] The new network will get a substantial amount of its program from TV Azteca of

Mexico. Univision relies more on foreign-produced Spanish-language entertainment programs, while Telemundo produces more domestic programming specifically designed for Hispanics in the United States. As yet, Hispanic television features relatively little news programming. A recent Ford Foundation study, however, reports that Hispanics are even more likely to get their news from television than the general U.S. population, for which television is already the most important news source.[7] So expect more news on Spanish-language television.

Radio: In several communities, Spanish floods the airwaves, sometimes even beating English-language stations in Arbitron Company ratings.[8] Although most of these stations feature entertainment in their programming, many also broadcast news, which is obtained from several networks: Cadena Radio Centro, UPI's Radio Noticias, the Spanish Information Service, and CNN's Radio Noticias. For example, CNN's Radio Noticias offers nearly six minutes of newscast at the top of each hour and separate regional reports for the eastern and western halves of the United States to some sixty stations in forty-three cities.[9]

Newspapers: The big story in Spanish-language newspapers is the battle between smaller Hispanic publishers, which have served local markets for years, and mainstream Anglo publishers seeking to enter the expanding Spanish-language market. Tito Duran, the president of the National Association of Hispanic Publishers, estimated the nationwide circulation of 329 Hispanic papers at about 10 million.[10] In the early 1990s, established metropolitan papers launched Spanish-language papers to compete for many of these readers. Examples included the Chicago Tribune Company, which started *Exito* in Miami and then published a sister paper in Chicago; the *Los Angeles Times' Nuestro Tiempo*; the *Fort-Worth Star-Telegram's La Estrella*; and the *Miami*

Herald's El Nuevo Herald. But *Nuestro Tiempo* was closed, *La Estrella* was scaled back, and *El Nuevo Herald* cut its staff. The problem seems to be that advertising is following the audience away from Spanish-language newspapers to television and radio.[11]

1. "Projections of the Resident Population by Race, Hispanic Origin, and Nativity: Middle Series, 2025 to 2045" (Washington, D.C.: Population Division, U.S. Census Bureau, 2000).
2. Jim Cooper, "Advertisers Rush into Growing Market," *Broadcasting and Cable*, 15 November 1993, p. 46.
3. Jami A. Fullerton, "Portrayal of Men and Women in U.S. Spanish-Language Television Commercials," *Journalism and Mass Communication Quarterly*, 77, 1 (Spring 2000), p. 128.
4. "Company Capsule: Univision Communications, Inc.," Hoover's Online <www.hoovers.com/co/capsule/2/0,2163,51512,00.html> December 21, 2000.
5. Christopher Stern, "Univision to Buy Diller TV Stations," *Washington Post*, 8 December 2000, p. E4.
6. "Telemundo Network Group, LLC: Perfil," corporate profile available at <www.telemundo.com/static/perfil.htm> 22 December 2000. Steve McClellan, "Room for *tres*?" *Broadcasting and Cable*, 4 December 2000, pp. 26–32.
7. Peter Viles, "Spanish Radio News: Is There Room for Another Network?" *Broadcasting and Cable*, 15 November 1993, pp. 42–43.
8. Tim Jones, "New Vision Likely for Channel 66," *Chicago Tribune*, 14 March 1994, Section 4, p. 1.
9. Ibid., p. 2.
10. M. L. Stein, "Boast of Success," *Editor & Publisher*, 12 February 1994, p. 13.
11. Allen R. Myerson, "Newspapers Cut Spanish-Language Publications," *New York Times*, 16 October 1995, p. C7.

New York Times v. *Sullivan*

Although the media are willing to encourage government action to promote equality at the cost of some personal freedom, they resist government attempts to infringe on freedom of the press to promote order.[96] A 1997 national survey commissioned by the *Chicago Tribune* and published on July 4 showed that the American public does not value freedom of speech and of the press as much as members of the media do. Nearly 60 percent of respondents favored censoring radio hosts who frequently refer to sex; 52 percent would prevent groups from advocating overthrowing the government; 50 percent would restrict material transmitted over the Internet; almost 50 percent would forbid militia or white supremacist groups to demonstrate in their community; and 27 percent actually agreed that the First Amendment goes too far in the rights it guarantees.[97] The *Tribune* responded with an editorial defending the First Amendment and its wording: "Congress shall make no law . . . abridging the freedom of speech, or the press."

The media's ability to report whatever they wish, whenever they wish certainly erodes efforts to maintain order. For example, sensational media coverage of terrorist acts gives terrorists the publicity they seek; portrayal of brutal killings and rapes on television encourages "copycat" crimes, committed "as seen on television"; and news stories about the burning of black churches in 1996 spawned "copycat" arsons. Freedom of the press is a noble value and one that has been important to democratic government. But we should not ignore the fact that democracies sometimes pay a price for pursuing it without qualification.

SUMMARY

The mass media transmit information to large, heterogeneous, and widely dispersed audiences through print and broadcasts. The mass media in the United States are privately owned and in business to make money, which they do mainly by selling space or air time to advertisers. Both print and electronic media determine which events are newsworthy largely on the basis of audience appeal. The rise of mass-circulation newspapers in the 1830s produced a politically independent press in the United States. In their aggressive competition for readers, those newspapers often engaged in sensational reporting, a charge sometimes leveled at today's media.

The broadcast media operate under technical, ownership, and content regulations imposed by the government; these tend to promote more even-handed treatment of political contests on radio and television than in newspapers and news magazines. The main function of the mass media is entertainment, but the media also perform the political functions of reporting news, interpreting news, influencing citizens' opinions, setting the political agenda, and socializing citizens about politics.

The major media maintain staffs of professional journalists in major cities around the world. Washington, D.C., hosts the biggest press corps in the world, but only a portion of those correspondents concentrate on the presidency. Because Congress is a more decentralized institution, it is covered in a more decentralized manner. What actually gets reported in the established media depends on the media's gatekeepers, the publishers and editors. Professional journalists follow rules for citing sources, and these also guide their reporting, but on the Internet and in talk radio, there are few rules concerning what is covered. We are entering an era in which the gatekeepers have less control over what poses as news, both in terms of what subjects are reported on and in terms of the veracity of the reports.

Although Americans today get more news from television than from newspapers, newspapers usually do a more thorough job of informing the public about politics. Despite heavy exposure to news in the print and electronic media, the ability of most people to retain much political information is shockingly low. The problem appears to be not in the media's ability to supply quality news coverage but in the lack of demand for it by the public. The media's most important effect on public opinion is in setting the country's political agenda. The role of the news media may be more important for affecting interactions among attentive policy elites than in influencing public opinion. The media play more subtle, contradictory roles in political socialization, both promoting and undermining certain political and cultural values.

Reporters from the national media tend to be more liberal than the public, as judged by their tendency to vote for Democratic candidates and by their own self-descriptions. Journalists' liberal leanings are checked somewhat by the conservative inclinations of their editors and publishers. However, if the media systematically demonstrate any pronounced bias in their news reporting, it is a bias against incumbents and front-runners, regardless of their party, rather than a bias in favor of liberal Democrats.

From the standpoint of majoritarian democracy, one of the most important roles of the media is to facilitate communication from the people to the government through the reporting of public opinion polls. The media zealously defend the freedom of the press, even to the point of encouraging disorder by granting extensive publicity to violent protests, terrorist acts, and other threats to order.

★ Selected Readings

Bennett, W. Lance. *News: The Politics of Illusion*, 3rd ed. New York: Longman, 1996. This is the third edition of a successful text that describes the news as being driven by economic interests and yet as an integral part of the political system as well.

Gerbner, George, Hamid Mowlana, and Herbert I. Schiller (eds.). *Invisible Crises: What Conglomerate Control of Media Means for America and the World*. Boulder, Colo.: Westview Press, 1996. A wide-ranging collection of studies concerning the concentration of media ownership; views the consequences of media concentration from the dark side.

Graber, Doris, Denis McQuail, and Pippa Norris (eds.). *The Politics of News, The News of Politics*. Washington, D.C.: CQ Press, 1998. Essays addressing the media–politics nexus from three perspectives: journalists, political actors, and the public voice. The volume also addresses the impact of new technologies.

Gunther, Richard, and Anthony Mughan (eds.). *Democracy and the Media: A Comparative Perspective*. Cambridge, UK: Cambridge University Press, 2000. A particularly cogent and detailed examination of the role played by the media in ten nations.

Lichter, S. Robert, and Richard E. Noyes. *Good Intentions Make Bad News: Why Americans Hate Campaign Journalism*. Lanham, Md.: Rowman & Littlefield, 1995. Argues that the "good intentions" of journalists to improve news coverage actually harm coverage. Contains numerous tables and graphs analyzing reporting content in the 1992 presidential campaign.

Page, Benjamin I. *Who Deliberates: Mass Media in Modern Democracy*. Chicago, Ill.: University of Chicago Press, 1996. Thoughtfully discusses and analyzes how the public "deliberates" through three specific case studies: the war with Iraq, the Los Angeles riots, and the failed nomination of Zoe Baird for attorney general.

Internet Exercises

1. *Like-mindedness on the Evening News?*

Does it really matter which network you watch to get your day's fill of national news? One way to find out is to access the Television News Archive at Vanderbilt University. The Archive describes itself as "the world's most available, extensive and complete archive of television news." Since 1968, the Archive has abstracted the evening newscasts of the major broadcast networks.

• Go to the Vanderbilt News Archive at **<tvnews. vanderbilt.edu/>** and follow the link to the site's collection of evening news abstracts. Browse the abstracts of the evening news broadcasts of ABC, CBS, CNN, and NBC for the week of May 10 through May 14, 1999.

• How does the news content provided on these four networks lend support to the argument that these major news outlets think alike when they put together their evening news programs? Is there some evidence of diversity in their presentations as well?

2. *"Anyone with a Modem . . ."*

Matt Drudge is perhaps the world's best known cyber-journalist. His Web site, *The Drudge Report*, reportedly receives thousands of hits per day, making it one of the most visited sources on the Internet for news and political information.

• Locate *The Drudge Report* at **<www.drudgereport. com/>,** and follow the link to a transcript of Matt Drudge's speech to the National Press Club. Read over the introductory remarks from National Press Club President Doug Harbrecht, and then the speech by Mr. Drudge. (In other words, you can stop reading when you get to the Q&A part of the talk.)

• What evidence do you find here that members of the traditional press corps and media find *The Drudge Report* to be a threat to the media as an institution? How is Mr. Drudge's approach to journalism more consistent with a majoritarian view of democracy than the mainstream media's, which Mr. Drudge would likely characterize as elitist?

chapter 7

Participation and Voting

★ **Democracy and Political Participation**

★ **Unconventional Participation**

Support for Unconventional Participation
The Effectiveness of Unconventional Participation
Unconventional Participation in America and the World

★ **Conventional Participation**

Supportive Behavior
Influencing Behavior
Conventional Participation in America

★ **Participating Through Voting**

Expansion of Suffrage
Voting on Policies
Voting for Candidates

★ **Explaining Political Participation**

Patterns of Participation over Time
The Standard Socioeconomic Explanation
Low Voter Turnout in America

★ **Participation and Freedom, Equality, and Order**

Participation and Freedom
Participation and Equality
Participation and Order

★ **Participation and the Models of Democracy**

Participation and Majoritarianism
Participation and Pluralism

THEY SEEMED LIKE ORDINARY FOLKS. That's how their suburban neighbors regarded the ten men and two women arrested in Phoenix, Arizona, on July 1, 1996. One worked in a doughnut shop. Another worked for the telephone company. Others painted houses or sold office equipment.[1] One had even run for political office (unsuccessfully). But to the arresting federal agents, they were the Viper Militia, a small, secret paramilitary organization charged with plotting to destroy several public buildings. Indeed, the agents found the suspects' homes stocked with an arsenal of weapons—in addition to the 140 guns, there were hand grenades, rocket launchers, gas masks, silencers, and homemade bombs.[2]

Although the Viper Militia represented the more extreme paramilitary groups in the United States, it was but one of many militia groups active in the 1990s. About two hundred militia units exist in Arizona alone, and hundreds more operate throughout the nation. They communicate through group media: newsletters, faxes, and the Internet.[3] In fact, militia activity on the Internet has stimulated the growth of anti-militia sites on the World Wide Web. One of the most prominent is "The Militia Watchdog." This site warns that activity on the Internet underestimates the militia movement, which relies heavily on newsletters, faxes, and videotapes. In addition, it lists scores of militia sites, including home pages for movements in dozens of states.[4]

Is involvement in a militia a form of political participation, or is it simply a form of recreation—playing war games in the woods? No doubt, some people are attracted to militias for fun and fellowship, but the militia movement also has a distinct political cast. It views the federal government as a threat to personal freedom. (This view of Washington was also held during the Reagan and Bush administrations, when many militias were formed.) Militia members even see conspiracies against freedom coming from the United Nations (which they think is planning to invade the United States), the Council of Foreign Relations (an academically oriented institution that publishes *Foreign Affairs*, a respected journal on international politics), and the Trilateral Commission (a group, headed by David Rockefeller, consisting of business, labor, academic, and media leaders from America, Europe, and Japan). The militia movement is deadly serious in its pledges to defend its view of freedom. Its exaltation of weapons is apparent in the "Minuteman Prayer," seen on a militia Web site:

194

Michigan Gothic

In the 1930s, Grant Wood's famous painting, "American Gothic," portrayed the austere, severe life of a farm couple in rural America. In the 1990s, a photographer signaled the changing times with this picture of an armed couple in the Michigan militia.

God grant me the serenity to accept the things I cannot change; the courage to change the things I can; and the superior firepower to make the difference.[5]

Although most people think of political participation primarily in terms of voting, there are other forms of political activity that are more robust than voting. Have militia members exceeded the boundaries of political participation, or are they simply defending freedom, in the tradition of the minutemen of the American Revolution? How politically active are Americans in general? How do they compare with citizens of other countries? How much and what kind of participation is necessary to sustain the pluralist and majoritarian models of democracy?

In this chapter, we try to answer these and other important questions about popular participation in government. We begin by studying participation in democratic government, distinguishing between conventional and unconventional participation. Then we evaluate the nature and extent of both types of participation in American politics. Next, we study the expansion of voting rights and voting as the major mechanism for mass participation in politics. Finally, we examine the extent to which the various forms of political participation serve the values of freedom, equality, and order and the majoritarian and pluralist models of democracy.

DEMOCRACY AND POLITICAL PARTICIPATION

Government ought to be run by the people. That is the democratic ideal in a nutshell. But how much and what kind of citizen participation is necessary for democratic government? Neither political theorists nor politicians, neither idealists nor realists, can agree on an answer. Champions of direct democracy believe that if citizens do not participate directly in government affairs, making government decisions themselves, they should give up all pretense of living in a democracy. More practical observers contend that people can govern indirectly, through their elected representatives. And they maintain that choosing leaders through elections—formal procedures for voting—is the only workable approach to democracy in a large, complex nation.

Elections are a necessary condition of democracy, but they do not guarantee democratic government. Before the collapse of communism, the former Soviet Union regularly held elections in which more than 90 percent of the electorate turned out to vote, but the Soviet Union certainly did not function as a democracy because there was only one party. Both the majoritarian and pluralist models of democracy rely on voting to varying degrees, but both models expect citizens to participate in politics in other ways. For example, they expect citizens to discuss politics, to form interest groups, to contact public officials, to campaign for political parties, to run for office, and even to protest government decisions.

political participation
Actions of private citizens by which they seek to influence or support government and politics.

We define **political participation** as "those actions of private citizens by which they seek to influence or to support government and politics."[6] This definition embraces both conventional and unconventional forms of political participation. In plain language, *conventional behavior* is behavior that is acceptable to the dominant culture in a given situation. Wearing a swimsuit at the beach is conventional; wearing one at a formal dance is not. Displaying campaign posters in front yards is conventional; spray-painting political slogans on buildings is not.

At times, figuring out whether a particular political act is conventional or unconventional is difficult. We find the following distinction useful in analyzing political participation:

conventional participation
Relatively routine political behavior that uses institutional channels and is acceptable to the dominant culture.

- **Conventional participation** is relatively routine behavior that uses the established institutions of representative government, especially campaigning for candidates and voting in elections.

unconventional participation
Relatively uncommon political behavior that challenges or defies established institutions and dominant norms.

- **Unconventional participation** is relatively uncommon behavior that challenges or defies established institutions or the dominant culture (and thus is personally stressful to participants and their opponents).

Voting and writing letters to public officials are examples of conventional political participation; staging sit-down strikes in public buildings and chanting slogans outside officials' windows are examples of unconventional participation. Certainly training with a militia is unconventional; the question is whether the activity is political or not. Experts contend that group participation is often a politicizing experience, developing skills in the individual that transfer to politics.[7] Political demonstrations can be conventional (carrying signs outside an abortion clinic) or unconventional (linking arms to prevent entrance). Various forms of unconventional participation are often used by powerless groups to gain political benefits while also working within the system.[8] Militia groups, however, blatantly reject the system.

Voting and other methods of conventional participation are important to democratic government. So are unconventional forms of participation. Let us look at both kinds of political participation in the United States.

UNCONVENTIONAL
PARTICIPATION

On Sunday, March 7, 1965, a group of about six hundred people attempted to march fifty miles from Selma, Alabama, to the state capitol at Montgomery. The marchers were demonstrating in favor of voting rights for blacks. (At the time, Selma had fewer than five hundred registered black voters, out of fifteen thousand who were eligible.)[9] Alabama governor George Wallace declared the march illegal and sent state troopers to stop it. The two groups met at the Edmund Pettus Bridge over the Alabama River at the edge of Selma. The peaceful marchers were disrupted and beaten by state troopers and deputy sheriffs—some on horseback—using clubs, bullwhips, and tear gas. The day became known as Bloody Sunday.

The march from Selma was a form of unconventional political participation. Marching fifty miles in a political protest is certainly not common; moreover, the march challenged the existing institutions that prevented blacks from voting. From the beginning, the marchers knew they were putting themselves in a dangerous situation, that they certainly would be taunted by whites along the way and could be physically hurt as well. But they had been prevented from participating conventionally—voting in elections—for many decades, and they chose this unconventional method to dramatize their cause.

The march ended in violence because Governor Wallace would not allow even this peaceful mode of unconventional expression. In contrast to some later demonstrations against the Vietnam War, this civil rights march posed no threat of violence. The brutal response to the marchers helped the rest of the nation understand the seriousness of the civil rights problem in the South. Unconventional participation is stressful and occasionally violent, but sometimes it is worth the risk.

Support for Unconventional Participation

Unconventional political participation has a long history in the United States. The Boston Tea Party of 1773, in which American colonists dumped three cargoes of British tea into Boston Harbor, was only the first in a long line of violent protests against British rule that eventually led to revolution. The minutemen who fought at Lexington in 1775 are also part of our proud history. Yet we know less about unconventional than conventional participation. The reasons are twofold: first, since it is easier to collect data on conventional practices, they are studied more frequently. Second, political scientists are simply biased toward institutionalized, or conventional, politics. In fact, some basic works on political participation explicitly exclude any behavior that is "outside the system."[10] One major study of unconventional political action asked people whether they had engaged in or approved of five types of political participation other than voting.[11] As shown in Figure 7.1, of the five activities, only signing petitions was clearly regarded as conventional, in the sense that the behavior was widely practiced.

The conventionality of two other forms of behavior was questionable. Only 15 percent had ever attended a demonstration, whereas 41 percent said that they would never demonstrate. The marchers in Selma, although peaceful, were surely demonstrating against the established order. If we

figure

7.1   What Americans Think Is Unconventional Political Behavior

A survey presented Americans with five different forms of political participation outside the electoral process and asked whether they "have done," "might do," or "would never do" any of them. The respondents disapproved of two forms overwhelmingly. Only signing petitions was widely done and rarely ruled out. Even attending demonstrations (a right guaranteed in the Constitution) was disapproved of by 44 percent of the respondents. Boycotting products was less objectionable and more widely practiced. According to this test, attending demonstrations and boycotting products are only marginally conventional forms of political participation. Joining strikes and occupying buildings are clearly unconventional activities for most Americans.

Source: 1990–91 World Values Survey. Data for the United States are available from the Inter-University Consortium for Political and Social Research. The weighted sample size was 1,837.

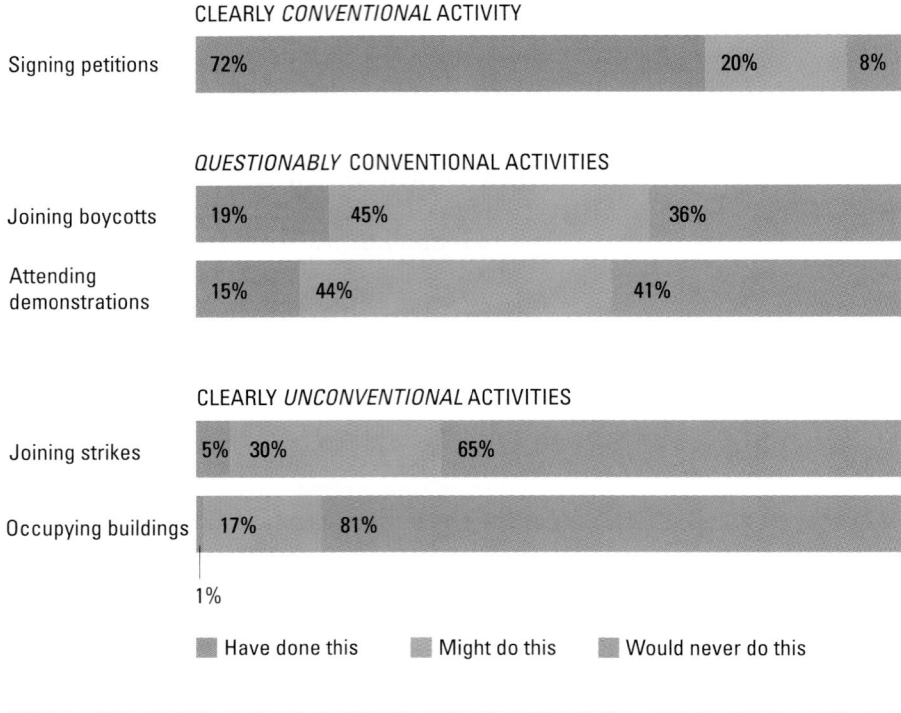

CLEARLY *CONVENTIONAL* ACTIVITY

Signing petitions   72%   20%   8%

QUESTIONABLY CONVENTIONAL ACTIVITIES

Joining boycotts   19%   45%   36%

Attending demonstrations   15%   44%   41%

CLEARLY *UNCONVENTIONAL* ACTIVITIES

Joining strikes   5%   30%   65%

Occupying buildings   17%   81%

1%

■ Have done this   ■ Might do this   ■ Would never do this

measure conventionality in terms of the proportion of people who disapprove of an action, we might argue that all demonstrations border on the unconventional. The same reasoning could be applied to boycotting products—for example, refusing to buy lettuce or grapes picked by nonunion farm workers. Demonstrations and boycotts are problem cases in deciding what is and is not conventional political participation.

The other two political activities listed in Figure 7.1 are clearly unconventional. In fact, when political activities interfere with people's daily lives (occupying buildings, for example), disapproval is nearly universal. When protesters demonstrating against the Vietnam War disrupted the 1968 Democratic National Convention in Chicago, they were clubbed by the city's police. Although the national television audience saw graphic footage of the confrontations and heard reporters' criticisms of the police's behavior, most viewers condemned the demonstrators, not the police.

The Effectiveness of Unconventional Participation

Vociferous antiabortion protests have discouraged many doctors from performing abortions, but they have not led to outlawing abortions. Does unconventional participation ever work (even when it provokes violence)? Yes. Antiwar protesters helped convince President Lyndon Johnson not to

Antiwar Protest, 1968

In August 1968, thousands of youthful antiwar protesters gathered in Chicago, where the Democrats were holding their national convention. Protests against the war had already forced President Lyndon Johnson not to seek reelection. Mayor Richard J. Daley vowed that the protesters would not disturb the impending nomination of Hubert Humphrey, Johnson's vice president. Daley's police kept the youths from demonstrating at the convention, but the resulting violence did not help Humphrey, who lost to Richard Nixon in an extremely close election. When the Democratic convention returned to Chicago in 1996, the new Mayor Daley (Richard M., the former mayor's son) faced a different situation and hosted a relatively peaceful convention.

Disturbances on College and University Campuses, 1967–1969

direct action
Unconventional participation that involves assembling crowds to confront businesses and local governments to demand a hearing.

Race Riots, 1965–1968

seek reelection in 1968, and they heightened public concern about U.S. participation in the Vietnam War. American college students who disrupted campuses in the late 1960s and early 1970s helped end the military draft in 1973, and although it was not one of their stated goals, they sped passage of the Twenty-sixth Amendment, which lowered the voting age to eighteen.

The unconventional activities of civil rights workers also produced notable successes. Dr. Martin Luther King, Jr., led the 1955 Montgomery bus boycott (prompted by Rosa Parks's refusal to surrender her seat to a white man), which sparked the civil rights movement. He used **direct action** to challenge specific cases of discrimination, assembling crowds to confront businesses and local governments and demanding equal treatment in public accommodations and government. The civil rights movement organized more than one thousand such newsworthy demonstrations nationwide—387 in 1965 alone.[12] And like the march in Selma, many of these protests provoked violent confrontations between whites and blacks.

Denied the usual opportunities for conventional political participation, minorities used unconventional politics to pressure Congress to pass a series of civil rights laws in 1957, 1960, 1964, and 1968—each one in some way extending national protection against discrimination by reason of race, color, religion, or national origin. (The 1964 act also prohibited discrimination in employment on the basis of sex.)

In addition, the Voting Rights Act of 1965 placed some state electoral procedures under federal supervision, protecting the registration of black voters and increasing the rate of black voter turnout (especially in the South, where much of the violence occurred). Black protest activity—both violent and nonviolent—has also been credited with increased welfare support for blacks in the South.[13] The civil rights movement showed that

THE BOONDOCKS   **by AARON MCGRUDER**

social change can occur, even when it faces violent opposition at first. In 1970, fewer than 1,500 blacks served as elected officials in the United States. In 2000, the number was more than 8,800.[14] However, racial divisions still persist across the nation.

Although direct political action and the politics of confrontation can work, using them requires a special kind of commitment. Studies show that direct action appeals most to those who both (1) distrust the political system and (2) have a strong sense of political efficacy—the feeling that they can do something to affect political decisions.[15] Whether this combination of attitudes produces behavior that challenges the system depends on the extent of organized group activity. The civil rights movement of the 1960s was backed by numerous organizations across the nation.

The decision to use unconventional behavior also depends on the extent to which individuals develop a group consciousness—identification with their group and awareness of its position in society, its objectives, and its intended course of action.[16] These characteristics were present among blacks and young people in the mid-1960s and are strongly present today among blacks and to a lesser degree among women. Indeed, some researchers contend that black consciousness has heightened both African Americans' distrust of the political system and their sense of individual efficacy, generating more political participation by poor blacks than by poor whites.[17] The National Organization for Women (NOW) and other women's groups have also heightened women's group consciousness, which may have contributed to their increased participation in politics, in both conventional and unconventional ways. Today, some white Christian males find a sense of belonging in local militias.

Unconventional Participation in America and the World

Although most Americans disapprove of using certain forms of participation to protest government policies, U.S. citizens are about as likely to take direct action in politics as citizens of European democracies. Surveys in 1990 and 1991 revealed that Americans claim to have participated in unconventional actions, such as demonstrations, boycotts, strikes, and occupying buildings, as much as or more than do British, German, and French citizens.[18] Contrary to the popular view that Americans are apathetic about politics, they are more likely to engage in political protests of various sorts than are citizens in other democratic countries.[19]

Ousting a President

In October 2000 a protester attacks the mansion gate of Philippine President Joseph Estrada, accused of robbing the public treasury for personal gain while failing to provide housing for the urban poor. In January 2001 he was arrested and succeeded by his vice-president, Gloria Macapagal-Arroyo.

This doesn't mean that citizens of other countries do not engage in unconventional participation. In fact, in recent years a truly international form of unconventional participation has developed and involves citizens of many countries coming together to protest the effects of globalization and the power of international institutions (see Politics in a Changing World 7.1). Some of the biggest mass protests of the past few years have been of this type.

Is something wrong with our political system if citizens resort to unconventional—and widely disapproved of—methods of political participation? To answer this question, we must first learn how much Americans use conventional methods of participation.

CONVENTIONAL PARTICIPATION

A practical test of the democratic nature of any government is whether citizens can affect its policies by acting through its institutions—meeting with public officials, supporting candidates, voting in elections. If people must operate outside government institutions to influence policymaking—as civil rights workers had to do in the South—the system is not democratic. Citizens should not have to risk their life and property to participate in politics, and they should not have to take direct action to force the government to hear their views. The objective of democratic institutions is to make political participation conventional—to allow ordinary citizens to engage in relatively routine, nonthreatening behavior to get the government to heed their opinions, interests, and needs.

In a democracy, for a group to gather at a statehouse or city hall to dramatize its position on an issue—say, a tax increase—is not unusual. Such a demonstration is a form of conventional participation. The group is not

★ **politics in a changing** world

7.1

International Debt and International Protest

More than one in five people in the world live in abject poverty today. In some parts of the world, such as sub-Saharan Africa, more than 40 percent of the population lives on less than $1 (U.S.) a day. The World Bank and the International Monetary Fund (IMF) are international institutions that play a key role in financing development throughout the world. By providing loans and economic advice to the governments of less developed nations, they have enabled some countries to build their industrial infrastructure and modernize their agricultural production.

However, these institutions are not without controversy. In recent years, critics have built an international protest movement to oppose the work of these institutions, charging that the loans come with austerity conditions attached that benefit lending nations at the expense of the developing nations. Because the decision-making process at the World Bank and the IMF is conducted behind closed doors, the public has little if any input into their operating practices. This secrecy has led opponents to pursue unconventional tactics, such as mass demonstrations.

When the IMF and the World Bank met in Washington, D.C., in April 2000, tens of thousands of protestors from around the globe converged on the U.S. capital in an attempt to shut down the meetings. A similar group had brought downtown Seattle to a standstill during the fall meetings of the World Trade Organization (WTO) in 1999. The protestors in both cities were a huge (though loosely formed) coalition of self-described anarchists, environmentalists, leftists, reformers, and poverty activists.

Although each group seemed to have its own emphasis and concern in joining the protests, they were spurred to unconventional participation by their inability to influence decisions through conventional means. As one protestor explained in an op-ed piece for the *Washington Post*, "Just as past revolutions have fought for political democracy, this movement aims to democratize economic decision-making at all levels so that the people who are most affected by economic policies have a voice in designing them."

Large-scale protests and demonstrations are much more common in Washington, D.C., than in Seattle, and the Washington police began preparing for the spring meetings of the IMF soon after the WTO debacle in Seattle. The protestors were unable to prevent the IMF from meeting, and the police arrested nearly thirteen hundred demonstrators during the three-day demonstration. Still, the protestors did achieve some of their goals. The demonstrations disrupted business in a significant part of downtown Washington, raised public awareness of the debate over IMF policies, and emboldened a new generation of activists in the United States and abroad.

Sources: "What on Earth? Outlook: Cloudy," *Washington Post,* 15 April 2000, p. A14; David Montgomery, "Demonstrators Are United by Zeal for 'Global Justice,'" *Washington Post,* 16 April 2000, p. A28; Juliette Beck, "Why We Are Protesting," *Washington Post,* 16 April 2000, p. B7; David Montgomery, "Protests End with Voluntary Arrests," *Washington Post,* 18 April 2000, p. A1.

powerless, and its members are not risking their personal safety by demonstrating. But violence can erupt between opposing groups demonstrating in a political setting, such as between pro-life and pro-choice groups. Circumstances, then, often determine whether organized protest is or is not conventional. In general, the less that the participants anticipate a threat, the more likely it is that the protest will be conventional.

Conventional political behaviors fall into two major categories: actions that show support for government policies and those that try to change or *influence* policies.

Supportive Behavior

supportive behavior
Actions that express allegiance to government and country.

Supportive behaviors are actions that express allegiance to country and government. When we recite the Pledge of Allegiance or fly the American flag on holidays, we are showing support for the country and, by implication, its political system. Such ceremonial activities usually require little effort, knowledge, or personal courage; that is, they demand little initiative on the part of the citizen. The simple act of turning out to vote is in itself a show of support for the political system. Other supportive behaviors—serving as an election judge in a nonpartisan election or organizing a holiday parade—demand greater initiative.

At times, people's perception of patriotism moves them to cross the line between conventional and unconventional behavior. In their eagerness to support the American system, they break up a meeting or disrupt a rally of a group they believe is radical or somehow "un-American." Radical groups may threaten the political system with wrenching change, but superpatriots pose their own threat. Their misguided excess of allegiance denies nonviolent means of dissent to others.[20]

Influencing Behavior

influencing behavior
Behavior that seeks to modify or reverse government policy to serve political interests.

Citizens use **influencing behaviors** to modify or even reverse government policy to serve political interests. Some forms of influencing behavior seek particular benefits from government; other forms have broad policy objectives.

Particular Benefits.   Some citizens try to influence government to obtain benefits for themselves, their immediate families, or close friends. For example, citizens might pressure their alderman to rebuild the curbs on their street or vote against an increase in school taxes, especially if they have no children. Serving one's self-interest through the voting process is certainly acceptable to democratic theory. Each individual has only one vote, and no single voter can wangle particular benefits from government through voting unless a majority of the voters agree.

Political actions that require considerable knowledge and initiative are another story. Individuals or small groups who influence government officials to advance their self-interest—for instance, to obtain a lucrative government contract—may secretly benefit without others knowing. Those who quietly obtain particular benefits from government pose a serious challenge to a democracy. Pluralist theory holds that groups ought to be

able to make government respond to their special problems and needs. On the other hand, majoritarian theory holds that government should not do what a majority does not want it to do. A majority of citizens might very well not want the government to do what any particular person or group seeks, if it is costly to other citizens.

Citizens often ask for special services from local government. Such requests may range from contacting the city forestry department to remove a dead tree in front of a house to calling the county animal control center to deal with a vicious dog in the neighborhood. Studies of such "contacting behavior" find that it tends not to be empirically related to other forms of political activity. In other words, people who complain to city hall do not necessarily vote. Contacting behavior is related to socioeconomic status: people of higher socioeconomic status are more likely to contact public officials.[21]

Americans demand much more of their local government than of the national government. Although many people value self-reliance and individualism in national politics, most people expect local government to solve a wide range of social problems. A study of residents of Kansas City, Missouri, found that more than 90 percent thought the city had a responsibility to provide services in thirteen areas, including maintaining parks, setting standards for new home construction, demolishing vacant and unsafe buildings, ensuring that property owners clean up trash and weeds, and providing bus service. The researcher noted that "it is difficult to imagine a set of federal government activities about which there would [be] more consensus."[22] Citizens can also mobilize against a project. Dubbed the "not in my back yard," or NIMBY, phenomenon, such a mobilization occurs when citizens pressure local officials to stop undesired projects from being located near their homes.

Finally, contributing money to a candidate's campaign is another form of influencing behavior. Here, too, the objective can be particular or broad benefits, although determining which is which can sometimes be difficult. For example, as discussed in Chapter 9, national law limits the amount of money that an individual or organization can contribute directly to a candidate's campaign for president, but there is no limit on the amount that can be given to either national party for "party-building" purposes.

Several points emerge from this review of "particularized" forms of political participation. First, approaching government to serve one's particular interests is consistent with democratic theory because it encourages participation from an active citizenry. Second, particularized contact may be a unique form of participation, not necessarily related to other forms of participation such as voting. Third, such participation tends to be used more by citizens who are advantaged in terms of knowledge and resources. Fourth, particularized participation may serve private interests to the detriment of the majority.

Broad Policy Objectives. We come now to what many scholars have in mind when they talk about political participation: activities that influence the selection of government personnel and policies. Here, too, we find behaviors that require little initiative (such as voting) and others that require high initiative (attending political meetings, persuading others how to vote).

Even voting intended to influence government policies is a low-initiative activity. Such "policy voting" differs from voting to show support or to gain special benefits in its broader influence on the community or society. Obviously, this distinction is not sharp: citizens vote for several reasons—a mix of allegiance, particularized benefits, and policy concerns. In addition to policy voting, many other low-initiative forms of conventional participation—wearing a campaign button, watching a party convention on television, posting a bumper sticker—are also connected with elections. In the next section, we focus on elections as a mechanism for participation. For now, we simply note that voting to influence policy is usually a low-initiative activity. As we discuss later, it actually requires more initiative to *register* to vote in the United States than to cast a vote on election day. With a computer, it is even easier to e-mail members of Congress than to vote.

Other types of participation to affect broad policies require high initiative. Running for office requires the most (see Chapter 9). Some high-initiative activities, such as attending party meetings and working in campaigns, are associated with the electoral process; others, such as attending legislative hearings and writing letters to Congress, are not. Although many nonelectoral activities involve making personal contact, their objective is often to obtain government benefits for some group of people—farmers, the unemployed, children, oil producers. In fact, studies of citizen contacts in the United States show that about two-thirds deal with broad social issues and only one-third are for private gain.[23]

Few people realize that using the court system is a form of political participation, a way for citizens to press for their rights in a democratic society. Although most people use the courts to serve their particular interests, some also use them, as we discuss shortly, to meet broad objectives. Going to court demands high personal initiative.[24] It also requires knowledge of the law or the financial resources to afford a lawyer.

class-action suit
A legal action brought by a person or group on behalf of a number of people in similar circumstances.

People use the courts for both personal benefit and broad policy objectives. A person or group can bring **class action suits** on behalf of other people in similar circumstances. Lawyers for the National Association for the Advancement of Colored People pioneered this form of litigation in the famous school desegregation case *Brown* v. *Board of Education* (1954).[25] They succeeded in getting the Supreme Court to outlaw segregation in public schools, not just for Linda Brown, who brought the suit in Topeka, Kansas, but for all others "similarly situated"—that is, for all other black students who wanted to attend desegregated schools. Participation through the courts is usually beyond the means of individual citizens, but it has proved effective for organized groups, especially those who have been unable to gain their objectives through Congress or the executive branch.

Individual citizens can also try to influence policies at the national level by participating directly in the legislative process. One way is to attend congressional hearings, which are open to the public and are occasionally held outside Washington. Especially since the end of World War II, the national government has sought to increase citizen involvement in creating regulations and laws by making information on government activities available to interested parties. For example, government agencies are required to publish all proposed and approved regulations in the daily *Federal Register* and to make government documents available to citizens on request.

Conventional Participation in America

You may know someone who has testified at a congressional or administrative hearing, but the odds are that you do not. Such participation is high-initiative behavior. Relatively few people—only those with high stakes in the outcome of a decision—are willing to participate in this way. How often do Americans contact government officials and engage in other forms of conventional political participation, compared with citizens in other countries?

The most common political behavior reported in a study of five countries was voting for candidates (see Compared with What? 7.1). On one hand, Americans are less likely to vote than are citizens in the other four countries studied. On the other hand, Americans are as likely (or substantially more likely) than those others to engage in all other forms of conventional political participation. As we have seen, the same pattern holds true for unconventional behaviors. Americans, then, are more apt to engage in nearly all forms of unconventional and conventional political participation, except voting.

Other researchers noted this paradox and wrote, "If, for example, we concentrate our attention on national elections we will find that the United States is the least participatory of [all] five nations." But looking at the other indicators, they found that "political apathy, by a wide margin, is lowest in the United States. Interestingly, the high levels of overall involvement reflect a rather balanced contribution of both . . . conventional and unconventional politics."[26] Clearly, low voter turnout in the United States constitutes a puzzle, to which we will return.

Balloting, Bali-Style ★

A polling station in Papua New Guinea, a member nation of the British Commonwealth. In the June 1997 general election for 109 members of parliament, there was an average of more than twenty candidates for each seat. Voters returned thirteen parties to parliament, the largest winning only sixteen seats. Forty members had no party affiliation.

Sources: Photo appeared in the *Chicago Tribune,* 17 June 1997, p. 13. Information on the election is from the Klapstan Press <www.klipsan. com/970422en.htm> and GeoCities Web sites <www.geocities.com/ ~derksen/election/country/pp.htm>.

PARTICIPATING THROUGH VOTING

The heart of democratic government lies in the electoral process. Whether a country holds elections—and if so, what kind—constitutes the critical difference between democratic and nondemocratic governments. Elections institutionalize mass participation in democratic government according to the three normative principles of procedural democracy discussed in Chapter 2: electoral rules specify *who* is allowed to vote, *how much* each person's vote counts, and *how many* votes are needed to win.

Again, elections are formal procedures for making group decisions. *Voting* is the act individuals engage in when they choose among alternatives in an election. **Suffrage** and **franchise** both mean the right to vote. By formalizing political participation through rules for suffrage and for counting ballots, electoral systems allow large numbers of people, who individually have little political power, to wield great power. Electoral systems decide collectively who governs and, in some instances, what government should do.

The simple act of holding elections is less important than the specific rules and circumstances that govern voting. According to democratic theory, everyone should be able to vote. In practice, however, no nation grants universal suffrage. All countries have age requirements for voting, and all disqualify some inhabitants on various grounds: lack of citizenship, criminal record, mental incompetence, and so forth. What is the record of enfranchisement in the United States?

suffrage
The right to vote. Also called the franchise.

franchise
The right to vote. Also called suffrage.

Expansion of Suffrage

The United States was the first country to provide for general elections of representatives through "mass" suffrage, but the franchise was far from universal. When the Constitution was framed, the idea of full adult suffrage

Can You Explain Why...
the eligibility for voting in national elections varied greatly by state in early elections?

★ **compared with what?**

7.1   Conventional Political Participation

A survey of respondents in five democratic industrialized nations found that Americans are far more likely than citizens in the other countries to engage in various forms of conventional political behavior—except voting. The findings clearly contradict the idea that Americans are politically apathetic. Citizens of the United States simply do not vote as much as other citizens in national elections, which says more about the nature of U.S. elections than about American citizens, who are active politically in other ways.

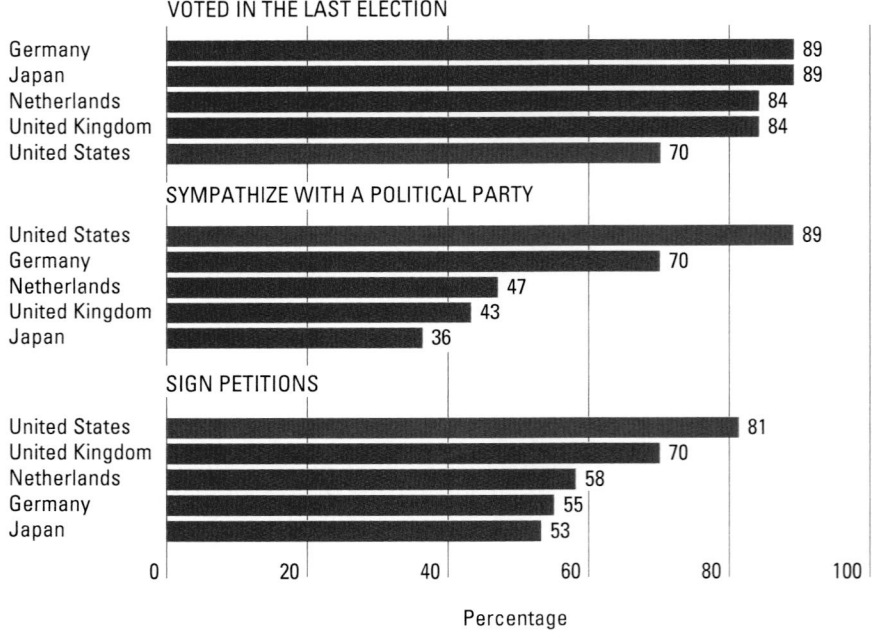

VOTED IN THE LAST ELECTION

Country	Percentage
Germany	89
Japan	89
Netherlands	84
United Kingdom	84
United States	70

SYMPATHIZE WITH A POLITICAL PARTY

Country	Percentage
United States	89
Germany	70
Netherlands	47
United Kingdom	43
Japan	36

SIGN PETITIONS

Country	Percentage
United States	81
United Kingdom	70
Netherlands	58
Germany	55
Japan	53

Percentage

was too radical to consider seriously. Instead, the framers left the issue of enfranchisement to the states, stipulating only that individuals who could vote for "the most numerous Branch of the State Legislature" could also vote for their representatives to the U.S. Congress (Article I, Section 2).

Initially, most states established taxpaying or property-holding requirements for voting. Virginia, for example, required ownership of twenty-five acres of settled land or five hundred acres of unsettled land. The original thirteen states began to lift such requirements after 1800. Expansion of the franchise accelerated after 1815, with the admission of new "western" states (Indiana, Illinois, Alabama), where land was more plentiful and widely owned. By the 1850s, the states had eliminated almost all

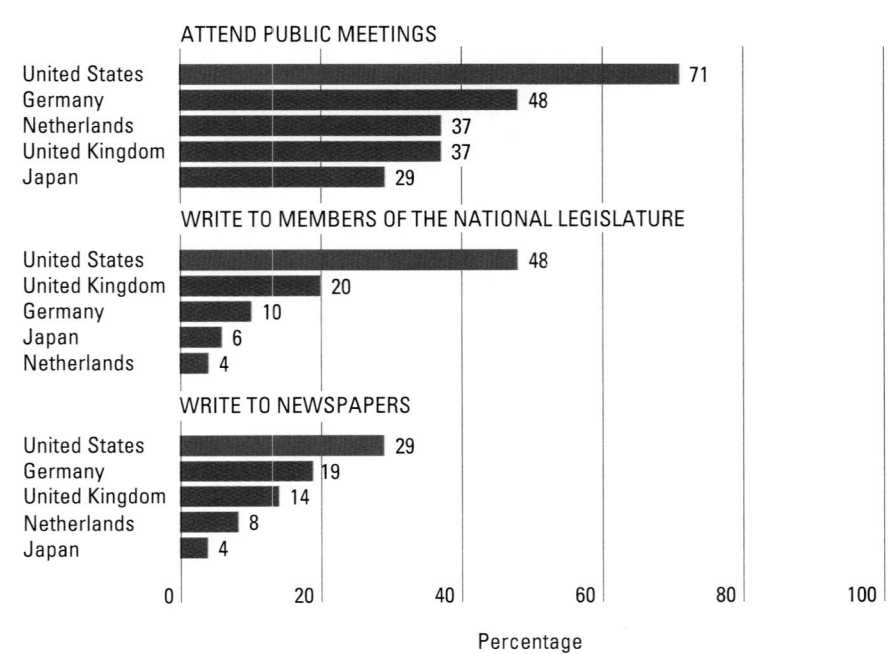

ATTEND PUBLIC MEETINGS

United States — 71
Germany — 48
Netherlands — 37
United Kingdom — 37
Japan — 29

WRITE TO MEMBERS OF THE NATIONAL LEGISLATURE

United States — 48
United Kingdom — 20
Germany — 10
Japan — 6
Netherlands — 4

WRITE TO NEWSPAPERS

United States — 29
Germany — 19
United Kingdom — 14
Netherlands — 8
Japan — 4

Percentage

Source: International Social Justice Project, a collaborative international research effort. The data for this chart, which were kindly provided by Antal Örkény at Eötvös Loránd University (ELTE) in Hungary, came from national surveys conducted in 1991 that were supported in whole or in part by the Institute for Research, University of Michigan; the Economic and Social Research Council (United Kingdom); the Deutsche Forschungsgemeinschaft; the Institute of Social Science, Chuo University (Japan); and the Dutch Ministry of Social Affairs. (The voter turnout figures for the Netherlands came from election reports.)

taxpaying and property-holding requirements, thus allowing the working class—at least its white male members—to vote. Extending the vote to blacks and women took longer.

The Enfranchisement of Blacks. The Fifteenth Amendment, adopted shortly after the Civil War, prohibited the states from denying the right to vote "on account of race, color, or previous condition of servitude." However, the states of the old Confederacy worked around the amendment by reestablishing old voting requirements (poll taxes, literacy tests) that worked primarily against blacks. Some southern states also cut blacks out of politics through a cunning circumvention of the amendment. Because

figure

7.2   Voter Registration in the South, 1960, 1980, and 1996

As a result of the Voting Rights Act of 1965 and other national actions, black voter registration in the eleven states of the old Confederacy nearly doubled between 1960 and 1980. In 1996, there was no difference between the voting registration rates of white and black voters in the Deep South.

Sources: Data for 1960 and 1980 are from U.S. Bureau of the Census, *Statistical Abstract of the United States, 1982–1983* (Washington, D.C.: U.S. Government Printing Office, 1983), p. 488; data for 1996 come from the 1996 American National Election Study.

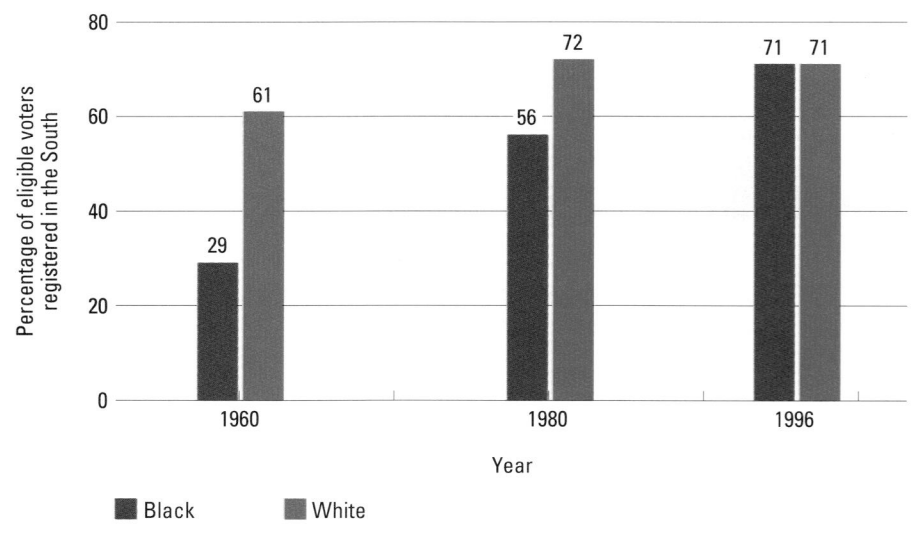

the amendment said nothing about voting rights in private organizations, these states denied blacks the right to vote in the "private" Democratic *primary* elections held to choose the party's candidates for the general election. Because the Democratic party came to dominate politics in the South, the "white primary" effectively disenfranchised blacks, despite the Fifteenth Amendment. Finally, in many areas of the South, the threat of violence kept blacks from the polls.

The extension of full voting rights to blacks came in two phases, separated by twenty years. In 1944, the Supreme Court decided in *Smith* v. *Allwright* that laws preventing blacks from voting in primary elections were unconstitutional, holding that party primaries are part of the continuous process of electing public officials.[27] The Voting Rights Act of 1965, which followed Selma's Bloody Sunday by less than five months, suspended discriminatory voting tests. It also authorized federal registrars to register voters in seven southern states, where less than half of the voting-age population had registered to vote in the 1964 election. For good measure, in 1966 the Supreme Court ruled in *Harper* v. *Virginia State Board of Elections* that state poll taxes are unconstitutional.[28] Although long in coming, these actions by the national government to enforce political equality in the states dramatically increased the registration of southern blacks (see Figure 7.2).

The Enfranchisement of Women.   The enfranchisement of women in the United States is a less sordid story but still nothing to be proud of. Women had to fight long and hard to win the right to vote. Until 1869, women could not vote anywhere in the world.[29] American women began to

Woman Suffrage Before 1920

The Fight for Women's Suffrage . . . and Against It

Militant suffragettes demonstrated outside the White House prior to ratification of the Nineteenth Amendment to the Constitution, which gave women the right to vote. Congress passed the proposed amendment in 1919, and it was ratified by the required number of states in time for the 1920 presidential election. Suffragettes' demonstrations were occasionally disrupted by men—and other women— who opposed extending the right to vote to women.

organize to obtain suffrage in the mid-1800s. Known then as *suffragettes,*[*] the early feminists initially had a limited effect on politics. Their first major victory did not come until 1869, when Wyoming, while still a territory, granted women the right to vote. No state followed suit until 1893, when Colorado enfranchised women.

In the meantime, the suffragettes became more active. In 1884, they formed the Equal Rights Party and nominated Belva A. Lockwood, a lawyer (who could not herself vote), as the first woman candidate for president.[30] Between 1896 and 1918, twelve other states gave women the vote. Most of these states were in the West, where pioneer women often departed from traditional women's roles. Nationally, the women's suffrage movement intensified, often resorting to unconventional political behaviors (marches, demonstrations), which occasionally invited violent attacks from men and even other women. In 1919, Congress finally passed the Nineteenth Amendment, which prohibits states from denying the right to vote "on account of sex." The amendment was ratified in 1920, in time for the November election.

Evaluating the Expansion of Suffrage in America. The last major expansion of suffrage in the United States took place in 1971, when the Twenty-sixth Amendment lowered the voting age to eighteen. For most of its history, the United States has been far from the democratic ideal of universal suffrage. The United States initially restricted voting rights to white male taxpayers or property owners, and wealth requirements lasted until the 1850s. Through demonstrations and a constitutional amendment, women won the franchise just seventy-nine years ago. Through civil war, constitutional amendments, court actions, massive demonstrations, and congressional action, blacks finally achieved full voting rights only three decades ago. Our record has more than a few blemishes.

But compared with other countries, the United States looks pretty democratic.[31] Women did not gain the vote on equal terms with men until 1921 in Norway; 1922 in the Netherlands; 1944 in France; 1946 in Italy,

---

[*] The term *suffragist* applied to a person of either sex who advocated extending the vote to women, while *suffragette* was reserved primarily for women who did so militantly.

Japan, and Venezuela; 1948 in Belgium; and 1971 in Switzerland. Women are still not universally enfranchised. In Kuwait, for example, the parliament narrowly voted in 1999 to reject women's suffrage.[32] Comparing the enfranchisement of minority racial groups is difficult, because most other democratic nations do not have a comparable racial makeup. We should note, however, that the indigenous Maori population in New Zealand won suffrage in 1867, but the aborigines in Australia were not fully enfranchised until 1961. In South Africa, blacks—who outnumber whites by more than four to one—were not allowed to vote freely in elections until 1994. With regard to voting age, nineteen of twenty-seven countries that allow free elections also have a minimum voting age of eighteen (none has a lower age), and eight have higher age requirements.

When judged against the rest of the world, the United States—which originated mass participation in government through elections—has as good a record of providing for political equality in voting rights as other democracies and a better record than many.

Voting on Policies

Disenfranchised groups have struggled to gain voting rights because of the political power that comes with suffrage. Belief in the ability of ordinary citizens to make political decisions and to control government through the power of the ballot box was strongest in the United States during the Progressive era, which began around 1900 and lasted until about 1925. **Progressivism** was a philosophy of political reform that trusted the goodness and wisdom of individual citizens and distrusted "special interests" (railroads, corporations) and political institutions (traditional political parties, legislatures). Such attitudes have resurfaced among the followers of the Reform Party and others who find this populist outlook appealing.

The leaders of the Progressive movement were prominent politicians (former president Theodore Roosevelt, Senator Robert La Follette of Wisconsin) and eminent scholars (historian Frederick Jackson Turner, philosopher John Dewey). Not content to vote for candidates chosen by party leaders, the Progressives championed the **direct primary**—a preliminary election, run by the state governments, in which the voters choose the party's candidates for the general election. Wanting a mechanism to remove elected candidates from office, the Progressives backed the **recall**—a special election initiated by a petition signed by a specified number of voters. Although about twenty states provide for recall elections, this device is rarely used. Only a few statewide elected officials have actually been unseated through recall.[33]

The Progressives also championed the power of the masses to propose and pass laws, approximating the citizen participation in policymaking that is the hallmark of direct democracy. They developed two voting mechanisms for policymaking that are still in use:

- A **referendum** is a direct vote by the people on either a proposed law or an amendment to a state constitution. The measures subject to popular vote are known as *propositions*. Twenty-four states permit popular referenda on laws, and all but Alabama require a referendum for a constitutional amendment. Most referenda are placed on the ballot by legislatures, not voters.

progressivism
A philosophy of political reform based upon the goodness and wisdom of the individual citizen as opposed to special interests and political institutions.

direct primary
A preliminary election, run by the state government, in which the voters choose each party's candidates for the general election.

recall
The process for removing an elected official from office.

referendum
An election on a policy issue.

initiative
A procedure by which voters can propose an issue to be decided by the legislature or by the people in a referendum. It requires gathering a specified number of signatures and submitting a petition to a designated agency.

- The **initiative** is a procedure by which voters can propose a measure to be decided by the legislature or by the people in a referendum. The procedure involves gathering a specified number of signatures from registered voters (usually 5 to 10 percent of the total in the state), then submitting the petition to a designated state agency. Twenty-four states provide for some form of voter initiative.

Figure 7.3 shows the West's affinity for these democratic mechanisms. Over 350 propositions have appeared on state ballots in general elections during the 1990s. In 2000, voters in forty-two states decided 204 initiatives or referenda. Of these, citizens placed 71 on the ballot, while state legislatures initiated 133.[34] The citizens of Oregon led the pack, placing 26 citizen-sponsored initiatives on the ballot—the highest number for a single state since North Dakota did so in 1932.[35] The Oregon initiatives included proposals to ban animal trapping, repeal the death penalty, and require background checks for customers at gun shows.[36] Across the country, some of the most frequent initiative topics included protecting animals (from hunting, trapping, or sport use), drug policy reform (drug treatment, asset forfeiture reform, and the medical use of marijuana), and education reform (primarily school choice). Nebraska became the nineteenth state to place term limits on members of the state legislature. Of the 71 citizen initiatives placed on the ballot nationwide, 48 percent passed, slightly above the one-hundred-year average of 41 percent.[37]

At times, many politicians oppose the initiatives that citizens propose and approve. This was true, for example, of term limits. A referendum can also work to the advantage of politicians, freeing them from taking sides on a hot issue. In 1998, for example, voters in Maine repealed a state law that barred discrimination against gays and lesbians in employment, housing, and public accommodations. In so doing, it became the first state to repeal a gay rights law.[38]

What conclusion can we draw about the Progressives' legacy of mechanisms for direct participation in government? One scholar who studied use of the initiative and referendum paints an unimpressive picture. He notes that an expensive "industry" developed in the 1980s that makes money circulating petitions, then managing the large sums of money needed to run a campaign to approve (or defeat) a referendum.[39] In 1998, opponents of a measure to allow casino gambling on Native American lands in California spent $25.8 million. This huge sum, however, pales in comparison to the $66.2 million spent during the campaign by the tribes that supported the measure. The initiative passed.[40]

Clearly, citizens can exercise great power over government policy through the mechanisms of the initiative and the referendum. What is not clear is whether these forms of direct democracy improve on the policies made by representatives elected for that purpose.

Voting for Candidates

We have saved for last the most visible form of political participation: voting to choose candidates for public office. Voting for candidates serves democratic government in two ways. First, citizens can choose the candidates they think will best serve their interests. If citizens choose

7.3   Westward Ho!

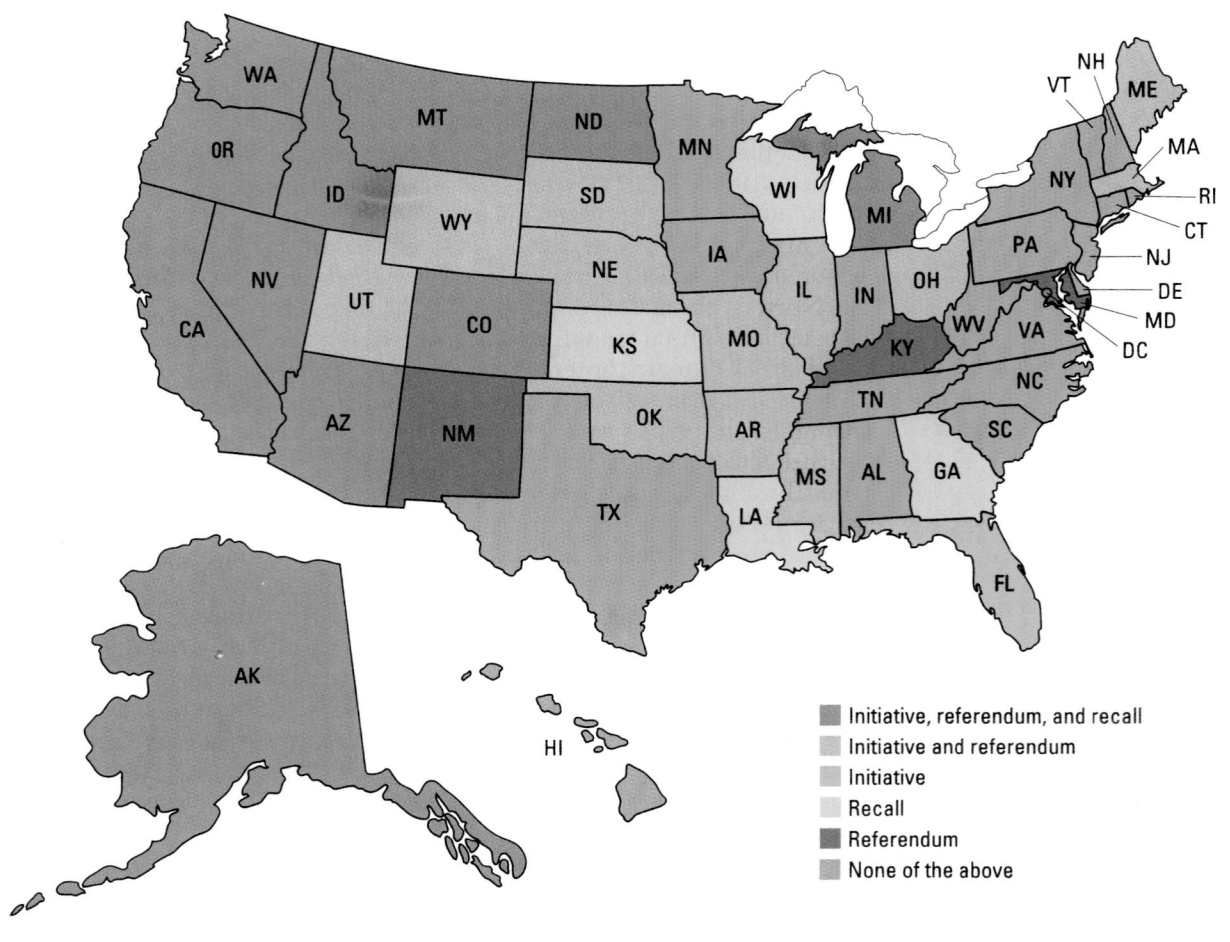

Initiative, referendum, and recall

Initiative and referendum

Initiative

Recall

Referendum

None of the above

This map shows quite clearly the western basis of the initiative, referendum, and recall mechanisms intended to place government power directly in the hands of the people. Advocates of "direct legislation" sought to bypass entrenched powers in state legislatures. Established groups and parties in the East dismissed them as radicals and cranks, but they gained the support of farmers and miners in the Midwest and West. The Progressive forces usually aligned with Democrats in western state legislatures to enact their proposals, often against Republican opposition.

Source: Reprinted by permission of the publisher from *Direct Democracy: The Politics of Initiative, Referendum, and Recall* by Thomas E. Cronin, Cambridge, Mass.: Harvard University Press: Copyright © 1989 by the Twentieth Century Fund, Inc. Updated from Initiative and Reform Institute, "Fact Sheet 1, Table 1.1," available on-line at <www.iandrinstitute.org/factsheets/fs1!2.htm>, 26 December 2000.

candidates that are "like themselves" in personal traits or party affiliation, elected officials should tend to think as their constituents do on political issues and automatically reflect the majority's views when making public policy.

Second, voting allows the people to reelect the officials they guessed right about and to kick out those they guessed wrong about. This function is very different from the first. It makes public officials accountable for their behavior through the reward-and-punishment mechanism of elections. It assumes that officeholders are motivated to respond to public opinion by the threat of electoral defeat. It also assumes that the voters (1) know what politicians are doing while they are in office and (2) participate actively in the electoral process. We look at the factors that underlie voting choice in Chapter 9. Here, we examine Americans' reliance on the electoral process.

In national politics, voters seem content to elect just two executive officers—the president and vice president—and to trust the president to appoint a cabinet to round out his administration. But at the state and local levels, voters insist on selecting all kinds of officials. Every state elects a governor (and forty-two elect a lieutenant governor). Forty elect an attorney general; thirty-five, a treasurer and a secretary of state; twenty-three, an auditor. The list goes on, down through superintendents of schools, secretaries of agriculture, controllers, boards of education, and public utilities commissioners.[41] Elected county officials commonly include commissioners, a sheriff, a treasurer, a clerk, a superintendent of schools, and a judge (often several). At the local level, voters elect all but about 600 of 15,300 school boards across the nation.[42] Instead of trusting state and local chief executives to appoint lesser administrators (as we do for more important offices at the national level), we expect voters to choose intelligently among scores of candidates they meet for the first time on a complex ballot in the polling booth.

In the American version of democracy, our laws recognize no limit to voters' ability to make informed choices among candidates and thus to control government through voting. The reasoning seems to be that elections are good; therefore, more elections are better, and the most elections are best. By this thinking, the United States clearly has the best and most democratic government in the world because it is the undisputed champion at holding elections. The author of a study that compared elections in the United States with elections in twenty-six other democracies concluded

> No country can approach the United States in the frequency and variety of elections, and thus in the amount of electoral participation to which its citizens have a right. No other country elects its lower house as often as every two years, or its president as frequently as every four years. No other country popularly elects its state governors and town mayors; no other has as wide a variety of nonrepresentative offices (judges, sheriffs, attorneys general, city treasurers, and so on) subject to election. . . . The average American is entitled to do far more electing—probably by a factor of three or four—than the citizen of any other democracy.[43]

However, we learn from Compared with What? 7.2 that the United States ranks at the bottom of twenty-seven countries in voter turnout in national elections. How do we square low voter turnout with Americans' devotion to elections as an instrument of democratic government? To complicate matters further, how do we square low voter turnout with the findings we mentioned earlier, which establish the United States as the leader among five Western democratic nations in both conventional and unconventional political participation, except for voting? Americans seem to participate at high levels in everything except elections.

Can You Explain Why...
Americans might be said to vote *more* than citizens in other countries?

★ **compared with what?**

7.2   Voter Turnout in Democratic Nations, 1975–1995

Americans participate as much as or more than citizens of other nations in all forms of conventional political behavior except voting. Voter turnout in American presidential elections ranks at the bottom of voting rates for twenty-seven countries with competitive elections. As discussed in the text, the facts are correct, but the comparison is not as damning as it appears.

Source: Inter-Parliamentary Union, *Chronicle of Parliamentary Elections and Developments* (Geneva: Switzerland, Vols. X–XXIX (1975–1995); U.S. Bureau of the Census, Current Population Reports, P20-453 and P20-466, *Voting and Registration in the Election of 1990 [and 1992]* (Washington, D.C.: U.S. Government Printing Office, 1991 [and 1993]), pp. viii, 10. The U.S. data are for all elections from 1976 to 1992, both presidential and nonpresidential election years. (Compared with What? 7.1 shows the percentage of respondents who *said* they voted, which is usually higher than actual voting turnout.)

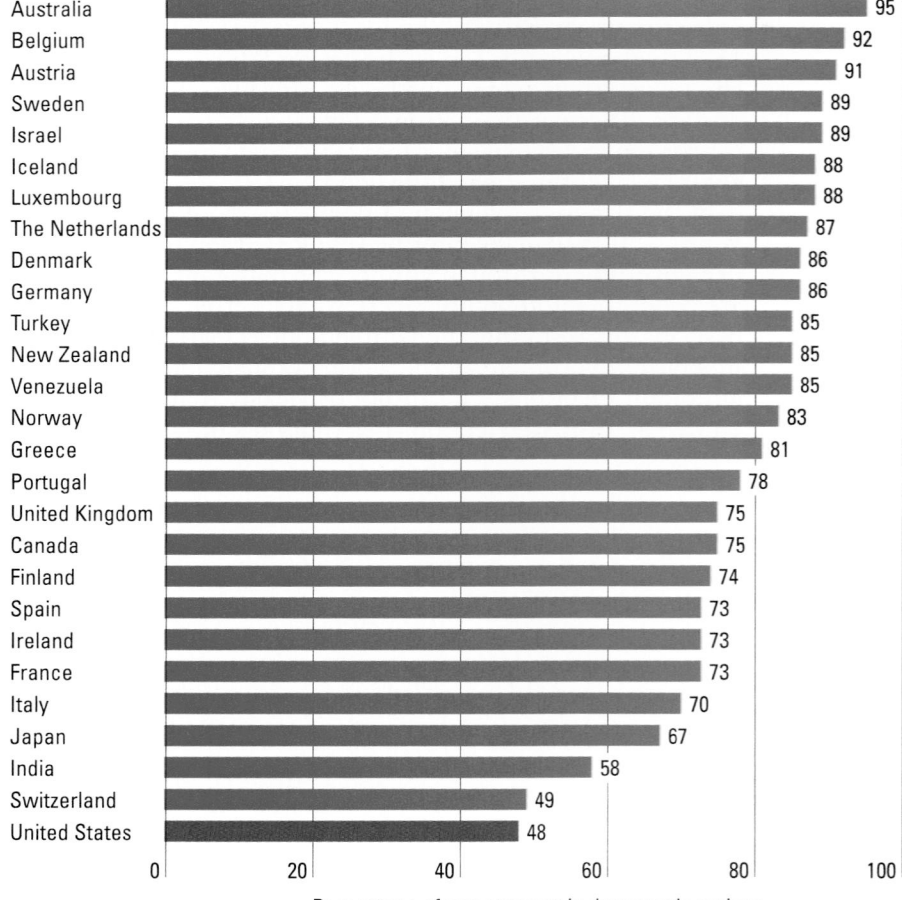

Country	Percentage
Australia	95
Belgium	92
Austria	91
Sweden	89
Israel	89
Iceland	88
Luxembourg	88
The Netherlands	87
Denmark	86
Germany	86
Turkey	85
New Zealand	85
Venezuela	85
Norway	83
Greece	81
Portugal	78
United Kingdom	75
Canada	75
Finland	74
Spain	73
Ireland	73
France	73
Italy	70
Japan	67
India	58
Switzerland	49
United States	48

Percentage of voter turnout in democratic nations

**EXPLAINING
POLITICAL
PARTICIPATION**

As you have seen, political participation can be unconventional or conventional, can require little or much initiative, and can serve to support the government or influence its decisions. Researchers have found that people who take part in some form of political behavior often do not take part in others. For example, citizens who contact public officials to obtain special benefits may not vote regularly, participate in campaigns, or even contact officials about broader social issues. In fact, because particularized contacting serves individual rather than public interests, it is not even considered political behavior by some people.

This section examines some factors that affect the more obvious forms of political participation, with particular emphasis on voting. The first task is to determine how much patterns of participation vary within the United States over time.

Patterns of Participation over Time

Did Americans become more politically apathetic in the 1990s than they were in the 1960s? The answer lies in Figure 7.4, which plots several measures of participation from 1952 through 2000. The graph shows little variation over time in the percentage of citizens who worked for candidates or attended party meetings. Interest in election campaigns and persuading people how to vote have actually tended to increase. Nevertheless, except for a spurt in 1992 due to Ross Perot's novel candidacy, voter turnout declined overall, sinking to 49 percent in 1996. This was the lowest turnout in a presidential election since 1924, when women first voted nationwide, and excepting 1924, the lowest since before the Civil War. Note that *the only line that shows a downward trend is voting in elections.* The plot has thickened. Not only is voter turnout low in the United States compared with that in other countries, but turnout has basically declined over time. Moreover, while voting has decreased, other forms of participation have remained stable or even increased. What is going on? Who votes? Who does not? Why? And does it really matter?

The Standard Socioeconomic Explanation

Researchers have found that socioeconomic status is a good indicator of most types of conventional political participation. People with more education, higher incomes, and white-collar or professional occupations tend to be more aware of the effect of politics on their lives, to know what can be done to influence government actions, and to have the necessary resources (time and money) to take action. So they are more likely to participate in politics than are people of lower socioeconomic status. This relationship between socioeconomic status and conventional political involvement is called the **standard socioeconomic model** of participation.[44]

standard socioeconomic model
A relationship between socioeconomic status and conventional political involvement: People with higher status and more education are more likely to participate than those with lower status.

Unconventional political behavior is less clearly related to socioeconomic status. Studies of unconventional participation in other countries have found that protest behavior is related to low socioeconomic status and especially to youth.[45] However, scattered studies of unconventional participation in the United States have found that protesters (especially blacks) are often of higher socioeconomic status than those who do not join in protests.[46]

figure

7.4   Electoral Participation in the United States over Time

Participation patterns from five decades show that in the 1980s Americans participated in election campaigns about as much or more than they did in the 1950s on every indicator except voting. The turnout rate dropped more than ten percentage points from 1952 to 2000. The graph shows little variation over time in the percentage of citizens who worked for candidates, attended party meetings, and tried to persuade people how to vote. In fact, interest in election campaigns tended to increase. Except for a spurt in 1992 due to Ross Perot's novel candidacy, however, voting turnout declined overall and sunk to 49 percent in 1996. This was the lowest in a presidential election since 1924, when women first voted nationwide. This long-term decline in turnout runs counter to the rise in educational level, a puzzle that is discussed in the text.

Source: Reprinted by permission of the publishers from *American National Election Studies Data Sourcebook, 1952–1978,* Warren Miller and Edward J. Schneider, eds. (Cambridge, Mass.: Harvard University Press). Copyright © 1980. Data after 1978 comes from subsequent National Election Studies.

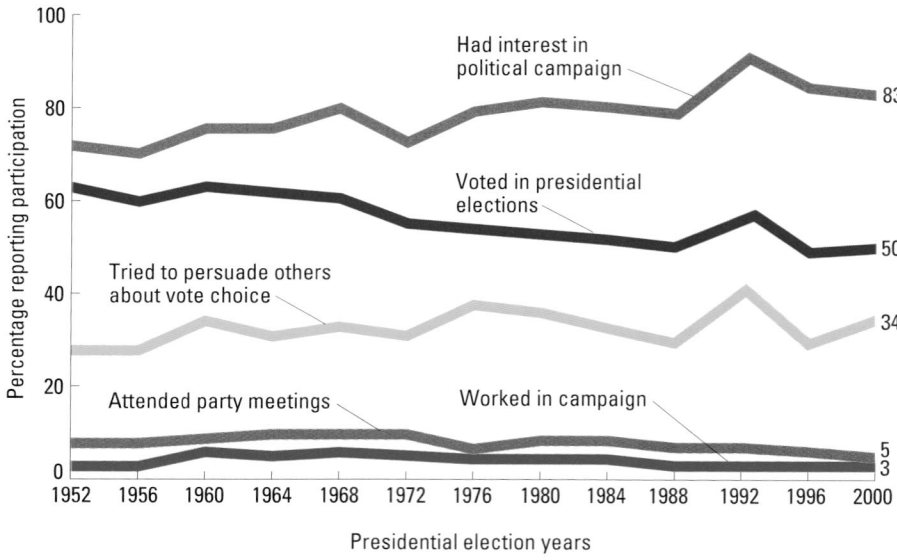

Obviously, socioeconomic status does not account for all the differences in the ways people choose to participate in politics, even for conventional participation. Another important variable is age. As just noted, young people are more likely to take part in political protests, but they are less likely to participate in conventional politics. Voting rates tend to increase as people grow older, until about age sixty-five, when physical infirmities begin to lower rates again.[47]

Two other variables—race and gender—have been related to participation in the past, but as times have changed, so have those relationships. Blacks, who had very low participation rates in the 1950s, now participate at rates comparable to whites, when differences in socioeconomic status are taken into account.[48] Women also exhibited low participation rates in the past, but gender differences in political participation have virtually disappeared.[49] (The one exception is in attempting to persuade others how to vote, which women are less likely to do than men.[50]) Recent research on the social context of voting behavior has shown that married men and women are more likely to vote than those of either sex living without a spouse.[51]

Of all the social and economic variables, education is the strongest single factor in explaining most types of conventional political participation. A recent major study on civic participation details the impact of education:

> It affects the acquisition of skills; it channels opportunities for high levels of income and occupation; it places individuals in institutional settings where they can be recruited to political activity; and it fosters psychological and cognitive engagement with politics.[52]

Figure 7.5 shows the striking relationship between level of formal education and various types of conventional political behavior. The strong

figure **7.5**

Effects of Education on Political Participation

Education has a powerful effect on political participation in the United States. These data from a 2000 sample show that level of education is directly related to five different forms of conventional political participation. (Respondents tend to overstate whether they voted.)

Source: This analysis was based on the 2000 National Election Study done by the Center for Political Studies, University of Michigan, and distributed by the Inter-University Consortium for Political and Social Research, Ann Arbor, Michigan.

Use the CROSSTABS computer program that accompanies this book to analyze the effects of other variables—such as gender, race, and region—on these measures of political participation. All the variables in Figure 7.5 are contained in the "Voters" data set.

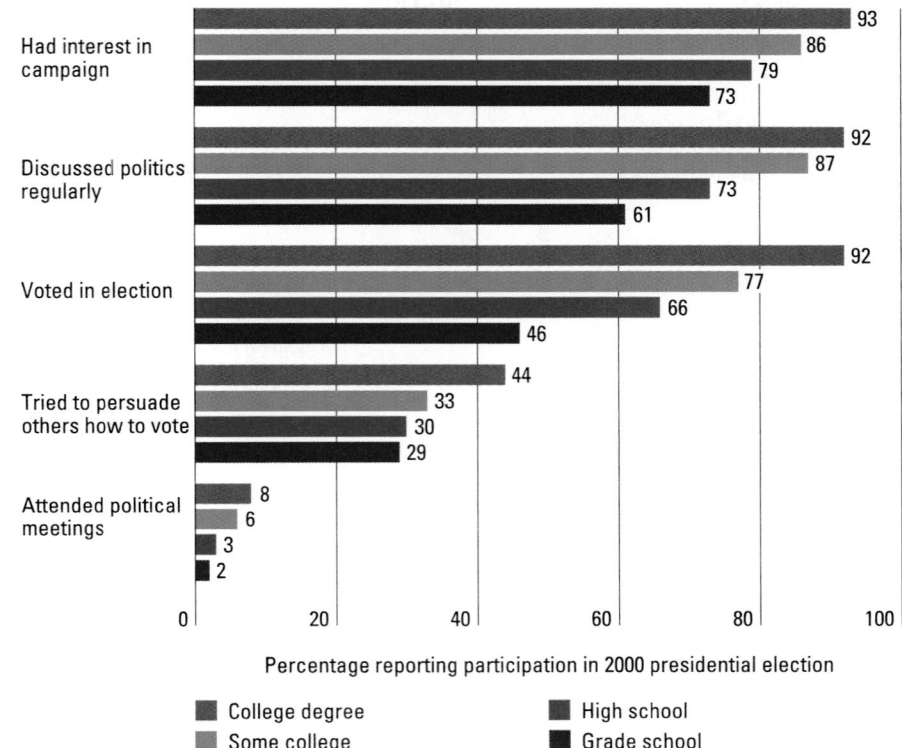

link between education and electoral participation raises questions about low voter turnout in the United States, both over time and relative to other democracies. The fact is that the proportion of individuals with college degrees is greater in the United States than in other countries. Moreover, that proportion has been increasing steadily. Why, then, is voter turnout in elections so low? And why has it been dropping over time?

Low Voter Turnout in America

Voting is a low-initiative form of participation that can satisfy all three motives for political participation—showing allegiance to the nation, obtaining particularized benefits, and influencing broad policy. How then do we explain the decline in voter turnout in the United States?

Can You Explain Why... lowering the voting age from 21 to 18 also lowered the national rate of voting turnout?

The Decline in Voting over Time. The graph of voter turnout in Figure 7.6 shows that the largest drop occurred between the 1968 and 1972 elections. During this period (in 1971, actually) Congress proposed and the states ratified the Twenty-sixth Amendment, which expanded the electorate by lowering the voting age from twenty-one to eighteen. Because people younger than twenty-one are much less likely to vote, their eligibility

figure

7.6   The Decline of Voter Turnout: An Unsolved Puzzle

Level of education is one of the strongest predictors of a person's likelihood of voting in the United States, and the percentage of citizens older than twenty-five with a high school education or more has grown steadily since the end of World War II. Nevertheless, the overall rate of voter turnout has gone down almost steadily in presidential elections since 1960. The phenomenon is recognized as an unsolved puzzle in American voting behavior.

Sources: "Percentage voting" data up to 1988 come from Michael Nelson, ed., *Congressional Quarterly's Guide to the Presidency* (Washington, D.C.: Congressional Quarterly, Inc., 1989), p. 170; data since 1988 come from U.S. Bureau of the Census, *Statistical Abstract of the United States, 1999* (Washington, D.C.: U.S. Government Printing Office, 1999), pp. 169, 301; and "Report: Gore Won Popular Vote by 539,897," *Washington Post,* 21 December 2000, p. A9.

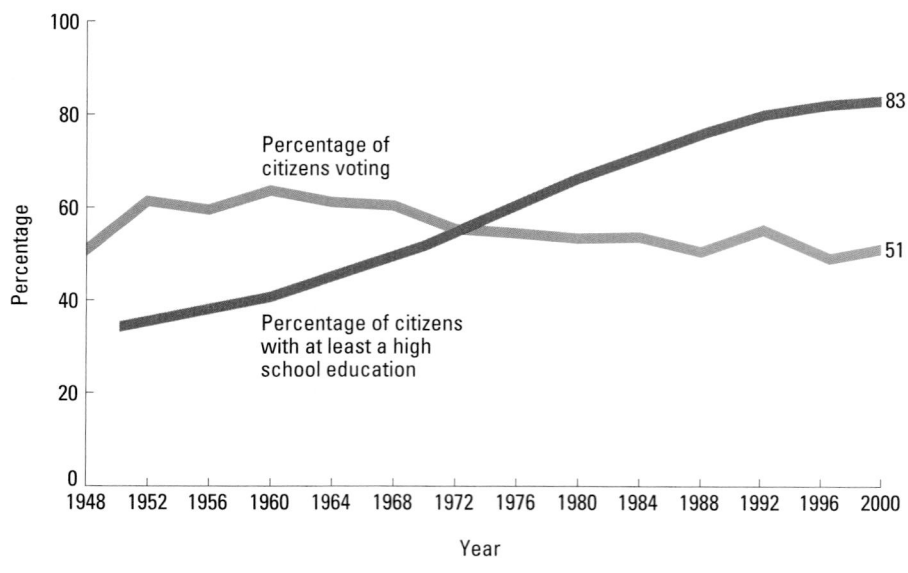

actually reduced the overall national turnout rate (the percentage of those eligible to vote who actually vote). To increase turnout of young people, an organization called "Rock the Vote" was formed in 1990 within the recording industry "to inform young Americans that their rights [to listen to racy and violent lyrics?] were in danger of being limited by a government in which they had little or no influence."[53] Some observers estimate that the enfranchisement of eighteen-year-olds accounts for about one or two percentage points in the total decline in turnout since 1952, but that still leaves more than ten percentage points to be explained.[54]

Why has voter turnout declined since 1968, while the level of education has increased? Many researchers have tried to solve this puzzle.[55] Some attribute most of the decline to changes in voters' attitudes toward politics. One major factor is the growing belief that government is not responsive to citizens and that voting does no good. One scholar refers to "a generalized withdrawal or disconnection from the political world, manifested most dramatically by declining psychological involvement in politics and a declining belief in government responsiveness."[56] Another is a change in attitude toward political parties, along with a decline in the extent and strength of party identification.[57] According to these psychological explanations, voter turnout in the United States is not likely to increase until the government does something to restore people's faith in the effectiveness of voting—with or without political parties. According to the age explanation, turnout in the United States is destined to remain a percentage point or two below its highs of the 1960s because of the lower voting rate of citizens younger than twenty-one.

★

Voting There . . . and Here

In the 1999 election in South Africa, citizens were willing to stand in the sun for hours to vote in their national election. In the United States, voter traffic is usually lighter, especially in a primary election. In Tupelo, Mississippi, election officials play games to pass the time between voters during the 2000 primary.

U.S. Turnout Versus Turnout in Other Countries. Scholars cite two factors to explain the low voter turnout in the United States compared with that in other countries. First are the differences in voting laws and administrative machinery.[58] In a few countries, voting is compulsory, and obviously turnout is extremely high. But other methods can encourage voting—declaring election days to be public holidays, providing a two-day voting period, making it easy to cast absentee ballots. The United States does none of these things.

Furthermore, nearly every other democratic country places the burden of registration on the government rather than on the individual voter. This is important. Voting in the United States is a two-stage process, and the first stage (going to the proper officials to register) has required more initiative than the second stage (going to the polling booth to cast a ballot). In most American states, the registration process has been separate from the voting process in terms of both time (usually voters had to register weeks in advance of an election) and geography (often voters had to register at the county courthouse, not their polling place). One researcher who studied three states (Minnesota, Maine, and Wisconsin) that allowed citizens to register and vote on the same day estimated that such practices nationwide would alone add five points to the turnout rate.[59] Moreover, registration procedures often have been obscure, requiring potential voters to call around to find out what to do. Furthermore, people who move (and roughly one-third of the U.S. population moves between presidential elections) have had to reregister. In short, although voting requires little initiative, registration usually has required high initiative. If we compute voter turnout on the basis of those who are registered to vote, about 87 percent of Americans vote—a figure that moves the United States to the middle (but not the top) of all democratic nations.[60]

To increase turnout, Congress in 1993 passed the so-called motor-voter law, which aimed to increase voter registration by requiring states to permit registration by mail and when obtaining or renewing a driver's license and by encouraging registration at other facilities, such as public assistance agencies. By the 1997–1998 election cycle, over half of all voter registration took place through motor vehicle agencies and other agencies specified in the motor-voter law. Although registration rose to its highest level for a congressional election since 1970, the voting rate in 1998 declined by almost 2.4 percent below the comparable 1994 election.[61]

Besides burdensome registration procedures, another factor usually cited to explain low turnout in American elections is the lack of political parties that mobilize the vote of particular social groups, especially lower-income and less-educated people. American parties do make an effort to get out the vote, but neither party is as closely linked to specific groups as are parties in many other countries, where certain parties work hand in hand with specific ethnic, occupational, or religious groups. Research shows that strong party-group links can significantly increase turnout.[62] One important study claims that "changing mobilization patterns by parties, campaigns, and social movements accounts for at least half of the decline in electoral participation since the 1960s."[63] Other research suggests that although well-funded, vigorous campaigns mobilize citizens to vote, the effect depends on the type of citizens and the nature of the election. Highly educated, low-income citizens are more likely to be stimulated to vote than are less-educated, high-income citizens, but lower-class citizens can be more easily mobilized to vote in presidential elections than in non-presidential elections.[64] Perhaps the increased turnout by black males in 1996—when a million more voted than in 1992—can be attributed to the mobilizing effects of the 1995 Million Man March. What else could account for black men's voting at a higher rate even as black women, white women, and white men all dropped below their 1992 rate?[65]

To these explanations for low voter turnout in the United States—the traditional burden of registration and the lack of strong party-group links—we add another. Although the act of voting requires low initiative, the process of learning about the scores of candidates on the ballot in American elections requires a great deal of initiative. Some people undoubtedly fail to vote simply because they feel inadequate to the task of deciding among candidates for the many offices on the ballot in U.S. elections.

Teachers, newspaper columnists, and public affairs groups tend to worry a great deal about low voter turnout in the United States, suggesting that it signifies some sort of political sickness—or at least that it gives us a bad mark for democracy. Some others who study elections closely seem less concerned.[66] One scholar argues:

> Turnout rates do not indicate the amount of electing—the frequency . . . , the range of offices and decisions, the "value" of the vote—to which a country's citizens are entitled. . . . Thus, although the turnout rate in the United States is below that of most other democracies, American citizens do not necessarily do less voting than other citizens; most probably, they do more.[67]

Despite such words of assurance, the nagging thought remains that turnout ought to be higher, so various organizations mount get-out-the-vote campaigns before elections. Civic leaders often back the campaigns because they value voting for its contribution to political order.

PARTICIPATION AND FREEDOM, EQUALITY, AND ORDER

As we have seen, Americans do participate in government in various ways and, to a reasonable extent, compared with citizens of other countries. What is the relationship of political participation to the values of freedom, equality, and order?

Down for the Count

Following the 2000 election, as the nation awaited the outcome of the presidential vote, Reverend Jesse Jackson spoke in Florida on the importance of counting every ballot.

Participation and Freedom

From the standpoint of normative theory, the relationship between participation and freedom is clear. Individuals should be free to participate in government and politics in the way they want and as much as they want. And they should be free not to participate as well. Ideally, all barriers to participation (such as restrictive voting registration and limitations on campaign expenditures) should be abolished—as should any schemes for compulsory voting. According to the normative perspective, we should not worry about low voter turnout because citizens should have the freedom not to vote as well as to vote.

In theory, freedom to participate also means that individuals should be able to use their wealth, connections, knowledge, organizational power (including sheer numbers in organized protests), or any other resource to influence government decisions, provided they do so legally. Of all these resources, the individual vote may be the weakest—and the least important—means of exerting political influence. Obviously, then, freedom as a value in political participation favors those with the resources to advance their own political self-interest.

Participation and Equality

The relationship between participation and equality is also clear. Each citizen's ability to influence government should be equal to that of every other citizen, so that differences in personal resources do not work against the poor or otherwise disadvantaged. Elections, then, serve the ideal of equality better than any other means of political participation. Formal rules for counting ballots—in particular, one person, one vote—cancel differences in resources among individuals.

At the same time, groups of people who have few resources individually can combine their votes to wield political power. Various European ethnic groups exercised this type of power in the late nineteenth and early twentieth centuries, when their votes won them entry to the sociopolitical system and allowed them to share in its benefits (see Chapter 5). More recently, blacks, Hispanics, homosexuals, and the disabled have used their voting power to gain political recognition. However, minorities often have had to use unconventional forms of participation to win the right to vote. As two major scholars of political participation put it, "Protest is the great equalizer, the political action that weights intensity as well as sheer numbers."[68]

Participation and Order

The relationship between participation and order is complicated. Some types of participation (pledging allegiance, voting) promote order and so are encouraged by those who value order; other types promote disorder and so are discouraged. Many citizens—men and women alike—even resisted giving women the right to vote for fear of upsetting the social order by altering the traditional roles of men and women.

Both conventional and unconventional participation can lead to the ouster of government officials, but the regime—the political system itself—is threatened more by unconventional participation. To maintain order, the government has a stake in converting unconventional participation to conventional participation whenever possible. We can easily imagine this tactic being used by authoritarian governments, but democratic governments also use it.

Think about the student unrest on college campuses during the Vietnam War. In private and public colleges alike, thousands of students stopped traffic, occupied buildings, destroyed property, boycotted classes, disrupted lectures, staged guerrilla theater, and behaved in other unconventional ways to protest the war, racism, capitalism, the behavior of their college presidents, the president of the United States, the military establishment, and all other institutions. (We are not exaggerating here. For example, students did all these things at Northwestern University in Evanston, Illinois, after members of the National Guard shot and killed four students at a demonstration at Kent State University in Ohio on May 4, 1970.)

Confronted by civil strife and disorder in the nation's institutions of higher learning, Congress took action. On March 23, 1971, it enacted and sent to the states the proposed Twenty-sixth Amendment, lowering the voting age to eighteen. Three-quarters of the state legislatures had to ratify the amendment before it became part of the Constitution. Astonishingly, thirty-eight states (the required number) complied by July 1, establishing a new speed record for ratification, cutting the old record nearly in half.[69] (Ironically, voting rights were not high on the list of students' demands.)

Testimony by members of Congress before the Judiciary Committee stated that the eighteen-year-old vote would "harness the energy of young people and direct it into useful and constructive channels," to keep students from becoming "more militant" and engaging "in destructive activities of a dangerous nature."[70] As one observer argued, the right to vote was extended to eighteen-year-olds not because young people demanded it but because "public officials believed suffrage expansion to be a means of institutionalizing youths' participation in politics, which would, in turn, curb disorder."[71]

PARTICIPATION AND THE MODELS OF DEMOCRACY

Ostensibly, elections are institutional mechanisms that implement democracy by allowing citizens to choose among candidates or issues. But elections also serve several other important purposes:[72]

- Elections socialize political activity. They transform what might otherwise consist of sporadic, citizen-initiated acts into a routine public function. That is, the opportunity to vote for change encourages citizens to refrain from demonstrating in the streets. This helps preserve government stability by containing and channeling away potentially disruptive or dangerous forms of mass political activity.

- Elections institutionalize access to political power. They allow ordinary citizens to run for political office or to play an important role in selecting political leaders. Working to elect a candidate encourages the campaign worker to identify problems or propose solutions to the newly elected official.

- Elections bolster the state's power and authority. The opportunity to participate in elections helps convince citizens that the government is responsive to their needs and wants, which reinforces its legitimacy.

Participation and Majoritarianism

Although the majoritarian model assumes that government responsiveness to popular demands comes through mass participation in politics, majoritarianism views participation rather narrowly. It favors conventional, institutionalized behavior—primarily, voting in elections. Because majoritarianism relies on counting votes to determine what the majority wants, its bias toward equality in political participation is strong. Clearly, a class bias in voting exists because of the strong influence of socioeconomic status on turnout. Simply put, better-educated, wealthier citizens are more likely to participate in elections, and get-out-the-vote campaigns cannot counter this distinct bias.[73] Because it favors collective decisions formalized through elections, majoritarianism has little place for motivated, resourceful individuals to exercise private influence over government actions.

Majoritarianism also limits individual freedom in another way: its focus on voting as the major means of mass participation narrows the scope of conventional political behavior by defining which political actions are "orderly" and acceptable. By favoring equality and order in political participation, majoritarianism goes hand in hand with the ideological orientation of communitarianism (see Chapter 1).

Participation and Pluralism

Resourceful citizens who want the government's help with problems find a haven in the pluralist model of democracy. A decentralized and organizationally complex form of government allows many points of access and accommodates various forms of conventional participation in addition to voting. For example, wealthy people and well-funded groups can afford to hire lobbyists to press their interests in Congress. In one view of pluralist democracy, citizens are free to ply and wheedle public officials to further their own selfish visions of the public good. From another viewpoint, pluralism offers citizens the opportunity to be treated as individuals when dealing with the government, to influence policymaking in special circumstances, and to fulfill (insofar as possible in representative government) their social potential through participation in community affairs.

SUMMARY

To have "government by the people," the people must participate in politics. Conventional forms of participation—contacting officials and voting in elections—come most quickly to mind. However, citizens can also participate in politics in unconventional ways—staging sit-down strikes in public buildings, blocking traffic, and so on. Most citizens disapprove of most forms of unconventional political behavior. Yet blacks and women used unconventional tactics to win important political and legal rights, including the right to vote.

People are motivated to participate in politics for various reasons: to show support for their country, to obtain particularized benefits for themselves or their friends, or to influence broad public policy. Their political actions may demand either little political knowledge or personal initiative, or a great deal of both.

The press often paints an unflattering picture of political participation in America. Clearly, the proportion of the electorate that votes in general elections in the United States has dropped and is far below that in other nations. The United States tends to show as much as or more citizen participation in politics than other nations, however, when a broad range of conventional and unconventional political behavior is considered. Voter turnout in the United States suffers by comparison with that of other nations because of differences in voter registration requirements. We also lack institutions (especially strong political parties) that increase voter registration and help bring those of lower socioeconomic status to the polls.

People's tendency to participate in politics is strongly related to their socioeconomic status. Education, one component of socioeconomic status, is the single strongest predictor of conventional political participation in the United States. Because of the strong effect of socioeconomic status, the political system is potentially biased toward the interests of higher-status people. Pluralist democracy, which provides many avenues for resourceful citizens to influence government decisions, tends to increase this bias. Majoritarian democracy, which relies heavily on elections and the concept of one person, one vote, offers citizens without great personal resources the opportunity to influence government decisions through elections.

Elections also serve to legitimize government simply by involving the masses in government through voting. Whether voting means anything depends on the nature of voters' choices in elections. The range of choices available is a function of the nation's political parties, the topic of the next chapter.

★ Selected Readings

Browning, Graeme, and Daniel J. Weitzner. *Electronic Democracy: Using the Internet to Influence American Politics.* Wilton, Conn.: On-line, 1996. A modern account of how to use the Internet for grassroots activism.

Conway, M. Margaret. *Political Participation in the United States,* 3d ed. Washington, D.C.: Congressional Quarterly Press, 2000. A straightforward but detailed overview, making use of psychological, economic, and educational explanations of the many forms of participation Americans employ.

Conway, M. Margaret, Gertrude A. Steuernagel, and David W. Ahern. *Women and Political Participation.* Washington, D.C.: Congressional Quarterly Press, 1997. A short but comprehensive study of women, American culture, and various forms of women's political activity.

Dalton, Russell J. *Citizen Politics in Western Democracies,* 2nd ed. Chatham, N.J.: Chatham House, 1996. Studies public opinion and behavior in the United States, Britain, Germany (west and east), and France. Two chapters compare conventional citizen action and protest politics in these countries.

George, John, and Laird Wilcox. *American Extremists: Militias, Supremacists, Klansmen, Communists, and Others.* Amherst, N.Y.: Prometheus Books, 1996. Explores segments of American society that have specialized in unconventional participation.

Grofman, Bernard, and Chandler Davidson, eds. *Controversies in Minority Voting: The Voting Rights Act in Perspective.* Washington, D.C.: Brookings Institution, 1992. Reviews the aims and accomplishments of the 1965 law that enforced voting rights for blacks in the South and some of its unintended consequences.

Rimmerman, Craig A. *The New Citizenship: Unconventional Politics, Activism, and Service.* Boulder, Colo.: Westview Press, 1997. Goes beyond voting to describe more active involvement in the political process, illustrating democratic theory with case studies.

Internet Exercises

1. *Raising a Ruckus*

The Ruckus Society, formed in October 1995, identifies its mission as providing "training in the skills of nonviolent civil disobedience to help environmental and human rights organizations achieve their goals.

- Go to the society's Web page at <**www.ruckus. org/**>. (Browsing the Action Gallery will allow you to see photos of some of the group's members at training sessions.) Follow the link to the group's collection of on-line training manuals, and skim through these two: "Media Manual" and "Scouting Manual."

- There are a variety of materials at Ruckus's site that describe forms of unconventional participation. How do the training manuals also illustrate that the society recognizes the importance of conventional institutions and tactics for helping it to further its mission?

2. *Social Capital and Voter Turnout*

C-SPAN is a public service station created by the nation's cable companies to provide coverage of the proceedings of the U.S. government and other forums where matters of public policy and politics are considered. One of the network's regular programs, Booknotes, profiles contemporary authors and their recent books. The program maintains a Web site located at <**www.booknotes.org/**>.

- In December of 2000, Harvard political scientist Robert Putnam appeared on the program to discuss his book *Bowling Alone: The Collapse and Revival of American Community.* Go to the Booknotes site and use the Online Archive feature to locate the transcript of this particular program.

- Read Professor Putnam's answer to moderator Brian Lamb's opening question about the theory of the book. Then locate the segment of their discussion (about three-fourths of the way through the program) where the two discuss Chapter 24, in which Putnam lays out his agenda for reviving the nation's stock of social capital.

- How might the nation's declining stock of social capital be a cause of declining voter turnout in the United States?

chapter 8

Political Parties

"AL GORE COST ME THE ELECTION," quipped Ralph Nader in December 2000.[1] In November's presidential election, Democrat Al Gore won 48.4 percent of 105 million votes to Republican George W. Bush's 47.9 percent. However, Gore won only twenty-one states with 267 electoral votes, and Bush won thirty with 271 votes—just one more than the 270 needed to win in the electoral college. For his part, Nadar won only 2.7 percent of the popular vote, carried no states, and got no electoral votes. But he undoubtedly took votes in some states that would have gone to Gore. Asked by CNN talk show host Larry King whether he had any regrets about the election, Nader said, "The regret is that I didn't get more votes."[2]

Many leaders of liberal environmental groups—groups whose causes Nader championed—did not appreciate his flippancy. Carl Pope, executive director of the Sierra Club warned Nader before the election that he could be "instrumental in electing" Bush. Afterward, Mike Casey, spokesperson for the Environmental Working Group, said that they "absolutely blame Ralph Nader directly" for Bush's victory. Rahm Emanuel, former adviser in the Clinton administration, summed up the rap against Nader: "Here's a guy who didn't get his money, didn't get his 5%, and did cost the election."[3]

Let's examine this last charge against Nader in the context of third-party politics in America. First, the 2000 campaign was not Nader's first run for the presidency. Idolized by the left for bashing corporate America, Nader accepted the Green Party's nomination in 1996 but told his nominators that he would not join the party ("I'm an independent"), would not run on its platform, and would neither raise nor accept any campaign financing.[4] Not surprisingly, Nader did not do well in the 1996 election. The Green Party candidate made the ballot in only twenty-two states and won only 685,040 votes—only 0.7 percent of the total.[5]

If the 1996 Green Party nomination had been thrust on an unwilling candidate, Nader willingly accepted its nomination with a purpose in 2000. He had no illusions of winning the presidency, but he aimed at getting 5 percent or more of the national vote, which would qualify the Green Party for federal funds and put it on track for becoming a viable third party. No longer professing to be "an independent," Nader hoped to build the Green Party "to play a watchdog role . . . to hold the two parties' feet to the fire."[6] Of the two major parties, Nader described them as "basically one corporate party wearing two heads and different makeup."[7] As for Gore losing to Bush in 2000, Nader said the nation would face "four more years of ignoring systemic injustice" under either candidate.[8]

★

An "Aye" for Bush?

Judge Robert Rosenberg, member of the election canvassing board in Broward County, Florida, inspects a disputed ballot cast for president on November 24, 2000, more than two weeks after the November 7 election.

In the 2000 presidential election, Nader appeared on the ballot in forty-six states, and he took 2,858,843 votes (2.7 percent). Was that enough to deny Gore the election? Most observers think so. Consider Florida, which Bush was credited with winning by 537 votes in a total of almost six million and where Nader won 97,488 votes. We can make informed guesses from Florida exit polls where Nader's votes might have gone in his absence. About half the Nader voters in Florida said they voted for Perot in 1996. The others split three to two for Clinton in 1996 over Republican candidate Bob Dole. If Gore had won only 51 percent of the 97,000 Nader voters, he would have picked up 1,950 votes—plenty to overcome his 537 vote defeat.[9] If Gore had won Florida's twenty-five electoral votes, he would have won the presidency.

Nader also seems to have cost Gore the four electoral votes of New Hampshire—where Nader took 3.9 percent of the vote. Bush won by only two percentage points (48.6 to 46.6), and over half the Nader voters in 2000 reported voting for Clinton in 1996.[10] So strong evidence indicates that Nader's candidacy attracted many voters who would have voted for Gore—if the Green Party candidate had not been on the ballot. Given the closeness of the presidential vote in these two states, one can reasonably argue that the Green Party prevented the Democratic Party from winning the presidency of the United States.

Studying the 2000 presidential election helps us understand why U.S. politics is dominated by a two-party system. The structure and dynamics of American politics work strongly against *any* third party, which cannot hope to win the presidency but can spoil a victory for one of the two major parties. The Democratic and Republican parties have dominated national and state politics for more than 125 years. Their domination is more complete than that of any pair of parties in any other democratic government. Although all democracies have some form of multiparty politics, very few have a stable two-party system—Britain being the most notable exception (see Compared with What? 8.1). Most people take our two-party system for granted, not realizing that it is arguably the most unique feature of American government.

Why do we have any political parties? What functions do they perform? How did we become a nation of Democrats and Republicans? Do these parties truly differ in their platforms and behavior? Are parties really necessary for democratic government, or do they just get in the way of citizens and their government? In this chapter, we will answer these questions by examining political parties, perhaps the most misunderstood element of American politics.

POLITICAL PARTIES AND THEIR FUNCTIONS

According to democratic theory, the primary means by which citizens control their government is voting in free elections. Most Americans agree that voting is important: of those surveyed after the 1996 presidential campaign, 86 percent felt that elections make the government "pay attention to what the people think."[11] Americans are not nearly as supportive of the role played by political parties in elections, however. When asked whether Perot should run for president in 1996 as "head of a third party which would also run candidates in state and local races" or "by himself as an independent candidate," 60 percent of a national sample favored his running without a party.[12]

★ **compared with what?**

8.1

Only Two to Tangle

Compared with party systems in other countries, the U.S. two-party system is unusual indeed. Most democracies have multiparty systems in which four or five parties win enough seats in the legislature to contest for government power. Even the few countries classified as having two-party systems have minor parties that regularly contest seats and win enough votes to complicate national politics. The United Kingdom is the most notable example of a country reputed to have a two-party system. The purity of the U.S. pattern shows clearly in these graphs of votes cast for party candidates running for the U.S. House compared with votes cast for party candidates running for the British House of Commons.

Sources: Thomas T. Mackie and Richard Rose, *The International Almanac of Electoral History,* 3rd ed. (Washington, D.C.: Congressional Quarterly Press, 1991); Elections Around the World, at <www.agora.stm.it/election/index.htm>; and *Congressional Quarterly Weekly Report,* 11 November 2000, pp. 2694–2703.

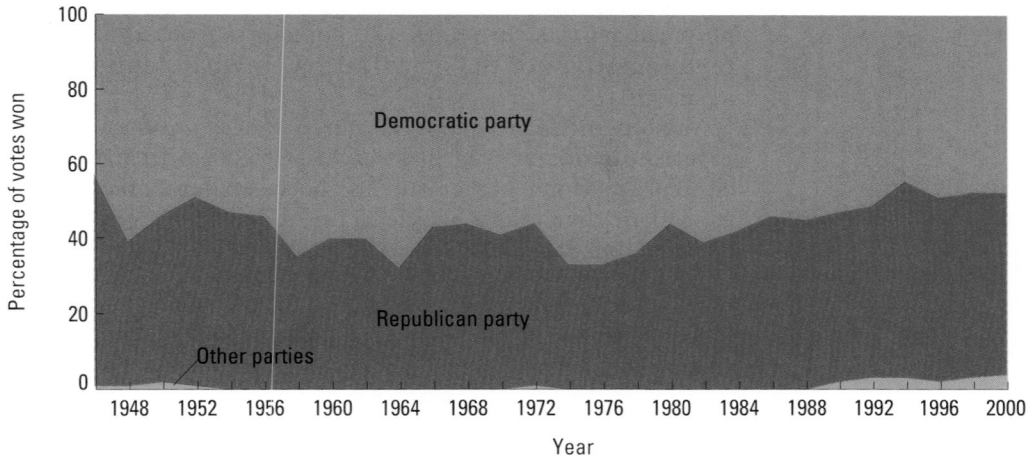

U.S. HOUSE OF REPRESENTATIVES

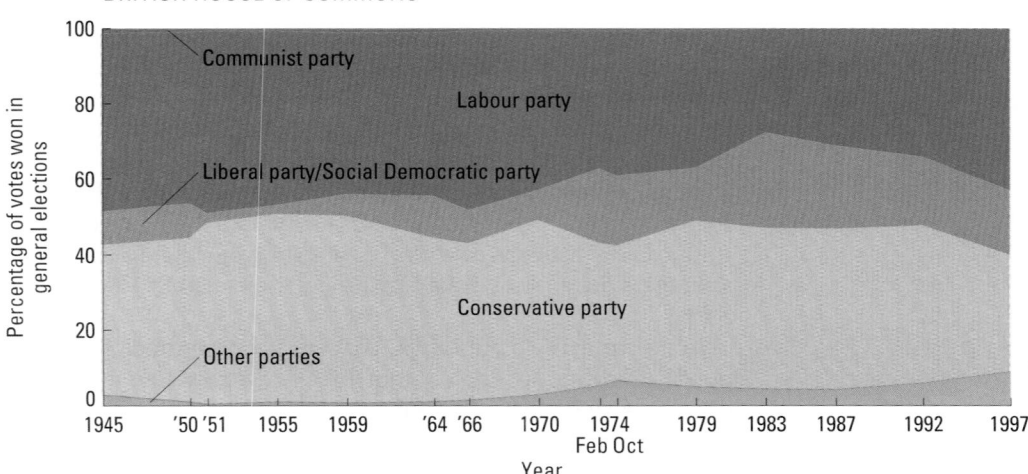

BRITISH HOUSE OF COMMONS

On the other hand, Americans are quick to condemn as "undemocratic" countries that do not regularly hold elections contested by political parties. In truth, Americans have a love-hate relationship with political parties. They believe that parties are necessary for democratic government; at the same time, they think parties are somehow obstructionist and not to be trusted. This distrust is particularly strong among younger voters. To better appreciate the role of political parties in democratic government, we must understand exactly what parties are and what they do.

What Is a Political Party?

political party
An organization that sponsors candidates for political office under the organization's name.

nomination
Designation as an official candidate of a political party.

A **political party** is an organization that sponsors candidates for political office *under the organization's name.* The italicized part of this definition is important. True political parties select individuals to run for public office through a formal **nomination** process, which designates them as the parties' official candidates. This activity distinguishes the Democratic and Republican parties from interest groups. The AFL-CIO and the National Association of Manufacturers are interest groups. They often support candidates, but they do not nominate them to run as their avowed representatives. If they did, they would be transformed into political parties. In short, the sponsoring of candidates, designated as representatives of the organization, is what defines an organization as a party.

Most democratic theorists agree that a modern nation-state cannot practice democracy without at least two political parties that regularly contest elections. In fact, the link between democracy and political parties is so firm that many people define *democratic government* in terms of competitive party politics.

Party Functions

political system
A set of interrelated institutions that links people with government.

Parties contribute to democratic government through the functions they perform for the **political system**—the set of interrelated institutions that link people with government. Four of the most important party functions are nominating candidates for election to public office, structuring the voting choice in elections, proposing alternative government programs, and coordinating the actions of government officials.

Nominating Candidates.   Without political parties, voters would confront a bewildering array of self-nominated candidates, each seeking votes on the basis of personal friendships, celebrity status, or name recognition. Parties can provide a form of quality control for their nominees through the process of peer review. Party insiders, the nominees' peers, usually know the strengths and faults of potential candidates much better than average voters and thus can judge their suitability for representing the party.

In nominating candidates, parties often do more than pass judgment on potential office seekers; sometimes, they go so far as to recruit talented individuals to become candidates. In this way, parties help not only to ensure a minimum level of quality among candidates who run for office but also to raise the quality of those candidates.

Structuring the Voting Choice.   Political parties also help democratic government by structuring the voting choice—reducing the number of candidates on the ballot to those who have a realistic chance of winning. Established parties—those with experience in contesting elections—acquire a following of loyal voters who guarantee the party's candidates a predictable base of votes. The ability of established parties to mobilize their supporters has the effect of discouraging nonparty candidates from running for office and of discouraging new parties from forming. Consequently, the realistic choice is between candidates offered by the major parties, reducing the amount of new information that voters need to make a rational decision. Contrast the voting decision in our stable two-party system (and the outcome) with the voter's task in the June 1999 Russian parliamentary election, in which twenty-six parties received measurable percentages of the vote and eleven won representation in the Federal Assembly.

Proposing Alternative Government Programs.   Parties also help voters choose among candidates by proposing alternative programs of government action—the general policies their candidates will pursue if they gain office. Even if voters know nothing about the qualities of the parties' candidates, they can vote rationally for the candidates of the party that has policies they favor. The specific policies advocated vary from candidate to candidate and from election to election. However, the types of policies advocated by candidates of one party tend to differ from those proposed by candidates of other parties. Although there are exceptions, candidates of the same party tend to favor policies that fit their party's underlying political philosophy, or ideology.

   In many countries, parties' names—such as Conservative and Socialist—reflect their political stance. The Democrats and Republicans have ideologically neutral names, but many minor parties in the United States have used their names to advertise their policies: the Prohibition Party, the Socialist Party, and even the Reform Party. The neutrality of the two major parties' names suggests that their policies are similar. This is not true. As we shall see, they regularly adopt very different policies in their platforms.

Coordinating the Actions of Government Officials.   Finally, party organizations help coordinate the actions of public officials. A government based on the separation of powers, such as that of the United States, divides responsibilities for making public policy. The president and the leaders of the House and Senate are not required to cooperate with one another. Political party organizations are the major means for bridging the separate powers to produce coordinated policies that can govern the country effectively. Parties do this in two ways. First, candidates' and officeholders' political fortunes are linked to their party organization, which can bestow and withhold favors. Second, and perhaps more important in the United States, members of the same party in the presidency, the House, and the Senate tend to share political principles and thus often voluntarily cooperate in making policy.

   So why do we have parties? One expert notes that successful politicians in the United States need electoral and governing majorities and that "no collection of ambitious politicians has long been able to think of a way to achieve their goals in this democracy save in terms of political parties."[13]

A HISTORY OF U.S. PARTY POLITICS

The two major U.S. parties are among the oldest in the world. In fact, the Democratic party, founded in 1828 but with roots reaching back to the late 1700s, has a strong claim to being the oldest party in existence. Its closest rival is the British Conservative Party, formed in 1832, two decades before the Republican party was organized in 1854. Several generations of citizens have supported the Democratic and Republican parties, and they are part of American history. They have become institutionalized in our political process.

The Preparty Period

Today we think of party activities as normal, even essential, to American politics. It was not always so. The Constitution makes no mention of political parties, and none existed when the Constitution was written in 1787. It was common then to refer to groups pursuing some common political interest as *factions*. Although factions were seen as inevitable in politics, they were also considered dangerous. One argument for adopting the Constitution—proposed in *Federalist* No. 10 (see Chapter 3 and the appendix)—was that its federal system would prevent factional influences from controlling the government.

Factions existed even under British rule. In colonial assemblies, supporters of the governor (and thus of the Crown) were known as *Tories* or *Loyalists,* and their opponents were called *Whigs* or *Patriots.* After independence, the arguments over whether to adopt the Constitution produced a different alignment of factions. Those who backed the Constitution were loosely known as *federalists,* their opponents as *antifederalists.* At this stage, the groups could not be called parties because they did not sponsor candidates for election.

electoral college
A body of electors chosen by voters to cast ballots for president and vice president.

Elections then were vastly different from elections today. The Constitution provided for the president and vice president to be chosen by an **electoral college**—a body of electors who met in the capitals of their respective states to cast their ballots. Initially, in most states the legislatures, not the voters, chose the electors (one for each senator and representative in Congress). Presidential elections in the early years of the nation, then, actually were decided by a handful of political leaders. (See Chapter 9 for a discussion of the electoral college in modern presidential politics.) Often they met in small, secret groups, called **caucuses,** to propose candidates for public office. Often these were composed of like-minded members of state legislatures and Congress. This was the setting for George Washington's election as the first president in 1789.

caucus
A closed meeting of the members of a political party to decide upon questions of policy and the selection of candidates for office.

We can classify Washington as a federalist because he supported the Constitution, but he was not a factional leader and actually opposed factional politics. His immense prestige, coupled with his political neutrality, left Washington unopposed for the office of president, and he was elected unanimously by the electoral college. During Washington's administration, however, the political cleavage sharpened between those who favored a stronger national government and those who wanted a less powerful, more decentralized national government.

The first group, led by Alexander Hamilton, proclaimed themselves *Federalists.* The second group, led by Thomas Jefferson, called themselves

Republicans. (Although they used the same name, they were not Republicans as we know them today.) The Jeffersonians chose the name Republicans to distinguish themselves from the "aristocratic" tendencies of Hamilton's Federalists. The Federalists countered by calling the Republicans the *Democratic Republicans,* attempting to link Jefferson's party to the disorder (and beheadings) spawned by the "radical democrats" in France during the French Revolution of 1789.

The First Party System: Federalists and Democratic Republicans

Washington's Farewell Address, 1796

Can You Explain Why...
President John Adams, a Federalist, had a vice president from a different political party?

Washington was reelected president unanimously in 1792, but his vice president, John Adams, was opposed by a candidate backed by the Democratic Republicans. This brief skirmish foreshadowed the nation's first major-party struggle over the presidency. Disheartened by the political split in his administration, Washington spoke out against "the baneful effects" of parties in his farewell address in 1796. Nonetheless, parties already existed in the political system, as Figure 8.1 shows. In the election of 1796, the Federalists supported Vice President John Adams to succeed Washington as president. The Democratic Republicans backed Thomas Jefferson for president but could not agree on a vice-presidential candidate. In the electoral college, Adams won seventy-one votes to Jefferson's sixty-eight, and both ran ahead of other candidates. At that time, the Constitution provided that the presidency would go to the candidate who won the most votes in the electoral college, with the vice presidency going to the runner-up. So Adams, a Federalist, had to accept Jefferson, a Democratic Republican, as his vice president. Obviously, the Constitution did not anticipate a presidential contest between candidates from opposing political parties.

The party function of nominating candidates emerged more clearly in the election of 1800. Both parties caucused in Congress to nominate candidates for president and vice president. The result was the first true party contest for the presidency. The Federalists nominated John Adams and Charles Pinckney; the Democratic Republicans nominated Thomas Jefferson and Aaron Burr. This time, the Democratic Republican candidates won. However, the new party organization worked too well. According to the Constitution, each elector had to vote by ballot for two persons. The Democratic Republican electors unanimously cast their two votes for Jefferson and Burr. The presidency was to go to the candidate with the most votes, but the top two candidates were tied!

Although Jefferson was the party's presidential candidate and Burr its vice-presidential candidate, the Constitution empowered the House of Representatives to choose either one of them as president. After seven days and thirty-six ballots, the House decided in favor of Jefferson.

The Twelfth Amendment, ratified in 1804, prevented a repeat of the troublesome election outcomes of 1796 and 1800. It required the electoral college to vote separately for president and vice president, implicitly recognizing that parties would nominate different candidates for the two offices.

The election of 1800 marked the beginning of the end for the Federalists, who lost the next four elections. By 1820, the Federalists were no more.

figure 8.1

Two-Party Systems in American History

Over time, the American party system has undergone a series of wrenching transformations. Since 1856, the Democrats and the Republicans have alternated irregularly in power, each party enjoying a long period of dominance.

Year	Left / third parties	Adams	Democratic-Republican / Democratic	Center third parties	National Republican / Whig / Republican	Era / System
1789						Washington unanimously elected president
1792						Washington unanimously reelected — PREPARTY PERIOD
1796	Federalist	Adams	Democratic Republican			FIRST PARTY SYSTEM
1800	—		Jefferson			
1804	—		Jefferson			
1808	—		Madison			
1812	—		Madison			
1816	—		Monroe			
1820			Monroe			"ERA OF GOOD FEELING"
1824			J.Q. Adams			
1828			Democratic Jackson		National Republican	SECOND PARTY SYSTEM
1832			Jackson		Whig	
1836			Van Buren		—	
1840			—		Harrison	
1844			Polk		—	
1848			—		Taylor	
1852			Pierce		—	
1856			Buchanan		Republican	THIRD PARTY SYSTEM
1860	Constitutional Union	Southern Democrat	—		Lincoln	
1864			—		Lincoln	
1868			—		Grant	
1872			—		Grant	
1876			—		Hayes	
1880			—		Garfield	
1884			Cleveland		—	
1888			—		Harrison	Rough Balance
1892			Cleveland		—	
1896			—	Populist	McKinley	
1900			—		McKinley	Republican Dominance
1904			—		Roosevelt, T.	
1908			—		Taft	
1912			Wilson	Progressive	—	
1916			Wilson		—	
1920			—		Harding	
1924			—		Coolidge	
1928			—		Hoover	
1932			Roosevelt, F. D.		—	Democratic Dominance
1936			Roosevelt, F. D.		—	
1940			Roosevelt, F. D.		—	
1944			Roosevelt, F. D.		—	
1948			Truman	States' Rights	—	
1952			—		Eisenhower	
1956			—		Eisenhower	
1960			Kennedy		—	
1964			Johnson		—	
1968			—	American Independent	Nixon	
1972			—		Nixon	
1976			Carter		—	
1980			—	Independent	Reagan	
1984			—		Reagan	
1988			—		Bush, G. H. W.	
1992			Clinton	Independent	—	
1996			Clinton	Reform	—	
2000			—	Green	Bush, G. W.	

The Democratic Republican candidate, James Monroe, was reelected in the first presidential contest without party competition since Washington's time. (Monroe received all but one electoral vote, which reportedly was cast against him so that Washington would remain the only president ever elected unanimously.) Ironically, the lack of partisan competition under Monroe, in what was dubbed "the Era of Good Feelings," also fatally weakened his party, the Democratic Republicans. Lacking competition, the Democratic Republicans neglected their function of nominating candidates. In 1824, the party caucus's nominee was challenged by three other Democratic Republicans, including John Quincy Adams and Andrew Jackson, who proved to be more popular candidates among the voters in the ensuing election.

Before 1824, the parties' role in structuring the popular vote was relatively unimportant because relatively few people were entitled to vote. But the states began to drop restrictive requirements for voting after 1800, and voting rights for white males expanded even faster after 1815 (see Chapter 7). With the expansion of suffrage, more states began to allow the voters, rather than Congress, to choose the presidential electors. The 1824 election was the first in which the voters selected the presidential electors in most states. Still, the role of political parties in structuring the popular vote had not yet developed fully.

Although Jackson won a plurality of both the popular vote and the electoral vote in 1824, he did not win the necessary majority in the electoral college. The House of Representatives again had to decide the winner. It chose the second-place John Quincy Adams (from the established state of Massachusetts) over the voters' choice, Jackson (from the frontier state of Tennessee). The factionalism among the leaders of the Democratic Republican Party became so intense that the party split in two.

The Second Party System: Democrats and Whigs

The Jacksonian faction of the Democratic Republican Party represented the common people in the expanding South and West, and its members took pride in calling themselves simply Democrats. Jackson ran again for the presidency as a Democrat in 1828, a milestone that marked the beginning of today's Democratic Party. That election was also the first "mass" election in U.S. history. Although voters had directly chosen many presidential electors in 1824, the total votes cast in that election numbered fewer than 370,000. By 1828, relaxed requirements for voting (and the use of popular elections to select presidential electors in more states) had increased the vote by more than 300 percent, to more than 1.1 million.

As the electorate expanded, the parties changed. No longer could a party rely on a few political leaders in the state legislatures to control the votes cast in the electoral college. Parties now needed to campaign for votes cast by hundreds of thousands of citizens. Recognizing this new dimension of the nation's politics, the parties responded with a new method for nominating presidential candidates. Instead of selecting candidates in a closed caucus of party representatives in Congress, the parties devised the **national convention**. At these gatherings, delegates from state parties across the nation would choose candidates for president and vice president and adopt a statement of policies called a **party platform**. The Anti-Masonic Party, which was the first "third" party in American history to

Can You Explain Why...
1828 is regarded as the first mass election in history?

national convention
A gathering of delegates of a single political party from across the country to choose candidates for president and vice president and to adopt a party platform.

party platform
The statement of policies of a national political party.

challenge the two major parties for the presidency, called the first national convention in 1831. The Democrats adopted the convention idea in 1832 to nominate Jackson for a second term, as did their new opponents that year, the National Republicans.

The label *National Republicans* applied to John Quincy Adams's faction of the former Democratic Republican Party. However, the National Republicans did not become today's Republican Party. Adams's followers called themselves National Republicans to signify their old Federalist preference for a strong national government, but the symbolism did not appeal to the voters, and the National Republicans lost to Jackson in 1832.

Elected to another term, Jackson began to assert the power of the nation over the states (acting more like a National Republican than a Democrat). His policies drew new opponents, who started calling him "King Andrew." A coalition made up of former National Republicans, Anti-Masons, and Jackson haters formed the Whig Party in 1834.[14] The name referred to the English Whigs, who opposed the powers of the British throne; the implication was that Jackson was governing like a king. For the next thirty years, Democrats and Whigs alternated in the presidency. However, the issues of slavery and sectionalism eventually destroyed the Whigs from within. Although the party had won the White House in 1848 and had taken 44 percent of the vote in 1852, the Whigs were unable to field a presidential candidate in the 1856 election.

The Current Party System: Democrats and Republicans

In the early 1850s, antislavery forces (including some Whigs and antislavery Democrats) began to organize. At meetings in Jackson, Michigan, and Ripon, Wisconsin, they recommended the formation of a new party, the Republican Party, to oppose the extension of slavery into the Kansas and Nebraska territories. This party, founded in 1854, continues as today's Republican Party.

The Republican Party entered its first presidential election in 1856. It took 33 percent of the vote, and its candidate (John Frémont) carried eleven states—all in the North. Then, in 1860, the Republicans nominated Abraham Lincoln. The Democrats were deeply divided over the slavery issue and actually split into two parties. The northern wing kept the Democratic Party label and nominated Stephen Douglas. The Southern Democrats ran John Breckinridge. A fourth party, the Constitutional Union Party, nominated John Bell. Lincoln took 40 percent of the popular vote and carried every northern state. Breckinridge won every southern state. But all three of Lincoln's opponents together still did not win enough electoral votes to deny him the presidency.

critical election
An election that produces a sharp change in the existing pattern of party loyalties among groups of voters.

electoral realignment
The change in voting patterns that occurs after a critical election.

The election of 1860 is considered the first of three critical elections under the current party system.[15] A **critical election** is marked by a sharp change in the existing patterns of party loyalty among groups of voters. Moreover, this change in voting patterns, which is called an **electoral realignment,** does not end with the election but persists through several subsequent elections.[16] The election of 1860 divided the country politically between the northern states, whose voters mainly voted Republican, and the southern states, which were overwhelmingly Democratic. The victory of the North over the South in the Civil War cemented Democratic loyalties in the South.

For forty years, from 1880 to 1920, no Republican presidential candidate won even one of the eleven states of the former Confederacy. The South's solid Democratic record earned it the nickname "the Solid South." The Republicans did not puncture the Solid South until 1920, when Warren G. Harding carried Tennessee. The Republicans later won five southern states in 1928, when the Democrats ran the first Catholic candidate, Al Smith. Republican presidential candidates won no more southern states until 1952, when Dwight Eisenhower broke the pattern of Democratic dominance in the South—ninety years after that pattern had been set by the Civil War.

Eras of Party Dominance Since the Civil War

two-party system
A political system in which two major political parties compete for control of the government. Candidates from a third party have little chance of winning office.

The critical election of 1860 established the Democratic and Republican parties as the dominant parties in our **two-party system.** In a two-party system, most voters are so loyal to one or the other of the major parties that independent candidates or candidates from a third party—which means any minor party—have little chance of winning office. Certainly that is true in presidential elections, as Perot found out in both 1992 and 1996. Third-party candidates tend to be most successful at the local or state level. Since the current two-party system was established, relatively few minor-party candidates have won election to the U.S. House, even fewer have won election to the Senate, and none have won the presidency.

The voters in a given state, county, or community are not always equally divided in their loyalties between the Republicans and the Democrats. In some areas, voters typically favor the Republicans, whereas voters in other areas prefer the Democrats. When one party in a two-party system *regularly* enjoys support from most voters in an area, it is called the *majority party* in that area; the other is called the *minority party*. Since the inception of the current two-party system, three periods have characterized the balance between the two major parties at the national level.

A Rough Balance: 1860–1894. From 1860 through 1894, the Grand Old Party (or GOP, as the Republican party is sometimes called) won eight of ten presidential elections, which would seem to qualify it as the majority party. However, some of its success in presidential elections came from its practice of running Civil War heroes and from the North's domination of southern politics. Seats in the House of Representatives are a better guide to the breadth of national support. An analysis shows that the Republicans and Democrats won an equal number of congressional elections, each controlling the chamber for nine sessions between 1860 and 1894.

A Republican Majority: 1896–1930. A second critical election, in 1896, transformed the Republican Party into a true majority party. Grover Cleveland, a Democrat, occupied the White House, and the country was in a severe depression. The Republicans nominated William McKinley, governor of Ohio and a conservative, who stood for a high tariff against foreign goods and sound money tied to the value of gold. Rather than tour the country seeking votes, McKinley ran a dignified campaign from his Ohio home.

William Jennings Bryan: When Candidates Were Orators

Today, televised images of a candidate waving his hands and shouting to an audience would look silly. But candidates once had to resort to such tactics to be effective with large crowds. One of the most commanding orators around the turn of the century was William Jennings Bryan (1860–1925), whose stirring speeches extolling the virtues of the free coinage of silver were music to the ears of thousands of westerners and southern farmers.

The Democrats, already in trouble because of the depression, nominated the fiery William Jennings Bryan. In stark contrast to McKinley, Bryan advocated the free and unlimited coinage of silver—which would mean cheap money and easy payment of debts through inflation. Bryan was also the nominee of the young Populist Party, an agrarian protest party that had proposed the free-silver platform Bryan adopted. Feature 8.1 explains that the book *The Wonderful Wizard of Oz*, which you probably know as a movie, was actually a Populist political fable.[17] Conservatives, especially businesspeople, were aghast at the Democrats' radical turn, and voters in the heavily populated Northeast and Midwest surged toward the Republican Party, many of them permanently. McKinley carried every northern state east of the Mississippi. The Republicans also won the House, and they retained their control of it in the next six elections.

The election of 1896 helped solidify a Republican majority in industrial America and forged a link between the Republican Party and business. In the subsequent electoral realignment, the Republicans emerged as a true majority party. The GOP dominated national politics—controlling the presidency, the Senate, and the House—almost continuously from 1896 until the Wall Street crash of 1929, which burst big business's bubble and launched the Great Depression.*

A Democratic Majority: 1932 to the Present?   The Republicans' majority status ended in the critical election of 1932 between incumbent president Herbert Hoover and the Democratic challenger, Franklin Delano Roosevelt. Roosevelt promised new solutions to unemployment and the economic crisis of the Depression. His campaign appealed to labor, middle-class

---

* *The only break in GOP domination was in 1912, when Teddy Roosevelt's Progressive Party split from the Republicans, allowing Democrat Woodrow Wilson to win the presidency and giving the Democrats control of Congress, and again in 1916, when Wilson was reelected.*

★★★

The Wizard of Oz: A Political Fable

Most Americans are familiar with *The Wizard of Oz* through the children's books or the 1939 motion picture, but few realize that the story was written as a political fable to promote the Populist movement around the turn of the century. Next time you see or read it, try interpreting the Tin Woodsman as the industrial worker, the Scarecrow as the struggling farmer, and the Wizard as the president, who is powerful only as long as he succeeds in deceiving the people. (Sorry, but in the book Dorothy's ruby slippers were only silver shoes.)

The Wonderful Wizard of Oz was written by Lyman Frank Baum in 1900, during the collapse of the Populist movement. Through the Populist party, Midwestern farmers, in alliance with some urban workers, had challenged the banks, railroads, and other economic interests that squeezed farmers through low prices, high freight rates, and continued indebtedness.

The Populists advocated government ownership of railroad, telephone, and telegraph industries. They also wanted silver coinage. Their power grew during the 1893 depression, the worst in U.S. history until then, as farm prices sank to new lows and unemployment was widespread.

In the 1894 congressional elections, the Populist party got almost 40 percent of the vote. It looked forward to winning the presidency, and the silver standard, in 1896. But in that election, which revolved around the issue of gold versus silver, Populist Democrat William Jennings Bryan lost to Republican William McKinley by 95 electoral votes. Bryan, a congressman from Nebraska and a gifted orator, ran again in 1900, but the Populist strength was gone.

Baum viewed these events in both rural South Dakota, where he edited a local weekly, and in urban Chicago, where he wrote *Oz*. He mourned the destruction of the fragile alliance between the Midwestern farmers (the Scarecrow) and the urban industrial workers (the Tin Woodsman). Along with Bryan (the Cowardly Lion, with a roar but little else), they had been taken down the yellow brick road (the gold standard) that led nowhere. Each journeyed to Emerald City seeking favors from the Wizard of Oz (the President). Dorothy, the symbol of Everyman, went along with them, innocent enough to see the truth before the others.

Along the way they met the Wicked Witch of the East, who, Baum tells us, had kept the little Munchkin people "in bondage for many years, making them slave for her night and day." She also had put a spell on the Tin Woodsman, once an independent and hard-working man, so that each time he swung his axe, it chopped off a different part of his body. Lacking another trade, he "worked harder than ever," becoming like a machine, incapable of love, yearning for a heart. Another witch, the Wicked Witch of the West, clearly symbolizes the large industrial corporations.

The small group heads toward Emerald City, where the Wizard rules from behind a papier-mâché façade. Oz, by the way, is the abbreviation for ounce, the standard measure for gold.

Like all good politicians, the Wizard can be all things to all people. Dorothy sees him as an enormous head. The Scarecrow sees a gossamer fairy. The Woodsman sees an awful beast, the Cowardly Lion "a ball of fire so fierce and glowing he could scarcely bear to gaze upon it."

Later, however, when they confront the Wizard directly, they see he is nothing more than "a little man, with a bald head and a wrinkled face."

"I have been making believe," the Wizard confesses. "I'm just a common man." But the Scarecrow adds, "You're more than that . . . you're a humbug."

"It was a great mistake my ever letting you into the Throne Room," admits the Wizard, a former ventriloquist and circus balloonist from Omaha.

This was Baum's ultimate Populist message. The powers-that-be survive by deception. Only people's ignorance allows the powerful to manipulate and control them. Dorothy returns to Kansas with the magical help of her silver shoes (the silver issue), but when she gets to Kansas she realizes her shoes "had fallen off in her flight through the air, and were lost forever in the desert." Still, she is safe at home with Aunt Em and Uncle Henry, simple farmers.

Source: Peter Dreier, "The Wizard of Oz: A Political Fable," *Today Journal,* 14 February 1986. Reprinted by permission of Pacific News Service <www.pacificnews.org>.

liberals, and new European ethnic voters. Along with Democratic voters in the Solid South, urban workers in the North, Catholics, Jews, and white ethnic minorities formed "the Roosevelt coalition." The relatively few blacks who voted at that time tended to remain loyal to the Republicans—"the party of Lincoln."

Roosevelt was swept into office in a landslide, carrying huge Democratic majorities with him into the House and Senate to enact his liberal activist programs. The electoral realignment reflected by the election of 1932 made the Democrats the majority party. Not only was Roosevelt reelected in 1936, 1940, and 1944, but Democrats held control of both houses of Congress in most sessions from 1933 through 1994. The only exceptions were Republican control of Congress in 1947 and 1948 (under President Truman); in 1953 and 1954 (under President Eisenhower); and of the Senate only in 1947 and 1948 and from 1981 to 1986 (under Reagan). In their smashing victory in the 1994 congressional elections, however, the Republicans gained control of Congress for the first time in forty years. Republicans retained control after the 1996 elections—the first time they took both houses in successive elections since Herbert Hoover was elected in 1928. Republicans took Congress again in 1998, but Democrats gained five House seats. Not since 1934 had a president's party won seats in a midterm election.

In presidential elections, however, the Democrats have not fared so well since Roosevelt. In fact, they won only six elections (Truman, Kennedy, Johnson, Carter, and Clinton twice), compared with the Republicans' eight victories (Eisenhower twice, Nixon twice, Reagan twice, and the two Bushes—father and later, his son). In 1996, Clinton became the first Democratic president since Roosevelt to be reelected—and the second president ever to be impeached.

Signs are strong that the coalition of Democratic voters forged by Roosevelt in the 1930s has already cracked. Certainly the South is no longer solid for the Democrats. Since 1952, the South has voted more consistently for Republican presidential candidates than for Democrats. Since the 1970s, this trend has extended to congressional candidates. Although party loyalty within regions has gradually shifted, the Democratic coalition of urban workers and religious and ethnic minorities still seems intact, if weakened. Instead of a full realignment, we seem to be in a period of **electoral dealignment,** in which party loyalties have become less important to voters as they cast their ballots. We examine the influence of party loyalty on voting in the next chapter, after we look at the operation of our two-party system.

electoral dealignment
A lessening of the importance of party loyalties in voting decisions.

THE AMERICAN TWO-PARTY SYSTEM

Our review of party history in the United States has focused on the two dominant parties. But we should not ignore the special contributions of certain minor parties, among them the Anti-Masonic Party, the Populists, and the Progressives of 1912. In this section, we study the fortunes of minor, or third, parties in American politics. We also will look at why we have only two major parties, explain how federalism helps the parties survive, and describe voters' loyalty to the two major parties today.

Minor Parties in America

Minor parties have always figured in party politics in America. Most minor parties in our political history have been one of four types:[18]

- *Bolter parties* are formed by factions that have split off from one of the major parties. Six times in the thirty-one presidential elections since the Civil War, disgruntled leaders have "bolted the ticket" and challenged their former parties. Bolter parties have occasionally won significant proportions of the vote. However, with the exception of Teddy Roosevelt's Progressive Party in 1912 and the possible exception of George Wallace's American Independent Party in 1968, bolter parties have not affected the outcome of presidential elections.

- *Farmer-labor parties* represent farmers and urban workers who believe that they, the working class, are not getting their share of society's wealth. The People's Party, founded in 1892 and nicknamed "the Populist Party," was a prime example of a farmer-labor party. The Populists won 8.5 percent of the vote in 1892 and also became the first third party since 1860 to win any electoral votes. Flushed by success, it endorsed William Jennings Bryan, the Democratic candidate, in 1896. When he lost, the party quickly faded. Farm and labor groups revived many Populist ideas in the Progressive Party in 1924, which nominated Robert La Follette for the presidency. Although the party won 16.6 percent of the popular vote, it carried only La Follette's home state of Wisconsin. The party died in 1925.

- *Parties of ideological protest* go further than farmer-labor parties in criticizing the established system. These parties reject prevailing doctrines and propose radically different principles, often favoring more government activism. The Socialist Party has been the most successful party of ideological protest. Even at its high point in 1912, however, it garnered only 6 percent of the vote, and Socialist candidates for president have never won a single state. In recent years, protest parties have tended to come from the right, arguing against govenment action in society. Such is the program of the Libertarian Party, which stresses freedom over order and equality. Libertarians have run candidates in every presidential election since 1972, but none has received more than 1.1 percent of the vote since 1980. In 1996 and 2000, the Green Party mounted a protest from the left, favoring government action to preserve the environment. In winning 2.7 percent of the vote in 2000, the Greens more than doubled the best showing of the Libertarian candidate for president, but Libertarian candidates for Congress were far more plentiful and successful (see Figure 8.2).

- *Single-issue parties* are formed to promote one principle, not a general philosophy of government. The Anti-Masonic parties of the 1820s and 1830s, for example, opposed Masonic lodges and other secret societies. The Free Soil Party of the 1840s and 1850s worked to abolish slavery. The Prohibition Party, the most durable example of a single-issue party, opposed the consumption of alcoholic beverages. Prohibition candidates consistently won from 1 to 2 percent of the vote in nine presidential elections between 1884 and 1916, and the party has run candidates in every presidential election since. Its candidate in 2000 was Earl Dodge of Denver, Colorado, who appeared on the ballot only in Colorado.

8.2   Party Candidates for the U.S. House in the 2000 Election

In 2000—as in recent elections—the Democratic and Republican parties ran candidates for the House of Representatives in more than 85 percent of the 435 congressional districts. Only the Libertarian Party, the best-organized minor party in the nation, came even close, running candidates in 248 districts. However, in 208 of those districts, the Libertarian candidates got less than 4 percent of the vote—often far less. Together, the other three minor parties ran only 155 candidates for the U.S. House. The closest a third-party candidate came to winning a seat in Congress was in Louisiana's 7th District, where (in the absence of a Republican) the Libertarian candidate won 16.7 percent of the vote against the incumbent Democrat's 83.3 percent. In Vermont, incumbent Bernard Sanders—who votes with Democrats in the House—won reelection as an Independent.

Source: Calculated from data reported in *Congressional Quarterly Weekly Report,* 11 November 2000, pp. 2694–2703.

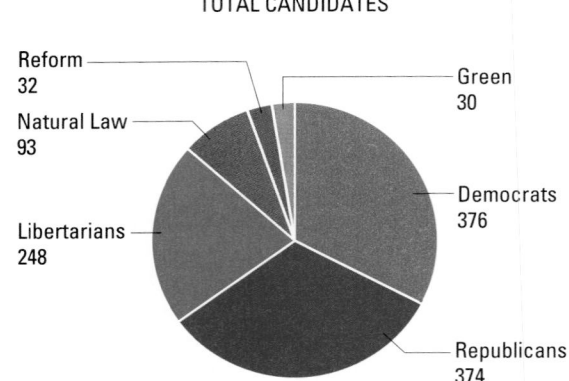

TOTAL CANDIDATES

Reform 32
Green 30
Natural Law 93
Democrats 376
Libertarians 248
Republicans 374

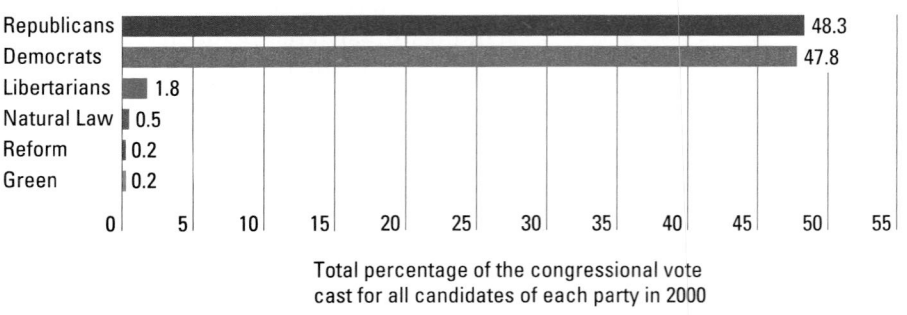

Republicans	48.3
Democrats	47.8
Libertarians	1.8
Natural Law	0.5
Reform	0.2
Green	0.2

Total percentage of the congressional vote cast for all candidates of each party in 2000

America has a long history of third parties operating on the periphery of our two-party system. Minor parties form primarily to express some voters' discontent with choices offered by the major parties and to work for their own objectives within the electoral system.[19] The Reform Party certainly reflected discontent with existing policies, but otherwise it resists classification. It did not bolt from an existing party, it did not have a farmer-labor base, it had no clear ideology, and it was not devoted to any single issue. Billionaire businessman Ross Perot created it for his 1996 presidential campaign, which relied on television to woo citizens previously uninvolved in partisan politics. The Reform Party won 8 percent of the vote in 1996, less than half of what Perot had won in 1992 as an independent. Neverthless, the party won enough votes to qualify for some $12 million in federal funds for the 2000 campaign. Perot then turned away from the party, however, and left others to fight for its leadership and its $12 million. Without its entrepreneur, the Reform Party quickly collapsed. Pat Buchanan, a seasoned ex-Republican partisan, wrested its nomination away from amateurs loyal to Perot. Segments split away from Buchanan's right-wing campaign, and the dispirited party won only 0.4 of 1 percent in 2000.

How have minor parties fared historically? As vote getters, they have not performed well. However, bolter parties have twice won more than 10 percent of the vote. More significantly, the Republican Party originated in 1854 as a single-issue third party opposed to slavery in the nation's new territories; in its first election, in 1856, the party came in second, displacing the Whigs. (Undoubtedly, the Republican exception to the rule has inspired the formation of other hopeful third parties.)

As policy advocates, minor parties have a slightly better record. At times, they have had a real effect on the policies adopted by the major parties. Women's suffrage, the graduated income tax, and the direct election of senators all originated with third parties.[20] Of course, third parties may fail to win more votes because their policies lack popular support. This was a lesson the Democrats learned in 1896, when they adopted the Populists' free-silver plank in their own platform. Both their candidate and their platform went down to defeat, hobbling the Democratic Party for decades.

Most important, minor parties function as safety valves. They allow those who are unhappy with the status quo to express their discontent within the system, to contribute to the political dialogue. Surely this was the function of Nader's candidacy and of the Green Party. If minor parties and independent candidates are indicators of discontent, what should we make of the numerous minor parties, detailed in Figure 8.3, that took part in the 2000 election? Not much. The number of third parties that contest elections is less important than the total number of votes they receive. Despite the presence of numerous minor parties in every presidential election, the two major parties usually collect more than 99 percent of the vote.

Why a Two-Party System?

The history of party politics in the United States is essentially the story of two parties that have alternating control of the government. With relatively few exceptions, Americans conduct elections at all levels within the two-party system. This pattern is unusual in democratic countries, where multiparty systems are more common. Why does the United States have only two major parties? The two most convincing answers to this question stem from the electoral system in the United States and the process of political socialization here.

In the typical U.S. election, two or more candidates contest each office, and the winner is the single candidate who collects the most votes, whether those votes constitute a majority or not. When these two principles of *single winners* chosen by a *simple plurality* of votes govern the election of the members of a legislature, the system (despite its reliance on pluralities rather than majorities) is known as **majority representation.** Think about how American states choose representatives to Congress. A state entitled to ten representatives is divided into ten congressional districts; each district elects one representative. Majority representation of voters through single-member districts is also a feature of most state legislatures.

Alternatively, a legislature might be chosen through a system of **proportional representation,** which awards legislative seats to each party in proportion to the total number of votes it wins in an election. Under this system, the state might hold a single statewide election for all ten seats,

majority representation
The system by which one office, contested by two or more candidates, is won by the single candidate who collects the most votes.

proportional representation
The system by which legislative seats are awarded to a party in proportion to the vote that party wins in an election.

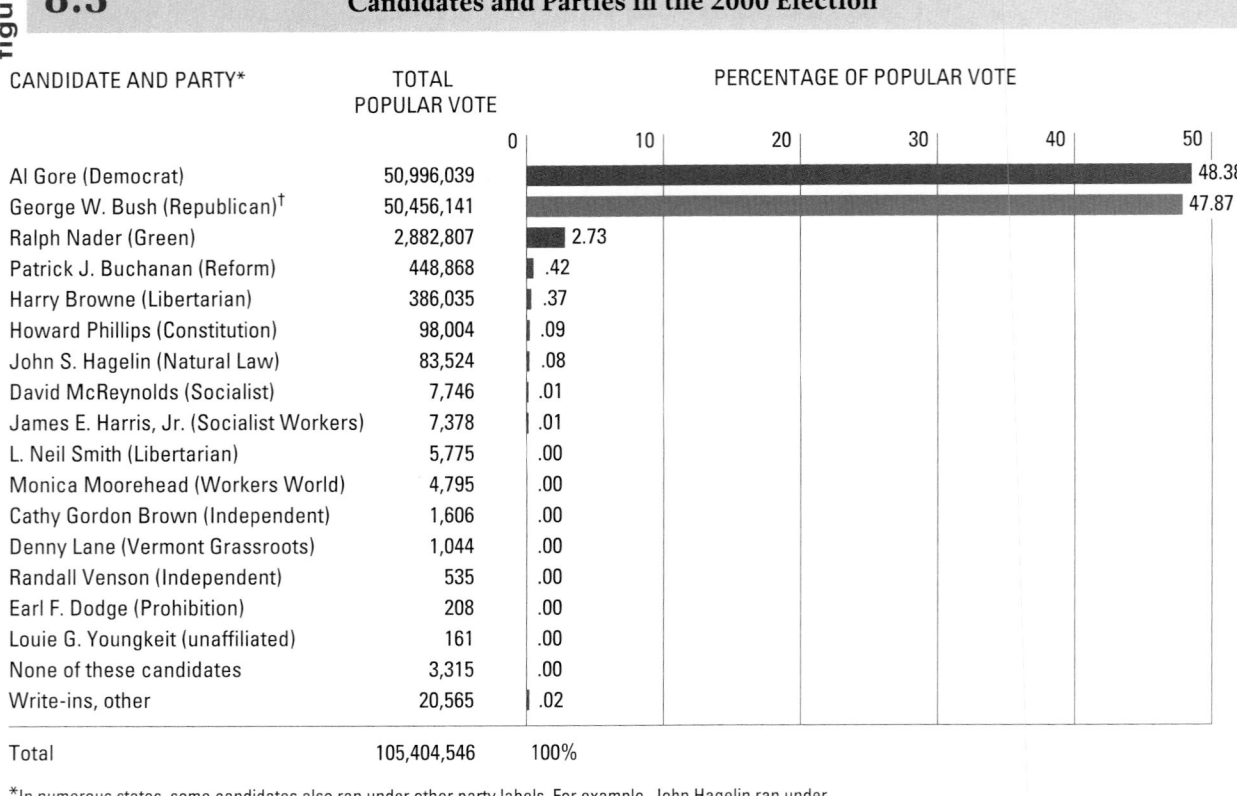

figure 8.3   **Candidates and Parties in the 2000 Election**

CANDIDATE AND PARTY*	TOTAL POPULAR VOTE	PERCENTAGE OF POPULAR VOTE
Al Gore (Democrat)	50,996,039	48.38
George W. Bush (Republican)[†]	50,456,141	47.87
Ralph Nader (Green)	2,882,807	2.73
Patrick J. Buchanan (Reform)	448,868	.42
Harry Browne (Libertarian)	386,035	.37
Howard Phillips (Constitution)	98,004	.09
John S. Hagelin (Natural Law)	83,524	.08
David McReynolds (Socialist)	7,746	.01
James E. Harris, Jr. (Socialist Workers)	7,378	.01
L. Neil Smith (Libertarian)	5,775	.00
Monica Moorehead (Workers World)	4,795	.00
Cathy Gordon Brown (Independent)	1,606	.00
Denny Lane (Vermont Grassroots)	1,044	.00
Randall Venson (Independent)	535	.00
Earl F. Dodge (Prohibition)	208	.00
Louie G. Youngkeit (unaffiliated)	161	.00
None of these candidates	3,315	.00
Write-ins, other	20,565	.02
Total	105,404,546	100%

*In numerous states, some candidates also ran under other party labels. For example, John Hagelin ran under the Reform Party label in five states, and Howard Phillips ran under various versions of the Constitution Party.

[†]Elected

Ralph Nader was not the only "third party" candidate in the 2000 presidential election. More than ten other candidates ran representing more than fifty parties. All of them together, however, captured less than 2 percent of the total vote. This is a complete accounting of all candidates who were listed on at least one state ballot.

Source: Federal Election Commission, "About Elections and Voting," available on February 27, 2001, at <http://www.fec.gov/elections.html>.

with each party presenting a rank-ordered list of ten candidates. Voters could vote for the party list they preferred, and the party's candidates would be elected from the top of each list, according to the proportion of votes won by the party. Thus, if a party got 30 percent of the vote in this example, its first three candidates would be elected.

Although this form of election may seem strange, many democratic countries (for example, the Netherlands, Israel, and Denmark) use it. Proportional representation tends to produce (or perpetuate) several parties because each can win enough seats nationwide to wield some influence in the legislature. In contrast, our system of elections forces interest groups of all sorts to work within the two major parties, for only one candidate in each race stands a chance of being elected under plurality voting. Therefore, the system tends to produce only two parties. Moreover, the two major parties benefit from state laws that automatically list candidates on the ballot if their party won a sizable percentage of the vote in the previous election. These laws discourage minor parties, which usually have to collect signatures to get on a state ballot.[21]

The rules of our electoral system may explain why only two parties tend to form in specific election districts, but why do the same two parties (Democratic and Republican) operate within every state? The contest for the presidency is the key to this question. A candidate can win a presidential election only by amassing a majority of electoral votes from across the entire nation. Presidential candidates try to win votes under the same party label in each state in order to pool their electoral votes in the electoral college. The presidency is a big enough political prize to induce parties to harbor uncomfortable coalitions of voters (southern white Protestants allied with northern Jews and blacks in the Democratic party, for example) just to win the electoral vote and the presidential election.

The American electoral system may force U.S. politics into a two-party mold, but why must the same two parties reappear from election to election? In fact, they do not. The earliest two-party system pitted the Federalists against the Democratic Republicans. A later two-party system involved the Democrats and the Whigs. More than 135 years ago, the Republicans replaced the Whigs in what is our two-party system today. But with modern issues so different from the issues then, why do the Democrats and Republicans persist? This is where political socialization comes into play. The two parties persist simply because they have persisted. After more than one hundred years of political socialization, the two parties today have such a headstart in structuring the vote that they discourage challenges from new parties. Of course, third parties still try to crack the two-party system from time to time, but most have had little success.

The Federal Basis of the Party System

Focusing on contests for the presidency is a convenient and informative way to study the history of American parties, but it also oversimplifies party politics to the point of distortion. By concentrating only on presidential elections, we tend to ignore electoral patterns in the states, where elections often buck national trends. Even during its darkest defeats for the presidency, a party can still claim many victories for state offices. Victories outside the arena of presidential politics give each party a base of support that keeps its machinery oiled and ready for the next contest.[22]

Party Identification in America

party identification
A voter's sense of psychological attachment to a party.

The concept of **party identification** is one of the most important in political science. It signifies a voter's sense of psychological attachment to a party (which is not the same thing as voting for the party in any given election). Scholars measure party identification simply by asking, "Do you usually think of yourself as a Republican, a Democrat, an independent, or what?"[23] Voting is a behavior; identification is a state of mind. For example, millions of southerners voted for Eisenhower for president in 1952 and 1956 but continued to consider themselves Democrats. Across the nation, more people identify with one of the two major parties than reject a party attachment. The proportions of self-identified Republicans, Democrats, and independents (no party attachment) in the electorate since 1952 are shown in Figure 8.4. Three significant points stand out:

- The number of Republicans and Democrats combined far exceeds the independents in every year.

- The number of Democrats consistently exceeds that of Republicans.

- The number of Democrats has shrunk over time, to the benefit of both Republicans and independents, and the three groups are now almost equal in size.

Although party identification predisposes citizens to vote for their favorite party, other factors may convince them to choose the opposition candidate. If they vote against their party often enough, they may rethink their party identification and eventually switch. Apparently, this rethinking has gone on in the minds of many southern Democrats over time. In 1952, about 70 percent of white southerners thought of themselves as Democrats, and fewer than 20 percent thought of themselves as Republicans. By 1996, white southerners were only 33 percent Democratic, whereas 33 percent were Republican and 34 percent were independent. Much of the nationwide growth in the proportion of Republicans and independents (and the parallel drop in the number of Democrats) stems from changes in party preferences among white southerners and from migration of northerners, which translated into substantial gains in the number of registered Republicans by 1996.[24]

Who are the self-identified Democrats and Republicans in the electorate? Figure 8.5 shows party identification by various social groups in 1996. The effects of socioeconomic factors are clear. People who have lower incomes and less education are more likely to think of themselves as Democrats than as Republicans. But the cultural factors of religion and race produce even sharper differences between the parties. Jews are strongly Democratic compared with other religious groups, and African Americans are also overwhelmingly Democratic. Finally, American politics has a gender gap: women tend to be more Democratic than men.

The influence of region on party identification has changed over time. Because of the high proportion of blacks in the South, it is still the most heavily Democratic region, followed closely by the Northeast. The Midwest and West have proportionately more Republicans. Despite the erosion of Democratic strength in the South, we still see elements of Roosevelt's old Democratic coalition of different socioeconomic groups. Perhaps the major change in that coalition has been the replacement of white European ethnic groups by blacks, attracted by the Democrats' backing of civil rights legislation in the 1960s.

Studies show that about half of all Americans adopt their parents' party. But it often takes time for party identification to develop. The youngest group of voters is most likely to be independent, but they have also identified increasingly with Republicans ever since the Reagan years (see Politics in a Changing America 8.1). The oldest group shows the greatest partisan commitment, reflecting the fact that citizens become more inter-

figure

8.4

Distribution of Party Identification, 1952–2000

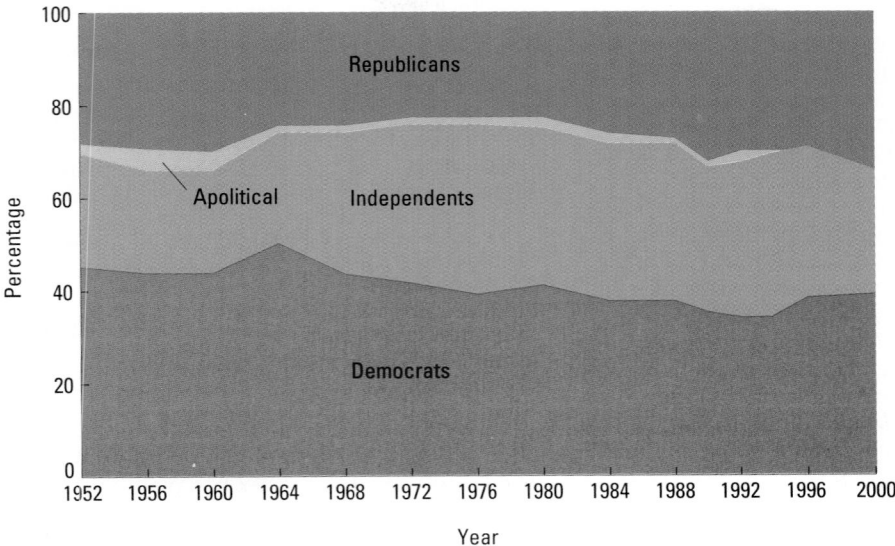

In every presidential election since 1952, voters across the nation have been asked, "Generally speaking, do you usually think of yourself as a Republican, a Democrat, an independent, or what?" Most voters think of themselves as either Republicans or Democrats, but the proportion of those who think of themselves as independents has increased over time. The size of the Democratic party's majority has also shrunk. Nevertheless, most Americans today still identify with one of the two major parties, and Democrats still outnumber Republicans.

Source: National Election Studies Guide to Public Opinion and Electoral Behavior, obtained at <www.umich.edu/~nes/nesguide/ toptables/tab2a_1.htm>, for data from 1952 to 1994, and the 1996 National Election Study, Center for Political Studies, University of Michigan, for 1996 data. Data for 2000 came from the *New York Times,* 12 November 2000, Section 4, p. 4.

ested in politics as they mature. Also, the youngest age group is most evenly divided between the parties. Some analysts believe this ratio of party identification among today's young voters will persist as they age, contributing to further erosion of the Democratic majority and perhaps greater electoral dealignment.

Americans tend to find their political niche and stay there.[25] The enduring party loyalty of American voters tends to structure the vote even before an election is held, even before the candidates are chosen. In Chapter 9 we will examine the extent to which party identification determines voting choice. But first we will look to see whether the Democratic and Republican parties have any significant differences between them.

PARTY IDEOLOGY AND ORGANIZATION

George Wallace, a disgruntled Democrat who ran for president in 1968 on the American Independent Party ticket, complained that "there isn't a dime's worth of difference" between the Democrats and Republicans. Humorist Will Rogers said, "I am not a member of any organized political party—I am a Democrat." Wallace's comment was made in disgust, Rogers's in jest. Wallace was wrong; Rogers was close to being right. Here we will dispel the myth that the parties do not differ significantly on issues and explain how they are organized to coordinate the activities of party candidates and officials in government.

figure

8.5   Party Identification by Social Groups

Respondents to a 2000 election survey were grouped by seven different socioeconomic criteria—income, education, religion, sex, race, region, and age—and analyzed according to their self-descriptions as Democrats, independents, or Republicans. All these factors had some effect on party identification, with region showing the least effect. As for age, its main effect was to reduce the proportion of independents as respondents grew older. Younger citizens, who tend to think of themselves as independents, are likely to develop an identification with one party or the other as they mature.

Source: Preliminary release, 2000 National Election Study, Center for Political Studies, University of Michigan.

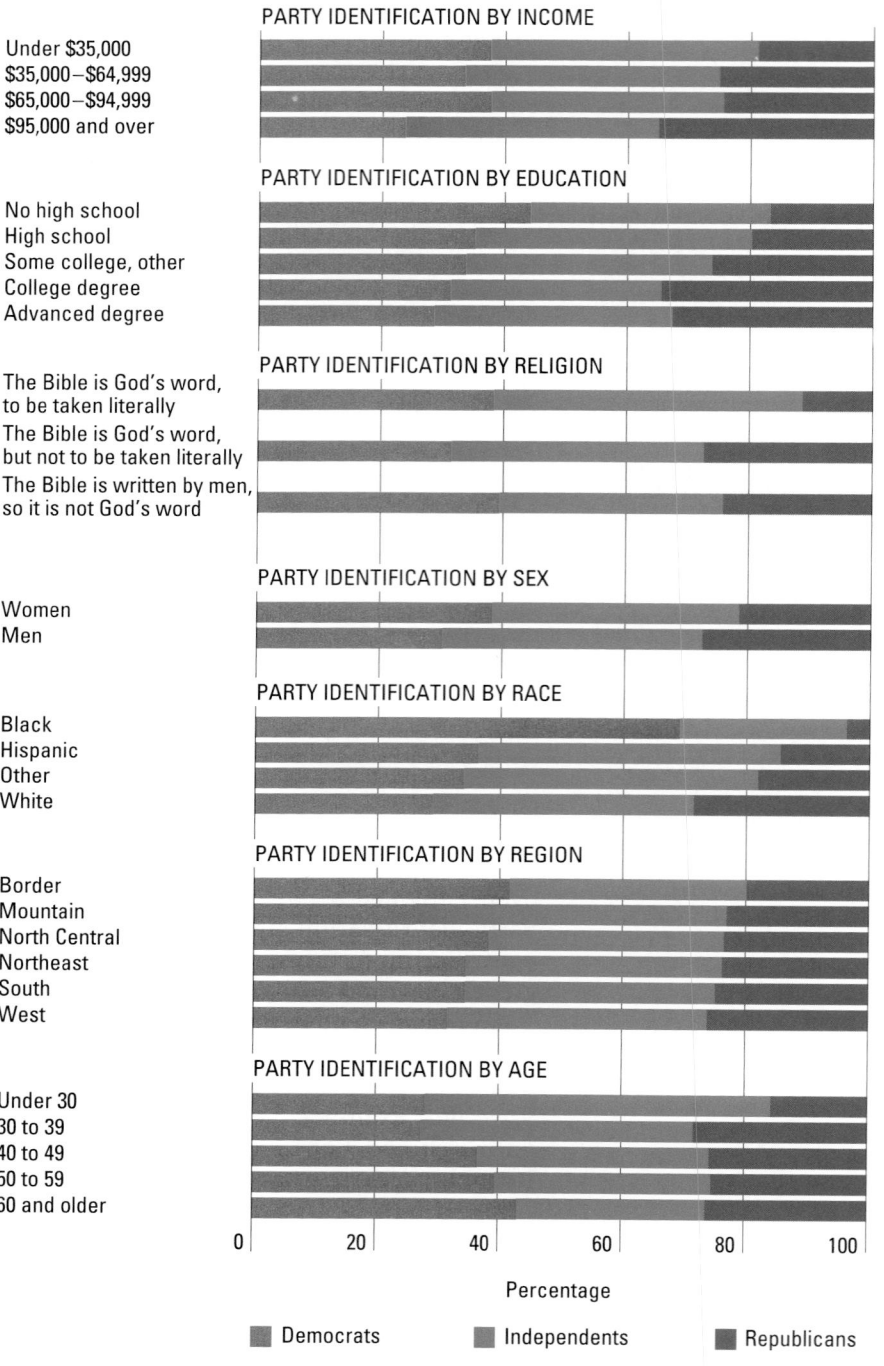

Differences in Party Ideology

George Wallace notwithstanding, there is more than a dime's worth of difference between the two parties. In fact, the difference amounts to many billions of dollars, the cost of the different government programs supported by each party. Democrats are more disposed to government spend-

8.1   The Changing Relationship Between Age and Party Identification

The relationship between age and party identification has changed dramatically during the past forty years. We can visualize this change by comparing Gallup surveys taken in 1952 and 1992. Both graphs show the percentage of Democratic identifiers minus the percentage of Republican identifiers for seventeen different four-year age groupings—ranging from eighteen- to twenty-one-year-olds to those eighty-two years of age and older. In 1952, the percentage of Democratic identifiers exceeded Republican identifiers by about fifteen points or more among younger and middle-aged voters, whereas the older age groups had far more Republicans than Democrats. By 1992, this pattern had reversed, with younger voters more likely to be Republicans and older voters (those who were young in 1952) retaining their Democratic sentiments. Note also that the overall relationship between age and party identification was substantially weaker in 1992 than in 1952.

Source: Everett Carll Ladd, "Age, Generation, and Party ID," *Public Perspective* (July–August 1992), pp. 15–16.

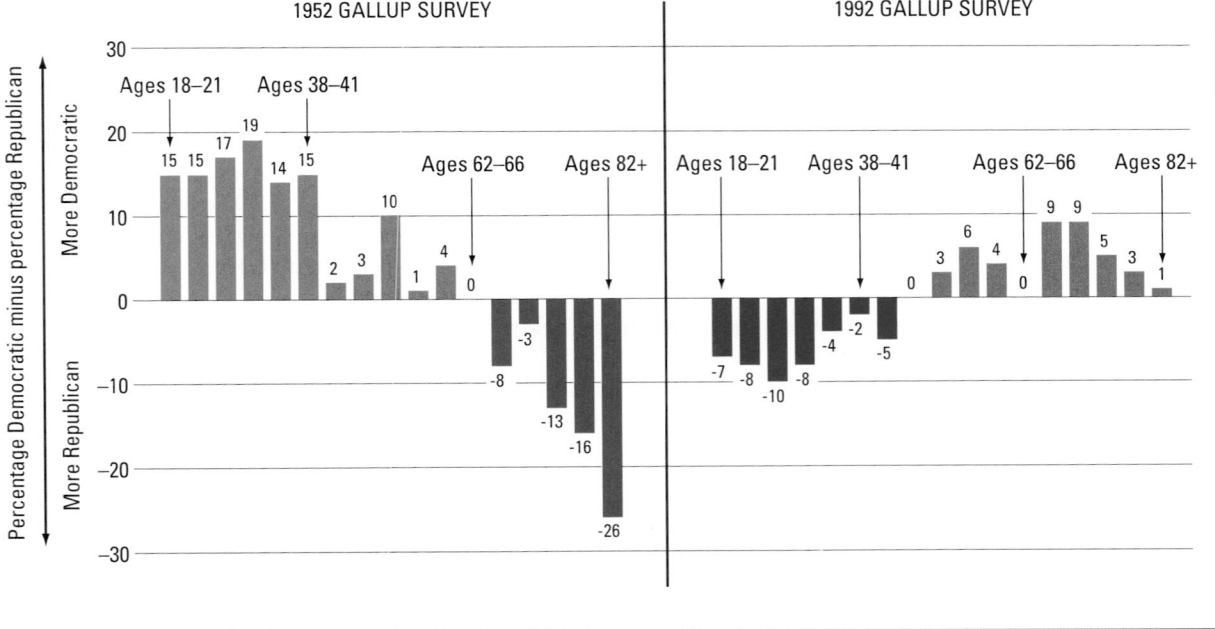

ing to advance social welfare (and hence to promote equality) than are Republicans. And social welfare programs cost money, a lot of money. Republicans decry massive social spending, but they are not averse to spending billions of dollars for the projects they consider important, among them national defense. Ronald Reagan portrayed the Democrats as big spenders, but his administration spent more than $1 trillion for defense. His Strategic Defense Initiative (the "Star Wars" missile defense program) cost billions before it was curtailed under the Democrats.[26]

President George W. Bush has promised to spend more on the military than the Democrats, including a missile defense program targeted against rogue nations.

Voters and Activists.   One way to examine the differences is to compare party voters with party activists. As shown in Figure 8.6, only 16 percent of Democratic voters described themselves as conservative, compared with 59 percent of Republican voters. As we discussed in Chapter 5, relatively few ordinary voters think about politics in ideological terms, but party activists often do. The ideological gap between the parties looms even larger when we focus on party activists on the left and right sides of Figure 8.6. Only 4 percent of the delegates to the 2000 Democratic convention described themselves as conservative, compared with 57 percent of the delegates to the Republican convention.

Platforms: Freedom, Order, and Equality.   Surveys of voters' ideological orientation may merely reflect differences in their personal self-image rather than actual differences in party ideology. For another test of party philosophy, we can look to the platforms adopted at party conventions. Although many people feel that party platforms don't matter very much, several scholars have demonstrated, using different approaches, that winning parties tend to carry out much of their platforms when in office.[27] One study matched the parties' platform statements from 1948 to 1985 against subsequent allocations of program funds in the federal budget. Spending priorities turned out to be quite closely linked to the platform emphases of the party that won control of Congress, especially if the party also controlled the presidency.[28]

Party platforms also matter a great deal to the parties' convention delegates—and to the interest groups that support the parties.[29] The wording of a platform plank often means the difference between victory and defeat for factions within a party. Delegates fight not only over ideas but also over words.

The platforms adopted by the Democratic and Republican conventions in 2000—while strikingly different in style and substance—did not differ as starkly as in 1996. The Republicans, who met first, produced a long document of almost 35,000 words—more than 10,000 words longer than the Democratic platform. As befits a conservative party, the Republicans mentioned *moral* or *morality* nine times compared to the Democrats' three. In contrast, the Democrats were big on *equal* and *equality*, mentioning those terms twelve times. The Republicans came close with nine mentions, but four of those were linguistic phrases, like *equally important*, while all twelve Democratic references were to policies or people.

By examining specific planks in the Republican platform, one sees that the Bush forces blunted the party's 1996 right-wing edge. The 2000 platform still opposed abortion, gay rights, and gun control; it still called for tax cuts, more military spending, and smaller government. But it would no longer abolish the Department of Education, or end funding for the arts, or deny citizenship to children born of illegal immigrants. It appears that Bush sought, through his party's platform, to position his campaign more toward the center—just as Clinton had done in 1992. That worked so well in 1992 and 1996 that Gore's forces did not tinker

figure

8.6 — Ideologies of Party Voters and Party Delegates in 2000

Contrary to what many people think, the Democratic and Republican parties differ substantially in their ideological centers of gravity. When citizens were asked to classify themselves on an ideological scale, more Republicans than Democrats described themselves as conservative. When delegates to the parties' national conventions were asked to classify themselves, the differences between the parties grew even sharper.

Source: Adam Clymer and Marjorie Connelly, "Poll Finds Delegates to the Left of Both Public and Party," *New York Times*, 14 August 2000, pp. 1 and 17.

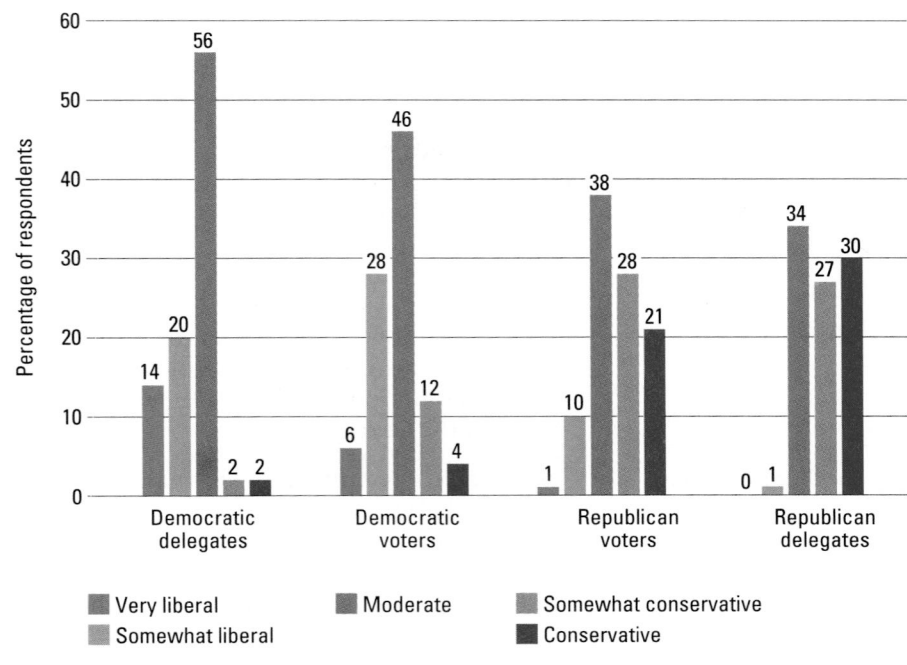

The "Voters" data in the CROSSTABS program contain variables on "Politics." Crosstabulate "Ideology" by "Party Identification" to learn how much those who identify with different parties also depart in their ideologies.

much with the formula in 2000. An analysis of the Democratic platform said that it reflected Clinton's "new Democrat" agenda, cutting "a middle path between welfare-state liberalism and laissez-faire Republicanism, advocating active but smaller government, fiscal discipline, free trade and tough crime policies."[30]

Different but Similar. The Democrats and the Republicans have very different ideological orientations. Yet many observers claim that the parties are really quite similar in ideology compared to the different parties of other countries. Specifically, both support capitalism; that is, both reject government ownership of the means of production (see Chapter 1). A study of Democratic and Republican positions on four economic issues— ownership of the means of production, the government's role in economic planning, redistribution of wealth, and providing for social welfare—found that Republicans consistently oppose increased government activity. Comparing these findings with data on party positions in thirteen other democracies, the researchers found about as much difference between the American parties as is usual within two-party systems. However, both American parties tend to be more conservative on economic matters than are parties in other two-party systems. In most multiparty systems, the presence of strong socialist and antisocialist parties ensures a much greater range of ideological choice than we find in our system, despite genuine differences between the Democrats and Republicans.[31]

National Party Organization

Most casual observers would agree with Will Rogers's description of the Democrats as an unorganized political party. It used to apply to the Republicans, too, but this has changed since the 1970s—at least at the national level. Bear in mind the distinction between levels of party structure. American parties parallel our federal system: they have separate national and state organizations (and virtually separate local organizations, in many cases).

At the national level, each major party has four main organizational components:

- *National convention.* Every four years, each party assembles thousands of delegates from the states and U.S. territories (such as Puerto Rico and Guam) in a national convention for the purpose of nominating a candidate for president. This presidential nominating convention is also the supreme governing body of the party. It determines party policy through the platform, formulates rules to govern party operations, and designates a national committee, which is empowered to govern the party until the next convention.

national committee
A committee of a political party composed of party chairpersons and party officials from every state.

- *National committee.* The **national committee,** which governs each party between conventions, is composed of party officials representing the states and territories, including the chairpersons of their party organizations. In 2000, the Republican National Committee (RNC) had about 150 members, consisting of the national committeeman, national committeewoman, and a chairperson from each state and from the District of Columbia, Guam, Puerto Rico, and the Virgin Islands. The Democratic National Committee (DNC) had approximately 450 elected and appointed members, including, in addition to the national committee members and party chairs, members representing auxiliary organizations. The chairperson of each national committee is chosen by the party's presidential nominee, then duly elected by the committee. If the nominee loses the election, the national committee usually replaces the nominee's chairperson.

party conference
A meeting to select party leaders and decide committee assignments, held at the beginning of a session of Congress by Republicans or Democrats in each chamber.

- *Congressional party conferences.* At the beginning of each session of Congress, the Republicans and Democrats in each chamber hold separate **party conferences** (the House Democrats call theirs a caucus) to select their party leaders and decide committee assignments. (Bernard Sanders, the lone independent member of Congress, asked to join the House Democratic Caucus but was excluded.) The party conferences deal only with congressional matters and have no structural relationship to each other and no relationship to the national committees.

congressional campaign committee
An organization maintained by a political party to raise funds to support its own candidates in congressional elections.

- *Congressional campaign committees.* Democrats and Republicans in the House and Senate also maintain separate **congressional campaign committees,** each of which raises its own funds to support its candidates in congressional elections. The separation of these organizations from the national committee tells us that the national party structure is loose; the national committee seldom gets involved with the election of any individual member of Congress. Moreover, even the congressional campaign organizations merely supplement the funds that senators and representatives raise on their own to win reelection.

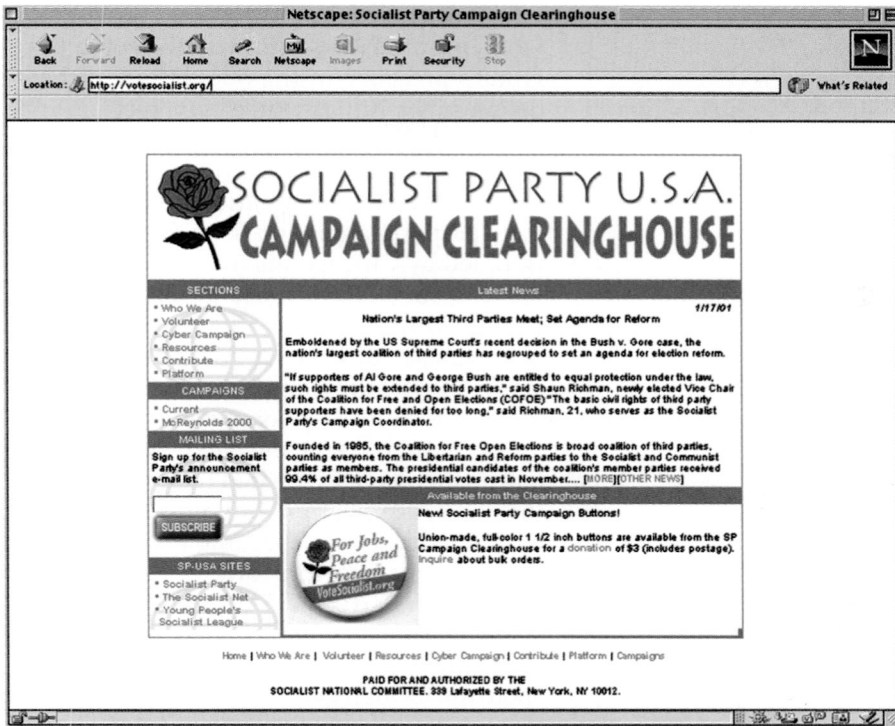

It is tempting to think of the national party chairperson as sitting at the top of a hierarchical party organization that not only controls its members in Congress but also issues orders to the state committees and on down to the local level. Few ideas could be more wrong.[32] The national committee has virtually no voice concerning congressional activity, and it exercises very little control over state and local campaigns. In fact, the RNC and DNC do not even really direct or control presidential campaigns. Candidates hire their own campaign staffs during the party primaries to win delegates who will support them for nomination at the party conventions. Successful nominees then keep their winning staffs to contest the general election. The main role of a national committee is to support its candidate's personal campaign staff in the effort to win.

In this light, the national committees appear to be relatively useless organizations. For many years, their role was essentially limited to planning for the next party convention. The committee would select the site, invite the state parties to attend, plan the program, and so on. In the 1970s, however, the roles of the DNC and RNC began to expand—but in different ways.

In response to street rioting by Vietnam War protesters during the 1968 Democratic convention, the Democrats created a special commission to introduce party reforms. In an attempt to open the party to broader participation and to weaken local party leaders' control over the process of selecting delegates, the McGovern-Fraser Commission formulated new guidelines for the selection of delegates to the 1972 Democratic convention. Included in these guidelines was the requirement that state parties take "affirmative action"—that is, see to it that their delegates included women, minorities, and young people "in reasonable relationship to the group's presence in the population of the state."[33] Many state parties rebelled at the imposition of sex, race, and age quotas. But the DNC threatened to deny seating at the 1972 convention to any state delegation that did not comply with the guidelines.

Never before had a national party committee imposed such rules on a state party organization, but it worked. Even the powerful Illinois delegation, led by Chicago mayor Richard Daley, was denied seating at the convention for violating the guidelines. And overall, women, blacks, and young voters gained dramatically in representation at the 1972 Democratic convention. Although the party has since reduced its emphasis on quotas, the gains by women and blacks have held up fairly well. The representation of young people, however, has declined substantially (as the young activists grew older). Many "regular" Democrats feared that the political activists who had taken over the 1972 convention would cripple the party organization. But most challengers were socialized into the party within a decade and became more open to compromise and more understanding of the organization's need to combat developments within the Republican Party.[34]

While the Democrats were busy with procedural reforms, the Republicans were making *organizational* reforms.[35] The RNC did little to open up its delegate selection process; Republicans were not inclined to impose quotas on state parties through their national committee. Instead, the RNC strengthened its fundraising, research, and service roles. Republicans acquired their own building and their own computer system, and in 1976 they hired the first full-time chairperson in the history of either national party. (Until then, the chairperson had worked part-time.) As RNC chairman, William Brock (formerly a senator from Tennessee) expanded the party's staff, launched new publications, held seminars, conducted election analyses, and advised candidates—things that national party committees in other countries had been doing for years.

The vast difference between the Democratic and Republican approaches to reforming the national committees shows in the funds raised by the DNC and RNC during election campaigns. During Brock's tenure as chairperson of the RNC, the Republicans raised three to four times as much money as the Democrats. Although the margin has narrowed, Republican party fundraising efforts are still superior. For the 1995–1996 election cycle, the Republicans' national, senatorial, and congressional committees raised $554 million, compared with $345 million raised by the comparable Democratic committees.[36] Although Republicans have traditionally raised more campaign money than Democrats, they no longer rely on a relatively few wealthy contributors. In fact, the Republicans received more of their funds in small contributions (less than $100), mainly through direct-mail solicitation, than the Democrats. In short, the RNC has recently been raising far more money than the DNC, from many more citizens, as part of its long-term commitment to improving its organizational services. Its efforts have also made a difference at the state and local levels.

State and Local Party Organizations

At one time, both major parties were firmly anchored by powerful state and local party organizations. Big-city party organizations, such as the Democrats' Tammany Hall in New York City and the Cook County Central Committee in Chicago, were called *party machines*. A **party machine** was a centralized organization that dominated local politics by controlling elections—sometimes by illegal means, often by providing jobs and social services to urban workers in return for their votes. The patronage and social service functions of party machines were undercut when the government expanded unemployment compensation, aid to families with dependent children, and other social services. As a result, most local party organizations lost their ability to deliver votes and thus to determine the outcome of elections. However, machines are still strong in certain areas. In Nassau County, New York, for example, suburban Republicans have shown that they can run a machine as well as urban Democrats.[37]

The individual state and local organizations of both parties vary widely in strength, but recent research has found that "neither the Republican nor Democratic party has a distinct advantage with regard to direct campaign activities."[38] Whereas once both the RNC and the DNC were dependent for their funding on "quotas" paid by state parties, now the funds flow the other way (see Figure 8.7). In the 1995–1996 election cycle, virtually every state party benefited greatly from the transfer of huge sums—more than $74 million from the DNC and over $66 million from the RNC.[39] In addition to money, state parties also received candidate training, poll data and research, and campaigning instruction.[40] The national committees have also taken a more active role in congressional campaigns.[41]

Decentralized but Growing Stronger

Although the national committees have gained strength over the past three decades, American political parties are still among the most decentralized parties in the world.[42] Not even the president can count on loyalty from the members (or even the officers) of his party. Consider the problem that confronted President Clinton after his resounding reelection in 1996. President Clinton sought legislation for authority to negotiate trade legislation that Congress could approve or disapprove, but not amend. Congress had given every president since Gerald Ford this so-called fast-track authority, and Republican leaders favored it as part of their free-trade philosophy. However, organized labor feared losing jobs to other countries and opposed giving Clinton this negotiating power. Richard Gephardt, leader of the Democractic minority in the House, took labor's side and led the fight against the president on this issue. Although Clinton supposedly headed the Democratic Party, Gephardt persuaded 80 percent of House Democrats to vote against the fast-track measure, denying the president a power he dearly wanted.[43] Clinton could do nothing to discipline his disobedient party lieutenant.

The absence of centralized power has always been the most distinguishing characteristic of American political parties. Moreover, the rise in the proportion of citizens who style themselves as independents suggests that our already weak parties are in further decline.[44] But there is evidence that

party machine
A centralized party organization that dominates local politics by controlling elections.

Typical State Party Organization

Can You Explain Why...
political parties have become more important in elections?

8.7   Changes in the Money Flow Between State and National Parties: 1950s Versus 1990s

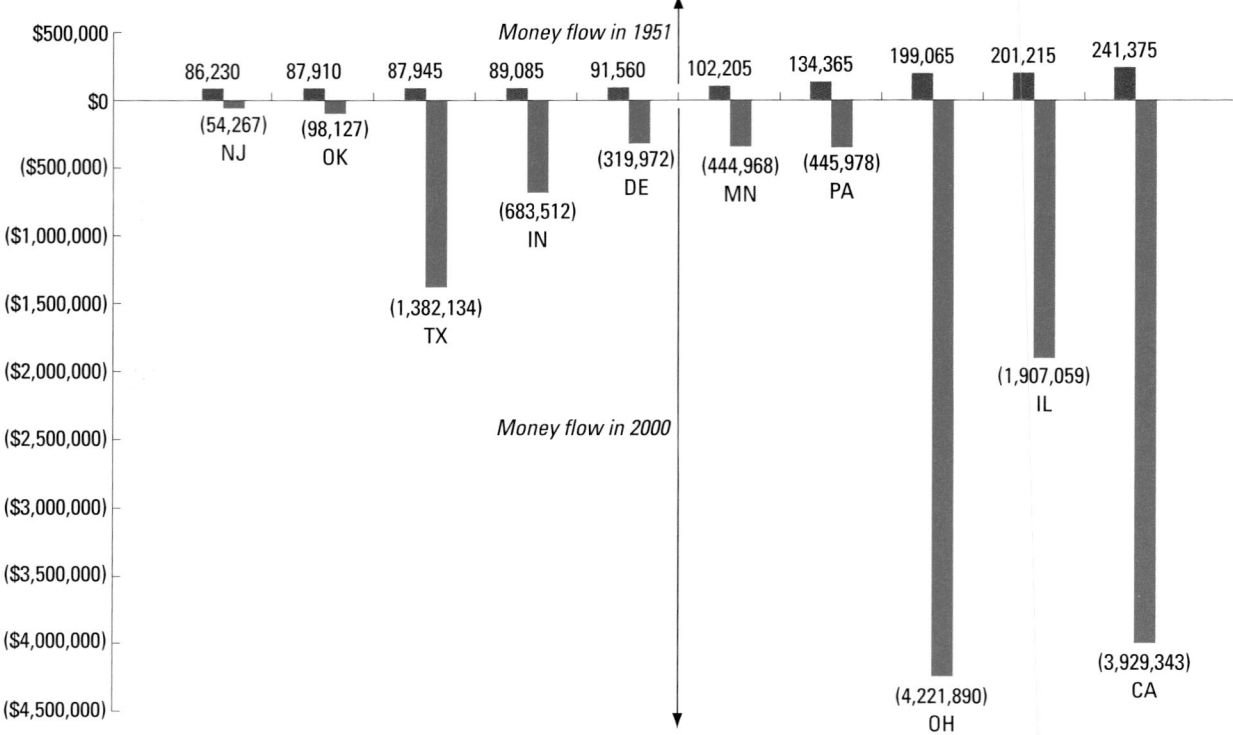

Amount of funds that the top ten state party organizations *gave to* the Republican National Committee in 1951.

Money flow in 1951

Money flow in 2000

Estimated amount of funds that the Republican National Committee transferred *downward* to state parties in 2000.

Changes over time in the money flows between the state party organizations and the national party committees clearly indicate changes in their power relationships. Traditionally, the national committees were funded by voluntary contributions from state parties, set as financial "quotas." Not all states met their quotas, and the Democratic National Committee chairman in the 1950s, Paul Butler, praised states that did in his monthly newsletter. Beginning in the 1960s, both national committees began to raise money from party supporters through direct mail solicitations. Both parties, but especially the Republicans, began to live off their own income and soon began to transfer money back to the states. This graph shows the extent to which the Republican National Committee changed from a taker of funds from the ten top state contributors in 1951 to a giver of funds to the same states in 1993.

Sources: The 1951 data come from a typewritten "Statement of Contributions by States Received During October 1951 and to Date," so the contributions for the year were almost complete. This statement resides in the files of the Republican National Committee at the U.S. National Archives in Washington, D.C. The data for 1993 are estimated from the Federal Election Commission News Release, "FEC Reports on Political Party Activity for 1993–94," 13 April 1995, p. 12. It includes both federal and non-federal funds. All data are expressed in constant 1987 dollars. The 1951 data were divided by .20 as a deflator and the 1993 data were divided by 1.2. The FEC data for 1993–94 were also divided in half because they were collected over two years; the 1951 data are for just one year. Thus, the 1993 data are estimates for one year based on two years of financial reporting.

our political parties, *as organizations*, are enjoying a period of resurgence. Both parties' national committees have never been better funded or more active in grassroots campaign activities.[45] And more votes in Congress are being decided along party lines—despite the Gephardt-Bonior and Gingrich mutinies. (See Chapter 11 for a discussion of the rise of party voting in Congress since the 1970s.) In fact, a specialist in congressional politics has concluded, "When compared to its predecessors of the last half-century, the current majority party leadership is more involved and more decisive in organizing the party and the chamber, setting the policy agenda, shaping legislation, and determining legislative outcomes."[46] However, the American parties have traditionally been so weak that these positive trends have not altered their basic character. American political parties are still so organizationally diffuse and decentralized that they raise questions about how well they link voters to the government.

THE MODEL OF RESPONSIBLE PARTY GOVERNMENT

responsible party government
A set of principles formalizing the ideal role of parties in a majoritarian democracy.

According to the majoritarian model of democracy, parties are essential to making the government responsive to public opinion. In fact, the ideal role of parties in majoritarian democracy has been formalized in the four principles of **responsible party government:**[47]

1. Parties should present clear and coherent programs to voters.

2. Voters should choose candidates on the basis of party programs.

3. The winning party should carry out its program once in office.

4. Voters should hold the governing party responsible at the next election for executing its program.

How well do these principles describe American politics? You've learned that the Democratic and Republican platforms are different and that they are much more ideologically consistent than many people believe. So the first principle is being met fairly well. To a lesser extent, so is the third principle: once parties gain power, they usually try to do what they said they would do. From the standpoint of democratic theory, the real question involves principles 2 and 4: do voters really pay attention to party platforms and policies when they cast their ballots? And if so, do voters hold the governing party responsible at the next election for delivering, or failing to deliver, on its pledges? To answer these questions, we must consider in greater detail the parties' role in nominating candidates and structuring the voters' choices in elections. At the conclusion of Chapter 9, we will return to evaluating the role of political parties in democratic government.

SUMMARY

Political parties perform four important functions in a political system: nominating candidates, structuring the voting choice, proposing alternative government programs, and coordinating the activities of government officials. Political parties have been performing these functions longer in the United States than in any other country. The Democratic Party, founded in 1828, is the world's oldest political party. When the Republican Party emerged as a major party after the 1856 election, our present two-party system emerged—the oldest party system in the world.

America's two-party system has experienced three critical elections, each of which realigned the electorate for years and affected the party balance in government. The election of 1860 established the Republicans as the major party in the North and the Democrats as the dominant party in the South. Nationally, the two parties remained roughly balanced in Congress until the critical election of 1896. This election strengthened the link between the Republican party and business interests in the heavily populated Northeast and Midwest and produced a surge in voter support that made the Republicans the majority party nationally for more than three decades. The Great Depression produced the conditions that transformed the Democrats into the majority party in the critical election of 1932. Until the Republicans won both houses in the 1994 election, the Democrats enjoyed almost uninterrupted control of Congress for six decades.

Minor parties have not enjoyed much electoral success in America, although they have contributed ideas to the Democratic and Republican platforms. The two-party system is perpetuated in the United States by the nature of our electoral system and by the political socialization process, which results in most Americans' identifying with either the Democratic or the Republican Party. The federal system of government has also helped the Democrats and Republicans survive defeats at the national level by sustaining them with electoral victories at the state level. The pattern of party identification has been changing in recent years: as more people are becoming independents and Republicans, the number of Democratic identifiers is dropping. Still, Democrats consistently outnumber Republicans, and together they both far outnumber independents.

The two major parties differ in their ideological orientations. Democratic identifiers and activists are more likely to describe themselves as liberal; Republican identifiers and activists tend to be conservative. The party platforms also reveal substantive ideological differences. The 2000 Democratic Party platform showed a more liberal orientation by stressing equality over freedom; the Republican platform was more conservative, concentrating on freedom but also emphasizing the importance of restoring social order. Organizationally, the Republicans have recently become the stronger party at both the national and state levels, and both parties are showing signs of resurgence. Nevertheless, both parties are still very decentralized compared with parties in other countries.

In keeping with the model of responsible party government, American parties do tend to translate their platform positions into government policy if elected to power. But, as we examine in Chapter 9, it remains to be seen whether citizens pay much attention to parties and policies when casting their votes. If not, American parties do not fulfill the majoritarian model of democratic theory.

★ Selected Readings

Aldrich, John H. *Why Parties? The Origin and Transformation of Political Parties in America.* Chicago, Ill.: University of Chicago Press, 1995. An original analysis of the formation of political parties that intertwines the ambitions of politicians, the problems of collective action, and the dilemmas in social choice.

Amy, Douglas J. *Real Choices, New Voices: The Case for Proportional Representation Elections in the United States.* New York: Columbia University Press, 1993. A critique of the majority election system in the United States and an argument for a fundamental change to the type of system widely used abroad in parliamentary systems.

Lowi, Theodore J., and Joseph Romance. *A Republic of Parties: Debating the Two-Party System.* Lanham, Md.: Rowman & Littlefield, 1998. A unique combination of arguments for and against the two-party system and key historical documents on American parties and party politics.

Reynolds, David. *Democracy Unbound: Progressive Challenges to the Two-Party System.* Boston, Mass.: South End Press, 1997. Describes how grassroots activists translate mass discontent into new people-driven parties.

Schattschneider, E. E. *Party Government.* New York: Holt, 1942. A clear and powerful argument for the cen-

tral role of political parties in a democracy according to the model of responsible party government; a classic book in political science.

Shea, Daniel M., and John C. Green (eds.). *The State of the Parties: The Changing Role of Contemporary American Parties,* 3rd ed. Lanham, Md.: Rowman & Littlefield, 1999. A valuable collection of empirical studies and theoretical analyses of American parties at the national and state levels. The articles document the increased activity of party organizations in election campaigns.

White, John Kenneth, and Daniel M. Shea. *New Party Politics: From Jefferson and Hamilton to the Information Age.* Boston, Mass.: Bedford/St. Martin's, 2000. A comprehensive text on American parties that incorporates technology into the practice of party politics.

Internet Exercises

1. *Ballot Access for Third Parties*

Third parties often have to battle established institutions in order to get their candidates listed on ballots in national and state elections. Ballot Access News is an on-line newsletter that describes what it calls the trials and tribulations of individuals who attempt to gain ballot access. The newsletter is located at <**www.ballot-access.org/**>.

• Go to the Ballot Access News Web site and link to the October 4, 1998, issue. There you will find a short story on a court challenge from a minor party candidate in Ohio who attempted to get on the ballot. After reading this piece, link to the January 1, 2000, issue for a follow-up report on the same case.

• Because they control state legislatures, and thus ballot access procedures, some observers argue that the major parties have conspired to make it difficult for minor parties to gain access to the ballot. How did Ohio's dual system of ballot access—which was successfully challenged, according to the Ballot Access News—lend support to these criticisms?

2. *Party Ideology in the U.S. Congress*

Professor Keith Poole is a political scientist at the University of Houston who has devoted much of his

career to studying the ideological orientations of the political parties in Congress. He maintains a Web site at <**voteview.uh.edu/**> with animations of some of his research based on a measurement that he has developed called "Nominate Scores." These scores essentially calculate the ideological orientations (i.e., liberal to conservative) of members of Congress based on their roll call voting record.

• Go to Professor Poole's site and follow the link to his Data Download page. There you will find a link to his General Data Collection, which includes animated "gif" files of Congress from the 1800s to the present. Run the "One Dimensional Animated Gif for the 46th to 105th Houses" file to observe how the ideological characteristics of the parties have changed over time.

• Based on the animation, what would be your overall conclusion about the ideological differences between the parties? Looking specifically at the periods from roughly 1954 to 1978 and 1988 to 1998, would you conclude that the parties have become more or less ideologically polarized? Explain your answer.

chapter 9

Nominations, Elections, and Campaigns

★ ★ ★ ★ ★ ★ ★ ★

IT TOOK JUST THIRTY-SIX DAYS in 2000 for Canada to call a federal election, conduct the entire campaign, and determine its head of government—thirty-six days from start to finish. It took thirty-six days in 2000 for the United States just to count the votes in its federal election and determine its head of government—and that was after four years of campaigning! Why the difference? The explanation lies in basic differences betweent the two countries' political and electoral systems.

Let's begin with some facts about the Canadian political system and its parliamentary form of government. Canada is led by a prime minister chosen by members in the elected house of parliament—the House of Commons. The party controlling the House selects the prime minister—much as the Republicans in the U.S. House chose Dennis Hastert as Speaker (see Chapter 11). Because a parliamentary system joins the executive and legislative powers, the House of Commons is the real government authority in Canada. So the prime minister becomes the head of government.[1] A prime minister is arguably more powerful than a president. Consider a prime minister's power to call an election, a power denied the president. Canadian governments are limited to five-year terms in office, but a prime minister can hold a general election earlier if the timing looks promising for the governing party. On the other hand, if the prime minister loses support of parliament, a general election is demanded to resolve the political problem.

Because Canadian elections are unpredictable, no party has time to prepare for them in advance. Because elections are timed to political needs, the campaign period is fixed and short. By Canadian law, a general election campaign lasts only thirty-six days. So, when Canadian Prime Minister Jean Chrétien decided on October 22, 2000, to ask for a general election, the date was fixed for November 27. Although this was one and a half years earlier than the five-year limit for his government, Chrétien was enjoying high approval ratings and hoped to increase the bare majority held by his Liberal Party in the 301-seat House of Commons.

Canada not only had a shorter election campaign, it counted its votes faster. Within hours after the polls closed, Canadians knew conclusively that Prime Minister Chrétien's gamble of an early election paid off, as the Liberal Party increased its margin to 57 percent of the seats. If members of the Canadian public didn't trust newspaper reports, they could view the results on the official "Elections Canada" Web site on election evening.[2]

If Canada holds its elections by the needs of politics, we hold ours by the movement of planets. In early November, after the earth has traveled four times around the sun, we hold a presidential election. The timing is entirely predictable but has little to do with political need. Predictability does carry some advantages for political stability, but it also has some negative consequences. A major one is the length of our presidential election campaigns. Presidential hopefuls in the Democratic Party began planning for the 2004 election as soon as Gore conceded to Bush on December 13—the day the election was decided, thirty-six days after the voting.

The delay in resolving the 2000 presidential election can't be blamed on the United States not having a parliamentary system like Canada's. It must be fixed on differences between voting in the two electoral systems. Of course, one difference is the size of the electorate. Over 105 million people voted in the U.S. election, compared with fewer than 13 million in the Canadian election. But the differences in total votes cast is even greater. As explained in Chapter 7, when Americans go to the polls in a general election, they are asked to decide among scores of candidates running for many different public offices at the local, state, and national levels. The election is general in the sense that it is inclusive of various levels of government. When Canadians go to the polls in a general election, they are asked *only* to choose among one small set of candidates running for a single seat in parliament. Their election is general only in the sense that all members of the House are up for election; there are *no other offices or issues on the ballot.* This difference leaps out when comparing the ballots for the United States and Canada (see Compared with What? 9.1).

This difference translates dramatically into enormous differences in total votes that are cast and that need to be counted in the two countries. The 13 million Canadians who voted in their 2000 federal election cast 13 million votes for parliamentary candidates. The 105 million Americans who went to the polls in 2000 cast over 1 *billion* votes. No wonder voting results for a general election are not available as quickly in the United States. Of course, the thirty-six-day delay in determining the president was due to the extremely close election in Florida, but Florida's problems in counting the votes can be attributed to the complexity of the ballot, designed to accommodate several offices.

In this chapter, we will describe the various methods that states use to count the billions of votes cast in each presidential election, as we probe more deeply into elections in the United States. We also consider the role of election campaigns and how they have changed over time. We study how candidates get nominated in the United States, and what factors are important in causing voters to favor one nominee over another. We also address these important questions: How well do election campaigns function to inform voters? How important is money in conducting a winning campaign? What are the roles of party identification, issues, and candidate attributes in influencing voters' choices and thus election outcomes? How do campaigns, elections, and parties fit into the majoritarian and pluralist models of democracy?

THE EVOLUTION
OF CAMPAIGNING

election campaign
An organized effort to persuade voters to choose one candidate over others competing for the same office.

Voting in free elections to choose leaders is the main way that citizens control government. As discussed in Chapter 8, political parties help structure the voting choice by reducing the number of candidates on the ballot to those who have a realistic chance of winning or who offer distinctive policies. An **election campaign** is an organized effort to persuade voters to choose one candidate over others competing for the same office. An effective campaign requires sufficient resources to acquire and analyze information about voters' interests, to develop a strategy and matching tactics for appealing to these interests, to deliver the candidate's message to the voters, and to get them to cast their ballots.[3]

In the past, political parties conducted all phases of the election campaign. As recently as the 1950s, just about fifty years ago, state and local party organizations "felt the pulse" of their rank-and-file members to learn what was important to the voters. They chose the candidates and then lined up leading officials to support them and to ensure big crowds at campaign rallies. They also prepared buttons, banners, and newspaper advertisements that touted their candidates, proudly named under the prominent label of the party. Finally, candidates relied heavily on the local precinct and county party organizations to contact voters before elections, to mention their names, to extol their virtues, and—most important—to make sure their supporters voted and voted correctly.

Today, candidates seldom rely much on political parties. How do candidates learn about voters' interests today? By contracting for public opinion polls, not by asking the party. How do candidates plan their campaign strategy and tactics now? By hiring political consultants to devise clever "sound bites" (brief, catchy phrases) that will catch voters' attention on television, not by consulting party headquarters. How do candidates deliver their messages to voters? By conducting media campaigns, not by counting on party regulars to canvass the neighborhoods.

Increasingly, election campaigns have evolved from being party centered to being candidate centered.[4] This is not to say that political parties no longer have a role to play in campaigns, for they do. As noted in Chapter 8, the Democratic National Committee now exercises more control over the delegate selection process than it did before 1972. Since 1976, the Republicans have greatly expanded their national organization and fundraising capacity. But whereas the parties virtually ran election campaigns in the past, now they exist mainly to support candidate-centered campaigns by providing services or funds to their candidates. Nevertheless, we will see that the party label is usually a candidate's prime attribute at election time.

Perhaps the most important change in American elections is that candidates don't campaign just to get elected anymore. It is now necessary to campaign for *nomination* as well. As we saw in Chapter 8, nominating candidates to run for office under the party label is one of the main functions of political parties. Party organizations once controlled that function. Even Abraham Lincoln served only one term in the House before the party transferred the nomination for his House seat to someone else.[5] For most important offices today, however, candidates are no longer nominated *by* the party organization but *within* the party. That is, party leaders

★ **compared with what?**

9.1   The Voter's Burden in the United States and Canada

No other country requires its voters to make as many decisions in a general election as the United States does. Compare these two facsimiles of official specimen ballots for the general elections in November 2000—one used in Canada and the other used in the United States. The long U.S. ballot is just a *portion* of the one that confronted voters in the city of Evanston, Illinois. In addition to the twenty-three different offices listed here, the full ballot also asked voters to check yes or no on the retention of seventy-seven incumbent judges. For good measure, Evanstonians were asked to vote on one statewide referendum and one city referendum. By contrast, the straightforward Canadian ballot (for the Notre-Dame-de-Grâce-Lachine district in Montreal) simply asked citizens to choose among a varied set of party candidates running for the House of Commons for that district. (Incidentally, the Liberal Party candidate won 61 percent of the vote.) No wonder counting the votes is so complicated in the United States and so simple in Canada.

Source: Information for the Canadian ballot was supplied by Rebecca Oliver, a resident of that district.

Candidate Party	
ETCOVITCH, Darrin Canadian Alliance	○
FABER, Grégoire Marijuana Party	○
GRAHAM, Katie Green Party	○
HOFFMAN, Rachel Marxist-Leninist Party	○
JENNINGS, Marlene Liberal Party	○
MEGYERY, Kathy Progressive Conservative Party	○
OUELLET, Jeannine Bloc Québécois	○
TOOMBS, Bruce New Democratic Party	○
WILSON, Michael Natural Law Party	○

OFFICIAL SPECIMEN BALLOT
General Election, Cook County, Illinois, Tuesday, November 7, 2000

FOR PRESIDENT AND VICE PRESIDENT OF THE UNITED STATES VOTE FOR ONE GROUP

Candidate	Party	
GEORGE W. BUSH AND DICK CHENEY	Republican	[]
AL GORE AND JOE LIEBERMAN	Democratic	[]
HARRY BROWNE AND ART OLIVIER	Libertarian	[]
RALPH NADER AND WINONA LaDUKE	Green	[]
JOHN HAGELIN AND NAT GOLDHABER	Reform	[]
PAT BUCHANAN AND EZOLA FOSTER	Independent	[]

FOR REPRESENTATIVE IN CONGRESS 9TH CONGRESSIONAL DISTRICT VOTE FOR ONE

DENNIS J. DRISCOLL	Republican	[]
JAN SCHAKOWSKY	Democratic	[]

FOR REPRESENTATIVE IN THE GENERAL ASSEMBLY 58TH REPRESENTATIVE DISTRICT VOTE FOR ONE

NO CANDIDATE	Republican	[]
JEFFREY M. SCHOENBERG	Democratic	[]

FOR COMMISSIONERS OF THE METROPOLITAN WATER RECLAMATION DISTRICT

DONALD G. HANSEN	Republican	[]
LOURDES G. MON	Republican	[]
JOSEPH M. "JOE" MAUN	Republican	[]
TERRENCE J. O'BRIEN	Democratic	[]
JAMES "JIM" HARRIS	Democratic	[]
HARRY "BUS" YOURELL	Democratic	[]

FOR COMMISSIONERS OF THE METROPOLITAN WATER RECLAMATION DISTRICT

Candidate	Party	
VARTAN SEFERIAN	Republican	[]
MARTIN A. SANDOVAL	Democratic	[]

FOR STATE'S ATTORNEY OF COOK COUNTY VOTE FOR ONE

DAVID R. GAUGHAN	Republican	[]
RICHARD A. DEVINE	Democratic	[]

FOR COOK COUNTY RECORDER OF DEEDS VOTE FOR ONE

ARTHUR D. SUTTON	Republican	[]
EUGENE "GENE" MOORE	Democratic	[]

FOR CLERK OF CIRCUIT COURT OF COOK COUNTY VOTE FOR ONE

NANCY F. MYNARD	Republican	[]
DOROTHY A. BROWN	Democratic	[]

FOR JUDGE OF THE SUPREME COURT 1ST JUDICIAL DISTRICT

NO CANDIDATE	Republican	[]
THOMAS R. FITZGERALD	Democratic	[]

FOR JUDGE OF THE APPELLATE COURT 1ST JUDICIAL DISTRICT

JOHN JOSEPH COYNE	Republican	[]
SHELVIN LOUISE MARIE HALL	Democratic	[]

FOR JUDGE OF THE CIRCUIT COURT COOK COUNTY JUDICIAL CIRCUIT

Candidate	Party	
NO CANDIDATE	Republican	[]
MATTHEW E. COGHLAN	Democratic	[]

FOR JUDGE OF THE CIRCUIT COURT COOK COUNTY JUDICIAL CIRCUIT

Candidate	Party	
NO CANDIDATE	Republican	[]
JOYCE M. MURPHY	Democratic	[]

FOR JUDGE OF THE CIRCUIT COURT COOK COUNTY JUDICIAL CIRCUIT

Candidate	Party	
NO CANDIDATE	Republican	[]
MARY MARGARET BROSNAHAN	Democratic	[]

FOR JUDGE OF THE CIRCUIT COURT COOK COUNTY JUDICIAL CIRCUIT

Candidate	Party	
NO CANDIDATE	Republican	[]
PAUL A. KARKULA	Democratic	[]

FOR JUDGE OF THE CIRCUIT COURT COOK COUNTY JUDICIAL CIRCUIT

Candidate	Party	
NO CANDIDATE	Republican	[]
R. SCOTT NEVILLE, JR.	Democratic	[]

FOR JUDGE OF THE CIRCUIT COURT COOK COUNTY JUDICIAL CIRCUIT

Candidate	Party	
NO CANDIDATE	Republican	[]
COLLEEN F. SHEEHAN	Democratic	[]

FOR JUDGE OF THE CIRCUIT COURT COOK COUNTY JUDICIAL CIRCUIT

Candidate	Party	
NO CANDIDATE	Republican	[]
DONNA PHELPS FELTON	Democratic	[]

FOR JUDGE OF THE CIRCUIT COURT COOK COUNTY JUDICIAL CIRCUIT

Candidate	Party	
NO CANDIDATE	Republican	[]
JOAN MARGARET O'BRIEN	Democratic	[]

FOR JUDGE OF THE CIRCUIT COURT COOK COUNTY JUDICIAL CIRCUIT

Candidate	Party	
NO CANDIDATE	Republican	[]
MARCIA MARAS	Democratic	[]

FOR JUDGE OF THE CIRCUIT COURT COOK COUNTY JUDICIAL CIRCUIT

Candidate	Party	
NO CANDIDATE	Republican	[]
MICHAEL T. HEALY	Democratic	[]

FOR JUDGE OF THE CIRCUIT COURT COOK COUNTY JUDICIAL CIRCUIT

Candidate	Party	
NO CANDIDATE	Republican	[]
THOMAS DAVID ROTI	Democratic	[]

FOR JUDGE OF THE CIRCUIT COURT COOK COUNTY JUDICIAL CIRCUIT

Candidate	Party	
NO CANDIDATE	Republican	[]
FRANCIS JOSEPH DOLAN	Democratic	[]

VOTE FOR ONE JUDGE OF THE CIRCUIT COURT COOK COUNTY JUDICIAL CIRCUIT 9TH SUBCIRCUIT

NO CANDIDATE	Republican	[]
JAMES R. EPSTEIN	Democratic	[]

seldom choose candidates; they merely organize and supervise the election process by which party *voters* choose the candidates. Because almost all aspiring candidates must first win a primary election to gain their party's nomination, those who would campaign for election must first campaign for nomination.

NOMINATIONS

The distinguishing feature of the nomination process in American party politics is that it usually involves an election by party voters. National party leaders do not choose their party's nominee for president or even its candidates for House and Senate seats. Virtually no other political parties in the world nominate candidates to the national legislature through party elections.[6] In more than half the world's parties, local party leaders choose legislative candidates, and their national party organization must usually approve these choices.

Democrats and Republicans nominate their candidates for national and state offices in varying ways across the country, because each state is entitled to make its own laws governing the nomination process. (This is significant in itself, for political parties in most other countries are largely free of laws stating how they must select their candidates.) We can classify nomination practices by the types of party elections held and the level of office sought.

Nomination for Congress and State Offices

primary election
A preliminary election conducted within a political party to select candidates who will run for public office in a subsequent election.

In the United States, most aspiring candidates for major offices are nominated through a **primary election,** a preliminary election conducted within the party to select its candidates. Forty-three states use primary elections alone to nominate candidates for all state and national offices, and primaries figure in the nomination processes of all the other states.[7] The nomination process, then, is highly decentralized, resting on the decisions of thousands, perhaps millions, of the party rank and file who participate in primary elections.

In both parties, only about half of the regular party voters (about one-quarter of the voting-age population) bother to vote in a given primary, although the proportion varies greatly by state and contest.[8] Early research on primary elections concluded that Republicans who voted in their primaries were more conservative than those who did not, whereas Democratic primary voters were more liberal than other Democrats. This finding led to the belief that primary voters tend to nominate candidates who are more ideologically extreme than the party as a whole would prefer. But other research, in which primary voters were compared with those who missed the primary but voted in the general election, reported little evidence that primary voters are unrepresentative of the ideological orientation of other party voters.[9] Some studies support another interpretation: although party activists who turn out for primaries and caucuses are not representative of the average party member, they subordinate their own views to select candidates "who will fare well in the general election."[10]

Can You Explain Why...
political parties favor closed rather than open primaries?

States hold different types of primary elections for state and congressional offices. The most common type (used by about forty states) is the

closed primary
A primary election in which voters must declare their party affiliation before they are given the primary ballot containing that party's potential nominees.

open primary
A primary election in which voters need not declare their party affiliation but must choose one party's primary ballot to take into the voting booth.

blanket primary
A primary election in which voters receive a ballot containing both parties' potential nominees and can help nominate candidates for all offices for both parties.

closed primary, in which voters must declare their party affiliation before they are given the primary ballot, which lists that party's potential nominees. A few states use the **open primary,** in which voters may choose either party's ballot to take into the polling booth. Four states use variations of the **blanket primary,** in which voters receive one or more ballots listing all parties' potential nominees for each office and can mark their ballots for any candidate, but only one for each office. The top vote-getter from each party advances to the general election. The state of Washington has used the blanket primary in this form since 1935, and Alaska adopted the same system. Under Louisiana's version of the blanket primary (devised when the state was solidly Democratic), a candidate who obtains a majority of the votes cast for that office in the primary is automatically elected without participating in the general election. (Usually the primary *was* the election.) In a 1996 referendum, California voters approved a blanket primary, with a new twist. The ballot listed all candidates and parties *in random order* for each office. Referring to this system as a "jungle" primary that would weaken every party's control over its nominations, both parties brought suit to invalidate it. In 2000, the Supreme Court agreed that the law placed a "severe and unnecessary" burden on the parties' rights of political association, and struck down the California variant of the blanket primary.

Most scholars believe that the type of primary held in a state affects the strength of its party organizations. Open primaries (and certainly blanket primaries and the jungle primary) weaken parties more than closed primaries, for they allow voters to float between parties rather than require them to work within one. But the differences among types of primaries are much less important than the fact that our parties have primaries at all—that parties choose candidates through elections. This practice originated in the United States and largely remains peculiar to us. Placing the nomination of party candidates in the hands of voters rather than party leaders is a key factor in the decentralization of power in American parties, which contributes more to pluralist than to majoritarian democracy.

Nomination for President

The decentralized nature of American parties is readily apparent in candidates' campaigns for the parties' nominations for president. Delegates attending the parties' national conventions, held the summer before the presidential election in November, nominate the presidential candidates. In the past, delegates chose their party's nominee right at the convention, sometimes after repeated balloting over several candidates who divided the vote and kept anyone from getting the majority needed to win the nomination. In 1920, for example, the Republican convention deadlocked over two leading candidates, after nine ballots. Party leaders then met in the storied "smoke-filled room" and compromised on Warren G. Harding, who won on the tenth. Harding was not among the leading candidates and had won only one primary (in his native Ohio). The last time that either party needed more than one ballot to nominate its presidential candidate was in 1952, when the Democrats took three ballots to nominate Adlai E. Stevenson. Although the Republicans took only one ballot that year to nominate Dwight Eisenhower, his nomination was contested by

---

feature 9.1

★

Changes in the Presidential Nomination Process

When President Lyndon Johnson abruptly announced in late March 1968 that he would not run for reelection, the door opened for his vice president, Hubert Humphrey. Humphrey felt it was too late to campaign in primaries against other candidates already in the race; nevertheless, he commanded enough support among party leaders to win the Democratic nomination. The stormy protests outside the party's convention against the "inside politics" of his nomination led to major changes in the way both parties have nominated their presidential candidates since 1968.

Presidential Nominating Process

Until 1968

Party-Dominated
The nomination decision is largely in the hands of party leaders. Candidates win by enlisting the support of state and local party machines.

Few Primaries
Most delegates are selected by state party establishments, with little or no public participation. Some primaries are held, but their results do not necessarily determine the nominee. Primaries are used to indicate candidates' "electability."

Short Campaigns
Candidates usually begin their public campaign early in the election year.

Since 1968

Candidate-Dominated
Campaigns are independent of party establishments. Endorsements by party leaders have little effect on nomination choice.

Many Primaries
Most delegates are selected by popular primaries and caucuses. Nominations are determined largely by voters' decisions at these contests.

Long Campaigns
Candidates begin laying groundwork for campaigns three or four years before the election. Candidates who are not well organized at least eighteen months before the election may have little chance of winning.

Senator Robert Taft, and Eisenhower won his nomination on the floor of the convention.

Although 1952 was the last year a nominating majority was constructed among delegates inside the hall, delegates to the Democratic convention in 1960 and the Republican convention in 1964 also resolved uncertain outcomes. Since 1972, both parties' nominating conventions have simply ratified the results of the complex process for selecting the convention delegates, as described in Feature 9.1. Most minor parties, like the Reform Party in 1996, still tend to use conventions to nominate their presidential candidates. Ironically, the more successful "third-party" candidates—like George Wallace in 1968, John Anderson in 1980, and Perot in 1992—nominated themselves.[11]

1996 National Party Conventions

Selecting Convention Delegates.   No national legislation specifies how the state parties must select delegates to their national conventions.

Until 1968
Easy Money
Candidates frequently raise large amounts of money quickly by tapping a handful of wealthy contributors. No federal limits on spending by candidates.

Limited Media Coverage
Campaigns are followed by print journalists and, in later years, by television. But press coverage of campaigns is not intensive and generally does not play a major role in influencing the process.

Late Decisions
Events early in the campaign year, such as the New Hampshire primary, are not decisive. States that pick delegates late in the year, such as California, frequently are important in selecting the nominee. Many states enter the convention without making final decisions about candidates.

Open Conventions
National party conventions sometimes begin with the nomination still undecided. The outcome is determined by maneuvering and negotiations among party factions, often stretching over multiple ballots.

Since 1968
Difficult Fundraising
Campaign contributions are limited to $1,000 per person, so candidates must work endlessly to raise money from thousands of small contributors. PAC contributions are important in primaries. Campaign spending is limited by law, both nationally and for individual states.

Media-Focused
Campaigns are covered intensively by the media, particularly television. Media treatment of candidates plays a crucial role in determining the nominee.

"Front-Loaded"
Early events, such as the Iowa caucuses and New Hampshire primary, are important. The nomination may be decided even before many major states vote. Early victories attract great media attention, which gives winners free publicity and greater fundraising ability.

Closed Conventions
The nominee is determined before the convention, which does little more than ratify the decision made in primaries and caucuses. Convention activities focus on creating a favorable media image of the candidate for the general election campaign.

Instead, state legislatures have enacted a bewildering variety of procedures, which often differ for Democrats and Republicans in the same state. The most important distinction in delegate selection is between the presidential primary and the local caucus.

A **presidential primary** is a special primary held to select delegates to attend a party's national nominating convention. In *presidential preference primaries* (used in all forty-two Democratic primaries in 2000 and in most of the forty-five Republican primaries), party supporters vote directly for the candidate they favor as their party's nominee for president. In each state primary, the candidates win delegates according to various formulas. Virtually all Democratic primaries are *proportional*, meaning that candidates win delegates in rough proportion to the votes they win. Specifically, candidates who win at least 15 percent of the vote divide the state's delegates in proportion to the percentage of their primary votes. In contrast,

presidential primary
A special primary election used to select delegates to attend the party's national convention, which in turn nominates the presidential candidate.

figure

9.1   Front-Loading the Delegate Selection Process

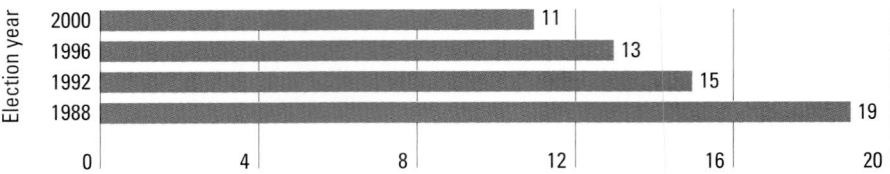

Number of weeks it took to choose 75% of the delegates to both party conventions

In 2000, more delegates were selected earlier in the nominating season than ever before. This was the consequence of states' jockeying for greater candidate and media attention. In 2000, thirty-four states held their primary or caucuses by March 18, when 63 percent of all Republican delegates had been selected.

Source: "The Primary Season," *Chicago Tribune*, 30 January 2000, p. 14.

local caucus
A method used to select delegates to attend a party's national convention. Generally, a local meeting selects delegates for a county-level meeting, which in turn selects delegates for a higher-level meeting; the process culminates in a state convention that actually selects the national convention delegates.

Can You Explain Why...
convention delegates are chosen increasingly earlier in recent election years?

front-loading
States' practice of moving delegate selection primaries and caucuses earlier in the calendar year to gain media and candidate attention.

most Republican primaries follow the *winner-take-all* principle, which gives all the state's delegates to the candidate who wins a plurality of its vote. Republicans in about ten states allocate delegates in proportion to the vote cast, and in about five states they vote in *delegate selection primaries*, voting for (theoretically) unpledged delegates rather than the candidates themselves.[12]

The **local caucus** method of delegate selection has several stages. It begins with local meetings, or caucuses, of party supporters to choose delegates to attend a larger subsequent meeting, usually at the county level. Most delegates selected in the local caucuses openly back one of the presidential candidates. The county meetings, in turn, select delegates to a higher level. The process culminates in a state convention, which actually selects the delegates to the national convention. Only nine states (but all four territories) relied mainly on the caucus process in 2000 (a few combined caucuses with primaries.)[13]

Primary elections (which were stimulated by the Progressive movement, discussed in Chapter 7) were first used to select delegates to nominating conventions in 1912. Heralded as a party "reform," primaries spread like wildfire. By 1916, a majority of delegates to both conventions were chosen through party elections, but presidential primaries soon dropped in popularity. From 1924 through 1960, rarely were more than 40 percent of the delegates to the national conventions chosen through primaries. Antiwar protests at the 1968 Democratic convention sparked rule changes in the national party that required more "open" procedures for selecting delegates. Voting in primaries seemed the most open procedure. By 1972, this method of selection accounted for about 60 percent of the delegates at both party conventions. Now the parties in over forty states rely on presidential primaries, which generate more than 80 percent of the delegates.[14] Because nearly all delegates selected in primaries are publicly committed to specific candidates, one can easily tell before a party's summer nominating convention who is going to be its nominee. Indeed, we have been learning the nominee's identity earlier and earlier, thanks to **front-loading** of delegate selection. This term describes the tendency during the last two decades for states to move their primaries and caucuses earlier in the calendar year to gain attention from the media and the candidates (see Figure 9.1).[15]

Campaigning for the Nomination. The process of nominating party candidates for president is a complex, drawn-out affair that has no parallel in any other nation. Would-be presidents announce their candidacy and begin campaigning many months before the first convention delegates are selected. Soon after one election ends, prospective candidates quietly begin lining up political and financial support for their likely race nearly four years later. This early, silent campaign has been dubbed the *invisible primary*.[16] Indeed, the 2000 race for the presidency began shortly after Clinton's reelection. Vice President Al Gore was first off the starting block. In mid-January 1997—only three months after the November election—he talked about campaigning for the election four years hence.[17] Although Gore said that he would keep his plans "under wraps until well after the 1998 congressional elections," he was silently preparing for the race.

Republican presidential hopefuls were not far behind Gore. By May 1997, former governor Lamar Alexander, senator John McCain, and publisher Steve Forbes had visited New Hampshire—all denying any political motive. Other Republican aspirants had already created campaign organizations or were speaking at fundraising events as prospective candidates. A veteran reporter said that White House hopefuls were "practically tripping over one another" in history's earliest "invisible" campaign.[18] By the summer of 1999, eight Republicans had registered exploratory campaign committees with the Federal Election Commission.[19]

By historical accident, two small states—Iowa and New Hampshire—have become the testing ground of candidates' popularity with party voters. Accordingly, each basks in the media spotlight once every four years. Both state legislatures are now committed to leading the delegate selection process, ensuring their states' share of national publicity and their bids for political history. The Iowa caucuses and the New Hampshire primary have served different functions in the presidential nominating process.[20] The contest in Iowa has traditionally tended to winnow out candidates rejected by the party faithful. The New Hampshire primary, held one week later, tests the Iowa front-runners' appeal to ordinary party voters, which foreshadows their likely strength in the general election.

Because voting takes little effort by itself, more citizens are likely to vote in primaries than to attend caucuses, which can last for hours. In 2000, about 7 percent of the voting age population participated in both parties' Iowa caucuses, whereas about 44 percent voted in both New Hampshire primaries.[21]

Until 1972, New Hampshire proudly claimed to be the first state that selected delegates to the parties' summer nominating conventions. It still qualifies as the first state to hold a primary election for selecting convention delegates, but New Hampshire now yields the spotlight every four years to Iowa, which decided in 1972 to hold caucuses even earlier for selecting convention delegates. The two states now have an informal pact: Iowa will hold the first caucuses and New Hampshire will hold the first primary. By being first, both small states make money from media spending, and both state legislatures are committed to lead the nation in their own method of delegate selection.[22] Challenged by front-loading in 2000, Iowa had to start as early as January 24 to be first to select delegates. New Hampshire followed with the nation's first primary on February 1. Conventional wisdom holds that a favorable showing in the Iowa caucuses helps candidates win the New Hampshire primary. That wisdom barely held true for the Democrats in 2000 and did not hold true for the Republicans.

By January, the Democratic contest had already narrowed to a two-horse race. Through his stature as vice president and his support from party leaders across the country, Al Gore had discouraged most other potential challengers. His only rival in 2000 was former Rhodes scholar, New York Knicks basketball star, and U.S. senator, Bill Bradley. Gore, the candidate of the party establishment, campaigned hard to win the Iowa caucuses, while Bradley concentrated his efforts on the New Hampshire primary. Gore swamped Bradley in Iowa with over 60 percent of the caucus votes, but Gore edged Bradley in New Hampshire by only 4 percentage points in a much larger primary vote. Although Bradley's close finish gave some hope to his campaign, a poor showing in the eleven primaries on March 7 ("Super Tuesday") forced the overmatched challenger to end his run on March 9.

On the Republican side, so many aspiring candidates threw their hats into the ring in the early stages that it's hard to keep count. Let's begin with the nine who competed in a media event straw poll held in Iowa in August 1999. Their identities and fates are depicted in Figure 9.2. From the beginning, George W. Bush enjoyed advantages over his rivals by being governor of Texas, son and namesake of a former president, and beneficiary of enormous campaign contributions. Only six of the nine Republican hopefuls in August survived to the Iowa caucuses five months later. Bush won Iowa handily over his closest rival, Steve Forbes, but—as in the Democratic caucuses— Bush's most potent rival, Senator John McCain, did not campaign much in Iowa and concentrated on New Hampshire (as did Bradley). In the New Hampshire primary one week later, McCain upset Bush, 49 to 30 percent. With nearly 80 percent of the New Hampshire vote going to these two candidates, the Republican contest was also reduced to a two-horse race. (The African-American candidate Alan Keyes, who seemed to enjoy campaigning despite winning few votes, did not formally withdraw until July 26.) In spite of McCain's victory in New Hampshire, his poor showing in the eleven

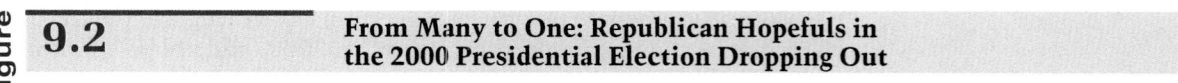

figure 9.2 | **From Many to One: Republican Hopefuls in the 2000 Presidential Election Dropping Out**

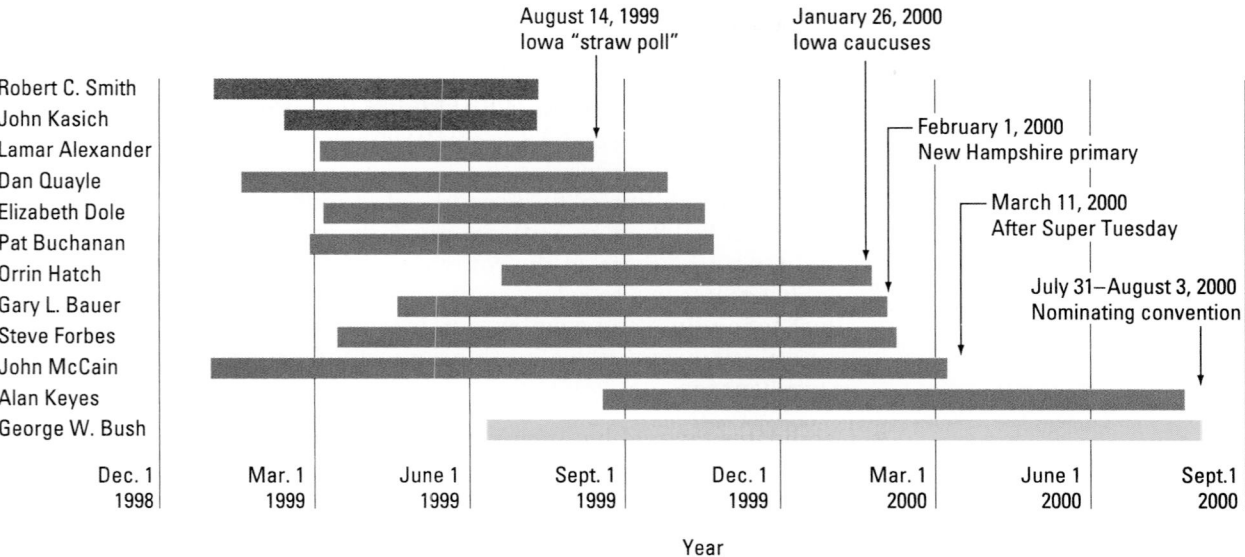

By early 1999, some prominent Republicans had already announced their intentions to run for their party's presidential nomination in 2000. George W. Bush did not formally announce his candidacy until June 12 in Iowa where, coincidentally, the offical nomination process would start in early 2000 with local party caucuses selecting delegates to the party's summer convention. To gain publicity and make money, Iowa Republicans held a straw poll on August 14, 1999. The poll was open to anyone willing to pay $25. Bush won the poll with 31 percent of the vote, ten points ahead of Steve Forbes. Elizabeth Dole was third with 14 percent. (McCain did not mount a serious contest to win that poll.) So the 23,685 people (not all of whom were Iowans), who paid $25 each, annointed these three as credible candidates a year before the Republican national convention.

primaries on March 7 ("Super Tuesday") also forced him to end his run on March 9.

By the second week in March, the Democrats and Republicans had chosen their candidates for the 2000 election—notwithstanding the fact that twenty-nine states still had not held primaries or caucuses to select their party delegates to the nominating conventions. Although changes in the nominating process introduced in 1972 had resulted in candidates being chosen prior to the nominating conventions (remember Feature 9.1), this was the earliest *ever* that both major parties had nominated their candidates for a presidential election.[23] Two intertwined factors seem to account for the quick resolution in 2000: (1) increased front-loading in the delegate selection process and (2) the greater need to raise large sums of money earlier to campaign effectively because of factor number one.

Over 36 million people (about 18 percent of the voting age population) voted in one of the presidential primaries in 2000, and about a half million participated in party caucuses.[24] Requiring prospective presidential candidates to campaign before many millions of party voters in primaries and hundreds of thousands of party activities in caucus states has several consequences:

- When no incumbent in the White House is seeking reelection, the presidential nominating process becomes contested in both parties. Because Vice President Gore decided to seek the Democratic nomination to succeed President Clinton, he discouraged serious campaigns from all challengers but Bill Bradley. Still, the nomination was Vice President Gore's to win, not to inherit. In the complex mix of caucus and primary methods that states use to select convention delegates, timing and luck can affect who wins, and even an outside chance of success ordinarily attracts a half dozen or so plausible contestants in either party lacking an incumbent president.

- Candidates favored by most party identifiers usually win their party's nomination. There have been only two exceptions to this rule since 1936, when poll data first became available: Adlai E. Stevenson in 1952 and George McGovern in 1972.[25] Both were Democrats; both lost impressively in the general election.

- Candidates who win the nomination do so largely on their own and owe little or nothing to the national party organization, which usually does not promote a candidate. In fact, Jimmy Carter won the nomination in 1976 against a field of nationally prominent Democrats, although he was a party outsider with few strong connections to the national party leadership.

ELECTIONS

general election
A national election held by law in November of every even-numbered year.

By national law, all seats in the House of Representatives and one-third of the seats in the Senate are filled in a **general election** held in early November in even-numbered years. Every state takes advantage of the national election to fill also some of the nearly five hundred thousand state and local offices across the country, which makes the election even more "general." When the president is chosen, every fourth year, the election is identified as a *presidential election.* The intervening elections are known as *congressional, midterm,* or *off-year elections.*

Presidential Elections and the Electoral College

In contrast to almost all other offices in the United States, the presidency does not go automatically to the candidate who wins the most votes. Instead, a two-stage procedure specified in the Constitution decides elections for the president; it requires selection of the president by a group (college) of electors representing the states. As mentioned in the opening vignette of Chapter 4, we elect a president not in a national election but in a *federal* election.

The Electoral College: Structure.   Surprising as it might seem, the term *electoral college* is not mentioned in the Constitution, nor is it readily found in books on American politics prior to World War II. One major dictionary defines a *college* as "a body of persons having a common purpose or shared duties."[26] The electors who choose the president of the United States became known as the electoral college largely during the twentieth century. Eventually, this term became incorporated into statutes relating to presidential elections, so it has assumed a legal basis.[27]

The Constitution (Article II, Section 1) says, "Each State shall appoint, in such Manner as the Legislature thereof may direct, a Number of Electors, equal to the whole Number of Senators and Representatives to which the State may be entitled in the Congress." Thus, each of the fifty states is entitled to one elector for each of its senators (100 total) and one for each of its representatives (435 votes total), totaling 535 electoral votes. In addition, the Twenty-third Amendment to the Constitution awarded three electoral votes (the minimum for any state) to the District of Columbia, although it elects no voting members of Congress. So the total number of electoral votes is 538. The Constitution specifies that a candidate needs a majority of electoral votes, or 270, to win the presidency.*

The 538 electoral votes are apportioned among the states according to their representation in Congress, which, in turn, depends on their population. Because of population changes recorded by the 2000 census, the distribution of electoral votes among the states will change between the 2000 and 2004 presidential elections. Figure 9.3 shows the distribution of electoral votes for the 2004 election, indicating which states have lost and gained electoral votes. The clear pattern is the systemic loss of people and electoral votes in the north central and eastern states and the gain in the western and southern states.

The Electoral College: Politics.   In 1789, the first set of presidential electors was chosen under the new Constitution. Only three states chose their electors by direct popular vote, while state legislatures selected electors in the others. Selection by state legislature remained the norm until 1792. Afterward, direct election by popular vote became more common, and by 1824 voters chose electors in eighteen of twenty-four states. Since 1860, all states have selected their electors through popular vote once they had entered the union.[28] If the Florida state legislature had carried through its plan in 2000 to select its delegates by the legislature, it would have had historical precedent, but pre–Civil War precedent.

Can You Explain Why...
the presidential election is
federal and not national?

Of course, the situation in Florida was itself unprecedented due to the extremely close election in 2000. Voters nationwide favored the Democratic candidate, Al Gore, by a plurality of approximately 500,000 votes out of 105 million cast. But the presidential election is a *federal* election. A candidate is not chosen president by national popular vote but by a majority of the

---

* *If no candidate receives a majority when the electoral college votes, the election is thrown into the House of Representatives. The House votes by state, with each state casting one vote. The candidates in the House election are the top three finishers in the general election. A presidential election has gone to the House only twice in American history, in 1800 and 1824, before a stable two-party system had developed.*

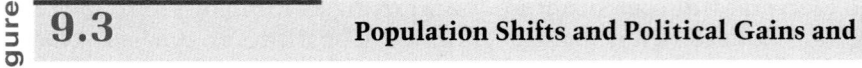

figure 9.3   **Population Shifts and Political Gains and Losses**

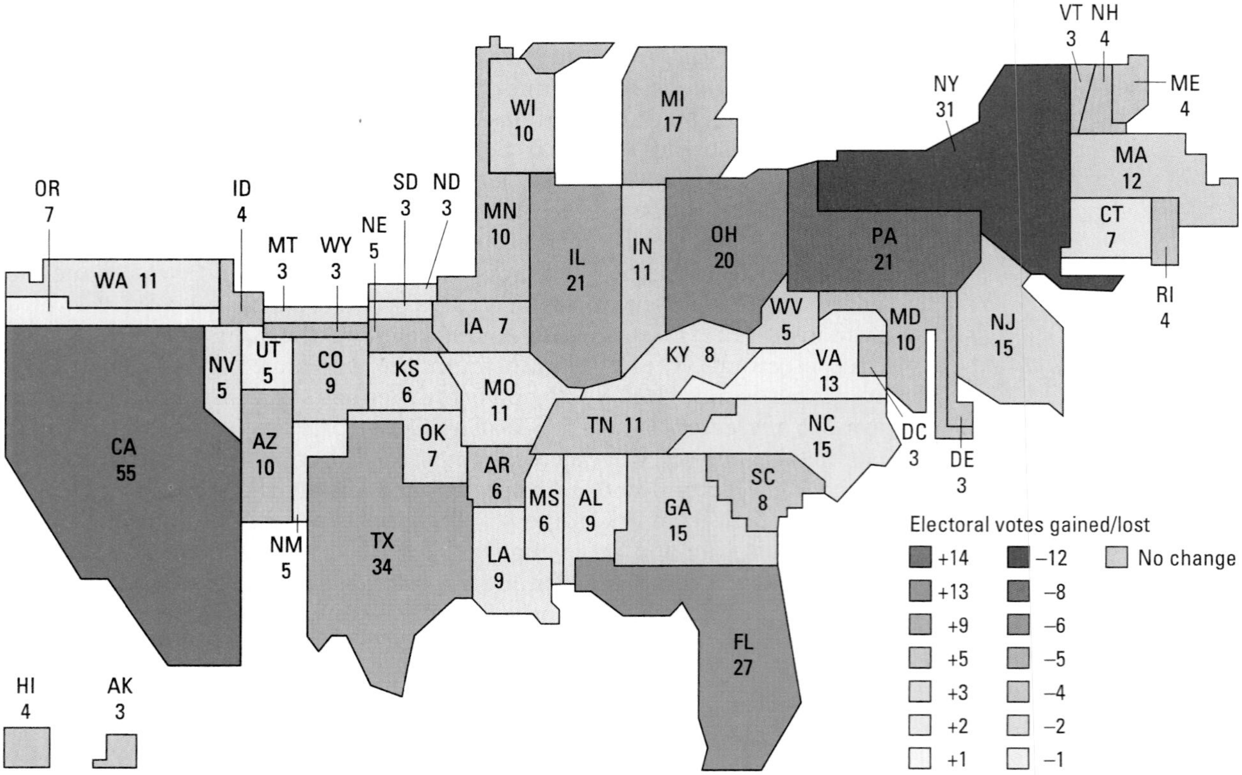

If the states were sized according to their electoral votes for the 2004 presidential election, the nation might resemble this map, on which states are drawn according to their population, based on the 2000 census. Each state has as many electoral votes as its combined representation in the Senate (always two) and the House (which depends on population). Although New Jersey is much smaller in area than Montana, New Jersey has far more people and is thus bigger in terms of "electoral geography." The coloring on this map shows the states that have gained electoral votes since 1960 (in shades of green) and those that have lost electoral votes (in shades of purple). States that have not had the number of their electoral votes changed since 1960 are blue. This map clearly reflects the drain of population (and seats in Congress) from the north central and eastern states to the western and southern states. California, with two senators and fifty-three representatives in the 2002 election, will have fifty-five electoral votes for presidential elections through 2010, when the next census will be taken.

states' electoral votes. In each state, the candidate who wins a plurality of its popular vote—whether by twenty votes or by 20,000 votes—wins *all* of the state's electoral votes. Gore and his Republican opponent, George W. Bush, ran close races in many states across the nation. Not counting Florida, Gore had won 267 electoral votes, just three short of the 270 he needed to claim the presidency.

During the ballot counting and recounting in Florida after the controversial 2000 presidential election, backers of rival candidates George W. Bush and Al Gore discuss the issues of the day.

But in Florida, which had twenty-five electoral votes in 2000, the initial vote count showed an extremely close race—with Bush ahead by the slimmest of margins. If Bush won Florida by even one vote, he could add its 25 electoral votes to the 246 he won in the other states, for a total of 271—just one more than the number needed to win the presidency. Gore trailed Bush by only about 2,000 votes, close enough to ask for a recount. But the recount proved difficult due to different ballots and different methods for counting them (see Figure 9.4). After more than a month of ballot counting, recounting, more recounting, lawsuits, court decisions—and the Republican legislature's threat to select the electors on its own to ensure Bush's victory—Bush was certified as the winner of Florida's 25 electoral votes by a mere 537 popular votes. So ended one of the most protracted, complicated, and intense presidential elections in American history.

The Electoral College: Abolish It? Between 1789 and 2000, about seven hundred proposals to change the electoral college scheme were introduced in Congress.[29] Historically, polls have found public opinion opposed to the electoral college.[30] Following the 2000 election, letters flooded into newspapers, urging anew that the system be changed, and even Hillary Rodham Clinton, soon after being elected senator of New York, announced her opposition to the electoral college.[31]

To evaluate the criticisms, one must first distinguish between the electoral "college" and the "system" of electoral votes. Strictly speaking, the electoral college is merely the set of individuals empowered to cast a state's electoral votes. In a presidential election, voters don't actually vote for a candidate; they vote for a slate of little-known electors (their names are rarely even on the ballot) pledged to one of the candidates. Most critics hold that the founding fathers argued for a body of electors because they

9.4   How America Votes

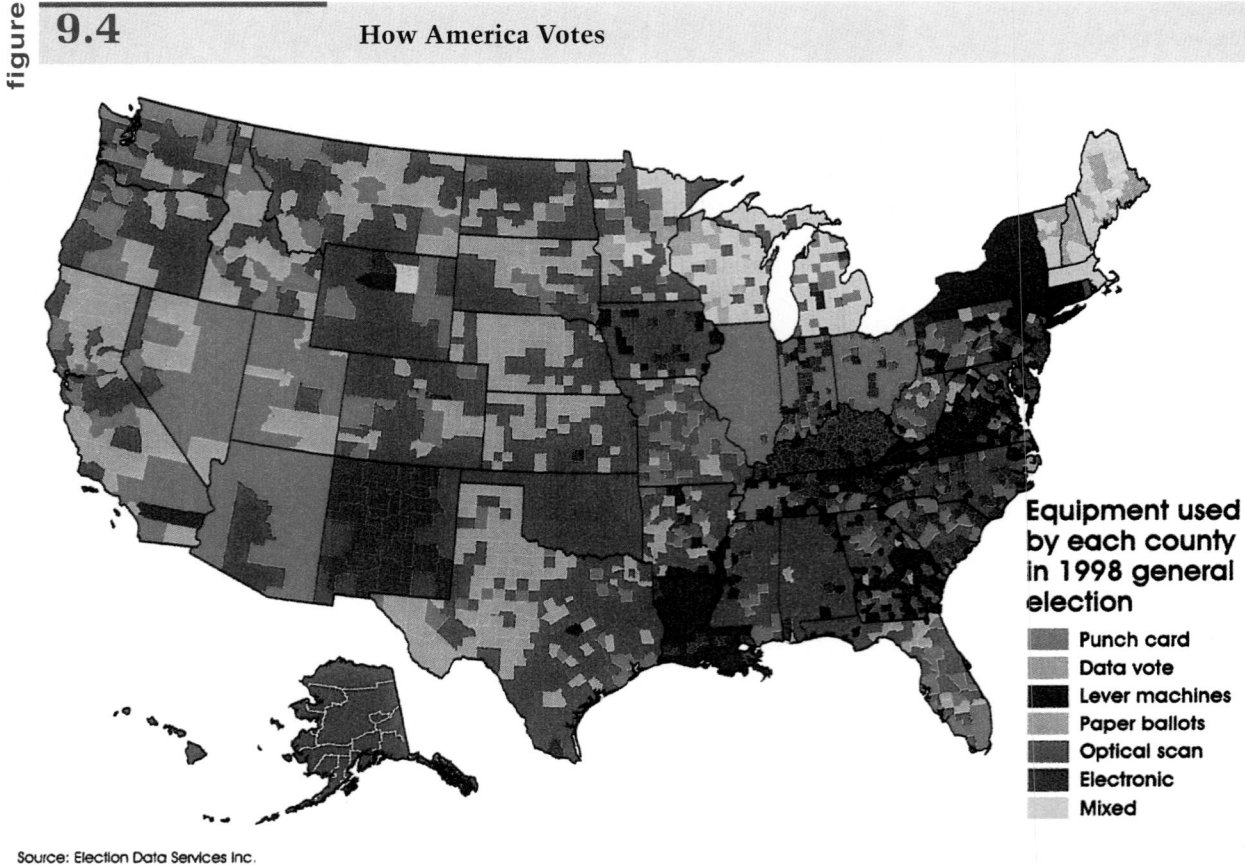

Equipment used
by each county
in 1998 general
election

- Punch card
- Data vote
- Lever machines
- Paper ballots
- Optical scan
- Electronic
- Mixed

Source: Election Data Services Inc.

This map shows the different methods used by the more than 3,000 counties in the United States to count the votes in the 1998 general election, the most recent one available. In 2000, as in 1998, about 20 percent of the nation's precincts used punch-card voting systems, which have been shown to result in somewhat more invalidated votes. No method is perfect, however, and each has certain strengths and weaknesses. As the map suggests, few states determine how its counties should count votes, which are necessarily cast at the local level. For their part, counties have more pressing needs for tax dollars than revamping their vote-counting methods. Despite public clamor for reforming the nation's electoral machinery, unless the state or national governments make money available for counties to buy new machines (optical scanners seem quite reliable), the map for 2004 will look much like this one.

Source: Anay Sostek, "Goodbye Mr. Chad," *Governing* (January 2001), p. 40; and Ford Fessenden, "New Focus on Punch-Card System," *New York Times*, 19 November 2000, p. 30.

did not trust people to vote directly for candidates. But one scholar contends that the device of independent electors was adopted by the Constitutional Convention as a compromise between those who favored having legislatures cast the states' electoral votes for president and those who favored direct popular election.[32] The electoral college allowed states to choose, and—as we have seen—all states gravitated to direct election of electors by 1860. Occasionally (but rarely), electors break their pledges

figure

9.5 The Popular Vote and the Electoral Vote

Strictly speaking, a presidential election is a federal election, not a national election. A candidate must win a majority (270) of the nation's total electoral vote (538). A candidate can win a plurality of the popular vote and still not win the presidency. Until 2000, the last time a candidate won most of the popular votes but did not win the presidency was in 1888. In every election between these two, the candidate who won a plurality of the popular vote won an even larger proportion of the electoral vote. So the electoral vote system magnified the winner's victory and thus increased the legitimacy of the president-elect. As we learned from the 2000 election, that result is not guaranteed.

Sources: Updated from Harold W. Stanley and Richard G. Niemi, *Vital Statistics on American Politics,* 2nd ed. (Washington, D.C.: Congressional Quarterly Press, 1990), pp. 104–106; and "Presidential Election," *Congressional Quarterly Weekly Report,* November 1992, p. 3549.

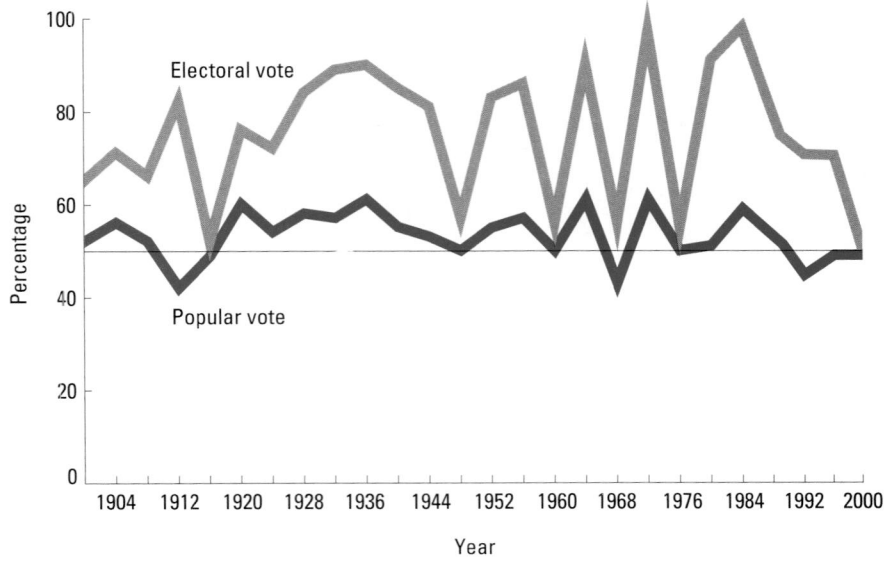

when they assemble to cast their written ballots at their state capitol in December (electors who do so are called "faithless electors"). Indeed, this happened in 2000, when Barbara Lett Simmons, a Democratic elector in Washington, D.C., cast a blank ballot to protest Washington's lack of a voting representative in Congress. (Simmons said that she would have voted for Gore if her vote were needed for him to win.)[33] Such aberrations make for historical footnotes, but they do not affect outcomes. Today, voters have good reason to oppose the need for a body of electors to translate their decision, and few observers defend the electoral college itself.

The more troubling criticism centers on the electoral vote *system,* which makes for a federal rather than a national election. Many reformers favor a majoritarian method for choosing the president—by nationwide direct popular vote. They argue that it is simply wrong to have a system that allows a candidate who wins the most popular votes nationally to lose the election. Until 2000, that situation had not happened for over 100 years—when Grover Cleveland won the popular vote but lost the presidency to Benjamin Harrison in the electoral college in 1888. During all intervening elections, the candidate winning a plurality of the popular vote also won a majority of the electoral vote. In fact, the electoral vote generally operated to magnify the margin of victory, as Figure 9.5 shows. Some scholars argued that this magnifying effect increased the legitimacy of presidents-elect who failed to win a majority of the popular vote, which happened in the elections of Kennedy, Nixon (first time), and Clinton (both times).

The 2000 election proved that today's defenders of the electoral vote system can no longer claim that a federal election based on electoral votes yields the same outcome as a national election based on the popular vote. However, three lines of argument support selecting a president by electoral votes rather than by popular vote. First, if one supports a federal form of government as embodied within the Constitution, then one may defend the electoral vote system because it gives small states more weight in the vote: they have two senators, the same as large states. Second, if one favors presidential candidates campaigning on foot and in rural areas (needed to win most states) rather than campaigning via television to the 100 most populous market areas, then one might favor the electoral vote system.[34] Third, if one does not want to see a nationwide recount in a close election (multiplying by fifty the counting problems in Florida), then one might want to keep the current system. So switching to selecting the president by popular vote has serious implications, which explains why Congress has not moved quickly to amend the Constitution.

Congressional Elections

In a presidential election, the candidates for the presidency are listed at the top of the ballot, followed by the candidates for other national offices and those for state and local offices. A voter is said to vote a **straight ticket** when she or he chooses the same party's candidates for all the offices. A voter who chooses candidates from different parties is said to vote a **split ticket.** About half of all voters admit to splitting their tickets, and the proportion of voters who chose a presidential candidate from one party and a congressional candidate from the other has increased from about 13 percent in 1952 to 25 percent in 1996.[35] In the 1970s and 1980s, the common pattern was to elect a Republican as president while electing mostly Democrats to Congress. This produced a divided government, with the executive and legislative branches controlled by different parties (see Chapter 12). In the 1990s, the electorate flipped the pattern, electing a Democratic president but Republican congresses.

Until the historic 1994 election, Democrats for decades had maintained a lock on congressional elections, winning a majority of House seats since 1954 and controlling the Senate for all but six years during that period. Republicans regularly complained that inequitable districts drawn by Democrat-dominated state legislatures had denied them their fair share of seats. For example, the Republicans won 46 percent of the congressional vote in 1992, but they won only 40 percent of the seats.[36] Despite the Republicans' complaint, election specialists note that this is the inevitable consequence of **first-past-the-post elections**—a British term for elections conducted in single-member districts that award victory to the candidate with the most votes. In all such elections worldwide, the party that wins the most votes tends to win more seats than projected by its percentage of the vote.* Thus in 1994, when Republicans got barely 50 percent of the House votes nationwide, they won 53 percent of the House seats. Gaining control of the House for the first time in forty years, they made no complaint. In 2000, an even closer election, the Republicans won 48.3 percent to the Democrats 47.8 percent of the votes, and the GOP took

straight ticket
In voting, a single party's candidates for all the offices.

split ticket
In voting, candidates from different parties for different offices.

first-past-the-post election
A British term for elections conducted in single-member districts that award victory to the candidate with the most votes.

* *If you have trouble understanding this phenomenon, think of a basketball team that scores, on average, 51 percent of the total points in all the games it plays. Such a team usually wins more than just 51 percent of its games because it tends to win the close ones.*

51 percent of the seats to keep control. (See Chapter 11 for an analysis of the 2000 congressional election.) These recent election results reveal no evidence of Democratic malapportionment of congressional districts. Both parties have enjoyed, and suffered, the mathematics of first-past-the-post elections.

CAMPAIGNS

As Barbara Salmore and Stephen Salmore have observed, election campaigns have been studied more through anecdotes than through systematic analysis.[37] These writers developed an analytical framework that emphasizes the political context of the campaign, the financial resources available for conducting the campaign, and the strategies and tactics that underlie the dissemination of information about the candidate.

The Political Context

The two most important structural factors that face each candidate planning a campaign are the office the candidate is seeking and whether he or she is the *incumbent* (the current officeholder, running for reelection) or the *challenger* (who seeks to replace the incumbent). Alternatively, the candidate can be running in an **open election,** which lacks an incumbent because of a resignation or death or constitutional requirement. Incumbents usually enjoy great advantages over challengers, especially in elections to Congress. As explained in Chapter 11, incumbents in the House of Representatives are almost impossible to defeat, historically winning more than 95 percent of the time. However, incumbent senators are somewhat more vulnerable. An incumbent president is also difficult to defeat—but not impossible, as George Bush learned in 1992.

open election
An election that lacks an incumbent.

Every candidate for Congress must also examine the characteristics of the state or district, including its physical size and the sociological makeup of its electorate. In general, the bigger and more populous the district or state and the more diverse the electorate, the more complicated and costly the campaign. Obviously, running for president means conducting a huge, complicated, and expensive campaign. Assured of being nominated at the Republican convention in Philadelphia at the end of July 2000, Governor Bush conducted a five-day campaign trip through six states, beginning in Arkansas and ending in Pennsylvania.[38] Right after the convention, Bush and his handpicked vice presidential candidate, Richard Cheney, campaigned together on a three-day train ride across Ohio, Michigan, and Illinois.[39] Immediately after the Democratic convention in Los Angeles two weeks later, Vice President Al Gore and his handpicked running mate, Senator Joe Lieberman, sailed down the Mississippi on the riverboat *Mark Twain,* stopping at towns in Wisconsin, Minnesota, Iowa, Illinois, and Missouri.[40]

Despite comments in the news about the decreased influence of party affiliation on voting behavior, the party preference of the electorate is an important factor in the context of a campaign. It is easier for a candidate to get elected when her or his party matches the electorate's preference, in part because raising the money needed to conduct a winning campaign is easier. Challengers for Congress, for example, get far less money from organized groups than do incumbents and must rely more on their personal funds and on raising money from individual donors. So where candidates are of the minority party, they have to overcome not only a voting bias but also a funding bias. Finally, significant political issues—such as economic recession, personal scandals, and war—not only affect a campaign but also can dominate it and even negate such positive factors as incumbency and the advantages of a strong economy. Ordinarily, a candidate like Vice President Al Gore would have benefited greatly from being part of a two-term presidential administration during an unprecedented period of prosperity. However, large segments of the electorate were deeply offended by the scandals surrounding President Clinton that culminated in his impeachment by the House of Representatives. Although Clinton was not convicted by the Senate, Vice President Gore made the strategic decision to avoid campaigning with the president and indeed requested that the president not campaign for him. Some feel that Gore made a strategic error that cost him the election. Surely his decision affected his campaign.

Financing

In talking about election campaigns, former House speaker Thomas ("Tip") O'Neill once said, "As it is now, there are four parts to any campaign. The candidate, the issues of the candidate, the campaign organization, and the money to run the campaign with. Without money you can forget the other three."[41] Money pays for office space, staff salaries, telephone bills, postage, travel expenses, campaign literature, and, of course, advertising in the mass media. Although a successful campaign requires a good campaign organization and a good candidate, enough money will buy the best campaign managers, equipment, transportation, research, and consultants—making the quality of the organization largely a function of money.[42] Although the equation is not quite as strong, when party sources promise ample campaign funds, good candidates become available. So from a cynical but practical viewpoint, campaign resources boil down to campaign funds.

Campaign financing is now heavily regulated by the national and state governments, and regulations vary according to the level of the office—national, state, or local. Even at the national level, differences in financing laws for presidential and congressional elections are significant.

Regulating Campaign Financing.   Strict campaign financing laws are relatively new to American politics. Early laws to limit campaign contributions and control campaign spending were flawed in one way or another, and none clearly provided for enforcement. In 1971, during the period of party reform, Congress enacted the Federal Election Campaign Act (FECA), which imposed stringent new rules for full reporting of campaign contributions and expenditures. The weakness of the old legislation soon became apparent. In 1968, before FECA was enacted, House and Senate candidates reported spending $8.5 million for their campaigns. In 1972, with FECA in force, the same number of candidates confessed to spending $88.9 million.[43]

FECA has been amended several times since 1971, usually to strengthen it. For example, the original law legalized political action committees, but a 1974 amendment limited the amounts they can contribute to election campaigns. (Political action committees are discussed in Chapter 10.) The

1974 amendment also created the **Federal Election Commission (FEC)** to implement the law. The FEC now enforces limits on financial contributions to national campaigns and requires full disclosure of campaign spending. The FEC also administers the public financing of presidential campaigns, which began with the 1976 election.

Financing Presidential Campaigns. Presidential campaigns have always been expensive, and at times the legality of the methods of raising funds to support them has been open to question. In the presidential election of 1972, the last election before the FEC took over the funding of presidential campaigns and the regulating of campaign expenditures, President Richard Nixon's campaign committee spent more than $65 million, some of it obtained illegally (for which campaign officials went to jail). In 1974, a new campaign finance law made public funds available to presidential candidates under certain conditions.

Candidates for each party's nomination for president can qualify for federal funding by raising at least $5,000 (in private contributions no greater than $250 each) in each of twenty states. The FEC matches these contributions up to one-half of a preset spending limit for the primary election campaign. Under the 1974 law, $10 million was the limit for spending in presidential primary elections. But by 2000, the limit was raised to $40.5 million by cost-of living provisions. Nevertheless, two candidates for the Republican nomination in 2000 declined to accept public funds. Wealthy publisher Steve Forbes said that he would pay his own way, and Texas Governor George W. Bush had already raised $50 million by September 1999.[44]

Both presidential nominees of the Democratic and Republican parties agreed to accept public funds for the 2000 general election campaign, and each was given up to $67.5 million.[45] Each major party also received public funds to pay for its convention ($13.5 million in 2000). Public funds go directly to each candidate's campaign committee, not to either party. But the FEC also limits what the national committees can spend on behalf of the nominees. In 2000, that limit was $13.7 million. And the FEC limits the amount individuals ($1,000) and organizations ($5,000) can contribute to presidential candidates during the nomination phase and to House and Senate candidates for the primary and general elections.

Since 1976, each major party's candidate has accepted public funds and the attendant spending limits for the general election. This has helped hold the amount officially spent by each campaign below Nixon's record expenditure of $65 million in 1972 dollars! Total campaign spending in 2000, however, was far more than the $67.5 million limit for each candidate. First, each national committee was permitted to spend that extra $13.7 million on behalf of its nominees. Second, the Democratic and Republican National Committees reported spending $513 million and $692 million, respectively, during the 1999–2000 election cycle for all their activities. Who can say how much of that general spending also benefited their presidential nominees?[46]

Originally, the 1974 legislation imposed spending limits both on monetary *contributions* by individuals and organizations to a candidate's campaign and on *expenses* incurred by individuals or organizations who campaigned, independently, on behalf of the candidate. In *Buckley* v. *Valeo* (1976), the Supreme Court distinguished between limits on contributions (which they upheld) and limits on independent expenditures (which they struck down). In its ruling, the Court likened citizens' independent expenditures to free speech, protected under the First Amendment. By equating spending money with speaking freely, the Court limited the possibilities for reforming campaign finance and opened the door to heavy spending by wealthy individuals and groups.

Public funding has had several effects on campaign financing. Obviously, it has limited campaign expenditures, and it has helped equalize the amounts spent by major party candidates in general elections. Also, it has strengthened the trend toward "personalized" presidential campaigns because federal funds are given to the candidate, not to the party orgniza-tion. Finally, public funding has forced candidates to spend a great deal of time seeking $1,000 contributions—a limit that has not changed since 1974, despite inflation that has more than doubled the FEC's spending limits. In the 1980s, however, both parties began to exploit a loophole in the law that allowed them to raise a virtually unlimited amount of **soft money:** funds to be spent for the entire ticket on party mailings, voter registration, and get-out-the-vote campaigns. During the 1999–2000 campaign cycle, each party raised over $250 million of such soft money.[47] The national committees channel soft money to state and local party committees for registration drives and other activities that are not exclusively devoted to the presidential candidates but nonetheless help them. The net effect of these "coordinated campaigns" has been to enhance the role of both the national and state parties in presidential campaigns.

soft money
Funds that are not raised and spent for a specific federal election campaign. Such funds are distinguished from "hard money," which is tied to specific campaigns and thus falls under government regulations.

You might think that a party's presidential campaign would be closely coordinated with the campaigns of its candidates for Congress. But remember that campaign funds go to the presidential candidate, not to the party, and that the national party organization does not run the presidential campaign. Presidential candidates may join congressional candidates in public appearances for mutual benefit, but presidential campaigns are usually isolated—financially and otherwise—from congressional campaigns.

At the end of the 1998 election campaign, many congressional candidates and both parties spoke piously about rewriting campaign finance laws, but little legislation came forth. The most prominent bill, sponsored by Republican Senator John McCain of Arizona and Democratic Senator Russell Feingold of Wisconsin, would have banned soft-money contributions and issue-advocacy ads that favored a given candidate. The bill received more support from Democrats than from Republicans, who saw it as limiting free speech. (Also, although they had criticized the system when they were out of power, Republicans found that it benefited them as incumbents.) After his spirited but unsuccessful run for the 2000 presidential nomination, Senator McCain promised that the McCain-Feingold bill, which had failed in two previous sessions of Congress, would be reintroduced in the session beginning 2001. This time, the bill overcame fierce opposition from Republican senators Mitch McConnell (Kentucky) and Trent Lott (Mississippi), the Republican majority leader, and passed the Senate for an uncertain fate in the House.[48]

Financing Congressional Elections.   Like the presidential election of the same year, the congressional elections of 2000 were the costliest in history. Congressional candidates spent more than $858 million, an increase of 39 percent from the 1997–1998 election cycle.[49] With the failure of campaign finance reform, candidates for congressional seats in 2000 further stretched the existing loopholes in laws restricting the raising and spending of campaign funds. The law already allowed multibillionaires to buy viability as presidential candidates. In 1992 wealthy Texan Ross Perot spent $65 million of his own money to run for president and won an eye-popping 19 percent of the vote. In 1996, newcomer publisher Steve Forbes bankrolled his way into the presidential primaries and returned in 2000 with some experience to accompany his money. Neither rich man won what they sought, but both bought their way into political credibility. At lower levels, some wealthy candidates have been more successful. Wall Street investor and liberal Democrat Jon S. Corzine spent $65 million on his way to winning the New Jersey race for U.S. senator in 2000—which amounts to about $20 for each of his 1.3 million votes.[50]

The rise of wealthy candidates for Congress has attracted systematic study. Looking at 1,548 major-party House candidates in 1996, Jennifer Steen found that incumbents almost never finance their own campaigns. Only about 12 percent of the incumbents she studied gave themselves more than $1,000. Three-quarters of all competitive nonincumbents, however, used more than $1,000 of their own money that year, and 15 percent used more than $100,000.[51] Although the use of personal wealth had a significant effect on the vote in the general election, it had *no* effect on the primary election. Steen's research demonstrates that campaign finance reform is more complicated than many people realize. Indeed, if you favor making it harder for congressional incumbents to be reelected, you might *not* want to support campaign finance reform that limits how much wealthy candidates can spend on their own campaigns.

Strategies and Tactics

In a military campaign, strategy is the overall scheme for winning the war, whereas tactics involve the conduct of localized hostilities. In an election campaign, strategy is the broad approach used to persuade citizens to vote for the candidate, and tactics determine the content of the messages and the way they are delivered. Three basic strategies, which campaigns may blend in different mixes, are as follows:

- *A party-centered strategy,* which relies heavily on voters' partisan identification as well as on the party's organization to provide the resources necessary to wage the campaign

- *An issue-oriented strategy,* which seeks support from groups that feel strongly about various policies

- *An image-oriented strategy,* which depends on the candidate's perceived personal qualities, such as experience, leadership ability, integrity, independence, trustworthiness, and the like[52]

The campaign strategy must be tailored to the political context of the election. Clearly, a party-centered strategy is inappropriate in a primary, because all contenders have the same party affiliation. Research suggests that a party-centered strategy is best suited to voters with little political

You Want Fries with Your Tax Cut?

Campaigning at a drug store in Grinnell, Iowa, Governor George W. Bush took short orders and served beefy promises about a Bush presidency.

knowledge.[53] How do candidates learn what the electorate knows and thinks about politics, and how can they use this information? Candidates today usually turn to pollsters and political consultants, of whom there are hundreds.[54] Well-funded candidates can purchase a "polling package" that includes

- A benchmark poll that provides "campaign information about the voting preferences and issue concerns of various groups in the electorate and a detailed reading of the image voters have of the candidates in the race"

- Focus groups, consisting of ten to twenty people "chosen to represent particular target groups the campaign wants to reinforce or persuade . . . led in their discussion by persons trained in small-group dynamics," giving texture and depth to poll results

- A trend poll "to determine the success of the campaigns in altering candidate images and voting preferences"

- Tracking polls that begin in early October, "conducting short nightly interviews with a small number of respondents, keyed to the variables that have assumed importance"[55]

Professional campaign managers can use information from such sources to settle on a strategy that mixes party affiliation, issues, and images in its messages.[56] In major campaigns, the mass media disseminates these messages to voters through news coverage and advertising.

Making the News.   Campaigns value news coverage by the media for two reasons: the coverage is free, and it seems objective to the audience. If news stories do nothing more than report the candidate's name, that is important, for name recognition by itself often wins elections. To get favorable coverage, campaign managers cater to reporters' deadlines and needs.[57]

Getting free news coverage is yet another advantage that incumbents enjoy over challengers, for incumbents can command attention simply by announcing political decisions—even if they had little to do with them. Members of Congress are so good at this, says one observer, that House members have made news organizations their "unwitting adjuncts."[58]

Campaigns vary in the effectiveness with which they transmit their messages via the news media. Effective tactics recognize the limitations of both the audience and the media. The typical voter is not deeply interested in politics and has trouble keeping track of multiple themes supported with details. By the same token, television is not willing to air lengthy statements from candidates. As a result, news coverage is often condensed to "sound bites" only a few seconds long.

The media often use the metaphor of a horse race in covering politics in the United States. One long-time student of the media contends that reporters both enliven and simplify campaigns by describing them in terms of four basic scenarios: *bandwagons, losing ground, the front-runner,* and *the likely loser.*[59] Once the opinion polls show weakness or strength in a candidate, reporters dust off the appropriate story line.

The more time the press spends on the horse race, the less attention it gives to campaign issues. In fact, recent studies have found that in some campaigns voters get more information from television ads than they do from television news.[60] Ads are more likely to be effective in campaigns below the presidential level because the voters know less about the candidates at the outset and there is little "free" news coverage of the campaigns.[61]

Advertising the Candidate. In all elections, the first objective of paid advertising is name recognition. The next is to promote candidates by extolling their virtues. Finally, campaign advertising can have a negative objective—to attack one's opponent. But name recognition is usually the most important. Studies show that many voters cannot recall the names of their U.S. senators or representatives, but they can recognize their names on a list—as on a ballot. Researchers attribute the high reelection rate for members of Congress mainly to high name recognition (see Chapter 11). Name recognition is the key objective during the primary season even in presidential campaigns, but other objectives become salient in advertising for the general election.

At one time, candidates for national office relied heavily on newspaper advertising; today, they overwhelmingly use the electronic media. Political ads convey more substantive information than many people believe, but the amount varies by campaign. In his comprehensive study of presidential campaign advertising, Darrell West found that the political ads in the 1984, 1988, and 1992 campaigns contained more references to the candidates' policy positions than to their personal qualities—although personal qualities were featured more than policy in 1996.[62] Other scholars have cautioned that the policy positions put forward in campaign ads may be misleading, however, if not downright deceptive.[63] West also found that more than half of the 1996 presidential campaign ads were negative in tone.[64] Not all negatively toned ads qualify as *attack ads,* those that advocate nothing positive. The term *contrast ads* describes those that both criticize an opponent but also advocate policies of the sponsoring candidate.[65]

A review of recent studies found that, ironically, both attack and contrast ads "actually carry more policy information than pure advocacy ads."[66]

The media often inflate the effect of prominent ads by reporting them as news, which means that citizens are about as likely to see controversial ads during the news as in the ads' paid time slots. Although negative ads do convey information, they also breed distrust of politics—as demonstrated in a major controlled study of political advertising: "In our experiments the effect of seeing a negative as opposed to a positive advertisement is to drop intentions to vote by nearly 5 percentage points." Although the authors' conclusion, "Negative advertising drives people away from the polls in large numbers," seems plausible, subsequent studies have failed to show that negative ads produce low voter turnout.[67]

Using New Media.   In the 2000 presidential campaign, both major candidates continued strategic use of new media, including talk and entertainment shows on television. Both Gore and Bush appeared on Oprah Winfrey's talk program, beamed out to a predominantly female viewing audience of about 7.5 million. One or both also showed up on *Live with Regis* and on Rosie O'Donnell's chat show. Then each candidate stayed up late with Leno and Letterman and did stints on *Saturday Night Live,* showing the public how "hip" they were.[68]

But the hottest media in 2000 was the Internet. Not only did the major and minor parties put up their own home pages, but so did the presidential candidates—including several just seeking the Republican nomination. There were "official" sites (endorsed by the candidates) and "unofficial" ones, sometimes created by supporters—and sometimes by opponents. There were so many false sites for candidates that Yahoo! created its own Web page listing candidate "parody pages."[69] Regardless of the political fun people had on the Internet, only 11 percent of the public said that they got most of their campaign news from that source—even when respondents were allowed two answers for "most." The public ranked the Internet far below television as their major source of campaign news (70 percent), below newspapers (39 percent), and even below radio (15 percent).[70] Concerning the 2000 election campaign, the Internet did not qualify as a medium for communication to the masses, but it was a superb medium for communicating among politically active groups (see Chapter 6 for the distinction).

The Internet allowed campaigns to communicate continually with activists on substantive issues, campaign appearances, requests for help, and requests for money. Senator McCain conducted the first presidential campaign fundraiser entirely on the Internet, collecting more the $1 million within forty-eight hours.[71] Candidates liked the Internet because it was fast, easy to use, and cheap—saving mailing costs and phone calls. Apart from candidates, party organizations also used the Internet to establish identity and cultivate supporters. Blessed with substantial financial resources, the two major parties maintained the most stable and resourceful Web sites.[72] Ever since the advent of computers in the 1950s, the national Republican Party has led the Democratic Party in adoption of new information technology, which may be due to the Republicans' link with business, or to their greater financial resources—probably both. In 2000, the Republican National Committee had fifteen people working with Internet technology, compared with only three at the Democratic National

Committee.[73] Despite some impressive applications in the 2000 campaign, politicians were just learning how to use the Internet, and Internet buffs were just learning how to approach politics. Internet coverage of Republican and Democratic nominating conventions, for example, fell short of expectations, and visits to political Web sites covering the conventions actually fell during the coverage.[74]

EXPLAINING VOTING CHOICE

Why do people choose one candidate over another? That is not easy to determine, but there are ways to approach the question. Individual voting choices can be analyzed as products of both long-term and short-term forces. Long-term forces operate throughout a series of elections, predisposing voters to choose certain types of candidates. Short-term forces are associated with particular elections; they arise from a combination of the candidates and issues of the time. Party identification is by far the most important long-term force affecting U.S. elections. The most important short-term forces are candidates' attributes and their policy positions.

Party Identification

Using the "Voters" data in the CROSSTABS program, analyze when respondents decided to vote ("time of vote decision") by strength of party identification. Who decides latest?

Ever since the presidential election of 1952, when the University of Michigan's National Election Studies began, we have known that more than half the electorate decides how to vote before the party conventions end in the summer.[75] And voters who make an early voting decision generally vote according to their party identification. Despite frequent comments in the media about the decline of partisanship in voting behavior, party identification again had a substantial effect on the presidential vote in 2000, as Figure 9.6 shows. About 91 percent of avowed Republicans voted for Bush, and 87 percent of Democrats voted for Gore. A plurality of independents also voted for Bush. This is a common pattern in presidential elections. The winner holds nearly all the voters who identify with his party. The loser holds most of his fellow Democrats or Republicans, but some percentage defects to the winner, a consequence of short-term forces—the candidates' attributes and the issues—surrounding the election. The winner usually gets most of the independents, who split disproportionately for him, also because of short-term forces.

Because Democrats outnumber Republicans, the Democrats should benefit. Why, then, have Republican candidates won more presidential elections since 1952 than Democrats? For one thing, Democrats do not turn out to vote as consistently as Republicans do. For another, Democrats tend to defect more readily from their party. Defections are sparked by the candidates' attributes and the issues, which have usually favored Republican presidential candidates since 1952.

In both 1992 and 1996, however, short-term forces in presidential politics clearly benefited the Democrat Clinton, first as the challenger and later as the incumbent. By winning in 1996, Clinton became the first Democratic president to be reelected to office since Franklin Delano Roosevelt in 1944. His electoral coattails, however, were not long enough or strong enough to wrest control of Congress from the Republicans.

figure   **9.6**   **Effect of Party Identification on the Vote, 2000**

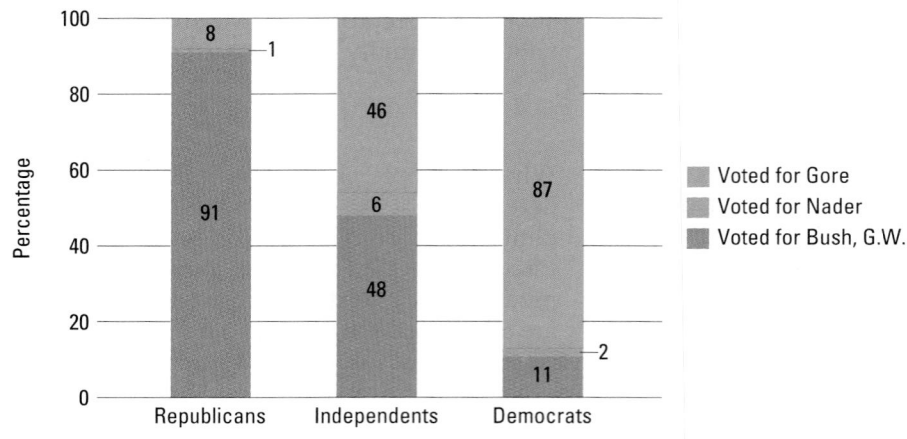

The 2000 election showed that party identification still plays a key role in voting behavior—even with an independent candidate in the contest. The chart shows the results of exit polls of thousands of voters as they left hundreds of polling places across the nation on election day. Voters were asked what party they identified with and how they voted for president. Those who identified with one of the two parties voted strongly for their party's candidate, whereas independent voters divided roughly evenly between Bush and Gore and were three times more likely to vote for Nader than Democratic voters were.

Source: Calculated from data given for 13,279 voters leaving the polls on election day. See Marjorie Connelly, "Who Voted: A Portrait of American Politics, 1976–2000," *New York Times,* 12 November 2000, Sect. 4, p. 4.

Issues and Policies

Candidates exploit issues that they think are important to voters. Challengers usually campaign by pointing out problems—unemployment, inflation, war, civil disorders, corruption—and promising to solve them. Incumbents compile a record in office (for better or worse) and thus try to campaign on their accomplishments. When Clinton campaigned for the presidency in 1992, his theme was on a sign in his campaign headquarters, "It's the economy, stupid." Clinton won by persuading voters that the economy was weak under incumbent President George Bush and by promising economic growth. He won reelection in 1996 by presiding over a strong economy (unemployment and inflation were at record lows and the stock market was at a record high) and over a nation at peace abroad and at home.

Heading into the 2000 campaign, the economy was even stronger and the nation was again peaceful at home and abroad—after a successful air campaign against Serbia that defeated President Milosevic's designs on Kosovo, a province of Yugoslavia. As vice president in the Clinton administration, Al Gore could legitimately share in these impressive accomplishments. According to conventional criteria for determining the outcome of presidential elections, Gore should have won in a walk over any Republican challenger. Scholars who build computer models to predict presidential elections almost unanimously predicted that Gore would succeed Clinton in the presidency.[76] All the factors seemed to be in line—except for those scandals about Clinton's womanizing and the House of Representative's pesky impeachment of the president (see Chapter 12).

As the Republican challenger in the 2000 presidential election, Governor George W. Bush was denied the usual domestic issues (bad economy) or foreign concerns (war in progress or impending) on which challengers attack the party in power. Nevertheless, money poured into his campaign and he promised to restore confidence and integrity in the White

Why Rick, How Nice of You!

During their televised debate in the 2000 New York senatorial campaign, Representative Rick Lazio walked over to hand his opponent, Hillary Rodham Clinton, a paper pledging both candidates to avoid using "soft money" in their campaigns. He asked her to sign it on the spot. Ms. Clinton was touched by his thoughtful gesture but felt that it was too much to accept, especially on television.

House. He figured that he could add enough Clinton-hating Democrats to that base to the win the election.

Understanding the thrust of Bush's campaign, Gore tried to distance himself from the president by naming as his running mate Senator Joe Lieberman—the earliest prominent Democrat to speak out against Clinton's moral shortcomings. That decision helped, but Gore distanced himself further by excluding Clinton from any public appearances in Gore's campaign and failing to link himself with the Clinton's considerable economic success. In the judgment of many analysts, these latter decisions probably hurt.[77]

Candidates' Attributes

Candidates' attributes are especially important to voters who lack good information about a candidate's past performance and policy stands—which means most of us. Without such information, voters search for clues about the candidates to try to predict their behavior in office.[78] Some fall back on their personal beliefs about religion, gender, and race in making political judgments. Such stereotypic thinking accounts for the patterns of opposition and support met by, among others, a Catholic candidate for president (John Kennedy), a woman candidate for vice president (Geraldine Ferraro in 1984), and a black contender for a presidential nomination (Jesse Jackson in 1984 and 1988). In 2000, the Democratic nominee for vice president, Joe Lieberman, became the first Jewish candidate on the presidential ticket of a major political party.

In a close election, such as the 2000 presidential election, almost any measurable factor can be identified as deciding the outcome. An almost indefinable factor, "personality," seemed to work in Bush's favor and arguably produced his victory. In a survey after the election, about 12 percent of the Bush voters said that what they liked most about him was his personality. Only 5 percent of the Gore voters liked that about him the most.[79] Bush just seemed more likable to most voters.

Evaluating the Voting Choice

Choosing among candidates according to their personal attributes might be an understandable approach, but it is not rational voting, according to democratic theory. According to that theory, citizens should vote according to the candidates' past performance and proposed policies. Voters who choose between candidates on the basis of their policies are voting on the issues, which fits the idealized conception of democratic theory. However, issues, candidates' attributes, and party identification all figure in the voting decision.

Unfortunately for democratic theory, most studies of presidential elections show that issues are less important to voters than either party identification or the candidates' attributes. One exception was in 1972, when voters perceived George McGovern as too liberal for their tastes and issue voting exceeded party identification.[80] In 2000, as usual, voting was determined mainly by party identification. However, when voters were asked whether they liked Bush or Gore more for their "stands on issues" than for their personality, leadership, or experience, there was a difference between the candidates. Most Bush voters (57 percent) liked his issue positions, the top five being his pro-life stance on abortion, tax cuts, social security, anti–gun control, and education. More Gore voters cited his attributes (mainly his experience) than his issue positions. Of the 42 percent who liked his stand on issues, the top issues were social security, education, environment, his pro-choice stand on abortion, and health care.[81]

Although party voting has declined somewhat since the 1950s, the relationship between voters' positions on the issues and their party identification is clearer and more consistent today. For example, Democratic Party identifiers are now more likely than Republican identifiers to describe themselves as liberal, and they are more likely than Republican identifiers to favor government spending for social welfare and abortion. The more closely party identification is aligned with ideological orientation, the more sense it makes to vote by party. Over the years, in fact, the alignment of party and ideology has increased in congressional voting such that the fit is almost perfect. Since 1981, the respected Washington weekly, *National Journal*, has analyzed the voting records of members of the House and Senate as predominantly liberal or conservative. Until the 1999 session of Congress, the *National Journal* always rated some Democrats as conservative and some Republicans as liberal. But its analysis of the 1999 votes found every Democratic senator to the left of every Republican, and only two Republicans and two Democrats out of over 400 members of the House who "crossed over" in ideological voting patterns.[82] In the absence of detailed information about candidates' positions on the issues, party labels are a handy indicator of those positions.[83]

Campaign Effects

If party identification is the most important factor in the voting decision and is also resistant to short-term changes, there are definite limits to the capacity of a campaign to influence the outcome of elections.[84] In a close election, however, just changing a few votes means the difference between victory and defeat, so a campaign can be decisive even if it has little overall effect.

The Television Campaign.   Because of the propensity of television news shows to offer only sound bites, candidates cannot rely on television news to get their message out. In 2000, remarks from the two major presidential candidates on network news programs averaged only seven seconds—the shortest since the count began in the 1988 election.[85] In truth, the networks devoted about as much airtime to the presidential campaign as in the past, but they did not give the candidates themselves much time to speak. In the average presidential campaign story, reporters spoke about 74 percent of the time compared with the candidates' 11 percent. No wonder that both candidates went on shows hosted by Oprah Winfrey, Regis Philbin, Jay Leno, and David Letterman—they got the chance to talk to the public! Both Gore and Bush got more airtime to themselves in their sole appearances on Letterman than they did on the network news for that month.[86]

Although candidates seek free coverage on news and entertainment programs, they fight their television campaigns principally through commercial advertisements. Both candidates hired professional consultants to plan their ad campaigns. As the motherlode for political consultants throughout the world (see Politics in a Changing World 9.1), the United States has plenty to supply. Gore followed the approach used in Clinton's successful campaigns, relying on Washington teams of Democratic media consultants who specialize in political advertising. Bush won the nomination using a Texas team of consultants, Maverick Media, but his campaign sought outside help from a Madison Avenue advertising firm, Young & Rubicam, to help with the general election. Together, they were labeled "the Park Avenue Posse."[87]

The important point about television advertising in the 2000 election campaign is how much of it there was. The parties and their candidates raised record amounts of money, which needed to be spent—an estimated $1 billion in television advertising alone.[88] At one time, spending on television advertisements could be justified in cost-benefit terms only for candidates seeking national or major statewide offices. This did not apply in 2000, where candidates were spending money for "whatever office, whatever level of government."[89] The 2000 election also saw more targeting of campaign expenditures in swing states, those where opinion polls showed close contests for winning the state and its electoral votes. Geographically, many swing states were in the Midwest and Pacific Northwest, where Bush and Gore each spent more than $5 million for airtime one month before the election in approximately twenty states.[90] In a radical departure from the past, presidential ads were placed almost exclusively on local stations rather than on the networks. Such precise targeting of political ads, not just on swing states but in specific media markets within those states,

★ politics in a changing world

9.1   The Americanization of Politics

Throughout most chapters in this book, we have discussed the process of globalization for its effects on American politics. Here we discuss the United States' effect on politics and governments in other countries. Foreign scholars have used the term *the Americanization of politics* to describe how politics elsewhere have been influenced by political developments in the United States. Bowler and Farrell note that at one level, "Americanization" simply refers to "the adoption of the latest tools, strategies, and techniques of professionally run campaigns in the United States." But at a deeper level, it represents emulating a "type of democratic politics where parties are weak, candidates are strong, and seemingly every kind of electoral expertise is available for hire on a contract basis." Bowler and Farrell found

political consultants in many countries practicing procedures and techniques in keeping with the "Americanization of politics." In 1998, the authors sent questionnaires to members of the International Association of Political Consultants (IAPC). Thirty-five members (about half of whom were Americans) reported that they had done election campaign work in countries outside Canada and the United States. The graph shows the regions of all countries where they said they worked.

Source: Shaun Bowler and David M. Farrell, "The Internationalization of Campaign Consultancy," in James A. Thurber and Candice J. Nelson (eds.), *Campaign Warriors: Political Consultants in Elections* (Washington, D.C.: Brookings Institution Press, 2000), p. 165.

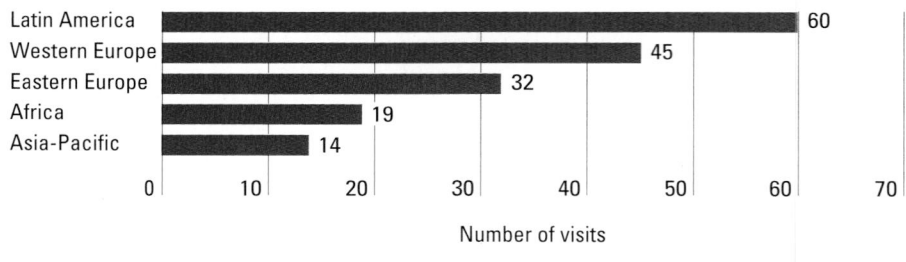

Number of visits

"gets you more bang for the buck," said a television trade spokesman.[91] Apparently, the advertising decisions and heavy spending helped voters make sense of the campaign. When voters were asked whether they "learned enough about the candidates and the issues to make an informed choice" among the candidates, 83 percent said they did—a substantially larger percentage than in the 1988, 1992, and 1996 presidential campaigns.[92]

The Presidential Debates.   In 1960, John F. Kennedy and Richard Nixon held the first televised presidential debate (thought to benefit Kennedy), but debates were not used again until 1976. Since then, candidate debates in some form have been a regular feature of presidential elections. Sitting presidents have been reluctant to debate except on their own terms. Perhaps Vice President Gore should also have been reluctant to debate, but he was eager to take on Governor Bush. The Bush campaign balked, fearing that their less experienced candidate might not hold his own. Bush was virtually forced into the three debates—and they may have been the single most important factor in his election. Before the debates, tracking polls in thirty-one states showed that Gore led in twenty-four of them. After the first debate, Bush led in twenty-eight. After the last one, Gore didn't lead in any.[93] Bush did not win over viewers by demonstrating superior knowledge of the issues; viewers simply found him to be more likable than Gore.

CAMPAIGNS, ELECTIONS, AND PARTIES

Election campaigns today tend to be highly personalized, candidate centered, and conducted outside the control of party organizations. The increased use of electronic media, especially television, has encouraged candidates to personalize their campaign messages; at the same time, the decline of party identification has decreased the power of party-related appeals. Although the party affiliations of the candidates and the party identifications of the voters jointly explain a good deal of electoral behavior, party organizations are not central to elections in America, and this situation has implications for democratic government.

Parties and the Majoritarian Model

According to the majoritarian model of democracy, parties link people with their government by making government responsive to public opinion. Chapter 8 outlined the model of responsible party government in a majoritarian democracy. This model holds that parties should present clear and coherent programs to voters, that voters should choose candidates according to the party programs, that the winning party should carry out its programs once in office, and that voters should hold the governing party responsible at the next election for executing its program. As noted in Chapter 8, the Republican and Democratic parties do follow the model because they formulate different platforms and tend to pursue their announced policies when in office. The weak links in this model of responsible party government are those that connect candidates to voters through campaigns and elections.

You have not read much in this book about the role of the party platform in nominating candidates, in conducting campaigns, or in explaining voters' choices. In nominating presidential candidates, basic party principles (as captured in the party platform) do interact with the presidential primary process, and the candidate who wins enough convention delegates through the primaries will surely be comfortable with any platform that her or his delegates adopt. But House and Senate nominations are rarely fought over the party platform. And usually, thoughts about party platforms are virtually absent from campaigning and from voters' minds when they cast their ballots.

Parties and the Pluralist Model

The way parties in the United States operate is more in keeping with the pluralist model of democracy than the majoritarian model. Our parties are not the basic mechanism through which citizens control their government; instead, they function as two giant interest groups. The parties' interests lie in electing and reelecting their candidates, in enjoying the benefits of public office. Except in extreme cases, the parties care little about the positions or ideologies favored by their candidates for Congress or state offices. One exception that proves the rule is the Republican Party's rejection of David E. Duke, the former Ku Klux Klan leader who in 1990 emerged as the party's nominee for senator in Louisiana. In a highly unusual move, national party leaders disowned Duke, and he lost the election. Otherwise, the parties are grateful for victories by almost any candidate running under their banner. In turn, individual candidates operate as entrepreneurs, running their own campaigns as they like, without party interference.

Some scholars believe that stronger parties would strengthen democratic government, even if they could not meet all the requirements of the responsible party model. Our parties already perform valuable functions in structuring the vote along partisan lines and in proposing alternative government policies, but stronger parties might also be able to play a more important role in coordinating government policies after elections. At present, the decentralized nature of the nominating process and of campaigning for office offers many opportunities for organized groups outside the parties to identify and back candidates who favor their interests. Although this is in keeping with pluralist theory, it is certain to frustrate majority interests on occasion.

SUMMARY

Campaigning has evolved from a party-centered to a candidate-centered process. The successful candidate for public office usually must campaign first to win the party nomination, then to win the general election. A major factor in the decentralization of American parties is their reliance on primary elections to nominate candidates. Democratic and Republican nominations for president are no longer actually decided in the parties' national conventions but are determined in advance through the complex process of selecting delegates pledged to particular candidates. Although candidates cannot win the nomination unless they have broad support within the party, the winners can legitimately say that they captured the nomination through their own efforts and that they owe little to the party organization.

The need to win a majority of votes in the electoral college structures presidential elections. Although a candidate can win a majority of the popular vote but lose in the electoral college, that had not happened in more than one hundred years until 2000. In fact, the electoral college usually magnifies the victory margin of the winning candidate. Since World War II, Republicans have usually won the presidency, whereas Democrats have usually controlled Congress; such divided government has interfered with party control of government.

In the general election, candidates usually retain the same staff that helped them win the nomination. The dynamics of campaign financing force candidates to rely mainly on their own resources or—in the case of presidential elections—on public funds. Party organizations now often contribute money to congressional candidates, but the candidates must still raise most of the money themselves. Money is essential in running a modern campaign for major office—for conducting polls and advertising the candidate's name, qualifications, and issue positions through the media. Candidates seek free news coverage whenever possible, but most must rely on paid advertising to get their message across. Ironically, voters also get most of their campaign information from advertisements. The trend in recent years has been toward negative advertising, which seems to work, although it contributes to voters' distaste for politics.

Voting choice can be analyzed in terms of party identification, candidates' attributes, and policy positions. Party identification is still the most important long-term factor in shaping the voting decision, but few candidates rely on it in their campaigns. Most candidates today run personalized campaigns that stress their attributes and policies.

The way that nominations, campaigns, and elections are conducted in America is out of keeping with the ideals of responsible party government that fit the majoritarian model of democracy. In particular, campaigns and elections do not function to link parties strongly to voters, as the model posits. American parties are better suited to the pluralist model of democracy, which sees them as major interest groups competing with lesser groups to further their own interests. At least political parties aspire to the noble goal of representing the needs and wants of most people. As we see in the next chapter, interest groups do not even pretend as much.

★ Selected Readings

Corrado, Anthony, Thomas E. Mann, Daniel R. Ortiz, Trevor Potter, and Frank J. Sorauf (eds.), *Campaign Finance Reform: A Sourcebook.* Washington, D.C.: The Brookings Institution, 1997. A rich collection of laws, court decisions, regulatory rulings, and analyses concerning this outwardly simple but very complex problem.

Faucheux, Ron. *The Road to Victory 2000: The Complete Guide to Winning Political Campaigns—Local, State and Federal,* 2nd ed. Dubuque, Iowa: Kendall/Hunt, 1998. The subtitle describes the book, which reprints important articles published in *Campaigns & Elections,* a magazine for political consultants.

Herrnson, Paul S. *Congressional Elections: Campaigning at Home and in Washington,* 3rd ed. Washington, D.C.: Congressional Quarterly Press, 2000. An up-to-date study of winning the nomination, preparing the general election campaign, and carrying it out.

Hrebenar, Ronald J., Matthew J. Burbank, and Robert C. Benedict. *Political Parties, Interest Groups, and Political Campaigns.* Boulder, Colo.: Westview Press, 1999. Discusses the links between interest groups and political parties and how they blend their mutual interests in backing common candidates.

Issacharpff, Samuel, Pamela S. Karlan, and Richard H. Pildes. *The Law of Democracy: Legal Structures of the Political Process.* Westbury, N.Y.: The Foundation Press, 1998. The authors are lawyers, but don't let that keep you from consulting this rich source on voting rights laws, regulation of political parties, voting systems, and money and politics. The book contains material by political scientists too.

Longley, Lawrence D., and Neal R. Pierce. *The Electoral College Primer 2000.* New Haven: Yale University Press, 1999. Written by critics of the electoral college, the book eerily speculates about a constitutional crisis in the 2000 election.

Mayer, William G., ed. *In Pursuit of the White House 2000: How We Choose Our Presidential Nominees.* Chatham, N.J.: Chatham House, 2000. A valuable set of studies, with plenty of data, on the nomination process, including the problems facing third-party candidates.

Menefee-Libey, David. *The Triumph of Campaign-Centered Politics*. New York: Chatham House, 2000. Emphasizes the consequences for campaigning of the decline of party identification within the electorate while also discussing an enlarged role for national parties in candidates' campaigns.

Thurber, James A., Candice J. Nelson, and David A. Dulio (eds.). *Crowded Airwaves: Campaign Advertising in Elections*. Washington, D.C.: Brookings Institution Press, 2000. A wide-ranging collection of studies by top scholars on negative advertising, the effects of advertising on voters' knowledge, and electoral behavior.

Internet Exercises

1. *Campaign 2000 on the Airwaves*

The Campaign Media Analysis Group (CMAG) is a private company that, through advanced satellite technology, monitors and collects all televised political and issue advertisements run in the nation's top seventy-five media markets. While most of the features on CMAG's Web site, <**www.politicsontv.com/**>, are available by subscription only, the group does publish a newsletter, "The CMAG Eye," that anyone can access on-line.

● Go to the CMAG site and follow the link to past editions of the newsletter. Click on the November/December 2000 edition, which provides summary discussion of the 2000 presidential and congressional elections. Skim over the contents of the newsletter, which also includes some entertaining examples of political advertisements run on behalf of presidential contenders George W. Bush, Al Gore, and Ralph Nader.

● How does the discussion in this newsletter illustrate the important role that television advertising played in campaigns for political offices in 2000? Be sure to cite a couple of specific examples in your answer.

2. *National Interest in Presidential and Congressional Elections*

The Federal Election Commission (FEC) is an independent regulatory agency created by Congress in 1975 to administer and enforce the Federal Election Campaign Act. The FEC gathers and makes available on its Web site a number of statistical databases on campaign spending, voter turnout, and election results. The site is located at <**www.fec.gov/**>.

● At the FEC's Elections and Voting page, you will find a variety of links to statistics about voter registration and turnout. Locate the link to data on voter turnout in presidential and congressional elections over the period from 1960 to 1996.

● What pattern do you notice in these data? What do you think explains the pattern?

chapter 10

Interest Groups

THE WORLD TRADE ORGANIZATION MEETING IN SEATTLE

THE WORLD TRADE ORGANIZATION MEETING IN SEATTLE may have seemed like an unlikely target for a riot. Prior to the December 1999 protests, relatively few Americans knew anything about the otherwise obscure organization headquartered in Geneva, Switzerland. The World Trade Organization (WTO) is composed of 135 member countries and is a forum for developing rules governing trade among nations. It takes on issues that involve a number of countries and thus it deals with complex problems that require an unusual level of cooperation. For example, one of the most troublesome issues facing world trade negotiators is agriculture. The United States wants countries of the European Union to reduce the subsidies that governments give to farmers. Since those subsidies give a price advantage to European farmers, they don't have to charge as much for their products. In turn, the European Union countries are apprehensive about bioengineered food products that come from the United States. They've pressed the WTO to write rules requiring the labeling of food products that contain any bioengineered element.

Most of the time the WTO works out of the limelight trying to negotiate modest agreements on narrow issues. Periodically, it holds a large-scale conference where all the member states can try to formulate rules that apply broadly to the world trading system. In simple terms, the WTO attempts to promote commerce between countries by reducing barriers to trade. Countries establish tariffs and other barriers to keep foreign companies from competing with domestic producers. They rationalize that the trade barriers they establish are an appropriate response to some unfair advantage possessed by foreign competitors. WTO supporters believe that free trade is preferable to a world mired in trade barriers because a free trading system promotes efficiency—those who can manufacture the best product at the lowest price will thrive and consumers will get the best prices in the marketplace.

Those who will be hurt by increased foreign competition are the most ardent foes of trade agreements. As the WTO summit in Seattle approached, American labor unions announced plans for large demonstrations in Seattle to protest poor working conditions and low wages in other countries. Even though President Clinton was a champion of free trade, labor had some leverage with his administration because of its steadfast support for the Democratic party. Although labor provided the greatest number of protestors in Seattle, other interest groups drowned out their voices. A colorful assortment of groups advocating a wide variety of causes, some of

Seattle Battle

Most Americans were baffled by the outburst of violence by anarchists raging at the World Trade Organization's meeting in Seattle. An area downtown was littered with broken glass and covered with graffiti and over six hundred protestors were arrested. These violent protests attracted a great deal of attention and relatively little notice was paid to more peaceful demonstrations by other groups.

which were only tangentially related to international trade, showed up in Seattle. Environmentalists were a strong presence; they wanted the United States to pressure other countries to protect animals and wilderness from economic expansion. The Milarepa Fund came to support a free Tibet. Médecins sans Frontières was there to lobby for cheaper AIDS drugs for those in developing countries.

The vast majority of the 40,000 protestors were there to protest peacefully. However, a contingent of anarchists—people who don't believe in government because it infringes on their freedom—surprised the Seattle city government with a violent and confrontational attempt to undermine the WTO. They smashed windows of downtown stores, trashing a Niketown and Starbucks, among others. A small but determined band of protestors fought with police, and the shocking and wild confrontation, more characteristic of the angry 1960s than the affluent 1990s, grabbed the nation's attention.

The WTO meeting in Seattle failed miserably and no new trade agreement was reached. It did not fail because of the protests; they were symptomatic of the problems facing the trade negotiators. Those pushing what would aid the majority—more foreign trade and more efficient economies— were decisively beaten by the forces of pluralism. Whether it be labor unions in the United States, farmers in France, software interests in India and Brazil, steel manufacturers in Japan, and environmentalists around the world, lots of interest groups don't want trade liberalization. Cumulatively, their opposition sunk a broad WTO agreement in Seattle.

Beyond the obvious self-interest of many economic sectors, opposition to further large-scale trade agreements comes from a fear of encroaching globalism. As international bodies like the WTO become more important and as each country becomes more interdependent with others around the world, there is a sense on the part of each nation that it is losing control of its own destiny.

World trade is an issue that combines traditional pluralist politics within countries with pluralism on a worldwide scale. In this chapter, we look at the central dynamic of pluralist democracy: the interaction of interest groups and government. In analyzing the process by which interest groups and lobbyists come to speak on behalf of different groups, we focus on several questions. How do interest groups form? Who do they represent? What tactics do they use to convince policymakers that their views are best for the nation? Is the interest group system biased in favor of certain types of people? If so, what are the consequences?

INTEREST GROUPS AND THE AMERICAN POLITICAL TRADITION

interest group
An organized group of individuals that seeks to influence public policy. Also called a *lobby*.

lobby
See *interest group*.

lobbyist
A representative of an interest group.

> **Can You Explain Why...**
> the government doesn't restrict interest groups lobbying for their own selfish needs?

An **interest group** is an organized body of individuals who share some political goals and try to influence public policy decisions. Among the most prominent interest groups in the United States are the AFL-CIO (representing labor union members), the American Farm Bureau Federation (representing farmers), the Business Roundtable (representing big business), and Common Cause (representing citizens concerned with reforming government). Interest groups are also called **lobbies,** and their representatives are referred to as **lobbyists.**

Interest Groups: Good or Evil?

A recurring debate in American politics concerns the role of interest groups in a democratic society. Are interest groups a threat to the well-being of the political system, or do they contribute to its proper functioning? A favorable early evaluation of interest groups can be found in the writings of Alexis de Tocqueville, a French visitor to the United States in the early nineteenth century. During his travels, Tocqueville marveled at the array of organizations he found, and he later wrote that "Americans of all ages, all conditions, and all dispositions, constantly form associations."[1] Tocqueville was suggesting that the ease with which we form organizations reflects a strong democratic culture.

Yet other early observers were concerned about the consequences of interest group politics. Writing in the *Federalist* papers, James Madison warned of the dangers of "factions," the major divisions in American society. In *Federalist* No. 10, written in 1787, Madison said it was inevitable that substantial differences would develop between factions. It was only natural for farmers to oppose merchants, tenants to oppose landlords, and so on. Madison further reasoned that each faction would do what it could to prevail over other factions, that each basic interest in society would try to persuade the government to adopt policies that favored it at the expense of others. He noted that the fundamental causes of faction were "sown in the nature of man."[2]

But Madison argued against trying to suppress factions. He concluded that factions can be eliminated only by removing our freedoms because "Liberty is to faction what air is to fire."[3] Instead, Madison suggested that relief from the self-interested advocacy of factions should come only through controlling the effects of that advocacy. The relief would be provided by a democratic republic in which government would mediate between opposing factions. The size and diversity of the nation as well as the structure of government would ensure that even a majority faction could never come to suppress the rights of others.[4]

How we judge interest groups—as "good" or "evil"—may depend on how strongly we are committed to freedom or equality (see Chapter 1). People dislike interest groups in general because they do not offer equal representation to all—some sectors of society are better represented than others. A survey of the American public showed that almost two-thirds of those polled regarded lobbying as a threat to American democracy.[5] Yet, as we'll demonstrate later, in recent years interest groups have enjoyed unparalleled growth; many new groups have formed, and old ones have expanded. Apparently we distrust interest groups as a whole, but we like those that represent our views. Stated more bluntly, we hate lobbies—except those that speak on our behalf.

The Roles of Interest Groups

The "evil" side of interest group politics is all too apparent. Each group pushes its own selfish interests, which, despite the group's claims to the contrary, are not always in the best interest of other Americans. The "good" side of interest group advocacy may not be so clear. How do the actions of interest groups benefit our political system?[6]

Representation. Interest groups represent people before their government. Just as a member of Congress represents a particular constituency, so does a lobbyist. A lobbyist for the National Association of Broadcasters, for example, speaks for the interests of radio and television broadcasters when Congress or a government agency is considering a relevant policy decision.

Whatever the political interest—the cement industry, social security, endangered species—it helps to have an active lobby operating in

figure

10.1   Group Stimulation

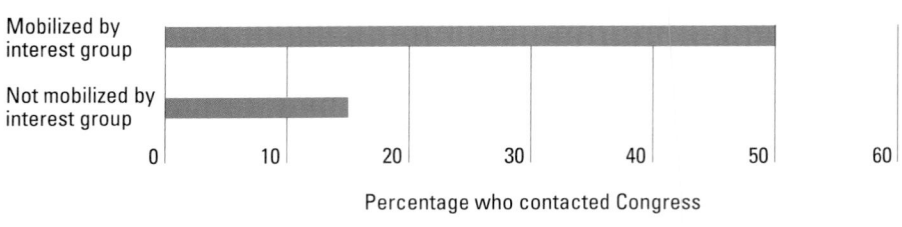

Percentage who contacted Congress

When President Clinton introduced a far-reaching health-care bill early in his administration, it set off a titanic struggle among interest groups. Groups wrote and phoned members asking them to write their legislators in Washington. A poll asked people if they had been contacted by a group and also if they had "called, or sent or faxed a letter" to their representative or senator. Those who had been contacted by a lobby were much more likely to have communicated with a member of Congress. (The figures are only for respondents in states where an interest group was running a letter-writing campaign.)

Source: Kenneth M. Goldstein, *Interest Groups, Lobbying, and Participation in America* (New York: Cambridge University Press, 1999), pp. 111 and 133.

In CROSSTABS, the variables "AFL-CIO" and "Christian Coalition" are ratings of all members of Congress by these two interest groups. How does Congress score on their scales?

agenda building
The process by which new issues are brought into the political limelight.

Washington. Members of Congress represent a multitude of interests, some of them conflicting, from their own districts and states. Government administrators, too, are pulled in different directions and have their own policy preferences. Interest groups articulate their members' concerns, presenting them directly and forcefully in the political process.

Participation.   Interest groups are also vehicles for political participation. They provide a means by which like-minded citizens can pool their resources and channel their energies into collective political action. People band together because they know it is much easier to get government to listen to a group than to an individual. One farmer fighting against a new pesticide proposal in Congress probably will not get very far, but thousands of farmers united in an organization stand a much better chance of getting policymakers to consider their needs. Interest groups not only facilitate participation, they stimulate it as well. By asking people to write their member of Congress or take other action, lobbies get people more involved in the political process than they otherwise would be (see Figure 10.1).

Education.   As part of their efforts to lobby government and to increase their membership, interest groups help educate their members, the public at large, and government officials. High-tech companies were slow to set up lobbying offices in Washington and to develop a mind-set within the corporate structure that communicating with people in government was part of their job. As more and more issues affecting the industry received attention from government, high-tech executives began to realize that policymakers didn't have a sufficient understanding of the rapidly changing industry. Leading computer companies like Microsoft, Cisco Systems, and Sun Microsystems have become more aggressive in seeking opportunities to discuss the industry with government officials.[7] To gain the attention of the policymakers they are trying to educate, interest groups need to provide them with information that is not easily obtained from other sources.[8]

Agenda Building.   In a related role, interest groups bring new issues into the political limelight through a process called **agenda building.** American society has many problem areas, but public officials are not addressing all of them. Through their advocacy, interest groups make the government aware of problems and then try to see to it that something is done to solve

figure

10.2   Labor Pains

As the economy has shifted from manufacturing to service industries, union membership has withered. The most heavily organized sector of the economy today is in fact the government itself, as teachers, postal workers, firefighters, and police have increasingly joined unions. But despite labor's decline, the AFL-CIO has remained an important player on the national scene, pushing for expanded family and medical leave, better wages for workers, and more flexible hours for working mothers.

Source: AFL-CIO Web site <www.aflcio.org>.

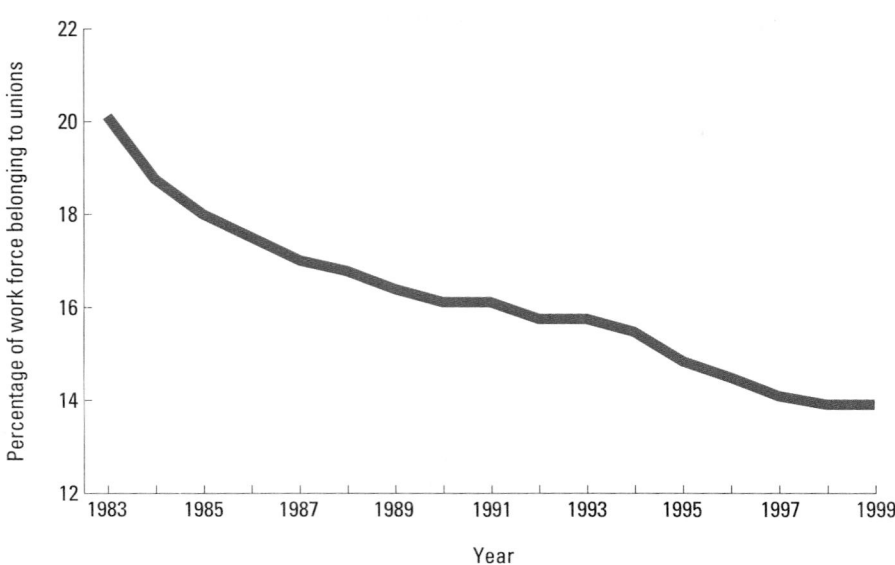

them. Labor unions, for example, have historically played a critical role in gaining attention for problems that were being systematically ignored. As Figure 10.2 shows, union membership has declined significantly over the years. Nevertheless, organized labor continues to have an impact on U.S. politics, a testament to its agenda-building power on issues like the living wage, a minimum wage that reflects the actual cost of living.[9]

program monitoring
Keeping track of government programs, usually by interest groups.

The Rise and Decline of Organized Labor

Program Monitoring.   Finally, interest groups engage in **program monitoring.** Lobbies follow government programs that are important to their constituents, keeping abreast of developments in Washington and in the communities where the policies are implemented. When a program is not operating as it should, concerned interest groups push administrators to change them in ways that promote the group's goals. They draw attention to agency officials' transgressions and even file suit to stop actions they consider unlawful. In 1999 housing and homeless advocacy groups complained to the Department of Housing and Urban Development (HUD) in Washington that New York City Mayor Rudolf Giuliani had held up HUD funds for the homeless because some of the service providers had criticized him. In response to the complaint, HUD took the money away from the New York City government and said that it would allocate the grants directly to organizations working with the homeless there.

Interest groups do, then, play some positive roles in their pursuit of self-interest. But we should not assume that the positive side of interest groups neatly balances the negative. Questions remain about the overall influence of interest groups on public policy making. Most important, are the effects of interest group advocacy being controlled, as Madison believed they should be?

HOW INTEREST GROUPS FORM

Do some people form interest groups more easily than others? Are some factions represented while others are not? Pluralists assume that when a political issue arises, interest groups with relevant policy concerns begin to lobby. Policy conflicts are ultimately resolved through bargaining and negotiation between the involved organizations and the government. Unlike Madison, who dwelled on the potential for harm by factions, pluralists believe interest groups are a good thing, that they further democracy by broadening representation within the system.

An important part of pluralism is the belief that new interest groups form as a matter of course when the need arises. David Truman outlines this idea in his classic work *The Governmental Process*.[10] He says that when individuals are threatened by change, they band together in an interest group. For example, if government threatens to regulate a particular industry, the firms that compose that industry will start a trade association to protect their financial well-being. Truman sees a direct cause-and-effect relationship in all of this: existing groups stand in equilibrium until some type of disturbance (such as falling wages or declining farm prices) forces new groups to form.

Truman's thinking on the way interest groups form is like the "invisible hand" notion of laissez-faire economics: self-correcting market forces will remedy imbalances in the marketplace. But in politics, no invisible hand, no force, automatically causes interest groups to develop. Truman's disturbance theory paints an idealized portrait of interest group politics in America. In real life, people do not automatically organize when they are adversely affected by some disturbance. A good example of "nonorganization" can be found in Herbert Gans's book *The Urban Villagers*.[11] Gans, a sociologist, moved into the West End, a low-income neighborhood in Boston, during the late 1950s. The neighborhood had been targeted for urban redevelopment; the city was planning to replace old buildings with modern ones. This meant that the people living there—primarily poor Italian Americans who very much liked their neighborhood—would have to move.

Being evicted is a highly traumatic experience, so the situation in the West End certainly qualified as a bona fide disturbance according to Truman's scheme of interest group formation. Yet the people of the West End barely put up a fight to save their neighborhood. They started an organization, but it attracted little support. Residents remained unorganized; soon they were moved, and buildings were demolished.

Disturbance theory clearly fails to explain what happened (or didn't happen) in Boston's West End. An adverse condition or change does not automatically mean that an interest group will form. What, then, is the missing ingredient? Political scientist Robert Salisbury says that the quality of interest group leadership may be the crucial factor.[12]

Interest Group Entrepreneurs

Salisbury likens the role of an interest group leader to that of an entrepreneur in the business world. An entrepreneur is someone who starts new enterprises, usually at considerable personal financial risk. Salisbury says that an **interest group entrepreneur,** or organizer, succeeds or fails for many of the same reasons a business entrepreneur succeeds or fails. The

interest group entrepreneur
An interest group organizer or leader.

★

There Goes the Neighborhood

When the city of Boston targeted its West End for urban renewal, residents did not organize to fight the decision. Wrecking balls soon demolished the neighborhood, clearing the way for various redevelopment projects, including high-rise housing.

interest group entrepreneur must have something attractive to "market" in order to convince people to join.[13] Potential members must be persuaded that the benefits of joining outweigh the costs. Someone starting a new union, for example, must convince workers that the union can win them wages high enough to more than offset membership dues. The organizer of an ideological group must convince potential members that the group can effectively lobby the government to achieve their particular goals.

The development of the United Farm Workers Union shows the importance of leadership in the formation of an interest group. The union is made up of men and women who pick crops in California and other parts of the country. The work is backbreaking, performed in the hot growing season. The pickers are predominantly poor, uneducated Mexican Americans.

Their chronically low wages and deplorable living conditions made the farm workers prime candidates for organization into a labor union. And throughout the twentieth century, various unions tried to organize the pickers. Yet, for many reasons, including distrust of union organizers, intimidation by employers, and lack of money to pay union dues, all failed. Then, in 1962, the late Cesar Chavez, a poor Mexican American, began to crisscross the central valley of California, talking to workers and planting the idea of a union. Chavez had been a farm worker himself (he first worked as a picker at the age of ten), and he was well aware of the difficulties that lay ahead for his newly organized union.

After a strike against grape growers failed in 1965, Chavez changed his tactic of trying to build a stronger union merely by recruiting a larger membership. Copying the civil rights movement, Chavez and his followers marched 250 miles to the state capitol in Sacramento to demand help from the governor. The march and other nonviolent tactics began to draw sympathy from people who had no direct involvement in farming. Seeing the movement as a way to help poor members of the church, the Catholic clergy was a major source of support. This support, in turn, gave the charismatic Chavez greater credibility, and his followers cast him in the role of

figure

10.3   Social Class and Interest Group Membership

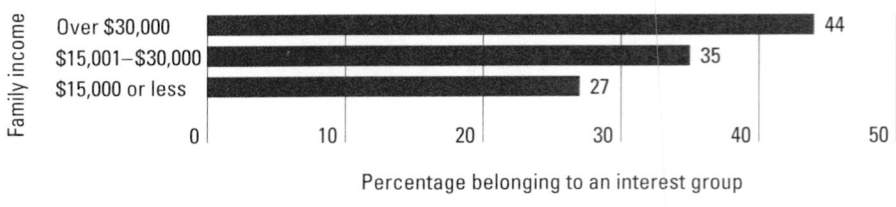

Membership in interest groups is clearly linked to social class. The higher their total family income, the more likely it is that individuals will belong to at least one political interest group. The data here come from a survey of citizens in five American cities (Birmingham, Alabama; Dayton, Ohio; Portland, Oregon; St. Paul, Minnesota; and San Antonio, Texas).

Source: Based on Jeffrey M. Berry, Kent E. Portney, and Ken Thomson, *The Rebirth of Urban Democracy* (Washington, D.C.: Brookings Institution, 1993). Used with permission.

spiritual as well as political leader. At one point, he fasted for twenty-five days to show his commitment to nonviolence. Democratic senator Robert Kennedy of New York, one of the most popular politicians of the day, joined Chavez when he broke his fast at a mass conducted on the back of a flatbed truck in Delano, California.[14]

Chavez subsequently called for a boycott, and a small but significant number of Americans stopped buying grapes. The growers, who had bitterly fought the union, were finally hurt economically. Under this and other economic pressures, they eventually agreed to recognize and bargain with the United Farm Workers. The union then helped its members with the wage and benefit agreements it was able to negotiate.

Who Is Being Organized?

Cesar Chavez is a good example of the importance of leadership in the formation of a new interest group. Despite many years of adverse conditions, efforts to organize the farm workers had failed. The dynamic leadership of Cesar Chavez is what seems to have made the difference.

But another important element is at work in the formation of interest groups. The residents of Boston's West End and the farm workers in California were poor, uneducated or undereducated, and politically inexperienced—factors that made it extremely difficult to organize them into interest groups. If they had been well-to-do, educated, and politically experienced, they probably would have banded together immediately. People who have money, are educated, and know how the system operates are more confident that their actions can make a difference.[15] Together, these attributes give people more incentive to devote their time and ample resources to organizing and supporting interest groups (see Figure 10.3).

Every existing interest group has its own history, but the three variables just discussed can help explain why groups may or may not become fully organized. First, an adverse change or disturbance can contribute to people's awareness that they need political representation. However, this alone does not ensure that an organization will form, and organizations have formed in the absence of a disturbance. Second, the quality of leadership is critical in the organization of interest groups. Some interest group entrepreneurs are more skilled than others at convincing people to join their organizations. Finally, the higher the socioeconomic level of potential members, the more likely they are to know the value of interest groups and to participate in politics by joining them.

Because wealthy and better-educated Americans are more likely to form and join lobbies, they seem to have an important advantage in the political process. Nevertheless, as the United Farm Workers' case shows, poor and uneducated people are also capable of forming interest groups. The question that remains, then, is not *whether* various opposing interests are represented but *how well* they are represented. Or, in terms of Madison's premise in *Federalist* No. 10, are the effects of faction—in this case, the advantages of the wealthy and well educated—being controlled? Before we can answer this question about how interest groups affect the level of political equality in our society, we need to turn our attention to the resources available to interest groups.

INTEREST GROUP RESOURCES

The strengths, capabilities, and influence of an interest group depend in large part on its resources. A group's most significant resources are its members, lobbyists, and money, including funds that can be contributed to political candidates. The sheer quantity of a group's resources is important, and so is the wisdom with which its resources are used.

Members

One of the most valuable resources an interest group can have is a large, politically active membership. If a lobbyist is trying to convince a legislator to support a particular bill, having a large group of members who live in the legislator's home district or state is tremendously helpful. A legislator who has not already taken a firm position on a bill might be swayed by the knowledge that voters back home are kept informed by interest groups of his or her votes on key issues.

Members give an organization not only the political muscle to influence policy but also financial resources. The more money an organization can collect through dues and contributions, the more people it can hire to lobby government officials and to monitor the policymaking process. The American Medical Association has considerable resources because its members—physicians—have high incomes and can pay expensive dues. The organization's wealth helped to make it a major player when President Clinton put comprehensive health-care reform at the top of his agenda.

Greater resources also allow an organization to communicate with its members more and to inform them better. And funding helps a group maintain its membership and attract new members.

Maintaining Membership. To keep the members it already has, an organization must persuade them that it is doing a good job in its advocacy. Most lobbies use a newsletter to keep members apprised of developments in government that relate to issues of concern to them. However, newsletters are more than a means of communicating news to members. Interest groups use them as a public relations tool to try to keep members believing that their lobby is playing a critical role in protecting their interests. Thus, the role the organization is playing in trying to influence government always receives prominent coverage in its newsletters.

Politically Armed

The National Rifle Association is the largest and most influential lobby working to protect the rights of gun owners. The organization's greatest resource is not its wealth or membership size (both quite large), but the fervent attitudes of its members. Some members are shown here at the NRA's annual convention. NRA supporters have such intense views about guns that even though polls show them to be in the minority, Congress pays close attention to the organization's preferences and rarely enacts gun control legislation.

Business, professional, and labor associations generally have an easier time holding on to members than do citizen groups, whose basis of organization is a concern for issues not directly related to their members' jobs. In many companies, corporate membership in a trade group constitutes only a minor business expense. Big individual corporations have no memberships as such, but they often open their own lobbying offices in Washington. They have the advantage of being able to use institutional financial resources to support their lobbying; they do not have to rely on voluntary contributions. Labor unions are helped in states that require workers to affiliate with the union that is the bargaining agent with their employer. In contrast, citizen groups base their appeal on members' ideological sentiments. These groups face a difficult challenge: issues can blow hot and cold, and a particularly hot issue one year may not hold the same interest to citizens the next.

Attracting New Members. All membership groups are constantly looking for new adherents to expand their resources and clout. Groups that rely on ideological appeals have a special problem because the competition in most policy areas is intense. People concerned about the environment, for example, can join a seemingly infinite number of local, state, and national groups.[16] The National Wildlife Federation, Environmental Action, the Environmental Defense Fund, the Natural Resources Defense Council, Friends of the Earth, the Wilderness Society, and the Sierra Club are just some of the national organizations that lobby on environmental issues. Groups try to distinguish themselves from competitors by concentrating on a few key issues and developing a reputation as the most involved and knowledgeable about them.[17] The Sierra Club, one of the oldest environmental groups, has long had a focus on protecting national parks. The names of newer groups, such as Clean Water Action and the National Toxics Campaign, reveal their substantive focus (and marketing strategy). Still, organizations in a crowded policy area must go beyond such differentiation and aggressively market themselves to potential contributors. Indeed, these groups are like businesses—their "profits" (their members and income) depend on their management's wisdom in allocating resources and in choosing which issues to work on.[18]

One common method of attracting new members is *direct mail*—letters sent to a selected audience to promote the organization and appeal for contributions. The key to direct mail is a carefully targeted audience. An organization can purchase a list of people who are likely to be sympathetic to its cause, or it can trade lists with a similar organization. A group trying to fight abortion, for instance, might use the subscription list from the conservative magazine *National Review*, whereas a pro-choice lobby might use that of the more liberal *New Republic*. The main drawbacks to direct mail are its expense and low rate of return. A response rate of 2 percent of those newly solicited is considered good. Groups usually lose money when prospecting for members from a mailing list they have rented from a direct mail broker, but they hope to recoup the money as the new members contribute again and again over time. Still, they have no assurance of this (see Politics in a Changing America 10.1). To maximize the chances of a good return, care and thought are given to the design and content of letters. Letters often try to play on the reader's emotions, to create the feeling that the reader should be personally involved in the struggle.[19]

Can You Explain Why... people don't join interest groups that advocate policies those same people strongly support?

free-rider problem
The situation in which people benefit from the activities of an organization (such as an interest group) but do not contribute to those activities.

The Free-Rider Problem. The need for aggressive marketing by interest groups suggests that getting people who sympathize with a group's goals actually to join and support it with their contributions is difficult. Economists call this difficulty the **free-rider problem,** but we might call it, more colloquially, the "let-George-do-it problem."[20] Funding for public television stations illustrates the dilemma. Almost all agree that public television, which survives in large part through viewers' contributions, is of great value. But only a fraction of those who watch public television contribute on a regular basis. Why? Because people can watch the programs whether they contribute or not. The free rider has the same access to public television as the contributor.

The same problem crops up for interest groups. When a lobbying group wins benefits, those benefits are not restricted to the members of the organization. For instance, if the Financial Services Forum convinces Congress to enact a policy benefiting the industry, all businesses in the financial services industry will benefit, not just those who actually pay the membership dues of the lobbying group. Thus, some executives may feel that their corporation doesn't need to spend the money to join this Financial Services Forum, even though they might benefit from the group's efforts; they prefer instead to let others shoulder the financial burden.

The free-rider problem increases the difficulty of attracting paying members, but it certainly does not make the task impossible. Many people realize that if everyone decides to let George do it, the job simply will not get done. Millions of Americans contribute to interest groups because they are concerned about an issue or feel a responsibility to help organizations that work on their behalf. Also, many organizations offer membership benefits that have nothing to do with politics or lobbying. Business **trade associations,** for example, are a source of information about industry trends and effective management practices; they organize conventions at

trade association
An organization that represents firms within a particular industry.

10.1   The Surprising Decline of the Christian Right

Fundamentalist Christians believe that modern society has turned away from basic moral principles, leading to serious social problems. In their eyes, liberal and moderate politicians have mistakenly tried to solve these problems with expensive, wasteful, and counterproductive social programs. Christian fundamentalists feel that what is needed instead is a return to strong family values.

Several citizen groups mobilized fundamentalist Christians into what appeared to be a powerful political movement. Advocacy organizations like the Christian Coalition, Focus on the Family, the Eagle Forum, and the Family Research Council work in Washington and at the grassroots to push for restrictions on abortion, prayer in school, and government financial support for religious schools.

These groups have generated considerable controversy because they claim to offer a Christian, moral point of view in the policy-making process. They have not hesitated to denounce politicians who disagree with them. Interest groups do this all the time, but these organizations imply that their point of view is closer to God's wishes and, thus, opponents are working against biblical precepts. While they may agree that the moral order of the country is in decline, some liberals regard the Christian groups as a dangerous threat to the nation's tradition of separation of church and state.

Many observers believed that Christian conservatives were on their way to becoming a dominant force in American politics. In the early 1990s the Christian Coalition, which is closely allied with the Republican party and is backed by the television evangelist Reverend Pat Robertson, emerged as the leading Christian lobby in Washington. Ralph Reed, the organization's youthful and telegenic lobbyist until he resigned in 1997, had considerable access to the Republican leadership in Congress.

Yet the Christian Coalition and other Christian conservative groups have been surprisingly unsuccessful in Washington. A recent study examined interest group participation in all domestic social and domestic economic issues that came before a single session of Congress. When citizen groups of the left are compared with citizen groups of the right, the results are striking. Liberal citizen

which members can learn, socialize, and occasionally find new customers or suppliers. An individual firm in the electronics industry may not care that much about the lobbying done by the Electronics Industries Association, but it may have a vital interest in the information about marketing and manufacturing that the organization provides. Successful interest groups are adept at supplying the right mix of benefits to their target constituency.[21]

Lobbyists

Part of the money raised by interest groups is used to pay lobbyists, who represent the organizations before the government. Lobbyists make sure that people in government know what their members want and that their organizations know what the government is doing. For example, when an administrative agency issues new regulations, lobbyists are right there to interpret the content and implications of the regulations for rank-and-file

groups were active on 65.9 percent of all issues, while conservative citizen groups participated on just 4.5 percent. For all the vaunted prowess of the Christian right groups, they appear to be largely on the sidelines when it comes to congressional policymaking.

In the past few years, the Christian Coalition has run into considerable trouble. When Reed left, he was replaced by former Reagan administration Secretary of the Interior Donald Hodel and former congressman Randy Tate. They tried to reorient the organization but failed and left the group. Contributions to the Christian Coalition have dropped significantly and it is $2 million in debt. The *New York Times* described the group as experiencing "financial and leadership turmoil."

Why have Christian lobbies fared so poorly? They are not false prophets—there are millions of Americans who share the political views espoused by these groups. Rather, the problem is that the Christian right groups are built almost entirely on direct mail. Mass mailings are sent to hundreds of thousands at a time, an extremely expensive way of raising money. The people who back the Christian

right lobbies tend to be middle-class individuals with modest incomes. Their donations are small and when those contributions fall below expectations, the very life of the organizations are threatened. This is what happened to the Moral Majority, which was the leading Christian group in the 1980s. Despite its notoriety, the group went bankrupt and closed its door after just a decade in operation.

The reason why the Christian groups don't lobby very much—and thus do a particularly poor job of representing their supporters—is that after paying their direct mail fundraising costs, they have little money with which to build a strong Washington office. In contrast, liberal citizen groups like environmental lobbies are thriving. They are popular with a more affluent constituency: suburban professionals who can afford to contribute more. They have also developed other important sources of income in addition to mail solicitations. There are, of course, wealthy conservatives, but they tend to be suburban businesspeople with more secular outlooks. They don't find organizations like the Christian Coalition appealing.

members. The Washington representative of an oil trade association was reading the *Federal Register* (a daily compendium of all new regulations issued by the government) as part of his daily routine when he noticed that the Federal Aviation Administration planned to issue new regulations requiring detailed flight plans by noncommercial aircraft. The policy would make rescue efforts for noncommercial planes easier, but the lobbyist realized that it could compromise the confidentiality surrounding the flights of company planes for aerial exploration for oil and gas. Anyone could obtain the filed flight plans. He notified the member companies, and their lobbying prevented the implementation of the regulations, precluding the possibility of competitors' getting hold of such secret data.[22]

Lobbyists can be full-time employees of their organization or employees of public relations or law firms who are hired on retainer. When hiring a lobbyist, an interest group looks for someone who knows her or his way around Washington. Lobbyists are valued for their experience and their

Can You Explain Why...
government is a training ground for lobbyists?

The Son Also Rises

It is no surprise that Tommy Boggs has built a career in the political world. His father, Hale Boggs, was a Democratic member of the House of Representatives and served as majority leader. After the senior Boggs died in a plane crash, his wife, Lindy, succeeded him in the House. Tommy Boggs turned away from electoral politics, however, and pursued a career as a lawyer-lobbyist in Washington. Enormously skillful and highly intelligent, Boggs has attracted many corporate clients to Patton, Boggs, and Blow, a law firm known for its lobbying prowess.

knowledge of how government operates. Often, they are people who have served in the legislative or executive branches or held a major party post, people who have firsthand experience with government. Tom Downey served as a member of the House of Representatives for close to twenty years. When Democrat Downey lost his New York seat to a Republican, he started his own lobbying firm. His connections to Congress and to the Clinton administration were crucial assets in attracting clients. Within a few years he had many lucrative clients, including Microsoft, Mobil Oil, TimeWarner, and Boeing. The Fuji film company paid him $360,000 to defend it in an administrative inquiry investigating charges that it blocked Kodak from the Japanese market.[23]

More than half of all lobbyists have some experience in government. The value of experience in the legislative or executive branch includes knowledge of the policymaking process, expertise in particular issues, and contacts with those still in government.[24] Contacts with former colleagues can be invaluable. As one lobbyist said of her former associates on Capitol Hill, "They know you, and they return your phone calls."[25] Lobbying is a lucrative profession, and good people with experience can easily make over $200,000 a year. The very best make considerably more.

Many lobbyists have law degrees and find their legal backgrounds useful in bargaining and negotiating over laws and regulations. Because of their location, many Washington law firms are drawn into lobbying. Expanding interest group advocacy has created a boom for Washington law firms. Corporations without their own Washington office rely heavily on law

Former member Bob Packwood left the Senate in disgrace in 1995 because of a series of sexual harassment charges. He started a lobbying firm and since that time he's built a very successful business. Clients are attracted to his connections to his former colleagues in the Senate. There are thousands of lobbyists in Washington, and those who are former legislators have a considerable advantage in getting their phone calls returned.

firms to lobby for them before the national government. Verner Liipfert Bernhard McPherson & Hand has 185 lawyers and lobbyists to serve corporate clients who need representation before Congress or an administrative agency.[26]

The most common image of a lobbyist is that of an arm twister, someone who spends most of his or her time trying to convince a legislator or administrator to back a certain policy. The stereotype of lobbyists also portrays them as people of dubious ethics because they trade on their connections and may hand out campaign donations to candidates for office. The campaign donations that interest groups make to congressional candidates justifiably create an unsavory image for lobbyists. Yet lobbying is a much maligned profession. The lobbyist's primary job is not to trade on favors or campaign contributions but to pass information on to policymakers. Lobbyists provide government officials and their staffs with a constant flow of data that support their organizations' policy goals. Lobbyists also try to build a compelling case for their goals, showing that the "facts" dictate that a particular change be made or avoided. What lobbyists are really trying to do, of course, is to convince policymakers that their data deserve more attention and are more accurate than those presented by other lobbyists.

Political Action Committees

An Explosion of PACs

political action committee (PAC)
An organization that pools campaign contributions from group members and donates those funds to candidates for political office.

One of the organizational resources that can make a lobbyist's job easier is a **political action committee (PAC).** PACs pool campaign contributions from group members and donate the money to candidates for political office. Under federal law, a PAC can give as much as $5,000 to a candidate for Congress for each separate election. A change in campaign finance law in 1974 led to a rapid increase in the number of PACs, and close to 4,000 PACs were active in the 2000 election.[27] The greatest growth came from corporations, most of which had been prohibited from operating PACs. There was also rapid growth in the number of nonconnected PACs, largely ideological groups that have no parent lobbying organization and are formed solely for the purpose of raising and channeling campaign funds. (Thus, a PAC can be the campaign-wing affiliate of an existing interest group or a wholly independent, unaffiliated group.) Most PACs are rather small, and most give less than $50,000 in total contributions during a two-year election cycle. There are many PACs, however, that are large enough to gain recognition for the issues they care about. In the 2000 election, seven Indian tribes gave over $100,000 to candidates for Congress (most of them Democrats). Native Americans' concerns include economic issues, Indian lands, and casino gambling (see Figure 10.4).[28]

Why do interest groups form PACs? The chief executive officer of one manufacturing company said his corporation had a PAC because "the PAC gives you access. It makes you a player."[29] Lobbyists believe that campaign contributions help significantly when they are trying to gain an audience with a member of Congress. Members of Congress and their staffers generally are eager to meet with representatives of their constituencies, but their time is limited. However, a member of Congress or staffer would find it difficult to turn down a lobbyist's request for a meeting if the PAC of the lobbyist's organization had made a significant campaign contribution in the last election.

Typically, PACs, like most other interest groups, are highly pragmatic organizations; pushing a particular political philosophy takes second place to achieving immediate policy goals.[30] Although many corporate executives strongly believe in a free-market economy, for example, their company PACs tend to hold congressional candidates to a much more practical standard. In recent elections corporate PACs as a group have given as much as 85 percent of their contributions to incumbents.[31] At the same time different sectors of the PAC universe may strongly favor one party or the other. Approximately nine out of every ten dollars that unions give go to Democrats, whether they be incumbents, challengers, or open seat candidates.[32] During the 2000 election energy companies and trade associations tried to help elect the Bush-Cheney ticket and congressional Republicans. Those in the energy business believed that the Republicans would be much more interested in developing new domestic sources of energy than the Democrats. Oil and gas companies gave $25.5 million to Republicans (78 percent of their total contributions). Utilities and mining concerns gave disproportionately to the Republicans as well. All these industries were pleased when President Bush unveiled his energy plan in the spring of 2001, as it emphasized deregulation and development of new resources.[33]

Interest groups can also contribute campaign funds through donations of "soft money," which is discussed in Chapter 9. Soft money is the unregulated gifts to political parties for party-building purposes, such as get-out-the-vote drives. Corporations and unions have donated large sums to both the Republican and Democratic parties in an effort to gain greater access and influence. Prior to the 2000 election, tobacco company executives planned a campaign to channel $7 million in soft money contributions to the Republican Party.[34]

Critics charge that contributions like these cannot help but influence public policy. Yet political scientists have not been able to document any consistent link between campaign donations and the way members of

figure

10.4 PACs Americana

Most PAC money comes from corporations, business trade groups, and professional associations. Labor unions contribute significantly as well. A much smaller proportion of all PAC contributions comes from citizen PACs, which form the bulk of the "nonconnected" category. Americans at the lower end of the economic spectrum are left out entirely. As former presidential candidate Bob Dole once put it, "There aren't any Poor PACs or Food Stamp PACs or Nutrition PACs or Medicare PACs."

Source: "FEC Releases Information on PAC Activity for 1997–98," Federal Election Commission press release, 8 June 1999.

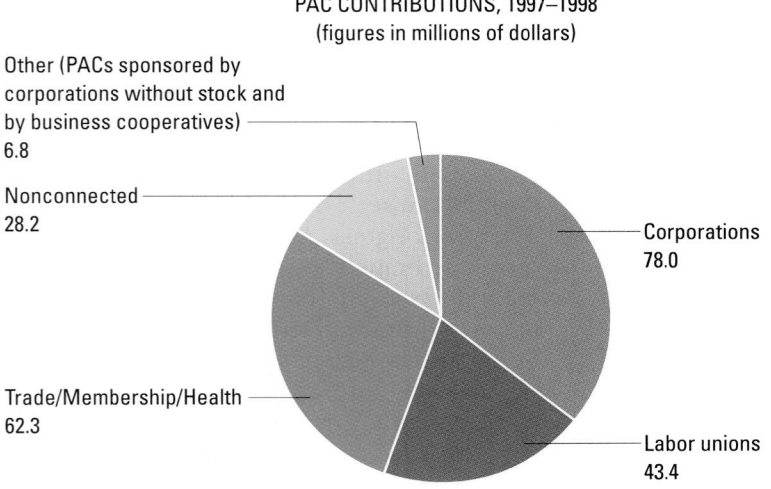

PAC CONTRIBUTIONS, 1997–1998
(figures in millions of dollars)

Other (PACs sponsored by corporations without stock and by business cooperatives)
6.8

Nonconnected
28.2

Trade/Membership/Health
62.3

Corporations
78.0

Labor unions
43.4

Congress vote on the floor of the House and Senate.[35] The problem is this: Do PAC contributions or soft-money donations from interest groups influence votes in Congress, or are they really just rewards for legislators who would vote for the group's interests anyway because of their long-standing ideology? How do we determine the answer to this question? Simply looking for the influence of PACs in the voting patterns of members of Congress may be shortsighted; influence can also be felt before bills get to the floor of the full House or Senate for a vote. Some recent, sophisticated research shows that PAC donations do seem to influence what goes on in congressional committees. As will be discussed in Chapter 11, committees are where the bulk of the work on legislation takes place. Lobbies with PACs have an advantage in the committee process and appear to gain influence because of the additional access they receive.[36]

Whatever the research shows, it is clear that the American public is suspicious of PACs and soft-money donors and regards them as problems in our political system. Large campaign contributions are seen as a means of securing privileges for those sectors of society with the resources to purchase additional access to Congress. But in a democracy, influence should not be a function of money; some citizens have little to give, yet their interests need to be protected. From this perspective, the issue is political equality—the freedom to give should not outweigh the need for equal political access for all sectors of society.

Strong arguments can also be made for retaining PACs. They offer a means for people to participate in the political system. They allow small givers to pool their resources and fight the feeling that one person cannot make a difference. Finally, PAC defenders also point out that prohibiting

PACs would amount to a restriction on the freedom of political expression. Because of the size of some soft-money gifts, these contributions are much harder to defend. (We take up the question of PACs and campaign finance reforms at the end of this chapter.)

LOBBYING TACTICS

When an interest group decides to try to influence the government on an issue, its staff and officers must develop a strategy, which may include several tactics aimed at various officials or offices. Together, these tactics should use the group's resources as effectively as possible.

Keep in mind that lobbying extends beyond the legislative branch. Groups can seek help from the courts and administrative agencies as well as from Congress. Moreover, interest groups may have to shift their focus from one branch of government to another. After a bill becomes a law, for example, a group that lobbied for the legislation will probably try to influence the administrative agency responsible for implementing the new law. Some policy decisions are left unresolved by legislation and are settled through regulations. Lobbies want to make sure regulatory decisions are as close to their group's preferences as possible.

We discuss three types of lobbying tactics here: those aimed at policymakers and implemented by interest group representatives (direct lobbying), those that involve group members (grassroots lobbying), and those directed at the public (information campaigns). We also examine the use of new high-tech lobbying tactics as well as cooperative efforts of interest groups to influence government through coalitions.

Direct Lobbying

direct lobbying
Attempts to influence a legislator's vote through personal contact with the legislator.

Direct lobbying relies on personal contact with policymakers. One survey of Washington lobbyists showed that 98 percent use direct contact with government officials to express their group's views.[37] This interaction occurs when a lobbyist meets with a member of Congress, an agency official, or a staff member. In their meetings, lobbyists usually convey their arguments by providing data about a specific issue. If a lobbyist from, for example, a chamber of commerce meets with a member of Congress about a bill the chamber backs, the lobbyist does not say (or even suggest), "Vote for this bill, or our people in the district will vote against you in the next election." Instead, the lobbyist might say, "If this bill is passed, we're going to see hundreds of new jobs created back home." The representative has no trouble at all figuring out that a vote for the bill can help in the next election.

Personal lobbying is a day-in, day-out process. It is not enough simply to meet with policymakers just before a vote or a regulatory decision. Lobbyists must maintain contact with congressional and agency staffers, constantly providing them with pertinent data. One lobbyist described his strategy in personal meetings with policymakers as rather simple and straightforward: "Providing information is the most effective tool. People begin to rely on you." Another lobbyist gave this advice: "You'd better bring good ideas and some facts, and they'd better be accurate."[38]

A tactic related to direct lobbying is testifying at committee hearings when a bill is before Congress. This tactic allows the interest group to put its views on record and to make them widely known when the hearing tes-

timony is published. Although testifying is one of the most visible parts of lobbying, it is generally considered window dressing. Most lobbyists believe that such testimony usually does little by itself to persuade members of Congress.

Another direct but somewhat different approach is legal advocacy. Using this tactic, a group tries to achieve its policy goals through litigation. Claiming some violation of law, a group will file a lawsuit and ask that a judge make a ruling that will benefit the organization. After the Food and Drug Administration (FDA) proposed regulations aimed at reducing smoking by minors, cigarette manufacturers counterattacked with a lawsuit filed in federal court. The tobacco industry believed the FDA had exceeded its authority, and it was concerned that if the regulations went unchallenged, the agency would take additional steps to restrict smoking.[39]

Grassroots Lobbying

grassroots lobbying
Lobbying activities performed by rank-and-file interest group members and would-be members.

Grassroots lobbying involves an interest group's rank-and-file members and may include people outside the organization who sympathize with its goals.[40] Grassroots tactics, such as letter-writing campaigns and protests, are often used in conjunction with direct lobbying by Washington representatives. Letters, telegrams, e-mail, faxes, and telephone calls from a group's members to their representatives in Congress or to agency administrators add to a lobbyist's credibility in talks with these officials. Policymakers are more concerned about what a lobbyist says when they know that constituents are really watching their decisions.

Group members—especially influential members (corporation presidents, local civic leaders)—occasionally go to Washington to lobby. But the most common grassroots tactic is letter writing. "Write your member of Congress" is not just a slogan for a civics test. Legislators are highly sensitive to the content of their mail. Interest groups often launch letter-writing campaigns through their regular publications or special alerts.[41]

They may even provide sample letters and the names and addresses of specific policymakers.

If people in government seem unresponsive to conventional lobbying
tactics, a group might resort to some form of political protest. A protest or
demonstration, such as picketing or marching, is designed to attract media
attention to an issue. Protesters hope that television and newspaper coverage will help change public opinion and make policymakers more receptive to their group's demands. Protests by advocates for the homeless in
Washington have included "splashing blood on the White House gates, un-
rolling mats across the White House drive and declaring it a homeless
shelter, [and] turning bags of cockroaches loose on the White House tour
to remind onlookers of the conditions under which many poor Americans
live."[42] The goal of each of these protests was to create a striking visual
image that would attract media attention; if reporters covered the protest,
people around the country would be exposed to the protestors' belief that
the government is doing far too little to help the homeless.

The main drawback to protesting is that policymaking is a long-term,
incremental process, and a demonstration is only short-lived. It is difficult
to sustain anger and activism among group supporters—to keep large
numbers of people involved in protest after protest. A notable exception
was the civil rights demonstrations of the 1960s, which were sustained
over a long period. National attention focused not only on the widespread
demonstrations but also on the sometimes violent confrontations between protesters and white law enforcement officers. For example, the use
of police dogs and high-power fire hoses against blacks marching in
Alabama in the early 1960s angered millions of Americans who saw films

of the confrontations on television. The protests were a major factor in stirring public opinion, which in turn hastened the passage of the Civil Rights Act of 1964 and the Voting Rights Act of 1965.

Information Campaigns

As the strategy of the civil rights movement shows, interest groups generally feel that public backing adds strength to their lobbying efforts. And because all interest groups believe they are absolutely right in their policy orientation, they believe that they will get that backing if they can only make the public aware of their position and the evidence supporting it. To this end, interest groups launch **information campaigns,** organized efforts to gain public backing by bringing their views to the public's attention. The underlying assumption is that public ignorance and apathy are as much a problem as the views of competing interest groups. Various means are used to combat apathy. Some are directed at the larger public; others are directed at smaller audiences with long-standing interest in an issue.

> **information campaign**
> An organized effort to gain public backing by bringing a group's views to public attention.

Public relations is one information-campaign tactic. A public relations campaign might involve sending speakers to meetings in various parts of the country, producing pamphlets and handouts, or taking out newspaper and magazine advertising. During the fight over the Clinton administration's health-care reform proposal during 1993 and 1994, the Health Insurance Association of America (HIAA) launched a television ad campaign designed to turn public opinion against the plan. These ads featured a fictional couple named Harry and Louise, who in a series of spots talked conversationally about the plan and pointed out its critical flaws. The ads were ubiquitous, and many felt they played a major role in defeating the plan. Yet surveys showed that the $14 million ad campaign had little impact on public opinion.[43] Given the costs of televised advertising and the difficulty of truly swaying public opinion through them, it's not surprising that few groups rely on paid television advertising as their primary weapon in advocacy campaigns.

Sponsoring research is another way interest groups press their cases. When a group believes that evidence has not been fully developed in a certain area, it may commission research on the subject. To publicize its belief that the government's agricultural policy unfairly favors large corporations and works against family farmers, the Environmental Working Group released a research report a week before the 2000 Iowa presidential caucuses. The report showed nearly half of $2 billion in aid to Iowa farmers went to just 12 percent of farm owners, while many small family farms "got less money than a welfare recipient."[44] By timing the release of the report to coincide with the imminent approach of the Iowa presidential caucuses, the liberal advocacy group hoped to maximize coverage by forcing the candidates campaigning around Iowa to respond to its findings.

High-Tech Lobbying

In recent years, Washington lobbies have added many high-tech tactics to their arsenals. Using such resources as direct mail, e-mail, faxes, polling, and the World Wide Web, lobbies have tried to find ways to expand their reach and increase their impact. The most conspicuous effect of high-tech lobbying is that it speeds up the political process. Using electronic communication, groups can quickly mobilize their constituents, who will in turn quickly contact policymakers about pending decisions. When the Clinton administration proposed that computer manufacturers be required to install a "clipper chip" in all the machines they sell, it set off alarms in the computer industry and among civil libertarians. (The chip would facilitate government access to encoded computerized communications, which are scrambled for security reasons.) Worrying that the clipper chip would lead to government spying, Computer Professionals for Social Responsibility and the Electronic Frontier Foundation used the Internet to build opposition to the proposal. Before the administration had a chance to make its case, 55,000 e-mail messages had been sent to Washington asking that the proposal be dropped. The administration did just that.[45]

The Web is also a tool for building a membership and even building new advocacy organizations. Hemophiliacs—people whose blood doesn't clot adequately and thus are at serious risk from bleeding—were traditionally represented by the National Hemophilia Foundation (NHF). The NHF has a close relationship with drug manufacturers, who in turn provide significant financial support to the group. This close relationship inhibited the organization from lobbying the government to force a reduction in drug prices. Through the Internet the small and geographically dispersed community of hemophiliacs was able to organize its own independent organizations.[46]

Although high-tech lobbying tactics facilitate direct communication between citizens and policymakers, which is to be applauded, there is a down side as well. Technology is expensive, so the introduction of such tactics favors groups that are wealthy and can best utilize them and citizens who own personal computers or have access to them at work. In short, high-tech tactics typically work to the advantage of those who are already well represented in the political process.[47]

Coalition Building

coalition building
The banding together of several interest groups for the purpose of lobbying.

A final aspect of lobbying strategy is **coalition building,** in which several organizations band together for the purpose of lobbying. Such joint efforts conserve or make more effective use of the resources of groups with similar views. Most coalitions are informal, ad hoc arrangements that exist only for the purpose of lobbying on a single issue. Coalitions most often form among groups that work in the same policy area and have similar constituencies, such as environmental groups or feminist groups. When an issue arises that several such groups agree on, they are likely to develop a coalition.

Yet coalitions often extend beyond organizations with similar constituencies and similar outlooks. Environmental groups and business groups are often thought of as dire enemies. But some businesses support the same goals as environmental lobbies because it is in their self-interest. For example, companies in the business of cleaning up toxic waste sites have worked with environmental groups to strengthen the Superfund program, the government's primary weapon for dealing with dangerous waste dumps.[48] Lobbyists see an advantage in having a diverse coalition. In the words of one health and education lobbyist, "If you have three hundred associations on a list, that's a pretty strong message."[49]

As we noted in Chapter 2, our political system is more pluralist than majoritarian. Policymaking is determined more by the interaction of groups with the government than by elections. The great advantage of majoritarianism is that it is built around the most elemental notion of fairness: what the government does is determined by what most of the people want.

How, then, do we justify the policy decisions made under a pluralist system? How do we determine whether they are fair? There is no precisely agreed-upon formula, but most people would agree with the following two simple notions. First, all significant interests in the population should be adequately represented by lobbying groups. That is, if a significant number of people with similar views have a stake in the outcome of policy decisions in a particular area, they should have a lobby to speak for them. If government makes policy that affects farmers who grow wheat, for example, then wheat farmers should have a lobby.

Second, government should listen to the views of all major interests as it develops policy. Lobbies are of little value unless policymakers are willing to listen to them. We should not require policymakers to balance perfectly all competing interests, however—some interests are diametrically opposed. Moreover, elections inject some of the benefits of majoritarianism into our system because the party that wins an election will have more say than its opponent in the making of public policy.

Membership Patterns

Public opinion surveys of Americans and surveys of interest groups in Washington can be used to determine who is represented in the interest group system. A clear pattern is evident: some sectors of society are much better represented than others. As noted in the earlier discussions of the Boston West Enders and the United Farm Workers, who is being organized makes a big difference. Those who work in business or in a profession, those with a high level of education, and those with high incomes are the most likely to belong to interest groups. Even middle-income people are much more likely to join interest groups than are those who are poor.

For example, one-third of those receiving veterans' benefits belong to an organization that works to protect and enhance veterans' benefits. A quarter of social security recipients are members of a group that works to protect that program. By contrast, less than 1 percent of food stamp recipients belong to a group that represents their interests in this program. Only about 2 percent of recipients of welfare are members of welfare rights groups.[50] Clearly, a **membership bias** is part of the pattern of who belongs to interest groups: certain types of people are much more likely to belong to interest groups than are others.

membership bias
The tendency of some sectors of society—especially the wealthy, the highly educated, professionals, and those in business—to organize more readily into interest groups.

Citizen Groups

Because the bias in interest group membership is unmistakable, should we conclude that the interest group system is biased? Before reaching that conclusion, we should examine another set of data. The actual population of interest groups in Washington surely reflects a class bias in interest group membership, but that bias may be modified in an important way. Some interest groups derive support from sources other than their membership. Thus, although they have no food stamp recipients as members, the Washington-based Food Research and Action Committee and the Community Nutrition Institute have been effective long-term advocates of the food stamp program. The Center for Budget and Policy Priorities and the Children's Defense Fund have no welfare recipients among their members, but they are highly respected Washington lobbies working on the problems of poor people. Poverty groups gain their financial support from philanthropic foundations, government grants, corporations, and wealthy individuals.

Groups such as these have played an important role in influencing policy on poor people's programs. Given the large numbers of Americans who are on programs such as food stamps, poor people's lobbies are not numerous enough.[51] Nevertheless, the poor are represented by these and other organizations (such as labor unions and health lobbies) that regard the poor as part of the constituency they must protect. In short, although the poor are somewhat underrepresented in our system, the situation is not nearly so bad as interest group membership patterns suggest.

Another part of the problem of membership bias has to do with free riders. The interests that are most affected by free riders are broad societal problems, such as the environment and consumer protection, in which literally everyone can be considered as having a stake in the outcome. We are all consumers, and we all care about the environment. But the greater the number of potential members of a group, the more likely it is that individuals will decide to be free riders because they believe that plenty of others can offer financial support to the organization. As noted earlier, business trade associations and professional associations do not have the same problem because they can offer many benefits that cannot be obtained without paying for membership.

Environmental and consumer interests have been chronically underrepresented in the Washington interest group community. In the 1960s, however, a strong citizen group movement emerged. **Citizen groups** are lobbying organizations built around policy concerns unrelated to members' vocational interests. People who join the Environmental Defense Fund join it because they care about the environment, not because it lobbies on issues related to their profession. If that group fights for stricter pollution control requirements, it doesn't further the financial interests of its members. The benefits to members are largely ideological and esthetic. In contrast, a corporation fighting the same stringent standards is trying to protect its economic interests. A law that requires a corporation to install expensive antipollution devices can reduce stockholders' dividends, depress salaries, and postpone expansion. Although both the environmental group and the corporation have valid reasons for their stands, their motives are different.

As Americans have become more affluent and more secure about the future of the economy and their own personal well-being, their interest in the kind of quality-of-life issues pursued by citizen groups has increased. Organizations pursuing environmental protection, consumer protection,

citizen group
Lobbying organization built around policy concerns unrelated to members' vocational interests.

figure

10.5   TV Stars

An analysis of close to a year's worth of nightly news programs on the television networks (like ABC's World News Tonight*) reveals that citizen groups receive more coverage than any other interest group sector. Moreover, coverage of citizen groups tends to be either positive or neutral, while business groups are treated less favorably.*

Source: Jeffrey M. Berry, *The New Liberalism* (Washington, D.C.: Brookings Institution, 1999), p. 122.

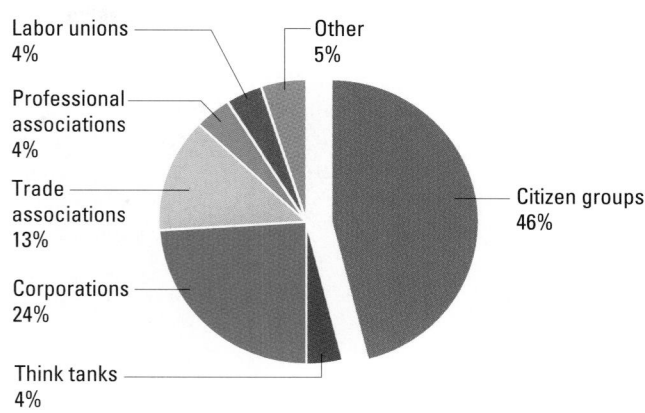

Labor unions 4%
Other 5%
Professional associations 4%
Citizen groups 46%
Trade associations 13%
Corporations 24%
Think tanks 4%

good government, family values, and equality for various groups in society have grown in number and collectively attracted millions of members. Since these groups are not motivated by financial gain the way that business, professional, and labor groups are, they have more credibility than other types of lobbying organizations. The national press gives them considerable coverage, reinforcing the ability of these groups to get their issues on the national agenda. One study showed that even though citizen groups constitute less than 5 percent of all Washington lobbies, they received almost half of all TV network news coverage of interest groups (see Figure 10.5). This success has been largely on the liberal side because environmental and consumer groups have had much more influence on Congress than the social conservative groups, which are considerably smaller and have much less money after their fundraising costs (recall Politics in a Changing America 10.1).[52]

Business Mobilization

Because a strong public interest movement has become an integral part of Washington politics, an easy assumption is that the bias in interest group representation in favor of business has been largely overcome. What must be factored in, however, is that business has become increasingly mobilized as well.[53] The 1970s and 1980s saw a vast increase in the number of business lobbies in Washington. Many corporations opened up Washington lobbying offices, and many trade associations headquartered elsewhere either moved to Washington or opened branch offices there.

   This mobilization was partly a reaction to the success of liberal citizen groups, which business tended to view as hostile to the free-enterprise system. The reaction of business also reflected the expanded scope of the national government. After the Environmental Protection Agency, the Consumer Product Safety Commission, OSHA, and other regulatory

Well-Fed Lobbyists

At first glance, the restaurant business may not seem to be an industry with serious political problems. Yet government regulation and taxation policies can significantly affect restaurant operations and profits. The National Restaurant Association, which employs these five lobbyists, is the trade association that represents restaurant owners and food and equipment manufacturers and distributors. Headquartered in Washington with a staff of 115 and a budget of $16 million, it is just one of the thousands of trade groups working to influence public policy in Washington.

agencies were created, many more companies found they were affected by federal regulations. And many corporations found that they were frequently reacting to policies that were already made rather than participating in their making. They saw representation in Washington—where the policymakers are—as critical if they were to obtain information on pending government actions soon enough to act on it. Finally, the competitive nature of business lobbying fueled the increase in business advocacy in Washington. This competition exists because legislation and regulatory decisions never seem to apply uniformly to all businesses; rather, they affect one type of business or one industry more than others.

The health-care industry is a case in point. Government regulation has become an increasingly important factor in determining health-care profits. Through reimbursement formulas for Medicare, Medicaid, and other health-care programs funded by Washington, the national government limits what providers can charge. As this regulatory influence grew, more and more health-care trade associations (like the American Hospital Association) and professional associations (like the American Nurses Association) came to view Washington lobbying as increasingly significant to the well-being of their members. In 1979 there were roughly 100 health-related groups lobbying in Washington. A little over a decade later, there were more than 700.[54]

The total number of organizations is far from a perfect indicator of interest group strength, however. The AFL-CIO, which represents millions of union members, is more influential than a two-person corporate listening post in Washington; nevertheless, as a rough indicator of interest group influence, the data show that business has an advantage in this country's interest group system.[55]

Access

At the outset of this discussion of interest group bias, we noted the importance of finding out not only which types of constituencies are represented by interest groups but also whether those in government listen to the various groups that approach them. The existence of an interest group makes little difference if the government systematically ignores it. Evidence shows that any particular policymaker or office of government can be highly selective in granting access to interest groups. The Reagan White House, for example, worked directly with only a small proportion of interest groups, and wealthy, conservative groups had much more access than others.[56]

The ideological compatibility between any given interest group and the policymaker it approaches certainly affects the likelihood that the policymaker will grant the group access and listen to what its lobbyists have to say. However, pluralists are convincing when they argue that the national government has many points of access, and virtually all lobbying organizations can find some part of that government that will listen to them. If liberal poverty lobbies are shut out of a conservative White House, liberal members of Congress will work with them. All forms of access are not of equal importance, and some organizations have wider access than others. Nevertheless, American government is generally characterized by the broad access it grants to interest groups (see Compared with What? 10.1).

Reform

If the interest group system is biased, should the advantages of some groups somehow be eliminated or reduced? This is hard to do. In an economic system marked by great differences in income, great differences in the degree to which people are organized are inevitable. Moreover, as Madison foresaw, limiting interest group activity is difficult without limiting fundamental freedoms. The First Amendment guarantees Americans the right to petition their government, and lobbying, at its most basic level, is a form of organized petitioning.

Still, some sectors of the interest group community may enjoy advantages that are unacceptable. If it is felt that the advantages of some groups are so great that they affect the equality of people's opportunity to be heard in the political system, then restrictions on interest group behavior can be justified on the grounds that the disadvantaged must be protected. Pluralist democracy is justified on exactly these grounds: all constituencies must have the opportunity to organize, and competition between groups as they press their case before policymakers must be fair.

Some critics charge that a system of campaign finance that relies so heavily on PACs undermines our democratic system. They claim that access to policymakers is purchased through the wealth of some constituencies. In the 2000 election, a small number of PACs individually contributed over $2 million in campaign funds to congressional candidates.[57] Around 67 percent of PAC contributions come from corporations, business trade associations, and professional associations (recall Figure 10.4).[58] It is not merely a matter of wealthy interest groups showering incumbents with donations; members of Congress aggressively solicit donations from

★ **compared with what?**

10.1   Pluralism Worldwide

A study of democracies around the world measured the degree to which interest groups operated independently of any formal link to government. Interest groups in political systems with low scores in this chart (like Norway) run the risk of being co-opted by policymakers because of their partnerships with government. These countries tend to have fewer groups but those groups are expected to work with government in a coordinated fashion. High scores indicate that the interest groups in those systems are clearly in a competitive position with other groups. Thus, countries with high scores (like the United States) are the most pluralistic.

Source: Arend Lijphart, *Patterns of Democracy* (New Haven, Conn.: Yale University Press, 1999), p. 177.

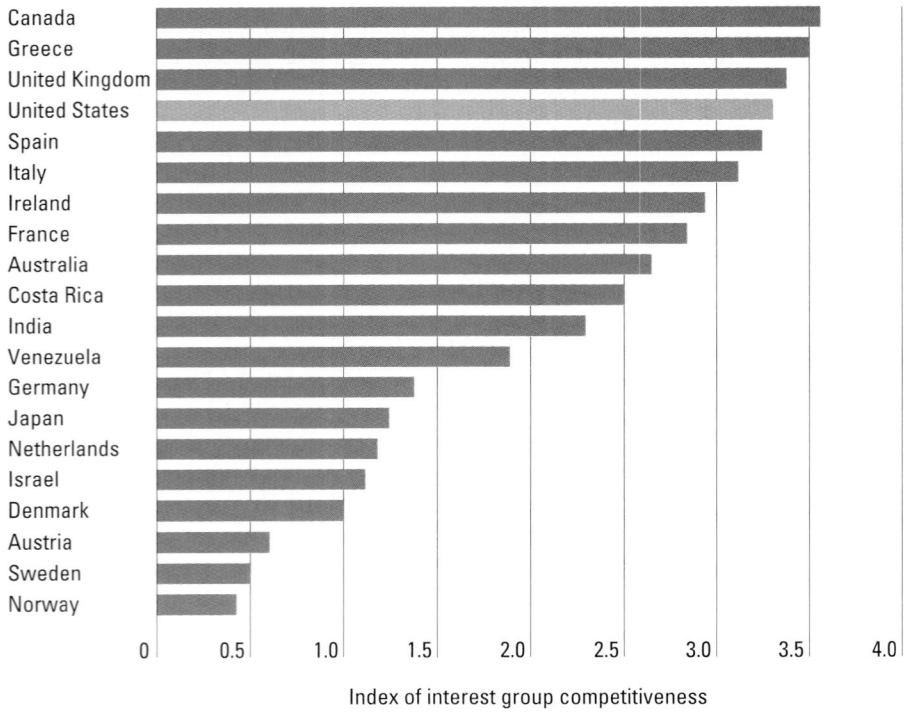

Index of interest group competitiveness

PACs. Although observers disagree on whether PAC money actually influences policy outcomes, agreement is widespread that PAC donations give donors better access to members of Congress.

The government has placed some restrictions on interest group campaign donations, however. During the 1970s, Congress put some important reforms into effect. Strong disclosure requirements now exist—the source of all significant contributions to candidates for national office is a matter of public record. Legislation also provides for public financing of presidential campaigns; taxpayer money goes in equal amounts to the presidential nominees of the major parties. In 1995 Congress passed some modest reforms outside the campaign finance area. Lobbyists are now subject to a strict registration requirement and must file reports every six months listing all their clients, the amount they spent on lobbying activities, and how much they were paid.[59] Another reform banned all gifts from lobbyists to legislators (with the exception of gifts of trivial value).[60]

Reformers have called for public financing of congressional elections to reduce the presumed influence of PACs on Congress. Public financing would restrict people's freedom to give to whom they want; the tradeoff is that it would also reduce political inequality. Other proposed approaches include reducing the amount individual PACs can give; limiting the overall amount of money any one candidate can accept from PACs; reducing the costs of campaigning by subsidizing the costs of commercials, printing, and postage; and giving tax incentives to individuals to contribute to candidates. However, incumbents usually find it easier to raise money from PACs than do challengers, so the incentive to leave the status quo intact is strong. And Republicans and Democrats have sharp, partisan differences over proposed PAC and soft-money reforms because each party believes that the other is trying to fashion a system that will somehow handicap the opposing party.

SUMMARY

Interest groups play many important roles in our political process. They are a means by which citizens can participate in politics, and they communicate their members' views to those in government. Interest groups differ greatly in the resources at their disposal and in the tactics they use to influence government. The number of interest groups has grown sharply in recent years.[61]

Despite the growth and change in the nature of interest groups, the fundamental problem identified by Madison more than 200 years ago endures. In a free and open society, groups form to pursue policies that favor them at the expense of the broader national interest. Madison hoped that the solution to the problem would come from the diversity of the population and the structure of our government.

To a certain extent, Madison's expectations have been borne out. The natural differences between groups have prevented a tyranny of any one faction. Yet the interest group system remains unbalanced, with some segments of society (particularly business, the wealthy, and the educated) considerably better organized than others. The growth of citizen groups has reduced the disparity somewhat, but significant inequalities remain in how well different interests are represented in Washington.

The inequities point to flaws in pluralist theory. There is no mechanism to automatically ensure that interest groups will form to speak for those who need representation. Likewise, when an issue arises and policymakers meet with interest groups that have a stake in the outcome, those groups may not equally represent all the constituencies that the policy changes will affect. The interest group system clearly compromises the principle of political equality stated in the maxim "one person, one vote." Formal political equality is certainly more likely to occur outside interest group politics, in elections between candidates from competing political parties—which better fits the majoritarian model of democracy.

Despite the inequities of the interest group system, little direct effort has been made to restrict interest group activity. Madison's dictum to avoid suppressing political freedoms, even at the expense of permitting interest group activity that promotes the selfish interests of narrow segments of the population, has generally guided public policy. Yet, as the problem of PACs demonstrates, government has had to set some restrictions on interest groups. Permitting PACs to give unlimited amounts to political candidates would undermine confidence in the system. Where to draw the line on PAC activity remains a thorny issue because there is little consensus on how to balance the conflicting needs of our society. Congress is one institution that must try to balance our diverse country's conflicting interests. In the next chapter, we will see how difficult this part of Congress's job is.

★ Selected Readings

Baumgartner, Frank R., and Beth L. Leech. *Basic Interests*. Princeton, N.J.: Princeton University Press, 1998. Offers a critical examination of interest group scholarship and prescribes future directions for the field.

Berry, Jeffrey M. *The Interest Group Society*, 3d ed. New York: Longman, 1997. An analysis of the growth of interest group politics.

Berry, Jeffrey M. *The New Liberalism*. Washington, D.C.: Brookings Institution, 1999. Documents the rising power of liberal citizen lobbies.

Biersack, Robert, Paul S. Herrnson, and Clyde Wilcox. *After the Revolution*. Boston, Mass.: Allyn & Bacon, 1999. Separate studies of various political action committees.

Cigler, Allan J., and Burdett A. Loomis, eds. *Interest Group Politics*, 5th ed. Washington, D.C.: Congressional Quarterly Press, 1998. This reader includes a selection of essays on lobbying groups.

Goldstein, Kenneth M. *Interest Groups, Lobbying, and Participation in America*. New York: Cambridge University Press, 1999. A study of the grassroots mobilization of interest group followers.

Internet Exercises

1. *Shifting Support*

The Center for Responsive Politics is a nonpartisan, nonprofit research group in Washington, D.C., that tracks the effects of money in politics. The center's home page is located at <**www.opensecrets.org/**>.

- Use the center's "Who's Giving" feature to read about the patterns of political giving from the following industries: defense, health professionals, and telephone utilities.

- What do you notice about the pattern of political giving in these three sectors before and after 1994? What do you think explains the pattern that you noticed?

2. *Interest Groups as Service Providers*

Three of the largest and most significant interest groups in the United States are the American Association of Retired Persons (AARP), the National Rifle Association (NRA), and the Sierra Club. While they engage in significant political activities, all three organizations do provide other services as well.

- Go to the Web sites of these groups at <**www.aarp. org/**>, <**www.nra.org/**>, <**www.sierraclub.org/**>. For each group, identify three activities that the group engages in or sponsors that you would characterize as "nonpolitical." Make a list of the activities that you have identified.

- How might these nonpolitical activities actually help to serve the political interests of the organization and its members?

Congress

HENRY HYDE, CHAIR OF THE HOUSE JUDICIARY COMMITTEE, strode purposely from the House side of the Capitol, across the rotunda to the Senate side. Accompanied by other Republican members of the committee, the gray-haired Hyde exhibited a solemn demeanor befitting the gravity of the occasion. Hyde carried with him two articles of impeachment alleging conduct by President William Jefferson Clinton deemed sufficient by the House to remove the president from office. When he reached secretary of the Senate Gary Sisco's office, Sisco was waiting for him. A bit player on this day of political theater, Sisco would receive the blue binder that Hyde was transporting. Not wanting to blow his lines, Hyde read from a small piece of blue stationery, explaining why he had come to the Senate. As Sisco took the binder, photographers captured the historic moment. With these articles of impeachment—an indictment, for all intents and purposes—delivered to Sisco, it was now the responsibility of the one hundred members of the Senate to sit as jurors in a trial.

For all the high drama of this moment, the American public remained unconvinced that Congress was doing the right thing in bringing the president to trial. What exactly had Clinton done? Quite simply, he had had a sexual relationship with a young White House intern, Monica Lewinsky, and then he and Lewinsky had tried to cover it up.[1]

Two articles of impeachment had been approved by a majority of the House. Article One said that in testimony before a federal grand jury, Clinton had "willfully provided perjurious, false and misleading testimony" concerning his relationship with Ms. Lewinsky. It also asserted that Clinton had given false testimony in a civil suit brought against him by Paula Jones, who claimed that when Clinton was governor of Arkansas and she was a state employee, he had crudely propositioned her. Article Two stated that Clinton had engaged in obstruction of justice, including encouraging Ms. Lewinsky to lie in an affidavit in the Jones lawsuit, and had taken actions designed to conceal evidence sought in that civil action.[2]

When the initial revelations about Clinton and Lewinsky had emerged months earlier, a Senate trial of the president seemed only a distant possibility. Americans did not clamor for Clinton's resignation or for impeachment. Republicans were not sure how far to take the Lewinsky matter. Three events had propelled the process forward. First, in September 1998, Independent Counsel Kenneth Starr delivered his report on Clinton to the House. Four years earlier, Starr had been hired to investigate allegations concerning the president's involvement in an Arkansas real estate development called Whitewater. Failing to turn up evidence of criminal wrongdoing in the Whitewater case, Starr refocused his investigation on the Lewinsky matter. The Starr report humiliated the president, making public salacious details of oral sex in the Oval Office taken from Ms. Lewinsky's grand jury testimony.

Second, as discussed later in this chapter, Republican congressional candidates did relatively poorly in the 1998 elections. Within a matter of days, Newt Gingrich was out as Speaker; GOP House members quickly coalesced around Louisiana's Bob Livingston as their next Speaker.[3] Within a matter of weeks Livingston was forced to resign the speakership—which he had yet to be formally elected to—because a news story revealed that he had been unfaithful to his wife. Dennis Hastert from Illinois was selected by Republicans to be their third Speaker in just a few months. Into this unstable leadership situation jumped Tom DeLay of Texas, who held the third-ranking position in the House party. DeLay, a virulent critic of Clinton and an effective and popular leader among Republicans, pushed and prodded his fellow House members to impeach the president.

Third, Hyde himself became a driving force behind impeachment. Unsure of himself at first, he failed in his efforts to build a bipartisan coalition in the Judiciary Committee.[4] This stood in stark contrast to the committee's response during Watergate, when a minority of the Republicans on the committee voted to recommend impeaching Nixon, a president of their own party. Adding to Hyde's frustration was the fact that the press had found out about a lengthy extramarital affair he had carried on in his forties. Hyde acknowledged the affair but dismissed it as a "youthful indiscretion." This remark invited ridicule and further undercut the impeachment effort: the Republicans lacked a congressional leader who could be seen as nonpartisan and command the respect necessary to guide the country to remove the president from office. Still, Hyde seized the moment after the election and worked with great diligence with other Republican members on the Judiciary Committee to push through the impeachment charges and to bring them to the floor for a vote by the full House of Representatives.

The party-line votes in the Judiciary Committee were repeated in the full House. By and large, Republicans voted for impeachment and Democrats against it. The House passed two of the four counts approved by the Judiciary Committee. Ostensibly, Hyde was the victor because he had successfully led the House to impeach the president—only the second time in history that that had happened. But though he had won the battle, he also knew that he had lost the war. Galling to the Republicans was the consistent support for the president in the public opinion polls. Just prior to the vote in the Senate, two-thirds of the public approved of Clinton's handling of his job as president while strongly disapproving of both Congress's handling of the impeachment process and of Special Prosecutor Starr.[5] The Senate needed a two-thirds majority to convict the president but could not muster even a simple majority for either count. The Clinton presidency survived.[6]

"I had a naive, utopian hope that as we documented the record, people who paid only passing attention would come to the conclusion that this was serious," said Hyde. "That never happened."[7] Hyde and his fellow Republicans believed that they had to act to preserve an appropriate moral

The President Must Stand Trial

On December 19, 1998, House Judiciary Chair Henry Hyde (right) led a delegation of Republican members of his committee to the Senate side of the Capitol. A trial of the president was formally initiated when Hyde handed the articles of impeachment adopted by the House to Gary Sisco, the secretary of the Senate (left). Hyde was a forceful advocate of impeachment, declaring that the House wanted "equal justice under the law, that's what we're fighting for."

code for the presidency. In their minds, Clinton and the Democrats were wrong to place so little value on preserving order. The American public, however, believed that the Republicans went too far and did not apply a proportionate punishment to the crime. In the end, Congress's final decision reflected the majority opinion (see Feature 11.1).

In the pages that follow, we'll examine more closely the relationship between members of Congress and their constituents, as well as the forces (such as political parties) that push legislators toward majoritarianism. We'll also focus on Congress's relations with the executive branch and analyze how the legislative process affects public policy. A starting point is to ask how the framers envisioned Congress.

THE ORIGIN AND POWERS OF CONGRESS

The framers of the Constitution wanted to keep power from being concentrated in the hands of a few, but they were also concerned with creating a union strong enough to overcome the weaknesses of the government that had operated under the Articles of Confederation. They argued passionately about the structure of the new government. In the end, they produced a legislative body that was as much of an experiment as the new nation's democracy.

The Great Compromise

The U.S. Congress has two separate and powerful chambers: the House of Representatives and the Senate. A bill cannot become law unless it is passed in identical form by both chambers. When drafting the Constitution during the summer of 1787, "the fiercest struggle for power" centered on representation in the legislature.[8] The small states wanted all the states to have equal representation. The more populous states wanted representation based on population; they did not want their power diluted. The Great Compromise broke the deadlock: the small states would receive equal representation in the Senate, but the number of each state's representatives in the House would be based on population, and the House would have the sole right to originate revenue-related legislation.

As the Constitution specifies, each state has two senators, and senators serve six-year terms of office. Terms are staggered, so that one-third of the Senate is elected every two years. When it was ratified, the Constitution directed that senators be chosen by the state legislatures. However, the Seventeenth Amendment, adopted in 1913, provided for the direct election of senators by popular vote. From the beginning, the people have directly elected members of the House of Representatives. They serve two-year terms, and all House seats are up for election at the same time.

There are 435 members of the House of Representatives. Because each state's representation in the House is in proportion to its population, the Constitution provides for a national census every ten years; population shifts are handled by the **reapportionment** (redistribution) of seats among the states after each census is taken. Since recent population growth has been centered in the Sunbelt, California, Texas, and Florida have gained seats while the Northeast and Midwest states have lost them. Each representative is elected from a particular congressional district within his or her state, and each district elects only one representative. The districts within a state must be roughly equal in population.

reapportionment
Redistribution of representatives among the states, based on population change. Congress is reapportioned after each census.

Duties of the House and Senate

Although the Great Compromise provided for considerably different schemes of representation for the House and Senate, the Constitution gives them similar legislative tasks. They share many important powers, among them the powers to declare war, raise an army and navy, borrow and coin money, regulate interstate commerce, create federal courts, establish rules for the naturalization of immigrants, and "make all Laws which shall be necessary and proper for carrying into Execution the foregoing Powers."

Of course, the constitutional duties of the two chambers are different in at least a few important ways. As noted earlier, the House alone has the right to originate revenue bills, a right that apparently was coveted at the Constitutional Convention. In practice, this power is of limited consequence because both the House and Senate must approve all bills—including revenue bills. As noted at the beginning of this chapter, the House of Representatives has the power of **impeachment,** the power formally to charge the president, vice president, and other "civil officers" of the national government with serious crimes. The Senate is empowered to act as a court to try impeachments, with the chief justice of the Supreme Court presiding. A two-thirds majority vote of the senators present is necessary for conviction. Prior to President Clinton's impeachment, only one sitting president, Andrew Johnson, had been impeached, and in 1868 the Senate came within a single vote of finding him guilty. The House Judiciary Committee voted to recommend impeachment of President Richard Nixon because of his involvement in the Watergate cover-up, but before the full House could vote, Nixon resigned from office.

impeachment
The formal charging of a government official with "treason, bribery, or other high crimes and misdemeanors."

The Constitution gives the Senate the power to approve major presidential appointments (such as to federal judgeships, ambassadorships, and cabinet posts) and treaties with foreign nations. The president is empowered to

feature 11.1

Was Impeachment the Best Way?

One of the most remarkable facets of the Clinton impeachment was that all of the major participants got burned by the fire. Even though he was eventually acquitted in the Senate, President Clinton was seriously and irreparably wounded by the impeachment. He is only the second American president to have been impeached by the House of Representatives. It is unclear how historians will ultimately judge the appropriateness of the House and Senate votes on Clinton's impeachment, but his affair with an intern half his age will forever tarnish his presidency.

Americans also judged Special Prosecutor Kenneth Starr harshly. Starr, a Republican, was never able to persuade the public that he was acting without partisan impulse. His self-righteous persona played poorly, and he seemed overly aggressive in his investigation, especially with tangential figures such as Monica Lewinsky's mother, whom he forced to testify against her daughter before a grand jury.

Leading Republican figures in Congress were hurt as well. Speaker Newt Gingrich resigned a few days after the Republicans' poor performance in the 1998 congressional election, which was widely regarded as a rebuke to the party for its efforts to impeach the president. As noted above, the party's chosen replacement, Bob Livingston, never actually became Speaker because shortly after his selection an article indicating that he had been unfaithful to his wife appeared. Livingston quickly resigned from Congress. Henry Hyde was greatly embarrassed by the revelations of his adultery, but he carried on in his position as Judiciary Committee chair. Trent Lott, the Senate majority leader, also received damaging publicity, with several articles noting that Lott had recently spoken before the Council of Conservative Citizens, a white supremacist organization. The *New Republic*, a liberal magazine, disclosed that House Whip Tom DeLay apparently had lied in a court deposition about his role in a pesticide company. Another Clinton antagonist, Georgia Representative Bob Barr, was embarrassed when it was revealed that he had paid for an abortion for one of his previous wives, even though he is an outspoken abortion opponent.

Republicans claimed that they were the subject of a witch hunt by journalists. To many Democrats it seemed like just retribution, given the unrelenting pursuit of Clinton by conservative publications and organizations throughout his presidency. Still, the Republicans are right in arguing that the press probably would not have pursued these stories had there been no GOP effort to impeach Clinton. For most Americans, the accusations of hypocrisy and immorality on both sides were further evidence of a political system gone awry.

The airing of politicians' personal lapses was only part of what contributed to Americans' frustration with the impeachment process. By the time the Senate voted to acquit the president, it had been more than a year since the Lewinsky story had first emerged. Most Americans wanted the impeachment to go away—and go away quickly. In fairness, the indictment and trial of a president should proceed not with speed but with all due deliberation, and Congress was right not to expedite the matter.

The broader issue, of course, is whether impeachment was the right instrument to deal with a

make treaties, but he must submit them to the Senate for approval by a two-thirds majority. Because of this requirement, the executive branch generally considers the Senate's sentiments when it negotiates a treaty. At times, a president must try to convince a doubting Senate of the worth of a particular treaty. Shortly after World War I, President Woodrow Wilson submitted to the Senate the Treaty of Versailles, which contained the

cover-up of a sexual indiscretion. Republicans were emphatic in pointing out that impeachment is the only tool the Constitution offers Congress for punishing the president. The Constitution lists "treason, bribery, or other high crimes and misdemeanors" as grounds for impeachment, but it offers no guidance as to what those terms mean.

Congressional Republicans believed that if Clinton was guilty of the allegations against him, those transgressions surely constituted "high crimes." We know that the framers were concerned about the abuse of power by the president and understood that it could take various forms. James Madison's account of the Constitutional Convention reports that Edmund Randolph, of Virginia, told his fellow delegates that "Guilt wherever found ought to be punished. The Executive will have great opportunity of abusing his power." Randolph's point was simple: no person should be above the law.

The framers were also concerned that the legislature might use its impeachment power unfairly to give it added leverage over the president. Charles Pinkney, of South Carolina, worried that impeachment would be used "as a rod over the Executive" and this could "effectually destroy his independence." In the end, however, the delegates felt that they needed to institute some provision for disciplining presidents who had committed serious crimes.

But if the need for an impeachment process is clear, the circumstances under which it should be set in motion remain murky. Aren't there other ways of disciplining a president outside of this constitutional provision? Conviction by the Senate requires that the president be removed from office, an extreme penalty for some transgressions. Many proposed that Congress censure Clinton, thus shaming him for his conduct but stopping short of this more dire punishment. Most Republicans in Congress believed censure was just a slap on the wrist and that legislators needed to do their constitutional duty by voting on impeachment.

Another possibility is to let the courts handle any alleged presidential transgressions that do not warrant impeachment. The Supreme Court ruled that President Clinton had to respond to the Paula Jones civil lawsuit while he was still in office. Some regard this as a troubling precedent because fighting the case was an enormous distraction for the president. One wag wondered what the costs to the nation would have been if Lincoln had been involved in a court suit when the Civil War broke out.

A related option is to let the courts deal with allegations against a president after he leaves office. However, this means justice will be delayed, as it would have been for Ms. Jones, who reached an out-of-court settlement with the president. After the Senate failed to convict Clinton, the Special Prosecutor's office raised the possibility of indicting him after he left office. However, on the day before his term ended, Clinton reached a plea agreement with the Special Prosecutor. In exchange for admitting that he had given false testimony, he was granted immunity from prosecution.

The dilemma that troubled the framers seems no easier to resolve today: how do we protect ourselves against presidents' violating the law without giving their opponents the opportunity to cripple them unfairly for political reasons?

charter for the proposed League of Nations. Wilson had attempted to convince the Senate that the treaty deserved its support; when the Senate refused to approve the treaty, Wilson suffered a severe setback.

Despite the long list of congressional powers stated in the Constitution, the question of what powers are appropriate for Congress has generated substantial controversy. For example, although the Constitution gives

figure

11.1   Incumbents: Life Is Good

Despite the public's dissatisfaction with Congress in general, incumbent representatives win reelection at an exceptional rate. Incumbent senators aren't quite as successful but still do well in reelection races. Voters seem to believe that their own representatives and senators don't share the same foibles that they attribute to the other members of Congress.

Sources: Norman J. Ornstein, Thomas E. Mann, and Michael J. Malbin, *Vital Statistics on Congress, 1999–2000* (Washington, D.C.: AEI Press, 2000), pp. 57–58; Emily Pierce, "Momentum Swing," *CQ Weekly*, 11 November 2000, pp. 2646–2647; and Gregory L. Giroux, "GOP Maintains Thin Edge," *CQ Weekly*, 11 November 2000, pp. 2652–2654.

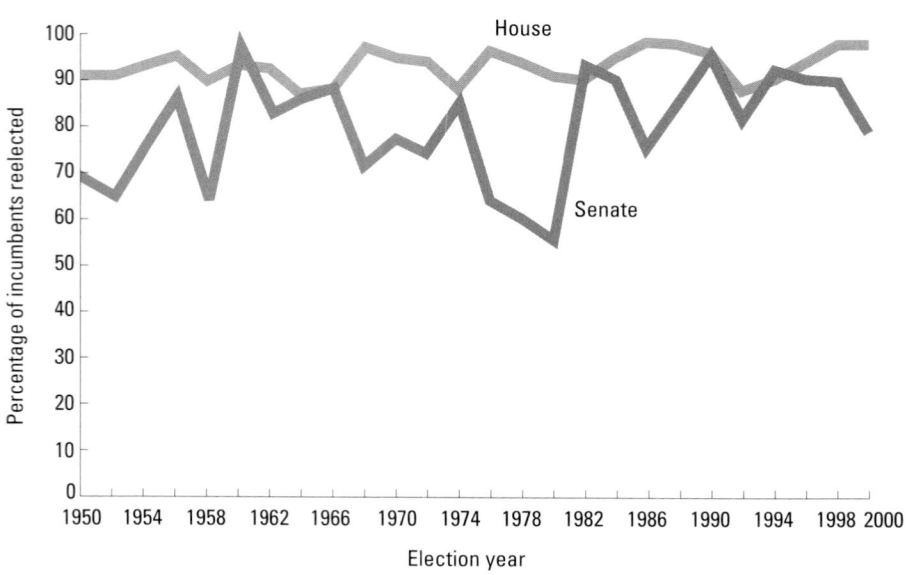

Congress the sole power to declare war, many presidents have initiated military action on their own. And at times, the courts have found that congressional actions have usurped the rights of the states.

ELECTING CONGRESS

If Americans are not happy with the job Congress is doing, they can use their votes to say so. With a congressional election every two years, the voters have frequent opportunities to express themselves.

The Incumbency Effect

incumbent
A current officeholder.

Can You Explain Why...
Americans hate the Congress but keep reelecting their own representative?

Congressional elections offer voters a chance to show their approval of Congress's performance, by reelecting **incumbents,** or to demonstrate their disapproval, by "throwing the rascals out." The voters do more reelecting than rascal throwing. The reelection rate is astonishingly high: in the majority of elections since 1950, more than 90 percent of all House incumbents have held on to their seats (see Figure 11.1). In some years, as few as a half-dozen incumbents have been defeated in the general election. Most House elections aren't even close; in recent elections, most House incumbents have won at least 60 percent of the vote. Senate elections are more competitive, but incumbents still have a high reelection rate.[9]

These findings may seem surprising, since the public does not hold Congress as a whole in particularly high esteem. Two-thirds of the American public tell pollsters that they disapprove of the job Congress is doing.[10] Close to 60 percent of Americans believe that at least half of all members of Congress are personally corrupt, a harsh indictment of the institution.[11] Although Americans feel disdain for Congress, they tend to distinguish the institution as a whole from their own members of Congress. Only 15 percent believe that their own representative is financially corrupt.[12] It is not entirely clear why Americans hate Congress so much given their satisfaction with their own members of the House and Senate. Scandals and campaign finance practices, especially the central role of political action committee (PAC) contributions, are another problem. Finally, American culture has traditionally held politicians in low esteem: we don't expect much from politicians, and we react sharply to their failings.[13]

Redistricting.   One explanation for the incumbency effect centers on redistricting, the way House districts are redrawn by state legislatures after a census-based reapportionment. It is entirely possible for them to draw the new districts to benefit the incumbents of one or both parties. Altering district lines for partisan advantage is commonly called **gerrymandering.**

gerrymandering
Redrawing a congressional district to intentionally benefit one political party.

But redistricting does not explain the incumbency effect in the House as a whole.[14] Redistricting may be very helpful for some incumbents, but it does not explain why more than 90 percent of House incumbents are routinely reelected. Nevertheless, politicians regard gerrymandering as an important factor in elections, and the political parties put considerable effort into trying to make sure that new boundaries are drawn in the most advantageous way.

Name Recognition.   Holding office brings with it some important advantages. First, incumbents develop significant name recognition among voters simply by being members of Congress. Congressional press secretaries help the name recognition advantage along through their efforts to get publicity for the activities and speeches of their bosses. The primary focus of such publicity seeking is on the local media back in the district—that's where the votes are. The local press, in turn, is eager to cover what local members of Congress are saying about the issues.

Another resource available to members of Congress is the *franking privilege*—the right to send mail free of charge. Mailings work to make constituents aware of their legislators' names, activities, and accomplishments. Periodic newsletters, for example, almost always highlight legislators' success at securing funds and projects for their district, such as money to construct a highway or a new federal building. Newsletters also "advertise for business," encouraging voters to phone or visit their legislators' district offices if they need help with a problem. Not surprisingly, legislators have taken advantage of the newest technology to extend their franking privilege. Rep. Bob Riley (R.-AL) recently sent a Christmas e-mail message to thousands of his constituents. When an accompanying icon was clicked, a short video featuring him appeared on the screen. Riley told viewers, "Hi. I'm Congressman Bob Riley. For my family, this is a special time of year . . . so I'd like to use this unique opportunity to wish you and your family all the best in the coming year."[15]

casework
Solving problems for constituents, especially problems involving government agencies.

Much of the work performed by the large staffs of members of Congress is **casework**—services for constituents such as tracking down a social security check or directing the owner of a small business to the appropriate federal agency. Constituents who are helped in this way usually remember who assisted them.

The Whip

Tom DeLay of Texas is the Republican majority whip in the House of Representatives, the third-ranking position in the party's House leadership hierarchy. DeLay's job as whip is to count votes on upcoming bills and to mobilize his fellow Republicans behind legislation favored by the party's leadership. He's a divisive figure, greatly admired by Republicans for his effectiveness and despised by Democrats, who regard him as excessively partisan.

Campaign Financing. It should be clear that anyone who wants to challenge an incumbent needs solid financial backing. Challengers must spend large sums of money to run a strong campaign with an emphasis on advertising—an expensive but effective way to bring their name and record to the voters' attention. But here, too, the incumbent has the advantage. Challengers find raising campaign funds difficult because they have to overcome contributors' doubts about whether they can win. In the 1998 elections, incumbents raised 68.5 percent of all money contributed to campaigns for election to the House. Only 19.2 percent went to challengers. (Those running for open seats received the rest.) Challengers to Senate incumbents did much better than their House counterparts, though still not nearly as well as the incumbents. Senate challengers received roughly one-third of all funds, compared with 55 percent for incumbents.[16]

PACs show a strong preference for incumbents (see Chapter 10). They tend not to want to risk offending an incumbent by giving money to a longshot challenger. The attitude of the American Medical Association's PAC is fairly typical. "We have a friendly incumbent policy," says its director. "We always stick with the incumbent if we agree with both candidates."[17] Over time, the financial advantage of incumbents over challengers has increased. The main reason is the "sophomore surge" as PACs rush to support the newest members when they prepare to run as incumbents for the first time.[18]

Successful Challengers. Clearly, the deck is stacked against challengers. As one analyst put it, "The typical House challenger is in a position similar to that of a novice athlete pitted against a world-class sprinter."[19] Yet some challengers do beat incumbents. How? The opposing party and unsympathetic PACs may target incumbents who seem vulnerable because of age, lack of seniority, a scandal, or unfavorable redistricting. Some incumbents appear vulnerable because they were elected by a narrow margin, or the ideological and partisan composition of their district does not favor their holding the seat. Vulnerable incumbents also bring out higher-quality challengers—individuals who have held elective office and are capable of raising adequate campaign funds. Such experienced challengers

Women of the Senate

Women are still far short of parity in representation in the Congress, but they have gained influence as their numbers and seniority have increased. The female members of the Senate at the beginning of 2001 are (from top left and around the circle): Blanche Lincoln (D.-AR), Jean Carnahan (D.-MO), Susan Collins (R.-ME), Patty Murray (D.-WA), Hillary Rodham Clinton (D.-NY), Kay Bailey Hutchison (R.-TX), Barbara Mikulski (D.-MD), Dianne Feinstein (D.-CA), Olympia Snowe (R.-ME), Barbara Boxer (D.-CA), Debbie Stabenow (D.-MI), Maria Cantwell (D.-WA), and Mary Landrieu (D.-LA).

Party Strength

are more likely to defeat incumbents than are amateurs with little background in politics.[20] The reason Senate challengers have a higher success rate than House challengers is that they are generally higher-quality candidates. Often they are governors or members of the House who enjoy high name recognition and can attract significant campaign funds because they are regarded as credible candidates.[21]

2000 Election. The prelude to the 2000 House and Senate elections was the highly unusual congressional election in 1998. The party controlling the White House—in this case, the Democrats—almost always loses House seats in the midterm election, as voters take out their disappointments with the president on candidates from his party. The president's party usually loses seats in the Senate too. In the previous midterm election (1994), the Republicans gained fifty-two House seats, almost twice the average pickup for the party not in control of the White House. The 1998 election also looked bad for the Democrats because of the Clinton-Lewinsky scandal. When the votes were counted, the results were stunning. The Democrats actually picked up five seats in the House and there was no overall change in the Senate. Due to the widespread expectation of Republican gains, the outcome was widely interpreted as a stinging defeat for the GOP.

Buoyed by their success in the 1998 election, the Democrats hoped to gain the seven seats they needed to give them a majority in the House of Representatives. The party faced a much bigger challenge in the Senate, where they needed a swing of five votes to give them a 51–49 majority in that chamber. They would have to defeat several Republican incumbents and take some open seats, while not losing many incumbent senators of their own.

The 2000 election was a bitter disappointment for House Democrats who, with peace and prosperity at their backs, managed to pick up just two seats. This left the Republicans in control by a slim 221–212 margin. (Two other members are independents.) Just six House incumbents lost their seats in the general election. In the Senate, the Democrats swept aside five Republican incumbents while losing just one of their own. The two parties ended up in a remarkable 50–50 tie, a shocking outcome for the Republicans, who expected to fare much better.

Since a Republican captured the presidency, House Democrats look forward to the midterm 2002 elections, when they hope that there will be a return to power with the usual pattern of the opposition party picking up seats. Of the one-third of the Senators who are up for reelection in 2002, there are many more Republicans whose terms are up than Democrats. If the deteriorating economic trends in 2001 continue, they will pose a problem for the Republicans in the 2002 elections.

Whom Do We Elect?

The people we elect (then reelect) to Congress are not a cross-section of American society. Most members of Congress are professionals—primarily lawyers, businesspeople, and educators.[22] Although nearly a third of the American labor force works in blue-collar jobs, someone currently employed as a blue-collar worker rarely wins a congressional nomination.

Women and minorities have long been underrepresented in elective office, although both groups have recently increased their representation in Congress significantly. There are currently fifty-nine women in the House of Representatives (14 percent), thirty-five African Americans (8 percent), and nineteen Hispanics (4 percent).[23] Other members of Congress don't necessarily ignore the concerns of women and minorities.[24] Yet many women and minorities believe that only members of their own group—people who have experienced what they have experienced—can truly represent their interests. This is a belief in **descriptive representation,** the view that a legislature should resemble the demographic characteristics of the population it represents.[25] (See Compared with What? 11.1 for a comparison of the representation of women in the world's national legislatures.)

During the 1980s, both Congress and the Supreme Court provided support for the principle of descriptive representation for blacks and Hispanic Americans. When Congress amended the Voting Rights Act in 1982, it encouraged the states to draw districts that concentrated minorities together, so blacks and Hispanic Americans would have a better chance of being elected to office. Supreme Court decisions also pushed the states to concentrate minorities in House districts.[26] After the 1990 census, states redrew House boundaries with the intent of creating districts with majority or near-majority minority populations. Some districts were very oddly shaped, snaking through their state to pick up black neighborhoods in various cities but leaving adjacent white neighborhoods to other districts. This effort led to a roughly 50 percent increase in the number of blacks elected to the House. Hispanic representation in the House also increased after redistricting created new districts with large concentrations of Hispanic American voters.

In a decision that surprised many, the Supreme Court ruled in 1993 that states' efforts to increase minority representation through **racial gerrymandering** could violate the rights of whites. In *Shaw* v. *Reno*, the majority ruled in a split decision that a North Carolina district that meandered

descriptive representation
A belief that constituents are most effectively represented by legislators who are similar to them in such key demographic characteristics as race, ethnicity, religion, or gender.

racial gerrymandering
The drawing of a legislative district to maximize the chances that a minority candidate will win election.

Shaw *v.* Reno

11.1 Women in Legislatures

The percentage of women in the world's national legislatures differs considerably from one country to another. Although the Western democracies have some of the highest percentages of women legislators, there is substantial variation here, too. For example, Sweden has over 40 percent women in its legislature, Italy has 15 percent, and Japan has less than 5 percent. The number of women does not seem to be a function of the structure of the legislature or the party system in these countries. Countries that are not democracies vary considerably as well. Clearly, each society's cultural expectations about the role of women are of paramount importance. The Scandinavian countries appear to be the most open to the full participation of women in politics.

Source: Inter-Parliamentary Union, on-line, updated May 15, 1998. <www.ipu.org/english/home.htm>

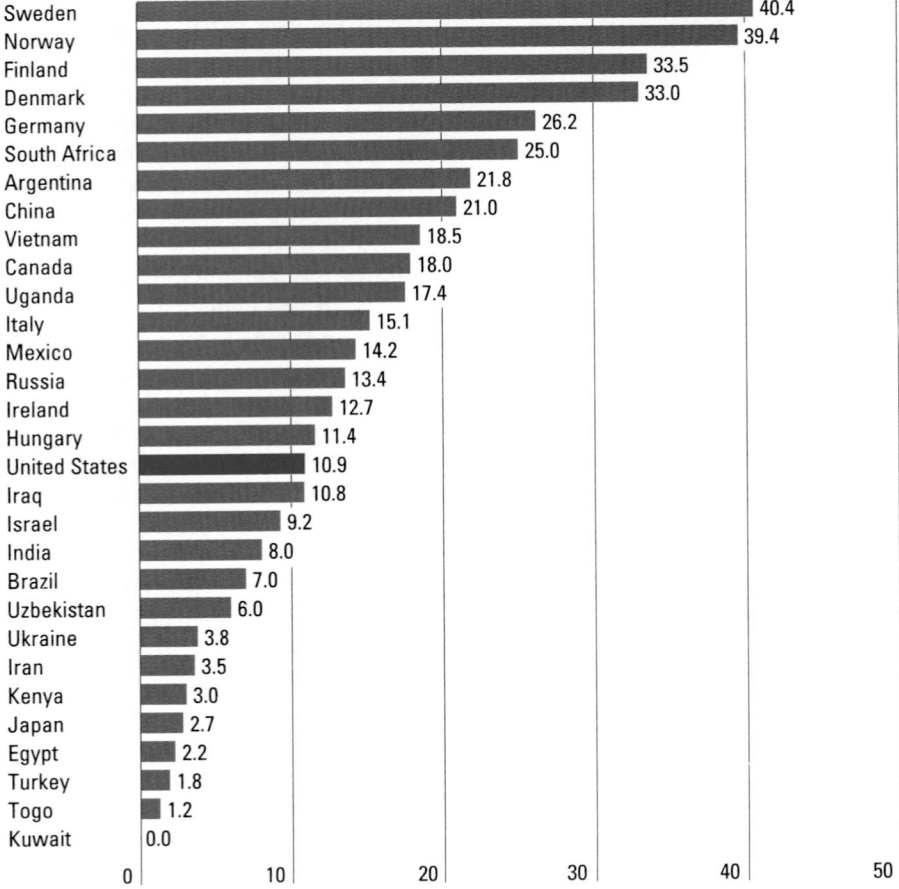

Percentage of women in lower house or single house

Country	Percentage
Sweden	40.4
Norway	39.4
Finland	33.5
Denmark	33.0
Germany	26.2
South Africa	25.0
Argentina	21.8
China	21.0
Vietnam	18.5
Canada	18.0
Uganda	17.4
Italy	15.1
Mexico	14.2
Russia	13.4
Ireland	12.7
Hungary	11.4
United States	10.9
Iraq	10.8
Israel	9.2
India	8.0
Brazil	7.0
Uzbekistan	6.0
Ukraine	3.8
Iran	3.5
Kenya	3.0
Japan	2.7
Egypt	2.2
Turkey	1.8
Togo	1.2
Kuwait	0.0

160 miles from Durham to Charlotte was an example of "political apartheid." (In some places, the Twelfth District was no wider than Interstate 85.) In effect, the Court ruled that racial gerrymandering segregated blacks from whites instead of creating districts built around contiguous communities.[27] In a 1995 case, *Miller* v. *Johnson*, the Supreme Court went even further in restricting the force of the Voting Rights Act. The Court's majority said that states should not draw district boundaries where race is the "predominant factor."[28] Thus, it is not merely the shape of the district that is suspect but the very intent to draw districts to favor an ethnic or racial group. If equality requires descriptive representation, then the Court's direction to states to move away from racial gerrymandering is a retreat from equality in Congress. In a later decision, the Supreme Court ruled that the "intensive and pervasive use of race" to protect incumbents and to promote political gerrymandering violated the Fourteenth Amendment and Voting Rights Act of 1965.[29]

Ironically, spreading black and Hispanic voters around more districts, rather than concentrating them in a relatively small number of them, might actually increase their influence. More representatives will have significant numbers of minority voters in their district and will have to consider their views as they contemplate their stand on the issues. Likewise, the Court decisions will probably have a small, but negative, effect on Republican electoral fortunes in the House. The GOP has benefited from having black and Hispanic voters, who are overwhelmingly Democratic, concentrated in districts designed to elect minority representatives. This has left the remaining districts not merely "whiter" but also more Republican than they would have otherwise been.[30]

The full force of these Supreme Court decisions will not be felt until the 2002 congressional elections. With the census complete at the end of the decade, states can now reapportion their House seats with their new population figures. Still, it is unclear just how much impact the new redistricting will have on minority representation. Many districts represented by African Americans or Hispanics already conform to recent Court decisions. Other minority representatives may win reelection even if newly drawn boundaries reduce the percentage of blacks and Hispanics living in their districts.

HOW ISSUES GET ON THE CONGRESSIONAL AGENDA

The formal legislative process begins when a member of Congress introduces a *bill*, a proposal for a new law. In the House, members drop bills in the "hopper," a mahogany box near the rostrum where the Speaker presides. Senators give their bills to a Senate clerk or introduce them from the floor.[31] But before a bill can be introduced to solve a problem, someone must perceive that a problem exists or that an issue needs to be resolved. In other words, the problem or issue somehow must find its way onto the congressional agenda. *Agenda* actually has two meanings in the vocabulary of political scientists. The first is that of a narrow, formal agenda, such as a calendar of bills to be voted on. The second meaning refers to the broad, imprecise, and unwritten agenda comprising all the issues an institution is considering. Here we use the term in the second, broader sense.

Many issues Congress is working on at any given time seem to have been around forever. Foreign aid, the national debt, and social security have come up in just about every recent session of Congress. Other issues emerge more suddenly, especially those that are the product of technological change. Genetically altered foods have recently become a controversial issue not only in the United States but around the world as well. In the Congress, consumer advocates have introduced legislation to require labeling of bioengineered food products. Members from farm areas have commissioned reports to show that such foods are safe. Once the technology was utilized to alter crops and food products, it was inevitable that Congress would have to place such a controversial issue on its agenda.[32]

New issues reach the congressional agenda in many ways. Sometimes a highly visible event focuses national attention on a problem. An explosion in a West Virginia mine in 1968 killed seventy-eight miners; Congress promptly went to work on laws to promote miners' safety.[33] Presidential support can also move an issue onto the agenda quickly. The media attention paid to the president gives him enormous opportunity to draw the nation's attention to problems he believes need some form of government action.

Within Congress, party leaders and committee chairs have the opportunity to move issues onto the agenda, but they rarely act capriciously, seizing upon issues without rhyme or reason. They often bide their time, waiting for other members of Congress to learn about an issue as they attempt to gauge the level of support for some kind of action. At times, the efforts of an interest group spark support for action, or at least awareness of an issue. When congressional leaders—or, for that matter, rank-and-file members—sense that the time is ripe for action on a new issue, they often are spurred on by the knowledge that sponsoring an important bill can enhance their own image. In the words of one observer, "Congress exists to do things. There isn't much mileage in doing nothing."[34]

THE DANCE OF LEGISLATION: AN OVERVIEW

The process of writing bills and getting them enacted is relatively simple, in the sense that it follows a series of specific steps. What complicates the process is the many different ways legislation can be treated at each step. Here, we examine the straightforward process by which laws are made. In the next few sections, we discuss some of the complexities of that process.

After a bill is introduced in either house, it is assigned to the committee with jurisdiction over that policy area (see Figure 11.2). A banking bill, for example, would be assigned to the Banking and Financial Services Committee in the House or to the Banking, Housing, and Urban Affairs Committee in the Senate. When a committee actively considers a piece of legislation assigned to it, the bill is usually referred to a specialized subcommittee. The subcommittee may hold hearings, and legislative staffers may do research on the bill. The original bill usually is modified or revised; if passed in some form, it is sent to the full committee. A bill approved by the full committee is reported (that is, sent) to the entire membership of the chamber, where it may be debated, amended, and either passed or defeated.

Bills coming out of House committees go to the Rules Committee before going before the full House membership. The Rules Committee attaches a rule to the bill that governs the coming floor debate, typically specifying the length of the debate and the types of amendments House members can offer. On major legislation, most rules are complex and quite

figure

11.2   The Legislative Process

The process by which a bill becomes law is subject to much variation. This diagram depicts the typical process a bill might follow. It is important to remember that a bill can fail at any stage because of lack of support.

HOUSE

Bill is introduced and assigned to a committee, which refers it to the appropriate . . .

Subcommittee
Subcommittee members study the bill, hold hearings, and debate provisions. If a bill is approved, it goes to the . . .

Committee
Full committee considers the bill. If the bill is approved in some form, it goes to the . . .

Rules Committee
Rules Committee issues a rule to govern debate on the floor. Sends it to the . . .

Full House
Full House debates the bill and may amend it. If the bill passes and is in a form different from the Senate version, it must go to a . . .

SENATE

Bill is introduced and assigned to a committee, which refers it to the appropriate . . .

Subcommittee
Subcommittee members study the bill, hold hearings, and debate provisions. If a bill is approved, it goes to the . . .

Committee
Full committee considers the bill. If the bill is approved in some form, it goes to the . . .

Full Senate
Full Senate debates the bill and may amend it. If the bill passes and is in a form different from the House version, it must go to a . . .

Conference Committee
Conference committee of senators and representatives meets to reconcile differences between bills. When agreement is reached, a compromise bill is sent back to both the . . .

Full House
House votes on the conference committee bill. If it passes in both houses, it goes to the . . .

Full Senate
Senate votes on the conference committee bill. If it passes in both houses, it goes to the . . .

President
President signs or vetoes the bill. Congress can override a veto by a two-thirds majority vote in both the House and Senate.

restrictive in terms of any amendments that can be offered. The Senate does not have a comparable committee, although restrictions on the length of floor debate can be reached through unanimous consent agreements (see the "Rules of Procedure" section later in the chapter).

Even if both houses of Congress pass a bill on the same subject, the Senate and House versions are typically different from each other. In that case, a conference committee, composed of legislators from both houses, works out the differences and develops a compromise version. This version goes back to both houses for another floor vote. If both chambers approve the bill, it goes to the president for his signature or veto.

When the president signs a bill, it becomes law. If the president **vetoes** (disapproves) the bill, he sends it back to Congress with his reasons for rejecting it. The bill becomes law only if Congress overrides the president's veto by a two-thirds vote in each house. If the president neither signs nor vetoes the bill within ten days (Sundays excepted) of receiving it, the bill becomes law. There is an exception here: if Congress adjourns within the ten days, the president can let the bill die through a **pocket veto,** by not signing it.

The content of a bill can be changed at any stage of the process in either house. Lawmaking (and thus policymaking) in Congress has many access points for those who want to influence legislation. This openness tends to fit within the pluralist model of democracy. As a bill moves through the dance of legislation,[35] it is amended again and again, in a search for a consensus that will get it enacted and signed into law. The process can be tortuously slow, and it is often fruitless. Derailing legislation is much easier than enacting it. The process gives groups frequent opportunities to voice their preferences and, if necessary, thwart their opponents. One foreign ambassador stationed in Washington aptly described the twists and turns of our legislative process this way: "In the Congress of the U.S., it's never over until it's over. And when it's over, it's still not over."[36]

veto
The president's disapproval of a bill that has been passed by both houses of Congress. Congress can override a veto with a two-thirds vote in each house.

pocket veto
A means of killing a bill that has been passed by both houses of Congress, in which the president does not sign the bill and Congress adjourns within ten days of the bill's passage.

COMMITTEES: THE WORKHORSES OF CONGRESS

Woodrow Wilson once observed that "Congress in session is Congress on public exhibition, whilst Congress in its committee-rooms is Congress at work."[37] His words are as true today as when he wrote them more than one hundred years ago. A speech on the Senate floor, for example, may convince the average citizen, but it is less likely to influence other senators. Indeed, few of them may even hear it. The real nuts and bolts of lawmaking go on in the congressional committees.

The Division of Labor Among Committees

The House and Senate are divided into committees for the same reason that other large organizations are broken into departments or divisions—to develop and use expertise in specific areas. At IBM, for example, different groups of people design computers, write software, assemble hardware, and sell the company's products. Each task requires an expertise that may have little to do with the others. Likewise, in Congress, decisions on weapons systems require a special knowledge that is of little relevance to decisions on reimbursement formulas for health insurance, for example. It makes sense for some members of Congress to spend more time examining defense issues, becoming increasingly expert on the topic as they do so, while others concentrate on health matters.

Eventually, all members of Congress have to vote on each bill that emerges from the committees. Those who are not on a particular committee depend on committee members to examine the issues thoroughly, to make compromises as necessary, and to bring forward a sound piece of legislation that has a good chance of being passed. Each member decides individually on the bill's merits. But once it reaches the House or Senate floor, members may get to vote on only a handful of amendments (if any at all) before they must cast their yea or nay for the entire bill.

Standing Committees.   There are several different kinds of congressional committees, but the **standing committee** is predominant. Standing committees are permanent committees that specialize in a particular area of legislation—for example, the House Judiciary Committee or the Senate Environment and Public Works Committee. Most of the day-to-day work of drafting legislation takes place in the eighteen standing Senate committees and twenty standing House committees. Typically, sixteen to twenty senators serve on each standing Senate committee, and an average of forty-two members serve on each standing committee in the House. The proportions of Democrats and Republicans on a standing committee are controlled by the majority party in each house. The majority party gives the minority a percentage of seats that, in theory, approximates the minority party's percentage in the entire chamber. However, the majority party usually gives itself enough of a cushion to ensure that it can control each committee. With the Senate at the beginning of the 107th Congress tied at fifty members for each party, Democrats asked for half the seats of each committee. Republicans claimed that they were really in the majority because Republican Vice President Dick Cheney is, constitutionally, the presiding officer of the Senate. In the end, the Democrats received half of each committee's seats but the ranking Republican got to be chairman.

With a few exceptions, standing committees are further broken down into subcommittees. The House Agriculture Committee, for example, has five subcommittees, among them one on specialty crops and another on livestock, dairy, and poultry. Subcommittees exist for the same reason parent committees exist: members acquire expertise by continually working within the same fairly narrow policy area. Typically, members of the subcommittee are the dominant force in the shaping of the content of a bill.[38]

Other Congressional Committees.   Members of Congress can also serve on joint, select, and conference committees. **Joint committees** are composed of members of both the House and the Senate. Like standing committees, the small number of joint committees are concerned with particular policy areas. The Joint Economic Committee, for instance, analyzes the country's economic policies. Joint committees are much weaker than standing committees because they are almost always restricted from reporting bills to the House or Senate. Thus, their role is usually that of fact-finding and publicizing problems and policy issues that fall within their jurisdiction.

A **select committee** is a temporary committee created for a specific purpose. Congress establishes select committees to deal with special circum-

standing committee
A permanent congressional committee that specializes in a particular legislative area.

joint committee
A committee made up of members of both the House and the Senate.

select committee
A temporary congressional committee created for a specific purpose and disbanded after that purpose is fulfilled.

stances or with issues that either overlap or fall outside the areas of expertise of standing committees. The Senate committee that investigated the Watergate scandal, for example, was a select committee, created for that purpose only.

A **conference committee** is also a temporary committee, created to work out differences between the House and Senate versions of a specific piece of legislation. Its members are appointed from the standing committees or subcommittees, from each house, that originally handled and reported the legislation. Depending on the nature of the differences and the importance of the legislation, a conference committee may meet for hours or for weeks on end. The conference committee for a complex defense bill had to resolve 2,003 separate differences between the two versions.[39] When the conference committee reaches a compromise, it reports the bill to both houses, which must then either approve or disapprove the compromise; they cannot amend or change it in any way. Only about 15 to 25 percent of all bills that eventually pass Congress go to a conference committee (although virtually all important or controversial bills do).[40] Committee or subcommittee leaders of both houses reconcile differences in other bills through informal negotiation.

conference committee
A temporary committee created to work out differences between the House and Senate versions of a specific piece of legislation.

Congressional Expertise and Seniority

Once appointed to a committee, a representative or senator has great incentive to remain on it and to gain expertise over the years. Influence in Congress increases with a member's expertise. Influence also grows in a more formal way, with **seniority,** or years of consecutive service, on a committee. In their quest for expertise and seniority, members tend to stay on the same committees. However, sometimes they switch places when they are offered the opportunity to move to one of the high-prestige committees (such as Ways and Means in the House or Finance in the Senate) or to a committee that handles legislation of vital importance to their constituents.

seniority
Years of consecutive service on a particular congressional committee.

Within each committee, the senior member of the majority party usually becomes the committee chair. Other senior members of the majority party become subcommittee chairs, whereas their counterparts from the minority party gain influence as ranking minority members. In the House and Senate combined, there are over 150 subcommittees, offering multiple opportunities for power and status. Unlike seniority, expertise does not follow simply from length of service. Ability and effort are critical factors, too. Senator Pete Domenici (R.-NM) has been a student of fiscal matters since he entered the Senate in 1973. As chair of the Senate Budget Committee during the Reagan years, when budget issues were at the center of national politics, he earned the respect of his peers for his considerable expertise in such a complex area of public policy. Today, he continues to exert considerable influence on budget matters because of the expertise he developed over the years.

After the Republicans gained control of the House in 1994, Speaker of the House Newt Gingrich made a major break with the seniority system by rejecting three Republicans who were in line to become committee chairs. Speakers had not appointed House committee chairs in this fashion since the first part of this century, when "Uncle Joe" Cannon ruled the

The Taxman Cometh

Congressional hearings are often staged like dramas, with villains' evil doings uncovered at the witness table by crusading heroes on the committee. When the Senate investigated alleged abuses by the Internal Revenue Service in 1997, it was especially easy to provide a bit of congressional theater. Legislators portrayed the agency's tax collectors as petty tyrants and ordinary, hard-working citizens as virtuous victims of a heartless bureaucracy. Pictured here is Nancy Jacobs of Bakersfield, California, who testified about her family's seventeen-year battle with the IRS over a debt owed by someone with a similar name.

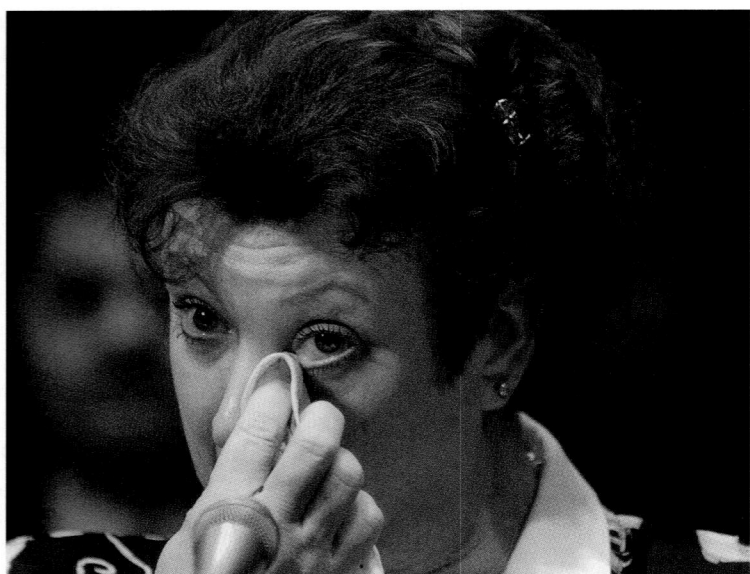

chamber with an iron fist.[41] Gingrich also instituted term limits for committee and subcommittee chairs, restricting their tenure to six years. House Republicans have continued with these policies and in January 2001, Speaker Hastert and his Steering Committee passed over members with the highest committee seniority to fill some vacant chairmanships. Marge Roukema of New Jersey, considered to be too moderate, was denied the chairmanship of the newly expanded banking committee. The job, instead, went to the less senior Michael Oxley of Ohio.

The way in which committees and subcommittees are led and organized within Congress is significant because much public policy decision making takes place there. The first step in drafting legislation is to collect information on the issue. Committee staffers research the problem, and committees hold hearings to take testimony from witnesses who have some special knowledge of the subject.

At times, committee hearings are more theatrical than informational, to draw public attention to them. When the House Judiciary Subcommittee on Administrative Law held hearings on alleged malpractice in military hospitals, for example, it did not restrict its list of witnesses to experts who had done relevant research. Instead, it called witnesses such as Dawn Lambert, a former member of the navy, who sobbed as she told the subcommittee that she had been left sterile by a misdiagnosis and a botched operation that had left a sponge and a green marker inside her. It was an irresistible story for the evening news, and it brought the malpractice problem in the military to light.[42]

The meetings at which subcommittees and committees actually debate and amend legislation are called *markup sessions.* The process by which committees reach decisions varies. Many committees have a strong tradition of deciding by consensus. The chair, the ranking minority member, and others in these committees work hard, in formal committee sessions and in informal negotiations, to find a middle ground on issues that divide committee members. In other committees, members exhibit strong ideological and partisan sentiments. However, committee and subcommittee leaders prefer to find ways to overcome inherent ideological and partisan divisions so that they can build compromise solutions that will appeal to the broader membership of their house. The skill of committee leaders in assembling coalitions that produce legislation that can pass on the floor of their house is critically important. When committees are mired in disagreement, they lose power. Since jurisdictions overlap, other committees may take more initiative in their common policy area. Committee disagreements also enhance the power of the executive branch, especially in foreign and defense policy, where the president has considerable latitude.[43]

Oversight: Following Through on Legislation

It is often said in Washington that knowledge is power. For Congress to retain its influence over the programs it creates, it must be aware of how the agencies responsible for them are administering them. To that end, legislators and their committees engage in **oversight,** the process of reviewing agencies' operations to determine whether they are carrying out policies as Congress intended.

oversight
The process of reviewing the operations of an agency to determine whether it is carrying out policies as Congress intended.

As the executive branch has grown and policies and programs have become increasingly complex, oversight has become more difficult. The sheer magnitude of executive branch operations is staggering. On a typical weekday, for example, agencies issue more than a hundred pages of new regulations. Even with the division of labor in the committee system, determining how good a job an agency is doing in implementing a program is no easy task.

Congress performs its oversight function in several different ways. The most visible is the hearing. Hearings may be part of a routine review or the by-product of information that reveals a major problem with a program or with an agency's administrative practices. Another way Congress keeps track of what departments and agencies are doing is by requesting reports on specific agency practices and operations. When President Clinton requested funds to help pay for the reconstruction of Bosnia, the chair of the Appropriations Subcommittee on Foreign Operations was willing to grant the money only if a key condition was met by the administration. Disturbed that Iranian soldiers who had come to fight on behalf of the Muslim population of Bosnia were still there after the peace accord was in place, the subcommittee chair insisted that the appropriations bill be amended to pressure the administration to take action. President Clinton was to report back to the committee and the Senate to certify that the Iranians had left. No money could be spent on Bosnian reconstruction until the committee received the certification.[44] But not all oversight is so formal or so mistrustful. A good deal of congressional oversight takes place informally, as there are ongoing contacts between committee and subcommittee leaders and agency administrators as well as between committee staffers and top agency staffers.

Congressional oversight of the executive branch has increased sharply since the early 1970s.[45] A primary reason for this increase is that Congress has given itself the staff necessary to watch over the growing federal government. In addition to significantly expanding the staffs of individual legislators and of House and Senate committees, Congress enhanced its analytical capabilities by creating the Congressional Budget Office and by strengthening the Government Accounting Office (GAO) and the Congressional Research Service of the Library of Congress.

Oversight is often stereotyped as a process in which angry legislators bring some administrators before the hot lights and television cameras at a hearing and proceed to dress them down for some recent scandal or mistake. Some of this does go on, but the pluralist side of Congress makes it likely that at least some members of a committee are advocates of the programs they oversee because those programs serve their constituents back home. Members of the House and Senate Agriculture Committees, for example, both Democrats and Republicans, want farm programs to succeed. Thus, most oversight is aimed at trying to find ways to improve programs and is not directed at efforts to discredit them.[46]

Majoritarian and Pluralist Views of Committees

Government by committee vests a tremendous amount of power in the committees and subcommittees of Congress—and especially their leaders. This is particularly true in the House, which has more decentralized patterns of influence than the Senate and is more restrictive about letting members amend legislation on the floor. Committee members can bury a bill by not reporting it to the full House or Senate. The influence of committee members extends even further, to the floor debate. Many of them also make up the conference committees charged with developing compromise versions of bills.

In some ways, the committee system enhances the force of pluralism in American politics. Representatives and senators are elected by the voters in their particular districts and states, and they tend to seek membership on the committees that make the decisions most important to their constituents. Members from farm areas, for example, want membership on the House and Senate Agriculture Committees. Westerners like to serve on the committees that deal with public lands and water rights. Urban liberals like the committees that handle social programs. As a result, committee members tend to represent constituencies with an unusually strong interest in the committee's policy area and are predisposed to write legislation favorable to those constituencies.

The committees have a majoritarian aspect as well. Although some committees have a surplus or shortage of legislators from particular kinds of districts or states, most committee members reflect the general ideological profiles of the two parties' congressional contingents. For example, Republicans on individual House committees tend to vote like all Republicans in the House. Moreover, even if a committee's views are not in line with those of the full membership, it is constrained in the legislation it writes because bills cannot become law unless they are passed by the parent chamber and by the other house. Consequently, in formulating legislation, committees anticipate what other representatives and senators will accept. The parties within each chamber also have means of rewarding members who are the most loyal to party priorities. Party committees and the party leadership within each chamber make committee assignments and respond to requests for transfers from less prestigious to more prestigious committees. Those who vote in line with the party get better assignments.[47]

LEADERS AND FOLLOWERS IN CONGRESS

Above the committee chairs is another layer of authority in the organization of the House and Senate. The Democratic and Republican leaders in each house work to maximize the influence of their own party while trying to keep their chamber functioning smoothly and efficiently. The operation of the two houses is also influenced by the rules and norms that each chamber has developed over the years.

The Leadership Task

Each of the two parties elects leaders in each of the two houses. In the House of Representatives, the majority party's leader is the **Speaker of the House,** who, gavel in hand, chairs sessions from the ornate rostrum at the front of the chamber. The Speaker's counterpart in the opposing party is the minority leader. The Speaker is a constitutional officer, but the Constitution does not list the Speaker's duties. The minority leader is not mentioned in the Constitution, but that post has evolved into an important party position in the House.

The Constitution makes the vice president of the United States the president of the Senate. But in practice the vice president rarely visits the Senate chamber, unless there is a possibility of a tie vote, in which case he can break the tie. The *president pro tempore* (president "for the time"), elected by the majority party, is supposed to chair the Senate in the vice president's absence, but by custom this constitutional position is entirely honorary.

The real power in the Senate resides in the **majority leader.** As in the House, the top position in the opposing party is that of minority leader. Technically, the majority leader does not preside over Senate sessions (members rotate in the president pro tempore's chair), but he or she does schedule legislation, in consultation with the minority leader. More broadly, party leaders play a critical role in getting bills through Congress. The most significant function that leaders play is steering the bargaining and negotiating over the content of legislation. When an issue divides their party, their house, the two houses, or their house and the White House, the leaders must take the initiative to work out a compromise.

Day in, day out, much of what leaders do is to meet with other members of their house to try to strike deals that will yield a majority on the floor. It is often a matter of finding out whether one faction is willing to give up a policy preference in exchange for another concession. Beyond trying to engineer tradeoffs that will win votes, the party leaders must persuade others (often powerful committee chairs) that theirs is the best deal possible. After serving his first years as Senate majority leader, Bob Dole (R.-KS) said he thought "majority pleader" was a more apt title.[48]

As recently as the 1950s, strong leaders dominated the legislative process. When he was Senate majority leader, Lyndon Johnson made full use of his intelligence, parliamentary skills, and forceful personality to direct the Senate. When he approached individual senators for one-on-one persuasion, "no one subjected to the 'Johnson treatment' ever forgot it."[49] In the contemporary Congress, however, it has been difficult for leaders to control rank-and-file members because they have independent electoral bases in their districts and states and receive the vast bulk of their campaign funds from nonparty sources. "There are no followers here," notes one observer.[50] Contemporary party leaders are coalition builders, not autocrats.

Speaker of the House
The presiding officer of the House of Representatives.

majority leader
The head of the majority party in the Senate; the second highest ranking member of the majority party in the House.

The Johnson Treatment

When he was Senate majority leader in the 1950s, Lyndon Johnson was well known for his style of interaction with other members. In this unusual set of photographs, we see him applying the "Johnson treatment" to Democrat Theodore Francis Green of Rhode Island. Washington journalists Rowland Evans and Robert Novak offered the following description of the treatment: "Its tone could be supplication, accusation, cajolery, exuberance, scorn, tears, complaint, the hint of threat. It was all of these together. It ran the gamut of human emotions. Its velocity was breathtaking and it was all in one direction. Interjections from the target were rare. Johnson anticipated them before they could be spoken. He moved in close, his face a scant millimeter from his target, his eyes widening and narrowing, his eyebrows rising and falling. From his pockets poured clippings, memos, statistics. Mimicry, humor, and the genius of analogy made The Treatment an almost hypnotic experience and rendered the target stunned and helpless" (Rowland Evans and Robert Novak, Lyndon B. Johnson: The Exercise of Power. *New York: New American Library, 1966, p. 104).*

With the opening of the 107th Congress in 2001, congressional leaders faced an unusually challenging situation. In the Senate, with each party controlling fifty seats, the Republicans were nominally in charge because Vice President Cheney could break ties. In May 2001 Senator James Jeffords of Vermont stunned the nation when he left the Republican party and said he would serve in the Senate as an independent. This threw control of the Senate to the Democrats. Democrat Tom Daschle became the Majority Leader and Republican Trent Lott the Minority Leader.

In the House, Speaker Hastert faces serious difficulties as well. With just a nine-vote margin, he must keep virtually all his members in line to pass legislation opposed by a unified Democratic Party. Among Republicans, both hard-right conservatives and the more centrist moderates can use the party's small margin as leverage to try to exact concessions from the leadership. Clearly Hastert will be forced to try to build bipartisan coalitions in the center of the ideological spectrum. This situation means cutting deals with the Democratic leadership. This is no small challenge in itself, and Hastert and his Democratic counterpart, minority leader Richard Gephardt of Missouri, have not worked well together and did not even speak to each other toward the end of the 106th Congress.

Rules of Procedure

The operations of the House and Senate are structured by both formal rules and informal norms of behavior. Rules in each chamber are mostly matters of parliamentary procedure. For example, they govern the scheduling of legislation, outlining when and how certain types of legislation can be brought to the floor. Rules also govern the introduction of floor amendments. In the House, amendments must be directly germane (relevant) to the bill at hand; in the Senate, except in certain, specified instances, amendments that are not germane to the bill at hand can be proposed.

As noted earlier, an important difference between the two chambers is the House's use of its Rules Committee to govern floor debate. Lacking a similar committee to act as a "traffic cop" for legislation approaching the floor, the Senate relies on unanimous consent agreements to set the starting time and length of debate. If one senator objects to such an agreement, it does not take effect. Senators do not routinely object to unanimous consent agreements, however, because they will need them when bills of their own await scheduling by the leadership. The rules facilitate cooperation among the competing interests and parties in each house so that legislation can be voted on. However, the rules are not neutral: they are a tool of the majority party and help it control the legislative process.[51]

If a senator wants to stop a bill badly enough, she or he may start a **filibuster** and try to talk the bill to death. By historical tradition, the Senate gives its members the right of unlimited debate. During a 1947 debate, Idaho Democrat Glen Taylor "spoke for $8\frac{1}{2}$ hours on fishing, baptism, Wall Street, and his children." The record for holding the floor belongs to Republican Senator Strom Thurmond of South Carolina, however, for a twenty-four-hour, eighteen-minute marathon.[52] In the House, no member is allowed to speak for more than an hour without unanimous consent.

After a 1917 filibuster by a small group of senators killed President Wilson's bill to arm merchant ships—a bill favored by a majority of senators—the Senate finally adopted **cloture,** a means of limiting debate. A petition signed by sixteen senators initiates a cloture vote. It now takes the votes of sixty senators to invoke cloture. Senators successfully invoked cloture when a filibuster by southern senators threatened passage of the far-reaching Civil Rights Act of 1964. There is considerable criticism of the filibuster, not simply because it can frustrate the majority in the Senate but also because it is often used against relatively minor legislation and gives a small group of committed senators far too much leverage on any single issue.[53] Yet there is no significant movement within the Senate to reform the rules of debate.

Norms of Behavior

Both houses have codes of behavior that help keep them running. These codes are largely unwritten norms, although some have been formally adopted as rules. Members of Congress recognize that they must eliminate (or minimize) personal conflict, lest Congress dissolve into bickering factions unable to work together. One of the most celebrated norms is that members show respect for their colleagues in public deliberations. During floor debate, bitter opponents still refer to one another in such terms as "my good friend, the senior senator from . . ." or "my distinguished colleague."

Members of Congress are only human, of course, and tempers occasionally flare. For example, when Democrat Barney Frank of Massachusetts was angered by what he thought were unusually harsh charges against the Democratic Party from Republican Robert Walker of Pennsylvania, Frank rose to ask the presiding officer if it was permissible to refer to Walker as a "crybaby." When he was informed that it was not, Frank sat down, having made his point without technically violating the House's code of behavior.[54] There are no firm measures of civility in Congress, but it seems to have declined in recent years.[55]

Probably the most important norm of behavior in Congress is that individual members should be willing to bargain with one another. Policymaking is a process of give and take; it demands compromise. And the cost of not compromising is high. When the first President Bush nominated Clarence Thomas to the Supreme Court, Senator Warren Rudman (R.-NH), like many

filibuster
A delaying tactic, used in the Senate, that involves speechmaking to prevent action on a piece of legislation.

cloture
The mechanism by which a filibuster is cut off in the Senate.

Can You Explain Why...
there is so much wheeling and dealing in the Congress?

A Firm Hand on the Gavel
Speaker of the House Dennis Hastert of Illinois leads with the barest of Republican majorities (nine votes). He has to work hard to keep Republicans united, which means finding common ground for the large number of conservatives and the small number of moderates that make up the party in the House. In the first few months of the new Bush administration, Hastert played a critical role in getting the president's tax proposal through the House and on to the Senate.

other senators, had serious reservations about Thomas's qualifications and character. When it was clear that the Thomas confirmation vote was going to be close, Rudman cut a deal: he'd vote for Thomas, but three of his long-time friends would be given federal judgeships.[56]

It is important to point out that members of Congress are not expected to violate their conscience on policy issues simply to strike a deal. They are expected, however, to listen to what others have to say and to make every effort to reach a reasonable compromise. Obviously, if they all stick rigidly to their own view, they will never agree on anything. Moreover, few policy matters are so clear-cut that compromise destroys one's position.

Some important norms have changed in recent years, most notably the notion that junior members of the House and Senate should serve apprenticeships and defer to their party and committee elders during their first couple of years in Congress. Aggressive, impatient, and ambitious junior legislators of both parties chafed at this norm, and it has weakened considerably in the past few decades. When seventy-three new Republicans entered the House after the GOP sweep in the 1994 elections, these freshmen served notice that they would use their size to change the way things were done in Congress. Said one GOP freshman, "We came here to be different and we are not going to be housebroken."[57] Over time the 1994 cohort began to act more like their elders but, nevertheless, this large group of freshmen destroyed what little was left of the apprenticeship norm.

THE LEGISLATIVE ENVIRONMENT

After legislation emerges from committee, it is scheduled for floor debate. How do legislators make up their minds on how to vote? In this section, we examine the broader legislative environment that affects decision making in Congress. More specifically, we look at the influence on legislators of political parties, the president, constituents, and interest groups. The first two influences, parties and the president, push Congress toward majoritarian democracy. The other two, constituents and interest groups, are pluralist influences on congressional policymaking.

Political Parties

The national political parties might appear to have limited resources at their disposal to influence lawmakers. They do not control the nominations of House and Senate candidates. Candidates receive the bulk of their funds from individual contributors and political action committees, not from the national parties. Nevertheless, the parties are strong forces in the legislative process. The party leaders and various party committees within each house can help or hinder the efforts of rank-and-file legislators to get on the right committees, get their bills and amendments considered, and climb on the leadership ladder themselves. Moreover, as we saw earlier, the Democrats and Republicans on a given committee tend to reflect the views of the entire party membership in the chamber. Thus, party members on a committee tend to act as agents of their party as they search for solutions to policy problems.[58]

Civil Rights Act of 1964

The most significant reason that the parties are important in Congress is, of course, that Democrats and Republicans have different ideological views. Both parties have diversity, but as Figure 11.3 illustrates, Democrats tend to vote one way and Republicans the other. The primary reason why partisanship has been rising since 1980 is that the parties are becoming more homogeneous.[59] The liberal wing of the Republican Party has practically disappeared, and the party is unified around a conservative agenda for America. Likewise, the conservative wing of the Democratic Party has declined. The changes for the Democrats had their origins in the civil rights movement. When the national Democratic Party embraced the civil rights movement in the 1960s, white southern conservatives began to gravitate to the Republicans. Southern Democratic legislators did their best to disassociate themselves from the national party and were generally able to retain their seats.[60] Over time, however, more and more southern House seats moved from the Democrats to the Republicans (see Figure 11.4). As the parties have sorted themselves out, their ideological wingspans have shrunk.

Some applaud this rising partisanship because it is a manifestation of majoritarianism. When congressional parties are more unified, it gives voters a stronger means of influencing public policy choices through their selection of representatives and senators. Others are skeptical of majoritarianism, believing that Congress is more productive and responsible when it relies on bipartisanship. In their view, parties that cooperate in searching for consensus will serve the nation better.

The President

Unlike members of Congress, the president is elected by voters across the entire nation. The president has a better claim, then, to representing the nation than does any single member of Congress. But it can also be argued that Congress as a whole has a better claim than the president to representing the majority of voters. In fact, when Congress and the president differ, opinion surveys sometimes show that Congress's position on a given bill more closely resembles the majority view; at other times, these surveys show that the president's position accords with the majority. Nevertheless, presidents capitalize on their popular election and usually act as though they are speaking for the majority.

figure

11.3   Rising Partisanship

The lines in this graph show the percentages of representatives and senators who voted with their party on party unity votes. (Party unity votes are those in which a majority of one party votes one way and a majority of the other party votes the opposite way.) The rising percentage of party unity votes in the last two decades indicates that congressional parties are more frequently at odds with each other. In a true majoritarian system, parties vote against each other on all key issues.

Sources: Norman J. Ornstein, Thomas E. Mann, and Michael J. Malbin, *Vital Statistics on Congress, 1999–2000* (Washington, D.C.: AEI Press, 2000), p. 201; *CQ Weekly*, various issues.

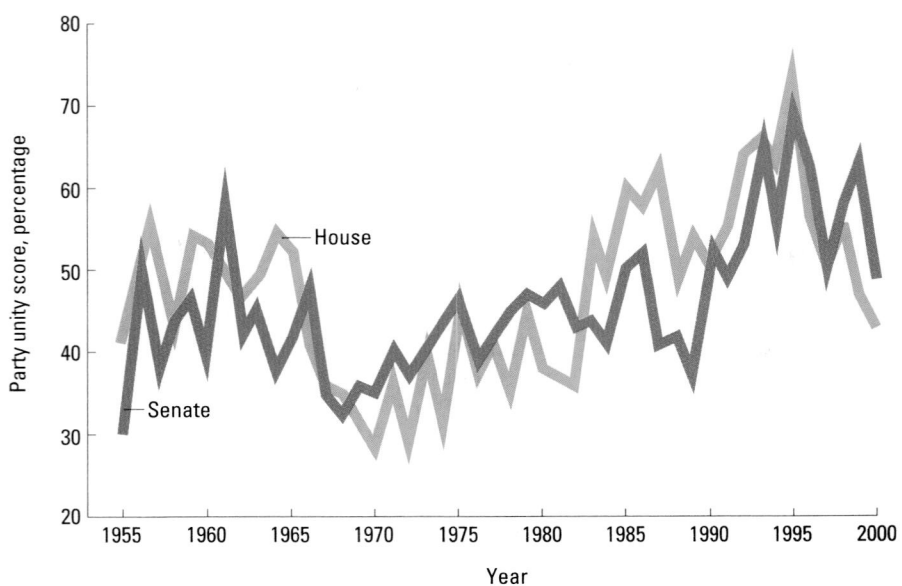

During the twentieth century, the public's expectations of what the president can accomplish in office grew enormously. We now expect the president to be our chief legislator: to introduce legislation on major issues and to use his influence to push bills through Congress. This is much different from our early history, when presidents felt constrained by the constitutional doctrine of separation of powers and had to have members of Congress work confidentially for them during legislative sessions.[61]

Today, the White House is openly involved not only in the writing of bills but also in their development as they wind their way through the legislative process. If the White House does not like a bill, it tries to work out a compromise with key legislators to have the legislation amended. On issues of the greatest importance, the president himself may meet with individual legislators to persuade them to vote a certain way. To monitor daily congressional activities and lobby for the administration's policies, hundreds of legislative liaison personnel work for the executive branch.

Although members of Congress grant presidents a leadership role in proposing legislation, they jealously guard the power of Congress to debate, shape, and pass or defeat any legislation the president proposes. Congress often clashes sharply with the president when his proposals are seen as ill-advised.

constituents
People who live and vote in a government official's district or state.

Constituents

Constituents are the people who live and vote in a legislator's district or state. Their opinions are a crucial part of the legislative decision-making

figure

11.4   Republicans Tilt South

Just as Republicans began to win more of their seats in the South, the Democrats began to make gains in the North. With fewer southern conservatives as members in the House, the Democrats were pulled to the left. Conversely, with more of their members from the South, the most conservative area of the country, and fewer from the North, House Republicans were pulled toward the right.

Source: Gary C. Jacobson, "Reversals of Fortune: The Transformation of U.S. House Elections in the 1990s," in *Continuity and Change in House Elections*, eds. David W. Brady, John F. Cogan, and Morris P. Fiorina (Stanford, Calif.: Stanford University Press and Hoover Institution Press, 2000), p. 19. Copyright 2000 by the Board of Trustees of the Leland Stanford Junior University. With the permission of Stanford University Press, <www.sup.org>.

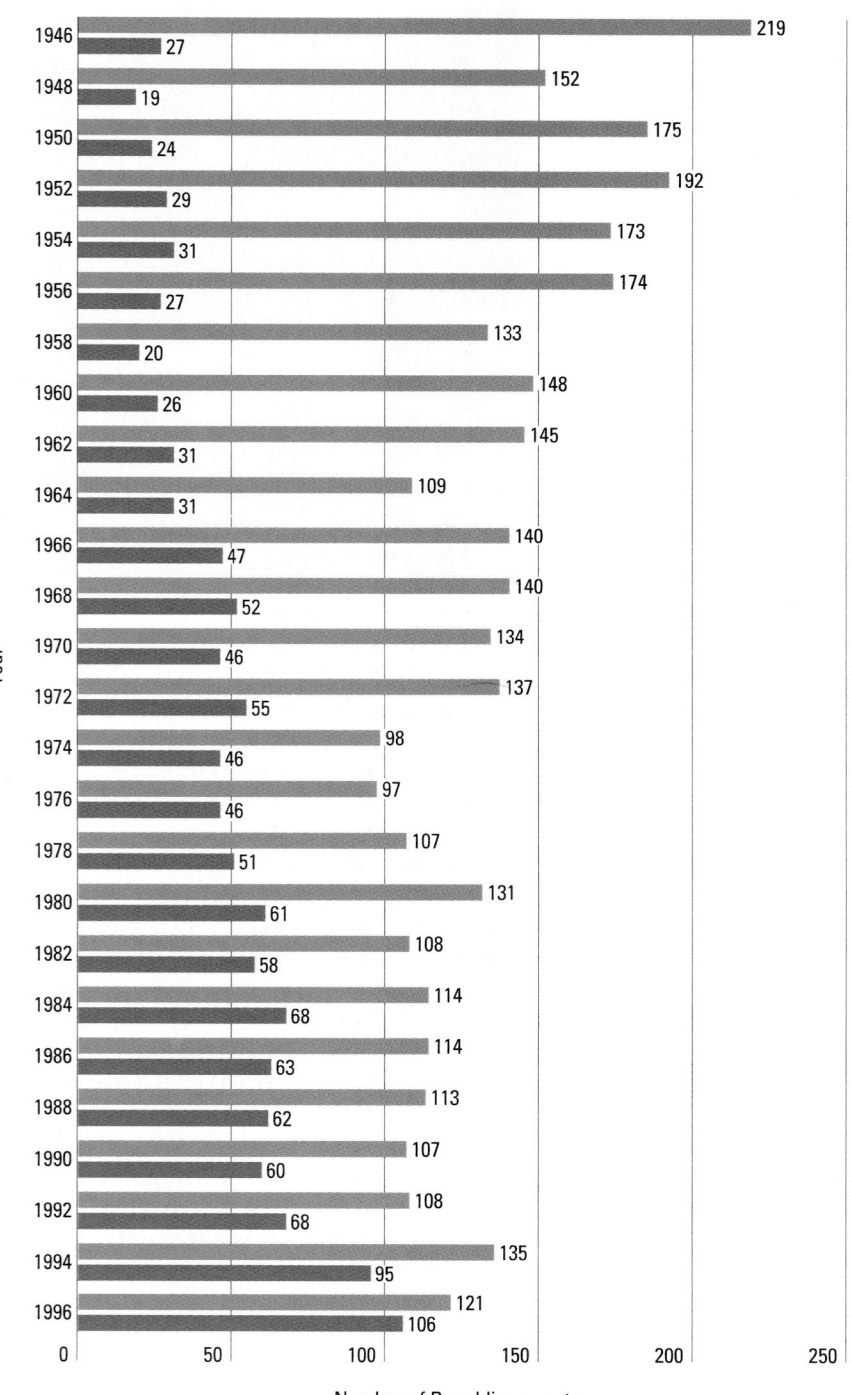

■ Other regions   ■ South, Plains, and Mountain West

Strange Bedfellows
Senator Orrin Hatch, a conservative Republican from Utah, and Senator Edward Kennedy, a liberal Democrat from Massachusetts, may at first glance seem like a mismatched pair to work together on legislation. Over the years, however, the two have developed a strong political partnership and personal friendship despite their obvious partisan and ideological differences. The two senators are shown here conferring at a Senate hearing on the dangers of teenage smoking. (Note the cancerous lung exhibited at the hearing.)

process. As much as members of Congress want to please their party's leadership or the president by going along with their preferences, they have to think about what the voters back home want. If they displease enough people by the way they vote, they might lose their seat in the next election.

Constituents' influence contributes to pluralism because the diversity of America is mirrored by the geographical basis of representation in the House and Senate. A representative from Los Angeles, for instance, may need to be sensitive to issues of particular concern to constituents whose backgrounds are Korean, Vietnamese, Hispanic, African American, or Jewish. A representative from Montana will have few such constituents but must pay particular attention to issues involving minerals and mining. A senator from Nebraska will give higher priority to agricultural issues than to urban issues. Conversely, a senator from New York will be sensitive to issues involving the cities. All these constituencies, enthusiastically represented by legislators who want to do a good job for the people back home, push and pull Congress in many different directions.

At all stages of the legislative process, the interests of the voters are on the minds of members of Congress. As they decide what to spend time on and how to vote, they weigh how different courses of action will affect their constituents' views of them.[62]

Interest Groups

As we pointed out in Chapter 10, interest groups are one way constituents influence Congress. Because they represent a vast array of vocational, regional, and ideological groupings within our population, interest groups exemplify pluralist politics. Interest groups press members of Congress to take a particular course of action, believing sincerely that what they prefer is also best for the country. Legislators, in turn, are attentive to interest groups, not because of an abstract commitment to pluralist politics but because these organizations represent citizens, some of whom live back home in their district or state. Lobbies are also sources of useful information and potentially of political support (and, in some instances, campaign contributions) for members of Congress.

Because the four external sources of influence on Congress—parties, the president, constituents, and interest groups—push legislators in both majoritarian and pluralist directions, Congress exhibits aspects of both pluralism and majoritarianism in its operations. We'll return to the conflict between pluralism and majoritarianism at the end of this chapter.

THE DILEMMA OF REPRESENTATION

When candidates for the House and Senate campaign for office, they routinely promise to work hard for their district's or state's interests. When they get to Washington, though, they all face a troubling dilemma: what their constituents want may not be what the people across the nation want.

Presidents and Shopping Bags

In doing the research for his book *Home Style*, political scientist Richard Fenno accompanied several representatives as they worked and interacted with constituents in their home district. On one of Fenno's trips, he was in an airport with a congressional aide, waiting for the representative's plane from Washington to land. When the representative arrived, he said, "I spent fifteen minutes on the telephone with the president this afternoon. He had a plaintive tone in his voice and he pleaded with me." His side of the issue had prevailed over the president's, and he was elated by the victory. When the three men reached the aide's car, the representative saw the back seat piled high with campaign paraphernalia: shopping bags printed with his name and picture. "Back to this again," he sighed.[63]

Every member of Congress lives in two worlds: the world of presidents and the world of personalized shopping bags. A typical week in the life of a representative means working in Washington, then boarding a plane and flying back to the home district. There the representative spends time meeting with individual constituents and talking to civic groups, church gatherings, business associations, labor unions, and the like. A survey of House members during a nonelection year showed that each made an average of thirty-five trips back to her or his district, spending an average of 138 days there.[64]

Members of Congress are often criticized for being out of touch with the people they are supposed to represent. This charge does not seem justified. Legislators work extraordinarily hard at keeping in touch with voters, at finding out what is on their constituents' minds. The problem is how to act on that knowledge.

Trustees or Delegates?

Are members of Congress bound to vote the way their constituents want them to vote, even if it means voting against their conscience? Some say no. They argue that legislators must be free to vote in line with what they think

The Majority Leaders
At the opening of the 107th Congress in 2001, Senate Republicans and Democrats had fifty members each. Since Vice President Dick Cheney can cast a vote to break a tie, Republican Trent Lott (right) of Mississippi remained nominally as the majority leader. After Senator James Jeffords left the Republican Party in May 2001, Democrat Tom Daschle of South Dakota became the majority leader and Lott the minority leader.

trustee
A representative who is obligated to consider the views of constituents but is not obligated to vote according to those views if he or she believes they are misguided.

delegate
A legislator whose primary responsibility is to represent the majority view of his or her constituents, regardless of his or her own view.

is best. This view has long been associated with the eighteenth-century English political philosopher Edmund Burke (1729–1797). Burke, who served in Parliament, told his constituents in Bristol that "you choose a member, indeed; but when you have chosen him, he is not a member of Bristol, but he is a member of *Parliament*."[65] Burke reasoned that representatives are sent by their constituents to vote as they think best. As **trustees,** representatives are obligated to consider the views of their constituents, but they are not obligated to vote according to those views if they think they are misguided.

Others hold that legislators are duty-bound to represent the majority view of their constituents, that they are **delegates** with instructions from the people at home on how to vote on critical issues. And delegates, unlike trustees, must be prepared to vote against their own policy preferences. During the fight over President Clinton's impeachment, Representative James Rogan of California knew that demographic changes were making his district less hospitable for a Republican like him. He knew that a majority of the voters back home weren't in favor of impeaching and removing Clinton from office. Rogan decided against acting as a delegate and instead voted his conscience to impeach the president. He also became one of the House managers who presented the case to the Senate. In the 2000 election, voters turned him out of office and replaced him with a Democrat.

Members of Congress are subject to two opposing forces, then. Although the interests of their districts encourage them to act as delegates, their interpretation of the larger national interest calls on them to be trustees. Given these conflicting role definitions, it is not surprising that Congress is not clearly either a body of delegates or one of trustees. Research has shown, however, that members of Congress are more apt to take the delegate role on issues that are of great concern to their constituents.[66] But much of the time, what constituents really want is not clear. Many issues are not highly visible back home. Some issues may cut across the constituency, affecting constituents in different ways. Or constituents may only partially understand them. For such issues, no delegate position is obvious.

PLURALISM, MAJORITARIANISM, AND DEMOCRACY

The dilemma that individual members of Congress face in adopting the role of either delegate or trustee has broad implications for the way our country is governed. If legislators tend to act as delegates, congressional policymaking is more pluralistic, and policies reflect the bargaining that goes on among lawmakers who speak for different constituencies. If, instead, legislators tend to act as trustees and vote their consciences, policymaking becomes less tied to the narrower interests of districts and states. But even here there is no guarantee that congressional decision making reflects majority interests. True majoritarian legislatures require a paramount role for political parties.

We end this chapter with a short discussion of pluralism versus majoritarianism in Congress. But first, to establish a frame of reference, we need to take a quick look at a more majoritarian type of legislature—the parliament.

Parliamentary Government

parliamentary system
A system of government in which the chief executive is the leader whose party holds the most seats in the legislature after an election or whose party forms a major part of the ruling coalition.

In our system of government, the executive and legislative functions are divided between a president and a congress, each elected separately. Most other democracies—for example, Britain and Japan—have parliamentary governments. In a **parliamentary system,** the chief executive is the legislative leader whose party holds the most seats in the legislature after an election or whose party forms a major part of the ruling coalition. For instance, in Great Britain, voters do not cast a ballot for prime minister. They vote only for their member of Parliament and thus influence the choice of prime minister only indirectly, by voting for the party they favor in the local district election. Parties are unified, and in Parliament, legislators vote for their party's position, giving voters a strong and direct means of influencing public policy.

In a parliamentary system, government power is highly concentrated in the legislature because the leader of the majority party is also the head of the government. Moreover, parliamentary legislatures are usually composed of only one house or have a second chamber that is much weaker than the other. (In the British Parliament, the House of Commons makes the decisions of government; the other chamber, the House of Lords, is largely an honorary debating club for distinguished members of society.) And parliamentary governments usually do not have a court that can invalidate acts of the parliament. Under such a system, the government is in the hands of the party that controls the parliament. With no separation of government powers, checks on government action are few. (The checks on the European Union Parliament are substantial, however; see Politics in a Changing World 11.1.) Overall these governments fit the majoritarian model of democracy to a much greater extent than a separation-of-powers system.

Pluralism Versus Majoritarianism in Congress

Can You Explain Why...
"pork" gets into the budget?

The U.S. Congress is often criticized for being too pluralist and not majoritarian enough. The federal budget deficit provides a case in point. Americans were deeply concerned about the big deficits that plagued our national budgets in recent years. And both Democrats and Republicans in Congress repeatedly called for reductions in those deficits. But when

★ **politics in a changing** w o r l d

11.1   A Legislature for Europe

As European integration moves forward, the European Parliament has taken on increasing importance. The European Parliament is the legislative arm of the European Union. As discussed in Chapter 4, the European Union (EU) represents the aspirations of member countries that believe that both their economies and their political power in international affairs will be enhanced by greater cooperation.

The fifteen countries of the European Union each elect legislators to the 626-member European Parliament. Populous Germany has ninety-nine members, France and Britain eighty-seven each, and tiny Luxembourg just six. As befitting an organization composed of so many different countries, the European Parliament carries out its business in several places. When all the members meet together—about one week a month—they gather in Strasbourg, France, where their debating chamber, the Hemicycle, is located. Roughly two weeks out of each month, members are involved in committee meetings, and those take place in Brussels, Belgium. The staff of the Parliament is headquartered in still a third location, in Luxembourg. The biggest job for the 3,500-person staff is interpretation and translation because there are eleven official languages of the European Parliament: Danish, Dutch, English, Finnish, French, German, Greek, Italian, Portuguese, Spanish, and Swedish. More official languages are sure to follow because the EU is preparing to admit many new European countries to its membership.

The members of the European Parliament are elected directly by voters in their home countries. They run as members of political parties and they're elected in a system of proportional representation, where each party above a minimum threshold gets a percentage of seats roughly corresponding to the percentage of the popular vote won. Once in the European Parliament, members sit not with all their countrymen but with members of their political grouping. There are currently eight groupings, each incorporating political parties of similar outlooks in the member countries. For example, one grouping is composed of the Green or pro-environment parties of Europe. Another encompasses socialist parties.

The European Parliament reflects not just the growing interdependence of European countries but the growing interdependence of the world. The Parliament offers greater leverage for Europe in the negotiations that are at the heart of contemporary world politics. The Parliament, for example, became involved in the banana war between the EU and the United States and other non-EU countries. The Parliament backed a system of tariffs and quotas to give advantage to producers from protectorates and former colonies of EU countries. The Parliament has also been forceful in denouncing human rights abuses in other areas of the world. The greater size and prestige of the European Parliament add stature to efforts to try to force other countries to behave in a responsible and humane fashion.

Although there is great potential for the European Parliament to become a central actor on the world's stage, its power remains restricted by its member countries. They've placed numerous, significant constraints on the Parliament's ability to act autonomously in European and international affairs. For example, the typical legislative process for bills before the Parliament requires that approval must also be gained from the Council of Ministers. The Council of Ministers is composed of the Cabinet secretaries of the member countries, and they meet in committees based on their area of expertise. For example, the health ministers of the countries meet to deliberate on EU Parliament legislation in the area of health policy. This process of codecision between the two bodies means that the European Parliament cannot diverge too far from what the ruling parties in the member countries want. Europe may be marching toward greater interdependence, but concerns about sovereignty and nationalism still weigh heavily in the capitals of the fifteen member countries of the European Union.

spending bills came before Congress, legislators' concern turned to what the bills would do for their district or state. Appropriations bills usually include pork barrel projects that benefit specific districts or states and further add to any deficit. In a recent transportation bill, House Democrat Nita Lowey got a $4.5 million bus facility for Westchester County in New York. Her Republican colleague from New York, James Walsh, got $7 million for buses and transportation projects for Syracuse. One legislator defended the money earmarked for his district by declaring, "This project is not pork. This project is a vital infrastructure necessity."[67]

Projects such as these get into the budget through bargaining among members; as we saw earlier in this chapter, congressional norms encourage it. Members of Congress try to win projects and programs that will benefit their constituents and thus help them at election time. To win approval of such projects, members must be willing to vote for other legislators' projects in turn. Such a system obviously promotes pluralism (and spending).

Critics have long contended that Congress would have to abandon pluralism before the country would ever achieve a balanced budget. By 2000, however, prosperity cured what politics couldn't. Over the course of the Clinton years, the booming economy and the skyrocketing stock market produced a windfall of additional tax revenues. Remarkably, attention turned from the budget deficit to the budget *surplus*. As the 107th Congress deals with the surplus through a likely combination of spending increases and tax cuts, pluralist politics will continue to be a driving force. Interest groups will push legislators to adopt policies that will give seniors prescription drug benefits, public schools more funding, and various industries new tax breaks.

It's easy to conclude that the consequence of pluralism in Congress is a lot of unnecessary spending and tax loopholes. Yet many different constituencies are well served by an appropriations process that allows for pluralism. For the low-income residents of Syracuse and Westchester County, bus service is vital to their livelihood. Middle-class people drive their cars to work and couldn't care less about their local bus system. But dishwashers, maids, and janitors pay taxes to fund the government, too, and they have a right to expect the government to care about the problems they have in getting to work.

Proponents of pluralism also argue that the makeup of Congress generally reflects that of the nation, that different members of Congress represent farm areas, oil and gas areas, low-income inner cities, industrial areas, and so on. They point out that America itself is pluralistic, with a rich diversity of economic, social, religious, and racial groups, and that even if one's own representatives and senators don't represent one's particular viewpoint, it's likely that someone in Congress does.

In the 104th Congress (1995–1996), House Republicans engaged in a bold experiment to try to inject more majoritarianism into the political system. During the 1994 campaign, most Republican candidates for Congress told voters they were committed to passing a platform of policy proposals they called the "Contract with America." If they took over control of the House from the Democrats, their "contract" with voters was their promise to enact these proposals. A Republican landslide that year gave the Republicans control and, under the leadership of Speaker Newt Gingrich, almost all the bills incorporating Contract promises passed the House of Representatives.

Ultimately this effort at majoritarian politics failed. Voters were generally unaware of the Contract with America during the campaign so they didn't really endorse it. Gingrich and House Republicans misjudged the electorate, believing voters were much more conservative than they were. Many of the Contract proposals died in the Senate, even though Republicans controlled that chamber too. Many Senate Republicans saw some of these proposals, such as some major regulatory reform bills that rolled back some environmental protections, as bad politics. Other bills made it through the Senate but were vetoed by President Clinton, who recognized that public opinion did not support the Republicans' objectives in their legislation. No more contracts were forthcoming from the Republicans in the subsequent elections.

Majoritarianism isn't completely absent in Congress. The rise in party unity discussed earlier reflects the increasing success of the congressional parties in defining political debate in terms of the basic philosophical divisions between them. Still, policymaking in the House and the Senate remains more pluralistic than majoritarian in nature.

SUMMARY

Congress writes the laws of the land and attempts to oversee their implementation. It helps to educate us about new issues as they appear on the political agenda. Most important, members of Congress represent us, working to see to it that interests from home and from around the country are heard throughout the policymaking process.

We count on Congress to do so much that criticism about how well it does some things is inevitable. However, certain strengths are clear. The committee system fosters expertise; representatives and senators who know the most about particular issues have the most influence over them. And the structure of our electoral system keeps legislators in close touch with their constituents.

Bargaining and compromise play important roles in the congressional policymaking process. Some find this disquieting. They want less deal making and more adherence to principle. This thinking is in line with the desire for a more majoritarian democracy. Others defend the current system, arguing that the United States is a large, complex nation, and the policies that govern it should be developed through bargaining among various interests.

There is no clear-cut answer to whether a majoritarian or a pluralist legislative system provides better representation for voters. Our system is a mix of pluralism and majoritarianism. It serves minority interests that might otherwise be neglected or even harmed by an unthinking or uncaring majority. At the same time, congressional parties work to represent the broader interests of the American people.

★ Selected Readings

Brady, David W., John F. Cogan, and Morris P. Fiorina (eds.). *Continuity and Change in House Elections.* Stanford, Calif.: Stanford University Press and Hoover Institution Press, 2000. An excellent collection of articles on various aspects of congressional elections.

Canon, David T. *Race, Redistricting, and Representation.* Chicago, Ill.: University of Chicago Press, 1999. Analyzes the difference in behavior between African-American legislators who run campaigns emphasizing "commonality rather than the politics of difference."

Fenno, Richard F., Jr. *Home Style.* Boston: Little, Brown, 1978. A classic analysis of how House members interact with constituents during visits to their home districts.

Herrnson, Paul S. *Congressional Elections*, 3rd ed. Washington, D.C.: CQ Press, 2000. Herrnson's study is a comprehensive look at congressional candidates and the electorate.

Loomis, Burdett A. (ed.). *Esteemed Colleagues.* Washington, D.C.: Brookings Institution Press, 2000. A set of essays examining declining civility in Congress as well as the institution's deliberative processes.

Reingold, Beth. *Representing Women.* Chapel Hill, N.C.: University of North Carolina Press, 2000. A look at the similarities and differences among male and female state legislators in Arizona and California.

Internet Exercises

1. Welfare Reform and the Legislative Process

Named in honor of President Thomas Jefferson and maintained by the Library of Congress, "Thomas" is perhaps the richest site on the Web for information about the United States Congress. The site is located at **<thomas.loc.gov/>**.

• Use the "Bill Summary and Status" feature of Thomas to search the legislation debated in the 104th Congress (1995–1996) for H.R. 4, a bill that was proposed to reform the nation's welfare system. Once you have located H.R. 4, review the bill's "Detailed Legislative Status" and "Floor/Executive Actions."

• How does the information that you found here illustrate (1) the role that committees play in developing legislation, (2) how bills can undergo significant changes even after committees have completed their work on them, and (3) the important role that the president plays in the legislative process?

2. Committees: The Workhorses of the Congress

• Go back to the Thomas Web site and peruse the home pages for the committees of the House and the Senate, noting the jurisdictions of the committees you have chosen to view. (Hint: If you look carefully, you'll find a good summary of House committee jurisdictions on the Thomas home page.)

• Note in particular the role and jurisdictions of the House and Senate appropriations committees.

• While the jurisdictional domains of these committees appear relatively short compared to the other committees in Congress, many members of Congress and Congress-watchers consider Appropriations one of (if not the) most powerful committees in either chamber. How can they be so powerful if the list describing their jurisdiction is so short?

chapter
12

★
★
★
★
★
★
★

The Presidency

I'M A UNITER, NOT A DIVIDER.

I'M A UNITER, NOT A DIVIDER. During the 2000 campaign, George W. Bush repeated this phrase like his personal mantra. He wanted to convey the idea that Al Gore couldn't work with both parties in Congress. Bush argued that little had been done during the eight years of Clinton-Gore and that partisanship had gotten out of hand. In Bush's mind, only he could solve this problem. He wasn't going to be president of only the groups of voters that supported him, nor was he going to be a president who ruled with a majority that overrode its opponents. Rather, he was going to be president of *all* the people.

It's a nice sentiment and good campaign rhetoric. Unfortunately for Bush, it's not much more than that. Indeed, all candidates for president voice similar platitudes during the campaign—Bush just said it more often and, seemingly, with more sincerity. In reality, presidents govern by taking the majority of voters that put them in office and then try to expand their support by adding different groups of voters attracted to particular policies. Even if they take over without majority control of the Congress, presidents can still draw legitimacy from the majority of voters that put them in office. And even if they don't get 50 percent or more of voters because of a third-party candidate, they almost always get a majority of the two-party vote.

But as George Bush took over the presidency, his party didn't completely control the Congress, he didn't win a majority of the voters overall, and he didn't even win a majority of the two-party vote. Democratic candidate Gore won a half million more votes than Bush did.

On January 20, 2001, as he drove up Pennsylvania Avenue to the Capitol to deliver his inaugural speech, Bush surely thought of the unifying theme he developed during the campaign and of the soothing words he would deliver to the nation after he took the oath of office from Chief Justice William Rehnquist. That day he told the nation, "this is my solemn pledge: I will work to build a single nation of justice and opportunity."[1]

For all the eloquent words and soaring visions, Bush knew that he faced serious problems in governing the nation, problems that derived from the unusual nature of his victory. Fully 40 percent of the public did not believe that he won the election legitimately.[2] In Congress the Republicans had a narrow nine-vote margin in the House of Representatives. In the Senate there was an inherently unstable situation, with each party controlling fifty seats. Many recent presidents have faced a Congress that their party didn't control and had been able to work productively with the legislative branch anyway. All it took was a willingness to compromise and Bush prided himself, justifiably, on his ability to work with the Democrats in the Texas legislature while he was governor there.[3]

Yet Bush knew that the Democrats in Congress were angry and were not particularly interested in being cooperative. While they've promised to work with the new president for the good of the country, theirs is a convenient rhetoric too. Many Democrats believe that the election was stolen from them, first by the Republican Party in Florida and then by a partisan Supreme Court. The Democrats were already looking forward to the 2002 midterm election, confident that they could gain a majority in the Senate and possibly take the House as well. Adding to Bush's challenge, he took office at a time when the economy was softening and energy prices skyrocketing.

Elections are about forming a majority to serve as the basis for governing. As he took the oath of office, however, Bush was nothing if not confident. He strongly believed he could lead effectively despite the unique nature of his election. After all, he's a uniter and not a divider.

In this chapter we will analyze presidential leadership, looking at how presidents try to muster majoritarian support for their goals. We'll also focus on several other important questions. What are the powers of the presidency? How is the president's advisory system organized? How does the separation of powers between the executive and legislative branches affect public policy making? Finally, what are the particular issues and problems that presidents face in foreign affairs?

THE CONSTITUTIONAL BASIS OF PRESIDENTIAL POWER

When the presidency was created, the colonies had just fought a war of independence; their reaction to British domination had focused on the autocratic rule of King George III. Thus, the delegates to the Constitutional Convention were extremely wary of unchecked power and were determined not to create an all-powerful, dictatorial presidency.

The delegates' fear of a powerful presidency was counterbalanced by their desire for strong leadership. The Articles of Confederation—which did not provide for a single head of state—had failed to bind the states together into a unified nation (see Chapter 3). In addition, the governors of the individual states had generally proved to be inadequate leaders because they had few formal powers. The new nation was conspicuously weak; its congress had no power to compel the states to obey its legislation. The delegates knew they had to create some type of effective executive office. Their task was to provide for national leadership without allowing opportunity for tyranny.

Initial Conceptions of the Presidency

Debates about the nature of the office began. Should there be one president or a presidential council or committee? Should the president be chosen by Congress and remain largely subservient to that body? The delegates gave initial approval to a plan that called for a single executive, chosen by Congress for a seven-year term and ineligible for reelection.[4] But some delegates continued to argue for a strong president who would be elected independently of the legislative branch.

The final structure of the presidency reflected the "checks and balances" philosophy that had shaped the entire Constitution. In the minds

We've Come to Praise Nixon and to Bury Him

Richard Nixon, who served as president between 1969 and 1974, died on April 22, 1994, and was buried a few days later with all living former presidents and their spouses in attendance. President Clinton, who had secretly consulted with Nixon after taking office, gave a generous eulogy and, in an allusion to Watergate, spoke to Nixon's place in history by suggesting that "the day of judging President Nixon on anything less than his entire life and career come to a close."

of the delegates, they had imposed important limits on the presidency through the powers specifically delegated to Congress and the courts. Those counterbalancing powers would act as checks, or controls, on presidents who might try to expand the office beyond its proper bounds.

The Powers of the President

The requirements for the presidency are set forth in Article II of the Constitution: the president must be a U.S.-born citizen, at least thirty-five years old, who has lived in the United States for a minimum of fourteen years. Article II also sets forth the responsibilities of presidents. In view of the importance of the office, the constitutional description of the president's duties is surprisingly brief and vague. This vagueness has led to repeated conflict about the limits of presidential power.

The delegates undoubtedly had many reasons for the lack of precision in Article II. One likely explanation was the difficulty of providing and at the same time limiting presidential power. Furthermore, the framers of the Constitution had no model—no existing presidency—on which to base their description of the office. And, ironically, their description of the presidency might have been more precise if they had had less confidence in George Washington, the obvious choice for the first president. According to one account of the Constitutional Convention, "when Dr. Franklin predicted on June 4 that 'the first man put at the helm will be a good one,' every delegate knew perfectly well who that first good man would be."[5] The delegates had great trust in Washington; they did not fear that he would try to misuse the office.

The major duties and powers that the delegates listed for Washington and his successors can be summarized as follows:

- *Serve as administrative head of the nation.* The Constitution gives little guidance on the president's administrative duties. It states merely that "the executive Power shall be vested in a President of the United

States of America" and that "he shall take Care that the Laws be faithfully executed." These imprecise directives have been interpreted to mean that the president is to supervise and offer leadership to various departments, agencies, and programs created by Congress. In practice, a chief executive spends much more time making policy decisions for his cabinet departments and agencies than enforcing existing policies.

- *Act as commander in chief of the military.* In essence, the Constitution names the president as the highest-ranking officer in the armed forces. But it gives Congress the power to declare war. The framers no doubt intended Congress to control the president's military power; nevertheless, presidents have initiated military action without the approval of Congress.[6] The entire Vietnam War was fought without a congressional declaration of war.

- *Convene Congress.* The president can call Congress into special session on "extraordinary Occasions," although this has rarely been done. He must also periodically inform Congress of "the State of the Union."

veto
The president's disapproval of a bill that has been passed by both houses of Congress. Congress can override a veto with a two-thirds vote in each house.

- *Veto legislation.* The president can **veto** (disapprove) any bill or resolution enacted by Congress, with the exception of joint resolutions that propose constitutional amendments. Congress can override a presidential veto with a two-thirds vote in each house.

- *Appoint various officials.* The president has the authority to appoint federal court judges, ambassadors, cabinet members, other key policymakers, and many lesser officials. Many appointments are subject to Senate confirmation.

- *Make treaties.* With the "Advice and Consent" of at least two-thirds of those senators voting at the time, the president can make treaties with foreign powers. The president is also to "receive Ambassadors," a phrase that presidents have interpreted to mean the right to recognize other nations formally.

- *Grant pardons.* The president can grant pardons to individuals who have committed "Offenses against the United States, except in Cases of Impeachment."

THE EXPANSION OF PRESIDENTIAL POWER

The framers' limited conception of the president's role has given way to a considerably more powerful interpretation. In this section, we look beyond the presidential responsibilities listed explicitly in the Constitution and examine the additional sources of power that presidents have used to expand the authority of the office. First, we look at the claims that presidents make about "inherent" powers implicit in the Constitution. Second, we turn to congressional grants of power to the executive branch. Third, we discuss the influence that comes from a president's political skills. Finally, we analyze how a president's popular support affects his political power.

Can You Explain Why...
presidential power today is so much greater than what's described in the Constitution?

The Inherent Powers

Several presidents have expanded the power of the office by taking actions that exceeded commonly held notions of the president's proper authority.

inherent powers
Authority claimed by the president that is not clearly specified in the Constitution. Typically, these powers are inferred from the Constitution.

These men justified what they had done by saying that their actions fell within the **inherent powers** of the presidency. From this broad perspective, presidential power derives not only from those duties clearly outlined in Article II but also from inferences that may be drawn from the Constitution.

When a president claims a power that has not been considered part of the chief executive's authority, he forces Congress and the courts either to acquiesce to his claim or to restrict it. When presidents succeed in claiming a new power, they leave to their successors the legacy of a permanent expansion of presidential authority. Assertions of inherent powers have often come at critical points in the nation's history. During the Civil War, for example, Abraham Lincoln issued several orders that exceeded the accepted limits of presidential authority. One order increased the size of the armed forces well beyond the congressionally mandated ceiling, although the Constitution gives only Congress the power "to raise and support Armies." And because military expenditures would then have exceeded military appropriations, Lincoln also acted to usurp the taxing and spending powers constitutionally conferred on Congress. In another order, Lincoln instituted a blockade of Southern ports, thereby committing acts of war against the Confederacy without the approval of Congress.

Lincoln said the urgent nature of the South's challenge to the Union forced him to act without waiting for congressional approval. His rationale was simple: "Was it possible to lose the nation and yet preserve the Constitution?"[7] In other words, Lincoln circumvented the Constitution to save the nation. Subsequently, Congress and the Supreme Court approved Lincoln's actions. That approval gave added legitimacy to the theory of inherent powers—a theory that over time has transformed the presidency.

Any president who lays claim to new authority runs the risk of being rebuffed by Congress or the courts and suffering political damage. After Andrew Jackson vetoed a bill reauthorizing a national bank, for example, he ordered William Duane, his secretary of the treasury, to withdraw all federal deposits and place them in state banks. Duane refused, claiming that he was under the supervision of both Congress and the executive branch; Jackson responded by firing him. The president's action angered many members of Congress, who believed that Jackson had overstepped his constitutional bounds; the Constitution does not actually state that a president may remove his cabinet secretaries. Although that prerogative is now taken for granted, Jackson's presidency was weakened by the controversy. His censure by the Senate was a slap in the face, and he was denounced even by members of his own party. It took many years for the president's right to remove cabinet officers to become widely accepted.[8]

Congressional Delegation of Power

delegation of powers
The process by which Congress gives the executive branch the additional authority needed to address new problems.

Presidential power grows when presidents successfully challenge Congress, but in many instances Congress willingly delegates power to the executive branch. As the American public pressures the national government to solve various problems, Congress, through a process called **delegation of powers,** gives the executive branch more responsibility to administer programs that address those problems. One example of delegation of congressional power occurred in the 1930s, during the Great Depression, when Congress gave Franklin Roosevelt's administration wide latitude to do what it thought was necessary to solve the nation's economic ills.

When Congress concludes that the government needs flexibility in its approach to a problem, the president is often given great freedom in how or when to implement policies. Richard Nixon was given discretionary authority to impose a freeze on wages and prices in an effort to combat escalating inflation. If Congress had been forced to debate the timing of the freeze, merchants and manufacturers would surely have raised their prices in anticipation of the event. Instead, Nixon was able to act suddenly, imposing the freeze without warning. (We discuss congressional delegation of authority to the executive branch in more detail in Chapter 13.)

At other times, however, Congress believes that too much power has accumulated in the executive branch, and it enacts legislation to reassert congressional authority. During the 1970s, many representatives and senators agreed that Congress's role in the American political system was declining, that presidents were exercising power that rightfully belonged to the legislative branch. The most notable reaction was the enactment of the War Powers Resolution (1973), which was directed at ending the president's ability to pursue armed conflict without explicit congressional approval.

The President's Power to Persuade

A president's influence in office comes not only from his assigned responsibilities but also from his political skills and from how effectively he uses the resources of his office. A classic analysis of the use of presidential resources is offered by Richard Neustadt in his book *Presidential Power.* Neustadt develops a model of how presidents gain, lose, or maintain their influence. His initial premise is simple enough: "Presidential power is the power to persuade."[9] Presidents, for all their resources—a skilled staff, extensive media coverage of presidential actions, the great respect the country holds for the office—must depend on others' cooperation to get things done. Harry Truman echoed Neustadt's premise when he said, "I sit here all day trying to persuade people to do the things they ought to have sense enough to do without my persuading them. . . . That's all the powers of the President amount to."[10]

Ability in bargaining, dealing with adversaries, and choosing priorities, according to Neustadt, separates above-average presidents from mediocre ones. A president must make wise choices about which policies to push and which to put aside until he can find more support. President Nixon described such decisions as a lot like poker. "I knew when to get out of a pot," said Nixon. "I didn't stick around when I didn't have the cards."[11] The president must decide when to accept compromise and when to stand on principle. He must know when to go public and when to work behind the scenes.

Often, a president faces a dilemma in which all the alternatives carry some risk. After Dwight Eisenhower took office in 1953, he had to decide how to deal with Joseph McCarthy, the Republican senator from Wisconsin who had been largely responsible for creating national hysteria over allegations about communists in government. McCarthy had made many wild, reckless charges, damaging several innocent people's careers by accusing them of communist sympathies. Many people expected Eisenhower to control McCarthy—not only because he was president but also because he was a fellow Republican. Yet Eisenhower, worrying about his own popularity, chose not to confront him. He used a "hidden hand" strategy, working behind the scenes to weaken McCarthy. Politically, Eisenhower seems to have made the right choice; McCarthy soon discredited himself.[12] However, Eisenhower's performance can be criticized as weak moral leadership. If he had publicly denounced the senator, he might have ended the McCarthy witch hunt sooner.

A president's political skills can be important in affecting outcomes in Congress. The chief executive cannot intervene in every legislative struggle. He must choose his battles carefully, then try to use the force of his personality and the prestige of his office to forge an agreement among differing factions. When President Lyndon Johnson needed House Appropriations chair George Mahon (D.-TX) to support him on an issue, he called Mahon on the phone and he emphasized the value of Mahon having a good long-term relationship with him. Speaking slowly to let every point sink in, Johnson told Mahon, "I know one thing. . . . I know I'm right on this. . . . I know I mean more to you, . . . and Lubbock [Texas], . . . and your district, . . . and your State, . . . and your grandchildren, than Charlie Halleck [the Republican House leader] does."[13] In terms of getting members to vote a certain way, presidential influence is best described as taking place "at the margins." That is, presidents do not have the power to move consistently large numbers of votes one way or the other. They can, however, affect some votes—perhaps enough to affect the outcome of a closely fought piece of legislation.[14]

Neustadt stresses that a president's influence is related to his professional reputation and prestige. When a president pushes hard for a bill that Congress eventually defeats or emasculates, the president's reputation is hurt. The public perceives him as weak or as showing poor judgment, and Congress becomes even less likely to cooperate with him in the future. President Clinton was clearly damaged by his failure to gain passage of his ambitious plan to reform the nation's health-care system. Yet presidents cannot easily avoid controversial bills, especially those meant to deliver on campaign promises. Clinton took risks with his strong support for controversial legislation such as NAFTA and handgun control measures, and he gained considerable respect for his efforts when these bills were enacted. One scholar describes the dilemma facing presidents this way: "If they risk big, they may gain big, but they are more likely to fail big. If they choose safe strategies, there is no doubt that they will be criticized for not seeking greater yields."[15]

The importance of bargaining skills and the informal nature of presidential power has become so central to the study of the executive branch that recently some political scientists have felt it necessary to remind us that presidents' formal powers are of consequence.[16] Presidents have the authority to order actions or policy changes in many areas. Harry Truman ordered the racial integration of the armed services and Bill Clinton ordered that gays and lesbians be permitted to serve (though not openly) in the military. The institutional resources of the presidency enhance each president's ability to accomplish his goals.[17]

The President and the Public

Neustadt's analysis suggests that a popular president is more persuasive than an unpopular one. A popular president has more power to persuade because he can use his public support as a resource in the bargaining process.[18] Members of Congress who know that the president is highly popular back home have more incentive to cooperate with the administration. If the president and his aides know that a member of Congress does not want to be seen as hostile to the president, they can apply more leverage to achieve a favorable compromise in a legislative struggle.

A familiar aspect of the modern presidency is the effort presidents devote to mobilizing public support for their programs. A president uses televised addresses (and the media coverage surrounding them), remarks to reporters, and public appearances to speak directly to the American people and convince them of the wisdom of his policies.

In recent years, presidents have increased their direct communication with the American people; as Figure 12.1 illustrates, the number of public presidential appearances has grown sharply since World War II. Obviously, modern technology has contributed to this growth. Nonetheless, the increase in public appearances and speeches represents something more than increased visibility for the president and his views. The power of the presidency has also changed fundamentally. During times when congressional leadership was weak and when political parties were in decline, expectations of the presidency grew. Over the years, Americans have come to expect more of the president in terms of setting the national agenda and offering leadership to the Congress.

Presidential popularity is typically at its highest during a president's first year in office. This "honeymoon period" affords the president a particularly good opportunity to use public support to get some of his programs through Congress.[19] When Ronald Reagan made a televised appeal for support for a legislative proposal during his first year in office, some members of Congress received calls and letters running ten to one in favor of the president. At the beginning of his second term, however, congressional offices typically received an equal number of negative and positive responses after a Reagan appeal.[20] Perhaps the positions he advocated were less attractive, but it was also clear that the public viewed Reagan with a more skeptical eye than it had four years earlier.

Several factors generally explain the rise and fall in presidential popularity. First, public approval of the job done by a president is affected by economic conditions, such as inflation and unemployment. Voters hold presidents responsible for the state of the economy, although much of what happens in the economy is beyond presidents' control. Second, a president is affected by unanticipated events of all types that occur during his administration.[21] When American embassy personnel were taken hostage in Teheran by militant anti-American Iranians, Jimmy Carter's popularity soared. This "rally 'round the flag" support for the president eventually gave way to frustration with his inability to gain the hostages' release, and Carter's popularity plummeted. The third factor that affects presidential popularity is American involvement in a war. Lyndon Johnson, for example, suffered a loss of popularity during his escalation of the American effort in Vietnam.[22]

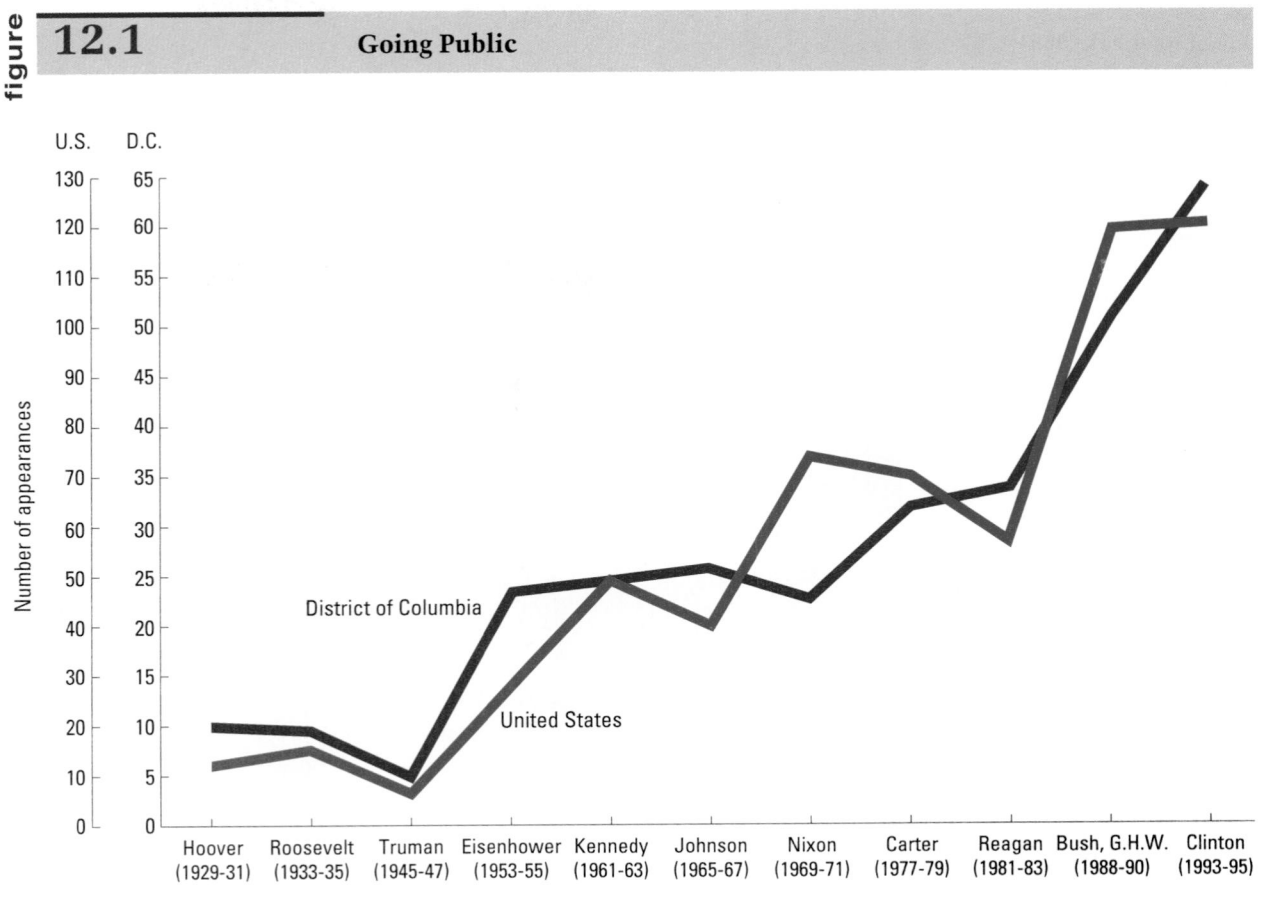

figure 12.1   Going Public

This graph depicts the average number of public appearances made in a year by presidents from 1929 to 1995.* The increase in presidential public appearances is driven in large part by the efforts of presidents to rally public support for their proposals and policies.

* Only the first three years of their first terms were examined; the fourth year was not tabulated in an effort to exclude appearances arranged with an eye toward an upcoming election. Gerald Ford's term is also excluded for this reason.

Source: From Samuel Kernell, *Going Public*, 3/e, p. 118. Copyright © 1997. Used by permission of CQ Press.

Presidents closely monitor their popularity because it is widely regarded as a basic report card on how well they are performing their duties. First-term presidents are especially concerned about their popularity because they are worried about their reelection prospects. Carter, Ford, and Bush, Sr., all unpopular at the time of their reelection campaign, were defeated in their efforts to win another term. A president's popularity can change dramatically during the course of a term. In the aftermath of the Gulf War, roughly nine in ten Americans approved of President Bush's performance in office. A month before the 1992 election, however, fewer than four in ten Americans approved of Bush.

Like Father, Like Son ★

The two George Bushes are the second set of father and son presidents. President John Quincy Adams (1825–1829) was the son of President John Adams (1797–1801). Two other pairs of presidents were related: Benjamin Harrison (1889–1893) was the grandson of William Henry Harrison (1841), and Theodore Roosevelt (1901–1909) and Franklin Roosevelt (1933–1945) were fifth cousins.

The strategy of leading by courting public opinion has considerable risks. It is not easy to move public opinion, and presidents who plan to use it as leverage in dealing with Congress are left highly vulnerable if public support for their position does not materialize. When Bill Clinton came into office, he was strongly predisposed toward governing by leading public opinion. His strategy worked poorly, though, because he was frequently unsuccessful in rallying the public to his side on issues crucial to his administration, such as national health insurance. After his first two years in office, he told an interviewer that the problems bedeviling his presidency were due to a failure to communicate: "What I've got to do is to spend more time communicating with the American people about what we've done and where we're going."[23] Communicating with the public is crucial to a modern president's success, but so too is an ability to form bipartisan coalitions in Congress and broad interest group coalitions. Clinton's administration suffered from shortcomings in these areas as well.[24]

Presidents' obsessive concern with public opinion can be defended as a means of furthering majoritarian democracy: the president tries to gauge what the people want so that he can offer policies that reflect popular preferences. As discussed in Chapter 2, responsiveness to the public's views is a bedrock principle of democracy, and presidents should respond to public opinion as well as try to lead it.[25] Some believe that presidents are too concerned about their popularity and are unwilling to champion unpopular causes or take principled stands that may affect their poll ratings.

Commenting on the presidential polls that first became widely used during his term, Harry Truman said, "I wonder how far Moses would have gone if he'd taken a poll in Egypt?"[26]

THE ELECTORAL CONNECTION

In his farewell address to the nation, Jimmy Carter lashed out at the interest groups that had plagued his presidency. Interest groups, he said, "distort our purposes because the national interest is not always the sum of all our single or special interests." Carter noted the president's singular responsibility: "The president is the only elected official charged with representing all the people."[27] Like all other presidents, Carter quickly recognized the dilemma of majoritarianism versus pluralism after he took office. The president must try to please countless separate constituencies while trying to do what is best for the whole country.

It is easy to stand on the sidelines and say that presidents should always try to follow a majoritarian path, pursuing policies that reflect the preferences of most citizens. However, simply by running for office, candidates align themselves with particular segments of the population. As a result of their electoral strategy, their identification with activists in their party, and their own political views, candidates come into office with an interest in pleasing some constituencies more than others.

As the election campaign proceeds, each candidate tries to win votes from different groups of voters through his stand on various issues. Because issue stances can cut both ways—attracting some voters but driving others away—candidates may try to finesse an issue by being deliberately vague. Candidates sometimes hope that voters will put their own interpretations on ambiguous stances. If the tactic works, the candidate will attract some voters without offending others. During the 1968 campaign, Nixon said he was committed to ending the war in Vietnam but gave few details about how he would accomplish that end. He wanted to appeal not only to those who were in favor of military pressure against the North Vietnamese but also to those who wanted quick military disengagement.[28]

Presidential Elections

mandate
An endorsement by voters. Presidents sometimes argue they have been given a mandate to carry out policy proposals.

But candidates cannot be deliberately vague about all issues. A candidate who is noncommittal on too many issues appears wishy-washy. And future presidents do not build their political careers without working strongly for and becoming associated with important issues and constituencies. Moreover, after the election is over, the winning candidate wants to claim that he has been given a **mandate,** or endorsement, by the voters to carry out the policies he campaigned on. Newly chosen presidents make a majoritarian interpretation of the electoral process, claiming that their election-day victory is an expression of the direct will of the people. For such a claim to be credible, the candidate must have emphasized some specific issues during the campaign and offered some distinctive solutions.

Mandates tend to be more rhetorical than real.[29] Although presidents claim that the votes they receive at the polls are expressions of support for their policy proposals, more dispassionate observers usually find it difficult to document concrete evidence of broad public support for the range of specific policies a winning candidate wants to pursue. As noted in the opening of this chapter, President George W. Bush entered office without even the illusion of a mandate. Consequently, in advocating his program,

table

12.1   Unified and Divided Party Control of Government, 1901–2002

Divided government exists when one party controls the White House and the other party controls one or both houses of Congress. Earlier in this century, divided government was rare. In recent years, however, it has become common.

Source: Updated from James A. Thurber, "An Introduction to Presidential-Congressional Rivalry," in *Rivals of Power*, ed. James A. Thurber, pp. 8–9. Copyright © 1996. Used by permission of CQ Press.

Year	President	Senate	House
1901–1903	R	R	R
1903–1905	R	R	R
1905–1907	R	R	R
1907–1909	R	R	R
1909–1911	R	R	R
1911–1913	R	R	D
1913–1915	D	D	D
1915–1917	D	D	D
1917–1919	D	D	D
1919–1921	D	R	R
1921–1923	R	R	R
1923–1925	R	R	R
1925–1927	R	R	R
1927–1929	R	R	R
1929–1931	R	R	R
1931–1933	R	R	D
1933–1935	D	D	D
1935–1937	D	D	D
1937–1939	D	D	D
1939–1941	D	D	D
1941–1943	D	D	D
1943–1945	D	D	D
1945–1947	D	D	D
1947–1949	D	R	R
1949–1951	D	D	D
1951–1953	D	D	D
1953–1955	R	R	R

divided government
The situation in which one party controls the White House and the other controls at least one house of Congress.

Can You Explain Why...
voters often select a president of one party and a House and/or Senate controlled by the other party?

he has emphasized national unity and bipartisanship instead of popular support. Even when a president wins a clear majority of the popular vote, the voters' public policy preferences can be muddy.

A central reason why it is difficult to read the president's political tea leaves from election results is that the president is elected independently of Congress. Often this leads to **divided government,** with one party controlling the White House and the other party controlling at least one house of Congress. This may seem politically schizophrenic, with the electorate saying one thing by electing a president from one party and another by its vote for legislators of the other party. This does not appear to bother the American people, however: polls often show that the public feels it is desirable for control of the government to be divided between Republicans and Democrats.[30]

While voters tell pollsters that they prefer divided government, whether they intentionally mark their ballot to try to bring that about is another— and very complicated—question. An individual can believe that it's better overall for the country if the Republicans control one branch and the

Year	President	Senate	House
1955–1957	R	D	D
1957–1959	R	D	D
1959–1961	R	D	D
1961–1963	D	D	D
1963–1965	D	D	D
1965–1967	D	D	D
1967–1969	D	D	D
1969–1971	R	D	D
1971–1973	R	D	D
1973–1975	R	D	D
1975–1977	R	D	D
1977–1979	D	D	D
1979–1981	D	D	D
1981–1983	R	R	D
1983–1985	R	R	D
1985–1987	R	R	D
1987–1989	R	D	D
1989–1991	R	D	D
1991–1993	R	D	D
1993–1995	D	D	D
1995–1997	D	R	R
1997–1999	D	R	R
1999–2001	D	R	R
2001–2003	R	Tied*	R

☐ Unified party control of government
☐ Divided party control of government

Initially, Republicans maintained nominal control because Vice President Cheney could break a tie. Democrats took control after Senator James Jeffords of Vermont announced, in May 2001, that he was leaving the Republican Party and would serve as an independent.

Democrats another, but that doesn't mean that person will vote with that idea as a guide. Political scientists who have tried to determine voters' intent on this basis do not agree about whether voters intentionally try to elect divided government.[31] As Table 12.1 shows, divided government has become more and more frequent.

Voters appear to use quite different criteria when choosing a president than they do when choosing congressional representatives. As one scholar has noted, "Presidential candidates are evaluated according to their views on national issues and their competence in dealing with national problems. Congressional candidates are evaluated on their personal character and experience and on their devotion to district services and local issues."[32]

Congressional independence is at the heart of why contemporary presidents work so hard to gain public support for their policies.[33] Without a strong base of representatives and senators who feel their election was tied to his, a president often feels that he needs to win in the court of public opinion. Favorable public opinion can help a president build consensus in a highly

---

★ **compared with what?**

12.1   A Landslide for Sharon but a Divided Israeli Parliament

Unlike the United States presidential election just a few months earlier, there was no question as to who won the February 2001 Israeli election. Challenger Ariel Sharon crushed incumbent Prime Minister Ehud Barak 62.5 to 37.4 percent. Despite his overwhelming landslide, Sharon's victory stood apart from his party's standing in the legislature. As in the United States, voters in Israel make separate selections for their executive leader (prime minister) and for their legislators. This contrasts with most parliamentary systems, where the prime minister is simply the leader of the majority party in the legislature.

In Israel the electoral system is designed so that usually the prime minister and the members of the Knesset (the legislature) will be chosen at the same time. A session of the Knesset can last four years, though a prime minister can dissolve it and call for early elections. Also, the Knesset can essentially dissolve itself by letting the government fall on a vote of no confidence. The 2001 contest was precipitated, however, when Barak resigned his prime ministership and a new election was necessary. Under these circumstances no accompanying legislative election was required, and after the election Sharon

inherited the same Knesset that Barak left behind.

To call Israel a multiparty system hardly does justice to the term. Seventeen different political parties hold seats in the current Knesset. There are no districts or states that candidates compete in—everyone runs on a nationwide basis. When voters go to the polls they cast a ballot for one party. If a party obtains enough votes to elect just one person to the Knesset, the person listed number one on that party's list goes to the parliament. The country uses a proportional representation system, so if a party gets 15 percent of the vote, it gets roughly 15 percent of the seats. An unusual feature of Israel's electoral system is its low threshold for a party to win seats. A party whose list wins just 1.5 percent of the national vote is guaranteed a seat in the legislature. Most parliamentary systems require a higher threshold to discourage small parties from splintering the legislature.

The Knesset has 120 members and a government is formed when at least 61 members commit to becoming part of the ruling coalition. Not surprisingly, forming a government out of seventeen parties is no small task. After the 2001 election, the largest party in the Knesset was Barak's Labor Party, which had just

---

gridlock
A situation in which government is incapable of acting on important issues, usually because of divided government.

independent legislative branch. Scholars are divided about the impact of divided government. One study showed that just as much significant legislation gets passed and signed into law when there is divided government as when one party controls both the White House and Congress.[34] Using different approaches, other scholars have shown that divided governments are in fact less productive than unified ones.[35] Despite these differences in the scholarly literature, political scientists generally don't believe that divided government produces **gridlock,** a situation in which government is incapable of acting on important policy issues.[36] There is a strong tradition of bipartisan policymaking in Congress that facilitates cooperation when the government is divided. The rising partisanship in Congress (recall Figure 11.3) may, however, make divided government more of a problem.

A parliamentary system, in which the legislative and executive branches are united, might seem the logical solution to the problem of

twenty-six seats. Sharon's own party, Likud, had only nineteen seats. Ten of the other parties had five seats or less, so forming a government is a process of building a coalition of strange bedfellows. Small parties of just a few members can exert enormous leverage over the government, demanding significant concessions from the prime minister even though their support nationwide is modest.

Although his margin of victory was impressive, Sharon still faces a bitterly divided country. The central issue in the election was Barak's bargaining with Palestinian leader

Yasser Arafat. Before the year 2000 was out, negotiations between the two, aided by the Clinton administration, moved the peace process tantalizingly close to a resolution over the most contentious issues. In September, Sharon ignited a firestorm of controversy when he led a large security detail to the grounds of the Aksa Mosque in Jerusalem's old city. This is the site where it is said that Muhammad ascended to heaven and it is revered by Muslims worldwide. The site is no less venerated by Jews, because it was the location of the first and second temples.

Sharon's inflammatory act led to violence by the Palestinians against Jews and violence by the Israeli government against Palestinians in response. Support for Barak and the peace process declined and with his government teetering, Barak decided to resign rather than call for new elections for both the Knesset and prime minister. The 72-year-old Sharon, with a long career in the military, was much more hawkish than Barak and promised to pull back what Barak had offered in peace proposals to Arafat. The voters clearly preferred Sharon's harder line. How this affects the peace process remains to be seen. With the structure of the Israeli electoral system and the current makeup of the Knesset, Sharon is traversing a high wire with no net below.

divided government. In parliamentary systems, however, the ruling government is sometimes internally divided because it is composed of a coalition of various political parties (see Compared with What? 12.1).

THE EXECUTIVE BRANCH ESTABLISHMENT

As the president tries to maintain the support of his electoral coalition for the policies he pursues, he draws on the extensive resources of the executive branch of government. The president has a White House staff that helps him formulate policy. The vice president is another resource; his duties within the administration vary according to his relationship with the president. The president's cabinet secretaries—the heads of the major departments of the national government—play a number of roles, including the critical function of administering the programs that fall within their jurisdictions. Effective presidents think strategically about how best to use the resources available to them. Each must find ways to organize structures and processes that best suit his management style.[37]

The Executive Office of the President

The president depends heavily on key aides. They advise him on crucial political choices, devise the general strategies the administration will follow in pursuing congressional and public support, and control access to the president to ensure that he has enough time for his most important tasks. Consequently, he needs to trust and respect these top staffers; many in a president's inner circle of assistants are long-time associates. The president's personal staff constitutes the White House Office.

Presidents typically have a chief of staff, who may be a first among equals or, in some administrations, the unquestioned leader of the staff. H. R. Haldeman, Richard Nixon's chief of staff, played the stronger role. He ran a highly disciplined operation, frequently prodding staff members to work harder and faster. Haldeman also felt that part of his role was to take the heat for the president by assuming responsibility for many of the administration's unpopular decisions: "Every president needs a son of a bitch, and I'm Nixon's."[38] Hamilton Jordan, President Carter's chief of staff, was at the other end of the spectrum: Carter did not give him the authority to administer the White House with a strong hand.

Presidents also have a national security adviser to provide daily briefings on foreign and military affairs and longer-range analyses of issues confronting the administration. The Council of Economic Advisers is also located in the White House. Senior domestic policy advisers help determine the administration's basic approach to areas such as health, education, and social services.

Below these top aides are the large staffs that serve them and the president. These staffs are organized around certain specialties. Some staff members work on political matters, such as communicating with interest groups, maintaining relations with ethnic and religious minorities, and managing party affairs. One staff deals exclusively with the media, and a legislative liaison staff lobbies the Congress for the administration. The large Office of Management and Budget (OMB) analyzes budget requests, is involved in the policymaking process, and examines agency management practices. This extended White House executive establishment, including the White House Office, is known as the **Executive Office of the President.** The Executive Office employs close to 1,600 individuals and has an annual budget of nearly $374 million.[39]

Executive Office of the President
The president's executive aides and their staffs; the extended White House executive establishment.

No one agrees about a "right way" for a president to organize his White House staff. Dwight Eisenhower, for example, a former general, wanted clear lines of authority and a hierarchical structure that mirrored a military command. One factor that influences how a president uses his senior staff is the degree to which he delegates authority to them. Carter immersed himself in the policymaking process to ensure that he made all the significant decisions himself. Early in his administration, he told his staff, "Unless there's a holocaust, I'll take care of everything the same day it comes in."[40]

When Bill Clinton took over the White House, he instituted a loose staff structure that gave many top staffers direct access to him. Clinton made a

A Heartbeat Away

Dick Cheney emerged quickly as a major influence in the new Bush administration and the President has relied on him in many areas. A principal responsibility has been to lead a task force developing the administration's energy policy. One nagging concern, however, has been Cheney's health. He's had a number of heart attacks, most recently right after the election in 2000.

surprising (and questionable) choice for his chief of staff, Mack McLarty. McLarty, a friend of Clinton since childhood and a successful Arkansas businessman, had no Washington experience. This appointment seemed to suggest that Clinton really wanted to be his own chief of staff, deeply involved in the nuts and bolts of White House policymaking. Indeed, as the White House planned the president's program during the first year, "Clinton found no detail too small for his attention."[41] McLarty was soon moved aside and new staff aides imposed a much more tightly run White House Office.

George W. Bush has a different management philosophy than Clinton. As governor of Texas, he spent relatively little time reading policy documents and making policy decisions. He was more willing to spend time on lobbying legislators to get his policies enacted.[42] Whether his presidential staff, led by Chief of Staff Andrew Card, will try to push him toward different priorities is unclear at this writing. Presidents must ensure that staff members feel comfortable telling him things he may not want to hear. Telling the president of the United States he is misguided on something is not an easy thing to do. George Stephanopoulos, a close aide to President Clinton, acknowledged frankly in his memoirs that he was too eager to ingratiate himself with Clinton because he saw himself in a competitive position with other staff aides. In retrospect, he realizes that he should have confronted Clinton early in the 1992 campaign about his infidelity. But says Stephanopoulos, "I needed Clinton to see me as his defender, not his interrogator, which made me, of course, his enabler."[43]

The Vice President

The vice president's primary function is to serve as standby equipment. Only a heartbeat from the presidency itself, vice presidents must be ready and able to take over the presidency if anything happens to the president during his term in office. Traditionally, vice presidents have not been used in any important advisory capacity. Instead, presidents tend to give them political chores—campaigning, fundraising, and "stroking" the party faithful. This is often the case because vice presidential candidates are chosen for reasons that have more to do with the political campaign than with governing the nation. Richard Nixon chose the little-known governor of Maryland, Spiro Agnew, to be his vice-presidential candidate and assigned Agnew to play the same role Nixon had under Dwight Eisenhower—that of a political hatchet man who went after the Democrats.

President Carter broke the usual pattern of relegating the vice president to political chores; he relied heavily on his vice president, Walter Mondale. Carter was wise enough to recognize that Mondale's experience in the Senate could be of great value to him, especially because Carter had never served in Congress. Al Gore played a significant role in the Clinton administration and was one of the president's most influential advisers. The new vice president, Dick Cheney, comes to the office with impressive qualifications as a former member of the House of Representatives, presidential chief of staff, Secretary of Defense, and head of Halliburton, a very large oil services corporation. It's clear that President Bush has a great deal of confidence in him and that he will be a major force within the administration.

The Cabinet

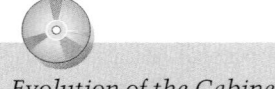

Evolution of the Cabinet

cabinet
A group of presidential advisers; the heads of the executive departments and other key officials.

Can You Explain Why...
we don't have cabinet government?

The president's **cabinet** is composed of the heads of the departments of the executive branch and a small number of other key officials, such as the head of the Office of Management and Budget and the ambassador to the United Nations. The cabinet has expanded greatly since George Washington formed his first cabinet, which included an attorney general and the secretaries of state, treasury, and war. Clearly, the growth of the cabinet to fourteen departments reflects the growth of government responsibility and intervention in areas such as energy, housing, and transportation.

In theory, the members of the cabinet constitute an advisory body that meets with the president to debate major policy decisions. In practice, however, cabinet meetings have been described as "vapid non-events in which there has been a deliberate non-exchange of information as part of a process of mutual nonconsultation."[44] One Carter cabinet member called the meetings "adult Show-and-Tell."[45] Why is this so? First, the cabinet has become rather large. Counting department heads, other officials of cabinet rank, and presidential aides, it is a body of at least twenty people—a size that many presidents find unwieldy for the give-and-take of political decision making. Second, most cabinet members have limited areas of expertise and simply cannot contribute much to deliberations in policy areas they know little about. The secretary of defense, for example, would probably be a poor choice to help decide important issues of agricultural policy. Third, the president often chooses cabinet members because of their reputations or to give his cabinet some racial, ethnic, geographic, gender, or religious balance, not because they are personally close to the president or easy for him to work with. Consider Clinton's attorney general, Janet Reno, for example. Although she was respected by the public for her independence, she had—at best—a prickly relationship with Clinton. Newspaper reports suggested that the president wanted to replace her after his 1996 victory, but she chose not to resign, and considering the number of investigations of the president then under way, he could not fire her.

Finally, modern presidents do not rely on the cabinet to make policy because they have such large White House staffs, which offer most of the advisory support they need. And in contrast to cabinet secretaries, who may

Cabinet Selections

Shortly before taking office President Bush (with Vice President Cheney at left) made a series of introductions of the new members of his cabinet. Pictured here are four of his choices (from right to left): Tommy Thompson (governor of Wisconsin), secretary of Health and Human Services; Anthony Principi (businessman and Vietnam veteran), secretary of Veterans Affairs; Gale Norton (former Colorado attorney general), secretary of the Interior; and Rod Paige (Houston superintendent of schools), secretary of Education.

be pulled in different directions by the wishes of the president and those of their clientele groups, staffers in the White House Office are likely to see themselves as being responsible to the president alone. Despite periodic calls for the cabinet to be a collective decision-making body, cabinet meetings seem doomed to be little more than academic exercises. In practice, presidents prefer the flexibility of ad hoc groups, specialized White House staffs, and the advisers and cabinet secretaries with whom they feel most comfortable.

More broadly, presidents use their personal staff and the large Executive Office of the President to centralize control over the entire executive branch. The vast size of the executive branch and the number and complexity of decisions that must be made each day pose a challenge for the White House. Each president must be careful to appoint people to top administration positions who are not merely competent but also passionate about the president's goals and skillful enough to lead others in the executive branch to fight for the president's program instead of their own agendas. Ronald Reagan was especially good at communicating to his top appointees clear ideological principles that they were to follow in shaping administration policy. To fulfill more of their political goals and policy preferences, modern presidents have given their various staffs more responsibility for overseeing decision making throughout the executive branch.[46]

THE PRESIDENT AS NATIONAL LEADER

With an election behind him and the resources of his office at hand, a president is ready to lead the nation. Although not every president's leadership is acclaimed, each president enters office with a general vision of how government should approach policy issues. During his term, a president spends much of his time trying to get Congress to enact legislation that reflects his general philosophy and specific policy preferences.

From Political Values . . .

Presidents differ greatly in their views of the role of government. Lyndon Johnson had a strong liberal ideology concerning domestic affairs. He believed that government has a responsibility to help disadvantaged Americans. Johnson described his vision of justice in his inaugural address:

Lyndon Jonnson's Inaugural Speech

> Justice was the promise that all who made the journey would share in the fruits of the land.
>
> In a land of wealth, families must not live in hopeless poverty. In a land rich in harvest, children just must not go hungry. In a land of healing miracles, neighbors must not suffer and die untended. In a great land of learning and scholars, young people must be taught to read and write.
>
> For [the] more than thirty years that I have served this nation, I have believed that this injustice to our people, this waste of our resources, was our real enemy. For thirty years or more, with the resources I have had, I have vigilantly fought against it.[47]

Johnson used *justice* and *injustice* as code for *equality* and *inequality*. He used them six times in his speech; he used *freedom* only twice. Johnson used his popularity, his skills, and the resources of his office to press for a "just" America—a "Great Society."

To achieve his Great Society, Johnson sent Congress an unprecedented package of liberal legislation. He launched projects such as the Job Corps (which created centers and camps offering vocational training and work experience to youths aged sixteen to twenty-one), Medicare (which provided medical care for the elderly), and the National Teacher Corps (which paid teachers to work in impoverished neighborhoods). Supported by huge Democratic majorities in Congress during 1965 and 1966, he had tremendous success getting his proposals through. Liberalism was in full swing.

In 1985, exactly twenty years after Johnson's inaugural speech, Ronald Reagan took his oath of office for the second time. Addressing the nation, Reagan reasserted his conservative philosophy. He emphasized freedom, using the term fourteen times, and failed to mention justice or equality once. In the following excerpts, we have italicized the term *freedom* for easy reference:

Ronald Reagan's Second Inaugural Speech

> By 1980, we knew it was time to renew our faith, to strive with all our strength toward the ultimate in individual *freedom* consistent with an orderly society. . . . We will not rest until every American enjoys the fullness of *freedom*, dignity, and opportunity as our birthright. . . . Americans . . . turned the tide of history away from totalitarian darkness and into the warm sunlight of human *freedom*. . . . Let history say of us, these were golden years—when the American Revolution was reborn, when *freedom* gained new life, when America reached for her best. . . . *Freedom* and incentives unleash the drive and entrepreneurial genius that are at the core of human progress. . . . From new *freedom* will spring new opportunities for growth. . . . Yet history has shown that peace does not come, nor will our *freedom* be preserved by goodwill alone. There are those in the world who scorn our vision of human dignity and *freedom*. . . . Human *freedom* is on the march, and nowhere more so than in our own hemisphere. *Freedom* is one of the deepest and noblest aspirations of the human spirit. . . . America must remain *freedom's* staunchest friend, for *freedom*

Different Visions

Lyndon Johnson and Ronald Reagan had strikingly different visions of American democracy and what their goals should be as president. Johnson was committed to equality for all and major civil rights laws are among the most important legacies of his administration. He's pictured here signing the 1964 Civil Rights Act. Reagan was devoted to reducing the size of government so as to enhance our freedom. He worked hard to reduce both taxes and spending.

is our best ally. . . . Every victory for human *freedom* will be a victory for world peace. . . . One people under God, dedicated to the dream of *freedom* that He has placed in the human heart.[48]

Reagan turned Johnson's philosophy on its head, declaring that "government is not the solution to our problem. Government *is* the problem." During his presidency, Reagan worked to undo many welfare and social service programs and cut funding for programs such as the Job Corps and food stamps. By the end of his term, there had been a fundamental shift in federal spending, with sharp increases in defense spending and "decreases in federal social programs [which] served to defend Democratic interests and constituencies."[49]

Although Johnson and Reagan had well-defined political philosophies and communicated a clear vision of where they wanted to lead the country, not all presidents move strongly toward one ideological position. George W. Bush's inaugural speech in 2001 struck the themes of equality and freedom about evenly. Interestingly, he talked more about civil society and community.[50] It's too early to tell whether this communitarian rhetoric will come to define his administration, but it's clear that he doesn't want to be confined by traditional conservative ideology.

. . . To Policy Agenda

The roots of particular policy proposals, then, can be traced to the more general political ideology of the president. Presidential candidates outline that philosophy of government during their campaign for the White House. As Figure 12.2 illustrates, when presidential candidates give their acceptance speech at their nominating convention, they are increasingly likely to discuss their policy goals in terms of appeals to different interest groups. Over time, presidential candidates have been increasingly likely to make appeals for support that reflect a pluralist view of American politics.

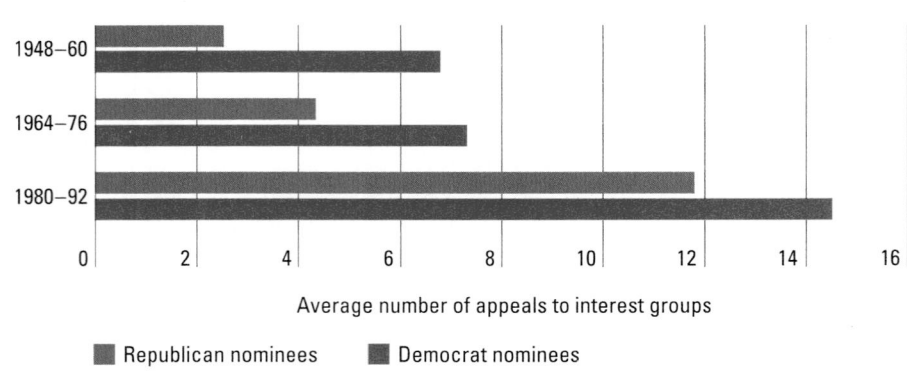

figure 12.2   Group Appeals

This graph shows the results of an analysis of the acceptance speeches of both Republican and Democratic presidential nominees from 1948 to 1992 at their national party conventions. It was noted each time the nominee appealed to an interest group constituency in this widely followed speech, and a summary count was produced. Interest group appeals are up sharply for both of the parties.

Average number of appeals to interest groups

■ Republican nominees   ■ Democrat nominees

Source: Jeffrey M. Berry and Deborah Schildkraut, "Citizen Groups, Political Parties, and Electoral Coalitions," in Anne Costain and Andrew McFarland, eds., *Social Movements and American Political Institutions* (Boulder, Colo.: Rowman and Littlefield, 1998), p. 145.

When the hot rhetoric of the presidential campaign meets the cold reality of what is possible in Washington, the newly elected president must make some hard choices about what to push for during the coming term. These choices are reflected in the bills the president submits to Congress, as well as in the degree to which he works for their passage. The president's bills, introduced by his allies in the House and Senate, always receive a good deal of initial attention. In the words of one Washington lobbyist, "When a president sends up a bill, it takes first place in the queue. All other bills take second place."[51]

The president's role in legislative leadership is largely a twentieth-century phenomenon. Not until the Budget and Accounting Act of 1921 did executive branch departments and agencies have to clear their proposed budget bills with the White House. Before this, the president did not even coordinate proposals for how much the executive branch would spend on all the programs it administered. Later, Franklin D. Roosevelt required that all major legislative proposals by an agency or department be cleared by the White House. No longer could a department submit a bill without White House support.[52]

Roosevelt's influence on the relationship between the president and Congress went far beyond this new administrative arrangement. With the nation in the midst of the Great Depression, Roosevelt began his first term in 1933 with an ambitious array of legislative proposals. During the first 100 days Congress was in session, it enacted fifteen significant laws, including the Agricultural Adjustment Act, the act creating the Civilian Conservation Corps, and the National Industrial Recovery Act. Never had a president demanded—and received—so much from Congress. Roosevelt's legacy was that the president would henceforth provide aggressive leadership of Congress through his own legislative program.

Chief Lobbyist

When Franklin D. Roosevelt and Harry Truman first became heavily involved in preparing legislative packages, political scientists typically described the process as one in which "the president proposes and

Congress disposes." In other words, once the president sends his legislation to Capitol Hill, Congress decides what to do with it. Over time, though, presidents have become increasingly active in all stages of the legislative process. The president is expected not only to propose legislation but also to make sure that it passes. Generally, a president has the most success at this task during his first year in office (see Figure 12.3).

The president's efforts to influence Congress are reinforced by the work of his legislative liaison staff. All departments and major agencies have legislative specialists as well. These department and agency people work with the White House liaison staff to coordinate the administration's lobbying on major issues.

The **legislative liaison staff** is the communications link between the White House and Congress. As a bill slowly makes its way through Congress, liaison staffers advise the president or a cabinet secretary on the problems that emerge. They specify what parts of a bill are in trouble and may have to be modified or dropped. They tell their boss what amendments are likely to be offered, which members of Congress need to be lobbied, and what the bill's chances for passage are with or without certain provisions. Decisions on how the administration will respond to such developments must then be reached. For example, when the Reagan White House realized that it was still a few votes short of victory on a budget bill in the House, it reversed its opposition to a sugar price-support bill. This attracted the votes of representatives from Louisiana and Florida, two sugar-growing states, for the budget bill. The White House would not call what happened a deal, but it noted that "adjustments and considerations" had been made.[53] Still, not all demands from legislators can be met. As one legislative liaison aide noted, "One of our problems is that we have to tell people 'no' a lot."[54]

A certain amount of the president's job consists of stereotypical arm twisting—pushing reluctant legislators to vote a certain way. Yet most day-in, day-out interactions between the White House and Congress tend to be more subtle, with the liaison staff trying to build consensus by working cooperatively with legislators. When a congressional committee is working on a bill, liaison people talk to committee members individually to see what concerns they have and to help fashion a compromise if some differ with the president's position. This type of quiet negotiation disappeared during the 1995–1996 session of Congress, when the new Republican majority in the House, heady with excitement at controlling the chamber for the first time in forty years, briefly let the government shut down on two occasions rather than bargain with the president. More typically, even when partisanship is running high, quiet negotiations continue.[55] For President Bush, a key task is to keep the conservative wing of the party on board while he cuts deals with centrist Democrats.[56]

The White House also works directly with interest groups in its efforts to build support for legislation. Presidential aides hope key lobbyists will activate the most effective lobbyists of all: the voters back home. Interest groups can quickly reach the constituents who are most concerned about a bill, using their communications network to mobilize members to write, call, or e-mail their members of Congress. There are so many interest groups in our pluralist political system that they could easily overload the White House with their demands. Consequently, except for those groups most important to the president, lobbies tend to be granted access only when the White House needs them to activate public opinion.[57]

12.3   Legislative Leadership

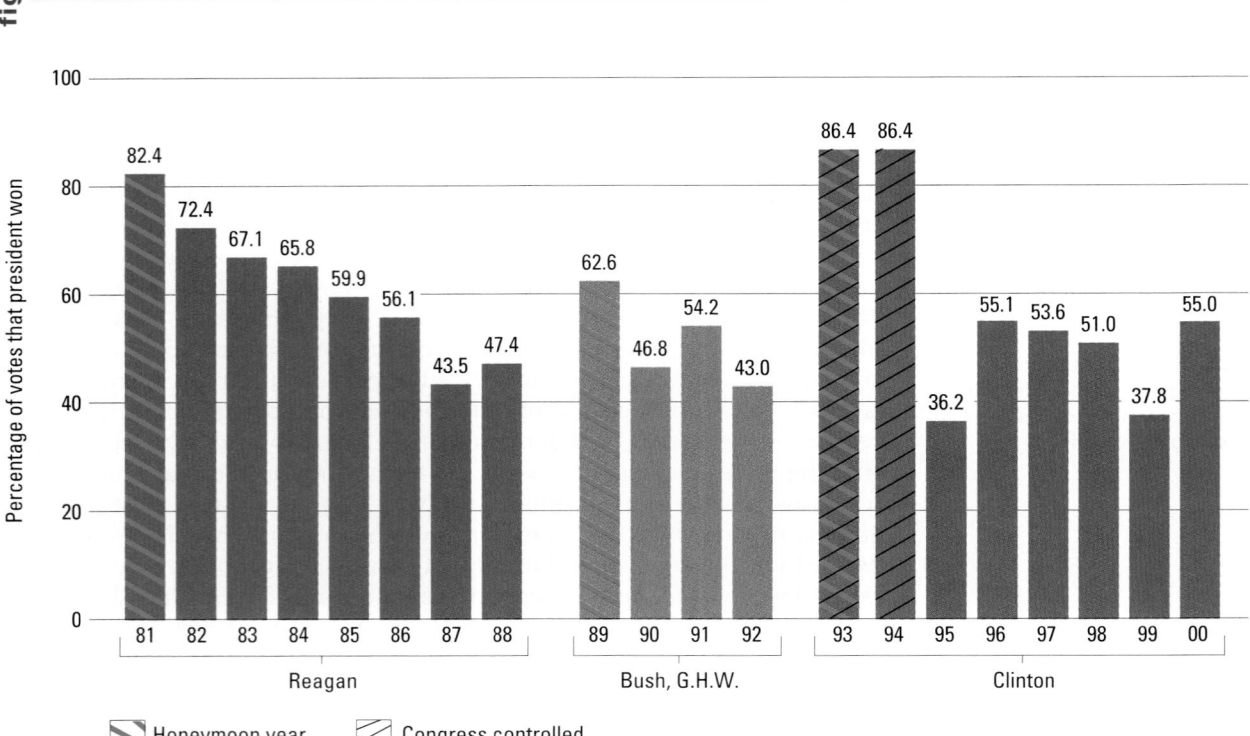

Presidents vary considerably in their ability to convince Congress to enact the legislation they send to Capitol Hill. Generally, presidents have their greatest success in Congress during their "honeymoon," the period immediately following their inauguration. As this figure demonstrates, Presidents Reagan, Bush, and Clinton all did well during their first year in office. President Clinton fared best, and in a sense he even had an extended honeymoon into his second year, but he was the only one of the three who sent legislation to a Congress controlled by his own party. Note the dramatic change in Clinton's fortunes in 1995, when he had to cope with a Republican Congress.

Source: *CQ Weekly*, various issues.

Although much of the liaison staff's work with Congress is done in a cooperative spirit, agreement cannot always be reached. When Congress passes a bill the president opposes, he may veto it and send it back to Congress; as we noted earlier, Congress can override a veto with a two-thirds majority of those voting in each house. Presidents use their veto power sparingly, but the threat that a president will veto an unacceptable bill increases his bargaining leverage with members of Congress. We have also seen that a president's leverage with Congress is related to his standing with the American people. The ability of the president and his liaison staff to bargain with members of Congress is enhanced when he is riding high in the public opinion polls and hindered when the public is critical of his performance.[58]

Party Leader

Part of the president's job is to lead his party. This is very much an informal duty, with no prescribed tasks. In this respect, American presidents are considerably different from European prime ministers, who are the formal leader of their party in the national legislature as well as the head of their government. In the American system, a president and members of his party in Congress can clearly take very different positions on the issues before them. When President Clinton reached agreement with Republican congressional leaders on a balanced budget deal, it provoked a great deal of controversy within the Democratic party. Many congressional Democrats refused to join in the balanced-budget celebration; they thought the president had betrayed the party's ideals by trimming Medicare and taxes on the wealthy. Barney Frank, a Democrat from Massachusetts, expressed the liberals' anger with the president's leadership by saying, "We addressed [an envelope] to the 'Democratic president of the United States.' It came back 'addressee unknown.'"[59] Because political parties in Europe tend to have strong national organizations, prime ministers have more reason to lead the party organization. In the United States, national party committees play a relatively minor role in national politics, although they are active in raising money for their congressional candidates (see Chapter 8).

The president himself has become the "fundraiser in chief" for his party. Since presidents have a vital interest in more members of their party being elected to the House and Senate, they have a strong incentive to spend time raising money for congressional candidates. All incumbent presidents travel frequently to fundraising dinners in different states where they are the main attraction. Donors will pay substantial sums—$1,000 a ticket is common—to go to such a dinner. In addition to helping elect more members of his party, a not so small by-product for the president is the gratitude of legislators. It's a lot harder to say no to a president's request for help on a bill when he spoke at your fundraiser during the last election.

THE PRESIDENT AS WORLD LEADER

The president's leadership responsibilities extend beyond Congress and the nation to the international arena. Each administration tries to further what it sees as the country's best interests in its relations with allies, adversaries, and the developing countries of the world. In this role, the president must be ready to act as diplomat and crisis manager.

Foreign Relations

From the end of World War II until the late 1980s, presidents were preoccupied with containing communist expansion around the globe. Truman and Korea, Kennedy and Cuba, Johnson and Nixon and Vietnam, and Reagan and Nicaragua are just some examples of presidents and the communist crosses

As a young politician, Richard Nixon was notorious for his staunch anticommunism. As president, however, he achieved a stunning reversal of U.S. policy toward the People's Republic of China. His trip there in 1972 signaled an end to the Cold War hostility between the United States and the communist regime.

they had to bear. Presidents not only used overt and covert military means to fight communism but also tried to reduce tensions through negotiations. President Nixon made particularly important strides in this regard, completing an important arms control agreement with the Soviet Union and beginning negotiations with the Chinese, with whom the United States had had no formal diplomatic relations.

With the collapse of communism in the Soviet Union and Eastern Europe, American presidents have entered a new era in international relations. The new presidential job description places much more emphasis on managing economic relations with the rest of the world. Trade relations are an especially difficult problem because presidents must balance the conflicting interests of foreign countries (many of them our allies), the interests of particular American industries, the overall needs of the American economy, and the demands of the legislative branch. President Clinton faced a particularly difficult dilemma when permanent normal trade relations with China came up for a vote in the Congress in 2000. Due to concern with human rights violations and other issues, a 1974 law required that each year Congress renew regular trade relations with China. If Congress did not pass such legislation, China would be subject to higher tariffs rather than the preferential trading rules most other U.S. trading partners received. An annual fight ensued over the legislation as critics of the Chinese regime tried to exact concessions from it as the price of renewal. As a means of promoting more trade with China and better relations with this important country, support grew for replacing the annual fight over renewal with permanent normal relations.

Many interests, especially farmers and manufacturers with goods to export to China, were intensely interested in permanent normal relations.[60]

Labor unions, worried about the price advantage that Chinese companies would have in the U.S. market because of the lower wages there, were adamantly opposed to changing the law. More Chinese imports would surely lead to fewer manufacturing jobs here in the United States. Organized labor is a mainstay of the Democratic Party and it was difficult for Clinton and congressional Democrats to work against their traditionally loyal allies. Clinton believed that increased trade was in the best long-term interests of the country and he worked skillfully to push the agreement through Congress.

The decline of communism has not enabled the president to ignore security issues. The world remains a dangerous place, and regional conflicts can still embroil the United States (see Politics in a Changing World 12.1). When Iraq invaded and quickly conquered Kuwait in August 1990, President Bush felt he had no choice but to respond firmly to protect our economic interests and to stand beside our Arab allies in the area. Bush worked the phones hard to get both Western and Arab leaders to join the United States in a coordinated military buildup in the area surrounding Kuwait. He had laid the groundwork for such cooperation with the heavy emphasis he had placed in the early months of his administration on building personal relationships with many important heads of state. It was, said one journalist, a "dazzling performance. In roughly four days, Bush organized the world against Saddam Hussein."[61]

Bush's impressive leadership of the twenty-eight-nation coalition continued in the months that followed. The coalition remained unified even through the difficult decision to go to war in January 1991, when the air campaign began. Bush played a key role in convincing the Israelis, who were not part of the coalition, to refrain from retaliating against Iraq after Israel came under attack from Scud missiles. (Iraq had hoped that by drawing Israel into the war, the United States' Arab allies would withdraw their support for the war because of their opposition to the Jewish state.) The successful ground war against Iraqi forces was a capstone to a remarkable foreign policy achievement.

Crisis Management

Periodically, the president faces a grave situation in which conflict is imminent or a small conflict threatens to explode into a larger war. Handling such episodes is a critical part of the president's job. Thus voters may make the candidates' personal judgment and intelligence primary considerations in how they cast their ballots. A major reason for Barry Goldwater's crushing defeat in the 1964 election was his warlike image. His bellicose rhetoric scared many Americans. Fearing that Goldwater would be too quick to resort to nuclear weapons, they voted for Lyndon Johnson instead.

A president must be able to exercise good judgment and remain cool in crisis situations. John Kennedy's behavior during the Cuban missile crisis of 1962 has become a model of effective crisis management. When the United States learned that the Soviet Union had placed missiles containing nuclear warheads in Cuba, U.S. government leaders saw those missiles as an unacceptable threat to this country's security. Kennedy asked a group of senior aides, including top people from the Pentagon, to advise

★ **politics in a changing** **world**

12.1   The Weight of the World

The world has become a more interdependent place, but it has not become any safer. Armed conflict remains all too common, and the collapse of the superpower rivalry between the United States and the former Soviet Union has not lessened pressure on the United States to use its power to stop warfare where it emerges around the globe. When conflict erupts, attention turns to the United States to see what it is prepared to do. Negotiation is always preferable, but in some cases, acting alone or with the United Nations or alliances, the United States has intervened with military force to end a war somewhere in the world.

During his time in office, President Clinton faced several difficult decisions involving the role of the United States and conflict abroad. Perhaps none was more agonizing than the fight in Kosovo. In January 1999, an ancient conflict in eastern Europe reignited. Serbia, a nation composed mainly of Eastern Orthodox Christians, was waging war against its own southern province, Kosovo, an area populated almost entirely by ethnic Albanian Muslims. The Serbian leader, Slobodan Milosevic, was also president of what remained of Yugoslavia, a formerly communist nation that had dwindled from six member republics to only two—Serbia and Montenegro. Kosovo had enjoyed considerable political freedom within Yugoslavia until 1989, when Milosevic took away its autonomy due to mistreatment of Serbian residents. The Kosovars resisted and eventually formed a guerilla movement, the Kosovo Liberation Army (KLA), to counter Serbian forces. Faced with a guerilla war, Milosevic responded with a brutal campaign of terror against the ethnic Albanians in Kosovo.

As the United States and other Western democracies learned more about what the Serbians were doing in Kosovo, they began to pressure Milosevic to accept a diplomatic solution to the growing crisis. To Milosevic and many other Serbs, Kosovo was a nonnegotiable issue. It was an historically important

region to Serbians, and to permit Kosovo to take even limited steps toward eventual independence was unthinkable. Milosevic's intransigence frustrated the Western allies; they didn't want to go to war against Yugoslavia, but they couldn't stand idly by and let the Serbs continue to slaughter unarmed civilians. When General Wesley Clark, the American head of NATO (the North Atlantic Treaty Organization) met with Milosevic on January 19, 1999, he showed him color photographs indicating that a massacre of Albanian Kosovars had taken place just three days earlier in the town of Racak. "This was not a massacre," Milosevic shouted at Clark. "This was staged [by the KLA]. These people are terrorists."

NATO, an alliance of nineteen countries formed after World War II to protect Western Europe's democracies from the Soviet bloc, was at a crossroads. What was its purpose, now that the communist East bloc had collapsed? Three formerly communist eastern European countries—Poland, Hungary, and the Czech Republic—were now members of NATO.

Believing that they had no choice, Clinton and the leaders of Britain, France, Germany, Italy, and the other NATO countries began bombing Serbia on March 25. The Serbs responded by forcing ethnic Albanians out of Kosovo. In the following weeks, hundreds of thousands of Kosovar Albanians crossed the border into the neighboring countries of Macedonia and Albania. This, of course, was just what Milosevic wanted: Kosovo without the Albanians. But the exodus of frightened Albanians, fleeing their villages at gunpoint with only the clothes on their backs and whatever they could carry, hardened Western opposition to Serbia's action.

The NATO bombing was massive in scope, and it inflicted enormous damage not only on Serbia's military but also on its economy. Major factories were destroyed, and the country's infrastructure—its roads, bridges, train

tracks, oil refineries, and the like—was decimated by NATO bombs.

Clinton resisted calls to introduce ground troops into Kosovo. He knew that Serbian troops could not defeat a NATO army, but it could inflict some casualties. The American people supported Clinton, and after six weeks public approval of the war effort was slightly higher than it was when the bombing first started. Clinton knew, however, that if Americans were killed in action, support could quickly vanish. He was also worried about damaging Vice President Gore's chances for winning the presidency. House Republicans voted down a resolution supporting the American effort in Yugoslavia, a stinging rebuke to Clinton. They wanted to make sure the conflict was seen as "Clinton's war." Thus if the war turned out badly, the GOP would be absolved of any responsibility.

Despite the increasingly heavy bombardment from the air, the Serbs hung on. Clinton came under criticism for publicly ruling out a ground invasion, right from the start. Meanwhile, a deep split in the NATO alliance developed. Britain came out in favor of a ground invasion, but Germany said it was adamantly opposed, and Italy said NATO should halt the bombing to see if that would bring Milosevic to the bargaining table. Clinton said NATO should be patient and stay the course: the bombing, he said, would work.

Clinton's instincts proved right. After close to three months of bombing and no sign of NATO's backing down, Milosevic conceded defeat and agreed to withdraw all his troops from Kosovo. NATO peacekeeping troops moved in, and the Albanian Kosovars began returning home. Unfortunately for Clinton, the American public didn't see the conflict as crucial to American interests, and there was no great national celebration when the war ended. Nevertheless, the victory was important, because it demonstrated that NATO was capable of maintaining the unity necessary to police rogue states in Europe. For the United States, the successful outcome was welcome proof that our military power could be used as a last resort to stop small wars before they became big wars.

him on feasible military and diplomatic responses. An armed invasion of Cuba and air strikes against the missiles were two options considered. In the end, Kennedy decided on a less dangerous response: a naval blockade of Cuba. Newly released tape recordings of Oval Office conversations confirm that Kennedy favored a less bellicose approach than his advisers did. He privately signaled Soviet leader Nikita Khrushchev that if the Soviet Union withdrew its missiles from Cuba, then the United States would remove American missiles from Turkey.[62] The Soviet Union thought better of prolonging its challenge to the United States and soon agreed to remove its missiles. For a short time, though, the world held its breath over the very real possibility of a nuclear war.

Are there guidelines for what a president should do in times of crisis or at other important decision-making junctures? Drawing on a range of advisers and opinions is certainly one. Not acting in unnecessary haste is another. A third is having a well-designed, formal review process that promotes thorough analysis and open debate.[63] A fourth guideline is rigorously examining the chain of reasoning that has led to the option chosen, to ensure that presumptions have not been subconsciously equated with what is actually known to be true. When Kennedy decided to back a CIA plan to sponsor a rebel invasion of Cuba by expatriates hostile to Fidel Castro, he never really understood that its chances for success were based on unfounded assumptions of immediate uprisings by the Cuban population.[64]

Still, these are rather general rules, and they provide no assurance that mistakes will not be made. Almost by definition, each crisis is a unique event. Sometimes all alternatives carry substantial risks. And almost always, time is of the essence. This was the situation when Cambodia captured the American merchant ship *Mayaguez* off its coast in 1975. Not wanting to wait until the Cambodian government moved the sailors inland, where there would be little chance of rescuing them, President Gerald Ford immediately sent in the Marines. Unfortunately, forty-one American soldiers were killed in the fighting, "all in vain because the American captives had shortly before the attack been released and sent across the border into Thailand."[65] Even so, Ford can be defended for making the decision he did; he did not know what the Cambodians would do. World events are unpredictable, and in the end presidents must rely on their own judgment in crisis situations.

PRESIDENTIAL CHARACTER

How does the public assess which presidential candidate has the best judgment and whether a candidate's character is suitable to the office? Americans must make a broad evaluation of the candidates' personalities and leadership styles. Although it's difficult to judge, character matters. One of Lyndon Johnson's biographers argues that Johnson had trouble extricating the United States from Vietnam because of insecurities about his masculinity. Johnson wanted to make sure he "was not forced to see himself as a coward, running away from Vietnam."[66] It's hard to know for sure whether this psychological interpretation is valid. Clearer, surely, is the tie between President Nixon's character and Watergate. Nixon had such an exaggerated fear of what his "enemies" might try to do to him that he created a climate in the White House that nurtured the Watergate break-in and subsequent cover-up.

The character issue dogged Bill Clinton since he began pursuing the presidency. During the 1992 campaign, questions emerged about his

Mom! Dad! I Got a Great Summer Internship . . . and the Boss Likes Me a Lot!

Revelation of the affair between President Clinton and White House intern Monica Lewinsky rocked the nation. Since she had lied in a legal deposition, denying the relationship, Lewinsky was vulnerable when the special prosecutor began investigating her. Her lawyers eventually reached an immunity deal with Kenneth Starr and Lewinsky gave a highly detailed account of her sexual encounters with the president to the Whitewater grand jury.

marital fidelity and he appeared to tacitly acknowledge unfaithfulness when he told an interviewer on CBS's *60 Minutes* that he was responsible for "causing pain in my marriage."[67] Although these charges in 1992 threatened to derail his run for the Democratic nomination, he continued his reckless behavior once in the White House, when he engaged in a sexual relationship with Monica Lewinsky, an intern half his age.

Clinton's behavior puzzled the American public. How can a man so gifted in many ways be so irresponsible in others? A look at Clinton's past offers some insight into the development of his character. Clinton's father, Bill Blythe, was an affable charmer. But he was also something of a sexual scoundrel, marrying at least three women (including two sisters) and fathering at least two children out of wedlock before he married Clinton's mother, Virginia Cassidy, in 1943. Blythe died in an auto accident shortly before his son was born. The future president's mother decided to remarry in 1950, despite knowing that her intended, Roger Clinton, was a philanderer. He was also abusive and an alcoholic. Little Bill called his stepfather Daddy and took his last name, but Roger Clinton showed little interest in the boy and never adopted him. By the time he was a teenager, the future president was physically protecting his mother from her husband's rages.[68]

After becoming president, Clinton faced accusations involving several different women. Paula Jones, a former Arkansas state employee, and Kathleen Willey, a former White House volunteer, claimed that Clinton made crude, unwanted sexual advances toward them. Clinton vigorously denied both accusations. Jones filed a well-publicized sexual harassment lawsuit against the president, but the case was eventually thrown out of court because there was no evidence that Jones had suffered any adverse repercussions on the job. She appealed the judge's decision to dismiss the case and, in an out-of-court settlement, Clinton agreed to pay Jones $850,000 in exchange for her dropping the lawsuit.

Clinton's affair with Lewinsky came to light after Whitewater special prosecutor Kenneth Starr received a tip that Clinton had lied in a deposition in the Paula Jones lawsuit. Starr had been appointed to investigate allegations that both Bill and Hillary Clinton had engaged in wrongdoing some years earlier, when they were members of a small partnership investing in undeveloped property in Arkansas. After four years of investigating the Clintons, Starr had yet to find convincing evidence of any illegality by either of the Clintons. When he told Attorney General Janet Reno of Clinton's possible perjury in the Jones lawsuit, Reno acceded to his request that he be given authority to inquire into this as well.

After investigating the matter for over six months, Starr formally recommended to Congress that they consider impeaching Clinton because, allegedly, he had perjured himself, obstructed justice, and encouraged others to perjure themselves. To buttress these claims, Starr's report included graphic descriptions of the sexual encounters between Clinton and Lewinsky. Clinton's response was twofold. First, he said that he hadn't lied in the Jones deposition when he denied having sex with Lewinsky, because they hadn't engaged in sexual intercourse—she had performed oral sex on him. Second, he finally acknowledged that he had had an "inappropriate" relationship with Lewinsky and that it was wrong. He offered a series of apologies both to his family and to the nation.

The American public was appalled by the revelations that their president was engaging in sexual activities with an intern in his private office in the White House. Many newspapers called for his resignation. Although Republicans were much harsher in their criticism of Clinton, Democrats were angry as well. As Chapter 11 noted, despite the disgust and anger the president's actions provoked among many Americans, most remained unconvinced that his behavior constituted an impeachable offense. The buoyant economy and the public's general satisfaction with Clinton's leadership strongly influenced the country's views on the matter. A common opinion was that sex outside of marriage, although immoral, is a private matter, and the issue should be left to Clinton and his wife to resolve between themselves.

After the Senate acquitted Clinton, it may have seemed that the president's nightmare was over. Yet there was still unfinished business from the Paula Jones lawsuit. Even though Clinton had reached an out-of-court settlement with Jones, Susan Webber Wright, the federal district court judge who heard the civil suit, held Clinton in contempt of court. Wright said that Clinton had lied to the court when he filed his deposition in the Jones case denying that he had had a sexual relationship with Monica Lewinsky. After his acquittal by the Senate, the special prosecutor's office held out the possibility that it would indict Clinton after he left office. On the day before his term ended Clinton reached a settlement with Special Prosecutor Robert Ray (who replaced Kenneth Starr) that spared him from possible indictment. Clinton admitted that he gave false testimony under oath, agreed to a fine of $25,000, and gave up his law license for five years.[69]

Clinton's disturbing character flaw calls into question whether he was fit to be president. Even though Lewinsky was a consensual partner, it was exploitive of Clinton to engage in sex with a young woman who was his employee. It was also reckless and impulsive—hardly desirable qualities in a president. There are security issues, too, as a president's mistress can blackmail him. (President Kennedy, who was chronically unfaithful to his wife while they lived in the White House, had an affair with the girlfriend of an organized crime boss.) At the same time, Clinton's many admirable qualities, especially his compassion, fairness, and intelligence, should not be overlooked. His lifelong concern for the disadvantaged made him especially popular with minorities and the poor. Sadly, though, Clinton's character flaws allowed him to turn an inappropriate relationship into the defining moment of his presidency.

SUMMARY

When the delegates to the Constitutional Convention met to design the government of their new nation, they had trouble shaping the office of the president. They struggled to find a balance—an office that was powerful enough to provide unified leadership but not so strong that presidents could use their powers to become tyrants or dictators. The initial conceptions of the presidency have slowly been transformed over time, as presidents have adapted the office to meet the nation's changing needs. The trend has been to expand presidential power. Some expansion has come from presidential actions taken under claims of inherent powers. Congress has also delegated a great deal of power to the executive branch, further expanding the role of the president.

Because the president is elected by the entire nation, he can claim to represent all citizens when proposing policy. Whether the presidency actually operates in a majoritarian manner depends on several factors—the individual president's perception of public opinion on specific issues, the relationship between public opinion and the president's political ideology, and the extent to which the president is committed to pursuing his values through his office.

The executive branch establishment has grown rapidly, and the White House has become a sizable bureaucracy. New responsibilities of the twentieth-century presidency were particularly noticeable in the area of legislative leadership. Now a president is expected to be a policy initiator for Congress, as well as a lobbyist who guides his bills through the legislative process.

The presidential "job description" for foreign policy has also changed considerably. Post–World War II presidents had been preoccupied with containing the spread of communism, but with the collapse of communism in the Soviet Union and Eastern Europe, international economic relations now loom largest as a priority for presidents. However, national security issues remain because regional conflicts can directly involve the interests of the United States.

★ Selected Readings

Campbell, Colin, and Bert A. Rockman, eds. *The Clinton Legacy*. New York: Chatham House, 2000. An early but astute "look back" at the Clinton presidency.

Edwards, George C., and Stephen J. Wayne. *Presidential Leadership*, 5th ed. New York: St. Martin's/Worth, 1999. A comprehensive text on the modern presidency.

Kernell, Samuel. *Going Public: New Strategies of Presidential Leadership*, 3rd ed. Washington, D.C.: Congressional Quarterly Press, 1997. In this volume, Kernell examines how presidents appeal to Americans beyond the Beltway for help in prodding Congress to pass their bills.

Neustadt, Richard E. *Presidential Power*, rev. ed. New York: Wiley, 1980. Neustadt's classic work examines the president's power to persuade.

Posner, Richard A. *An Affair of State*. Cambridge, Mass.: Harvard University Press, 1999; and Jeffrey Toobin, *A Vast Conspiracy*. New York: Touchstone, 1999. Together these two books offer a broad view of the Clinton sexual scandal and its aftermath. Posner's book is a legal analysis of the investigation and impeachment, while Toobin focuses on the politics surrounding the episode.

Skowronek, Stephen. *The Politics Presidents Make*. Cambridge, Mass.: Harvard University Press, 1993. A sweeping, magisterial analysis of the cycles of presidential history.

Internet Exercises

1. *"Presidency" versus "President"*

History and Politics Out Loud is a searchable archive of politically important audio materials, which includes excerpts from presidential speeches and conversations. The site is located at <**www.hpol.org**>.

• Go to History and Politics Out Loud and listen to President John F. Kennedy's reflections on the Cuban Missile Crisis from October 18, 1962.

• How does this audio recording of President Kennedy illustrate the difference between what many people think of as "the President" and what political scientists and historians often call "the Presidency"?

2. *The President's Many Hats*

The *Weekly Compilation of Presidential Documents (WCPD)*, published by the Office of the Federal Register, contains statements, messages, and other presidential materials released by the White House during the preceding week. Essentially, whenever the president utters words in public or acts in an official capacity, it is recorded and compiled in this publication, which is eventually reprinted as the Public Papers of the President. All of the editions of the *WCPD* for President Clinton's tenure are maintained on the Web by the National Archives and Records Administration at <**www.access.gpo.gov/nara/nara003.html**>.

• Go to this Web site and retrieve the tables of contents of the five issues of the *WCPD* for March 1999. (See the "Helpful Hints" link on the Web page for instructions on how to do this.)

• How do the activities listed in these tables of contents illustrate the many roles that the president plays, such as policy leader, political and party leader, and potential shaper of public opinion?

The Bureaucracy

A FEW MINUTES AFTER VALUJET FLIGHT 592 TOOK OFF from the Miami airport and headed north, smoke began to fill the cabin. The pilot turned the plane around to return to Miami, but before it could reach the airport, the plane lost power and took a nosedive into an alligator-infested swamp in the Everglades. None of the 109 on board survived.

Plane crashes are shocking, not just because of the carnage but because commercial airline crashes are so rare. Travel on the major air carriers is commonly thought to be the safest form of transportation. Even more shocking than the crash was the revelation that the Federal Aviation Administration (FAA), the regulatory agency charged with setting, monitoring, and enforcing airline safety standards, had previously documented a poor maintenance record by ValuJet. Yet the agency had done little to force ValuJet to improve its repair and record-keeping practices. After the crash, a high-ranking Department of Transportation official said she had stopped flying ValuJet some time ago "because of its many mishaps."[1]

The cause of the crash appears to have been some used oxygen canisters, which can heat up to 430 degrees in flight and must be packed according to strict safety standards. ValuJet was not authorized to carry such cargo, and the canisters were loaded by mistake. Why weren't correct procedures followed? Beyond the individual errors in judgment are the financial pressures brought on the airlines by deregulation. Until the late 1970s, airline pricing was oligopolistic, with common fares approved by the government. Today, airlines compete vigorously, and many cut-rate start-ups like ValuJet have taken market share away from major carriers like United, American, and Delta.

Many of the new low-cost carriers save money by buying or leasing used aircraft with considerable mileage on them. Another cost-cutting measure is to farm out maintenance work to subcontractors who can do the work more cheaply. Indeed, it was a subcontractor who loaded the fatal canisters onto flight 592. This has made the FAA's work more difficult because its work force has not expanded to match the increasing number of companies running or servicing commercial airlines.[2]

But why is this so? Why doesn't the FAA just add inspectors and write more regulations to improve its monitoring of carriers and subcontractors? Americans surely want commercial airliners to be as safe as possible. Yet, at the same time that Americans want government to reduce the risks of everyday life, there is also great pressure to cut the budget and shrink the size of government. Less than four months before the ValuJet crash,

Flight to Oblivion

After ValuJet flight 592 crashed into the Everglades, the FAA was roundly criticized for failing to do a better job of monitoring airline maintenance and safety standards. After reviewing its own performance, the FAA announced that it was taking steps to improve its supervision of maintenance subcontractors, such as Sabretech, the company that worked for ValuJet at the time of the crash. In September 1996 ValuJet, reorganized as AirTran, began flying again.

President Clinton declared in his State of the Union address that "the era of big government is over."[3] As we'll explore in this chapter, Americans don't want big government, but they want the services big government provides. The controversy over the bureaucracy's role is not just a function of majoritarian opinion that is contradictory; it is also due to the fact that majoritarianism is often pitted against pluralism. One reason the FAA didn't take more concerted action against ValuJet prior to the crash is that any government rebuke of the carrier would have jeopardized the company's future. (After the crash, the FAA did force the company to suspend its service.) More broadly, one of the FAA's responsibilities is to promote the airline industry, and it is thus lobbied heavily on both business and safety issues by large and small carriers alike. Beyond our focus on pluralist and majoritarian dynamics in bureaucratic politics, we'll also look closely at why Americans dislike government so much. Many people believe that bureaucracies are unresponsive to what the public wants. Finally, we will discuss reforms that might make government work better.

ORGANIZATION MATTERS

bureaucracy
A large, complex organization in which employees have specific job responsibilities and work within a hierarchy of authority.

bureaucrat
An employee of a bureaucracy, usually meaning a government bureaucracy.

A nation's laws and policies are administered, or put into effect, by various departments, agencies, bureaus, offices, and other government units, which together are known as its *bureaucracy.* **Bureaucracy** actually means any large, complex organization in which employees have specific job responsibilities and work within a hierarchy of authority. The employees of these government units, who are quite knowledgeable within their narrow areas, have become known somewhat derisively as **bureaucrats.**

We study bureaucracies because they play a central role in the governments of modern societies. In fact, organizations are a crucial part of any society, no matter how elementary. For example, a preindustrial tribe is an organization. It has a clearly defined leader (a chief), senior policymakers

Profiling America

One of the bureaucracy's many tasks is collecting information. Various agencies gather vitally important statistics, such as the unemployment rate and the crime rate. Each decade the Bureau of the Census does a count of the nation's population and compiles a statistical profile of America. Much of the census is now done through the mail but census takers still do some door-to-door work.

(elders), a fixed division of labor (some hunt, some cook, some make tools), an organizational culture (religious practices, initiation rituals), and rules of governance (what kind of property belongs to families and what belongs to the tribe). How that tribe is organized is not merely a quaint aspect of its evolution; it is critical to the survival of its members in a hostile environment.

The organization of modern government bureaucracies also reflects their need to survive. The environment in which modern bureaucracies operate, filled with conflicting political demands and the ever-present threat of budget cuts, is no less hostile than that of preindustrial tribes. The way a given government bureaucracy is organized also reflects the particular needs of its clients. The bottom line, however, is that the manner in which any bureaucracy is organized affects how well it can accomplish its tasks.

A major study of America's schools vividly demonstrates the importance of organization. After studying a large number of high schools around the country, two political scientists tried to determine what makes some better than others. They used the test scores of students to measure the achievement level of each school. Because some high schools' students are much better prepared to begin with than others', the authors compared similar schools. In other words, schools in low-income neighborhoods where entering students had average or below-average reading scores were compared with similar schools, not with schools in wealthy suburban neighborhoods where entering students had above-average reading scores. When similar schools were compared in terms of improvements in student performance, it was evident that the students in some schools achieved more than the students in other schools. Why?

The authors' statistical tests led them to conclude that the differences in student performance were a result of the way the schools were organized. The biggest influence on the effectiveness of a school's organization was its level of autonomy within its district. Schools that had more control over hiring, curriculum, and discipline did better in terms of student achievement. This freedom seemed to allow for strong leadership, which helped the schools develop coherent goals and build staffs strongly supportive of those goals.[4]

Clearly, organization matters. The ways in which bureaucracies are structured to perform their work directly affect their ability to accomplish their tasks. Unfortunately, "if organization matters, it is also the case that there is no one best way of organizing."[5] Although greater autonomy may improve the performance of public schools, it may not improve other kinds of organizations. If a primary goal of a state social welfare agency, for example, is to treat its clients equally, to provide the same benefits to people with the same needs and circumstances, then giving local offices a lot of individual autonomy is not a good approach. The study of bureaucracy, then, centers around finding solutions to the many different kinds of problems faced by large government organizations.

THE DEVELOPMENT OF THE BUREAUCRATIC STATE

A common complaint voiced by Americans is that the national bureaucracy is too big and tries to accomplish too much. To the average citizen, the national government may seem like an octopus—its long arms reach just about everywhere. Ironically, compared to other western democracies, the size of the United States government is proportionally smaller (see Compared with What? 13.1).

Federal Expenditures for State and Local Governments

The Growth of the Bureaucratic State

American government seems to have grown unchecked during this century. As one observer noted wryly, "The assistant administrator for water and hazardous materials of the Environmental Protection Agency [presides] over a staff larger than Washington's entire first administration."[6] Yet even during George Washington's time, bureaucracies were necessary. No one argued then about the need for a postal service to deliver mail or a treasury department to maintain a system of currency.

However, government at all levels (national, state, and local) has grown enormously in the twentieth century,[7] for several major reasons. A principal cause of government expansion is the increasing complexity of society. George Washington did not have an assistant administrator for water and hazardous materials because he had no need for one. The National Aeronautics and Space Administration (NASA) was not necessary until rockets were invented.

Another reason government has grown is that the public's attitude toward business has changed. Throughout most of the nineteenth century, there was little or no government regulation of business. Business was generally autonomous, and any government intervention in the economy that might limit that autonomy was considered inappropriate. This attitude began to change toward the end of the nineteenth century, as more Americans became aware that the end product of a laissez-faire approach was not always highly competitive markets that benefited consumers. Instead, businesses sometimes formed oligopolies, such as the infamous "sugar trust," a small group of companies that controlled virtually the entire sugar market.

★ **compared with what?**

13.1   Not So Big by Comparison

When the United States is viewed against the other western democracies, our government turns out to be relatively small. Measuring the size of government is difficult, but one way is to calculate the proportion of all of a nation's workers who are employed by their government.

The primary reason why the size of the bureaucracies in other democracies is larger in comparison to the United States is that they offer a much more extensive array of welfare and social service benefits to their citizens.

These countries tend to have generous pension, health, and unemployment benefits. These benefits do not come cheaply, however; residents of the other advanced industrialized countries tend to pay much higher taxes than do Americans. There's no free lunch. In recent years, budget pressures have forced European governments to try to trim their spending.

Source: Alan R. Ball and B. Guy Peters, *Modern Politics and Government*, 6th ed. (New York: Chatham House, 2000), p. 221.

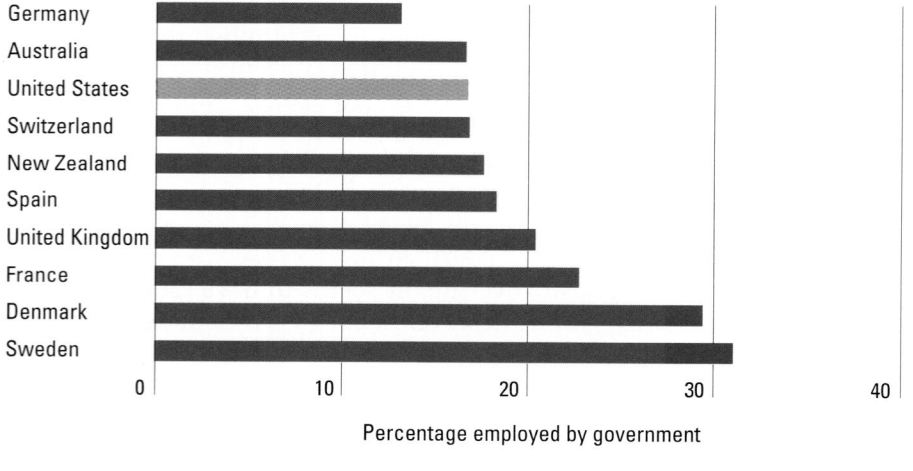

Percentage employed by government

Gradually, government intervention came to be accepted as necessary to protect the integrity of markets. And if government was to police unfair business practices effectively, it needed administrative agencies. During the twentieth century, new bureaucracies were organized to regulate specific industries. Among them are the Securities and Exchange Commission (SEC), which oversees securities trading, and the Food and Drug Administration (FDA), which tries to protect consumers from unsafe food, drugs, and cosmetics. Through bureaucracies such as these, government has become a referee in the marketplace, developing standards of fair trade, setting rates, and licensing individual businesses for operation. As new problem areas have emerged, government has added new agencies, further expanding the scope of its activities. During the 1960s, for instance, Ralph Nader made the public aware that certain design flaws in automobiles made them unnecessarily dangerous. For example, sharp,

Secretary Martinez

Cabinet secretaries wear many hats. Principally, they are responsible to the president, carrying out the broad outlines of policy decided upon by the White House. At the same time, they advise the White House on programs involving their department. They must also be responsive to client groups—the lobbies that are affected by the programs administered by the department. Finally, they must be sensitive to congressional preferences. Secretary of Housing and Urban Development Mel Martinez explains some of his plans to a congressional committee.

Mr. Martinez

protruding dashboard knobs caused a car's interior to be dangerous on impact. Congress responded to public demands for change by creating the National Highway Traffic Safety Administration in 1966.

General attitudes about government's responsibilities in the area of social welfare have changed, too. An enduring part of American culture is the belief in self-reliance. People are expected to overcome adversity on their own, to succeed on the basis of their own skills and efforts. Yet certain segments of our population are believed to deserve government support, either because we particularly value their contribution to society or have come to believe that they cannot realistically be expected to overcome adversity on their own.[8]

This belief goes as far back as the nineteenth century. The government provided pensions to Civil War veterans because they were judged to deserve financial support. Later, programs to help mothers and children were developed.[9] Further steps toward income security came in the wake of the Great Depression, when the Social Security Act became law, creating a fund that workers pay into and then collect income from during old age. In the 1960s, the government created programs designed to help minorities. As the government made these new commitments, it also made new bureaucracies or expanded existing ones.

Finally, government has grown because ambitious, entrepreneurial agency officials have expanded their organizations and staffs to take on added responsibilities.[10] Each new program leads to new authority. Larger budgets and staffs, in turn, are necessary to support that authority. In the wake of the collapse of communism, the budgets of the Defense Department and various security agencies came under pressure from those who believed those parts of the government could shrink a little. To bolster itself against the budget cutters, the CIA volunteered its spy satellites to monitor environmental quality around the world.[11] Agency administrators saw expanding the agency's mission as a key to survival in a time of government austerity.

figure

13.1   Bureaucrats at Work

Although the national government has been downsizing in recent years, it still employs a large number of workers. As this graph indicates, the Department of Defense is by far the largest bureaucracy within the federal government. That over 1 million civilian workers are employed in just two departments, Defense and Veterans Affairs, is a reflection of the centrality of war and the Cold War in American politics during the twentieth century. At the opposite end of the spectrum is the tiny Department of Education, with under 5,000 employees, despite all the rhetoric about the need to improve education.

Source: U.S. Bureau of the Census, *Statistical Abstract of the United States, 1999* (Washington, D.C.: U.S. Government Printing Office, 1999), p. 363.

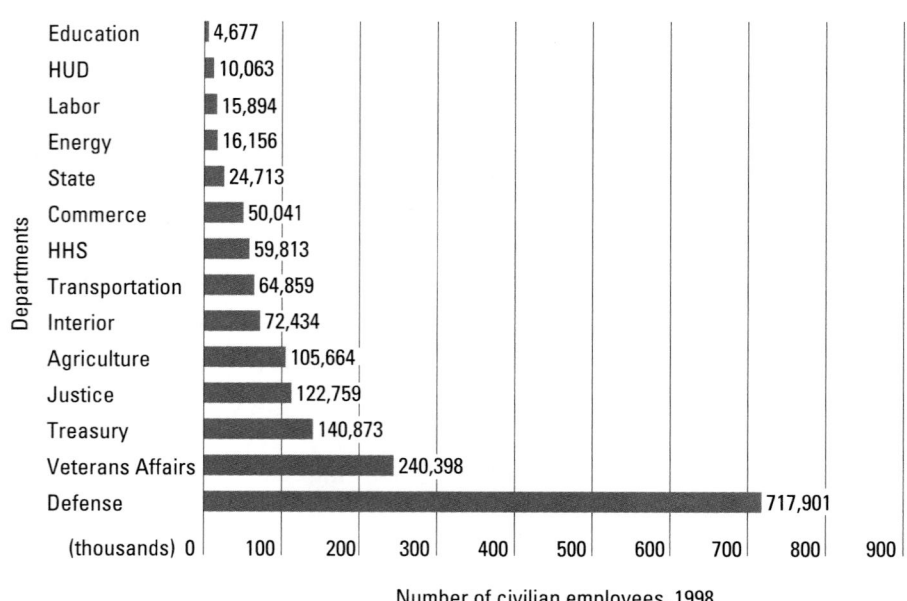

Number of civilian employees, 1998

Department	Number
Education	4,677
HUD	10,063
Labor	15,894
Energy	16,156
State	24,713
Commerce	50,041
HHS	59,813
Transportation	64,859
Interior	72,434
Agriculture	105,664
Justice	122,759
Treasury	140,873
Veterans Affairs	240,398
Defense	717,901

Can We Reduce the Size of Government?

When candidates for Congress and the presidency campaign, they typically "run against the government"—even if they are incumbents. Government is unpopular: Americans have little confidence in its capabilities and feel that it wastes money and is out of touch with the people. Americans want a smaller government that costs less and performs better.

Most of the national government is composed of large bureaucracies, so if government is to become smaller, bureaucracies will have to be eliminated or reduced in size. Everyone wants to believe that government can be shrunk just by eliminating unnecessary bureaucrats. Although efficiencies can be found, serious budget cuts also require serious reductions in programs. Not surprisingly, presidents and members of Congress face a tough job when they try to cut specific programs. Across-the-board cuts are not often a viable option because there is tremendous variation in the number of workers employed by each cabinet-level department (see Figure 13.1). As will be discussed more fully in Chapter 17, in recent years the national government has engaged in a bit of a shell game, modestly reducing the number of bureaucrats (which is popular) without reducing government programs (which is politically risky). The government has accomplished this sleight of hand by turning over the jobs of the former bureaucrats to private contractors who do the same job but are not technically government employees.[12]

For many years, most change came from the pressure to reduce budget deficits. Republican presidents Reagan and Bush and Republicans in

figure

13.2   Don't Cut Taxes!

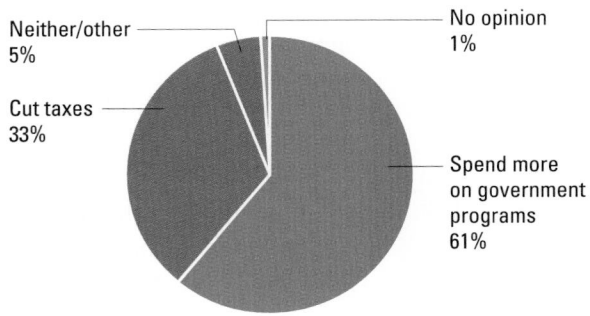

With a budget surplus for the first time in decades, policymakers must now decide what to do with it. Americans may say that they do not like big government or paying taxes, but when a recent Gallup Poll asked a random sample of U.S. adults what they would do with a national budget surplus, almost twice as many preferred spending more on government programs to cutting taxes. The favorite areas for additional money were social security, Medicare, and public education.

Source: *Gallup Poll* <www.gallup.com/poll/indicators/indtaxes3.asp>

Congress (sometimes in the majority) pushed hard to shrink the government but had limited success. Still, budget pressures kept the rate of growth down and some bureaucracies were subjected to serious cuts. Toward the end of the Clinton era, though, the booming economy produced so much tax revenue that the budget deficit turned into projected surpluses.

Not only has the budget surplus reduced pressure to cut the size of the bureaucracy but the strength of the American economy has led politicians to feel comfortable in arguing for an enhanced role for government. When he began campaigning for the presidency in 2000, George W. Bush emphasized his support for a broad tax cut. Voters displayed modest support for a tax cut but demonstrated more interest in increased spending for important programs (see Figure 13.2). Bush was soon arguing for new programs, especially in the area of education, which he promised to make a priority if elected.[13] His promise to bolster the Department of Education was a dramatic change from President Reagan's promise to terminate it.

The Department of Education survived the Reagan era budget cutting because, like all government bureaucracies, it performs a service of value to some sector of society. Even though bankers as a group favor laissez-faire capitalism, the principles of a free market, and minimal government intervention, few bankers voiced such preferences when the savings and loan industry collapsed in the late 1980s. A noninterventionist government could have stood by and done nothing, but inaction would have had a disastrous effect on the U.S. financial system—in this case, free-market corrections to the problem looked like a very unattractive option. Bankers became more concerned about order than freedom and were happy to see the government mount a rescue effort. A new bureaucracy, the Resolution Trust Corporation, was created to administer the medicine to the sick patient. Big government got even bigger.

Bankers are far from the only group that wants to be protected by the national government. Builders profit from programs offered by the U.S. Department of Housing and Urban Development. Labor unions want a vigorous Occupational Safety and Health Administration. Interest groups that have a stake in an agency almost always resist efforts to cut back its scope.

The tendency for big government to endure reflects the tension between majoritarianism and pluralism. Even when the public as a whole wants a smaller national government, that sentiment can be undermined by the strong desire of different segments of society for government to continue performing some valuable function for them. Lobbies that represent these segments work strenuously to convince Congress and the administration that certain agencies' funding is vital and that any cuts ought to come out of other agencies' budgets. At the same time, those other agencies are also working to protect themselves and to garner support.

BUREAUS AND BUREAUCRATS

We often think of the bureaucracy as a monolith. In reality, the bureaucracy in Washington is a disjointed collection of departments, agencies, bureaus, offices, and commissions—each a bureaucracy in its own right.

Evolution of the Cabinet

The Organization of Government

By examining the basic types of government organizations, we can better understand how the executive branch operates. In our discussion, we pay particular attention to the relative degree of independence of these organizations and to their relationship with the White House.

department
The biggest unit of the executive branch, covering a broad area of government responsibility. The heads of the departments, or secretaries, form the president's cabinet.

Departments. **Departments** are the biggest units of the executive branch, covering broad areas of government responsibility. As noted in Chapter 12, the secretaries (heads) of the departments, along with a few other key officials, form the president's cabinet. The current cabinet departments are State, Treasury, Defense, Interior, Agriculture, Justice, Commerce, Labor, Health and Human Services, Housing and Urban Development, Transportation, Energy, Education, and Veterans Affairs. Each of these massive organizations is broken down into subsidiary agencies, bureaus, offices, and services.

independent agency
An executive agency that is not part of a cabinet department.

Independent Agencies.   Within the executive branch are also many **independent agencies** that are not part of any cabinet department. Instead, they stand alone and are controlled to varying degrees by the president. Some, among them the CIA, are directly under the president's control. Others, such as the Federal Communications Commission, are structured as **regulatory commissions.** Each commission is run by a small number of commissioners (usually an odd number, to prevent tied votes) appointed to fixed terms by the president. Some commissions were formed to guard against unfair business practices. Others were formed to protect the public from unsafe products. Although presidents don't have direct control over these regulatory commissions, they can strongly influence their direction through their appointments of new commissioners.

regulatory commission
An agency of the executive branch of government that controls or directs some aspect of the economy.

government corporation
A government agency that performs services that might be provided by the private sector but that involve either insufficient financial incentive or are better provided when they are somehow linked with government.

Government Corporations.   Finally, Congress has also created a small number of **government corporations.** The services these executive branch agencies perform theoretically could be provided by the private sector, but Congress has decided that the public is better served by these organizations' having some link with the government. For example, the national government maintains the postal service as a government corporation because it feels that Americans need low-cost, door-to-door service for all kinds of mail, not just for profitable routes or special services. In some instances, the private sector does not have enough financial incentive to provide an essential service. This is the case with the financially troubled Amtrak train line.

The Civil Service

The national bureaucracy is staffed by nearly 2.8 million civilian employees, who account for about 2.1 percent of the U.S. work force.[14] Americans have a tendency to stereotype all government workers as faceless paper pushers, but the public work force is actually quite diverse. Government workers include forest rangers, FBI agents, typists, foreign service officers, computer programmers, policy analysts, public relations specialists, security guards, librarians, administrators, engineers, plumbers, and people from literally hundreds of other occupations.

An important feature of the national bureaucracy is that most of its workers are hired under the requirements of the **civil service.** The civil service was created after the assassination of President James Garfield, who was killed by an unbalanced and dejected job seeker. Congress responded by passing the Pendleton Act (1883), which established the Civil Service Commission (now the Office of Personnel Management). The objective of the act was to reduce patronage—the practice of filling government positions with the president's political allies or cronies. The civil service fills jobs on the basis of merit and sees to it that workers are not fired for political reasons. Over the years, job qualifications and selection procedures have been developed for most government positions.

The vast majority of the national government's workers are employed outside Washington. One reason for this decentralization is to make government offices accessible to the people they serve. The Social Security Administration, for example, has to have offices within a reasonable distance of most Americans, so that its many clients have somewhere to take their questions, problems, and paperwork. Decentralization is also a way to distribute jobs and income across the country. The headquarters of the Centers for Disease Control could easily have been located in Washington, but it is in Atlanta. Likewise, NASA's headquarters for space flights is located in Houston. Members of Congress, of course, are only too happy to place some of the "pork" back home, so that their constituents will credit them with the jobs and money that government installations create.

civil service
The system by which most appointments to the federal bureaucracy are made, to ensure that government jobs are filled on the basis of merit and that employees are not fired for political reasons.

*Growth of Classified
Civil Service*

Presidential Control over the Bureaucracy

Civil service and other reforms have effectively insulated the vast majority of government workers from party politics. An incoming president can appoint only about 3,000 people to jobs in his administration—fewer than 1 percent of all executive branch employees.[15] Still, presidential appointees fill the top policymaking positions in government. Each new president, then, establishes an extensive personnel review process to find appointees who are both politically compatible and qualified in their field. Although the president selects some people from his campaign staff, most political appointees have not been campaign workers. Instead, cabinet secretaries, assistant secretaries, agency heads, and the like, tend to be drawn directly from business, universities, and government itself.

★

Gus the Gorilla Gets a Checkup

Americans typically picture bureaucrats as sitting behind desks, filling out endless forms, and—most likely—creating yards of red tape for some hapless citizen. Yet many government jobs bear no relationship to this stereotype. In this picture, these bureaucrats (veterinarians at the National Zoo in Washington, D.C.) are administering an EKG to a 448-pound (and heavily sedated) gorilla named Gus as part of a study to learn why great apes, like their human cousins, develop heart disease as they age.

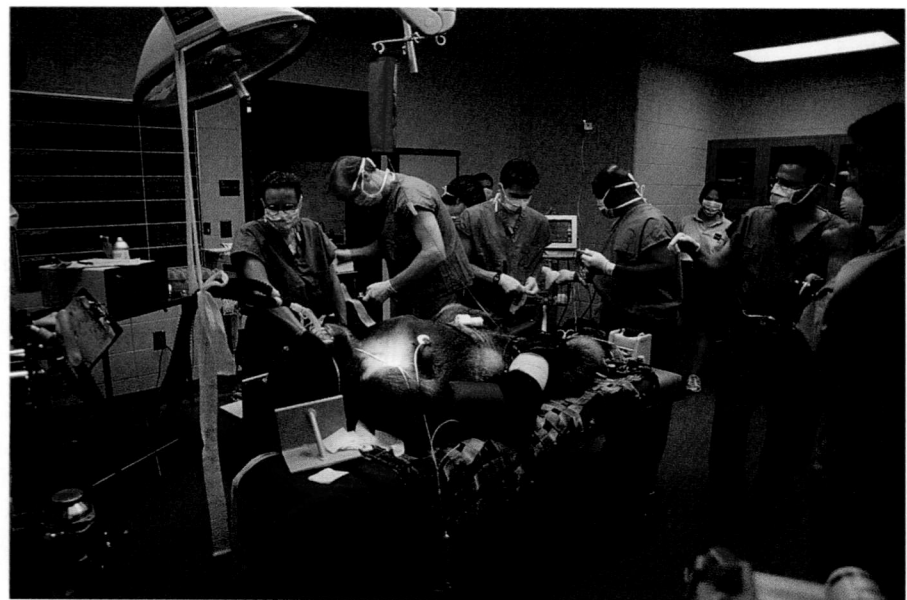

Because so few of their own appointees are in each department and agency, presidents often believe that they do not have enough control over the bureaucracy. Republican presidents have also worried that the civil service would be hostile to their objectives because they assume that career bureaucrats have a liberal Democratic bias.

Presidents find that the bureaucracy is not always as responsive as they might like, for several reasons. Principally, pluralism can pull agencies in a direction other than that favored by the president. The Department of Transportation may want to move toward more support for mass transit, but politically it cannot afford to ignore the preferences of highway builders. An agency administrator must often try to broker a compromise between conflicting groups rather than pursue a position that holds fast and true to the president's ideology. Bureaucracies must also follow—at least in general terms—the laws governing the programs they are entrusted with, even if the president doesn't agree with some of those statutes.

Even when the statutes offer some flexibility, presidents can be frustrated by the bureaucracy when they try to push an agency toward one of the available options. During the early 1990s, there was a "credit crunch" as banks ostensibly cut back on loans to customers without the safest credit rating. In hindsight, it's not clear that bank lending practices changed that much during this period. At the time, anecdotal evidence suggested that credit markets tightened because government examiners were forcing individual banks to put more of their funds into their capital reserves as security against loans gone bad. This practice led to calls from both the Bush and Clinton administrations for bank examiners to relax this requirement so that more funds would be available for lending.

Three agencies, the Federal Deposit Insurance Corporation, the Federal Reserve, and the Office of the Comptroller of the Currency, supervise the nation's 12,500 commercial banks. Each has a different jurisdiction, depending on the chartering of the banks, and each sends examiners into the field to inspect the books at individual lending institutions. The examiners are highly trained professionals who are civil servants and, thus, are not appointed by the president. They resisted what they regarded as political pressure from the White House and continued to err on the side of caution when confronted by a difficult case. Their auditing work is complex and it's hard for political superiors to contradict their findings. They were also able to resist pressure from the White House because some in Congress were pressuring the political appointees who led these agencies to resist calls for relaxing the standards traditionally followed by examiners. No changes in examination practices emerged and whatever tightness there might have been in lending eased as the economy became increasingly robust.[16]

Although government bureaucracies may sometimes frustrate the president, by and large their policies move in the direction set by the White House. When President Clinton took office, he appointed Bruce Babbitt to head the Department of the Interior, which manages federally owned land. Babbitt's credentials as an environmentalist were impressive: not only had he compiled a strong record as governor of Arizona, he had also served as president of the League of Conservation Voters. As interior secretary, Babbitt usually sided with environmentalists wanting to preserve and protect public lands rather than with developers and ranchers interested in making profits through mining, logging, and grazing. For example, in one of his most widely cited speeches, Babbitt emphatically defended the Endangered Species Act by saying the nation was compelled by its religious heritage "to protect the whole of creation."[17] His management of the Interior Department contrasts sharply with Reagan and Bush appointees, whose decisions tilted strongly toward business interests. Some industries found it difficult to adjust to the changes at Interior during the Babbitt years. When Babbitt rebuked oil and gas lobbyists for minimizing the dangers of global warming, these companies lashed back, charging Babbitt with stifling dissent and stepping "seriously out of line."[18]

Presidential appointments to leadership positions in bureaucracy are important not only because of their policy implications but because they are a chance to broaden opportunity for advancement for traditionally underrepresented groups. President Clinton promised during his first campaign for the White House that he would appoint people who would reflect the diversity of America. Twenty-five percent of his top political appointees were African Americans, Hispanics, Asians, or Native Americans. Thirty percent of his appointees to top positions in the White House and agencies were women (see Politics in a Changing America 13.1). Clinton's record of women and minority appointments was significantly higher than that of his predecessor, George Bush. As one scholar concluded, Clinton "succeeded to a quite remarkable extent" in making his administration resemble the broader population.[19]

ADMINISTRATIVE POLICYMAKING: THE FORMAL PROCESSES	Many Americans wonder why agencies sometimes actually make policy rather than merely carry it out. Administrative agencies are, in fact, authoritative policymaking bodies, and their decisions on substantive issues are legally binding on the citizens of this country.

★ **politics in a changing** **america**

13.1   Does Gender Make a Difference?

When the U.S. Forest Service was sued for discriminating against women employees, it signed a consent decree pledging to hire enough women at each level of the organization so that its employment mix would be similar to the gender composition of the rest of the American work force. It moved quickly to hire more women in all types of jobs.

It is easy to applaud the Forest Service for tackling discrimination within its ranks, thus creating more opportunities for women. Clearly, it makes a difference for women, who can now compete more fairly for better jobs with increased responsibility and better pay. But does it make a difference in how the Forest Service operates? Does employing more women have an impact on the Forest Service's policy decisions? After all, the primary job of the Forest Service is to manage publicly owned forests—is there a distinctly "feminine" approach to managing trees?

Research demonstrates that men and women in the Forest Service are different in important ways. A survey of those working for the agency shows that women are decidedly more concerned about environmental protection. Women in the Forest Service are more likely to believe that there are limits to the number of people the earth can sup-

port, that the balance of nature is easily upset, that economic growth should be "steady-state," and that humans are abusing the environment.

The Forest Service must balance the needs of consumers for wood products with the desire of Americans to have our forests preserved for generations to come. But if a larger percentage of employees entering the Forest Service believe we need to do more to protect the environment, then the existing balance between development and preservation is likely to be challenged.

The influx of women into the agency is too recent to measure whether these attitudes have carried over into new policies. Furthermore, basic policy is set by Congress and by the president's appointees who run the agency. Inevitably, though, the different mix of men and women within the Forest Service is going to affect policy, just as adding a lot more liberals or conservatives to an agency would change it. The National Forest Products Association, a trade group of businesses that develop or use public-forest resources, has warned its members that "the sharp changes in the demographic characteristics of Forest Service employees will lead to further deemphasis on commodity production and to

---

Can You Explain Why...
agencies make policy rather than just carry out the policies that Congress sets?

administrative discretion
The latitude that Congress gives agencies to make policy in the spirit of their legislative mandate.

Administrative Discretion

What are executive agencies set up to do? To begin with, cabinet departments, independent agencies, and government corporations are creatures of Congress. Congress creates a new department or agency by enacting a law that describes the organization's mandate, or mission. As part of that mandate, Congress grants the agency the authority to make certain policy decisions. Congress recognized long ago that it has neither the time nor the technical expertise to make all policy decisions. Ideally, it sets general guidelines for policy and expects agencies to act within those guidelines. The latitude that Congress gives agencies to make policy in the spirit of their legislative mandate is called **administrative discretion.** When this discretion is granted to agencies, it is also indirectly granted to the White House because it is the president who appoints agency heads.

increasing emphasis accorded to non–timber resource values." In other words, more women in the agency means a different out-look on how to manage the nation's forests.

Source: Greg Brown and Charles C. Harris, "The Implications of Work Force Diversification in the U.S. Forest Service," *Administration and Society* 25 (May 1993), pp. 85–113.

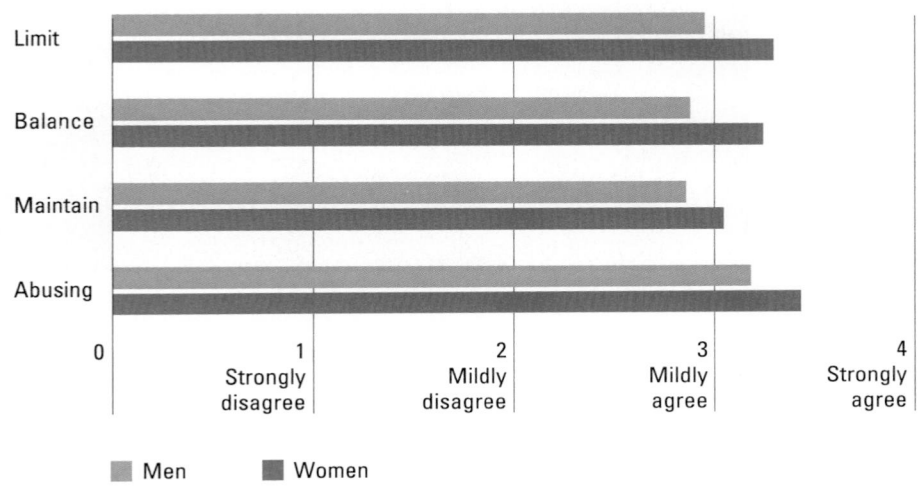

Average response based on placement of respondents on a four-point scale.
Limit = We are approaching the limit of the number of people the earth can support.
Balance = The balance of nature is very delicate and easily upset.
Maintain = To maintain a healthy economy we will have to develop a "steady-state" economy, where industrial growth is controlled.
Abusing = Humankind is severely abusing the environment.

In 1999 the Occupational Safety and Health Administration (OSHA) issued proposed regulations designed to reduce workplace injuries due to repetitive stress. For example, if workers lifting boxes develop back prob-lems, their employers would have to develop new procedures to reduce such injuries. OSHA was never specifically instructed by Congress to develop such rules, but rather it used its discretionary authority under the law that gives OSHA the general power to issue regulations to pro-mote worker safety. Business groups bitterly denounced the proposed regulations because they believed they would cost companies money by making it easier for workers to claim that any of their musculoskeletal problems are their employer's responsibility.[20] The Clinton adminis-tration, sympathetic to labor, issued the regulations anyway. With the change in administrations after the 2000 election, Republicans in Congress and President Bush worked together to undo the regulations.

Helping Workers or Hurting Business?

The controversial nature of regulation is illustrated by the fight over the Occupational Safety and Health Administration's effort to institute a comprehensive set of ergonomic rules. Labor unions want government to do whatever it can to prevent workers from getting hurt on the job. Some solutions are relatively inexpensive, such as ergonomically correct computer keyboards to prevent carpal tunnel syndrome. Other remedies, argue business groups, are much too expensive, and government should let management and labor work out their own solutions.

They agreed with business's view and a law was enacted invalidating the new rules.

Critics of the bureaucracy frequently complain that agencies are granted too much discretion. In his book *The End of Liberalism*, Theodore Lowi argues that Congress commonly gives vague directives in its initial enabling legislation instead of truly setting guidelines.[21] Congress charges agencies with protecting "the public interest" but leaves them to determine on their own what policies best serve the public. Lowi and other critics believe that members of Congress delegate too much of their responsibility for difficult policy choices to appointed administrators.

Congress often is vague about its intent when setting up a new agency or program. At times, a problem is clear-cut, but the solution is not; yet Congress is under pressure to act. So it creates an agency or program to show that it is concerned and responsive, but it leaves it to administrators to develop specific solutions. For example, the 1934 legislation that established the FCC recognized a need for regulation in the burgeoning radio industry. The growing number of stations and overlapping frequencies would soon have made it impossible to listen to the radio. But Congress avoided tackling several sticky issues by giving the FCC the ambiguous directive that broadcasters should "serve the public interest, convenience, and necessity."[22] In other cases, several obvious solutions to a problem may be available, but lawmakers cannot agree on which is best. Compromise wording is often ambiguous, papering over differences and ensuring conflict over administrative regulations as agencies try to settle lingering policy disputes.

The wide latitude Congress gives administrative agencies often leads to charges that the bureaucracy is out of control, a power unto itself. But such claims are frequently exaggerated. Administrative discretion is not a fixed commodity. Congress has the power to express its displeasure by reining in agencies with additional legislation. If Congress is unhappy with an agency's actions, it can pass laws invalidating specific policies.[23] As noted above, this is what happened with the workplace safety regulations.[24] A second powerful tool is Congress's control over the budget. Congress can influence an agency because it has the power to cut budgets and to reorder agency priorities through its detailed appropriations legislation.

In general, then, the bureaucracy is not out of control. But Congress has chosen to limit its own oversight in one area—domestic and international security. Both the FBI and the CIA have enjoyed a great deal of freedom from formal and informal congressional constraints because of the legitimate need for secrecy in their operations. During the years that the legendary J. Edgar Hoover ran the FBI (1924–1972), it was something of a rogue elephant, independent of both Congress and the president. Politicians were afraid of Hoover, who was not above keeping files on them and using those files to increase his power. At Hoover's direction, the FBI spied on Martin Luther King, Jr., and once sent King a tape recording with embarrassing revelations gathered by bugging his hotel rooms. The anonymous letter accompanying the tape suggested that King save himself further embarrassment by committing suicide.[25]

Rule Making

Agencies exercise their policymaking discretion through formal administrative procedures, usually rule making. **Rule making** is the administrative process that results in the issuance of regulations.[26] **Regulations** are rules that guide the operation of government programs. When an agency issues regulations, it is using the discretionary authority granted to it by Congress to implement a program or policy enacted into law.

Because they are authorized by congressional statutes, regulations have the effect of law. The policy content of regulations is supposed to follow from the intent of enabling legislation. After Congress enacted the Nutrition Labeling and Education Act, for example, the FDA drew up regulations to implement the policy guidelines set forth in the law. One part of the law says that producers of foods and food supplements can make health claims for their products only when "significant scientific agreement" exists to support those claims. Following that principle, the FDA proposed regulations requiring manufacturers of vitamins and dietary supplements to substantiate the health claims they make for their products on their labels. Clearly, the FDA was following the intent of a law enacted by Congress.

Regulations are first published as proposals, to give all interested parties an opportunity to comment on them and to try to persuade the agency to adopt, alter, or withdraw them. When the FDA issued its proposed regulations on vitamins and health supplements, the industry fought them vigorously. Aware that many of their health claims could not be substantiated and that it would be expensive to finance scientific studies to try to prove their assertions, the manufacturers asked Congress for relief. Although it was responsible for the legislation authorizing the regulations, Congress passed a one-year moratorium on the proposed rules. Congress seemed to want to have it both ways, ensuring the integrity of food and drugs while protecting the business interests of industry

rule making
The administrative process that results in the issuance of regulations by government agencies.

regulations
Administrative rules that guide the operation of a government program.

Can You Explain Why...
Americans want less "red tape," but bureaucracies keep producing more and more regulations?

constituents. When the moratorium expired, however, the FDA announced plans to reissue the regulations.[27]

The regulatory process is controversial because regulations often require individuals and corporations to act against their own self-interest. In this case, the producers of vitamins and dietary supplements resented the implication that they were making false claims and reminded policymakers that they employ many people to make products that consumers want. However, the FDA must balance its desire not to put people out of work through overregulation with its concern that people not be misled or harmed by false labeling.

| ADMINISTRATIVE POLICYMAKING: INFORMAL POLITICS | When an agency is considering a new regulation and all the evidence and arguments have been presented, how does an administrator reach a decision? Because policy decisions typically address complex problems that lack a single satisfactory solution, they rarely exhibit mathematical precision and efficiency. |

The Science of Muddling Through

In his classic analysis of policymaking, "The Science of Muddling Through," Charles Lindblom compared the way policy might be made in the ideal world with the way it is formulated in the real world.[28] The ideal, rational decision-making process, according to Lindblom, begins with an administrator's tackling a problem by ranking values and objectives. After the objectives are clarified, the administrator thoroughly considers all possible solutions to the problem. The administrator comprehensively analyzes alternative solutions, taking all relevant factors into account. Finally, the administrator chooses the alternative that is seen as the most effective means of achieving the desired goal and solving the problem.

Lindblom claims that this "rational-comprehensive" model is unrealistic. To begin with, policymakers have great difficulty defining precise values and goals. Administrators at the U.S. Department of Energy, for example, want to be sure that supplies of home heating oil are sufficient each winter. At the same time, they want to reduce dependence on foreign oil. Obviously, the two goals are not fully compatible. How should these administrators decide which goal is more important? And how should they relate them to the other goals of the nation's energy policy?

Real-world decision making parts company with the ideal in another way: the policy selected cannot always be the most effective means to the desired end. Even if a tax at the pump is the most effective way to reduce gasoline consumption during a shortage, motorists' anger would make this theoretically "right" decision politically difficult. So the "best" policy is often the one on which most people can agree. However, political compromise may mean that the government is able to solve only part of a problem.

Finally, critics of the rational-comprehensive model point out that policymaking can never be based on truly comprehensive analyses. A secretary of energy cannot possibly find the time to read a comprehensive study of all alternative energy sources and relevant policy considerations for the future. A truly thorough investigation of the subject would produce thou-

Of Hijabs and Turbans

New guidelines protect the religious rights of federal workers. Muslim women may don head scarves, called hijabs, and Sikh men may wear turbans (as pictured here) while on the job. Employees may keep Bibles and Korans on their desks for use at lunch time, hang religious art in their cubicles, and even proselytize in the office if such attention is clearly welcomed by their colleagues.

sands of pages of text. Instead, administrators usually rely on short staff memos that outline a limited range of feasible solutions to immediate problems. Time is of the essence, and problems are often too pressing to wait for a complete study.

incrementalism
Policymaking characterized by a series of decisions, each instituting modest change.

In short, policymaking tends to be characterized by **incrementalism,** with policies and programs changing bit by bit, step by step.[29] Decision makers are constrained by competing policy objectives, opposing political forces, incomplete information, and the pressures of time. They choose from a limited number of feasible options that are almost always modifications of existing policies rather than wholesale departures from them.

Because policymaking proceeds by means of small modifications of existing policies, it is easy to assume that incrementalism describes a process that is intrinsically conservative, sticking close to the status quo. Yet even if policymaking moves in small steps, those steps may all be in the same direction. Over time, a series of incremental changes can significantly alter a program.[30]

The Culture of Bureaucracy

How an agency makes decisions and performs its tasks is greatly affected by the people who work there—the bureaucrats. Americans often find their interactions with bureaucrats frustrating because bureaucrats are inflexible (they go by the book) or lack the authority to get things done. Top administrators, too, can become frustrated with the bureaucrats who work for them.

Why do people act bureaucratically? Individuals who work for large organizations cannot help but be affected by the culture of bureaucracy. Modern bureaucracies develop explicit rules and standards to make their operations more efficient and guarantee fair treatment for their clients.

norms
An organization's informal, unwritten rules that guide individual behavior.

But within each organization, **norms** (informal, unwritten rules of behavior) also develop and influence the way people act on the job. Norms at the IRS, for example, have long encouraged an adversarial relationship with taxpayers. Officials reinforced this tendency within the agency by ranking district offices according to the amount of money they collected from the public. To make sure their offices met their expected quotas, district supervisors sometimes looked the other way when agents blatantly harassed citizens, or even subtly encouraged them to pursue illegal tactics to force citizens to pay up. This picture of the internal operations of the IRS emerged from a hearing before the Senate Finance Committee in 1997. After mistreated taxpayers aired their grievances on nationwide television and agents testified about flagrant abuses by the IRS, acting commissioner Michael P. Dolan began dismantling the quota system and apologized to the American people for the agency's transgressions.[31]

Bureaucracies are often influenced in their selection of policy options by the prevailing customs, attitudes, and expectations of the people working within them. Departments and agencies commonly develop a sense of mission, where a particular objective or a means for achieving it is emphasized. The Army Corps of Engineers, for example, is dominated by engineers who define the agency's objective as protecting citizens from floods by building dams. There could be other objectives, and there are certainly other methods of achieving this one, but the engineers promote the solutions that fit their conception of what the agency should be doing. As one study concluded, "When asked to generate policy proposals for review by their political superiors, bureaucrats are tempted to bias the search for alternatives so that their superiors wind up selecting the kind of program the agency wants to pursue."[32]

Bureaucrats go by the book because the "book" is actually the law they administer, and they are obligated to enforce the law. The regulations under those laws are often broad standards intended to cover a range of behavior. Yet sometimes those laws and regulations don't seem to make sense. Take the case of Tommy McCoy, who was the batboy for the Savannah Cardinals, a farm team for the major league Atlanta Braves. An investigator for the Department of Labor discovered that Tommy was only fourteen years old and he was working at the night games of the Cardinals. Child labor laws forbid fourteen-year-olds from working past 7:00 P.M. on school nights, and the Department of Labor inspector threatened to fine the team unless they stopped employing Tommy. The Cardinals went to bat for Tommy, scheduling a "Save Tommy's Job" night at the stadium. The publicity about Tommy's imminent firing made the Department of Labor look ridiculous. When ABC News asked Secretary of Labor Robert Reich to comment on the situation, he knew he was facing a public relations disaster. But when he asked his staff how they could permit Tommy to keep his job, he was told, "There's nothing we can do. The law is the law."[33]

Reich overrode his staff, deciding that new regulations would exempt batboys and batgirls. That may seem to be a happy ending to a story of a bureaucracy gone mad, but it's not that simple. Child labor laws are important—before this country had such laws, children were exploited in factories that paid them low wages and subjected them to unsanitary working conditions. The exploitation of child labor is still a problem in many parts of the world. It made sense for Congress to pass a law to forbid child labor abuses, and it made sense for the Department of Labor to write a blanket regulation that forbids work after 7:00 P.M. for all children fourteen and under. The alternative was to try to determine an evening curfew for every type of job that a youngster might have. Although Reich's exemption made sense from a public relations point of view, it was nonsensical as public policy. How about kids working as peanut vendors at the Cardinals' games? Why didn't Reich write a new regulation exempting them as well? And if he wrote an exemption for children who worked for a baseball team, how about children who scoop ice cream at the local creamery? Why should Tommy McCoy be treated with favoritism?

Bureaucrats often act bureaucratically because they are trying to apply the laws of this country in a manner that treats everyone equally. Sometimes, as in the case of Tommy McCoy, equal application of the law doesn't seem to make sense. Yet it would be unsettling if government employees interpreted rules as they please. Americans expect to be treated equally before the law, and bureaucrats work with that expectation in mind.

PROBLEMS IN IMPLEMENTING POLICY

implementation
The process of putting specific policies into operation.

One of the questions in the IDEAlog program that accompanies this textbook deals with the issue of pornography. How did you answer that question in the self-test?

The development of policy in Washington is the end of one phase of the policymaking cycle and the beginning of another. After policies have been developed, they must be implemented. **Implementation** is the process of putting specific policies into operation. Ultimately, bureaucrats must convert policies on paper into policies in action. It is important to study implementation because policies do not always do what they were designed to do.

Implementation may be difficult because the policy to be carried out is not clearly stated. Policy directives to bureaucrats sometimes lack clarity and leave them with too much discretion. When Congress learned that the National Endowment for the Arts (NEA) provided a grant for a museum exhibition that included a photo of a crucifix submerged in a glass of urine, some conservatives became enraged at the agency because they felt it was using tax funds to support obscene art. After a bitter fight in Congress, a compromise required that NEA grants be restricted to works that fall within "general standards of decency." But what exactly is a "general standard of decency"? It was left to the NEA—with an administrator hostile to the very idea of a decency standard—to figure it out.[34]

Implementation can also be problematic because of the sheer complexity of some government endeavors. Take, for example, the government's Superfund program to clean up toxic waste sites. When the EPA cleans up a site itself, the cleanup takes an average of eight years to complete. Yet this is not a program that works badly because of malfeasance by administrators. Superfund cleanups pose complex engineering, political, and financial problems. Inevitably, regional EPA offices and key actors on the local level must engage in considerable negotiations at each stage of the process.[35] The more organizations and levels of government involved, the more difficult it is to coordinate implementation.

Policymakers can create implementation difficulties by ignoring the administrative capabilities of an agency they have chosen to carry out a program. Earlier it was noted that in the late 1990s, Congress was angered by

Overloaded Agency

Few bureaucracies receive as much criticism as the Internal Revenue Service. Its budget has not kept pace with the demands placed on it. This, in turn, has made it more difficult for the IRS to effectively respond to the criticism it receives. Due to financial constraints, the IRS now does fewer audits and some wonder if tax compliance has suffered because of the diminishing chances that taxpayers' returns will be reviewed.

the IRS, which it believed was overly harsh in treating those with tax problems and those they were auditing. To punish the IRS, it froze the agency's budget. The agency found itself forced to reduce its staffing to free up funds to pay for upgrades of its computer system, which couldn't handle the workload. As a result of having fewer tax agents, IRS collections fell off. For a six-month period, garnishments of paychecks of individuals who hadn't paid their taxes fell from 1.8 million two years earlier to less than 500,000. Congress had assumed that the IRS could still do what was necessary to collect all the taxes that were fairly due, but it was naïve to think that the agency wouldn't eventually buckle under growing demand and fewer resources.[36]

Ironically, although one of the central criticisms of the bureaucracy is that agencies are given too much discretion in developing policies under the laws they are given to administer, another common criticism is that there is not enough discretion available to lower-level bureaucrats. Often the agency officials doing the actual implementing in schools, hospitals, and other local settings find that their agency's programs have become "encrusted with rules."[37] Some see this as causing inflexibility, with local bureaucrats unable to fashion solutions most appropriate to the specific context.[38] For example, using the discretionary authority granted them by Congress, Clinton administration officials in the U.S. Department of Agriculture (USDA) decided to issue new dietary guidelines for school lunches. The new regulations limited fat in the lunches for any given week to 30 percent of total calories. School chefs implemented these guidelines in different ways, but then the USDA decided that it wanted the chefs to reach the 30 percent level by using specified amounts of particular foods. As school system employees, the chefs in this instance were the front-line bureaucrats, but they couldn't implement a simple policy in the way they saw fit. The chefs believed they knew best what kids are most likely to eat.[39]

Obstacles to effective implementation can create the impression that nothing the government does succeeds, but programs can and do work. Problems in implementation demonstrate why patience and continual analysis are necessary ingredients of successful policymaking. To return to a term we used earlier, implementation is by its nature an *incremental* process, in which trial and error eventually lead to policies that work.

REFORMING THE BUREAUCRACY: MORE CONTROL OR LESS?

As we saw at the beginning of this chapter, organization matters. How bureaucracies are designed directly affects how effective they are in accomplishing their tasks. People in government constantly tinker with the structure of bureaucracies, trying to find ways to improve their performance. Administrative reforms have taken many different approaches in recent years as criticism of government has mounted. Like those before it, the Clinton administration proposed many management changes to save the taxpayers money and streamline the bureaucracy.[40] Led by Vice President Al Gore, the Reinventing Government initiative put forth 800 proposals, "ranging from a top-to-bottom overhaul of the civil-service system to elimination of the subsidy for mohair."[41] During the 2000 campaign for president, however, neither George W. Bush nor Al Gore said much about reforming the bureaucracy. The budget surplus lifted much of the pressure to wring efficiencies from the bureaucracy, and the candidates' focus instead turned to new programs, like a prescription drug benefit for seniors.

A central question that surrounds much of the debate over bureaucratic reform is whether we need to establish more control over the bureaucracy or less. There is no magic solution that will work for every type of bureaucracy: less control may be best for public schools, but the NEA may need more direction by Congress if it is to retain the public's confidence. Those who advocate less government control extol the virtues of letting consumer preferences and popular opinion play more of a role in the workings of government and the economy. Those who believe that the problem is to reform government without reducing its role look for a way to enhance government performance by improving management. We will look at both broad approaches.

Deregulation

regulation
Government intervention in the workings of business to promote some socially desired goal.

deregulation
A bureaucratic reform by which the government reduces its role as a regulator of business.

Many people believe that government is too involved in **regulation,** intervening in the natural working of business markets to promote some social goal. For example, government might regulate a market to ensure that products pose no danger to consumers. Through **deregulation,** the government reduces its role and lets the natural market forces of supply and demand take over. Conservatives have championed deregulation because they see freedom in the marketplace as the best route to an efficient and growing economy. Indeed, nothing is more central to capitalist philosophy than the belief that the free market will efficiently promote the balance of supply and demand. Considerable deregulation took place in the 1970s

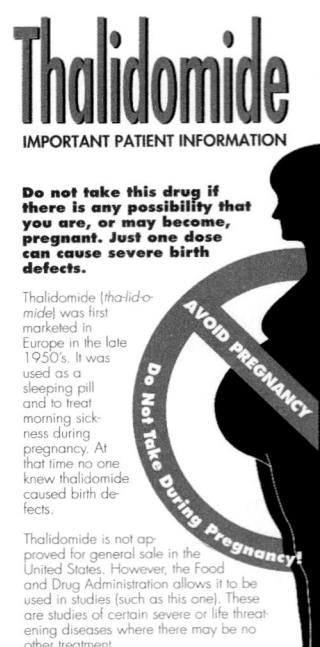

Thalidomide

IMPORTANT PATIENT INFORMATION

Do not take this drug if there is any possibility that you are, or may become, pregnant. Just one dose can cause severe birth defects.

Thalidomide (tha-lid-o-mide) was first marketed in Europe in the late 1950's. It was used as a sleeping pill and to treat morning sickness during pregnancy. At that time no one knew thalidomide caused birth defects.

Thalidomide is not approved for general sale in the United States. However, the Food and Drug Administration allows it to be used in studies (such as this one). These are studies of certain severe or life threatening diseases where there may be no other treatment.

AVOID PREGNANCY
Do Not Take During Pregnancy!

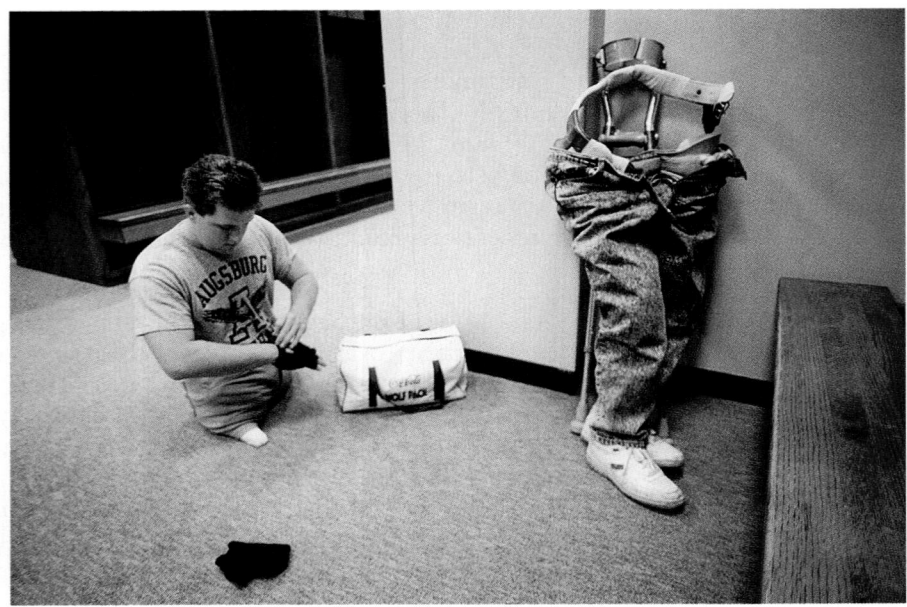

★

The Return of Thalidomide

The United States was spared the thalidomide disaster because of the skepticism of Frances Kelsey, a Food and Drug Administration doctor who refused to allow thalidomide to be prescribed here. In 1997, however, the FDA decided to permit the use of thalidomide to treat leprosy, although the dangers to pregnant women remain. Shown here is an adult thalidomide victim, as well as one of the FDA stickers designed to prevent women from taking this drug during pregnancy.

and 1980s, notably in the airline, trucking, financial services, and telecommunications industries.

In telecommunications, for example, consumers used to have no choice in choosing a long-distance vendor—one could call on the Bell system or not call at all. After an out-of-court settlement broke up the Bell system in 1982, AT&T was awarded the right to sell the long-distance services that had previously been provided by that system, but it now had to face competition from other long-distance carriers, like MCI and Sprint. Consumers have benefited from the competition and, more recently, competition has opened up for local phone service as well.

Deciding on an appropriate level of deregulation is particularly difficult for health and safety issues. Companies within a particular industry may legitimately claim that health and safety regulations are burdensome, making it difficult for them to earn sufficient profits or compete effectively with foreign manufacturers. But the drug-licensing procedures used by the FDA illustrate the potential danger of deregulating such policy areas. The thorough and lengthy process that the FDA uses to evaluate drugs has as its ultimate validation the thalidomide case. The William S. Merrill Company purchased the license to market this sedative, already available in Europe, and filed an application with the FDA in 1960. The company then began a protracted fight with an FDA bureaucrat, Dr. Frances Kelsey, who was assigned to evaluate the thalidomide application. She demanded that the company abide by all FDA drug-testing requirements, despite the fact that the drug was already in use in other countries. She and her superiors resisted pressure from the company to bend the rules a little and expedite approval. Before Merrill had conducted all the FDA tests, news came pouring in from Europe that some women who had taken thalidomide during pregnancy were giving birth to babies without arms, legs, or ears. Strict adherence to government regulations protected Americans from the same tragic consequences.

Nevertheless, the pharmaceutical industry has been highly critical of the FDA, claiming that its licensing procedures are so complex that drugs of great benefit are kept from the marketplace for years, with people suffering from diseases and denied access to new treatments.[42] Manufacturers claim that there is a "drug lag" and point to the fact that many more new medicines are introduced in Great Britain than in the United States. They have encouraged the FDA to adopt faster procedures to save the industry substantial research and development costs and to speed valuable drugs into the hands of seriously ill Americans. The FDA has resisted doing anything that would compromise what it sees as necessary precautions.

In recent years, however, the AIDS epidemic has brought about some concessions from the FDA. Although AIDS is incurable, drugs have been found to help patients deal with various symptoms of the disease and to lengthen their lives. The FDA has issued new rules expediting the availability of experimental drugs and, more generally, the FDA has adopted a somewhat speedier timetable for clinical tests of new drugs.[43] In legislation passed in 1997, Congress stipulated that patients with any life-threatening illness, not just AIDS or cancer, can have their doctors petition to use a drug still under investigation by the FDA. In addition, new drugs and vaccines designed for diseases with no effective treatment can be placed on an FDA fast-track list for quick review.[44]

The conflict over how far to take deregulation reflects the traditional dilemma of choosing between freedom and order. A strong case can be made for deregulated business markets, in which free and unfettered competition benefits consumers and promotes productivity. The strength of capitalist economies comes from the ability of individuals and firms to compete freely in the marketplace, and the regulatory state places restrictions on this freedom. But without regulation, nothing ensures that marketplace participants will act responsibly.

Monitoring, Accountability, and Responsiveness

total quality management (TQM)
A management philosophy emphasizing listening closely to customers, breaking down barriers between parts of an organization, and continually improving quality.

Bureaucracies must also strive to be responsive to the public, to provide services in an efficient and accessible manner. Presidents and agency administrators always have a plan to improve the performance of the executive branch. It's unfair to call these reform programs fads, but there is a certain cyclical nature to changes in management philosophy. At times, the dominant vision is making the government smaller or less intrusive (as with deregulation). Other times, the emphasis is on fighting waste in government, which can often lead to additional staffing because agencies hire auditors and lawyers to monitor more strictly what the agency is doing.[45] Clinton's Reinventing Government initiative was built on a management method known as **total quality management (TQM).** Although initially directed at improving the quality of manufacturing, it is now being adapted to organizations (such as government bureaucracies) that provide services as their "product." The principles of TQM include listening to the customer, relying on teamwork, focusing on continually improving quality, breaking down barriers between parts of organizations, and engaging in participatory management.[46]

Most Americans believe that government has a long way to go toward treating its clients like "customers." As one manual on TQM in government asked, "When was the last time you felt like a 'valued customer' when you encountered a government bureaucracy?"[47] Government, of course, does not have to treat people as customers, because its customers cannot go to the competition—government has a monopoly over most everything it does.

As the Clinton administration drew to a close, a major scholarly assessment of the Reinventing Government initiative concluded that it achieved some important successes, earning *"a solid grade of B"* in the evaluator's mind.[48] The initiative's performance varied widely along all its wide-ranging goals. Particularly notable is the progress made in "customer service." Many agencies developed new ways to treat their clients with efficiency and respect. A periodic business survey of consumer sentiment bears this finding out. A measure of customer satisfaction gives government a score of 68.6 (out of 100), not too far below the score of 73 for the private sector. These scores range widely depending on the specific agency, with the Social Security Administration scoring 82 and the Federal Aviation Administration 58 (see Figure 13.3). Business shows this same variation. For example, Northwest Airlines scores badly at 53, while luxury car maker BMW gets 86.[49]

Although it's certainly desirable for government to think imaginatively about how to treat its customers better, there is a real limit to analogizing government performance to that of firms in the marketplace. Are the Department of Agriculture's customers the farmers who want the agency to spend a lot of money providing them with services and subsidies, or are they the taxpayers who want the agency to minimize the amounts spent by government? The broad decision of what services an agency offers is really up to Congress, which creates the programs each agency must implement.

Still, the effort to improve service delivery goes on. A major initiative to hold agencies accountable for their performance is the **Government Performance and Results Act.** Passed by Congress, it requires each agency "to create strategic plans describing overall goals and objectives [and] performance plans describing quantifiable measures of agency and program performance."[50] Beginning in 2000, the law required that agencies begin to publish reports with performance data on each measure established. It is too early to tell if the law is improving government performance, but it's difficult to quantify many of the outputs of government agencies. What is the value to be placed on saving an endangered species?

Government Performance and Results Act
A law requiring each government agency to implement quantifiable standards to measure its performance in meeting stated program goals.

SUMMARY

As the scope of government activity has grown during the twentieth century, so too has the bureaucracy. The executive branch has evolved into a complex set of departments, independent agencies, and government corporations. The way in which the various bureaucracies are organized matters a great deal because their structure affects their ability to carry out their tasks.

figure

13.3   Passing Grades for Some Government Agencies

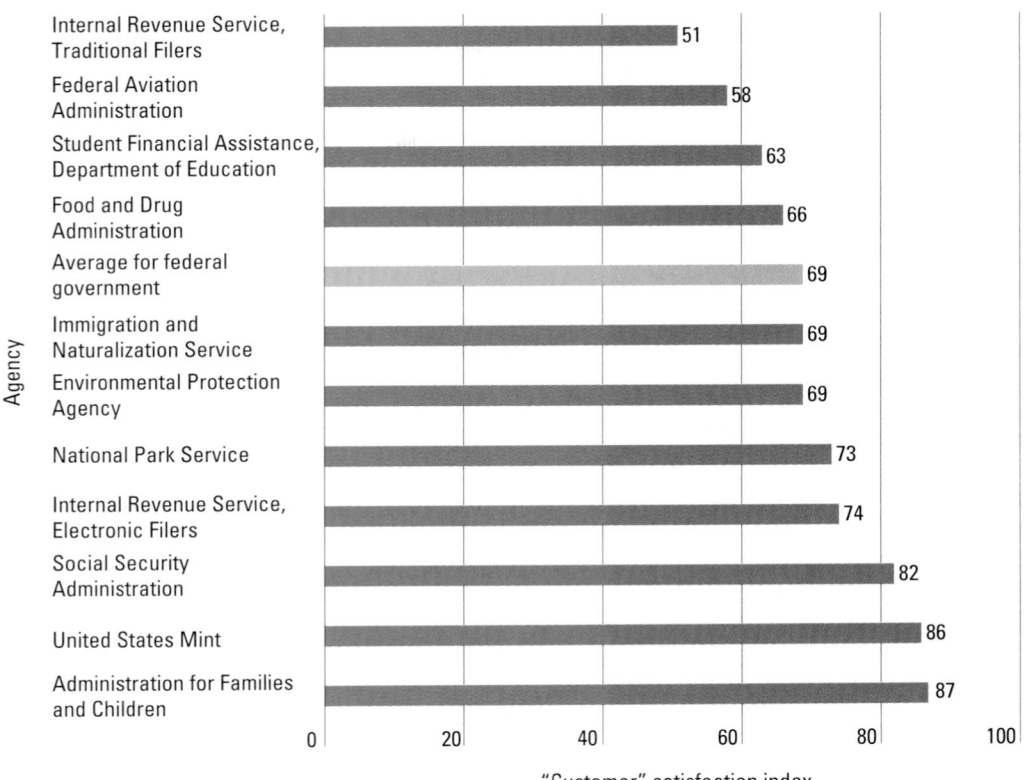

A quarterly survey by the business school at the University of Michigan questions Americans about their satisfaction with the products and services they purchase from major corporations. In an interesting comparison, one of their surveys included thirty different agencies of the national government. Some of those scores are listed here. One very positive result for government is that 60 percent of the sample said that service by the government had improved over the previous two years.

Source: Sarah Lueck, "Survey Measures Satisfaction with Federal Services," *Wall Street Journal,* 13 December 1999, p. A2.

Through the administrative discretion granted them by Congress, these bodies make policy decisions by making rules that have the force of law. In making policy choices, agency decision makers are influenced by their external environment, especially the White House, Congress, and interest groups. Internal norms and the need to work cooperatively with others both inside and outside their agencies also influence decision makers.

The most serious charge facing the bureaucracy is that it is unresponsive to the will of the people. In fact, the White House, Congress, interest groups, and public opinion act as substantial controls on the bureaucracy. Still, to many Americans, the bureaucracy seems too big, too costly, and too intrusive. Reducing the size and scope of bureaucratic activity is difficult because pluralism characterizes our political system. The entire executive branch may appear too large, and each of us can point to agencies that we believe should be reduced or eliminated. Yet each bureaucracy has its supporters. The Department of Agriculture performs vital services for farmers. Unions care a great deal about the Department of Labor. Scholars want the National Science Foundation protected. And home builders do not want Housing and Urban Development programs cut back. Bureaucracies survive because they provide important services to groups of people, and those people—no matter how strong their commitment to shrinking the government—are not willing to sacrifice their own benefits.

Plans for reforming the bureaucracy to make it work better are not in short supply. Proponents of deregulation believe our economy would be more productive if we freed the marketplace from the heavy hand of government supervision. Opponents believe that deregulation involves considerable risk and that we ought to be careful in determining which markets and business practices can be subjected to less government supervision. Government bureaucracies must be able to monitor the behavior of people inside and outside government and supervise business practices in a wide range of industries. However, most people continue to believe that the overall management of bureaucracies is poor and that government needs to be more customer-driven.

★ Selected Readings

Harris, Richard A., and Sidney M. Milkis. *The Politics of Regulatory Change*, 2nd ed. New York: Oxford University Press, 1996. A study of how political change affected policymaking at the Federal Trade Commission and the Environmental Protection Agency.

Kerwin, Cornelius M. *Rulemaking: How Government Agencies Write Law and Make Policy*, 2nd ed. Washington, D.C.: Congressional Quarterly Press, 1999. An inside look at how agencies write regulations to carry out the laws they must administer.

Kettl, Donald F. *Reinventing Government: A Fifth-Year Report Card.* Washington, D.C.: Brookings Institution Press, 1998. A sober, judicious evaluation of the Clinton-Gore initiative to make government more customer-oriented.

Kettl, Donald F., Patricia W. Ingraham, Ronald P. Sanders, and Constance Horner. *Civil Service Reform: Building a Government That Works.* Washington, D.C.: Brookings Institution Press, 1996. A brief, bipartisan look at educating and recruiting a new generation of civil servants to help "build the bridge to the twenty-first century."

Light, Paul C. *Tides of Reform.* New Haven, Conn.: Yale University Press, 1997. When it comes to administrative reform, what goes around comes around.

Light, Paul C. *The True Size of Government.* Washington, D.C.: Brookings Institution Press, 1999. Figuring out how many people actually work for the government isn't as simple as it may seem.

Osborne, David, and Ted Gaebler. *Reinventing Government.* New York: Plume Books, 1993. Although it makes the process of administrative reform seem too simple, this is a valuable guide to making government more entrepreneurial and customer-driven.

Reich, Robert B. *Locked in the Cabinet.* New York: Vintage, 1998. A wry, self-effacing account of what it's like to run a large bureaucracy.

Internet Exercises

1. *Overseeing the bureaucracy*

The Central Intelligence Agency is one of the most well known and controversial bureaucracies in the United States government. Go to the Frequently Asked Questions page on the CIA's Web site at <**www.cia.gov/cia/public_affairs/faq.html**>. Read the answers provided to the questions about the agency's mission and powers, its relationship to the elected branches of government, its relationship with the American public, and its figures on its workforce and operating budget.

- Based on the information found at its Web site, can you think of at least one significant reason why the CIA might be a difficult agency for the rest of government (and the general public) to monitor?

2. *Food safety*

Have you ever wondered where that nutrition label on your packaged food comes from? If you scan your shelves, you'll find that no matter what the item, the labeling is almost identical. That uniformity is due to regulations that have been developed by the Food and Drug Administration (FDA), a government agency that describes itself as "the nation's foremost consumer protection agency." Go to the FDA's Frequently Asked Questions page at <**vm.cfsan.fda.gov/~dms/qa-top.html**>. In the Topics List window, click on the link for Food Labeling.

- If you see "sugar free" on a label, can you be sure that the product contains no sugar? Is "fresh" food literally right off the vine?

- Because there are so many kinds of foods, setting safety guidelines for the nation's food producers may seem like a challenging task, and many producers find themselves in situations that would make it impossible for them to comply with safety regulations. Is there any evidence on this page that the FDA has recognized and attempted to address this potential problem?

The Courts

"ARE YOU SAYING WHAT I THINK YOU'RE SAYING?" asked a disbelieving Governor George W. Bush in the early morning hours of November 8, 2000. "Let me make sure I understand. You're calling me back to retract your concession?"

"You don't have to get snippy about it!" replied Vice President Al Gore. Just forty-five minutes earlier, Gore had conceded the closely contested presidential race to Bush. "Circumstances have changed since I first called you," said Gore. "The state of Florida is too close to call."[1]

The 2000 presidential election hinged on the results in Florida. Bush maintained a narrow lead of 1,725 votes, so narrow as to cast in doubt the true winner. Gore was ahead in the national popular vote by more than 300,000 votes of the more than 100 million cast. But elections for president do not hinge on the popular vote; they depend on the electoral college vote (see Chapter 10). Florida would cast all of its twenty-five electoral votes for the candidate who won the most popular votes in that state. If Bush kept his razor-thin lead in Florida, he would have 271 electoral votes, just one more than the minimum to claim victory. If Gore moved into the lead in Florida, he would be the victor, with 292 electoral votes.

On the day after the election, William Daley, Gore's campaign chairman, declared: "Until the results in Florida are official, our campaign continues."[2] The campaign continued in a new venue: the courts. Judges in the United States exercise enormous power. By transforming the electoral dispute into a legal dispute, the campaign for the presidency moved to the judicial branch, where different rules and actors would achieve resolution.

Democrats immediately dispatched a planeload of lawyers to Florida to consider their options. Republican lawyers soon followed. Over the next thirty-six days, teams of lawyers on both sides would parry and thrust in a rash of lawsuits in state and federal courts and rely on the separate and overlapping allocation of power between state and nation to resolve the presidential election.

Florida was now in the spotlight. Given the small margin of victory— less than 2,000 votes—Florida's election law required a recount. The recount produced a much slimmer margin—930 votes—but a similar outcome for Bush. A surprising number of votes for president had been disallowed, however, because voters had cast votes for two or more candidates (these are called overvotes) or for no candidate at all (these are called undervotes). Many of these disallowed ballots were cast in counties with large Democratic majorities. With the margin of victory paper-thin, rea-

"Our consideration is limited to the present circumstances."

In Bush v. Gore, *a sharply divided U.S. Supreme Court resolved the 2000 presidential election. The Court reached its controversial decision in record time (about 36 hours), forcing some justices and many of their clerks to work through the night. The majority said that the ruling should not be viewed as a precedent-setter for other equal-protection claims. Critics say that may be wishful thinking.*

soned the Democrats, it was possible that errors in the vote-counting process could reverse the results. Moreover, overseas absentee ballots still had not been tallied. There were enough such ballots to cast the results one way or the other. Since members of the military, who tend to support Republican candidates, cast many of these ballots, counting the overseas ballots could bolster the Bush lead.

Given the fast-approaching deadline established by the Florida legislature to report or "certify" the results officially, the Democrats protested the vote counting in court. The Democratic strategy was to assert that all the votes had not been counted and that the obligation of government was to count every vote. The Republicans replied that every legitimate vote had been counted—twice—and each time, Bush was the winner. Florida state law permits hand recounts. The Gore team seized on this approach, focusing on a few select counties, to determine whether or not the overvotes or undervotes signaled an intent to support one candidate or another. In largely Democratic Palm Beach and Broward counties, local officals ordered a complete hand recount of all the votes.

Threatened with the possibility that a full hand recount could reverse the result of the original count and machine recount, the Bush team requested that federal courts stop the hand recount. The lengthy hand recount process, they argued, would violate the conditions in Florida state law for officially certifying the results. The Democrats, looking at the same Florida voting rules, argued in the Florida courts that the state law was riddled with inconsistencies and that the overall policy was to determine the intent of the voters, even if the effort to do so took additional time.

Through a fast-paced series of legal cases, the matter reached the Florida Supreme Court. Its seven justices (all Democratic appointees), in an effort to harmonize conflicting state voting statutes, ruled unanimously to include the hand recounts and to push back the time required for the state to certify the election outcome. To Republicans, this action was a blatant attempt to rewrite the rulebook after the game was over. When the new deadline for certification arrived and with some hand recounts still underway, Florida elected officials (who were Republicans) certified George W. Bush as the winner by 537 votes. Meanwhile, the Bush team had sought and won review in the Supreme Court of the United States, arguing that the Florida Supreme Court rewrote the rules by improperly extending the certification deadline. Within a few days, the Supreme Court unanimously declined to reach the major issue of the recount. Instead, it set aside the Florida Supreme Court decision and requested a clarifying ruling with regard to possible conflicts with federal law and the U.S. Constitution.[3]

The Democrats were down but not out. Although the *protest* period ended with the official certification of the vote, Florida law permitted candidates to *contest* the election results following certification. In a new lawsuit, the Gore team sought a complete hand recount of all votes in the disputed counties. Following a marathon court hearing, a Florida trial judge denied the request for a hand recount. Not yet finished, the Democrats appealed once more to the Florida Supreme Court. In a breathtaking 4–3 decision, the Florida justices ordered an immediate, complete manual recount for all ballots in the state where no vote for president was recorded by machine, a total of 45,000 votes out of more than 6 million votes cast. It also ordered the inclusion of additional undervotes for Gore, reducing Bush's lead to 193.[4]

With their margin of victory eroding with every decision, the Republicans countered with another appeal to the Supreme Court of the United States. Acting on an emergency request, the deeply divided court temporarily halted the recount on the ground that such action would produce irreparable harm; it also set the case for a hearing.[5] In this round of arguments, the Bush team maintained that the vote recount procedures were standardless—they varied within and across counties—and therefore violated the Constitution's Fourteenth Amendment guarantee of equal protection. The Gore team argued the importance of counting every vote and deferring to the wisdom of the Florida courts.

Just one day after hearing arguments, the justices acted decisively and controversially when the Supreme Court invoked its role as umpire in the extra-inning game of presidential politics. While in substantial agreement (7–2) that the state vote-counting procedures violated the equal protection guarantee of the Fourteenth Amendment, the justices split 5–4 on the remedy. The majority (all conservatives) declared that the time had run out on the recounting of disputed votes. The minority (moderates and liberals) maintained that the recounts should have continued.[6] In words that reflected the sharp partisan tone of the court's action, dissenting Justice John Paul Stevens wrote:

> Although we may never know with complete certainty the identity of the winner of this year's Presidential election, the identity of the loser is perfectly clear. It is the Nation's confidence in the judge as an impartial guardian of the rule of law.

The following day, Vice President Al Gore made his third and final telephone call to Governor George W. Bush, conceding the election while strongly disagreeing with the Supreme Court's ruling. The game was over.

This extraordinary election illustrates the powerful role of the judiciary in American politics. A surprisingly assertive (and conservative) Supreme Court majority ended the controversy and short-circuited a constitutional crisis, avoiding a drawn-out battle in Congress regarding the proper winner of the 2000 election. In the name of the Constitution, the justices trumped the Florida courts, raising the specter that the nation's highest court acted out of partisanship rather than impartiality.

The power of the courts to shape public policy, including the extraordinary circumstance of the 2000 election creates a difficult probem for democratic theory. According to that theory, the power to make law and the power to determine the outcome of elections reside only in the people or their elected representatives. When judges undo the work of elected majorities (as some have charged in the 2000 election), they risk depriving the people of the right to make the laws or to govern themselves.

Court rulings—especially Supreme Court rulings—extend far beyond any particular case. Judges are students of the law, but they remain human beings. They have their own opinions about the values of freedom, order, and equality. And although all judges are constrained by statutes and precedents from imposing their personal will on others through their decisions, some judges are more prone than others to interpreting the law in light of those beliefs.

America's courts are deeply involved in the life of the country and its people. Some courts, such as the Supreme Court, make fundamental policy decisions vital to the preservation of freedom, order, and equality. Through checks and balances, the elected branches link the courts to democracy, and the courts link the elected branches to the Constitution. But does it work? Can the courts exercise political power within the pluralist model? Or are judges simply sovereigns in black robes, making decisions independent of popular control? In this chapter, we try to answer these questions by exploring the role of the judiciary in American political life.

NATIONAL JUDICIAL SUPREMACY

Section 1 of Article III of the Constitution creates "one supreme Court." The founders were divided on the need for other national courts, so they deferred to Congress the decision to create a national court system. Those who opposed the creation of national courts believed that such a system would usurp the authority of state courts.[7] Congress considered the issue in its first session and, in the Judiciary Act of 1789, gave life to a system of federal (that is, national) courts that would coexist with the courts in each state but be independent of them. Federal judges would also be independent of popular influences because the Constitution provided for their virtual lifetime appointment.

In the early years of the republic, the federal judiciary was not a particularly powerful branch of government. It was especially difficult to recruit and keep Supreme Court justices. They spent much of their time as individual traveling judges ("riding circuit"); disease and poor transportation were everyday hazards. The justices met as the Supreme Court only for a few weeks in February and August.[8] John Jay, the first chief justice, refused to resume his duties in 1801 because he concluded that the Court could

Chief Justice John Marshall

John Marshall (1755–1835) clearly ranks as the Babe Ruth of the Supreme Court. Both Marshall and the Bambino transformed their respective games and became symbols of their institutions. Scholars now recognize both men as originators—Marshall of judicial review, and Ruth of the modern age of baseball.

not muster the "energy, weight, and dignity" to contribute to national affairs.[9] Several distinguished statesmen refused appointments to the Court, and several others, including Oliver Ellsworth, the third chief justice, resigned. But a period of profound change began in 1801 when President John Adams appointed his secretary of state, John Marshall, to the position of chief justice.

Judicial Review of the Other Branches

Shortly after Marshall's appointment, the Supreme Court confronted a question of fundamental importance to the future of the new republic: if a law enacted by Congress conflicts with the Constitution, which should prevail? The question arose in the case of *Marbury* v. *Madison* (1803), which involved a controversial series of last-minute political appointments.

The case began in 1801, when an obscure Federalist, William Marbury, was designated a justice of the peace in the District of Columbia. Marbury and several others were appointed to government posts created by Congress in the last days of John Adams's presidency, but the appointments were never completed. The newly arrived Jefferson administration had little interest in delivering the required documents; qualified Jeffersonians would welcome the jobs.

To secure their jobs, Marbury and the other disgruntled appointees invoked an act of Congress to obtain the papers. The act authorized the Supreme Court to issue orders against government officials. Marbury and the others sought such an order in the Supreme Court against the new secretary of state, James Madison, who held the crucial documents.

Marshall observed that the act of Congress invoked by Marbury to sue in the Supreme Court conflicted with Article III of the U.S. Constitution, which did not authorize such suits. In February 1803, the Court delivered its opinion.*

Must the Court follow the law or the Constitution? The High Court held, in Marshall's forceful argument, that the Constitution was "the fundamental and paramount law of the nation" and that "an act of the legislature, repugnant to the constitution, is void." In other words, when an act of the legislature conflicts with the Constitution—the nation's highest law—that act is invalid. Marshall's argument vested in the judiciary the power to weigh the validity of congressional acts:

> It is emphatically the province and duty of the judicial department to say what the law is. Those who apply the rule to particular cases, must of necessity expound and interpret that rule. . . . So if a law be in opposition to the constitution; if both the law and the constitution apply to a particular case, so that the court must either decide that case conformably to the law, disregarding the constitution; or conformably to the constitution, disregarding the law; the court must determine which of these

---

* *Courts publish their opinions in volumes called reporters. Today, the* United States Reports *is the official reporter for the U.S. Supreme Court. For example, the Court's opinion in the case of* Brown v. *Board of Education is cited as 347 U.S. 483 (1954). This means that the opinion in* Brown *begins on page 483 of Volume 347 in* United States Reports. *The citation includes the year of the decision, in this case, 1954.*

Before 1875, the official reports of the Supreme Court were published under the names of private compilers. For example, the case of Marbury v. *Madison is cited as 1 Cranch 137 (1803). This means that the case is found in Volume 1, compiled by reporter William Cranch, starting on page 137, and that it was decided in 1803.*

conflicting rules governs the case. This is of the very essence of judicial duty.[10]

The decision in *Marbury* v. *Madison* established the Supreme Court's power of **judicial review**—the power to declare congressional acts invalid if they violate the Constitution.* Subsequent cases extended the power to cover presidential acts as well.[11]

judicial review
The power to declare government acts invalid because they violate the Constitution.

Marshall expanded the potential power of the Supreme Court to equal or exceed the power of the other branches of government. Should a congressional act (or, by implication, a presidential act) conflict with the Constitution, the Supreme Court claimed the power to declare the act void. The judiciary would be a check on the legislative and executive branches, consistent with the principle of checks and balances embedded in the Constitution. Although Congress and the president may sometimes wrestle with the constitutionality of their actions, judicial review gave the Supreme Court the final word on the meaning of the Constitution.

The exercise of judicial review—an appointed branch's checking of an elected branch in the name of the Constitution—appears to run counter to democratic theory. But in nearly two hundred years of practice, the Supreme Court has invalidated only about 150 provisions of national law. Only a small number have had great significance for the political system.[12] (The Court produced important invalidations during the last five years, however, voiding provisions of the Brady gun-control law and the Violence Against Women Act, and the entire Communications Decency Act, Religious Freedom Restoration Act, Indian Land Consolidation Act, and the Gun-Free School Zone Act.) Moreover, there are mechanisms to override judicial review (constitutional amendments) and to control excesses of the justices (impeachment). In addition, the Court can respond to the continuing struggle among competing interests (a struggle that is consistent with the pluralist model) by reversing itself.

Judicial Review of State Government

The establishment of judicial review of national laws made the Supreme Court the umpire of the national government. When acts of the national government conflict with the Constitution, the Supreme Court can declare those acts invalid. But suppose state laws conflict with the Constitution, national laws, or federal treaties: can the U.S. Supreme Court invalidate them as well?

The Court answered in the affirmative in 1796. The case involved a British creditor who was trying to collect a debt from the state of Virginia.[13] Virginia law canceled debts owed to British subjects, yet the Treaty of Paris (1783), in which Britain formally acknowledged the independence of the colonies, guaranteed that creditors could collect such debts. The Court ruled that the Constitution's supremacy clause (Article VI), which embraces national laws and treaties, nullified the state law.

The states continued to resist the yoke of national supremacy. Advocates of strong states' rights conceded that the supremacy clause ob-

* *The Supreme Court had earlier upheld an act of Congress in* Hylton v. United States *(3 Dallas 171 [1796]).* Marbury v. Madison *was the first exercise of the power of a court to invalidate an act of Congress.*

ligates state judges to follow the Constitution when state law conflicts with it; however, they maintained that the states were bound only by their own interpretation of the Constitution. The Supreme Court said no, ruling that it had the authority to review state court decisions that called for the interpretation of national law.[14] National supremacy required the Supreme Court to impose uniformity on national law; otherwise, the Constitution's meaning would vary from state to state. The people, not the states, had ordained the Constitution, and the people had subordinated state power to establish a viable national government. In time, the Supreme Court would use its judicial review power in nearly 1,200 instances to invalidate state and local laws, on issues as diverse as abortion, the death penalty, the rights of the accused, and reapportionment.[15]

The Exercise of Judicial Review

These early cases, coupled with other historic decisions, established the components of judicial review:

- The power of the courts to declare national, state, and local laws invalid if they violate the Constitution

- The supremacy of national laws or treaties when they conflict with state and local laws

- The role of the Supreme Court as the final authority on the meaning of the Constitution

Can You Explain Why...
the Supreme Court's power to invalidate unconstitutional laws might be construed as antidemocratic?

This political might—the power to undo decisions of the representative branches of the national and state governments—lay in the hands of appointed judges, people who were not accountable to the electorate. Did judicial review square with democratic government?

Alexander Hamilton had foreseen and tackled the problem in *Federalist* No. 78. Writing during the ratification debates surrounding the adoption of the Constitution (see Chapter 3), Hamilton maintained that despite the power of judicial review, the judiciary would be the weakest of the three branches of government because it lacked "the strength of the sword or the purse." The judiciary, wrote Hamilton, had "neither FORCE nor WILL, but only judgment."

Although Hamilton was defending legislative supremacy, he argued that judicial review was an essential barrier to legislative oppression.[16] He recognized that the power to declare government acts void implied the superiority of the courts over the other branches. But this power, he contended, simply reflects the will of the people, declared in the Constitution, as opposed to the will of the legislature, expressed in its statutes. Judicial independence, guaranteed by lifetime tenure and protected salaries, frees judges from executive and legislative control, minimizing the risk of their deviating from the law established in the Constitution. If judges make a mistake, the people or their elected representatives have the means to correct the error, through constitutional amendments and impeachment.

Their lifetime tenure does free judges from the direct influence of the president and Congress. And although mechanisms to check judicial power are in place, these mechanisms require extraordinary majorities and are rarely used. When they exercise the power of judicial review, then, judges can and occasionally do operate counter to majoritarian rule by

---

★ compared with what?

14.1   Judicial Review

The U.S. Constitution does not explicitly give the Supreme Court the power of judicial review. In a controversial interpretation, the Court inferred this power from the text and structure of the Constitution. Other countries, trying to avoid political controversy over the power of their courts to review legislation, explicitly define that power in their constitutions. For example, Japan's constitution, inspired by the American model, went beyond it in providing that "the Supreme Court is the court of last resort with power to determine the constitutionality of any law, order, regulation, or official act."

The basic objection to the American form of judicial review is an unwillingness to place federal judges, who are usually appointed for life, above representatives elected by the people. Some constitutions explicitly deny judicial review. For example, Article 84 of the Belgian constitution (revised in 1994) firmly asserts that "the authoritative interpretation of laws is solely the prerogative of the Legislative authority."

The logical basis of judicial review—that government is responsible to a higher authority—can take interesting forms in other countries. In some, judges can invoke an authority higher than the constitution—God, an ideology, or a code of ethics. For example,

both Iran and Pakistan provide for an Islamic review of all legislation. (Pakistan also has the American form of judicial review.)

By 1992, about seventy countries—most in Western Europe, Latin America, Africa, and the Far East—had adopted some form of judicial review. Australia, Brazil, Canada, India, Japan, and Pakistan give their courts a full measure of judicial review power. Australia and Canada come closest to the American model of judicial review, but the fit is never exact. And wherever courts exercise judicial review, undoing it requires extraordinary effort. For example, in Australia the federal parliament has no recourse after a law is declared unconstitutional by the high court but to redraft the offending act in a manner prescribed by the court. In the United States, overruling judicial review by the Supreme Court would require a constitutional amendment.

Governments with a tradition of judicial review share some common characteristics: stability, competitive political parties, distribution of power (akin to separation of powers), a tradition of judicial independence, and a high degree of political freedom. Is judicial review the cause or the consequence of these characteristics? More likely than not, judicial review contributes to stability, judicial independence, and political freedom. And separa-

---

invalidating the actions of the people's elected representatives. (See Compared with What? 14.1 for a discussion of the nature of judicial review in other governments, democratic and nondemocratic.)

THE ORGANIZATION OF COURTS

The American court system is complex, partly as a result of our federal system of government. Each state runs its own court system, and no two states' courts are identical. In addition, we have a system of courts for the national government. The national, or federal, courts coexist with the state courts (see Figure 14.1). Individuals fall under the jurisdiction of both court systems. They can sue or be sued in either system, depending mostly on what their case is about. Litigants file nearly all cases (99 percent) in state courts.[17]

tion of powers, judicial independence, and political freedom contribute to the effectiveness of judicial review.

Some constitutional courts possess extraordinary power compared with the American model. The German constitutional court, for example, has the power to rectify the failure of the nation's lawmakers to act. In 1975, for example, the German constitutional court nullified the legalization of abortion and declared that the government had a duty to protect unborn human life against all threats. The court concluded that the German constitution required the legislature to enact legislation protecting the fetus.

Some judges take their power at face value. South Africa created a constitutional court in 1995 and gave it powers on a par with the legislative and executive branches. In its first major decision, the court's eleven appointed justices abolished the death penalty, a decades-old practice that placed South Africa among the nations with the highest rate of capital punishment. "Everyone, including the most abominable of human beings, has a right to life, and capital punishment is therefore unconstitutional," declared the court's president.

The Supreme Court of India offers an extreme example of judicial review. In 1967, the court held that the Indian parliament could not change the fundamental rights sections of the country's constitution, even by constitutional amendment. The parliament then amended the constitution to secure its power to amend the constitution. The Supreme Court upheld the amendment but declared that any amendments that attacked the "basic structure" of the constitution would be invalid. In India, the Supreme Court is truly supreme.

Switzerland's Supreme Federal Tribunal is limited by the country's constitution to ruling on the constitutionality of cantonal laws (the Swiss equivalent of our state laws). It lacks the power to nullify laws passed by the national assembly. Through a constitutional initiative or a popular referendum, the Swiss people may exercise the sovereign right to determine the constitutionality of federal law. In Switzerland, the people are truly supreme.

Sources: Henry J. Abraham, *The Judicial Process,* 7th ed. (New York: Oxford University Press, 1998), pp. 229–334; Chester J. Antineau, *Adjudicating Constitutional Issues* (London: Oceana, 1985), pp. 1–6; Jerold L. Waltman and Kenneth M. Holland, *The Political Role of Law Courts in Modern Democracies* (New York: St. Martin's Press, 1988), pp. 46, 99–100; Robert L. Hardgrave, Jr., and Stanley A. Kochanek, *India: Government and Politics in a Developing Nation,* 5th ed. (New York: Harcourt Brace Jovanovich, 1993), p. 102; Howard W. French, "South Africa's Supreme Court Abolishes Death Penalty," *New York Times,* 7 June 1995, p. A3.

Some Court Fundamentals

Simplicity and Complexity in the State Court Systems

Courts are full of mystery to citizens uninitiated in their activities. Lawyers, judges, and seasoned observers understand the language, procedures, and norms associated with legal institutions. Let's start with some fundamentals.

Typical Process of Criminal Trials

Criminal and Civil Cases.   A crime is a violation of a law that forbids or commands an activity. Criminal laws are created, amended, and repealed by state legislatures. These laws and the punishments for violating them are recorded in each state's penal code. Some crimes—murder, rape, arson—are on the books of every state. Others—sodomy between consenting adults is one example—are considered crimes in certain states but not all. Because crime is a violation of public order, the government

figure **14.1** The Federal and State Court Systems, 1998–1999

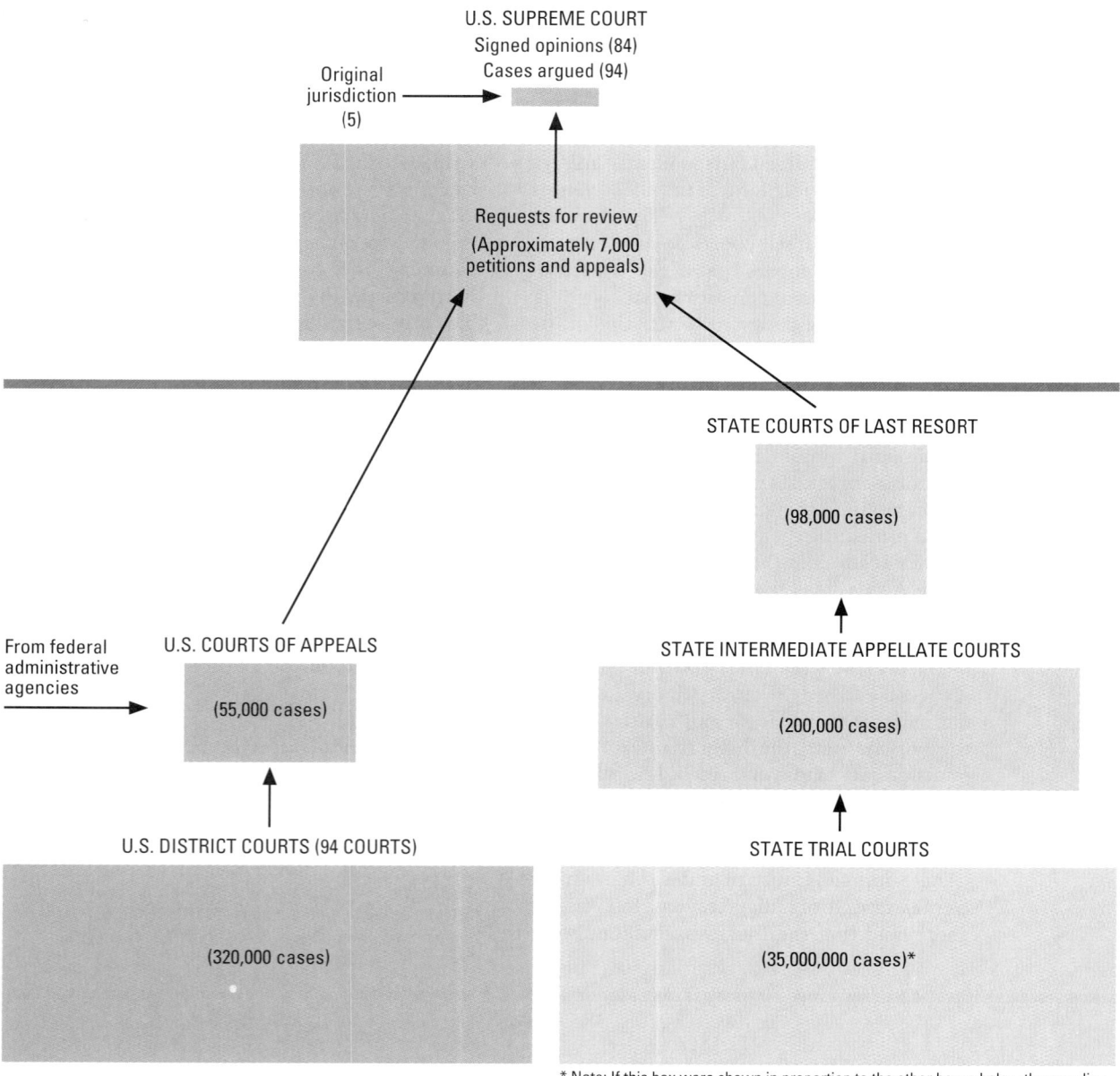

U.S. SUPREME COURT
Signed opinions (84)
Cases argued (94)

Original jurisdiction (5)

Requests for review (Approximately 7,000 petitions and appeals)

STATE COURTS OF LAST RESORT

(98,000 cases)

STATE INTERMEDIATE APPELLATE COURTS

(200,000 cases)

From federal administrative agencies

U.S. COURTS OF APPEALS

(55,000 cases)

U.S. DISTRICT COURTS (94 COURTS)

(320,000 cases)

STATE TRIAL COURTS

(35,000,000 cases)*

* Note: If this box were shown in proportion to the other boxes below the gray line the actual size would be approximately 3 feet wide × 1 foot high.

The federal courts have three tiers: district courts, courts of appeals, and the Supreme Court. The Supreme Court was created by the Constitution; all other federal courts were created by Congress. State courts dwarf federal courts, at least in terms of caseload. There are more than 100 state cases for every federal case filed. The structure of state courts varies from state to state; usually, there are minor trial courts for less serious cases, major trial courts for more serious cases, intermediate appellate courts, and supreme courts. State courts were created by state constitutions.

Sources: National Center for State Courts, "State Court Caseload Statistics," Annual Report, 1998 (Williamsburg, Va.: National Center for State Courts, 2000); William H. Rehnquist, "The 1999 Year-End Report on the Federal Judiciary" (Dec. 31, 1999), <www.uscourts.gov/>.

criminal case
A court case involving a crime, or violation of public order.

civil case
A court case that involves a private dispute arising from such matters as accidents, contractual obligations, and divorce.

*Typical Process of
Civil Trials*

common (judge-made) law
Legal precedents derived from previous judicial decisions.

prosecutes **criminal cases.** Maintaining public order through the criminal law is largely a state and local function. Criminal cases brought by the national government represent only a small fraction of all criminal cases prosecuted in the United States. In theory, the national penal code is limited by the principle of federalism. The code is aimed at activities that fall under the delegated and implied powers of the national government, enabling the government, for example, to criminalize tax evasion or the use of computers and laser printers to counterfeit money, bank checks, or even college transcripts.

Fighting crime is popular, and politicians sometimes outbid one another in their efforts to get tough on criminals. National crime-fighting measures have begun to usurp areas long viewed to be under state authority. Since 1975, Congress has added hundreds of new federal criminal provisions covering a wide range of activities once thought to be within the states' domain, including carjacking, willful failure to pay child support, and crossing state lines to engage in gang-related street crime.[18]

Courts decide both criminal and civil cases. **Civil cases** stem from disputed claims to something of value. Disputes arise from accidents, contractual obligations, and divorce, for example. Often, the parties disagree over tangible issues (possession of property, custody of children), but civil cases can involve more abstract issues, too (the right to equal accommodations, compensation for pain and suffering). The government can be a party to civil disputes, called on to defend its actions or to allege wrongdoing.

Procedures and Policymaking.   Most civil and criminal cases never go to trial. In most criminal cases, the defendant's lawyer and the prosecutor plea-bargain, negotiating the severity and number of charges to be brought against the defendant. In a civil case, one side may only be using the threat of a lawsuit to exact a concession from the other. Often, the parties settle their dispute because of the uncertainties involved in litigation. Settlement can occur even at the level of the Supreme Court. For example, in 1997 the Court was scheduled to hear a case involving a white teacher who had been laid off so that a black teacher could be retained. School officials acknowledged that both teachers were equally qualified. The case provided the Court an opportunity to rule on the use of race in affirmative action programs. Civil rights groups, fearing that they would lose the case, negotiated a settlement with the white teacher, who dropped her lawsuit in exchange for a $433,500 payment.[19]

When cases do not settle, they end with an *adjudication*, a court judgment resolving the parties' claims and enforced by the government. When trial judges adjudicate cases, they may offer written reasons to support their decisions. When the issues or circumstances of cases are novel, judges may publish *opinions*, explanations justifying their rulings.

Judges make policy in two different ways. The first is through their rulings on matters that no existing legislation addresses. Such rulings set precedents that judges rely on in future, similar cases. We call this body of rules the **common**, or **judge-made, law.** The roots of the common law lie in the English legal system. Contracts, property, and torts (injuries or wrongs to the person or property of another) are common-law domains. The second area of judicial lawmaking involves the application of statutes enacted by legislatures. The judicial interpretation of legislative acts is called *statutory construction*. The proper application of a statute is not always clear from its wording. To determine how a statute should be applied, judges look for the legislature's intent, reading reports of committee hearings and debates. If these sources do not clarify the statute's meaning, the court does so. With or without legislation to guide them, judges look to the relevant opinions of higher courts for authority to decide the issues before them.

The federal courts are organized in three tiers, as a pyramid. At the bottom of the pyramid are the **U.S. district courts,** where litigation begins. In the middle are the **U.S. courts of appeals.** At the top is the Supreme Court of the United States. To *appeal* means to take a case to a higher court. The courts of appeals and the Supreme Court are appellate courts; with few exceptions, they only review cases that have already been decided in lower courts. Most federal courts hear and decide a wide array of civil and criminal cases.

U.S. district court
A court within the lowest tier of the three-tiered federal court system; a court where litigation begins.

U.S. court of appeals
A court within the second tier of the three-tiered federal court system, to which decisions of the district courts and federal agencies may be appealed for review.

The U.S. District Courts

There are ninety-four federal district courts in the United States. Each state has at least one district court, and no district straddles more than one state.[20] In 2000, there were 646 full-time federal district judgeships, and they received over 320,000 new criminal and civil cases.[21]

The district courts are the entry point for the federal court system. When trials occur in the federal system, they take place in the federal district courts. Here is where witnesses testify, lawyers conduct cross-examinations, and judges and juries decide the fate of litigants. More than one judge may sit in each district court, but each case is tried by a single judge, sitting alone. U.S. magistrate-judges assist district judges, but they lack independent judicial authority. Magistrate-judges have the power to hear and decide minor offenses and to conduct preliminary stages of more serious cases. District court judges appoint magistrate-judges for eight-year (full-time) or four year (part-time) terms. In 1999, there were 454 full-time and 62 part-time magistrate-judges.[22]

Sources of Litigation.   Today, the authority of U.S. district courts extends to

- Federal criminal cases, as defined by national law (for example, robbery of a nationally insured bank or interstate transportation of stolen securities)

- Civil cases, brought by individuals, groups, or the government, alleging violation of national law (for example, failure of a municipality to implement pollution-control regulations required by a national agency)

- Civil cases brought against the national government (for example, a vehicle manufacturer sues the motor pool of a government agency for its failure to take delivery of a fleet of new cars)

- Civil cases between citizens of different states, when the amount in controversy exceeds $75,000 (for example, when a citizen of New York sues a citizen of Alabama in a U.S. district court in Alabama for damages stemming from an auto accident that occurred in Alabama)

"The Wright Call"

*Judge Susan Webber Wright is
a federal district court judge
in Little Rock, Arkansas. She
studied law at the University
of Arkansas with (then)
Professor Bill Clinton. Wright,
a Republican, presided in a
civil case brought by Paula
Corbin Jones against
President Bill Clinton for
sexual misconduct when
Clinton was Arkansas's governor. Wright sided with the
president's request to delay
the case but the U.S. Supreme
Court overturned her decision. Wright threw the case
out entirely in 1998 following
a deposition by President
Clinton. (Jones and Clinton
later settled the matter.) Little
more than a year later, Wright
found that the president had
given intentionally false testimony tainting the proceedings. She rebuked Clinton,
holding him in civil contempt,
an ignominious "first" for any
American president.*

*U.S. Circuit Courts
of Appeals*

The U.S. Courts of Appeals

All cases resolved in a U.S. district court and all decisions of federal administrative agencies can be appealed to one of the thirteen U.S. courts of
appeals. These courts, with 179 full-time judgeships, received nearly
55,000 new cases in 2000.[23] Each appeals court hears cases from a geographic area known as a *circuit*. The U.S. Court of Appeals for the Seventh
Circuit, for example, is located in Chicago; it hears appeals from the U.S.
district courts in Illinois, Wisconsin, and Indiana. The United States is divided into twelve circuits.*

Appellate Court Proceedings. Appellate court proceedings are public,
but they usually lack courtroom drama. There are no jurors, witnesses, or
cross-examinations; these are features only of the trial courts. Appeals are
based strictly on the rulings made and procedures followed in the trial
courts. Suppose, for example, that in the course of a criminal trial, a U.S.
district judge allows the introduction of evidence that convicts a defendant but was obtained under questionable circumstances. The defendant
can appeal on the ground that the evidence was obtained in the absence of
a valid search warrant and so was inadmissible. The issue on appeal is the
admissibility of the evidence, not the defendant's guilt or innocence. If the
appellate court agrees with the trial judge's decision to admit the evidence,
the conviction stands. If the appellate court disagrees with the trial judge
and rules that the evidence is inadmissible, the defendant must be retried
without the incriminating evidence or be released.

The courts of appeals are regional courts. They usually convene in
panels of three judges to render judgments. The judges receive written

* *The thirteenth court, the U.S. Court of Appeals for the Federal Circuit, is not a regional court; it specializes in appeals involving patents, contract claims against the national government, and federal employment cases.*

arguments known as briefs (which are also sometimes submitted in trial courts). Often, the judges hear oral arguments and question the lawyers to probe their arguments.

Precedents and Making Decisions.   Following review of the briefs and, in many appeals, oral arguments, the three-judge panel will meet to reach a judgment. One judge attempts to summarize the panel's views, although each judge remains free to disagree with the judgment or the reasons for it. When an appellate opinion is published, its influence can reach well beyond the immediate case. For example, a lawsuit turning on the meaning of the Constitution produces a ruling, which then serves as a **precedent** for subsequent cases; that is, the decision becomes a basis for deciding similar cases in the same way. Thus, judges make public policy to the extent that they influence decisions in other courts. Although district judges sometimes publish their opinions, it is the exception rather than the rule. At the appellate level, however, precedent requires that opinions be written.

> **precedent**
> A judicial ruling that serves as the basis for the ruling in a subsequent case.

Making decisions according to precedent is central to the operation of our legal system, providing continuity and predictability. The bias in favor of existing decisions is captured by the Latin expression **stare decisis,** which means "let the decision stand." But the use of precedent and the principle of *stare decisis* do not make lower-court judges cogs in a judicial machine. "If precedent clearly governed," remarked one federal judge, "a case would never get as far as the Court of Appeals: the parties would settle."[24]

> **stare decisis**
> Literally, let the decision stand; decision making according to precedent.

Judges on the courts of appeals direct their energies to correcting errors in district court proceedings and interpreting the law (in the course of writing opinions). When judges interpret the law, they often modify existing laws. In effect, they are making policy. Judges are politicians in the sense that they exercise political power, but the black robes that distinguish judges from other politicians signal constraints on their exercise of power.

> **Can You Explain Why...**
> the same national law might sometimes have different meanings in different parts of the country?

Uniformity of Law.   Decisions by the courts of appeals ensure a measure of uniformity in the application of national law. For example, when similar issues are dealt with in the decisions of different district judges, the decisions may be inconsistent. The courts of appeals harmonize the decisions within their region so that laws are applied uniformly.

The regional character of the courts of appeals undermines uniformity somewhat because the courts are not bound by the decisions of other circuits. A law may be interpreted differently in different courts of appeals. For example, the Internal Revenue Code imposes identical tax burdens on similar individuals. But thanks to the regional character of the courts of appeals, national tax laws may be applied differently throughout the United States. The percolation of cases up through the federal system of courts virtually guarantees that, at some point, two or more courts of appeals, working with similar sets of facts, are going to interpret the same law differently. However, the problem of conflicting decisions in the intermediate appellate courts can be corrected by review in the Supreme Court, where policymaking, not error correction, is the paramount goal.

THE SUPREME COURT   Above the west portico of the Supreme Court building are inscribed the words EQUAL JUSTICE UNDER LAW. At the opposite end of the building, above the east portico, are the words JUSTICE THE GUARDIAN

OF LIBERTY. The mottos reflect the Court's difficult task: achieving a just balance among the values of freedom, order, and equality. Consider how these values came into conflict in two controversial issues the Court has faced in recent years.

Flag burning as a form of political protest pits the value of order, or the government's interest in maintaining a peaceful society, against the value of freedom, including the individual's right to vigorous and unbounded political expression. In two flag-burning cases, the Supreme Court affirmed constitutional protection for unbridled political expression, including the emotionally charged act of desecrating a national symbol.[25]

School desegregation pits the value of equality (in this case, equal educational opportunities for minorities) against the value of freedom (the right of parents to send their children to neighborhood schools). In *Brown v. Board of Education,* the Supreme Court carried the banner of racial equality by striking down state-mandated segregation in public schools. The decision helped launch a revolution in race relations in the United States. The justices recognized the disorder their decision would create in a society accustomed to racial bias, but in this case, equality clearly outweighed freedom. Twenty-four years later, the Court was still embroiled in controversy over equality when it ruled that race could be a factor in university admissions (to diversify the student body), in the *Bakke* case.[26] Having secured equality for blacks, the Court then had to confront the charge that it was denying whites the freedom to compete for admission. The controversy continued in 1995 as a new majority of conservative justices limited race-based preferences in government policies.[27] Since then, the Court has declined to hear new cases on this subject.

The Supreme Court makes national policy. Because its decisions have far-reaching effects on all of us, it is vital that we understand how it reaches those decisions. With this understanding, we can better evaluate how the Court fits within our model of democracy.

Access to the Court

There are rules of access that must be followed to bring a case to the Supreme Court. Also important is a sensitivity to the justices' policy and ideological preferences. The notion that anyone can take a case all the way to the Supreme Court is true only in theory, not fact.

original jurisdiction
The authority of a court to hear a case before any other court does.

The Supreme Court's cases come from two sources. A few arrive under the Court's **original jurisdiction,** conferred by Article III, Section 2, of the Constitution, which gives the Court the power to hear and decide "all Cases affecting Ambassadors, other public Ministers and Consuls, and those in which a State shall be Party." Cases falling under the Court's original jurisdiction are tried and decided in the Court itself; the cases begin and end there. For example, the Court is the first and only forum in which legal disputes between states are resolved. The Court hears few original jurisdiction cases today, however, usually referring them to a special master, often a retired judge, who reviews the parties' contentions and recommends a resolution that the justices are free to accept or reject.

appellate jurisdiction
The authority of a court to hear cases that have been tried, decided, or reexamined in other courts.

Most cases enter the Supreme Court from the U.S. courts of appeals or the state courts of last resort. This is the Court's **appellate jurisdiction.** These cases have been tried, decided, and reexamined as far as the law permits in other federal or state courts. The Court exercises judicial power

figure

14.2   Access to and Decision Making in the U.S. Supreme Court

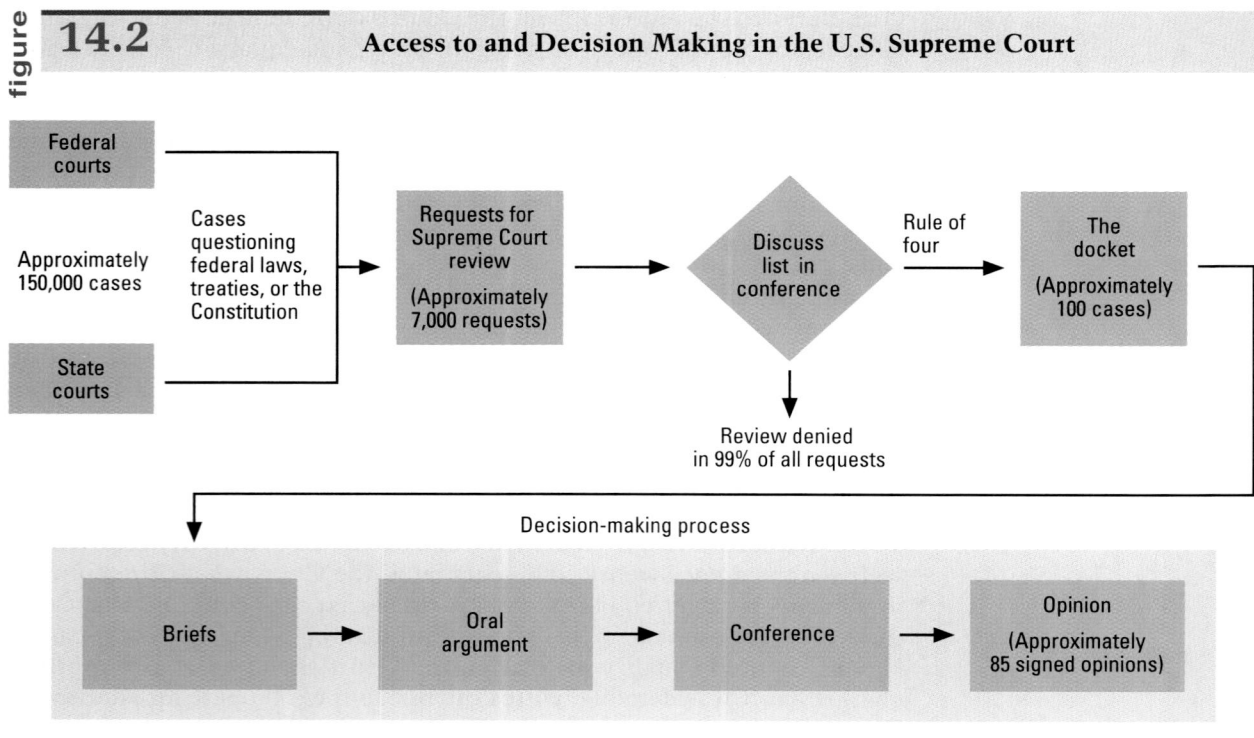

State and national appeals courts churn out thousands of decisions each year. Only a fraction end up on the Supreme Court's docket. This chart sketches the several stages leading to a decision from the High Court.

Source: William H. Rehnquist, "The 1999 Year-End Report on the Federal Judiciary," *The Third Branch: Newsletter of the Federal Courts*, Vol. 32, Number 1, January 2000. Available on-line at <http://www. uscourts.gov/ttb/jan2000.html>.

federal question
An issue covered by the constitution, national laws, or U.S. treaties.

docket
A court's agenda.

under its appellate jurisdiction only because Congress gives it the authority to do so. Congress may change (and, perhaps, eliminate) the Court's appellate jurisdiction. This is a powerful but rarely used weapon in the congressional arsenal of checks and balances.

Litigants in state cases who invoke the Court's appellate jurisdiction must satisfy two conditions. First, the case must have reached the end of the line in the state court system. Litigants cannot jump at will from a state to the national arena of justice. Second, the case must raise a **federal question**, an issue covered by the Constitution, federal laws, or national treaties. But even cases that meet both these conditions do not necessarily reach the High Court.

Since 1925, the Court has exercised substantial (today, nearly complete) control over its **docket**, or agenda (see Figure 14.2). The Court selects a handful of cases (less than one hundred) for consideration from the seven thousand or more requests filed each year. These requests take the form of petitions for *certiorari*, in which a litigant seeking review asks the Court "to become informed" of the lower-court proceeding. For the vast majority of cases, the Court denies the petition for *certiorari*, leaving the decision of the lower court undisturbed. No explanations accompany these denials, so they have little or no value as court rulings.

rule of four
An unwritten rule that requires at least four justices to agree that a case warrants consideration before it is reviewed by the Supreme Court.

The Court grants a review only when four or more justices agree that a case warrants full consideration. This unwritten rule is known as the **rule of four.** With advance preparation by their law clerks, who screen petitions and prepare summaries, all nine justices make these judgments at secret conferences held twice a week.[28] During the conferences, justices vote on previously argued cases and consider which new cases to add to the docket. The chief justice circulates a "discuss list" of worthy petitions. Cases on the list are then subject to the rule of four. Though it takes only four votes to place a case on the docket, it may ultimately take an enormous leap to garner a fifth and deciding vote on the merits of the appeal. This is especially true if the Court is sharply split ideologically. Thus, a minority of justices in favor of an appeal may oppose review if they are not confident the outcome will be to their satisfaction.[29]

The Solicitor General

Why does the Court decide to hear certain cases but not others? The best evidence scholars have adduced suggests that agenda setting depends on the individual justices, who vary in their decision-making criteria, and on the issues raised by the cases. Occasionally, justices will weigh the ultimate outcome of a case when granting or denying review. At other times, justices will grant or deny review based on disagreement among the lower courts or because delay in resolving the issues would impose alarming economic or social costs.[30] The solicitor general plays a vital role in the Court's agenda setting.

solicitor general
The third highest ranking official of the U.S. Department of Justice, and the one who represents the national government before the Supreme Court.

The **solicitor general** represents the national government before the Supreme Court, serving as the hinge between an administration's legal approach and its policy objectives. Appointed by the president, the solicitor general is the third-ranking official in the U.S. Department of Justice (after the attorney general and the deputy attorney general). President Clinton appointed three solicitor generals. The last to serve was Seth P. Waxman.

By a razor-thin vote in 2001, the Senate confirmed President George W. Bush's nomination of Theodore B. Olson as his solicitor general. Olson had rescued Bush's presidential bid by arguing before the justices in December 2000 that the ballot counting in Florida should stop.

The solicitor general's duties include determining whether the government should appeal lower-court decisions; reviewing and modifying, when necessary, the briefs filed in government appeals; and deciding whether the government should file an **amicus curiae brief*** in any appellate court.[31] The objective is to create a cohesive program for the executive branch in the federal courts.

amicus curiae brief
A brief filed (with the permission of the court) by an individual or group that is not a party to a legal action but has an interest in it.

Solicitors general play two different, occasionally conflicting, roles. First, they are advocates for the president's policy preferences; second, as officers of the Court, they traditionally defend the institutional interests of the national government.

Solicitors general usually act with considerable restraint in recommending to the Court that a case be granted or denied review. By recommending only cases of general importance, they increase their credibility

---

* *Amicus curiae is Latin for "friend of the court." Amicus briefs can be filed with the consent of all the parties or with the permission of the Court. They allow groups and individuals who are not parties to the litigation but have an interest in it to influence the Court's thinking and, perhaps, its decision.*

★

The Supreme Court, 2000 Term: The Starting Lineup

The justices of the Supreme Court of the United States, pictured from left to right: Clarence Thomas, Antonin Scalia, Sandra Day O'Connor, Anthony Kennedy, David Souter, Stephen Breyer, John Paul Stevens, Chief Justice William Rehnquist, Ruth Bader Ginsburg.

and their influence. Rex E. Lee, who was solicitor general from 1981 to 1985, acknowledged in an unusually candid interview that he had refused to make arguments that members of the Reagan administration had urged on him: "I'm not the pamphleteer general; I'm the solicitor general. My audience is not 100 million people; my audience is nine people. . . . Credibility is the most important asset that any solicitor general has."[32]

By contrast, President G. H. W. Bush's solicitor general, Kenneth Starr, reluctantly but vigorously argued that the justices should uphold an act of Congress designed to curb flag burning, although the Court had struck down a similar Texas law the year before. "There was no doubt at all in my mind that the constitutionality of the statute could appropriately be defended," recalled Starr. "Once Congress passes a law, our duty is to defend it. That is perhaps the most fundamental duty of this office."[33] Starr lost— the Court struck down the prohibition.

By carefully selecting the cases it presses, the solicitor general's office usually maintains a very impressive record of wins in the Supreme Court. Solicitors general are a "formidable force" in the process of setting the Supreme Court's agenda.[34] Their influence in bringing cases to the Court and arguing them there has earned them the informal title of "the tenth justice."

Decision Making

Once the Court grants review, attorneys submit written arguments (briefs). Oral arguments, typically limited to thirty minutes for each side, usually follow. From October through April, the justices spend four hours a day, five or six days a month, hearing arguments. Experience seems to help. Like the solicitor general, seasoned advocates enjoy a greater success rate, regardless of the party they represent.[35] The justices like crisp, concise, conversational presentations; they disapprove of attorneys who read from a prepared text. Some justices are aggressive, relentless questioners who frequently interrupt the lawyers; others are more subdued. In a recent free speech case, an attorney who offered an impassioned plea on the facts of the case was soon "awash in a sea of judicial impatience that at times seemed to border on anger. . . . 'We didn't take this case to determine who said what in the cafeteria,'" snapped one justice.[36]

Court protocol prohibits the justices from addressing one another directly during oral arguments, but they often debate obliquely through the questions they pose to the attorneys. The justices reach no collective decision at the time of oral arguments. They reach a tentative decision only after they have met in conference.

Our knowledge of the dynamics of decision making on the Supreme Court is all secondhand. Only the justices attend the Court's Wednesday and Friday conferences. By tradition, the justices first shake hands, a gesture of harmony. The chief justice then begins the presentation of each case with a discussion of it and his vote, which is followed by a discussion and vote from each of the other justices, in order of their seniority on the Court. Justice Antonin Scalia, who joined the Court in 1986, remarked that "not much conferencing goes on." By *conferencing*, Scalia meant efforts to persuade others to change their view by debating points of disagreement. "To call our discussion of a case a conference," he said, "is really something of a misnomer. It's much more a statement of the views of each of the nine Justices, after which the totals are added and the case is assigned" for an opinion.[37]

Judicial Restraint and Judicial Activism.   How do the justices decide how to vote on a case? According to some scholars, legal doctrines and previous decisions explain their votes. This explanation, which is consistent with the majoritarian model, anchors the justices closely to the law and minimizes the contribution of their personal values. This view is embodied in the concept of **judicial restraint,** which maintains that legislators, not judges, should make the laws. Judges are said to exercise judicial restraint when they hew closely to statutes and previous cases in reaching their decisions. Other scholars contend that the value preferences and resulting ideologies of the justices provide a more powerful interpretation of their voting.[38] This view is embodied in the concept of **judicial activism,** which maintains that judges should interpret laws loosely, using their power to promote their preferred social and political goals. Judges are said to be activists when they are apt to interpret existing laws and rulings with little regard to precedent and to interject their own values into court decisions, a pattern more consistent with the pluralist model.

The terms *judicial restraint* and *judicial activism* describe different relative degrees of judicial assertiveness. Judges acting according to an extreme model of judicial restraint would never question the validity of duly enacted laws but would defer to the superiority of other government institutions in construing the laws. Judges acting according to an extreme model of judicial activism would be an intrusive and ever-present force that would dominate other government institutions. Actual judicial behavior lies somewhere between these two extremes.

In recent history, many activist judges have tended to support liberal values, thus linking judicial activism with liberalism. But the critical case of *Bush* v. *Gore* suggests to many critics that conservative jurists can also be judicial activists, promoting their preferred political goals. Had a majority

judicial restraint
A judicial philosophy whereby judges adhere closely to statutes and precedents in reaching their decisions.

judicial activism
A judicial philosophy whereby judges interpret existing laws and precedents loosely and interject their own values in court decisions.

Justice Ginsburg & Company

Justice Ruth Bader Ginsburg meets with one of her four law clerks. Justices assign a range of responsibilities to their clerks, from memo preparation to opinion drafting. The typical clerkship lasts a year, though it may seem much longer at times because of the demanding work schedule. Despite the absence of overtime pay, there is no shortage of applications from the best graduates of the best law schools.

deferred to the Florida courts on the issue of the recount, the decision would have been hailed as an example of judicial restraint. But overturning the Florida courts and delivering a victory for the Republicans has labeled the majority in *Bush* v. *Gore* as conservative judicial activists.

judgment
The judicial decision in a court case.

Judgment and Argument. The voting outcome is the **judgment,** the decision on who wins and who loses. The justices often disagree, not only on the winner and loser but also on the reasons for their judgment. This should not be surprising, given nine independent minds and issues that can be approached in several ways. Voting in the conference does not end the justices' work or resolve their disagreements. Votes remain tentative until the Court issues an opinion announcing its judgment.

After voting, the justices in the majority must draft an opinion setting out the reasons for their decision. The **argument** is the kernel of the opinion—its logical content, as distinct from supporting facts, rhetoric, and procedures. If all justices agree with the judgment and the reasons supporting it, the opinion is unanimous. Agreement with a judgment for different reasons than those set forth in the majority opinion is called a **concurrence.** Or a justice can **dissent** if she or he disagrees with a judgment. Both concurring and dissenting opinions may be drafted, in addition to the majority opinion.

argument
The heart of a judicial opinion; its logical content separated from facts, rhetoric, and procedure.

concurrence
The agreement of a judge with the court's majority decision, for a reason other than the majority reason.

dissent
The disagreement of a judge with a majority decision.

The Opinion. After the conference, the most senior justice in the majority decides which justice will write the majority opinion. He or she may consider several factors in assigning the crucial opinion-writing task, including the prospective author's workload, expertise, public opinion, and (above all) ability to hold the majority together. (Remember, at this point, the votes are only tentative.) On the one hand, if the drafting justice holds an extreme view on the issues in a case and is not able to incorporate the views of more moderate colleagues, those justices may withdraw their votes. On the other hand, assigning a more moderate justice to draft an opinion could weaken the argument on which the opinion rests. Opinion-writing assignments can also be punitive. Justice Harry Blackmun once commented, "If one's in the doghouse with the Chief [former Chief Justice Warren Burger], he gets the crud."[39]

Opinion writing is the justices' most critical function. It is not surprising, then, that they spend much of their time drafting opinions. The justices usually call on their law clerks—top graduates of the nation's elite law schools—to help them prepare opinions and carry out other tasks. The commitment can be daunting. According to one close Court observer, the clerks shoulder much of the writing responsibility for most of the justices.[40]

The writing justice distributes a draft opinion to all the justices; the other justices read it, then circulate their criticisms and suggestions. An opinion may have to be rewritten several times to accommodate colleagues who remain unpersuaded by the draft. Justice Felix Frankfurter was a perfectionist; some of his opinions went through thirty or more drafts. Justices can change their votes, and perhaps alter the judgment, until the decision is officially announced. And the justices announce their decisions only when they are ready. Often, the most controversial cases pile up as coalitions on the Court vie for support or sharpen their criticisms. When the Court announces a decision, the justices who wrote the opinion read or summarize their views in the courtroom. Printed and electronic copies of the opinion, known as *slip opinions*, are then distributed to interested parties and the press.

Justices in the majority frequently try to muffle or stifle dissent to encourage institutional cohesion. Since the mid-1940s, however, unity has been more difficult to obtain.[41] Gaining agreement from the justices today is akin to negotiating with nine separate law firms. It may be more surprising that the justices ever agree. In 1997, for example, the Court spoke unanimously in only about one-third of all opinions.[42] Nevertheless, the justices must be keenly aware of the slender foundation of their authority, which rests largely on public respect. That respect is tested whenever the Court ventures into areas of controversy. Banking, slavery, and Reconstruction policies embroiled the Court in controversy in the nineteenth century. Freedom of speech and religion, racial equality, and the right to privacy have led the Court into controversy in the twentieth century.

Strategies on the Court

The Court is more than the sum of its formal processes. The justices exercise real political power. If we start with the assumption that the justices attempt to stamp their own policy views on the cases they review, we should expect typical political behavior from them. Cases that reach the Supreme Court's docket pose difficult choices. Because the justices are grappling with conflict on a daily basis, they probably have well-defined ideologies that reflect their values. Scholars and journalists have attempted to pierce the veil of secrecy that shrouds the Court from public view and analyze the justices' ideologies.[43]

The beliefs of most justices can be located on the two-dimensional model of political values discussed in Chapter 1 (see Figure 1.2). Liberal justices, such as John Paul Stevens and Ruth Bader Ginsburg, choose freedom over order and equality over freedom. Conservative justices—Antonin Scalia and

Justices Ruth Bader Ginsburg (left) and Sandra Day O'Connor (right) are occasional allies on the issues of abortion and gender equality. But O'Connor parts company with Ginsburg and tends to side with Chief Justice William Rehnquist (center) on matters dealing with racial equality and federalism. The justices are pictured here in the conference room of the Supreme Court building.

Clarence Thomas, for example—choose order over freedom and freedom over equality. These choices translate into clear policy preferences.

As in any group of people, the justices also vary in their intellectual ability, advocacy skills, social graces, temperament, and the like. For example, Chief Justice Charles Evans Hughes (1930–1941) had a photographic memory and came to each conference armed with well-marked copies of Supreme Court opinions. Few justices could keep up with him in debates. Then, as now, justices argue for the support of their colleagues, offering information in the form of drafts and memoranda to explain the advantages and disadvantages of voting for or against an issue. And justices make occasional, if not regular, use of friendship, ridicule, and appeals to patriotism to mold their colleagues' views.

A justice might adopt a long-term strategy of encouraging the appointment of like-minded colleagues to marshal additional strength on the Court. Chief Justice (and former president) William Howard Taft, for example, bombarded President Warren G. Harding with recommendations and suggestions whenever a Court vacancy was announced. Taft was especially determined to block the appointment of anyone who might side with the "dangerous twosome," Justices Oliver Wendell Holmes and Louis D. Brandeis. Taft said he "must stay on the Court in order to prevent the Bolsheviki from getting control."[44]

The Chief Justice

The chief justice is only one of nine justices, but he has several important functions based on his authority. Apart from his role in forming the docket and directing the Court's conferences, the chief justice can also be a social leader, generating solidarity within the group. Sometimes, a chief justice can embody intellectual leadership. Finally, the chief justice can provide policy leadership, directing the Court toward a general policy position. Perhaps only John Marshall could lay claim to possessing social, intellectual, and policy leadership. Warren E. Burger, who resigned as chief justice in 1986, was reputed to be a lackluster leader in all three areas.[45]

When presiding at the conference, the chief justice can control the discussion of issues, although independent-minded justices are not likely to acquiesce to his views. Moreover, justices today rarely engage in a debate of the issues in the conference. Rather, they use their law clerks as ambassadors between justices' chambers and, in effect, "run the Court without talking to one another."[46]

JUDICIAL RECRUITMENT	Neither the Constitution nor national law imposes formal requirements for appointment to the federal courts. Once appointed, district and appeals judges must reside in the district or circuit to which they are appointed.

The president appoints judges to the federal courts, and all nominees must be confirmed by majority vote in the Senate. Congress sets, but cannot lower, a judge's compensation. In 2001, salaries were as follows:

Chief justice of the Supreme Court	$186,300
Associate Supreme Court justices	178,300
Courts of appeals judges	153,900
District judges	145,100
Magistrate-judges	133,492

By comparison, in 2000 the average salary of a state supreme court judge was $116,184. The average for a state trial judge was $104,369.[47] In more than half the states, the governor appoints the state judges, often in consultation with judicial nominating commissions. In many of these states, voters decide whether the judges should be retained in office. Other states select their judges by partisan, nonpartisan, or (rarely) legislative election.[48] In some states, nominees must be confirmed by the state legislature. Contested elections for judgeships are unusual. In Chicago, where judges are elected, even highly publicized and widespread criminal corruption in the courts failed to unseat incumbents. Most voters paid no attention whatsoever.

The Appointment of Federal Judges

The Constitution states that federal judges shall hold their commission "during good Behaviour," which in practice means for life.* A president's judicial appointments, then, are likely to survive his administration, providing a kind of political legacy. The appointment power assumes that the president is free to identify candidates and appoint judges who favor his policies. President Franklin D. Roosevelt had appointed nearly 75 percent of all sitting federal judges by the end of his twelve years in office. In contrast, President Ford appointed fewer than 13 percent in his three years in office. Presidents Reagan and Bush together appointed more than 60 percent of all federal judges. During his administration, President Clinton appointed more than 40 percent of the 852 federal judges at all levels.

Only twelve federal judges have been impeached. Of these, seven were convicted in the Senate and removed from office. Three judges were impeached by the Senate in the 1980s. In 1992, Alcee Hastings became the first such judge to serve in Congress.

Judicial selection was not a major priority for the Clinton administration and many appointments languished. In contrast, the George W. Bush administration has signaled its commitment to appoint federal judges with extraordinary speed. Within the first one hundred days of the new administration, fifteen White House and Justice Department aides interviewed more than fifty candidates and emphasized filling appellate court vacancies with conservative candidates who held to a limited role for federal judges.[49]

Judicial vacancies occur when sitting judges resign, retire, or die. Vacancies also arise when Congress creates new judgeships to handle increasing case loads. In both cases, the president nominates a candidate, who must be confirmed by the Senate. The president has the help of the Justice Department, which screens candidates before the formal nomination, subjecting serious contenders to FBI investigation. The department and the Senate vie for control in the approval of district and appeals court judges.

The "Advice and Consent" of the Senate.   For district and appeals court vacancies, the appointment process hinges on the nominee's acceptability to the senior senator in the president's party from the state in which the vacancy arises. The senator's influence is greater for appointments to district court than for appointments to the courts of appeals.

senatorial courtesy
A practice whereby the Senate will not confirm for a lower federal court judgeship a nominee who is opposed by the senior senator in the president's party in the nominee's state.

This practice, called **senatorial courtesy,** forces presidents to share the nomination power with members of the Senate. The Senate will not confirm a nominee who is opposed by the senior senator from the nominee's state if that senator is a member of the president's party. The Senate does not actually reject the candidate. Instead, the chairman of the Senate Judiciary Committee, which reviews all judicial nominees, will not schedule a confirmation hearing, effectively killing the nomination.

Although the Justice Department is still sensitive to senatorial prerogatives, senators can no longer submit a single name to fill a vacancy. The department searches for acceptable candidates and polls the appropriate senator for her or his reaction to them. President G. H. W. Bush asked Republican senators to seek more qualified female and minority candidates. Bush made progress in developing a more diverse bench, and President Clinton accelerated the change.[50]

The Senate Judiciary Committee conducts a hearing for each judicial nominee. The chairman exercises a measure of control in the appointment process that goes beyond senatorial courtesy. If a nominee is objectionable to the chairman, he or she can delay a hearing or hold up other appointments until the president and the Justice Department find an alternative. Such behavior does not win a politician much influence in the long run, however. So committee chairmen are usually loathe to place obstacles in a president's path, especially when they may want presidential support for their own policies and constituencies.

The American Bar Association.   The American Bar Association (ABA), the biggest organization of lawyers in the United States, was involved in screening candidates for the federal bench from 1946 until 1997.[51] Its role was defined by custom, not law. At the president's behest, the ABA's Standing Committee on the Federal Judiciary routinely rated prospective appointees, using a three-value scale: "well qualified," "qualified," and "not qualified."

Presidents did not always agree with the committee's judgment, in part because its objections were sometimes motivated by disagreements with a candidate's political views. Occasionally, a candidate deemed "not qualified" was nominated and even appointed, but the overwhelming majority of appointees to the federal bench between 1946 and 1997 had the ABA's blessing. From 1997 to 2001, the Republican-controlled Senate eliminated the ABA's officially sanctioned role in the confirmation process. President George W. Bush further distanced the ABA from the selection process in 2001 by declining to give the Association advance notice of possible judicial nominees. But blunting Bush's move, Senator Patrick Leahy (D.-VT), chairman of the Senate Judiciary Committee, declared in 2001 that judicial nominees would not receive a hearing until the ABA had conducted its assessment.[52]

Recent Presidents and the Federal Judiciary

President Jimmy Carter had two objectives in making his judicial appointments. First, Carter wanted to base judicial appointments on merit, to appoint judges of higher quality than his predecessors had done. Carter's second objective was to make the judiciary more representative of the general population. He appointed substantially more blacks, women, and Hispanics to the federal bench than did any of his predecessors or his immediate successors. (Nearly all Carter judges were Democrats.)

Early in his administration, it was clear that President Reagan did not share Carter's second objective. Although Reagan generally heeded senatorial recommendations for the district courts and, like Carter, held a firm rein on appointments to the appeals courts, the differences were strong. Only 2 percent of Reagan's appointments were blacks and only 8 percent were women; in contrast, 14 percent of Carter's appointments were blacks and 16 percent were women (see Figure 14.3). Four percent of Reagan judges were Hispanics, compared to 6 percent of Carter judges. Bush's record on women and minority appointments was better than Reagan's.

Clinton's appointments stood in stark contrast to his conservative predecessors'. For the first time in history, more than half of a president's judicial appointments were women or minorities. Clinton's chief judge selector, Assistant Attorney General Eleanor Acheson, followed through on Clinton's campaign pledge to make his appointees "look like America."

The racial and ethnic composition of the parties themselves helps to explain much of the variation between the appointments of presidents of different parties. It seems clear that political ideology, not demographics, lies at the heart of judicial appointments. Reagan and Bush sought nominees with particular policy preferences who would leave their stamp on the judiciary well into the twenty-first century. Clinton was animated by the same goal. The Reagan-Bush legacy is considerable. They appointed more than half of all judges sitting today.[53] When it comes to ideological preferences as revealed by judicial choices, Carter's judges take the cake. A review of more than 25,000 federal court decisions from 1968 to 1995 concluded that Carter-appointed judges were the most liberal, whereas Reagan- and Bush-appointed judges were the least liberal. (Carter had an advantage in his efforts to mold the bench because his appointees were reviewed by a Democratic-led Senate. Reagan, Bush, and Clinton, for the most part, contended with a Senate in the hands of the opposing party.) Clinton-appointed judges are less liberal than Carter's but decidedly more liberal than the legacy of Nixon, Ford, Reagan, or Bush.[54] One general rule seems clear: presidents are likely to appoint judges who share similar values.

figure 14.3   Diversity on the Federal Courts

To what extent should the courts reflect the diverse character of the population? President Jimmy Carter sought to make the federal courts more representative of the population by appointing more blacks, Hispanics, and women. Ronald Reagan's appointments reflected neither the lawyer population nor the population at large. Bush's appointments were somewhat more representative than Reagan's on race and gender criteria. Clinton's nominees represent a dramatic departure in appointments, especially in terms of race and gender.

Sources: U.S. Bureau of the Census, *Statistical Abstract of the United States, 1997* (Washington, D.C.: U.S. Government Printing Office, 2000), Table No. 644, on-line at <http://www.census.gov/statab/www/part1.html>; and "Federal Judges Biographical Database," on-line at <http://air.fjc.gov/history/judges_frm.html>.

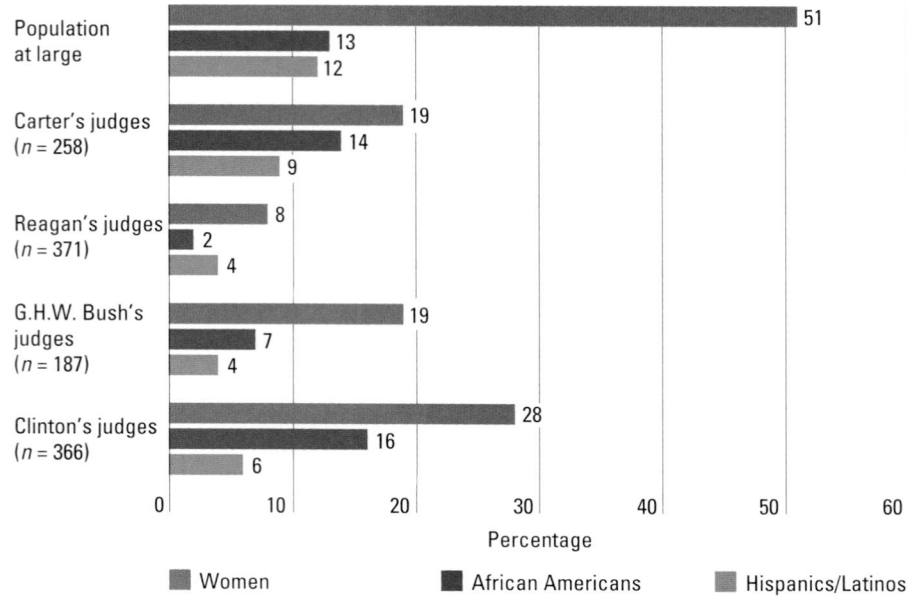

Appointment to the Supreme Court

The announcement of a vacancy on the High Court usually causes quite a stir. Campaigns for Supreme Court seats are commonplace, although the public rarely sees them. Hopefuls contact friends in the administration and urge influential associates to do the same on their behalf. Some candidates never give up hope. Judge John J. Parker, whose nomination to the Court was defeated in 1930, tried in vain to rekindle interest in his appointment until he was well past the age—usually the early sixties—that appointments are made.[55]

The president is not shackled by senatorial courtesy when it comes to nominating a Supreme Court justice. However, appointments to the Court attract more intense public scrutiny than do lower-level appointments, effectively narrowing the president's options and focusing attention on the Senate's advice and consent.

Of the 146 men and two women nominated to the Court, twenty-eight—or about one in five—have failed to receive Senate confirmation. Only five such fumbles occurred in the twentieth century, the last one during the Reagan administration. The most important factor in the rejection of a nominee is partisan politics. Thirteen candidates lost their bids for appointment because the presidents who nominated them were considered likely to become lame ducks: the party in control of the Senate anticipated victory for its candidate in an upcoming presidential race and sought to deny the incumbent president an important political appointment.[56] The most recent nominee to be rejected on partisan and ideological grounds was Judge Robert H. Bork.

Sixteen of the twenty-two successful Supreme Court nominees since 1950 have had prior judicial experience in federal or state courts. This tendency toward "promotion" from within the judiciary may be based on the idea that a judge's previous opinions are good predictors of his or her future opinions on the High Court. After all, a president is handing out a powerful lifetime appointment; it makes sense to want an individual who is sympathetic to his views. Federal or state court judges holding lifetime appointments are likely to state their views frankly in their opinions. In contrast, the policy preferences of High Court candidates who have been in legal practice or in political office can only be guessed at, based on the conjecture of professional associates or on speeches they have given to local Rotary Clubs, on the floor of a legislature, and the like.

President Clinton made his mark on the Court in 1993 when Associate Justice Byron R. White announced his retirement. Clinton chose Ruth Bader Ginsburg for the vacancy; she had been an active civil rights litigator, a law professor, and a federal judge. Some Court watchers described her as the Thurgood Marshall of women's rights because of her tireless efforts to enhance the legal status of women. In the 1970s, she argued several key cases before the Supreme Court. Ginsburg's Senate confirmation hearing revealed little of her constitutional philosophy beyond her public record. Some Republican senators tried to coax greater specificity from her broad affirmations of constitutional principles. Ginsburg declined their implicit invitation to reveal her constitutional value preferences. She cruised through to a 96–3 confirmation vote in the Senate.

Justice Harry Blackmun's resignation in 1994 gave Clinton a second opportunity to leave his imprint on the Court. After six weeks of deliberation, Clinton chose federal appeals judge Stephen G. Breyer for the coveted appointment. Breyer's moderate pragmatic views made him a consensus candidate. He sailed through tame confirmation hearings to take his place as the 108th justice.

Ginsburg and Breyer have tended to avoid ideological extremes. In close cases decided from 1996 through 2000, they remained part of a moderate-to-liberal minority. But that minority may become smaller if President George W. Bush, as expected, has one or more opportunities to appoint additional Republicans to the nation's highest court. You can bet that the fight for the Court's ideological future will be as intense as any confirmation contest in recent memory. Democrats in the closely divided Senate will be quick to recall the role played by the Supreme Court in resolving the 2000 presidential election. "Whoever gets it [a Supreme Court nomination] is going to go through hell," predicted one Republican leader.[57]

THE CONSEQUENCES OF JUDICIAL DECISIONS

plea bargain
A defendant's admission of guilt in exchange for a less severe punishment.

Judicial rulings represent the tip of the iceberg in terms of all the legal conflicts and disputes that arise in this country. Most cases never surface in court. The overwhelming majority of lawsuits end without a court judgment. Many civil cases are settled, or the parties give up, or the courts dismiss the suits because they are beyond the legitimate bounds of judicial resolution. Most criminal cases end in a **plea bargain,** with the defendant admitting his or her guilt in exchange for a less severe punishment. Only about 10 percent of criminal cases in the federal district courts are tried; an equally small percentage of civil cases are adjudicated.

Furthermore, the fact that a judge sentences a criminal defendant to ten years in prison or a court holds a company liable for $11 billion in damages does not guarantee that the defendant will lose his or her freedom or the company will give up any assets. In the case of the criminal defendant, the road of seeking an appeal following trial and conviction is well traveled and, if nothing else, serves to delay the day when he or she must go to prison. In civil cases, as well, an appeal may be filed to delay the day of reckoning.

Supreme Court Rulings: Implementation and Impact

When the Supreme Court makes a decision, it relies on others to implement it, to translate policy into action. How a judgment is implemented depends in good measure on how it was crafted. Remember that the justices, in preparing their opinions, must work to hold their majorities together, to gain greater, if not unanimous, support for their arguments. This forces them to compromise in their opinions, to moderate their arguments, which introduces ambiguity into many of the policies they articulate. Ambiguous opinions affect the implementation of policy. For example, when the Supreme Court issued its order in 1955 to desegregate public school facilities "with all deliberate speed,"[58] judges who opposed the Court's policy dragged their feet in implementing it. In the early 1960s, the Supreme Court prohibited prayers and Bible reading in public schools. Yet state court judges and attorneys general reinterpreted the High Court's decision to mean that only compulsory prayer or Bible reading was unconstitutional, and that state-sponsored voluntary prayer or Bible reading was acceptable.[59]

Can You Explain Why... racial school segregation persisted for nearly two decades after the Court declared it illegal in *Brown* v. *Board of Education* (1954)?

Because the Supreme Court confronts issues freighted with deeply felt social values or fundamental political beliefs, its decisions have influence beyond the immediate parties in a dispute. The Court's decision in *Roe* v. *Wade*, legalizing abortion, generated heated public reaction. The justices were barraged with thousands of angry letters. Groups opposing abortion vowed to overturn the decision; groups favoring the freedom to obtain an abortion moved to protect the right they had won. Within eight months of the decision, more than two dozen constitutional amendments had been introduced in Congress, although none managed to carry the extraordinary majority required for passage. Still, the antiabortion faction achieved a modest victory with the passage of a provision forbidding the use of national government funds for abortions except when the woman's life is in jeopardy. (Since 1993, the exception has also included victims of rape or incest.)

Opponents of abortion have also directed their efforts at state legislatures, hoping to load abortion laws with enough conditions to discourage women from terminating their pregnancies. For example, one state required that women receive detailed information about abortions, then wait at least twenty-four hours before consenting to the procedure. The information listed every imaginable danger associated with abortion and included a declaration that fathers are liable to support their children financially. A legal challenge to these new restrictions reached the Supreme Court, and in 1989, it abandoned its strong defense of abortion rights.[60] The Court continued to support a woman's right to abortion, but in yet another legal challenge in 1992, it recognized the government's power to further limit the exercise of that right.[61]

Public Opinion and the Supreme Court

Democratic theorists have a difficult time reconciling a commitment to representative democracy with a judiciary that is not accountable to the electorate yet has the power to undo legislative and executive acts. The difficulty may simply be a problem for theorists, however. The policies coming from the Supreme Court, although lagging years behind public opinion, rarely seem out of line with the public's ideological choices.[62] Surveys in several controversial areas reveal that an ideologically balanced Court seldom departs from majority sentiment or trends.[63] Chief Justice Rehnquist reflected as much in a recent decision upholding suspects' protections, known as the Miranda warnings, during police questioning (see Chapter 15). In his opinion for the Court, Rehnquist recognized that "Miranda has become embedded in routine police practice to the point where the warnings have become part of our national culture."[64]

The evidence supports the view that the Supreme Court reflects public opinion at least as often as other elected institutions. In a comprehensive study comparing 146 Supreme Court rulings with nationwide opinion polls from the mid-1930s through the mid-1980s, the Court reflected public opinion majorities or pluralities in more than 60 percent of its rulings.[65] The fit is not perfect, however. The Court parted company with public opinion in a third of its rulings. For example, the Court has clearly defied the wishes of the majority for decades on the issue of school prayer. Most Americans today do not agree with the Court's position. And so long as the public continues to want prayer in schools, the controversy will continue.

There are at least three explanations for the Court's reflecting majority sentiment. First, the modern Court has shown deference to national laws and policies, which typically echo national public opinion. Second, the Court moves closer to public opinion during periods of crisis. And third, rulings that reflect the public view are subject to fewer changes than rulings that depart from public opinion.

Finally, the evidence also supports the view that the Court seldom influences public opinion. Americans have little factual knowledge of the Court. According to a recent survey, more than half of all Americans can't name a single justice, although two-thirds can correctly identify the Three Stooges.[66] It is not surprising that the Court enjoys only moderate popularity and that its decisions are not much noticed by the public. With few exceptions, there is no evidence of shifting public opinion before and after a Supreme Court ruling.[67]

The Court's decision in *Bush* v. *Gore* will provide critics with fodder for years to come. However, the public seems content with the outcome and realistic in its assessment of the process by which it was reached. The Gallup Organization polled seven thousand Americans between November 7, 2000 (Election Day), and December 18, 2000 (the weekend following the resolution of the election). The findings reveal the following: no erosion in confidence following the Court's decision in *Bush* v. *Gore*; assurance that the Court was the best institution to make a final decision to resolve the Florida controversy—much more so than the Florida state courts, the Florida state legislature, or the U.S. Congress; and a belief that the Court was more influenced by the legal issues before them than by their own desires to see Bush as president.[68] However, a slight majority of Americans also said that they believed the Supreme Court justices were influenced by their own personal feelings in the matter. Despite the barrage of criticism, the Court weathered the controversy with no sustainable damage to its integrity.

THE COURTS AND MODELS OF DEMOCRACY

How far should judges stray from existing statutes and precedents? Supporters of the majoritarian model would argue that the courts should adhere to the letter of the law, that judges must refrain from injecting their own values into their decisions. If the law places too much (or not enough) emphasis on equality or order, the elected legislature, not the courts, can change the law. In contrast, those who support the pluralist model maintain that the courts are a policymaking branch of government. It is thus legitimate for the individual values and interests of judges to mirror group interests and preferences and for judges to attempt consciously to advance group interests as they see fit. However, when, where, and how to proceed are difficult questions for judges at all levels (see Politics in a Changing America 14.1).

class action
A procedure by which similarly situated litigants may be heard in a single lawsuit.

The argument that our judicial system fits the pluralist model gains support from a legal procedure called a **class action.** A class action is a device for assembling the claims or defenses of similarly situated individuals so that they can be heard in a single lawsuit. A class action makes it possible for people with small individual claims and limited financial resources to aggregate their claims and resources and thus make a lawsuit viable. The class action also permits the case to be tried by representative parties, with the judgment binding on all. Decisions in class action suits can have broader impact than decisions in other types of cases. Since the 1940s, class action suits have been the vehicles through which groups have asserted claims involving civil rights, legislative apportionment, and environmental problems. For example, schoolchildren have sued (through their parents) under the banner of class action to rectify claimed racial discrimination on the part of school authorities, as in *Brown* v. *Board of Education.*

Abetting the class action is the resurgence of state supreme courts' fashioning policies consistent with group preferences. Informed Americans often look to the U.S. Supreme Court for protection of their rights and liberties. In many circumstances, that expectation is correct. But state courts may serve as the staging areas for legal campaigns to change the law in the nation's highest court. They also exercise substantial influence over the policies that affect citizens daily, including the rights and liberties enshrined in state constitutions, statutes, and common law.[69]

Furthermore, state judges need not look to the U.S. Supreme Court for guidance on the meaning of certain state rights and liberties. If a state court chooses to rely solely on national law in deciding a case, that case is reviewable by the U.S. Supreme Court. But a state court can avoid review by the U.S. Supreme Court by basing its decision solely on state law or by plainly stating that its decision rests on both state and federal law. If the U.S. Supreme Court is likely to render a restrictive view of a constitutional right and the judges of a state court are inclined toward a more expansive view, the state judges can use the state ground to avoid Supreme Court review. In a period when the nation's highest court is moving in a

14.1 No Constitutional Right to Die

In June 1997, the Supreme Court ended its long silence on the constitutionality of a right to suicide, rejecting two separate challenges to state laws prohibiting assisted suicide. In 1996, the U.S. Court of Appeals for the Ninth Circuit relied on the Supreme Court's abortion decisions to strike down a Washington State law against aiding or abetting suicide. The circuit court reasoned from the High Court's abortion rulings that the Fourteenth Amendment's due process clause protects the individual's right "to define one's own concept of existence, of meaning, of the universe, and of the mystery of life." The Supreme Court, however, in *Washington* v. *Glucksberg*, unanimously rejected the circuit court's reasoning, in no uncertain terms. Chief Justice Rehnquist's opinion for the Court stressed that suicide is not a "fundamental right" that is "deeply rooted in our legal tradition." Unlike abortion, suicide has been all but universally condemned in the law.

In another 1996 decision, the U.S. Court of Appeals for the Second Circuit adopted a different line of reasoning to invalidate a New York law banning physician-assisted suicide. The court held that the law violated the Fourteenth Amendment's equal protection clause because it treated those who needed a physician's help to administer lethal doses of prescription drugs (which is criminalized by

law) differently from those who can demand removal of life-support systems (which is allowed under prior Supreme Court cases). In June 1997, the Supreme Court unanimously rejected this argument in *Vacco* v. *Quill*. Chief Justice Rehnquist's opinion for the Court held that the New York law does not result in like cases being treated differently. It creates no suspect classifications; anyone has the right to refuse treatment, and nobody has the right to assisted suicide. "The distinction between letting a patient die and making that patient die is important, logical, rational, and well established," Rehnquist wrote. Furthermore, the chief justice argued, the state has compelling reasons to criminalize assisted suicide.

The Supreme Court displayed an acute awareness of the ongoing debate in the states about assisted suicide. Because the Court determined only that the U.S. Constitution does not protect a right to assisted suicide, the states may still establish such a right by statute or state constitutional amendments. Only Oregon, under its Death with Dignity Act, has established a limited right to assisted suicide.

Sources: Washington v. *Glucksberg,* 117 S.Ct. 2258 (1997); *Vacco* v. *Quill,* 117 S.Ct. 2293 (1997); *Compassion in Dying* v. *Washington,* 79 F.3d 790 (9th Cir. 1996); *Quill* v. *Vacco,* 80 F.3d 716 (2d Cir. 1996).

Can You Explain Why...
the U.S. Supreme Court may be powerless to review certain decisions made by state supreme courts?

decidedly conservative direction, some state courts have become safe havens for liberal values. And individuals and groups know where to moor their policies.

The New Jersey Supreme Court has been more aggressive than most state supreme courts in following its own liberal constitutional path. It has gone further than the U.S. Supreme Court in promoting equality at the expense of freedom by prohibiting discrimination against women by private employers and by striking down the state's public school financing system, which had perpetuated vast disparities in public education within the state. The court has also preferred freedom over order in protecting the right to terminate life-support systems and in protecting free speech against infringement.[70] The New Jersey judges have charted their own

Courtly Demeanor ★

The New York Court of Appeals is the highest court in the state. Although it is bound by the decisions of the U.S. Supreme Court when defining and limiting national constitutional rights, it may rely on provisions of the state constitution to extend protections to individuals beyond those granted by the Supreme Court. For example, the New York court requires police to follow stricter procedures during car searches than those required by the U.S. Supreme Court.

path, despite the similarity in language between sections of the New Jersey Constitution and the U.S. Constitution. And the New Jersey judges have parted company with their national "cousins" even when the constitutional provisions at issue were identical.

For example, the U.S. Supreme Court ruled in 1988 that warrantless searches of curbside garbage are constitutionally permissible. Both the New Jersey Constitution and the U.S. Constitution bar unreasonable searches and seizures. Yet, in a 1990 decision expanding constitutional protections, the New Jersey court ruled that police officers need a search warrant before they can rummage through a person's trash. The court claimed that the New Jersey Constitution offers a greater degree of privacy than the U.S. Constitution. Because the decision rested on an interpretation of the state constitution, the existence of a similar right in the national charter had no bearing. The New Jersey court cannot act in a more restrictive manner than the U.S. Supreme Court allows, but it can be—and is—less restrictive.[71] State supreme courts can turn to their own state constitutions to "raise the ceiling of liberty above the floor created by the federal Bill of Rights."[72]

When judges reach decisions, they pay attention to the views of other courts—and not just those above them in the judicial hierarchy. State and federal court opinions are the legal storehouse from which judges regularly draw their ideas. Often the issues that affect individual lives—property, family, contracts—are grist for state courts, not federal courts. For example, when a state court faces a novel issue in a contract dispute, it will look at how other state courts have dealt with the problem. (Contract disputes are not a staple of the federal courts.) And if courts in several states have addressed an issue and the direction of the opinion is largely one-sided, the weight and authority of those opinions may move the court in that direction.[73] Courts that confront new issues with cogency and clarity are likely to become leaders of legal innovation.

State courts have become renewed arenas for political conflict, with litigants—individually or in groups—vying for their preferred policies. The multiplicity of the nation's court system, with overlapping state and national responsibilities, provides alternative points of access for individuals and groups to present and argue their claims. This description of the courts fits the pluralist model of government.

SUMMARY

The power of judicial review, claimed by the Supreme Court in 1803, placed the judiciary on an equal footing with Congress and the president. The principle of checks and balances can restrain judicial power through several means, such as constitutional amendments and impeachment. But restrictions on that power have been infrequent, leaving the federal courts to exercise considerable influence through judicial review and statutory construction.

The federal court system has three tiers. At the bottom are the district courts, where litigation begins and most disputes end. In the middle are the courts of appeals. At the top is the Supreme Court. The ability of judges to make policy increases as they move up the pyramid from trial courts to appellate courts to the Supreme Court.

The Supreme Court, free to draft its agenda through the discretionary control of its docket, harmonizes conflicting interpretations of national law and articulates constitutional rights. It is helped at this crucial stage by the solicitor general, who represents the executive branch of government before the High Court. The solicitor general's influence with the justices affects their choice of cases to review.

Political allegiance and complementary values are necessary conditions for appointment by the president to the coveted position of judge. The president and senators from the same party share appointment power in the case of federal district and appellate judges. The president has more leeway in nominating Supreme Court justices, although all nominees must be confirmed by the Senate.

Courts inevitably fashion policy, for each of the states and for the nation. They provide multiple points of access for individuals to pursue their preferences and so fit the pluralist model of democracy. Furthermore, the class action enables people with small individual claims and limited financial resources to pursue their goals in court, reinforcing the pluralist model.

Judges confront both the original and the modern dilemmas of government. The impact of their decisions can extend well beyond a single case. Some democratic theorists are troubled by the expansion of judicial power. But today's courts fit within the pluralist model and usually are in step with what the public wants.

As the U.S. Supreme Court heads in a more conservative direction, some state supreme courts have become safe havens for more liberal policies on civil rights and civil liberties. The state court systems have overlapping state and national responsibilities, offering groups and individuals many access points to present and argue their claims.

★ Selected Readings

Baum, Lawrence. *American Courts: Process and Policy*, 4th ed. Boston: Houghton Mifflin, 1998. A comprehensive review of trial and appellate courts in the United States that addresses their activities, describes their procedures, and explores the processes that affect them.

Coffin, Frank M. *On Appeal: Court, Lawyering, and Judging*. New York: Norton, 1994. A close look at the workings of a federal appellate court and the ways in which its chief judge reaches decisions.

Epstein, Lee, and Jack Knight. *The Choices Justices Make*. Washington, D.C.: CQ Press, 1997. Argues that Supreme Court justices are policymakers who strategically select courses of action by weighing not only their own preferences but also the actions they expect from their colleagues on the Court and in Congress, and from the president.

Friedman, Lawrence M. *American Law: An Introduction*, 2nd ed. New York: Norton, 1998. A clear, highly readable introduction to the bewildering complexity of the law. Explains how law is made and administered.

Goldman, Sheldon. *Picking Federal Judges: Lower Court Selection from Roosevelt Through Reagan.* New Haven, Conn.: Yale University Press, 1997. Goldman provides a historically rich account of how Presidents Roosevelt through Reagan selected federal district and appellate court judges. A wealth of data and illuminating interviews with key actors describe not only the process of selection, and how it has changed over time, but also what types of judges, demographically and ideologically, each president sought to appoint.

Perry, H. W., Jr. *Deciding to Decide: Agenda Setting in the United States Supreme Court.* Cambridge, Mass.: Harvard University Press, 1991. Through interviews with Supreme Court justices and their former and current clerks, Perry provides a rich account, replete with amusing and enlightening excerpts from his interviews, of how the Supreme Court arrives at its docket.

Rosenberg, Gerald. *The Hollow Hope.* Chicago: University of Chicago Press, 1991. Argues that the Supreme Court has not been a successful national policymaker in areas in which it is commonly thought to have been influential, such as civil rights, abortion and women's rights, the environment, and the criminal justice system.

Internet Exercises

1. Supreme Courts of Other Nations

While many nations of the world have courts of last resort, or "supreme" courts, there is significant variation in how they are structured and organized. One interesting example is the supreme court of Estonia, a former republic of the Soviet Union, whose Web site you can find on the Internet at <**www.nc.ee/**>. From the English version of this Web site, read through the following five topics about Estonia's supreme court: (1) History, (2) Composition, (3) Chambers, (4) Ad Hoc Panel, and (5) Appeals Selection.

- How is the supreme court of Estonia like the U.S. Supreme Court?

- How is it like the U.S. Congress?

2. FDR on Reorganizing the Judiciary

Go to the History and Politics Out Loud Web site, <**www.hpol.org/**>, and locate President Franklin Roosevelt's fireside chat on the reorganization of the judiciary. Listen to the chat beginning at the point when FDR states, "The American people have learned from the depression," up until "But, at the same time, we must have Judges who will bring to the Courts a present-day sense of the Constitution—Judges who will retain in the Courts the judicial functions of a court, and reject the legislative powers which the courts have today assumed."

- According to Roosevelt, how was the Court affecting his New Deal program?

- Based on his speech, explain why you think Roosevelt was in favor of or against an active judiciary.

3. Oral Arguments in Bush v. Gore

Listen to the oral arguments in *Bush* v. *Gore* at <**oyez.org/election/00-949.portraits.ram**>. This will take about ninety minutes. Consider the following questions in small groups.

- Early in the argument, the justices peppered each of the three attorneys with questions regarding the Court's jurisdiction. Why is this questioning important?

- As you listen to the questions from the justices to the attorneys, consider what seems to interest the justices most. Is it the Court's prior decisions (precedents), the Court's supervisory power over the Florida courts, or the issues revolving around the policy that may emanate from their decision?

- How would you describe the role of humor in such tension-filled proceedings?

4. Constitutional Courts Cross-Nationally

The Constitutional Court of the Republic of Slovenia maintains an interesting cross-national database of how different countries handle the issue of constitutional judicial review. To find the database, point your browser to <**www.us-rs.com/en/index.html**>.

- Follow the link to "comparisons," and study the five tables that are provided.

- How would you describe the general overall pattern that you see in the first table? According to that table, how many countries do not have a system of constitutional judicial review? What do your answers to these two questions suggest about the general power of constitutional judicial review around the world?

Order and Civil Liberties

JAKE BAKER, A NINETEEN-YEAR-OLD LINGUISTICS STUDENT at the University of Michigan, posted shockingly explicit sex stories to an electronic bulletin board, one of the thousands of newsgroups that form the worldwide collection of networked information called Usenet. Baker wrote fictional fantasies that frequently included rape and violence to women and girls. In one story in which Baker graphically described the torture, rape, and murder of a woman, he gave the victim the name of a classmate at the University of Michigan.[1] Baker's stories could be read by millions of people every day. Some read them and moved on. Others were appalled and complained.

A computer operator in Washington, D.C., thought it was the grossest thing he had ever read on-line. He e-mailed University of Michigan officials that one of their students might be dangerous. Five thousand miles away, a sixteen-year-old girl in Russia read one of Baker's stories and showed it to her father. He in turn alerted an American attorney and Michigan alumnus who was working in Moscow, who thought that Baker's stories had gone beyond bad taste. He also contacted university officials. Media attention soon followed.

When the clamor rose, university officials acted. They visited Baker in his dorm room. He admitted writing the stories, waived his right to an attorney, and provided his e-mail password so officials could read his electronic mail. Shortly thereafter, the university president suspended Baker without a hearing. He was told to pack his bags and leave the university immediately.[2]

The Federal Bureau of Investigation and the Justice Department contemplated a criminal prosecution. Had Baker committed a crime? If so, what was it? Writing fiction is not a crime, even when it describes harmful acts. However, after reading his private e-mail, prosecutors decided to charge Baker with making threats to kill or kidnap in electronic messages transmitted via the Internet to a correspondent in Canada. U.S. commerce law prohibits the interstate or international transmission of threats to injure or kidnap a victim. Baker became the first person charged with making e-mail threats via the Internet. The law carries a penalty of up to five years of imprisonment. Baker was detained in jail for twenty-nine days while a federal judge contemplated releasing him on bail.

The government prosecuted Baker to maintain order—that is, to ensure the peace and safety of the community. The government viewed Baker's private correspondence as evidence of a threat of imminent harm. Baker's

Freedom's Embrace

*Jake Baker, a college under-
graduate, stood accused of
criminal conduct in 1995 after
he posted messages about his
shockingly explicit fantasies
on the Internet. Baker was
embraced by his mother when
he was released on bail after
spending twenty-nine days in
jail.*

attorney, joined by the American Civil Liberties Union, urged dismissal of
the government's case. They maintained that the free speech clause of the
First Amendment protected Baker from government action. A federal
judge, Avern Cohn, sat at the center of the controversy, holding in the
balance Baker's freedom and the community's demand for order. (We will
examine the outcome of the case later in this chapter.)

How well do the courts respond to clashes that pit freedom against order
or freedom against equality? Are freedom, order, or equality ever unconditional? In this chapter, we explore some value conflicts that the judiciary
has resolved. You will be able to judge from the decisions in these cases
whether American government has met the challenge of democracy by
finding the appropriate balance between freedom and order and between
freedom and equality.

The value conflicts described in this chapter revolve around claims or
entitlements that rest on law. Although we concentrate here on conflicts
over constitutional issues, the Constitution is not the only source of people's rights. Government at all levels can—and does—create rights through
laws written by legislatures and regulations issued by bureaucracies.

We begin this chapter with the Bill of Rights and the freedoms it protects. Then we take a closer look at the role of the First Amendment in the
original conflict between freedom and order. Next we turn to the
Fourteenth Amendment and the limits it places on the states. Then we
examine the Ninth Amendment and its relationship to issues of personal
autonomy. Finally, we examine the threat to the democratic process when
judges transform policy issues into constitutional issues. In Chapter 16,
we will look at the Fourteenth Amendment's promise of equal protection,
which sets the stage for the modern dilemma of government: the struggle
between freedom and equality.

THE BILL OF RIGHTS

You may remember from Chapter 3 that at first the framers of the Constitution did not include a list of individual liberties—a bill of rights—in the national charter. They believed that a bill of rights was not necessary, because the Constitution spelled out the extent of the national government's power. But during the ratification debates, it became clear that the omission of a bill of rights was the most important obstacle to the adoption of the Constitution by the states. Eventually, the First Congress approved twelve amendments and sent them to the states for ratification. In 1791, the states ratified ten of the twelve amendments, and the nation had a bill of rights.

The Bill of Rights imposed limits on the national government but not on the state governments.* During the next seventy-seven years, litigants pressed the Supreme Court to extend the amendments' restraints to the states, but the Court refused until well after the adoption of the Fourteenth Amendment in 1868. Before then, protection from repressive state government had to come from state bills of rights.

The U.S. Constitution guarantees Americans numerous liberties and rights. In this chapter we explore a number of them. We will define and distinguish civil liberties and civil rights. (On some occasions, we will use the terms interchangeably.) **Civil liberties,** sometimes referred to as "negative rights," are freedoms that are guaranteed to the individual. The guarantees take the form of restraints on government. For example, the First Amendment declares that "Congress shall make no law . . . abridging the freedom of speech." Civil liberties declare what the government cannot do.

civil liberties
Freedoms guaranteed to individuals.

In contrast, civil rights, sometimes called "positive rights," declare what the government must do or provide. **Civil rights** are powers and privileges that are guaranteed to the individual and protected against arbitrary removal at the hands of the government or other individuals. The right to vote and the right to a jury trial in criminal cases are civil rights embedded in the Constitution. Today, civil rights also embrace laws that further certain values. The Civil Rights Act of 1964, for example, furthered the value of equality by establishing the right to nondiscrimination in public accommodations and the right to equal employment opportunity. (See Feature 15.1 for examples of positive and negative rights in U.S. and U.N. contexts.) Civil liberties are the subject of this chapter; we discuss civil rights and their ramifications in Chapter 16.

civil rights
Powers or privileges guaranteed to individuals and protected from arbitrary removal at the hands of government or individuals.

The Bill of Rights lists both civil liberties and civil rights. When we refer to the rights and liberties of the Constitution, we mean the protections that are enshrined in the Bill of Rights and in the first section of the Fourteenth Amendment.[3] The list includes freedom of religion, freedom of speech and of the press, the rights to assemble peaceably and to petition the government, the right to bear arms, the rights of the criminally accused, the requirement of due process, and the equal protection of the laws.

FREEDOM OF RELIGION

Congress shall make no law respecting an establishment of religion, or prohibiting the free exercise thereof.

Religious freedom was important to the colonies and later to the states. That importance is reflected in its position among the ratified amend-

---

* *Congress considered more than one hundred amendments in its first session. One that was not approved would have limited the power of the states to infringe on the rights of conscience, speech, press, and jury trial in criminal cases. James Madison thought this amendment was the "most valuable" of the list, but it failed to muster a two-thirds vote in the Senate.*

feature 15.1
Examples of Positive and Negative Rights: Constitutional Rights and Human Rights

	United States Constitution	United Nations Universal Declaration of Human Rights
Civil liberties, or "negative rights"	Congress ***shall make no law*** . . . abridging the freedom of speech, or of the press. (First Amendment) Excessive bail ***shall not be*** required, nor excessive fines imposed, nor cruel and unusual punishments inflicted. (Eighth Amendment)	***No one shall be*** held in slavery or servitude; slavery and the slave trade shall be prohibited in all their forms. (Article 4) ***No one shall be*** subjected to arbitrary arrest, detention or exile. (Article 9)
Civil rights, or "positive rights"	In all criminal prosecutions, the accused shall enjoy ***the right to*** a speedy and public trial, . . . and to have the assistance of counsel for his defense. (Sixth Amendment)	Everyone has ***the right to*** a standard of living adequate for the health and well-being of himself and of his family, including food, clothing, housing and medical care and necessary social services, and the right to security in the event of unemployment, sickness, disability, widowhood, old age or other lack of livelihood in circumstances beyond his control. (Article 25.1) Everyone has ***the right to*** work, to free choice of employment, to just and favourable conditions of work and to protection against unemployment. (Article 23.1)

establishment clause
The first clause in the First Amendment, which forbids government establishment of religion.

free-exercise clause
The second clause in the First Amendment, which prevents the government from interfering with the exercise of religion.

ments that we know as the Bill of Rights: first, in the very first amendment. The First Amendment guarantees freedom of religion in two clauses: the **establishment clause** prohibits laws establishing religion; the **free-exercise clause** prevents the government from interfering with the exercise of religion. Together, they ensure that the government can neither promote nor inhibit religious beliefs or practices.

Sacrificing Rights

Animal sacrifice is a central ritual in the Afro-Caribbean–based religion of Santeria. The Miami suburb of Hialeah banned such sacrifices, and a Santeria church in Hialeah challenged the local law. In a 1993 ruling, the Supreme Court sided with the church. Animal sacrifice for religious purposes is protected by the First Amendment free-exercise clause.

At the time of the Constitutional Convention, many Americans, especially in New England, maintained that government could and should foster religion, specifically Protestantism. However, many more Americans agreed that this was an issue for state governments, that the national government had no authority to meddle in religious affairs. The religion clauses were drafted in this spirit.[4]

The Supreme Court has refused to interpret the religion clauses definitively. The result is an amalgam of rulings, the cumulative effect of which is that freedom to believe is unlimited, but freedom to practice a belief can be limited. Religion cannot benefit directly from government actions (for example, government cannot make contributions to churches or synagogues), but it can benefit indirectly from those actions (for example, government can supply books on secular subjects for use in all schools—public, private, and parochial).

America is the most religious nation in the developed world.[5] Most Americans identify with a particular religious faith, and 40 percent attend church in a typical week. The vast majority believe in God, a judgment day, and life after death. Majoritarians might argue, then, that government should support religion. They would agree that the establishment clause bars government support of a single faith, but they might maintain that government should support all faiths. Such support would be consistent with what the majority wants and true to the language of the Constitution. In its decisions, the Supreme Court has rejected this interpretation of the establishment clause, leaving itself open to charges of undermining democracy. Those charges may be true with regard to majoritarian democracy, but the Court can justify its protection in terms of the basic values of democratic government.

The Establishment Clause

The provision that "Congress shall make no law respecting an establishment of religion" bars government sponsorship or support of religious activity. The Supreme Court has consistently held that the establishment clause requires government to maintain a position of neutrality toward religions and to maintain that position in cases that involve choices between religion and nonreligion. However, the Court has never interpreted the clause as barring all assistance that incidentally aids religious institutions.

Government Support of Religion. In 1879, the Supreme Court contended, quoting Thomas Jefferson's words, that the establishment clause erected "a wall of separation between church and State."[6] That wall was breached somewhat in 1947, when the justices upheld a local government program that provided free transportation to parochial school students.[7] The breach seemed to widen in 1968, when the Court held constitutional a government program in which parochial school students borrowed state-purchased textbooks.[8] The objective of the program, reasoned the majority, was to further educational opportunity. The students, not the schools, borrowed the books, and the parents, not the church, realized the benefits.

Lemon v. Kurtzman

But in 1971, in ***Lemon v. Kurtzman,*** the Court struck down a state program that would have helped pay the salaries of teachers hired by parochial schools to give instruction in secular subjects.[9] The justices proposed a three-pronged test for determining the constitutionality of government programs and laws under the establishment clause:

- They must have a secular purpose (such as lending books to parochial school students).

- Their primary effect must not be to advance or inhibit religion.

- They must not entangle the government excessively with religion.

The program in the *Lemon* case did not satisfy the last prong. The government would have had to monitor the program constantly, thus ensuring an excessive entanglement with religion. The "*Lemon* test," as it became known, governed the Supreme Court's interpretation of such cases for twenty-five years. Then, in 1997, the Court dramatically loosened its application of the test in a case reminiscent of the one that gave rise to it.

Agostini v. *Felton* involved the use of public school teachers to teach congressionally mandated remedial courses to disadvantaged students in New York parochial schools. This time, the Court emphasized that only government *neutrality* toward religion was required by the First Amendment. Moreover, only *excessive* entanglements will be deemed to violate the establishment clause. By a vote of 5–4, it held that religion was neither hindered nor helped by parochial schools' using public school teachers at taxpayer expense to teach secular subjects.[10] Although the opinion was narrowly written, the Court appears to have lowered the wall separating church and state.

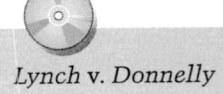

Lynch v. Donnelly

Does the display of religious artifacts on public property violate the establishment clause? In *Lynch* v. *Donnelly* (1984), the Court said no, by a vote of 5–4.[11] At issue was a publicly funded nativity scene on public property, surrounded by commercial symbols of the Christmas season such as Santa and his sleigh. Although he conceded that a crèche has religious significance, Chief Justice Warren E. Burger, writing for the majority, maintained that the display had a legitimate secular purpose: the celebration of a national holiday. Second, the display did not have the primary effect of benefiting religion; the religious benefits were "indirect, remote and incidental." And third, the display led to no excessive entanglement of religion and government. The justices hinted at a relaxation of the establishment clause by asserting their "unwillingness to be confined to any single test or criterion in this sensitive area." The upshot of *Lynch* was an "acknowledgment" of the religious heritage of the majority of Americans, although the Christmas holiday is a vivid reminder to religious minorities and the nonreligious of their separateness from the dominant Christian culture.

The *Lynch* decision led to a proliferation of cases testing the limits of government-sponsored religious displays. In 1989, a divided Court approved the display of a menorah while rejecting the display of a crèche.[12] The menorah appeared on the steps of the main entrance to a government building, alongside a Christmas tree and a sign reading "Salute to Liberty." The crèche appeared in a courthouse during the Christmas season. A majority found that the crèche display violated the second prong of the *Lemon* test but could not agree on the reasons for validating the menorah display. In such circumstances, the justices become vulnerable to the charge that they serve as constitutional "interior designers," imposing their own value preferences when they cannot fully explain why one religious image passes muster but another does not.

School Prayer.   The Supreme Court has consistently equated prayer in public schools with government support of religion. In 1962, it struck down the daily reading of this twenty-two-word nondenominational prayer in New York's public schools: "Almighty God, we acknowledge our dependence upon Thee, and we beg Thy blessings upon us, our parents, our teachers and our country." Justice Hugo L. Black, writing for a 6–1 majority, held that official state approval of prayer was an unconstitutional attempt on the part of the state to establish a religion. This decision, in *Engel v. Vitale*, drew a storm of protest that has yet to subside.[13]

Engel v. Vitale

The following year, the Court struck down a state law calling for daily Bible reading and recitation of the Lord's Prayer in Pennsylvania's public schools.[14] The school district defended the reading and recitation on the grounds that they taught literature, perpetuated traditional institutions, and inculcated moral virtues. But the Court held that the state's involvement violated the government's constitutionally imposed neutrality in matters of religion.

A new school prayer issue arose in 1992 when the Court struck down the offering of nonsectarian prayers at official public school graduations. In a 5–4 decision, the Court held that government involvement creates "a state-sponsored and state-directed religious exercise in a public school."[15] The justices said that the establishment clause means that government may not conduct a religious exercise in the context of a school event.

School prayer persists despite Court opinions to the contrary. In 1996, a federal judge ordered the public schools in rural Pontotoc County,

Seeking Divine Inspiration

Prior to kickoff, the Yorktown High School football team in Arlington, Virginia, stops for a moment of silence. Student-led prayers at public high school football games now run afoul of the Constitution's Establishment Clause. But players may use a moment of silence—to pray for victory or review key plays or do nothing at all—consistent with the current constitutional rules of the game.

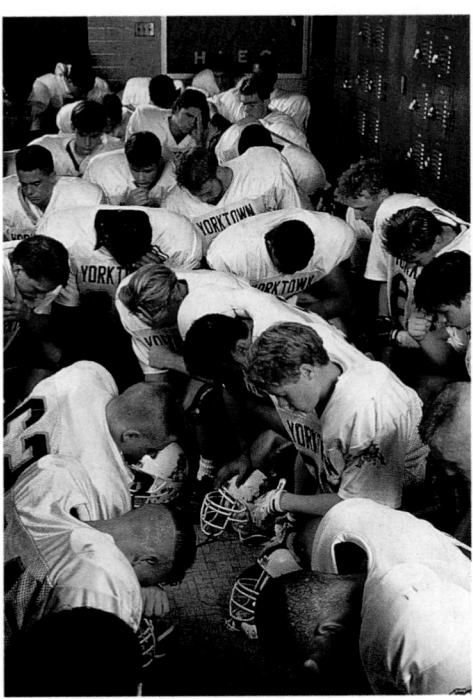

Wallace v. Jaffree

Mississippi, to stop allowing student-led prayers over the intercom, classroom prayers before lunch, and Bible classes taught by instructors chosen and paid by local churches. A single family—transplants from Wisconsin—endured years of harassment and ostracism resulting from its objections to the long-standing policy of allowing prayer in the schools. In 1996, federal judge Neal Biggers, Jr., ordered the school district to end the practices. "The Bill of Rights was created to protect the minority from tyranny by the majority," Biggers declared.[16]

In 2000, the football gridiron was the latest battlefield in the conflict over school prayer. By a 6–3 vote, the Supreme Court struck down the practice of organized, student-led prayer at public high school football games. To insulate the elected school board from charges that the prayers represented school policy, the students voted whether or not to offer "invocations" and then voted to select the student to deliver them. But the school board's sponsorship of such prayers and the election mechanism could not ensure victory. The majority maintained that "the delivery of a pre-game prayer had the improper effect of coercing those present to participate in an act of religious worship." It reaffirmed that "fundamental rights may not be submitted to vote; they depend on the outcome of no elections."[17]

It is clear that the Constitution bars school prayer. But does it also bar silent meditation in school? In *Wallace* v. *Jaffree* (1985), the Court struck down a series of Alabama statutes requiring a moment of silence for meditation or voluntary prayer in elementary schools.[18] In a 6–3 decision, the Court renewed its use of the *Lemon* test and reaffirmed the principle of government neutrality between religion and nonreligion. The Court found that the purpose of the statute was to endorse religion; however, a majority of the justices hinted that a straightforward moment-of-silence statute that steered clear of religious endorsements might pass constitutional muster.

Religious training during public school is out-of-bounds, but religious training after school now passes constitutional muster. In 2001, the Supreme Court ruled that public schools must open their doors to after-school religious activities on the same basis as other after-school programs such as the debate club. To do otherwise would constitute viewpoint discrimination in violation of the Free Speech Clause of the First Amendment.

The establishment clause creates a problem for government. Support for all religions at the expense of nonreligion seems to pose the least risk to social order. Tolerance of the dominant religion at the expense of other religions risks minority discontent, but support for no religion (neutrality between religion and nonreligion) risks majority discontent.

The Free-Exercise Clause

The free-exercise clause of the First Amendment states that "Congress shall make no law . . . prohibiting the free exercise [of religion]." The Supreme Court has struggled to avoid absolute interpretations of this restriction and thus avoid its complement, the establishment clause. An example: suppose Congress grants exemptions from military service to individuals who have religious scruples against war. These exemptions could be construed as a violation of the establishment clause because they favor some religious groups over others. But if Congress forced conscientious objectors to fight—to violate their religious beliefs—the government would run afoul of the free-exercise clause. In fact, Congress has granted military draftees such exemptions. But the Supreme Court has avoided a conflict between the establishment and free-exercise clauses by equating religious objection to war with any deeply held humanistic opposition to it. This solution leaves unanswered a central question: does the free-exercise clause require government to grant exemptions from legal duties that conflict with religious obligations, or does it guarantee only that the law will be applicable to religious believers without discrimination or preference?[19]

In the free-exercise cases, the justices have distinguished religious beliefs from actions based on those beliefs. Beliefs are inviolate, beyond the reach of government control. But the First Amendment does not protect antisocial actions. Consider conflicting values about working on the Sabbath and using drugs as religious sacraments.

strict scrutiny
A standard used by the Supreme Court in deciding whether a law or policy is to be adjudged constitutional or not. To pass strict scrutiny, the law or policy must be justified by a "compelling governmental interest" as well as being the least restrictive means for achieving that interest.

Working on the Sabbath.   The modern era of free-exercise thinking began with **Sherbert v. Verner** (1963). Adeil Sherbert, a Seventh-Day Adventist, lost her mill job because she refused to work on Saturday, her Sabbath. She filed for unemployment compensation and was referred to another job, which she declined, because it also required Saturday work. Because she declined the job, the state disqualified her from receiving unemployment benefits. In a 7–2 decision, the Supreme Court ruled that the disqualification imposed an impermissible burden on Sherbert's free exercise of religion. The First Amendment, declared the majority, protects observance as well as belief. A neutral law that burdens the free exercise of religion is subject to **strict scrutiny.** This means that the law may be upheld only if the government can demonstrate that the law is justified by a "compelling

Sherbert v. *Verner*

governmental interest" and is the least restrictive means for achieving that interest.[20] And only rarely can government muster enough evidence to demonstrate a compelling interest.

The *Sherbert* decision prompted religious groups and individual believers to challenge laws that conflict with their faith. We have seen how conflicts arise from the imposition of penalties for refusing to engage in religiously prohibited conduct. But conflicts may also arise from laws that impose penalties for engaging in religiously motivated conduct.[21]

Using Drugs as Sacraments. Partaking of illegal substances as part of a religious sacrament forces believers to violate the law. For example, the Rastafarians and members of the Ethiopian Zion Coptic church smoke marijuana in the belief that it is the body and blood of Christ. Obviously, taking to an extreme the freedom to practice religion can result in a license to engage in illegal conduct. And even when such conduct stems from deeply held convictions, government resistance to it is understandable. The inevitable result is a clash between religious freedom and social order.

The courts used the compelling-government-interest test for many years, and on that basis invalidated most laws restricting free exercise. But in 1990 the Supreme Court abruptly and unexpectedly rejected its long-standing rule, tipping the balance in favor of social order. In *Employment Division* v. *Smith*, two members of the Native American Church sought an exemption from an Oregon law that made the possession or use of peyote a crime.[22] (Peyote is a cactus that contains the hallucinogen mescaline. Native Americans have used it for centuries in their religious ceremonies.) Oregon did not prosecute the two church members for their use or possession of peyote. Rather, the state rejected their applications for unemployment benefits after they were dismissed from their drug-counseling jobs for using peyote. Oregon believed it had a compelling interest in proscribing the use of certain drugs according to its own drug laws.

Justice Antonin Scalia, writing for the 6–3 majority, examined the conflict between freedom and order through the lens of majoritarian democratic thought. He observed that the Court has never held that an individual's religious beliefs excuse him or her from compliance with an otherwise valid law prohibiting conduct that government is free to regulate. Allowing exceptions to every state law or regulation affecting religion "would open the prospect of constitutionally required exemptions from civic obligations of almost every conceivable kind." Scalia cited as examples compulsory military service, payment of taxes, vaccination requirements, and child-neglect laws. The Court rejected the strict scrutiny standard, declaring that laws indirectly restricting religious practices are acceptable; only laws aimed at religious groups are constitutionally prohibited.

The decision brought in its wake scores of government actions infringing on religious exercise. One such case involved unauthorized autopsies. Several religions proscribe the mutilation of the human body; they view autopsies as a form of mutilation. Many Jews, Navajo Indians, and Hmong (an immigrant group from Laos) hold this belief. For the Hmong, an autopsy means that the deceased's spirit will never be free. Yet Rhode Island performed an autopsy on a Hmong without regard to the family's religious beliefs. Because the autopsy rule did not target a religious group, the family had no recourse against the shame of government mutilation of their loved one. The demands of social order triumphed over the spirit of religious freedom.

The political response to *Employment Division* v. *Smith* was an example of pluralism in action. An unusual coalition of religious and nonreligious groups (including the National Association of Evangelicals, the American Civil Liberties Union, the National Islamic Prison Foundation, and B'nai B'rith) organized to restore the more restrictive strict scrutiny test. At first the coalition failed to rouse much public interest in a case involving the use of hallucinogenic drugs. But as government infringements on religious practice mounted, public interest and legislative reaction soon meshed.

Spanning the theological and ideological spectrum, the alliance regained in Congress what it had lost in the Supreme Court. In 1993, President Bill Clinton signed into law the Religious Freedom Restoration Act (RFRA). This enormously popular law, passed unanimously by the House and by a margin of 97–3 in the Senate, requires the government to satisfy the strict scrutiny standard before it can institute measures that interfere with religious practices. The victory was short-lived, however, because in June 1997 the Supreme Court struck back, declaring the act unconstitutional in *City of Boerne* v. *Flores.*[23]

The case began when the Catholic archbishop of San Antonio, Patrick Flores, sued the city of Boerne, Texas. The city had denied the archbishop's church a building permit for a planned expansion because the church, built in 1923, was located in a city historic district and was deemed a historic landmark. Flores argued that the city's decision inhibited his parishioners' free exercise of religion because, without the renovations, the church would be too small to accommodate its growing parish. The trial court ruled in the city's favor, but the church, relying on the RFRA, won a reversal on appeal.

The Supreme Court, in a 6–3 decision, overturned the appeals court, declaring that Congress lacked the power to change the meaning of the Constitution's free-exercise clause when it enacted the RFRA. Thus, the strict scrutiny standard imposed by the RFRA no longer binds government actions, and the precedent established in *Employment Division* v. *Smith* is once again the law of the land.

FREEDOM OF EXPRESSION

> Congress shall make no law . . . abridging the freedom of speech, or of the press; or the right of the people peaceably to assemble, and to petition the Government for a redress of grievances.

James Madison introduced the original versions of the speech clause and the press clause of the First Amendment in the House of Representatives in June 1789. One early proposal provided that "the people shall not be deprived of their right to speak, to write, or to publish their sentiments, and the freedom of the press, as one of the great bulwarks of liberty, shall be inviolable." That version was rewritten several times, then merged with the religion and peaceable assembly clauses to yield the First Amendment.

The original House debates on the proposed speech and press clauses are not informative. There is no record of debate in the Senate or in the states

prior restraint
Censorship before publication.

during ratification. But careful analysis of other records supports the view that the press clause prohibited only the imposition of **prior restraint**— censorship before publication. Publishers could not claim protection from punishment if works they had already published were later deemed improper, mischievous, or illegal.

The spare language of the First Amendment seems perfectly clear: "Congress shall make no law . . . abridging the freedom of speech, or of the press." Yet a majority of the Supreme Court has never agreed that this "most majestic guarantee" is absolutely inviolable.[24] Historians have long debated the framers' intentions regarding these **free-expression clauses,** the press and speech clauses of the First Amendment. The dominant view is that the clauses confer a right to unrestricted discussion of public affairs.[25] Other scholars, examining much the same evidence, conclude that few, if any, of the framers clearly understood the clause; moreover, they insist that the First Amendment does not rule out prosecution for seditious statements (statements inciting insurrection).[26]

free-expression clauses
The press and speech clauses of the First Amendment.

The license to speak freely does not move multitudes of Americans to speak out on controversial issues. Americans have woven subtle restrictions into the fabric of our society: the risk of criticism or ostracism by family, peers, or employers tends to reduce the number of people who test the limits of free speech to individuals ready to bear the burdens. As Mark Twain once remarked, "It is by the goodness of God that in our country we have three unspeakably precious things: freedom of speech, freedom of conscience, and the prudence never to practice either of them."[27]

Today, the clauses are deemed to bar most forms of prior restraint (consistent with the framers' understanding) as well as after-the-fact prosecution for political and other discourse. The Supreme Court has evolved two approaches to the resolution of claims based on the free-expression clauses. First, government can regulate or punish the advocacy of ideas, but only if it can prove an intent to promote lawless action and demonstrate that a high probability exists that such action will occur. Second, government may impose reasonable restrictions on the means for communicating ideas, restrictions that can incidentally discourage free expression.

Suppose, for example, that a political party advocates nonpayment of personal income taxes. Government cannot regulate or punish that party for advocating tax nonpayment because the standards of proof—that the act be directed at inciting or producing imminent lawless action and that the act be likely to produce such action—do not apply. But government can impose restrictions on the way the party's candidates communicate what they are advocating. Government can bar them from blaring messages from loudspeakers in residential neighborhoods at 3 A.M.

clear and present danger test
A means by which the Supreme Court has distinguished between speech as the advocacy of ideas, which is protected by the First Amendment, and speech as incitement, which is not protected.

Freedom of Speech

The starting point for any modern analysis of free speech is the **clear and present danger test,** formulated by Justice Oliver Wendell Holmes in the Supreme Court's unanimous decision in *Schenck* v. *United States* (1919). Charles T. Schenck and his fellow defendants were convicted under a federal criminal statute for attempting to disrupt World War I military recruitment by distributing leaflets claiming that conscription was

Schenck v. *United States*

unconstitutional. The government believed this behavior threatened the public order. At the core of the Court's opinion, as Holmes wrote, was the view that

> the character of every act depends upon the circumstances in which it is done. . . . The most stringent protection of free speech would not protect a man in falsely shouting fire in a theatre, and causing a panic. . . . The question in every case is whether the words used are used in such circumstances and are of such a nature as to create *a clear and present danger* that they will bring about the substantive evils that Congress has a right to prevent. It is a question of proximity and degree. When a nation is at war many things that might be said in time of peace are such a hindrance to its effort that their utterance will not be endured so long as men fight, and that no court could regard them as protected by any constitutional right [emphasis added].[28]

Because the actions of the defendants in Schenck were deemed to create a clear and present danger to the United States at that time, the Supreme Court upheld the defendants' convictions. The clear and present danger test helps to distinguish the advocacy of ideas, which is protected, from incitement, which is not. However, Holmes later frequently disagreed with a majority of his colleagues in applying the test.

In an often-quoted dissent in *Abrams* v. *United States* (1919), Holmes revealed his deeply rooted resistance to the suppression of ideas. The majority had upheld Jacob Abrams's criminal conviction for distributing leaflets that denounced the war and U.S. opposition to the Russian Revolution. Holmes wrote,

Abrams v. *United States*

> When men have realized that time has upset many fighting faiths, they may come to believe . . . that the ultimate good desired is better reached by free trade in ideas—that the best test of truth is the power of the thought to get itself accepted in the competition of the market, and that truth is the only ground upon which their wishes safely can be carried out. That at any rate is the theory of our Constitution.[29]

In 1925, the Court issued a landmark decision in *Gitlow* v. *New York*.[30] Benjamin Gitlow was arrested for distributing copies of a "left-wing manifesto" that called for the establishment of socialism through strikes and working-class uprisings of any form. Gitlow was convicted under a state criminal anarchy law; Schenck and Abrams had been convicted under a federal law. For the first time, the Court assumed that the First Amendment speech and press provisions applied to the states through the due process clause of the Fourteenth Amendment. Still, a majority of the justices affirmed Gitlow's conviction. Justices Holmes and Louis D. Brandeis argued in dissent that Gitlow's ideas did not pose a clear and present danger. "Eloquence may set fire to reason," conceded the dissenters. "But whatever may be thought of the redundant discourse before us, it had no chance of starting a present conflagration."

Gitlow v. *New York*

The protection of advocacy faced yet another challenge in 1948, when eleven members of the Communist Party were charged with violating the Smith Act, a federal law making the advocacy of force or violence against the United States a criminal offense. The leaders were convicted, although the government introduced no evidence that they had actually urged people to

Alien Restoration Act of 1940 (Smith Act)

commit specific violent acts. The Supreme Court mustered a majority for its decision to uphold the convictions under the act, but it could not get a majority to agree on the reasons in support of that decision. The biggest bloc, of four justices, announced the plurality opinion in 1951, arguing that the government's interest was substantial enough to warrant criminal penalties.[31] The justices interpreted the threat to the government to be the gravity of the advocated action, "discounted by its improbability." In other words, a single soap-box orator advocating revolution stands little chance of success. But a well-organized, highly disciplined political movement advocating revolution in the tinderbox of unstable political conditions stands a greater chance of success. In broadening the meaning of "clear and present danger," the Court held that the government was justified in acting preventively rather than waiting until revolution was about to occur.

By 1969, the pendulum had swung back in the other direction: the justices began to put more emphasis on freedom. That year, in ***Brandenburg v. Ohio,*** a unanimous decision extended the freedom of speech to new limits.[32] Clarence Brandenburg, the leader of the Ohio Ku Klux Klan, had been convicted under a state law for advocating racial strife at a Klan rally. His comments, which had been filmed by a television crew, included threats against government officials.

Brandenburg v. *Ohio*

The Court reversed Brandenburg's conviction because the government had failed to prove that the danger was real. The Court went even further and declared that threatening speech is protected by the First Amendment unless the government can prove that such advocacy is "directed to inciting or producing imminent lawless action and is likely to incite or produce such action." The ruling offered wider latitude for the expression of political ideas than ever before in the nation's history.

Symbolic Expression.   Symbolic expression, or nonverbal communication, generally receives less protection than pure speech. But the courts have upheld certain types of symbolic expression. ***Tinker v. Des Moines Independent County School District*** (1969) involved three public school students who wore black arm bands to school to protest the Vietnam War. Principals in their school district had prohibited the wearing of arm bands on the ground that such conduct would provoke a disturbance; the district suspended the students. The Supreme Court overturned the suspensions. Justice Abe Fortas declared for the majority that the principals had failed to show that the forbidden conduct would substantially interfere with appropriate school discipline:

Tinker v. *Des Moines Independent County School District*

> Undifferentiated fear or apprehension of disturbance is not enough to overcome the right to freedom of expression. Any departure from absolute regimentation may cause trouble. Any variation from the majority's opinion may inspire fear. Any word spoken, in class, in the lunchroom, or on the campus, that deviates from the views of another person may start an argument or cause a disturbance. But our Constitution says we must take this risk.[33]

The flag is an object of deep veneration in our society, yet its desecration is also a form of symbolic expression protected by the First Amendment. In 1989, a divided Supreme Court struck down a Texas law that barred the desecration of venerated objects. Congress then enacted the Flag Protection Act of 1989 in an attempt to overcome the constitutional flaws of the Texas decision. Gregory Johnson, whose 1984 flag burning in Texas led to the Court's 1989 decision, joined other protesters and burned an American flag on the steps of the Capitol in October 1989, in a test of the new national law.

The Supreme Court nullified the federal flag-burning statute in *United States* v. *Eichman* (1990). The Court was not persuaded that the new law was distinguishable from its Texas cousin. By a vote of 5–4, the justices reaffirmed First Amendment protection for all expressions of political ideas. The vote was identical to the Texas case, with conservative justices Anthony M. Kennedy and Scalia joining with the liberal wing to forge an unusual majority. The majority placed the same emphasis on freedom that it had in the Texas case, including a quotation from its earlier opinion: " 'If there is a bedrock principle underlying the First Amendment, it is that the Government may not prohibit the expression of an idea simply because society finds the idea itself offensive or disagreeable.' Punishing desecration of the flag dilutes the very freedom that makes this emblem so revered, and worth revering."[34]

In this opinion, the Court majority relied on the substantive conception of democratic theory, which embodies the principle of freedom of speech. Yet a May 1990 poll revealed that most people wanted to outlaw flag burning as a means of political expression and that a clear majority favored a constitutional amendment to that end.[35] (Such an amendment won Senate approval in 1990, but it fell thirty-four votes shy of the required two-thirds majority in the House.) The procedural interpretation of democratic theory holds that government should do what the people want. In the case of flag burning, the people are apparently willing to abandon the principle of freedom of speech embodied in the substantive view of democracy.

Although offensive to the vast majority of Americans, flag burning is a form of political expression. But suppose the conduct in question does not embody a political idea. May government ever legitimately ban that conduct? Consider the case of three nude dancers in JR's Kitty Kat Lounge, a South Bend, Indiana, strip joint, who sought to block the enforcement of an Indiana law that bans all public nudity. If nude dancing is merely conduct, government has the latitude to control or even ban it. But if nude dancing is expression, government action to prohibit it runs afoul of the First Amendment.

The distinction between conduct and expression masks underlying value conflicts. Control advocates who sought to promote social order argued that the statute attempted to promote public decency and morality. Expression advocates who sought to promote a form of freedom argued that the dancers provided entertainment, communicating eroticism and sensuality. In 1991, a sharply divided Supreme Court upheld the state prohibition in the interest of "protecting societal order and morality," so long as the prohibition does not target the erotic message of the performance, a form of expression entitled to some protection under the First Amendment.[36]

Order Versus Free Speech: Fighting Words and Threatening Expression. Fighting words are a notable exception to the protection of free speech. In *Chaplinsky* v. *New Hampshire* (1942), a Jehovah's Witness, convicted under a state statute for calling a city marshal a "God-damned racketeer"

Chaplinsky v.
New Hampshire

fighting words
Speech that is not protected by the First Amendment because it inflicts injury or tends to incite an immediate disturbance of the peace.

and "a damned fascist" in a public place, appealed to the Supreme Court.[37] The Supreme Court upheld Chaplinsky's conviction on the theory that **fighting words**—words that "inflict injury or tend to incite an immediate breach of the peace"—do not convey ideas and thus are not subject to First Amendment protection.

The Court sharply narrowed the definition of *fighting words* just seven years later. Arthur Terminiello, a suspended Catholic priest from Alabama and a vicious anti-Semite, addressed the Christian Veterans of America, a right-wing extremist group, in a Chicago hall. Terminiello called the jeering crowd of 1,500 angry protesters outside the hall "slimy scum" and ranted on about the "communistic, Zionistic" Jews of America, evoking cries of "kill the Jews" and "dirty kikes" from his listeners. The crowd outside the hall heaved bottles, bricks, and rocks, while the police attempted to protect Terminiello and his listeners inside. Finally, the police arrested Terminiello for disturbing the peace.

Terminiello's speech was far more incendiary than Walter Chaplinsky's. Yet the Supreme Court struck down Terminiello's conviction on the ground that provocative speech, even speech that stirs people to anger, is protected by the First Amendment. "Freedom of speech," wrote Justice William O. Douglas in the majority opinion, "though not absolute . . . is nevertheless protected against censorship or punishment, unless shown likely to produce a clear and present danger of a serious substantive evil that rises far above public inconvenience, annoyance, or unrest."

This broad view of protection brought a stiff rebuke in Justice Jackson's dissenting opinion:

Can You Explain Why...
too much free speech could actually destroy the freedom of speech?

> The choice is not between order and liberty. It is between liberty with order and anarchy without either. There is danger that, if the Court does not temper its doctrinaire logic with a little practical wisdom, it will convert the constitutional Bill of Rights into a suicide pact.[38]

The times seem to have caught up with the idealism that Jackson criticized in his colleagues. In ***Cohen v. California*** (1971), a nineteen-year-old department store worker expressed his opposition to the Vietnam War by wearing a jacket in the hallway of a Los Angeles county courthouse emblazoned with the words FUCK THE DRAFT. STOP THE WAR. The young man, Paul Cohen, was charged in 1968 under a California statute that prohibits "maliciously and willfully disturb[ing] the peace and quiet of any neighborhood or person [by] offensive conduct." He was found guilty and sentenced to thirty days in jail. On appeal, the U.S. Supreme Court reversed Cohen's conviction.

Cohen v. California

The Court reasoned that the expletive he used, while provocative, was not directed at anyone in particular; besides, the state presented no evidence that the words on Cohen's jacket would provoke people in "substantial numbers" to take some kind of physical action. In recognizing that "one man's vulgarity is another's lyric," the Supreme Court protected two elements of speech: the emotive (the expression of emotion) and the cognitive (the expression of ideas).[39]

The Supreme Court will confront these kinds of questions again as challenges to intimidating speech on the World Wide Web make their way through the nation's legal system. One recent case in particular provides an example of what might be on the horizon as the clash between free speech and social order takes new forms. In 1999, a federal trial court ordered a coalition of antiabortion advocates to pay Planned Parenthood and a group of doctors over $100 million for issuing threats to kill, harm, or intimidate the doctors, in violation of the Freedom of Access to Clinic Entrances Act. The antiabortion advocates maintained a Web site that contained Old West–style "wanted" posters of doctors who were known to perform abortions. The site included the doctors' names and, for some, their home addresses, license-plate numbers, and names of their immediate family members. Three doctors on the list who had been killed had their names displayed with a line drawn through them. The court also issued a permanent injunction closing the Web site. Two years later a federal appeals court unanimously set aside the verdict on free speech grounds.[40]

Recall the government's prosecution of Jake Baker for transmitting threats to injure or kidnap over the Internet. Baker's prosecution involved pure speech, so it was subject to First Amendment limits. The task involved distinguishing true threats, which are punishable, from constitutionally protected speech, which is not punishable. True threats must be unequivocal, unconditional, immediate, and specific as to the person threatened.

Judge Cohn threw out the indictment before the case reached a trial. The charges against Baker failed to meet the "true threat" standard. "Discussion of desires, alone," reasoned Cohn, "is not tantamount to threatening to act on those desires." In the absence of a threat to act, Baker's communications were protected by the First Amendment.[41]

Though Jake Baker has his freedom, the demand for social order on the Internet has significant support. In 1996, Congress passed the Communications Decency Act, which made it a crime for a person knowingly to circulate "patently offensive" sexual material to Internet sites accessible to those under eighteen years old. Is this an acceptable way to protect children from offensive material (perhaps like Baker's stories), or is it a muzzle on free speech? A federal court quickly declared the act unconstitutional. In an opinion of over 200 pages, the court observed that "just as the strength of the Internet is chaos, so the strength of our liberty depends on the chaos and cacophony of the unfettered speech the First Amendment protects."[42]

The Supreme Court upheld the lower court's ruling in June 1997 in ***Reno v. ACLU***.[43] The Court's nearly unanimous opinion was a broad affirmation of free speech rights in cyberspace, arguing that the Internet was more analogous to print media than to television, and thus even indecent material on the Internet was entitled to First Amendment protection. Globalization, however, may put the brakes on the liberating forces of cyberspace (see Politics in a Changing World 15.1).

Free Speech Versus Order: Obscenity.   The Supreme Court has always viewed obscene material—whether in words, music, books, magazines, or films—as being outside the bounds of constitutional protection, which means that states may regulate or even ban obscenity. However, difficulties arise in determining what is obscene and what is not. In *Roth* v. *United States* (1957), Justice William J. Brennan, Jr., outlined a test for judging a work as obscene: "Whether to the average person, applying contemporary community standards, the dominant theme of the material taken as a whole appeals to prurient interest."[44] (*Prurient* means having a tendency to incite lustful thoughts.) Yet a definition of obscenity has proved elusive; no objective test seems adequate. Justice Potter Stewart

★

Superstar or Antichrist?

To his legions of loyal fans, Marilyn Manson is a superstar. To Manson's long list of critics—including government officials—he is the Antichrist, in the form of a skinny kid from Florida. Government efforts to ban Manson's concerts have proved unsuccessful, thanks to the First Amendment's protection of free expression.

Miller v. California

will long be remembered for his solution to the problem of identifying obscene materials. He declared that he could not define it. "But," he added, "I know it when I see it."[45]

In ***Miller v. California*** (1973), its most recent major attempt to clarify constitutional standards governing obscenity, the Court declared that a work—a play, film, or book—is obscene and may be regulated by the government if (1) the work taken as a whole appeals to prurient interests; (2) the work portrays sexual conduct in a patently offensive way; and (3) the work taken as a whole lacks serious literary, artistic, political, or scientific value.[46] Local community standards govern application of the first and second prongs of the *Miller* test.

Feminism, Free Expression, and Equality. Historically, civil liberties have conflicted with demands for social order. However, civil liberties can also conflict with demands for equality. In the 1980s, city officials in Indianapolis, Indiana—influenced by feminist theorists—invoked Fourteenth Amendment equality principles to justify legislation restricting freedom of expression. Specifically, they argued that pornography is sex discrimination.[47]

The ordinance focused on pornography and its effect on women's status and treatment. It defined pornography as the graphic, sexually explicit subordination of women in words or pictures that present women as "sexual objects who experience pleasure in being raped" or as "sexual objects of domination, conquest, violation, exploitation, possession, or use, or [in] postures or positions of servility or submission or display." The ordinance rested on three findings:

● That pornography is a form of discrimination that denies equal opportunities in society.

★ **politics in a changing** w o r l d

15.1   Freedom Versus Order in Cyberspace

The year 2000 will likely be remembered as the year when governments started to regulate cyberspace in earnest. In Britain, the Regulation of Investigatory Powers Act now gives the police broad access to e-mail and other on-line communications. South Korea has outlawed access to gambling Web sites. The United States has passed a law requiring schools and libraries that receive federal funds for Internet connections to install software on their computers that will block material harmful to the young. And a French court ordered the Internet portal firm Yahoo! to find some way of preventing French users from seeing the Nazi memorabilia posted on its American sites or face a daily fine of Fr 100,000 ($13,000). Yahoo! is fighting the case, even though it has now stopped sales of Nazi memorabilia.

The case could be a preview of things to come. Under a new European Union (EU) law, for example, European consumers may now sue EU-based Internet sites in their own countries, and the rule may well be extended internationally. The United States has just endorsed the gist of the Council of Europe's cybercrime treaty, which aims to harmonize laws against hacking, Internet fraud, and child pornography.

The Council of Europe—a group of forty-one countries that includes all fifteen members of the European Union—is putting the finishing touches to the world's first international treaty on cybercrime. The United States, which has also been involved in the negotia-

tions, supports the treaty's main points. Signatories to the agreement must have laws on their books that allow, for instance, quick seizure of incriminating computer data and its distribution to authorities in other countries.

Although negotiations began three years ago, the treaty was made public in April 2000, in its twenty-second draft. Internet advocacy groups were only recently able to get involved. To them, the treaty is a document that "threatens the rights of the individual while extending the power of police authorities." The treaty also exemplifies the risk that governments, especially democratic ones, run when they try to assert their authority in the on-line world. The legal tools and technologies they develop, though useful in that context, may well be abused not only by them but also by authoritarian governments. The means used by France to fight antisemitism on the Web could also be used to prevent people living in less democratic countries from getting the information they need to strive for basic freedoms.

All this is a far cry from what leading Internet thinkers prophesied only five years ago. "You [governments] have no moral right to rule us nor do you possess any methods of enforcement we have true reason to fear," proclaimed John Perry Barlow in his 1996 Declaration of Independence of Cyberspace. Libertarian thinking also ran through early Internet scholarship. David Post and David Johnson, law professors at Temple University

- That pornography is central in creating and maintaining gender as a category of discrimination.

- That pornography is a systematic practice of exploitation and subordination based on sex, imposing differential harms on women.

The ordinance then banned pornographic material according to the following arguments. (1) The government's interest in promoting equality outweighs any First Amendment protections of expression. (2) Pornog-

and Georgetown University, respectively, argued in that same year that cyberspace was a distinct place that needed laws and legal institutions entirely of its own.

To treat cyberspace differently seemed logical. Because data are sent around the Internet in small packets, each of which can take a different route, the flow of information is hard to stop, even if much of the network is destroyed. This built-in resilience appealed to the Internet's original sponsor, the U.S. Defense Department, and made it the medium of choice for civil libertarians. "The Internet," runs their favorite motto, "interprets censorship as damage and routes around it."

Many on-line experts argue that, since the Internet does away with geographical boundaries, it also does away with territorially based laws. The transmission of data is almost instant, regardless of where sender and receiver are. Today individuals as well as multinational companies can decide in which country to base their Web sites, thus creating competition between jurisdictions. For example, the United States, thanks to its constitutional guarantee of the right to free speech, has become a safe haven for hundreds of German neo-Nazi sites that are illegal under German law.

Yet, for all that, governments are not completely helpless in cyberspace. They have some potentially powerful tools at their disposal. Filtering is one. Software installed on a PC, in an Internet service provider's equipment or in gateways that link one country with the rest of the on-line world, can block access to certain sites. China, for instance, has essentially covered its territory with an intranet isolated from the rest of the on-line world by software that blocks access to sites with unwanted content. Although clever surfers can find ways to tunnel through the "Great Firewall," it keeps the majority from straying too far on-line. Most Chinese, in any case, get on the Internet from work or a public place, where the state can control the software and track what users do and where they risk being seen if they go to an illegal site.

Nor do governments always need new technology to impose their regulatory muscle. They can also rely on human intervention, just as Yahoo! now intends to do to ban auctions of Nazi and Ku Klux Klan items on its site. Although it is coy about details, the company says that it will use software to filter out objectionable material and human reviewers to decide borderline cases.

On the Internet, the struggle between freedom and state control will rage for some time. But if recent trends in on-line regulation prove anything, it is that technology is being used by both sides in this battle and that freedom is by no means certain to win. The Internet could indeed become the most liberating technology since the printing press—but only if governments let it.

raphy affects thoughts—it works by socializing, by establishing the expected and permissible; depictions of subordination tend to perpetuate subordination, and this leads to affronts to women and to the continuation of lower pay at work, insult and injury at home, and battery and rape in the streets. (3) Since pornography conditions society to subordinate women, an ordinance regulating pornographic expression will help control the resulting unacceptable conduct.

According to the ordinance, works depicting sexual encounters premised on equality are lawful no matter how sexually explicit. And works that treat women in the disapproved way—as sexually submissive or as enjoying humiliation—are unlawful no matter how significant the literary, artistic, or political qualities of the work. U.S. District Judge Sarah Evans Barker declared the ordinance unconstitutional, stating that it went beyond prohibiting what the law has deemed unprotected expression (such as child pornography) to suppress otherwise protected expression.

Judge Barker thus confronted the tradeoff between equality and freedom in a pluralist democracy. Interest groups that use the democratic process to carve out exceptions to the First Amendment benefit at the expense of everyone's rights. Although efforts to restrict behavior that leads to the humiliation and degradation of women may be necessary and desirable, "free speech, rather than being the enemy," wrote Judge Barker, "is a long-tested and worthy ally. To deny free speech in order to engineer social change in the name of accomplishing a greater good for one sector of our society erodes the freedom of all."[48]

This novel effort to recast an issue of freedom versus order as one of freedom versus equality remains a theory. Barker's decision protected freedom. Her judgment was affirmed by the U.S. Court of Appeals in 1985 and affirmed without argument by the Supreme Court in 1986. In 1988, the citizens of Bellingham, Washington, approved by referendum an ordinance similar to the one in Indianapolis, but a federal district judge invalidated it in 1989. The Massachusetts legislature introduced a narrower version in 1992. In the next confrontation—and, in a pluralist democracy, there will surely be others—equality may prove the victor.

Freedom of the Press

The First Amendment guarantees that government "shall make no law . . . abridging the freedom . . . of the press." Although the free press guarantee was originally adopted as a restriction on the national government, since 1931 the Supreme Court has held that it applies to state and local governments as well.

The ability to collect and report information without government interference was (and still is) thought to be essential to a free society. The print media continue to use and defend the freedom conferred on them by the framers. However, the electronic media have had to accept some government regulation stemming from the scarcity of broadcast frequencies (see Chapter 6).

New York Times v. Sullivan

Defamation of Character.   Libel is the written defamation of character.* A person who believes his or her name and character have been harmed by false statements in a publication can institute a lawsuit against the publication and seek monetary compensation for the damage. Such a lawsuit can impose limits on freedom of expression; at the same time, false statements impinge on the rights of individuals. In a landmark decision in **New York Times v. Sullivan** (1964), the Supreme Court declared that freedom of the press takes precedence—at least when the defamed individual is a public official.[49] The Court unanimously agreed that the First Amendment

---

* *Slander is the oral defamation of character. The durability of the written word usually means that libel is a more serious accusation than slander.*

protects the publication of all statements—even false ones—about the conduct of public officials, except statements made with actual malice (with knowledge that they are false or in reckless disregard for their truth or falsity). Citing John Stuart Mill's 1859 treatise *On Liberty*, the Court declared that "even a false statement may be deemed to make a valuable contribution to public debate, since it brings about the 'clearer perception and livelier impression of truth, produced by its collision with error.'"

Three years later, the Court extended this protection to apply to suits brought by any public figure, whether a government official or not. **Public figures** are people who assume roles of prominence in society or thrust themselves to the forefront of public controversies—including officials, actors, writers, television personalities, and others. These people must show actual malice on the part of the publication that printed false statements about them. Because the burden of proof is so great, few plaintiffs prevail. And freedom of the press is the beneficiary.

What if the damage inflicted is not to one's reputation but to one's emotional state? Government seeks to maintain the prevailing social order, which prescribes proper modes of behavior. Does the First Amendment restrict the government in protecting citizens from behavior that intentionally inflicts emotional distress? This issue arose in a parody of a public figure in *Hustler* magazine. The target was the Reverend Jerry Falwell, a Baptist televangelist who founded the Moral Majority and organized conservative Christians into a political force. The parody had Falwell—in an interview—discussing a drunken, incestuous rendezvous with his mother in an outhouse, saying, "I always get sloshed before I go out to the pulpit." Falwell won a $200,000 award for "emotional distress." The magazine appealed, and the Supreme Court confronted the issue of social order versus free speech in 1988.[50]

In a unanimous decision, the Court overturned the award. In his sweeping opinion for the Court, Chief Justice William H. Rehnquist gave wide latitude to the First Amendment's protection of free speech. He observed that "graphic depictions and satirical cartoons have played a prominent role in public and political debate" throughout the nation's history and that the First Amendment protects even "vehement, caustic, and sometimes unpleasantly sharp attacks." Free speech protects criticism of public figures, even if the criticism is outrageous and offensive.

Prior Restraint and the Press.   As discussed above, in the United States, freedom of the press has primarily meant protection from prior restraint, or censorship. The Supreme Court's first encounter with a law imposing prior restraint on a newspaper was in *Near* v. *Minnesota* (1931).[51] In Minneapolis, Jay Near published a scandal sheet in which he attacked local officials, charging that they were in league with gangsters.[52] Minnesota officials obtained an injunction to prevent Near from publishing his newspaper, under a state law that allowed such action against periodicals deemed "malicious, scandalous, and defamatory."

The Supreme Court struck down the law, declaring that prior restraint places an unacceptable burden on a free press. Chief Justice Charles Evans Hughes forcefully articulated the need for a vigilant, unrestrained press: "The fact that the liberty of the press may be abused by miscreant purveyors of scandal does not make any the less necessary the immunity of the

public figures
People who assume roles of prominence in society or thrust themselves to the forefront of public controversy.

press from previous restraint in dealing with official misconduct." Although the Court acknowledged that prior restraint may be permissible in exceptional circumstances, it did not specify those circumstances, nor has it yet done so.

Consider another case, which occurred during a war, a time when the tension between government-imposed order and individual freedom is often at a peak. In 1971, Daniel Ellsberg, a special assistant in the Pentagon's Office of International Security Affairs, delivered portions of a classified U.S. Department of Defense study to the *New York Times* and the *Washington Post*. By making the documents public, he hoped to discredit the Vietnam War and thereby end it. The U.S. Department of Justice sought to restrain the *Times* and the *Post* from publishing the documents, which became known as the Pentagon Papers, contending that their publication would prolong the war and embarrass the government. The case was quickly brought before the Supreme Court, which delayed its summer adjournment to hear oral arguments.

New York Times v. *United States*

Three days later, in a 6–3 decision in **New York Times v. United States** (1971), the Court concluded that the government had not met the heavy burden of proving that immediate, inevitable, and irreparable harm would follow publication of the documents.[53] The majority expressed its view in a brief, unsigned opinion; individual and collective concurring and dissenting views added nine additional opinions to the decision. Two justices maintained that the First Amendment offers absolute protection against government censorship, no matter what the situation. But the other justices left the door ajar for the imposition of prior restraint in the most extreme and compelling of circumstances. The result was hardly a ringing endorsement of freedom of the press, nor was it a full affirmation of the public's right to all the information that is vital to the debate of public issues.

Freedom of Expression Versus Maintaining Order.   The courts have consistently held that freedom of the press does not override the requirements of law enforcement. A grand jury called on a Louisville, Kentucky, reporter who had researched and written an article about drug-related activities to identify people he had seen in possession of marijuana or in the act of processing it. The reporter refused to testify, maintaining that freedom of the press shielded him from this inquiry. In a closely divided decision, the Supreme Court in 1972 rejected this position.[54] The Court declared that no exception, even a limited one, is permissible to the rule that all citizens have a duty to give their government whatever testimony they are capable of giving.

A divided Supreme Court reiterated in 1978 that journalists are not protected from the demands of law enforcement. The Court upheld a lower court's warrant to search a Stanford University campus newspaper office for photographs of a violent demonstration. The investigation of criminal conduct seems to be a special area—one in which the Court is not willing to provide the press with extraordinary protections.[55]

The Supreme Court again confronted the conflict between free expression and order in 1988.[56] The principal of a St. Louis high school had deleted articles on divorce and teenage pregnancy from the school's newspaper on the ground that the articles invaded the privacy of the students and families who were the focus of the stories. Three student editors filed suit in federal court, claiming that the principal had violated their First Amendment rights. They argued that the principal's censorship interfered with the newspaper's function as a public forum, a role protected by the First Amendment. The principal maintained that the newspaper was just an extension of classroom instruction and thus was not protected by the First Amendment.

In a 5–3 decision, the Court upheld the principal's actions in sweeping terms. Educators may limit speech within the confines of the school curriculum and speech that might seem to bear the approval of the school, provided their actions serve any "valid educational purpose." The majority justices maintained that "students in public school do not 'shed their constitutional rights to freedom of expression at the schoolhouse gate,'" but recent Court decisions suggest that students do lose certain rights—including elements of free expression—when they pass through the public school portals.

The Rights to Assemble Peaceably and to Petition the Government

The final clause of the First Amendment states that "Congress shall make no law . . . abridging . . . the right of the people peaceably to assemble, and to petition the Government for a redress of grievances." The roots of the right of petition can be traced to the Magna Carta, the charter of English political and civil liberties granted by King John at Runnymede in 1215. The right of peaceable assembly arose much later. The framers meant that the people have the right to assemble peaceably *in order to* petition the government. Today, however, the right to assemble peaceably is equated with the right to free speech and a free press, independent of whether or not the government is petitioned. Precedent has merged these rights and made them indivisible.[57] Government cannot prohibit peaceful political meetings and cannot brand as criminals those who organize, lead, and attend such meetings.[58]

The clash of interests in cases involving these rights illustrates the continuing nature of the effort to define and apply fundamental principles. The need for order and stability has tempered the concept of freedom. And when freedom and order conflict, the justices of the Supreme Court, who are responsible only to their consciences, strike the balance. Such clashes are certain to occur again and again. Freedom and order conflict when public libraries become targets of community censors, when religious devotion interferes with military service, when individuals and groups express views or hold beliefs at odds with majority sentiment. Conflicts between freedom and order, and between minority and majority viewpoints, are part and parcel of politics and government, here and abroad. Is freedom increasing or declining worldwide? See Compared with What? 15.1.

THE RIGHT TO BEAR ARMS

The Second Amendment declares

> A well-regulated militia being necessary to the security of a free State, the right of the people to keep and bear arms shall not be infringed.

This amendment has created a hornet's nest of problems for gun-control advocates and their opponents. Gun-control advocates assert that the amendment protects the right of the states to maintain *collective* militias.

15.1   Freedom Rebounding

Each year, Freedom House researchers analyze the state of freedom around the world. Using a seven-point scale, they rank nations from 1 (the greatest degree of freedom) to 7 (the least degree of freedom). In countries rated 1, the press is a free outlet for the expression of political opinions, especially when the intent of that expression is to affect the political process legitimately. In addition, in these countries no major medium serves as a simple conduit for government propaganda. The courts protect the individual; people cannot be punished for their opinions; there is respect for private rights and wants in people's education, occupation, religion, and residence; and law-abiding citizens do not fear for their lives because of their political activities.

Moving down the scale from 2 to 7, we see a steady loss of civil freedoms. Compared with those in nations rated 1, the police and courts in nations rated 2 have more authoritarian traditions or a less institutionalized or secure set of liberties. Nations rated 3 or higher may have political prisoners and varying forms of censorship. Often, their security services torture prisoners. States rated 6 almost always have political prisoners. Here the mainstream media are usually completely under government supervision; there is no right to assembly; and often, there are narrow restrictions on travel, on where people may live, and on the occupations they may pursue. However, at level 6 there may still be relative freedom within private conversations, especially in homes; demonstrations against the government can or do occur; and underground literature circulates. At 7 on the scale, there is pervasive fear; there is little independent expression, even in private; and there is almost no public expression of opposition to the government. Imprisonment and execution are swift and sure.

In 2000, a country was considered free if it scored between 1 and 2.5 ($n = 85$), partly free if it scored between 3 and 5.5 ($n = 60$), and not free if it scored between 5.5 and 7 ($n = 47$). While the overall number of people living in nations considered free or partially free grew by only

---

Gun-use advocates assert that the amendment protects the right of *individuals* to own and use guns. There are good arguments on both sides.

Federal firearms regulations did not come into being until Prohibition, so the Supreme Court had little to say on the matter before then. In 1939, however, a unanimous Court upheld a 1934 federal law requiring the taxation and registration of machine guns and sawed-off shotguns. The Court held that the Second Amendment protects a citizen's right to own ordinary militia weapons; sawed-off shotguns did not qualify for protection.[59]

Restrictions on gun ownership (for example, registration and licensing) have passed constitutional muster. However, outright prohibitions on gun ownership (for example, a ban on handguns) might run afoul of the amendment. After all, Madison and others supported the amendment based on the view that armed citizens provided a bulwark against tyranny. However, some scholars argue that modern circumstances should confine the amendment to the preservation of state militias, relinquishing the right of individuals to possess modern lethal weapons.[60]

marginal amounts in 2000, twenty-four nations did improve their freedom score during this year, compared with seventeen that got worse. The proportion of people who are free today stands at roughly 39 percent, double the

lowest level of 19 percent recorded in 1994.

Source: Adrian Karatnycky et al., *Freedom in the World, 1999–2000* (New York: Freedom House, 2001) <www.freedomhouse.org/survey/2000/karat.html>. Copyright © 2001. Reprinted by permission of Freedom House.

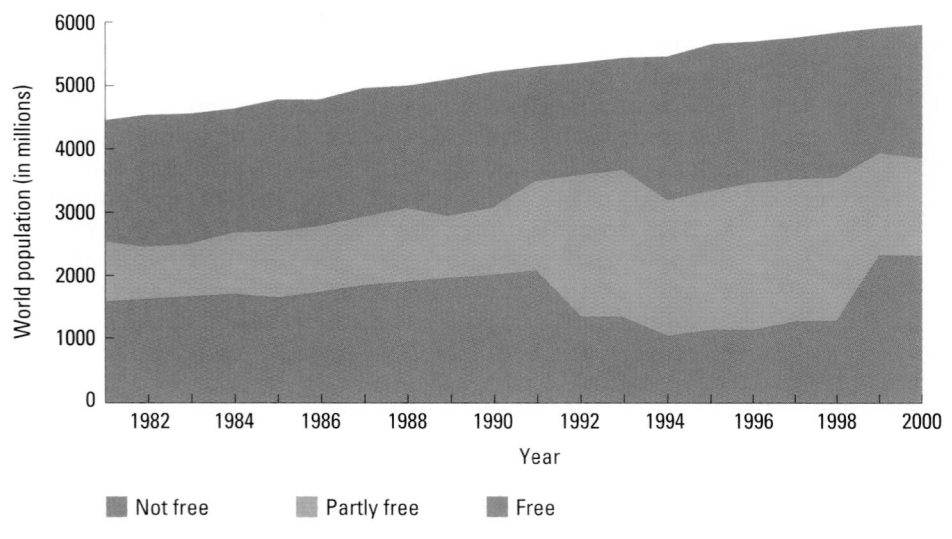

APPLYING THE BILL OF RIGHTS TO THE STATES

bill of attainder
A law that pronounces an individual guilty of a crime without a trial.

ex post facto law
A law that declares an action to be criminal after it has been performed.

obligation of contracts
The obligation of the parties to a contract to carry out its terms.

The major purpose of the Constitution was to structure the division of power between the national government and the state governments. Even before it was amended, the Constitution set some limits on both the nation and the states with regard to citizens' rights. It barred both governments from passing **bills of attainder,** laws that make an individual guilty of a crime without a trial. It also prohibited them from enacting **ex post facto laws,** laws that declare an action a crime after it has been performed. And it barred both nation and states from impairing the **obligation of contracts,** the obligation of the parties in a contract to carry out its terms.

Although initially the Bill of Rights seemed to apply only to the national government, various litigants pressed the claim that its guarantees also applied to the states. In response to one such claim, Chief Justice John Marshall affirmed what seemed plain from the Constitution's language and "the history of the day" (the events surrounding the Constitutional Convention): the provisions of the Bill of Rights served only to limit national authority. "Had the framers of these amendments intended them to be limitations on the powers of the state governments," wrote Marshall, "they would have . . . expressed that intention."[61]

Change came with the Fourteenth Amendment, which was adopted in 1868. The due process clause of that amendment is the linchpin that holds the states to the provisions of the Bill of Rights.

The Fourteenth Amendment: Due Process of Law

> *Section 1.* . . . No State shall make or enforce any law which shall abridge the privileges or immunities of citizens of the United States; nor shall any State deprive any person of life, liberty, or property, without due process of law. . . .

Most freedoms protected in the Bill of Rights today function as limitations on the states. And many of the standards that limit the national government serve equally to limit state governments. The changes have been achieved through the Supreme Court's interpretation of the due process clause of the Fourteenth Amendment: "nor shall any State deprive any person of life, liberty, or property, without due process of law." The clause has two central meanings. First, it requires the government to adhere to appropriate procedures. For example, in a criminal trial, the government must establish the defendant's guilt beyond a reasonable doubt. Second, it forbids unreasonable government action. For example, at the turn of the century, the Supreme Court struck down a state law that forbade bakers from working more than sixty hours a week. The justices found the law unreasonable under the due process clause.

The Supreme Court has used the first meaning of the due process clause as a sponge, absorbing or incorporating the procedural specifics of the Bill of Rights and spreading or applying them to the states. The history of due process cases reveals that unlikely litigants often champion constitutional guarantees and that freedom is not always the victor.

The Fundamental Freedoms

In 1897, the Supreme Court declared that the states are subject to the Fifth Amendment's prohibition against taking private property without providing just compensation.[62] The Court reached that decision by absorbing the prohibition into the due process clause of the Fourteenth Amendment, which explicitly applies to the states. Thus, one Bill of Rights protection—but only that one—applied to both the states and the national government, as illustrated in Figure 15.1. In 1925, the Court assumed that the due process clause protected the First Amendment speech and press liberties from impairment by the states.[63]

Palko v. *Connecticut*

The inclusion of other Bill of Rights guarantees within the due process clause faced a critical test in ***Palko v. Connecticut*** (1937).[64] Frank Palko had been charged with homicide in the first degree. He was convicted of second-degree murder, however, and sentenced to life imprisonment. The state of Connecticut appealed and won a new trial; this time, Palko was found guilty of first-degree murder and sentenced to death. Palko appealed the second conviction on the ground that it violated the protection against

15.1   The Incorporation of the Bill of Rights

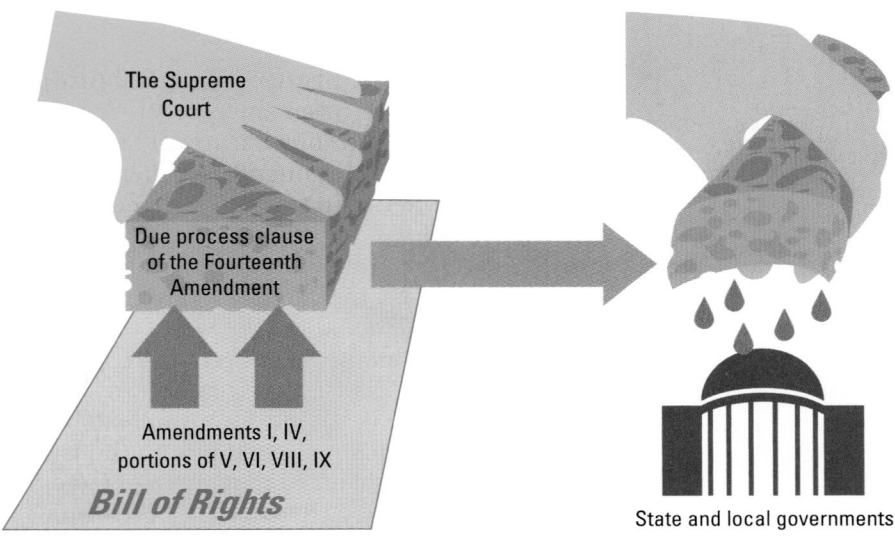

The Supreme Court has used the due process clause of the Fourteenth Amendment as a sponge, absorbing most—but not all—of the provisions in the Bill of Rights and applying them to state and local governments. All provisions in the Bill of Rights apply to the national government.

The Supreme Court

Due process clause of the Fourteenth Amendment

Amendments I, IV, portions of V, VI, VIII, IX

Bill of Rights

State and local governments

double jeopardy guaranteed to him by the Fifth Amendment. This protection applied to the states, he contended, because of the Fourteenth Amendment's due process clause.

The Supreme Court upheld Palko's second conviction. In his opinion for the majority, Justice Benjamin N. Cardozo formulated principles that were to guide the Court's actions for the next three decades. He reasoned that some Bill of Rights guarantees—such as freedom of thought and speech—are fundamental and that these fundamental rights are absorbed by the Fourteenth Amendment's due process clause and are therefore applicable to the states. These rights are essential, argued Cardozo, because "neither liberty nor justice would exist if they were sacrificed." Trial by jury and other rights, although valuable and important, are not essential to liberty and justice and therefore are not absorbed by the due process clause. "Few would be so narrow or provincial," Cardozo claimed, "as to maintain that a fair and enlightened system of justice would be impossible" without these other rights. In other words, only certain provisions of the Bill of Rights—the "fundamental" provisions—were absorbed into the due process clause and made applicable to the states. Because protection against double jeopardy was not one of them, Palko died in Connecticut's gas chamber in 1938.

The next thirty years saw slow but perceptible change in the standard for determining whether a Bill of Rights guarantee was fundamental. The reference point changed from the idealized "fair and enlightened system of justice" in *Palko* to the more realistic "American scheme of justice" thirty years later.[65] Case after case tested various guarantees that the Court found to be fundamental. By 1969, when *Palko* was finally overturned, the Court had found most of the Bill of Rights applicable to the states.

Criminal Procedure: The Meaning of Constitutional Guarantees

"The history of liberty," remarked Justice Frankfurter, "has largely been the history of observance of procedural safeguards."[66] The safeguards embodied in the Fourth through Eighth Amendments to the Constitution specify how government must behave in criminal proceedings. Their application to the states has reshaped American criminal justice in the past thirty years in two stages. The first stage was the judgment that a guarantee asserted in the Bill of Rights also applied to the states. The second stage required that the judiciary give specific meaning to the guarantee. The courts could not allow the states to define guarantees themselves without risking different definitions from state to state—and thus differences among citizens' rights. If rights are fundamental, their meaning cannot vary. But life is not quite so simple under the U.S. Constitution. The concept of federalism is sewn into the constitutional fabric, and the Supreme Court has recognized that there may be more than one way to prosecute the accused while heeding his or her fundamental rights.

Consider, for example, the right to a jury trial in criminal cases, which is guaranteed by the Sixth Amendment. This right was made obligatory for the states in *Duncan* v. *Louisiana* (1968). The Supreme Court later held that the right applied to all nonpetty criminal cases, those in which the penalty for conviction was more than six months' imprisonment.[67] But the Court did not require that state juries have twelve members, the number required for federal criminal proceedings. The Court permits jury size to vary from state to state, although it has set the minimum number at six. Furthermore, it has not imposed on the states the federal requirement of a unanimous jury verdict. As a result, even today many states do not require unanimous verdicts for criminal convictions. Some observers question whether criminal defendants in these states enjoy the same rights as defendants in unanimous-verdict states.

In contrast, the Court left no room for variation in its definition of the fundamental right to an attorney, also guaranteed by the Sixth Amendment. Clarence Earl Gideon was a penniless vagrant accused of breaking into and robbing a pool hall. (The "loot" he was charged with taking was mainly change from vending machines.) Because Gideon could not afford a lawyer, he asked the state to provide him with legal counsel for his trial. The state refused and subsequently convicted Gideon and sentenced him to five years in the Florida State Penitentiary. From his cell, Gideon appealed to the U.S. Supreme Court, claiming that his conviction should be struck down because the state had denied him his Sixth Amendment right to counsel. (Gideon was also without counsel in this appeal; he filed a handwritten "pauper's petition" with the Court after studying law texts in the prison library. When the Court agreed to consider his case, he was assigned a prominent Washington attorney, Abe Fortas, who later became a Supreme Court justice.)[68]

In its landmark decision in ***Gideon*** v. ***Wainwright*** (1963), the Court set aside Gideon's conviction and extended to defendants in state courts the

Gideon v. *Wainwright*

Sixth Amendment right to counsel.[69] The state retried Gideon, who this time had the assistance of a lawyer, and the court found him not guilty.

In subsequent rulings that stretched over more than a decade, the Court specified at which points in the course of criminal proceedings a defendant is entitled to a lawyer (from arrest to trial, appeal, and beyond). These pronouncements are binding on all states. In state as well as federal proceedings, the government must furnish legal assistance to those who do not have the means to hire their own attorney.

During this period the Court also came to grips with another procedural issue: informing suspects of their constitutional rights. Without this knowledge, procedural safeguards are meaningless. Ernesto Miranda was arrested in Arizona in connection with the kidnapping and rape of an eighteen-year-old woman. After the police questioned him for two hours and the woman identified him, Miranda confessed to the crime. An Arizona court convicted him on the basis of that confession—although he was never told that he had the right to counsel and the right not to incriminate himself. Miranda appealed his conviction, which was overturned by the Supreme Court in 1966.[70]

The Court based its decision in *Miranda* v. *Arizona* on the Fifth Amendment privilege against self-incrimination. According to the Court, the police had forced Miranda to confess during in-custody questioning, not with physical force but with the coercion inherent in custodial interrogation without counsel. The Court said that warnings are necessary to dispel that coercion. The Court does not require warnings if a person is only held in custody without being questioned or is only questioned without being arrested. But in *Miranda*, the Court found the combination of custody and interrogation sufficiently intimidating to require warnings before questioning. These statements are known today as the **Miranda warnings:**

- You have the right to remain silent.

- Anything you say can be used against you in court.

- You have the right to talk to a lawyer of your own choice before questioning.

- If you cannot afford to hire a lawyer, a lawyer will be provided without charge.

In each area of criminal procedure, the justices have had to grapple with two steps in the application of constitutional guarantees to criminal defendants: the extension of a right to the states and the definition of that right. In *Duncan*, the issue was the right to jury trial, and the Court allowed variation in all states. In *Gideon*, the Court applied the right to counsel uniformly in all states. Finally, in *Miranda*, the Court declared that all governments—national, state, and local—have a duty to inform suspects of the full measure of their constitutional rights. In one of its most important cases in 2000, the Court reaffirmed this protection in a 7–2 decision, holding that *Miranda* had "announced a constitutional rule" that Congress could not undermine through legislation.[71]

The problems in balancing freedom and order can be formidable. A primary function of government is to maintain order. What happens when the government infringes upon individuals' freedom for the sake of order?

Miranda v. *Arizona*

Miranda warnings
Statements concerning rights that police are required to make to a person before he or she is subjected to in-custody questioning.

Wolf v. *Colorado*

exclusionary rule
The judicial rule that states that evidence obtained in an illegal search and seizure cannot be used in trial.

Mapp v. *Ohio*

Consider the guarantee in the Fourth Amendment: "The right of the people to be secure in their persons, houses, papers, and effects, against unreasonable searches and seizures, shall not be violated." The Court made this right applicable to the states in *Wolf* v. *Colorado* (1949).[72] Following the reasoning in *Palko,* the Court found that the core of the amendment—security against arbitrary police intrusion—is a fundamental right and that citizens must be protected from illegal searches by state and local governments. But how? The federal courts had long followed the **exclusionary rule,** which holds that evidence obtained from an illegal search and seizure cannot be used in a trial. And of course, if that evidence is critical to the prosecution, the case dissolves. But the Court refused to apply the exclusionary rule to the state courts. Instead, it allowed the states to decide on their own how to handle the fruits of an illegal search. The decision in *Wolf* stated that obtaining evidence by illegal means violated the Constitution and that states could fashion their own rules of evidence to give effect to this constitutional decree. The states were not bound by the exclusionary rule.

The justices considered the exclusionary rule again twelve years later, in *Mapp* v. *Ohio.*[73] An Ohio court had found Dolree Mapp guilty of possessing obscene materials after an admittedly illegal search of her home for a fugitive. The Ohio Supreme Court affirmed her conviction, and she appealed to the U.S. Supreme Court. Mapp's attorneys argued for a reversal based primarily on freedom of expression, contending that the First Amendment protected the confiscated materials. However, the Court elected to use the decision in *Mapp* to give meaning to the constitutional guarantee against unreasonable search and seizure. In a 6–3 decision, the justices declared that "all evidence obtained by searches and seizures in violation of the Constitution is, by [the Fourth Amendment], inadmissible in a state court." Ohio had convicted Mapp illegally; the evidence should have been excluded.

The decision was historic. It placed the exclusionary rule under the umbrella of the Fourth Amendment and required all levels of government to operate according to the provisions of that amendment. Failure to do so could result in the dismissal of criminal charges against guilty defendants.

Mapp launched a divided Supreme Court on a troubled course of determining how and when to apply the exclusionary rule. For example, the Court has continued to struggle with police use of sophisticated electronic eavesdropping devices and searches of movable vehicles. In each case, the justices have confronted a rule that appears to handicap the police and to offer freedom to people whose guilt has been established by the illegal evidence. In the Court's most recent pronouncements, order has triumphed over freedom.

The struggle over the exclusionary rule took a new turn in 1984, when the Court reviewed *United States* v. *Leon.*[74] In this case, the police obtained a search warrant from a judge on the basis of a tip from an informant of unproved reliability. The judge issued a warrant without firmly establishing probable cause to believe the tip. The police, relying on the warrant, found large quantities of illegal drugs. The Court, by a vote of 6–3, established the **good faith exception** to the exclusionary rule. The justices held that the state could introduce at trial evidence seized on the basis of a mistakenly issued search warrant. The exclusionary rule, argued the majority, is not a right but a remedy against illegal police conduct. The rule is

good faith exception
An exception to the Supreme Court exclusionary rule, holding that evidence seized on the basis of a mistakenly issued search warrant can be introduced at trial if the mistake was made in good faith, that is, if all the parties involved had reason at the time to believe that the warrant was proper.

costly to society. It excludes pertinent valid evidence, allowing guilty people to go unpunished and generating disrespect for the law. These costs are justifiable only if the exclusionary rule deters police misconduct. Such a deterrent effect was not a factor in *Leon:* the police acted in good faith. Hence, the Court decided, there is a need for an exception to the rule.

In 1988, the justices ruled 6–2 that police may search through garbage bags and other containers that people leave outside their houses. The case resulted from an investigation of a man police suspected of narcotics trafficking. The police obtained his trash bags from the local garbage collector; the bags contained evidence of narcotics, which then served as the basis for obtaining a search warrant for his house. That search revealed quantities of cocaine and hashish and led to criminal charges. The lower courts dismissed the drug charges on the ground that the warrant was based on an unconstitutional search. By overturning that ruling, the Supreme Court further eroded the Fourth Amendment's protection of individual privacy.[75]

The exclusionary rule continues to divide the Supreme Court. In 1990, the justices again reaffirmed the rule, but only by a bare 5–4 majority.[76] The current Supreme Court lineup has a more conservative bent, which suggests that the battle over the exclusionary rule has not ended.

Mapp and all the cases that followed it forced the Court to confront the classic dilemma of democracy: the choice between freedom and order. If the justices tip the scale too far toward freedom, guilty parties might go free and perhaps break the law again. If they choose excessive order, however, they might give official sanction to police conduct that violates the Constitution.

THE NINTH AMENDMENT AND PERSONAL AUTONOMY

Can You Explain Why... there is a constitutional right to privacy even though the word *privacy* is never mentioned in the Constitution?

Griswold v. *Connecticut*

The enumeration in the Constitution, of certain rights, shall not be construed to deny or disparage others retained by the people.

The working and history of the Ninth Amendment remain an enigma; the evidence supports two different views. The amendment may protect rights that are not enumerated, or it may simply protect state governments against the assumption of power by the national government.[77] The meaning of the amendment was not an issue until 1965, when the Supreme Court used it to protect privacy, a right that is not enumerated in the Constitution.

Controversy: From Privacy to Abortion

In *Griswold* **v.** *Connecticut* (1965), the Court struck down, by a vote of 7–2, a seldom-enforced Connecticut statute that made the use of birth control devices a crime.[78] Justice Douglas, writing for the majority, asserted that the "specific guarantees in the Bill of Rights have penumbras [partially illuminated regions surrounding fully lit areas]" that give "life and substance" to broad, unspecified protections in the Bill of Rights. Several specific guarantees in the First, Third, Fourth, and Fifth Amendments create a zone of privacy, Douglas argued, and this zone is protected by the Ninth Amendment and is applicable to the states by the due process clause of the Fourteenth Amendment.

Three justices gave further emphasis to the relevance of the Ninth Amendment, which, they contended, protects fundamental rights derived from those specifically enumerated in the first eight amendments. This view contrasted sharply with the position expressed by the two dissenters, Justices Black and Stewart. In the absence of some specific prohibition, they argued, the Bill of Rights and the Fourteenth Amendment do not allow judicial annulment of state legislative policies, even if those policies are abhorrent to a judge or justice.

Griswold established the principle that the Bill of Rights as a whole creates a right to make certain intimate, personal choices, including the right of married people to engage in sexual intercourse for reproduction or pleasure. This zone of personal autonomy, protected by the Constitution, was the basis of a 1973 case that sought to invalidate state antiabortion laws. But rights are not absolute, and in weighing the interests of the individual against the interests of the government, the Supreme Court found itself caught up in a flood of controversy that has yet to subside.

Roe v. Wade

In **Roe v. Wade** (1973), the Court, in a 7–2 decision, declared unconstitutional a Texas law making it a crime to obtain an abortion except for the purpose of saving the woman's life.[79]

Justice Harry A. Blackmun, who wrote the majority opinion, could not point to a specific constitutional guarantee to justify the Court's ruling. Instead, he based the decision on the right to privacy protected by the due process clause of the Fourteenth Amendment. In effect, state abortion laws were unreasonable and hence unconstitutional. The Court declared that in the first three months of pregnancy, the abortion decision must be left to the woman and her physician. In the interest of protecting the woman's health, states may restrict but not prohibit abortions in the second three months of pregnancy. Finally, in the last three months of pregnancy, states may regulate or even prohibit abortions to protect the life of the fetus, except when medical judgment determines that an abortion is necessary to save the woman's life. In all, the Court's ruling affected the laws of forty-six states.

The dissenters—Justices Byron R. White and Rehnquist—were quick to assert what critics have frequently repeated since the decision: the Court's judgment was directed by its own dislikes, not by any constitutional compass. In the absence of guiding principles, they asserted, the majority justices simply substituted their views for the views of the state legislatures whose abortion regulations they invalidated.[80] In a 1993 television interview, Blackmun insisted that "*Roe* versus *Wade* was decided . . . on constitutional grounds."[81] It was as if Blackmun were trying, by sheer force of will, to turn back twenty years' worth of stinging objections to the opinion he had crafted.

The composition of the Court shifted under President Ronald Reagan. His elevation of Rehnquist to chief justice in 1986 and his appointment of Scalia in 1986 and Kennedy in 1988 raised new hope among abortion foes and old fears among advocates of choice.

A perceptible shift away from abortion rights materialized in *Webster* v. *Reproductive Health Services* (1989). The case was a blockbuster, attracting voluminous media coverage. *Webster* also set a record for the number of amicus briefs submitted on behalf of individuals and organizations with an interest in the outcome. (The number of briefs—seventy-eight—surpassed the old record of fifty-eight set in the landmark affirmative action case *Regents of the University of California* v. *Bakke* in 1978.)

Webster v. Reproductive Health Services

In *Webster*, the Supreme Court upheld the constitutionality of a Missouri law that denied the use of public employees or publicly funded facilities in the performance of an abortion unless the woman's life was in danger.[82] Furthermore, the law required doctors to perform tests to determine whether fetuses twenty weeks and older could survive outside the womb. This was the first time that the Court upheld significant government restrictions on abortion.

The justices issued five opinions, but no single opinion captured a majority. Four justices (Blackmun, Brennan, Thurgood Marshall, and John Paul Stevens) voted to strike down the Missouri law and hold fast to *Roe*. Four justices (Kennedy, Rehnquist, Scalia, and White) wanted to overturn *Roe* and return to the states the power to regulate abortion. The remaining justice—Sandra Day O'Connor—avoided both camps. Her position was that state abortion restrictions are permissible provided they are not "unduly burdensome." She voted with the conservative plurality to uphold the restrictive Missouri statute on the ground that it did not place an undue burden on women's rights. But she declined to reconsider (and overturn) *Roe*.

The Court has since moved cautiously down the road toward greater government control of abortion. In 1990, the justices split on two state parental notification laws. The Court struck down a state requirement that compelled unwed minors to notify both her parents before having an abortion. In another case, however, the Court upheld a state requirement that a physician notify one parent of a pregnant minor of her intent to have an abortion. In both cases, the justices voiced widely divergent opinions, revealing a continuing division over abortion.[83]

The abortion issue pits freedom against order. The decision to bear or beget children should be free from government control. Yet government has a legitimate interest in protecting and preserving life, including fetal life, as part of its responsibility to maintain an orderly society. Rather than choose between freedom and order, the majority on the Court has loosened constitutional protections of abortion rights and cast the politically divisive issue into the state legislatures, where elected representatives can thrash out the conflict.

Many groups defending or opposing abortion have now turned to state legislative politics to advance their policies. This approach will force candidates for state office to debate the abortion issue and then translate electoral outcomes into legislation that restricts or protects abortion. If the abortion issue is deeply felt by Americans, pluralist theory would predict that the strongest voices for or against abortion will mobilize the greatest support in the political arena.

With a clear conservative majority, the Court seemed poised to reverse *Roe* in 1992. But a new coalition—forged by Reagan and Bush appointees O'Connor, Souter, and Kennedy—reaffirmed *Roe* yet tolerated additional restrictions on abortions. In *Planned Parenthood* v. *Casey*, a bitterly divided bench opted for the O'Connor "undue burden" test. Eight years later, in 2000, O'Connor sided with a coalition of liberal and moderate justices in a 5–4 decision striking down a Nebraska law that had banned the so-called partial-birth abortion, illustrating the Court's continuing and deep division on the abortion issue.[84]

Presidential values, as reflected in the appointment of Supreme Court justices, have left an imprint on the abortion controversy. Justices appointed by presidents Reagan and Bush weakened abortion as a constitutional right. But President Clinton's High Court appointments of Ruth Bader Ginsburg and Stephen G. Breyer in 1993 and 1994 added two liberal votes to a conservative Court and made good on a Clinton campaign promise to protect women's access to abortion from further assault. (Ginsburg replaced White, who had opposed *Roe* v. *Wade* from its inception. Breyer replaced Blackmun, the principal author of the *Roe* opinion.)

Although Ginsburg ducked most questions at her confirmation hearings, she was forthright in her judgment that the Constitution protects a woman's right to choose. But Ginsburg offered objections of her own to the Court's reasoning on abortion. She seemed unpersuaded by the "right to privacy" roots of *Roe*. Instead, she saw a woman's right to abortion as rooted in the equal protection clause of the Fourteenth Amendment.[85]

Breyer, a self-described pragmatist, made clear his view that a woman's right to an abortion is now settled law. Interestingly, Breyer's research as a Supreme Court law clerk in 1965 contributed to the right-to-privacy decision in *Griswold* v. *Connecticut*.

Personal Autonomy and Sexual Orientation

The right-to-privacy cases may have opened a Pandora's box of divisive social issues. Does the right to privacy embrace private homosexual acts between consenting adults? Consider the case of Michael Hardwick, who was arrested in 1982 in his Atlanta bedroom while having sex with another man. In a standard approach to prosecuting homosexuals, Georgia charged him under a state criminal statute with the crime of sodomy, which means oral or anal intercourse. The police said that they had gone to his home to arrest him for failing to pay a fine for drinking in public. Although the prosecutor dropped the charges, Hardwick sued to challenge the law's constitutionality. He won in the lower courts, but the state pursued the case.

The conflict between freedom and order lies at the core of the case. "Our legal history and our social traditions have condemned this conduct uniformly for hundreds and hundreds of years," argued Georgia's attorney. Constitutional law, he continued, "must not become an instrument for a change in the social order." Hardwick's attorney, a noted constitutional scholar, said that government must have a more important reason than "majority morality to justify regulation of sexual intimacies in the privacy of the home." He maintained that the case involved two precious freedoms: the right to engage in private sexual relations and the right to be free from government intrusion in one's home.[86]

More than half the states have eliminated criminal penalties for private homosexual acts between consenting adults. The rest still outlaw homosexual sodomy, and many outlaw heterosexual sodomy as well. As a result, homosexual rights groups and some civil liberties groups followed Hardwick's case closely. Fundamentalist Christian groups and defenders of traditional morality expressed deep interest in the outcome, too.

Bowers v. *Hardwick*

In a bitterly divided ruling in 1986, the Court held in ***Bowers* v. *Hardwick*** that the Constitution does not protect homosexual relations between consenting adults, even in the privacy of their own homes.[87] The logic of the findings in the privacy cases involving contraception and abortion would seem to have compelled a finding of a right to personal autonomy—a right to make personal choices unconstrained by government—in this case as well. But the 5–4 majority maintained that only heterosexual choices—whether and whom to marry, whether to conceive a child, whether to have an abortion—fall within the zone of privacy established by the Court in its earlier rulings. "The Judiciary necessarily takes to itself further authority to govern the country without express constitutional authority" when it expands the list of fundamental rights not rooted in the language or design of the Constitution, wrote Justice White, the author of the majority opinion.

The arguments on both sides of the privacy issue are compelling. This makes the choice between freedom and order excruciating for ordinary citizens and Supreme Court justices alike. At the conference to decide the merits of the *Hardwick* case, Justice Lewis Powell cast his vote to extend privacy rights to homosexual conduct. Later, he joined with his conservative colleagues, fashioning a new majority. Four years after the *Hardwick* decision, Powell revealed another change of mind: "I probably made a mistake," he declared, speaking of his decision to vote with the conservative majority.[88]

Issues around sexual orientation have shifted toward the states, where various groups continue to assert their political power. At one point, the Hawaii courts were poised to be the first in the nation to approve gay marriages. But this effort was foiled in 1997 when the state legislature voted to put a state constitutional amendment on the ballot reaffirming traditional marriage. The amendment passed. In anticipation of state-approved same-sex unions, Congress moved affirmatively in 1996 to bar the effects of homosexual marriage through passage of the Defense of Marriage Act. President Clinton signed the bill into law. The law defines marriage as a union between people of opposite sexes and declares that states are not

Everyone's Irish on St. Patrick's Day

Despite a new militancy on the part of gay and lesbian activists, the quest for national constitutional protection of homosexual rights halted with the Supreme Court's 1986 decision upholding state laws against sodomy. In response, many activists have shifted their efforts from the national level to state and local arenas. Here, activists air their views during New York City's St. Patrick's Day parade.

obliged to recognize gay marriages performed elsewhere. (The Constitution's full faith and credit clause would otherwise impose a duty on all the states to enforce the legal acts of every other state.) The law does not ban such unions; it only protects states from having to recognize homosexual marriage sanctioned by other states. Thirty-five states now bar the recognition of same-sex marriages.

Some states have been innovators in legitimizing homosexuality. Vermont has led the way. In 2000, the state legislature approved same-sex "unions" but not same-sex marriages. The difference between a union and a marriage may prove to be a distinction without a difference. It should encourage groups for and against such intimate choices to push or oppose similar legislation in their own states.

The pluralist model provides one solution for groups dissatisfied with rulings from the nation's highest court. State courts and state legislatures have demonstrated their receptivity to positions that are probably untenable in the federal courts. However, state-by-state decisions offer little comfort to Americans who believe the U.S. Constitution protects them in their most intimate decisions and actions, regardless of where they reside.

CONSTITUTIONALIZING PUBLIC POLICIES

The effects of the *Griswold* and *Roe* decisions are more fundamental and disturbing for democracy than the surface issues of privacy and personal autonomy. By enveloping a policy in the protection of the Constitution, the courts remove that policy from the legislative arena, where the people's will can be expressed through the democratic process.

As the abortion controversy demonstrates, the courts can place under the cloak of the Constitution a host of public policies that the democratic process once debated and resolved. By giving a policy constitutional protection (as the Court did with abortion), judges assume responsibilities that have traditionally been left to the elected branch to resolve. If we trust appointed judges to serve as guardians of democracy, we have no reason to fear for the democratic process. But if we believe that democratic solutions are necessary to resolve such questions, our fears may be well grounded. The controversy will continue as the justices wrestle among themselves and with their critics over whether the Constitution authorizes them to fill the due process clause with fundamental values that cannot easily be traced to constitutional text, history, or structure.

Although the courts may be "the chief guardians of the liberties of the people," they ought not have the last word, argued the great jurist Learned Hand, because

> a society so riven that the spirit of moderation is gone, no court can save;
> . . . a society where that spirit flourishes, no court need save; . . . in a society which evades its responsibilities by thrusting upon the courts the nurture of that spirit, that spirit in the end will perish.[89]

SUMMARY

Using the "Voters" data in the CROSSTABS program, analyze issue variables (e.g., abortion, school prayer, the death penalty) by ideology. Do value preferences match policy positions?

When they established the new government of the United States, the states and the people compelled the framers, through the Bill of Rights, to protect their freedoms. In interpreting these ten amendments, the courts, especially the Supreme Court, have taken on the task of balancing freedom and order.

The First Amendment protects several freedoms: freedom of religion, freedom of speech and of the press, and the freedom to assemble peaceably and to petition the government. The establishment clause demands government neutrality toward religions and between the religious and the nonreligious. According to judicial interpretations of the free-exercise clause, religious beliefs are inviolable, but the Constitution does not protect antisocial actions in the name of religion. Extreme interpretations of the religion clauses could bring the clauses into conflict with each other.

Freedom of expression encompasses freedom of speech, freedom of the press, and the right to assemble peaceably and to petition the government. Freedom of speech and freedom of the press have never been held to be absolute, but the courts have ruled that the Bill of Rights gives them far greater protection than other freedoms. Exceptions to free speech protections include some forms of symbolic expression, fighting words, and obscenity. Press freedom has enjoyed broad constitutional protection because a free society depends on the ability to collect and report information without government interference. The rights to assemble peaceably and to petition the government stem from the guarantees of freedom of speech and of the press. Each freedom is equally fundamental, but the right to exercise them is not absolute.

The adoption of the Fourteenth Amendment in 1868 extended the guarantees of the Bill of Rights to the states. The due process clause became the vehicle for applying specific provisions of the Bill of Rights—one at a time, case after case—to the states. The designation of a right as fundamental also called for a definition of that right. The Supreme Court has tolerated some variation from state to state in the meaning of certain constitutional rights. The Court has also imposed a duty on governments to inform citizens of their rights so that they are equipped to exercise them.

As it has fashioned new fundamental rights from the Constitution, the Supreme Court has become embroiled in controversy. The right to privacy served as the basis for the right of women to terminate a pregnancy, which in turn suggested a right to personal autonomy. The abortion controversy is still raging, and the justices appear to have called a halt to the extension of personal privacy in the name of the Constitution.

In the meantime, judicial decisions raise a basic issue. By offering constitutional protection to certain public policies, the courts may be threatening the democratic process, the process that gives the people a say in government through their elected representatives. One thing is certain: the challenge of democracy requires the constant balancing of freedom and order.

★ Key Cases

Lemon v. *Kurtzman*
Sherbert v. *Verner*
Brandenburg v. *Ohio*
Tinker v. *Des Moines Independent County School District*

Cohen v. *California*
Reno v. *ACLU*
Miller v. *California*
New York Times v. *Sullivan*
New York Times v. *United States*

Palko v. *Connecticut*
Gideon v. *Wainwright*
Griswold v. *Connecticut*

Roe v. *Wade*
Bowers v. *Hardwick*

★ Selected Readings

Carter, Stephen L. *The Culture of Disbelief: How American Law and Politics Trivialize Religious Devotion.* New York: Basic Books, 1993. In this wide-ranging, thoughtful work, Carter argues that Americans can simultaneously preserve separation of church and state, embrace American spirituality, and avoid treating believers with disdain.

Garrow, David. *Liberty & Sexuality: The Right to Privacy and the Making of* Roe v. Wade. New York: Macmillan, 1994. This is a comprehensive, historical narrative of the fundamental right to sexual privacy.

Levy, Leonard W. *The Establishment Clause: Religion and the First Amendment.* New York: Macmillan, 1986. This searching study of the establishment clause claims that the view that government can assist all religions is historically groundless. Levy argues that it is unconstitutional for government to provide aid to any religion.

Lewis, Anthony. *Make No Law: The Sullivan Case and the First Amendment.* New York: Random House, 1991. This is an enlightening study of a great constitutional decision. Lewis illuminates the history and evolution of the First Amendment guarantees of free expression and free press.

Polenberg, Richard. *Fighting Faiths.* New York: Alfred A. Knopf, 1987. By focusing on the famous case of *Abrams* v. *United States,* a noted historian examines anarchism, government surveillance, freedom of speech, and the impact of the Russian Revolution on American liberals.

Powe, Lucas A. *The Warren Court and American Politics.* Cambridge, Mass.: The Belknap Press of Harvard University Press, 2000. Studying the Supreme Court as a political institution, Powe argues that the Warren Court was revolutionary because it imposed national liberal-elite values on outlier groups—the white South, rural America, and areas of Roman Catholic dominance

Smolla, Rodney A. *Free Speech in an Open Society.* New York: Alfred A. Knopf, 1993. A lucid examination covering a wide range of contemporary problems in free speech, such as flag burning, hate speech, and new technologies.

Internet Exercises

1. *Flag Burning and Symbolic Speech*

The Oyez Project is the most comprehensive multimedia database on the U.S. Supreme Court. It provides access to selected oral arguments conducted before the Court. One of the most interesting cases of the 1980s was *Texas* v. *Johnson* (1989), which considered whether flag burning was constitutional.

- Go to the Oyez Web site, **<oyez.northwestern.edu/>**, and search for the *Texas* v. *Johnson* (1989) case.

- Listen to the following segments of the oral argument: Time 0:00–6:10 and time 38:55–43:25.

- Identify at least three different examples of what might constitute "flag desecration" in these segments of the oral argument. Based on the discussion, how does one of the justices suggest that burning a flag might actually increase its power as a national symbol? What is the Texas attorney's response to this claim?

2. *Hate Crimes and the First Amendment*

One of the Federal Bureau of Investigation's (FBI) responsibilities is to investigate and prosecute individuals who commit hate crimes. These activities are part of the FBI's Civil Rights Program, which is designed to "enforce federal civil rights statutes and to ensure that the protected civil rights of all inhabitants are not abridged."

- Go to the FBI's home page at **<www.fbi.gov/>** and follow the link to the bureau's "Programs and Initiatives," where you can find information on the Civil Rights Program and the FBI's enforcement of hate crime statutes.

- Read the FBI's discussion of hate crimes, in particular its explanation of how the law defines a hate crime, and the bureau's summaries of the four federal statutes that outline the FBI's jurisdiction in this area.

- How could someone use the First Amendment to argue that one or more of these hate crime statutes is unconstitutional? How could someone use the First Amendment to argue that the statutes are consistent with the Constitution, and indeed required to protect the civil liberties of the nation's citizens?

Equality and Civil Rights

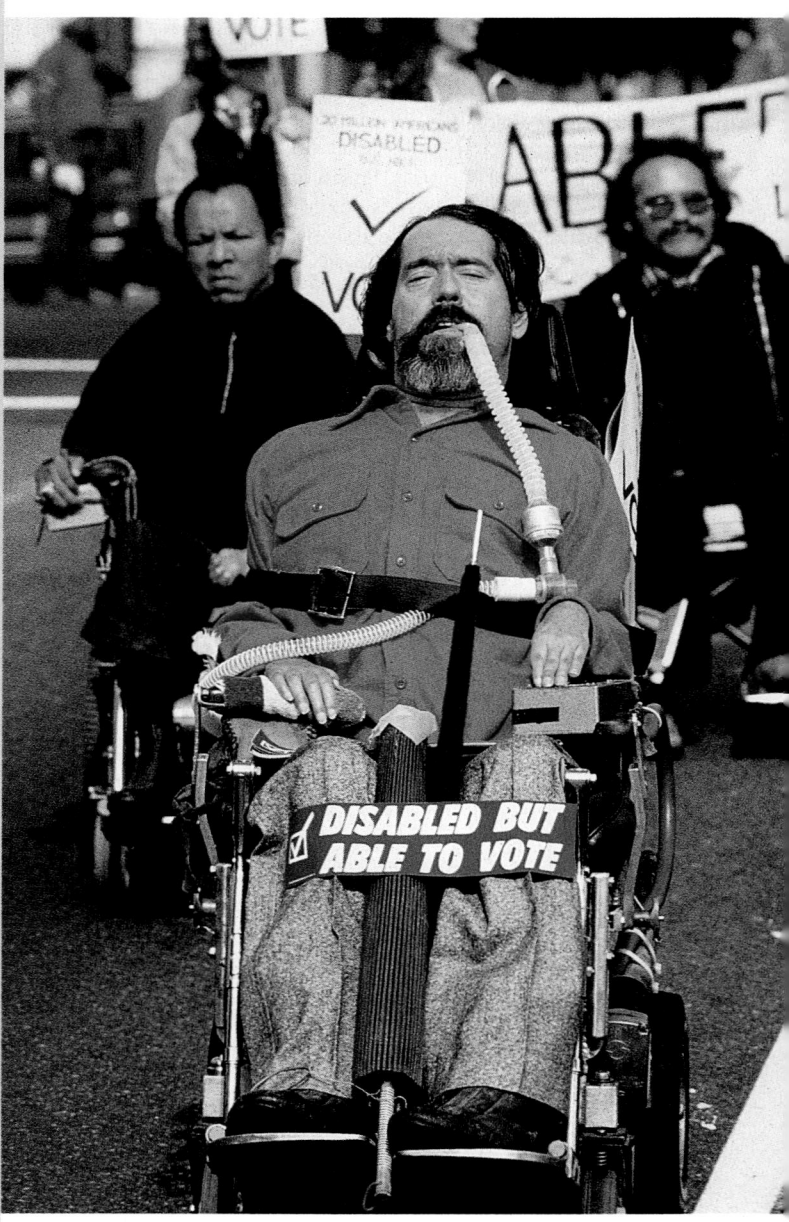

RACIAL DISCRIMINATION still persists in 2000, the U.S. State Department found—not in South Africa or Germany or Japan or Russia, but in the United States! Why should the U.S. State Department, charged with executing *foreign* policy, issue an official report on American racial discrimination, an issue of domestic concern? The answer is globalization. The United States was bound by a United Nations treaty signed by President Clinton in 1994. Under the terms of the treaty, the United States is obligated to report its civil rights performance with the aim "to adopt all necessary measures for speedily eliminating racial discrimination in all its forms and manifestations, and to prevent and combat racist doctrines and practices in order to promote understanding between races and to build an international community free from all forms of racial segregation and racial discrimination."[1]

The State Department race-relations report card gave the United States high marks for making great strides in race and ethnic relations. However, "[t]he path towards true racial equality has been uneven, and substantial barriers must still be overcome," the report declared. It was uncharacteristically candid in its catalog of racial abuses:

- The persistence of attitudes, policies, and practices reflecting a legacy of segregation, ignorance, stereotyping, discrimination, and disparities in opportunity and achievement.

- Inadequate enforcement of existing antidiscrimination laws.

- Economic disadvantage: persons belonging to minority groups appear in disproportionate numbers at the bottom of the income distribution curve.

- Persistent discrimination in employment and labor relations.

- Continued segregation and discrimination in housing, public accommodation, and consumer goods. Even where civil rights laws prohibit segregation and discrimination in these areas, such practices continue.

- Lack of access to business capital and credit markets.

- Lack of access to technology and high-technology skills.

- Lack of educational opportunities.

- Discrimination in the criminal justice system.[2]

Since our founding as a nation, advocates for greater social, political, and economic equality have relied on legal, moral, political, and spiritual authority to end racial discrimination. Under the new treaty, advocates may appeal to international authority in the quest to end the blight of racial and other forms of bias.

Why does racial and other forms of unlawful discrimination persist in the United States despite laudable efforts to end it? The answer may appear deceptively simple. Laws and policies—and now treaties—that aim to end unlawful discrimination achieve their objectives by promoting equality. And the promotion of equality conflicts with demands for freedom. The conflict between freedom and equality intensifies when we recognize that Americans advocate competing conceptions of equality.

TWO CONCEPTIONS OF EQUALITY

Americans want equality, at least in principle. Public support for the principle of equal treatment increased dramatically from the 1940s to the 1990s. Today, more than nine in ten Americans support equal treatment for all in schools, public accommodations, housing, employment, and public transportation. However, Americans are far less united in their approach to implementing this principle.[3]

equality of opportunity
The idea that each person is guaranteed the same chance to succeed in life.

Most Americans support **equality of opportunity,** the idea that people should have an equal chance to develop their talents and that effort and ability should be rewarded equitably. This form of equality offers all individuals the same chance to get ahead; it glorifies personal achievement and free competition and allows everyone to play on a level field where the same rules apply to all. Special recruitment efforts aimed at identifying qualified minority or female job applicants, for example, ensure that everyone has the same chance starting out. Low-bid contracting illustrates equality of opportunity because every bidder has the same chance to compete for work.

equality of outcome
The concept that society must ensure that people are equal, and governments must design policies to redistribute wealth and status to achieve economic and social equality.

Americans are far less committed to **equality of outcome,** which means greater uniformity in social, economic, and political power among different social groups. For example, schools and businesses aim at equality of outcome when they allocate admissions or jobs on the basis of race, gender, or disability, which are unrelated to ability. (Some observers refer to these allocations as *quotas,* whereas others call them *goals.* The difference is subtle. A quota *requires* that a specified, proportional share of some benefit go to a favored group. A goal *aims* for proportional allocation of benefits, without requiring it.) The government seeks equality of outcome when it adjusts the rules to handicap some bidders or applicants and favor others. The vast majority of Americans, however, consistently favor low-bid contracting and merit-based admissions and employment over preferential treatment.[4] Quota- or goal-based policies muster only modest support in national opinion polls, ranging from 10 to 30 percent of the population, depending on how poll questions are worded.[5]

Some people believe that equality of outcome can occur in today's society only if we restrict the free competition that is the basis of equality of opportunity. Supreme Court Justice Harry Blackmun articulated this controversial position: "In order to get beyond racism, we must first take account of race. There is no other way. And in order to treat some persons equally, we must treat them differently."[6]

Can You Explain Why...
government policies to guarantee equality of outcome
tend to be more controversial
than those guaranteeing
equality of opportunity?

Quota policies generate the most opposition because they confine competition and create barriers to personal achievement. Quotas limit advancement for some individuals and ensure advancement for others. They alter the results by taking into account factors unrelated to ability. Equal outcomes policies that benefit minorities, women, or the disabled at the expense of whites, men, or the able-bodied create strong opposition because quotas seem to be at odds with individual initiative. In other words, equality clashes with freedom. To understand the ways government resolves this conflict, we have to understand the development of civil rights in this country.

The history of civil rights in the United States is primarily a story of a search for social and economic equality. This search has persisted for more than a century and is still going on today. It began with the battle for civil rights for black citizens, whose prior subjugation as slaves had roused the passions of the nation and brought about its bloodiest conflict, the Civil War. The struggle of blacks has been a beacon lighting the way for Native Americans, Hispanic Americans, women, the disabled, and homosexuals. Each of these groups has confronted **invidious discrimination.** Discrimination is simply the act of making or recognizing distinctions. When making distinctions among people, discrimination may be benign (that is, harmless) or invidious (harmful). Sometimes this harm has been subtle, and sometimes it has been overt. Sometimes it has even come from other minorities. Each group has achieved a measure of success in its struggle by pressing its interests on government, even challenging it. These challenges and the government's responses to them have helped shape our democracy.

Remember that **civil rights** are powers or privileges guaranteed to the individual and protected from arbitrary removal at the hands of the government or other individuals. Sometimes, people refer to civil rights as "positive rights" (see Feature 15.1 for examples). (Rights need not be confined to humans. Some advocates claim that animals have rights, too.) In this chapter, we will concentrate on the rights guaranteed by the constitutional amendments adopted after the Civil War and by laws passed to enforce those guarantees. Prominent among them is the right to equal protection of the laws. This right remained a promise rather than a reality well into the twentieth century.

invidious discrimination
Discrimination against persons or groups that works to their harm and is based on animosity.

civil rights
Powers or privileges guaranteed to individuals and protected from arbitrary removal at the hands of government or individuals.

THE CIVIL WAR AMENDMENTS

The Civil War amendments were adopted to provide freedom and equality to black Americans. The Thirteenth Amendment, ratified in 1865, provided that

> neither slavery nor involuntary servitude . . . shall exist within the United States, or any place subject to their jurisdiction.

The Fourteenth Amendment was adopted three years later. It provides first that freed slaves are citizens:

> All persons born or naturalized in the United States, and subject to the jurisdiction thereof, are citizens of the United States and of the State wherein they reside.

As we saw in Chapter 15, it also prohibits the states from abridging the "privileges or immunities of citizens of the United States" or depriving "any person of life, liberty, or property, without due process of law." The amendment then goes on to guarantee equality under the law, declaring that no state shall

> deny to any person within its jurisdiction the equal protection of the laws.

The Fifteenth Amendment, adopted in 1870, added a measure of political equality:

> The right of citizens of the United States to vote shall not be denied or abridged by the United States or by any State on account of race, color, or previous condition of servitude.

American blacks were thus free and politically equal—at least according to the Constitution. But for many years, the courts sometimes thwarted the efforts of the other branches to protect their constitutional rights.

Congress and the Supreme Court: Lawmaking Versus Law Interpreting

black codes
Legislation enacted by former slave states to restrict the freedom of blacks.

Civil Rights Act of 1866

Civil Rights Act of 1875

In the years after the Civil War, Congress went to work to protect the rights of black citizens. In 1866, lawmakers passed a civil rights act that gave the national government some authority over the treatment of blacks by state courts. This legislation was a response to the **black codes**, laws enacted by the former slave states to restrict the freedom of blacks. For example, vagrancy and apprenticeship laws forced blacks to work and denied them a free choice of employers. One section of the 1866 act that still applies today grants all citizens the right to make and enforce contracts; the right to sue others in court (and the corresponding ability to be sued); the duty and ability to give evidence in court; and the right to inherit, purchase, lease, sell, hold, or convey property. Later, in the Civil Rights Act of 1875, Congress attempted to guarantee blacks equal access to public accommodations (streetcars, inns, parks, theaters, and the like).

Although Congress enacted laws to protect the civil rights of black citizens, the Supreme Court weakened some of those rights. In 1873, the Court ruled that the Civil War amendments had not changed the relationship between the state and national governments.[7] State citizenship and national citizenship remained separate and distinct. According to the Court, the Fourteenth Amendment did not obligate the states to honor the rights guaranteed by U.S. citizenship. (In a 1999 case, *Saenz* v. *Roe*, the Court resurrected the amendment's privileges or immunities clause as protection against overreaching state and local governments.)

In subsequent years, the Court's decisions narrowed some constitutional protections for blacks. In 1876, the justices limited congressional attempts to protect the rights of blacks.[8] A group of Louisiana whites had used violence and fraud to prevent blacks from exercising their basic constitutional rights, including the right to assemble peaceably. The justices held that the rights allegedly infringed on were not nationally protected rights and that therefore Congress was powerless to punish those who violated them. On the very same day, the Court ruled that the Fifteenth Amendment did not guarantee all citizens the right to vote; it simply listed grounds that could not be used to deny that right.[9] And in 1883, the Court struck down the public accommodations section of the Civil Rights

Act of 1875.[10] The justices declared that the national government could prohibit only *government* action that discriminated against blacks; private acts of discrimination or acts of omission by a state were beyond the reach of the national government. For example, a state law excluding blacks from jury service was an unlawful abridgment of individual rights. However, a person who refused to serve blacks in a private club was outside the control of the national government because the discrimination was a private—not a governmental—act. The Court refused to see racial discrimination as an act that the national government could prohibit. In many cases the justices tolerated racial discrimination. In the process they abetted **racism,** the belief that there are inherent differences among the races that determine people's achievement and that one's own race is superior to and thus has a right to dominate others.

racism
A belief that human races have distinct characteristics such that one's own race is superior to, and has a right to rule, others.

The Court's decisions gave the states ample room to maneuver around civil rights laws. In the matter of voting rights, for example, states that wanted to bar black men from the polls simply used nonracial means to do so. One popular tool was the **poll tax,** first imposed by Georgia in 1877. This was a tax of $1 or $2 on every citizen who wanted to vote. The tax was not a burden for most whites. But many blacks were tenant farmers, deeply in debt to white merchants and landowners; they just did not have any extra money for voting. Other bars to black suffrage included literacy tests, minimum education requirements, and a grandfather clause that restricted suffrage to men who could establish that their grandfathers were eligible to vote before 1867 (three years before the Fifteenth Amendment declared that race could not be used to deny individuals the right to vote).[11] White southerners also used intimidation and violence to keep blacks from the polls.

poll tax
A tax of $1 or $2 on every citizen who wished to vote, first instituted in Georgia in 1877. Although it was no burden on most white citizens, it effectively disenfranchised blacks.

The Roots of Racial Segregation

racial segregation
Separation from society because of race.

From well before the Civil War, **racial segregation** had been a way of life in the South: blacks lived and worked separately from whites. After the war, southern states began to enact Jim Crow laws to reinforce segregation. (*Jim Crow* was a derogatory term for a black person.) Once the Supreme Court took the teeth out of the Civil Rights Act of 1875, such laws proliferated. They required blacks to live in separate (generally inferior) areas and restricted them to separate sections of hospitals; separate cemeteries; separate drinking and toilet facilities; separate schools; and separate sections of streetcars, trains, jails, and parks. Each day, in countless ways, they were reminded of the inferior status accorded them by white society.

In 1892, Homer Adolph Plessy—who was seven-eighths Caucasian—took a seat in a "whites-only" car of a Louisiana train. He refused to move to the car reserved for blacks and was arrested. Plessy argued that Louisiana's law mandating racial segregation on its trains was an unconstitutional infringement on both the privileges and immunities guaranteed by the Fourteenth Amendment and its equal protection clause. The Supreme Court disagreed. The majority in ***Plessy* v. *Ferguson*** (1896) upheld state-imposed racial segregation.[12] They based their decision on what came to be known as the **separate-but-equal doctrine,** which held that separate facilities for blacks and whites satisfied the Fourteenth Amendment as long as they were equal. The lone dissenter was John Marshall Harlan

separate-but-equal doctrine
The concept that providing separate but equivalent facilities for blacks and whites satisfies the equal protection clause of the Fourteenth Amendment.

Separate and Unequal

The Supreme Court gave constitutional protection to racial separation on the theory that states could provide "separate but equal" facilities for blacks. But racial separation meant unequal facilities, as these two water fountains dramatically illustrate. The Supreme Court struck a fatal blow against the separate-but-equal doctrine in its landmark 1954 ruling in Brown v. Board of Education.

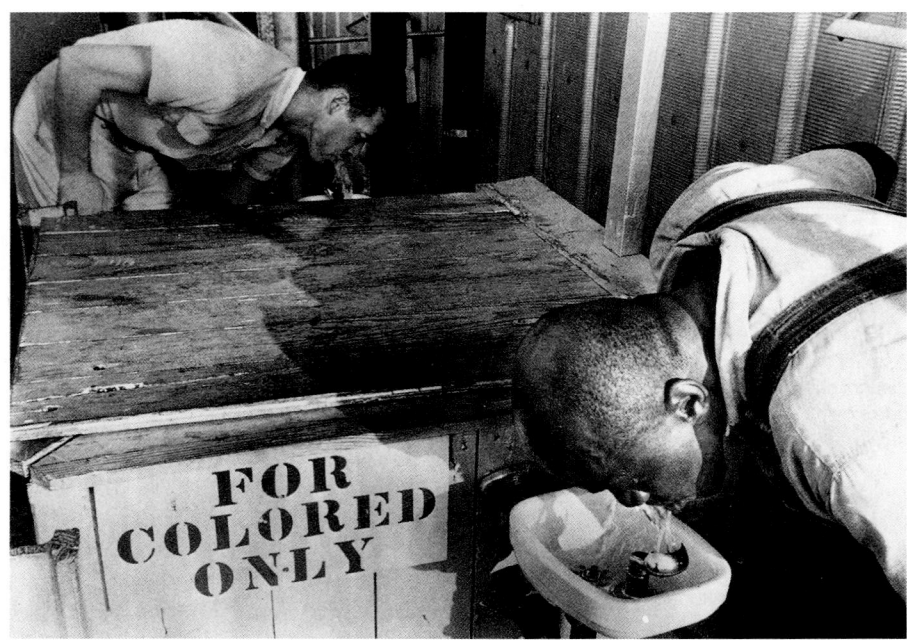

(the first of two distinguished justices with the same name). Harlan, who envisioned a "color-blind Constitution," wrote this in his dissenting opinion:

> We boast of the freedom enjoyed by our people above all other peoples. But it is difficult to reconcile that boast with a state of the law which, practically, puts the brand of servitude and degradation upon a large class of our fellow citizens, our equals before the law. The thin disguise of "equal" accommodations for passengers in railroad coaches will not mislead anyone, or atone for the wrong this day done.[13]

Three years later, the Supreme Court extended the separate-but-equal doctrine to the schools.[14] The justices ignored the fact that black educational facilities (and most other "colored-only" facilities) were far from equal to those reserved for whites.

By the end of the nineteenth century, legal racial segregation was firmly entrenched in the American South. Although constitutional amendments and national laws to protect equality under the law were in place, the Supreme Court's interpretation of those amendments and laws rendered them ineffective. Several decades would pass before any change was discernible.

THE DISMANTLING OF SCHOOL SEGREGATION

Denied the right to vote and to be represented in the government, blacks sought access to power through other parts of the political system. The National Association for the Advancement of Colored People (NAACP), founded in 1909 by W. E. B. Du Bois and others, both black and white, with the goal of ending racial discrimination and segregation, took the lead in the campaign for black civil rights. The plan was to launch a two-pronged legal and lobbying attack on the separate-but-equal doctrine: first by pressing for fully equal facilities for blacks, then by proving the unconstitutionality of segregation. The process would be a slow one, but the strategies involved did not require a large organization or heavy financial backing; at the time, the NAACP had neither.*

Pressure for Equality . . .

By the 1920s, the separate-but-equal doctrine was so deeply ingrained in American law that no Supreme Court justice would dissent from its continued application to racial segregation. But a few Court decisions offered hope that change would come. In 1935, Lloyd Gaines graduated from Lincoln University, a black college in Missouri, and applied to the state law school. The law school rejected him because he was black. Missouri refused to admit blacks to its all-white law school; instead, the state's policy was to pay the costs of blacks admitted to out-of-state law schools. With the support of the NAACP, Gaines appealed to the courts for admission to the University of Missouri Law School. In 1938, the U.S. Supreme Court ruled that he must be admitted.[15] Under the *Plessy* ruling, Missouri could not shift to other states its responsibility to provide an equal education for blacks.

Two later cases helped reinforce the requirement that segregated facilities must be equal in all major respects. One was brought by Heman Sweatt, again with the help of the NAACP. The all-white University of Texas Law School had denied Sweatt entrance because of his race. A federal court ordered the state to provide a black law school for him; the state responded by renting a few rooms in an office building and hiring two black lawyers as teachers. Sweatt refused to attend the school and took his case to the Supreme Court.[16]

The second case raised a related issue. A doctoral program in education at the all-white University of Oklahoma had refused George McLaurin admission because he was black. The state had no equivalent program for blacks. McLaurin sought a federal court order for admission and, under pressure from the decision in *Gaines,* the university amended its procedures and admitted McLaurin "on a segregated basis." It restricted the sixty-eight-year-old McLaurin to hastily designated "colored-only" sections of a few rooms. With the help of the NAACP, McLaurin appealed this obvious lack of equal facilities to the Supreme Court.[17]

The Court ruled on *Sweatt* and *McLaurin* in 1950. The justices unanimously found that the facilities in each case were inadequate: the separate "law school" provided for Sweatt did not approach the quality of the white state law school, and the restrictions placed on McLaurin's interactions with other students would result in an inferior education. Their respective state universities had to give both Sweatt and McLaurin full student status. But the Court avoided reexamining the separate-but-equal doctrine.

. . . And Pressure for Desegregation

These decisions—especially *McLaurin*—suggested to the NAACP that the time was right for an attack on segregation itself. In addition, public attitudes toward race relations were slowly changing from the predominant

---

* *In 1939, the NAACP established an offshoot, the NAACP Legal Defense and Education Fund, to work on legal challenges while the parent organization concentrated on lobbying.*

Anger Erupts in Little Rock

In 1957, the Little Rock, Arkansas, school board attempted to implement court-ordered desegregation. Nine blacks were to be admitted to Little Rock Central High School. Governor Orval Faubus ordered the National Guard to bar their attendance. A mob blocked a subsequent attempt by the students. Finally, President Dwight D. Eisenhower ordered federal troops to escort the students to the high school. Among them was fifteen-year-old Elizabeth Eckford (right). She was surrounded by a large crowd of boys and girls, men and women, soldiers and police officers. She held her head high, her eyes fixed straight ahead, while Hazel Brown (left) angrily taunted her. This image seared the nation's conscience. The violence and hostility led the school board to seek a postponement of the desegregation plan. The Supreme Court, meeting in special session, affirmed the Brown *decision and ordered the plan to proceed. Years later, Hazel Brown apologized for her hateful display. Brown and Eckford are now reconciled friends.*

desegregation
The ending of authorized segregation, or separation by race.

Brown v. Board of Education

racism of the nineteenth and early twentieth centuries toward greater tolerance. Black groups had fought with honor—albeit in segregated military units—in World War II. Blacks and whites were working together in unions and in service and religious organizations. Social change and court decisions suggested that government-imposed segregation was vulnerable.

President Harry S Truman risked his political future with his strong support of blacks' civil rights. In 1947, he established the President's Committee on Civil Rights. The committee's report, issued later that year, became the agenda for the civil rights movement during the next two decades. It called for national laws prohibiting racially motivated poll taxes, segregation, and brutality against minorities and for guarantees of voting rights and equal employment opportunity. In 1948, Truman ordered the **desegregation** (the dismantling of authorized racial segregation) of the armed forces.

In 1947, the U.S. Department of Justice had begun to submit briefs to the courts in support of civil rights. The department's most important intervention probably came in ***Brown v. Board of Education.***[18] This case was the culmination of twenty years of planning and litigation on the part of the NAACP to invalidate racial segregation in public schools.

Linda Brown was a black child whose father tried to enroll her in a white public school in Topeka, Kansas. The white school was close to Linda's home; the walk to the black school meant that she had to cross a dangerous set of railroad tracks. Brown's request was refused because of Linda's race. A federal district court found that the black public school was, in all major respects, equal in quality to the white school; therefore, according to the *Plessy* doctrine, Linda was required to go to the black public school. Brown appealed the decision.

Brown v. *Board of Education* reached the Supreme Court in late 1951. The justices delayed argument on the sensitive case until after the 1952 national election. *Brown* was merged with four similar cases into a class action, a device for combining the claims or defenses of similar individuals so that they can be tried in a single lawsuit (see Chapter 14). The class action was supported by the NAACP and coordinated by Thurgood Marshall, who would later become the first black justice to sit on the Supreme Court. The five cases squarely challenged the separate-but-equal doctrine. By all tangible measures (standards for teacher licensing, teacher-pupil ratios, library facilities), the two school systems in each case—one white, the other black—were equal. The issue was legal separation of the races.

On May 17, 1954, Chief Justice Earl Warren, who had only recently joined the Court, delivered a single opinion covering four of the cases. Warren spoke for a unanimous Court when he declared that "in the field of public education the doctrine of 'separate but equal' has no place. Separate educational facilities are inherently unequal,"[19] depriving the plaintiffs of the equal protection of the laws. Segregated facilities generate in black children "a feeling of inferiority . . . that may affect their hearts and minds in a way unlikely ever to be undone."[20] In short, the nation's highest court found that state-imposed public school segregation violated the equal protection clause of the Fourteenth Amendment.

A companion case to *Brown* challenged the segregation of public schools in Washington, D.C.[21] Segregation there was imposed by Congress. The equal protection clause protected citizens only against state violations; no equal protection clause restrained the national government. It was unthinkable for the Constitution to impose a lesser duty on the national government than on the states. In this case, the Court unanimously decided that the racial segregation requirement was an arbitrary deprivation of liberty without due process of law, a violation of the Fifth Amendment. In short, the concept of liberty encompassed the idea of equality.

The Court deferred implementation of the school desegregation decisions until 1955. Then, in **Brown v. Board of Education II,** it ruled that school systems must desegregate "with all deliberate speed" and assigned the task of supervising desegregation to the lower federal courts.[22]

Brown v. Board of Education II

Some states quietly complied with the *Brown* decree. Others did little to desegregate their schools. And many communities in the South defied the Court, sometimes violently. Some white business and professional people formed "white citizens' councils." The councils put economic pressure on blacks who asserted their rights, by foreclosing on their mortgages and denying them credit at local stores. Georgia and North Carolina resisted desegregation by paying tuition for white students attending private schools. Virginia and other states ordered that desegregated schools be closed.

This resistance, along with the Supreme Court's "all deliberate speed" order, placed a heavy burden on federal judges to dismantle what was the fundamental social order in many communities.[23] Gradual desegregation under *Brown* was in some cases no desegregation at all. In 1969, a unanimous Supreme Court ordered that the operation of segregated school systems must stop "at once."[24]

Two years later, the Court approved several remedies to achieve integration, including busing, racial quotas, and the pairing or grouping of noncontiguous school zones. In *Swann* v. *Charlotte-Mecklenburg County*

No More Pencils, No More Books

In 1994, 60 percent of California voters passed a referendum called Proposition 187. It bars illegal immigrants from receiving nonemergency health care, welfare, and public education. Some public school teachers (pictured here) viewed the law as another form of invidious discrimination, and protested the requirement that they report illegal immigrant students to state and national authorities. In 1999, Governor Gray Davis decided not to enforce the public education ban.

de jure segregation
Government-imposed segregation.

de facto segregation
Segregation that is not the result of government influence.

Schools, the Supreme Court affirmed the right of lower courts to order the busing of children to ensure school desegregation.[25] But these remedies applied only to **de jure segregation,** government-imposed segregation (for example, government assignment of whites to one school and blacks to another within the same community). Court-imposed remedies did not apply to **de facto segregation,** segregation that is not the result of government action (for example, racial segregation resulting from residential patterns).

The busing of schoolchildren came under heavy attack in both the North and the South. Desegregation advocates saw busing as a potential remedy in many northern cities, where schools had become segregated as white families left the cities for the suburbs. This "white flight" had left inner-city schools predominantly black and suburban schools almost all white. Public opinion strongly opposed the busing approach, and Congress sought to impose limits on busing as a remedy to segregation. In 1974, a closely divided Court ruled that lower courts could not order busing across school district boundaries unless each district had practiced racial discrimination or school district lines had been deliberately drawn to achieve racial segregation.[26] This ruling meant an end to large-scale school desegregation in metropolitan areas.

THE CIVIL RIGHTS MOVEMENT

Although the NAACP concentrated on school desegregation, it also made headway in other areas. The Supreme Court responded to NAACP efforts in the late 1940s by outlawing whites-only primary elections in the South, declaring them to be in violation of the Fifteenth Amendment. The Court also declared segregation on interstate bus routes to be unconstitutional and desegregated restaurants and hotels in the District of Columbia.

Despite these and other decisions that chipped away at existing barriers to equality, states still were denying black citizens political power, and segregation remained a fact of daily life.

Dwight D. Eisenhower, who became president in 1953, was not as concerned about civil rights as his predecessor had been. He chose to stand above the battle between the Supreme Court and those who resisted the Court's decisions. He even refused to reveal whether he agreed with the Court's decision in *Brown* v. *Board of Education.* "It makes no difference," Eisenhower declared, because "the Constitution is as the Supreme Court interprets it."[27]

Eisenhower did enforce school desegregation when the safety of schoolchildren was involved, but he appeared unwilling to do much more to advance racial equality. That goal seemed to require the political mobilization of the people—black and white—in what is now known as the **civil rights movement.**

Black churches served as the crucible of the movement. More than places of worship, they served hundreds of other functions. In black communities, the church was "a bulletin board to a people who owned no organs of communication, a credit union to those without banks, and even a kind of people's court."[28] Some of its preachers were motivated by fortune, others by saintliness. One would prove to be a modern-day Moses.

Civil Disobedience

Rosa Parks, a black woman living in Montgomery, Alabama, sounded the first call to action. That city's Jim Crow ordinances were tougher than those in other southern cities, where blacks were required to sit in the back of the bus while whites sat in the front, both races converging as the bus filled with passengers. In Montgomery, however, bus drivers had the power to define and redefine the floating line separating blacks and whites: drivers could order blacks to vacate an entire row to make room for one white or order blacks to stand even when some seats were vacant. Blacks could not walk through the white section to their seats in the back; they had to leave the bus after paying their fare and reenter through the rear.[29] In December 1955, Parks boarded a city bus on her way home from work and took an available seat in the front of the bus; she refused to give up her seat when the driver asked her to do so and was arrested and fined $10 for violating the city ordinance.

Montgomery's black community responded to Parks's arrest with a boycott of the city's bus system. A **boycott** is a refusal to do business with a company or individual as an expression of disapproval or a means of coercion. Blacks walked or carpooled or stayed at home rather than ride the city's buses. As the bus company moved close to bankruptcy and downtown merchants suffered from the loss of black business, city officials began to harass blacks, hoping to frighten them into ending the boycott. But Montgomery's black citizens now had a leader—a charismatic twenty-six-year-old Baptist minister named Martin Luther King, Jr.

King urged the people to hold out, and they did. A year after the boycott began, a federal court ruled that segregated transportation systems violated the equal protection clause of the Constitution. The boycott had proved to be an effective weapon.

civil rights movement
The mass mobilization during the 1960s that sought to gain equality of rights and opportunities for blacks in the South and to a lesser extent in the North, mainly through nonviolent unconventional means of participation. Martin Luther King, Jr., was the leading figure and symbol of the civil rights movement, but it was powered by the commitment of great numbers of people, black and white, of all sorts and stations in life.

boycott
A refusal to do business with a firm, individual, or nation as an expression of disapproval or as a means of coercion.

A Modern-Day Moses

Martin Luther King, Jr., was a Baptist minister who believed in the principles of nonviolent protest practiced by India's Mohandas ("Mahatma") Gandhi. This photograph, taken in 1963 in Baltimore, captures the crowd's affection for King, the man many thought would lead them to a new Canaan of racial equality. King, who won the Nobel Peace Prize in 1964, was assassinated in 1968 in Memphis, Tennessee.

civil disobedience
The willful but nonviolent breach of laws that are regarded as unjust.

In 1957, King helped organize the Southern Christian Leadership Conference (SCLC) to coordinate civil rights activities. King was totally committed to nonviolent action to bring racial issues into the light. To that end, he advocated **civil disobedience,** the willful but nonviolent breach of unjust laws.

One nonviolent tactic was the sit-in. On February 1, 1960, four black freshmen from North Carolina Agricultural and Technical College in Greensboro sat down at a whites-only lunch counter. They were refused service by the black waitress, who said, "Fellows like you make our race look bad." The freshmen stayed all day and promised to return the next morning to continue what they called a "sit-down protest." Other students soon joined in, rotating shifts so that no one missed classes. Within two days, eighty-five students had flocked to the lunch counter. Although abused verbally and physically, the students would not move. Finally, they were arrested. Soon people held similar sit-in demonstrations throughout the South and then in the North.[30] The Supreme Court upheld the actions of the demonstrators, although the unanimity that had characterized its earlier decisions was gone. (In this decision, three justices argued that even bigots had the right to call on the government to protect their property interests.)[31]

The Civil Rights Act of 1964

In 1961, a new administration, headed by President John F. Kennedy, came to power. At first Kennedy did not seem to be committed to civil rights. His stance changed as the movement gained momentum and as more and more whites became aware of the abuse being heaped on sit-in demonstra-

*Civil Rights Act
of 1964*

tors, freedom riders (who protested unlawful segregation on interstate bus routes), and those who were trying to help blacks register to vote in southern states. Volunteers were being jailed, beaten, and killed for advocating activities among blacks that whites took for granted.

In late 1962, President Kennedy ordered federal troops to ensure the safety of James Meredith, the first black to attend the University of Mississippi. In early 1963, Kennedy enforced the desegregation of the University of Alabama. In April 1963, television viewers were shocked to see civil rights marchers in Birmingham, Alabama, attacked with dogs, fire hoses, and cattle prods. (The idea of the Birmingham march was to provoke confrontations with white officials in an effort to compel the national government to intervene on behalf of blacks.) Finally, in June 1963, Kennedy asked Congress for legislation that would outlaw segregation in public accommodations.

Two months later, Martin Luther King, Jr., joined in a march on Washington, D.C. The organizers called the protest "A March for Jobs and Freedom," signaling the economic goals of black America. More than 250,000 people, black and white, gathered peaceably at the Lincoln Memorial to hear King speak. "I have a dream," the great preacher extemporized, "that my little children will one day live in a nation where they will not be judged by the color of their skin but by the content of their character."[32]

Congress had not yet enacted Kennedy's public accommodations bill when he was assassinated on November 22, 1963. His successor, Lyndon B. Johnson, considered civil rights his top legislative priority. Within months, Congress enacted the Civil Rights Act of 1964, which included a vital provision barring segregation in most public accommodations. This congressional action was, in part, a reaction to Kennedy's death. But it was also almost certainly a response to the brutal treatment of blacks throughout the South.

Congress had enacted civil rights laws in 1957 and 1960, but they dealt primarily with voting rights. The 1964 act was the most comprehensive legislative attempt ever to erase racial discrimination in the United States. Congress acted after the longest debate in Senate history and only after the first successful use of cloture, a procedure used to end a filibuster.

Among its many provisions, the act

Can You Explain Why...
some people would argue that the 1964 Civil Rights Act had a wider impact than *Brown* v. *Board of Education*?

- Entitled all persons to "the full and equal enjoyment" of goods, services, and privileges in places of public accommodation, without discrimination on the grounds of race, color, religion, or national origin

- Established the right to equality in employment opportunities

- Strengthened voting rights legislation

- Created the Equal Employment Opportunity Commission (EEOC) and charged it with hearing and investigating complaints of job discrimination*

- Provided that funds could be withheld from federally assisted programs administered in a discriminatory manner

* *Since 1972, the EEOC has had the power to institute legal proceedings on behalf of employees who allege that they have been victims of illegal discrimination.*

The last of these provisions had a powerful effect on school desegregation when Congress enacted the Elementary and Secondary Education Act in 1965. That act provided for billions of federal dollars for the nation's schools; the threat of losing that money spurred local school boards to formulate and implement new plans for desegregation.

The 1964 act faced an immediate constitutional challenge. Its opponents argued that the Constitution does not forbid acts of private discrimination—the position the Supreme Court itself had taken in the late nineteenth century. But this time, a unanimous Court upheld the law, declaring that acts of discrimination impose substantial burdens on interstate commerce and thus are subject to congressional control.[33] In a companion case, Ollie McClung, the owner of a small restaurant, had refused to serve blacks. McClung maintained that he had the freedom to serve whomever he wanted in his own restaurant. The justices, however, upheld the government's prohibition of McClung's racial discrimination on the ground that a substantial portion of the food served in his restaurant had moved in interstate commerce.[34] Thus, the Supreme Court vindicated the Civil Rights Act of 1964 by reason of the congressional power to regulate interstate commerce rather than on the basis of the Fourteenth Amendment. Since 1937, the Court had approved ever-widening authority to regulate state and local activities under the commerce clause. It was the most powerful basis for the exercise of congressional power in the Constitution.

President Johnson's goal was a "great society." Soon a constitutional amendment and a series of civil rights laws were in place to help him meet his goal:

- The Twenty-fourth Amendment, ratified in 1964, banned poll taxes in primary and general elections for national office.

- The Economic Opportunity Act of 1964 provided education and training to combat poverty.

- The Voting Rights Act of 1965 empowered the attorney general to send voter registration supervisors to areas in which fewer than half the eligible minority voters had been registered. This act has been credited with doubling black voter registration in the South in only five years.[35]

- The Fair Housing Act of 1968 banned discrimination in the rental and sale of most housing.

The Continuing Struggle over Civil Rights

In the decades that followed, it became clear that civil rights laws on the books do not ensure civil rights in action. In 1984, for example, the Supreme Court was called on to interpret a law forbidding sex discrimination in schools and colleges that receive financial assistance from the national government: must the entire institution comply with the regulations, or only those portions of it that receive assistance?

In *Grove City College* v. *Bell*, the Court ruled that government educational grants to students implicate the institution as a recipient of government funds; therefore, it must comply with government nondiscrimination provisions. However, only the specific department or program receiving the funds (in Grove City's case, the financial aid program), not the whole institution, was barred from discriminating.[36] Athletic departments rarely receive such government funds, so colleges had no obligation to provide equal opportunity for women in their sports programs.

The *Grove City* decision had widespread effects because three other important civil rights laws were worded similarly. The implication was that any law barring discrimination on the basis of race, sex, age, or disability would be applicable only to programs receiving federal funds, not to the entire institution. So a university laboratory that received federal research grants could not discriminate, but other departments that did not receive federal money could. The effect of *Grove City* was to frustrate enforcement of civil rights laws. In keeping with pluralist theory, civil rights and women's groups shifted their efforts to the legislative branch.

Congress reacted immediately, exercising its lawmaking power to check the law-interpreting power of the judiciary. Congress can revise national laws to counter judicial decisions; in this political chess game, the Court's move is hardly the last one. Legislators protested that the Court had misinterpreted the intent of the antidiscrimination laws, and they forged a bipartisan effort to make that intent crystal clear: if any part of an institution gets federal money, no part of it can discriminate. Their work led to the Civil Rights Restoration Act, which became law in 1988 despite a presidential veto by Ronald Reagan.

Although Congress tried to restore and expand civil rights enforcement, the Supreme Court weakened it again. The Court restricted minority contractor set-asides of state public works funds, an arrangement it had approved in 1980. (A set-aside is a purchasing or contracting provision that reserves a certain percentage of funds for minority-owned contractors.) The five-person majority held that past societal discrimination alone cannot serve as the basis for rigid quotas.[37]

Buttressed by Republican appointees, the Supreme Court continued to narrow the scope of national civil rights protections in a string of decisions that suggested the ascendancy of a new conservative majority more concerned with freedom than equality.[38] To counter the Court's changing interpretations of civil rights laws, liberals turned to Congress to restore and enlarge earlier Court decisions by writing them into law. The result was a comprehensive new civil rights bill. President George Bush vetoed a 1990 version, asserting that it would impose quotas in hiring and promotion. But a year later, after months of debate, Bush signed a similar measure. The Civil Rights Act of 1991 reversed or altered twelve Court decisions that had narrowed civil rights protections. The new law clarified and expanded earlier legislation and increased the costs to employers for intentional, illegal discrimination. Continued resentment generated by equal outcomes policies would move the battle back to the courts, however.

Racial Violence and Black Nationalism

Increased violence on the part of those who demanded their civil rights and those who refused to honor them marked the middle and late 1960s. Violence against civil rights workers was confined primarily to the South, where volunteers continued to work for desegregation and to register black voters. Among the atrocities that incensed even complacent whites were the bombing of dozens of black churches; the slaying of three young civil rights workers in Philadelphia, Mississippi, in 1964 by a group of whites, among them deputy sheriffs; police violence against demonstrators marching peacefully from Selma, Alabama, to Montgomery in 1965; and the assassination of Martin Luther King, Jr., in Memphis in 1968.

Black violence took the form of rioting in northern inner cities. Civil rights gains had come mainly in the South. Northern blacks had the vote and were not subject to Jim Crow laws, yet most lived in poverty. Unemployment was high, opportunities for skilled jobs were limited, and earnings were low. The segregation of blacks into the inner cities, although not sanctioned by law, was nevertheless real; their voting power was minimal because they constituted a small minority of the northern population. The solid gains made by southern blacks added to their frustration. Beginning in 1964, northern blacks took to the streets, burning and looting. Riots in 168 cities and towns followed King's assassination in 1968, and many were met with violent responses from urban police forces and the National Guard.

The lack of progress toward equality for northern blacks was an important factor in the rise of the black nationalist movement in the 1960s. The Nation of Islam, or Black Muslims, called for separation from whites rather than integration and for violence in return for violence. Malcolm X was their leading voice, until he distanced himself from the Muslims shortly before his assassination by fellow Muslims in 1965. The militant Black Panther party generated fear with its denunciation of the values of white America. In 1966, Stokely Carmichael, then chairman of the Student Nonviolent Coordinating Committee (SNCC), called on blacks to assert "We want black power" in their struggle for civil rights. Organizations that had espoused integration and nonviolence now argued that blacks needed power more than white friendship.

The movement had several positive effects. Black nationalism instilled and promoted pride in black history and black culture. By the end of the decade, U.S. colleges and universities were beginning to institute black studies programs. More black citizens were voting than ever before, and their voting power was evident: increasing numbers of blacks were winning election to public office. In 1967, Cleveland's voters elected Carl Stokes, the first black mayor of a major American city. And by 1969, black representatives were able to form the Congressional Black Caucus. These achievements were incentives for other groups that also faced barriers to equality.

CIVIL RIGHTS FOR OTHER MINORITIES	

CIVIL RIGHTS FOR OTHER MINORITIES

Recent civil rights laws and court decisions protect members of all minority groups. The Supreme Court underscored the breadth of this protection in an important decision in 1987.[39] The justices ruled unanimously that the Civil Rights Act of 1866 (known today as Section 1981) offers broad protection against discrimination to all minorities. Previously, members of white ethnic groups could not invoke the law in bias suits. Under the 1987 decision, members of any ethnic group—Italian, Iranian, Chinese, Norwegian, or Vietnamese, for example—can recover money damages if they prove they have been denied a job, excluded from rental housing, or subjected to another form of discrimination prohibited by the law. The 1964 Civil Rights Act offers similar protections but specifies strict procedures for filing suits that tend to discourage litigation. Moreover, the remedies in most cases are limited. In job discrimination, for example, back pay and reinstatement are the only remedies. Section

1981 has fewer hurdles and allows litigants to seek punitive damages (damages awarded by a court as additional punishment for a serious wrong). In some respects, then, the older law is a more potent weapon than the newer one in fighting discrimination.

Clearly, the civil rights movement has had an effect on all minorities. However, the United States has granted equality most slowly to nonwhite minorities. Here we examine the civil rights struggles of four groups—Native Americans, Hispanic Americans, the disabled, and homosexuals.

Native Americans

During the eighteenth and nineteenth centuries, the U.S. government took Indian lands, isolated Native Americans on reservations, and denied them political and social rights. The government's dealings with the Indians were often marked by violence and broken promises. The agencies responsible for administering Indian reservations kept Native Americans poor and dependent on the national government.

The national government switched policies at the beginning of the twentieth century, promoting assimilation instead of separation. The government banned the use of native languages and religious rituals; it sent Indian children to boarding schools and gave them non-Indian names. In 1924, Indians received U.S. citizenship. Until that time, they had been considered members of tribal nations whose relations with the U.S. government were determined by treaties. The Native American population suffered badly during the Depression, primarily because the poorest Americans were affected most severely but also because of the inept administration of Indian reservations. (Today, Indians make up less than 1 percent of the population.) Poverty persisted on the reservations well after the Depression was over, and Indian land holdings continued to shrink through the 1950s and into the 1960s—despite signed treaties and the religious significance of portions of the lands they lost. In the 1960s, for example, a part of the Hopi Sacred Circle, which is considered the source of all life in the Hopi tribal religion, was strip-mined for coal.

Anger bred of poverty, unemployment, and frustration with an uncaring government exploded in militant action in late 1969, when several American Indians seized Alcatraz Island, an abandoned island in San Francisco Bay. The group cited an 1868 Sioux treaty that entitled them to unused federal lands; they remained on the island for a year and a half. In 1973, armed members of the American Indian Movement seized eleven hostages at Wounded Knee, South Dakota, the site of an 1890 massacre of 200 Sioux (Lakota) by U.S. cavalry troops. They remained there, occasionally exchanging gunfire with federal marshals, for seventy-one days, until the government agreed to examine the treaty rights of the Oglala Sioux.[40]

In 1946, Congress enacted legislation establishing an Indian claims commission to compensate Native Americans for land that had been taken from them. In the 1970s, the Native American Rights Fund and other groups used that legislation to win important victories in the courts. The tribes won the return of lands in the Midwest and in the states of Oklahoma, New Mexico, and Washington. In 1980, the Supreme Court ordered the national government to pay the Sioux $117 million plus interest for the Black Hills of South Dakota, which had been stolen from them a century before. Other cases, involving land from coast to coast, are still pending.

The special status accorded Indian tribes in the Constitution has proved attractive to a new breed of Indian leaders. As we discussed in Chapter 4, some of the 557 recognized tribes have successfully instituted casino gambling on their reservations, even in the face of state opposition to their plans. The tribes pay no taxes on their profits, which has helped them make gambling a powerful engine of economic growth for themselves and has given a once impoverished people undreamed-of riches and responsibilities. Congress has allowed these developments, provided that the tribes spend their profits on Indian assistance programs.

It is important to remember that throughout American history, Native Americans have been coerced physically and pressured economically to assimilate into the mainstream of white society. The destiny of Native Americans as viable groups with separate identities depends in no small measure on curbing their dependence on the national government.[41] The wealth created by casino gambling and other ventures funded with gambling profits may prove to be Native Americans' most effective weapon for regaining their heritage.

Hispanic Americans

Many Hispanic Americans have a rich and deep-rooted heritage in America, but until the 1920s that heritage was largely confined to the southwestern states, particularly California. Then, unprecedented numbers of Mexican and Puerto Rican immigrants came to the United States in search of employment and a better life. Business people who saw in them a source of cheap labor welcomed them. Many Mexicans became farm workers, but both groups settled mainly in crowded, low-rent, inner-city districts: the Mexicans in the Southwest, the Puerto Ricans primarily in New York City. Both groups formed their own barrios, or neighborhoods, within the cities, where they maintained the customs and values of their homelands.

Like blacks who had migrated to northern cities, most new Latino immigrants found poverty and discrimination. And, like poor blacks and Native Americans, they suffered disproportionately during the Depression. About one-third of the Mexican American population (mainly those who had been migratory farm workers) returned to Mexico during the 1930s.

World War II gave rise to another influx of Mexicans, who this time were primarily courted to work farms in California. But by the late 1950s, most farm workers—blacks, whites, and Hispanics—were living in poverty. Those Hispanic Americans who lived in cities fared little better. Yet millions of Mexicans continued to cross the border into the United States, both legally and illegally. The effect was to depress wages for farm labor in California and the Southwest.

In 1965, Cesar Chávez led a strike of the United Farm Workers union against growers in California. The strike lasted several years and eventually, in combination with a national boycott, resulted in somewhat better pay, working conditions, and housing for farm workers.

In the 1970s and 1980s, the Hispanic American population continued to grow. The 20 million Hispanics living in the United States in the 1970s were still mainly Puerto Rican and Mexican American, but they were joined by immigrants from the Dominican Republic, Colombia, Cuba, and Ecuador. Although civil rights legislation helped them to an extent, they were among the poorest and least educated groups in the United States. Their problems were similar to those faced by other non-whites, but most also had to overcome the further difficulty of learning and using a new language.

One effect of the language barrier is that voter registration and voter turnout among Latinos are lower than among other groups. The creation of nine Hispanic-majority congressional districts ensured a measure of representation. These majority minority districts remain under scrutiny as a result of Supreme Court decisions prohibiting race-based districting (see Chapter 11). Also, voter turnout depends on effective political advertising, and Hispanics are not targeted as often as other groups with political messages that they can understand. But despite these stumbling blocks, Latinos have started to exercise a measure of political power.

Hispanics occupy positions of power in national and local arenas. Hispanics or Latinos constitute 9 percent of the population and 4 percent of Congress. The 107th Congress (2001 to 2003) convened with a diverse group of nineteen Hispanic House members (sixteen Democrats and three Republicans). The National Hispanic Caucus of State Legislators, which has 250 members, is an informal bipartisan group dedicated to voicing and advancing issues affecting Hispanic Americans. The group's president, Ephraín González, Jr. (D.-NY), has observed that "We're coming together [in Washington, D.C.] to work in a more united fashion. We've got 435 representatives, 100 senators and more than 3,000 staff members we have to educate about our communities' needs."[42]

Disabled Americans

Americans with Disabilities Act of 1990, Sections 101, 102, 301, and 304

Minority status is not confined to racial and ethnic groups. After more than two decades of struggle, 43 million disabled Americans gained recognition in 1990 as a protected minority with the enactment of the Americans with Disabilities Act (ADA).

The law extends the protections embodied in the Civil Rights Act of 1964 to people with physical or mental disabilities, including people with AIDS, recovering alcoholics, and drug abusers. It guarantees them access to employment, transportation, public accommodations, and communication services.

The roots of the disabled rights movement stem from the period after World War II. Thousands of disabled veterans returned to a country and a society that were insensitive to their needs. Institutionalization seemed the best way to care for the disabled, but this approach came under increasing fire as the disabled and their families sought care at home.

Advocates for the disabled found a ready model in the existing civil rights laws. Opponents argued that the changes mandated by the 1990 law (such as access for those confined to wheelchairs) could cost billions of dollars, but supporters replied that the costs would be offset by an equal or greater reduction in federal aid to disabled people, who would rather be working.

The law's enactment set off an avalanche of job discrimination complaints filed with the national government's discrimination watchdog agency, the EEOC. By 1999, the EEOC had received almost 126,000 ADA-related complaints. Curiously, most complaints came from already employed people, both previously and recently disabled. They charged that their employers failed to provide reasonable accommodations as required by the new law. The disabilities cited most frequently were back problems, mental illness, heart trouble, neurological disorders, and substance abuse.

A deceptively simple question lies at the heart of many ADA suits: what is the meaning of *disability*? The deliberately vague language of the statute has thrust the courts into the role of providing needed specificity, a path that politicians have feared to tread.[43]

A change in the nation's laws, no matter how welcome, does not ensure a change in people's attitudes. Laws that end racial discrimination do not extinguish racism, and laws that ban biased treatment of the disabled cannot mandate their acceptance. But civil rights advocates predict that bias against the disabled, like similar biases against other minorities, will wither as the disabled become full participants in society.

Homosexual Americans

June 27, 1969, marked the beginning of an often overlooked movement for civil rights in the United States. On that Friday evening, plainclothes officers of the New York City police force raided a gay bar in Greenwich Village known as the Stonewall Inn. The police justified the raid because of their suspicions that Stonewall had been operating without a proper liquor license. In response, hundreds of citizens took to the streets in protest. Violent clashes and a backlash against the police involving hundreds of people ensued for several nights, during which cries of "Gay power!" and "We want freedom!" could be heard. The event became known as the Stonewall Riots and served as the touchstone for the gay liberation movement in the United States.[44]

Stonewall led to the creation of several political interest groups that have fought for the civil liberties and civil rights of members of the gay and lesbian communities. One in particular, the National Gay and Lesbian Task Force (NGLTF), successfully lobbied the U.S. Civil Service Commission in 1973 to allow gay people to serve in public employment. More recently, in 1999, the NGLTF founded the Legislative Lawyering Project, designed to work for progressive legislation at both the federal and state levels. Another organization, the Human Rights Campaign, founded in 1980, today boasts a membership of over 360,000. One of its current priorities is to seek passage of an employment nondiscrimination act to prevent U.S. citizens from being fired from their jobs for being perceived as gay.

Although once viewed as being on the fringe of American society, the gay community today maintains a significant presence in national politics. Now three openly gay members serve in the U.S. Congress: Representative Barney Frank of Massachusetts and Representative Tammy Baldwin of Wisconsin, both Democrats, and Representative Jim Kolbe of Arizona, a Republican. Even though they have encountered strong resistance from conservatives, members of the Log Cabin Republicans, the nation's largest gay and lesbian Republican organization, helped to muster over 1 million votes for George W.

"On my honor, I will do my best . . ."

The Boy Scout oath calls for duty to God and country, a commitment to help other people, and a vow to keep physically strong, mentally awake, and morally straight. This proved James Dale's undoing. Dale was a distinguished Eagle Scout (Dale is pictured on the left with his Eagle Scout mentor). He was serving as an assistant scoutmaster for a troop in Matawan, New Jersey, when the Scout leadership fired him after learning he was gay. Dale sued the Scouts and won in state court but lost in the U.S. Supreme Court in 2000.

Bush in the 2000 election; exit polls indicated that this represented roughly one-quarter of the gay and lesbian vote nationwide.[45]

Gays and lesbians have made significant progress since the early 1970s, but they still have a long way to go to enjoy the complete menu of civil rights now written into laws that protect other minority groups. In addition to some of the civil liberties concerns noted in Chapter 15, gays and lesbians are still unable to serve openly in the U.S. military, despite attempts by the Clinton administration to improve conditions through its "don't ask, don't tell" policy, which some observers maintain has actually made things worse for homosexuals in uniform. Because domestic partner benefits are not recognized uniformly across the United States, same-sex partners are unable to take full advantage of laws that allow citizens to leave their personal estates to family members. And finally, they often cannot sign onto their partner's health-care plans (except when company policies allow it); heterosexual couples enjoy this employment benefit almost without exception.

The 2000 Supreme Court decision, ***Boy Scouts of America* v. *Dale***, illustrated both the continuing legal struggles of gays and lesbians for civil rights and the modern conflict between freedom and equality. James Dale began his involvement in scouting in 1978 and ten years later achieved the esteemed rank of Eagle Scout. In 1989, he applied to and was accepted for the position of assistant scoutmaster of Troop 73 in New Jersey. Shortly thereafter, in 1990, the Boy Scouts revoked Dale's membership in the organization when it learned that he had become a campus activist with the Rutgers University Lesbian/Gay Alliance. The Boy Scouts argued that because homosexual conduct was inconsistent with its mission, the organization enjoyed the right to revoke his membership. Dale argued that the Scouts' actions violated a New Jersey law that prohibited discrimination on the basis of sexual orientation in places of public accommodation. The Court resolved this conflict in a narrow 5–4 decision and sided with the Scouts. The majority opinion, authored by Chief Justice William H. Rehnquist, maintained that New Jersey's public accommodations law violated the Boy Scouts' freedom of association, outweighing Dale's claim for equal treatment. The dissenters, led by Justice John Paul Stevens, maintained that equal treatment outweighed free association. They reasoned that allowing Dale to serve as an assistant scoutmaster did not impose serious burdens on the Scouts or force the organization "to communicate any message that it does not wish to endorse."[46]

GENDER AND EQUAL RIGHTS: THE WOMEN'S MOVEMENT

Together with unconventional political activities such as protests and sit-ins, conventional political tools such as the ballot box and the lawsuit have brought minorities in America a measure of equality. The Supreme Court—once responsible for perpetuating inequality for blacks—has expanded the array of legal tools available to all minorities to help them achieve social equality. Women, too, have benefited from this change.

Protectionism

protectionism
The notion that women must be protected from life's cruelties; until the 1970s, the basis for laws affecting women's civil rights.

Until the early 1970s, laws that affected the civil rights of women were based on traditional views of the relationship between men and women. At the heart of these laws was **protectionism**—the notion that women must be sheltered from life's harsh realities. Thomas Jefferson, author of the Declaration of Independence, believed that "were our state a pure democracy there would still be excluded from our deliberations women, who, to prevent deprivation of morals and ambiguity of issues, should not mix promiscuously in gatherings of men."[47] And "protected" they were, through laws that discriminated against them in employment and other areas. With few exceptions, women were also "protected" from voting until early in the twentieth century.

The demand for women's rights arose from the abolition movement and later was based primarily on the Fourteenth Amendment's prohibition of laws that "abridge the privileges or immunities of citizens of the United States." However, the courts consistently rebuffed challenges to protectionist state laws. In 1873, the Supreme Court upheld an Illinois statute that prohibited women from practicing law. The justices maintained that the Fourteenth Amendment had no bearing on a state's authority to regulate admission of members to the bar. In a concurring opinion, Justice Joseph P. Bradley articulated the common protectionist belief that women were unfit for certain occupations: "Man is, or should be, woman's protector and defender. The natural and proper timidity and delicacy which belongs to the female sex evidently unfits it for many of the occupations of civil life."[48]

Protectionism reached a peak in 1908, when the Court upheld an Oregon law limiting the number of hours women could work.[49] The decision was rife with assumptions about the nature and role of women, and it gave wide latitude to laws that "protected" the "weaker sex." It also led to protectionist legislation that barred women from working more than forty-eight hours a week and from working at jobs that required them to lift more than thirty-five pounds. (The average work week for men was sixty hours or longer.) In effect, women were locked out of jobs that called for substantial overtime (and overtime pay); instead, they were shunted to jobs that men believed suited their abilities.

Protectionism can take many forms. Some employers hesitate to place women at risk in the workplace. Some have excluded women capable of bearing children from jobs that involve exposure to toxic substances that could harm a developing fetus. Usually, such jobs offer more pay to compensate for their higher risk. Although they too face reproductive risks from toxic substances, men have faced no such exclusions.

In 1991, the Supreme Court struck down a company's fetal protection policy in strong terms. The Court relied on amendments to the 1964 Civil Rights Act providing for only a very few, narrow exceptions to the principle that, unless some workers differ from others in their ability to work, they must be treated the same as other employees. "In other words," declared the majority, "women as capable of doing their jobs as their male counterparts may not be forced to choose between having a child and having a job."[50]

Political Equality for Women

With a few exceptions, women were not allowed to vote in this country until 1920. In 1869, Francis and Virginia Minor sued a St. Louis, Missouri, registrar for not allowing Virginia Minor to vote. In 1875, the Supreme Court held that the Fourteenth Amendment's privileges and immunities clause did not confer the right to vote on all citizens or require that the states allow women to vote.[51]

The decision clearly slowed the movement toward women's suffrage, but it did not stop it. In 1878, Susan B. Anthony, a women's rights activist, convinced a U.S. senator from California to introduce a constitutional amendment requiring that "the right of citizens of the United States to vote shall not be denied or abridged by the United States or by any State on account of sex." The amendment was introduced and voted down several times over the next twenty years. Meanwhile, as noted in Chapter 7, a number of states—primarily in the Midwest and West—did grant limited suffrage to women.

The movement for women's suffrage became a political battle to amend the Constitution. In 1917, police arrested 218 women from twenty-six states when they picketed the White House, demanding the right to vote. Nearly one hundred went to jail, some for days, others for months. Hunger strikes and forced feedings followed. The movement culminated in the adoption in 1920 of the **Nineteenth Amendment,** which gave women the right to vote. Its wording was that first suggested by Anthony.

Meanwhile, the Supreme Court continued to act as the benevolent protector of women. Women entered the work force in significant numbers during World War I and did so again during World War II, but they received lower wages than the men they replaced. Again, the justification was the "proper" role of women as mothers and homemakers. Because society expected men to be the principal providers, it followed that women's

Can You Explain Why...
some women in the United States were able to vote many years before the adoption of the Nineteenth Amendment in 1920?

Woman Suffrage Before 1920

Nineteenth Amendment
The amendment to the Constitution, adopted in 1920, that assures women of the right to vote.

earnings were less important to the family's support. This thinking perpetuated inequalities in the workplace. Economic equality was closely tied to social attitudes. Because society expected women to stay at home, the assumption was that they needed less education than men did. Therefore, they tended to qualify only for low-paying, low-skilled jobs with little chance for advancement.

Prohibiting Sex-Based Discrimination

The movement to provide equal rights to women advanced a step with the passage of the Equal Pay Act of 1963. That act required equal pay for men and women doing similar work. However, state protectionist laws still had the effect of restricting women to jobs that men usually did not want. Where employment was stratified by sex, equal pay was an empty promise. To remove the restrictions of protectionism, women needed equal opportunity for employment. They got it in the Civil Rights Act of 1964 and later legislation.

The objective of the Civil Rights Act of 1964 was to eliminate racial discrimination in America. The original wording of Title VII of the act prohibited employment discrimination based on race, color, religion, and national origin—but not gender. In an effort to scuttle the provision during House debate, Democrat Howard W. Smith of Virginia proposed an amendment barring job discrimination based on sex. Smith's intention was to make the law unacceptable; his effort to ridicule the law brought gales of laughter to the debate. But Democrat Martha W. Griffiths of Michigan used Smith's strategy against him. With her support, Smith's amendment carried, as did the act.[52] Congress extended the jurisdiction of the EEOC to cover cases of invidious sex discrimination, or **sexism.**

sexism
Invidious sex discrimination.

Presidential authority also played a crucial role in the effort to eliminate sexism. In 1965, President Johnson issued an executive order that required federal contractors to take affirmative action in hiring and employment and to practice nondiscrimination with regard to race, color, religion, and national origin. Three years later, he amended the order to include gender as well. The result was new opportunity for women.

Subsequent women's rights legislation was motivated by the pressure for civil rights, as well as by a resurgence of the women's movement, which had subsided in 1920 after the adoption of the Nineteenth Amendment. One particularly important law was Title IX of the Education Amendments of 1972, which prohibited sex discrimination in federally aided education programs. Another boost to women came from the Revenue Act of 1972, which provided tax credits for child care expenses. In effect, the act subsidized parents with young children so that women could enter or remain in the work force. However, the high-water mark in the effort to secure women's rights was the Equal Rights Amendment, as we shall explain shortly.

Stereotypes Under Scrutiny

After nearly a century of protectionism, the Supreme Court began to take a closer look at gender-based distinctions. In 1971, it struck down a state law that gave men preference over women in administering the estate of a person who died without naming an administrator.[53] The state maintained that the law reduced court workloads and avoided family battles; however, the Court dismissed those objections, because they were not important enough to justify making gender-based distinctions between individuals. Two years later, the justices declared that paternalism operated to "put women not on a pedestal, but in a cage."[54] They then proceeded to strike down several laws that either prevented or discouraged departures from "proper" sex roles. In 1976, the Court finally developed a workable standard for reviewing such laws: gender-based distinctions are justifiable only if they serve some important government purpose.[55]

The objective of the standard is to dismantle laws based on sexual stereotypes while fashioning public policies that acknowledge relevant differences between men and women. Perhaps the most controversial issue is the idea of "comparable worth," which requires employers to pay comparable wages for different jobs, filled predominantly by one sex or the other, that are of about the same worth to the employer. Absent new legislation, the courts remain reluctant and ineffective vehicles for ending wage discrimination.[56]

The courts have not been reluctant to extend to women the *constitutional* guarantees won by blacks. In 1994, the Supreme Court extended the Constitution's equal protection guarantee by forbidding the exclusion of potential jurors on the basis of their sex. In a 6–3 decision, the justices held that it is unconstitutional to use gender, and likewise race, as a criterion for determining juror competence and impartiality. "Discrimination in jury selection," wrote Justice Harry A. Blackmun for the majority, "whether based on race or on gender, causes harm to the litigants, the community, and the individual jurors who are wrongfully excluded from participation in the judicial process."[57] The 1994 decision completed a constitutional revolution in jury selection that began in 1986 with a bar against juror exclusions based on race.

In 1996, the Court spoke with uncommon clarity when it declared that the men-only admissions policy of the Virginia Military Institute (VMI), a state-supported military college, violated the equal protection clause of the Fourteenth Amendment. Virginia defended the school's policy on the ground that it was preserving diversity among America's educational institutions.

In an effort to meet women's demands to enter VMI—and to stave off continued legal challenges—Virginia established a separate-but-equal institution called the Virginia Women's Institute for Leadership (VWIL). The program was housed at Mary Baldwin College, a private liberal arts college for women, and students enrolled in VWIL received the same financial support as students at VMI.

The presence of women at VMI would require substantial changes in the physical environment and the traditional close scrutiny of the students. Moreover, the presence of women would, in itself, alter the manner in which cadets interacted socially. Was the uniqueness of VMI worth preserving at the expense of women who could otherwise meet the academic, physical, and psychological stress imposed by the VMI approach?

In a 7–1 decision, the High Court voted no. Writing for a six-member majority in **United States v. Virginia,** Justice Ruth Bader Ginsburg applied a demanding test she labeled "skeptical scrutiny" to official acts that deny individuals rights or responsibilities based on their sex. "Parties who seek to defend gender-based government action," she wrote, "must demonstrate an 'exceedingly persuasive justification' for that action." Ginsburg declared that "women seeking and fit for a VMI-quality education cannot be offered anything less, under the State's obligation to afford them genuinely equal protection." Ginsburg went on to note that the VWIL program offered no cure for the "opportunities and advantages withheld from women who want a VMI education and can make the grade."[58] The upshot is that distinctions based on sex are almost as suspect as distinctions based on race.

Three months after the Court's decision, VMI's board of directors finally voted 9–8 to admit women. This ended VMI's distinction as the last government-supported single-sex school. However, school officials made few allowances for women. Buzz haircuts and fitness requirements remained the standard for all students. "It would be demeaning to women to cut them slack," declared VMI's superintendent.[59]

The Equal Rights Amendment

Equal Rights Amendment (ERA)
A failed constitutional amendment first introduced by the National Women's Party in 1923, declaring that "equality of rights under the law shall not be denied or abridged by the United States or any State on account of sex."

Policies protecting women, based largely on gender stereotypes, have been woven into the legal fabric of American life. This protectionism has limited the freedom of women to compete with men socially and economically on an equal footing. However, the Supreme Court has been hesitant to extend the principles of the Fourteenth Amendment beyond issues of race. When judicial interpretation of the Constitution imposes a limit, then only a constitutional amendment can overcome it.

The National Women's Party, one of the few women's groups that did not disband after the Nineteenth Amendment was enacted, first introduced the proposed **Equal Rights Amendment (ERA)** in 1923. The ERA declared that "equality of rights under the law shall not be denied or abridged by the United States or any State on account of sex." It remained bottled up in committee in every Congress until 1970, when Representative Martha Griffiths filed a discharge petition to bring it to the House floor for a vote. The House passed the ERA, but the Senate scuttled it by attaching a section calling for prayer in the public schools.

A national coalition of women's rights advocates generated enough support to get the ERA through Congress in 1972. Its proponents then had seven years to get the amendment ratified by thirty-eight state legislatures, as required by the Constitution. By 1977, they were three states short of that goal, and three states had rescinded their earlier ratification. Then, in an unprecedented action, Congress extended the ratification deadline. It didn't help. The ERA died in 1982, still three states short of adoption.

Why did the ERA fail? There are several explanations. Its proponents mounted a national campaign to generate approval, while its opponents organized state-based anti-ERA campaigns. ERA proponents hurt their cause by exaggerating the amendment's effects; such claims only gave ammunition to the amendment's opponents. For example, the puffed-up claim that the amendment would make wife and husband equally responsible for their family's financial support caused alarm among the undecided. As the opposition grew stronger, especially from women who wanted to maintain their traditional role, state legislators began to realize that supporting the amendment involved risk. Given the exaggerations and counterexaggerations, lawmakers ducked. Because it takes an extraordinary majority to amend the Constitution, it takes only a committed minority to thwart the majority's will.

Despite its failure, the movement to ratify the ERA produced real benefits. It raised the consciousness of women about their social position, spurred the formation of the National Organization for Women (NOW) and other large organizations, contributed to women's participation in politics, and generated important legislation affecting women.[60]

The failure to ratify the ERA stands in stark contrast to the quick enactment of many laws that now protect women's rights. Such legislation had little audible opposition. If years of racial discrimination called for government redress, then so did years of gender-based discrimination. Furthermore, laws protecting women's rights required only the amending of civil rights bills or the enactment of similar bills.

Some scholars argue that, for practical purposes, the Supreme Court has implemented the equivalent of the ERA through its decisions. It has struck down distinctions based on sex and held that stereotyped generalizations about sexual differences must fall.[61] In recent rulings, the Court has held that states may require employers to guarantee job reinstatement to women who take maternity leave, that sexual harassment in the workplace is illegal, and that the existence of a hostile work environment may be demonstrated by a reasonable perception of abuse rather than by proven psychological injury.[62]

But the Supreme Court can reverse its decisions, and legislators can repeal statutes. Without an equal rights amendment, argue some feminists, the Constitution will continue to bear the sexist imprint of a document written by men for men. Until the ERA becomes part of the Constitution, said veteran feminist Betty Friedan, "We are at the mercy of a Supreme Court that will interpret equality as it sees fit."[63]

AFFIRMATIVE ACTION: EQUAL OPPORTUNITY OR EQUAL OUTCOME?

affirmative action
Any of a wide range of programs, from special recruitment efforts to numerical quotas, aimed at expanding opportunities for women and minority groups.

In his vision of a Great Society, President Johnson linked economic rights with civil rights and equality of outcome with equality of opportunity. "Equal opportunity is essential, but not enough," he declared. "We seek not just legal equity but human ability, not just equality as a right and a theory but equality as a fact and equality as a result."[64] This commitment led to affirmative action programs to expand opportunities for women, minorities, and the disabled.

Affirmative action is a commitment by a business, employer, school, or other public or private institution to expand opportunities for women, blacks, Hispanic Americans, and members of other minority groups. Affirmative action aims to overcome the effects of present and past discrimination. It embraces a range of public and private programs, policies, and procedures, including special recruitment, preferential treatment, and quotas in job training and professional education, employment, and the awarding of government contracts. The point of these programs is to move beyond equality of opportunity to equality of outcome.

Establishing numerical goals (such as designating a specific number of places in a law school for minority candidates or specifying that 10 percent of the work on a government contract must be subcontracted to minority-owned companies) is the most aggressive form of affirmative action, and it generates more debate and opposition than any other aspect of the civil

Civil Rights Groups Dodge Teacher's Bullet

Sharon Taxman, a Piscataway, New Jersey, high school teacher, sued her school board in 1989 when, in a downsizing choice between two equally qualified teachers, it invoked "diversity" as the reason to lay her off in favor of a black teacher. The lower courts sided with Taxman but the school board, supported by the Clinton administration, appealed to the Supreme Court, which granted review. Fearing a precedent-setting judgment that would further curtail the use of racial preferences, the Black Leadership Forum—a hastily devised coalition of twenty-one black civic, fraternal, and civil rights groups— pitched in with a generous financial settlement in late 1997, offering Taxman an inflation-adjusted deal she could not refuse.

rights movement. Advocates claim that such goal setting for college admissions, training programs, employment, and contracts will move minorities, women, and the disabled out of their second-class status. President Johnson explained why aggressive affirmative action was necessary:

> You do not take a person who for years has been hobbled by chains, liberate him, bring him up to the starting line of a race, and then say, "You are free to compete with all the others," and still justly believe that you have been completely fair. Thus, it is not enough just to open the gates of opportunity; all our citizens must have the ability to walk through those gates.[65]

Arguments for affirmative action programs (from increased recruitment efforts to quotas) tend to use the following reasoning: certain groups have historically suffered invidious discrimination, denying them educational and economic opportunities. To eliminate the lasting effects of such discrimination, the public and private sectors must take steps to provide access to good education and jobs. If the majority once discriminated to hold groups back, discriminating to benefit those groups is fair. Therefore, quotas are a legitimate means to provide a place on the ladder to success.[66]

Affirmative action opponents maintain that quotas for designated groups necessarily create invidious discrimination (in the form of reverse discrimination) against individuals who are themselves blameless. Moreover, they say, quotas lead to admission, hiring, or promotion of the less qualified at the expense of the well qualified. In the name of equality, such policies thwart individuals' freedom to succeed.

Government-mandated preferential policies probably began in 1965 with the creation of the Office of Federal Contract Compliance. Its purpose was to ensure that all private enterprises doing business with the federal government complied with nondiscrimination guidelines. Because so many companies do business with the federal government, a large portion of the American economy became subject to these guidelines. In

1968, the guidelines required "goals and timetables for the prompt achievement of full and equal employment opportunity." By 1971, they called for employers to eliminate "underutilization" of minorities and women, which meant that employers had to hire minorities and women in proportion to the government's assessment of their availability.[67]

Preferential policies are seldom explicitly legislated. More often, such policies are the result of administrative regulations, judicial rulings, and initiatives in the private sector to provide a remedial response to specific discrimination or to satisfy new legal standards for proving nondiscrimination. Quotas or goals enable administrators to assess changes in hiring, promotion, and admissions policies. Racial quotas are an economic fact of life today. Employers engage in race-conscious preferential treatment to avoid litigation. Cast in value terms, equality trumps freedom. Do preferential policies in other nations offer lessons for us? See Compared with What? 16.1 to learn the answer.

Reverse Discrimination

The Supreme Court confronted an affirmative action quota program for the first time in ***Regents of the University of California v. Bakke.***[68] Allan Bakke, a thirty-five-year-old white man, had twice applied for admission to the University of California Medical School at Davis. He was rejected both times. The school had reserved sixteen places in each entering class of one hundred for qualified minority applicants, as part of the university's affirmative action program, in an effort to redress long-standing and unfair exclusion of minorities from the medical profession. Bakke's qualifications (college grade point average and test scores) exceeded those of all of the minority students admitted in the two years his applications were rejected. Bakke contended, first in the California courts, then in the Supreme Court, that he was excluded from admission solely on the basis of his race. He argued that the equal protection clause of the Fourteenth Amendment and the Civil Rights Act of 1964 prohibited this reverse discrimination.

The Court's decision in *Bakke* contained six opinions and spanned 154 pages. But even after careful analysis of the decision, discerning what the Court had decided was difficult: no opinion had a majority. One bloc of four justices opposed the medical school's plan, contending that any racial quota system endorsed by the government violated the Civil Rights Act of 1964. A second bloc of four justices supported the plan, arguing that the government may use a racial classification scheme, provided it does not demean or insult any racial group and only to remedy the disadvantages imposed on minorities by racial prejudice. Justice Lewis F. Powell, Jr., agreed with parts of both arguments. With the first bloc, he argued that the school's rigid use of racial quotas violated the equal protection clause of the Fourteenth Amendment. With the second bloc, he contended that the use of race was permissible as one of several admissions criteria. Powell cast the deciding vote ordering the medical school to admit Bakke. (He now practices medicine in Minnesota.) Despite the confusing multiple opinions, the Court signaled its approval of affirmative action programs in education that use race as a *plus* factor (one of many such factors) but not as *the* factor (one that alone determines the outcome). Thus, the Court managed to minimize white opposition to the goal of equality (by finding for Bakke) while extending gains for racial minorities through affirmative action.

16.1   How Other Nations Struggle with Affirmative Action

Americans are not alone in their disagreements over affirmative action. Controversies, even bloodshed, have arisen in other countries where certain groups of citizens are treated preferentially by the government over others. One study found several common patterns among countries that had enacted preferential policies. Although begun as temporary measures, preferential policies tended to persist and even to expand to include more groups. The policies usually sought to improve the situation of disadvantaged groups as a whole, but they often benefited the better-off members of such groups more so than the worse-off members. Finally, preferential policies tended to increase antagonisms among different groups within a country.

Of course, there were variations across countries in terms of who benefited from such policies, what types of benefits were bestowed, and even in the names the policies were given. As in the United States, preferential policies in Canada and Australia are called "affirmative action" measures. In India, however, such policies carry the label "positive discrimination." But that isn't the only way India differs from the United States when it comes to preferential policies.

Although India is the world's largest democracy, its society is rigidly stratified into groups called castes. Though the government forbade caste-based discrimination, members of the lower castes (the lowest being the "untouchables") were historically restricted to the least prestigious and lowest paying jobs. To improve their status, India has set aside government jobs for the lower castes, who make up half of India's population of 1 billion. India now reserves 27 percent of government jobs for the lower castes and an additional 23 percent for untouchables and remote tribe members. Gender equality has also improved since a 1993 constitutional amendment that set aside one-third of all seats in local government councils for women. Even the country's 15 million eunuchs, who work as prostitutes or as dancing partners or guards for Moslem

---

Although the Court sent a mixed message, *Bakke* may have achieved tangible benefits. The number of minority physicians in the United States doubled in the decade after the decision. Moreover, minority physicians tended to relocate to areas that had critical health-care shortages. They also tended to serve significantly larger proportions of poor patients, regardless of the patient's race or ethnicity.[69]

Other cases followed. In 1979, the Court upheld a voluntary affirmative action plan that gave preferences to blacks in an employee training program.[70] Five years later, however, the Court held that affirmative action did not exempt minorities (typically the most recently hired employees) from traditional work rules, which generally specify that the last hired are the first fired. Layoffs must proceed by seniority, declared the Court, unless minority employees can demonstrate that they are actually victims of discrimination.[71]

women, may soon have government jobs set aside for them. (In late 1997, activists began legal proceedings to force the government to set job quotas for eunuchs.)

Positive discrimination in India has intensified tensions between the lower and upper castes. In 1990, soon after the new quotas were established, scores of young upper-caste men and women set themselves ablaze in protest. And when Indian courts issued a temporary injunction against the positive discrimination policies, lower-caste terrorists bombed a train and killed dozens of people. Political conflict continues to this day as India's upper-caste members grow increasingly bitter about losing their once-exclusive access to well-paying government jobs in an economy that is not expanding rapidly enough to satisfy its citizenry. And today poor people who are not members of the lower castes seek in vain for government benefits as if they were lower caste themselves.

India's experience with positive discrimination has implications for majoritarian and pluralist models of democracy. All governments broker conflict to varying degrees. Under a majoritarian model, group demands could lead quickly to conflict and instability because majority rule leaves little room for compromise. A pluralist model allows different groups to get a piece of the pie. By parceling out benefits, pluralism mitigates disorder in the short term. But in the long term, repeated demands for increased benefits can spark instability. A vigorous pluralist system should provide acceptable mechanisms (legislative, executive, bureaucratic, judicial) to vent such frustrations and yield new allocations of benefits.

Sources: Trudy Rubin, "Will Democracy Survive in India?" *The Record* (New Jersey), 19 January 1998, p. A12; Alex Spillius, "India's Old Warriors to Launch Rights Fight," *The Daily Telegraph*, 20 October 1997, p. 12; Robin Wright, "World's Leaders: Men, 187, Women, 4," *Los Angeles Times*, 30 September 1997, p. A1; "Indian Eunuchs Demand Government Job Quotas," *Agence France Presse*, 22 October 1997; Juergen Hein and M.V. Balaji, "India's First Census of New Millennium Begins on February 9," *Deutsche Presse-Agentur*, 7 February 2001.

Sexism can cut both ways, against both women and men. Overcoming sexism may inadvertently create invidious discrimination against men. In 1974, the transportation agency of Santa Clara, California, promoted Diane Joyce to the position of road dispatcher over Paul Johnson. Both candidates were qualified for the job. The agency took into account the sex of the applicants in making the promotion decision. Because none of the employees at the level of dispatcher were women, the agency decided to give the job to Joyce. Johnson claimed that the agency impermissibly took into account the sex of the applicants, in violation of Title VII of the Civil Rights Act of 1964, which declares that employers cannot "limit, segregate or classify" workers and thus deprive "any individual of employment opportunities."

In a 6–3 vote, the Supreme Court affirmed the promotion procedures in 1987. Writing for the majority in ***Johnson v. Transportation Agency, Santa Clara County,*** Justice William J. Brennan, Jr., argued that in light of *Bakke* it was not unreasonable to consider sex as one factor among many in making promotion decisions. Moreover, the agency's actions did not create an absolute barrier to the advancement of men.[72]

The most crippling jolt to some forms of affirmative action came in 1995. The Supreme Court struck a sharp blow to the legal foundations of government policies that award benefits on the basis of race, signaling an end to equal outcomes policies. The issue was the constitutionality of set-aside programs using federal highway funds for minority contractors. Was the special advantage for minority contractors a violation of equal treatment for white contractors under the Fifth Amendment? Writing for a 5–4 majority in ***Adarand Constructors* v. *Peña,*** Justice Sandra Day O'Connor declared that such programs must be subject to the most searching judicial inquiry (what the Court calls "strict scrutiny") and must be "narrowly tailored" to achieve a "compelling government interest."[73] Few, if any, programs can satisfy the Court's stringent requirements for constitutionality.

The Court sent the case back to the trial court so that it could evaluate the facts in light of the strict scrutiny approach. The trial court held the subcontractor provisions of the highway act unconstitutional. A federal appeals court reversed that decision, finding that the government had met the compelling interest and narrow tailoring standards. The matter remains in litigation. The High Court decision nevertheless casts doubt on billions of dollars in government contracts earmarked for minority- or women-owned firms.[74]

Quota policies remain under serious threat from several quarters. Relying on the *Adarand* case, a federal appeals court in 1996 rejected the use of race or ethnicity as the determining factor for admission to the University of Texas Law School.[75] (In the absence of race-based criteria, few minorities would have been admitted.) In 2000, a federal trial court in Michigan chose a different path, upholding the University of Michigan's point advantage for black and Hispanic applicants.[76] These two cases—and others—set the stage for a possible showdown in the Supreme Court.

Meanwhile, the governing board of the University of California vacillated on its race-based admissions policy. And legislative movements in more than a dozen states aim to curtail or eliminate racial preferences in educational admissions and financial aid. Colorado, for example, has begun to offer college scholarships on the basis of need rather than race.[77]

The biggest showdown to date regarding the future of affirmative action occurred during the 1996 elections. California voters were asked to approve or reject a ballot initiative to amend the state constitution as follows:

> Neither the State of California, nor any of its political subdivisions or agents, shall use race, sex, color, ethnicity or national origin as a criterion for either discriminating against, or granting preferential treatment to, any individual or group in the operation of the State's system of public employment, public education or public contracting.

Most states have agreed that ending affirmative action in college admissions would deepen social inequality by denying minority citizens access to higher education. Six states are now contemplating the abandonment of race-sensitive admissions policies, but they have discovered that the only way to enlarge the minority presence in college is to improve dramatically the public schools that most black and Latino students attend. These states are watching California, Texas, and Florida, where percentage systems have been introduced to replace affirmative action. Under these sys-

★

**Michigan Wolverines Tackle
Affirmative Action**

*The University of Michigan
has summoned a creative
defense for affirmative action,
relying on academic studies
purporting to demonstrate the
benefits of racial diversity. In
lawsuits motivated by
Michigan philosophy professor
Carl Cohen (left), plaintiffs
like Barbara Grutter (right)
are challenging the race-based
admissions preferences of
Michigan's highly ranked law
school. The University has an
uphill battle. It lost in federal
court in 2001. But it is too
soon to count the Wolverines
out. The matter is likely to be
resolved in the last quarter of
play: in the U.S. Supreme
Court.*

tems, students who achieve a specified ranking in their high school graduating classes are guaranteed admission to state colleges.[78]

Meanwhile, the Clinton administration chose to staunch its losses
rather than terminate its quota and set-aside programs. ("Mend them,
don't end them," Clinton averred.) This new approach produced a new policy in 1998. Under this plan, minority-owned firms are allowed to bid as
much as 10 percent more and still win competitive contracts. But the
firms must show that their share of federal contract business is smaller
than their share of the market for their goods and services. Surveys in
some industries, such as trucking, show that minority-owned firms receive fewer federal contracts than their share in the private sector. But in
other industries, such as food processing, these new affirmative action
rules will not apply because minority-owned businesses receive about the
same share of federal contracts as they get from the private sector.

The Politics of Affirmative Action

A comprehensive review of nationwide surveys conducted over the past
twenty years reveals an unsurprising truth: that blacks favor affirmative
action programs and whites do not. Women and men do not differ on this
issue. The gulf between the races was wider in the 1970s than it is today,
but the moderation results from shifts among blacks, not whites. Perhaps
the most important finding is that "whites' views have remained essentially unchanged over twenty-five years."[79]

★ **politics in a changing** **a m e r i c a**

16.1   Preferences, Out; Extra Effort, In

Americans are divided over affirmative action. But what is the source of this divide? Some critics of affirmative action suggest that it is rooted in objections to preferences. Some defenders of affirmative action claim that objections to the use of preferences mask deep-seated racial prejudice.

To unlock these questions, Professor James H. Kuklinski and six colleagues used a novel experiment in a 1991 national survey of white Americans' racial attitudes. The respondents were randomly divided into two groups. Respondents in each group were then asked slightly different versions of the same question:

1. Some people say that because of past discrimination, qualified blacks should be given *preference* in university admissions. Others say that this is wrong because it discriminates against whites. How do you feel—are you in favor of or opposed to giving qualified blacks preference in admission to colleges and universities?

2. Some people say that because of past discrimination, an *extra effort* should be made to make sure that qualified blacks are considered for university admissions. Others say that this is wrong because it discriminates against whites. How do you feel—are you in favor of or opposed to making an extra effort to make sure qualified blacks are considered for admission to colleges and universities?

The first question mentions *preference;* the second question substitutes *extra effort.* If whites' objections to affirmative action are rooted in a lack of concern for blacks or outright prejudice, then there should be little difference in the responses to the two different questions. Alternatively, if the element of *preference* is crucial, then responses should differ across the two questions.

The pair of bar graphs reveal that only 25 percent of white Americans favor preferential treatment, but 60 percent endorse extra effort. In other words, U.S. whites overwhelmingly reject affirmative action if it involves preferences, but a clear majority of them support going the extra mile to ensure that all blacks meriting assistance receive it.

Source: James H. Kuklinski et al., "Racial Prejudice and Attitudes Toward Affirmative Action," *American Journal of Political Science,* 41 (April 1997), pp. 402–419.

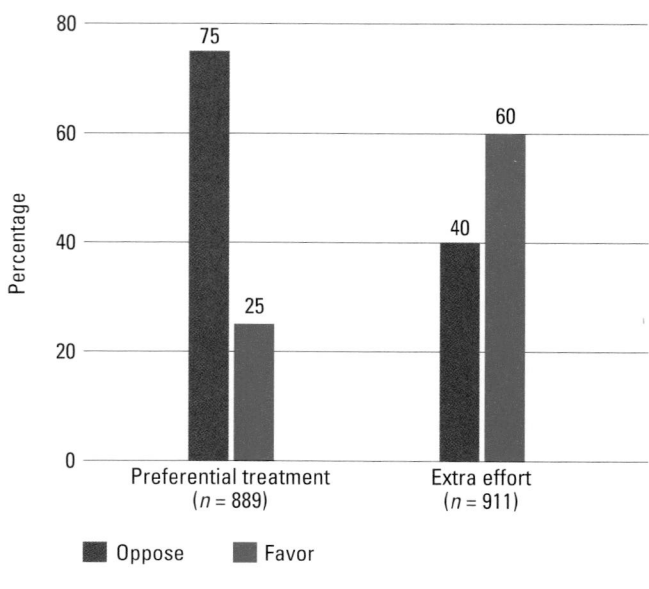

How do we account for the persistence of equal outcomes policies? A majority of Americans have consistently rejected explicit race or gender preferences for the awarding of contracts, employment decisions, and college admissions, regardless of the groups such preferences benefit. Nevertheless, preference policies have survived and thrived under both Democrats and Republicans because they are attractive. They encourage unprotected groups to strive for inclusion. The list of protected groups has expanded beyond African Americans to include Hispanic Americans, Native Americans, Asian Pacific Americans, Subcontinental Asian Americans, women, and gays. Politicians have a powerful motive—votes—to expand the number of protected groups and the benefits such policies provide.

Recall that affirmative action programs began as temporary measures, ensuring a "jump start" for minorities shackled by decades or centuries of invidious discrimination. For example, forty years ago, minority racial identity was a fatal flaw on a medical or law school application. Today it is viewed as an advantage, encouraging applicants to think in minority-group terms. Thinking in group terms and conferring benefits on such ground generates hostility from members of the majority, who see the deck stacked against them for no other reason than their race. It is not surprising that affirmative action has become controversial, since many Americans view it as a violation of their individual freedom.

Recall Lyndon Johnson's justification for equal outcomes policies. Though free to compete, a person once hobbled by chains cannot run a fair race. Americans are willing to do more than remove the chains. They will support special training and financial assistance for those who were previously shackled. The hope is that such efforts will enable once-shackled runners to catch up with those who have forged ahead. But Americans stop short at endorsing equal outcomes policies because they predetermine the results of the race.[80]

The conflict between freedom and equality will continue as other individuals and groups press their demands through litigation and legislation. The choice will depend on whether and to what extent Americans still harbor deep-seated racial prejudice. We explore this issue in Politics in a Changing America 16.1.

SUMMARY

Americans want equality, but they disagree on the extent to which government should guarantee it. At the heart of this conflict is the distinction between equal opportunities and equal outcomes. Today, its resolution has global implications.

Congress enacted the Civil War amendments—the Thirteenth, Fourteenth, and Fifteenth Amendments—to provide full civil rights to black Americans. In the late nineteenth century, however, the Supreme Court interpreted the amendments very narrowly, declaring that they did not restrain individuals from denying civil rights to blacks and that they did not apply to the states. The Court's rulings had the effect of denying the vote to most blacks and of institutionalizing racism, making racial segregation a fact of daily life.

Through a series of court cases spanning two decades, the Court slowly dismantled segregation in the schools. The battle for desegregation culminated in the *Brown* cases in 1954 and 1955, in which a now-supportive Supreme Court declared segregated schools to be inherently unequal and therefore unconstitutional. The Court also ordered the desegregation of all schools and upheld the use of busing to do so.

Gains in other spheres of civil rights came more slowly. The motivating force was the civil rights movement, led by Martin Luther King, Jr., until his assassination in 1968. King believed strongly in civil disobedience and nonviolence, strategies that helped secure for blacks equality in voting rights, public accommodations, higher education, housing, and employment opportunity.

Civil rights activism and the civil rights movement worked to the benefit of all minority groups—in fact, they benefited all Americans. Native Americans obtained some redress for past injustices. Hispanic Americans came to recognize the importance of group action to achieve economic and political equality. Disabled Americans won civil rights protections enjoyed by African Americans and others. And civil rights legislation removed the protectionism that was, in effect, legalized discrimination against women in education and employment. Homosexuals aim to follow the same path, but their quest for equality has been trumped by occasional conflicts with freedom.

Despite legislative advances in the area of women's rights, the states did not ratify the Equal Rights Amendment. Still, the struggle for ratification produced several positive results, heightening awareness of women's roles in society and mobilizing their political power. And legislation and judicial rulings implemented much of the amendment's provisions in practice. The Supreme Court now judges sex-based discrimination with "skeptical scrutiny," meaning that distinctions based on sex are almost as suspect as distinctions based on race.

Government and business instituted affirmative action programs to counteract the results of past discrimination. These provide preferential treatment for women, minorities, and the disabled in a number of areas that affect individuals' economic opportunity and well-being. In effect, such programs discriminate to remedy earlier discrimination. When programs make race the determining factor in awarding contracts, offering employment, or granting admission to educational institutions, the courts will be skeptical of their validity. Notwithstanding congressional efforts to reverse some Supreme Court decisions, a conservative majority on the Court has emerged to roll back the equality-preferring policies of the more liberal bench that held sway through the 1980s.

We can guarantee equal outcomes only if we restrict the free competition that is an integral part of equal opportunity. Many Americans object to policies that restrict individual freedom, such as quotas and set-asides that arbitrarily change the outcome of the race. The challenge of pluralist democracy is to balance the need for freedom with demands for equality.

★ Key Cases

Plessy v. *Ferguson*
Brown v. *Board of Education*
Brown v. *Board of Education II*

Boy Scouts of America v. *Dale*
United States v. *Virginia*
Regents of the University of California v. *Bakke*

Johnson v. *Transportation Agency, Santa Clara County*

Adarand Constructors v. *Peña*

★ Selected Readings

Branch, Taylor. *Parting the Waters: America in the King Years, 1954–1963*. New York: Simon & Schuster, 1988. A riveting, Pulitzer Prize–winning narrative history and biography of the King years.

Branch, Taylor. *Pillar of Fire: America in the King Years, 1963–65*. New York: Simon & Schuster, 1998. The second volume of this prize-winning narrative.

Landsberg, Brian K. *Enforcing Civil Rights: Race, Discrimination and the Department of Justice.* Lawrence: University of Kansas Press, 1997. Landsberg, who worked as an attorney in the Civil Rights Division of the Department of Justice from 1964 to 1988, provides an insider's account of the development of that office and the strategies it adopted to prosecute successfully those who violated the civil rights of black Americans.

Lyons, Oren, et al. *Exiled in the Land of the Free: Democracy, Indian Nations, and the U.S. Constitution.* Santa Fe, N.M.: Clear Light, 1992. A collection of essays exploring the relationship of Indians to the Constitution, how Indian traditions influenced the Constitution's creation, and how constitutional interpretation has affected Indian lives.

Mansbridge, Jane J. *Why We Lost the ERA*. Chicago, Ill.: University of Chicago Press, 1986. A valuable study of organizations pitted for and against the Equal Rights Amendment in Illinois.

Sniderman, Paul M., and Thomas Piazza. *The Scar of Race.* Cambridge, Mass.: Belknap Press of Harvard University Press, 1993. The authors of this insightful study argue that the problems of race cannot be reduced to racism. On many racial issues, white Americans are open to argument and persuasion, even though they disagree on racial policies.

Thernstrom, Abigail, and Stephan Thernstrom. *America in Black and White: One Nation, Indivisible*. New York: Simon & Schuster, 1997. The authors provide a political, historical, and social history of race relations in the United States over the past half-century or so, detailing the great economic and educational gains made by African Americans. They argue that most of the progress occurred before the 1960s and that reliance on preferential policies has not been important to blacks' progress.

Internet Exercises

1. *Racial Profiling*

Justice Talking is a public radio program created by the Annenberg Public Policy Center at the University of Pennsylvania and designed to examine cases and controversies that appear before the nation's courts. Recently, *Justice Talking* addressed the issue of racial profiling and considered whether it constituted overt discrimination or a legitimate tool to stop crime.

• Go to the *Justice Talking* site, **<justicetalking.org>** and follow the site's link to an index of its past shows. There you will find the program entitled "Driving While Black: Racial Profiling on America's Highways."

• Listen to these two portions of the broadcast: 0:00–2:35 and 20:00–26:15.

• How does the controversy of racial profiling illustrate the tension between the nation's interest in maintaining order and in protecting citizens' civil rights?

2. Regents of the University of California *v.* Bakke *(1978)*

Regents of the University of California v. *Bakke* (1978), also known as *Bakke,* is one of the most significant U.S. Supreme Court decisions on the question of affirmative action in university admissions. Audio of the announcement of the Court's opinion is available on the Internet from the Oyez Project's Web site.

• Go to the Oyez site at **<www.oyez.org>**, and find the Bakke decision.

• Activate the Real Audio announcement of the Court's opinion with transcript to listen to (and read along with) excerpts of the remarks from the following justices: Stevens (13:15–20:30) and Blackmun (39:45–41:15 and 44:00–50:20).

• Aside from their disagreement in the overall outcome, Stevens and Blackmun approached this case in fundamentally different ways. What was so different about how they reached their respective decisions?

17

Policymaking

★ ★ ★ ★ ★ ★ ★ ★

"HELLO DOLLY!" heralded the newspaper headlines, announcing a most unusual birth. In February 1997, Scottish scientists stunned the world with the news that they had cloned a sheep named Dolly—the first mammal ever cloned and an exact replica of its mother. While Dolly placidly munched her dinner, religious, government, and academic leaders were thrown into turmoil as they pondered the implications of potential human cloning. In a bout of speculation that seemed far better suited to an episode of *Star Trek* than to newspaper headlines, scientists predicted a human clone might be possible within seven years.

Even if a human clone could be physically produced in a laboratory, was it morally right to make a carbon copy of another human being? Thirty years ago, Joshua Lederberg, an American Nobel laureate in genetics, had broached the subject. He thought the idea was exciting, as humanity could clone its best and brightest people for all time. Also, the human genetics pool could be made predictable, with undesirable traits weeded out. Lederberg suggested other uses for human cloning as well. If a child were brain damaged in an accident, the parents could have a replacement made of their beloved offspring. Or if someone needed a bone marrow transplant to win a fight against leukemia, an identical infant could be reproduced to save the original.[1]

Critics of cloning wondered whether creating a replica of another individual is truly possible. Even if a Thomas Jefferson or a Leonardo Da Vinci were genetically reproduced, would the copy really be the same as the original? Could a Leonardo take root anywhere except in Renaissance Florence? To what extent had the flowering of Jefferson's brilliance depended on the ideas of the Enlightenment and the leisure provided by a slave economy? No one can say for sure what roles time and place, family nurturing, and education play in the making of a genius or whether genes alone are enough to create a prodigy. Although the risks to humanity may seem minimal in testing such "nature versus nurture" theories with a clone of a Mother Teresa, what is to prevent a Stalin or a Hitler from being copied?

Another concern is that the diversity of the human gene pool could be lost over time. What is popular and desirable in one era of human history may be unpopular and out of fashion in another era. Ancient China valued Mandarins, scholars who served as bureaucrats, but Nazi Germany prized blond, blue-eyed warriors. Individuals of historical renown have sometimes been more admired by later generations than by their contemporaries. Recall the fates of Socrates, Joan of Arc, and Gandhi.

Double Take

The arrival of Dolly (pictured on the left with two cloned friends), the first mammal to be cloned in a laboratory, touched off a storm of controversy about genetic engineering. Public opinion polls discovered that most Americans opposed human cloning, and even Ian Wilmut, the embryologist who had created Dolly, disliked the idea. Ideas that just a short while ago had seemed possible only in science fiction were suddenly public issues in need of resolution by government officials.

Would the best and the brightest of any generation be picked for cloning, or is it more likely that the wealthiest and most powerful would be selected? For example, can anyone really imagine the Roman Empire cloning a Christian martyr ahead of the emperor or Henry VIII preferring a duplicate of any Tudor subject to one of himself?

Additionally, human cloning could threaten the philosophical underpinnings of democracy. Americans believe that every individual is unique and possesses inalienable rights bestowed by his or her creator. Each person's distinct genetic makeup bolsters this individuality and our belief in the preciousness of a single life. Mass-producing human clones, in the eyes of University of Chicago professor Leon Kass, "is profoundly dehumanizing, no matter how good the product." Moreover, he asserts, "human equality, freedom and dignity" will be jeopardized if even one human clone is made.[2]

With Dolly's arrival, President Clinton quickly began hammering out a policy to deal with this revolutionary advance in technology. First, he issued an executive order forbidding the use of federal money for cloning research and then handed the task of debating the legal and ethical ramifications of cloning to the National Bioethics Commission. Panel chairman Harold Shapiro, president of Princeton University, thought the issues involved were remarkably difficult because they "go to the very nature of what it means to be human."[3] In response to the commission's recommendations, President Clinton appealed for a five-year moratorium on all attempts to duplicate a human life. Over 64,000 scientists agreed to honor the president's request, but in December 1997, Dr. Richard Seed stated that he would defy the voluntary ban and try to produce the first human clone. In reaction to this announcement, President Clinton declared human cloning to be an affront "to our cherished concepts of faith and humanity" and urged Congress to outlaw it in the United States.[4]

The president's remarks touched a responsive chord with the public and politicians alike, as most Americans appeared to share the president's deep distaste for cloning. According to one public opinion poll, over 90 percent of Americans would not want to clone themselves, and almost three-quarters thought human cloning violated God's will.[5] In Congress there also seemed to be growing interest in addressing this issue. Not only were members concerned about the ramifications of a full-fledged human clone, but Representative Vernon Ehlers, a Republican from Michigan, also wanted to prohibit the creation of human embryos that would briefly be used for medical research and then allowed to die. The FDA got into the act by warning Dr. Seed that his laboratory would be closed if he proceeded without the agency's permission.

While officials grappled with the issue, scientists began to wonder if their freedom to experiment was being too rigidly proscribed. The International Embryo Transfer Society, a professional organization that includes Ian Wilmut, the scientist who produced Dolly, explained that animal cloning was helping develop new herds of genetically superior farm animals and could provide animals capable of producing medicines. There are now cloned lambs that have been altered so that their milk will carry a drug.[6] The American Society for Reproductive Medicine thought scientists needed to help write the new laws because most politicians are unfamiliar with the fine points of laboratory research. In Florida, for example, a bill was introduced to make the "cloning of human DNA" a felony, but this procedure is common and would have halted the state's biomedical industry.[7] Once legislators understood the consequences of the suggested language, the bill was withdrawn.

The case of Dolly illustrates how rapid technological change can suddenly thrust a new issue onto the public agenda. Of course, many other factors can also push an issue forward: a heinous crime, the courageous determination of an individual, a miscarriage of justice, Mother Nature—the list of possibilities is more or less endless. How do policy issues arise, and what happens to them once they catch the public's attention? Previous chapters have focused on individual institutions of government. Here we focus on government more broadly and ask how policymaking takes place across institutions. We first identify different types of public policies and then analyze the stages in the policymaking process. Because different institutions and different levels of government (national, state, and local) frequently work on the same issues, policymaking is often fragmented. How can better coordination be achieved? We then look at policymaking communities and ask how the complex relationships among the various participants structure the policymaking process.

GOVERNMENT PURPOSES AND PUBLIC POLICIES

public policy
A general plan of action adopted by the government to solve a social problem, counter a threat, or pursue an objective.

In Chapter 1, we noted that virtually all citizens are willing to accept limitations on their personal freedom in return for various benefits of government. We defined the major purposes of government as maintaining order, providing public benefits, and promoting equality. Different governments place different values on each broad purpose, and those differences are reflected in their public policies. A **public policy** is a general plan of action adopted by a government to solve a social problem, counter a threat, or pursue an objective.

At times, governments choose not to adopt a new policy to deal with a troublesome situation; instead, they just "muddle through," hoping the problem will go away or diminish in importance. This, too, is a policy decision because it amounts to choosing to maintain the status quo. Sometimes government policies are carefully developed and effective. Sometimes they are hastily drawn and ineffective, even counterproductive. But careful planning is no predictor of success. Well-constructed policies may result in total disaster, and quick fixes may work just fine.

Whatever their form and effectiveness, however, all policies have this in common: they are the means by which government pursues certain goals in specific situations. People disagree about public policies because they disagree about one or more of the following elements: the goals government should have, the means it should use to meet them, and how the situation at hand should be perceived.

How do policymakers attempt to achieve their goals? As a starting point, we will divide all governmental approaches to solving problems into four broad types: we can analyze public policies according to whether they prohibit, protect, promote, or provide.

Some policies are intended to prohibit behaviors that endanger society. All governments outlaw murder, robbery, and rape. Governments that emphasize order tend to favor policies of prohibition, which instruct people in what they must not do (drink liquor, have abortions, use illegal drugs).

Government policies can also protect certain activities, business markets, or special groups of citizens. For example, taxes were once levied on colored margarine (a butter substitute) to reduce its sales and protect the dairy industry from competition. Regulations concerning the testing of new drugs are intended to protect citizens from harmful side effects; government rules about safety in the workplace are enacted to protect workers. Although governments argue that these kinds of regulations serve the public good, some people believe that most protective legislation is unwarranted government interference.

Policies can also promote social activities that are important to the government. One way that government promotes is by persuasion. For instance, our government has used advertising to urge people to buy bonds or to join the army. When policymakers really want to accomplish a goal they have set, they can be quite generous. To promote railroad construction in the 1860s, Congress granted railroad companies huge tracts of public land as rights-of-way through western states.

The government also promotes activities through tax breaks. Because it amounts to a loss of government revenue, the technical term for this form of government promotion is a *tax expenditure*. For example, the government encourages people to buy their own home by allowing them to deduct the interest they pay on their mortgage from their taxable income. In 2000, this tax expenditure cost the national government nearly $55 billion.[8] And of course, churches and private educational institutions typically pay no property taxes to state and local governments.

Finally, public policies can provide benefits directly to citizens, either collectively or selectively. Collective benefits are facilities or services that all residents share (mail service, roads, schools, street lighting, libraries, parks). Selective benefits go to certain groups of citizens (poor people, farmers, veterans, college students). Collective benefits can be difficult to deliver because they require either the construction of facilities (roads, dams, sewer systems) or the creation of organizations (transportation agencies, power companies, sanitation departments) to provide them. Many selective benefits are simply payments to individuals in the form of food stamps, subsidies, pensions, and loans. The payments are made because the recipients are particularly needy or powerful, or both.

In sum, the notion of policy is a many-splendored thing. Government has many different means at its disposal for pursuing particular goals. Those means and goals, in turn, are shaped by the specific situations that surround a problem at the time. Policies aimed at specific problems are not static; means, goals, and situations change.

THE POLICYMAKING PROCESS

We distinguish between government policies according to their approach not simply to create an inventory of problem-solving methods but also to emphasize the relationship between policy and process. By process we mean the configuration of participants involved, the procedures used for decision making, and the degree of cooperation or conflict usually present. The premise is simple: different kinds of policies affect the political process in different ways.

The Effect of Policy

One basic reason for the various policymaking processes is that different approaches to public policy affect people in different ways. If a policy proposal affects a well-organized constituency adversely, that constituency will fight it aggressively. During the 1999–2000 Congress, environmentalists and their allies in the House of Representatives worked hard to revise existing law to increase the average gas mileage of new automobiles. Average gas mileage has actually dropped from twenty-six miles per gallon (mpg) in 1988 to twenty-four mpg in 2000. This is primarily due to increased sales of SUVs and minivans, which get less mileage than cars but are not subject to the same government mileage requirements as cars. Automobile manufacturers fought the proposal because they make more money from larger, heavier vehicles, and they believe that they will soon have new technologies that will reduce the amount of gasoline consumed. In this instance, the automakers succeeded with their arguments and the environmentalists' bill was withdrawn in the face of certain defeat.[9]

The pluralist nature of our policymaking system often leads to compromise between different sectors on opposing sides of an issue. Action for Children's Television and other organizations promoting children's educational programming have long pressured the Federal Communications Commission (FCC) to require broadcasters to air more high-quality shows for young viewers. The National Association for Broadcasters, representing 1,400 local TV stations, fought against such rules. The broadcasters wanted the freedom to put on the kind of programming that they feel works best for their individual stations. It was a protracted fight, but after the Clinton White House pressured the broadcasters, a compromise was reached that requires each television station to show three hours of regularly scheduled children's programming each week.[10]

Whether a policy is intended to prohibit, protect, promote, or provide does not fully predict the level of public involvement it will generate, the degree to which it will mobilize affected constituencies, or the degree of competition it will spark between organizations working on different sides of the same issue. But by being aware of the kind of approach the government proposes to take on an issue, we can begin to understand which factors are going to influence policymaking. If a well-entrenched set of interest groups is ready to fight a policy that would prohibit one activity, a solution emphasizing promotion of another, countervailing activity might be more feasible politically.

A government may use more than one approach to a problem, not only because some alternatives engender less opposition than others but also because public policy problems can be quite complex. One approach will not always ameliorate all manifestations of a problem. For example, crimes committed by teenagers—especially violent crimes—have risen dramatically in recent years. Between 1985 and 1995, juvenile arrests for murder went up 96 percent. There are lots of competing theories to account for this rise, and an equal number of suggestions for solving the problem. Some blame the increase on the breakdown of the family or at least on a lack of parental supervision between the critical hours of 3:00 and 7:00 P.M., when most teenage crime occurs. According to this view, more counseling, family interventions, and after-school programs like athletics and Boys and Girls Clubs (to keep youngsters off the streets and out of trouble) should help reduce crime. For others, the root cause is that teenagers are treated too leniently when they get into minor trouble. If teens were held accountable for small offenses, this view contends, perhaps they would think twice about the consequences before graduating to bigger crimes. The policy preference is to make sure no crime, no matter how petty, goes unpunished and to try more juveniles as adults. Still others think that the rising crime rate is directly related to increased drug use. According to this group, getting people off drugs and into treatment programs has to be part of any serious effort to reduce the crime problem in America.[11] Different communities and states vary widely in how they have approached crime, and sharp differences are evident among nations as well (see Compared with What? 17.1).

When officials have a choice in how to address a problem, they consider how each approach would affect policymaking. Is the best approach one that is likely to generate a lot of conflict between opposing groups? If so, will it be possible to enact a new policy, or is the conflict likely to scuttle new proposals, leaving the status quo intact? In short, when policymakers weigh new policy options, they carefully consider the effect of each approach on those most directly affected.

One very controversial issue is the death penalty. Using the IDEAlog program, compare your position to that of the American population as a whole.

A Policymaking Model

Clearly, different approaches to solving policy problems affect the policymaking process, but common patterns do underlie most processes. Political scientists have produced many models of the policymaking process to distinguish the different types of policy, such as our framework of policies that prohibit, protect, promote, or provide. They also distinguish different stages of the policymaking process and try to identify patterns in the way people attempt to influence decisions and in the way decisions are reached.

We can separate the policymaking process into four stages: agenda setting, policy formulation, implementation, and policy evaluation.[12] Figure

---

★ **compared with what?**

17.1 Japan: Shame on Crime

There may be crime everywhere, but there's certainly not the same amount of crime everywhere. Comparative statistics on incarceration show vast differences between countries. Particularly striking is Japan, which has an extremely low crime rate and has only thirty-seven people in prison per 100,000 residents. Analysts cite a number of reasons. Japan bans handguns, and in a recent, typical year there were only thirty-eight murders nationwide. More people are shot each *day* in the United States. Japanese prisons are particularly odious. The cells are tiny cubicles, and many prisoners are forbidden to speak. The Japanese police force is unusually effective

and solves 37 percent of crimes, compared to just 20 percent in the United States.

Probably the most important factor, though, is the shame associated with crime. In Japan, a convicted criminal is subject to severe ostracism. Someone who commits a serious crime, such as murder, is likely to be disowned by his family, who may refuse to see him even after his release from prison. Japan is a society that clearly values order, and those who violate the strong taboo against criminal activity are judged harshly and isolated.

Source: Nicholas Kristof, "Japanese Say No to Crime: Tough Methods at a Price," *New York Times*, 14 May 1995, p. 1.

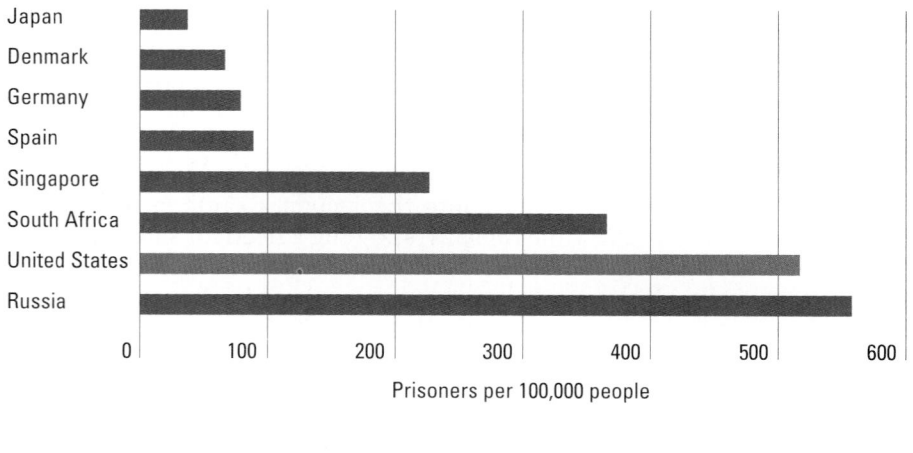

Prisoners per 100,000 people

17.1 shows the four stages in sequence. Note, however, that the process does not end with policy evaluation. As you will see, policymaking is a circular process; the end of one phase is really the beginning of another.

agenda setting
The stage of the policymaking process during which problems get defined as political issues.

Agenda Setting. **Agenda setting** is the part of the process in which problems are defined as political issues. Many problems confront Americans in their daily lives, but government is not actively working to solve them all. Consider social security, for example. Today the old-age insurance program seems a hardy perennial of American politics, but it was not created until the New Deal. The problem of poverty among the elderly did not suddenly arise during the 1930s—there had always been poor people of all ages—but that is when inadequate income for the elderly was defined as a

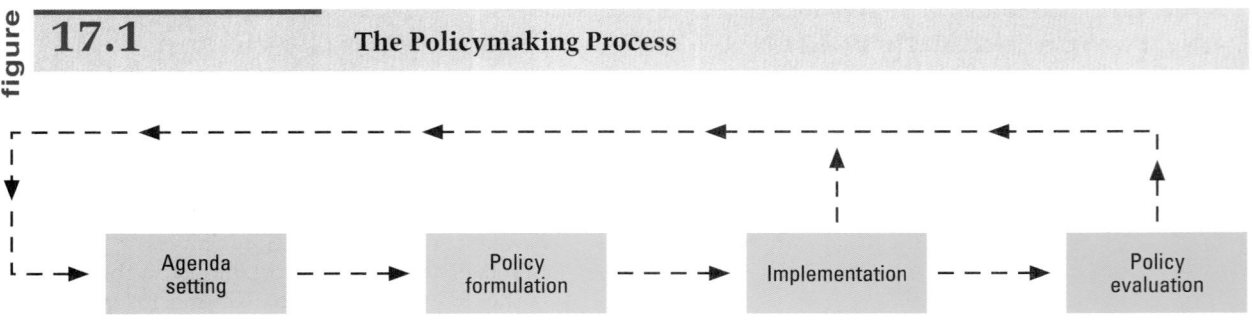

figure 17.1   The Policymaking Process

This model, one of many possible ways to depict the policymaking process, shows four policymaking stages. Feedback on program operations and performance from the last two stages stimulates new cycles of the process.

political problem. During this time people began arguing that it was government's responsibility to create a system of income security for the aged rather than leaving old people to fend for themselves.

When the government begins to consider acting on an issue it has previously ignored, we say that the issue has become part of the political agenda. Usually when we use *agenda* in this context, we are simply referring to the entire set of issues before all the institutions of government. (There is no formal list of issues for the entire political system; the concept of an agenda for the system is merely a useful abstraction.)

Why does an existing social problem become redefined as a political problem? There is no single reason; many different factors can stimulate new thinking about a problem. Sometimes, highly visible events or developments push issues onto the agenda. Examples include great calamities (such as a terrible oil spill, showing a need for safer tankers), the effects of technology (such as air pollution, requiring clean-air regulations), or irrational human behavior (such as airline hijackings, pointing to the need for greater airport security).[13] The probability that a certain problem will move onto the agenda is also affected by who controls the government and by broad ideological shifts. After President Bush (senior) went on television to announce his War on Drugs campaign, the proportion of Americans who said in surveys that drugs were the nation's most important problem more than doubled. As the administration's interest in the issue waned, the public went back to viewing drugs as it had before Bush's speech.[14]

As noted above, and as illustrated by the opening vignette about cloning, technology is one of the major factors explaining the rise of new issues. New discoveries and applications emerge quickly, and government finds itself without a policy to regulate adequately the problems produced by new products brought to market. The technology allowing individuals to download music from Web sites went quickly from the minds of computer programmers to the active transmittal of digital music. Companies like MP3.com and Napster allowed people to hear and download music produced by other companies—music that was copyrighted by those recording firms. Were MP3.com and Napster violating copyright law by their actions? Recording companies like TimeWarner, Bertelsmann, and EMI thought so. Rather than wait for Congress or an agency to figure out what

★

Nabbing Napster

Napster founder Shawn Fanning speaks at a press conference to defend his company after a court had ruled against it. One of the most outspoken critics of Napster and the free downloading of copyrighted music is the band Metallica (the group's James Hetfield is pictured here). This complicated set of issues emerged on the nation's political agenda suddenly, with the development of the technology used by Napster.

to do, they sued the Web-based companies they believed were stealing their music. A court decision against MP3.com helped to spur royalty agreements between some of the companies and these Internet sites.[15] An additional problem arising from the Internet is that one country can't regulate content on Web sites in other countries (see Politics in a Changing World 17.1).

Political scientists analyze the agenda of a particular political institution over time to try to understand political change. In looking at Congress, for example, the number of hearings held on different issue areas can be measured over time to document how some sectors of society succeed in getting their concerns addressed. As Figure 17.2 illustrates, change over time can be quite significant. Health care has always been of critical importance, but the government's role in health policy has expanded significantly and Congress spends more and more time on an array of different health matters.[16] One of the sharpest trends is the increased amount of time and resources that Congress has devoted to quality of life issues, such as environmental protection and consumer protection. Such issues involve protecting wildlife and wilderness, ensuring the integrity of markets so that consumers are not taken advantage of, establishing the rights of vulnerable segments of society, and reforming the procedures of government so that it works better.[17]

Part of the politics of agenda building is not just which new issues emerge and which issues decline in visibility, but the way the substantive problem at the heart of an issue is conceived. **Issue definition** is the way we think about a problem.[18] As individuals, our conception of an issue is influenced by our own values and the way we see the political world. However, issue definition is strongly shaped by interest groups and politicians as they try to cast their views in an advantageous light. For example, the pro-life movement was very successful in casting late-term abortions

issue definition
Our conception of the problem at hand.

17.1 Odds Are Against Regulating This Industry

Gambling in the United States is nominally illegal; that is, it's illegal unless it's done at any of the many places where it is legal: race tracks, Atlantic City, casinos on Indian reservations, convenience stores, riverboats on the Mississippi, and the whole state of Nevada. In truth, gambling is not so much illegal as it is regulated. The sin taxes levied on legalized gambling allow government to keep other—and more politically difficult—taxes slightly lower.

The gambling industry is changing, however, and government is getting cut out of the action. More and more gambling sites are being set up offshore, outside our borders, and are serving an eager clientele inside the United States. The new technology of the Internet has outrun the capacity of any nation's government to regulate the gambling that Web sites facilitate. In 1961, before the Internet, the U.S. government passed a law making it illegal to transmit bets over phone lines or wire within this country or between the United States and other countries. Even though this law is applicable to Internet gambling, applying it effectively is something else. In the Caribbean country of Antigua, online gambling is not only legal, the government actively recruits companies to set up shop there. (Antigua gets a nice piece of the action: an annual licensing fee of $75,000 to $100,000 for each business.)

Technologically, it's quite simple to set up a gambling site. One clever cyberspace entrepreneur, Ron Tarter, franchises gambling sites. All the betting goes through his "back office" in Antigua, but the franchise holders each get a percentage of the take. One franchisee told the *Wall Street Journal* he makes "as much as $2,500 a month from five virtual betting joints—which cost him just $5 a month each to run." Tarter has more than 1,000 franchisees up and running and many more are in the works.

For the consumer, placing a bet couldn't be simpler. Give the Web site your credit card number and let the fun begin. Do you want the Dolphins with 3 points over the Jets for a cool $100? Just click a box. Do you want to play the slots? The mouse becomes your handle, so spin away. If you like poker, play a few hands of Caribbean stud.

Offshore gambling lacks the ambiance of the MGM Grand in Las Vegas or Foxwoods in Connecticut, but you just can't beat it for convenience. For people who have trouble with gambling, it may be a little too convenient. For many, gambling is a serious addiction, although gamblers can find plenty of places to bet without logging on to the Internet. Still, offshore gambling may be one of those uses of the Internet that seems like a step backward, not forward.

The Internet is not erasing the sovereign boundaries of the nation state, but it is testing them. There's no effective regulation by the United States or by any world body of the gambling that transpires between living rooms in this country and servers sitting in an air-conditioned room in Antigua. The betting is that there won't be any effective regulation anytime soon.

Source: Michael Allen, "Offshore Sports Bookmakers Find Internet a Winner," *Wall Street Journal*, 4 August 2000, p. B4; and Michael Allen, "Internet Casinos Proliferate Unchecked," *Wall Street Journal*, 23 August 2000, p. A14.

as partial birth abortions. This issue definition evokes a gruesome image of the actual procedure, and the opponents of abortion have succeeded in gaining widespread use of this term. Those on the other side of the issue prefer that these abortions be referred to as late-term abortions or by a more neutral sounding medical term. This example illustrates not only

figure

17.2

A Changing Agenda

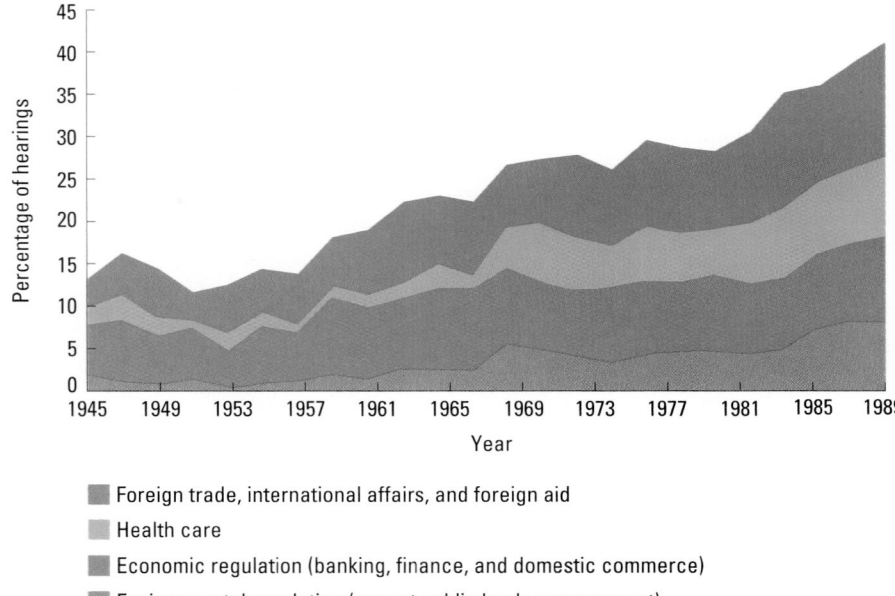

The general stability of the political system should not obscure the very real changes in the composition of the political agenda. Just after World War II, environmental regulation, economic regulation, health care, and foreign trade accounted for just under 15 percent of the congressional agenda. Almost fifty years later, these issues formed around 40 percent of the agenda.

Source: Frank R. Baumgartner and Beth L. Leech, "Where Is the Public in Public Policy?" paper presented at the conference on Political Participation: Building a Research Agenda, Princeton University, October 2000, p. 10.

■ Foreign trade, international affairs, and foreign aid

■ Health care

■ Economic regulation (banking, finance, and domestic commerce)

■ Environmental regulation (except public lands management)

how important issue definition is, but that not everyone accepts the same definition.

When interest groups believe that it would be better if an issue of concern were defined differently, they can try to change it.[19] In the language of Washington, they can try to change the spin on the story. This is hard to do, however, because there is no coordinating mechanism that determines how we define problems. Even a wealthy group that can buy a lot of advertising has an uphill struggle to change the way a problem is broadly perceived. For most issues, issue definition remains relatively constant over time, changing in incremental ways, if at all.[20] When an issue definition is changed by some outside event or technological breakthrough, the political implications can be dramatic. For years the nuclear power industry convinced Congress that the primary issue concerning nuclear power was America's growing demand for energy. After the Three Mile Island nuclear power plant in Pennsylvania had a dangerous accident, plant safety became an overriding concern in Congress despite an extensive effort by the industry to downplay the problem.[21]

policy formulation
The stage of the policymaking process during which formal proposals are developed and adopted.

Policy Formulation. **Policy formulation** is that stage of the policymaking process in which formal policy proposals are developed and officials decide whether to adopt them. The most obvious kind of policy formulation is the proposal of a measure by the president or the development of legislation by Congress. Administrative agencies also formulate policy, through the regulatory process. Courts formulate policy, too, when their decisions

A Winning Team

The Supreme Court's power to formulate policy has never been illustrated more dramatically than when it declared in 1954 that segregation in public schools is unconstitutional. The team of litigators that won this momentous case was (left to right) George E. C. Hayes, Thurgood Marshall, and James Nabrit, Jr.

establish new interpretations of the law. We usually think of policy formulation as a formal process with a published document (a statute, regulation, or court opinion) as the final outcome. In some instances, however, policy decisions are not published or otherwise made explicit. Presidents and secretaries of state may not always fully articulate their foreign policy decisions, for example, because they want some wiggle room for adapting policy to changing conditions.

Although policy formulation is depicted in Figure 17.1 as one stage, it can actually take place over several separate stages. For example, the Americans with Disabilities Act was enacted by Congress to protect the civil rights of those who are blind, deaf, wheelchair-bound, otherwise physically disabled, or mentally ill. Then the Architectural and Transportation Barriers Compliance Board issued administrative regulations specifying standards for complying with the act. For instance, at least 5 percent of the tables in a restaurant must be accessible to those with disabilities, and at least half the drinking fountains on every floor in an office building must be accessible to those in wheelchairs.[22] In addition, the Justice Department issued guidelines for those who want to bring legal complaints against the government for failing to implement the act properly.[23]

As noted in Chapter 13, policy formulation tends to be *incremental*. As policies are being debated, the starting point is the existing policy in that area, and if new policy is adopted, it is usually a modification of what was in place previously. Figure 17.1 depicts how this process works. At the very end of the Clinton administration, the Forest Service adopted a new set of regulations that banned the construction of new roads into one-third of all the national forests. This change effectively banned any logging in these areas because roads are necessary to take the timber out.[24] On one level this new departure was important because it marked a change in the way the Forest Service calculated the costs and benefits of logging versus the preservation of wilderness. On another level, however, this policy had its roots in policies on wilderness formulated in the late 1970s by the Carter administration.[25] In another twist, the Bush administration announced it was going to review the new regulations and further changes seem likely.

Keep in mind that policy formulation is only the development of proposals designed to solve a problem. Some issues reach the agenda and stimulate new proposals but then fail to win enactment because political opposition mobilizes. In the early 1980s, for example, a movement arose to freeze the development of nuclear weapons. Although a freeze resolution gained significant support in Congress, it never gained enough votes to pass. The nuclear freeze movement quickly withered away and disappeared from sight. Thus, the move from proposal to policy requires the approval of some authoritative, policymaking body.

implementation
The process of putting specific policies into operation.

Implementation.   Policies are not self-executing; **implementation** is the process by which they are carried out. When regulations are issued by agencies in Washington, some government bodies must then put those policies into effect. This may involve notifying the intended targets of agency actions of new or changed regulations. In the case of the Americans with Disabilities Act, for example, the owners of office buildings would probably not have repositioned their water fountains simply because Washington published new regulations. Administrative bodies at the regional, state, or local level had to inform them of the rules, give them a timetable for compliance, communicate the penalties for noncompliance, be available to answer questions that emerged, and report to Washington on how well the regulations were working.

For the national government, a key issue in implementation is how much discretion should be given to the state and local officials who have the responsibility for carrying out the policy. After officials in Washington enact a law and write the subsequent regulations, people outside Washington typically must implement the policy. The agents may be local officials, state administrators, or federal bureaucrats headquartered in regional offices around the country. Those who implement programs are often given considerable discretion in how to apply general policies to specific, local situations. The discretion can give agents flexibility to tailor situations to local conditions, but it can also mean that people affected by the programs are treated differently depending on where they live. The Ryan White CARE Act, which provides funds to help states and cities cope with their AIDS caseload, is a case in point.

Congress enacted the Ryan White Act to support several different programs for AIDS-related services. Each of these services, such as treatment of those already infected, early intervention, counseling, and specialized care for children, were defined only broadly in the legislation. Local bureaucracies and nonprofits were given discretion in deciding how the programs would operate, who would get services, and who would have administrative responsibility for them. In some cities, this broad discretion had some positive results. In Denver, AIDS services had been largely focused on direct services from medical practitioners. A requirement to receive Ryan White money led to the creation there of an inclusive planning council. Community organizations in Denver were placed on the council,

Are You With Me?

Prior to his inauguration George W. Bush met with leaders of America's technology industries for a two-day economic summit. Ostensibly he wanted to hear what was on their minds and to get their suggestions for new policies. More importantly, he used the occasion to draw attention to the first item on his agenda: passage of a large tax cut. These high-tech CEOs were highly supportive of the Bush plan.

and they persuaded medical professionals to allocate some of the AIDS money to them so that they could provide services. These community-based services resulted in shorter hospital stays because AIDS patients could receive a broader range of care on an outpatient basis in their neighborhoods. This, in turn, saved money because these outpatient services were less expensive that those provided at a hospital. This kind of creativitiy and efficiency was surely what was in the minds of the legislators who wrote the Ryan White Act.

Yet the discretion at the local level led to some problems with the implementation of the Ryan White Act as well. With little in the way of federal standards, different cities made different decisions on important administrative questions. Some cities counted an AIDS client receiving services in two different programs as two different patients. Since funding from Washington was heavily determined on a per capita basis, such double counting led to considerably larger budgets. This and other related problems led to serious inequity in the amount of money being provided to each AIDS sufferer. An audit of the program found that San Francisco was getting more than $6,000 per living AIDS patient, while Milwaukee was getting about $1,000. This was certainly not what Congress had in mind when it designed the Ryan White Act.[26]

Although it may sound highly technical, implementation is very much a political process. It involves a great deal of bargaining and negotiation among different groups of people in and out of government. The difficulty of implementing complex policies in a federal system, with multiple layers of government, that is also a pluralistic system, with multiple competing interests, seems daunting. Yet there are incentives for cooperation, not the least of which is to avoid blame if a policy fails. (We will discuss coordination in more detail later in the chapter.)

Can You Explain Why...
the end of the policymaking
process is also the beginning?

policy evaluation
Analysis of a public policy so as to
determine how well it is working.

Policy Evaluation. How does the government know whether a policy is working? In some cases, success or failure may be obvious, but at other times experts in a specific field must tell government officials how well a policy is working. **Policy evaluation** is the analysis of the results of public policy. Although there is no one method of evaluating policy, evaluation tends to draw heavily on approaches used by academics, including cost-effectiveness analysis and various statistical methods designed to provide concrete measurements of program outcomes. Although technical, the studies can be quite influential in decisions on whether to continue, expand, alter, reduce, or eliminate programs. The continuing stream of negative evaluations of programs designed to bring jobs to the unemployed has clearly reduced political support for such policies.[27]

Evaluating public policy is extremely difficult. The most pertinent data are not always available, predicting trends may require making problematic assumptions, and policy analysts may have biases that influence their research. Sometimes, the data are unclear and subject to differing interpretations. One interesting case involved weaponry used in the Persian Gulf War. For the first time, the United States made extensive use of "smart bombs"—bombs that are electronically guided to their targets instead of being dropped the old-fashioned way with visual sighting of targets. During the war the Pentagon touted the effectiveness of these weapons, showing the American public dramatic videotapes of smart bombs hitting targets in Iraq. One tape showed a smart bomb aimed so accurately that it went down the air shaft of a Baghdad building. Some early independent assessments at the end of the war were positive, and one study concluded that "The criticism that America's weapons were too complex and fragile to work in war was dispelled."[28] Later, a thorough and dispassionate study by Congress's General Accounting Office demonstrated that those tapes showed the exceptions and not the rule. Its systematic comparison of smart bombs and "dumb bombs" showed no difference in their accuracy. This was a critically important finding because smart bombs are much more expensive than conventional bombs. Although smart bombs accounted for only 8 percent of the ordnance used in the Gulf War, they consumed 84 percent of the money spent on munitions.[29] This is the kind of policy evaluation that is most useful: directly comparing different ways of achieving the same goal, and determining the relative effectiveness and efficiency of each approach.

feedback
Information received by policymakers about the effectiveness of
public policy.

Evaluation is part of the policymaking process because it helps to identify problems and issues that arise from current policy. In other words, evaluation studies provide **feedback** to policymakers on program performance. (The dotted line in Figure 17.1 represents a feedback loop. Problems that emerge during the implementation stage also provide feedback to policymakers.) By drawing attention to emerging problems, policy evaluation influences the political agenda. For instance, you may recall our discussion of oversight in Chapter 11. When congressional committees perform oversight duties, they are evaluating policy with an eye toward identifying issues they will have to deal with in subsequent legislation. Thus, we have come full circle. The end of the process—evaluating whether the policy is being implemented as it was envisioned when it was formulated—is the beginning of a new cycle of public policymaking.

**A MULTIPLICITY
OF PARTICIPANTS**

The policymaking process encompasses many different stages and includes many different participants at each stage. Here we examine some forces that pull the government in different directions and make problem solving less coherent than it might otherwise be. In the next section, we look at some structural elements of American government that work to coordinate competing and sometimes conflicting approaches to the same problems.

Multiplicity and Fragmentation

fragmentation
In policymaking, the phenomenon of attacking a single problem in different and sometimes competing ways.

A single policy problem may be attacked in different and sometimes competing ways by government for many reasons. At the heart of this **fragmentation** of policymaking is the fundamental nature of government in America. The separation of powers divides authority among the branches of the national government, and federalism divides authority among the national, state, and local levels of government. These multiple centers of power are, of course, a primary component of pluralist democracy. Different groups try to influence different parts of the government; no one entity completely controls policymaking.

The fragmentation of policymaking is illustrated by policymaking concerning day care. Sixty percent of women with children under six are in the labor force, so the need for high-quality, affordable day care is acute. It's easy for politicians to agree with such homilies as "children are our future," but one would never know they feel that way from the government's approach to the care of its youngest citizens. The national government plays only a modest role in the area of day care, and communities and states vary widely in the degree to which they regulate day care, if they regulate it at all. In the United States there are approximately 80,000 day care centers and close to 670,000 homes providing family day care.[30] Some of this care is clearly substandard, and there is no coherent approach for ensuring that children receive care that is safe and stimulating. Studies show that day care that is regulated is of clearly higher quality, but there is little prospect in the near future that the state and national governments will institute greater coherence and coordination in day-care policy.[31]

Fragmentation is often the result of competing goals espoused by different parts of the government. Political leaders espouse the importance of energy independence, but this goal conflicts with other government policies. Relatively mild winters hid a growing problem with natural gas supplies, which became evident in the winter of 2000–2001. Natural gas prices shot up as increasing demand chased a relatively stable supply.

Why hadn't natural gas production kept up with demand? Although part of the reason has to do with changes in the energy industry, different parts of the national government manifest conflicting objectives. The broad policy of the government is to promote the use of natural gas because it is a cleaner (less polluting) fuel. Yet environmental concerns have made new exploration difficult as there is a strong sentiment to preclude drilling in wilderness and forest areas, and it's nearly impossible to drill new sites adjacent to inhabited areas. The Bureau of Land Management in the Department of Interior and the Forest Service in the Department of Agriculture have established substantial obstacles to new exploration. At the same time, the Environmental Protection Agency has worked to reduce

It Takes a Village to Raise a Child

The growing percentage of women in the labor force with young children has sharply increased the demand for day care. The majority of providers offer care in their homes. Some of this care, such as that pictured here, is of high quality, but much of it is unregulated and is not subject to any kind of outside review. One study estimates that two-thirds of all home day-care providers are operating illegally by not informing licensing agencies that they have a home day-care business.

emissions from coal-fired plants, thus reducing the incentives for businesses to invest in new coal plants. Likewise, the Department of Energy has made it more difficult to build new nuclear or hydroelectric facilities. In short, the overall effect of energy policy was to increase demand for natural gas by moving America away from other energy supplies, while making it more difficult for energy companies to explore for new gas fields.[32]

Congress is characterized by the same diffusion of authority. In the area of illegal drugs, seventy-five separate House and Senate committees and subcommittees claim some jurisdiction, and the committees jealously guard their prerogatives.[33]

The multiplicity of institutional participants is partly the product of the complexity of public policy issues. Controlling illegal drugs is not one problem but a number of different, interrelated problems. Drug treatment questions, for example, have little in common with questions related to the smuggling of drugs into the country. Still, the responsibilities of agencies and committees do overlap. Why are responsibilities not parceled out more precisely to clarify jurisdictions and eliminate overlap? Such reorganizations create winners and losers, and agencies fearing the loss of jurisdiction over an issue become highly protective of their turf.

The Pursuit of Coordination

How does the government overcome fragmentation so that it can make its public policies more coherent? Coordination of different elements of government is not impossible, and fragmentation often creates a productive pressure to rethink jurisdictions.

One common response to the problem of coordination is the formation of interagency task forces within the executive branch. Their common goal is to develop a broad policy response that all relevant agencies will endorse. Such task forces include representatives of all agencies claiming responsibility for a particular issue. They attempt to forge good policy as well as goodwill among competing agencies. President Lyndon Johnson's expansive War on Poverty incorporated several new policy initiatives that cut across many existing departments and agencies. He relied heavily on interagency task forces to work through the jurisdiction issues between different parts of government and to make a range of decisions about program design and administration.

Sometimes, the executive branch attempts to reassign jurisdictions among its agencies, although certain players may resist the loss of their turf. Reorganization of jurisdictions is more common within than across agencies. A shift across agencies is likely to require White House involvement. Nevertheless, the president and his aides sometimes orchestrate such restructurings, which may involve creating a new agency to assume control over other, existing agencies or programs. With congressional approval, President Richard Nixon created the Environmental Protection Agency (EPA) in 1970 to coordinate fifteen programs administered by five other parts of the executive branch.[34]

The Office of Management and Budget (OMB) also fosters coordination within the executive branch. OMB can do much more than review budgets and look for ways to improve management practices. The Reagan administration used OMB to clear regulations before they were proposed publicly by the administrative agencies. It initiated OMB's regulatory review role to centralize control of the executive branch. Reagan's successor, George Bush, created the President's Council on Competitiveness to review regulations before agencies implemented them. Led by his vice president, Dan Quayle, the council rejected regulations that it regarded as detrimental to the economy.[35] The virtue of centralized control by the White House through such instruments as OMB and the Council on Competitiveness is that the administration can ensure that its objectives are carried out and not compromised by agencies eager to please interest groups that give them political support. Critics say that such White House control excludes many relevant groups from the policymaking process.

Over its history, Congress has repeatedly made efforts to promote greater coordination among all its disparate, decentralized parts. This is especially true in the area of budgeting, where individual committee preferences have to be balanced with overall budget goals. The most obvious answer to insufficient coordination is to strengthen the hand of the leadership, but stronger leadership conflicts with the preference of committee chairs (as well as rank and file) who do not want their own individual freedom and authority diminished. As agendas change with the emergence of new issues, the overlap in committee jurisdictions grows worse. As noted above with the case of illegal drugs, many committees and subcommittees can claim some jurisdiction over the same problem.

Due to the power of individual committee chairs, it is difficult for the House and the Senate to make significant reorganizations of their committee systems. Instead, reorganization comes about incrementally as individual chairs try to expand their jurisdictions, or conflict erupts between committees and new jurisdictional boundaries are negotiated.[36] At the beginning of 2001, the Republican leadership in the House reorganized the Banking Committee and the Commerce Committee. The Commerce Committee had long held jurisdiction over the securities and insurance industries. Changes in the financial services industry has led to many conglomerates doing business in banking, securities, and insurance rather than in just one. To provide greater coordination in these areas, the Banking Committee was given jurisdiction over securities and insurance to go along with its authority over banking; it was renamed the Financial Services Committee. The Commerce Committee was left with a narrower (but still substantial) jurisdiction.[37]

Finally, the policy fragmentation created by federalism may be solved when an industry asks the national government to develop a single regulatory policy. Often, the alternative is for that industry to try to accommodate the different regulatory approaches used in various states. Although an industry may prefer no regulation at all, it generally prefers one master to fifty.

The effect of pluralism on the problem of coordination is all too evident. In a decentralized, federal system of government with large numbers of interest groups, fragmentation is inevitable. Beyond the structural factors is the natural tendency of people and organizations to defend their base of power. Government officials understand, however, that mechanisms of coordination are necessary so that fragmentation does not overwhelm policymaking. Mechanisms such as interagency task forces, reorganizations, and White House review can bring some coherence to policymaking.

THE NONPROFIT SECTOR

nonprofits
Organizations that are not part of government or business and cannot distribute profits to shareholders or to anyone else.

Can You Explain Why...
government programs aren't always administered by the government?

In the earlier discussion of implementation and the example about the AIDS effort in Denver, we noted that some community-based organizations became important participants in the policymaking process. Organizations that were not officially part of the government were receiving government funds and using them to implement a government program, in this case, providing services to those with AIDS. These organizations are **nonprofits**. Nonprofits are neither governmental organizations nor private sector organizations. They are voluntary organizations and, as the term *nonprofit* denotes, they may not distribute profits to shareholders or to anyone else.

There are many different types of nonprofits, but when we use the term, we are usually referring to organizations that are considered "public charities" by the Internal Revenue Service. They are not charities in the sense that they necessarily have to distribute money or goods to the needy but rather that they perform some public good. The greatest number of nonprofits are involved in social services.[38] Such organizations might distribute meals, offer after-school activities to low-income children, administer shelters for abused women or runaway children, or provide hospice care for the terminally ill. Obviously these are vitally important services, and all communities are highly dependent on their nonprofits. As one scholar notes, they are "the glue that holds civil society together."[39]

Not all the nonprofits that qualify as public charities are social service providers. Other nonprofits include symphony orchestras, PTAs, Little Leagues, museums, and foundations. All of these groups provide something valuable to society by engaging people in their communities, offering them a chance to appreciate art, creating opportunities for volunteering, and providing recreation to children and adults alike. These activities enrich

Growing Role for Nonprofits

As government has tried to shrink, the role of nonprofits has expanded. One of the advantages of nonprofits is that they draw on a substantial amount of volunteer labor, including this retiree delivering meals to frail elderly. Volunteers can't entirely replace government funding, however, and many social service programs operated by nonprofits are paid for by state and federal money.

society, and it's important to design policies to encourage people to become involved in nonprofits.[40] Nonprofits are rewarded for these valuable endeavors with tax deductibility for donors. Individuals who contribute money to public charity nonprofits can deduct that money from their taxes. This tax break encourages people to give money because government is essentially subsidizing the contribution. (Recall the earlier discussion of tax expenditures—tax provisions that cause a loss of government revenue.)

The typical nonprofit is supported by a mix of private and government funds. One of the advantages for government from using nonprofits to administer social service programs is that substantial amounts of funding come from contributions made by individuals. Even though the government is subsidizing those contributions through the tax deductibility of donations, the government still benefits by not having to pay for all those services itself.

The government also gets more social services than would be the case if there were no nonprofits and the government had to provide more direct services through its bureaucracies at the national, state, and local levels. Government is under substantial pressure to keep expenditures down. Indeed, nonprofits are growing in importance because government has found it desirable to shift more administration of social services onto this sector (see Figure 17.3).[41] This allows government to appear to cut the size of government by reducing the number of bureaucrats while at the same time not angering people who depend on social services.[42]

Nonprofits have the additional advantage of being innovative and extending their services in ways the government would be unlikely to. Take, for example, the Idaho Youth Ranch located in Rupert, Idaho. This is a residential facility for at-risk youth that serves both boys and girls. It's a particularly imaginative treatment program, combining a school and a working ranch that raises horses. In addition to their schoolwork, the young people there do chores around the ranch, participate in 4-H programs, and are involved in community service. The Idaho Youth Ranch is

Source: C. Eugene Steuerle and Virginia Hodgkinson, "Meeting Social Needs: Comparing the Resources of the Independent Sector and Government," in *Nonprofits and Government*, eds. Elizabeth T. Boris and C. Eugene Steuerle (Washington, D.C.: Urban Institute, 1999), pp. 77–78.

figure

17.3 **The Nonprofit Sector**

Employment by nonprofits has grown as a proportion of all workers, while government employment has shrunk. The number of people employed by nonprofits, including volunteers and part-time workers as well as full-time workers, is over 17 million. The nonprofit sector produces about 7 percent of the nation's economic output (gross domestic product).

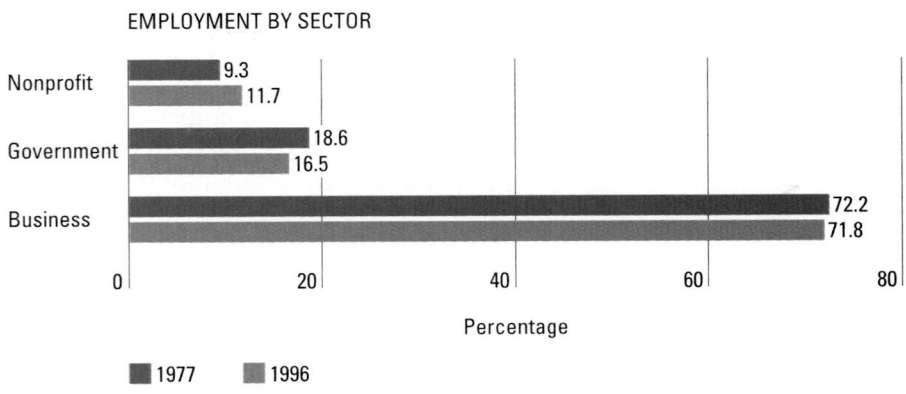

supported by funds from the state, private contributions, and from various other sources.[43] The state of Idaho could run a facility on its own to serve troubled youths, but it's unlikely that it would decide to create a 500-acre ranch as its treatment site. Due to budget limitations, the state would be more likely to create something more austere and limited in its scope.

Nonprofits may sound too good to be true, and in a sense they are because they can't do all that we might like them to. Policymakers have often claimed that the nonprofit sector could provide the safety net that protects Americans when they are in serious need of support. President Reagan said that his budget cuts wouldn't damage the safety net because philanthropy and nonprofits would fill the gap. His assurances were overly optimistic.

Given the importance of nonprofits in providing social services, it's clear that they have a role to play in developing policy as well as in implementing it. In many policy areas, they've become part of the policymaking communities that dominate the debate over the political issues relevant to their concerns. We turn now to an examination of those policy communities.

ISSUE NETWORKS

We have emphasized how different kinds of issues can affect the policymaking process in different ways and how government officials cope with the problems of fragmentation and coordination. We want to extend these themes by focusing more closely on interest groups. Within any issue area, a number—often a very large number—of interest groups try to influence policy decisions. Representatives from these organizations interact with each other and with government officials on a recurring basis. The ongoing interaction produces both conflict and cooperation.

Government by Policy Area

We noted earlier that policy formulation takes place across different institutions. Participants from these institutions do not patiently wait their turn as policymaking proceeds from one institution to the next. Rather, they try to influence policy at whatever stage they can. Suppose that Congress is considering amendments to the Clean Air Act. Because Congress does not function in a vacuum, the other parts of government that will be affected by the legislation participate in the process, too. The EPA has an interest in the outcome because it will have to administer the law. The White House is concerned about any legislation that affects such vital sectors of the economy as the steel and coal industries. As a result, officials from both the EPA and the White House work with members of Congress and the appropriate committee staffs to try to ensure that their interests are protected. At the same time, lobbyists representing corporations, trade associations, and environmental groups do their best to influence Congress, agency officials, and White House aides. Trade associations might hire public relations firms to sway public opinion toward their industry's point of view. Experts from think tanks and universities might be asked to testify at hearings or to serve in an informal advisory capacity in regard to the technical, economic, and social effects of the proposed amendments.

The various individuals and organizations that work in a particular policy area form a loosely knit community. More specifically, those "who share expertise in a policy domain and who frequently interact constitute an issue network."[44] The boundaries and membership of an **issue network** are hardly precise, but in general terms such networks include members of Congress, committee staffers, agency officials, lawyers, lobbyists, consultants, scholars, and public relations specialists. This makes for a large number of participants—in a broad policy area, the number of interest group organizations alone is usually in the dozens, if not hundreds.[45]

Not all of the participants in an issue network have a working relationship with all the others. Indeed, some may be chronic antagonists. Others tend to be allies. For example, environmental groups will coalesce in trying to influence a clean air bill but are likely to be in opposition to business groups. The common denominator for friends and foes in an issue network is their expertise in that particular policy area.

Political scientists have long analyzed policymaking by issue area. In the 1950s, policy communities were typically much smaller, with a few key committee or subcommittee chairs, a top agency official, and a couple of lobbyists from the principal trade groups negotiating behind the scenes to settle important policy questions. Political scientists used to call such small, tightly knit policy communities *iron triangles*. Iron triangles were thought to be relatively autonomous and to operate by consensus. The explosion in the number of interest groups and the growth of government and overlapping jurisdictions put an end to iron triangles. Today, policy communities are much more open and much more conflictual issue networks.

Policy Expertise

Although issue networks are fluid communities, easily entered by new interest group participants, there is nevertheless one significant barrier to admission. One must have the necessary expertise to enter the community of activists and politicians that influence policymaking in an issue area. Expertise has always been important, but "more than ever, policymaking is becoming an intramural activity among expert issue watchers."[46]

issue network
A shared-knowledge group consisting of representatives of various interests involved in some particular aspect of public policy.

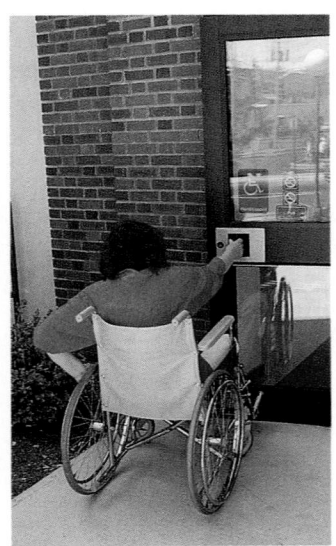

★

Opening the Door to Access

*Implementation of the
Americans with Disabilities
Act was enormously challenging, as regulations written in
Washington had to be put into
effect in every community
across the country. Policymaking is incremental and
step-by-step the access section
of the law has been successfully implemented in office
buildings, grocery stores, post
offices, restaurants, shopping
malls, banks, and many other
kinds of facilities.*

in-and-outer
A participant in an issue network
who has a good understanding of
the needs and problems of others
in the network and can easily
switch jobs within the network.

Consider Medicare, for example. The program is crucial to the health
of the elderly, and with millions of baby boomers rapidly approaching
retirement age, it needs to be restructured to make sure there will be
enough money available to care for them all. But to enter the political debate on this issue requires specialized knowledge. What is the difference
between a "defined benefit" and a "defined contribution," or between a
"provider-sponsored organization" and a "health maintenance organization"? Which needs to be reformed first, "Medicare Part A" or "Medicare
Part B"? Without getting into "portability" or "capitated" arrangements,
is it better to have "medical savings accounts" or "fee for service" plans?[47]

The members of an issue network speak the same language. They can
participate in the negotiation and compromise of policymaking because
they can offer concrete, detailed solutions to the problems at hand. They
understand the substance of policy, the way Washington works, and one
another's viewpoints.

One reason participants in an issue network have such a good understanding of the needs and problems of others in the network is that job
switches within policy communities continue to be common. When someone wants to leave her or his current position but remain in Washington,
the most obvious place to look for a new job is within the same policy field.
For these **in-and-outers,** knowledge and experience remain relevant to a
particular issue network, no matter which side of the fence they are on.

A common practice—and one that is the focus of much criticism—is to
work in government for a number of years, build up knowledge of a policy
area, and then take a lobbying job. Law firms, consulting firms, public relations firms, and trade associations generally pay much higher salaries
than the government does. And they pay not just for experience and know-
how but also for connections within government. Alan Wm. Wolff gained
valuable experience working for the Office of the Special Trade Representative in the executive branch. He worked on various foreign trade conflicts and then parlayed his valuable government experience into a
lucrative job with the Washington office of Dewey, Ballantine, a nationally known law firm. There he represents clients such as Kodak and the
American Iron and Steel Institute, trying to get his former employer to
take action against foreign companies allegedly engaging in illegal trade
practices. For his valuable time, clients are charged $450 an hour.[48]

In short, experience in government not only gives individuals expertise in
an issue area, it also gives them contacts with those who remain in the executive or legislative branches and who retain authority over policy. Although
not everyone who leaves government for the private sector will command
Wolff's half a million dollars or more a year in salary, it is very common for
high-ranking officials to leave government for jobs that pay considerably
higher than what they were earning. Indeed, people who take high-level government jobs often do so at some cost to their income. One survey of political
appointees to top government jobs showed that 55 percent said they had made
a financial sacrifice to move into government. Yet roughly 50 percent indicated that government service enhanced their subsequent earning power.[49]

One constraint on in-and-outers is the Ethics in Government Act of
1978, which specifies that senior executive branch officials cannot lobby
their former agency for a year after leaving the government. Critics have
complained, however, that in-and-outers have not found this requirement
much of an inhibition and that some former executive branch officials

figure 17.4   The Price of a Decent Used Car?

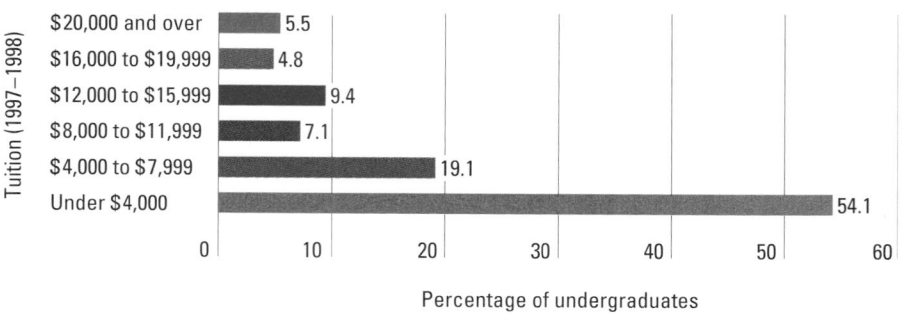

Percentage of undergraduates

Tuition (1997–1998)

$20,000 and over	5.5
$16,000 to $19,999	4.8
$12,000 to $15,999	9.4
$8,000 to $11,999	7.1
$4,000 to $7,999	19.1
Under $4,000	54.1

Using experts to devise policy can be fraught with unexpected pitfalls, as members of Congress discovered recently. As this figure indicates, during the 1997–1998 academic year, nearly half of all undergraduates attending a four-year college or university paid more than $4,000 for tuition alone. Congressional Republicans set up a commission to recommend ways to contain the upward march of the cost of tuition, but the experts failed to see a problem. When the panel concluded that most students at public institutions annually pay "about what a decent used car would cost," infuriated Republicans insisted the commission try again. On their second try, commission members agreed that tuition is high and that its growth should be slowed, but they asserted that students get their money's worth.

Sources: Sue Kirchhoff, "Commission on College Costs Back to Drawing Board," *Congressional Quarterly Weekly Report,* 20 December 1997, p. 3129. The chart is from the College Entrance Examination Board, "Distribution of Full-Time Undergraduates at Four-Year Institutions by Tuition Charged, 1997–1998," Exhibit 3, from <www.collegeboard.org>, 26 January 1998. Copyright © 1998 by the College Entrance Examination Board. All rights reserved.

Can You Explain Why...
government doesn't always do what the experts tell it to do?

have had little trouble getting around it. Nothing prevents a former offical from directing other lobbyists or from using their knowledge of how the White House operates to their firms' advantage. Moreover, the limitation lasts only a relatively short time.

Issue Networks and Democracy

Are issue networks making the government too fragmented? Are some issue networks beyond popular control? Has the increasing complexity of public policy given technical experts too much policymaking authority?

These questions relate to the broad issues raised in Chapter 2. For many years, political scientists have described American democracy as a system in which different constituencies work energetically to influence policies of concern to them. Policymaking is seen as responding to these groups rather than to majority will. This is a considerably different conception of democracy than the more traditional perspective, that policies reflect what most people want. It is a pluralist, not a majoritarian, view of American government.

In a number of ways, issue networks promote pluralist democracy. They are open systems, populated by a wide range of interest groups. Decision making is not centralized in the hands of a few key players; policies are formulated in a participatory fashion. But there is still no guarantee that all relevant interests are represented, and those with greater financial resources have an advantage. Nevertheless, issue networks provide access to government for a diverse set of competing interests and thus further the pluralist ideal.[50]

For those who prefer majoritarian democracy, however, issue networks are an obstacle to achieving their vision of how government should operate. The technical complexity of contemporary issues makes it especially difficult for the public at large to exert control over policy outcomes. When we think of the complexity of issues such as nuclear power, toxic wastes, air pollution, poverty, drug abuse, and so on, it is easy to understand why majoritarian democracy is so difficult to achieve. The more complex the issue, the more elected officials must depend on a technocratic elite for policy guidance. And technical expertise, of course, is a chief characteristic of participants in issue networks (see Figure 17.4).

At first glance, having technical experts play a key role in policymaking may seem highly desirable. After all, who but the experts should be making decisions about toxic wastes? This works to the advantage of government bureaucracies, which are full of people hired for their technical expertise. But governmental dependence on technocrats also helps interest groups, which use policy experts to maximize their influence with government. Seen in this light, issue networks become less appealing. Interest groups—at least those with which we do not personally identify—are seen as selfish. They pursue policies that favor their constituents rather than the national interest.

Although expertise is an important factor in bringing interest groups into the decision-making process, it is not the only one. Americans have a fundamental belief that government should be open and accessible to "the people." If some constituency has a problem, they reason, government ought to listen to it. However, the practical consequence of this view is a government that is open to interest groups.

Finally, although issue networks promote pluralism, keep in mind that majoritarian influences on policymaking are still significant. The broad contours of public opinion can be a dominant force on highly visible issues. Policymaking on civil rights, for example, has been sensitive to shifts in public opinion. Elections, too, send messages to policymakers about the most widely discussed campaign issues. What issue networks have done, however, is facilitate pluralist politics in policy areas in which majoritarian influences are weak.

SUMMARY

Government tries to solve problems through a variety of approaches. Some public policies prohibit, some protect, some promote, and some provide. The approach chosen can significantly affect the policymaking process.

Although there is much variation in the policymaking process, we can conceive of it as consisting of four stages. The first stage is agenda setting, the process by which problems become defined as political issues worthy of government attention. Once people in government feel that they should be doing something about a problem, an attempt at policy formulation will follow. All three branches of the national government formulate policy. Once policies have been formulated and ratified, administrative units of government must implement them. Finally, once policies are being carried out, they need to be evaluated. Implementation and program evaluation influence agenda building because program shortcomings become evident during these stages. Thus, the process is really circular, with the end often marking the beginning of a new round of policymaking.

Our policymaking system is also characterized by forces that push it toward fragmentation and by institutional structures intended to bring some element of coordination to government. The multiplicity of participants in policymaking, the diffusion of authority within both Congress and the executive branch, the separation of powers, and federalism are chief causes of conflict and fragmentation in policymaking.

Policymaking in many areas can be viewed as an ongoing process of interaction within issue networks composed of actors inside and outside government. Each network provides a way to communicate and exchange information and ideas about a particular policy area. In a network, lobbying coalitions form easily and dissolve rapidly as new issues arise. Issue networks place a high premium on expertise, as public policy problems have grown more and more complex.

Political scientists view issue networks with some concern. The networks unquestionably facilitate the representation of many interests in the policymaking process, but they do so at a price. They allow well-organized, aggressive constituencies to prevail over the broader interests of the nation. Once again, the majoritarian and pluralist models of democracy conflict. It is easy to say that the majority should rule. But in the real world, the majority tends to be far less interested in many issues than are the constituencies most directly affected by them. It is also easy to say that those most affected by issues should have the most influence. But experience teaches us that such influence leads to policies that favor the well represented at the expense of those who should be at the bargaining table but are not.

★ Selected Readings

Anderson, James E. *Public Policymaking,* 4th ed. Boston: Houghton Mifflin, 2000. A brief overview of the policymaking system.

Aron, Joan. *Licensed to Kill? The Nuclear Regulatory Commission and the Shoreham Power Plant.* Pittsburgh: University of Pittsburgh Press, 1998. A case study that looks at the risks that come with modern technology and inept policymaking.

Boris, Elizabeth T., and C. Eugene Steuerle. *Nonprofits and Government.* Washington, D.C.: Urban Institute, 1999. An excellent collection of essays on the multifaceted relationship between government and the third sector.

Castles, Francis G. *Comparative Public Policy.* Cheltenham, United Kingdom: Edward Elgar, 1999. Castles compares the development of various policies in the western democracies in the second half of the twentieth century.

Vig, Norman J., and Michael Kraft, eds. *Environmental Policy,* 4th ed. Washington, D.C.: CQ Press, 2000. Covers a wide range of environmental issues and policymaking dilemmas.

Weaver, R. Kent. *Ending Welfare as We Know It.* Washington, D.C.: Brookings Institution, 2000. An impressive, comprehensive study of the transformation of basic welfare policy.

Internet Exercises

1. *Coordinating Immigration Enforcement*
The Immigration and Naturalization Service (INS), an agency of the U.S. Department of Justice, is responsible for administering immigration-related services and enforcing immigration laws and regulations

- Go to the INS Web site at <**www.ins.gov**> and follow the link to the INS's description of law enforcement and border management. Look in detail at how the agency describes its activities related to "interior enforcement," which includes strategies, investigations, and custody and removals.

- How are some of the INS's interior enforcement activities similar to activities pursued by state and local law enforcement agencies? What kinds of coordination issues might these similarities raise?

2. *Regulation and Issue Networks*
In August 2000, facing fifty separate lawsuits and a federal investigation, Bridgestone/Firestone recalled 6.5 million of its tires that were vulnerable to tread failures. Less than six months later, the federal government was prepared to issue new regulations on tire safety. Citi-

zens and interested observers can gather information on these and other new regulations in *The Federal Register*, the government's official daily publication for rules, proposed rules, and notices of federal agencies and organizations. Before issuing new regulations, federal agencies are required to post them in the *Register* and solicit public comments.

- Go to the Government Printing Office Web site, **<www.access.gpo.gov>**, and use its "GPO Access" feature to link to the on-line version of *The Federal Register*.

- Look up the words "tire safety" in the December 1, 2000, edition of the *Register* to locate a description of proposed new tire regulations of the National Highway Traffic Safety Commission (NHTSC).

- What action by the elected branches of government motivated the secretary of transportation and the NHTSC to issue these regulations? In what way were the secretary and the NHTSC trying to assist consumers with these regulations? Identify four specific groups within the transportation issue network that were likely to take an interest in these proposed regulations.

Economic Policy

TEN THOUSAND ANTIGLOBALIZATION DEMONSTRATORS converged on Melbourne, Australia, in September 2000, drawn there to oppose the political and economic aims of the Asia-Pacific Economic Forum, which was meeting in a luxurious Melbourne hotel. Stunned convention delegates could only watch as the protestors formed a human chain around the hotel complex, delaying the start of the meeting by about an hour.

The Melbourne protest—less violent and less infamous than similar protests in Seattle, Prague, and Washington, D.C.—nevertheless had several factors in common with the other antiglobalization demonstrations of 2000. For one thing, it was partly organized by some of the same activists, who keep in touch via the Internet and organize rallies on a rapidly escalating number of Web sites (ironically, using some of the same tools that have made the globalization of world trade such a controversial issue).[1]

The Seattle, Prague, Washington, and Melbourne demonstrators were also protesting the same development: not war or political repression, but the globalized economy, embodied by entities such as the World Trade Organization (WTO), the World Bank, and the International Monetary Fund (IMF). These organizations are the principal actors overseeing and encouraging the transition to global free markets and free trade. Recognizing that the rise of global trade and multinational corporations and the increasingly free flow of money and investments across borders have eroded the power of national governments and central banks to control their own economies, these antiglobalization activists are increasingly willing to act on a global scale. As one activist put it, "Voting for national representatives . . . achieves nothing, because they have scant power."[2]

Despite the recent string of protests, however, globalization is not particularly new. Consider the case of the United States, a nation of immigrants. During the nineteenth century, 60 million people left Europe in search of a new life. They settled in Australia, North America, and South America; so many came to the United States that in 1900, the census reported that 14 percent of Americans were foreign born. In early 2000, that figure was slightly over 10 percent, with over half coming from Latin America.[3] And the percentage of the gross national product (GNP) devoted to exports in the United States is today virtually the same as it was at the beginning of the twentieth century.

So why the protests? Globalization today is far less likely to take the form of emigration and immigration flows across national borders. And it is less prominent in the form of global trade. Of much greater importance are global capital flows of investment dollars. Such flows affect employment patterns in widely disparate countries, standards of living for the poor, the value of stocks and bonds in market exchanges from Europe to Asia, and macroeconomic conditions of inflation and recession.

Since the end of the Cold War, economic orthodoxy has held that countries should liberalize trade, create independent central banks to stabilize money supplies, restrain public spending (especially deficit spending), privatize state property, and spend more on health and education.[4] But the resulting benefits have been both elusive and unevenly distributed. Consider the following: since 1987, adoption of orthodox economic policies worldwide has led to growth and the reduction of poverty in only three underdeveloped regions: East Asia and the Pacific, the Middle East and North Africa, and South Asia. Poverty rates have actually increased in Eastern Europe and Central Asia, Latin America and the Caribbean, and subsaharan Africa.[5]

The global economic crisis of 1997, caused by a panic in the Thai economy, demonstrated that no country's economy is immune from external shocks. That fact makes managing the domestic economy of the United States ever more difficult. How much control can government really exercise over the economy through the judicious use of economic theory? How is the national budget formulated, and why did the deficit grow so large and prove so difficult to control? What effects do government taxing and spending policies have on the economy and on economic equality? As we shall see, no one person or organization controls the American economy; multiple actors have a say in economic conditions. And not all of these actors are public.

THEORIES OF ECONOMIC POLICY

Government attempts to control the economy rely on theories about how the economy responds to government taxing and spending policies. How policymakers tax and spend depends on their beliefs about (1) how the economy functions and (2) the proper role of government in the economy. The American economy is so complex that no policymaker knows exactly how it works. Policymakers rely on economic theories to explain its functioning, and there are nearly as many theories as there are economists. Unfortunately, different theories (and economists) often predict different outcomes. One source of differing predictions is the different assumptions that underlie competing economic theories. Another problem is the differences between abstract theories and the real world. Still, despite the disagreement among economists, a knowledge of basic economics is necessary to understand how government approaches public policy.

We are concerned here with economic policy in a market economy—one in which the prices of goods and services are determined through the interaction of sellers and buyers (that is, through supply and demand). This kind of economy is typical of the consumer-dominated societies of Western Europe and the United States. A nonmarket economy relies on government planners to determine both the prices of goods and the amounts that are produced. The old Soviet economy is a perfect example. In a nonmarket economy, the government owns and operates the major means of production.

Economists Getting Data for Predictions

The forecast you get depends on the economist you ask.

THE ECONOMISTS

Market economies are loosely called *capitalist economies:* they allow private individuals to own property; to sell goods for profit in free, or open, markets; and to accumulate wealth, called *capital.* Market economies often exhibit a mix of government and private ownership. For example, Britain has had considerably more government-owned enterprises (railroads, broadcasting, and housing) than has the United States. Competing economic theories differ largely on how free they say the markets should be—in other words, on government's role in directing the economy.

Laissez-Faire Economics

The French term *laissez faire,* introduced in Chapter 1 and discussed again in Chapter 13, describes the absence of government control. The economic doctrine of laissez faire likens the operation of a free market to the process of natural selection. Economic competition weeds out the weak and preserves the strong. In the process, the economy prospers and everyone eventually benefits.

Advocates of laissez-faire economics are fond of quoting Adam Smith's *The Wealth of Nations.* In this 1776 treatise, Smith argued that each individual, pursuing his own selfish interests in a competitive market, was "led by an invisible hand to promote an end which was no part of his intention." Smith's "invisible hand" has been used for two centuries to justify the belief that the narrow pursuit of profits serves the broad interests of society. Strict advocates of laissez faire maintain that government interference with business tampers with the laws of nature, obstructing the workings of the free market.

Keynesian Theory

economic depression
A period of high unemployment and business failures; a severe, long-lasting downturn in a business cycle.

inflation
An economic condition characterized by price increases linked to a decrease in the value of the currency.

One problem with laissez-faire economics is its insistence that government should do little about **economic depressions** (periods of high unemployment and business failures) or raging **inflation** (price increases that decrease the value of currency). Inflation is ordinarily measured by the consumer price

business cycle
Expansions and contractions of business activity, the first accompanied by inflation and the second by unemployment.

aggregate demand
The money available to be spent for goods and services by consumers, businesses, and government.

productive capacity
The total value of goods and services that can be produced when the economy works at full capacity.

gross domestic product (GDP)
The total value of the goods and services produced by a country during a year.

Keynesian theory
An economic theory stating that the government can stabilize the economy—i.e., can smooth business cycles—by controlling the level of aggregate demand, and that the level of aggregate demand can be controlled by means of fiscal and monetary policies.

fiscal policies
Economic policies that involve government spending and taxing.

monetary policies
Economic policies that involve control of, and changes in, the supply of money.

deficit financing
The Keynesian technique of spending beyond government income to combat an economic slump. Its purpose is to inject extra money into the economy to stimulate aggregate demand.

Council of Economic Advisers (CEA)
A group that works within the executive branch to provide advice on maintaining a stable economy.

index (CPI), which Feature 18.1 explains. Since the beginning of the Industrial Revolution, capitalist economies have suffered through many cyclical fluctuations. The United States has experienced more than fifteen of these **business cycles**—expansions and contractions of business activity, the first stage accompanied by inflation and the second stage by unemployment. No one had a theory that really explained these cycles until the Great Depression of the 1930s.

That was when John Maynard Keynes, a British economist, theorized that business cycles stem from imbalances between aggregate demand and productive capacity. **Aggregate demand** is the income available to consumers, business, and government to spend on goods and services. **Productive capacity** is the total value of goods and services that can be produced when the economy is working at full capacity. The value of the goods and services actually produced is called the **gross domestic product (GDP).** When demand exceeds productive capacity, people are willing to pay more for available goods, which leads to price inflation. When productive capacity exceeds demand, producers cut back on their output of goods, which leads to unemployment. When many people are unemployed for an extended period, the economy is in a depression. Keynes theorized that government could stabilize the economy (and smooth out or eliminate business cycles) by controlling the level of aggregate demand.

Keynesian theory holds that aggregate demand can be adjusted through a combination of fiscal and monetary policies. **Fiscal policies,** which are enacted by the president and Congress, involve changes in government spending and taxing. When demand is too low, according to Keynes, government should either spend more itself, hiring people and thus giving them money, or cut taxes, giving people more of their own money to spend. When demand is too great, the government should either spend less or raise taxes, giving people less money to spend. **Monetary policies,** which are largely determined by the Federal Reserve Board, involve changes in the money supply and operate less directly on the economy. Increasing the amount of money in circulation increases aggregate demand and thus increases price inflation. Decreasing the money supply decreases aggregate demand and inflationary pressures.

Despite some problems with the assumptions of Keynesian theory, capitalist countries have widely adopted it in some form.[6] At one time or another, virtually all have used the Keynesian technique of **deficit financing**—spending in excess of tax revenues—to combat an economic slump. The objective of deficit financing is to inject extra money into the economy to stimulate aggregate demand. Most deficits are financed with funds borrowed through the issuing of government bonds, notes, or other securities. The theory holds that deficits can be paid off with budget surpluses after the economy recovers.

Because Keynesian theory requires government to play an active role in controlling the economy, it runs counter to laissez-faire economics. Before Keynes, no administration in Washington would shoulder responsibility for maintaining a healthy economy. In 1946, the year Keynes died, Congress passed an employment act establishing "the continuing responsibility of the national government to . . . promote maximum employment, production and purchasing power." It also created the **Council of Economic Advisers (CEA)** within the Executive Office of the President to

feature 18.1

The Consumer Price Index

Inflation in the United States is usually measured in terms of the consumer price index, which is calculated by the U.S. Bureau of Labor Statistics. The CPI is based on prices paid for food, clothing, shelter, transportation, medical services, and other items necessary for daily living. Data are collected from eighty-five areas across the country, from nearly sixty thousand homes and almost twenty thousand businesses. To maintain its accuracy, the CPI is reviewed approximately every ten years.

The CPI is not a perfect yardstick. One problem is that it does not differentiate between inflationary price increases and other price increases. A Ford sedan bought in 1987, for instance, is not the same as a Ford sedan bought in 1997. To some extent, the price difference reflects improvements in quality as well as a decrease in the value of the dollar. The CPI is also slow to reflect changes in purchasing habits. Wash-and-wear clothes were tumbling in the dryer for several years before the government agreed to include them as an item in the index.

These are minor issues compared with the weight given over time to the cost of housing. Until 1983, 26 percent of the CPI was attributed to the cost of purchasing and financing a home. This formula neglected the realities that many people rent and that few people buy a home every year. A better measure of the cost of shelter is the cost of renting equivalent housing. Using this method of calculating the cost of shelter, the weight given to housing in the CPI dropped from 26 percent to 14 percent.

The government uses the CPI to make cost-of-living adjustments in civil service and military pension payments and social security benefits. Many union wage contracts with private businesses are indexed (tied) to the CPI. Because the CPI tends to rise each year, so do payments that are tied to it. In a way, indexing payments to the CPI promotes both the growth of government spending and inflation itself. The United States is one of the few nations that also ties its tax brackets to a price index, which reduces government revenues by eliminating the effect of inflation on taxpayer incomes.

Despite its faults, the CPI is at least a consistent measure of prices, and it is likely to continue as the basis for adjustments to wages, benefits, and payments affecting millions of people.

Sources: Adapted from David S. Moore, *Statistics: Concepts and Controversies,* 2nd ed. (New York: Freeman, 1985), pp. 238–241. Used by permission of W. H. Freeman. Also see U.S. Bureau of the Census, U.S. Department of Commerce, *Statistical Abstract of the United States, 1990* (Washington, D.C.: U.S. Government Printing Office, 1990), pp. 465–466; Robert D. Hershey, Jr., "An Inflation Index Is Said to Overstate the Case," *New York Times,* 11 January 1994, pp. C1–C2; and David Wessel, "Why the CPI Fix Looks So Likely," *Wall Street Journal,* 11 December 1995, p. 1.

advise the president on maintaining a stable economy. The CEA normally consists of three economists (usually university professors) appointed by the president with Senate approval. Aided by a staff of about twenty-five people (mostly economists), the CEA helps the president prepare his annual economic report, also a provision of the 1946 act. The chair of the CEA is usually a prominent spokesperson for the administration's economic policy.

The Employment Act of 1946, which reflected Keynesian theory, had a tremendous effect on government economic policy. Many people believe it was the primary source of "big government" in America. Even Richard Nixon, a conservative president, admitted that "we are all Keynesians now," by accepting government responsibility for the economy.

Fed Head

Alan Greenspan, chairman of the Federal Reserve Board, heads the central banking operation of the United States on appointment by the president for a four-year term. Initially appointed in 1987 by Reagan, Greenspan was reappointed by Bush and Clinton (twice). He may remain a fixture in Washington for some time, for his current term lasts until July, 2004.

monetarists
Those who argue that government can effectively control the performance of an economy only by controlling the supply of money.

Federal Reserve System
The system of banks that acts as the central bank of the United States and controls major monetary policies.

Monetary Policy

Although most economists accept Keynesian theory in its broad outlines, they depreciate its political utility. Some especially question the value of fiscal policies in controlling inflation and unemployment. They argue that government spending programs take too long to enact in Congress and to implement through the bureaucracy. As a result, jobs are created not when they are needed but years later, when the crisis may have passed and government spending needs to be reduced.

Also, government spending is easier to start than to stop because the groups that benefit from spending programs tend to defend them even when they are no longer needed. A similar criticism applies to tax policies. Politically, it is much easier to cut taxes than to raise them. In other words, Keynesian theory requires that governments be able to begin and end spending quickly and to cut and raise taxes quickly. But in the real world, these fiscal tools are easier to use in one direction than the other.

Recognizing these limitations of fiscal policies, **monetarists** argue that government can control the economy's performance effectively only by controlling the nation's money supply. Monetarists favor a long-range policy of small but steady growth in the amount of money in circulation rather than frequent manipulation of monetary policies.

Monetary policies in the United States are under the control of the **Federal Reserve System,** which acts as the country's central bank. Established in 1914, the Fed is not a single bank but a system of banks. At the top of the system is the board of governors, seven members appointed by the president for staggered terms of fourteen years. The president designates one member of the board to be its chairperson, who serves a four-year term that extends beyond the president's term of office. This complex arrangement was intended to make the board independent of the president and even of Congress. An independent board, the reasoning went, would be able to make financial decisions for the nation without regard to their political implications.

The Fed controls the money supply, which affects inflation, in three ways. It can change the *reserve requirement,* which is the amount of cash that member banks must keep on deposit in their regional Federal Reserve bank. An increase in the reserve requirement reduces the amount of money banks have available to lend. The Fed can also change its *discount rate,* the interest rate that member banks have to pay to borrow money from a Federal Reserve bank. A lower rate encourages member banks to borrow and lend more freely. Finally, the Fed can *buy and sell government securities* (such as U.S. Treasury notes and bonds) on the open market. When it buys securities, it pays out money, putting more money into circulation; when it sells securities, the process works in reverse. These transactions influence the federal funds rate, which banks charge one another for overnight loans. Again, a lower federal funds rate encourages borrowing and lending money.

Basic economic theory holds that interest rates should be raised when the economy is growing too quickly (this restricts the flow of money, thus avoiding inflation) and lowered when the economy is sluggish (thus increasing the money flow to encourage spending and economic growth). The Federal Reserve Board (the Fed), not the president, controls interest rates. (Indeed, the Fed was created to be independent of presidential control.) This makes the Fed chairman a critical player in economic affairs.

The Brass Golden Dollar

In 2000, the United States Mint issued a "golden dollar" coin—the same size as the old Susan B. Anthony silver-colored dollar coin, which it replaces. The new coin is made of manganese brass, a golden-colored material composed of 77 percent copper, 12 percent zinc, 7 percent manganese, and 4 percent nickel. The new coin's face depicts a young Shoshone interpreter named Sacajawea who assisted the Lewis and Clark expedition from 1804 through 1806. Why a dollar coin? The vending industry wants it.

Can You Explain Why...
a president is not directly responsible for the nation's interest rates?

Historically, the Fed has adjusted interest rates to combat inflation rather than to stimulate economic growth.[7] (A former Fed chairman once said its task was "to remove the punch bowl when the party gets going.")[8] But in 1998, the Fed—and Greenspan—oversaw an economy with low inflation, low unemployment, *and* strong growth. As one economics commentator wrote, "What more could a Federal Reserve chairman want?"[9]

Although the president is formally responsible for the state of the economy and although voters hold him accountable for the economy, the president neither determines interest rates (the Fed does) nor controls spending (Congress does). In this respect, President Clinton has suffered the same restrictions as his twentieth-century predecessors. All have had to work with a Fed that was made independent of both the president and Congress, and all have had to deal with the fact that Congress ultimately controls spending. These restrictions on presidential authority are consistent with the pluralist model of democracy, but a president held responsible for the economy may not appreciate that theoretical argument.

The Fed's activities are essential parts of the government's overall economic policy, but they lie outside the direct control of the president. This can create problems in coordinating economic policy. For example, the president might want the Fed to lower interest rates to stimulate the economy, but the Fed might resist for fear of inflation. Such policy clashes can pit the chair of the Federal Reserve Board directly against the president. So presidents typically court the Fed chair, even one appointed by a president of the other party.

Although the Fed's economic policies are not perfectly insulated from political concerns, they are sufficiently independent that the president is not able to control monetary policy without the Fed's cooperation. This means that the president cannot be held completely responsible for the state of the economy—even though traditionally most Americans have held him almost totally responsible. In fact, political scientists who study presidential elections suggest that economic conditions play an important, though not always decisive, role in determining which candidate wins. As a generalization, a strong economy favors the incumbent party. When people are optimistic about the economic future and feel that they are doing well, they typically see no reason to change the party controlling the White House. But when conditions are bad or worsening, voters often decide to seek a change. For example, Bill Clinton rode to victory in 1992 over the incumbent president, George Bush, by constantly reminding himself that the central issue of the campaign could be summarized quite succinctly: "It's the economy, stupid!"

But economic conditions do not always determine the winner of a presidential election. The 2000 election is a case in point. To the dismay of many Democrats, Al Gore lost the election despite the strongest economy in over a century (and relative world peace). Gore sought to remind voters of the strong economy and to claim credit for it. He repeatedly accused his opponent, George W. Bush, of risking economic prosperity by offering a large, "risky" tax cut that threatened to return the budget to deficit levels, eat up the surplus, and cause an economic recession. Ultimately, voters in 2000 chose not to give entire credit for the strong economy to the Democrats and decided to change control of the White House from the Democrats to the Republicans.

Part of this decision can be explained by the fact that the economic expansion of the late 1990s lasted for so many years. Some scholars believe that many voters simply decided that a continuously growing economy was "normal," so they no longer gave the Clinton-Gore administration credit for it. The prolonged economic boom had also prompted millions of citizens to invest in the stock market, many of them for the first time (see Politics in a Changing America 18.1). As a result, they became more knowledgeable about the workings of the economy; instead of giving the Clinton-Gore administration all the credit for the economic boom, they also credited Alan Greenspan and the Fed. Indeed, Alan Greenspan became one of the most famous men in the nation—and the world.

In his role as Federal Reserve Board chairman, Alan Greenspan has played a vital role in preserving economic stability, not only in the American economy but also in economic conditions worldwide. When the economy of Thailand collapsed in 1997, the effects were felt throughout Asia. A regional economy that had once been referred to as the Asian Tiger now fell into a deep and lasting recession. The effects spread quickly to Eastern Europe and especially Russia, as nervous investors pulled back their capital from emerging markets and invested in the safer economies of Western Europe and the United States.

This rapid capital flow out of developing countries threatened global economic stability and raised the specter of a worldwide economic depression. Greenspan responded by aggressively cutting the interest rate charged by the Federal Reserve to member banks in the United States. This action, in turn, lowered market interest rates to corporations and consumers alike. As a result, the American economy took an upswing, effectively countering the global recessionary effects of Asian and Eastern European economic downturns. Greenspan maintained this policy throughout 1997 and 1998 until the threat of global recession had passed.

Beginning in late 1999, Greenspan changed course and began to raise interest rates in order to slow down the American economy, which had begun showing signs of inflationary pressures. Warning investors in the American stock market that prices were unrealistically high, Greenspan

★ politics in a changing america

18.1 The Democratization of the Stock Market

Once, only the very rich in America bought stocks or bonds and watched the stock market returns on the evening news. Indeed, the stereotype of the Wall Street investor used to be a rich, old, overweight man smoking a cigar and dressed in striped pants and tails. But the invention of mutual funds, the legislative authorization of 401(k) plans and other personal investment plans for retirement savings, Roth IRAs (tax-free individual retirement accounts), and double-digit rates of return on investments have enticed millions of middle-class Americans into the stock market. In the second half of the 1990s, investors could expect a 20 percent rate of return on their stock portfolio, compared to a paltry 2 or 3 percent on their savings account and perhaps 5 or 6 percent on certificates of deposit or federal savings bonds.

This democratization of stock holding has had important political effects. Now a president concerned about his own or his party's reelection prospects has to worry not only about the unemployment rate but also the Dow Jones Industrial Average (an index that tracks the stock prices of thirty of the largest, most frequently traded U.S. companies), the Standard and Poor's 500, and the NASDAQ (a stock exchange specializing in newer, high-technology firms). This change has put additional constraints on the options that a president may use to manage the nation's economy. With more than half of American families investing in the stock market, a sharp decline in the Dow Jones or NASDAQ

can be every bit as politically damaging today as double-digit unemployment used to be in earlier generations (and would be still).

At the turn of the millennium, investors were left in a state of nervous anticipation. Having suffered through shocks from the collapse of the Asian and Russian economies in mid- to late 1997, investors saw rapid increases in stock prices and values until February 2000. At that point, the "irrational exuberance" (to use Greenspan's phrase) for high-tech stocks cooled as earnings declined or disappeared and the Federal Reserve Board raised interest rates to slow the economy's rate of growth. Greenspan and other Federal Reserve Board governors became concerned that the high rates of growth in the American economy were unsustainable over the long run without triggering inflation. Hence, during 1999 the Fed began to raise interest rates. This rate increase put a squeeze on corporate profits as companies had to pay more to borrow funds for expansion. In early 2001, the NASDAQ had lost almost one-third of its value over the previous year, seriously affecting investors' retirement accounts and personal investment portfolios.

Thus, when President Bush took office in 2001, shoring up the economy had to be one of his top priorities. Whether or not he will be successful—and whether or not he will be blamed if the economy slips into a recession—remains to be seen.

first tried to "talk prices down" by commenting publicly on the market's "irrational exuberance." When talking did not slow the rapid increase in stock prices, particularly in high tech or dot.com stocks, Greenspan and the Federal Reserve began raising interest rates incrementally throughout 2000.

By the end of 2000, the American economy began showing signs of slowing down. Inflationary price increases for goods and services ended, consumer confidence (a measure of likely purchases) declined, holiday sales were disappointing, and the stock market fell. Content that the inflationary pressures in the American economy were under control and that the growth rate of the economy was now at a lower and sustainable level, Greenspan changed course again in early 2001 and dropped interest rates a full half percentage point. The hope was that this management of the Federal Reserve loan rate would bring the American economy to a "soft landing" and put the country back on track to continued prosperity. Whether this hope is correct or not depends on whether the Federal Reserve predicted the course of the economy accurately; some analysts fear that the Fed kept interest rates too high for too long and that the current period of economic growth is about to end in a recession. Only time will tell.

Supply-Side Economics

supply-side economics
Economic policies aimed at increasing the supply of goods (as opposed to increasing demand), consisting mainly of tax cuts for possible investors and less regulation of business.

When Reagan came to office in 1981, he embraced a school of thought called **supply-side economics** to deal with the double-digit inflation that the nation was experiencing. Keynesian theory argues that inflation results when consumers, businesses, and governments have more money to spend than there are goods and services to buy. The standard Keynesian solution is to reduce demand (for example, by increasing taxes). Supply-siders argue that inflation can be lowered more effectively by increasing the supply of goods. (That is, they stress the supply side of the economic equation.) Specifically, they favor tax cuts to stimulate investment (which, in turn, leads to the production of more goods) and less government regulation of business (again, to increase productivity—which they hold will yield more, not less, government revenue). Supply-siders also argue that the rich should receive larger tax cuts than the poor because the rich have more money to invest. The benefits of increased investment will then "trickle down" to working people in the form of additional jobs and income.

In a sense, supply-side economics resembles laissez-faire economics because it prefers less government regulation and less taxation. Supply-siders believe that government interferes too much with the efforts of individuals to work, save, and invest. Inspired by supply-side theory, Reagan proposed (and got) massive tax cuts in the Economic Recovery Tax Act of 1981. The act reduced individual tax rates by 23 percent over a three-year period and cut the marginal tax rate for the highest income group from 70 to 50 percent. Reagan also launched a program to deregulate business. According to supply-side theory, these actions would generate extra government revenue, making spending cuts unnecessary. Nevertheless, Reagan also cut funding for some domestic programs, including Aid to Families with Dependent Children. Contrary to supply-side theory, he also proposed hefty increases in military spending. This blend of tax cuts, deregulation, cuts in spending for social programs, and increases in spending for defense became known, somewhat disparagingly, as *Reaganomics*.

How well did Reaganomics work? Although it reduced inflation and unemployment (aided by a sharp decline in oil prices) and worked largely as expected in the area of industry deregulation, Reaganomics failed massively to reduce the budget deficit. Contrary to supply-side theory, the 1981 tax cut was accompanied by a massive drop in tax revenues. Shortly after taking office, Reagan promised that his economic policies would balance the national budget by 1984, but lower tax revenues and higher defense spending produced the largest budget deficits ever, as shown in Figure 18.1.[10] In fact, budget deficits continued until 1998, when a booming U.S. economy generated the first budget surplus since 1969.

PUBLIC POLICY AND THE BUDGET

What Is the Budget?

To most people—college students included—the national budget is B-O-R-I-N-G. To national politicians, it is an exciting script for high drama. The numbers, categories, and percentages that numb normal minds cause politicians' nostrils to flare and their hearts to pound. The budget is a battlefield on which politicians wage war over the programs they support.

Control of the budget is important to members of Congress because they are politicians, and politicians want to wield power, not watch someone else wield it. Also, the Constitution established Congress, not the president, as the "first branch" of government and the people's representatives. Unfortunately for Congress, the president has emerged as the leader in shaping the budget. Although Congress often disagrees with presidential spending priorities, it has been unable to mount a serious challenge to presidential authority by presenting a coherent alternative budget.

Today, the president prepares the budget, and Congress approves it. This was not always the case. Before 1921, Congress prepared the budget under its constitutional authority to raise taxes and appropriate funds. The budget was formed piecemeal by enacting a series of laws that originated in the many committees involved in the highly decentralized process of raising revenue, authorizing expenditures, and appropriating funds. Executive agencies even submitted their budgetary requests directly to Congress, not to the president. No one was responsible for the big picture—the budget as a whole. The president's role was essentially limited to approving revenue and appropriations bills, just as he approved other pieces of legislation.

Congressional budgeting (such as it was) worked well enough for a nation of farmers, but not for an industrialized nation with a growing population and an increasingly active government. Soon after World War I, Congress realized that the budget-making process needed to be centralized. With the Budget and Accounting Act of 1921, it thrust the responsibility for preparing the budget onto the president. The act established the Bureau of the Budget to help the president write "his" budget, which had to be submitted to Congress each January. Congress retained its constitutional authority to raise and spend funds, but now Congress would begin its work with the president's budget as its starting point. And all executive agencies' budget requests had to be funneled for review through the Bureau of the Budget (which became the Office of Management and Budget in 1970); those consistent with the president's overall economic and legislative program were incorporated into the president's budget.

The Nature of the Budget

The national budget is complex. But its basic elements are not beyond understanding. We begin with some definitions. The *Budget of the United States Government* is the annual financial plan that the president is

figure

18.1   Budget Deficits and Surpluses Over Time

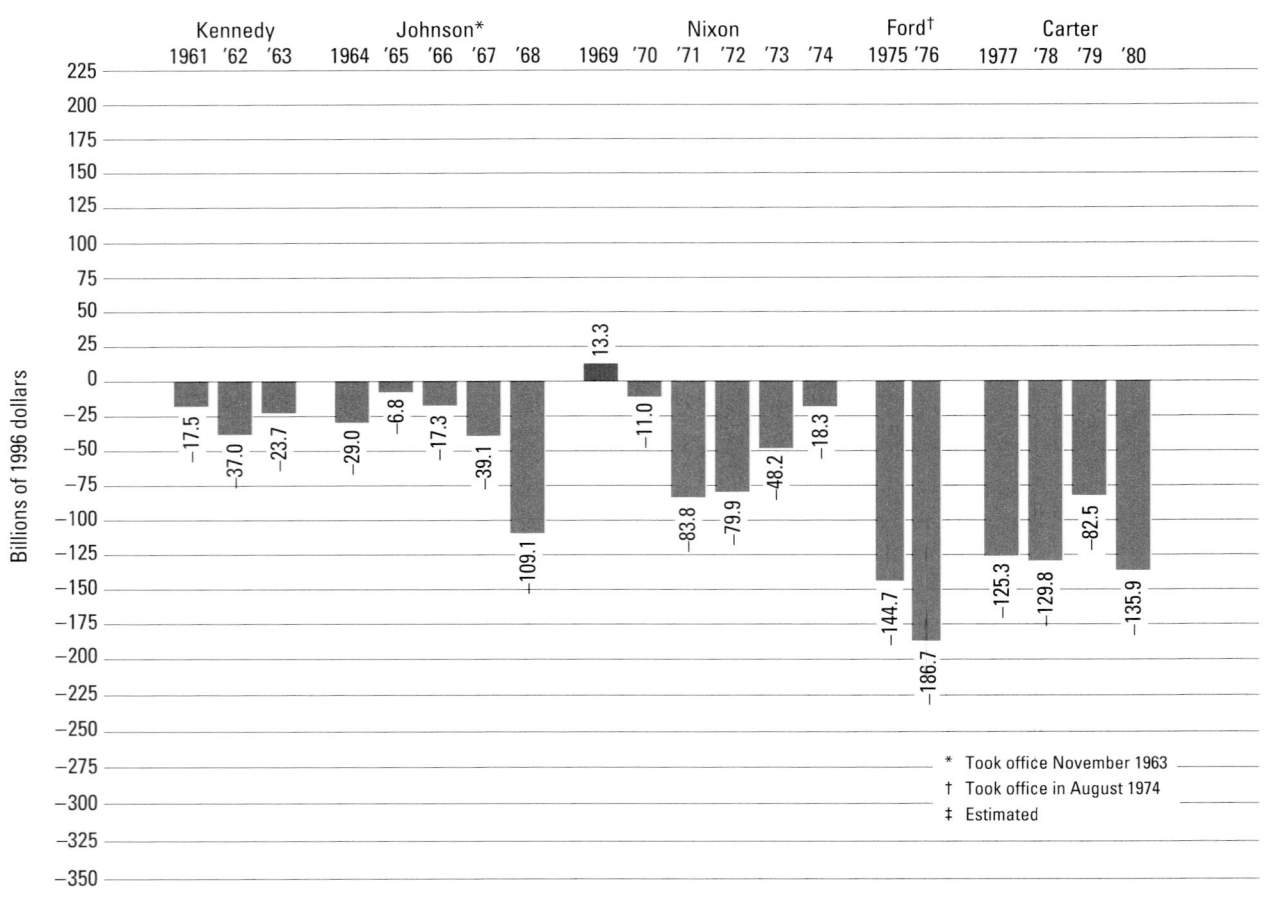

*   Took office November 1963
†   Took office in August 1974
‡   Estimated

In his first inaugural address, President Reagan said, "You and I, as individuals, can, by borrowing, live beyond our means, but only for a limited period of time. Why, then, should we think that collectively, as a nation, we're not bound by that same limitation?" But borrow he did. Reagan's critics charged that the budget deficits under his administration—more than $1.3 trillion—exceeded the total deficits of all previous presidents. But this charge does not take inflation into account. A billion dollars in the 1990s is worth much less than it was a century ago or even ten years ago.

fiscal year (FY)

The twelve-month period from October 1 to September 30 used by the government for accounting purposes. A fiscal-year budget is named for the year in which it ends.

required to submit to Congress at the start of each year. It applies to the next **fiscal year (FY)**, the interval the government uses for accounting purposes. Currently, the fiscal year runs from October 1 to September 30. The budget is named for the year in which it *ends*, so the FY 2002 budget applies to the twelve months from October 1, 2001, to September 30, 2002.

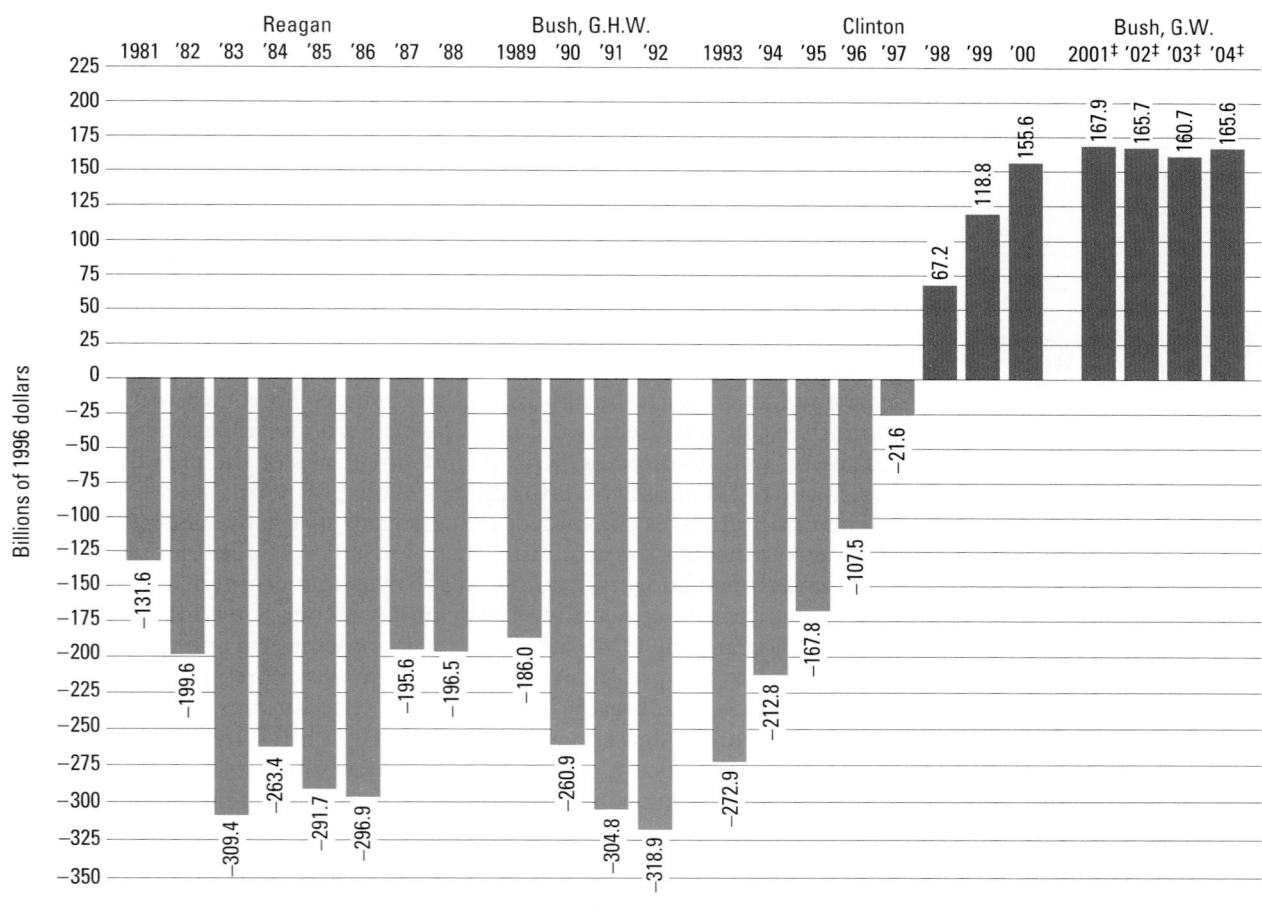

A fairer way to calculate deficits and surpluses is in constant dollars—dollars whose value has been standardized to a given year. This chart shows the actual deficits and surpluses in 1996 dollars incurred under presidential administrations from Eisenhower to Bush. Even computed this way, Reagan's deficits were enormous—especially for a president who claimed to oppose government borrowing. The deficit grew to be as large under Bush before being reduced and eventually eliminated under Clinton.

Source: Executive Office of the President, *Budget of the United States Government, Fiscal Year 2001: Historical Tables* (Washington, D.C.: U.S. Government Printing Office, 2000), p. 364.

budget authority
The amounts that government agencies are authorized to spend for their programs.

budget outlays
The amounts that government agencies are expected to spend in the fiscal year.

receipts
For a government, the amount expected or obtained in taxes and other revenues.

Broadly, the budget defines **budget authority** (how much government agencies are authorized to spend on programs); **budget outlays,** or expenditures (how much they are expected to spend); and **receipts** (how much is expected in taxes and other revenues). President Clinton's FY 2000 budget contained authority for expenditures of $1,781 billion, but it provided for outlays of "only" $1,766 billion. His budget also anticipated receipts of

$1,883 billion, leaving an estimated *surplus* of $117 billon—the difference between receipts and outlays.

Clinton's FY 2001 budget, with appendices, was thousands of pages long and weighed several pounds. (The president's budget document contains more than numbers. It also explains individual spending programs in terms of national needs and agency objectives, and it analyzes proposed taxes and other receipts.) Each year, the publication of the president's budget is anxiously awaited by reporters, lobbyists, and political analysts eager to learn his plans for government spending in the coming year.

Preparing the President's Budget

Office of Management and Budget (OMB)
The budgeting arm of the Executive Office; prepares the president's budget.

The budget that the president submits to Congress each winter is the end product of a process that begins the previous spring under the supervision of the **Office of Management and Budget (OMB).** OMB is located within the Executive Office of the President and is headed by a director appointed by the president with the approval of the Senate. The OMB, with a staff of more than five hundred, is the most powerful domestic agency in the bureaucracy, and its director, who attends meetings of the president's cabinet, is one of the most powerful figures in government.

The OMB initiates the budget process each spring by meeting with the president to discuss the economic situation and his budgetary priorities. It then sends broad budgeting guidelines to every government agency and requests their initial projection of how much money they will need for the next fiscal year. The OMB assembles this information and makes recommendations to the president, who then develops more precise guidelines describing how much each is likely to get. By summer, the agencies are asked to prepare budgets based on the new guidelines. By fall, they submit their formal budgets to the OMB, where budget analysts scrutinize agency requests, considering both their costs and their consistency with the president's legislative program. A lot of politicking goes on at this stage, as agency heads try to circumvent the OMB by pleading for their pet projects with presidential advisers and perhaps even the president himself. Unlike presidents Reagan and Bush, who basically delegated economic policy to others in their administrations, Clinton was more involved in the process and made more of the big decisions himself.

Political negotiations over the budget may extend into the early winter—often until it goes to the printer. The voluminous document looks very much like a finished product, but the figures it contains are not final. In giving the president the responsibility for preparing the budget in 1921, Congress simply provided itself with a starting point for its own work. And even with this headstart, Congress has a hard time disciplining itself to produce a coherent, balanced budget.

Passing the Congressional Budget

The president's budget must be approved by Congress. Its process for doing so is a creaky conglomeration of traditional procedures overlaid with structural reforms from the 1970s, external constraints from the 1980s, and changes introduced by the 1990 Budget Enforcement Act. The cumbersome process has had difficulty producing a budget according to Congress's own timetable.

The Traditional Procedure: The Committee Structure.   Traditionally, the tasks of budget making were divided among a number of committees—a process that has been retained. Three types of committees are involved in budgeting:

tax committees
The two committees of Congress responsible for raising the revenue with which to run the government.

authorization committees
Committees of Congress that can authorize spending in their particular areas of responsibility.

appropriations committees
Committees of Congress that decide which of the programs passed by the authorization committees will actually be funded.

- **Tax committees** are responsible for raising the revenues to run the government. The Ways and Means Committee in the House and the Finance Committee in the Senate consider all proposals for taxes, tariffs, and other receipts contained in the president's budget.

- **Authorization committees** (such as the House Armed Services Committee and the Senate Banking, Housing, and Urban Affairs Committee) have jurisdiction over particular legislative subjects. The House has about twenty committees that can authorize spending, and the Senate about fifteen. Each pores over the portions of the budget that pertain to its area of responsibility. However, in recent years power has shifted from the authorization committees to the appropriations committees.

- **Appropriations committees** decide which of the programs approved by the authorization committees will actually be funded (that is, given money to spend). For example, the House Armed Services Committee might propose building a new line of tanks for the army, and it might succeed in getting this proposal enacted into law. But the tanks will never be built unless the appropriations committees appropriate funds for that purpose. Thirteen distinct appropriations bills are supposed to be enacted each year to fund the nation's spending.

Two serious problems are inherent in a budgeting process that involves three distinct kinds of congressional committees. First, the two-step spending process (first authorization, then appropriation) is complex; it offers wonderful opportunities for interest groups to get into the budgeting act in the spirit of pluralist democracy. Second, because one group of legislators in each house plans for revenues and many other groups plan for spending, no one is responsible for the budget as a whole. In the 1970s, Congress added a new committee structure that combats the pluralist politics inherent in the old procedures and allows budget choices to be made in a more majoritarian manner, by votes in both chambers. In the 1980s, Congress tried to force itself to balance the budget by setting targets. In 1990, Congress tried again to patch the leaks in the budget boat with additional reforms. Here is a brief account of these developments.

Reforms of the 1970s: The Budget Committee Structure.   Congress surrendered considerable authority in 1921 when it gave the president the responsibility of preparing the budget. During the next fifty years, attempts by Congress to regain control of the budgeting process failed because of jurisdictional squabbles between the revenue and appropriations committees. The Budget and Impoundment Control Act of 1974 fashioned a typically political solution to the problems of wounded egos and competing

budget committees
One committee in each house of Congress that supervises a comprehensive budget review process.

Congressional Budget Office (CBO)
The budgeting arm of Congress, which prepares alternative budgets to those prepared by the president's OMB.

jurisdictions, which had frustrated previous attempts to change the budget-making process. All the tax and appropriations committees (and chairpersons) were retained, but new House and Senate budget committees were superimposed over the old committee structure. The **budget committees** supervise a comprehensive budget review process, aided by the Congressional Budget Office. The **Congressional Budget Office (CBO),** with a staff of more than two hundred, has acquired a budgetary expertise equal to that of the president's OMB, so it can prepare credible alternative budgets for Congress.

At the heart of the 1974 reforms was a timetable for the congressional budgeting process. The budget committees are supposed to propose an initial budget resolution that sets overall revenue and spending levels, broken down into twenty-one different "budget functions," such as national defense, agriculture, and health. By April 15, both houses are supposed to have agreed on a single budget resolution to guide their work on the budget during the summer. The appropriations committees are supposed to begin drafting the thirteen appropriations bills by May 15 and complete them by June 30. Throughout, the levels of spending set by majority vote in the budget resolution are supposed to constrain pressures by special interests to increase spending.

Congress implemented this basic process in 1975, and it worked reasonably well for the first few years. Congress was able to work on and structure the budget as a whole rather than in pieces. But the process broke down during the Reagan administration, when the president submitted annual budgets with huge deficits. The Democratic Congress adjusted Reagan's spending priorities away from the military and toward social programs, but it refused to propose a tax increase to reduce the deficit without the president's cooperation. At loggerheads with the president, Congress encountered increasing difficulty in enacting its budget resolutions according to its own timetable.

Lessons of the 1980s: Gramm-Rudman.   Alarmed by the huge deficits in Reagan's budgets, frustrated by his refusal to raise taxes, and stymied by their own inability to cut the deficit, members of Congress were ready to try almost anything. Republican senators Phil Gramm of Texas and Warren Rudman of New Hampshire were joined by Democrat Ernest Hollings of South Carolina in a drastic proposal to force a balanced budget by gradually eliminating the deficit. Soon known simply as **Gramm-Rudman,** this 1985 act mandated that the budget deficit be lowered to a specified level each year until the budget was balanced by FY 1991. If Congress did not meet the deficit level in any year, the act would trigger across-the-board budget cuts. In 1986, the very first year under Gramm-Rudman, Congress failed to meet its deficit target, and few members liked the 4.3 percent sliced from every domestic and defense program (except those exempted, such as social security). Unable to make the deficit meet the law again in 1987, Congress and the president simply changed the law to match the deficit. Gramm-Rudman showed that Congress lacked the will to force itself to balance the budget by an orderly plan of deficit reduction.

Gramm-Rudman
Popular name for an act passed by Congress in 1985 that, in its original form, sought to lower the national deficit to a specified level each year, culminating in a balanced budget in FY 1991. New reforms and deficit targets were agreed on in 1990.

Reforms of the 1990s: Balanced Budgets.   When the 1990 recession threatened another huge deficit for FY 1991, Congress and President Bush

Budget Enforcement Act (BEA)
A 1990 law that distinguished between mandatory and discretionary spending.

mandatory spending
In the Budget Enforcement Act of 1990, expenditures required by previous commitments.

discretionary spending
In the Budget Enforcement Act of 1990, authorized expenditures from annual appropriations.

entitlement
A benefit to which every eligible person has a legal right and that the government cannot deny.

pay-as-you-go
In the Budget Enforcement Act of 1990, the requirement that any tax cut or expansion of an entitlement program must be offset by a tax increase or other savings.

agreed on a new package of reforms and deficit targets in the **Budget Enforcement Act (BEA)** of 1990. Instead of defining annual deficit targets, the BEA defined two types of spending: **mandatory spending** and **discretionary spending.** Spending is mandatory for **entitlement** programs (such as social security and veterans' pensions) that provide benefits to individuals legally entitled to them (see Chapter 19) and cannot be reduced without changing the law. This is not true of discretionary spending, which are expenditures authorized by annual appropriations, such as for the military. For the first time, the law established **pay-as-you-go** restrictions on mandatory spending: any proposed expansion of an entitlement program must be offset by cuts to another program or by a tax increase. Similarly, any tax cut must be offset by a tax increase somewhere else or by spending cuts.[11] Also for the first time, the law imposed limits, or "caps," on discretionary spending. To get the Democratic Congress to pass the BEA, Bush accepted some modest tax increases. Just two years earlier, however, Bush had accepted his party's nomination for president with the vow, "Read my lips: no new taxes." Consequently, he faced a rebellion from members of his own party in Congress, who bitterly opposed the tax increase. Indeed, the tax hike may have cost him reelection in 1992.

Although Bush paid a heavy price for the BEA, the 1990 law did limit discretionary spending and slowed unfinanced entitlements and tax cuts. Clinton's 1993 budget deal, which barely squeaked by Congress, made even more progress in reducing the deficit. It retained the limits on discretionary spending and the pay-as-you-go rules from the 1990 act and combined spending cuts and higher revenues to cut the accumulated deficits from 1994 to 1998 by $500 billion. The 1993 law worked better than expected, and the deficit declined to $22 billion in 1997.[12]

Balanced Budget Act (BBA)
A 1997 law that promised to balance the budget by 2002.

The 1990 and 1993 budget agreements, both of which encountered strong opposition in Congress, helped pave the way for the historic **Balanced Budget Act (BBA)** that President Clinton and Congress negotiated in 1997. The BBA accomplished what most observers thought was beyond political possibility. It not only led to the balanced budget it promised but actually produced a budget surplus ahead of schedule—the first surplus since 1969.

Once annual budget deficits were eliminated and surpluses began to accumulate, the two major parties differed sharply in the 2000 presidential campaign on what to do with the surpluses. The Republicans advocated large, across-the-board tax cuts to return the surplus to the taxpayers (and to maintain spending discipline in the federal government). Democrats pointed to unmet social needs, like social security reform, prescription drug coverage for the elderly, and universal health coverage for children, as the best use of the surpluses. Given the popularity of tax cuts with the public, Democrats agreed on a smaller tax cut than that advocated by Republicans and on cuts targeted to middle and lower income earners only. As the American economy slowed down in the second half of 2000 and as projected budget surpluses increased, Democrats signaled a willingness to compromise with newly elected president George W. Bush on the size of tax cuts. But the two parties will likely continue to disagree on the distribution of tax cuts (across-the-board versus targeted) and on the use of the remaining surplus both to decrease the national debt and to fund new social spending programs.

You are looking inside the Brookhaven Service Center in New York, one of the ten centers operated by the Internal Revenue Service to process tax forms and taxpayer requests. This is the aptly titled "extracting and sorting area."

TAX POLICIES

So far, we have been concerned mainly with the spending side of the budget, for which appropriations must be enacted each year. The revenue side of the budget is governed by overall tax policy, which is designed to provide a continuous flow of income without annual legislation. A major text on government finance says that tax policy is sometimes changed to accomplish one or more of several objectives:

- To adjust overall revenue to meet budget outlays

- To make the tax burden more equitable for taxpayers

- To help control the economy by raising taxes (thus decreasing aggregate demand) or by lowering taxes (thus increasing demand)[13]

Tax Reform

Tax reform proposals are usually so heavily influenced by interest groups looking for special benefits that they end up working against their original purpose. However, Reagan's proposals in the 1980s met with relatively few major changes, and in 1986 Congress passed one of the most sweeping tax reform laws in history. The new policy reclaimed a great deal of revenue by eliminating many deductions for corporations and wealthy citizens. That revenue was supposed to pay for a general reduction in tax rates for individual citizens. By eliminating many tax brackets, the new tax policy approached the idea of a flat tax—one that requires everyone to pay at the same rate.

A flat tax has the appeal of simplicity, but it violates the principle of **progressive taxation,** under which the rich pay proportionately higher taxes than the poor. The ability to pay has long been a standard of fair taxation,

progressive taxation
A system of taxation whereby the rich pay proportionately higher taxes than the poor; used by governments to redistribute wealth and thus promote equality.

and surveys show that citizens favor this idea in the abstract.[14] In practice, however, they have different opinions, as we will see. Nevertheless, governments rely on progressive taxation to redistribute wealth and thus promote economic equality.

Can You Explain Why...
a flat tax may not be a fair tax?

In general, the greater the number of tax brackets, the more progressive a tax can be. Before Reagan proposed his tax reforms in 1986, there were fourteen tax brackets, ranging from 11 percent to 50 percent. After the law took effect in 1988, there were only two rates—15 and 28 percent. In 1990, Bush was forced to violate his pledge of "no new taxes" by creating a third tax rate, 31 percent, for those with the highest incomes. Clinton created a fourth level, 40 percent, in 1993, moving toward a more progressive tax structure, although still less progressive than before 1986.

Comparing Tax Burdens

No one likes to pay taxes, so politicians find it popular to criticize the agency that collects taxes—the Internal Revenue Service. In 1998, after citizens testified before Congress about abuses of the IRS, lawmakers of both parties rushed to defend the people against that villainous bureaucracy. Within months, the House had written a bill to prevent IRS abuses. Among its other curbs, the bill shifted the burden of proof from the taxpayer to the IRS in many tax court cases and made it easier for taxpayers who win a case to have their costs reimbursed. Democrats and Republicans alike wanted to be recorded as champions of the people, and the House passed the bill by the lopsided vote of 402 to 8. The Senate quickly followed by a vote of 96 to 2, sending the bill to a willing president for signature.

Not only the IRS, but the income tax itself—and taxes in general—are popular targets for U.S. politicians who campaign on getting government off the backs of the people. Is the tax burden on American citizens truly too heavy? Compared with what? One way to compare tax burdens is to examine taxes over time in the same country; another is to compare taxes in different countries at the same time. By comparing taxes over time in the United States, we find that the total tax burden on U.S. citizens has indeed been growing. For the average family, the percentage of income that went to all national, state, and local taxes doubled, to 23 percent, between 1953 and 1993.[15]

However, neither the national government nor the national income tax accounts for the bulk of that increase. First, national taxes as a percentage of the gross national product have changed very little during the last thirty years; it is the state and local tax burden that has doubled in size.[16] Second, the income tax has not been the main culprit in the increasing tax bite at the national level; the proportion of national budget receipts contributed by income taxes has remained fairly constant since the end of World War II. The largest increases have come in social security taxes, which have risen steadily to pay for the government's single largest social welfare program, aid to the elderly (see Chapter 19).

Another way to compare tax burdens is to examine tax rates in different countries. Despite Americans' complaints about high taxes, the U.S. tax burden is not large compared with that of other democratic nations. As shown in Compared with What? 18.1, Americans' taxes are quite low in

★ **compared with what?**

18.1   Tax Burdens in Twenty-five Countries

All nations tax their citizens, but some nations impose a heavier tax burden than do others. This graph compares tax burdens in 1998 in twenty-five countries as a percentage of gross domestic product (GDP), which is the market value of goods produced inside the country by workers, businesses, and government. The percentages include national, state, and local taxes and social security contributions. By this measure, the U.S. government extracts less in taxes from its citizens than do the governments of almost every other democratic nation. At the top of the list stand Sweden and Denmark, well known as states that provide heavily for social welfare.

Source: U.S. Bureau of the Census, *U.S. Department of Commerce Statistical Abstract of the United States, 2000* (Washington, D.C.: U.S. Government Printing Office, 2000), p. 847.

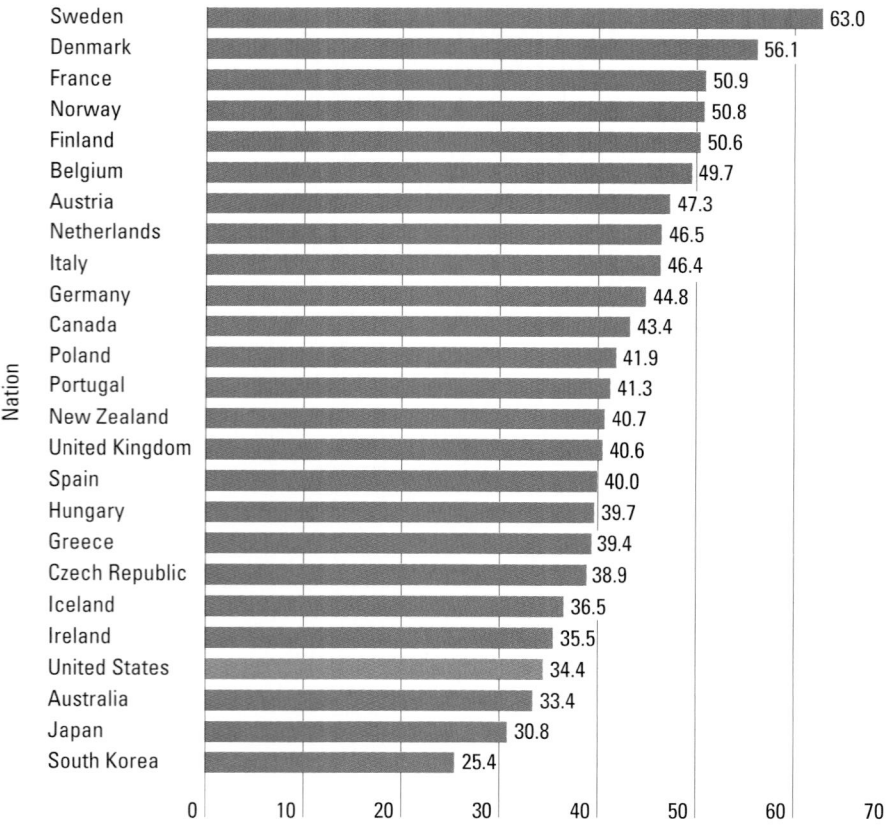

Nation	Tax revenues as percentage of GDP
Sweden	63.0
Denmark	56.1
France	50.9
Norway	50.8
Finland	50.6
Belgium	49.7
Austria	47.3
Netherlands	46.5
Italy	46.4
Germany	44.8
Canada	43.4
Poland	41.9
Portugal	41.3
New Zealand	40.7
United Kingdom	40.6
Spain	40.0
Hungary	39.7
Greece	39.4
Czech Republic	38.9
Iceland	36.5
Ireland	35.5
United States	34.4
Australia	33.4
Japan	30.8
South Korea	25.4

general compared with those in twenty-four other democratic nations. Primarily because they provide their citizens with more generous social benefits (such as health care and unemployment compensation), almost every democratic nation on Earth taxes more heavily than the United States does.

SPENDING POLICIES

The national government spends hundreds of billions of dollars every year. Where does the money go? Figure 18.2 shows how the $1.8 trillion in spending authority for 2001 contained in President Clinton's FY 2001 budget was broken down, by eighteen major governmental functions. The largest amount (23 percent of the total budget) was earmarked for social security.

Until FY 1993, the largest spending category was national defense, but military spending dropped into second place after the collapse of communism. The third largest line, income security, encompasses various programs that provide a social safety net, including unemployment compensation, food for low-income parents and children, help for the blind and disabled, and assistance for the homeless. Medicare and health, the next-largest categories, together account for nearly 20 percent of all budgetary outlays, which underscores the importance of controlling the costs of health care. The fifth-largest category was interest on the accumulated national debt, which alone consumes about 11 percent of all national government spending.

To understand current expenditures, it is a good idea to examine national expenditures over time, as in Figure 18.3. The effect of World War II is clear: spending for national defense rose sharply after 1940, peaked at about 90 percent of the budget in 1945, and fell to about 30 percent in peacetime. The percentage allocated to defense rose again in the early 1950s, reflecting rearmament during the Cold War with the Soviet Union. Thereafter, the share of the budget devoted to defense decreased steadily (except for the bump during the Vietnam War in the late 1960s), until the trend was reversed by the Carter administration in the 1970s and then shot upward during the Reagan presidency. Defense spending significantly decreased under Bush and continued to go down under Clinton.

Government payments to individuals (e.g., social security checks) consistently consumed less of the budget than national defense until 1971. Since then, payments to individuals have accounted for the largest portion of the national budget, and they have been increasing. Net interest payments have also increased substantially in recent years, reflecting the rapidly growing national debt. Pressure from payments for national defense, individuals, and interest on the national debt has squeezed all other government outlays.

One might expect government expenditures to increase steadily, roughly matching the rate of price inflation; however, national spending has far outstripped inflation. Figure 18.4 graphs government receipts and outlays as a percentage of gross domestic product (GDP), which eliminates the effect of inflation. It shows that national spending has increased from about 15 percent of GDP soon after World War II to just over 20 percent in the mid-1990s, before dropping slightly after 1998. The reason for the

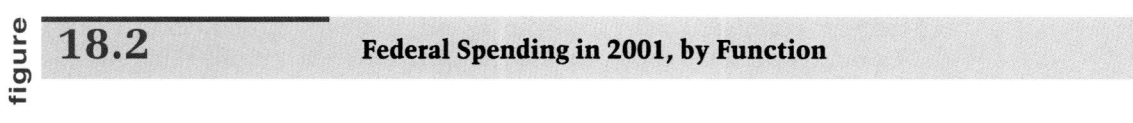

figure **18.2**   **Federal Spending in 2001, by Function**

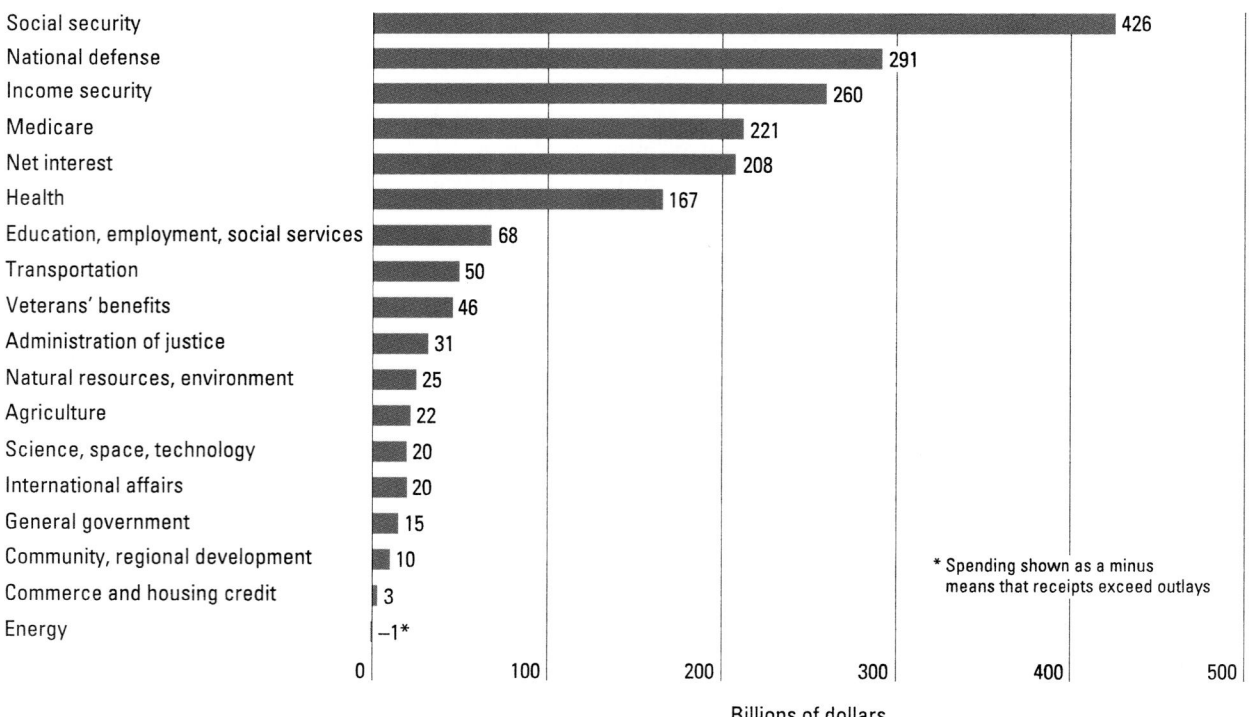

Billions of dollars

Federal budget authorities and outlays are organized into about twenty categories, some of which are mainly for bookkeeping purposes. This graph shows expected outlays for each of eighteen substantive functions for the year 2001 in Clinton's FY 2001 budget. The final budget differed somewhat from this distribution because Congress amended some of the president's spending proposals. The graph makes clear the huge differences among spending categories. Nearly 40 percent of government outlays are for social security and income security—that is, payments to individuals. Health costs (including Medicare) account for just over 20 percent more, slightly more than national defense, and net interest consumes about 11 percent. This leaves relatively little for transportation, agriculture, justice, science, and energy—matters often regarded as important centers of government activity—which fall under the heading of "discretionary spending."

Source: Executive Office of the President, *Budget of the United States Government, Fiscal Year 2001* (Washington, D.C.: U.S. Government Printing Office, 2000).

recent drop is simple: although government spending has increased in recent years, the nation's GDP has increased even faster.

There are two major explanations for the general trend of increasing government spending. One is bureaucratic, the other political.

18.3   National Government Outlays over Time

This chart plots the percentage of the annual budget devoted to four major expense categories over time. It shows that significant changes have occurred in national spending since 1940. During World War II, defense spending consumed more than 80 percent of the national budget. Defense again accounted for most national expenditures during the Cold War of the 1950s. Since then, the military's share of expenditures has declined, while payments to individuals (mostly in the form of social security benefits) have increased dramatically. Also, as the graph shows, the proportion of the budget paid in interest on the national debt has increased substantially since the 1970s.

Source: Executive Office of the President, *Budget of the United States Government, Fiscal Year 2001: Historical Tables* (Washington, D.C.: U.S. Government Printing Office, 2000).

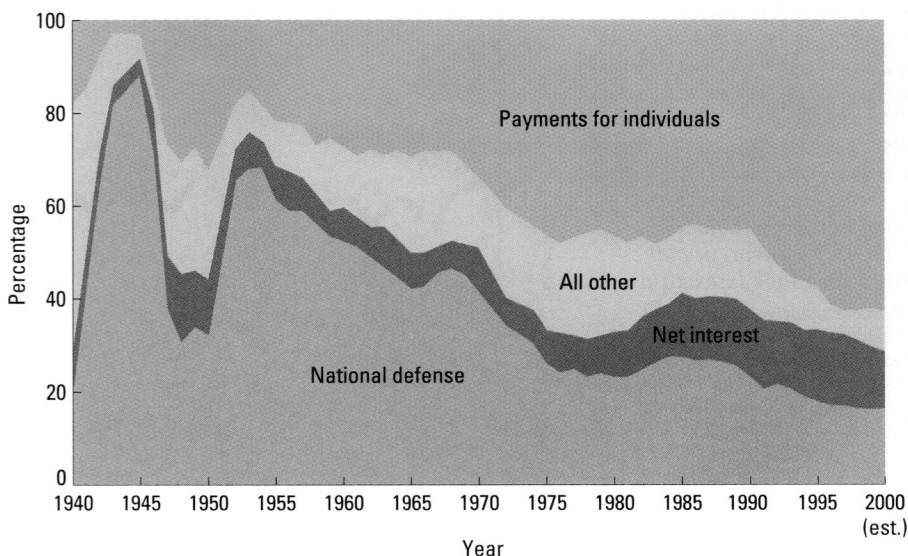

incremental budgeting
A method of budget making that involves adding new funds (an increment) onto the amount previously budgeted (in last year's budget).

Incremental Budgeting . . .

The bureaucratic explanation for spending increases involves **incremental budgeting:** bureaucrats, in compiling their funding requests for the following year, traditionally ask for the amount they got in the current year plus some incremental increase to fund new projects. Because Congress has already approved the agency's budget for the current year, it pays little attention to the agency's current size (the largest part of its budget) and focuses instead on the extra money (the increment) requested for the next year. As a result, few agencies are ever cut back, and spending continually goes up.

Incremental budgeting produces a sort of bureaucratic momentum that continually pushes up spending. Once an agency is established, it attracts a clientele that defends its existence and supports the agency's requests for extra funds to do more year after year. Because budgeting is a two-step process, agencies that get cut back in the authorizing committees sometimes manage (assisted by their interest group clientele) to get funds restored in the appropriations committees—and if not in the House, then perhaps in the Senate. So incremental budgeting and the congressional budget-making process itself are ideally suited to pluralist politics.

. . . And Uncontrollable Spending

Certain government programs are effectively immune to budget reductions, because they have been enacted into law and are enshrined in politics. For example, social security legislation guarantees certain benefits to

18.4   Government Outlays and Receipts as a Percentage of GDP

In this graph, outlays and receipts are each expressed as a percentage of GDP. The area between the two lines represents years of surpluses or (more often) deficits. Because the graph portrays outlays and receipts in the context of economic growth (as some economists favor), it makes the deficit look less alarming.

Source: Executive Office of the President, *Budget of the United States Government, Fiscal Year 2001: Historical Tables* (Washington, D.C.: U.S. Government Printing Office, 2000), p. 3.

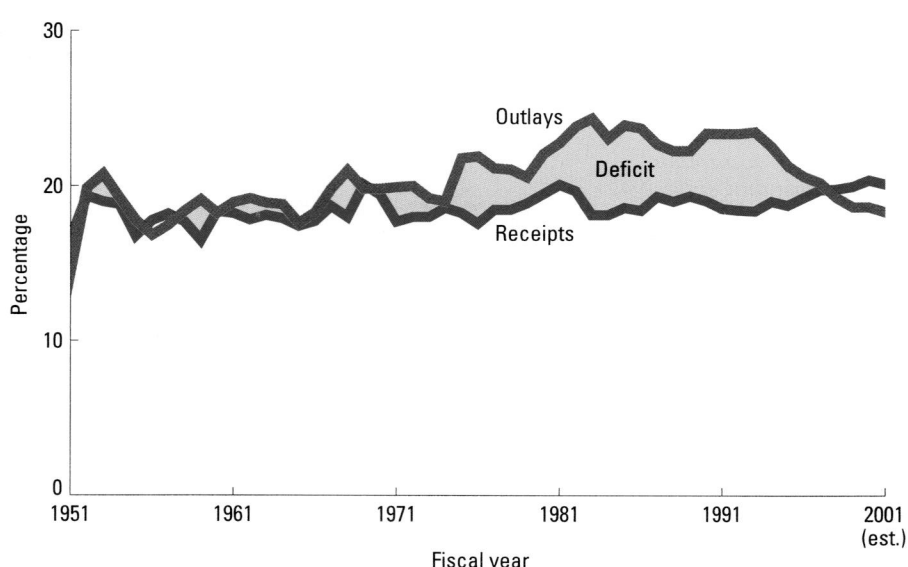

uncontrollable outlay
A payment that government must make by law.

The "Voters" data in the CROSSTABS program contains responses to questions asked about increasing or decreasing government spending in several different areas. Analyze the responses according to the voters' "Personal Traits" to see who favors what programs.

program participants when they retire. Medicare and veterans' benefits also entitle citizens to certain payments. Because these payments have to be made under existing law, they represent **uncontrollable outlays.** In Clinton's FY 1999 budget, over two-thirds of all budget outlays were uncontrollable or relatively uncontrollable—mainly payments to individuals under social security, Medicare, and public assistance; interest on the national debt; and farm price supports. About half of the rest went for defense, leaving about 17 percent in domestic discretionary spending.

To be sure, Congress could change the laws to abolish entitlement payments, and it does modify them through the budgeting process. But politics argues against large-scale reductions. What spending cuts would be acceptable to or even popular with the public? At the most general level, voters favor cutting government spending, but they tend to favor maintaining "government programs that help needy people and deal with important national problems."[17] Substantial majorities favor spending the same or even more on social security, Medicare, education, job training, programs for poor children, and the military. In fact, when a national poll asked whether respondents favored "increasing, decreasing, or keeping about the same level" of government spending for thirteen different purposes—food stamps, welfare, AIDS research, foreign aid, student loans, help for the homeless, immigration control, social security, environmental programs, public schools, crime prevention, child care, and support for the poor—a majority favored less spending in only two areas, welfare and foreign aid.[18] Support was strongest for cutting foreign aid, which makes up only about

1 percent of the budget and thus would not offer much savings. Even when asked whether they favored cuts in spending to reduce their taxes, almost 65 percent said they did not.

In truth, a perplexed Congress, trying to reduce the budget deficit, faces a public that favors funding most programs at even higher levels than those favored by most lawmakers.[19] Moreover, spending for the most expensive of these programs—social security and Medicare—is uncontrollable. Americans have grown accustomed to certain government benefits, but they do not like the idea of raising taxes to pay for them.

TAXING, SPENDING, AND ECONOMIC EQUALITY

As we noted in Chapter 1, the most controversial purpose of government is to promote equality, especially economic equality. Economic equality comes about only at the expense of economic freedom, for it requires government action to redistribute wealth from the rich to the poor. One means of redistribution is government tax policy, especially the progressive income tax. The other instrument for reducing inequalities is government spending through welfare programs. The goal in both cases is not to produce equality of outcome; it is to reduce inequalities by helping the poor.

The national government introduced an income tax in 1862 to help finance the Civil War. That tax was repealed in 1871, and a new tax imposed in 1893 was declared unconstitutional by the Supreme Court. The Sixteenth Amendment (1913) gave the government the power to levy a tax on individual incomes, and it has done so every year since 1914.[20] From 1964 to 1981, people who reported taxable incomes of $100,000 or more paid a top marginal tax rate of 70 percent (except during the Vietnam War), whereas those with lower incomes paid taxes at progressively lower rates. (Figure 18.5 shows how the top rate has fluctuated over the years.) At about the same time, the government launched the War on Poverty as part of President Johnson's Great Society initiative. His programs and their successors are discussed at length in Chapter 19. For now, let us look at the overall effect of government spending and tax policies on economic equality in America.

Government Effects on Economic Equality

We begin by asking whether government spending policies have any measurable effect on income inequality. Economists refer to government payments to individuals through social security, unemployment insurance, food stamps, and other programs, such as agricultural subsidies, as **transfer payments.** Transfer payments need not always go to the poor. In fact, one problem with the farm program is that the wealthiest farmers have often received the largest subsidies.[21] Nevertheless, most researchers have determined that transfer payments have had a definite effect on reducing income inequality.

A study of government policies from 1966 to 1985 found that families in the lowest tenth of the population in terms of income paid 33 percent of their income in national, state, and local taxes but also received payments from all levels of government that almost equaled their earned income.[22]

transfer payment
A payment by government to an individual, mainly through social security or unemployment insurance.

figure

18.5   **The Ups and Downs of National Tax Rates**

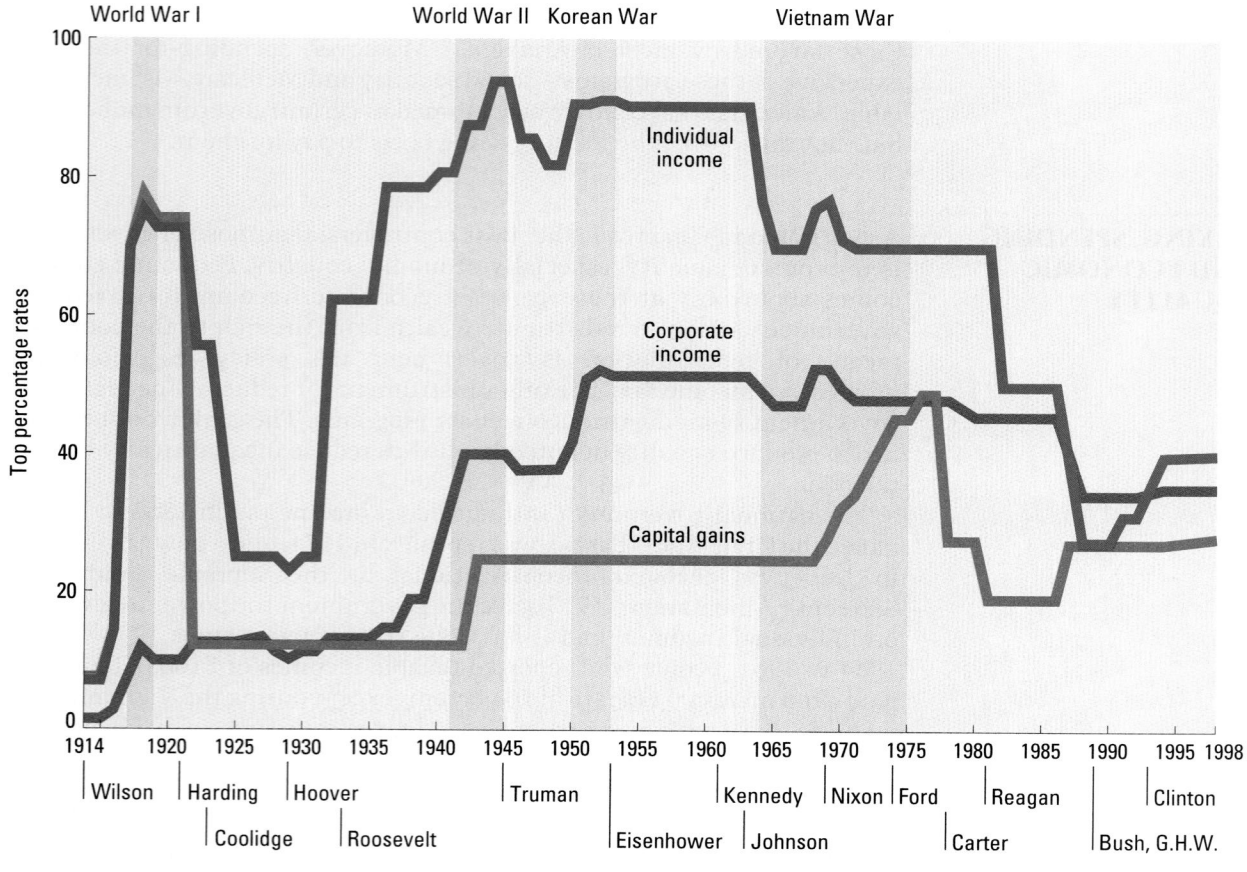

In 1913, the Sixteenth Amendment empowered the national government to collect taxes on income. Since then, the government has levied taxes on individual and corporate income and on capital gains realized by individuals and corporations from the sale of assets, such as stocks or real estate. This chart of the top marginal tax rates shows that they have fluctuated wildly over time, from less than 10 percent to more than 90 percent. (They tend to be highest during periods of war.) During the Reagan administration, the maximum individual income tax rate fell to the lowest level since the Coolidge and Hoover administrations in the late 1920s and 1930s. The top rate increased slightly for 1991, to 31 percent, as a result of a law enacted in 1990, and it jumped to 39.6 percent for 1994 under Clinton's 1993 budget package.

Source: *Wall Street Journal*, 18 August 1986, p. 10. Reprinted by permission of the *Wall Street Journal*, Dow Jones & Company, Inc., 1986. All rights reserved. Additional data from *Congressional Quarterly Weekly Report*, 3 November 1990, pp. 3714–3715; "Tax Law Update," published by Merrill Lynch, 1993; and Scott Kaplan, C.P.A., Paul Brown & Co.

So the lowest income group enjoyed a net benefit from government because of transfer payments. Another study, covering 1979 to 1988, found that transfer payments nearly cut in half the percentage of families with children that were below the official poverty line.[23] Both studies found that tax policies had little effect on the redistribution of income. From 1966 to 1985, ironically, families in the top 1 percent of income paid proportionately less of their income in taxes (about 28 percent) than did people in the lowest-income group.[24] The tax burden has grown even greater for younger generations of Americans.

Can You Explain Why...
lower income people pay a higher percentage of their income in taxes than higher income people do?

How can people in the lowest income group pay a higher percentage of their income in taxes than do those in the very highest group? The answer has to do with the combination of national, state, and local tax policies. Only the national income tax is progressive, with rates rising as income rises. The national payroll tax, which funds social security and Medicare, is highly regressive: its effective rate decreases as income increases beyond a certain point. Everyone pays social security at the same rate (6.2 percent in 2001), but this tax is levied on only the first $80,400 of a person's income (in 2001). There is no social security tax at all on wages over that amount. So the effective rate of the social security tax is higher for lower income groups than for the very top group.

Most state and local sales taxes are equally regressive. Poor and rich usually pay the same flat rate on their purchases. But the poor spend almost everything they earn on purchases, which are taxed, whereas the rich are able to save. A study showed that the effective sales tax rate for the lowest income group was thus about 7 percent, whereas that for the top 1 percent was only 1 percent.[25]

In general, the nation's tax policies at all levels have historically favored not only the wealthy but also those who draw their income from capital (wealth) rather than labor.[26] For example:

- The tax on income from the sale of real estate or stocks (called *capital gains*) has typically been lower than the highest tax on income from salaries.

- The tax on earned income (salaries and wages) is withheld from paychecks by employers under national law; the tax on unearned income (interest and dividends) is not.

- There is no national tax at all on investments in certain securities, including municipal bonds (issued by local governments for construction projects).

Effects of Taxing and Spending Policies over Time

In 1966, at the beginning of President Johnson's Great Society programs, the poorest fifth of American families received 4 percent of the nation's income after taxes and transfer payments, whereas the richest fifth received 46 percent. In 1999, after many billions of dollars had been spent on social programs, the income gap between the rich and poor had actually *grown*, as illustrated in Figure 18.6. This is true despite the facts that many households in the lowest category had about one-third more earners, mainly women, going to work, and that the average American worked eighty-three more hours (two full work weeks) per year than in 1980.[27]

figure   **18.6**   **Distribution of Family Income over Time**

During the past three decades, the 20 percent of U.S. families with the highest incomes received over 45 percent of all income. This distribution of income is one of the most unequal among Western nations. At the bottom end of the scale, the poorest 20 percent of families received less than 5 percent of total family income.

Sources: For the 1966 data, Joseph A. Pechman, *Who Paid the Taxes, 1966–1985?* (Washington, D.C.: Brookings Institution, 1985), p. 74; for the 1999 data, Isaac Shapiro and Robert Greenstein, *The Widening Income Gulf* (Washington, D.C.: Center on Budget and Policy Priorities, 1999), at <http://www.cbpp.org/9-4-99tax-rep.htm>.

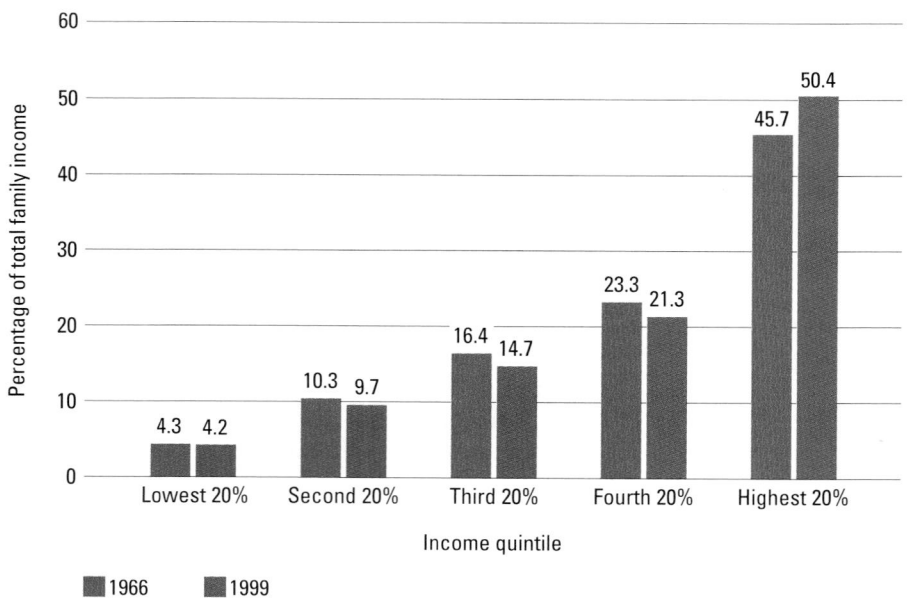

In a capitalist system, some degree of inequality is inevitable. Is there some mechanism that limits how much economic equality can be achieved and prevents government policies from further equalizing income, no matter what is tried? To find out, we can look to other democracies to see how much equality they have been able to sustain. A recent study of sixteen western democracies found that the gap in after-tax income between the rich (those at the 90th percentile of the income scale) and the poor (those at the 10th percentile) was greater in the United States than in any other country.[28] The comparison suggests that our society has measurably more economic inequality than others. The question is, why?

Democracy and Equality

Although the United States is a democracy that prizes political equality for its citizens, its record in promoting economic equality is not as good. In fact, its distribution of wealth—which includes not only income but also ownership of savings, housing, automobiles, stocks, and so on—is strikingly unequal. According to the Federal Reserve, the wealthiest 1 percent of American families control almost 40 percent of the nation's household wealth.[29] Moreover, the distribution of wealth among ethnic groups is alarming. The typical white family has an annual income of about 1.5 times that of both blacks and Hispanics.[30] If democracy means government "by the people," why aren't the people sharing more equally in the

Under the Overpass

Tax cuts are not likely to help this homeless family living under I-95 near Miami, Florida.

nation's wealth? If one of the supposed purposes of government is to promote equality, why are government policies not working that way?

One scholar theorizes that interest group activity in a pluralist democracy distorts government's efforts to promote equality. His analysis of pluralism sees "corporations and organized groups with an upper-income slant as exerting political power over and above the formal one-man-one-vote standard of democracy."[31] Even Clinton's budget for FY 1998, which was ostensibly designed to cut taxes for the middle class, produced large tax savings for the top income group and numerous tax breaks for interest groups.[32] As you learned in Chapters 10 and 17, the pluralist model of democracy rewards those groups that are well organized and well funded.

What would happen if national tax policy were determined according to principles of majoritarian rather than pluralist democracy? Perhaps not much, if public opinion is any guide. The people of the United States are not eager to redistribute wealth by increasing the only major progressive tax, the income tax. If national taxes must be raised, Americans strongly favor a national sales tax over increased income taxes.[33] But a sales tax is a flat tax, paid by rich and poor at the same rate, and it would have a regressive effect on income distribution, promoting inequality. The public also prefers a weekly $10 million national lottery to an increase in the income tax.[34] Because the poor are willing to chance more of their income on winning a fortune through lotteries than are rich people, lotteries (run by about forty states) also contribute to wealth inequality.[35]

Although most citizens tend to favor the idea that the rich should pay more (inherent in the concept of progressive taxation), they respond differently when asked specific questions about what amount of taxation "would be fair" for people of different incomes. In a 1995 survey, the average respondent thought that it would be fair to pay no more than 19 percent of *his or her own* income in all taxes combined: local, state, and national. When asked what would be the highest fair rate for a family making $200,000 a year, the median response was only 25 percent. Moreover, this was the median rate *regardless* of the respondents' income level, race, age, or party![36] The professor conducting the survey describes this remarkable consensus on a tax rate "ceiling" as "the most extraordinary finding in the history of domestic-policy polling in the United States."[37] Ironically, people making $200,000 already pay about 39 percent in total taxes—far more than most people think just. One wonders whether most citizens realize that their own taxes would increase for the same services if the rich did not pay progressively more than what the public thinks is just. For example, Clinton's 1993 tax increase, which raised the rate for people with incomes beginning at $115,000 from 31 to 36 percent and also created a new 39.6 percent bracket for incomes above $250,000, produced $31 billion in additional revenue over the 1992 rates. This additional revenue helped reduce the budget deficit.

Majoritarians might argue that most Americans fail to understand the inequities of the national tax system, which hides regressiveness in sales taxes and social security taxes. However, majoritarians cannot argue that the public demands "fairer" tax rates that take from richer citizens to help poorer ones. If the public did, the lowest income families might receive a greater share of the national income than they do. Instead, economic policy is determined mainly through a complex process of pluralist politics that returns nearly half the national income into the hands of only 20 percent of the nation's families.

SUMMARY

There are conflicting theories about how market economies work best. Laissez-faire economics holds that the government should keep its hands off the economy. Keynesian theory holds that government should take an active role in dealing with inflation and unemployment, using fiscal and monetary policies to produce desired levels of aggregate demand. Monetarists believe fiscal policies are unreliable; they opt instead to use the money supply to affect aggregate demand. Supply-side economists, who had an enormous influence on economic policy during the Reagan administration, focus on controlling the supply of goods and services rather than the demand for them. The remarkable growth of the U.S. economy in the mid- to late 1990s led economists of all schools to question some of their key principles. And the continuing process of globalization has eroded any government's ability to manage its own economy completely.

Congress alone prepared the budget until 1921, when it thrust the responsibility onto the president. After World War II, Congress tried unsuccessfully to regain control of the process. Later, Congress managed to restructure the process under the House and Senate budget committees. The new process worked well until it confronted the huge budget deficits of the 1980s. Because so much of the budget involves military spending and uncontrollable payments to individuals, balancing the budget by reducing what remains—mainly spending for nonentitlement domestic programs—was regarded as impossible. Unwilling to accept responsibility for passing a tax increase, Congress passed the Gramm-Rudman deficit-reduction law in 1985. Under that law, deficits were to be reduced in stages, through automatic across-the-board cuts if necessary, until the budget was balanced by

FY 1991. The deficit problem proved so intractable, however, that Congress had to amend the law in 1987 to extend the deadline to 1993—and the budget still wasn't balanced. When the Republicans gained control of Congress in 1995, they abandoned the informal policy of incremental budgeting and drastically cut spending on discretionary programs.

Although President Bush promised "no new taxes" when he was campaigning for office in 1988, he had to acknowledge the need for revenue increases to cut the deficit and was forced to accept the Budget Enforcement Act of 1990, which raised the income tax. This act modified the budgeting procedure and made it easier to meet the Gramm-Rudman targets, but Bush suffered in his reelection campaign for breaking his pledge. The act also amended the sweeping tax reform bill of 1986, which had eliminated tax loopholes and drastically reduced the number of tax brackets. The new law added a third bracket, at 31 percent, which was much lower than the top rate before 1986. In 1993, President Clinton narrowly won approval of a fourth bracket, at 40 percent. Responding to increased revenue and a hold on spending, the deficit declined. Aided by a growth economy, Clinton engineered taxing and spending changes in 1997 that produced a budget surplus in FY 1998—the first surplus since 1969.

Despite public complaints about high taxes, current U.S. tax rates are lower than those in most other major countries and lower than they have been since the Depression. But even with the heavily progressive tax rates of the past, the national tax system did little to redistribute income. Government transfer payments to individuals have helped reduce some income inequalities, but the distribution of income is less equal in the United States than in most major western nations.

Pluralist democracy as practiced in the United States has allowed well-organized, well-financed interest groups to manipulate tax and spending policies to their benefit. The result is that a larger and poorer segment of society is paying the price. Taxing and spending policies in the United States are tipped in the direction of freedom rather than equality.

★ Selected Readings

Axelrod, Donald. *Budgeting for Modern Government,* 2nd ed. New York: St. Martin's Press, 1995. A thorough explanation of the process of public budgeting, from agency requests to the finished budget. Excellent in evaluating criticisms and proposing reforms.

Eisner, Robert. *The Great Deficit Scares: The Federal Budget, Trade, and Social Security.* New York: Century Foundation Press, 1997. Eisner is one of the few prominent economists who think that a budget deficit is not as serious a problem as the public has been led to believe. He argues that the deficit is calculated improperly, not allowing for capital assets.

Penny, Timothy J., and Steven E. Schier. *Payment Due: A Nation in Debt, A Generation in Trouble.* Boulder, Colo: Westview Press, 1996. A former member of Congress (Penny) and a scholar collaborate in analyzing the problems in reducing the deficit and the consequences for America if we do not.

Stein, Herbert. *On the Other Hand . . . Reflections on Economics, Economists, and Politics.* Washington, D.C.: American Enterprise Institute, 1995. The chairman of President Nixon's Council of Economic Advisers, Herbert Stein, examines controversies over economic growth, employment, taxes, and deficits, and the ideas of economists whose theories have influenced economic practice.

Wetterau, Bruce. *Congressional Quarterly's Desk Reference on the Federal Budget.* Washington, D.C.: Congressional Quarterly Press, 1998. Another in CQ's series of comprehensive reference books on American politics.

Internet Exercises

1. *Budgeting in a Federal System*

Thanks to the development of the Web, the federal government can now make an amazing amount of information about its annual budget instantly available to the public. You can find information about the president's proposed budget for the most recent fiscal year, as well as budgets from past years, from the Office of Management and Budget (OMB) at **<www.gpo.gov/ usbudget/>**.

• Go to the OMB's budget page and follow the link to the budget documents that accompany the Fiscal Year 2001 budget. From there you will find a publication called Historical Tables, which outlines long-term trends in government spending. In this resource, locate Table 4.2, Percentage Distribution of Outlays by Agency: 1962–2005. Study the relative distribution of funds, and the changes in agency allocations over time.

• How could one use these numbers to illustrate the division of labor in the nation's federal system?

2. *National Banker: The Federal Reserve System*

Even though its members are not elected by the public, the members of the Federal Reserve System, including its chairman, Alan Greenspan, wield tremendous power over the nation's economy. The Fed maintains twelve regional reserve banks, one of which is located in Chicago. You can find the Chicago Fed on the Internet at **<www.chicagofed.org/>**.

• At the Chicago Fed's home page, you will find a link to information about the Fed. Following that link will lead you to a page that connects to a brief on-line tour of the Chicago Fed, which includes some discussion of the system as a whole. Navigate your way through the four main parts of the tour.

• Based on the information in the tour, the Fed appears to behave both like a competitive private business and an agent of the government. What are some examples of each behavior that the tour describes?

Domestic Policy

LORI FURLOW HAD HIT ROCK BOTTOM by the time she was twenty years old. Her addiction to methamphetamines had caused her weight to drop to eighty-six pounds, she had suffered a heart attack, and in a desperate (although successful) attempt to pass a court-ordered urinalysis test, she once drank several bottles of vinegar. As she put it, "Spandex would fall off me. You could smell meth coming out of my pores." She supported herself and her daughters by manufacturing meth and collecting welfare checks.[1]

Rita Davis, along with her twelve brothers and sisters, was raised by a sexually abusive father who removed his children from school so he could home-school them. She eventually was able to read at the seventh-grade level, got married, and had a son at age thirty-one. Despite weighing 325 pounds, the result of an eating disorder stemming from her childhood abuse, she helped support her son by delivering newspapers. But the progress she had made unraveled after her husband left her when her son was two years old. Unable to find work because of her limited education and physical problems, Rita Davis applied for welfare benefits.

When President Bill Clinton fulfilled his campaign pledge to "end welfare as we know it," by signing into law the Temporary Assistance to Needy Families (TANF) Act of 1996, people like Lori Furlow and Rita Davis held their breath. What would become of them?

Americans scorned the old welfare system, viewing it as plagued by fraud and abuse. They blamed the system for creating generations of welfare dependents. The new welfare system, which we discuss in greater detail later in this chapter, places state governments at the center of welfare reform. State governors and legislatures, freed substantially from national guidelines but still using national government money, are now responsible for crafting eligibility requirements, defining welfare program services, and establishing benefit levels for their citizens.

Fortunately, Lori Furlow and Rita Davis live in Oregon. Because the national government's grants to states under TANF are calculated based on their pre-1996 welfare expenditures, the more generous a state was under the old system, the more money it now receives. Today Oregon receives from the national government about $6,600 for each family that was on welfare at the time the law was changed. That figure is 60 percent higher than the national average of $4,100 per family.[2]

As soon as TANF took effect, Lori Furlow started receiving letters from her local welfare office, informing her that she must begin attending a job-preparation class to continue receiving full benefits. She paid attention to the notices only after the office docked her monthly welfare check $50.

Jobs to Go

The Job Corps is the only national residential job training and education program for at-risk youth ages 16 to 24. It serves as a source of entry-level workers for the home building industry. Job Corps offers young people industry-validated, up-to-date skills training, as well as world-of-work and social skills tips that teach young people how to act on the job site. Job Corps is a public-private partnership.

The office threatened further cuts if Lori failed to comply with the training program. Eventually, she received job training and successfully completed a year-long residential drug rehabilitation program. She now holds a state clerical job, making $18,000 a year. For Lori, the reduced checks were a powerful motivator: "It all finally culminated—the burnout, the guilt, the fear. . . . I think the sanction's a real wake-up call."

Rita Davis's problem was not a lack of motivation. Rather, she faced health problems and had limited skills. Rita tried to get jobs with many temporary employment agencies; all were receptive on the phone but would turn her down once they saw her. After exceptional efforts by a job-placement counselor who recognized Rita's knack for numbers, an accounting agency hired her. The counselor worked out an agreement by which the state of Oregon paid most of Rita's salary for six months, in lieu of making welfare payments. When Davis's boss at the accounting agency threatened to fire her, complaining that her body odor was driving customers away, the same counselor helped her seek medical attention and brought her shampoos and deodorants to try out. The intervention worked. Rita's employer was pleased with the outcome and quickly promoted her to bookkeeper. "She's even better than some professionals I've had," he said. And although Rita still faces a daily struggle to maintain her new life, working is now a source of comfort to her. "I love this job," she says. "Somebody is able to look past my size and see me. I've wondered why it took so long."

These success stories represent the best hopes of the nation's recent experiment with welfare reform, which has been one of the most significant public policy changes to occur in decades. (**Public policy** is a general plan of action adopted by government to solve a social problem, counter a threat, or pursue an objective.) Whether from expulsions from the welfare rolls, threats of expulsions, or the robust economy, welfare case loads have been falling dramatically throughout the United States. Not every story is

public policy

A general plan of action adopted by the government to solve a social problem, counter a threat, or pursue an objective.

a happy one, though. TANF is just one policy providing economic support to the needy in America. It is complemented by several other state and federal programs, which produce various results.

In Chapter 17 we examined the policymaking process in general; in this chapter we look at specific domestic public policies, government plans of action targeting concerns internal to the United States. These are among the most enduring and costly programs that the government has launched on behalf of its citizens. Four key questions guide our inquiry: What are the origins and politics of specific domestic policies? What are the effects of those policies once they are implemented? Why do some policies succeed and others fail? Finally, are disagreements about policy really disagreements about values?

Public policies sometimes seem as numerous as fast-food restaurants, offering something for every appetite and budget. With such a wide range of policies worth exploring, you may be wondering why we plan to spend much of this chapter discussing social insurance, public assistance, health care, and education. These policies deserve special consideration for four reasons. First, government expenditures in these areas represent more than half the national budget and one-tenth of our gross domestic product (the total market value of all goods and services produced in this country during a year). In 1997, of every dollar spent by the national government, 58 cents went to direct payments to individuals.[3] All citizens ought to know how their resources are allocated and why. Regrettably, the public has limited and distorted knowledge about national government spending. For example, only one in four Americans knows that the government spends more for social security than for national defense.[4] Second, one goal of social welfare policies is to alleviate some consequences of economic inequality. Nevertheless, poverty remains a fixture of American life, and we must try to understand why. Third, these policies pose some vexing questions involving the conflicts between freedom and order and between freedom and equality. Fourth, with the eclipse of Cold War tensions, social welfare issues (along with the economy) have moved to the forefront of voters' concerns. In the 2000 presidential election, education, the economy, health care, and social security (in that order) were the most influential issues in deciding voters' choice among the candidates.[5]

This chapter concentrates on policies based on the authority of the national government to tax and spend for the general welfare. But it is important to recognize that state and local governments play a vital role in shaping and directing the policies that emanate from Washington. For example, with TANF the national government largely abandoned setting standards for the allocation of welfare benefits. Now the states impose their own standards for recipients.[6]

GOVERNMENT POLICIES AND INDIVIDUAL WELFARE

The most controversial purpose of government is to promote social and economic equality. To do so may conflict with the freedom of some citizens because it requires government action to redistribute income from rich to poor. This choice between freedom and equality constitutes the modern dilemma of government; it has been at the center of many conflicts in U.S. public policy since World War II. On one hand, most Americans believe that government should help the needy. On the other hand, they do not want to sacrifice their own standard of living to provide government handouts to those whom they may perceive as shiftless and lazy.

The Growth of the American Welfare State

Using the "Voters" data in the CROSSTABS program, analyze issue variables (e.g., government services, ensuring that everyone has a job, health insurance) by trust in government. Does trust in government tend to go hand in hand with some issues but not with others?

welfare state
A nation in which the government assumes responsibility for the welfare of its citizens, redistributing income to reduce social inequality.

social welfare programs
Government programs that provide the minimum living standards necessary for all citizens.

At one time, governments confined their activities to the minimal protection of people and property—to ensuring security and order. Now, however, almost every modern nation may be characterized as a **welfare state,** serving as the provider and protector of individual well-being through economic and social programs. **Social welfare programs** are government programs designed to provide the minimum living conditions necessary for all citizens. Income for the elderly, health care, public assistance, and education are among the concerns addressed by government social welfare programs.

Social welfare policy is based on the premise that society has an obligation to provide for the basic needs of its members. In an unusual national survey targeting the poor and nonpoor, both sectors agreed that government should protect its citizens against risks they are powerless to combat. Americans expressed a clear conviction that money and wealth ought to be more evenly shared.[7] The term *welfare state* describes this protective role of government.

The recent history of U.S. government spending in support of social welfare policies is illustrated in Figure 18.3. In 1960, 26 percent of the national budget went to payments for individuals. In 1970, 33 percent of the budget went to payments for individuals. And in 1980, more than 40 percent went to individuals. By 1985, spending for individuals had fallen off by a few percentage points. But the latest data, for 1999, show that nearly 60 percent of national spending goes to direct payments to individuals or grants in support of individuals. The elderly have been the principal beneficiaries. The national government clearly remains a provider of social welfare, despite changes in administrations.

America today is far from being a welfare state on the order of Germany or Great Britain; those nations provide many more medical, educational, and unemployment benefits to their citizens than does the United States. However, the United States does have several social welfare functions. To understand social welfare policies in the United States, you must first understand the significance of a major event in U.S. history—the Great Depression—and the two presidential plans that extended the scope of the government, the New Deal and the Great Society.

Great Depression
The longest and deepest setback the American economy has ever experienced. It began with the stock market crash on October 12, 1929, and did not end until the start of World War II.

The Great Depression. Throughout its history, the U.S. economy has experienced alternating good times and hard times, generally referred to as business cycles (see Chapter 18). The **Great Depression** was, by far, the longest and deepest setback that the American economy has ever experienced. It began with the stock market crash of 1929 (on October 29, a day known as Black Tuesday) and did not end until the start of World War II. By 1932, one out of every four U.S. workers was unemployed, and millions more were underemployed. No other event has had a greater effect on the thinking and the institutions of government in the twentieth century.

In the 1930s, the forces that had stemmed earlier business declines were no longer operating. There were no more frontiers, no growth in export

A Human Tragedy

The Great Depression made able-bodied Americans idle. By 1933, when President Herbert Hoover left office, about one-fourth of the labor force was out of work. Private charities were swamped with the burden of feeding the destitute. The hopeless men pictured here await a handout from a wealthy San Francisco matron known as the "White Angel" who provided resources for a bread line.

Principal New Deal Acts During Hundred Days Congress, 1933

New Deal
The measures advocated by the Roosevelt administration to alleviate the Depression.

markets, no new technologies to boost employment. Unchecked, unemployment spread like an epidemic. And the crisis fueled itself. Workers who lost their source of income could no longer buy the food, goods, and services that kept the economy going. Thus, private industry and commercial farmers tended to produce more than they could sell profitably. Closed factories, surplus crops, and idle workers were the consequences.

The industrialized nations of Europe were also hit hard. The value of U.S. exports fell, and the value of imports increased; this led Congress to impose high tariffs, which strangled trade and fueled the Depression. From 1929 to 1932, more than 44 percent of the nation's banks failed when unpaid loans exceeded the value of bank assets. Farm prices fell by more than half in the same period. Marginal farmers lost their land, and tenant farmers succumbed to mechanization. The uprooted—tens of thousands of dispossessed farm families—headed West with their possessions atop their cars and trucks in a hopeless quest for opportunity.

The New Deal.   In his speech accepting the presidential nomination at the 1932 Democratic National Convention, Franklin Delano Roosevelt (then governor of New York) made a promise: "I pledge you, I pledge myself to a new deal for the American people." Roosevelt did not specify what his **New Deal** would consist of, but the term was later applied to measures undertaken by the Roosevelt administration to stem the Depression. Some scholars regard these measures as the most imaginative burst of do-

Later Major New Deal Measures, 1933–1939

mestic policy in the nation's history. Others see them as the source of massive government growth without matching benefits.

President Roosevelt's New Deal was composed of two phases. The first, which ended in 1935, was aimed at boosting prices and lowering unemployment through programs like the Civilian Conservation Corps (CCC), which provided short-term jobs for young men. The second phase, which ended in 1938, was aimed at aiding the forgotten people: the poor, the aged, unorganized working men and women, and farmers. The hallmark of this second phase is the social security program.

Poverty and unemployment persisted, however, despite the best efforts of the Democrats. By 1939, 17 percent of the work force (more than 9 million people) were still unemployed. Only World War II was able to provide the economic surge needed to yield lower unemployment and higher prices, the elusive goals of the New Deal.

Roosevelt's overwhelming popularity did not translate into irresistibly popular policy or genuine popularity for government. Public opinion polls revealed that Americans were divided over New Deal policies through the early 1940s. Eventually, the New Deal became the status quo, and Americans grew satisfied with it. But Americans remained wary of additional growth in the power of the national government.[8]

Economists still debate whether the actual economic benefits of the New Deal reforms outweighed their costs. It is clear, however, that New Deal policies initiated a long-range trend toward government expansion. And another torrent of domestic policymaking burst forth three decades later.

The Great Society. John F. Kennedy's election in 1960 brought to Washington a corps of public servants sensitive to the needs of the poor and minorities. This raised expectations that national government policies would benefit these groups. But Kennedy's razor-thin margin of victory was far from a mandate to improve the plight of the poor and dispossessed.

In the aftermath of Kennedy's assassination in November 1963, his successor, Lyndon Baines Johnson, received enormous support for a bold policy program designed to foster equality. In his 1965 State of the Union address, President Johnson offered his own version of the New Deal, the **Great Society**—a broad array of programs designed to redress political, social, and economic inequality. In contrast to the New Deal, few if any of Johnson's programs were aimed at short-term relief; most were targeted at chronic ills requiring a long-term commitment by the national government.

A vital element of the Great Society was the **War on Poverty.** The major weapon in this war was the Economic Opportunity Act (1964); its proponents promised that it would eradicate poverty in ten years. The act encouraged a variety of local community programs to educate and train people for employment. Among them were college work-study programs, summer employment for high school and college students, loans to small businesses, a domestic version of the Peace Corps (called VISTA, for Volunteers in Service to America), educational enrichment for preschoolers, and legal services for the poor. It offered opportunity: a hand up, rather than a handout.

Great Society
President Lyndon Johnson's broad array of programs designed to redress political, social, and economic inequality.

War on Poverty
A part of President Lyndon Johnson's Great Society program, intended to eradicate poverty within ten years.

The act also established the Office for Economic Opportunity (OEO), which was the administrative center of the War on Poverty. Its basic strategy was to involve the poor themselves in administering antipoverty programs, in the hope that they would know which programs would best serve their needs. The national government channeled money directly to local community action programs. This approach avoided the vested interests of state and local government bureaucrats and political machines. But it also led to new local controversies by shifting the control of government funds from local politicians to other groups. (In one notorious example, the Blackstone Rangers, a Chicago street gang, received funds for a job-training program.)

The War on Poverty eventually faded as funding was diverted to the Vietnam War. Although it achieved little in the way of income redistribution, it did lead to one significant change: it made the poor aware of their political power. Some candidates representing the poor ran for political office, and officeholders paid increased attention to the poor. The poor also found that they could use the legal system to their benefit. For example, with legal assistance from the OEO, low-income litigants were successful in striking down state laws requiring a minimum period of residency before people could receive public assistance.[9]

Public Assistance

public assistance
Government aid to individuals who can demonstrate a need for that aid.

Public assistance is what most people mean when they use the terms *welfare* or *welfare payments*; it is government aid to individuals who demonstrate a need for that aid. Although much public assistance is directed toward those who lack the ability or the resources to provide for themselves or their families, the poor are not the only recipients of welfare. Corporations, farmers, and college students are among the many recipients of government aid in the form of tax breaks, subsidized loans, and other benefits.

entitlements
Benefits to which every eligible person has a legal right and that the government cannot deny.

Public assistance programs instituted under the Social Security Act are known today as *categorical assistance programs*. They include (1) old-age assistance for the needy elderly not covered by old-age pension benefits, (2) aid to the needy blind, (3) aid to needy families with dependent children, and (4) aid to the totally and permanently disabled. Adopted initially as stopgap measures during the Depression, these programs have become **entitlements**—benefits to which every eligible person has a legal right and that the government cannot deny. They are administered by the states, but the bulk of the funding comes from the national government's general tax revenues. Because the states also contribute to the funding of their public assistance programs, the benefits vary widely from state to state.

poverty level
The minimum cash income that will provide for a family's basic needs; calculated as three times the cost of a market basket of food that provides a minimally nutritious diet.

Poverty and Public Assistance.   Until 1996, the national government imposed national standards on state welfare programs. It distributed funds to each state based on the proportion of its population that was living in poverty. That proportion is determined on the basis of a federally defined **poverty level**, or poverty threshold, which is the minimum cash income that will provide for a family's basic needs. The poverty level varies by family size and is calculated as three times the cost of a minimally nutritious diet for a given number of people over a given time period. (The threshold is computed in this way because research suggests that poor families of three or more persons spend approximately one-third of their income on food.*)

The poverty level is fairly simple to apply, but it is only a rough measure for distinguishing the poor from the nonpoor. Using it is like using a wrench as a hammer: it works, but not very well. We attach importance to the poverty level figure, despite its inaccuracies, because measuring poverty is a means of measuring how the American promise of equality stands up against the performance of our public policies. In 1999, the government calculated that more than 32 million people, or nearly 12 percent of the population, were living in poverty in the United States.[10]

The use of the poverty line as a social indicator also reflects a fundamental ambiguity in the notion of equality. Consider, for example, that greater equality of incomes can be achieved in two completely different ways: those lowest in the income distribution could be raised up by increasing their income, or those at the top could be brought down by the government taking a greater share of their income. Doing the latter alone would not help the worst off at all if the money taken from the wealthiest were not transferred to the poorest. Using a concept like the poverty line, which reflects a social commitment that no citizen should live below a certain standard, helps ensure that our progress toward equality does improve the absolute condition of the least well off among us.

The poverty level is adjusted each year to reflect changes in consumer prices. In 2001, the poverty threshold for a family of four was a cash income below $17,650.[11] This is income *before* taxes. If the poverty threshold were defined as disposable income (income *after* taxes), the proportion of the population categorized as living in poverty would increase.

Some critics believe that factors other than income should be considered in computing the poverty level. Assets (home, cars, possessions), for example, are excluded from the definition. Also, the computation fails to take into account noncash benefits such as food stamps, health benefits (Medicaid), and subsidized housing. Presumably, the inclusion of these noncash benefits as income would reduce the number of individuals seen as living below the poverty level.

The poverty rate in the United States has declined since the mid-1960s (see Politics in a Changing America 19.1). It rose again slightly in the 1980s, then declined, and now is about 12 percent. In 1995, the poverty rate for blacks fell below 30 percent (where it remains), the lowest level since the government started to record poverty data in the 1960s. Still, poverty retains a hold on the American population.

Poverty was once a condition of old age. Social security changed that. Today, poverty is still related to age, but in the opposite direction: it is largely a predicament of the young. Twenty percent of persons younger than eighteen live in poverty.[12]

The evidence from the 1980s and 1990s, however, offers reassurance to both conservatives and liberals. Both before-tax and after-tax income grew in absolute terms; inequality also grew in the same period (see Chapter 18). Changes in families and household composition suggest several plausible explanations for this increased gulf between the haves and the have-nots.

Although it has been the source of endless debate, today's definition of poverty retains remarkable similarity to its precursors. As early as 1795, a group of English magistrates "decided that a minimum income should be the cost of a gallon loaf of bread, multiplied by three, plus an allowance for each dependent." See Alvin L. Schorr, "Redefining Poverty Levels," New York Times, 9 May 1984, p. 27.

feminization of poverty
The term applied to the fact that a growing percentage of all poor Americans are women or the dependents of women.

The rising number of double-worker households may explain income growth. Growth in the number of elderly people—who have substantially lower incomes—tends to increase income inequality. Growth in the number of persons living alone (or with nonrelatives)—who typically have much lower incomes than households composed of families—also increases income inequality. In addition, the growth in the number of female-headed households contributes to income inequality. About half of such households are in the lowest income group, as described in Politics in a Changing America 19.1. Researchers have labeled this trend toward greater poverty among women the **feminization of poverty,** as a growing percentage of all poor Americans are women or dependents of women.[13]

It is relatively easy to draw a portrait of the poor. It is much more difficult to craft policies that move them out of destitution. Critics of social welfare spending, led by libertarian scholar Charles Murray, argue that antipoverty policies have made poverty more attractive by removing incentives to work. They believe that policies aimed at providing for the poor have actually promoted poverty.

Another explanation, proposed by liberal thinker William Julius Wilson, maintains that the failure of government policies to reduce poverty rests on changes in racial attitudes. In the 1960s, racial barriers kept the black middle class in the same urban neighborhoods as poor blacks. Their presence provided social stability, role models, and strong community institutions and businesses. Then the decline of racial barriers allowed middle-class blacks to move out of the inner cities. As a result, the inner cities became increasingly poor and increasingly dependent on welfare.[14]

Welfare Reform: Major Changes, Uncertain Consequences.   A spirit of equality—equality of opportunity—motivated the reforms of the 1960s, many of which carried over to the 1970s. But Ronald Reagan's overwhelming election in 1980 and his landslide reelection in 1984 forced a reexamination of social welfare policy. Reagan professed support for the "truly needy" and for preserving a "reliable safety net of social programs," by which he meant the core programs begun in the New Deal. Nevertheless, his administration abolished several social welfare programs and redirected others.

In a dramatic departure from his predecessors (Republicans as well as Democrats), Reagan shifted emphasis from economic equality to economic freedom. He questioned whether government alone should continue to be responsible for guaranteeing the economic and social well-being of less fortunate citizens. And he maintained that, to the extent that government should bear this responsibility, state and local governments could do so more efficiently than the national government.

Congress blocked some of the president's proposed cutbacks, and many Great Society programs remained in force, although with less funding. Overall spending on social welfare programs (as a proportion of the gross national product) fell to about mid-1970s levels. But the dramatic growth in the promotion of social welfare that began with the New Deal ended with the Reagan administration. It remained in repose during the Bush administration.

In the 1992 and 1996 elections, candidates for all offices turned up the rhetoric regarding the future of public assistance to the poor. In 1996, the Republican-led Congress sought a fundamental revision of the welfare sys-

★ **politics in a changing** **a m e r i c a**

19.1 The Feminization of Poverty

When we examine the composition of poor families, especially over the past twenty-five years, we observe a dramatic and disturbing trend. One in every two poor Americans resides in a family in which a woman is the sole householder, or head of the household (see graph). Thirty years ago, only one in every four poor people lived in such a family. What accounts for this dramatic upward shift in the proportion of female-headed poor families?

The twentieth century brought extraordinary changes for women. Women won the right to vote and to own property. Women also gained a measure of legal and social equality (see Chapter 16). But increases in the rates of divorce, marital separation, and adolescent pregnancy have cast more and more women into the head-of-household role. Caring for children competes with women's ability to work. Affordable child care is out of reach for many single parents. In the absence of a national child care policy, single women with young children face limited employment opportunities and lower wages in comparison to full-time workers. These factors and others contribute to the "feminization of poverty," the fact that a growing percentage of all poor Americans are women or the dependents of women.

Sources: Barbara Ehrenreich and Frances Fox Piven, "The Feminization of Poverty," *Dissent* (Spring 1984), 162–170; Harrell R. Rodgers, Jr., *Poor Women, Poor Families: The Economic Plight of America's Female-Headed Households*, 2nd ed. (Armonk, N.Y.: M. E. Sharpe, 1990).

Source for data: U.S. Bureau of the Census, U.S. Department of Commerce, *Poverty in the United States, 1999,* Current Population Reports, Series P-60, No. 210 (Washington, D.C.: U.S. Government Printing Office, 2000).

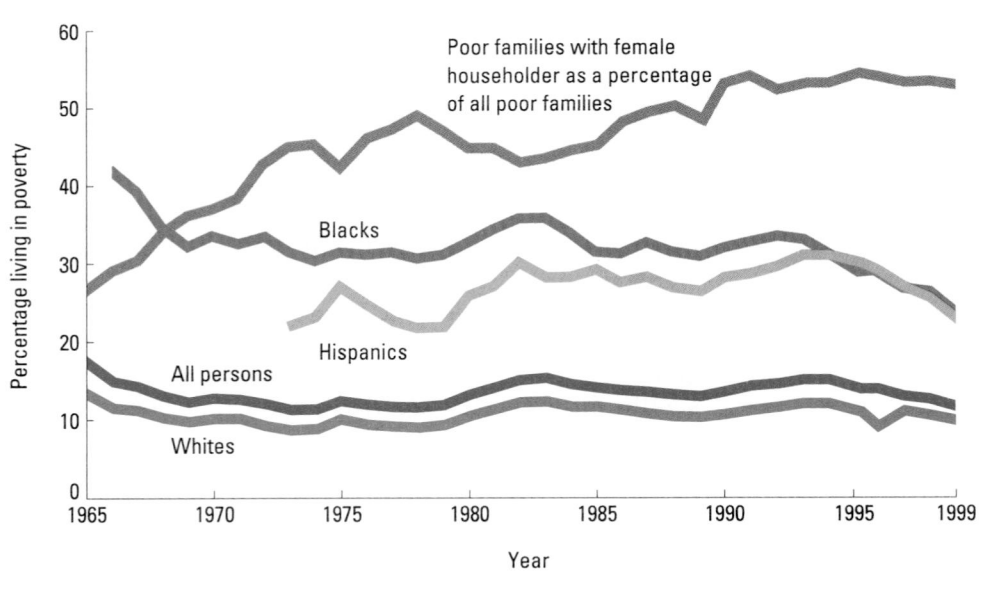

tem and managed to enlist the president in their cause. When President Clinton signed the **Temporary Assistance for Needy Families Act (TANF)** into law on August 22, 1996, he joined forces with the Republican-led Congress "to end welfare as we know it." The act abolished the sixty-one-year-old Aid to Families with Dependent Children (AFDC) program,

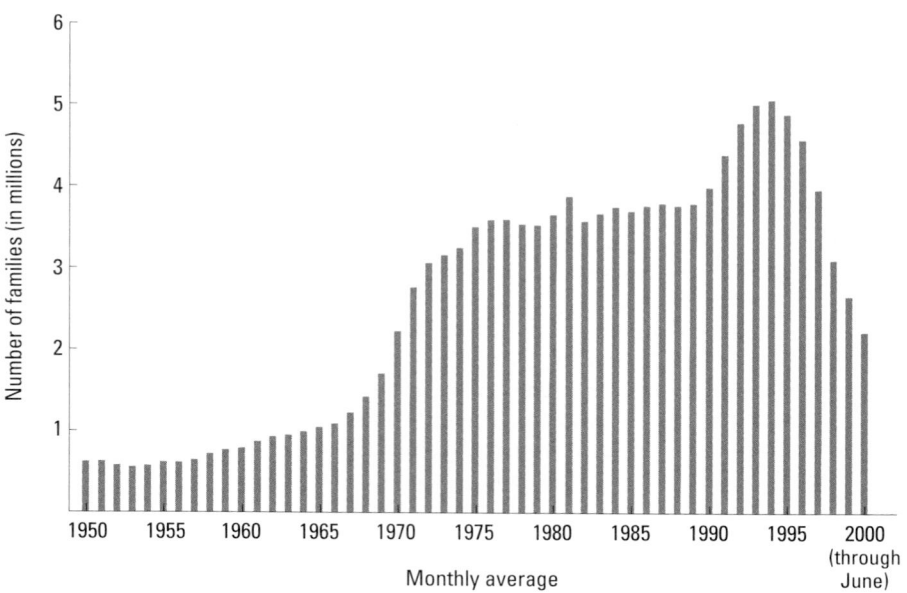

figure 19.1

Families on Welfare, 1950–2000

Beginning in the 1950s, the number of families on welfare skyrocketed as divorce and single motherhood increased. The welfare rolls stabilized during the late 1970s and 1980s but again lurched upward in the early 1990s. The sharp decline in the last few years represents the "end of welfare as we know it" by legislation and the demand for workers fueled by a strong domestic economy.

Source: U.S. Welfare Caseload Information, <www.acf.dhhs.gov/news/stats/3697.htm>.

Temporary Assistance for Needy Families Act (TANF)
A 1996 national act that abolished the long-time welfare policy, AFDC (Aid for Families with Dependent Children). TANF gives the states much more control over welfare policy.

which had provided a federal guarantee of cash assistance that had kept millions of citizens afloat during difficult times.

Critics of the program had complained that for some recipients floating had become a way of life and that government aid discouraged individuals from swimming on their own. Although originally established with widowed mothers in mind, at a time when divorce and out-of-wedlock births were rare, AFDC grew rapidly beginning in the 1960s as divorce and single motherhood increased (see Figure 19.1). By the time AFDC was abolished, 4 million adults and almost 9 million children were on the welfare rolls, and 24 million Americans were receiving food stamps. The end of AFDC significantly changed the lives of more than one-fifth of American families.

Under the new plan, adult recipients of welfare payments have to become employed within two years. The law places the burden of job creation on the states. Families can receive no more than a total of five years of benefits in a lifetime, and the states can set a lower limit. In addition, most immigrants who arrived after the bill was signed are no longer eligible for the majority of federal benefits and services, although most states have elected to step in and provide these benefits and services themselves. Even before signing the bill, Clinton had granted waivers permitting states to offer extensions beyond the five-year limit, as long as recipients continue to look for work. Republicans countered that such waivers effectively undermined the law.[15] In practice, however, there are no mechanisms for monitoring current welfare recipients at the national level, and until such a system is implemented, recipients can skirt the work requirements by moving from state to state.

Under the old entitlement system, benefits varied dramatically from state to state. The basic monthly benefit for a family varied from a low of $187 in Mississippi to a high of $655 in Vermont.[16] Nonetheless, for the 328 House members and 74 senators who voted for the bill (Republicans heavily in favor, Democrats split), devolving power to the states proved a prime force in the reform effort. President Clinton's own desire to permit states to act as laboratories for welfare reform provided ample ammunition for advocates of change. When the bill was signed into law, some forty-five states had already begun experimenting with their welfare system.[17] Clinton and others had heaped praise on such experiments as Wisconsin's "W-2" plan ("Wisconsin Works"), which Republican governor Tommy Thompson put into effect in 1998. Its pilot program had seen some success in dropping the state's welfare case load but an accurate assessment remains years away. As a result of his success in Wisconsin, Thompson was appointed secretary of Health and Human Services in George W. Bush's administration.

How have the states been affected by the welfare reform bill of 1996? As envisioned, there are now fifty new welfare systems under the plan of block, or lump-sum, grants to the states. Some state officials were concerned by the stringent work requirements imposed by the new law and confused by some of its provisions. As Jack Tweedie, a welfare policy specialist at the National Conference of State Legislatures, put it, "The word is *confusion*." States are unclear about the definition of "work." For example, some states regard job *training* as work, but the aim of the legislation is to achieve *employment*. In addition, states will be forced to make difficult decisions in allocating the yearly total of $16.4 billion in block grants, a figure that will remain unchanged until 2002, with no adjustments for inflation or population shifts.[18]

Many policymakers were concerned with the dramatic nature of the changes. For many Democratic Party loyalists, the president had taken his position of "New Democrat" too far. But Clinton stated that "the nature of the poverty population is so different now that I am convinced we have got to be willing to experiment, to try to work to find ways to break the cycle of dependency." And, rare in the age of partisanship, many Republicans agreed.[19]

Which side is right? Although it is far too early to answer that question definitively, the early experience with welfare reform has produced some surprising results. One is how quickly the welfare rolls have fallen. On average, the welfare rolls in the states fell about 18 percent in the first year of reform. This statistic masks wide state-by-state variation, however. Hawaii's rolls have actually increased, by over 15 percent, whereas Idaho's and Wyoming's case loads have fallen by over 60 percent. A significant cause of these large decreases are new rules in thirty-three states, stripping welfare recipients of cash benefits for not complying with program requirements, such as seeking a job, receiving job training, remaining drug free, or not being convicted of a crime.[20]

These falling case loads represent a financial boon to the states because they will receive the same amount from the federal government through the year 2002, regardless of fluctuations in their case loads. Furthermore, critics contend that such a system fosters a "race to the bottom," in which states compete to offer the fewest benefits under the strictest rules, thus encouraging dependent residents to leave and discouraging other states' residents from relocating.

Given the dramatically falling case loads, few reports have surfaced of former beneficiaries being driven to hunger or suffering other extreme hardships. One explanation is that in the especially strong national economy of the late 1990s, roughly half of those who left welfare have found jobs. For the other half, many are turning to family and friends for support, and some maintain their eligibility under other government benefit programs. This is not to say, however, that there have been no cases of hardship. Some cities have experienced increased applications for homeless shelters in the wake of reform. We will face the real test of these reforms when the economy weakens (as the business cycle assures us it will) and the needy use up their lifetime benefits. Although Wisconsin promises its needy residents that they will be supported with state funds for as long as they comply with program requirements, this promise is an exception, not the rule. Twenty states have set limits even shorter than five years, and ten states have set limits of just two years.

The transfer of responsibility for welfare to the states is being watched closely by many. Will the impoverished be able to keep their heads above water, or will they be left to sink? Will inequality be reduced, or will it be exacerbated? Millions of lives will be altered as the welfare experiment plays out in the fifty states.

SOCIAL INSURANCE

social insurance
A government-backed guarantee against loss by individuals without regard to need.

Insurance is a device for protecting against loss. Since the late nineteenth century, there has been a growing tendency for governments to offer **social insurance,** which is government-backed protection against loss by individuals, regardless of need. The most common forms of social insurance offer health protection and guard against losses from worker sickness, injury, and disability; old age; and unemployment. The first example of social insurance in the United States was workers' compensation. Beginning early in the twentieth century, most states created systems of insurance that compensated workers who lost income because they were injured in the workplace.

Social insurance benefits are distributed to recipients without regard to their economic status. Old-age benefits, for example, are paid to workers—rich or poor—provided that they have enough covered work experience and they have reached the required age. In most social insurance programs, employees and employers contribute to a fund from which employees later receive payments. *

Social insurance programs are examples of entitlements. National entitlement programs consume about half of every dollar of government spending; the largest entitlement program is social security.

SOCIAL SECURITY

social security
Social insurance that provides economic assistance to persons faced with unemployment, disability, or old age. It is financed by taxes on employers and employees.

Social security is social insurance that provides economic assistance to people faced with unemployment, disability, or old age; it is financed by taxes on employers and employees. Initially, social security benefits were distributed only to the aged, the unemployed, and surviving spouses—

---

* *Examine your end-of-year W2 wage and tax statement. It should indicate your contribution to Social Security Tax (SST) and Medicare Tax (MT). SST supports disability, survivors', and retirement benefits. In 2001, it was 6.2 percent of the first $80,400 earned. MT pays for Medicare benefits. In 2001, it was 1.45 percent of all wages. Employers provide matching contributions to SST and MT.*

most of whom were widows—with dependent children. Today, social security also provides medical care for the elderly and income support for the disabled.

Origins of Social Security

The idea of social security came late to the United States. As early as 1883, Germany enacted legislation to protect workers against the hazards of industrial life. Most European nations adopted old-age insurance after World War I; many provided income support for the disabled and income protection for families after the death of the principal wage earner. In the United States, however, the needs of the elderly and the unemployed were left largely to private organizations and individuals. Although twenty-eight states had old-age assistance programs by 1934, neither private charities nor state and local governments—nor both together—could cope with the prolonged unemployment and distress that resulted from the Great Depression. It became clear that a national policy was necessary to deal with a national crisis.

The first important step came on August 14, 1935, when President Franklin Roosevelt signed the **Social Security Act;** that act is the cornerstone of the modern American welfare state. The act's framers developed three approaches to the problem of dependence. The first provided social insurance in the form of old-age and surviving-spouse benefits and cooperative state-national unemployment assistance. To ensure that the elderly did not retire into poverty, it created a program to provide income to retired workers. Its purpose was to guarantee that the elderly would have a reliable base income after they stopped working. (Most Americans equate social security with this program.) An unemployment insurance program, financed by employers, was also created to provide payments for a limited time to workers who were laid off or dismissed for reasons beyond their control.

The second approach provided aid to the destitute in the form of grants-in-aid to the states. The act represented the first permanent national commitment to provide financial assistance to the needy aged, needy families with dependent children, the blind, and (since the 1950s) the permanently and totally disabled. By the 1990s, the disabled category had grown to include the learning-disabled and the drug- and alcohol-dependent.

The third approach provided health and welfare services through federal aid to the states. Included were health and family services for disabled children and orphans and vocational rehabilitation for the disabled.

How Social Security Works

Old-age retirement revenue goes into its own *trust fund* (each social security program has a separate fund). The fund is administered by the Social Security Administration, which became an independent government agency in 1995. Trust fund revenue can be spent only for the old-age benefits program. Benefits, in the form of monthly payments, begin when an employee reaches retirement age, which today is sixty-five. (People can retire as early as age sixty-two but with reduced benefits.) The age at which full benefits are paid will increase gradually to sixty-seven after the year 2000.

Social Security Act
The law that provided for social security and is the basis of modern American social welfare.

Can You Explain Why...
many younger Americans fear they will never get any social security benefits, even though they have been paying into the system?

Many Americans believe that each person's social security contributions are set aside specifically for his or her retirement, like a savings account.[21] But social security doesn't operate quite like that. Instead, the social security taxes collected today pay the benefits of today's retirees. Thus, social security (and social insurance in general) is not a form of savings; it is a pay-as-you-go tax system. Today's workers support today's elderly.

When the social security program began, it had many contributors and few beneficiaries. The program could thus provide relatively large benefits with low taxes. In 1937, for example, the tax rate was 1 percent, and the social security taxes of nine workers supported each beneficiary. As the program matured and more people retired or became disabled, the ratio of workers to recipients decreased. In 1999, the social security system paid benefits of $386 billion to almost 45 million people and collected tax revenue from 152 million, a ratio of slightly more than three workers for every beneficiary. By 2030, the ratio will decline to two workers for every beneficiary.[22]

The solvency of the social security program will soon be tested. As the baby boomer generation retires, beginning in about 2010, politicians will face an inevitable dilemma: lower benefits and generate the ire of retirees or raise taxes and generate the ire of taxpayers. To put off this day of reckoning, policymakers built up the trust funds' assets in anticipation of the growth in the number of retirees. But the assets will be exhausted by 2029 (see Figure 19.2).

At one time, federal workers, members of Congress, judges, and even the president were omitted from the social security system. Today there are few exceptions. Universal participation is essential for the system to operate, because it is a tax program, not a savings program. If participation were not compulsory, there would not be enough revenue to provide benefits to current retirees. Government—the only institution that can coerce—requires all employees and their employers to contribute, thereby imposing restrictions on freedom.

Those people who currently pay into the system will receive retirement benefits financed by future participants. As with a pyramid scheme or a chain letter, success depends on the growth of the base. If the birthrate remains steady or grows, future wage earners will be able to support today's contributors when they retire. If the economy expands, there will be more jobs, more income, and a growing wage base to tax for increased benefits to retirees. But suppose the birthrate falls, or unemployment rises and the economy falters? Then contributions could decline to the point at which benefits exceed revenues. The pyramidal character of social security is its Achilles' heel.

Who Pays? Who Benefits?

"Who pays?" and "Who benefits?" are always important questions in government policymaking, and they continue to shape social security policy. In 1968, the Republican Party platform called for automatic increases in social security payments as the cost of living rose. The theory was simple: as the cost of living rises, so should retirement benefits; otherwise, benefits are paid in "shrinking dollars" that buy less and

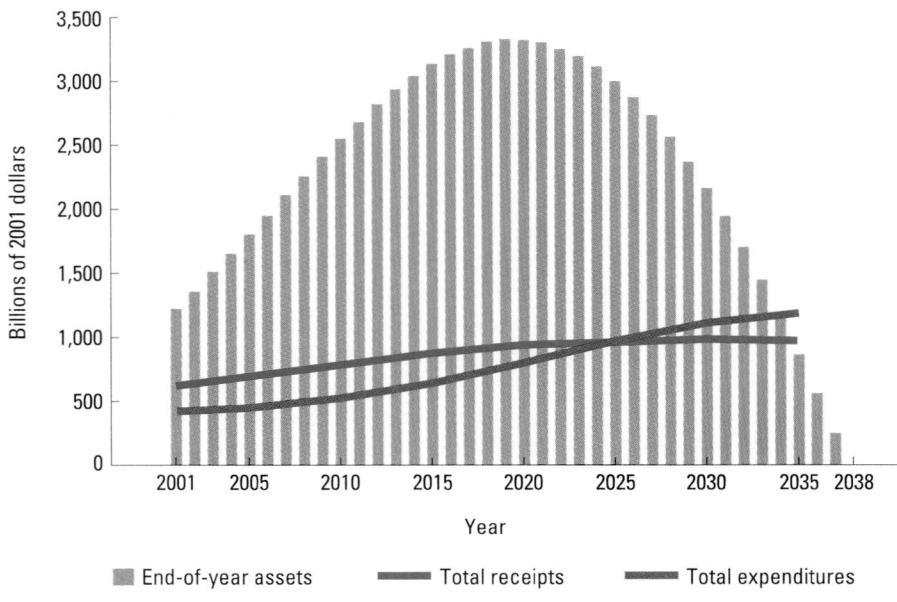

figure 19.2   **Day of Reckoning**

Social security tax revenues now exceed benefits paid out. But by 2012 or so, benefits will exceed receipts. With bankruptcy of the system looming so predictably, the debate over change boils down to two questions that politicians politely decline to answer: How soon will the national government change the current system, and how much will it change it?

Source: The 2001 Annual Report of the Board of Trustees of the Federal Old-Age and Survivors Insurance and Disability Insurance Trust Funds (March 19, 2001) <www.ssa.gov/OACT/TR/TR01/>.

---

less. Cost-of-living adjustments (COLAs) became a political football in 1969 as Democrats and Republicans tried to outdo each other by suggesting larger increases for retirees. The result was a significant expansion in benefits, far in excess of the cost of living. The beneficiaries were the retired, who were beginning to flex their political muscle. Politicians knew that alienating this constituency could lose them an election.[23]

In 1972, Congress adopted automatic adjustments in benefits and in the dollar amount of contributors' wages subject to tax, so that revenue would expand as benefits grew. This approach set social security on automatic pilot. When most economists criticized the COLA as overly generous, Congress tempered it. The 2001 COLA was 3.5 percent.

When stagflation (high unemployment coupled with high inflation) took hold in the 1970s, it jeopardized the entire social security system. Stagflation gripped the social security system in an economic vise: unemployment meant a reduction in revenue; high inflation meant automatically growing benefits. This one-two punch drained social security trust fund reserves to critically low levels in the late 1970s and early 1980s. Meanwhile, other troubling factors were becoming clear. A lower birthrate meant that in the future, fewer workers would be available to support the pool of retirees. And the number of retirees would grow, as average life spans lengthened and the baby-boom generation retired. Higher taxes—an unpopular political move—loomed as one alternative. Another was to pay for social security out of general revenues—that is, income taxes. Social security would then become a public assistance program, similar to welfare. In 1983, shortly before existing social security benefit funds would have become exhausted, Congress and President Reagan agreed to a solution that called for two painful adjustments: increased taxes and reduced benefits.

Social Security Reform

The changes enacted in 1983 prolonged the life of the social security system. However, future economic conditions will determine its success or failure. Concern over the future survival of social security is reflected in public opinion polls. Slightly less than half (49 percent) of nonretired Americans questioned think that social security will be able to pay them a benefit when they retire, and less than one-fifth (17 percent) count on social security as their main source of retirement income.[24]

In the 2000 presidential election campaign, both major parties sought to capitalize on social security reform as an issue. The Republicans argued that if the system is not changed, the country will be faced with "three bitter choices": raising taxes, reducing benefits, or adding to the national debt. As an alternative, Republicans proposed a plan that would allow individual workers to invest their own payroll taxes in the stock market in hopes of earning a higher rate of return than currently paid to the social security trust funds. However, people who wanted to stay in the current social security system could choose to do so.[25] In short, the Republicans hoped to avoid either raising payroll taxes or cutting benefits by increasing the rate of growth of trust fund monies. But their plan depends, of course, on the stock market continuing to grow at historically unprecedented rates. Note also that the Republicans are relying on choice and freedom as values in their proposed reforms.

The 2000 Democratic platform also proposed a private investment program, but theirs would be in addition to the existing program rather than a part or a reform of it. The principal goal of the Democrats' plan was to ensure the solvency of social security by committing the current federal budget surplus to strengthening the trust funds and to make the program more fair "for widows, widowers, and mothers." Called Retirement Savings Plus, the Democrats' program would "let Americans save and invest on top of the foundation of social security's guaranteed benefit. Under this plan, the federal government would match individual contributions with tax credits, with the hardest pressed working families getting the most assistance."[26] The Democrats' reference to fairness and to greater help for the hardest pressed clearly indicates their commitment to greater equality as a value.

It is far too early to tell how reform of social security will proceed, given the closeness of the 2000 presidential contest and the even partisan balance in Congress. Public opinion polls show that 65 percent of Americans favor the Republican plan for private investment of payroll taxes; however, support for the proposal declines sharply with increasing age of the respondent.[27] This is an important qualifier, however, because as a group, older Americans exercise enormous political power. People at or over retirement age now make up 32 percent of the potential electorate, and voter turnout among older Americans is reported to be about twice that of younger people.[28]

HEALTH CARE

It is hard to imagine a modern welfare state that does not protect the health of its population. Yet the United States is the only major industrialized nation without a universal health-care system. Government programs to provide health care include both Medicare (for the elderly) and Medicaid (for the qualifying poor.)

Medicare

In 1962, the Senate considered extending social security benefits to provide hospitalization and medical care for the elderly. In opposing the extension, Democratic senator Russell Long of Louisiana declared, "We are not staring at a sweet old lady in bed with her kimono and nightcap. We are looking into the eyes of the wolf that ate Red Riding Hood's grandma."[29] Long was concerned that costs would soar without limit. Other opponents echoed the fears of the American Medical Association (AMA), which saw virtually any form of government-provided medical care as a step toward government control of medicine. Long and his compatriots won the battle that day. Three years later, however, the Social Security Act was amended to provide **Medicare,** health care for all people aged sixty-five and older.

Medicare
A health-insurance program for all persons older than sixty-five.

Origins of Medicare.   As early as 1945, public opinion clearly supported some form of national health insurance. However, that idea became entangled in Cold War politics—the growing crusade against communism in America.[30] The AMA, representing the nation's physicians, mounted and financed an all-out campaign to link national health insurance (so-called socialized medicine) with socialism; the campaign was so successful that the prospect of a national health-care policy vanished.

Both proponents and opponents of national health insurance tried to link their positions to deeply rooted American values: advocates emphasized equality and fairness; opponents stressed individual freedom. In the absence of a clear mandate on the kind of insurance (publicly funded or private) the public wanted, the AMA was able to exert its political influence to prevent any national insurance at all.[31]

By 1960, however, the terms of the debate had changed. It no longer focused on the clash between freedom and equality. Now the issue of health insurance was cast in terms of providing assistance to the aged, and a ground swell of support forced it onto the national agenda.[32]

The Democratic victory in 1964 and the advent of President Johnson's Great Society made some form of national health-care policy almost inevitable. On July 30, 1965, Johnson signed a bill that provided a number of health benefits to the elderly and the poor. Fearful of the AMA's power to punish its opponents, the Democrats had confined their efforts to a compulsory hospitalization insurance plan for the elderly (known today as Part A of Medicare). In addition, the bill contained a version of an alternative Republican plan that called for voluntary government-subsidized insurance to cover physician's fees (known today as Part B of Medicare). A third program, added a year later, is called **Medicaid;** it provides medical

Medicaid
A need-based comprehensive medical and hospitalization program.

aid to the poor through federally assisted state health programs. Medicaid is a need-based comprehensive medical and hospitalization program: if you are poor, you qualify. Medicaid today is the second largest social insurance program in the United States. (Social security is first.) Medicaid covers 41 million people, at a cost of $142 billion in 1998.[33]

Medicare Today.   Part A of Medicare is compulsory insurance that covers certain hospital services for people aged sixty-five and older. Workers pay a tax; retirees pay premiums deducted from their social security payments. Payments for necessary services are made by the national government directly to participating hospitals and other qualifying facilities. In 1999, nearly 39 million people were enrolled in Part A, and the government paid $129 billion in benefits.[34]

Part B of Medicare is a voluntary program of medical insurance for people aged sixty-five and older who pay the premiums. The insurance covers the services of physicians and other qualifying providers. In 1999, 37 million people were enrolled; the government spent more than $81 billion for Part B benefits, of which about $20 billion came from enrollees. The difference of $61 billion comes from general tax revenue. In 2001, the monthly premium for this insurance was $50.00.[35]

Medicare costs continue to increase at rates in excess of the cost of living. Consequently, government has sought to contain those costs. One attempt at cost containment makes use of economic incentives in the hospital treatment of Medicare patients. The plan seems to have had the desired economic benefits, but it raises questions about possibly endangering the health of elderly patients. Previously, Medicare payments to hospitals were based on the length of a patient's stay: the longer the stay, the more revenue the hospital earned. This approach encouraged longer, more expensive hospital stays because the government was paying the bill. In 1985, however, the government switched to a new payment system under which hospitals are paid a fixed fee based on the patient's diagnosis. If the patient's stay costs more than the fee schedule allows, the hospital pays the difference. On the other hand, if the hospital treats a patient for less than the fixed fee, the hospital reaps a profit. This new system provides an incentive for hospitals to discharge patients sooner, perhaps in some cases before they are completely well.

Health-Care Reform

Nearly everyone maintains that the U.S. health-care system needs fixing. Let's consider the two main problems.

First, many Americans have no health insurance. In 1997, 43 million Americans—that's about 16 percent of the nonelderly population—were uninsured on any given day. They are uninsured because either their employers do not provide health insurance or the cost of health insurance is prohibitive for them. In 1993, the average annual family premium for employer-based group health insurance was $5,200, which was more than double the average premium in 1988. Compounding the problem is the fact that a job change or job loss often entails losing one's health insurance coverage.

Second, the cost of health care is rising faster than the cost of living. The United States spends far more money on health care than does any other nation. In 1997, total expenditures on health care in the United States (all government and private spending) came to almost $1.1 trillion, or about 14 percent of the gross domestic product. The Congressional Budget Office estimates that in 2007, total expenditures will slightly exceed $2 trillion, or about 16 percent of GDP.[36] Furthermore, the benefits of higher health-care spending may be elusive (see Compared with What? 19.1).

The American public remains divided on the remedy. The Clinton administration held firm to its objective of universal coverage, but none of the proposed approaches to this end has gained the support of a majority of Americans. Moreover, there is no clear sense of how to pay for the increased cost that any plan will entail. Half the public is prepared to pay higher taxes to ensure universal coverage, but the only taxes that generate strong support are "sin" taxes on alcohol and cigarettes. Yet these taxes are insufficient to pay for the comprehensive coverage Americans want. In summarizing the array of data on health-care reform, a commentator remarked, "We want the government to reform our health-care system, but we lack a shared vision of what that system should be or how to achieve it."[37]

The two central problems of health care give rise to two key goals and a familiar dilemma. First, any reform should democratize health care—that is, it should make health care available to everyone. But by providing broad access to medical care, we will increase the amount we spend on such care. Second, any reform must control the ballooning cost of health care. But controlling costs requires restricting the range of procedures and providers available to patients. Thus, the health-care issue goes to the heart of the modern dilemma of government: we must weigh greater equality in terms of universal coverage and cost controls against a loss of freedom in markets for health care and in choosing a doctor.

★ compared with what?

19.1 Health Spending and Its Possible Effects

In 1997, the United States spent nearly 14 percent of its gross domestic product (GDP, the total market value of all goods and services produced in this country during the year) on health care. This amount was substantially more than any other large-population nation.

Most of American health care spending was in the private sector. *Public health* spending is far less, both as a proportion of the GDP and in comparison to other nations.

What does health spending achieve? Measures of health spending outcomes are too numerous

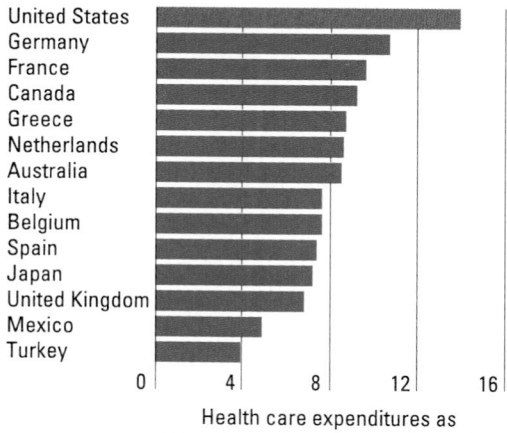

Health Expenditures by Country, 1997

Total health-care expenditures as a percentage of the gross domestic product.

Source: *1999 Statistical Abstract of the United States*, p. 838.

The dilemma of controlling costs without inhibiting the freedom to choose one's doctor applies not just to public health care, however. The same financial pressures affecting Medicare and Medicaid have also affected privately provided health coverage. Over the last quarter of a century, the health insurance industry has undergone tremendous change.

Most Americans used to carry what was called catastrophic care insurance, which provided hospital coverage for serious illnesses only. As the cost of medical care ballooned, numerous scholars and health-care providers realized that preventing illness through regular physical examinations and appropriate lifestyle changes was far cheaper than curing ill-

for inclusion here. Let's focus on just one: longevity. With only two exceptions (Mexico and Turkey), life expectancy in large-population nations reveals very little variation. Babies born in Mexico in 1999 can expect to live on average to age 72. Babies born in Japan and Australia in 1999 can expect to live on average to age 80. Despite the fact that Americans outspend other nations on health care, the payoff in life expectancy has not yet been realized.

Expectation of life at birth (1999)

Life Expectancy in 1999

The United States spends more of its wealth, as a percentage of its gross domestic product, on health-related expenditures than does any other country. This spending has not bought a high return, at least not in life expectancy. Children born in 1999 in the countries listed above can expect to live between 70 and 80 years. Though the differences between countries are small, the United States ranks toward the bottom of the list.

Source: *1999 Statistical Abstract of the United States*, p. 836. Excludes countries with populations less than 10 million in 1999.

nesses after onset. Thus, health insurance providers began to offer extended coverage of routine, preventive care in return for limiting an individual's freedom to choose when and what type of medical specialist to see.

These new types of insurance fell into two main categories: health maintenance organizations (HMOs) or preferred provider organizations (PPOs). In either case, insurance benefits now covered routine office visits for preventive care (sometimes with a modest copayment by the patient) in return for restricted access to more expensive, specialized care. The success of these new plans, and the transformation of the health-care industry, is reflected in the following facts: in 1993, 55 percent of insured

Golden Oldies Rock

Getting old is unavoidable but there is still hope for staying young. George Bernard Shaw declared that the secret to life was "to die young as late as possible." Thanks to improved health care and a rising standard of living, Americans are living longer. The baby-boom generation will soon be entering retirement with an increasing burden for their needs placed on younger working Americans.

Americans carried traditional, catastrophic coverage; 22 percent used HMOs; and 14 percent used PPOs. By 2000, 34 percent of those insured carried HMO coverage, 31 percent were enrolled in PPOs, and 25 percent carried traditional catastrophic coverage.[38]

This transformation in coverage has met with general public approval; while 54 percent of Americans are satisfied with the quality of health care generally in the United States, 82 percent are satisfied with their own health care. But there are differences in the levels of satisfaction. Those with PPO or traditional coverage report higher levels of satisfaction than those with HMO coverage (although 71 percent of the latter report being satisfied with their own coverage).

Given that the most common form of medical insurance is the HMO and that HMO customers have the lowest level of satisfaction among those insured, it is not surprising that there is pressure for some sort of government regulation of the health insurance industry. During the 2000 presidential campaign, both parties offered to support a patients' bill of rights, though Republicans and Democrats differed on the details. Republicans embraced the concept that the traditional patient-doctor relationship must be preserved, with treatment decisions being made by caregivers and not administrators or accountants. When a patient is denied treatment of his or her own choice, Republicans promised a rapid appeals process within the insurance company.[39] Democrats also endorsed a patients' bill of rights, but theirs guaranteed the right to appeal decisions to an outside board and the right to sue when patients are unfairly denied coverage.[40]

Another major topic of public debate is prescription drug care coverage. The American population is aging and as pharmaceutical companies develop a greater range of medications to treat a wider range of diseases, the cost of prescription drugs has become a political issue. Because prescriptions are most widely used by the aged and the chronically ill, there is considerable pressure to add prescription drug care coverage to the existing Medicare and Medicaid programs. How to pay for this potentially very expensive coverage without tax increases or additional burdens on the federal budget is a question yet to be answered.

EDUCATION

Since Horace Mann introduced mandatory public schooling in Massachusetts in the second quarter of the nineteenth century, public elementary and secondary schools have been a highly visible part of local government. National involvement in education, however, has been of more recent origin.

Education and Equality

Elementary and Secondary Education Act of 1965

Head Start
A child development program serving low-income children and their families.

An important part of Lyndon Johnson's Great Society was the traditional American belief that social and economic equality could be attained through equality of educational opportunity. The Elementary and Secondary Education Act of 1965 provided direct national government aid for the first time to local school districts, based on the number of low-income families in each district. An important federal initiative under this act is **Head Start,** a child development program serving low-income children and their families. Head Start aims to prepare disadvantaged youth for school by offering various preschool activities.

Average per-pupil educational expenditures by all levels of government, adjusted for inflation, have grown from $3,774 in 1970 to $6,915 in 1999 in the United States. Yet the promised improvements in social and economic equality have been elusive. While educational achievement improved, particularly for African Americans, until about 1990, after that year the gap in educational achievement between white Americans and black Americans began to grow again. And educational achievement in an information-based economy is closely linked to earning potential. For example, among employed men who were thirty-one to thirty-six years old in 1993, African Americans earned 68 percent of what whites earned. However, for African American males who scored above the fiftieth percentile in an educational achievement assessment, their earnings were 96 percent of the white average.[41]

Concern over educational achievement is not limited to issues of social equality at home. In an increasingly competitive global economy with fewer barriers to international investment and plant relocation, countries are competing to offer—and attract—highly educated and skilled workers. Thus, education has moved to the forefront of the public agenda. Public opinion polls during the 2000 election year showed that one-half of the American electorate believed education to be an "extremely important" issue; no other issue was rated to be as important by American voters.[42]

Increased citizen interest in education as an issue stems in part from growing unease with educational outcomes. Sixty-one percent of the public, when asked in August 2000, said they were either "somewhat dissatisfied" or "completely dissatisfied" with the quality of American education; this result is a ten-point increase in response to the same question one year earlier.[43] This increasing dissatisfaction has given rise to various school

Who Knows C++?

Starting young is a good idea. Computers in the classroom were the exception ten years ago. Now, they are familiar components in the standard array of educational tools. It is not uncommon for students—even very young students—to know more than their teachers when it comes to computing. Some educational reformers hinge anticipated improvements on improved computing use and access to the World Wide Web.

reform initiatives in the states, including teacher certification testing, student achievement testing, school vouchers, charter schools, and school finance reform.

Education Reform

The national debate over education reform in the United States is taking place against the backdrop of two fundamental facts: the limited role of the national government in primary and secondary education, and the relatively high level of satisfaction most parents have with their local schools. As recently as 1999, federal expenditures on primary and secondary education, including Head Start, amounted to just 7 percent of total expenditures on public primary and secondary education. And in election year 2000, 78 percent of parents of school-age children declared themselves either "completely satisfied" or "somewhat satisfied" with the quality of their child's education. Primary and secondary education is still predominantly a local responsibility, and most parents express satisfaction with their local school at the same time they express dissatisfaction with the nation's educational system.

At the center of the current debate over education is the dilemma of freedom versus equality. The American belief in equality is heavily weighted toward equality of opportunity, and equality of opportunity depends on equal access to a good education. At the same time, the American belief in freedom is perhaps nowhere expressed more vigorously than in the freedom to choose both where to live and what one's children will be taught in school.

As with health-care reform, both Republicans and Democrats made education reform a campaign issue in the 2000 election campaign. Republicans tied educational reform and improvement to strengthening accountability and empowering parents. Appealing to the value of freedom, the Republican platform called for five key changes, including raising academic standards through increased local control and accountability to parents, and allowing families (especially low-income families) greater flexibility in choosing which schools their children attend.[44] In fact, four of the five key changes proposed by Republicans appeal to freedom of choice and parental control as solutions to the dissatisfaction with American education.

By contrast, during the 2000 election campaign, Democrats proposed education reforms that would guarantee "equality of opportunity for all regardless of socioeconomic status." The Democratic platform made eight specific recommendations, including requiring all teachers to pass a competency exam, making affordable preschool available to all families, improving technology in the classroom and teaching all students computer skills, and allowing parents more freedom to choose which public schools their children attend.[45]

Whereas the Republican platform stressed choice in four of its five proposals, choice was mentioned in only one of the Democratic platform reforms. The Democrats instead stressed either equality of access or equality of achievement in almost all of their reform principles. As the challenges we face grow in technological and scientific sophistication, the dilemmas of education reform will become more pressing. The questions of who will pay for reform (and how much) as well as who will benefit (and in what terms: freedom or equality) promise not to go away soon.

BENEFITS AND FAIRNESS

As we have seen, the national government provides many Americans with benefits. There are two kinds of benefits: cash, such as a retiree's social security check, and noncash, such as food stamps. Some benefits are conditional. **Means-tested benefits** impose an income test to qualify. For example, free or low-cost school lunch programs and Pell college grants are available to households that have an income that falls below a designated threshold. **Non-means-tested benefits** impose no such income test; benefits such as Medicare and social security are available to all, regardless of income.

> **Can You Explain Why...**
> even very rich people are eligible for some government benefits?

Some Americans question the fairness of non-means-tested benefits. After all, benefits are subsidies, and some people need them more than others do. If the size of the benefit pie remains fixed, imposing means tests on more benefits has real allure. For example, all elderly people now receive the same Medicare benefits, regardless of their income. Fairness advocates maintain that the affluent elderly should shoulder a higher share of Medicare costs, shifting more benefits to the low-income elderly.

means-tested benefits
Conditional benefits provided by government to individuals whose income falls below a designated threshold.

non-means-tested benefits
Benefits provided by government to all citizens, regardless of income; Medicare and social security are examples.

If the idea of shifting benefits gains support in the future, reform debates will focus on the income level below which a program will apply. Thus, the question of fairness is one more problem for policymakers to consider as they try to reform social insurance, health-care, and education programs.

SUMMARY

In this chapter, we have examined domestic policy, a general plan of action adopted by the government to solve a social problem, counter a threat, or pursue an objective within the country's own borders. Often, disagreements about public policy are disagreements about values. Some of the oldest and most costly domestic policies, such as social security and Medicare, pose choices between freedom and equality.

Many domestic policies that provide benefits to individuals and promote economic equality were instituted during the Great Depression. Today, the government plays an active role in providing benefits to the poor, the elderly, and the disabled. The object of these domestic policies is to alleviate conditions that individuals are powerless to prevent. This is the social welfare function of the modern state. The call for health-care reform is a reflection of the modern dilemma of democracy: universal coverage and cost controls versus a loss of freedom in health-care choices. Incremental reforms in 1996 broadened coverage but fell far short of providing quality health care for all Americans.

Government confers benefits on individuals through social insurance and public assistance. Social insurance is not based on need; public assistance (welfare) hinges on proof of need. In one form of social insurance—old-age benefits—a tax on current workers pays retired workers' benefits. Aid for the poor, by contrast, comes from the government's general tax revenues. Although the current welfare system has few defenders, clear solutions to the problem of welfare dependence have yet to emerge.

Programs to aid the elderly and the poor have been gradually transformed into entitlements, or rights that accrue to eligible persons. These government programs have reduced poverty among some groups, especially the elderly. However, poverty retains a grip on certain segments of the population. Social and demographic changes have feminized poverty, and there is little prospect of reversing that trend soon.

Bill Clinton and a Republican-led Congress reformed the welfare system. The biggest entitlement program (AFDC) is gone. Thanks to TANF, individual state programs will substitute for a single national policy. Work requirements and time limits on welfare may break the cycle of dependency, but the reforms run the risk of endangering the neediest among us. Time and experience will tell whether this grand experiment will produce better outcomes.

In contrast to social insurance and public assistance programs, the federal government's involvement in education is of relatively recent origin, dating from the Great Society initiatives of the 1960s. Even today, education remains largely a state and local endeavor, with the federal government providing less than 10 percent of the funds for primary and secondary education. Traditionally, the federal government's education policy has centered around providing equal access to a good education for all Americans, but recently Republicans have proposed reforms that would shift the focus toward increased freedom and choice for families. Democratic reform proposals, on the other hand, stress programs that would promote equality of opportunity for all citizens. Thus, education policy today poses a choice between freedom and equality.

Some government subsidy programs provide means-tested benefits, for which eligibility hinges on income. Non-means-tested benefits are available to all, regardless of income. As the demand for such benefits exceeds available resources, policymakers have come to question their fairness. Subsidies for rich and poor alike are the basis for a broad national consensus. A departure from that consensus in the name of fairness may very well be the next challenge of democracy.

★ Selected Readings

Bennett, Linda L. M., and Stephen Earl Bennett. *Living with Leviathan: Americans Coming to Terms with Big Government.* Lawrence: University Press of Kansas, 1990. An analysis of public opinion about the powers and responsibilities of national government, from Franklin Roosevelt to Ronald Reagan.

Ellwood, David T. *Poor Support: Poverty in the American Family.* New York: Basic Books, 1988. Ellwood agrees with Murray's analysis (see below) but argues for incentives to break the grip of poverty. Ellwood's ideas have been part of the Clinton's administration's effort to "end welfare as we know it."

Goldberg, Gertrude Schaffner, and Eleanor Kremen, eds. *The Feminization of Poverty: Only in America?* New York: Greenwood, 1990. This comparative study of poverty among females in seven capitalist and socialist countries argues that the feminization of poverty is not unique to the United States.

Katz, Michael B. *The Undeserving Poor: From the War on Poverty to the War on Welfare.* New York: Pantheon, 1989. A historical overview of the ideas and assumptions that shaped policies toward the poor from the 1960s through the 1980s.

Murray, Charles. *Losing Ground.* New York: Basic Books, 1985. An assessment of American social policy from 1950 to 1980. Murray argues that by attempting to remove the barriers to the good life for the poor, policymakers have created a poverty trap. Controversial in its day, Murray's analysis is taken as received wisdom today.

Wilson, William Julius. *The Truly Disadvantaged: The Inner City, the Underclass, and Public Policy.* Chicago, Ill.: University of Chicago Press, 1987. Wilson argues that the decay of the inner city cannot be explained by racism alone and targets the class structure of ghetto neighborhoods as the most important factor in a complex web of reasons.

Internet Exercises

1. *Passing the Food Stamp Program*

The Social Security Administration maintains an online collection of President Lyndon B. Johnson's phone conversations regarding the development of some of his Great Society Programs. The site is located at **<www.ssa.gov/history/lbj.html>**.

• Go to this site and listen to tape number WH6404.09 (3020), in which Johnson discusses his feelings on his administration's proposal to create the food stamp program.

• Based on LBJ's conversation, how might one argue that the food stamp program was crafted with many interests, not just the interest of the poor, in mind?

2. *National Health Care*

Physicians for a National Health Program (PNHP) describes itself as a "single-issue organization advocating a universal, comprehensive single-payer national health care program." The organization maintains a Web site, which is located at **<www.pnhp.org/>**.

• Go to the PNHP Web site and review its mission statement. Then follow the group's "basic information" link to obtain a fact sheet on the single-payer national health program that it supports.

• How does this reform proposal differ from the current health-care programs—Medicare and Medicaid—that the United States has today? What evidence from the past suggests that, politically, the single-payer approach would be an extremely difficult one to pass in the United States?

"TURNER DONATION HELPS U.S. Trim U.N. Payment," said the newspaper headline in late December 2000. Ted Turner, the billionaire founder of CNN, gave $34 million to the State Department to break a financial logjam in the United Nations and a political impasse in the U.S. Senate.[1] Why did a private citizen have to bail out the richest nation in the world, the world's only superpower, and the founder and home of the United Nations—an organization of some 130 member nations?

This question invites a short answer but needs a deeper explanation. First, the short answer. The "Republican revolution" in the 1994 congressional elections gave Republicans control of the House and Senate for the first time in four decades, and Republican Senator Jesse Helms became chair of the Foreign Relations Committee. Helms was well known for his conservative social views, opposing abortion and favoring prayer in school. He also had conservative views on foreign affairs, opposing foreign aid programs and American involvement in foreign peacekeeping activities. Thus, Helms balked at paying U.S. bills for U.N. peacekeeping, and our U.N. debt jumped from under $0.5 billion in 1994 to over $1.2 billion in 1995.[2] The United States became both the United Nations' largest donor nation and its largest debtor nation.

In 1997, Senator Helms and Democratic Senator Joseph Biden, ranking member of the Foreign Relations Committee, sponsored legislation to pay a large part of the debt to the United Nations, but only if it cut staff, slashed its budget, and also reduced the U.S. share from 25 percent to 20 percent.[3] The U.S. share had already dropped substantially since the United Nations' founding in 1946, when the United States paid about 39 percent of its budget. The U.S. share remained about the same for a decade and then dropped to 33 percent. In 1972 it was fixed at 25 percent, where it remained.[4] Was the 1972 assessment of 25 percent still "fair" in 2000? If one judged according to the relative wealth of nations, it might seem so, for the United States had 26 percent of the world gross national product in the 1990s.[5] Most U.N. member nations, even our allies, said that the United States should pay up without trying to dictate terms.

Helms and others who favored a reduced U.S. contribution to the United Nations complained about more than its basic 25 percent assessment for the general budget. Starting in 1973, the United Nations began to assess its members separately for military peacekeeping missions, and the U.S. share came to 31 percent of those costs.[6] As the United Nations became more involved in peacekeeping missions, this two-tiered method of assessment resulted in the United States paying considerably more than 25 percent of the United Nations' overall budget.

The dispute between Senator Helms and the United Nations came to a head in early 2000, when he bluntly addressed the Security Council: "If the United Nations respects the sovereign rights of the American people and serves them as an effective tool of diplomacy, it will earn and deserve their respect." But he said that Americans have "grown increasingly frustrated with what they feel is a lack of gratitude" and warned the Security Council not to expect further U.S. contributions without significant changes at the risk of "eventual U.S. withdrawal."[7] Many representatives of member nations bristled at Helms's reference to the U.N. as a "tool" of U.S. diplomacy that lacked "gratitude" for American contributions. The Dutch representative condemned "withholding money that is due under a treaty obligation."[8]

Such was the backdrop for Ted Turner's donation of $34 million, which allowed a compromise on the first major overhaul of U.N. financing since 1972. The deal reduced the U.S. share of the administrative budget to 22 percent and its share of the peacekeeping budget to about 27 percent.[9] Cutting the U.S. share meant that other nations had to pay more. The fifteen members of the European Union, who collectively already paid more than their share of the world's GNP and refused any major increase, agreed to pay slightly more. Eighteen developing countries with growing economies, especially South Korea, Singapore, and Brazil, swallowed most of the U.S. cut.[10] Still, a $34 million shortfall remained for the 2001 U.N. budget—which private citizen Ted Turner paid to allow the deal to go through. U.N. Secretary-General Kofi Annan called the Christmas Eve agreement "the best possible seasonal gift."[11] Senator Helms allowed that it was "a real leap forward," although it did not "resolve all the issues" in financing.[12]

The final cost of this deal remains to be tallied. Clearly, the United States saved money but it lost goodwill among nations with which it must interact in an increasingly global world. This brings us to the deeper explanation of how a private citizen came to bat for the United States at the United Nations—a step that involves Ted Turner's commitment to his political values. Three years earlier, Turner gave the U.N. $1 *billion* (roughly one-third of his wealth) for causes "like refugees, cleaning up land mines, peacekeeping, UNICEF for the children, for diseases."[13] Whereas Senator Helms viewed the United Nations as an instrument of U.S. foreign policy—which reflects his conservative attitudes in foreign affairs—Ted Turner valued it as an organization that bypassed national governments and dealt directly with world problems—which reflects his liberal ideology in international affairs.

How do these ideological labels relate to the ideological framework described in Chapter 1 and that run throughout this book? The two-dimensional framework for analyzing ideological attitudes in American politics proposed in Chapter 1 can be readily adapted to international affairs, as shown in Figure 20.1. According to this typology, Ted Turner is an international liberal, while Senator Helms fits in the international conservative category. As suggested in this opening vignette, U.S. foreign pol-

Using the "Voters" data in CROSSTABS, analyze the public's support for government spending on "Defense" and "Foreign Aid." Are there any differences in government spending by party? How can you explain what you find?

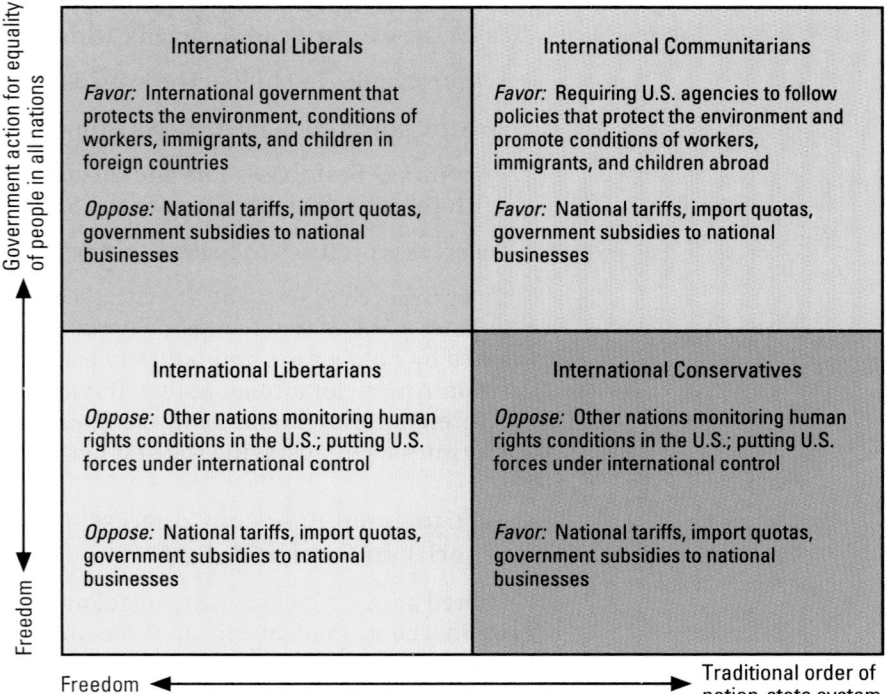

figure

20.1 A Two-Dimensional Framework of International Ideologies

As in Figure 1.2 in Chapter 1, the four ideological types here are defined by the values that they favor in balancing the values of freedom and order and freedom and equality in international affairs. In this typology, however, order is tied to the defense of national sovereignty within the traditional nation-state system of international relations.

International Liberals

Favor: International government that protects the environment, conditions of workers, immigrants, and children in foreign countries

Oppose: National tariffs, import quotas, government subsidies to national businesses

International Communitarians

Favor: Requiring U.S. agencies to follow policies that protect the environment and promote conditions of workers, immigrants, and children abroad

Favor: National tariffs, import quotas, government subsidies to national businesses

International Libertarians

Oppose: Other nations monitoring human rights conditions in the U.S.; putting U.S. forces under international control

Oppose: National tariffs, import quotas, government subsidies to national businesses

International Conservatives

Oppose: Other nations monitoring human rights conditions in the U.S.; putting U.S. forces under international control

Favor: National tariffs, import quotas, government subsidies to national businesses

Government action for equality of people in all nations ↑

Freedom ↓

Freedom ←——————→ Traditional order of nation-state system

---

icy is affected by members of Congress and even private individuals and organizations. Although a president may be held accountable for foreign affairs, many others are also involved. We begin our discussion of global policy by establishing the constitutional bases of governmental authority for making foreign policy.

MAKING FOREIGN POLICY: THE CONSTITUTIONAL CONTEXT

A nation's **foreign policy** is its general plan to defend and advance national interests, especially its security against foreign threats. The Constitution mentions the word *foreign* in only five places. Four are in the section dealing with Congress, which is entrusted to "regulate commerce among foreign nations"; to "regulate the value . . . of foreign coins"; to approve any gift or title to a government official "from any king, prince, or foreign state"; and to approve "any compact or agreement" between a state and "a foreign power" in time of war. The fifth mention gives the courts jurisdiction over cases arising "between a state . . . and foreign states. . . ." The Constitution never mentions *foreign* in its Article describing the executive branch, and yet the presidency has emerged as the dominant actor in foreign policy. Why?

foreign policy
The general plan followed by a nation in defending and advancing its national interests, especially its security against foreign threats.

Constitutional Bases of Presidential Authority in Foreign Policy

One must read between the lines of the Constitution to understand how presidents have derived their authority in foreign policy. The Constitution creates the executive in Article II, which provides that the president

- is commander in chief of the armed forces.

- has the power to make treaties (subject to the consent of the Senate).

- appoints U.S. ambassadors and the heads of executive departments (also with the advice and consent of the Senate).

- receives (or refuses to receive) ambassadors from other countries.

Over time, the president has parlayed these constitutional provisions—plus laws passed by Congress, Supreme Court decisions, and precedents created by bold action and political acceptance—to emerge as the leading actor in American foreign policy. But as in a play, there are other actors in the foreign policy drama, and Congress plays a strong supporting role—sometimes even upstaging the star performer.

Constitutional Bases of Congressional Authority in Foreign Policy

As noted above, Congress already claims most references to the word *foreign* in the Constitution, and—as in the case of the presidency—the Constitution gives Congress additional powers to use in foreign policy without mentioning the term. Specifically, the Constitution establishes that the Congress is empowered to

- legislate.

- declare war.

- raise revenue and dispense funds.

- support, maintain, govern, and regulate the army and navy.

- call out the state militias to repel invasions.

- regulate commerce with foreign nations.

- define and punish piracy and offenses against the law of nations.

The most salient power for foreign policy on this list is the power to declare war, but Congress has used this power only five times. It has relied more on its other powers to influence foreign policy. Using its legislative power, Congress can involve the nation in programs of international scope or limit the actions of the executive branch. Probably most important, Congress has used the power of the purse to provide funds for the activities it supports—and to prohibit funds for those it opposes. (As discussed in the opening vignette, Congress's frustration over the U.S. role in the United Nations led to its refusal to pay the U.S. accumulated debt.)

The Constitution also ascribes some powers to the Senate alone, which has made the U.S. Senate the leading chamber of Congress on foreign policy issues. The Constitution requires that the Senate

- give advice and consent to treaties made by the president.

- give advice and consent to the appointment of ambassadors and various other public officials involved in foreign policy.

The Senate has used its special powers to check presidential initiatives in foreign policy. Whereas only the president can *make* treaties, the Senate can *break* treaties—in the sense of rejecting those made by the president.

The Senate and Major Treaties. In truth, the Senate rarely defeats a treaty, having defeated only twenty-one of the thousands it has considered.[14] Some of the defeats have been historically significant, however, establishing the Senate as a force in foreign policy. A hard-hearted Senate demonstrated its veto power to Democratic President Woodrow Wilson in 1919. At the end of World War I, Wilson proposed and championed a plan for an international organization—the League of Nations—to eliminate future wars. To enter the League, however, Wilson's treaty had to be approved by two-thirds of the Senate. Wilson, an idealistic, international liberal, was opposed by a group of mostly Republican, internationally conservative senators. After eight months of debate, the Senate rejected his treaty and the United States never joined the League of Nations (which failed to prevent a second world war).

Charter of the United Nations (1949)

In the early days of World War II, President Franklin D. Roosevelt and British Prime Minister Winston Churchill revived Wilson's idea for collective security and proposed a new international organization—the United Nations—after the war. By the time the U.N. treaty went to the Senate in the summer of 1945, Roosevelt had died. It fell to Democratic President Harry Truman, who was mindful of Wilson's failure with the League of Nations, to win acceptance of the U.N. treaty by a Republican-controlled Senate. In public hearings on the treaty, several representatives of isolationist groups spoke against it, fearing loss of sovereignty to a world government.[15] But both parties in Congress now widely accepted U.S. international involvement, and Republican Senator Arthur H. Vandenberg, chair of the Foreign Relations Committee, led his party and the Senate to approve the treaty by a vote of 89 to 2 after only five days of debate. Without the Senate's approval, the United States would not have entered the United Nations.

The twenty-first and most recent treaty rejection by the Senate occurred October 13, 1999, on the Comprehensive Nuclear Test Ban Treaty. This treaty, signed by President Clinton in 1996, would have effectively outlawed all nuclear weapons testing. Almost all arms control agreements since Eisenhower's administration have been proposed by presidents of both parties, but they have been opposed by conservatives of both parties in Congress. Although Senator Helms and other conservatives led the fight against this treaty, even moderate Republicans were concerned about cheating by other nations. In the vote, the treaty failed to get the required two-thirds majority. All Democratic senators voted for it, and all but four Republicans voted against.[16] Governmental leaders around the world reacted angrily at the defeat of a treaty that had been decades in the making. One overseas newspaper editorialized, "If the United States, the sole superpower, refuses stubbornly to ratify a global nuclear test ban treaty that will make the world safer for all, why on earth would any other country want to do it?"[17] In the United States, Senator Jon Kyl (R.-AZ) said that the treaty rejection shows "that our constitutional democracy, with its shared powers and checks and balances, is alive and well."[18]

Skirting the Senate Through Executive Agreements.   An **executive agreement** is a pact between heads of countries concerning their joint activities. The Supreme Court has ruled that executive agreements are within the inherent powers of the president and have the legal status of treaties.[19] Executive agreements must conform to the Constitution, existing treaties, and the laws of Congress.[20] Like treaties, executive agreements have the force of law; unlike treaties, they do not require Senate approval. Until 1972 the texts of these agreements did not even have to be reported to Congress. Legislation passed that year required the president to send copies to the House and Senate Foreign Relations committees. This requirement has not seriously affected the use of executive agreements, which has escalated dramatically, outnumbering treaties by about ten to one since the 1930s.[21]

executive agreement
A pact between the heads of two countries.

Most executive agreements deal with minor bureaucratic business that would not interest a busy Senate. On occasion, presidents have resorted to executive agreements on important issues that were unlikely to win Senate consent. In 1992, President Bush negotiated an accord with Canada and Mexico that would facilitate free trade among the three countries by reducing national tariffs on imported goods. This plan, which reflected the free market international libertarian ideology, was widely favored by economists, but it was bitterly opposed by trade protectionists and international conservatives. Labor unions, who especially feared loss of manufacturing jobs to Mexico, were at the core of conservative opposition to the accord.

Although Bush was a Republican president backed by free-trade Republicans in the Senate, he worried that the accord, if embodied in a treaty, would fail to get two-thirds support in the Senate due to labor union pressure on Democratic senators. So Bush chose to frame it as an executive agreement—the North American Free Trade Agreement, or NAFTA.[22] He had to send the agreement to Congress for enabling legislation, but it required only simple majorities in both houses to pass. Bush expected to be reelected in 1992, but he was defeated by Bill Clinton, who inherited the pending NAFTA legislation.

President Clinton touted himself as a "new Democrat," and he was closer to Bush on free trade than to the traditional core of the Democratic party. Bucking organized labor, Clinton spoke passionately about free trade being good for the nation and shepherded NAFTA through passage in each chamber with more support from Republicans than from Democrats. In 1993, President Clinton signed the NAFTA agreement negotiated by President Bush.

Can You Explain Why...
NAFTA was not framed as an international treaty?

Constitutional Roots of Statutory Powers in Foreign Policy

Within the framework of the powers the Constitution grants to the executive, Congress has conferred other responsibilities to the presidency through laws—and creative presidents have even expanded on these grants of authority. For example, Congress has allowed the presidency certain leeway on use of *discretionary funds*—large sums of cash that may be spent on unforeseen needs to further the national interest. In January 1995, President Clinton used such emergency authority to loan up to $20 billion to Mexico to prevent its bankruptcy. The bailout worked, and Mexico repaid the loan with interest.[23] Similarly, the president's *transfer authority,* or the reprogramming of funds, allows him to take money that Congress has approved for one purpose and to spend it on something else. The executive branch also has control over the disposal of excess government stocks, including surplus or infrequently used equipment. The Central Intelligence Agency (CIA) has been an important beneficiary of excess stock disposal.

As commander in chief of the armed forces, several presidents have committed American troops in emergency situations, thus involving the United States in undeclared wars. America's undeclared wars, police actions, and similar interventions have outnumbered its formal, congressionally declared wars by about forty to one. Since the last declared war ended in 1945, over 100,000 American members of the military have died in locations ranging from Korea and Vietnam to Grenada, Somalia, and the Persian Gulf.

War Powers Resolution (1973)

Reacting to the undeclared Vietnam War, Congress passed the War Powers Resolution, which required that the president "consult" with Congress in "every possible instance" before involving U.S. troops in hostilities. In addition, the president must notify Congress within forty-eight hours of committing troops to a foreign intervention. Once troops have been deployed, they may not stay for more than sixty days without congressional approval (although the president may take up to thirty days more to remove them "safely"). President Nixon vetoed the War Powers Resolution as an unwarranted restriction on the president's constitutional authority, but it was approved over his veto. Some critics of the legislation claimed that it did not restrict presidential power as much as extend a free hand to wage war for up to sixty days.[24] The actual impact of the War Powers Resolution is probably quite minimal. Nixon's successors in the White House have all questioned its constitutionality, and no president has ever been punished for violating its provisions. At the time of the Persian Gulf crisis, Congress passed a resolution authorizing the use of force and avoided a showdown between the branches over this thorny issue. The issue arose again in 1999, when Clinton announced air attacks on Serbia in response to its invasion of Kosovo. Although Clinton promised not to use U.S. ground troops against Serbia, Republican leaders in Congress invoked the War Powers Resolution to take up the president's commitment of the U.S. military in the conflict. Like all other presidents before him, Clinton refused to recognize congressional limits on his authority as commander in chief. Congress itself failed to act conclusively to limit the president's authority in that conflict.[25]

As presidents have expanded their role in the foreign policy drama, the Senate sought to enlarge its part, interpreting quite broadly its power to "advise and consent" on presidential appointments to offices involved in foreign affairs. Senators have used confirmation hearings as opportunities to investigate and prod the administration. For example, the Foreign Relations Committee, chaired by Senator Jesse Helms (R.-NC), used the power of confirmation to deny the Mexican ambassadorship to William Weld, a former Republican governor of Massachusetts, who was more liberal than Helms and many other Republicans on social issues. In proposing his own ambassadorial appointments, President George W. Bush presumably will propose ambassadors whom the Senate finds more acceptable and thus will encounter fewer obstacles in conducting foreign policy. In nominating John Negroponte as U.N. ambassador, Bush picked a publishing executive and retired career diplomat—someone sure to win Senate confirmation.

MAKING FOREIGN POLICY: ORGANIZATION AND CAST

Although American foreign policy originates within the executive branch, the organizational structure for policymaking is created and funded by Congress and is subject to congressional oversight. When the United States acquired its superpower status after World War II, Congress overhauled the administration of foreign policy with the 1947 National Security Act, which established three new organizations—the Department of Defense, the National Security Council, and the CIA—to join the Department of State in the organizational structure.

The Department of State

During its very first session in 1789, Congress created a Department of Foreign Affairs as the government's first executive department. Within two months it was renamed the State Department, as it has remained.[26] The State Department helps formulate American foreign policy and then executes and monitors it throughout the world. The department's head, the secretary of state, is the highest ranking official in the cabinet; he is also, in theory at least, the president's most important foreign policy adviser. However, some chief executives, like John Kennedy, preferred to act as their own secretary of state and have thus appointed relatively weak figures to the post. Others, such as Dwight Eisenhower, appointed stronger individuals (John Foster Dulles) to the post. Presidents often come to the Oval Office promising to rely on the State Department and its head to play a leading role in formulating and carrying out foreign policy. The reality that emerges is usually somewhat different and prompts analysts to bemoan the chronic weakness of the department.[27]

By nominating former general Colin L. Powell to be secretary of state, President George W. Bush may have signaled that the State Department will play a greater role in foreign policy than it did under most previous secretaries, including the last secretary of state, Madeline Albright, in the Clinton administration. General Powell served for four years as chairman of the Joint Chiefs of Staff under presidents Bush and Clinton. A forceful man and motivational speaker, he's expected to limit the use of the U.S. military in peacekeeping operations, in keeping with what's become known as the Powell Doctrine: "Define your objective. Bring massive force to bear. Take on only those battles you are sure you can win, and line up public support before you start."[28] (To which Albright, then U.N. ambassador, reportedly said, "What's the point of having this superb military that you've always been talking about if we can't use it?")[29]

Like other executive departments, the State Department is staffed by political appointees and permanent employees selected under the civil service merit system. Political appointees include deputy secretaries and undersecretaries of state and some—but not all—ambassadors. Permanent employees include approximately four thousand foreign service officers, home and abroad, who staff and service U.S. embassies and consulates throughout the world. They have primary responsibility for representing America to the world and caring for American citizens and interests abroad. Although the foreign service is highly selective (fewer than two hundred of the fifteen thousand candidates who take the annual examination are appointed), the State Department is often charged with lacking initiative and creativity. Critics claim that bright young foreign service officers quickly realize that conformity is the best path to career advancement.[30]

A serious problem facing the State Department is its lack of a strong domestic constituency to exert pressure in support of its policies. The Department of Agriculture, by contrast, can mobilize farmers to support its activities; the Department of Defense can count on help from defense industries and veterans' groups. In a pluralist democracy, the lack of a natural constituency is a serious drawback for an agency or department. Exacerbating this problem is the changing character of global political issues. As economic and social issues emerge in foreign affairs, executive agencies with pertinent domestic policy expertise have become more involved in shaping global policy.

The Department of Defense

In 1947, Congress replaced two venerable cabinet-level departments—the War Department and the Department of the Navy—with the Department of Defense, intending to promote unity and coordination among the armed forces and to provide the modern bureaucratic structure needed to manage America's greatly expanded peacetime military. In keeping with the U.S. tradition of civilian control of the military, the new department was given a civilian head—the secretary of defense—a cabinet member with authority over the military. Later reorganizations of the department (in 1949 and 1958) have given the secretary greater budgetary powers; control of defense research; and the authority to transfer, abolish, reassign, and consolidate functions among the military services.

The power wielded by the defense secretary often depends on the individual secretary's own vision of the job and willingness to use the tools available. Strong secretaries of defense, including Robert McNamara (under Kennedy and Johnson), Melvin Laird (under Nixon), James Schlesinger (under Nixon and Ford), and Caspar Weinberger (under Reagan) have wielded significant power. For his new administration, President George W. Bush nominated Donald Rumsfeld, an experienced Washington government official, as secretary of defense. Rumsfeld served in Congress, was ambassador to NATO, and was White House chief of staff under President Ford, under whom he also served as the nation's youngest secretary of defense. So he returned to head the Department of Defense a second time and is likely to be a strong voice in Bush's administration, one strong enough to counter Secretary of State Powell.

Below the secretary are the civilian secretaries of the army, navy, and air force; below them are the military commanders of the individual branches of the armed forces. These military leaders make up the Joint Chiefs of Staff. The Joint Chiefs meet to coordinate military policy among the different branches; they also serve as the primary military advisers to the president, the secretary of defense, and the National Security Council, helping to shape policy positions on matters such as alliances, plans for nuclear and conventional war, and arms control and disarmament.

The National Security Council

The National Security Council (NSC) is made up of a group of advisers who help the president mold a coherent approach to foreign policy by integrating and coordinating details of domestic, foreign, and military affairs that relate to national security. The statutory members of the NSC include the president, the vice president, and the secretaries of state and defense. NSC discussions can cover a wide range of issues, such as how to deal with changes in Eastern Europe or the formulation of U.S. policy in the Middle East. In theory, at least, NSC discussions offer the president an opportunity to solicit advice and allow key participants in the foreign policy–making process to keep abreast of the policies and capabilities of other departments.

In practice, the role played by the NSC has varied considerably under different presidents. Truman and Kennedy seldom met with it; Eisenhower and Nixon brought it into much greater prominence. During the Nixon administration, the NSC was critically important in making foreign policy. Much of this importance derived from Nixon's reliance on Henry Kissinger, his assistant for national security affairs (the title of the head of the NSC staff). Soon after his election was settled, President George W. Bush nominated Condoleezza Rice as head of his NSC. Although only forty-six years old, Professor Rice was not a newcomer to the NSC. From 1989 to 1991, she served Bush's father as the top Russian expert on the NSC before she returned to teaching political science at Stanford. In Bush's 2000 election campaign, Rice was his top national security adviser and someone who, as Bush said, "can explain foreign policy matters to me in a way I can understand."[31] So she's expected to be within his foreign policy inner circle.

The CIA and the Intelligence Community

Before World War II, the United States had no permanent agency specifically charged with gathering intelligence (that is, information) about the actions and intentions of foreign powers. In 1941, poor American intelligence procedures contributed to the success of the Japanese surprise attack on Pearl Harbor. After the war, when America began to play a much greater international role and the ice began to form during the Cold War, Congress created the Central Intelligence Agency to collect such information. The departments of defense, state, energy, and the treasury also possess intelligence-related agencies, which together with the CIA make up the "intelligence community."

The CIA's charter charges it with collecting, analyzing, evaluating, and circulating intelligence relating to national security matters. Most of these activities are relatively noncontroversial. By far the bulk of material obtained by the CIA comes from readily available sources: statistical abstracts, books, and newspapers. The agency's Intelligence Directorate is responsible for these overt (open) activities in collecting and processing information.

The charter also empowers the CIA "to perform such other functions and duties related to intelligence affecting the national security as the National Security Council shall direct." This vague clause has been used by the agency as its legal justification for the covert (secret) activities undertaken in foreign countries by its Operations Directorate. These activities have included espionage, coups, assassination plots, wiretaps, interception of mail, and infiltration of protest groups.

A key dilemma posed by the CIA and the intelligence community concerns the role of covert activities. Covert operations raise both moral and legal questions for a democracy. Allen Dulles, President Eisenhower's CIA director, once called these operations "an essential part of the free world's struggle against communism." But are they equally important in a post–Cold War world? Can they be reconciled with the principle of checks and balances in American government? Obviously, when the government engages in clandestine actions that the public knows nothing about, the people are not able to hold their government accountable for its actions. Is the intelligence community needed at all in the post–Cold War world? One analyst argues that "the Cold War may be over, but the U.S. need for accurate information about the world remains acute."[32] Such commentators see a new role for the intelligence community, addressing issues such as terrorism, drug trafficking, nuclear proliferation, and possibly even U.S. economic security.

As former head of the CIA in the Ford administration, George Bush (senior) had felt that the intelligence function should be above partisan politics. In fact, he proposed to president-elect Jimmy Carter that he stay in his job, but Carter declined the offer.[33] It fell to Bush's son, President George W. Bush, to deliver on his father's idea. By retaining George J. Tenet, a registered Democrat, as head of the CIA, the younger Bush also fulfilled his 2000 campaign promise to appoint a Democrat to a cabinet-level job; however, CIA Director Tenet is unlikely to be within President Bush's foreign policy inner circle.

Other Parts of the Foreign Policy Bureaucracy

The last few decades have witnessed a proliferation in the number of players on the foreign policy stage. Due to globalization and the interdependence of social, environmental, and economic issues with political matters, many departments and agencies other than those described above now find themselves involved in global policy. For some, foreign affairs constitute their chief concern. The Agency for International Development (AID) oversees aid programs to nations around the globe. In doing so, AID works with a full range of other departments and agencies, including the Defense Department, the CIA, the Peace Corps, and the Department of Agriculture. The United States Information Agency (USIA), which has more than two hundred offices in over one hundred countries, provides educational and cultural materials about the United States. The U.S. Arms Control and Disarmament Agency (ACDA) is charged with promoting, negotiating, and verifying arms control, nonproliferation, and disarmament policies and agreements. ACDA is the agency responsible for integrating arms control issues into U.S. foreign policy. In an effort to save funds and to coordinate functions, ACDA and USIA were incorporated into the State Department in 1999. AID remained a separate agency but fell under the authority of the secretary of state. As of early 2000, the merger produced no savings but at least a one-time cost of an additional $219 million.[34]

Other departments and agencies primarily concerned with domestic issues have become more active in the foreign policy arena. For example, the Department of Agriculture provides agricultural assistance to other countries and promotes American farm products abroad. Likewise, the Department of Commerce tries to expand overseas markets for nonagricultural U.S. goods. In addition, the Department of Commerce administers export control laws to prevent other nations from gaining access to American technologies connected with national security (such as computers and military equipment). As trade has become a more important aspect of foreign policy, the role of the Commerce Department in promoting American business abroad has also grown. The Department of Energy monitors nuclear weapons programs internationally and works with foreign governments and international agencies such as the International Atomic Energy Agency to coordinate international energy programs. Recently it has also supported American energy companies trying to do business abroad.

An array of government corporations, independent agencies, and quasi-governmental organizations also participate in the foreign policy arena. These include the National Endowment for Democracy, an independent nonprofit organization, funded by Congress, to promote democracy in other countries; the Export-Import Bank, a government corporation that subsidizes the export of American products; and the Overseas Private Investment Corporation, an independent agency that helps American companies invest abroad.

This list of bureaucratic entities with foreign policy interests is by no means exhaustive, but it does suggest the complexity of the foreign policy–making machinery. Furthermore, as social and economic issues become more prominent on the global policy agenda, we can expect an increase in the involvement of agencies not traditionally preoccupied with foreign policy. Finally, states and localities have also begun to pay attention to international matters. Most state governments now have separate offices, bureaus, or divisions for promoting the export of state goods and attracting overseas investment into their state.[35] All this suggests that the line between domestic and foreign policy will become even more blurred.

A REVIEW OF U.S. FOREIGN POLICY

Presidents come to office with an ideological orientation for interpreting and evaluating international events, and they tend to be more internationalist than isolationist in their orientation. Presidents also tend to fill the offices of secretary of state, secretary of defense, national security adviser, and director of the CIA with individuals who are tuned to the presidential wavelength. However, presidents must accept advice and receive consent from members of Congress, who tend to be more isolationist in their orientations. The political result is the nation's foreign policy. Of course, foreign policies change according to presidential and congressional views of "national interests" and to whatever actions are thought appropriate for defending and advancing those interests. In reviewing America's role in foreign affairs, it is helpful to structure the review in terms of presidents and the shorthand labels attached to the nation's policies during their administrations.

Emerging from Isolationism

isolationism
A foreign policy of withdrawal from international political affairs.

For most of the nineteenth century, the limits of American interests were those staked out by the Monroe Doctrine of 1823, in which the United States rejected European intervention in the Western Hemisphere and agreed not to involve itself in European politics. Throughout the 1800s, U.S. presidents practiced a policy of **isolationism,** or withdrawal from the political entanglements of Europe. American isolationism was never total, however. As the nineteenth century wore on, the United States continued its expansion from coast to coast and also became a regional power that was increasingly involved in the affairs of nations in the Pacific and Latin America. Still, America's defense establishment and foreign policy commitments remained limited.

World War I was the United States' first serious foray into European politics. The rhetoric that surrounded our entry into the war in 1917—"to make the world safe for democracy"—gave an idealistic tone to America's effort to advance its own interest in freedom of the seas. Such moralism has often characterized America's approach to international politics, and

The Monroe Doctrine— U.S. Policy in the Americas

U.S. Hegemony in the Caribbean and Latin America

The Same in Any Language

These three World War I posters (from Germany, Great Britain, and the United States) were used to persuade men to join the army. Interestingly, they all employed the same psychological technique—pointing at viewers to make each individual feel the appeal personally.

Cold War
A prolonged period of adversarial relations between the two superpowers, the United States and the Soviet Union. During the Cold War, which lasted from the late 1940s to the late 1980s, many crises and confrontations brought the superpowers to the brink of war, but they avoided direct military conflict with each other.

containment
The basic U.S. policy toward the Soviet Union during the Cold War, according to which the Soviets were to be contained within existing boundaries by military, diplomatic, and economic means, in the expectation that the Soviet system would decay and disintegrate.

it was certainly reflected in Wilson's plan for U.S. entry into the League of Nations to prevent future wars. When the Senate failed to ratify the treaty needed for entry, America's brief moment of internationalism ended. Until World War II, America continued to define its security interests narrowly and needed only a small military establishment to defend them.

World War II dramatically changed America's orientation toward the world. The United States emerged from the war a superpower, and its national security interests extended across the world. The country did not withdraw into isolationism again but instead confronted a new rival—its wartime ally, the Soviet Union. In the fight against Hitler, the Soviets overran much of Eastern Europe. In the aftermath of the war, the Soviets solidified their control over these lands, spreading their communist ideology. To Americans, Soviet communism appeared to destroy freedom, and the possibility of continued Soviet expansion in Europe threatened international order. European conflicts had drawn the United States into war twice in twenty-five years. American foreign policy experts believed that the Soviets, if left unchecked, might soon do it again.

Cold War and Containment

To frustrate Soviet expansionist designs, Americans prepared to wage a new kind of war: not an actual shooting war, or "hot war," but a **Cold War,** characterized by suspicion, rivalry, mutual ideological revulsion, and a military buildup between the two superpowers, but no shooting. The United States waged its Cold War on a policy of **containment,** or holding Soviet power in check.[36]

The policy of containment had military, economic, and political dimensions. Militarily, the United States committed itself to high defense expenditures, including maintaining a large fighting force with troops stationed around the world. Economically, the United States backed the

The North Atlantic Treaty (1949)

North Atlantic Treaty Organization (NATO)
An organization including nations of Western Europe, the United States, and Canada, created in 1949 to defend against Soviet expansionism. With the Soviet threat in Western Europe diminished or eliminated, the purposes and membership of NATO are under examination.

nation building
A policy once thought to shore up Third World countries economically and democratically, thereby making them less attractive targets for Soviet opportunism.

establishment of an international economic system that relied on free trade, fixed currency exchange rates, and America's ability to act as banker for the world. This system, plus an aid program to rebuild Europe (the Marshall Plan), fueled recovery and reduced the economic appeal of communism. Politically, the United States forged numerous alliances against Soviet aggression. The first treaty of alliance (1949) created the **North Atlantic Treaty Organization (NATO),** dedicated to the defense of member countries in Europe and North America. In addition, the United States tried to use international institutions such as the United Nations as instruments of containment. Because the Soviets had veto power in the U.N. Security Council, the United States was rarely able to use the United Nations as anything more than a sounding board to express anti-Soviet feelings.

In the first decades of the Cold War, the United States relied heavily on its superiority in nuclear weapons to implement a policy of nuclear deterrence. It discouraged Soviet expansion by threatening to use nuclear weapons to retaliate against Soviet power, which had also acquired nuclear capabilities. By the late 1960s, both nations' nuclear technology had reached the level where they could destroy each other totally. From this situation came the policy of mutual assured destruction (MAD)—a first strike from either nation would result in the complete annihilation of both sides.

In the 1950s and 1960s, many countries in the developing world were gaining independence from colonial control imposed by western nations. By the late 1950s, the Soviets were paying close attention to these developing nations. They offered to help forces involved in what they called wars of national liberation—that is, wars fought to end colonialism. To counter the Soviets, the United States followed policies aimed at **nation building** in the developing countries, the so-called Third World. These measures were designed to strengthen the opponents of communism in newly emerging nations by promoting democratic reforms and shoring up their economies.

Vietnam and the Challenge to the Cold War Consensus

Soviet support for a war of national liberation came into conflict with American nation building in Vietnam. There, the United States tried to strengthen noncommunist institutions in South Vietnam to prevent a takeover by Soviet-backed forces from North Vietnam and their communist allies in the south, the Viet Cong. The Cold War turned hot in Vietnam by the mid-1960s. Over 58,000 American lives were lost during the protracted fighting, until the United States withdrew in 1973. The Vietnam War badly damaged the Cold War consensus on containment, both abroad and at home. Some American critics complained that the government lacked the will to use enough military force to win the war. Others argued that America relied too much on military force to solve what were really political problems. Still others objected that America was intervening in a civil war rather than blocking Soviet expansion. In short, Americans disagreed passionately on what to do in Vietnam and how to do it. Eventually, after signing a peace agreement in 1973, the

United States pulled its forces out of Vietnam, and in 1975, north and south were forcibly united under a communist regime.

Even as the war in Vietnam wore on, President Nixon and his chief foreign policy adviser (and later secretary of state), Henry Kissinger, overhauled American foreign policy under the **Nixon Doctrine.** Now the United States would intervene only where "it makes a real difference and is considered in our interest."[37] As a student of nineteenth-century diplomatic history, Kissinger believed that peace prevailed then because the great nations of Europe maintained a balance of power among themselves. Nixon and Kissinger sought to create a similar framework for peace among the world's most powerful nations in the late twentieth century. To this end, they pursued a policy of **détente** (a relaxing of tensions between rivals) with the Soviet Union and ended decades of U.S. hostility toward the communist People's Republic of China. The brief period of détente saw the conclusion of a major arms agreement, the Strategic Arms Limitation Treaty (SALT I), in 1972. This pact limited the growth of strategic nuclear weapons. The thaw in the Cold War also witnessed greater cooperation between the United States and the Soviet Union in other spheres, including a joint space mission.

President Jimmy Carter's stance on foreign policy differed substantially from that of his predecessors. From 1977 to 1979, he tended to downplay the importance of the Soviet threat. He saw revolutions in Nicaragua and Iran as products of internal forces rather than of Soviet involvement. In contrast to Nixon and Kissinger, Carter was sometimes criticized as being overly idealistic. He emphasized human rights, leveling criticism at both friends and enemies with poor human rights records. He usually leaned toward open rather than secret diplomacy. Nonetheless, his greatest foreign policy achievement, the Camp David accords, which brought about peace between Egypt and Israel, resulted from closed negotiations he arranged between Egyptian president Anwar Sadat and Israeli premier Menachem Begin.

In many ways, Carter's foreign policy reflected the influence of the Vietnam syndrome, a crisis of confidence that resulted from America's failure in Vietnam and the breakdown of the Cold War consensus about America's role in the world. For example, his administration deemphasized the use of military force but could offer no effective alternatives when Iranians took American diplomats hostage and when the Soviets invaded Afghanistan.

The End of the Cold War

Carter's successor, Ronald Reagan, came to the Oval Office untroubled by the Vietnam syndrome. He believed that the Soviets were responsible for most of the evil in the world. Attributing instability in Central America, Africa, and Afghanistan to Soviet meddling, he argued that the best way to combat the Soviet threat was to renew and demonstrate American military strength—a policy of **peace through strength.** Increased defense spending was focused on major new weapons systems, such as the Strategic Defense Initiative (or "Star Wars" program), a new space-based missile defense system. The Reagan administration argued that its massive military buildup was both a deterrent and a bargaining chip to use in talks with the Soviets. During this period, the Cold War climate once again grew chilly.

Nixon Doctrine
Nixon's policy, formulated with assistance from Henry Kissinger, that restricted U.S. military intervention abroad absent a threat to its vital national interests.

détente
A reduction of tensions. This term is particularly used to refer to a reduction of tensions between the United States and the Soviet Union in the early 1970s during the Nixon administration.

peace through strength
Reagan's policy of combatting communism by building up the military, including aggressive development of new weapons systems.

Things changed when Mikhail Gorbachev came to power in the Soviet Union in 1985. Gorbachev wished to reduce his nation's commitments abroad so it could concentrate its resources on needed domestic reforms. By the end of Reagan's second term, the United States and the Soviet Union had concluded agreements outlawing intermediate-range nuclear forces (the INF Treaty) and providing for a Soviet military pullout from Afghanistan.[38]

In 1989, not long after Reagan left office, the Berlin wall was torn down, symbolizing the end of the Cold War. The conventional view is that the Cold War ended and America won.[39] Some believe that communism collapsed because of Reagan's policies. Others insist that the appeal of western affluence, Gorbachev's own new thinking, and a shared interest in overcoming the nuclear threat led to the end of the Cold War.[40] Still others argue that both superpowers had lost by spending trillions of dollars on defense while neglecting other sectors of their economies.[41] Regardless of its explanation, the end of the Soviet threat raised the question about what would shape American foreign policy.

Foreign Policy Without the Cold War

When George Bush became president in 1989, he came with strong foreign policy credentials: U.N. ambassador, director of the CIA, ambassador to China—as well as vice president. He soon faced a classic national security challenge when Iraq invaded Kuwait. Not only did Iraq attack an American friend, but it risked cutting off our supply of oil. Bush emphasized multilateral action and the use of international organizations like the United Nations. To oppose Saddam Hussein, he built a coalition of nations that included America's western allies, the Soviet Union, Eastern European states, many Arab states, and other developing countries. The United States also won approval for a series of actions against Iraq from the U.N. Security Council. During the Cold War, most major crises pitted U.S.-backed nations against states supported by the Soviet Union, so the Security Council usually proved ineffective because one of the two powers could veto the other's action. However, the two superpowers cooperated against Saddam in this post–Cold War crisis.

enlargement and engagement
Clinton's policy, following the collapse of communism, of increasing the spread of market economies and increasing the United States' role in global affairs.

Iraq's invasion of Kuwait constituted a visible, vital threat to U.S. interests and galvanized Americans in support of President Bush's military action to repel the invasion. President Clinton, who had come to the White House with no foreign policy experience, enjoyed no galvanizing challenge and struggled to provide clear, coherent foreign policy leadership. Clinton's presidential campaign emphasized domestic concerns, but he soon found that messy crises in Somalia, Bosnia, Haiti, and then Kosovo absorbed much of his time (see Compared with What 20.1).

The Clinton administration replaced the Cold War policy of containment with a policy of **enlargement and engagement.** "Enlargement" meant increasing the number of democracies with market economies and also adding to the membership of NATO. "Engagement" meant rejecting isolationism and striving to achieve greater flexibility in a chaotic global era. But critics worried that the policy did not provide adequate guidelines about when, where, and why the United States should be engaged.[42] Even when Clinton acted in concert with NATO to stop the genocidal violence

✖ Using the "Congress" data in CROSSTABS, analyze the votes in Congress on limiting troops sent to Bosnia and expanding NAFTA (the North American Free Trade Agreement). Which party favored placing limits on the use of troops and which favored expanding NAFTA?

20.1   War in the Twentieth and Twenty-first Centuries

The last major multinational war of the twentieth century was truly remarkable, as wars go. The NATO air campaign against Serbian forces in Kosovo began on March 24, 1999, and ended on June 10, having achieved its major objective: the withdrawal of Serbian troops from the province. During these seventy-eight days, NATO hit Serbia and Kosovo with 23,000 bombs and missiles. As 40,000 Serbian troops withdrew from Kosovo, 50,000 NATO troops from five countries—Britain, France, Germany, Italy, and the United States—entered to take positions in separate zones of the province. Russia also supplied a small occupying force. Approximately 800,000 Albanian refugees flooded back into their ravaged homeland, and approximately 100,000 frightened Kosovo Serbs fled to Serbia. This strange war ended in a strange victory for NATO. Although it achieved its objective of driving out Serb forces, it failed to protect Kosovo Albanian inhabitants from the brunt of Serbia's "ethnic cleansing"— wholesale extermination or deportation of an unwelcome people. Moreover, NATO appeared to have committed itself to policing Kosovo for years, and Serbia's leader, Slobodan Milosevic, claimed victory for standing up for Serbian values against the combined might of the nineteen nations in the world's most powerful military alliance.

This war at the close of the twentieth century set several precedents that may influence future wars:

- It was the first war conducted and won entirely by air strikes by one side.

- It was the first multinational war in Europe in which there were no combat deaths on one side.

- It was the first hostile military action ever undertaken by NATO, the fifty-year-old

military alliance formed to defend Western democracies against the Soviet threat.

- It was the first multinational war fought openly and genuinely for humanitarian values rather than national self-interest.

Why did NATO decide to go to war against Slobodan Milosevic, president of Yugoslavia, and his Serbian forces in Kosovo? Prior to 1989, Kosovo was one of two "autonomous provinces" among the six republics in the Socialist Federal Republic of Yugoslavia (SFRY). Most of the SFRY's more than 22 million people were ethnic Serbs and Eastern Orthodox Christians. The Republic of Serbia was the SFRY's largest member republic, and the Serbian capital, Belgrade, was also the federal capital of Yugoslavia.

Kosovo was given autonomous status within Serbia by Josip Tito, the communist dictator who held the Yugoslav federation together for thirty-five years following World War II. The province's population was almost 90 percent Albanian and spoke a different language (Albanian) and practiced a different religion (Islam) than the rest of the Serbian republic. In 1989, after the majority Albanians in Kosovo clashed with the minority Serbs living there, Milosevic moved to revoke the province's autonomous status and bring it under Belgrade's control.

The other republics in the SFRY saw this move as part of Milosevic's call for a "Greater Serbia." Alarmed by the threat of Serbian nationalism, Slovenia, Croatia, and part of Bosnia-Herzegovina split from the SFRY in the early 1990s and won independence after bloody battles with Serbian forces and between Serbian and non-Serbian civilians. The Albanians in Kosovo pressed Milosevic to restore their autonomy; more radical Kosovars formed the Kosovo Liberation Army to seek full independence rather than mere autonomy within Serbia.

Milosevic's forces responded with brutal repression in Kosovo—as they had done in the other republics when they first threatened to secede. By 1998, the western media had filed numerous reports of Serbian atrocities against Kosovar Albanians, and by early 1999, additional Serbian troops were massing just over the Kosovo border. Thousands of Albanians were forced out of the country on foot, while others were crowded onto buses or trains and deported. Photos of hordes of refugees streaming out of Albania recalled similar forced relocations during World War II.

Anticipating a catastrophic "ethnic cleansing" of Albanians in Kosovo, the western powers decided to act more decisively this time than they had from 1992 to 1995, when majority ethnic groups in the seceding republics of Yugoslavia had slaughtered minority ethnic groups. Western nations pushed both sides to attend a peace conference in Rambouillet, France, in February 1999. The West proposed restoring autonomy to Ko-

sovo, to be enforced by NATO peacekeepers. Some Albanian Kosovars balked at these terms, wanting independence instead, but they eventually agreed to them. The Serbs refused both autonomy for Kosovo and NATO enforcement, which they said would violate their sovereignty. When diplomatic pressure on Milosevic failed to produce headway, NATO decided to use force. On March 24, bombs began falling on Serbia.

NATO's secretary general, Javier Solana, insisted that the air campaign, which killed relatively few civilians but destroyed much of Serbia's infrastructure, was fought to defend human values. Twenty-first century Europe would not tolerate the twentieth century brutality of "ethnic cleansing."[1]

What questions does the last war of this century leave for wars in the next century? Former Air Force general and Bush administration national security adviser Brent Scowcroft sees fundamental questions for our foreign policy.

- Is it OK to violate the sovereignty of a country for humanitarian purposes?

- Is it OK to threaten or destroy a state to protect a minority within that state?

- If the atrocities in Kosovo were beyond the pale and demanded a response by the United States, are not atrocities in Sudan equally reprehensible? In Sierra Leone?

- What is our standard for behavior on issues of humanitarian concern?[2]

The American people, as well as their government, must grapple with these questions in the years to come.

1. Craig R. Whitney, "Bombing Ends as Serbs Begin Pullout," *New York Times*, 11 June 1999, p. 1.
2. Terry Atlas, "Lessons of Kosovo May Be Fleeting," *Chicago Tribune*, 13 June 1999, p. 8.

in Kosovo, his policy was criticized. Nevertheless, Clinton himself drew praise for his efforts to end the fighting in Northern Ireland and for working to broker a peaceful end to the Israeli-Palestinian conflict. By the end of 2000, Clinton's personal achievements allowed him to be warmly welcomed in Vietnam when he made the first visit of a U.S. president to our former bitter foe from the communist era.

Entering the presidency in 2001, George W. Bush had something in common with Bill Clinton—no experience. In President Bush's case, however, he recruited two leading figures from his father's 1990 triumph over Iraq in the Persian Gulf War. His vice president, Richard Cheney, had been his father's secretary of defense, and the younger Bush's secretary of state, Colin Powell, served as his father's chairman of the Joint Chiefs of Staff. Both certainly had foreign policy experience in the old-fashioned sense of defending U.S. interests through military means. It remains to be seen how well they deal with global policy.

From Foreign Policy to Global Policy

The end of the Cold War and the process of globalization have resulted in a fundamental shift in the nature of foreign policy. For the first time, U.S. foreign policy has taken on a truly *global* focus. We apply the term **global policy,** like foreign policy, to a general plan to defend and advance national interests, but global policy embraces a broader view of national interests. Whereas foreign policy focuses on security against foreign threats (mainly military but also economic threats), global policy adds social and environmental concerns to matters of national interest. Whereas foreign policy typically deals with disputes between leaders, ideologies, or states, global policy confronts more silent, cumulative effects of billions of individual choices made by people everywhere on the globe. Inevitably, global policy requires global action. The players are no longer competing alliances among nations but international organizations that cooperate on a worldwide scale.

Even the Reagan administration, which claims credit for ending the Cold War, did not do well on issues outside the East-West confrontation. Until the mid-1960s, nations in the U.N. General Assembly had usually supported U.S. positions in their votes. As the United Nations expanded its membership to include many newly independent states, however, the United States and its Western European allies frequently found themselves outvoted. Under Reagan, the United States reduced its commitment to international institutions such as the United Nations and the World Court when they acted in ways that ran counter to American interests. For example, the United States began to drag its feet on paying its U.N. assessments, briefly withdrew from the International Labor Organization, and rejected the jurisdiction of the World Court in cases involving U.S. activities in Nicaragua.

The United States did act as a world leader under President Bush (senior) during the Gulf War, but that was when the world needed a cop. When the international political agenda shifted toward issues such as world trade, world poverty, the environment, human rights, and emerging democracy, American leadership was less evident—and less accepted. Now that the

global policy
Like foreign policy, it's a plan for defending and advancing national interests, but—unlike foreign policy—it includes social and environmental concerns among national interests.

★

Enemies Behind Them

In 1988, President Ronald Reagan spoke at Moscow State University in front of a larger-than-life bust of Lenin, leader of the Russian Revolution and symbol of the nation we opposed during the Cold War. In 2000, President Bill Clinton spoke at a ceremony in Hanoi, in front of a colossal bust of Ho Chi Minh, leader of the Viet Cong, who defeated the United States in the Vietnam War. These scenes suggest the healing power of time.

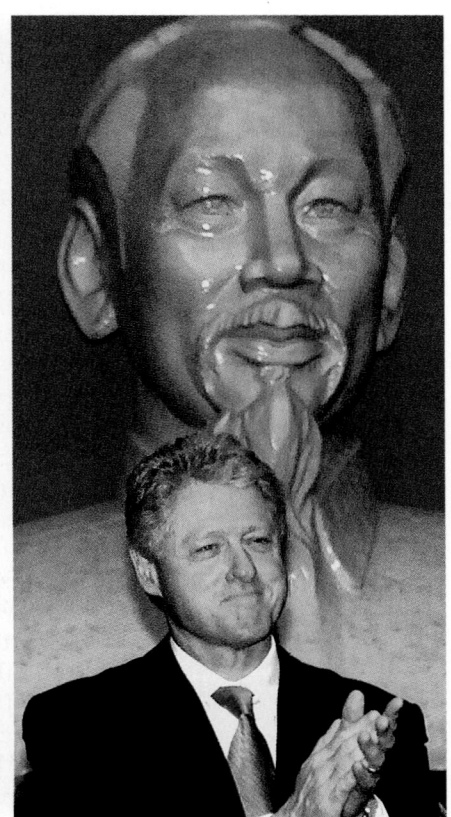

Cold War is over, other goals, such as promoting economic prosperity and preserving environmental quality, receive increased attention as important components of our national interest.

GLOBAL POLICY ISSUE AREAS

intermestic
Issues in which international and domestic concerns are mixed.

Global issues like world poverty and environmental degradation have always existed, but they have been put on the policy agendas of nations as a result of the process of globalization, the increased interdependence among nations. Nations today understand not only that their economies are tied to one another, but the air we breathe, the illnesses we contract, and even the climate we experience can be affected by events in other countries. Consequently, global policy deals with **intermestic** problems—those that blend international and domestic concerns. Because global policy requires global action, domestic policies and practices become subject to policies and rules of international organizations. Conservative opponents of international organizations regard this global interaction as compromising their nation's sovereignty. Compared with foreign policy, global policy not only presents different challenges to policymaking, but those challenges threaten the very concept of sovereignty that lies at the basis of national interest in traditional foreign policy. In this section, we choose to study only three broad topics within global interdependence: investment and trade, human rights and foreign aid, and the environment. International approaches to all topics involve salient threats to the sovereignty of the nations that take on global policies.

Investment and Trade

At the end of World War II, the United States dominated the world's economy. Half of all international trade involved the United States, and the dollar played a key role in underwriting economic recovery in Europe and Asia. America could not expect to retain forever the economic dominance it enjoyed in the late 1940s and 1950s, but the United States was able to invest heavily abroad even through the 1970s, prompting European concern that both profits and control of European-based firms would drain away to America.

During the Cold War, the economically dominant United States often made tactical use of economic policy in foreign policy. To shore up anti-Soviet forces in Western Europe and Japan, the United States lowered trade barriers for those countries, without receiving equal access to their markets. Meanwhile, the United States forbade the export to communist countries of products with possible military uses.[43] These policies were thought to produce security gains that outweighed their economic costs. In the 1980s, however, the situation began to reverse itself. A combination of tax cuts and defense spending increases created gaping deficits in the federal budget. These deficits were partly financed by selling U.S. treasury obligations to foreigners at high rates of interest. As investors from abroad bought up American government debt, the value of the dollar soared. This made American goods very expensive on the world market and foreign goods relatively cheap for Americans. The result was a shift in our balance of trade—the United States began to import more than it exported. And we continued to borrow heavily. With the recession in the late 1980s and declining interest rates, foreign firms became less interested in investing in the United States. As the flow of foreign capital into the United States slowed, American economic problems deepened.

As the United States became entangled in the global web of international finance, it also became more closely tied to other countries through international trade. In 1970, the value of U.S. foreign trade came to 11.2 percent of the nation's GDP; by 1997, it had reached 28.8 percent.[44] As foreign trade becomes more important to the American economy, policymakers face alternative responses. Among them are *free trade, fair trade, managed trade,* and *protectionism*. A true **free trade** policy would allow for the unfettered operation of the free market—nations would not impose tariffs or other barriers to keep foreign goods from being sold in their countries. All trading partners would benefit under free trade, which would allow the principle of **comparative advantage** to work unhindered. According to this principle, all trading nations gain when each produces goods it can make comparatively cheaply and then trades them to obtain funds for the items it can produce only at a comparatively higher cost.

Although the United States has not embraced a pure form of free trade, it has generally favored a liberal international trade regime in the last decades of the twentieth century. (In this case, the word *liberal* is used in

free trade
An economic policy that allows businesses in different nations to sell and buy goods without paying tariffs or other limitations.

comparative advantage
A principle of international trade that states that all nations will benefit when each nation specializes in those goods that it can produce most efficiently.

Globalization Brings Joy to the World!

There's something sad about this Cambodian monk holding this plastic bottle of a dishwashing detergent in a country that suffers a shortage of safe drinking water. Although about 30 percent of Cambodia's people live on less than a dollar per day, that percentage is down from almost 50 percent in 1990 (World Bank's "Presentation of the East Asia and Pacific Regional Brief," March 29, 2001). It's not clear yet how much of this is due to globalization and whether the infusion of western culture will ultimately benefit Cambodia.

fair trade
Trade regulated by international agreements outlawing unfair business practices.

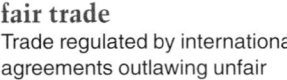
Can You Explain Why...
"free trade" is not necessarily "fair trade"?

its classic sense to mean "free.") American critics of free-trade policies complain that free trade has too often been a one-way street. America's trading partners could sell their goods in the United States while restricting their own markets through an array of tariffs and nontariff barriers (NTBs)—regulations that make importation of foreign goods difficult or impossible by outlining stringent criteria that an imported product must meet in order to be offered for sale. The Japanese, for example, have been criticized for excessive use of NTBs. In one instance, American-made baby bottles were barred from the Japanese market because the bottles provided gradation marks in ounces as well as centiliters.[45]

Although the United States has sought to make trade more free by reducing tariff and nontariff barriers, Americans do not want only freedom in the world market; they want order, too. Policymakers committed to the idea of **fair trade** have worked to create order through international agreements outlawing unfair business practices. These practices include bribery; pirating intellectual property such as software, CDs, and films; and "dumping," a practice in which a country sells its goods below cost in order to capture the market for its products in another country. The World Trade Organization (WTO) was created in 1995 to regulate trade among member nations. Headquartered in Geneva, Switzerland, it has a staff of 500 to administer trade agreements signed by its 140 member nations and ratified in their parliaments. According to the WTO, "These agreements are the legal ground-rules for international commerce. Essentially, they are contracts, guaranteeing member countries important trade rights. They also bind governments to keep their trade policies within agreed limits."[46] Originally, conservatives in the United States feared that the WTO's dispute settlement authority could be used to erode America's sovereignty and international trading position. Indeed, the WTO has ruled that some U.S. laws have violated its regulations, but the rulings were highly technical and with limited impact. For example, in early 2000, the WTO ruled against certain tax breaks to American exporters, and the United States offered to change its tax laws.[47] More recently, the

WTO has been criticized also from the left (e.g., by Ralph Nader) for its secretive decision making and for neglecting labor rights and environmental concerns in making purely business decisions.[48]

Free trade and fair trade are not the only approaches to trade that American policymakers consider. America began the 1980s as the world's leading creditor and ended the decade as the world's leading debtor. For years the nation has run up huge balance-of-payments deficits with other nations. By far, the largest of these deficits has been with Japan. The trade acts mentioned above are ways the United States has tried to redress trade imbalances. Another method is **managed trade,** in which the government intervenes in trade policy in order to achieve a specific result—a clear departure from a free-trade system. Under the Reagan, Bush, and Clinton administrations, the United States negotiated agreements with Japan that established guarantees or numerical benchmarks to give American firms a larger share of the Japanese market for various products, including semiconductors and auto parts.

Domestic political pressure often bears on trade issues. Although free traders claim that the principle of comparative advantage ensures that eliminating trade barriers would make everyone better off in the long run, their opponents argue that imports threaten American industries and jobs. To guard against these hazards, **protectionists** want to retain barriers to free trade. For example, most unions and many small manufacturers opposed NAFTA. They believed that if tariffs were removed, Mexico, with its low labor costs, would be able to undersell American producers and thus run them out of business or force them to move their operations to Mexico. Either alternative threatened American jobs. At the same time, many Americans were eager to take advantage of new opportunities in a growing Mexican market for goods and services. They realized that protectionism can be a double-edged sword. Countries whose products are kept out of the United States retaliate by refusing to import American goods. And protectionism enormously complicates the process of making foreign policy. It is a distinctly unfriendly move toward nations that may be our allies.

Human Rights, Poverty, and Foreign Aid

NATO's campaign against ethnic cleansing in the Balkans made clear that the western democracies would go to war to protect human rights. This is especially true of America, which has long championed democracy and human rights. Support for moral ideals such as freedom, democracy, and human rights fits well with U.S. interests. These elements of liberal democracy permeate our political culture, and we relate better to nations who share them. But the relationship between America's human rights policy goals and its economic policy goals has often been problematic.

For example, in studying the potential for growth in exports, the Clinton administration identified ten rapidly growing markets that seemed especially promising for the United States. These big emerging markets (BEMs) include the Chinese economic area (the People's Republic of China, Taiwan, and Hong Kong), Indonesia, India, South Korea, Mexico, Brazil, Argentina, South Africa, Turkey, and Poland. These nations have large areas and populations, are growing rapidly, are influential in their region,

---

managed trade
Government intervention in trade policy in order to achieve a specific result.

protectionists
Those who wish to prevent imports from entering the country and therefore oppose free trade.

★ **politics in a changing** w o r l d

20.1 Population Growth in World Regions, 1950–2050

American foreign policy has traditionally had a European focus. In the early part of the twentieth century, Europe alone produced World War I. By the middle of the century, World War II spread across the world, due to the rise of an Asian power, Japan. As we enter the twenty-first century, we should study the population growth graphs to see where the people will be. Note that the growth lines for Europe (and North America) are virtually flat.

U.S. global policy in the twenty-first century will have to deal with the tremendous population increase in Asia (and even Africa)—and with the rise of China, with a population of over 1.2 billion, as a world superpower.

Source: Adapted from data published in *World Population Prospects, 1950–2050. The 1996 Edition (Annex I and II).* United Nations Population Division, 1997. Data available at <www.iiasa.ac.at/Research/LUC/Papers/gkhl/tab1_2.htm> on February 22, 2001.

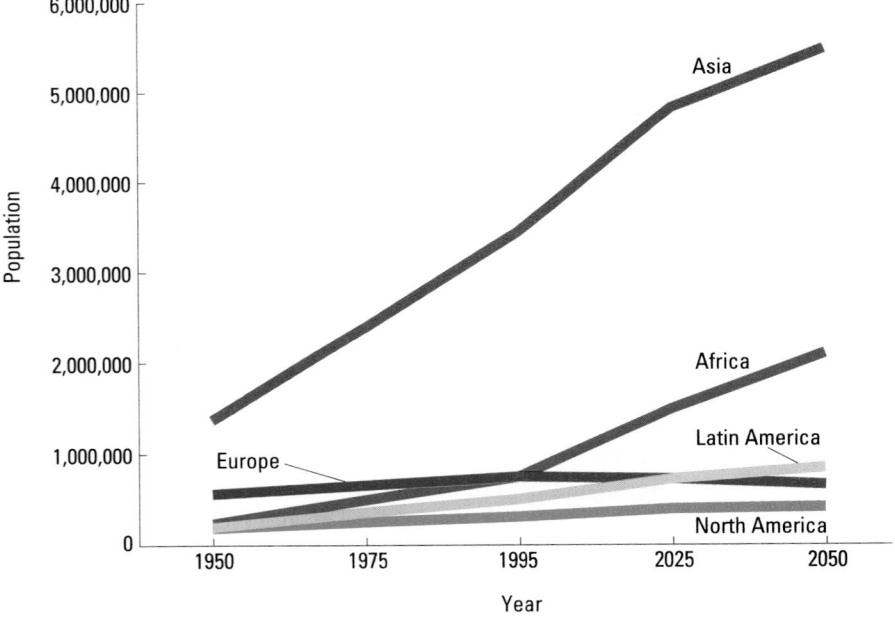

and buy the types of goods and services America has to sell (see Politics in a Changing World 20.1). The Commerce Department has taken the lead in helping American businesses win contracts in these nations.[49] But engagement with these countries raises questions that go beyond America's economic interests. Some of the BEMs have dubious records in the areas of human rights, workers' rights, and child labor. Some are lax about environmental standards, intellectual property protection, or nuclear nonproliferation. To what extent should development of commercial ties with these nations override other policy objectives?

In addition to granting nations favorable trade terms, the United States has other economic tools available to help pursue its policy objectives. These include development aid, debt forgiveness, and loans with favorable credit terms. Assistance to developing countries also takes the form of donations of American goods, which directly benefits the American businesses that supply the products. Inequality between rich nations and poor nations is growing. Figures show an increasing gap in income between the industrialized states of the north and the nonindustrialized states of the south.[50] This income gap between nations provokes arguments in international politics, just as issues of social inequality motivates those who favor social equality for minorities in domestic politics. Many people believe it is unjust for the developed world to enjoy great wealth while people in the global South, or Third World, are deprived. Sheer self-interest may also motivate policymakers to address this problem. Great disparities in wealth between the developed and developing nations may lead to political instability and disorder and thus threaten the interests of the industrially developed democracies. Recently, Russia and the countries of Eastern Europe have begun to compete with the Third World for development dollars, and American lawmakers have taken into account the need to ensure political stability and to bring about a successful transition to democracy in the former communist states. As a result, between 1991 and 1995, $15 billion in aid and credits were supplied to Russia and other newly independent states.[51]

Although foreign aid serves both humanitarian and political ends, in times of fiscal austerity it is an easy target for budget cutters. Foreign aid tends to be unpopular, partly because foreign aid recipients do not vote in American elections and also because American citizens overestimate what the nation spends on aid. In repeated national surveys, about half the respondents believe that at least 15 percent of the federal budget went to foreign aid. Half thought it would be appropriate to devote 5 percent of the budget to foreign aid and that 3 percent would be too little. In actuality, less than 1 percent of the federal budget goes to foreign aid.[52] Figure 20.2 shows how America's aid to developing countries stacks up against the contributions of other developed nations.

In the last month of his administration, Clinton overrode objections from conservative Republican senators and his own advisers in the Defense Department by signing the treaty to establish the International Criminal Court, the world's first standing court with jurisdiction over individuals facing charges of genocide, war crimes, and other crimes against humanity. The armed services feared that American troops abroad could be vulnerable to prosecution as a result of military operations. Aware of the opposition, Clinton had refused to sign the treaty in 1998 when it had been negotiated. He signed it only on the last day that nations could sign without ratification, which might enable the United States, as an original party to the treaty, to influence the court's evolution. Clinton said that he would not submit the treaty to the Senate or recommend doing so to his successor. Still, Senator Helms called the action "a blatant attempt by a lame-duck president to tie the hands of his successor. Well, I have a message for the outgoing president: This decision will not stand."[53]

figure

20.2   Aid to Developing Countries

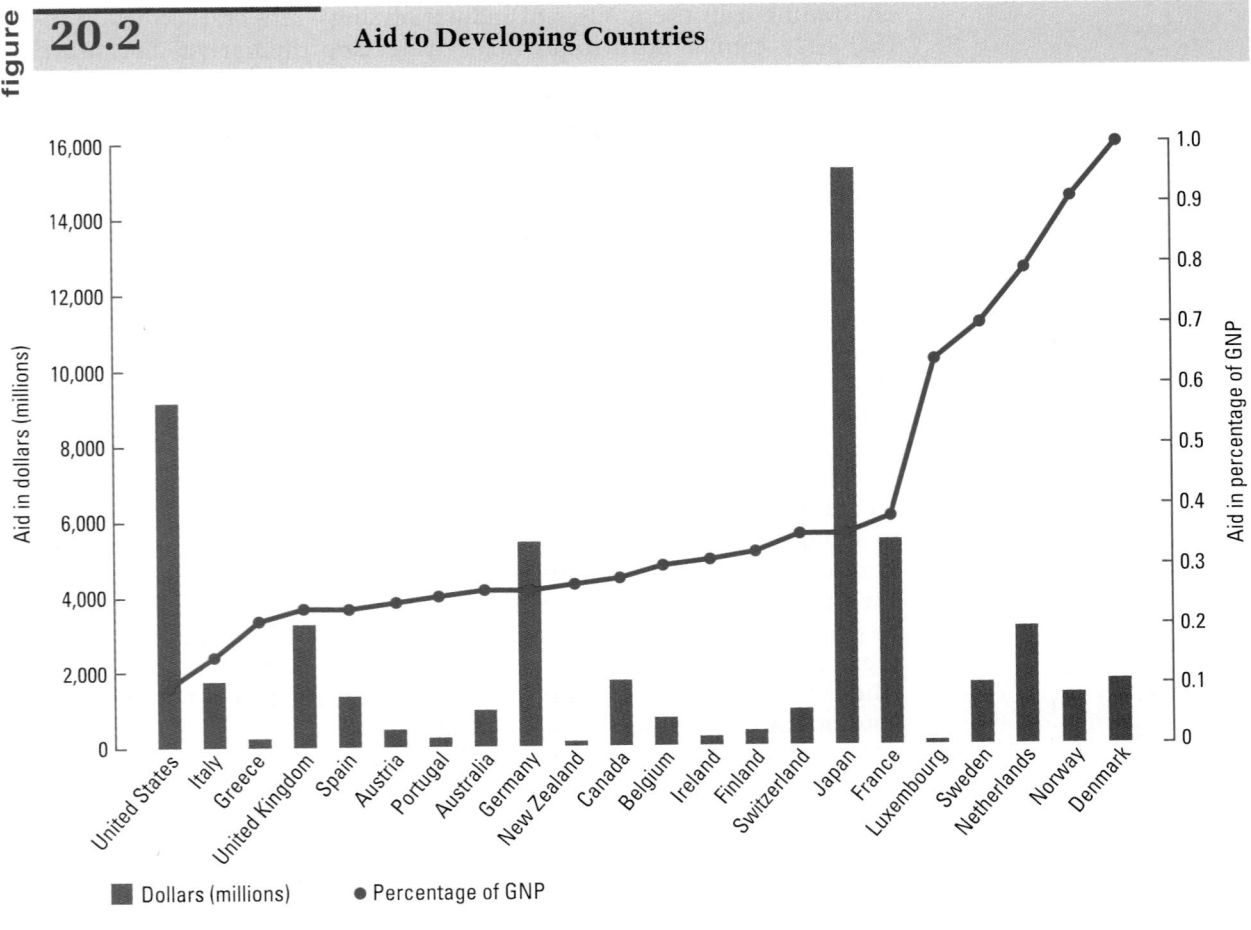

This graph compares U.S. aid to developing countries with the aid given by twenty-two member countries of the Development Assistance Committee of the Organization of Economic Cooperation and Development (OECD). These figures are reported for Official Development Assistance, a standard measure of grants and loans to a designated list of recipient nations. The data show the amount of aid in absolute dollars given by a country (the United States gives the second most) and then breaks these dollar amounts into the percentage of a country's gross national product, GNP (with the nations ranked from most to least). Although the United States gives the second most in dollars to assist developing countries, it gives the least in the percentage of its wealth.

Source: Department of Economic and Social Affairs, *World Economic and Social Survey 2000* (New York: The United Nations, 2000), p. 57.

The Environment

Environmental issues pose new and vexing challenges for foreign policy makers. The value conflict of freedom versus order, which we have seen in domestic politics, surfaced in the international arena. In the prototypic example, wealthy industrialized nations—which polluted the world environment in the process of industrializing—tell Third World nations that *they* cannot burn fossil fuels to develop themselves because that would further pollute the environment. Leaders in developing countries do not appreciate limits on their freedom to industrialize, limits that serve the developed world's definition of global order.

The United States, universally recognized as being the richest, most powerful nation on Earth, often drew attacks from developed and underdeveloped nations alike for claiming special privileges in international agreements widely accepted by other nations. The 1992 United Nations Conference on Environment and Development in Rio de Janiero, popularly known as the Earth Summit, illustrates both the worldwide acknowledgment of new issues in global politics and the problematic position of the United States. The Earth Summit produced the Biodiversity Treaty, which aimed at conserving the earth's diverse biological resources through development of national strategies for conservation, creation of protected areas, and protection of ecosystems and natural habitats. Although environmental problems were made clearer to the world at Rio, the steps put forth there to solve them were not acceptable to the United States. President Bush (senior) feared that the Biodiversity Treaty placed too many limits on U.S. patent rights in biotechnology and failed to protect U.S. intellectual property rights, and he refused to sign it. In the view of the Bush administration, the measures proposed at Rio would threaten the U.S. economy. Although Clinton signed the treaty and sent it to the Senate, it was not put up for a vote, so the United States is not a party to it.

Can You Explain Why...
The United States does not observe the 1992 Biodiversity Treaty, although the president signed it?

A similar problem occurred with the 1997 understanding on global warming worked out by 170 nations in Kyoto, Japan. It committed three dozen industrialized nations to reducing their combined greenhouse gas emissions by at least 5 percent of their 1990 levels by 2012. However, the specific rules for meeting these national targets were not worked out in the Kyoto agreement. In late 2000, when the United States proposed counting its forest lands as sinks to help meet its target of 7 percent reduction, the treaty talks failed. The industrialized nations in Europe had no forests and instead had to reduce greenhouse gases at the source: mainly tailpipes and smokestacks.[54] A representative for the European Union rejected the American proposal, saying, "We didn't come here to trade away the work done at Kyoto."[55] So even in the Clinton administration, which was more receptive to international concerns about environmental problems, domestic politics prevented that round of talks on controlling global warming from succeeding.

THE PUBLIC AND GLOBAL POLICY

The president and Congress have always considered public opinion when making foreign policy: both had to face the public's wrath if blamed for policy failures. Historically, the public has paid little attention to traditional concerns of foreign policy—alliances, military bases abroad, and general diplomacy. Except for issues of war and peace, other matters of national security, and the spread of communism, public opinion on foreign policy seldom affected domestic politics in any major way.

Today, globalization has made nations more interdependent in economic and social spheres, and major events in other countries can have a direct impact on life in the United States. If gangsters in Russia and China cooperate with mobs in Nigeria and Italy, the United States will soon experience an increase in smuggled aliens, drugs, and counterfeit goods.[56] The globalized media immediately communicate foreign affairs to the American audience. If the economy collapses in Asian countries, we'll feel it on Wall Street literally within hours. At the beginning of the new millennium, one might expect the U.S. public to pay much more attention to foreign affairs now than it did twenty-five years ago. Alas, this is not so.

The Public and the Majoritarian Model

To assess the state of public knowledge of and interest in foreign affairs, we draw on a 1998 survey by the Chicago Council on Foreign Relations—the sixth in a series of surveys begun in 1974 and repeated every five years.[57] In 1998, a random sample of 1,507 Americans was augmented by a sample of 379 knowledgeable individuals selected from Congress, academia, business, the media, labor unions, and churches. The study permits comparisons of public attitudes over time and comparisons of public opinion with leaders' opinions. As in the six previous surveys, the 1998 survey found that only about 30 percent of the public was "very interested" in news of other countries, and only about half was very interested in news of U.S. relations with other countries. In each survey, the public was more interested in national news and most interested in news of their local community.[58]

While the public's interest in news about foreign affairs changed little since 1974, there was a steady increase in the percentage who thought that "the U.S. plays a more important and powerful role as a world leader today than it did ten years ago." Despite the clear increase over time in the perceived importance of the United States as a world leader, only about a steady 60 percent of the public favored an active part for the United States in world affairs. In contrast, in each survey, over 95 percent of the leader sample favored an active part for the United States.[59]

For the first time, the 1998 survey asked specifically about globalization: whether "the increasing connections of our economy with others around the world" is "mostly good or mostly bad for the United States." Most of the public (54 percent) thought that globalization was mostly good, but 11 percent of the public had not even heard about it. Virtually all the leaders ventured an opinion on globalization, and 87 percent thought it was mostly good for the United States. Although globalization and free trade usually go hand in hand, nearly half the public and about one-third of the leaders felt that tariffs were necessary for the United States—mainly for protecting manufacturing jobs. Giving economic aid to other countries was favored by only about 50 percent of the public and about 90 percent of the leaders.[60]

Both groups were asked how the United States should respond to international crises. Nearly three-quarters of the public thought that "the U.S. should not take action alone if it does not have the support of its allies," but leaders were split almost evenly on this question. Asked whether the United States "should take part in U.N. international peacekeeping forces in troubled parts of the world," a strong majority (57 percent) thought it should, but only 48 percent felt that the United States should pay the "back dues and assessments it owes the United Nations" (38 percent said no).[61] So Senator Helms was feeling the public's pulse by

The Ideal War

Global media coverage of international conflict has introduced public constraints on military decisions. This may be good in the sense of limiting military casualties, but it may compromise the broader pursuit of national interests.

withholding payment of U.S. debt to the United Nations and forcing a reduction in U.S. dues, as discussed at the beginning of the chapter.

One clear message that emerges from the study of public opinion toward U.S. involvement in international crises is the low level of support for using American troops abroad: "In 1998 none of the potential foreign military conflicts posed in the survey found majority support among the public for using U.S. troops."[62] The sample of leaders, however, was more inclined to commit military force. In general, the public seems less likely to expose American troops to danger for reasons of global altruism—such as promoting human rights abroad, promoting democratic governments, or protecting weaker nations against aggression.[63] In the abstract, the public supports an active role for the United States in international affairs, with two conditions. First, public support fades when troops might be needed to support that role. Second, the public is more apt to support pursuing our national interest defined in terms of national security, rather than our global interest defined in broader terms. One analysis of the public's ranking of foreign policy goals concluded:

> The ranking appears to be more in step with the political philosophy of isolationists such as . . . Pat Buchanan than with the grounds President Clinton outlined for U.S. involvement in Kosovo. At the top of Americans' list of foreign policy goals is preventing the spread of nuclear weapons, followed by stemming the flow of drugs into the U.S. and protecting American jobs. Combatting terrorism and securing energy supplies also rank highly, with more than 60% rating these as very important goals. Defending our allies' security, defending human rights, and protecting weaker nations from aggression rank in the bottom half of the list of seventeen items tested.[64]

So the data suggest that if the nation's foreign policy were made according to the majoritarian model and followed public opinion more closely, the United States would remain involved in foreign affairs, but its foreign policy would be more narrowly oriented toward national security interests, with an isolationist coloring.

Interest Groups and the Pluralist Model

What would be the nature of policies in a global society made under the pluralist model, in which government responds to competing groups? Ordinary citizens can become interested in foreign affairs when they learn how events in foreign lands can affect their economic interests or values. Often, citizens learn from the more knowledgeable leaders of groups to which they belong. Both labor and business leaders in the auto industry may urge their followers to favor import restrictions on Japanese cars. Church leaders may warn of religious persecution abroad. Aroused citizens often have their positions argued to lawmakers in Washington by group representatives.

As described in Chapter 10, thousands of interest groups maintain offices in Washington. Even foreign firms, groups, and governments have hired lobbying firms to represent their interests in the U.S. capital. In 1996 the Palestine Liberation Organization opened an office on K Street, where vast numbers of lobbying groups are located. Among other groups in their neighborhood are Sinn Fein, the Ulster Unionists, the Liberal Democratic Party of Russia, the Bahrain Freedom Movement, the Kashmir American Council, and the National Council of Resistance of Iran.[65]

The influence of these groups varies, depending on the issue. Interest groups are more effective at maintaining support for the status quo than at bringing about policy changes.[66] Because global policies often respond to new events abroad, one might expect these policies to form with little impact from interest groups. However, lobbying is also more effective when it deals with noncrisis issues of little importance to the public at large and that can take place behind the scenes. Because the public has little interest in foreign affairs, interest groups can wield a great deal of influence on global policies outside matters of national security.

Passage of the 2000 China trade bill illustrates the pluralist model in action. The bill's roots can be traced to the presidency of Ronald Reagan, who favored free trade with China as a strategy for breaking down its communist system. President Clinton endorsed the idea and made the China trade bill a centerpiece of his administration. Early in his 2000 presidential campaign, Governor George W. Bush came out in support of the bill and urged Republicans in Congress to support it, saying, "This trade agreement is the work of 13 years and of three administrations" (one of which was his father's).[67]

The bill itself embodied a comprehensive 250-page agreement characterized by technical and complex provisions. The U.S. objective was to change the balance of trade with China: we bought large amounts of Chinese goods but the Chinese bought little from the United States. For its part, China agreed to phase out import quotas and to reduce its tariffs on U.S. goods from 24.6 to 9.4 percent. In return, the United States promised (1) to support China's entry into the World Trade Organization (WTO) and (2) to ask Congress to extend normal trade relations (NTR) status to China on a permanent basis. China already had NTR status (i.e., China enjoyed the same trade terms as other nations), but it was extended on an annual basis, each year producing debate about whether the communist nation deserved such status.[68]

Are you asleep yet? Well, the China trade bill certainly did not keep the public awake. At the height of Congress's attention to the bill, only 46 percent of respondents in a national survey said that they had heard about it.[69] It was the kind of technical, complex bill that interested only certain segments of the public with a real or symbolic stake in the outcome, such as trade groups, human rights groups, specific businesses, labor unions, and lawyers (always lawyers). Lobbying on all sides was intense. Those favoring the bill included the Business Roundtable, the major lobbying arm of big business, and the U.S. Chamber of Commerce, which asked small-business executives in swing districts to pitch the deal to their House members. The Business Coalition for U.S.-China Trade gave weekly awards for grassroots campaigning efforts, and one winner was the Electronics Industry Alliance, which gave free T-shirts to those who signed a letter supporting the bill and supplied their zip code for electronic mailing to their representative in Congress.[70]

Those opposed to the bill included most labor unions, which denied that they wanted only to protect American jobs. They opposed the China trade bill, they said, because it did nothing to protect the rights and safety of Chinese workers. Incidentally, lax labor standards in China could invite U.S. companies to relocate there.[71] Opposition also came from religious groups, which argued that China "tortures and kills priests and nuns," and from human rights groups, which denounced "Slave State Red China."[72]

The bill passed the House in late May 2000 by a surprisingly large margin of 237 to 197. This bill, backed by a Democratic president, was supported by about 75 percent of Republicans and opposed by 65 percent of Democrats. (It cleared the Senate in September by a vote of 83 to 15, with both parties supporting it about equally.)

Passage of the China trade bill clearly fit the pluralist model of democracy, not the majoritarian model. The public knew little about the bill, and those who did were divided about its merits.[73] But interested groups openly competed in presenting their arguments to members of Congress, which then decided, or, as one seasoned reporter put it, "Members vote their districts":

> That is, they vote their districts if their constituents have an interest, and a trade bill is a singular foreign policy measure because the question of jobs gained and lost commands attention from lawmakers and constituents not much concerned about the rest of the world.[74]

SUMMARY

The ideological orientations of key players on the stage affect the nation's global policy. The president is the leading actor, but Congress, and especially the U.S. Senate, is a strong contributor. With shared responsibility among Congress, the executive branch, and various agencies, foreign policy can change from drama to farce if the cast is not reading from the same script. For two decades following World War II, from which America emerged as a superpower, there was a clear consensus: communism was the threat, and the goal was to contain Soviet expansion. The Vietnam War challenged that consensus, and Democrats and Republicans began to argue over foreign policy. In the post–Cold War era, international issues and domestic concerns have become more closely entwined as a result of globalization, and foreign policy became embraced within broader issues of global policy. Strict notions of national sovereignty eroded as international organizations emerged to deal with global policies. Generally speaking, the majoritarian model of democratic policymaking does not fit well with foreign policy, and even less with global policy, because most citizens do not pay much attention to foreign affairs. Opinion leaders are closely attuned to globalization, however, and global policy tends to be hammered out on the anvil of competing groups, according to the pluralist model.

★ Selected Readings

Falk, Richard. *Predatory Globalization: A Critique.* Williston, Vt.: Blackwell, 1999. A penetrating critique of the globalization of trade and politics by one of the nation's leading scholars on foreign affairs.

Gaubatz, Kurt Taylor. *Elections and War: The Electoral Incentive in the Democratic Politics of War and Peace.* Stanford, Calif.: Stanford University Press, 1999. Analyzes the impact of domestic politics on international politics, and vice versa.

Giddens, Anthony. *Runaway World: How Globalization Is Reshaping Our Lives.* New York: Routledge, 2000. Shows how global forces affect daily life, including local culture, traditions, families, and politics.

Hardt, Michael, and Antonio Negri. *Empire.* Cambridge, Mass.: Harvard University Press, 2000. Views globalization as "a new global form of sovereignty" in which various national and supranational organizations are united under the "empire."

Kissinger, Henry. *Years of Renewal.* New York: Simon & Schuster, 1999. The concluding volume of Kissinger's memoirs provides a riveting description of statecraft during the Nixon and Ford administrations.

Internet Exercises

1. *Promoting Democracy Through Nongovernmental Organizations*

The government of the United States has vast administrative resources for conducting global policy. Still, these official agents of the government are sometimes ill equipped to handle certain activities. In those cases, the United States often turns to nongovernmental organizations, or NGOs, to help it achieve its policy objectives. One in particular, created in 1983, is the National Endowment for Democracy (NED), which can be found on the Internet at <**www.ned.org/**>.

• Go to the NED Web site and click the About link to see a brief description of the Endowment, which includes a message from its president. Then click on the collection of Frequently Asked Questions, and pay particular attention to the three that describe the NED's relationship to the U.S. government.

• How is the NED intimately linked to the U.S. government, even though it is an independent organization? How might the NED's independent status make it better able to address certain issues or situations in which official government involvement might be ineffective or even harmful?

2. *Disease as a National Security Issue*

In spring 2000, President Clinton declared that the United States considered the global AIDS crisis to be a threat to its national security. One organization that has tracked the development of the disease around the world is the Joint United Nations Programme on HIV/AIDS, also known as UNAIDS. This affiliate of the United Nations maintains a Web site at <**www.unaids.org/**>.

• Go to the UNAIDS site and use the search function to locate its December 2000 report on the global HIV/AIDS epidemic. Click on the report and review the bulleted global overview that runs from pages 4–5. Then backtrack to the page where you accessed the report and click on the Graphics—December 2000 feature for a short slide show on the global spread of the epidemic.

• Based on this information, list at least two reasons for President Clinton's identification of the HIV/AIDS epidemic as a possible threat to the national security of the United States.

The Declaration of Independence
July 4, 1776

The unanimous Declaration of the thirteen United States of America

When in the course of human events, it becomes necessary for one people to dissolve the political bands which have connected them with another, and to assume, among the powers of the earth the separate and equal station to which the Laws of Nature and of Nature's God entitle them, a decent respect to the opinions of mankind requires that they should declare the causes which impel them to the separation.

We hold these truths to be self-evident, that all men are created equal, that they are endowed by their Creator with certain unalienable rights, that among these are life, liberty, and the pursuit of happiness. That to secure these rights, governments are instituted among men, deriving their just powers from the consent of the governed. That whenever any form of government becomes destructive of these ends, it is the right of the people to alter or to abolish it, and to institute new government, laying its foundation on such principles, and organizing its power in such form, as to them shall seem most likely to effect their safety and happiness. Prudence, indeed, will dictate that governments long established should not be changed for light and transient causes; and accordingly all experience hath shown, that mankind are more disposed to suffer, while evils are sufferable, than to right themselves by abolishing the forms to which they are accustomed. But when a long train of abuses and usurpations, pursuing invariably the same object evinces a design to reduce them under absolute despotism, it is their right, it is their duty, to throw off such government, and to provide new guards for their future security. Such has been the patient sufferance of these Colonies; and such is now the necessity which constrains them to alter their former

systems of government. The history of the present King of Great Britain is a history of repeated injuries and usurpations, all having in direct object the establishment of an absolute tyranny over these States. To prove this, let facts be submitted to a candid world.

He has refused his assent to laws, the most wholesome and necessary for the public good.

He has forbidden his governors to pass laws of immediate and pressing importance, unless suspended in their operation till his assent should be obtained; and, when so suspended, he has utterly neglected to attend to them.

He has refused to pass other laws for the accommodation of large districts of people, unless those people would relinquish the right of representation in the legislature, a right inestimable to them, and formidable to tyrants only.

He has called together legislative bodies at places unusual, uncomfortable, and distant from the depository of their public records, for the sole purpose of fatiguing them into compliance with his measures.

He has dissolved representative houses repeatedly, for opposing, with manly firmness, his invasions on the rights of the people.

He has refused for a long time, after such dissolutions, to cause others to be elected; whereby the legislative powers, incapable of annihilation, have returned to the people at large for their exercise; the State remaining, in the meantime exposed to all the dangers of invasions from without and convulsions within.

He has endeavored to prevent the population of these States; for that purpose obstructing the laws for naturalization of foreigners; refusing to pass others to encourage their migration hither, and raising the conditions of new appropriations of lands.

He has obstructed the administration of justice, by refusing his assent to laws for establishing judiciary powers.

He has made judges dependent on his will alone, for the tenure of their offices, and the amount and payment of their salaries.

He has erected a multitude of new offices, and sent hither swarms of officers to harass our people, and eat out their substance.

He has kept among us, in times of peace, standing armies, without the consent of our legislatures.

He has affected to render the military independent of and superior to the civil power.

He has combined with others to subject us to a jurisdiction foreign to our constitution, and unacknowledged by our laws; giving his assent to their acts of pretended legislation:

For quartering large bodies of armed troops among us:

For protecting them, by a mock trial, from punishment for any murders which they should commit on the inhabitants of these states:

A1

For cutting off our trade with all parts of the world:

For imposing taxes on us without our consent:

For depriving us, in many cases, of the benefits of trial by jury:

For transporting us beyond seas, to be tried for pretended offenses:

For abolishing the free system of English laws in a neighboring province, establishing therein an arbitrary government, and enlarging its boundaries, so as to render it at once an example and fit instrument for introducing the same absolute rule into these Colonies:

For taking away our Charters, abolishing our most valuable laws, and altering fundamentally the forms of our governments:

For suspending our own Legislatures, and declaring themselves invested with power to legislate for us in all cases whatsoever.

He has abdicated government here, by declaring us out of his protection and waging war against us.

He has plundered our seas, ravaged our coasts, burned our towns, and destroyed the lives of our people.

He is at this time transporting large armies of foreign mercenaries to complete the works of death, desolation, and tyranny, already begun with circumstances of cruelty and perfidy scarcely paralleled in the most barbarous ages, and totally unworthy the head of a civilized nation.

He has constrained our fellow-citizens taken captive on the high seas to bear arms against their country, to become the executioners of their friends and brethren, or to fall themselves by their hands.

He has excited domestic insurrection among us, and has endeavored to bring on the inhabitants of our frontiers the merciless Indian savages, whose known rule of warfare is an undistinguished destruction of all ages, sexes, and conditions.

In every stage of these oppressions we have petitioned for redress in the most humble terms: our repeated petitions have been answered only by repeated injury. A prince whose character is thus marked by every act which may define a tyrant, is unfit to be the ruler of a free people.

Nor have we been wanting in our attentions to our British brethren. We have warned them, from time to time, of attempts by their Legislature to extend an unwarrantable jurisdiction over us. We have reminded them of the circumstances of our emigration and settlement here. We have appealed to their native justice and magnanimity, and we have conjured them by the ties of our common kindred to disavow these usurpations, which would inevitably interrupt our connections and correspondence. They too have been deaf to the voice of justice and of consanguinity. We must, therefore, acquiesce in the necessity, which denounces our separation, and hold them, as we hold the rest of mankind, enemies in war, in peace friends.

We, therefore, the Representatives of the United States of America, in General Congress assembled, appealing to the Supreme Judge of the world for the rectitude of our intentions, do, in the name, and by the authority of the good people of these Colonies, solemnly publish and declare, That these United Colonies are, and of right ought to be, FREE AND INDEPENDENT STATES; that they are absolved from all allegiance to the British Crown, and that all political connection between them and the State of Great Britain is, and ought to be, totally dissolved; and that, as Free and Independent States they have full power to levy war, conclude peace, contract alliances, establish commerce, and do all other acts and things which independent States may of right do. And for the support of this declaration, with a firm reliance on the protection of Divine Providence, we mutually pledge to each other our lives, our fortunes and our sacred honor.

JOHN HANCOCK
and fifty-five others

Articles of Confederation

Whereas the Delegates of the United States of America in Congress assembled did on the fifteenth day of November in the Year of our Lord One Thousand Seven Hundred and Seventy seven, and in the Second Year of the Independence of America agree to certain articles of Confederation and perpetual Union between the States of Newhampshire, Massachusetts-Bay, Rhode Island and Providence Plantations, Connecticut, New York, New Jersey, Pennsylvania, Delaware, Maryland, Virginia, North-Carolina, South-Carolina and Georgia in the Words following, viz. "Articles of Confederation and perpetual Union between the states of Newhampshire, Massachusetts-Bay, Rhode Island and Providence Plantations, Connecticut, New-York, New-Jersey, Pennsylvania, Delaware, Maryland, Virginia, North-Carolina, South-Carolina and Georgia."

Article I The Stile of this confederacy shall be "The United States of America."

Article II Each state retains its sovereignty, freedom and independence, and every power, jurisdiction and right, which is not by this Confederation expressly delegated to the United States, in Congress assembled.

Article III The said states hereby severally enter into a firm league of friendship with each other, for their common defence, the security of their liberties, and their mutual and general welfare, binding themselves to assist each other, against all force offered to, or attacks made upon them, or any of them, on account of religion, sovereignty, trade, or any other pretence whatever.

Article IV The better to secure and perpetuate mutual friendship and intercourse among the people of the different states in this union, the free inhabitants of each of these states, paupers, vagabonds and fugitives from justice excepted, shall be entitled to all privileges and immunities of free citizens in the several states; and the people of each state shall have free ingress and regress to and from any other state, and shall enjoy therein all the privileges of trade and commerce, subject to the same duties, impositions and restrictions as the inhabitants thereof respectively, provided that such restriction shall not extend so far as to prevent the removal of property imported into any state, to any other state of which the owner is an inhabitant; provided also that no imposition, duties or restriction shall be laid by any state, on the property of the united states, or either of them.

If any person guilty of, or charged with treason, felony, or other high misdemeanor in any State, shall flee from justice, and be found in any of the United States, he shall upon demand of the Governor or executive power, of the State from which he fled, be delivered up and removed to the state having jurisdiction of his offence.

Full faith and credit shall be given in each of these States to the records, acts and judicial proceedings of the courts and magistrates of every other State.

Article V For the more convenient management of the general interests of the United States, delegates shall be annually appointed in such manner as the legislature of each State shall direct, to meet in Congress on the first Monday in November, in every year, with a power reserved to each State, to recall its delegates, or any of them, at any time within the year, and to send others in their stead, for the remainder of the year.

No State shall be represented in Congress by less than two, nor by more than seven members; and no person shall be capable of being a delegate for more than three years in any term of six years; nor shall any person, being a delegate, be capable of holding any office under the United States, for which he, or another for his benefit receives any salary, fees or emolument of any kind.

Each State shall maintain its own delegates in a meeting of the States, and while they act as members of the committee of the States.

In determining questions in the United States, in Congress assembled, each State shall have one vote.

Freedom of speech and debate in Congress shall not be impeached or questioned in any court, or place out of Congress, and the members of Congress shall be protected in their persons from arrests and imprisonments, during the time of their going to and from, and attendance on Congress, except for treason, felony, or breach of the peace.

Article VI No State without the consent of the United States in Congress assembled, shall send any embassy to, or receive any embassy from, or enter into any conference, agreement, or alliance or treaty with any king, prince or state; nor shall any person holding any office of profit or trust under the United States, or any of them, accept of any present, emolument, office or title of any kind whatever from any king, prince or foreign state; nor shall the United States in Congress assembled, or any of them, grant any title of nobility.

No two or more states shall enter into any treaty, confederation or alliance whatever between them, without the consent of the United States in Congress assembled, specifying accurately the purposes for which the same is to be entered into, and how long it shall continue.

No State shall lay any imposts or duties, which may interfere with any stipulations in treaties, entered into by the United States in Congress assembled, with any king, prince or state, in pursuance of any treaties already proposed by Congress, to the courts of France and Spain.

No vessels of war shall be kept up in time of peace by any State, except such number only, as shall be deemed necessary by the United States in Congress assembled, for the defence of such State or its trade; nor shall any body of forces be kept up by any State, in time of peace, except such number only, as in the judgment of the United States in Congress assembled, shall be deemed requisite to garrison the forts necessary for the defence of such State; but every State shall always keep up a well regulated and disciplined militia, sufficiently armed and accoutred, and shall provide and constantly have ready for use, in public stores, a due number of field-pieces and tents, and a proper quantity of arms, ammunition and camp equipage.

No State shall engage in any war without the consent of the United States in Congress assembled, unless such State be actually invaded by enemies, or shall have received certain advice of a resolution being formed by some nation of Indians to invade such State, and the danger is so imminent as not to admit of a delay, till the United States in Congress assembled can be consulted: nor shall any State grant commissions to any ships or vessels of war, nor letters of marque or reprisal, except it be after a declaration of war by the United States in Congress assembled, and then only against the kingdom or state and the subjects thereof, against which war has been so declared, and under such regulations as shall be established by the United States in Congress assembled, unless such State be infested by pirates, in which case vessels of war may be fitted out for that occasion, and kept so long as the danger shall continue, or until the United States in Congress assembled shall determine otherwise.

Article VII When land forces are raised by any state for the common defence, all officers of or under the rank of colonel shall be appointed by the legislature of each State respectively by whom such forces shall be raised, or in such manner as such State shall direct; and all vacancies shall be filled up by the State which first made the appointment.

Article VIII All charges of war and all other expences that shall be incurred for the common defence or general welfare, and allowed by the United States in Congress assembled, shall be defrayed out of a common treasury, which shall be supplied by the several States, in proportion to the value of all land within each State, granted to or surveyed for any person, as such land and the buildings and improvements thereon shall be estimated according to such mode as the United States in Congress assembled, shall from time to time direct and appoint.

The taxes for paying that proportion shall be laid and levied by the authority and direction of the legislatures of the several States within the time agreed upon by the United States in Congress assembled.

Article IX The United States in Congress assembled, shall have the sole and exclusive right and power of determining on peace and war, except in the cases mentioned in the sixth article—of sending and receiving ambassadors—entering into treaties and alliances, provided that no treaty of commerce shall be made whereby the legislative power of the respective States shall be restrained from imposing such imposts and duties on foreigners, as their own people are subjected to, or from prohibiting the exportation or importation of any species of goods or commodities whatsoever—of establishing rules for deciding in all cases, what captures on land or water shall be legal, and in what manner prizes taken by land or naval forces in the service of the United States shall be divided or appropriated—of granting letters of marque and reprisal in times of peace—appointing courts for the trial of piracies and felonies committed on the high seas and establishing courts for receiving and determining finally appeals in all cases of captures, provided that no member of Congress shall be appointed a judge of any of the said courts.

The United States in Congress assembled shall also be the last resort on appeal in all disputes and differences now subsisting or that hereafter may arise between two or more States concerning boundary, jurisdiction or any other cause whatever; which authority shall always be exercised in the manner following:—Whenever the legislative or executive authority or lawful agent of any State in controversy with another shall present a petition to Congress, stating the matter in question and praying for a hearing, notice thereof shall be given by order of Congress to the legislative or executive authority of the other State in controversy, and a day assigned for the appearance of the parties by their lawful agents, who shall then be directed to appoint by joint consent, commissioners or judges to constitute a court for hearing and determining the matter in question: but if they cannot agree, Congress shall name three persons out of each of the United States, and from the list of such persons each party shall alternately strike out one, the petitioners beginning, until the number shall be reduced to thirteen; and from that number not less than seven, nor more than nine names as Congress shall direct, shall in the presence of Congress be drawn out by lot, and the persons whose names shall be so drawn or any five of them, shall be commissioners or judges, to hear and finally determine the controversy, so always as a major part of the judges who shall hear the cause shall agree in the determination: and if either party shall neglect to attend at the day appointed, without showing reasons, which Congress shall judge sufficient, or being present shall refuse to strike, the Congress shall proceed to nominate three persons out of each State, and the Secretary of Congress shall strike in behalf of such party absent or refusing; and the judgment and sentence of the court to be appointed, in the manner before prescribed, shall be final and conclusive; and if any of the parties shall refuse to submit to the authority of such court, or to appear to defend their claim or cause, the court shall nevertheless proceed to pronounce sentence or judgment, which shall in like manner be final and decisive, the judgment or sentence and other proceedings being in either case transmitted to Congress, and lodged among the acts of Congress for the security of the parties concerned: provided that every commissioner, before he sits in judgment, shall take an oath to be administered by one of the judges of the Supreme or Superior Court of the State, where the cause shall be tried, *"well and truly to hear and determine the matter in question, according to the best of his judgment, without favour, affection or hope of reward,"* provided also that no State shall be deprived of territory for the benefit of the United States.

All controversies concerning the private right of soil claimed under different grants of two or more States, whose jurisdictions as they may respect such lands, and the States which passed such grants are adjusted, the said grants or either of them being at the same time claimed to have originated antecedent to such settlement of jurisdiction, shall on the petition of either party to the Congress of the United States, be finally determined as near as may be in the same manner as is before prescribed for deciding disputes respecting territorial jurisdiction between different States.

The United States in Congress assembled shall also have the sole and exclusive right and power of regulating the alloy and value of coin struck by their own authority, or by that of the respective States—fixing the standard of weights and measures throughout the United States—regulating the trade and managing all affairs with the Indians, not members of any of the States, provided that the legislative right of any State within its own limits be not infringed or violated—establishing and regulating post-offices from one State to another, throughout all the United States, and exacting such postage on the papers passing through the same as may be requisite to defray the expences of the said office—appointing all officers of the land forces, in the service of the United States, excepting regimental officers—appointing all the officers of the naval forces, and commissioning all officers whatever in the service of the United States—making rules for the government and regulation of the said land and naval forces, and directing their operations.

The United States in Congress assembled shall have authority to appoint a committee, to sit in the recess of Congress, to be denominated "A Committee of the States," and to consist of one delegate from each State; to appoint such other committees and civil officers as may be necessary for managing the general affairs of the United States under their direction; and to appoint one of their number to preside, provided that no person be allowed to serve in the office of president more than one year in any term of three years—to ascertain the necessary sums of money to be raised for the service of the

United States, and to appropriate and apply the same for defraying the public expences—to borrow money, or emit bills on the credit of the United States, transmitting every half-year to the respective States an account of the sums of money so borrowed or emitted—to build and equip a navy—to agree upon the number of land forces, and to make requisitions from each State for its quota, in proportion to the number of white inhabitants in such State; which requisition shall be binding, and thereupon the legislature of each State shall appoint the regimental officers, raise the men and clothe, arm and equip them in a soldier-like manner, at the expence of the United States, and the officers and men so clothed, armed and equipped shall march to the place appointed, and within the time agreed on by the United States in Congress assembled; but if the United States in Congress assembled shall, on consideration of circumstances, judge proper that any State should not raise men, or should raise a smaller number than its quota, and that any other State should raise a greater number of men than the quota thereof, such extra number shall be raised, officered, clothed, armed and equipped in the same manner as the quota of such State, unless the legislature of such State shall judge that such extra number cannot be safely spared out of the same, in which case they shall raise, officer, clothe, arm and equip as many of such extra number as they judge can be safely spared: and the officers and men so clothed, armed and equipped, shall march to the place appointed, and within the time agreed on by the United States in Congress assembled.

The United States in Congress assembled shall never engage in a war, nor grant letters of marque and reprisal in time of peace, nor enter into any treaties or alliances, nor coin money, nor regulate the value thereof, nor ascertain the sums and expences necessary for the defence and welfare of the United States, or any of them, nor emit bills, nor borrow money on the credit of the United States, nor appropriate money, nor agree upon the number of vessels of war, to be built or purchased, or the number of land or sea forces to be raised, nor appoint a commander-in-chief of the army or navy, unless nine States assent to the same; nor shall a question on any other point, except for adjourning from day to day be determined, unless by the votes of a majority of the United States in Congress assembled.

The Congress of the United States shall have power to adjourn to any time within the year, and to any place within the United States, so that no period of adjournment be for a longer duration than the space of six months, and shall publish the journal of their proceedings monthly, except such parts thereof relating to treaties, alliances or military operations as in their judgment require secrecy; and the yeas and nays of the delegates of each State on any question shall be entered on the journal, when it is desired by any delegate; and the delegates of a State, or any of them, at his or their request shall be furnished with a transcript of the said journal, except such parts as are above excepted, to lay before the legislatures of the several States.

Article X The Committee of the States, or any nine of them, shall be authorized to execute, in the recess of Congress, such of the powers of Congress as the United States in Congress assembled, by the consent of nine States, shall from time to time think expedient to vest them with; provided that no power be delegated to the said Committee, for the exercise of which, by the Articles of Confederation, the voice of nine States in the Congress of the United States assembled is requisite.

Article XI Canada, acceding to this Confederation, and joining in the measures of the United States, shall be admitted into, and entitled to all the advantages of this union; but no other colony shall be admitted into the same, unless such admission be agreed to by nine States.

Article XII All bills of credit emitted, monies borrowed and debts contracted by, or under the authority of Congress, before the assembling of the United States, in pursuance of the present Confederation, shall be deemed and considered as a charge against the United States, for payment and satisfaction whereof the said United States, and the public faith are hereby solemnly pledged.

Article XIII Every State shall abide by the determinations of the United States in Congress assembled, on all questions which by this Confederation are submitted to them. And the Articles of this Confederation shall be inviolably observed by every State, and the Union shall be perpetual; nor shall any alteration at any time hereafter be made in any of them; unless such alteration be agreed to in a Congress of the United States, and be afterwards confirmed by the legislatures of every State.

AND WHEREAS it hath pleased the Great Governor of the World to incline the hearts of legislatures we respectively represent in Congress to approve of and to authorize us to ratify the said Articles of Confederation and perpetual Union. KNOW YE that we the under-signed delegates, by virtue of the power and authority to us given for that purpose, do by these presents, in the name and in behalf of our respective constituents, fully and entirely ratify and confirm each and every of the said Articles of Confederation and perpetual Union, and all and singular the matters and things therein contained: and we do further solemnly plight and engage the faith of our respective constituents that they shall abide by the determinations of the United States in Congress assembled, on all questions which by the said Confederation are submitted to them. And that the Articles thereof shall be inviolably observed by the States we respectively represent, and that the Union shall be perpetual. In Witness whereof we have hereunto set our hands in Congress. Done at Philadelphia in the state of Pennsylvania the ninth day of July, in the year of our Lord one Thousand seven Hundred and Seventy-eight, and in the third year of the independence of America.

The Constitution of the United States of America*

(Preamble: outlines goals and effect)

We the people of the United States, in order to form a more perfect Union, establish Justice, insure domestic Tranquility, provide for the common defence, promote the general Welfare, and secure the Blessings of Liberty to ourselves and our Posterity, do ordain and establish this Constitution for the United States of America.

Article I (The legislative branch)

(Powers vested)

Section 1 All legislative Powers herein granted shall be vested in a Congress of the United States, which shall consist of a Senate and a House of Representatives.

(House of Representatives: selection, term, qualifications, apportionment of seats, census requirement, exclusive power to impeach)

Section 2 The House of Representatives shall be composed of Members chosen every second Year by the people of the several States, and the Electors in each State shall have the Qualifications requisite for Electors of the most numerous Branch of the State Legislature.

No person shall be a Representative who shall not have attained to the Age of twenty five Years, and been seven Years a Citizen of the United States, and who shall not, when elected, be an Inhabitant of that State in which he shall be chosen.

Representatives and direct Taxes shall be apportioned among the several States which may be included within this Union, according to their respective numbers, *which shall be determined by adding to the whole Number of free Persons, including those bound to Service for a Term of Years and excluding Indians not taxed, three-fifths of all other Persons.* The actual Enumeration shall be made within three Years after the first Meeting of the Congress of the United States, and within every subsequent Term of ten Years, in such Manner as they shall by Law direct. The number of Representatives shall not exceed one for every thirty Thousand, but each State shall have at Least one Representative; *and until such enumeration shall be made, the State of New Hampshire shall be entitled to choose three, Massachusetts eight, Rhode Island and Providence Plantations one, Connecticut five, New York six, New Jersey four, Pennsylvania eight, Delaware one, Maryland six, Virginia ten, North Carolina five, South Carolina five, and Georgia three.*

When vacancies happen in the Representation from any State, the Executive Authority thereof shall issue Writs of Election to fill such Vacancies.

The House of Representatives shall chuse their Speaker and other Officers; and shall have the sole Power of Impeachment.

*Passages no longer in effect are printed in italic type.

(Senate: selection, term, qualifications, exclusive power to try impeachments)

Section 3 The Senate of the United States shall be composed of two Senators from each State, *chosen by the Legislature thereof,* for six years; and each Senator shall have one Vote.

Immediately after they shall be assembled in Consequence of the first Election, they shall be divided as equally as may be into three Classes. The Seats of the Senators of the first Class shall be vacated at the Expiration of the second Year, of the second Class at the expiration of the fourth Year, and of the third Class at the expiration of the sixth Year, so that one-third may be chosen every second Year; *and if Vacancies happen by Resignation or otherwise, during the Recess of the Legislature of any State, the Executive thereof may make temporary Appointments until the next meeting of the legislature, which shall then fill such Vacancies.*

No person shall be a Senator who shall not have attained to the Age of thirty Years, and been nine Years a Citizen of the United States, and who shall not, when elected, be an Inhabitant of that State for which he shall be chosen.

The Vice-President of the United States shall be President of the Senate, but shall have no Vote, unless they be equally divided.

The Senate shall choose their other officers, and also a President pro tempore, in the absence of the Vice-President, or when he shall exercise the Office of President of the United States.

The Senate shall have the sole Power to try all impeachments. When sitting for that purpose, they shall be on Oath or Affirmation. When the President of the United States is tried, the Chief Justice shall preside: and no Person shall be convicted without the Concurrence of two-thirds of the members Present.

Judgment in Cases of Impeachment shall not extend further than to removal from the Office, and disqualification to hold and enjoy any Office of honor, Trust or Profit under the United States: but the Party convicted shall nevertheless be liable and subject to Indictment, Trial, Judgment and Punishment, according to Law.

(Elections)

Section 4 The Times, Places and Manner of holding Elections for Senators and Representatives shall be prescribed in each State by the Legislature thereof; but the Congress may at any time by Law make or alter such regulations, except as to the Places of chusing Senators.

The Congress shall assemble at least once in every Year, and such meeting *shall be on the first Monday in December, unless they shall by Law appoint a different Day.*

(Powers and duties of the two chambers: rules of procedure, power over members)

Section 5 Each House shall be the Judge of the Elections, Returns and Qualifications of its own

Members, and a Majority of each shall constitute a Quorum to do Business; but a smaller Number may adjourn from day to day, and may be authorized to compel the Attendance of absent Members, in such Manner, and under such Penalties as each House may provide.

Each House may determine the Rules of its proceedings, punish its Members for disorderly behaviour, and with the Concurrence of two thirds, expel a Member.

Each House shall keep a Journal of its Proceedings, and from time to time publish the same, excepting such Parts as may in their Judgment require Secrecy; and the Yeas and Nays of the Members of either House on any question shall, at the Desire of one fifth of those Present, be entered on the Journal.

Neither House, during the Session of Congress, shall, without the Consent of the other, adjourn for more than three days, nor to any other Place than that in which the two Houses shall be sitting.

(Compensation, privilege from arrest, privilege of speech, disabilities of members)

Section 6 The Senators and Representatives shall receive a Compensation for their services, to be ascertained by Law, and paid out of the Treasury of the United States. They shall in all Cases, except Treason, Felony and Breach of the Peace, be privileged from Arrest during their Attendance at the Session of their respective Houses, and in going to and returning from the same; and for any Speech or Debate in either House, they shall not be questioned in any other Place.

No Senator or Representative shall, during the Time for which he was elected, be appointed to any civil office under the Authority of the United States, which shall have been created, or the Emoluments whereof shall have been increased, during such time; and no Person holding any Office under the United States, shall be a Member of either House during his Continuance in Office.

(Legislative process: revenue bills, approval or veto power of president)

Section 7 All bills for raising Revenue shall originate in the House of Representatives; but the Senate may propose or concur with Amendments as on other Bills.

Every Bill which shall have passed the House of Representatives and the Senate, shall, before it become a Law, be presented to the President of the United States; if he approve he shall sign it, but if not he shall return it with Objections to that House in which it originated, who shall enter the Objections at large on their journal, and proceed to reconsider it. If after such Reconsideration two thirds of that House shall agree to pass the Bill, it shall be sent, together with the Objections, to the other House, by which it shall likewise be reconsidered, and, if approved by two thirds of that house, it shall become a Law. But in all such Cases the Votes of both Houses shall be determined by yeas and Nays, and the Names of the Persons voting for and against the Bill shall be entered on the journal of each

House respectively. If any Bill shall not be returned by the President within ten Days (Sundays excepted) after it shall have been presented to him, the Same shall be a Law, in like Manner as if he had signed it, unless the Congress by their Adjournment prevent its Return, in which Case it shall not be a Law.

Every Order, Resolution, or Vote to which the Concurrence of the Senate and House of Representatives may be necessary (except on a question of Adjournment) shall be presented to the President of the United States; and before the Same shall take Effect, shall be approved by him, or being disapproved by him, shall be repassed by two thirds of the Senate and House of Representatives, according to the Rules and Limitations prescribed in the Case of a Bill.

(Powers of Congress enumerated)

Section 8 The Congress shall have Power
To lay and collect Taxes, Duties, Imposts, and Excises, to pay the Debts and provide for the common Defence and general Welfare of the United States; but all Duties, Imposts and Excises shall be uniform throughout the United States;

To borrow Money on the credit of the United States;

To regulate Commerce with foreign Nations, and among the several States, and with the Indian tribes;

To establish an uniform Rule of Naturalization, and uniform Laws on the subject of Bankruptcies throughout the United States;

To coin Money, regulate the Value thereof, and of foreign Coin, and fix the Standard of Weights and Measures;

To provide for the Punishment of counterfeiting the Securities and current Coin of the United States;

To establish Post Offices and post Roads;

To promote the Progress of Science and useful Arts by securing for limited Times to Authors and Inventors the exclusive Right to their respective Writings and Discoveries;

To constitute Tribunals inferior to the supreme Court;

To define and punish Piracies and Felonies committed on the high Seas, and offenses against the Law of Nations;

To declare War, grant Letters of Marque and Reprisal, and make Rules concerning Captures on Land and Water;

To raise and support Armies, but no Appropriation of Money to that Use shall be for a longer Term than two Years;

To provide and maintain a Navy;

To make rules for the Government and Regulation of the land and naval Forces;

To provide for calling forth the Militia to execute the Laws of the Union, suppress Insurrections, and repel Invasions;

To provide for organizing, arming, and disciplining the Militia, and for governing such Part of them as may be employed in the Service of the United States, reserving to the States respectively the Appointment of the

Officers, and the Authority of training the Militia according to the discipline prescribed by Congress;

To exercise exclusive Legislation in all Cases whatsoever, over such District (not exceeding ten Miles square) as may, by cession of particular States, and the Acceptance of Congress, become the Seat of Government of the United States, and to exercise like Authority over all places purchased by the Consent of the Legislature of the State in which the Same shall be, for Erection of Forts, Magazines, Arsenals, dock-Yards, and other needful Buildings;—And

(Elastic clause)

To make all Laws which shall be necessary and proper for carrying into Execution the foregoing Powers, and all other powers vested by this Constitution in the Government of the United States, or in any Department or Officer thereof.

(Powers denied Congress)

Section 9 *The Migration or Importation of such persons as any of the States now existing shall think proper to admit, shall not be prohibited by the Congress prior to the Year 1808; but a Tax or duty may be imposed on such Importation, not exceeding $10 for each Person.*

The Privilege of the Writ of Habeas Corpus shall not be suspended, unless when in Cases of Rebellion or Invasion the public Safety may require it.

No Bill of Attainder or ex post facto Law shall be passed.

No Capitation, or other direct, Tax shall be laid, unless in Proportion to the Census or Enumeration herein before directed to be taken.

No Tax or Duty shall be laid on Articles exported from any State.

No Preference shall be given by any Regulation of Commerce or Revenue to the Ports of one State over those of another; nor shall Vessels bound to, or from, one State, be obliged to enter, clear, or pay Duties in another.

No Money shall be drawn from the Treasury, but in Consequence of Appropriations made by Law; and a regular Statement and Account of the receipts and Expenditures of all public Money shall be published from time to time.

No Title of Nobility shall be granted by the United States: And no Person holding any Office or Profit or trust under them, shall, without the Consent of the Congress, accept of any present, Emolument, Office, or Title, of any kind whatever, from any King, Prince, or foreign State.

(Powers denied the states)

Section 10 No State shall enter into any Treaty, Alliance, or Confederation; grant Letters of Marque and Reprisal; coin Money; emit Bills of Credit; make any Thing but gold and silver Coin a Tender in Payment of Debts; pass any Bill of Attainder, ex post facto law, or

Law impairing the obligation of Contracts, or grant any Title of Nobility.

No State shall, without the Consent of Congress, lay any Imposts or Duties on Imports or Exports, except what may be absolutely necessary for executing its inspection Laws: and the net Produce of all duties and imposts, laid by any State on Imports or Exports, shall be for the Use of the Treasury of the United States; and all such Laws shall be subject to the Revision and Controul of the Congress.

No State shall, without the consent of Congress, lay any Duty of Tonnage, keep Troops or Ships of War in time of Peace, enter into any Agreement or Compact with another State, or with a foreign Power, or engage in War, unless actually invaded, or in such imminent Danger as will not admit of delay.

Article II (The executive branch)

(The president: power vested, term, electoral college, qualifications, presidential succession, compensation, oath of office)

Section 1 The executive Power shall be vested in a President of the United States of America. He shall hold his office during the Term of four Years, and, together with the Vice President, chosen for the same Term, be elected as follows:

Each State shall appoint, in such Manner as the Legislature thereof may direct, a Number of Electors, equal to the whole Number of Senators and Representatives to which the State may be entitled in the Congress; but no Senator or Representative, or Person holding an Office of Trust or Profit under the United States, shall be appointed an Elector.

The Electors shall meet in their respective States, and vote by Ballot for two Persons, of whom one at least shall not be an inhabitant of the same State with themselves. And they shall make a List of all the Persons voted for, and of the Number of Votes for each: which List they shall sign and certify, and transmit sealed to the Seat of Government of the United States, directed to the President of the Senate. The President of the Senate shall, in the presence of the Senate and House of Representatives, open all the Certificates, and the Votes shall then be counted. The Person having the greatest Number of Votes shall be the President, if such Number be a Majority of the whole number of Electors appointed; and if there be more than one who have such Majority, and have an equal Number of Votes, then the House of Representatives shall immediately chuse by Ballot one of them for President; and if no Person have a Majority, then from the five highest on the List said House shall in like Manner chuse the President. But in chusing the President the Votes shall be taken by States, the Representation from each State having one Vote; a quorum for this purpose shall consist of a Member or Members from two thirds of the States, and a Majority of all the States shall be necessary to a Choice. In every Case, after the Choice of the President, the person having the greatest Number of Votes of the

Electors shall be the Vice President. But if there should remain two or more who have equal Votes, the Senate shall chuse from them by Ballot the Vice President.

The Congress may determine the Time of chusing the Electors and the Day on which they shall give their Votes; which Day shall be the same throughout the United States.

No person except a natural born Citizen, or a Citizen of the United States at the time of the Adoption of this Constitution, shall be eligible to the Office of President; neither shall any Person be eligible to that Office who shall not have attained to the age of thirty-five Years, and been fourteen Years a Resident within the United States.

In cases of the Removal of the President from Office or of his Death, Resignation, or Inability to discharge the Powers and Duties of the said Office, the same shall devolve on the Vice President, and the Congress may by law provide for the case of Removal, Death, Resignation, or inability, both of the President and Vice President, declaring what Officer shall then act as President, and such Officer shall act accordingly, until the Disability be removed, or a President shall be elected.

The President shall, at stated Times, receive for his Services, a Compensation, which shall neither be increased nor diminished during the Period for which he shall have been elected, and he shall not receive within that Period any other emolument from the United States, or any of them.

Before he enter on the Execution of his Office, he shall take the following Oath or Affirmation:—"I do solemnly swear (or affirm) that I will faithfully execute the Office of the President of the United States, and will to the best of my Ability preserve, protect and defend the Constitution of the United States."

(Powers and duties: as commander in chief, over advisers, to pardon, to make treaties and appoint officers)

Section 2 The President shall be Commander in Chief of the Army and Navy of the United States, and of the Militia of the several States, when called into the actual service of the United States; he may require the Opinion, in writing, of the principal Officer in each of the executive Departments, upon any Subject relating to the Duties of their respective Offices, and he shall have Power to grant Reprieves and Pardons for Offences against the United States, except in Cases of Impeachment.

He shall have Power, by and with the Advice and Consent of the Senate, to make Treaties, provided two-thirds of the Senators present concur; and he shall nominate, and by and with the Advice and Consent of the Senate, shall appoint Ambassadors, other public Ministers and Consuls, Judges of the supreme Court, and all other Officers of the United States, whose Appointments are not herein otherwise provided for, and which shall be established by Law: but Congress may by Law vest the Appointment of such inferior Officers, as they think proper, in the President alone, in the courts of Law, or in the Heads of Departments.

The President shall have Power to fill up all Vacancies that may happen during the Recess of the Senate, by granting Commissions which shall expire at the end of their next Session.

(Legislative, diplomatic, and law-enforcement duties)

Section 3 He shall from time to time give to the Congress Information of the State of the Union, and recommend to their Consideration such Measures as he shall judge necessary and expedient; he may, on extraordinary Occasions, convene both Houses, or either of them, and in Case of Disagreement between them, with Respect to the Time of Adjournment, he may adjourn them to such Time as he shall think proper; he shall receive Ambassadors and other public Ministers; he shall take Care that the Laws be faithfully executed, and shall Commission all the Officers of the United States.

(Impeachment)

Section 4 The President, Vice President and all civil Officers of the United States shall be removed from Office on Impeachment for, and on Conviction of, Treason, Bribery, or other high Crimes and Misdemeanors.

Article III (The judicial branch)

(Power vested; Supreme Court; lower courts; judges)

Section 1 The judicial Power of the United States shall be vested in one supreme Court, and in such inferior Courts as the Congress may from time to time ordain and establish. The Judges, both of the supreme and inferior Courts, shall hold their Offices during good Behaviour, and shall, at stated Times, receive for their Services a Compensation which shall not be diminished during their Continuance in Office.

(Jurisdiction; trial by jury)

Section 2 The judicial Power shall extend to all Cases, in Law and Equity, arising under this Constitution, the Laws of the United States, and Treaties made, or which shall be made, under their Authority;—to all Cases affecting Ambassadors, other public Ministers and Consuls;—to all Cases of admiralty and maritime Jurisdiction;—to Controversies to which the United States shall be a Party;—to controversies between two or more States;—*between a State and Citizens of another State;*—between Citizens of different States—between Citizens of the same State claiming Lands under grants of different States, and between a State, or the Citizens thereof, and foreign States, Citizens or Subjects.

In all cases affecting Ambassadors, other public Ministers and Consuls, and those in which a State shall be Party, the supreme Court shall have original

Jurisdiction. In all the other Cases before mentioned, the supreme Court shall have appellate Jurisdiction, both as to Law and Fact, with such Exceptions, and under such Regulations, as the Congress shall make.

The Trial of all Crimes, except in cases of Impeachment, shall be by Jury; and such Trial shall be held in the State where said Crimes shall have been committed; but when not committed within any State, the Trial shall be at such Place or Places as the Congress may by Law have directed.

(Treason: definition, punishment)

Section 3 Treason against the United States shall consist only in levying War against them, or in adhering to their Enemies, giving them Aid and Comfort. No Person shall be convicted of Treason unless on the Testimony of two Witnesses to the same overt Act, or on confession in open Court.

The Congress shall have power to declare the Punishment of Treason, but no Attainder of Treason shall work Corruption of Blood, or Forfeiture except during the Life of the Person attainted.

Article IV (States' relations)

(Full faith and credit)

Section 1 Full Faith and Credit shall be given in each State to the public Acts, Records, and judicial Proceedings of every other State. And the Congress may by general laws prescribe the Manner in which such Acts, Records, and Proceedings shall be proved, and the Effect thereof.

(Interstate comity, rendition)

Section 2 The Citizens of each State shall be entitled to all Privileges and Immunities of Citizens in the several States.

A Person charged in any State with Treason, Felony, or other Crime, who shall flee from Justice, and be found in another State, shall on Demand of the executive Authority of the State from which he fled, be delivered up, to be removed to the State having Jurisdiction of the Crime.

No person held to Service or Labor in one State, under the Laws thereof, escaping into another, shall, in consequence of any Law or Regulation therein, be discharged from such Service or Labor, but shall be delivered up on Claim of the Party to whom such Service or Labor may be due.

(New states)

Section 3 New States may be admitted by the Congress into this Union; but no new State shall be formed or erected within the Jurisdiction of any other State; nor any State be formed by the Junction of two or more States, or parts of States, without the Consent of the Legislatures of the States concerned as well as of the Congress.

The Congress shall have Power to dispose of and make all needful Rules and Regulations respecting the Territory or other Property belonging to the United States; and nothing in this Constitution shall be so construed as to Prejudice any Claims of the United States, or of any particular State.

(Obligations of the United States to the states)

Section 4 The United States shall guarantee to every State in this Union a Republican Form of Government, and shall protect each of them against Invasion; and on Application of the Legislature, or of the Executive (when the Legislature cannot be convened), against domestic Violence.

Article V (Mode of amendment)

The Congress, whenever two-thirds of both Houses shall deem it necessary, shall propose Amendments to this Constitution, or, on the Application of the Legislatures of two-thirds of the several States, shall call a Convention for proposing Amendments, which, in either Case, shall be valid to all Intents and Purposes, as part of this Constitution, when ratified by the legislatures of three-fourths of the several States, or by Conventions in three-fourths thereof, as the one or the other Mode of Ratification may be proposed by the Congress; Provided *that no Amendment which may be made prior to the Year One thousand eight hundred and eight shall in any Manner affect the first and fourth clauses in the Ninth Section of the first Article;* and that no State, without its Consent, shall be deprived of its equal suffrage in the Senate.

Article VI (Prior debts; supremacy of Constitution; oaths of office)

All Debts contracted and Engagements entered into, before the Adoption of this Constitution, shall be as valid against the United States under this Constitution, as under the Confederation.

This Constitution, and the Laws of the United States which shall be made in Pursuance thereof; and all Treaties made, or which shall be made, under the Authority of the United States, shall be the supreme Law of the Land; and the judges in every State shall be bound thereby, anything in the Constitution or Laws of any State to the Contrary notwithstanding.

The Senators and Representatives before mentioned, and the Members of the several State Legislatures, and all executive and judicial Officers, both of the United States and of the several States, shall be bound by Oath or Affirmation to support this Constitution; but no religious test shall ever be required as a Qualification to any Office or public Trust under the United States.

Article VII (Ratification)

The ratification of the Conventions of nine States shall be sufficient for the Establishment of this Constitution between the States so ratifying the Same.

Done in Convention by the Unanimous Consent of the States present, the seventeenth day of September in the Year of our Lord one thousand seven hundred and eighty-seven and of the Independence of the United States of America the twelfth. In WITNESS whereof We have hereunto subscribed our Names.

GEORGE WASHINGTON
and thirty-seven others

Amendments to the Constitution

(The first ten amendments—the Bill of Rights—were adopted in 1791.)

Amendment I (Freedom of religion, speech, press, assembly)

Congress shall make no law respecting an establishment of religion, or prohibiting the free exercise thereof; or abridging the freedom of speech, or of the press; or the right of the people peaceably to assemble, and to petition the Government for a redress of grievances.

Amendment II (Right to bear arms)

A well-regulated militia being necessary to the security of a free State, the right of the people to keep and bear arms shall not be infringed.

Amendment III (Quartering of soldiers)

No Soldier shall, in time of peace, be quartered in any house without the consent of the Owner, nor in time of war, but in a manner to be prescribed by law.

Amendment IV (Searches and seizures)

The right of the people to be secure in their persons, houses, papers, and effects, against unreasonable searches and seizures, shall not be violated, and no Warrants shall issue but upon probable cause, supported by Oath or affirmation, and particularly describing the place to be searched, and the persons or things to be seized.

Amendment V (Rights of persons: grand juries; double jeopardy; self-incrimination; due process; eminent domain)

No person shall be held to answer for a capital, or otherwise infamous crime, unless on a presentment or indictment of a Grand Jury, except in cases arising in the land or naval forces, or in the Militia, when in actual service in time of War or public danger; nor shall any person be subject for the same offense to be twice put in jeopardy of life or limb; nor shall be compelled in any criminal case to be a witness against himself, nor be deprived of life, liberty, or property, without due process of law; nor shall private property be taken for public use without just compensation.

Amendment VI (Rights of accused in criminal prosecutions)

In all criminal prosecutions, the accused shall enjoy the right to a speedy and public trial, by an impartial jury of the State and district wherein the crime shall have been committed, which district shall have been previously ascertained by law, and to be informed of the nature and cause of the accusation; to be confronted with the witnesses against him; to have compulsory process for obtaining Witnesses in his favor, and to have the assistance of counsel for his defence.

Amendment VII (Civil trials)

In Suits at common law, where the value in controversy shall exceed twenty dollars, the right of trial by jury shall be preserved, and no fact tried by a jury shall be otherwise reexamined in any Court of the United States, than according to the rules of the common law.

Amendment VIII (Punishment for crime)

Excessive bail shall not be required, nor excessive fines imposed, nor cruel and unusual punishments inflicted.

Amendment IX (Rights retained by the people)

The enumeration in the Constitution, of certain rights, shall not be construed to deny or disparage others retained by the people.

Amendment X (Rights reserved to the states)

The powers not delegated to the United States by the Constitution, nor prohibited by it to the States, are reserved to the States respectively, or to the people.

Amendment XI (Suits against the states; adopted 1798)

The Judicial power of the United States shall not be construed to extend to any suit in law or equity, commenced or prosecuted against one of the United States by Citizens of another state, or by Citizens or Subjects of any Foreign State.

Amendment XII (Election of the president; adopted 1804)

The electors shall meet in their respective States, and vote by ballot for President and Vice-President, one of whom, at least, shall not be an inhabitant of the same state with themselves; they shall name in their ballots the person voted for as President, and in distinct ballots the person voted for as Vice-President, and they shall make distinct lists of all persons voted for as President, and of all persons voted for as Vice-President, and of the number of votes for each, which lists they shall sign and certify, and transmit sealed to the seat of government of the United States, directed to the President of the Senate;—the President of the Senate shall, in the presence of the Senate and House of Representatives, open all the certificates and the votes shall then be counted;—the person having the greatest number of votes for President shall be the President, if such number be a majority of the whole number of electors appointed; and if no person have such majority, then from the persons having the highest numbers not exceeding three on the list of those voted for as President, the House of Representatives shall choose immediately, by ballot, the President. But in choosing the President, the votes shall be taken by States, the representation from each State having one vote; a quorum for this purpose shall consist of a member or members from two-thirds of the States, and a majority of all the States shall be necessary to a choice. And if the House of Representatives shall not choose a President whenever the right of choice shall devolve upon them, before *the fourth day of March* next following, then the Vice-President shall act as President, as in the case of the death or other constitutional disability of the President.—The person having the greatest number of votes as Vice-President shall be the Vice-President, if such number be a majority of the whole number of electors appointed; and if no person have a majority, then from the two highest numbers on the list the Senate shall choose the Vice-President; a quorum for the purpose shall consist of two-thirds of the whole number of Senators, and a majority of the whole number shall be necessary to a choice. But no person constitutionally ineligible to the office of President shall be eligible to that of Vice-President of the United States.

Amendment XIII (Abolition of slavery; adopted 1865)

Section 1 Neither slavery nor involuntary servitude, except as a punishment for crime whereof the party shall have been duly convicted, shall exist within the United States, or any place subject to their jurisdiction.

Section 2 Congress shall have power to enforce this article by appropriate legislation.

Amendment XIV (Adopted 1868)

(Citizenship rights; privileges and immunities; due process; equal protection)

Section 1 All persons born or naturalized in the United States, and subject to the jurisdiction thereof, are citizens of the United States and of the State wherein they reside. No State shall make or enforce any law which shall abridge the privileges or immunities of citizens of the United States; nor shall any State deprive any person of life, liberty, or property, without due process of law; nor deny to any person within its jurisdiction the equal protection of the laws.

(Apportionment of representation)

Section 2 Representatives shall be apportioned among the several States according to their respective numbers, counting the whole number of persons in each State, excluding Indians not taxed. But when the right to vote at any election for the choice of Electors for President and Vice-President of the United States, Representatives in Congress, the Executive and Judicial officers of a State, or the members of the Legislature thereof, is denied to any of the male inhabitants of such State, being twenty-one years of age and citizens of the United States, or in any way abridged, except for participation in rebellion, or other crime, the basis of representation therein shall be reduced in the proportion which the number of such male citizens shall bear to the whole number of male citizens twenty-one years of age in such State.

(Disqualification of Confederate officials)

Section 3 No person shall be a Senator or Representative in Congress, or Elector of President and Vice-President, or hold any office, civil or military, under the United States, or under any State, who, having previously taken an oath, as a member of Congress, or as an officer of the United States, or as a member of any State legislature, or as an executive or judicial officer of any State, to support the Constitution of the United States, shall have engaged in insurrection or rebellion against the same, or given aid or comfort to the enemies thereof. Congress may, by a vote of two-thirds of each house, remove such disability.

(Public debts)

Section 4 The validity of the public debt of the United States, authorized by law, including debts incurred for payment of pensions and bounties for services in suppressing insurrection or rebellion, shall not be questioned. But neither the United States nor any State shall assume or pay any debt or obligation incurred in aid of insurrection or rebellion against the United States, or any claim for the loss of emancipation of any slave; but all such debts, obligations, and claims shall be held illegal and void.

(Enforcement)

Section 5 The Congress shall have power to enforce, by appropriate legislation, the provisions of this article.

Amendment XV (Extension of right to vote; adopted 1870)

Section 1 The right of citizens of the United States to vote shall not be denied or abridged by the United States or by any State on account of race, color, or previous condition of servitude.

Section 2 The Congress shall have power to enforce this article by appropriate legislation.

Amendment XVI (Income tax; adopted 1913)

The Congress shall have power to lay and collect taxes on incomes, from whatever source derived, without apportionment among the several States, and without regard to any census or enumeration.

Amendment XVII (Popular election of senators; adopted 1913)

Section 1 The Senate of the United States shall be composed of two Senators from each State, elected by the people thereof, for six years; and each Senator shall have one vote. The electors in each State shall have the qualifications requisite for electors of the most numerous branch of the State legislatures.

Section 2 When vacancies happen in the representation of any State in the Senate, the executive authority of such State shall issue writs of election to fill such vacancies: Provided, that the Legislature of any State may empower the executive thereof to make temporary appointments until the people fill the vacancies by election as the Legislature may direct.

Section 3 This amendment shall not be so construed as to affect the election or term of any Senator chosen before it becomes valid as part of the Constitution.

Amendment XVIII (Prohibition of intoxicating liquors; adopted 1919, repealed 1933)

Section 1 After one year from the ratification of this article the manufacture, sale or transportation of intoxicating liquors within, the importation thereof into, or the exportation thereof from the United States and all territory subject to the jurisdiction thereof, for beverage purposes, is hereby prohibited.

Section 2 The Congress and the several States shall have concurrent power to enforce this article by appropriate legislation.

Section 3 This article shall be inoperative unless it shall have been ratified as an amendment to the Constitution by the legislatures of the several States, as provided by the Constitution, within seven years from the date of the submission thereof to the States by the Congress.

Amendment XIX (Right of women to vote; adopted 1920)

Section 1 The right of citizens of the United States to vote shall not be denied or abridged by the United States or by any State on account of sex.

Section 2 The Congress shall have power to enforce this article by appropriate legislation.

Amendment XX (Commencement of terms of office; adopted 1933)

Section 1 The terms of the President and Vice-President shall end at noon on the 20th day of January, and the terms of Senators and Representatives at noon on the 3d day of January, of the years in which such terms would have ended if this article had not been ratified; and the terms of their successors shall then begin.

Section 2 The Congress shall assemble at least once in every year, and such meetings shall begin at noon on the 3d day of January, unless they shall by law appoint a different day.

(Extension of presidential succession)

Section 3 If, at the time fixed for the beginning of the term of the President, the President-elect shall have died, the Vice-President-elect shall become President. If a President shall not have been chosen before the time fixed for the beginning of his term, or if the President-elect shall have failed to qualify, then the Vice-President-elect shall act as President until a President shall have qualified; and the Congress may by law provide for the case wherein neither a President-elect nor a Vice-President-elect shall have qualified, declaring who shall then act as President, or the manner in which one who is to act shall be selected, and such persons shall act accordingly until a President or Vice-President shall have qualified.

Section 4 The Congress may by law provide for the case of the death of any of the persons from whom the House of Representatives may choose a President whenever the right of choice shall have devolved upon them, and for the case of the death of any of the persons from whom the Senate may choose a Vice-President whenever the right of choice shall have devolved upon them.

Section 5 Sections 1 and 2 shall take effect on the 15th day of October following the ratification of this article.

Section 6 This article shall be inoperative unless it shall have been ratified as an amendment to the

Constitution by the Legislatures of three-fourths of the several States within seven years from the date of its submission.

Amendment XXI (Repeal of Eighteenth Amendment; adopted 1933)

Section 1 The eighteenth article of amendment to the Constitution of the United States is hereby repealed.

Section 2 The transportation or importation into any State, Territory, or Possession of the United States for delivery or use therein of intoxicating liquors, in violation of the laws thereof, is hereby prohibited.

Section 3 This article shall be inoperative unless it shall have been ratified as an amendment to the Constitution by conventions in the several States, as provided in the Constitution, within seven years from the date of submission thereof to the States by the Congress.

Amendment XXII (Limit on presidential tenure; adopted 1951)

Section 1 No person shall be elected to the office of President more than twice, and no person who has held the office of President, or acted as President, for more than two years of a term to which some other person was elected President shall be elected to the office of President more than once. But this article shall not apply to any person holding the office of President when this article was proposed by the Congress, and shall not prevent any person who may be holding the office of President, or acting as President, during the term within which this article becomes operative from holding the office of President or acting as President during the remainder of such term.

Section 2 This article shall be inoperative unless it shall have been ratified as an amendment to the Constitution by the legislatures of three-fourths of the several States within seven years from the date of its submission to the States by the Congress.

Amendment XXIII (Presidential electors for the District of Columbia; adopted 1961)

Section 1 The District constituting the seat of Government of the United States shall appoint in such manner as the Congress may direct:

A number of electors of President and Vice President equal to the whole number of Senators and Representatives in Congress to which the District would be entitled if it were a State, but in no event more than the least populous State; they shall be in addition to those appointed by the States, but they shall be considered for the purposes of the election of President and Vice President, to be electors appointed by a State; and they shall meet in the District and perform such duties as provided by the twelfth article of amendment.

Section 2 The Congress shall have the power to enforce this article by appropriate legislation.

Amendment XXIV (Poll tax outlawed in national elections; adopted 1964)

Section 1 The right of citizens of the United States to vote in any primary or other election for President or Vice President, for electors for President or Vice President, or for Senator or Representative in Congress, shall not be denied or abridged by the United States or any State by reason of failure to pay any poll tax or other tax.

Section 2 The Congress shall have the power to enforce this article by appropriate legislation.

Amendment XXV (Presidential succession; adopted 1967)

Section 1 In case of the removal of the President from office or of his death or resignation, the Vice President shall become President.

(Vice presidential vacancy)

Section 2 Whenever there is a vacancy in the office of the Vice President, the President shall nominate a Vice President who shall take office upon confirmation by a majority vote of both Houses of Congress.

Section 3 Whenever the President transmits to the President pro tempore of the Senate and the Speaker of the House of Representatives his written declaration that he is unable to discharge the powers and duties of his office, and until he transmits to them a written declaration to the contrary, such powers and duties shall be discharged by the Vice President as Acting President.

(Presidential disability)

Section 4 Whenever the Vice President and a majority of either the principal officers of the executive departments or of such other body as Congress may by law provide, transmit to the President pro tempore of the Senate and the Speaker of the House of Representatives their written declaration that the President is unable to discharge the powers and duties of his office, the Vice President shall immediately assume the powers and duties of the office as Acting President.

Thereafter, when the President transmits to the President pro tempore of the Senate and the Speaker of the House of Representatives his written declaration that no inability exists, he shall resume the powers and duties of his office unless the Vice President and a majority of either the principal officers of the executive department(s) or of such other body as Congress may by law provide, transmit within four days to the President pro tempore of the Senate and the Speaker of the House of Representatives their written declaration that the President is unable to discharge the powers and duties of his office. Thereupon Congress shall decide the issue, assembling within forty-eight hours for that purpose if not in session. If the Congress, within twenty-one days after receipt of the latter written declaration, or, if Congress is not in session, within twenty-one days after Congress is required to assemble, determines by two-thirds vote of both Houses that the President is unable to discharge the powers and duties of his office, the Vice President shall continue to discharge the same as Acting President; otherwise, the President shall resume the powers and duties of his office.

Amendment XXVI (Right of eighteen-year-olds to vote; adopted 1971)

Section 1 The right of citizens of the United States, who are eighteen years of age or older, to vote shall not be denied or abridged by the United States or by any State on account of age.

Section 2 The Congress shall have power to enforce this article by appropriate legislation.

Amendment XXVII (Congressional pay raises; adopted 1992)

No law, varying the compensation for the services of the Senators and Representatives shall take effect, until an election of Representatives shall have intervened.

Federalist No. 10   1787

To the People of the State of New York: Among the numerous advantages promised by a well-constructed Union, none deserves to be more accurately developed than its tendency to break and control the violence of faction. The friend of popular governments never finds himself so much alarmed for their character and fate, as when he contemplates their propensity to this dangerous vice. He will not fail, therefore, to set a due value on any plan which, without violating the principles to which he is attached, provides a proper cure for it. The instability, injustice, and confusion introduced into the public councils, have, in truth, been the mortal diseases under which popular governments have everywhere perished; as they continue to be the favourite and fruitful topics from which the adversaries to liberty derive their most specious declamations. The valuable improvements made by the American constitutions on the popular models, both ancient and modern, cannot certainly be too much admired; but it would be an unwarrantable partiality, to contend that they have as effectually obviated the danger on this side, as was wished and expected. Complaints are everywhere heard from our most considerate and virtuous citizens, equally the friends of public and private faith, and of public and personal liberty, that our governments are too unstable; that the public good is disregarded in the conflicts of rival parties; and that measures are too often decided, not according to the rules of justice, and the rights of the minor party, but by the superior force of an interested and overbearing majority. However anxiously we may wish that these complaints had no foundation, the evidence of known facts will not permit us to deny that they are in some degree true. It will be found, indeed, on a candid review of our situation, that some of the distresses under which we labor have been erroneously charged on the operation of our governments; but it will be found, at the same time, that other causes will not alone account for many of our heaviest misfortunes; and, particularly, for that prevailing and increasing distrust of public engagements, and alarm for private rights, which are echoed from one end of the continent to the other. These must be chiefly, if not wholly, effects of the unsteadiness and injustice, with which a factious spirit has tainted our public administrations.

By a faction, I understand a number of citizens, whether amounting to a majority or minority of the whole, who are united and actuated by some common impulse of passion, or of interest, adverse to the rights of other citizens, or to the permanent and aggregate interests of the community.

There are two methods of curing the mischiefs of faction: The one, by removing its causes; the other, by controlling its effects.

There are again two methods of removing the causes of faction: The one, by destroying the liberty which is essential to its existence; the other, by giving to every citizen the same opinions, the same passions, and the same interests.

It could never be more truly said, than of the first remedy, that it was worse than the disease. Liberty is to faction what air is to fire, an ailment without which it instantly expires. But it could not be a less folly to abolish liberty, which is essential to political life, because it nourishes faction, than it would be to wish the annihilation of air, which is essential to animal life, because it imparts to fire its destructive agency.

The second expedient is as impracticable, as the first would be unwise. As long as the reason of man continues fallible, and he is at liberty to exercise it, different opinions will be formed. As long as the connection subsists between his reason and his self-love, his opinions and his passions will have a reciprocal influence on each other; and the former will be objects to which the latter will attach themselves. The diversity in the faculties of men, from which the rights of property originate, is not less an insuperable obstacle to an uniformity of interests. The protection of these faculties is the first object of government. From the protection of different and unequal faculties of acquiring property, the possession of different degrees and kinds of property immediately results; and from the influence of these on the sentiments and views of the respective proprietors, ensues a division of the society into different interests and parties.

The latent causes of faction are thus sown in the nature of man; and we see them everywhere brought into different degrees of activity, according to the different circumstances of civil society. A zeal for different opinions concerning religion, concerning government, and many other points, as well as of speculation as of practice; an attachment to different leaders ambitiously contending for preeminence and power; or to persons of other descriptions whose fortunes have been interesting to the human passions, have, in turn, divided mankind into parties, inflamed them with mutual animosity, and rendered them much more disposed to vex and oppress each other, than to cooperate for their common good. So strong is this propensity of mankind, to fall into mutual animosities, that where no substantial occasion presents itself, the most frivolous and fanciful distinctions have been sufficient to kindle their unfriendly passions and excite their most violent conflicts. But the most common and durable source of factions has been the various and unequal distribution of property. Those who hold and those who are without property have ever formed distinct interests in society. Those who are creditors, and those who are debtors, fall under alike discrimination. A landed interest, a manufacturing interest, a mercantile interest, a moneyed interest, with many lesser interests, grow up of necessity in civilized nations, and divide them into different classes, actuated by different sentiments and views. The regulation of these various and interfering interests forms the principal task of modern legislation, and involves the spirit of the party and faction in the necessary and ordinary operations of the government.

No man is allowed to be a judge in his own cause; because his interest will certainly bias his judgment, and, not improbably, corrupt his integrity. With equal, nay with greater reason, a body of men are unfit to be both judges and parties at the same time; yet what are many of the most important acts of legislation, but so many judicial determinations, not indeed concerning the right of single persons, but concerning the rights of large bodies of citizens? And what are the different classes of legislators, but advocates and parties to the causes which they determine? Is a law proposed concerning private debts? It is a question to which the creditors are parties on one side, and the debtors on the other. Justice ought to hold the balance between them. Yet the parties are, and must be, themselves the judges; and the most numerous party, or, in other words, the most powerful faction, must be expected to prevail. Shall domestic manufactures be encouraged, and in what degree, by restrictions on foreign manufactures? are questions which would be differently decided by the landed and the manufacturing classes; and probably by neither with a sole regard to justice and the public good. The apportionment of taxes, on the various descriptions of property, is an act which seems to require the most exact impartiality; yet there is, perhaps, no legislative act, in which greater opportunity and temptation are

given to a predominant party to trample on the rules of justice. Every shilling, with which they overburden the inferior number, is a shilling saved to their own pockets.

It is in vain to say, that enlightened statesmen will be able to adjust these clashing interests, and render them all subservient to the public good. Enlightened statesmen will not always be at the helm: nor, in many cases, can such an adjustment be made at all, without taking into view indirect and remote considerations, which will rarely prevail over the immediate interest which one party may find in disregarding the rights of another, or the good of the whole.

The inference to which we are brought is, that the *causes* of faction cannot be removed; and that relief is only to be sought in the means of controlling its *effects*.

If a faction consists of less than a majority, relief is supplied by the republican principle, which enables the majority to defeat its sinister views, by regular vote. It may clog the administration, it may convulse the society; but it will be unable to execute and mask its violence under the forms of the constitution. When a majority is included in a faction, the form of popular government, on the other hand, enables it to sacrifice to its ruling passion or interest, both the public good and the rights of other citizens. To secure the public good, and private rights, against the danger of such a faction, and at the same time to preserve the spirit and the form of popular government, is then the great object to which our inquiries are directed. Let me add, that it is the great desideratum by which alone this form of government can be rescued from the opprobrium under which it has so long labored, and be recommended to the esteem and adoption of mankind.

By what means is this object attainable? Evidently by one of two only. Either the existence of the same passion or interest in a majority, at the same time, must be prevented; or the majority, having such coexistent passion or interest, must be rendered, by their number and local situation, unable to concert and carry into effect schemes of oppression. If the impulse and the opportunity be suffered to coincide, we well know that neither moral nor religious motives can be relied on as an adequate control. They are not found to be such on the injustice and violence of individuals, and lose their efficacy in proportion to the number combined together; that is, in proportion as their efficacy becomes needful.

From this view of the subject, it may be concluded, that a pure democracy, by which I mean a society consisting of a small number of citizens, who assemble and administer the government in person, can admit of no cure for the mischiefs of faction. A common passion or interest will, in almost every case, be felt by a majority of the whole; a communication and concert, results from the form of government itself; and there is nothing to check the inducements to sacrifice the weaker party, or an obnoxious individual. Hence, it is, that such democracies have ever been spectacles of turbulence and contention; have ever been found incompatible with personal security, or the rights of property; and have in general been as short in their lives, as they have been violent in their deaths. Theoretic politicians, who have patronized this species of government, have erroneously supposed, that by reducing mankind to a perfect equality in their political rights, they would, at the same time, be perfectly equalized and assimilated in their possessions, their opinions, and their passions.

A republic, by which I mean a government in which the scheme of representation takes place, opens a different prospect, and promises the cure for which we are seeking. Let us examine the points in which it varies from pure democracy, and we shall comprehend both the nature of the cure and the efficacy which it must derive from the union.

The two great points of difference, between a democracy and a republic, are: first, the delegation of the government, in the latter, to a small number of citizens, elected by the rest; secondly, the greatest number of citizens, and greater sphere of country, over which the latter may be extended.

The effect of the first difference is, on the one hand, to refine and enlarge the public views, by passing them through the medium of a chosen body of citizens, whose wisdom may best discern the true interest of their country, and whose patriotism and love of justice, will be least likely to sacrifice it to temporary or partial considerations. Under such a regulation, it may well happen, that the public voice, pronounced by the representatives of the people, will be more consonant to the public good, than if pronounced by the people themselves, convened for the purpose. On the other hand, the effect may be inverted. Men of factious tempers, of local prejudices, or of sinister designs, may by intrigue, by corruption, or by other means, first obtain the suffrages, and then betray the interest of the people. The question resulting is, whether small or extensive republics are most favourable to the election of proper guardians of the public weal; and it is clearly decided in favour of the latter by two obvious considerations.

In the first place, it is to be remarked that, however small the republic may be, the representatives must be raised to a certain number, in order to guard against the cabals of a few; and that however large it may be, they must be limited to a certain number, in order to guard against the confusion of a multitude. Hence, the number of representatives in the two cases not being in proportion to that of the constituents, and being proportionally greatest in the small republic, it follows, that if the proportion of fit characters be not less in the large than in the small republic, the former will present a greater option, and consequently a greater probability of a fit choice.

In the next place, as each representative will be chosen by a greater number of citizens in the large than in the small republic, it will be more difficult for unworthy candidates to practise with success the vicious arts, by which elections are too often carried; and the suffrages of the people being more free, will be more likely to centre in men who possess the most attractive merit, and the most diffusive and established characters.

It must be confessed that in this, as in most other cases, there is a mean, on both sides of which inconveniences will be found to lie. By enlarging too much the number of electors, you render the representatives too little acquainted with all their local circumstances and lesser interests; as by reducing it too much, you render him unduly attached to these, and too little fit to comprehend and pursue great and national objects. The federal Constitution forms a happy combination being referred to the national, the local and particular to the state legislatures.

The other point of difference is, the greater number of citizens, and extent of territory, which may be brought within the compass of republican, than of democratic government; and it is this circumstance principally which renders factious combinations less to be dreaded in the former, than in the latter. The smaller the society, the fewer probably will be the distinct parties and interests composing it; the fewer the distinct parties and interests, the more frequently will a majority be found of the same party; and the smaller the number of individuals composing a majority, and the smaller the compass within which they are placed, the more easily will they concert and execute their plans of oppression. Extend the sphere and you take in a greater variety of parties and interests; you make it less probable that a majority of the whole will have a common motive to invade the rights of other citizens; or if such a common motive exists, it will be more difficult for all who feel it to discover their own strength, and to act in unison with each other. Besides other impediments, it may be remarked, that where there is a consciousness of unjust or dishonourable purposes, communication is always checked by distrust, in proportion to the number whose concurrence is necessary.

Hence, it clearly appears, that the same advantage, which a republic has over a democracy, in controlling the effects of faction, is enjoyed by a large over a small republic,—is enjoyed by the Union over the States composing it. Does this advantage consist in the substitution of representatives whose enlightened views and virtuous sentiments render them superior to local prejudices, and to schemes of injustice? It will not be denied that the representation of the Union will be most likely to possess these requisite endowments. Does it consist in the greater security afforded by a greater variety of parties, against the event of any one party being able to outnumber and oppress the rest? In an equal degree does the increased variety of parties, comprised within the Union, increase the security? Does it, in fine, consist in the greater obstacles opposed to the concert and accomplishment of the secret wishes of an unjust and interested majority? Here, again, the extent of the Union gives it the most palpable advantage.

The influence of factious leaders may kindle a flame within their particular States, but will be unable to spread a general conflagration through the other States. A religious sect may degenerate into a political faction in a part of the confederacy; but the variety of sects dispersed over the entire face of it, must secure the national councils against any danger from that source. A rage for paper money, for an abolition of debts, for an equal division of property, or for any other improper or wicked project, will be less apt to pervade the whole body of the Union than a particular member of it; in the same proportion as such a malady is more likely to taint a particular county or district, than an entire State.

In the extent and proper structure of the Union, therefore, we behold a republican remedy for the diseases most incident to republican government. And according to the degree of pleasure and pride we feel in being republicans, ought to be our zeal in cherishing the spirit, and supporting the character of Federalists.

JAMES MADISON

Federalist No. 51   1788

To the People of the State of New York: To what expedient, then, shall we finally resort for maintaining in practice the necessary partition of power among the several departments, as laid down in the Constitution? The only answer that can be given is, that as all these exterior provisions are found to be inadequate, the defect must be supplied, by so contriving the interior structure of the government, as that its several constituent parts may, by their mutual relations, be the means of keeping each other in their proper places. Without presuming to undertake a full development of this important idea, I will hazard a few general observations, which may perhaps place it in a clearer light, and enable us to form a more correct judgment of the principles and structure of the government planned by the convention.

In order to lay a due foundation for that separate and distinct exercise of the different powers of government, which to a certain extent, is admitted on all hands to be essential to the preservation of liberty, it is evident that each department should have a will of its own; and consequently should be so constituted, that the members of each should have as little agency as possible in the appointment of the members of the others. Were this principle rigorously adhered to, it would require that all the appointments for the supreme executive, legislative, and judiciary magistracies, should be drawn from the same fountain of authority, the people, through channels, having no communication whatever with one another. Perhaps such a plan of constructing the several departments would be less difficult in practice than it may in contemplation appear. Some difficulties, however, and some additional expense would attend the execution of it. Some deviations, therefore, from the principle must be admitted. In the constitution of the judiciary department in particular, it might be inexpedient to insist rigorously on the principle; first, because peculiar qualifications being essential in the members, the primary consideration ought to be to select that mode of choice, which best secures these qualifications; secondly, because the permanent tenure by which the appointments are held in that department, must soon destroy all sense of dependence on the authority conferring them.

It is equally evident that the members of each department should be as little dependent as possible on those of the others, for the emoluments annexed to their offices. Were the executive magistrate, or the judges, not independent of the legislature in this particular, their independence in every other would be merely nominal.

But the great security against a gradual concentration of the several powers in the same department, consists in giving to those who administer each department, the necessary constitutional means, and personal motives, to resist encroachments of the others. The provision for defense must in this, as in all other cases, be made commensurate to the danger of attack. Ambition must be made to counteract ambition. The interest of the man must be connected with the constitutional rights of the place. It may be a reflection on human nature, that such devices should be necessary to control the abuses of government. But what is government itself, but the greatest of all reflections on human nature? If men were angels, no government would be necessary. If angels were to govern men, neither external nor internal controls on government would be necessary. In framing a government which is to be administered by men over men, the great difficulty lies in this: you must first enable the government to control the governed; and in the next place, oblige it to control itself. A dependence on the people is, no doubt, the primary control on the government; but experience has taught mankind the necessity of auxiliary precautions.

This policy of supplying by opposite and rival interests, the defect of better motives, might be traced through the whole system of human affairs, private as well as public. We see it particularly displayed in all the subordinate distributions of power, where the constant aim is to divide and arrange the several offices in such a manner as that each may be a check on the other—that the private interest of every individual, may be a sentinel over the public rights. These inventions of prudence cannot be less requisite in the distribution of the supreme powers of the State.

But it is not possible to give to each department an equal power of self-defense. In republican government, the legislative authority necessarily predominates. The remedy for this inconveniency is to divide the legislature into different branches; and to render them by different modes of election, and different principles of action, as little connected with each other, as the nature of their common functions, and their common dependence on the society, will admit. It may even be necessary to guard against dangerous encroachments by still further precautions. As the weight of the legislative authority requires that it should be thus divided, the weakness of the executive may require, on the other hand, that it should be fortified. An absolute negative, on the legislature, appears, at first view, to be the natural defence with which the executive magistrate should be armed. But perhaps it would be neither altogether safe nor alone sufficient. On ordinary occasions, it might not be exerted with the requisite firmness, and on extraordinary occasions it might be perfidiously abused. May not this defect of an absolute negative be supplied by some qualified connection between this weaker department, and the weaker branch of the stronger department, by which the latter may be led to support the constitutional rights of the former, without being too much detached from the rights of its own department?

If the principles on which these observations are founded be just, as I persuade myself they are, and they be applied as a criterion, to the several State constitutions, and to the federal Constitution, it will be found, that if the latter does not perfectly correspond with them, the former are infinitely less able to bear such a test.

There are, moreover, two considerations particularly applicable to the federal system of America, which place that system in a very interesting point of view.

First. In a single republic, all the power surrendered by the people is submitted to the administration of a single government; and usurpations are guarded against by a division of the government into distinct and separate departments. In the compound republic of America, the power surrendered by the people, is first divided between two distinct governments, and then the portion allotted to each, subdivided among distinct and separate departments. Hence a double security arises to the rights of the people. The different governments will control each other, at the same time that each will be controlled by itself.

Second. It is of great importance in a republic, not only to guard the society against the oppression of its rulers; but to guard one part of the society against the injustice of the other part. Different interests necessarily exist in different classes of citizens. If a majority be united by a common interest, the rights of the minority will be insecure. There are but two methods of providing against this evil: The one by creating a will in the community independent of the majority—that is, of the society itself; the other, by comprehending in the society so many separate descriptions of citizens as will render an unjust combination of a majority of the whole very improbable, if not impracticable. The first method prevails in all governments possessing an hereditary or self-appointed authority. This at best is but a precarious security; because a power independent of the society may as well espouse the unjust views of the major, as the rightful interests of the minor party, and may possibly be turned against both parties. The second method will be exemplified in the federal republic of the United States. Whilst all authority in it will be derived from and dependent on the society, the society itself will be broken into so many parts, interests and classes of citizens, that the rights of individuals or of the minority, will be in little danger from interested combinations of the majority. In a free government, the security for civil rights must be the same as for religious rights. It consists in the one case in the multiplicity of sects. The degree of security in both cases will depend on the number of interests and sects; and this may be presumed to depend on the extent of country and number of people comprehended under the same government. This view of the subject must particularly recommend a proper federal system to all the sincere and considerate friends of republican government, since it shows that in exact proportion as the territory of the Union may be formed into more circumscribed Confederacies, or States, oppressive combinations of a majority will be facilitated; the best security under the republican forms, for the rights of every class of citizens, will be diminished; and consequently, the stability and independence of some member of the government, the only other security, must be proportionally increased. Justice is the end of government. It is the end of civil society. It ever has been, and ever will be pursued, until it be obtained, or until liberty be lost in the pursuit. In a society under the forms of which the stronger faction can readily unite and oppress the weaker, anarchy may as truly be said to reign, as in a state of nature where the weaker individual is not secured against the violence of the stronger; and as, in the latter state, even the stronger individuals are prompted, by the uncertainty of their condition, to submit to a government which may protect the weak as well as themselves, so in the former state, will the more powerful factions or parties be gradually induced, by a like motive, to wish for a government which will protect all parties, the weaker as well as the more powerful. It can be little doubted, that if the State of Rhode Island was separated from the Confederacy and left to itself, the insecurity of rights under the popular form of government within such narrow limits would be displayed by such reiterated oppressions of factious majorities that some power altogether independent of the people would soon be called for by the voice of the very factions whose misrule had proved the necessity of it. In the extended republic of the United States, and among the great variety of interests, parties and sects which it embraces, a coalition of a majority of the whole society could seldom take place on any other principles than those of justice and the general good; whilst there being thus less danger to a minor from the will of the major party, there must be less pretext, also, to provide for the security of the former, by introducing into the government a will not dependent on the latter, or, in other words, a will independent of the society itself. It is no less certain than it is important, notwithstanding the contrary opinions which have been entertained, that the larger the society, provided it lie within a practicable sphere, the more duly capable it will be of self-government. And happily for the *republican cause,* the practicable sphere may be carried to a very great extent, by a judicious modification and mixture of the *federal principle.*

JAMES MADISON

Presidents of the United States

President	Party	Term
1. George Washington (1732–1799)	Federalist	1789–1797
2. John Adams (1734–1826)	Federalist	1797–1801
3. Thomas Jefferson (1743–1826)	Democratic-Republican	1801–1809
4. James Madison (1751–1836)	Democratic-Republican	1809–1817
5. James Monroe (1758–1831)	Democratic-Republican	1817–1825
6. John Quincy Adams (1767–1848)	Democratic-Republican	1825–1829
7. Andrew Jackson (1767–1845)	Democratic	1829–1837
8. Martin Van Buren (1782–1862)	Democratic	1837–1841
9. William Henry Harrison (1773–1841)	Whig	1841
10. John Tyler (1790–1862)	Whig	1841–1845
11. James K. Polk (1795–1849)	Democratic	1845–1849
12. Zachary Taylor (1784–1850)	Whig	1849–1850
13. Millard Fillmore (1800–1874)	Whig	1850–1853
14. Franklin Pierce (1804–1869)	Democratic	1853–1857
15. James Buchanan (1791–1868)	Democratic	1857–1861
16. Abraham Lincoln (1809–1865)	Republican	1861–1865
17. Andrew Johnson (1808–1875)	Union	1865–1869
18. Ulysses S. Grant (1822–1885)	Republican	1869–1877
19. Rutherford B. Hayes (1822–1893)	Republican	1877–1881
20. James A. Garfield (1831–1881)	Republican	1881
21. Chester A. Arthur (1830–1886)	Republican	1881–1885
22. Grover Cleveland (1837–1908)	Democratic	1885–1889
23. Benjamin Harrison (1833–1901)	Republican	1889–1893
24. Grover Cleveland (1837–1908)	Democratic	1893–1897
25. William McKinley (1843–1901)	Republican	1897–1901
26. Theodore Roosevelt (1858–1919)	Republican	1901–1909
27. William Howard Taft (1857–1930)	Republican	1909–1913
28. Woodrow Wilson (1856–1924)	Democratic	1913–1921
29. Warren G. Harding (1865–1923)	Republican	1921–1923
30. Calvin Coolidge (1871–1933)	Republican	1923–1929
31. Herbert Hoover (1874–1964)	Republican	1929–1933
32. Franklin Delano Roosevelt (1882–1945)	Democratic	1933–1945
33. Harry S Truman (1884–1972)	Democratic	1945–1953
34. Dwight D. Eisenhower (1890–1969)	Republican	1953–1961
35. John F. Kennedy (1917–1963)	Democratic	1961–1963
36. Lyndon B. Johnson (1908–1973)	Democratic	1963–1969
37. Richard M. Nixon (1913–1994)	Republican	1969–1974
38. Gerald R. Ford (b. 1913)	Republican	1974–1977
39. Jimmy Carter (b. 1924)	Democratic	1977–1981
40. Ronald Reagan (b. 1911)	Republican	1981–1989
41. George H. W. Bush (b. 1924)	Republican	1989–1993
42. Bill Clinton (b. 1946)	Democratic	1993–2001
43. George W. Bush (b. 1946)	Republican	2001–

Twentieth and Twenty-First Century Justices of the Supreme Court

Justice*	Term of Service	Years of Service	Life Span	Justice*	Term of Service	Years of Service	Life Span
Oliver W. Holmes	1902–1932	30	1841–1935	Wiley B. Rutledge	1943–1949	6	1894–1949
William R. Day	1903–1922	19	1849–1923	Harold H. Burton	1945–1958	13	1888–1964
William H. Moody	1906–1910	3	1853–1917	*Fred M. Vinson*	1946–1953	7	1890–1953
Horace H. Lurton	1910–1914	4	1844–1914	Tom C. Clark	1949–1967	18	1899–1977
Charles E. Hughes	1910–1916	5	1862–1948	Sherman Minton	1949–1956	7	1890–1965
Willis Van Devanter	1911–1937	26	1859–1941	*Earl Warren*	1953–1969	16	1891–1974
Joseph R. Lamar	1911–1916	5	1857–1916	John Marshall Harlan	1955–1971	16	1899–1971
Edward D. White	1910–1921	11	1845–1921	William J. Brennan, Jr.	1956–1990	34	1906–1997
Mahlon Pitney	1912–1922	10	1858–1924	Charles E. Whittaker	1957–1962	5	1901–1973
James C. McReynolds	1914–1941	26	1862–1946	Potter Stewart	1958–1981	23	1915–1985
Louis D. Brandeis	1916–1939	22	1856–1941	Byron R. White	1962–1993	31	1917–
John H. Clarke	1916–1922	6	1857–1930	Arthur J. Goldberg	1962–1965	3	1908–1990
William H. Taft	1921–1930	8	1857–1945	Abe Fortas	1965–1969	4	1910–1982
George Sutherland	1922–1938	15	1862–1942	Thurgood Marshall	1967–1991	24	1908–1993
Pierce Butler	1922–1939	16	1866–1939	*Warren E. Burger*	1969–1986	17	1907–1995
Edward T. Sandford	1923–1930	7	1865–1930	Harry A. Blackmun	1970–1994	24	1908–
Harlan F. Stone	1925–1941	16	1872–1946	Lewis F. Powell, Jr.	1972–1987	15	1907–1998
Charles E. Hughes	1930–1941	11	1862–1948	William H. Rehnquist	1972–1986	14	1924–
Owen J. Roberts	1930–1945	15	1875–1955	John P. Stevens	1975–	—	1920–
Benjamin N. Cardozo	1932–1938	6	1870–1938	Sandra Day O'Connor	1981–	—	1930–
Hugo L. Black	1937–1971	34	1886–1971	*William H. Rehnquist*	1986–	—	1924–
Stanley F. Reed	1938–1957	19	1884–1980	Antonin Scalia	1986–	—	1936–
Felix Frankfurter	1939–1962	23	1882–1965	Anthony M. Kennedy	1988–	—	1936–
William O. Douglas	1939–1975	36	1898–1980	David H. Souter	1990–	—	1939–
Frank Murphy	1940–1949	9	1890–1949	Clarence Thomas	1991–	—	1948–
Harlan F. Stone	1941–1946	5	1872–1946	Ruth Bader Ginsburg	1993–	—	1933–
James F. Byrnes	1941–1942	1	1879–1972	Stephen G. Breyer	1994–	—	1938–
Robert H. Jackson	1941–1954	13	1892–1954				

* The names of chief justices are printed in italic type.

Party Control of the Presidency, Senate, and House of Representatives   1901–2001

Congress	Years	President	Senate D	R	Other*	House D	R	Other*
57th	1901–1903	McKinley T. Roosevelt	31	55	4	151	197	9
58th	1903–1905	T. Roosevelt	33	57	—	178	208	—
59th	1905–1907	T. Roosevelt	33	57	—	136	250	—
60th	1907–1909	T. Roosevelt	31	61	—	164	222	—
61st	1909–1911	Taft	32	61	—	172	219	—
62d	1911–1913	Taft	41	51	—	228	161	1
63d	1913–1915	Wilson	51	44	1	291	127	17
64th	1915–1917	Wilson	56	40	—	230	196	9
65th	1917–1919	Wilson	53	42	—	216	10	6
66th	1919–1921	Wilson	47	49	—	190	240	3
67th	1921–1923	Harding	37	59	—	131	301	1
68th	1923–1925	Coolidge	43	51	2	205	225	5
69th	1925–1927	Coolidge	39	56	1	183	247	4
70th	1927–1929	Coolidge	46	49	1	195	237	3
71st	1929–1931	Hoover	39	56	1	167	267	1
72d	1931–1933	Hoover	47	48	1	220	214	1
73d	1933–1935	F. Roosevelt	60	35	1	319	117	5
74th	1935–1937	F. Roosevelt	69	25	2	319	103	10
75th	1937–1939	F. Roosevelt	76	16	4	331	89	13
76th	1939–1941	F. Roosevelt	69	23	4	261	164	4
77th	1941–1943	F. Roosevelt	66	28	2	268	162	5
78th	1943–1945	F. Roosevelt	58	37	1	218	208	4
79th	1945–1947	Truman	56	38	1	242	190	2
80th	1947–1949	Truman	45	51	—	188	245	1
81st	1949–1951	Truman	54	42	—	263	171	1
82d	1951–1953	Truman	49	47	—	234	199	1
83d	1953–1955	Eisenhower	47	48	1	211	221	—
84th	1955–1957	Eisenhower	48	47	1	232	203	—
85th	1957–1959	Eisenhower	49	47	—	233	200	—
86th**	1959–1961	Eisenhower	65	35	—	284	153	—
87th**	1961–1963	Kennedy	65	35	—	263	174	—
88th	1963–1965	Kennedy Johnson	67	33	—	258	177	—

Sources: Department of Commerce, Bureau of the Census, *Statistical Abstract of the United States* (Washington, D.C.: U.S. Government Printing Office, 1980), p. 509, and *Members of Congress Since 1789*, 2d ed. (Washington, D.C.: Congressional Quarterly Press, 1981), pp. 176–177. Adapted from Barbara Hinckley, *Congressional Elections* (Washington, D.C.: Congressional Quarterly Press, 1981), pp. 144–145.
* Excludes vacancies at beginning of each session.
** The 437 members of the House in the 86th and 87th Congresses is attributable to the at-large representative given to both Alaska (January 3, 1959) and Hawaii (August 2, 1959) prior to redistricting in 1962.

Party Control of the Presidency, Senate, and House of Representatives   1901–2001 *(continued)*

Congress	Years	President	Senate			House		
			D	R	Other*	D	R	Other*
89th	1965–1967	Johnson	68	32	—	295	140	—
90th	1967–1969	Johnson	64	36	—	247	187	—
91st	1969–1971	Nixon	57	43	—	243	192	—
92d	1971–1973	Nixon	54	44	2	254	180	—
93d	1973–1975	Nixon Ford	56	42	2	239	192	1
94th	1975–1977	Ford	60	37	2	291	144	—
95th	1977–1979	Carter	61	38	1	292	143	—
96th	1979–1981	Carter	58	41	1	276	157	—
97th	1981–1983	Reagan	46	53	1	243	192	—
98th	1983–1985	Reagan	45	55	—	267	168	—
99th	1985–1987	Reagan	47	53	—	252	183	—
100th	1987–1989	Reagan	54	46	—	257	178	—
101st	1989–1991	Bush, G. H. W.	55	45	—	262	173	—
102d	1991–1993	Bush, G. H. W.	56	44	—	276	167	—
103d	1993–1995	Clinton	56	44	—	256	178	1
104th	1995–1997	Clinton	47	53	—	204	230	1
105th	1997–1999	Clinton	45	55	—	206	228	—
106th	1999–2001	Clinton	45	55	—	211	223	—
107th	2001–	Bush, G. W.	50	49	1	210	221	2

administrative discretion   The latitude that Congress gives agencies to make policy in the spirit of their legislative mandate. (13)

affirmative action   Any of a wide range of programs, from special recruitment efforts to numerical quotas, aimed at expanding opportunities for women and minority groups. (16)

agenda building   The process by which new issues are brought into the political limelight. (10)

agenda setting   The stage of the policymaking process during which problems get defined as political issues. (17)

aggregate demand   The money available to be spent for goods and services by consumers, businesses, and government. (18)

amicus curiae brief   A brief filed (with the permission of the court) by an individual or group that is not a party to a legal action but has an interest in it. (14)

anarchism   A political philosophy that opposes government in any form. (1)

appellate jurisdiction   The authority of a court to hear cases that have been tried, decided, or reexamined in other courts. (14)

appropriations committees   Committees of Congress that decide which of the programs passed by the authorization committees will actually be funded. (18)

argument   The heart of a judicial opinion; its logical content separated from facts, rhetoric, and procedure. (14)

Articles of Confederation   The compact among the thirteen original states that established the first government of the United States. (3)

attentive policy elites   Leaders who follow news in specific policy areas. (6)

authorization committees   Committees of Congress that can authorize spending in their particular areas of responsibility. (18)

autocracy   A system of government in which the power to govern is concentrated in the hands of one individual. Also called *monarchy*. (2)

Balanced Budget Act (BBA)   A 1997 law that promised to balance the budget by 2002. (18)

big emerging markets (BEMs)   Rapidly growing international markets that are especially promising for the United States. (20)

bill of attainder   A law that pronounces an individual guilty of a crime without a trial. (15)

Bill of Rights   The first ten amendments to the Constitution. They prevent the national government from tampering with fundamental rights and civil liberties, and emphasize the limited character of national power. (3)

bimodal distribution   A distribution (of opinions) that shows two responses being chosen about as frequently as each other. (5)

black codes   Legislation enacted by former slave states to restrict the freedom of blacks. (16)

blanket primary   A primary election in which voters receive a ballot containing both parties' potential nominees and can help nominate candidates for all offices for both parties. (9)

block grant   A grant-in-aid awarded for general purposes, allowing the recipient great discretion in spending the grant money. (4)

boycott   A refusal to do business with a firm, individual, or nation as an expression of disapproval or as a means of coercion. (16)

budget authority   The amounts that government agencies are authorized to spend for their programs. (18)

budget committees   One committee in each house of Congress that supervises a comprehensive budget review process. (18)

Budget Enforcement Act (BEA)   A 1990 law that distinguished between mandatory and discretionary spending. (18)

budget outlays   The amounts that government agencies are expected to spend in the fiscal year. (18)

bureaucracy   A large, complex organization in which employees have specific job responsibilities and work within a hierarchy of authority. (13)

bureaucrat   An employee of a bureaucracy, usually meaning a government bureaucracy. (13)

business cycle   Expansions and contractions of business activity, the first accompanied by inflation and the second by unemployment. (18)

cabinet   A group of presidential advisers; the heads of the executive departments and other key officials. (12)

capitalism   The system of government that favors free enterprise (privately owned businesses operating without government regulation). (1)

casework   Solving problems for constituents, especially problems involving government agencies. (11)

categorical grant   A grant-in-aid targeted for a specific purpose either by formula or by project. (4)

caucus   A closed meeting of the members of a political party to decide upon questions of policy and the selection of candidates for office. (8)

checks and balances   A government structure that gives each branch some scrutiny and control over the other branches. (3)

citizen group   Lobbying organization built around policy concerns unrelated to members' vocational interests. (10)

civil case   A court case that involves a private dispute arising from such matters as accidents, contractual obligations, and divorce. (14)

civil disobedience   The willful but nonviolent breach of laws that are regarded as unjust. (16)

civil liberties   Freedoms guaranteed to individuals. (15)

civil rights   Powers or privileges guaranteed to individuals and protected from arbitrary removal at the hands of government or individuals. (15, 16)

civil rights movement   The mass mobilization during the 1960s that sought to gain equality of rights and opportunities for blacks in the South and to a lesser extent in the North, mainly through nonviolent unconventional means of participation. Martin Luther King, Jr., was the leading figure and symbol of the civil rights movement, but it was powered by the commitment of great numbers of people, black and white, of all sorts and stations in life. (16)

civil service   The system by which most appointments to the federal bureaucracy are made, to ensure that government jobs are filled on the basis of merit and that employees are not fired for political reasons. (13)

A25

class action A procedure by which similarly situated litigants may be heard in a single lawsuit. (14)

class-action suit A legal action brought by a person or group on behalf of a number of people in similar circumstances. (7)

clear and present danger test A means by which the Supreme Court has distinguished between speech as the advocacy of ideas, which is protected by the First Amendment, and speech as incitement, which is not protected. (15)

closed primary A primary election in which voters must declare their party affiliation before they are given the primary ballot containing that party's potential nominees. (9)

cloture The mechanism by which a filibuster is cut off in the Senate. (11)

coalition building The banding together of several interest groups for the purpose of lobbying. (10)

Cold War A prolonged period of adversarial relations between the two superpowers, the United States and the Soviet Union. During the Cold War, which lasted from the late 1940s to the late 1980s, many crises and confrontations brought the superpowers to the brink of war, but they avoided direct military conflict with each other. (20)

commerce clause The third clause of Article I, Section 8, of the Constitution, which gives Congress the power to regulate commerce among the states. (4)

common (judge-made) law Legal precedents derived from previous judicial decisions. (14)

communism A political system in which, in theory, ownership of all land and productive facilities is in the hands of the people, and all goods are equally shared. The production and distribution of goods are controlled by an authoritarian government. (1)

communitarians Those who are willing to use government to promote both order and equality. (1)

comparative advantage A principle of international trade that states that all nations will benefit when each nation specializes in those goods that it can produce most efficiently. (20)

concurrence The agreement of a judge with the court's majority decision, for a reason other than the majority reason. (14)

confederation A loose association of independent states that agree to cooperate on specified matters. (3)

conference committee A temporary committee created to work out differences between the House and Senate versions of a specific piece of legislation. (11)

Congressional Budget Office (CBO) The budgeting arm of Congress, which prepares alternative budgets to those prepared by the president's OMB. (18)

congressional campaign committee An organization maintained by a political party to raise funds to support its own candidates in congressional elections. (8)

conservatives Those who are willing to use government to promote order but not equality. (1)

constituents People who live and vote in a government official's district or state. (11)

containment The basic U.S. policy toward the Soviet Union during the Cold War, according to which the Soviets were to be contained within existing boundaries by military, diplomatic, and economic means, in the expectation that the Soviet system would decay and disintegrate. (20)

conventional participation Relatively routine political behavior that uses institutional channels and is acceptable to the dominant culture. (7)

cooperative federalism A view that holds that the Constitution is an agreement among people who are citizens of both state and nation, so there is little distinction between state powers and national powers. (4)

Council of Economic Advisers (CEA) A group that works within the executive branch to provide advice on maintaining a stable economy. (18)

county government The government unit that administers a county. (4)

criminal case A court case involving a crime, or violation of public order. (14)

critical election An election that produces a sharp change in the existing pattern of party loyalties among groups of voters. (8)

Declaration of Independence Drafted by Thomas Jefferson, the document that proclaimed the right of the colonies to separate from Great Britain. (3)

de facto segregation Segregation that is not the result of government influence. (16)

deficit financing The Keynesian technique of spending beyond government income to combat an economic slump. Its purpose is to inject extra money into the economy to stimulate aggregate demand. (18)

de jure segregation Government-imposed segregation. (16)

delegate A legislator whose primary responsibility is to represent the majority view of his or her constituents, regardless of his or her own view. (11)

delegation of powers The process by which Congress gives the executive branch the additional authority needed to address new problems. (12)

deliberative democracy That model of democracy in which citizens and their elected representatives exercise reasoned and full debate on questions of public policy. (2)

democracy A system of government in which, in theory, the people rule, either directly or indirectly. (2)

democratic socialism A socialist form of government that guarantees civil liberties such as freedom of speech and religion. Citizens determine the extent of government activity through free elections and competitive political parties. (1)

democratization A process of transition as a country attempts to move from an authoritarian form of government to a democratic one. (2)

department The biggest unit of the executive branch, covering a broad area of government responsibility. The heads of the departments, or secretaries, form the president's cabinet. (13)

deregulation A bureaucratic reform by which the government reduces its role as a regulator of business. (13)

descriptive representation A belief that constituents are most effectively represented by legislators who are similar to them in such key demographic characteristics as race, ethnicity, religion, or gender. (11)

desegregation The ending of authorized segregation, or separation by race. (16)

détente A reduction of tensions. This term is particularly used to refer to a reduction of tensions between the United States and the Soviet Union in the early 1970s during the Nixon administration. (20)

direct action Unconventional participation that involves assembling crowds to confront businesses and local governments to demand a hearing. (7)

direct lobbying Attempts to influence a legislator's vote through personal contact with the legislator. (10)

direct primary A preliminary election, run by the state government, in which the voters choose each party's candidates for the general election. (7)

discretionary spending In the Budget Enforcement Act of 1990, authorized expenditures from annual appropriations. (18)

dissent The disagreement of a judge with a majority decision. (14)

divided government The situation in which one party controls the White House and the other controls at least one house of Congress. (12)

docket A court's agenda. (14)

dual federalism A view that holds the Constitution is a compact among sovereign states, so that the powers of the national government are fixed and limited. (4)

economic depression A period of high unemployment and business failures; a severe, long-lasting downturn in a business cycle. (18)

elastic clause The last clause in Section 8 of Article 1 of the Constitution, which gives Congress the means to execute its enumerated powers. This clause is the basis for Congress's implied powers. Also called the *necessary and proper clause.* (4)

election campaign An organized effort to persuade voters to choose one candidate over others competing for the same office. (9)

electoral college A body of electors chosen by voters to cast ballots for president and vice president. (8)

electoral dealignment A lessening of the importance of party loyalties in voting decisions. (8)

electoral realignment The change in voting patterns that occurs after a critical election. (8)

elite theory The view that a small group of people actually makes most of the important government decisions. (2)

enlargement and engagement Clinton's policy, following the collapse of communism, of increasing the spread of market economies and increasing the United States' role in global affairs. (20)

entitlement A benefit to which every eligible person has a legal right and that the government cannot deny. (18, 19)

enumerated powers The powers explicitly granted to Congress by the Constitution. (3)

equality of opportunity The idea that each person is guaranteed the same chance to succeed in life. (1, 16)

equality of outcome The concept that society must ensure that people are equal, and governments must design policies to redistribute wealth and status to achieve economic and social equality. (1, 16)

equal opportunities rule Under the Federal Communications Act of 1934, the requirement that if a broadcast station gives or sells time to a candidate for any public office, it must make available an equal amount of time under the same conditions to all other candidates for that office. (6)

Equal Rights Amendment (ERA) A failed constitutional amendment first introduced by the National Women's Party in 1923, declaring that "equality of rights under the law shall not be denied or abridged by the United States or any State on account of sex." (16)

establishment clause The first clause in the First Amendment, which forbids government establishment of religion. (15)

exclusionary rule The judicial rule that states that evidence obtained in an illegal search and seizure cannot be used in trial. (15)

executive agreement A pact between the heads of two countries. (20)

executive branch The law-enforcing branch of government. (3)

Executive Office of the President The president's executive aides and their staffs; the extended White House executive establishment. (12)

ex post facto law A law that declares an action to be criminal *after* it has been performed. (15)

extraordinary majorities Majorities greater than that required by majority rule, that is, greater than 50 percent plus one. (3)

fair trade Trade regulated by international agreements outlawing unfair business practices. (20)

Federal Communications Commission (FCC) An independent federal agency that regulates interstate and international communication by radio, television, telephone, telegraph, cable, and satellite. (6)

Federal Election Commission (FEC) A federal agency that oversees the financing of national election campaigns. (9)

federalism The division of power between a central government and regional governments. (3, 4)

federal question An issue covered by the constitution, national laws, or U.S. treaties. (14)

Federal Reserve System The system of banks that acts as the central bank of the United States and controls major monetary policies. (18)

feedback Information received by policymakers about the effectiveness of public policy. (17)

feminization of poverty The term applied to the fact that a growing percentage of all poor Americans are women or the dependents of women. (19)

fighting words Speech that is not protected by the First Amendment because it inflicts injury or tends to incite an immediate disturbance of the peace. (15)

filibuster A delaying tactic, used in the Senate, that involves speechmaking to prevent action on a piece of legislation. (11)

first-past-the-post election A British term for elections conducted in single-member districts that award victory to the candidate with the most votes. (9)

fiscal policies Economic policies that involve government spending and taxing. (18)

fiscal year (FY) The twelve-month period from October 1 to September 30 used by the government for accounting purposes. A fiscal-year budget is named for the year in which it ends. (18)

food stamp program A federally funded program that increases the purchasing power of needy families by providing them with coupons they can use to purchase food. (19)

foreign policy The general plan followed by a nation in defending and advancing national interests, especially its security against foreign threats. (20)

formula grant A categorical grant distributed according to a particular formula, which specifies who is eligible for the grants and how much each eligible applicant will receive. (4)

fragmentation In policymaking, the phenomenon of attacking a single problem in different and sometimes competing ways. (17)

franchise   The right to vote. Also called *suffrage*. (7)

freedom from   Immunity, as in *freedom from want*. (1)

freedom of   An absence of constraints on behavior, as in *freedom of speech*, or *freedom of religion*. (1)

free-exercise clause   The second clause in the First Amendment, which prevents the government from interfering with the exercise of religion. (15)

free-expression clauses   The press and speech clauses of the First Amendment. (15)

free-rider problem   The situation in which people benefit from the activities of an organization (such as an interest group) but do not contribute to those activities. (10)

free trade   An economic policy that allows businesses in different nations to sell and buy goods without paying tariffs or other limitations. (20)

front-loading   States' practice of moving delegate selection primaries and caucuses earlier in the calendar year to gain media and candidate attention. (9)

gatekeepers   Media executives, news editors, and prominent reporters who direct the flow of news. (6)

general election   A national election held by law in November of every even-numbered year. (9)

gerrymandering   Redrawing a congressional district to intentionally benefit one political party. (11)

globalization   The increasing interdependence of citizens and nations across the world. (1)

global policy   Like foreign policy, it's a plan for defending and advancing national interests, but—unlike foreign policy—it includes social and environmental concerns among national interests. (20)

good faith exception   An exception to the Supreme Court exclusionary rule, holding that evidence seized on the basis of a mistakenly issued search warrant can be introduced at trial if the mistake was made in good faith, that is, if all the parties involved had reason at the time to believe that the warrant was proper. (15)

government   The legitimate use of force to control human behavior; also, the organization or agency authorized to exercise that force. (1)

government corporation   A government agency that performs services that might be provided by the private sector but that involve either insufficient financial incentive or are better provided when they are somehow linked with government. (13)

Government Performance and Results Act   A law requiring each government agency to implement quantifiable standards to measure its performance in meeting stated program goals. (13)

Gramm-Rudman   Popular name for an act passed by Congress in 1985 that, in its original form, sought to lower the national deficit to a specified level each year, culminating in a balanced budget in FY 1991. New reforms and deficit targets were agreed on in 1990. (18)

grant-in-aid   Money provided by one level of government to another, to be spent for a given purpose. (4)

grassroots lobbying   Lobbying activities performed by rank-and-file interest group members and would-be members. (10)

Great Compromise   Submitted by the Connecticut delegation to the Constitutional Convention of 1787, and thus also known as the *Connecticut Compromise*, a plan calling for a bicameral legislature in which the House of Representatives would be apportioned according to population and the states would be represented equally in the Senate. (3)

Great Depression   The longest and deepest setback the American economy has ever experienced. It began with the stock market crash on October 12, 1929, and did not end until the start of World War II. (19)

Great Society   President Lyndon Johnson's broad array of programs designed to redress political, social, and economic inequality. (19)

gridlock   A situation in which government is incapable of acting on important issues, usually because of divided government. (12)

gross domestic product (GDP)   The total value of the goods and services produced by a country during a year. (18)

group media   Communications technologies, such as the fax and the Internet, used primarily within groups of people of common interests. (6)

Head Start   A child development program serving low-income children and their families. (19)

high politics   A term used to describe strategic and security issues in global politics. Traditionally, policymakers involved in global politics were expected to give greater priority to these issues than to issues of low politics such as socioeconomic or welfare issues . (20)

home rule   The right to enact and enforce legislation locally. (4)

horse race journalism   Election coverage by the mass media that focuses on which candidate is ahead, rather than on national issues. (6)

impeachment   The formal charging of a government official with "treason, bribery, or other high crimes and misdemeanors." (11)

implementation   The process of putting specific policies into operation. (13, 17)

implied powers   Those powers that Congress requires in order to execute its enumerated powers. (3, 4)

in-and-outer   A participant in an issue network who has a good understanding of the needs and problems of others in the network and can easily switch jobs within the network. (17)

incremental budgeting   A method of budget making that involves adding new funds (an increment) onto the amount previously budgeted (in last year's budget). (18)

incrementalism   Policymaking characterized by a series of decisions, each instituting modest change. (13)

incumbent   A current officeholder. (11)

independent agency   An executive agency that is not part of a cabinet department. (13)

inflation   An economic condition characterized by price increases linked to a decrease in the value of the currency. (18)

influencing behavior   Behavior that seeks to modify or reverse government policy to serve political interests. (7)

information campaign   An organized effort to gain public backing by bringing a group's views to public attention. (10)

infotainment   The practice of mixing journalism with theater, employed by some news programs. (6)

inherent powers   Authority claimed by the president that is not clearly specified in the Constitution. Typically, these powers are inferred from the Constitution. (12)

initiative   A procedure by which voters can propose an issue to be decided by the legislature or by the people in a referendum. It requires gathering a specified number of signatures and submitting a petition to a designated agency. (7)

interest group An organized group of individuals that seeks to influence public policy. Also called a *lobby*. (2, 10)

interest group entrepreneur An interest group organizer or leader. (10)

intermestic Issues in which international and domestic concerns are mixed. (20)

invidious discrimination Discrimination against persons or groups that works to their harm and is based on animosity. (16)

isolationism A foreign policy of withdrawal from international political affairs. (20)

issue definition Our conception of the problem at hand. (17)

issue network A shared-knowledge group consisting of representatives of various interests involved in some particular aspect of public policy. (17)

joint committee A committee made up of members of both the House and the Senate. (11)

judgment The judicial decision in a court case. (14)

judicial activism A judicial philosophy whereby judges interpret existing laws and precedents loosely and interject their own values in court decisions. (14)

judicial branch The branch of government that interprets laws. (3)

judicial restraint A judicial philosophy whereby judges adhere closely to statutes and precedents in reaching their decisions. (14)

judicial review The power to declare government acts invalid because they violate the Constitution. (3, 14)

Keynesian theory An economic theory stating that the government can stabilize the economy—i.e., can smooth business cycles—by controlling the level of aggregate demand, and that the level of aggregate demand can be controlled by means of fiscal and monetary policies. (18)

laissez faire An economic doctrine that opposes any form of government intervention in business. (1)

legislative branch The lawmaking branch of government. (3)

legislative liaison staff Those people who compose the communications link between the White House and Congress, advising the president or cabinet secretaries on the status of pending legislation. (12)

liberals Those who are willing to use government to promote freedom but not order. (1)

libertarianism A political ideology that is opposed to all government action except as necessary to protect life and property. (1)

libertarians Those who are opposed to using government to promote either order or equality. (1)

lobby See *interest group*.

lobbyist A representative of an interest group. (10)

local caucus A method used to select delegates to attend a party's national convention. Generally, a local meeting selects delegates for a county-level meeting, which in turn selects delegates for a higher-level meeting; the process culminates in a state convention that actually selects the national convention delegates. (9)

low politics A term used to describe socioeconomic or welfare issues. Traditionally, policymakers involved in global politics were expected to place less emphasis on these issues than on issues of high politics such as strategic and security issues. (20)

majoritarian model of democracy The classical theory of democracy in which government by the people is interpreted as government by the majority of the people. (2)

majority leader The head of the majority party in the Senate; the second highest ranking member of the majority party in the House. (11)

majority representation The system by which one office, contested by two or more candidates, is won by the single candidate who collects the most votes. (8)

majority rule The principle—basic to procedural democratic theory—that the decision of a group must reflect the preference of more than half of those participating; a simple majority. (2)

managed trade Government intervention in trade policy in order to achieve a specific result. (20)

mandate A requirement that a state undertake an activity or provide a service, in keeping with minimum national standards. (4)

mandate An endorsement by voters. Presidents sometimes argue they have been given a mandate to carry out policy proposals. (12)

mandatory spending In the Budget Enforcement Act of 1990, expenditures required by previous commitments. (18)

mass media The means employed in mass communication, often divided into print media and broadcast media. (6)

means-tested benefits Conditional benefits provided by government to individuals whose income falls below a designated threshold. (19)

media event A situation that is so "newsworthy" that the mass media are compelled to cover it; candidates in elections often create such situations to garner media attention. (6)

Medicaid A need-based comprehensive medical and hospitalization program. (19)

Medicare A health-insurance program for all persons older than sixty-five. (19)

membership bias The tendency of some sectors of society—especially the wealthy, the highly educated, professionals, and those in business—to organize more readily into interest groups. (10)

minority rights The benefits of government that cannot be denied to any citizens by majority decisions. (2)

Miranda warnings Statements concerning rights that police are required to make to a person before he or she is subjected to in-custody questioning. (15)

monetarists Those who argue that government can effectively control the performance of an economy only by controlling the supply of money. (18)

monetary policies Economic policies that involve control of, and changes in, the supply of money. (18)

municipal government The government unit that administers a city or town. (4)

national committee A committee of a political party composed of party chairpersons and party officials from every state. (8)

national convention A gathering of delegates of a single political party from across the country to choose candidates for president and vice president and to adopt a party platform. (8)

national sovereignty "A political entity's externally recognized right to exercise authority over its affairs." (1)

nation building A policy once intended to shore up Third World countries economically and democratically, thereby making them less attractive targets for Soviet opportunism. (20)

necessary and proper clause The last clause in Section 8 of Article I of the Constitution, which gives Congress the means to execute its enumerated powers. This clause is the basis for Congress's implied powers. Also called the *elastic clause.* (3)

New Deal The measures advocated by the Roosevelt administration to alleviate the Depression. (19)

"new" ethnicity A newer outlook on the people comprising America's "melting pot," with focus on race. (5)

New Jersey Plan Submitted by the head of the New Jersey delegation to the Constitutional Convention of 1787, a set of nine resolutions that would have, in effect, preserved the Articles of Confederation by amending rather than replacing them. (3)

newsworthiness The degree to which a news story is important enough to be covered in the mass media. (6)

Nineteenth Amendment The amendment to the Constitution, adopted in 1920, that assures women of the right to vote. (16)

Nixon Doctrine Nixon's policy, formulated with assistance from Henry Kissinger, that restricted U.S. military intervention abroad absent a threat to its vital national interests. (20)

nomination Designation as an official candidate of a political party. (8)

non-means-tested benefits Benefits provided by government to all citizens, regardless of income; Medicare and social security are examples. (19)

nonprofits Organizations that are not part of government or business and cannot distribute profits to shareholders or to anyone else. (17)

nontariff barrier (NTB) A regulation that outlines the exact specifications an imported product must meet in order to be offered for sale. (20)

norm An organization's informal, unwritten rules that guide individual behavior. (13)

normal distribution A symmetrical bell-shaped distribution (of opinions) centered on a single mode, or most frequent response. (5)

North Atlantic Treaty Organization (NATO) An organization including nations of Western Europe, the United States, and Canada, created in 1949 to defend against Soviet expansionism. With the Soviet threat in Western Europe diminished or eliminated, the purposes and membership of NATO are under examination. (20)

nullification The declaration by a state that a particular action of the national government is not applicable to that state. (4)

obligation of contracts The obligation of the parties to a contract to carry out its terms. (15)

Office of Management and Budget (OMB) The budgeting arm of the Executive Office; prepares the president's budget. (18)

"old" ethnicity An older outlook on the people comprising America's "melting pot," with focus on religion and country of origin. (5)

oligarchy A system of government in which power is concentrated in the hands of a few people. (2)

open election An election that lacks an incumbent. (9)

open primary A primary election in which voters need not declare their party affiliation but must choose one party's primary ballot to take into the voting booth. (9)

opinion schema A network of organized knowledge and beliefs that guides a person's processing of information regarding a particular subject. (5)

order The rule of law to preserve life and protect property. Maintaining order is the oldest purpose of government. (1)

original jurisdiction The authority of a court to hear a case before any other court does. (14)

oversight The process of reviewing the operations of an agency to determine whether it is carrying out policies as Congress intended. (11)

parliamentary system A system of government in which the chief executive is the leader whose party holds the most seats in the legislature after an election or whose party forms a major part of the ruling coalition. (11)

participatory democracy A system of government where rank-and-file citizens rule themselves rather than electing representatives to govern on their behalf. (2)

party conference A meeting to select party leaders and decide committee assignments, held at the beginning of a session of Congress by Republicans or Democrats in each chamber. (8)

party identification A voter's sense of psychological attachment to a party. (8)

party machine A centralized party organization that dominates local politics by controlling elections. (8)

party platform The statement of policies of a national political party. (8)

pay-as-you-go In the Budget Enforcement Act of 1990, the requirement that any tax cut or expansion of an entitlement program must be offset by a tax increase or other savings. (18)

peace through strength Reagan's policy of combatting communism by building up the military, including aggressive development of new weapons systems. (20)

plea bargain A defendant's admission of guilt in exchange for a less severe punishment. (14)

pluralist model of democracy An interpretation of democracy in which government by the people is taken to mean government by people operating through competing interest groups. (2)

pocket veto A means of killing a bill that has been passed by both houses of Congress, in which the president does not sign the bill and Congress adjourns within ten days of the bill's passage. (11)

police power The authority of a government to maintain order and safeguard citizens' health, morals, safety, and welfare. (1)

policy evaluation Analysis of a public policy so as to determine how well it is working. (17)

policy formulation The stage of the policymaking process during which formal proposals are developed and adopted. (17)

political action committee (PAC) An organization that pools campaign contributions from group members and donates those funds to candidates for political office. (10)

political agenda A list of issues that need government attention. (6)

political equality Equality in political decision making: one vote per person, with all votes counted equally. (1, 2)

political ideology A consistent set of values and beliefs about the proper purpose and scope of government. (1)

political participation Actions of private citizens by which they seek to influence or support government and politics. (7)

political party An organization that sponsors candidates for political office under the organization's name. (8)

political socialization The complex process by which people acquire their political values. (5)

political system A set of interrelated institutions that links people with government. (8)

poll tax A tax of $1 or $2 on every citizen who wished to vote, first instituted in Georgia in 1877. Although it was no burden on most white citizens, it effectively disenfranchised blacks. (16)

poverty level The minimum cash income that will provide for a family's basic needs; calculated as three times the cost of a market basket of food that provides a minimally nutritious diet. (19)

precedent A judicial ruling that serves as the basis for the ruling in a subsequent case. (14)

preemption The power of Congress to enact laws by which the national government assumes total or partial responsibility for a state government function. (4)

presidential primary A special primary election used to select delegates to attend the party's national convention, which in turn nominates the presidential candidate. (9)

primary election A preliminary election conducted within a political party to select candidates who will run for public office in a subsequent election. (9)

prior restraint Censorship before publication. (15)

procedural democratic theory A view of democracy as being embodied in a decision-making process that involves universal participation, political equality, majority rule, and responsiveness. (2)

productive capacity The total value of goods and services that can be produced when the economy works at full capacity. (18)

program monitoring Keeping track of government programs, usually by interest groups. (10)

progressive taxation A system of taxation whereby the rich pay proportionately higher taxes than the poor; used by governments to redistribute wealth and thus promote equality. (18)

progressivism A philosophy of political reform based upon the goodness and wisdom of the individual citizen as opposed to special interests and political institutions. (7)

project grant A categorical grant awarded on the basis of competitive applications submitted by prospective recipients. (4)

proportional representation The system by which legislative seats are awarded to a party in proportion to the vote that party wins in an election. (8)

protectionism The notion that women must be protected from life's cruelties; until the 1970s, the basis for laws affecting women's civil rights. (16)

protectionists Those who wish to prevent imports from entering the country and therefore oppose free trade. (20)

public assistance Government aid to individuals who can demonstrate a need for that aid. (19)

public figures People who assume roles of prominence in society or thrust themselves to the forefront of public controversy. (15)

public goods Benefits and services, such as parks and sanitation, that benefit all citizens but are not likely to be produced voluntarily by individuals. (1)

public opinion The collected attitudes of citizens concerning a given issue or question. (5)

public policy A general plan of action adopted by the government to solve a social problem, counter a threat, or pursue an objective. (17, 19)

racial gerrymandering The drawing of a legislative district to maximize the chances that a minority candidate will win election. (11)

racial segregation Separation from society because of race. (16)

racism A belief that human races have distinct characteristics such that one's own race is superior to, and has a right to rule, others. (16)

reapportionment Redistribution of representatives among the states, based on population change. Congress is reapportioned after each census. (11)

reasonable access rule An FCC rule that requires broadcast stations to make their facilities available for the expression of conflicting views or issues by all responsible elements in the community. (6)

recall The process for removing an elected official from office. (7)

receipts For a government, the amount expected or obtained in taxes and other revenues. (18)

referendum An election on a policy issue. (7)

regulation Government intervention in the workings of business to promote some socially desired goal. (13)

regulations Administrative rules that guide the operation of a government program. (13)

regulatory commission An agency of the executive branch of government that controls or directs some aspect of the economy. (13)

representative democracy A system of government where citizens elect public officials to govern on their behalf. (2)

republic A government without a monarch; a government rooted in the consent of the governed, whose power is exercised by elected representatives responsible to the governed. (3)

republicanism A form of government in which power resides in the people and is exercised by their elected representatives. (3)

responsible party government A set of principles formalizing the ideal role of parties in a majoritarian democracy. (8)

responsiveness A decision-making principle, necessitated by representative government, that implies that elected representatives should do what the majority of people wants. (2)

restraint A requirement laid down by act of Congress, prohibiting a state or local government from exercising a certain power. (4)

rights The benefits of government to which every citizen is entitled. (1)

rule making The administrative process that results in the issuance of regulations by government agencies. (13)

rule of four An unwritten rule that requires at least four justices to agree that a case warrants consideration before it is reviewed by the Supreme Court. (14)

school district An area for which a local government unit administers elementary and secondary school programs. (4)

select committee A temporary congressional committee created for a specific purpose and disbanded after that purpose is fulfilled. (11)

self-interest principle The implication that people choose what benefits them personally. (5)

senatorial courtesy A practice whereby the Senate will not confirm for a lower federal court judgeship a nominee who is opposed by the senior senator in the president's party in the nominee's state. (14)

seniority Years of consecutive service on a particular congressional committee. (11)

separate-but-equal doctrine The concept that providing separate but equivalent facilities for blacks and whites satisfies the equal protection clause of the Fourteenth Amendment. (16)

separation of powers The assignment of law-making, law-enforcing, and law-interpreting functions to separate branches of government. (3)

sexism Invidious sex discrimination. (16)

skewed distribution An asymmetrical but generally bell-shaped distribution (of opinions); its mode, or most frequent response, lies off to one side. (5)

social contract theory The belief that the people agree to set up rulers for certain purposes and thus have the right to resist or remove rulers who act against those purposes. (3)

social equality Equality in wealth, education, and status. (1)

social insurance A government-backed guarantee against loss by individuals without regard to need. (19)

socialism A form of rule in which the central government plays a strong role in regulating existing private industry and directing the economy, although it does allow some private ownership of productive capacity. (1)

social security Social insurance that provides economic assistance to persons faced with unemployment, disability, or old age. It is financed by taxes on employers and employees. (19)

Social Security Act The law that provided for social security and is the basis of modern American social welfare. (19)

social welfare Government programs that provide the minimum living standards necessary for all citizens. (19)

socioeconomic status Position in society, based on a combination of education, occupational status, and income. (5)

soft money Funds that are not raised and spent for a specific federal election campaign. Such funds are distinguished from "hard money," which is tied to specific campaigns and thus falls under government regulations. (9)

solicitor general The third highest ranking official of the U.S. Department of Justice, and the one who represents the national government before the Supreme Court. (14)

sovereign A nation that owes obedience to no power or law other than its own. (20)

Speaker of the House The presiding officer of the House of Representatives. (11)

special district A government unit created to perform particular functions, especially when those functions are best performed across jurisdictional boundaries. (4)

split ticket In voting, candidates from different parties for different offices. (9)

stable distribution A distribution (of opinions) that shows little change over time. (5)

standard socioeconomic model A relationship between socioeconomic status and conventional political involvement: People with higher status and more education are more likely to participate than those with lower status. (7)

standing committee A permanent congressional committee that specializes in a particular legislative area. (11)

stare decisis Literally, let the decision stand; decision making according to precedent. (14)

states' rights The idea that all rights not specifically conferred on the national government by the Constitution are reserved to the states. (4)

straight ticket In voting, a single party's candidates for all the offices. (9)

strict scrutiny A standard used by the Supreme Court in deciding whether a law or policy is to be adjudged constitutional or not. To pass strict scrutiny, the law or policy must be justified by a "compelling governmental interest" as well as being the least restrictive means for achieving that interest. (15)

substantive democratic theory The view that democracy is embodied in the substance of government policies rather than in the policymaking procedure. (2)

suffrage The right to vote. Also called the *franchise.* (7)

supply-side economics Economic policies aimed at increasing the supply of goods (as opposed to increasing demand), consisting mainly of tax cuts for possible investors and less regulation of business. (18)

supportive behavior Actions that express allegiance to government and country. (7)

supremacy clause The clause in Article VI of the Constitution that asserts that national laws take precedence over state and local laws when they conflict. (3)

tax committees The two committees of Congress responsible for raising the revenue with which to run the government. (18)

television hypothesis The belief that television is to blame for the low level of citizens' knowledge about public affairs. (6)

Temporary Assistance for Needy Families Act (TANF) A 1996 national act that abolished the long-time welfare policy, AFDC (Aid for Families with Dependent Children). TANF gives the states much more control over welfare policy. (19)

totalitarianism A political philosophy that advocates unlimited power for the government to enable it to control all sectors of society. (1)

total quality management (TQM) A management philosophy emphasizing listening closely to customers, breaking down barriers between parts of an organization, and continually improving quality. (13)

trade association An organization that represents firms within a particular industry. (10)

transfer payment A payment by government to an individual, mainly through social security or unemployment insurance. (18)

trustee A representative who is obligated to consider the views of constituents but is not obligated to vote according to those views if he or she believes they are misguided. (11)

two-party system A political system in which two major political parties compete for control of the government. Candidates from a third party have little chance of winning office. (8)

two-step flow of communication The process in which a few policy elites gather information and then inform their more numerous followers, mobilizing them to apply pressure to government. (6)

uncontrollable outlay A payment that government must make by law. (18)

unconventional participation Relatively uncommon political behavior that challenges or defies established institutions and dominant norms. (7)

universal participation The concept that everyone in a democracy should participate in governmental decision making. (2)

U.S. Court of Appeals A court within the second tier of the three-tiered federal court system, to which decisions of the district courts and federal agencies may be appealed for review. (14)

U.S. district court A court within the lowest tier of the three-tiered federal court system; a court where litigation begins. (14)

veto The president's disapproval of a bill that has been passed by both houses of Congress. Congress can override a veto with a two-thirds vote in each house. (11, 12)

Virginia Plan A set of proposals for a new government, submitted to the Constitutional Convention of 1787; included separation of the government into three branches, division of the legislature into two houses, and proportional representation in the legislature. (3)

War on Poverty A part of President Lyndon Johnson's Great Society program, intended to eradicate poverty within ten years. (19)

War Powers Resolution An act of Congress that limits the president's ability to wage undeclared war. (20)

welfare state A nation in which the government assumes responsibility for the welfare of its citizens, redistributing income to reduce social inequality. (19)

Chapter 1 / Freedom, Order, or Equality? / pp. 1–28

1. "Love Bug' Cops Lack Applicable Law; Philippines Investigators Planned to Charge Fraud; Top Lawyer Says It's Not Applicable," Manila, Philippines, posted 8:54 A.M. EDT May 18, 2000 http://www.toronto.globaltv.com/ca/technology/stories/techology-20000518-125427.html. See also "Charges Filed in Love Bug Virus," updated 6-29-00 http://nectculture.about.com/internet/netculture/library/blvirusupdate.htm

2. Ted Bridis, "Study by FBI Is Confident in 'Carnivore,'" *Wall Street Journal,* 21 November 2000, p. A4; Drew Clark, "FBI Defends E-mail Monitoring System," *National Journal's Technology Daily,* 25 July 2000, http://www.govexec.com/dailyfed/c700/072500td.htm.

3. Sarah Lyall, "British Authorities May Get Wide Power to Decode E-Mail," *New York Times,* 19 July 2000, p. A3; D. Ian Hooper, "E-Mail Tool's Capability Worries Privacy Experts," *Chicago Tribune,* 18 November 2000, p. 6; John Schwartz, "Wiretapping System Works on Internet, Review Finds," *New York Times,* 22 November 2000, p. A17.

4. National Telecommunications and Information Administration, *Falling Through the Net: Towards Digital Inclusion* (Washington, D.C.: U.S. Department of Commerce, A Report on American Access to Technology Tools, October 2000).

5. Center for Political Studies, Institute for Social Research, *American National Election Study, 2000* (Ann Arbor, University of Michigan).

6. Thomas Biersteker and Cynthia Weber (eds.), *State Sovereignty as Social Construct* (Cambridge: Cambridge University Press, 1996), p. 12. For a definition of sovereignty at the national level, see Bernard Crick, "Sovereignty," in *International Encyclopedia of the Social Sciences,* Volume 15 (New York: Macmillan and the Free Press, 1968), p. 77. Elsewhere in the same encyclo-pedia, David Apter in "Government," Volume 6, links sovereignty to "a national autonomous community," p. 215.

7. William T. R. Fox and Annette Baker Fox, "International Politics," in David L. Sills (ed.), *International Encyclopedia of the Social Sciences,* Volume 8 (New York: The Macmillan Company and the Free Press, 1968), pp. 50–53.

8. Judith Miller, "Sovereignty Isn't So Sacred Anymore," *New York Times,* 18 April 1999, Section 4, p. 4.

9. Stephanie Strom, "Fund for Wartime Slaves Set Up in Japan," *New York Times,* 30 November 2000, p. A14.

10. Roger Cohen, "A European Identity: National-State Losing Ground," *New York Times,* 14 January 2000, p. A3.

11. Barbara Crossette, "Parsing Degrees of Atrocity Within the Logic of Law," *New York Times,* 8 July 2000, p. A15; Steven Lee Myers, "U.S. Signs Treaty for World Court to Try Atroc-ities," *New York Times,* 1 January 2001, p. 1.

12. Charles M. Madigan and Colin McMahon, "A Slow, Painful Quest for Justice," *Chicago Tribune,* 7 September 1999, pp. 1, 8.

13. Tom Hundley, "Europe Seeks to Convert U.S. on Death Penalty," *Chicago Tribune,* 26 June 2000, p. 1; Salim Muwakkil, "The Capital of Capital Punishment," *Chicago Tribune,* 12 July 1999, p. 18.

14. 1977 Constitution of the Union of Soviet Socialist Republics, Article 11, in *Constitutions of Countries of the World,* ed. A. P. Blaustein and C. H. Flanz (Dobbs Ferry, N.Y.: Oceana, 1971).

15. Karl Marx and Friedrich Engels, *Critique of the Gotha Programme* (New York: International Publishers, 1938), p. 10. Originally written in 1875 but published in 1891.

16. See the argument in Amy Gutman, *Liberal Equality* (Cambridge, England: Cambridge University Press, 1980), pp. 9–10.

17. See John H. Schaar, "Equality of Opportunity and Beyond," in *Equality,* NOMOS IX, eds. J. Roland Pennock and John W. Chapman (New York: Atherton Press, 1967), pp. 228–249.

18. Lyndon Johnson, "To Fulfill These Rights," commencement address at Howard University, 4 June 1965. Available at <oyez.nwu.edu/history-outloud/lhj/civil-rights/>.

19. Jean Jacques Rousseau, *The Social Contract and Discourses,* trans. G. D. H. Cole (New York: Dutton, 1950), p. 5.

20. Marist College, Marist Institute for Public Opinion Poll, 21–23 April 1997. Found at <www.mipo.marist.edu/docs/usapolls/9705CRI.HTM>.

21. Michael A. Lev, "Vicious Crimes Taking Root in China's Changing Society," *Chicago Tribune,* 5 November 2000, pp. 1, 13.

22. Centers for Disease Control and Prevention (CDC). *HIV/AIDS Surveillance Report* 1999, 11 (no. 2): 1–44.

23. Alessandra Stanley, "Russian TV, Freed of Communism, Gilds It," *New York Times,* 30 December 1995, p. 1.

24. Milton Friedman, *Capitalism and Freedom* (Chicago: University of Chicago Press, 1962).

25. Joseph Khan, "Anarchism, the Creed That Won't Stay Dead," *New York Times,* 5 August 2000, p. A15.

26. Steven Erlanger, "Czech Police and Army Get Ready for Protest at I.M.F. World Bank Meeting," *New York Times,* 12 August 2000, p. A3.

27. Flynn McRoberts, "Oregon City Is Cradle to Latest Generation of Anarchist Protesters," *Chicago Tribune,* 12 August 2000, p. 4.

28. The communitarian category was labeled "populist" in the first four editions of this book. We have relabeled it for two reasons. First, we believe that *communitarian* is more descriptive of the category. Second, we recognize that the term *populist* has been used increas-ingly to refer to the political styles of candidates such as Pat Buchanan and Ralph Nader. In this sense, a populist appeals to mass resentment against those in power. Given the debate over what *populist* really means, we have decided to use *communitarian,* a less familiar term with fewer connotations. See Michael Kazin, *The Populist Persuasion: An American History* (New York: Basic Books, 1995).

29. The communitarian movement was founded by a group of ethicists and social scientists who met in Washington, D.C., in 1990 at the invita-tion of sociologist Amitai Etzioni and political theorist William Galsron to discuss the declining state of morality and values in the United States. Etzioni became the leading spokesperson for the movement. See his *Rights and the Common Good: The Communitarian Perspective* (New York: St. Martin's

Press, 1995), pp. iii–iv. The communitarian political movement should be distinguished from communitarian thought in political philosophy, which is associated with theorists such as Alasdair MacIntyre, Michael Sandel, and Charles Taylor, who wrote in the late 1970s and early 1980s. In essence, communitarian theorists criticized liberalism, which stressed freedom and individualism, as excessively individualistic. Their fundamental critique was that liberalism slights the values of community life. See Allen E. Buchanan, "Assessing the Communitarian Critique of Liberalism," *Ethics*, 99 (July 1989), pp. 852–882, and Patrick Neal and David Paris, "Liberalism and the Communitarian Critique: A Guide for the Perplexed," *Canadian Journal of Political Science*, 23 (September 1990), pp. 419–439. Communitarian philosophers attacked liberalism over the inviolability of civil liberties. In our framework, such issues involve the tradeoff between freedom and order. Communitarian and liberal theorists differ less concerning the tradeoff between freedom and equality. See William R. Lund, "Communitarian Politics and the Problem of Equality," *Political Research Quarterly*, 46 (September 1993), pp. 577–600. But see also Susan Hekman, "The Embodiment of the Subject: Feminism and the Communitarian Critique of Liberalism," *Journal of Politics*, 54 (November 1992), pp. 1098–1119.

30. Etzioni, *Rights and the Common Good*, p. iv, and Etzioni, "Communitarian Solutions/What Communitarians Think," *The Journal of State Government*, 65 (January–March), pp. 9–11. For a critical, review of the communitarian program, see Jeremiah Creedon, "Communitarian Manifesto," *Utne Reader* (July–August 1992), pp. 38–40.

31. Etzioni, "Communitarian Solutions/What Communitarians Think," p. 10. Dana Milbank, "Catchword for Bush Ideology; 'Communitarianism' Finds Favor," *Washington Post*, 1 February 2001, A1. See also Lester Thurow, "Communitarian vs. Individualistic Capitalism," in Etzioni, *Rights and the Common Good*, pp. 277–282. Note, however, that government's role in dealing with issues of social and economic inequality is far less developed in communitarian writings than is its role in dealing with issues of order. In the same volume, an article by David Osborne, "Beyond Left and Right: A New Political Paradigm" (pp. 283–290), downplays the role of government in guaranteeing entitlements.

32. Etzioni, *Rights and the Common Good*, p. 17.

33. *Ibid.*, p. 22.

34. On the philosophical similarities and differences between communitarianism and socialism, see Alexander Koryushkin and Gerd Meyer (eds.), *Communitarianism, Liberalism, and the Quest for Democracy in Post-Communist Societies* (St. Petersburg: St. Petersburg University Press, 1999).

Chapter 2 / Majoritarian or Pluralist Democracy? / pp. 29–53

1. Michael Janofsky, "Both Sides See Momentum in Congress for Gun Control," *New York Times*, 15 November 2000, p. A14.

2. "Guns, Continued," Gallup Poll (April 2000). Found at www.gallup.com//poll/indicators/indguns3.asp.

3. Kenneth Janda, "What's in a Name? Party Labels Across the World," in *The CONTA Conference: Proceedings of the Conference of Conceptual and Terminological Analysis of the Social Sciences*, ed. F. W. Riggs (Frankfurt: Indeks Verlage, 1982), pp. 46–62.

4. Richard F. Fenno, Jr., *The President's Cabinet* (New York: Vintage, 1959), p. 29.

5. Robert A. Dahl, *Democracy and Its Critics* (New Haven: Yale University Press, 1989), pp. 13–23.

6. Jeffrey M. Berry, Kent E. Portney, and Ken Thomson, *The Rebirth of Urban Democracy* (Washington, D.C.: Brookings Institution, 1993).

7. Philip O'Connor, "Chicago's Success Story a Decade After Reform," *Kansas City Star*, 30 May 1999, p. B1.

8. Jean Jacques Rousseau, *The Social Contract*, 1762. Reprint (Hammondsworth, England: Penguin, 1968), p. 141.

9. Berry, Portney, and Thomson, *Rebirth*, p. 77.

10. See James A. Stimson, Michael B. MacKuen, and Robert S. Erikson, "Dynamic Representation," *American Political Science Review*, 89 (September 1995), pp. 543–565.

11. See C. B. Macpherson, *The Real World of Democracy* (New York: Oxford University Press, 1975), pp. 58–59.

12. Thomas E. Cronin, *Direct Democracy* (Cambridge, Mass.: Harvard University Press, 1989), p. 47.

13. Elisabeth R. Gerber, *The Populist Paradox: Interest Group Influence and the Promise of Direct Legislation* (Princeton: Princeton University Press, 1999).

14. Meredith Goad, "Doctors Urge Voters to Reject Question 1," *Portland Press Herald*, 3 November 2000, p. 1A; Michael O'D Moore, *Bangor Daily News*, 8 November 2000; Beth Daley, "Maine Ballot Questions Linger," *Boston Globe*, 9 November 2000, p. B6; and "Suicide Voted Down," *Wall Street Journal*, 10 November 2000, p. A18.

15. Kevin Cullen, "Tony Blair Hits Bump on Road to Devolution," *Boston Globe*, 21 September 1997, p. 1

16. Jack Citrin, "Who's the Boss? Direct Democracy and Popular Control of Government," in *Broken Contract?* ed. Stephen C. Craig (Boulder, Colo.: Westview, 1996), p. 271.

17. "Reform: More Direct Democracy," *Public Perspective* 9 (February/March 1998), p. 45.

18. M. Margaret Conway, *Political Participation in the United States*, 3rd ed. (Washington, D.C.: Congressional Quarterly Press, 2000), pp. 50 and 210.

19. Joseph M. Bessette, *The Mild Voice of Reason: Deliberative Democracy and American National Government* (Chicago: University of Chicago Press, 1994).

20. Benjamin I. Page and Robert Y. Shapiro, *The Rational Public* (Chicago: University of Chicago Press, 1992), p. 387.

21. See Robert A. Dahl, *Dilemmas of Pluralist Democracy* (New Haven, Conn.: Yale University Press, 1982), p. 5.

22. Robert A. Dahl, *Pluralist Democracy in the United States* (Chicago: Rand McNally, 1967), p. 24.

23. Jeffrey M. Berry, *The New Liberalism* (Washington, D.C.: Brookings Institution, 1999).

24. Robert D. Putnam, *Bowling Alone* (New York: Simon and Schuster, 2000).

25. The classic statement on elite theory is C. Wright Mills, *The Power Elite* (New York: Oxford University Press, 1956).

26. Michael Useem, *The Inner Circle* (New York: Oxford University Press, 1984). On a broader level, see Charles Lindblom, *Politics and Markets* (New York: Basic Books, 1977).

27. Robert A. Dahl, *Who Governs?* (New Haven, Conn.: Yale University Press, 1961).

28. Clarence N. Stone, *Regime Politics* (Lawrence: University of Kansas Press, 1989).

29. John P. Heinz, Edward O. Laumann, Robert L. Nelson, and Robert H. Salisbury, *The Hollow Core* (Cambridge, Mass.: Harvard University Press, 1993).

30. Peter Bachrach and Morton S. Baratz, "Two Faces of Power," *American Political Science Review*, 56 (December 1962), pp. 947–952; and John Gaventa, *Power and Powerlessness* (Urbana: University of Illinois Press, 1980).

31. See, for example, Dan Clawson, Alan Neustatdl, and Denise Scott, *Money Talks* (New York: Basic Books, 1992).

32. Kay Lehman Schlozman and John T. Tierney, *Organized Interests and American Politics* (New York: Harper & Row, 1986).

33. Arend Lijphart, *Democracies* (New Haven, Conn.: Yale University Press, 1984).

34. *Africa Demos*, 3 (May 1996) 5, pp. 1 and 27; and Michael Bratton and Nicholas van de Walle, "Popular Protest and Political Reform in Africa," *Comparative Politics*, 24 (July 1992), pp. 419–442.

35. The classic treatment of the conflict between freedom and order in democratizing countries is Samuel P. Huntington, *Political Order in Changing Societies* (New Haven, Conn.: Yale University Press, 1968).

36. Benjamin R. Barber, "Jihad vs. McWorld," *Atlantic Monthly*, March 1992, p. 53.

37. Tony Smith, America's Mission: *The United States and the Worldwide Struggle for Democracy in the Twentieth Century* (Princeton: Princeton University Press, 1994).

38. James Fowler, "The United States and South Korean Democratization," *Political Science Quarterly* 114 (Summer 1999), pp. 265–288.

39. Susan J. Pharr and Robert D. Putnam, eds., *Disaffected Democracies* (Princeton: Princeton University Press, 2000).

40. Rita Jalai and Seymour Martin Lipset, "Racial and Ethnic Conflicts: A Global Perspective," *Political Science Quarterly*, 107 (Winter 1992–93), p. 588.

41. E. E. Schattschneider, *The Semi-Sovereign People* (New York: Holt, Rinehart, & Winston, 1960), p. 35.

42. Citrin, "Who's the Boss?" pp. 286–287.

Chapter 3 / The Constitution / pp. 54–93

1. Carl Bernstein and Bob Woodward, *All the President's Men* (New York: Warner, 1975); Stanley I. Kutler, *The Wars of Watergate* (New York: Alfred A. Knopf, 1990).

2. Bernstein and Woodward, *All the President's Men*, p. 30.

3. *The Encyclopedia of American Facts and Dates* (New York: Crowell, 1979), p. 946.

4. Richard B. Morris, ed., *Encyclopedia of American History* (New York: Harper & Row, 1976), p. 544.

5. Laurence H. Tribe, "And the Winner is . . . ," *New York Times*, 12 February 1999, p. A27.

6. Gallup Organization, *Gallup Poll Monthly*, June 1992, pp. 2–3.

7. Samuel Eliot Morison, *Oxford History of the American People* (New York: Oxford University Press, 1965), p. 172.

8. Richard Walsh, *Charleston's Sons of Liberty: A Study of the Artisans, 1763–1789* (Columbia: University of South Carolina Press, 1959).

9. Mary Beth Norton, *Liberty's Daughters* (Boston: Little, Brown, 1980), pp. 155–157.

10. Morison, *Oxford History*, p. 204.

11. John Plamentz (rev. ed. by M. E. Plamentz and Robert Wokler), *Man and Society*, Vol. 1: From the Middle Ages to Locke (New York: Longman, 1992), pp. 216–218.

12. Pauline Maier, *American Scripture: Making the Declaration of Independence* (New York: Knopf, 1997), pp. 133–134.

13. Charles H. Metzger, S. J., *Catholics and the American Revolution: A Study in Religious Climate* (Chicago: Loyola University Press, 1962).

14. Extrapolated from U.S. Department of Defense, *Selected Manpower Statistics, FY 1982* (Washington, D.C.: U.S. Government Printing Office, 1983), Table 2-30, p. 130; and U.S. Bureau of the Census, *1985 Statistical Abstract of the United States* (Washington, D.C.: U.S. Government Printing Office, 1985), Tables 1 and 2, p. 6.

15. Joseph T. Keenan, *The Constitution of the United States* (Homewood, Ill.: Dow-Jones-Irwin, 1975).

16. David P. Szatmary, *Shays' Rebellion: The Making of an Agrarian Insurrection* (Amherst: University of Massachusetts Press, 1980), pp. 82–102.

17. As cited in Morison, *Oxford History*, p. 304.

18. "The Call for the Federal Constitutional Convention, Feb. 21, 1787" in Edward M. Earle (ed.), *The Federalist* (New York: Modern Library), p. 577.

19. Robert H. Jackson, *The Struggle for Judicial Supremacy* (New York: Alfred A. Knopf, 1941), p. 8.

20. John Dickinson of Delaware, as quoted in Morison, *Oxford History*, p. 270.

21. Catherine Drinker Bowen, *Miracle at Philadelphia* (Boston: Little, Brown, 1966), p. 122.

22. Forrest McDonald, *Novus Ordo Seclorum: The Intellectual Origins of the Constitution* (Lawrence: University Press of Kansas, 1985), pp. 205–209.

23. Donald S. Lutz, "The Preamble to the Constitution of the United States," *This Constitution*, 1 (September 1983), pp. 23–30.

24. See also Charles O. Jones, "The Separated Presidency—Making It Work in Contemporary Politics," in *The New American Political System*, 2nd ed., Anthony King (Washington, D.C.: American Enterprise Institute, 1990).

25. Charles A. Beard, *An Economic Interpretation of the Constitution of the United States* (New York: Macmillan, 1913).

26. Leonard W. Levy, *Constitutional Opinions* (New York: Oxford University Press, 1986), p. 101.

27. Robert E. Brown, *Charles Beard and the Constitution* (Princeton, N.J.: Princeton University Press, 1956); Levy, *Constitutional Opinions*, pp. 103–104; and Forrest McDonald, *We the People: Economic Origins of the Constitution* (Chicago: University of Chicago Press, 1958).

28. Compare Eugene D. Genovese, *The Political Economy of Slavery: Studies in the Economics and Society of the Slave South* (Middletown, Conn.: Wesleyan University Press, 1989); and Robert William Fogel, *Without Contract or Consent: The Rise and Fall of American Slavery* (New York: W. W. Norton, 1989).

29. Robert A. Goldwin, Letter to the Editor, *Wall Street Journal*, 30 August 1993, p. A11.

30. Bernard Bailyn, *Faces of Revolution: Personalities and Themes in the Struggle for American Independence* (New York: Alfred A. Knopf, 1990), pp. 221–222.

31. Walter Berns, *The First Amendment and the Future of Democracy* (New York: Basic Books, 1976), p. 2.

32. Herbert J. Storing, ed., *The Complete Anti-Federalist*, 7 vols. (Chicago: University of Chicago Press, 1981).

33. Alexis de Tocqueville, *Democracy in America*, 1835–1839, Reprint, eds. J. P. Mayer and Max Lerner (New York: Harper & Row, 1966), p. 102.

34. Russell L. Caplan, *Constitutional Brinkmanship: Amending the Constitution by National Convention*

(New York: Oxford University Press, 1988), p. 162.

35. Richard L. Berke, "1789 Amendment Is Ratified but Now the Debate Begins," *New York Times*, 8 May 1992, p. A1.

36. The interpretation debate is fully explored in John H. Garvey and T. Alexander Aleinikoff, *Modern Constitutional Theory: A Reader*, 2d ed. (Minneapolis, Minn.: West Publishing Co., 1991).

37. The International Institute for Democracy (ed.), *The Rebirth of Democracy: 12 Constitutions of Central and Eastern Europe*, 2nd ed. Revised (The Netherlands: Council of Europe, 1996).

38. Jerold L. Waltman, *Political Origins of the U.S. Income Tax* (Jackson: University Press of Mississippi, 1985), p. 10.

Chapter 4 / Federalism / pp. 94–123

1. *Bush* v. *Gore*, 531 U.S. ___ (2000).

2. Taylor Branch, *Parting the Waters: America in the King Years, 1954–63* (New York: Simon & Schuster, 1988), Chap. 17.

3. Daniel J. Elazar, "Opening the Third Century of American Federalism: Issues and Prospects," *Annals of the American Academy of Political and Social Sciences*, 509 (May 1990), p. 14.

4. William H. Stewart, *Concepts of Federalism* (Lanham, Md.: University Press of America, 1984).

5. Edward Corwin, *The Passing of Dual Federalism*, 36 *University of Virginia Law Review* 4 (1950).

6. See Daniel J. Elazar, *The American Partnership* (Chicago, Ill.: University of Chicago Press, 1962); and Morton Grodzins, *The American System* (Chicago, Ill.: Rand McNally, 1966).

7. Sam Howe Verhovek, "States Are Already Providing Glimpse at Welfare's Future," *New York Times*, 21 September 1995, p. A1.

8. Martha Derthick, "The Enduring Features of American Federalism," *The Brookings Review*, Summer 1989, p. 35.

9. *South Carolina* v. *Katzenbach*, 383 U.S. 301 (1966).

10. Raoul Berger, *Federalism: The Founders' Design* (Norman: University of Oklahoma Press, 1987), pp. 61–62.

11. *United States* v. *Lopez*, 514 U.S. 549 (1995).

12. *United States* v. *Morrison*, 120 S. Ct. 1740 (2000).

13. *Seminole Tribe of Florida* v. *Florida*, 517 U.S. 44 (1996).

14. *Budget of the United States Government, FY 1998 Historical Tables* (Washington, D.C.: U.S. Government Printing Office, 1998), Table 12.1.

15. Advisory Commission on Intergovernmental Relations, *Characteristics of Federal Grant-in-Aid Programs to State and Local Governments: Grants Funded FY 1993* (Washington, D.C.: U.S. Government Printing Office, 1994), Table 2, p. 5.

16. *South Dakota* v. *Dole*, 483 U.S. 203 (1987).

17. "President Signs off on Wilson Bridge Funds," *Washington Times*, p. C4.

18. *McCulloch* v. *Maryland*, 4 Wheat. 316 (1819).

19. *Dred Scott* v. *Sandford*, 19 How. 393, 426 (1857).

20. James T. Patterson, *The New Deal and the States: Federalism in Transition* (Princeton, N.J.: Princeton University Press, 1969).

21. *United States* v. *Darby*, 312 U.S. 100 (1941).

22. Ronald Reagan, "Statement on Signing Executive Order Establishing the Presidential Advisory Committee on Federalism," 1981 Pub. Papers 341, 8 April 1981.

23. *Alden* v. *Maine* (98-436), *Florida* v. *College Savings Bank* (98-531), and *College Savings Bank* v. *Florida* (98-149).

24. Joseph F. Zimmerman, *Contemporary American Federalism: The Growth of National Power* (New York: Praeger, 1992), Chap. 4.

25. W. John Moore, "Stopping the States," *The National Journal*, vol. 22 (21 July 1990), pp. 1758+.

26. Lorianne Denne, "Food Labeling Bill Is a Fine Idea—But Scary, Too," *Puget Sound Business Journal*, vol. 11 (12 November 1990), Section 1, p. 13; Elaine S. Povich, "New Food Labeling Rules Get Stuck in States-Rights Dispute," *Chicago Tribune*, 23 March 1990, Business Section, p. 1.

27. *Crosby* v. *National Foreign Trade Council*, 530 U.S. 363 (2000).

28. National Governors' Association, Policy Positions, July 2000, <http://www.nga.org/Pubs/Policies/HR/hr16.asp>.

29. John Abell, "Clinton Says Bush Not Credible on Jobs Creation," *Reuter Library Report* (31 August 1992), NEXIS.

30. "Unfunded Federal Mandates," *Congressional Digest*, March 1995, p. 68.

31. Albert Hunt, "Federalism Debate Is as Much About Power as About Principle," *Wall Street Journal*, 19 January 1995, p. A17.

32. David Rogers, "Republicans' Move to Curb 'Unfunded Mandates' for States, Localities Has Its Own Complications," *Wall Street Journal*, 10 January 1995, p. A22.

33. U.S. Bureau of the Census, *Statistical Abstract of the United States: 1993* (Washington, D.C.: U.S. Government Printing Office, 1993), Table 466, p. 291.

34. Rebecca M. Blank, *It Takes a Nation: A New Agenda for Fighting Poverty* (New York and Princeton, N.J.: Russell Sage Foundation and Princeton University Press); John D. Donahue, *Disunited States* (New York: Basic Books, 1997); Paul E. Peterson and Mark C. Rom, *Welfare Magnets: A New Case for a National Standard* (Washington, D.C.: Brookings Institution, 1990).

35. *U.S. Term Limits* v. *Thornton*, 514 U.S. 779 (1995).

36. Ronald L. Watts (1999), *Comparing Federal Systems* (2nd ed.) (Montreal and Kingston, Canada: McGill-Queen's University Press), p. 4.

37. *Book of the States, 1992–93*, p. 246; *Book of the States, 1994–95*, p. 356.

38. Alice Rivlin, *Reviving the American Dream: The Economy, the States, and the Federal Government* (Washington, D.C.: Brookings Institution, 1992).

39. Michael A. Pagano and Ann O'M. Bowman, "The State of American Federalism, 1992–93" *Publius* 23 (Summer 1993), pp. 1–22.

Chapter 5 / Public Opinion and Political Socialization / pp. 124–158

1. Brooke A. Masters, "Missteps on Road to Injustice," *Washington Post*, 1 December 2000, pp. A1, A10.

2. DeNeen L. Brown, "Fighting for Survival on Death Row," *Washington Post*, 1 July 1990, accessed via <http://www.washingtonpost.com/ac2/wp-dyn/A99979-1990Jul2>.

3. Masters, "Missteps," p. A10.

4. Brooke A. Masters, "DNA Clears Inmate in 1982 Slaying," *Washington Post*, 3 October 2000, p. A1.

5. Mark Gillespie, "Americans Favor DNA 'Second Chance' Testing for Convicts," Gallup Poll Releases, 1 June 2000. Available on-line at <http://www.gallup.com/poll/releases/pr000601b.asp>.

6. Jeffrey M. Jones, "Slim Majority of Americans Think Death Penalty Applied Fairly in This Country," *Gallup Poll Monthly*, June 2000, pp. 64–67.

7. Gallup Organization, *Gallup Report*, 280 (January 1989), 27.

8. Warren Weaver, Jr., "Death Penalty a

300-Year Issue in America," *New York Times*, 3 July 1976.

9. *Furman* v. *Georgia*, 408 U.S. 238 (1972).

10. *Gregg* v. *Georgia*, 248 U.S. 153 (1976).

11. Tracy L. Snell, "Bureau of Justice Statistics Bulletin: Capital Punishment 1998" (Washington, D.C.: Office of Justice Programs, U.S. Department of Justice, 1999), pp. 11–12. Revised on-line 6 January 2000 at <http://www.ojp. usdoj.gov/bjs/pub/pdf/cp98.pdf>.

12. Gallup Organization, *Gallup Monthly Poll* (June 1991), p. 41.

13. *Ibid.*, p. 42.

14. E. Wayne Carp, "If Pollsters Had Been Around During the American Revolution" (letter to the editor), *New York Times*, 17 July 1993, p. 10.

15. Sidney Verba, "The Citizen as Respondent: Sample Surveys and American Democracy," *American Political Science Review*, 90 (March 1996), p. 3.

16. Nine national surveys taken from 1971 through 1988 found that an average of 61 percent of Americans disapproved of the ruling in *Abington School District* v. *Schempp*, 374 U.S. 203 (1963). See Richard Niemi, John Mueller, and Tom Smith, *Trends in Public Opinion: A Compendium of Survey Data* (New York: Greenwood Press, 1989), p. 263.

17. Jeffrey Schmalz, "Poll Finds an Even Split on Homosexuality's Cause," *New York Times*, 5 March 1993, p. A11.

18. Warren E. Miller and Santa A. Traugott, *American National Election Studies Sourcebook, 1952–1986* (Cambridge, Mass.: Harvard University Press, 1989), pp. 94–95. See Niemi, Mueller, and Smith, *Trends*, p. 19, for later years.

19. Tom W. Smith and Paul B. Sheatsley, "American Attitudes Toward Race Relations," *Public Opinion* 7 (October/November 1984), p. 15.

20. *Ibid.*, p. 83.

21. Steven A. Peterson, *Political Behavior: Patterns in Everyday Life* (Newbury Park, Calif.: Sage, 1990), pp. 28–29. For the importance of early learning for political attitudes, see also Jon A. Krosnick and Duane F. Alwin, "Aging and Susceptibility to Attitude Change," *Journal of Personality and Social Psychology*, 57 (1989), 416–423.

22. Paul Allen Beck, "The Role of Agents in Political Socialization," in *Handbook of Political Socialization Theory and Research*, ed. Stanley Allen Renshon (New York: Free Press, 1977), pp. 117–118.

23. W. Russell Neuman, *The Paradox of Mass Politics: Knowledge and Opinion in the American Electorate* (Cambridge, Mass.: Harvard University Press, 1986), pp. 113–114. See also Richard G. Niemi and Jane Junn, "Civics Courses and the Political Knowledge of High School Seniors," paper prepared for presentation at the annual meeting of the American Political Science Association, Washington, D.C., September 1993. They found that a favorable home environment (for example, having reading and reference material at home) related significantly to factual knowledge in a high school civics test.

24. M. Kent Jennings and Richard G. Niemi, *The Political Character of Adolescence: The Influence of Families and Schools* (Princeton, N.J.: Princeton University Press, 1974), p. 39. See also Stephen E. Frantzich, *Political Parties in the Technological Age* (New York: Longman, 1989), p. 152. Frantzich presents a table showing that more than 60 percent of children in homes in which both parents have the same party preference will adopt that preference. When parents are divided, the children tend to be divided among Democrats, Republicans, and independents.

25. In a panel study of parents and high school seniors in 1965 and in 1973, some years after their graduation, Jennings and Niemi found that 57 percent of children shared their parents' party identification in 1965, but only 47 percent did by 1973. See Jennings and Niemi, *Political Character*, pp. 90–91. See also Robert C. Luskin, John P. McIver, and Edward G. Carmines, "Issues and the Transmission of Partisanship," *American Journal of Political Science* 33 (May 1989), pp. 440–458. They found that children are more likely to shift between partisanship and independence than to "convert" to the other party. When conversion occurs, it is more likely to be based on economic issues than on social issues.

26. Robert D. Hess and Judith V. Torney, *The Development of Political Attitudes in Children* (Chicago: Aldine, 1967). But other researchers disagree. See Jerry L. Yeric and John R. Todd, *Public Opinion: The Visible Politics* (Itasca, Ill.: F. E. Peacock, 1989), pp. 45–47, for a summary of the issues. For a critical evaluation of the early literature on political socialization, see Pamela Johnston Conover, "Political Socialization: Where's the Politics?" in *Political Science: Looking to the Future,*

Volume 3: *Political Behavior*, ed. William Crotty (Evanston, Ill.: Northwestern University Press, 1991), pp. 125–152.

27. David Easton and Jack Dennis, *Children in the Political System* (New York: McGraw-Hill, 1969).

28. Jarol B. Manheim, *The Politics Within* (New York: Longman, 1982), pp. 83,125–151.

29. Richard Niemi and Jane Y. Junn, "Civics Courses and the Political Knowledge of High School Seniors," paper prepared for presentation at the annual meeting of the American Political Science Association, Washington, D.C., September 1993.

30. Edith J. Barrett, "The Political Socialization of Inner-City Adolescents," paper prepared for presentation at the annual meeting of the American Political Science Association, Washington, D.C., September 1993.

31. M. Kent Jennings, "Political Knowledge Over Time and Across Generations," *Public Opinion Quarterly* 60 (Summer 1996), pp. 239, 241.

32. Janie S. Steckenrider and Neal E. Cutler, "Aging and Adult Political Socialization: The Importance of Roles and Transitions," in *Political Learning in Adulthood: A Sourcebook of Theory and Research*, ed. Roberta S. Sigel (Chicago: University of Chicago Press, 1989), pp. 56–88.

33. See Robert Huckfeldt and John Sprague, "Networks in Context: The Social Flow of Information," *American Political Science Review* 81 (December 1987), 1197–1216. The authors' study of voting in neighborhoods in South Bend, Indiana, found that residents who favored the minority party were acutely aware of their minority status.

34. Theodore M. Newcomb et al., *Persistence and Social Change: Bennington College and Its Students After Twenty-Five Years* (New York: Wiley, 1967); and Duane F. Alwin, Ronald L. Cohen, and Theodore M. Newcomb, *Political Attitudes over the Life Span: The Bennington Women after Fifty Years* (Madison: University of Wisconsin Press, 1991).

35. M. Kent Jennings and Gregory Marcus, "Yuppie Politics," *Institute of Social Research Newsletter*, August 1986.

36. See Roberta S. Sigel, ed., *Political Learning in Adulthood: A Sourcebook of Theory and Research* (Chicago: University of Chicago Press, 1989).

37. Pew Center for the People and the Press, *In Retrospect: Public Opinions*

1997 (Washington, D.C.: Pew Research Center, 1997), p. 18.

38. The wording of this question is criticized by R. Michael Alvarez and John Brehm in "When Core Beliefs Collide: Conflict, Complexity, or Just Plain Confusion?" a paper prepared for delivery at the annual meeting of the American Political Science Association, Washington, D.C., September 1993, p. 9. They argue that using the phrase "personal choice" (which they call a core value) triggers the psychological effect of reactance, or the feeling that a freedom has been removed. But this core value is precisely our focus in this analysis. Alvarez and Brehm favor using instead the battery of six questions on abortion that have been used in the General Social Survey. Those six questions are also used in Elizabeth Adell Cook, Ted G. Jelen, and Clyde Wilcox, *Between Two Absolutes: Public Opinion and the Politics of Abortion* (Boulder, Colo.: Westview, 1992). Those interested primarily in analyzing various attitudes toward abortion probably should use data from the General Social Survey.

39. Although some people view the politics of abortion as "single issue" politics, the issue has broader political significance. In their book on the subject, Cook, Jelen, and Wilcox say, "Although embryonic life is one important value in the abortion debate, it is not the only value at stake." They contend that the politics is tied to alternative sexual relationships and traditional roles of women in the home, which are "social order" issues. See *Between Two Absolutes*, pp. 8–9.

40. *Ibid.*, p. 50.

41. The increasing wealth in industrialized societies may or may not be replacing class conflict with conflict over values. See the exchange between Ronald Inglehart and Scott C. Flanagan, "Value Change in Industrial Societies," *American Political Science Review* 81 (December 1987), pp. 1289–1319.

42. Nathan Glazer, "The Structure of Ethnicity," *Public Opinion* 7 (October/November 1984), p. 4.

43. For a review of these studies, see Robert S. Erikson, Norman R. Luttbeg, and Kent L. Tedin, *American Public Opinion*, 3d ed. (New York: Macmillan, 1988).

44. Steven A. Holmes, "Census Sees a Profound Ethnic Shift in U.S.," *New York Times*, 14 March 1996, p. A8.

45. Glazer, "Structure of Ethnicity," p. 5.

46. National Election Study for 1994,

an election survey conducted by the Center for Political Studies at the University of Michigan.

47. See David C. Leege and Lyman A. Kellstedt, eds., *Rediscovering the Religious Factor in American Politics* (Armonk, N.Y.: M. E. Sharpe, 1993) for a comprehensive examination of religion in political life that goes far beyond the analysis here.

48. "The Diminishing Divide . . . American Churches, American Politics," news release, 25 June 1996 (Washington, D.C.: Pew Research Center for the People & the Press), pp. 1 and 12. See also Lyman A. Kellstedt, "Religion, the Neglected Variable: An Agenda for Future Research on Religion and Political Behavior," in Leege and Kellstedt, *Rediscovering the Religious Factor*, p. 273.

49. John Robinson, "The Ups and Downs and Ins and Outs of Ideology," *Public Opinion* 7 (February/March 1984), p. 12.

50. For a more positive interpretation of ideological attitudes within the public, see William G. Jacoby, "The Structure of Ideological Thinking in the American Electorate," paper presented at the Annual Meeting of the American Political Science Association, Washington, D.C., September 1993. Jacoby applies a new method to survey data for the 1984 and 1988 elections and concludes "that there is a systematic, cumulative structure underlying liberal-conservative thinking in the American public" (p. 1).

51. Quoted in Marjorie Connelly, "A 'Conservative' Is (Fill in the Blank)," *New York Times*, 3 November 1996, Section 4, p. 5.

52. Angus Campbell, Philip E. Converse, Warren E. Miller, and Donald E. Stokes, *The American Voter* (New York: Wiley, 1960), Chap. 10.

53. Connelly, "A 'Conservative' Is (Fill in the Blank)."

54. *Ibid.*

55. See William G. Jacoby, "Levels of Conceptualization and Reliance on the Liberal-Conservative Continuum," *Journal of Politics* 48 (May 1986), pp. 423–432. We also know that certain political actors, such as delegates to national party conventions, hold far more consistent and durable beliefs than the public. See M. Kent Jennings, "Ideological Thinking Among Mass Publics and Political Elites," *Public Opinion Quarterly* 56 (Winter 1992), pp. 419–441.

56. National Election Study, 1996.

57. However, citizens can have ideo-

logically consistent attitudes toward candidates and perceptions about domestic issues without thinking about politics in explicitly liberal and conservative terms. See William G. Jacoby, "The Structure of Liberal-Conservative Thinking in the American Public," paper prepared for presentation at the annual meeting of the Midwest Political Science Association, 1990.

58. Pamela Johnston Conover, "The Origins and Meaning of Liberal-Conservative Self-identifications," *American Journal of Political Science* 25 (November 1981), pp. 621–622, 643.

59. A relationship between liberalism and political tolerance was found by John L. Sullivan et al., "The Sources of Political Tolerance: A Multivariate Analysis," *American Political Science Review* 75 (March 1981), p. 102. See also Robinson, "Ups and Downs," pp. 13–15.

60. Herbert Asher, *Presidential Elections and American Politics* (Homewood, Ill.: Dorsey, 1980), pp. 14–20. Asher also constructs a two-dimensional framework, distinguishing between "traditional New Deal" issues and "new lifestyle" issues.

61. John E. Jackson, "The Systematic Beliefs of the Mass Public: Estimating Policy Preferences with Survey Data," *Journal of Politics* 45 (November 1983), pp. 840–865.

62. Milton Rokeach also proposed a two-dimensional model of political ideology grounded in the terminal values of freedom and equality. See *The Nature of Human Values* (New York: Free Press, 1973), especially Chap. 6. Rokeach found that positive and negative references to the two values permeate the writings of socialists, communists, fascists, and conservatives and clearly differentiate the four bodies of writing from one another (pp. 173–174). However, Rokeach built his two-dimensional model around only the values of freedom and equality; he did not deal with the question of freedom versus order.

63. William S. Maddox and Stuart A. Lilie, *Beyond Liberal and Conservative: Reassessing the Political Spectrum* (Washington, D.C.: Cato Institute, 1984), p. 68. From 1993 to 1996, the Gallup Organization, in conjunction with CNN and *USA Today*, has asked national samples two questions: (1) whether individuals or government should solve our country's problems, and (2) whether the government should promote traditional values. Gallup constructed a similar ideological typology from responses to these questions and found a similar distribution of the population into four groups. See Gallup's "Final Top Line" for 12–15 January 1996, pp. 30–31.

64. See Neuman, *Paradox*, p. 81. See also Aaron Wildavsky, "Choosing Preferences by Constructing Institutions: A Cultural Theory of Preference Formation," *American Political Science Review* 81 (March 1987), p. 13.

65. The same conclusion was reached in a major study of British voting behavior. See Hilde T. Himmelweit, et al., *How Voters Decide* (New York: Academic Press, 1981), pp. 138–141. See also Wildavsky, "Choosing Preferences," p. 13.

66. In our framework, opposition to abortion is classified as a communitarian position. However, the Communitarian movement led by Amitai Etzioni adopted no position on abortion. (Personal communication from Vanessa Hoffman by e-mail, in reply to my query of 5 February 1996.)

67. But a significant literature is developing on the limitations of self-interest in explaining political life. See Jane J. Mansbridge, ed., *Beyond Self-interest* (Chicago: University of Chicago Press, 1990).

68. Wildavsky, "Choosing Preferences," pp. 3–21.

69. David O. Sears and Carolyn L. Funk, "Self-interest in Americans' Political Opinions," in Mansbridge, *Beyond Self-interest*, pp. 147–170.

70. Two researchers who compared the public's knowledge on various topics in 1989 with its knowledge of the same topics in the 1940s and 1950s found similar levels of knowledge across the years. They point out, however, "That knowledge has been stable during a period of rapid changes in education, communication, and the public role of women seems paradoxical." They suspect, but cannot demonstrate, that the expected increase in knowledge did not materialize because of a decline in the public's interest in politics over time. See Michael X. Delli Carpini and Scott Keeter, "Stability and Change in the U.S. Public's Knowledge of Politics," *Public Opinion Quarterly* 55 (Winter 1991), p. 607.

71. Darren K. Carlson, "Who's Who? Gallup Polls the Public on Prominent Public Figures," *Gallup Poll Monthly*, January 2000, p. 63. Frank Newport, "Americans Don't Necessarily Like Russia, but Tend to See Russia's Relationship to U.S. as Friendly," *Gallup*

Poll Monthly, June 2000, p. 42. Richard Morin, "Who's in Control? Many Don't Know or Care," *Washington Post*, 29 January 1996, p. A6.

72. Benjamin I. Page and Robert Y. Shapiro, *The Rational Public* (Chicago: University of Chicago Press, 1992).

73. *Ibid.*, p. 45.

74. *Ibid.*, p. 385. The argument for a rational quality in public opinion by Page and Shapiro was supported by Stimson's massive analysis of swings in the liberal-conservative attitudes of the U.S. public from 1956 to 1990. Analyzing more than one thousand attitude items, he found that the public mood had already swung away from liberalism when Ronald Reagan appeared on the scene to campaign for president as a conservative. See James A. Stimson, *Public Opinion in America: Moods, Cycles, & Swings* (Boulder, Colo.: Westview, 1992).

75. See R. Michael Alvarez and John Brehm, "When Core Beliefs Collide"; and Scott L. Althaus, "Opinion Polls, Information Effects, and Political Equality: Exploring Ideological Biases in Collective Opinion," *Political Communication*, 13 (January-March 1996), pp. 3–21.

76. Michael X. Delli Carpini and Scott Keeter, *What Americans Know About Politics and Why It Matters* (New Haven, Conn.: Yale University Press, 1996).

77. *Ibid.*, p. 269.

78. *Ibid.*, p. 271.

79. There is evidence that the educational system and parental practices hamper the ability of women to develop their political knowledge. See Linda L. M. Bennett and Stephen Earl Bennett, "Enduring Gender Differences in Political Interests," *American Politics Quarterly* 17 (January 1989), pp. 105–122.

80. Neuman, *Paradox*, p. 81.

81. Pamela Johnston Conover and Stanley Feldman, "How People Organize the Political World: A Schematic Model," *American Journal of Political Science* 28 (February 1984), p. 96. For an excellent review of schema structures in contemporary psychology—especially as they relate to political science—see Reid Hastie, "A Primer of Information-Processing Theory for the Political Scientist," in *Political Cognition*, ed. Richard R. Lau and David O. Sears (Hillsdale, N.J.: Erlbaum, 1986), pp. 11–39.

82. John Hurwitz and Mark Peffley, "How Are Foreign Policy Attitudes

Structured? A Hierarchical Model," *American Political Science Review* 81 (December 1987), pp. 1099–1220.

83. Richard L. Allen, Michael C. Dawson, and Ronald E. Brown, "A Schema-Based Approach to Modeling an African-American Racial Belief System," *American Political Science Review* 83 (June 1989), pp. 421–441.

84. See Milton Lodge and Ruth Hamill, "A Partisan Schema for Political Information Processing," *American Political Science Review* 80 (June 1986), pp. 505–519.

85. Arthur Sanders, *Making Sense Out of Politics* (Ames: Iowa State University Press, 1990).

86. Lee Sigelman, "Disarming the Opposition: The President, the Public, and the INF Treaty," *Public Opinion Quarterly* 54 (Spring 1990), p. 46.

87. Benjamin I. Page, Robert Y. Shapiro, and Glenn R. Dempsey, "What Moves Public Opinion?" *American Political Science Review* 81 (March 1987), pp. 23–43.

88. Michael Margolis and Gary A. Mauser, *Manipulating Public Opinion: Essays on Public Opinion as a Dependent Variable* (Pacific Grove, Calif.: Brooks/Cole, 1989).

Chapter 6 / The Media / pp. 159–192

1. Peter Finn, "Neo-Nazi Web Sites Moving to U.S.," *Washington Post*, 21 December 2000, p. A1.

2. *Ibid.*

3. Kevin W. Hula, *Lobbying Together: Interest Group Coalitions in Legislative Politics* (Washington, D.C.: Georgetown University Press, 1999), p. 91.

4. *Ibid.*, p. 90.

5. \ H. Stempel III, Thomas Hargrove, and Joseph P. Bernt, "Relation of Growth of Use of the Internet to Changes in Media Use from 1995 to 1999," *Journalism and Mass Communication Quarterly*, 77, 1 (Spring 2000), p. 71.

6. Robert Neuwirth, "Getting an Eyeful," *Editor and Publisher*, 11 December 2000, p. ill.

7. A man who shot a state trooper in Austin, Texas, in 1992 blamed his action on antipolice rap music from a Shakur album he was listening to before he was stopped by the trooper. See "Rap Music Blamed in Trooper's Killing," *Chicago Tribune*, 3 June 1993, p. 13.

8. S. N. D. North, *The Newspaper and Periodical Press* (Washington, D.C.: U.S. Government Printing Office, 1884), p. 27. This source provides much of the information reported here about newspapers and magazines before 1880.

9. Editor and Publisher, *International Year Book, 1997* (New York: Editor & Publisher Co., 1997), p. xxiii.

10. In 1950, a total of 1,772 daily papers had a circulation of 53.8 million; in 1993, a total of 1,556 papers had a circulation of 59.8 million. The number of newspapers per capita was 0.35 in 1950 and 0.23 in 1993. See Harold W. Stanley and Richard G. Niemi (eds.), *Vital Statistics on American Politics*, 5th ed. (Washington, D.C.: Congressional Quarterly Press, 1995), p. 50.

11. Mark Fitzgerald, "Latest FAS-FAX Report: It Sinks!" *Editor and Publisher*, 6 November 2000, p. 14.

12. Benjamin I. Page, *Who Deliberates: Mass Media in Modern Democracy* (Chicago: University of Chicago Press, 1996), p. 106.

13. Douglas Kellner, *Television and the Crisis of Democracy* (Boulder, Colo.: Westview Press, 1990), pp. 225–248.

14. Howard Kurtz, *Hot Air: All Talk, All the Time* (New York: Times Books, 1996). See also Michael Traugott, et al., "The Impact of Talk Radio on Its Audience," paper prepared for presentation at the annual meeting of the Midwest Political Science Association, Chicago, 1996. This study demonstrates that listening to talk radio increases people's attention to political news.

15. Dana R. Ulloth, Peter L. Klinge, and Sandra Eells, *Mass Media: Past, Present, Future* (St. Paul, Minn.: West, 1983), p. 278.

16. Daily fax assaults against the Clinton campaign in the 1992 election season are discussed in Jacob Weisberg, "True Fax: Mary Matalin, Vindicated," *New Republic*, 5 June 1993, pp. 11–12.

17. Robin Wright, "Hyper Democracy: Washington Isn't Dangerously Disconnected from the People; the Trouble May Be It's Too Plugged In," *Time*, 23 January 1995, pp. 14–31.

18. Rich Lowry, "Fax Populi: Armed with Computers and Fax Machines, Grass-Roots Organizations Are Shaking Up the Liberal Establishment," *National Review*, 7 November 1994, pp. 50–54. *Fax Congress Now* is a computer program designed to facilitate faxing government officials; see *Macworld*, May 1995, p. 48. The percentage of homes with fax machines comes from Steve Lohr, "The Great Unplugged Masses Confront the Future," *New York Times*, 21 January 1996, Section 4, p. 1.

19. Fittingly, this history of the Internet came from the Discovery Channel Online Web site at <www.discovery.com/DCO/doc/1012/world/technology/internet/inet1.5.html>.

20. John December, Neil Randall, and Wes Tatters, *Discover the World Wide Web with Your Sportster* (Indianapolis, Ind.: Sams.net Publishing, 1995), pp. 11–12.

21. Janny Scott, "A Media Race Enters Waters Still Uncharted," *New York Times*, 1 February 1998, pp. 1, 17. A search of the Internet for "Paula Jones" produced 6,674 "hits" only three days after Clinton gave his deposition in her lawsuit. A search one week later produced 7,808 and over 200 hits were in foreign language sources, indicating the worldwide nature of the Web. The first search was performed on January 20 and the second on January 26. Both searches used the AltaVista search engine.

22. Jon Bigness, "Clinton's Crisis, Internet's Boom," *Chicago Tribune*, 30 January 1998, Section 3, pp. 1, 4.

23. Steve Lohr, "European TV's Vast Growth: Cultural Effect Stirs Concern," *New York Times*, 16 March 1989, p. 1.

24. U.S. Bureau of the Census, *Statistical Abstract of the United States, 1996* (Washington D.C.: U.S. Government Printing Office, 1996), pp. 561, 566.

25. Stephen Seplow and Jonathan Storm, "TV at 50: Dominating Americans' Free Time," *St. Paul Pioneer Press*, 28 December 1997, pp. 1, 8A; and Pew Research Center for the People and the Press, "TV News Viewership Declines," *News Release*, 13 May 1996, p. 64.

26. Doris A. Graber, *Mass Media and American Politics* (Washington, D.C.: Congressional Quarterly Press, 1984), pp. 78–79. See also W. Lance Bennett, *News: The Politics of Illusion*, 3d ed. (White Plains, N.Y.: Longman, 1996), Chap. 2.

27. Kenneth R. Clark, "Network Audience Share at Record Low," *Chicago Tribune*, 30 November 1990, section 3, p. 1.

28. *Editor & Publisher International Yearbook* (New York: Editor & Publisher Company, 1996).

29. Kelvin Childs, "End the Cross-Owner Ban," *Editor & Publisher*, 28 June 1997, p. 11.

30. "Measuring a Combined Viacom/CBS Against Other Media Giants," *New York Times*, 8 September 1999, p. C15. "Viacom, Inc.: The Facts," 21 December 2000, available on-line at <http://www.viacom.com/thefacts.tin>.

31. Joseph Turow, *Media Industries: The Production of News and Entertainment* (New York: Longman, 1984), p. 18. Our discussion of government regulation draws heavily on this source.

32. Bill McConnell, "Now Opening: AOL-TW," *Broadcasting & Cable*, 18 December 2000, p. 12.

33. Mark Crispin Miller, "Free the Media," *The Nation*, 3 June 1996, pp. 9–15.

34. Bill Carter, "F.C.C. Will Permit Owning 2 Stations in Big TV Markets," *New York Times*, 6 August 1999, pp. A1, C5.

35. Jared Sandberg, "Federal Judges Block Censorship on the Internet," *Wall Street Journal*, 13 June 1996, p. B1.

36. Paige Albiniak, "Court Scraps Reply Rules," *Broadcasting & Cable*, 16 October 2000, pp. 6–7. Stephen Labaton, "In Test, F.C.C. Lifts Requirement on Broadcasting Political Replies," *New York Times*, 5 October 2000, pp. A1, A27.

37. Graber, *Mass Media*, p. 110.

38. Robert Entman, *Democracy Without Citizens: Media and the Decay of American Politics* (New York: Oxford University Press, 1989), pp. 103–108.

39. S. Robert Lichter and Richard E. Noyes, *Good Intentions Make Bad News* (Lanham, Md.: Rowman & Littlefield, 1995), p. 26, note 9.

40. Michael Nelson (ed.), *Guide to the Presidency* (Washington, D.C.: Congressional Quarterly Press, 1989), p. 729.

41. *Ibid.*, p. 735.

42. Graber, *Mass Media*, p. 241.

43. Warren Weaver, "C-Span on the Hill: 10 Years of Gavel to Gavel," *New York Times*, 28 March 1989, p. 10; and Francis X. Clines, "C-Span Inventor Offers More Politics Up Close," *New York Times*, 31 March 1996, p. 11.

44. Bennett, *News: The Politics of Illusion*, p. 26.

45. Quote attributed to Sandra Mims Rowe, president of the American Society of Newspaper Editors, in Janny Scott, "A Media Race Enters Waters Still Uncharted," *New York Times*, 1 February 1998, p. 1.

46. Bill Kovach, "The Brewing Backlash," *Chicago Tribune*, 1 February 1998, Section 2, p. 1; and Scott, "A Media Race Enters Waters Still Uncharted."

47. Austin Ranney, *Channels of Power: The Impact of Television on American Politics* (New York: Basic Books, 1983), p. 46.

48. Doris A. Graber, *Mass Media and*

American Politics, 3d ed. (Washington, D.C.: Congressional Quarterly Press, 1989), p. 237. See also Janet Hook, "Most of Us Don't Have a Clue About How Congress Works," *Chicago Tribune*, 10 June 1993, section 1, p. 17.

49. Markle Presidential Election Watch, "Networks Yawned, Public Shrugged at Campaign '96," November 1996. Found at <www.markle.org/J95327pr3.html>.

50. "America's Watching: Public Attitudes Toward Television," pamphlet published in New York by the Network Television Association and the National Association of Broadcasters, 1995, pp. 17–18.

51. Pew Research Center for the People and the Press, "TV News Viewership Declines," press release, 13 May 1996, p. 1.

52. Pew Research Center for the People and the Press, *Scene 96: Take 2* (Washington, D.C.: Pew Charitable Trusts, 1996), p. 6.

53. Debra Gersh Hernandez, "Profile of the News Consumer," *Editor & Publisher*, 18 January 1997, p. 6.

54. Linda L. M. Bennett and Stephen Earl Bennett, "Enduring Gender Differences in Political Interests," *American Politics Quarterly* 17 (January 1989), pp. 105–122, especially pp. 116–117.

55. Times Mirror Center for the People and the Press, "The American Media," 15 July 1990. This fits with findings by Stephen Earl Bennett in "Trends in Americans' Political Information, 1967–1987," *American Politics Quarterly* 17 (October 1989), pp. 422–435. Bennett found that race was significantly related to level of political information in a 1967 survey but not in a 1987 survey.

56. Pew Research Center for the People and the Press, "Americans Only a Little Better Off, but Much Less Anxious," *Press Release*, 23 May 1997, p. 5.

57. One seasoned journalist argues instead that the technology of minicams and satellites has set back the quality of news coverage. Now a television crew can fly to the scene of a crisis and immediately televise information without knowing much about the local politics or culture, which was not true of the old foreign correspondents. See David R. Gergen, "Diplomacy in a Television Age: The Dangers of Teledemocracy," in *The Media and Foreign Policy*, ed. Simon Serfaty (New York: St. Martin's Press, 1990), p. 51.

58. Bennett, "Trends in Americans' Political Information." Bennett's find-

ings are supported by a national poll in 1990 that found only 40 percent of the sample had read a newspaper "yesterday," compared with 71 percent in 1965. Times-Mirror Center for the People and the Press, "The American Media," p. 100. Two researchers who compared the public's level of knowledge in 1989 with answers to the same questions in the 1940s and 1950s found similar levels of knowledge across the years but added, "That knowledge has been stable during a period of rapid changes in education, communication, and the public role of women seems paradoxical." They suspect, but cannot demonstrate, that the lack of expected increase is because of a decline in political interest over time. See Michael X. Delli Carpini and Scott Keeter, "Stability and Change in the U.S. Public's Knowledge of Politics," *Public Opinion Quarterly* 55 (Winter 1991), pp. 583–612.

59. W. Russell Neuman, Marion R. Just, and Ann N. Crigler, *Common Knowledge: News and the Construction of Political Meaning* (Chicago: University of Chicago Press, 1992), p. 10. See also Hernandez, "Profile of the News Consumer," p. 7; respondents who said that newspapers were their primary source of information correctly answered more factual questions than those who used other media.

60. Doris A. Graber, *Processing the News: How People Tame the Information Tide*, 2d ed. (New York: Longman, 1988), pp. 166–169.

61. Neuman, Just, and Crigler, *News and the Contruction of Political Meaning*.

62. *Ibid.*, pp. 86–87.

63. *Ibid.*, pp. 106–107.

64. *Ibid.*, p. 113.

65. Laurence Parisot, "Attitudes About the Media: A Five-Country Comparison," *Public Opinion* 10 (January/February 1988), p. 60.

66. The statistical difficulties in determining media effects owing to measurement error are discussed in Larry M. Bartels, "Messages Received: The Political Impact of Media Exposure," paper prepared for delivery at the annual meeting of the American Political Science Association, Washington, D.C., September 1993. According to Bartels, "More direct and convincing demonstrations of significant opinion changes due to media exposure will require data collections spanning considerably longer periods of time" (p. 27).

67. "Clinton Gets a Bounce: Most People Who Watched Give His State of Union Speech High Marks," 27 January

1998, CNN/Time All-Politics Web site <www.allpolitics.com>. The Nielsen estimates of total number of viewers was 53.1 million, reported in the anonymous news item, "Clinton's Troubles Built TV Ratings," *New York Times*, 29 January 1998, p. A19.

68. Benjamin I. Page, Robert Y. Shapiro, and Glenn R. Dempsey, "What Moves Public Opinion?" *American Political Science Review* 81 (March 1987), p. 31.

69. Donald L. Jordan, "Newspaper Effects on Policy Preferences," *Public Opinion Quarterly* 57 (Summer 1993), pp. 191–204. Interestingly, Bartels's study of media effects in the 1980 presidential election, which used very different methodology, found that "the average impact of newspaper exposure across a wide range of candidate and issue perceptions was only about half as large as the corresponding impact of television news exposure" (Bartels, "Messages Received," p. 26).

70. Daniel J. Wakin, "Report Calls Networks' Election Night Coverage a Disaster," *New York Times*, 3 February 2001, p. A8.

71. Tim Jones, "Tonight: Murder, Mayhem . . . and Second Thoughts," *Chicago Tribune*, 6 July 1997, Section 5, pp. 1, 9. See also Mark Fitzgerald, "Local TV Lacks Substance," *Editor & Publisher*, 24 May 1997, pp. 8–9.

72. Everett C. Ladd, "Crime and Punishment," *Public Perspective* (June-July 1997), p. 11.

73. *Ibid.*, pp. 35–37.

74. Lawrie Mifflin, "Crime Falls, but Not on TV," *New York Times*, 6 July 1997, Section 4, p. 4.

75. Ladd, "Crime and Punishment," p. 10.

76. W. Russell Neuman, "The Threshold of Public Attention," *Public Opinion Quarterly* 54 (Summer 1990), pp. 159–176.

77. David E. Harrington, "Economic News on Television: The Determinants of Coverage," *Public Opinion Quarterly* 53 (Spring 1989), pp. 17–40.

78. Entman, *Democracy Without Citizens*, p. 86.

79. *Ibid.*, pp. 47–48.

80. A panel study of ten- to seventeen-year-olds during the 1988 presidential campaign found that the campaign helped these young people crystallize their party identifications and their attitudes toward the candidates but had little effect on their political ideology and views on central campaign issues. See David O. Sears, Nicholas A. Valentino, and Rick Kosterman, "Domain Specificity in the Effects of Political Events on Preadult Socialization," paper prepared for delivery at the annual meeting of the American Political Science Association, Washington, D.C., September 1993.

81. Richard Zoglin, "Is TV Ruining Our Children?" *Time,* 5 October 1990, p. 75. Moreover, much of what children see are advertisements. See "Study: Almost 20% of Kid TV Is Ad-Related," *Chicago Tribune,* 22 April 1991, p. 11. See also Stephen Seplow and Jonathan Storm, "Reviews Mixed on Television's Effect on Children," *St. Paul Pioneer Press,* 28 December 1997, p. 9A.

82. John J. O'Connor, "Soothing Bromides? Not on TV," *New York Times,* 28 October 1990, Arts & Leisure section, pp. 1, 35. Some people watch *The X-Files* because it involves sinister government activities. See Alanna Nash, "Confused or Not, the X-Philes Keep Coming," *New York Times,* 11 January 1998, p. 41.

83. Douglas Kellner, *Television and the Crisis of Democracy* (Boulder, Colo.: Westview Press, 1990), p. 17.

84. James Fallows, *Breaking the News: How the Media Undermine American Democracy* (New York: Pantheon Books, 1996).

85. These facts come from the web page "ASNE Survey: Journalists Say They're Liberal," found at <www.asne.org/kiosk/editor/97.jan-feb/dennis4.htm>. The research project is described in American Society of Editors, "Newspaper Journalists Examined in Major Study," *News Release,* 10 April 1997. Available at <www.asne.org/kiosk/newsworkforc.htm>.

86. Markle Presidential Election Watch, "Networks Yawned, Public Shrugged at Campaign '96," press release data, November 1996, found at <www.markle.org/J95327pr3. html>.

87. *The People, The Press, & Their Leaders* (Washington, D.C.: Times-Mirror Center for the People and the Press, 1995).

88. "Bird in the Hand for Bush," *Editor & Publisher,* 6 November 2000, pp. 24–27.

89. Michael Robinson and Margaret Sheehan, *Over the Wire and on TV: CBS and UPI in Campaign '80* (New York: Russell Sage Foundation, 1983).

90. Michael J. Robinson, "The Media in Campaign '84: Part II; Wingless, Toothless, and Hopeless," *Public Opinion* 8 (February/March 1985), p. 48.

91. Maura Clancey and Michael J.

Robinson, "General Election Coverage: Part I," *Public Opinion* 7 (December/January 1985), p. 54.

92. Todd Shields, "Media Accentuates the Negative," *Editor & Publisher,* 27 November 2000, p. 12.

93. Stanley Rothman and S. Robert Lichter, "Elite Ideology and Risk Perception in Nuclear Energy Policy," *American Political Science Review* 81 (June 1987), p. 393.

94. For a historical account of efforts to determine voters' preferences before modern polling, see Tom W. Smith, "The First Straw? A Study of the Origin of Election Polls," *Public Opinion Polling* 54 (Spring 1990), pp. 21–36. See also Chapter 4 in Susan Herbst, *Numbered Voices: How Opinion Polling Has Shaped American Politics* (Chicago: University of Chicago Press, 1993).

95. Michael W. Traugott, "Public Attitudes About News Organizations, Campaign Coverage, and Polls," in *Polling and Presidential Election Coverage,* p. 135.

96. Schneider and Lewis, "Views on the News," p. 11. For similar findings from a 1994 study, see Times-Mirror Center for the People and the Press, "Mixed Message about Press Freedom on Both Sides of the Atlantic," press release of 16 March 1994, p. 65. See also Patterson, "News Decisions," p. 21.

97. Charles M. Madigan and Bob Secter, "Second Thoughts on Free Speech," *Chicago Tribune,* 4 July 1997, pp. 1, 18, 20.

Chapter 7 / Participation and Voting / pp. 193–227

1. V. Dion Haynes, "Normal Folks Held in Arizona Militia Plot," *Chicago Tribune,* 4 July 1996, p. 1.

2. Patricia King, "'Vipers' in the 'Burbs," *Newsweek.* 15 July 1996, p. 23.

3. Haynes, p. 1.

4. This imformation is taken from the Link section of "The Militia Watch-dog" at <www.militia-watchdog.org>.

5. Cited in "Minuteman Press Online," obtained at <www.afn.org/~mpress/page1.html> on July 6, 1996. The "Restoring America" militia site can be found at <www.rechmgmt.com/restore/resotre.html>.

6. Lester W. Milbrath and M. L. Goel, *Political Participation,* (Chicago, Ill.: Rand McNally, 1977), p. 2.

7. See Sidney Verba, Kay Lehman Scholozman, and Henry E. Brady, *Voice*

and Equality: Civic Voluntarism in American Politics* (Cambridge, Mass.: Harvard University Press, 1995), pp. 40–42. In a highly publicized article, Robert D. Putnam argued that participation in politics in the United States has suffered because our nation is losing the "social capital" that is based on active participation in community life. For example, Americans are "bowling alone"—that is, they are still bowling, but not in organized leagues." See his "Bowling Alone: America's Declining Social Capital," *Journal of Democracy,* 6 (January 1995), pp. 65–78. Putnam's analysis inspired related critical observations on contemporary society, but it also sparked criticism of his data and his argument. For an empirical rebuttal, see Everett C. Ladd, "The Data Just Don't Show Erosion of America's 'Social Capital'!" *Public Perspective,* 7 (June–July 1996), pp. 1, 5–22.

8. Michael Lapsky, "Protest as a Political Resource," *American Political Science Review* 62 (December 1968), p. 1145.

9. William E. Schmidt, "Selma Marchers Mark 1965 Clash," *New York Times,* 4 March 1985.

10. See Sidney Verba and Norman H. Nie, *Participation in America: Political Democracy and Social Equality* (New York: Harper & Row, 1972), p. 3.

11. Russell J. Dalton, *Citizen Politics,* 2nd ed. (Chatham, N.J.: Chatham House, 1996).

12. Jonathan D. Casper, *Politics of Civil Liberties* (New York: Harper & Row, 1972), p. 90.

13. David C. Colby, "A Test of the Relative Efficacy of Political Tactics," *American Journal of Political Science* 26 (November 1982), pp. 741–753. See also Frances Fox Piven and Richard Cloward, *Poor People's Movements* (New York: Vintage, 1979)

14. Raoul V. Mowatt, "Voting Act Heralded 35 Years Later," *Chicago Tribune,* 5 August 2000, p. 5.

15. Stephen C. Craig and Michael A. Magiotto, "Political Discontent and Political Action," *Journal of Politics* 43 (May 1981), pp. 514–522. But see Mitchell A. Seligson, "Trust Efficacy and Modes of Political Participation: A Study of Costa Rican Peasants," *British Journal of Political Science* 10 (January 1980), pp. 75–98, for a review of studies that came to different conclusions.

16. Arthur H. Miller et al., "Group Consciousness and Political Participation," *American Journal of Political Science* 25 (August 1981), p.

495. See also Susan J. Carroll, "Gender Politics and the Socializing Impact of the Women's Movement," in *Political Learning in Adulthood: A Sourcebook of Theory and Research,* ed. Roberta S. Sigel (Chicago, Ill.: University of Chicago Press, 1989), p. 307.

17. Richard D. Shingles, "Black Consciousness and Political Participation: The Missing Link," *American Political Science Review* 75 (March 1981), pp. 76–91. See also Lawrence Bobo and Franklin D. Gilliam, Jr., "Race, Sociopolitical Participation, and Black Empowerment," *American Political Science Review* 84 (June 1990), pp. 377–393; and Jan Leighley, "Group Membership and the Mobilization of Political Participation," *Journal of Politics,* 58 (May 1996), pp. 447–463.

18. Dalton, *Citizen Politics,* p. 65.

19. M. Kent Jennings, Jan W. van Deth, et al., *Continuities in Political Action: A Longitudinal Study of Political Orientations in Three Western Democracies* (New York: Walter de Gruyter, 1990).

20. See James L. Gibson, "The Policy Consequences of Political Intolerance: Political Repression During the Vietnam War Era," *Journal of Politics* 51 (February 1989), pp. 13–35. Gibson found that individual state legislatures reacted quite differently in response to antiwar demonstrations on college campuses, but the laws passed to discourage dissent were not related directly to public opinion within the state.

21. See Verba and Nie, *Participation in America,* p. 69. Also see John Clayton Thomas, "Citizen-Initiated Contacts with Government Agencies: A Test of Three Theories," *American Journal of Political Science* 26 (August 1982), pp. 504–522; and Elaine B. Sharp, "Citizen-Initiated Contacting of Government Officials and Socioeconomic Status: Determining the Relationship and Accounting for It," *American Political Science Review* 76 (March 1982), pp. 109–115.

22. Elaine B. Sharp, "Citizen Demand Making in the Urban Context," *American Journal of Political Science* 28 (November 1984), pp. 654–670, especially pp. 654 and 665.

23. Verba and Nie, *Participation in America,* p. 67; and Sharp, "Citizen Demand Making," p. 660.

24. See Joel B. Grossman et al., "Dimensions of Institutional Participation: Who Uses the Courts and How?" *Journal of Politics* 44 (February 1982), pp. 86–114; and Frances Kahn

Zemans, "Legal Mobilization: The Neglected Role of the Law in the Political System," *American Political Science Review* 77 (September 1983), pp. 690–703.

25. *Brown* v. *Board of Education,* 347 U.S. 483 (1954).

26. Max Kaase and Alan Marsh, "Political Action: A Theoretical Perspective," in Samuel H. Barnes and Max Kaase (eds.), *Political Action: Mass Participation in Five Western Democracies* (Beverly Hills, Calif.: Sage Publications, 1979), p. 168.

27. *Smith* v. *Allwright,* 321 U.S. 649 (1944).

28. *Harper* v. *Virginia State Board of Elections,* 383 U.S. 663 (1966).

29. Everett Carll Ladd, *The American Polity* (New York: W. W. Norton, 1985), p. 392.

30. Gorton Carruth and associates, eds., *The Encyclopedia of American Facts and Dates* (New York: Crowell, 1979), p. 330. For an eye-opening account of women's contribution to politics before gaining the vote, see Robert J. Dinkin, *Before Equal Suffrage: Women in Partisan Politics from Colonial Times to 1920* (Westport, Conn., Greenwood Press, 1995).

31. Ivor Crewe, "Electoral Participation," in *Democracy at the Polls: A Comparative Study of Competitive National Elections,* ed. David Butler, Howard R. Penniman, and Austin Ranney (Washington, D.C.: American Enterprise Institute, 1981), pp. 219–223.

32. Diana Elias, "Kuwait Parliament Rejects Women's Suffrage by Slim Margin," *Chicago Tribune,* 1 December 1999, p. 12.

33. Thomas E. Cronin, *Direct Democracy: The Politics of Initiative, Referendum, and Recall* (Cambridge, Mass.: Harvard University Press, 1989), p. 127.

34. Initiative and Reform Institute, "IRI 2000 General Election Post Election Report," on-line at <http://www.ballotwatch.org/2000 postanalysis.htm>, December 26, 2000.

35. Sam Howe Verhovek, "A Ballot Full of Voter Initiatives Becomes an Issue Itself in Oregon," *New York Times,* 25 October 2000, p. A1.

36. "Ballot Initiatives Hit New High in Oregon," *New York Times,* 16 July 2000, p. A18.

37. Initiative and Reform Institute, "IRI 2000 General Election Post Election Report."

38. "Gay Rights Law Faces Reversal in

Maine Vote," *Chicago Tribune,* 11 January 1998, p. 16.

39. David B. Magleby, *Direct Legislation: Voting on Ballot Propositions in the United States* (Baltimore, Md.: Johns Hopkins University Press, 1984), p. 59. See also Ernest Tollerson, "In 90's Ritual, Hired Hands Carry Democracy's Petitions," *New York Times,* 9 July 1996, p. 1.

40. David S. Broder, "A Snake in the Grass Roots," *Washington Post,* 26 March 2000, pp. B1–B2.

41. *The Book of the States 1996–97,* vol. 28 (Lexington, Ky.: Council of State Governments, 1996), p. 150.

42. *Chicago Tribune,* 10 March 1985.

43. Crewe, "Electoral Participation," p. 232. Several scholars have successfully explained variations in voting turnout across nations with only a few institutional and contextual variables. (See G. Bingham Powell, Jr., "American Voter Turnout in Comparative Perspective," *American Political Science Review* 80 (March 1986), pp. 17–43; and Robert W. Jackman, "Political Institutions and Voter Turnout in the Industrial Democracies," *American Political Science Review* 81 (June 1987), pp. 405–423.) However, this work has been criticized on methodological grounds and also for failing to explain successfully two deviant cases, the United States and Switzerland, both of which have low voter turnout. (See Wolfgang Hirczy, "Comparative Turnout: Beyond Cross-National Regression Models," paper prepared for presentation at the annual meeting of the American Political Science Association, Chicago, September 1992.)

44. Verba and Nie, *Participation in America,* p. 13.

45. Max Kaase and Alan Marsh, "Distribution of Political Action," in *Political Action,* p. 186. Dalton, *Citizen Politics,* p. 80.

46. Milbrath and Goel, *Political Participation,* pp. 95–96. Dalton, *Citizen Politics,* p. 80.

47. Verba and Nie, *Participation in America,* p. 148. For a concise summary of the effect of age on voting turnout, see Michael M. Gant and Norman R. Luttbeg, *American Electoral Behavior* (Itasca, Ill.: F. E. Peacock, 1991), pp. 103–104.

48. Richard Murray and Arnold Vedlitz, "Race, Socioeconomic Status, and Voting Participation in Large Southern Cities," *Journal of Politics* 39 (November 1977), pp. 1064–1072; and Verba and Nie, *Participation in*

America, p. 157. See also Bobo and Gilliam, "Race, Sociopolitical Participation, and Black Empowerment." Their study of 1987 national survey data with a black over-sample found that African Americans participated more than whites of comparable socioeconomic status in cities in which the mayor's office was held by an African American.

49. William H. Flanigan and Nancy H. Zingale, *Political Behavior of the American Electorate*, 8th ed. (Washington, D.C.: Congressional Quarterly Press, 1994), pp. 41–43.

50. Ronald B. Rapoport, "The Sex Gap in Political Persuading: Where the 'Structuring Principle' Works," *American Journal of Political Science* 25 (February 1981), pp. 32–48. Perhaps surprisingly, research fails to show any relationship between a wife's role in her marriage and her political activity. See Nancy Burns, Kay Lehman Schlozman, and Sidney Verba, "The Public Consequences of Private Inequality: Family Life and Citizen Participation," *American Political Science Review* 91 (June 1997), 373–389.

51. Bruce C. Straits, "The Social Context of Voter Turnout," *Public Opinion Quarterly* 54 (Spring 1990), pp. 64–73.

52. Sidney Verba, Kay Lehman Scholzman, and Henry E. Brady, *Voice and Equality: Civic Voluntarism in American Politics* (Cambridge, Mass.: Harvard University Press, 1995), p. 433.

53. Obtained on July 11, 1996, from "Rock the Vote" home page at <www.rockthevote.org/and/RockVote/INSIDERTV/155/15_5_1.html>.

54. Stephen D. Shaffer, "A Multivariate Explanation of Decreasing Turnout in Presidential Elections, 1960–1976," *American Journal of Political Science* 25 (February 1981), pp. 68–95; and Paul R. Abramson and John H. Aldrich, "The Decline of Electoral Participation in America," *American Political Science Review* 76 (September 1981), pp. 603–620. However, one scholar argues that this research suffers because it looks only at voters and non-voters in a single election. When the focus shifts to people who vote sometimes but not at other times, the models do not fit so well. See M. Margaret Conway and John E. Hughes, "Political Mobilization and Patterns of Voter Turnout," paper prepared for delivery at the annual meeting of the American Political Science Association,

Washington, D.C., September 1993.

55. Apparently, Richard A. Brody was the first scholar to pose this problem as a puzzle. See his "The Puzzle of Political Participation in America," in Anthony King, ed., *The New American Political System* (Washington, D.C.: American Enterprise Institute, 1978), pp. 287–324. Since then, a sizable literature has attempted to explain the decline in voter turnout in the United States. Some authors have claimed to account for the decline with just a few variables, but their work has been criticized for being too simplistic. See Carol A. Cassel and Robert C. Luskin, "Simple Explanations of Turnout Decline," *American Political Science Review* 82 (December 1988), pp. 1321–1330. They contend that most of the post–1960 decline is still unexplained. If it is any comfort, voter turnout in Western European elections has seen a somewhat milder decline, and scholars have not been very successful at explaining it, either. See Richard S. Flickinger and Donley T. Studlar, "The Disappearing Voters? Exploring Declining Turnout in Western European Elections," *West European Politics* 15 (April 1992), pp. 1–16.

56. Ruy A. Teixeira, *The Disappearing American Voter* (Washington, D.C.: Brookings Institution, 1992), p. 57.

57. Abramson and Aldrich, "Decline of Electoral Participation," p. 519; and Shaffer, "Multivariate Explanation," pp. 78, 90.

58. The negative effect of registration laws on voter turnout is argued in Frances Fox Piven and Richard Cloward, "Government Statistics and Conflicting Explanations of Nonvoting," *PS: Political Science and Politics* 22 (September 1989), pp. 580–588. Their analysis was hotly contested in Stephen Earl Bennett, "The Uses and Abuses of Registration and Turnout Data: An Analysis of Piven and Cloward's Studies of Nonvoting in America," *PS: Political Science and Politics* 23 (June 1990), pp. 166–171. Bennett showed that turnout declined 10 to 13 percent after 1960, despite efforts to remove or lower legal hurdles to registration. For their reply, see Frances Fox Piven and Richard Cloward, "A Reply to Bennett," *PS: Political Science and Politics* 23 (June 1990), pp. 172–173. You can see that reasonable people can disagree on this matter.

59. Mark J. Fenster, "The Impact of Allowing Day of Registration Voting on Turnout in U.S. Elections from 1960 to 1992: A Research Note," *American*

Politics Quarterly 22 (January 1994), pp. 74–87.

60. David Glass, Peverill Squire, and Raymond Wolfinger, "Voter Turnout: An International Comparison," *Public Opinion* 6 (December/January 1984), p. 52. Wolfinger says that because of the strong effect of registration on turnout, most rational choice analyses of voting would be better suited to analyzing turnout of only registered voters. See Raymond E. Wolfinger, "The Rational Citizen Faces Election Day," *Public Affairs Report* 6 (November 1992), p. 12.

61. Federal Election Commission, *The Impact of the National Voter Registration Act of 1993 on the Administration of Elections for Federal Office 1997–1998* (Washington, D.C.: Federal Election Commission, 1999), available on-line at <http://www.fec.gov/pages/9798NVRAexec.htm>, 28 December 2000.

62. Recent research finds that "party contact is clearly a statistically and substantively important factor in predicting and explaining political behavior." See Peter W. Wielhouwer and Brad Lockerbie, "Party Contacting and Political Participation, 1952–1990," paper prepared for delivery at the annual meeting of the American Political Science Association, Chicago, 1992, p. 14. Of course, parties strategically target the groups that they want to see vote in elections. See Peter W. Wielhouwer, "Strategic Canvassing by Political Parties, 1952–1990," *American Review of Politics*, 16 (Fall 1995), pp. 213–238.

63. Steven J. Rosenstone and John Mark Hansen, *Mobilization, Participation, and Democracy in America* (New York: Macmillan Publishing Company, 1993), p. 213.

64. See Robert A. Jackson, "Voter Mobilization in the 1986 Midterm Election," *Journal of Politics* 55 (November 1993), pp. 1081–1099; and Kim Quaile Hill and Jan E. Leighley, "Political Parties and Class Mobilization in Contemporary United States Elections," *American Journal of Political Science*, 40 (August 1996), pp. 787–804.

65. Michael K. Frisby, "Both Parties Take Stock of Jump in Black Male Turnout," *Wall Street Journal*, 13 February 1997, p. A20.

66. See Charles Krauthammer, "In Praise of Low Voter Turnout," *Time*, 21 May 1990, p. 88. Krauthammer says, "Low voter turnout means that people see politics as quite marginal to their lives, as neither salvation nor ruin. . . . Low voter turnout is a leading indicator of contentment." A major study in 1996 that compared 1,000 likely *non*-voters with 2,300 likely voters found that 24 percent of the non-voters said they "hardly ever" followed public affairs, versus 5 percent of likely voters. See Dwight Morris, "No-Show '96: Americans Who Don't Vote," Summary Report to the Medill News Service and WTTW Television, Northwestern University School of Journalism, 1996.

67. Crewe, "Electoral Participation," p. 262.

68. Samuel H. Barnes and Max Kaase, *Political Action*, p. 532.

69. *1971 Congressional Quarterly Almanac* (Washington, D.C.: Congressional Quarterly Press, 1972), p. 475.

70. Benjamin Ginsberg, *The Consequences of Consent: Elections, Citizen Control, and Popular Acquiescence* (Reading, Mass.: Addison-Wesley, 1982), p. 13.

71. Ginsberg, *Consequences of Consent*, pp. 13–14.

72. *Ibid.*, pp. 6–7.

73. Some people have argued that the decline in voter turnout during the 1980s served to increase the class bias in the electorate because people of lower socioeconomic status stayed home. But recent research has concluded that "class bias has not increased since 1964" (p. 734, Jan E. Leighley and Jonathan Nagler, "Socioeconomic Class Bias in Turnout, 1964–1988: The Voters Remain the Same," *American Political Science Review* 86 [September 1992], pp. 725–736). Nevertheless, Rosenstone and Hansen say, "the economic inequalities in political participation that prevail in the United States today are as large as the racial disparities in political participation that prevailed in the 1950s. America's leaders today face few incentives to attend to the needs of the disadvantaged," in *Mobilization, Participation, and Democracy in America*, p. 248.

Chapter 8 / Political Parties / pp. 228–261

1. Shailagh Murray, "Nader's Cause Could Pay for His Spoiler Role," *Wall Street Journal*, 9 December 2000, p. A17.

2. "Nader Has No Regrets About Running Against Gore," Reuters, 15 December 2000, distributed via e-mail by <campaigns@listbot.com>.

3. Murray, "Nader's Cause Could Pay for His Spoiler Role."

4. B. Drummond Ayers, Jr., "Ralph Nader Is Nominated for President, but Vows He Will Ignore His Party's Platform," *New York Times*, 20 August 1996, p. A10.

5. *The Rhodes Cook Letter*, Vol. 1, No. 3 (October 2000), p. 5. Published electronically at <rhodescook.com>.

6. "Nader Brushes Off Spoiler Role," <http://campaigns.listbot.com>.

7. "Nader Calls the Major Parties One Unit 'Wearing Two Heads,'" 6 April 2000, <campaigns@listbot.com>.

8. Adam Clymer, "Nader Sees Greens Building Status as a Major Party," *New York Times*, 18 November 2000, p. A16.

9. These estimates were calculated from data tabulated for 1,818 voters in Florida who were asked how they voted after leaving the polling station. The tabulation was posted on the CNN web site at <http://www.cnn.com/ELECTION/2000/epolls/FL/P000.html>.

10. These estimates were calculated from data tabulated for 1,232 voters in New Hampshire who were asked how they voted after leaving the polling station. The tabulation was posted on the CNN web site at <http://www.cnn.com/ELECTION/2000/epolls/NH/P000.html>.

11. Center for Political Studies of the Institute for Social Research, *American National Election Study 1996* (Ann Arbor: University of Michigan, 1996).

12. David W. Moore, "Perot Supporters: For the Man, Not a Third Party," *Gallup Organization Newsletter Achive* 60, 7 August 1995; the Gallup Organization's Web page at <www.gallup.com/newsletter/aug95/>.

13. John H. Aldrich, *Why Parties? The Origin and Transformation of Political Parties in America* (Chicago, Ill.: University of Chicago Press, 1995), p. 296.

14. Richard B. Morris (ed.), *Encyclopedia of American History* (New York: Harper & Row, 1976), p. 209.

15. See Jerome M. Clubb, William H. Flanigan, and Nancy H. Zingale, *Partisan Realignment: Voters, Parties, and Government in American History*, Vol. 108 (Beverly Hills, Calif.: Sage, 1980), p. 163.

16. See Gerald M. Pomper, "Classification of Presidential Elections," *Journal of Politics* 29 (August 1967), pp. 535–566.

17. For a more extensive treatment, see Henry M. Littlefield, "The Wizard of Oz: Parable on Populism," *American Quarterly* 16 (Spring 1964), pp. 47–58.

18. The discussion that follows draws heavily on Austin Ranney and Willmoore Kendall, *Democracy and the American Party System* (New York: Harcourt, Brace, 1956), Chs. 18 and 19.

19. J. David Gillespie, *Politics at the Periphery: Third Parties in a Two-Party America* (Columbia, S.C.: University of South Carolina Press, 1993). Surveys of public attitudes toward minor parties are reported in Christian Coller, "Trends: Third Parties and the Two-Party System," *Public Opinion Quarterly* 60, (Fall 1996), 431–449.

20. Rosenstone, Behr, and Lazarus, *Third Parties in America*, p. 8.

21. State laws and court decisions may systematically support the major parties, but the U.S. Supreme Court seems to hold a more neutral position toward major and minor parties. See Lee Epstein and Charles D. Hadley, "On the Treatment of Political Parties in the U.S. Supreme Court, 1900–1986," *Journal of Politics* 52 (May 1990), pp. 413–432; and E. Joshua Rosenkranz, *Voter Choice 96: A 50-State Report Card on the Presidential Elections* (New York: New York University School of Law, Brennan Center for Justice, 1996), p. 24.

22. See James Gimpel, *National Elections and the Autonomy of American State Party Systems* (Pittsburgh, Pa.: University of Pittsburgh Press, 1996).

23. Measuring the concept of party identification has had its problems. For recent insights into the issues, see R. Michael Alvarez, "The Puzzle of Party Identification," *American Politics Quarterly* 18 (October 1990), pp. 476–491; and Donald Philip Green and Bradley Palmquist, "Of Artifacts and Partisan Instability," *American Journal of Political Science* 34 (August 1990), pp. 872–902.

24. Rhodes Cook, "GOP Shows Dramatic Growth, Especially in the South," *Congressional Quarterly Weekly Report*, 13 January 1996, pp. 97–100.

25. There is some dispute over how stable party identification really is, when the same respondents are asked about their party identification over a period of several months during an election campaign. The research literature is reviewed in Brad Lockerbie, "Change in Party Identification: The Role of Prospective Economic Evaluations," *American Politics Quarterly* 17 (July 1989), pp. 291–311. Lockerbie agrues that respondents change their party identification according to whether they think a party will help them personally in the future.

But see also Green and Palmquist, "Of Artifacts and Partisan Instability."

26. Bill Keller, "As Arms Buildup Eases, U.S. Tries to Take Stock," *New York Times*, 14 May 1985; Ed Gillespie and Bob Schellhas, *Contract with America* (New York: Times Books, 1994), p. 107.

27. See for example, Gerald M. Pomper, *Elections in America* (New York: Dodd, Mead, 1968); Benjamin Ginsberg, "Election and Public Policy," *American Political Science Review* 70 (March 1976), pp. 41–50; and Jeff Fishel, *Presidents and Promises* (Washington, D.C.: Congressional Quarterly Press, 1985).

28. Ian Budge and Richard I. Hofferbert, "Mandates and Policy Outputs: U.S. Party Platforms and Federal Expenditures," *American Political Science Review* 84 (March 1990), pp. 111–131.

29. See Terri Susan Fine, "Economic Interests and the Framing of the 1988 and 1992 Democratic and Republican Party Platforms," *The American Review of Politics*, 16 (Spring 1995), 79–93.

30. James Dao, "Platform Is Centrist, Like G.O.P.'s, but Differs in Details," *New York Times*, 14 August 2000, pp. A1 and A16.

31. Robert Harmel and Kenneth Janda, *Parties and Their Environments: Limits to Reform?* (New York: Longman, 1982), pp. 27–29. See also John Huber and Ronald Inglehart, "Expert Interpretations of Party Space and Party Locations in 42 Societies," *Party Politics* 1 (January 1995), pp. 73–111; and Alan Ware, *Political Parties and Party Systems* (New York: Oxford University Press, 1996), Ch. 1.

32. See Ralph M. Goldman, *The National Party Chairmen and Committees: Factionalism at the Top* (Armonk, N.Y.: M. E. Sharpe, 1990). The subtitle is revealing.

33. William Crotty and John S. Jackson III, *Presidential Primaries and Nominations* (Washington, D.C.: Congressional Quarterly Press, 1985), p. 33.

34. Debra L. Dodson, "Socialization of Party Activists: National Convention Delegates, 1972–1981," *American Journal of Political Science* 34 (November 1990), pp. 1119–1141.

35. Phillip A. Klinkner, "Party Culture and Party Behavior," in Shea and Green, *The State of the Parties*, pp. 275–287; and Phillip A. Klinkner, *The Losing Parties: Out-Party National Committees, 1956–1993* (New Haven, Conn.: Yale University Press, 1994).

36. Reports posted by the Federal Election Commission on its web site at <www.fec.gov/finance/finmenu.htm>.

37. Dan Barry, "Republicans on Long Island Master Science of Politics," *New York Times*, 8 March 1996, p. A1S. Recent research suggests that when *both* parties have strong organizations at the county level, the public has more favorable attitudes toward the parties. See John J. Coleman, "Party Organization Strength and Public Support for Parties," *American Journal of Political Science* 40 (August 1996), pp. 805–824.

38. John Frendreis, Alan R. Gitelson, Gregory Flemming, and Anne Layzell, "Local Political Parties and Legislative Races in 1992," in Shea and Green, *The State of the Parties*, p. 139.

39. Report posted by the Federal Election Commission on its Web site at <www.fec.gov/finance/narsrate.htm>.

40. Robert Biersack, "Hard Facts and Soft Money: State Party Finance in the 1992 Federal Elections," in Shea and Green, *The State of the Parties*, p. 114.

41. Paul S. Herrnson, "Party Stategy and Campaign Activities in the 1992 Congressional Elections," pp. 83–106.

42. See the evidence presented in Harmel and Janda, *Parties and Their Environments*, Ch. 5.

43. See John M. Broder and Lizette Alvarez, "President and Party Sound Like Couple in Need of Therapy," *New York Times*, 15 November 1997, pp. A1, A8.

44. Martin P. Wattenberg, *The Decline of American Political Parties, 1952–1994* (Cambridge, Mass.: Harvard University Press, 1996).

45. In 1996, the Democratic National Committee mounted an unprecedented drive to organize up to 60,000 precinct captains in twenty states, while the new Republican candidate for U.S. senator from Illinois, Al Salvi, fired his own campaign manager and replaced him with someone from the National Republican Senatorial Campaign Committee. See Sue Ellen Christian, "Democrats Will Focus on Precincts," *Chicago Tribune*, 29 June 1996; and Michael Dizon, "Salvi Fires Top Senate Race Aides," *Chicago Tribune*, 24 May 1996, Section 2, p. 3.

46. Barbara Sinclair, "The Congressional Party: Evolving Organizational, Agenda-Setting, and Policy Roles," in *Parties Respond*, p. 227.

47. The model is articulated most clearly in a report by the American Political Science Association, "Toward a More Responsible Two-Party System," *American Political Science Review* 44 (September 1950), Part II. See also Gerald M. Pomper, "Toward a More Responsible Party System? What, Again?" *Journal of Politics* 33 (November 1971), pp. 916–940. See also the seven essays in the symposium, "Divided Government and the Politics of Constitutional Reform," *PS: Political Science & Politics*, 24 (December 1991), pp. 634–657.

Chapter 9 / Nominations, Elections, and Campaigns / pp. 262–300

1. The Canadian parliament has a Senate, but it is an appointive body with limited legislative powers—like the British House of Lords.

2. "Elections Canada is the non-partisan agency responsible for the conduct of federal elections and referendums. In accordance with our mandate from Parliament, we devote a good deal of effort to making information about the federal electoral system widely available to all Canadians. This Web site is part of that effort and we intend to make it a valuable and accessible resource for everyone interested in elections. The site was completely rebuilt in September 2000 to place it firmly on the leading edge of Internet-based electoral information. On election night, for example, everyone can now receive a simultaneous on-line compilation of the results from several electoral districts of their choice." Go to <http://www.elections.ca/>.

3. This is essentially the framework for studying campaigns set forth in Barbara C. Salmore and Stephen A. Salmore, *Candidates, Parties, and Campaigns: Electral Politics in America*, 2nd ed. (Washington, D.C.: Congressional Quarterly Press, 1989).

4. Menefree-Libey, David, *The Triumph of Campaign-Centered Politics* (New York: Chatham House Publishers, 2000).

5. Stephen E. Frantzich, *Political Parties in the Technological Age* (New York: Longman, 1989), p. 105.

6. Michael Gallagher, "Conclusion," in Michael Gallagher and Michael Marsh (eds.), *Candidate Selection in Comparative Perspective: The Secret Garden of Politics* (London: Sage, 1988), p. 238. See also Malcolm E. Jewell, "Primary Elections," in Richard Rose (ed.), *International Encyclopedia of Elections* (Washington, D.C.: CQ Press, 2000), p. 224.

7. *The Book of the States, 1996–97*, vol. 31 (Lexington, Ky.: Council of State Governments, 1996), pp. 157–158.

8. Malcolm E. Jewell and David M.

Olson, *Political Parties and Elections in American States*, 3rd ed. (Chicago, Ill.: Dorsey Press, 1988), pp. 108–112. For data on turnout in the Republican primaries and caucuses in 1996, see "Guide to the 1996 Republican National Convention," *Congressional Quarterly Supplement to Weekly Report Number 31*, 3 August 1996, pp. 62–63.

9. See John G. Geer, "Assessing the Representativeness of Electorates in Presidential Elections," *American Journal of Political Science* 32 (November 1998), pp. 929–945; and Barbara Norrander, "Ideological Representativeness of Presidential Primary Voters," *American Journal of Political Science* 33 (August 1989), pp. 570–587.

10. James A. McCann, "Presidential Nomination Activists and Political Representation: A View from the Active Minority Studies," in William G. Mayer (ed.), *In Pursuit of the White House: How We Choose Our Presidential Nominees* (Chatham, N.J.: Chatham House, 1996), p. 99.

11. Emmet T. Flood and William C. Mayer, "Third-Party and Independent Candidates: How They Get on the Ballot, How They Get Nominated," in Mayer, *In Pursuit of the White House*, pp. 311–313.

12. This information was drawn from tables reporting the "Presidential Nominating Calendar" for the two parties in *National Journal*, 5 February 2000, pp. 379–380; and from "The Green Papers" Web site on the 2000 election. It existed on 13 January 2001 at <http://www.thegreenpapers.com/PCC/Tabul.html>.

13. *Ibid.*, pp. 2485–2487. For a description of how caucuses operate and how differently they work in the two parties, see William G. Mayer, "Caucuses: How They Work, What Difference They Make," in Mayer, *In Pursuit of the White House*, pp. 105–157.

14. Harold W. Stanley and Richard C. Niemi, *Vital Statistics on American Politics, 1999–2000* (Washington, D.C.: Congressional Quarterly Press, 2000), p. 62.

15. States may achieve additional publicity from this move, but it is doubtful that it gives them more influence over the nomination process. See Andrew E. Busch, "New Features of the 2000 Nominating Process: Republican Reforms, Front-Loading's Second Wind, and Early Voting," in William G. Mayer (ed.), *In Pursuit of the White House: How We Choose Our*

Presidential Nominees (Chatham, N.J.: Chatham House, 2000), pp. 57–86.

16. Arthur T. Hadley, *The Invisible Primary* (Englewood Cliffs, N.J.: Prentice-Hall, 1976). For a recent test of some of Hadley's assertions, see Emmett H. Buell, Jr., "The Invisible Primary," in Mayer, *In Pursuit of the White House* (1996), pp. 1–43.

17. R. W. Apple, Jr. "Gore Is Crossing Starting Line for Year 2000," *New York Times*, 19 January 1997, p. 12.

18. Jerry Gray, "Gephardt Takes to the Road, and Speculation on 2000 Follows," *New York Times*, 29 March 1997, p. 7.

19. Richard L. Berke "Six Months After Vote, Campaigns Have Begun," *New York Times*, 11 May 1997, p. 14.

20. Gary R. Orren and Nelson W. Polsby (eds.), *Media and Momentum: The New Hampshire Primary and Nomination Politics* (Chatham, N.J.: Chatham House, 1987), p. 23.

21. "Few Voices, Speaking Loudly," *New York Times*, 3 February 2000, p. A22.

22. Richard L. Berke, "Two States Retain Roles in Shaping Presidential Race," *New York Times*, 29 November 1999, p. 1; Leslie Wayne, "Iowa Turns Its Presidential Caucuses into a Cash Cow, and Milks Furiously," *New York Times*, 5 January 2000, p. A 16.

23. "Looking Back: Heading up the Ticket," *New York Times*, 15 March 2000, p. A18. This chart portrays the times at which candidates were selected since 1972. Before that, one or both candidates were not effectively chosen until the summer nominating conventions.

24. Will Lester, "Primary Turnout Higher Than in '96 but Still Low," Associated Press e-mail message from campaigns.listbot.com (undated).

25. See James R. Beniger, "Winning the Presidential Nomination: National Polls and State Primary Elections, 1936–1972," *Public Opinion Quarterly* 40 (Spring 1976), pp. 22–38.

26. *The American Heritage Dictionary of the English Language*, 4th Edition (Boston, Mass.: Houghton Mifflin Company, 2000), p. 362. Indeed, the entry on "Electoral College" in the 1989 *Oxford English Dictionary* does not note any usage in American politics up to 1875, when it cites a reference in connection with the Germanic Diet.

27. References to the electoral college in the *U.S. Code* can be found conveniently at the National Archives and Records Administration Web site, <http://www.nara.gov/fedreg/elctcoll/provis.html#top>.

28. Michael Nelson, *Congressional Quarterly's Guide to the Presidency* (Washington, D.C.: Congressional Quarterly Press, 1989), pp. 155–156. Colorado selected its presidential electors through the state legislature in 1876, but that was the year it entered the union.

29. Shlomo Slonim, "The Electoral College at Philadelphia: The Evolution of an Ad Hoc Congress for the Selection of a President," *Journal of American History* 73 (June 1986), p. 35. For a recent critique and proposal for reform, see David W. Abbott and James P. Levine, *Wrong Winner: The Coming Debacle in the Electoral College* (New York: Praeger, 1991). For a reasoned defense, see Walter Berns (ed.), *After the People Vote: A Guide to the Electoral College* (Washington, D.C.: American Entreprise Institute, 1992).

30. Gallup News Service, "Americans Have Historically Favored Changing Way Presidents Are Elected," *Poll Releases*, 10 November 2000, available on 7 January 2001 at <www.gallup.com/poll/releases/pr001110.asp>. See also Frank Newport, "Americans Support Proposal to Eliminate Electoral College System," *Poll Releases*, 5 January 2001, available on 16 January 2001 at <www.gallup.com/poll/releases/pr010105.asp>.

31. See, for example, the set of letters to the editor of the *New York Times*, 20 December 2000, p. A26.

32. Walter Berns (ed.), *After the People Vote: A Guide to the Electoral College* (Washington, D.C.: American Entreprise Institute, 1992), pp. 45–48. The framers had great difficulty deciding how to allow both the people and the states to participate in selecting the president. This matter was debated on twenty-one different days before they compromised on the electoral college, which Slonim says, "in the eyes of its admirers . . . represented a brilliant scheme for successfully blending national and federal elements in the selection of the nation's chief executive," p. 58.

33. David Stout, "The Electors Vote, and the Surprises Are Few," *New York Times*, 19 December 2000, p. A23.

34. See Alexis Simendinger, James A. Barnes, and Carl M. Cannon, "Pondering a Popular Vote," *National Journal*, 18 November 2000, pp. 3650–3656.

35. Harold W. Stanley and Richard G. Niemi, *Vital Statistics on American Politics*, 2nd ed. (Washington, D.C.: Congressional Quarterly Press, 1990), p. 132; and the 1992 and 1996 National Election Studies, Center for Political Studies, University of Michigan.

36. Rhodes Cook, "House Republicans Scored a Quiet Victory in '92," *Congressional Quarterly Weekly Report*, 17 April 1993, p. 966.

37. Salmore and Salmore, *Candidates, Parties, and Campaigns*, p. 1.

38. Judy Keen, "Bush Draws Crowds on His Way to Philly," *USA Today*, 31 July 2000. Available on 14 January 2001 at <www.usatoday.com/news/conv/034.htm>.

39. Anonymous, "Bush and Cheney Head to Midwest," *USA Today*, 31 July 2001. Available on 14 January 2001 at <www.usatoday.com/news/e98/e2453.htm>.

40. Martin Kasindorf, "Gore Tries to Win over Midwest Voters," *USA Today*, 31 July 2000. Available on 14 January 2001 at <www.usatoday.com/news/conv/313.htm>.

41. Quoted in E. J. Dionne, Jr., "On the Trail of Corporation Donations," *New York Times*, 6 October 1980.

42. Salmore and Salmore, *Candidates, Parties, and Campaigns*, p. 11. See also David Himes, "Strategy and Tactics for Campaign Fund-Raising," in James A. Thurber and Candice J. Nelson (eds.), *Campaigns and Elections: American Style* (Boulder, Colo.: Westview Press, 1995), pp. 62–77.

43. Federal Election Commission, "The First Ten Years: 1975–1985" (Washington, D.C.: Federal Election Commission), 14 April 1985, p. 1.

44. "Bush Reaches $50 Million Mark," *USA Today*, 2 September 2000. Available on 15 January 2001 at <www.usatoday.com/news/e98/e269.htm>.

45. "FEC Announces 2000 Presidential Spending Limits," News Release (Washington, D.C.: Federal Election Commission), 1 March 2000.

46. "Party Fundraising Escalates," News Release (Washington, D.C.: Federal Election Commission), 12 January 2001, p. 1.

47. *Ibid.*

48. Tom Squitieri, "McCain Pushes for Finance Reform," *USA Today*, 5 January 2001. Available on 15 January 2001 at <www.usatoday.com/news/washdc/2001-01-04-mccain.htm>.

49. "Congressional Financial Activity Soars for 2000," Federal Election Commission *News Release*, 9 January 2001.

50. "Corzine Spent $20 per Vote on Election Day," *USA Today*, 8 November 2000. Available on 15 January 2001 at <www.usatoday.com/news/vote2000/nj/main01.htm>.

51. Jennifer A. Steen, "Self-Financed Candidates in the 1996 Congressional Elections," paper presented at the annual meeting of the Western Political Science Association, March 19–21, 1998, Los Angeles. Steen's analysis involved 493 nonincumbents in competitive House races. In a personal communication, she said, "It obviously helps a candidate to have more money to spend, but a dollar raised is in some sense more valuable than a dollar self-financed. Purchasing power is the same, but the process of fund-raising adds value to a campaign that writing a personal check does not" (e-mail message, 28 February 1998).

52. Salmore and Salmore, *Candidates, Parties, and Campaigns*, p. 11.

53. David Moon, "What You Use Depends on What You Have: Information Effects on the Determinants of Electoral Choice," *American Politics Quarterly* 18 (January 1990), pp. 3–24.

54. See the "Marketplace: Political Products and Services" section in monthly issues of the magazine *Campaigns & Elections*. These classified ads list scores of names, addresses, and telephone numbers for people who supply "political products and services"—from "campaign schools" to "voter files and mailing lists."

55. Salmore and Salmore, *Candidates, Parties, and Campaigns*, pp. 115–116.

56. Read the fine set of studies on campaign consultants at work in James A. Thurber and Candice J. Nelson (eds.), *Campaign Warriors: The Role of Political Consultants in Elections* (Washington, D.C.: Brookings Institution Press, 2000).

57. James Warren, "Politicians Learn Value of Sundays—Too Well," *Chicago Tribune*, 22 October 1990, p.1.

58. Timothy E. Cook, *Making Laws and Making News: Media Strategies in the U.S. House of Representatives* (Washington, D.C.: Brookings Institution, 1989). Recent research into media effects on Senate and House elections finds that in low-information elections, which characterize House more than Senate elections, the media coverage gives an advantage to incumbents, particularly among independent voters. See Robert Kirby Goidel, Todd G. Shields, and Barry Tadlock, "The Effects of the Media in United States Senate and House Elections: A Comparative Analysis," paper presented at the annual meeting of the American Political Science Association, Washington, D.C., September 1993.

59. Ann N. Crigler, Marion R. Just, and Timothy E. Cook, "Local News, Network News and the 1992 Presidential Campaign," paper presented at the annual meeting of the American Political Science Association, Washington, D.C., September 1993, p. 9.

60. Stephen Ansolabehere and Shanto Iyengar, *Going Negative: How Political Advertisements Shrink and Polarize the Electorate* (New York: Free Press, 1995), p. 145.

61. Darrell M. West, *Air Wars: Television Advertising in Election Campaigns 1952–1996*, 2nd ed., Washington, D.C.: Congressional Quarterly Press, 1998), p. 108.

62. *Ibid.*, p. 46.

63. This theme runs throughout Kathleen Hall Jamieson's *Dirty Politics: Deception, Distraction, and Democracy* (New York: Oxford University Press, 1992). See also John Boiney, "You Can Fool All of the People . . . Evidence on the Capacity of Political Advertising to Mislead," paper presented at the annual meeting of the American Political Science Association, Washington, D.C., September 1993.

64. West, *Air Wars*, p. 59.

65. Kathleen Hall Jamieson, Paul Waldman, and Susan Sheer, "Eliminate the Negative? Categories of Analysis for Political Advertisements," in James A. Thurber, Candice J. Nelson, and David A. Dulio (eds.), *Crowded Airwaves: Campaign Advertising in Elections* (Washington, D.C.: Brookings Institution Press, 2000), p. 49.

66. David A. Dulio, Candice J. Nelson, and James A. Thurber, "Summary and Conclusions," in James A. Thurber, Candice J. Nelson, and David A. Dulio (eds.), *Crowded Airwaves: Campaign Advertising in Elections* (Washington, D.C.: Brookings Institution Press, 2000). p. 172.

67. Ansolabehere and Iyengar, *Going Negative*, p. 112. West, however, takes issue with the Ansolabehere and Iyengar analysis, saying that turnout is more dependent on mistrust than on negativity of ads. See West, *Air Wars*, pp. 63–64. West's position is upheld by Steven E. Finkel and John G. Geer, "Spot Check: Casting Doubt on the Demobilizing Effect of Attack Advertising," *American Journal of Political Science*, 42 (April 1988), pp. 573–595.

68. Martha T. Moore, "Talk Shows Become a Campaign Staple," *USA Today*, 20 September 2000. Available on 15 January 2001 at <www.usatoday.com/news/e98/c2737.htm>.

69. The URL (as of 15 January 2001 is <dir.yahoo.com/Government/U_S_

Government/Politics/Humor/1996_ Presidential_Election/Candidate_ Parodies/>.

70. Pew Research Center, "Despite Uncertain Outcome, Campaign 2000 Highly Rated," *News Release,* 16 November 2000, p. 18.

71. Frank James, "E-Campaigns Grow Up," *Chicago Tribune,* 11 February 2000, p. 3. See also Tina Kelley, "Candidate on the Stump Is Surely on the Web," *New York Times,* 19 October 1999, p. 1.

72. Bob Kolasky, "Both Parties Use the Net to Revive Their Relevance," *Inter@active Week,* 3 July 2000, pp. 34–36.

73. Neil Munro, "The New Wired Politics," *National Journal,* 22 April 2000, pp. 1260–1263.

74. Leslie Wayne, "Online Coverage Fell Short of the Hype," *New York Times,* 19 August 2000, p. A10.

75. See the Web site for the National Election Studies at <http://www.umich. edu/~nes/nesguide/nesguide.htm>.

76. Robert G. Kaiser, "Is This Any Way to Pick a Winner?" *Washington Post,* 26 May 2000, p. A01.

77. Susan Page, "Ten Lessons Learned from the Campaign," *USA Today,* 8 November 2000. Available on 15 January 2001 at <www.usatoday.com/news/ vote2000/lessons.htm>.

78. Pamela Johnston Conover and Stanley Feldman, "Candidate Perception in an Ambiguous World: Campaigns, Cues, and Inference Processes," *American Journal of Political Science* 33 (November 1989), pp. 912–940.

79. Pew Research Center, "Endnotes on Campaign 2000: Some Final Observations on Voter Opinions."

80. Michael M. Gant and Norman R. Luttbeg, *American Electoral Behavior* (Itasca, Ill.: Peacock, 1991), pp. 63–64. The literature on the joint effects of party, issues, and candidates is quite involved. See also David W. Romero, "The Changing American Voter Revisited: Candidate Evaluations in Presidential Elections, 1952–1984," *American Politics Quarterly* 17 (October 1989), pp. 409–421. Romero contends that research that finds a new American voter who votes according to issues is incorrectly looking at standardized rather than unstandardized regression coefficients.

81. All these factors were named by more than 10 percent of Bush voters as what they liked most about him. Pew Research Center, "Endnotes on Campaign 2000: Some Final Observations on Voter Opinions."

Available on 16 January 2001 at <www. people-press.org/endnote00qe.htm>.

82. Richard E. Cohen, "A Congress Divided," *National Journal,* 5 February 2000, p. 382.

83. Conover and Feldman, "Candidate Perception," p. 938.

84. Party identification has been assumed to be relatively resistant to short-term campaign effects, but see Dee Allsop and Herbert F. Weisberg, "Measuring Change in Party Identification in an Election Campaign," *American Journal of Political Science* 32 (November 1988), pp. 996–1017. They conclude that partisanship is more volatile than we have thought.

85. These figures come from the Center for Media and Public Affairs, which monitored television news coverage throughout the 2000 presidential campaign. See CMPA, "Journalists Monopolize TV Election News," press release, 30 October 2000. Available on 16 January 2001 at <www.cmpa.com/ pressrel/electpr10.htm>.

86. *Ibid.*

87. Jackie Calmes, "Bush Advisors Seek Help from Madison Avenue Talent," *Wall Street Journal,* 30 May 2000, p. A28.

88. Ceci Connolly and Dana Milbank, "Campaigns Fuel a Frenzy of TV Spots," *Washington Post,* 27 October 2000, p. A1. See also Don Van Natta, Jr., "A $3 Billion Record, but Does Anyone Care?" *New York Times,* 23 January 2000, Sect. 4, p. 1.

89. Wayne Leslie, "Political Consultants Thrive in the Cash-Rich New Politics," *New York Times,* 24 October 2000. Available on 16 January 2001 at <www.nytimes.com/2000/10/24/ politics/24DONA.html>.

90. Martha T. Moore, "Bush, Gore Ads Aimed at Swing States," *USA Today,* 22 August 2000. Available on 16 January 2001 at <www.usatoday.com/news/e98/ e2466.htm>.

91. Kathy Chen, "In Campaign 2000, Local Stations Are Winning Big," *Wall Street Journal,* 3 November 2000, p. B1.

92. Pew Research Center, "Despite Uncertain Outcome, Campaign 2000 Highly Rated," news release, 16 November 2000, p. 17.

93. Susan Page, "Ten Lessons Learned from the Campaign," p. 2.

Chapter 10 / Interest Groups / pp. 301–332

1. Alexis de Tocqueville, *Democracy in America, 1835–1839,* Reprint, ed.

Richard D. Heffner (New York: Mentor Books, 1956), p. 79.

2. *The Federalist Papers* (New York: Mentor Books, 1961), p. 79.

3. *Ibid.,* p. 78.

4. See Robert A. Dahl, *A Preface to Democratic Theory* (Chicago: University of Chicago Press, 1956), pp. 4–33.

5. Alan Rosenthal, *The Third House* (Washington, D.C.: Congressional Quarterly, 1993), p. 7.

6. This discussion follows from Jeffrey M. Berry, *The Interest Group Society* (New York: Longman, 1997), pp. 6–8.

7. John Simons and John Harwood, "For the Tech Industry, Market in Washington is Toughest to Crack," *Wall Street Journal,* 5 March 1998, p. A1.

8. John Mark Hansen, *Gaining Access* (Chicago: University of Chicago Press, 1991), pp. 11–17.

9. Steven Greenhouse, "The Most Innovative Figure in Silicon Valley? Maybe This Labor Organizer," *New York Times,* 14 November 1999, p. 26.

10. David B. Truman, *The Governmental Process* (New York: Alfred A. Knopf, 1951).

11. Herbert Gans, *The Urban Villagers* (New York: Free Press, 1962).

12. Robert H. Salisbury, "An Exchange Theory of Interest Groups," *Midwest Journal of Political Science* 13 (February 1969), pp. 1–32.

13. See Mancur Olson, Jr., *The Logic of Collective Action* (New York: Schocken, 1968).

14. Peter Matthiessen, *Sal Si Puedes* (New York: Random House, 1969); and John G. Dunne, *Delano,* rev. ed. (New York: Farrar, Strauss & Giroux, 1971).

15. Kay Lehman Schlozman, Sidney Verba, and Henry E. Brady, "Civic Participation and the Equality Problem," in *Civic Engagement in American Democracy,* eds. Theda Skocpol and Morris Fiorina (Washington, D.C.: Brookings Institution, 1999), pp. 427–459.

16. Ronald G. Shaiko, *Voices and Echoes for the Environment* (New York: Columbia University Press, 1999).

17. William P. Browne, "Organized Interests and Their Issue Niches: A Search for Pluralism in a Policy Domain," *Journal of Politics* 52 (May 1990), pp. 477–509.

18. Christopher Boerner and Jennifer Chilton Kallery, *Restructuring Environmental Big Business,* Occasional Paper No. 146, Center for the Study of American Business, Washington

University, St. Louis, Mo., December 1994; and Christopher J. Bosso, "The Color of Money: Environmental Groups and the Pathologies of Fund Raising," in *Interest Group Politics*, 4th ed., ed. Allan J. Cigler and Burdett A. Loomis (Washington, D.C.: Congressional Quarterly, 1995), pp. 101–130.

19. R. Kenneth Godwin, *One Billion Dollars of Influence* (Chatham, N.J.: Chatham House, 1988), pp. 1–34.

20. See Olson, *Logic*.

21. David C. King and Jack L. Walker, "The Provision of Benefits by Interest Groups in the United States," *Journal of Politics* 54 (May 1992), pp. 394–426.

22. Edward O. Laumann and David Knoke, *The Organizational State* (Madison: University of Wisconsin Press, 1987), p. 3. Cited in Robert H. Salisbury, "The Paradox of Interest Groups in Washington—More Groups, Less Clout," in *The New American Political System*, 2d ed., ed. Anthony King (Washington, D.C.: American Enterprise Institute, 1990), p. 226.

23. David Grann, "Beltway Boy," *New Republic*, 9 August 1999, pp. 21–22.

24. John P. Heinz, Edward O. Laumann, Robert L. Nelson, and Robert H. Salisbury, *The Hollow Core* (Cambridge, Mass.: Harvard University Press, 1993), pp. 105–155.

25. Jeffrey H. Birnbaum, *The Lobbyists* (New York: Times Books, 1992), pp. 128–129.

26. Jeffrey H. Birnbaum, "The Power 25: The Influence Merchants," *Fortune*, December 7, 1998, at <www.pathfinder.com/fortune/1998/981207/the1.html>.

27. "FEC Issues Semi-Annual Federal PAC Count," Federal Election Commission press release, 14 January 2000.

28. Karen Foerstel, "Gaming Profits Help Tribes Build Influence," *CQ Weekly*, 12 May 2001, pp. 1085–1087.

29. Dan Clawson, Alan Neustadl, and Denise Scott, *Money Talks* (New York: Basic Books, 1992), p. 1.

30. On how different PACs approach the tradeoff between pragmatism and ideology, see Robert Biersack, Paul S. Herrnson, and Clyde Wilcox, eds., *After the Revolution* (Needham Heights, Mass.: Allyn & Bacon, 1999).

31. "FEC Releases Information on PAC Activity for 1997–98," Federal Election Commission Press Release, 8 June 1999.

32. *Ibid.*

33. Jim VandeHei, "Democrats Take Aim at Bush Weak Spot: Administration's Ties to Energy Industry," *Wall Street Journal*, 16 May 2001, p. A24.

34. Jeffrey Taylor, "GOP to Get 'Soft Money' Tobacco Aid," *Wall Street Journal*, 7 January 2000, p. A16. See also David B. Magleby, *Outside Money* (Lanham, Md.: Rowman & Littlefield, 2000).

35. See John R. Wright, *Interest Groups and Congress* (Boston: Allyn & Bacon, 1996), pp. 136–145; and Mark Smith, *American Business and Political Power* (Chicago, Ill.: University of Chicago Press, 2000), pp. 115–141.

36. Marie Hojnacki and David Kimball, "The Contribution and Lobbying Strategies of PAC Sponsors in Committee," paper delivered at the annual meeting of the American Political Science Association, Boston, September 1998; John R. Wright, "Contributions, Lobbying, and Committee Voting in the U.S. House of Representatives," *American Political Science Review* 84 (June 1990), pp. 417–438; and Richard L. Hall and Frank W. Wayman, "Buying Time: Money Interests and the Mobilization of Bias in Congressional Committees," *American Political Science Review*, 84 (September 1990), pp. 797–820.

37. Kay Lehman Schlozman and John T. Tierney, *Organized Interests and American Democracy* (New York: Harper & Row, 1986), p. 150.

38. Berry, *The Interest Group Society*, p. 166.

39. Yumiko Ono, "Tobacco Firms Rush to Counterattack Despite Signs of Dissension in Ranks," *Wall Street Journal*, 14 August 1995, p. A3.

40. Ken Kollman, *Outside Lobbying* (Princeton, N.J.: Princeton University Press, 1998).

41. Kenneth M. Goldstein, *Interest Groups, Lobbying, and Participation in America* (New York: Cambridge University Press, 1999).

42. Douglas R. Imig, *Poverty and Power* (Lincoln: University of Nebraska Press, 1996), p. 88.

43. Darrell M. West, Diane J. Heith, and Chris Goodwin, "Harry and Louise Go to Washington," *Journal of Health Policy, Politics and Law* 21 (Spring 1996), pp. 35–68.

44. Bruce Ingersoll, "Iowa Farm Aid Helped Rich Most, Study Says," *Wall Street Journal*, 14 January 2000, p. A2.

45. Graeme Browning, "Zapping the Capitol," *National Journal*, 22 November 1994, p. 2449.

46. Lori A. Brainard and Patricia D. Siplon, "Activism for the Future: Using the Internet to Reshape Grassroots Victims Organizations," paper delivered at the annual meeting of the American

Political Science Association, Boston, September 1998.

47. Berry, *The Interest Group Society*, pp. 135–137.

48. Marc K. Landy and Mary Hague, "Private Interests and Superfund," *Public Interest* 108 (Summer 1992), pp. 97–115.

49. Kevin Hula, "Rounding Up the Usual Suspects: Forging Interest Group Coalitions in Washington," paper delivered at the annual meeting of the Midwest Political Science Association, Chicago, April 1993, p. 29.

50. Sidney Verba, Kay Lehman Schlozman, Henry Brady, and Norman H. Nie, "Citizen Activity: Who Participates? What Do They Say?" *American Political Science Review* 87 (June 1993), p. 311.

51. Imig, *Poverty and Power*.

52. Jeffrey M. Berry, *The New Liberalism* (Washington, D.C.: Brookings Institution, pp. 120–130.

53. Schlozman and Tierney, *Organized Interests*, pp. 58–87.

54. Jonathan Rauch, *Demosclerosis* (New York: Times Books, 1994), p. 91.

55. Frank R. Baumgartner and Beth L. Leech, "The Business Advantage in the Washington Lobbying Community," paper presented at the annual meeting of the Midwest Political Science Association, Chicago, April 1999.

56. Mark A. Peterson, "The Presidency and Organized Interests: White House Patterns of Interest Group Liaison," *American Political Science Review* 86 (September 1992), pp. 612–625.

57. "Top 50 PACs by Contributions to Candidates through June, 2000," Federal Election Commission, <www.fec.gov/press/paccon1800.htm>.

58. "FEC Releases Information on PAC Activity for 1997–98."

59. Adam Clymer, "Congress Passes Bill to Disclose Lobbyists' Roles," *New York Times*, 30 November 1995, p. A1.

60. Eric Schmitt, "Order for Lobbyists: Hold the Gravy," *New York Times*, 11 February 1996, p. 30.

61. See Jonathan Rauch, *Demosclerosis* (New York: Times Books, 1994).

Chapter 11 / Congress / pp. 333–369

1. Despite the recent nature of these events, two very good books on the Clinton impeachment have already emerged. Richard A. Posner's *An Affair of State* (Cambridge, Mass.: Harvard University Press, 1999) is a legal analysis of the issues raised by the impeachment and trial of Clinton. The journalistic history is offered by Jeffrey Toobin, *A Vast Conspiracy* (New York: Random House, 1999).

2. "The Articles of Impeachment," *CQ Weekly,* 9 January 1999, p. 47.

3. Jeffrey L. Katz, "Shakeup in the House," *CQ Weekly,* 7 November 1998, pp. 2989–2992.

4. See Dan Carney, "Hyde Leads Impeachment Drive in Growing Isolation," *CQ Weekly,* 5 December 1998, pp. 3247–3249.

5. Richard L. Berke with Janet Elder, "Damaged by Trial, Senate's Standing Sinks in New Poll," *New York Times,* 3 February 1999, p. A1; and James Bennet with Janet Elder, "Despite Intern, President Stays in Good Graces," *New York Times,* 24 February 1999, p. A1.

6. Clinton was later found to be in contempt of court for providing false testimony in a deposition in the Paula Jones lawsuit. John M. Broder and Neil A. Lewis, "Clinton Is Found to Be in Contempt in Jones Lawsuit," *New York Times,* 13 April 1999, p. A1.

7. Paul A. Gigot, "Hyde on His Mistakes—and Ours," *Wall Street Journal,* 12 February 1999, p. A16.

8. Clinton Rossiter, *1787: The Grand Convention* (New York: Mentor, 1968), p. 158.

9. Norman J. Ornstein, Thomas E. Mann, and Michael J. Malbin, *Vital Statistics on Congress, 1999–2000* (Washington, D.C.: AEI Press, 2000), pp. 57–58.

10. Albert R. Hunt, "In Congress, Some Things Never Change," *Wall Street Journal,* 28 March 1996, p. A15.

11. "The Critique of Congress," *American Enterprise* 3 (May–June 1992), p. 101.

12. "Ethics," *American Enterprise* 3 (November–December 1992), p. 84.

13. John R. Hibbing and Elizabeth Theiss-Morse, "What the Public Dislikes About Congress," in *Congress Reconsidered,* 6th ed., eds. Lawrence C. Dodd and Bruce I. Oppenheimer (Washington, D.C.: Congressional Quarterly, 1997), pp. 61–80.

14. Gary C. Jacobson, "Reversal of Fortune: The Transformation of U.S. House Elections in the 1990s," in *Continuity and Change in House Elections,* eds. David W. Brady, John F. Cogan, and Morris P. Fiorina (Stanford, Calif.: Stanford University Press and Hoover Institution Press, 2000), pp. 10–38.

15. Glenn R. Simpson, "Now Showing on an E-Mail Screen Near You: Your Congressman, Produced by Joe Taxpayer," *Wall Street Journal,* 7 January 2000, p. A16.

16. "FEC Reports on Congressional Fundraising for 1997–98," Federal Election Commission press release, 18 April 1999, p. 14.

17. Larry Sabato, *PAC Power* (New York: Norton, 1984), p. 72.

18. Stephen Ansolabehere and James M. Snyder, Jr., "Money and Office: The Sources of Incumbency Advantage in Congressional Campaign Finance," in Brady, Cogan, and Fiorina, *Continuity and Change in House Elections,* pp. 65–86.

19. Paul S. Herrnson, *Congressional Elections,* 3rd ed. (Washington, D.C.: CQ Press, 2000), p. 231.

20. Gary C. Jacobson and Samuel Kernell, *Strategy and Choice in Congressional Elections* (New Haven, Conn.: Yale University Press, 1983). See also L. Sandy Maisel et al., "Re-Exploring the Weak-Challenger Hypothesis: The 1994 Candidate Pools," in *Midterm: Elections of 1994 in Context,* ed. Philip A. Klinkner (Boulder, Colo.: Westview Press, 1996), pp. 137–155.

21. Jonathan S. Krasno, *Challengers, Competition, and Reelection* (New Haven, Conn.: Yale University Press, 1994).

22. Ornstein, Mann, and Malbin, *Vital Statistics on Congress, 1999–2000,* pp. 20–21 and 26–27.

23. "Houses Divided: The 107th Congress," *Boston Globe,* 21 January 2001, p. E2.

24. See Beth Reingold, *Representing Women* (Chapel Hill, N.C.: University of North Carolina Press, 2000).

25. Hanna Fenichel Ptikin, *The Concept of Representation* (Berkeley: University of California Press, 1967), pp. 60–91; and Jane Mansbridge, Should Blacks Represent Blacks and Women Represent Women? A Contingent 'Yes,'" *Journal of Politics* 61 (August 1999), pp. 628–657.

26. Carol M. Swain, *Black Faces, Black Interests* (Cambridge, Mass.: Harvard University Press, 1993), p. 197.

27. *Shaw* v. *Reno,* 509 U.S. 630 (1993).

28. *Miller* v. *Johnson,* 115 S.Ct. 2475 (1995).

29. *Bush* v. *Vera,* 116 S.Ct. 1941 (1996).

30. See David Lublin, *The Paradox of Representation* (Princeton, N.J.: Princeton University Press, 1997). On the political behavior of African-American representatives elected from these districts, see David T. Canon, *Race, Redistricting, and Representation* (Chicago, Ill.: University of Chicago Press, 1999).

31. Walter J. Oleszek, *Congressional Procedures and the Policy Process,* 5th ed. (Washington, D.C.: CQ Press, 2001).

32. Adriel Bettelheim, "Reluctant Congress Drafted into Bioengineering Battle," *CQ Weekly,* 22 April 2000, pp. 938–944.

33. Roger W. Cobb and Charles D. Elder, *Participation in American Politics,* 2nd ed. (Baltimore, Md.: Johns Hopkins University Press, 1983), pp. 64–65.

34. John W. Kingdon, *Agendas, Alternatives, and Public Policies* (Boston, Mass.: Little, Brown, 1984), p. 41.

35. It was Woodrow Wilson who described the legislative process as the "dance of legislation." Eric Redman used the phrase for the title of his case study, *The Dance of Legislation* (New York: Touchstone, 1973).

36. David Shribman, "Canada's Top Envoy to Washington Cuts Unusually Wide Swath," *Wall Street Journal,* 29 July 1985, p. 1.

37. Woodrow Wilson, *Congressional Government* (Boston, Mass.: Houghton Mifflin, 1885), p. 79.

38. Richard L. Hall and C. Lawrence Evans, "The Power of Subcommittees," *Journal of Politics* 52 (May 1990), p. 342.

39. Lawrence D. Longley and Walter J. Oleszek, *Bicameral Politics* (New Haven, Conn.: Yale University Press, 1989), p. 10.

40. Ibid., p. 4.

41. Karen Foerstel, "Gingrich Flexes His Power in Picking Panel Chiefs," *Congressional Quarterly Weekly Report,* 7 January 1995, p. 3326.

42. Philip M. Boffey, "Lawmakers Vow a Legal Recourse for Military Malpractice Victims," *New York Times,* 9 July 1985, p. A14.

43. James M. Lindsay, *Congress and the Politics of U.S. Foreign Policy* (Baltimore, Md.: Johns Hopkins University Press, 1994), pp. 53–75.

44. Carroll J. Doherty and Pat Towell, "Senate Restricts Bosnia Aid Until Iranians Leave," *Congressional Quarterly Weekly Report,* 16 March 1996, p. 713.

45. Joel D. Aberbach, *Keeping a Watchful Eye* (Washington, D.C.: Brookings Institution, 1990), p. 44.

46. Aberbach, *Keeping a Watchful Eye,* pp. 162–183.

47. Gary W. Cox and Mathew D. McCubbins, *Legislative Leviathan* (Berkeley: University of California Press,

1993); and Keith Krehbiel, *Information and Legislative Organization* (Ann Arbor: University of Michigan Press, 1992).

48. Andy Plattner, "Dole on the Job," *Congressional Quarterly Weekly Report*, 29 June 1985, p. 1270.

49. Roger H. Davidson, "Senate Leaders: Janitors for an Untidy Chamber?" in *Congress Reconsidered*, 3d ed., ed. Lawrence C. Dodd and Bruce Oppenheimer (Washington, D.C.: Congressional Quarterly Press, 1985), p. 228.

50. Dan Carney, "Transforming the Nation by Fits and Starts," *CQ Weekly*, 29 January 2000, p. 166.

51. Cox and McCubbins, *Legislative Leviathan*.

52. Charles O. Jones, *The United States Congress* (Homewood, Ill.: Dorsey Press, 1982), p. 322.

53. See Keith Krehbiel, *Pivotal Politics* (Chicago, Ill.: University of Chicago Press, 1998).

54. Deborah Baldwin, "Pulling Punches," *Common Cause* (May–June 1985), p. 22.

55. Eric M. Uslaner, "Is the Senate More Civil Than the House?" in *Esteemed Colleagues*, ed. Burdett A. Loomis (Washington, D.C.: Brookings Institution Press, 2000), pp. 32–55.

56. John Milne, "Memoir: Rudman Had Doubt About Thomas," *Boston Globe*, 12 April 1996, p. 29.

57. Jackie Koszczuk, "Freshmen: New, Powerful Voice," *Congressional Quarterly Weekly Report*, 28 October 1995, p. 3254.

58. Cox and McCubbins, *Legislative Leviathan*; D. Roderick Kiewiet and Mathew D. McCubbins, *The Logic of Delegation* (Chicago, Ill.: University of Chicago Press, 1991); and Krehbiel, *Information and Legislative Organization*.

59. Dan Carney, "As Hostilities Rage on the Hill, Partisan-Vote Rate Soars," *Congressional Quarterly Weekly Report*, 27 January 1996, pp. 199–201; and Jacobson, "Reversal of Fortune."

60. See James Glaser, *Race, Campaign Politics, and the Realignment in the South* (New Haven, Conn.: Yale University Press, 1996).

61. James Sterling Young, *The Washington Community* (New York: Harcourt, Brace, 1964).

62. R. Douglas Arnold, *The Logic of Congressional Action* (New Haven, Conn.: Yale University Press, 1990).

63. Richard F. Fenno, Jr., *Home Style* (Boston, Mass.: Little, Brown, 1978), p. xii.

64. *Ibid.*, p. 32.

65. Louis I. Bredvold and Ralph G. Ross (eds.), *The Philosophy of Edmund Burke* (Ann Arbor: University of Michigan Press, 1960), p. 148.

66. Warren E. Miller and Donald E. Stokes, "Constituency Influence in Congress," *American Political Science Review* 57 (March 1963), pp. 45–57.

67. Michael Wines, "Watch Out with That Budget Ax. My District NEEDS That Dam," *New York Times*, 30 July 1995, Section 4, p. 7.

Chapter 12 / The Presidency / pp. 370–404

1. "Bush Speech," *New York Times*, 21 January 2001, p. 13.

2. Janet Elder, "Poll Shows Americans Divided Over Election, Indicating That Bush Must Build Public Support," *New York Times*, 18 December 2000, p. A21.

3. Nicholas D. Kristof, "A Master of Bipartisanship with No Taste for Details," *New York Times*, 16 October 2000, p. A1.

4. Clinton Rossiter, *1787: The Grand Convention* (New York: Mentor, 1968), p. 148.

5. *Ibid.*, pp. 190–191.

6. See Louis Fisher, *Presidential War Power* (Lawrence: University Press of Kansas, 1995).

7. Wilfred E. Binkley, *President and Congress*, 3rd ed. (New York: Vintage, 1962), p. 155.

8. Richard M. Pious, *The American Presidency* (New York: Basic Books, 1979), pp. 60–63.

9. Richard E. Neustadt, *Presidential Power* (New York: John Wiley, 1980), p. 10.

10. *Ibid.*, p. 9.

11. Chad Roedemeier, "Nixon Kept Softer Self Off Limits, Tape Shows," *Boston Globe*, 8 July 2000, p. A4.

12. Fred I. Greenstein, *The Hidden-Hand Presidency* (New York: Basic Books, 1982), pp. 155–227.

13. Terry Sullivan, "I'll Walk Your District Barefoot," paper delivered at the M.I.T. Conference on the Presidency, Cambridge, Mass., 29 January 2000, p. 6.

14. George C. Edwards III, *At the Margins* (New Haven, Conn.: Yale University Press, 1989). See also Jon R. Bond and Richard Fleisher, *The President in the Legislative Arena* (Chicago, Ill.: University of Chicago Press, 1990).

15. Bert Rockman, "Leadership Style and the Clinton Presidency," in *The Clinton Presidency: First Appraisals*, ed.

Colin Campbell and Bert A. Rockman (Chatham, N.J.: Chatham House, 1996), p. 328.

16. Terry M. Moe and William G. Howell, "Unilateral Action and Presidential Power," *Presidential Studies Quarterly* 29 (December 1999), pp. 850–872.

17. Kenneth R. Mayer and Thomas J. Weko, "The Institutionalization of Power," in *Presidential Power: Forging the Presidency for the Twenty-First Century*, eds. Robert Y. Shapiro, Martha Joynt Kumar, Lawrence R. Jacobs (New York: Columbia University Press, 2000), pp. 178–208.

18. See Edwards, *At the Margins*, pp. 101–125.

19. Richard A. Brody, *Assessing the President* (Stanford, Calif.: Stanford University Press, 1991), pp. 27–44.

20. Darrell M. West, *Congress and Economic Policymaking* (Pittsburgh, Pa.: University of Pittsburgh Press, 1987), p. 33.

21. Paul Brace and Barbara Hinckley, *Follow the Leader* (New York: Basic Books, 1992).

22. Charles W. Ostrom and Dennis M. Simon, "Promise and Performance: A Dynamic Model of Presidential Popularity," *American Political Science Review* 79 (June 1985), pp. 334–358.

23. George C. Edwards III, "Frustration and Folly: Bill Clinton and the Public Presidency," in *The Clinton Presidency*, p. 255.

24. Mark A. Peterson, "Clinton and Organized Interests: Splitting Friends, Unifying Enemies," in *The Clinton Legacy*, eds. Colin Campbell and Bert A. Rockman (New York: Chatham House, 2000), pp. 140–168.

25. Jeffrey E. Cohen, *Presidential Responsiveness and Public Policy-Making* (Ann Arbor: University of Michigan Press, 1999); and Lawrence C. Jacobs and Robert Y. Shapiro, *Politicians Don't Pander* (Chicago, Ill.: University of Chicago Press, 2000).

26. David McCullough, *Truman* (New York: Simon and Schuster, 1992), p. 914.

27. "Prepared Text of Carter's Farewell Address," *New York Times*, 15 January 1981, p. B10.

28. Benjamin I. Page, *Choices and Echoes in Presidential Elections* (Chicago, Ill.: University of Chicago Press, 1978).

29. Robert A. Dahl, "Myth of the Presidential Mandate," *Political Science Quarterly* 105 (Fall 1990), pp. 355–372.

30. "Two Cheers for United Government," *American Enterprise* 4 (January–February 1993), pp. 107–108.

31. Morris Fiorina, *Divided Government*, 2d ed. (Needham Heights, Mass.: Allyn & Bacon, 1996), p. 153.

32. Gary C. Jacobson, "Meager Patrimony: The Reagan Era and Republican Representation in Congress," in *Looking Back at the Reagan Presidency*, ed. Larry Berman (Baltimore, Md.: Johns Hopkins University Press, 1990), p. 300.

33. See, generally, Charles O. Jones, *The Presidency in a Separated System* (Washington, D.C.: Brookings Institution, 1994).

34. David R. Mayhew, *Divided We Govern* (New Haven, Conn.: Yale University Press, 1991); and David R. Mayhew, "The Return to Unified Government Under Clinton: How Much of a Difference in Lawmaking," in *The New American Politics*, ed. Bryan D. Jones (Boulder, Colo.: Westview Press, 1995), pp. 111–121.

35. See Sean Kelley, "Divided We Govern: A Reassessment," *Polity* 25 (Spring 1993), pp. 475–484; and George Edwards, Andrew Barrett, and Jeffrey Peake, "The Legislative Impact of Divided Government: What *Failed* to Pass in Congress," n.d., Center for Presidential Studies, Texas A&M University.

36. See Sarah H. Binder, "The Dynamics of Legislative Gridlock, 1947–96," *American Political Science Review* 93 (September 1999), pp. 519–534.

37. See generally, Bradley H. Patterson, *The White House Staff* (Washington, D.C.: Brookings Institution Press, 2000).

38. Jeb Stuart Magruder, *An American Life* (New York: Atheneum, 1974), p. 58, quoted in Benjamin I. Page and Mark Petracca, *The American Presidency* (New York: McGraw-Hill, 1983), p. 171.

39. *Statistical Abstract of the United States*, 1999 (on-line at <www.census.gov/prod/99pubs/99statab/sec10.pdf>).

40. Paul J. Quirk, "Presidential Competence," in *The Presidency and the Political System*, 5th ed., ed. Michael Nelson (Washington, D.C.: CQ Press, 1998), p. 174.

41. Bob Woodward, *The Agenda* (New York: Simon & Schuster, 1994), p. 127.

42. Kristof, "A Master of Bipartisanship with No Taste for Details."

43. George Stephanopoulos, *All Too Human* (Boston, Mass.: Back Bay Books, 1999), p. 61.

44. Edward Weisband and Thomas M.

Franck, *Resignation in Protest* (New York: Penguin, 1975), p. 139, quoted in Thomas E. Cronin, *The State of the Presidency*, 2nd ed. (Boston, Mass.: Little, Brown, 1980), p. 253.

45. Griffin B. Bell with Ronald J. Ostrow, *Taking Care of the Law* (New York: Morrow, 1982), p. 45.

46. Terry M. Moe, "The Politicized Presidency," in *The New Direction in American Politics*, ed. John E. Chubb and Paul E. Peterson (Washington, D.C.: Brookings Institution, 1985), pp. 235–271.

47. *Public Papers of the President, Lyndon B. Johnson, 1965*, vol. 1 (Washington, D.C.: Government Printing Office, 1966), p. 72.

48. "Transcript of Second Inaugural Address by Reagan," *New York Times*, 22 January 1985, p. 72.

49. Kevin Phillips, *The Politics of Rich and Poor* (New York: Random House, 1990), p. 88.

50. "Bush Speech," p. 13.

51. John W. Kingdon, *Agendas, Alternatives, and Public Policies* (Boston, Mass.: Little, Brown, 1984), p. 25.

52. Richard E. Neustadt, "Presidency and Legislation: The Growth of Central Clearance," *American Political Science Review* 48 (September 1954), pp. 641–671.

53. Seth King, "Reagan, in Bid for Budget Votes, Reported to Yield on Sugar Prices," *New York Times*, 27 June 1981, p. A1.

54. Barbara Sinclair, "The President as Legislative Leader," in *The Clinton Legacy*, p. 75.

55. Roger H. Davidson and Colton C. Campbell, "The Senate and the Executive," in *Esteemed Colleagues*, ed. Burdett A. Loomis (Washington, D.C.: Brookings Institution, 2000), pp. 194–219.

56. "Special Report," *CQ Weekly*, 16 December 2000, pp. 2842–2856.

57. Jeffrey M. Berry and Kent E. Portney, "Centralizing Regulatory Control and Interest Group Access: The Quayle Council on Competitiveness," in *Interest Group Politics*, 4th ed., ed. Allan J. Cigler and Burdett A. Loomis (Washington, D.C.: Congressional Quarterly Press, 1994), pp. 319–347.

58. The extent to which popularity affects presidential influence in Congress is difficult to determine with any precision. For an overview of this issue, see Jon R. Bond, Richard Fleisher, and Glen S. Katz, "An Overview of the Empirical Findings on Presidential-Congressional Relations," in *Rivals for

Power*, ed. James A. Thurber (Washington, D.C.: Congressional Quarterly Press, 1996), pp. 103–139.

59. George Hager, "Clinton, GOP Congress Strike Historic Budget Agreement," *Congressional Quarterly Weekly Report*, 3 May 1997, p. 996.

60. Lori Nitschke, "Agriculture Has Muscle in China Free-Trade Fight," *CQ Weekly*, 4 March 2000, pp. 444–448.

61. Fred Barnes, "Hour of Power," *New Republic*, 3 September 1990, p. 12.

62. Ernest R. May and Philip D. Zelikow (eds.), *The Kennedy Tapes: Inside the White House During the Cuban Missile Crisis* (Cambridge, Mass.: Harvard University Press, 1997), pp. 498–499, 501, 512–513, 663–666.

63. John P. Burke and Fred I. Greenstein, *How Presidents Test Reality* (New York: Russell Sage Foundation, 1989).

64. Richard E. Neustadt and Ernest R. May, *Thinking in Time* (New York: Free Press, 1986), p. 143.

65. Theodore J. Lowi, *The Personal President* (Ithaca, N.Y.: Cornell University Press, 1985), p. 185.

66. Doris Kearns, *Lyndon Johnson and the American Dream* (New York: Signet, 1977), p. 363.

67. Dan Balz, "Clinton Concedes Marital Wrongdoing," *Washington Post*, 27 January 1992, p. A1.

68. David Maraniss, *First in His Class* (New York: Simon and Schuster, 1995), especially pp. 24–41.

69. Neil A. Lewis, "Existing Job, Clinton Accepts Immunity Deal," *New York Times*, 20 January 2001, p. A1.

Chapter 13 / The Bureaucracy / pp. 405–433

1. Adam Bryant, "Crash Stirs Up Safety Debate in U.S. Agency," *New York Times*, 15 May 1996, p. A1.

2. Adam Bryant, "F.A.A. Struggles as Airlines Turn to Subcontracts," *New York Times*, 2 June 1996, p. 1.

3. Alison Mitchell, "Clinton Offers Challenge to Nation, Declaring, 'Era of Big Government Is Over,'" *New York Times*, 24 January 1996, p. A1.

4. John E. Chubb and Terry M. Moe, *Politics, Markets, and America's Schools* (Washington, D.C.: Brookings Institution, 1990).

5. James Q. Wilson, *Bureaucracy* (New York: Basic Books, 1989), p. 25.

6. Bruce D. Porter, "Parkinson's Law Revisited: War and the Growth of American Government," *Public Interest* 60 (Summer 1980), p. 50.

7. See, generally, Ballard C. Campbell, *The Growth of American Government* (Bloomington: Indiana University Press, 1995).

8. See Anne Schneider and Helen Ingram, "Social Construction of Target Populations: Implications for Politics and Policy," *American Political Science Review* 87 (June 1993), pp. 334–347.

9. Theda Skocpol, *Protecting Soldiers and Mothers: The Political Origins of Social Policy in the United States* (Cambridge, Mass.: Harvard University Press, 1992).

10. Paul C. Light, *Thickening Government* (Washington, D.C.: Brookings Institution, 1995).

11. William J. Broad, "U.S. Will Deploy Its Spy Satellites on Nature Mission," *New York Times*, 27 November 1995, p. A1.

12. Paul C. Light, *The True Size of Government* (Washington, D.C.: Brookings Institution, 1999).

13. Frank Bruni, "Bush Signaling a Readiness to Go His Own Way as an Unconventional Republican," *New York Times*, 3 April 2000, p. A15.

14. U.S. Bureau of the Census, *Statistical Abstract of the United States, 1999* (Washington, D.C.: U.S. Government Printing Office, 1999), 364.

15. Patricia Wallace Ingraham, *The Foundation of Merit* (Baltimore, Md.: Johns Hopkins University Press, 1995), p. 9.

16. Todd T. Kunioka, "Bank Supervision and the Limits of Political Influence over Bureaucracy," *Public Administration Review* 59 (July/August 1999), pp. 303–313.

17. Bruce Babbitt, "Between the Flood and the Rainbow. Our Covenant: To Protect the Whole of Creation," *Vital Speeches of the Day* (Mt. Pleasant, S.C.: City News Publishing Co., 1996), p. 281.

18. "Babbitt and Climate Change," *Oil and Gas Journal*, 18 August 1997, p. 13.

19. Joel D. Aberbach, "A Reinvented Government, or the Same Old Government," in *The Clinton Legacy*, Colin Campbell and Bert A. Rockman, eds. (New York: Chatham House, 2000), pp. 199–120.

20. James C. Benton, "Proposed Ergonomics Rules Rub GOP the Wrong Way," *CQ Weekly*, 27 November 1999, p. 2843; and Phil Kuntz, "Proposed OSHA Rules for Workplace Injuries Make Companies Ache," *Wall Street Journal*, 18 September 2000, p. A1.

21. Theodore J. Lowi, Jr., *The End of Liberalism*, 2nd ed. (New York: Norton, 1979).

22. Doris A. Graber, *Mass Media and American Politics*, 3rd ed. (Washington, D.C.: Congressional Quarterly Press, 1989), p. 51.

23. Jeffrey M. Berry, *Feeding Hungry People* (New Brunswick, N.J.: Rutgers University Press, 1984).

24. Rebecca Adams, "GOP-Business Alliance Yields Swift Reversal of Ergonomics Rules," *CQ Weekly*, 10 March 2001, pp. 535–539.

25. David J. Garrow, *Bearing the Cross* (New York: Morrow, 1986), pp. 373–374.

26. See, generally, Cornelius M. Kerwin, *Rulemaking*, 2nd ed. (Washington, D.C.: Congressional Quarterly, 1999).

27. Marian Burros, "F.D.A. Is Again Proposing to Regulate Vitamins and Supplements," *New York Times*, 15 June 1993, p. A25.

28. Charles E. Lindblom, "The Science of Muddling Through," *Public Administration Review* 19 (Spring 1959), pp. 79–88.

29. See Michael T. Hayes, *Incrementalism and Public Policy* (White Plains, N.Y.: Longman, 1992).

30. Andrew Weiss and Edward Woodhouse, "Reframing Incrementalism: A Constructive Response to the Critics," *Policy Sciences* 25 (August 1992), pp. 255–273.

31. "Battles with the IRS," *Congressional Quarterly Weekly Report*, 27 September 1997, p. 2299; "IRS Overhaul," *Congressional Quarterly Weekly Report*, 20 December 1997, p. 3119.

32. Jonathan Bendor, Serge Taylor, and Roland Van Gaalan, "Stacking the Deck: Bureaucratic Mission and Policy Design," *American Political Science Review* 81 (Spring 1987), p. 874.

33. Robert B. Reich, *Locked in the Cabinet* (New York: Vintage, 1998), pp. 115–118.

34. John Frohnmeyer, *Leaving Town Alive* (Boston: Houghton Mifflin, 1993).

35. Thomas W. Church and Robert T. Nakamura, *Cleaning Up the Mess* (Washington, D.C.: Brookings Institution, 1993).

36. David Cay Johnston, "Fearing for Jobs, I.R.S. Workers Relax Effort to Get Unpaid Taxes," *New York Times*, 18 May 1999, p. A1.

37. Gerald Garvey, *Facing the Bureaucracy: Living and Dying in a Public Agency* (San Francisco, Calif.: Jossey-Bass, 1993), p. 190.

38. See Philip K. Howard, *The Death of*

Common Sense (New York: Warner Books, 1994).

39. Eric Schmitt, "Agriculture Dept. Rebuffed on School Lunches," *New York Times*, 15 May 1996, p. A17.

40. For a general discussion, see Paul C. Light, *The Tides of Reform* (New Haven, Conn.: Yale University Press, 1997).

41. Jeffrey H. Birnbaum and Paulette Thomas, "Clinton Moves to Streamline Government," *Wall Street Journal*, 8 September 1993, p. A2.

42. Peter H. Stone, "Ganging Up on the FDA," *National Journal*, 18 February 1995, pp. 410–414.

43. David Vogel, "AIDS and the Politics of Drug Lag," *Public Interest* 96 (Summer 1989), pp. 73–85.

44. Lori Nitschke, "Senate Bill Aims to Speed Review of Drugs, Medical Devices by FDA," *Congressional Quarterly Weekly Report*, 27 September 1997, p. 2312.

45. Light, *The Tides of Reform*.

46. A good, short introduction to TQM in government is James E. Swiss, "Adapting Total Quality Management to Government," *Public Administration Review* 52 (July–August 1992), pp. 356–362.

47. David Osborne and Ted Gaebler, *Reinventing Government* (New York: Plume Books, 1993), p. 166.

48. Donald F. Kettl, *Reinventing Government: A Fifth Year Report Card* (Washington, D.C.: Brookings Institution, 1998), p. vii.

49. Sarah Lueck, "Survey Measures Satisfaction with Federal Services," *Wall Street Journal*, 13 December 1999, p. A2.

Chapter 14 / The Courts / pp. 434–468

1. David Von Drehle, "The Night That Would Not End," *Washington Post*, 9 November 2000, p. A1.

2. Sara Fritz, Bill Adair, and David Ballingrud, "Florida Finish," *St. Petersburg Times*, 8 November 2000, p. 3A.

3. Bush v. *Palm Beach County Canvassing Board*, 531 U.S. ___ (2000).

4. *Gore and Lieberman* v. *Harris*, No. SC00-2431 (Supreme Court of Florida).

5. *Bush* v. *Gore*, No. 00-949 (00A504) (granting a stay in SC00-2431).

6. Bush v. Gore, 531 U.S. ___ (2000).

7. Felix Frankfurter and James M. Landis, *The Business of the Supreme Court* (New York: Macmillan, 1928), pp. 5–14; and Julius Goebel, Jr., *Antecedents and Beginnings to 1801,* vol. 1 of *The History of the Supreme Court of the United States* (New York: Macmillan, 1971).

8. Maeva Marcus, ed., *The Justices on Circuit, 1795–1800*, vol. 3 of *The Documentary History of the Supreme Court of the United States, 1789–1800* (New York: Columbia University Press, 1990).

9. Robert G. McCloskey, *The United States Supreme Court* (Chicago, Ill.: University of Chicago Press, 1960), p. 31.

10. *Marbury* v. *Madison*, 1 Cranch 137 at 177, 178 (1803).

11. Interestingly, the term *judicial review* dates only to 1910; it was apparently unknown to Marshall and his contemporaries. Robert Lowry Clinton, *Marbury* v. *Madison and Judicial Review* (Lawrence: University Press of Kansas, 1989), p. 7.

12. Henry J. Abraham, *The Judicial Process*, 6th ed. (New York: Oxford University Press, 1993), pp. 274–279. Lee Epstein et al., *The Supreme Court Compendium* (Washington, D.C.: Congressional Quarterly Press, 1994), Table 2-12.

13. *Ware* v. *Hylton*, 3 Dallas 199 (1796).

14. *Martin* v. *Hunter's Lessee*, 1 Wheat. 304 (1816).

15. *Constitution of the United States of America: Annotated and Interpreted* (Washington, D.C.: U.S. Government Printing Office, 1987) and supplements.

16. Garry Wills, *Explaining America: The Federalist* (Garden City, N.Y.: Doubleday, 1981), pp. 127–136.

17. *State Justice Institute News*, 4 (Spring 1993), p. 1.

18. William P. Marshall, "Federalization: A Critical Overview," 44 *DePaul Law Review* 719 (1995), 722–723.

19. Abby Goodnough, "Financial Details Are Revealed in Affirmative Action Settlement," *New York Times*, 6 December 1997, p. B-5.

20. Charles Alan Wright, *Handbook on the Law of Federal Courts*, 3rd ed. (St. Paul, Minn.: West, 1976), p. 7.

21. William H. Rehnquist, "2000 Year-End Report on the Federal Judiciary," *The Third Branch* 33, 1 (January 2001), pp. 1–5.

22. Federal Magistrate Judges Association at <http://www.fedjudge.org/>.

23. Mecham, "Judicial Business of the United States Courts," pp. 16 and 23, on-line at <www.uscourts.gov/judbus 1999/contents.html>.

24. Linda Greenhouse, "Precedent for Lower Courts: Tyrant or Teacher?" *New York Times*, 29 January 1988, p. B7.

25. *Texas* v. *Johnson*, 491 U.S. 397 (1989); *United States* v. *Eichman*, 496 U.S. 310 (1990).

26. *Regents of the University of California* v. *Bakke*, 438 U.S. 265 (1978).

27. *Adarand Constructors* v. *Peña*, 515 U.S. ____ (1995); *Miller* v. *Johnson*, ____ U.S. ____ (1995).

28. "Reading Petitions Is for Clerks Only at High Court Now," *Wall Street Journal*, 11 October 1990, p. B7.

29. H. W. Perry, Jr., *Deciding to Decide: Agenda Setting in the United States Supreme Court* (Cambridge, Mass.: Harvard University Press, 1991); Linda Greenhouse, "Justice Delayed; Agreeing Not to Agree," *New York Times*, 17 March 1996, Sect. 4, p. 1.

30. Perry, *Deciding to Decide*; Gregory A. Caldiera and John R. Wright, "The Discuss List: Agenda Building in the Supreme Court," 24 *Law & Society Review* 807 (1990).

31. Doris M. Provine, *Case Selection in the United States Supreme Court* (Chicago, Ill.: University of Chicago Press, 1980), pp. 74–102.

32. Elder Witt, *A Different Justice: Reagan and the Supreme Court* (Washington, D.C.: Congressional Quarterly Press, 1986), p. 133.

33. Neil A. Lewis, "Solicitor General's Career Advances at Intersection of Law and Politics," *New York Times*, 1 June 1990, p. A11.

34. Perry, *Deciding to Decide*, p. 286.

35. Kevin T. McGuire, "Repeat Players in the Supreme Court: The Role of Experienced Lawyers in Litigation Success," *Journal of Politics* 57 (1995), pp. 187–196.

36. Michael Kirkland, *Court Hears "Subordinate" Speech Debate*, UPI, 1 December 1993, available in NEWSNET News Bulletin Board. The oral argument in the case, *Waters* v. *Churchill*, can be found at <oyez.at.nwu.edu/cases/92–1450/>.

37. "Rising Fixed Opinions," *New York Times*, 22 February 1988, p. 14. See also Linda Greenhouse, "At the Bar," *New York Times*, 28 July 1989, p. 21.

38. Jeffrey A. Segal and Harold J. Spaeth, *The Supreme Court and the Attitudinal Model* (Cambridge, England: Cambridge University Press, 1993).

39. Stuart Taylor, Jr., "Lifting of Secrecy Reveals Earthy Side of Justices," *New York Times*, 22 February 1988, p. A16.

40. Glen Elasser, "Courting Justice," *Chicago Tribune*, 6 June 1990, Tempo, p. 1.

41. Thomas G. Walker, Lee Epstein, and William J. Dixon, "On the Mysterious Demise of Consensual Norms in the United States Supreme Court," *Journal of Politics* 50 (1988), pp. 361–389.

42. "The Supreme Court, 1996 Term," 111 *Harvard Law Review* 433, Table IC (1997).

43. See, for example, Walter F. Murphy, *Elements of Judicial Strategy* (Chicago, Ill.: University of Chicago Press, 1964), and Bob Woodward and Scott Armstrong, *The Brethren* (New York: Simon & Schuster, 1979).

44. Henry J. Abraham, *Justices and Presidents: A Political History of Appointments to the Supreme Court*, 2nd ed. (New York: Oxford University Press, 1985), pp. 183–185.

45. Stephen L. Wasby, *The Supreme Court in the Federal Judicial System*, 3rd ed. (Chicago, Ill.: Nelson-Hall, 1988), p. 241.

46. Linda Greenhouse, "At the Bar," *New York Times*, 28 July 1989, p. 21.

47. National Center for State Courts, "Survey of Judicial Salaries," Vol. 26, No. 1 (Winter 2000) <www.ncsc.dni.us/is/winter2000.pdf>.

48. Lawrence Baum, *American Courts: Process and Policy*, 3rd ed. (Boston, Mass.: Houghton Mifflin, 1994), pp. 114–129.

49. Neil A. Lewis, "President Moves Quickly on Judgeships," *New York Times*, 11 March 2001, Section 1, p. 18.

50. Paul Barrett, "More Minorities, Women Named to U.S. Courts," *Wall Street Journal*, 23 December 1993, p. B1; Sheldon Goldman and Elliot Slotnick, "Clinton's Second Term Judiciary: Picking Judges Under Fire," *Judicature*, Vol. 82, No. 6 (May/June 1999), pp. 264–284.

51. Wasby, *Supreme Court*, pp. 107–110.

52. Neil A. Lewis, "In Setting Priorities, Democrats Give Up Confirmation Battle," *New York Times*, 25 May 2001, p. A1.

53. Sheldon Goldman, "Judicial Selection Under Clinton: A Midterm Examination," 78 *Judicature* 276 (1995). Professor Goldman kindly provided additional data from the 104th Congress.

54. Ronald Stidham, Robert A. Carp, and Donald R. Songer, "The Voting Behavior of Judges Appointed by President Clinton," paper presented at the annual meeting of the Southwestern Political Science Association, Houston, Texas, March 1996.

55. Peter G. Fish, "John J. Parker," in *Dictionary of American Biography*, supp. 6, 1956–1980 (New York: Scribner's, 1980), p. 494.

56. *Congressional Quarterly's Guide to the U.S. Supreme Court*, 2nd ed. (Washington, D.C.: Congressional Quarterly Press, 1990), pp. 655–656.

57. Stuart Taylor, Jr., "The Supremes: *Bush* v. *Gore* May Be Just the Beginning," *Newsweek*, December 25, 2000/January 1, 2001, p. 50.

58. *Brown* v. *Board of Education II*, 349 U.S. 294 (1955).

59. Charles A. Johnson and Bradley C. Canon, *Judicial Policies: Implementation and Impact* (Washington, D.C.: Congressional Quarterly Press, 1984).

60. *Webster* v. *Reproductive Health Services*, 492 U.S. 490 (1989).

61. *Planned Parenthood* v. *Casey*, 505 U.S. ___ (1992).

62. Alexander M. Bickel, *The Least Dangerous Branch* (Indianapolis, Ind.: Bobbs-Merrill, 1962); and Robert A. Dahl, "*Decision-Making in a Democracy: The Supreme Court as a National Policy-Maker,*" 6 *Journal of Public Law* 279 (1962).

63. William Mishler and Reginal S. Sheehan, "The Supreme Court as a Countermajoritarian Institution? The Impact of Public Opinion on Supreme Court Decisions," *American Political Science Review* 87 (1993), pp. 87–101.

64. 530 U.S. 428 (2000).

65. Thomas R. Marshall, *Public Opinion and the Supreme Court* (Boston, Mass.: Unwin Hyman, 1989).

66. Richard Morin, "Unconventional Wisdom," *Washington Post*, 8 October 1995, p. C5.

67. Marshall, *Public Opinion and the Supreme Court*, pp. 192–193; Gerald N. Rosenberg, *The Hollow Hope: Can Courts Bring About Social Change?* (Chicago, Ill.: University of Chicago Press, 1991).

68. The Gallup Organization, "The Florida Recount Controversy from the Public's Perspective: 25 Insights" (December 22, 2000), on-line at <http://www.gallup.com/poll/releases/pr001222b.asp>.

69. William J. Brennan, Jr., "State Supreme Court Judge Versus United States Supreme Court Justice: A Change in Function and Perspective," 19 *University of Florida Law Review* 225 (1966).

70. G. Alan Tarr and M. C. Porter, *State Supreme Courts in State and Nation* (New Haven, Conn.: Yale University Press, 1988), pp. 206–209.

71. Dennis Hevesi, "New Jersey Court Protects Trash from Police Searches," *New York Times*, 19 July 1990, p. A9.

72. Kermit L. Hall, "The Canon of American Constitutional History in Comparative Perspective (keynote address) 5, p. 14, Supreme Court Historical Society, Washington, D.C., February 16, 2001).

73. Baum, *American Courts*, pp. 319–347.

Chapter 15 / Order and Civil Liberties / pp. 469–509

1. *United States* v. *Baker and Gonda*, 890 F. Supp. 1375 (1995).

2. Charles Platt, *Anarchy Online* (New York: Harper Prism, 1997).

3. Learned Hand, *The Bill of Rights* (Boston, Mass.: Atheneum, 1958), p. 1.

4. Leonard W. Levy, *The Establishment Clause: Religion and the First Amendment* (New York: Macmillan, 1986); Leo Pfeffer, *Church, State, and Freedom* (Boston, Mass.: Beacon, 1953); and Leonard W. Levy, "The Original Meaning of the Establishment Clause of the First Amendment," in *Religion and the State*, ed. James E. Wood, Jr. (Waco, Tex.: Baylor University Press, 1985), pp. 43–83.

5. Garry Wills, *Under God: Religion and American Politics* (New York: Simon & Schuster, 1990); Barry A. Kosmin and Seymour P. Lachman, *One Nation Under God: Religion in Contemporary American Society* (New York: Harmony Books, 1993).

6. *Reynolds* v. *United States*, 98 U.S. 145 (1879).

7. *Everson* v. *Board of Education*, 330 U.S. 1 (1947).

8. *Board of Education* v. *Allen*, 392 U.S. 236 (1968).

9. *Lemon* v. *Kurtzman*, 403 U.S. 602 (1971).

10. *Agostini* v. *Felton*, 96 U.S. 552 (1997).

11. *Lynch* v. *Donnelly*, 465 U.S. 668 (1984).

12. *County of Allegheny* v. *ACLU Greater Pittsburgh Chapter*, 492 U.S. 573 (1989).

13. *Engle* v. *Vitale*, 370 U.S. 421 (1962).

14. *Abington School District* v. *Schempp*, 374 U.S. 203 (1963).

15. *Lee* v. *Weisman*, 505 U.S. (1992).

16. *Herdahl* v. *Pontotoc County School District, No. 3*, 1996 U.S. Dist. LEXIS 7671 (N.D. Miss. W.D.) (3 June 1996).

17. *Sante Fe Independent School District* v. *Doe*, 530 U.S. 290 (2000), quoting *West Virginia Bd. of Ed.* v. *Barnette*, 319 U.S. 624, 638 (1943).

18. *Wallace* v. *Jaffree*, 472 U.S. 38 (1985).

19. Michael W. McConnell, "The Origins and Historical Understanding of the Free Exercise of Religion," 103 *Harvard Law Review* 1409, 1990.

20. *Sherbert* v. *Verner*, 374 U.S. 398 (1963).

21. McConnell, *Origins and Historical Understanding*.

22. *Employment Division* v. *Smith*, 494 U.S. 872 (1990).

23. *City of Boerne* v. *Flores*, 95 U.S. 2074 (1997).

24. Laurence Tribe, *Treatise on American Constitutional Law*, 2nd ed. (St. Paul, Minn.: West, 1988), p. 566.

25. Zechariah Chafee, *Free Speech in the United States* (Cambridge, Mass.: Harvard University Press, 1941).

26. Leonard W. Levy, *The Emergence of a Free Press* (New York: Oxford University Press, 1985).

27. Mark Twain, *Following the Equator* (Hartford, Conn.: American Publishing, 1897).

28. *Schenck* v. *United States*, 249 U.S. 47 (1919).

29. *Abrams* v. *United States*, 250 U.S. 616 (1919).

30. *Gitlow* v. *New York*, 268 U.S. 652 (1925).

31. *Dennis* v. *United States*, 341 U.S. 494 (1951).

32. *Brandenburg* v. *Ohio*, 395 U.S. 444 (1969).

33. *Tinker* v. *Des Moines Independent County School District*, 393 U.S. 503 at 508 (1969).

34. *United States* v. *Eichman*, 496 U.S. 310 (1990).

35. Linda Greenhouse, "Supreme Court Voids Flag Law," *New York Times*, 12 June 1990, p. A1.

36. *Barnes* v. *Glen Theatre*, 501 U.S. 560 (1991).

37. *Chaplinsky* v. *New Hampshire*, 315 U.S. 568 (1942).

38. *Terminiello* v. *Chicago*, 337 U.S. 1.

39. *Cohen* v. *California*, 403 U.S. 15 ___ (1971).

40. Sam Howe Verhovek, "Creators of Anti-Abortion Web Site Told to Pay Millions," *New York Times*, February 3, 1999, p. A9; *Planned Parenthood, Inc.* v. *American Coalition of Life Activists*, 41 F. Supp. 2d 1030 (D. OR) (1999); Howard Mintz, "Appeals Court Reverses $107 Million Judgment Against Anti-Abortion Web Site," *San Jose Mercury News*, 29 March 2001.

41. *United States* v. *Baker and Gonda*, 890 F. Supp. 1375 (1995).

42. *ACLU* v. *Reno* (1996 U.S. Dist. LEXIS) (June 12, 1996).

43. *Reno* v. *ACLU*, 96 U.S. 511 (1997).

44. *Roth* v. *United States*, 354 U.S. 476 (1957).

45. *Jacobellis* v. *Ohio*, 378 U.S. 184 (1964).

46. *Miller* v. *California*, 413 U.S. 15 (1973).

47. Donald Alexander Downs, *The New Politics of Pornography* (Chicago, Ill.: University of Chicago Press, 1989), pp. 95–143.

48. *American Booksellers Ass'n* v. *Hudnut*, 598 F. Supp. 1316 (1984).

49. *New York Times* v. *Sullivan*, 376 U.S. 254 (1964).

50. *Hustler Magazine* v. *Falwell*, 485 U.S. 46 (1988).

51. *Near* v. *Minnesota*, 283 U.S. 697 (1931).

52. For a detailed account of *Near*, see Fred W. Friendly, *Minnesota Rag* (New York: Random House, 1981).

53. *New York Times* v. *United States*, 403 U.S. 713 (1971).

54. *Branzburg* v. *Hayes*, 408 U.S. 665 (1972).

55. *Zurcher* v. *Stanford Daily*, 436 U.S. 547 (1978).

56. *Hazelwood School District* v. *Kuhlmeier*, 484 U.S. 260 (1988).

57. *United States* v. *Cruikshank*, 92 U.S. 542 (1876); *Constitution of the United States of America: Annotated and Interpreted* (Washington, D.C.: U.S. Government Printing Office, 1973), p. 1031.

58. *DeJonge* v. *Oregon*, 299 U.S. 353 (1937).

59. *United States* v. *Miller*, 307 U.S. 174 (1939).

60. Laurence H. Tribe and Michael C. Dorf, *On Reading the Constitution* (Cambridge, Mass.: Harvard University Press, 1991), p. 10.

61. *Barron* v. *Baltimore*, 32 U.S. (7 Pet.) 243 (1833).

62. *Chicago B. & Q. R.* v. *Chicago*, 166 U.S. 226 (1897).

63. *Gitlow* v. *New York*, 268 U.S. at 666 (1925).

64. *Palko* v. *Connecticut*, 302 U.S. 319 (1937).

65. *Duncan* v. *Louisiana*, 391 U.S. 145 (1968).

66. *McNabb* v. *United States*, 318 U.S. 332 (1943).

67. *Baldwin* v. *New York*, 399 U.S. 66 (1970).

68. Anthony Lewis, *Gideon's Trumpet* (New York: Random House, 1964).

69. *Gideon* v. *Wainwright*, 372 U.S. 335 (1963).

70. *Miranda* v. *Arizona*, 384 U.S. 436 (1966).

71. *Dickerson* v. *United States*, 530 U.S. 428 (2000).

72. *Wolf* v. *Colorado*, 338 U.S. 25 (1949).

73. *Mapp* v. *Ohio*, 367 U.S. 643 (1961).

74. *United States* v. *Leon*, 468 U.S. 897 (1984).

75. *California* v. *Greenwood*, 486 U.S. 35 (1988).

76. *James* v. *Illinois*, 493 U.S. 307 (1990).

77. Paul Brest, *Processes of Constitutional Decision-making* (Boston, Mass.: Little, Brown, 1975), p. 708.

78. *Griswold* v. *Connecticut*, 381 U.S. 479 (1965).

79. *Roe* v. *Wade*, 410 U.S. 113 (1973).

80. See John Hart Ely, "The Wages of Crying Wolf: A Comment on *Roe* v. *Wade*," 82 *Yale Law Journal* 920 (1973).

81. Interview with Justice Harry Blackmun, ABC's "Nightline," 2 December 1993.

82. *Webster* v. *Reproductive Health Services*, 492 U.S. 490 (1989).

83. *Hodgson* v. *Minnesota*, 497 U.S. 417 (1990); *Ohio* v. *Akron Center for Reproductive Health*, 497 U.S. 502 (1990).

84. *Steinberg* v. *Carhart*, 530 U.S. 914 (2000).

85. Ruth Bader Ginsburg, "Some Thoughts on Autonomy and Equality in Relation to *Roe* v. *Wade*," 63 *North Carolina Law Review* 375 (1985).

86. Stuart Taylor, "Supreme Court Hears Case on Homosexual Rights," *New York Times*, 1 April 1986, p. A-24.

87. *Bowers* v. *Hardwick*, 478 U.S. 186 (1986).

88. Linda Greenhouse, "Washington Talk: When Second Thoughts Come Too Late," *New York Times*, 5 November 1990, p. A9.

89. Learned Hand, "The Contribution of an Independent Judiciary to Civilization," in *The Spirit of Liberty: Papers and Addresses of Learned Hand*, ed. Irving Dilliard, 3rd ed. (New York: Alfred A. Knopf, 1960), p. 164.

Chapter 16 / Equality and Civil Rights / pp. 510–547

1. International Convention on the Elimination of All Forms of Racial Discrimination, <http://www.unhchr.ch/html/menu3/b/d_icerd.htm> (October 21, 1994).

2. Initial Report of the United States of America to the United Nations Committee on the Elimination of Racial Discrimination, September 2000, <http: //www.state.gov/www/global/human _rights/cerd_report/cerd_intro.html>.

3. Howard Schuman, Charlotte Steeh, and Lawrence Bobo, *Racial Attitudes in America: Trends and Interpretations* (Cambridge, Mass.: Harvard University Press, 1985); Sidney Verba and Gary R. Orren, *Equality in America: The View from the Top* (Cambridge, Mass.: Harvard University Press, 1985), especially pp. 1–51; Jack Citrin, "Affirmative Action in the People's Court," *The Public Interest* 122, 1996, pp. 39–48.

4. Citrin, pp. 40–41; Sam Howe Verhovek, "In Poll, Americans Reject Means but Not Ends of Racial Diversity," *New York Times*, December 14, 1997, Sect. 1, p. 1; National Election Studies Guide to Public Opinion and Electoral Behavior, "Aid to Blacks and Minorities, 1970–1998," <www.umich.edu/~nes/ nesguide/toptable/tab4b_4.htm>.

5. David W. Moore, "Americans Today Are Dubious About Affirmative Action," *The Gallup Poll Monthly*, March 1995, pp. 36–38; Charlotte Steeh and Maria Krysan, "Affirmative Action and the Public, 1970–1995," *Public Opinion Quarterly* 60, 1996, pp. 128–158; Gallup Poll, October 25–28, 2000. "Would you vote . . . for or against a law which would allow your state to give preferences in job hiring and school admission on the basis of race?" For, 13 percent; against, 85 percent; no opinion, 2 percent.

6. *Regents of the University of California* v. *Bakke*, 438 U.S. 265, 407 (1978).

7. *The Slaughterhouse Cases*, 83 U.S. 36 (1873).

8. *United States* v. *Cruikshank*, 92 U.S. 542 (1876).

9. *United States* v. *Reese*, 92 U.S. 214 (1876).

10. *Civil Rights Cases*, 109 U.S. 3 (1883).

11. Mary Beth Norton et al., *A People and a Nation: A History of the United States*, 3rd ed. (Boston, Mass.: Houghton Mifflin, 1990), p. 490.

12. *Plessy* v. *Ferguson*, 163 U.S. 537 (1896).

13. *Plessy*, 163 U.S. at 562 (Harlan, J., dissenting).

14. *Cummings* v. *County Board of Education*, 175 U.S. 528 (1899).

15. *Missouri ex rel. Gaines* v. *Canada*, 305 U.S. 337 (1938).

16. *Sweatt* v. *Painter*, 339 U.S. 629 (1950).

17. *McLaurin* v. *Oklahoma State Regents*, 339 U.S. 637 (1950).

18. *Brown* v. *Board of Education*, 347 U.S. 483 (1954).

19. *Brown* v. *Board of Education*, 347 U.S. 483, 495 (1954).

20. *Brown* v. *Board of Education*, 347 U.S. 483, 494 (1954).

21. *Bolling* v. *Sharpe*, 347 U.S. 497 (1954).

22. *Brown* v. *Board of Education II*, 349 U.S. 294 (1955).

23. Jack W. Peltason, *Fifty-Eight Lonely Men*, rev. ed. (Urbana: University of Illinois Press, 1971).

24. *Alexander* v. *Holmes County Board of Education*, 396 U.S. 19 (1969).

25. *Swann* v. *Charlotte-Mecklenburg County Schools*, 402 U.S. 1 (1971).

26. *Milliken* v. *Bradley*, 418 U.S. 717 (1974).

27. Richard Kluger, *Simple Justice* (New York: Alfred A. Knopf, 1976), p. 753.

28. Taylor Branch, *Parting the Waters: America in the King Years, 1955–1963* (New York: Simon & Schuster, 1988), p. 3.

29. *Ibid.*, p. 14.

30. *Ibid.*, p. 271.

31. *Bell* v. *Maryland*, 378 U.S. 226 (1964).

32. Norton et al., *People and a Nation*, p. 943.

33. *Heart of Atlanta Motel* v. *United States*, 379 U.S. 241 (1964).

34. *Katzenbach* v. *McClung*, 379 U.S. 294 (1964).

35. But see Abigail M. Thernstrom, *Whose Vote Counts? Affirmative Action and Minority Voting Rights* (Cambridge, Mass.: Harvard University Press, 1987).

36. *Grove City College* v. *Bell*, 465 U.S. 555 (1984).

37. *Richmond* v. *J.A. Croson Co.*, 488 U.S. 469 (1989).

38. *Martin* v. *Wilks*, 490 U.S. 755 (1989); *Wards Cove Packing Co.* v. *Atonio*, 490 U.S. 642 (1989); *Patterson* v. *McLean Credit Union*, 491 U.S. 164 (1989); *Price Waterhouse* v. *Hopkins*, 490 U.S. 228 (1989); *Lorance* v. *AT&T Technologies*, 490 U.S. 900 (1989); and *EEOC* v. *Arabian American Oil Co.*, 499 U.S. 244 (1991).

39. *Saint Francis College* v. *Al-Khazraji*, 481 U.S. 604 (1987).

40. Dee Brown, *Bury My Heart at Wounded Knee: An Indian History of the American West* (New York: Holt, Rinehart & Winston, 1971).

41. Francis Paul Prucha, *The Great Father: The United States Government and the American Indian*, vol. 2 (Lincoln: University of Nebraska Press, 1984).

42. Jonathan J. Higuera, "Block Grants Worry Latino Legislators," <www.latinolink.com/hisbl16e.html> (1995).

43. Lisa J. Stansky, "Opening Doors," *ABA Journal*, 1996, pp. 66–69.

44. "Stonewall and Beyond: Lesbian and Gay Culture," the on-line edition of a Columbia University Libraries exhibition held from May 25 to September 17, 1994, <www.columbia.edu/cu/libraries/events/sw25/>.

45. "With Election Not Yet Determined, Bush-Cheney Captures 25% of Gay Vote Despite Gay Press Predictions of Single-Digit Support," 8 November 2000, <www.lcr.org/press/20001108oped.htm>. Exit poll results are available from ABC News (www.abcnews.go.com/sections/politics/2000vote/general/exitpoll_hub.html) and CNN (www.cnn.com/ELECTION/2000/results/index.epolls.html).

46. *Boy Scouts of America* v. *Dale*, 530 U.S. 610 (2000).

47. Cited in Martin Gruberg, *Women in American Politics* (Oshkosh, Wisc.: Academic Press, 1968), p. 4.

48. *Bradwell* v. *Illinois*, 83 U.S. 130 (1873).

49. *Muller* v. *Oregon*, 208 U.S. 412 (1908).

50. *International Union, United Automobile, Aerospace and Agricultural Implement Workers of America* v. *Johnson Controls, Inc.*, 499 U.S. 187 (1991).

51. *Minor* v. *Happersett*, 88 U.S. 162 (1875).

52. John H. Aldrich et al., *American Government: People, Institutions, and Policies* (Boston, Mass.: Houghton Mifflin, 1986), p. 618.

53. *Reed* v. *Reed*, 404 U.S. 71 (1971).

54. *Frontiero* v. *Richardson*, 411 U.S. 677 (1973).

55. *Craig* v. *Boren*, 429 U.S. 190 (1976).

56. Paul Weiler, "The Wages of Sex: The Uses and Limits of Comparable Worth," 99 *Harvard Law Review* 1728, 1986; Paula England, *Comparable Worth: Theories and Evidence* (New York: Aldine de Gruyter, 1992).

57. *J.E.B.* v. *Alabama ex rel. T.B.*, 511 U.S. 127 (1994).

58. *United States* v. *Virginia*, slip op. 94–1941 and 94–2107 (decided June 26, 1996).

59. Mike Allen, "Defiant V.M.I. to Admit Women but Will Not Ease Rules for Them," *New York Times*, 22 September 1996, Section 1, p. 1.

60. Jane J. Mansbridge, *Why We Lost the ERA* (Chicago, Ill.: University of Chicago Press, 1986).

61. Melvin I. Urofsky, *A March of Liberty* (New York: Alfred A. Knopf, 1988), p. 902.

62. *Harris* v. *Forklift Systems*, 510 U.S. 17 (1993).

63. *Time*, 6 July 1987, p. 91.

64. *Facts on File* 206B2 (4 June 1965).

65. As quoted in Melvin I. Urofsky, *A Conflict of Rights: The Supreme Court and Affirmative Action* (New York: Scribner's, 1991), p. 17.

66. *Ibid.*, p. 29.

67. Thomas Sowell, *Preferential Policies: An International Perspective* (New York: Morrow, 1990), pp. 103–105.

68. *Regents of the University of California* v. *Bakke*, 438 U.S. 265 (1978).

69. Steven N. Keith, Robert M. Bell, and Albert P. Williams, *Assessing the Outcome of Affirmative Action in Medical Schools* (Santa Monica, Calif.: Rand, 1987).

70. *United Steelworkers of America, AFL-CIO* v. *Weber*, 443 U.S. 193 (1979).

71. *Firefighters* v. *Stotts*, 467 U.S. 561 (1984).

72. *Johnson* v. *Transportation Agency, Santa Clara County*, 480 U.S. 616 (1987).

73. *Adarand Constructors, Inc.* v. *Peña*, 518 U.S. 200 (1995).

74. "Death by Judges? Affirmative Action," *The Economist*, 17 June 1995, p. 28; Peter Behr, "Small Business, Less Preference," *Washington Post*, 31 July 2000, p. F10.

75. *Hopwood* v. *Texas*, 78 F. 3d 932 (1996).

76. *Gratz* v. *Bollinger*, 122 F. Supp. 2d 811 (USDC, E.D. Mich.) (2000).

77. William H. Honan, "Moves to End Affirmative Action Gain Support Nationwide," *New York Times*, 31 March 1996, p. 30; James Brooke, "Colorado Bases College Aid on Need Rather Than Race," *New York Times*, 16 January 1996, p. A8.

78. "After Affirmative Action," *New York Times*, 20 May 2000, p. A14.

79. Stephen Earl Bennett et al., *Americans' Opinions About Affirmative Action* (Cincinnati, Ohio: University of Cincinnati, Institute for Policy Research, 1995), p. 4; Lawrence Bobo, "Race and Beliefs about Affirmative Action," in David O. Sears, Jim Sidanius, and Lawrence Bobo (eds.), *Racialized Politics: The Debate about Racism in America* (Chicago, Ill.: University of Chicago Press, 2000).

80. Seymour Martin Lipset, "Two Americas, Two Systems: Whites, Blacks, and the Debate Over Affirmative Action," *The New Democrat*, May–June 1995.

Chapter 17 / Policymaking / pp. 548–575

1. Allen Verhey, "Theology After Dolly: Cloning and the Human Family," *Chris-*

tian Century, 19 March 1997, p. 285.

2. Leon R. Kass, "The Wisdom of Repugnance: Why We Should Ban the Cloning of Humans," *The New Republic*, 2 June 1997, p. 23.

3. "Clinton Urges Ban on Cloning of Humans," *The Christian Century*, 18 June 1997, p. 583.

4. Brian McGrory, "President Asks for Human Clone Ban," *Boston Sunday Globe*, 11 January 1998, p. 1.

5. These Time/CNN poll results by Yankelovitch Partners, Inc., from 26–27 February 1997, were published in Jeffrey Kluger, "Will We Follow the Sheep?" *Time*, 10 March 1997, p. 71.

6. Richard Saltus, "Embryo Scientists Seek Voice on Cloning," *Boston Globe*, 20 January 1998, pp. 1, 6.

7. "FDA Warns Would-Be Cloners Not to Attempt It on Humans," *Boston Globe*, 20 January 1998, p. 6.

8. U.S. Bureau of the Census, *Statistical Abstract of the United States, 1999* (Washington, D.C.: Government Printing Office, 1999), p. 352.

9. Jeff Plungis, "GOP Again Blocks Changes in Fuel Efficiency Standards," *CQ Weekly*, 20 May 2000, pp. 1173–1175.

10. Lawrie Mifflin, "TV Broadcasters Agree to 3 Hours of Children's Educational Programs a Week," *New York Times*, 30 July 1996, p. A8.

11. Dan Carney, "Differences Not Standing in Way of Juvenile Crime Effort," *Congressional Quarterly Weekly Report*, 12 April 1997, pp. 845, 848–849; "Experts and Lawmakers Disagree on Stemming Juvenile Crime," *Congressional Quarterly Weekly Report*, 12 April 1997, pp. 846–847.

12. The policymaking process can be depicted in many ways. Another approach, a bit more elaborate than this, is described in James E. Anderson, *Public Policymaking*, 3rd ed. (Boston, Mass.: Houghton Mifflin, 1997), pp. 39–41.

13. Roger W. Cobb and Charles D. Elder, *Participation in American Politics*, 2nd ed. (Baltimore, Md.: Johns Hopkins University Press, 1983), p. 14.

14. Bryan D. Jones, *Reconceiving Decision-Making in Democratic Politics* (Chicago, Ill.: University of Chicago Press, 1994), pp. 107–108.

15. Martin Peers, "MP3.com Has Infringed on Copyrights of Five Record Firms, Judge Decides," *Wall Street Journal*, 1 May 2000, p. A3; and "Rock Musicians Warn Legislators of Internet Piracy Peril," *New York Times*, 12 July 2000, p. C2.

16. Frank R. Baumgartner and Beth L.

Leech, "Where Is the Public in Public Policy?" paper presented at the conference on Political Participation: Building a Research Agenda, Princeton University, October 2000.

17. Jeffrey M. Berry, *The New Liberalism* (Washington, D.C.: Brookings Institution, 1999).

18. David A. Rochefort and Roger W. Cobb, *The Politics of Problem Definition* (Lawrence: University Press of Kansas, 1994), p. vii.

19. William H. Riker, *The Art of Political Manipulation* (New Haven, Conn.: Yale University Press, 1986).

20. Frank R. Baumgartner, Jeffrey M. Berry, Marie Hojnacki, David C. Kimball, and Beth L. Leech, "Advocacy and Policy Argumentation," paper delivered at the annual meeting of the American Political Science Association, Washington, D.C., September 2000.

21. Frank R. Baumgartner and Bryan D. Jones, *Agendas and Instability in American Politics* (Chicago, Ill.: University of Chicago Press, 1993), pp. 59–82.

22. Robert Pear, "U.S. Proposes Rules to Bar Obstacles for the Disabled," *New York Times*, 22 January 1991, p. A1.

23. Peter C. Bishop and Augustus J. Jones, Jr., "Implementing the Americans with Disability Act: Assessing the Variables of Success," *Public Administration Review* 53 (March–April 1993), p. 126.

24. Douglas Jehl, "Road Ban Set for One-Third of U.S. Forests," *New York Times*, 5 January 2001, p. A1.

25. Jeffrey M. Berry, "Effective Advocacy for Nonprofits," paper presented at the Urban Institute, Washington, D.C., September 2000, pp. 8–9.

26. Patricia D. Siplon, "Washington's Response to the AIDS Epidemic," *Policy Studies Journal*, 27:4 (1999), p. 805.

27. Margaret Weir, *Politics and Jobs* (Princeton, N.J.: Princeton University Press, 1992).

28. Michael R. Gordon and Bernard E. Trainor, *The Generals' War* (Boston, Mass.: Little, Brown, 1995), p. 475.

29. Tim Weiner, "'Smart' Weapons Were Overrated, Study Concludes," *New York Times*, 9 July 1996, p. A1.

30. William T. Gormley, *Everybody's Children* (Washington, D.C.: Brookings Institution, 1995), pp. 3–5.

31. *Ibid*, p. 81.

32. Alexei Barrionuevo, John J. Fialka, and Rebecca Smith, "How Federal Policies, Industry Shifts Created a Natural Gas Crunch," *Wall Street Journal*, 3 January 2001, p. A1.

33. John E. Yang and Paul M. Barrett,

"Drug Issue Triggers Washington Habit: Turf Wars in Congress, Administration," *Wall Street Journal*, August 11, 1989, p. A5.

34. Alfred Marcus, "Environmental Protection Agency," in *The Politics of Regulation*, ed. James Q. Wilson (New York: Basic Books, 1980), p. 267.

35. Jeffrey M. Berry and Kent E. Portney, "Centralizing Regulatory Control and Interest Group Access: The Quayle Council on Competitiveness," in *Interest Group Politics*, 4th ed., eds. Allan J. Cigler and Burdett A. Loomis (Washington, D.C.: Congressional Quarterly Press, 1995), pp. 319–347.

36. David C. King, *Turf Wars* (Chicago, Ill.: University of Chicago Press, 1997).

37. Karen Foerstel with Alan K. Ota, "Early Grief for GOP Leaders in New Committee Rules," *CQ Weekly*, 6 January 2001, pp. 11–12.

38. Lester M. Salamon, *Partners in Public Service* (Baltimore, Md.: Johns Hopkins University Press, 1995), p. 62.

39. William Gorham, "Foreword," in *Nonprofits and Government*, eds. Elizabeth T. Boris and C. Eugene Steuerle (Washington, D.C.: Urban Institute, 1999), p. xi.

40. See Robert D. Putnam, *Bowling Alone* (New York: Simon and Schuster, 2000).

41. C. Eugene Steuerle and Virginia Hodgkinson, "Meeting Social Needs: Comparing the Resources of the Independent Sector and Government," in *Nonprofits and Government*, pp. 72–98.

42. Paul C. Light, *The True Size of Government* (Washington, D.C.: Brookings Institution, 1999).

43. <http://www.youthranch.org>.

44. Jeffrey M. Berry, *The Interest Group Society*, 3rd ed. (New York: Longman, 1997), p. 187.

45. John P. Heinz, Edward O. Laumann, Robert L. Nelson, and Robert H. Salisbury, *The Hollow Core* (Cambridge, Mass.: Harvard University Press, 1993).

46. Hugh Heclo, "Issue Networks and the Executive Establishment," in *The New American Political System*, ed. Anthony King (Washington, D.C.: American Enterprise Institute, 1978), p. 105.

47. Steve Langdon, "On Medicare, Negotiators Split over Policy, Not Just Figures," *Congressional Quarterly Weekly Report*, 22 February 1997, pp. 488–490.

48. Ben Wildavsky, "Wolff at the Door," *National Journal*, 5 August 1995, pp. 1994–1997.

49. Carl Brauer, "Tenure, Turnover, and Postgovernment Employment

Trends of Presidential Appointees," in *The In-and-Outers*, ed. G. Calvin MacKenzie (Baltimore, Md.: Johns Hopkins University Press, 1993), p. 62.

50. Jeffrey M. Berry, "Subgovernments, Issue Networks, and Political Conflict," in *Remaking American Politics*, eds. Richard A. Harris and Sidney M. Milkis (Boulder, Colo.: Westview Press, 1989), pp. 239–260.

Chapter 18 / Economic Policy / pp. 576–608

1. Uli Schmetzer, "World Trade Targeted Down Under," *Chicago Tribune*, 12 September 2000, p. 1.

2. Roger Cohen, "Growing up and Getting Practical Since Seattle," *New York Times*, 24 September 2000, Sect. 4, p. 1.

3. Lisa Lollock, *The Foreign-Born Population in the United States: March 2000* (Washington, D.C.: U.S. Government Printing Office, 2001), p. 1.

4. Joseph Kahn, "Redrawing the Map," *New York Times*, 25 June 2000, Sect. 4, p. 5.

5. *Ibid.*

6. Lawrence Malkin, "In Financial Markets, All Eyes Are on the Fed," *International Herald Tribune*, 17 May 1994, pp. 1, 4.

7. David Wessel, "Common Interest: The President and Fed Appear to Be in Step on Latest Rate Rise," *Wall Street Journal*, 7 February 1994, p. A1. See also Lawrence Malkin, "Markets Satisfied as U.S. Rates Rise," *International Herald Tribune*, 18 May 1994, pp. 1, 6; "Fed Chief Tries to Ease Fears in Senate on Rates," *International Herald Tribune*, 28–29 May 1994, p. 11.

8. Peter Passell, "The Fed Is Trapped Between Expectation and Reality," *New York Times*, 7 May 1998, p. C2.

9. N. Gregory Mankiw, "Symposium on Keynesian Economics Today," *Journal of Economic Perspectives*, 7 (Winter 1993), pp. 3–4. In his preface to four articles in the symposium, Mankiw says, "The literature that bears the label 'Keynesian' is broad, and it does not offer a single vision of how the economy behaves."

10. Jonathan Rauch, Lawrence J. Haas, and Bruce Stokes, "Payment Deferred," *National Journal*, 14 May 1988, p. 1256.

11. For a concise discussion of the 1990 budget reforms, see James A. Thurber, "Congressional-Presidential Battles to Balance the Budget," in James A. Thurber (ed.), *Rivals for Power: Presidential-Congressional Relations*

(Washington, D.C.: Congressional Quarterly Press, 1996), pp. 196–202.

12. *A Citizen's Guide to the Federal Budget*, <http://www.access.gpo.gov/su_docs?budget99/guide/guide04.html>.

13. Richard A. Musgrave and Peggy B. Musgrave, *Public Finance in Theory and Practice*, 2nd ed. (New York: McGraw-Hill, 1976), p. 42.

14. Michael L. Roberts, Peggy A. Hite, and Cassie F. Bradley, "Understanding Attitudes Toward Progressive Taxation," *Public Opinion Quarterly*, 58 (Summer 1994), pp. 167–168. See also David W. Moore and Frank Newport, "Public Lukewarm on Flat Tax," *The Gallup Poll Monthly*, January 1996, pp. 18–20.

15. Advisory Commission on Intergovernmental Relations, *Significant Features of Fiscal Federalism, 1981–1982* (Washington, D.C., 1983), p. 54; and David E. Rosenbaum, "A New Heave in Tax Tug-of-War," *New York Times*, 8 December 1992, p. C1.

16. Lawrence Mishel and David M. Frankel, *The State of Working America*, 1990–91 ed. (Washington, D.C.: Economic Policy Institute, 1990), p. 62. In 1994, however, many states enacted tax reductions, both to improve their tax climate to attract business and in reaction to the improving national economy. See Tom Redburn, "Many States Moving to Ease Property Tax Burdens," *New York Times*, 17 March 1994, p. A9.

17. Times-Mirror Center for the People & the Press, "Voter Anxiety Dividing GOP: Energized Democrats Backing Clinton," press release of 14 November 1995, p. 88.

18. These questions were asked in the 1996 National Election Survey.

19. Fay Lomax Cook et al., *Convergent Perspectives on Social Welfare Policy: The Views from the General Public, Members of Congress, and AFDC Recipients* (Evanston, Ill.: Center for Urban Affairs and Policy Research, Northwestern University, 1988), Table 4-1.

20. B. Guy Peters, *The Politics of Taxation: A Comparative Perspective* (Cambridge, Mass.: Basil Blackwell, 1991), p. 228.

21. David S. Cloud, "Farm Bloc on the Defensive as Bills Move to Floor," *Congressional Quarterly Weekly Report*, 14 July 1990, pp. 2209–2212.

22. Joseph A. Pechman, *Who Paid the Taxes, 1966–1985?* (Washington, D.C.: Brookings Institution, 1985).

23. Mishel and Frankel, *State of Working America*, pp. 178–179. The

proportion of people living below the poverty line is also less if one uses the consumption of commodities as the measure of well-being instead of before-tax income. See Daniel T. Slesnick, "Gaining Ground: Poverty in the Postwar United States," *Journal of Political Economy* 101 (1993), pp. 1–38.

24. But the rich received only 1 percent of their income in transfer payments, suffering a net loss from government. See Pechman, *Who Paid the Taxes?* p. 53. Families in the top 1 percent of income actually had their effective national tax rate drop from 31.7 percent in 1980 to 24.9 percent in 1985, before they were raised to 28.8 percent in 1992 after the 1990 tax increase. See Sylvia Nasar, "One Group Saw Relief: Richest 1%," *New York Times*, 1 October 1992, p. C2.

25. Pechman, *Who Paid the Taxes?* p. 80.

26. *Ibid.*, p. 73.

27. Mishel and Frankel, *State of Working America*, pp. 37–39. See also Gary Burtless, ed., *A Future of Lousy Jobs? The Changing Structure of U.S. Wages* (Washington, D.C.: Brookings Institution, 1990), for discussions of the rise in women's earnings and the decline in lower-scale men's earnings. Other researchers have found that women's earnings have also accounted for increases in "the rich." See Sheldon Danziger, Peter Gottschalk, and Eugene Smolensky, "How the Rich Have Fared, 1973–87," *American Economic Association, Papers and Proceedings* 79 (May 1989), pp. 310–314; R. C. Longworth, "Middle-Wage Earners Lagging," *Chicago Tribune*, 6 September 1999, p. 3.

28. Keith Bradsher, "Widest Gap in Incomes? Research Points to U.S.," *New York Times*, 27 October 1995, p. C2.

29. Keith Bradsher, "Gap in Wealth in U.S. Called Widest in West," *New York Times*, 17 April 1995, p. 1; Keith Bradsher, "Rich Control More of U.S. Wealth, Study Says, as Debts Grow for Poor," *New York Times*, 22 June 1996, p. 17.

30. U.S. Bureau of the Census, *Statistical Abstract of the United States, 1999*, <http://www.census.gov/prod/99pubs/99statab/sec14.pdf>.

31. Benjamin I. Page, *Who Gets What from Government?* (Berkeley: University of California Press, 1983), p. 213.

32. David Wessel, "Budget Seeks to Raise U.S. Living Standards and Reduce Inequality," *Wall Street Journal*, 7 February 1997, p.1; David Cay Johnston, "'97 Middle-Class Tax Relief Benefits

Wealthy First," *New York Times*, 4 May 1997, p. 17; and Lizette Alvarez, "Buried in the Tax-Cut Bill, Dozens of Breaks for Small Interest Groups," 29 June 1997.

33. *Public Opinion* 8 (February–March 1985), p. 27. Data from the National Conference of State Legislatures shows that states raised income taxes by $8.2 billion from 1990 through 1993, which had a greater impact on wealthy than on poor residents. But from 1994 to 1997, the states reduced income taxes by $9.8 billion. In contrast, sales and excise taxes, which weigh more on those with lower incomes, were raised by $11.7 billion from 1990 through 1993 and cut by only $200 million from 1994 to 1997. See David Cay Johnston, "Taxes Are Cut, and Rich Get Richer," *New York Times*, 5 October 1997, p. 16.

34. James Sterngold, "Muting the Lotteries' Perfect Pitch," *New York Times*, national edition, 14 July 1996, Sect. 4, p. 1.

35. "Taxes: What's Fair?" *Public Perspective*, 7 (April–May 1996), pp. 40–41. Similar findings were found in experiments involving undergraduate students in advanced tax classes at two public universities; see Roberts, Hite, and Bradley, "Understanding Attitudes Toward Progressive Taxation."

36. Rachel Wildavsky, "How Fair Are Our Taxes?" *Wall Street Journal*, 10 January 1996, p. A10.

37. Associated Press, "Well-to-Do Paid 16% More in Taxes in '93, Study Says," *New York Times*, 17 April 1995, p. C4.

Chapter 19 / Domestic Policy / pp. 609–637

1. Jason DeParle, "The Drawer People," *New York Times*, 20 November 1997, p. A1. (All facts came from this article, except where noted otherwise.)

2. *Ibid.* For national average figure, see Jason DeParle, "What About Mississippi?" *New York Times*, 16 October 1997, p. A1.

3. U.S. Social Security Administration, *Social Security Bulletin, Annual Statistical Supplement*, 1993, Table 3.A.1, p. 128; *Budget of the United States Government, FY 1995*, Historical Table 3.1, p. 42.

4. "The People, Press & Economics," in *A Times Mirror Multi-National Study of Attitudes Toward U.S. Economic Issues* (The Gallup Organization, May 1989).

5. "Education: A Vital Issue in Election 2000," 2 October 2000, <gallup.com/poll /releases/pr001002.asp>.

6. Thomas J. Anton, *American Federalism and Public Policy* (Philadelphia, Pa.: Temple University Press, 1989).

7. I. A. Lewis and William Schneider, "Hard Times: The Public on Poverty," *Public Opinion* 8 (June–July 1985), p. 2.

8. Linda L. M. Bennett and Stephen Earl Bennett, *Living with Leviathan: Americans Coming to Terms with Big Government* (Lawrence: University Press of Kansas, 1990), pp. 21–24.

9. *Shapiro* v. *Thompson*, 394 U.S. 618 (1969).

10. *1999 Current Population Reports*, Series P-60, No. 210, September 2000. <www.census.gov/prod/2000 pubs/ p60–210.pdf>

11. *Federal Register*, Vol. 66, No. 33, 16 February 2001, pp. 10695–10697.

12. U.S. Bureau of the Census, U.S. Department of Commerce, *Poverty in the United States, 1997*. Current Population Reports, Series P-60, No. 201 (September 1998).

13. U.S. Bureau of the Census, U.S. Department of Commerce, *Current Population Reports: Money Income and Poverty Status in the United States, 1989*, Series P-60, No. 168, pp. 5–7 (1990); Bureau of the Census, *Poverty in the United States*, 1992 Series P-60, No. 185, p. xvii (1993).

14. William Julius Wilson, *The Truly Disadvantaged: The Inner City, the Underclass, and Public Policy* (Chicago, Ill.: University of Chicago Press, 1987).

15. Francis X. Clines, "Clinton Signs Bill Cutting Welfare," *New York Times*, 23 August 1996, p. A1.

16. George J. Church, "Ripping Up Welfare," *Time*, 12 August 1996, p. 21.

17. Peter T. Kilborn, "With Welfare Overhaul Now Law, States Grapple with the Consequences," *New York Times*, 23 August 1996, p. A10.

18. *Ibid.*

19. Christopher Ogden, "Bye-Bye, American Pie," *Time*, 12 August 1996, p. 17.

20. Jason DeParle, "Success and Frustration, as Welfare Rules Change," *New York Times*, 30 December 1997, p. A1.

21. Paul C. Light, *Artful Work: The Politics of Social Security Reform* (New York: Random House, 1985), p. 63.

22. Annual Statistical Supplement, 2000, Highlights and Trends <www.ssa. gov/statistics/Supplement/2000/ highlights.pdf>.

23. Martha Derthick, *Policymaking for Social Security* (Washington, D.C.:

Brookings Institution, 1979), pp. 346–347.

24. Gallup Poll Topics: A–Z—Social Security/Medicare, n.d., <gallup.com/ poll/indicators/indsocialsecurity. asp>.

25. Retirement Security and Quality Health Care: Our Pledge to America, n.d., <www.rnc.org/2000/ 2000platform5>.

26. *The 2000 Democratic National Platform: Prosperity, Progress, and Peace* (Washington, D.C.: Democratic National Committee, 2000), p. 6.

27. Gallup Poll Topics: A–Z—Social Security/Medicare, n.d., <http://gallup. com/poll/indicators/indsocialsecurity. asp>.

28. U.S. Bureau of the Census, U.S. Department of Commerce, *Statistical Abstract of the United States, 1995* (Washington, D.C.: U.S. Government Printing Office, 1995), p. 289.

29. Derthick, *Policymaking*, p. 335.

30. Paul Starr, *The Social Transformation of American Medicine* (New York: Basic Books, 1982), pp. 279–280.

31. *Ibid.*, p. 287.

32. Theodore Marmor, *The Politics of Medicare* (Chicago, Ill.: Aldine, 1973).

33. Annual Statistical Supplement, 2000, Highlights and Trends <http://www.ssa.gov/statistics/ supplement/2000/highlights.pdf>.

34. *Ibid.*

35. *Ibid.*

36. Congressional Budget Office, *The Economic and Budget Outlook: Fiscal Years 1998–2007, A Report to the Senate and House Committees on the Budget* (Washington, D.C.: U.S. Government Printing Office, January 1997), p. 126.

37. Bob Blendon, "The Gridlock Is Us," *New York Times*, 12 June 1994, Sect. 4, p. 3.

38. Chris Chambers, *Americans Largely Satisfied with Own Health Care, and HMO Users Only Slightly Less Satisfied Than Those with Other Forms of Health Care Coverage*, http://www.gallup.com/poll/realeases/ pr000920.asp (20 September 2000).

39. *Retirement Security and Quality Health Care: Our Pledge to America*, n.d., <http://www.rnc.org/2000/ 2000platform5>; see "Improving the Quality of Health Care."

40. *The 2000 Democratic National Platform: Prosperity, Progress, and Peace* (Washington, D.C.: Democratic National Committee, 2000) p. 29.

41. Christopher Jencks and Meredith Phillips, eds., *The Black-White Test*

Score Gap (Washington, D.C.: Brookings Institution Press, 1998), p. 6.

42. Alec Gallup, *Education: A Vital Issue in Election 2000*, 2 October 2000, <http://www.gallup.com/poll/releases/pr00l002.asp>.

43. *Ibid.*

44. *Education and Opportunity: Leave No American Behind*, n.d., <http://www.rnc.org/2000/2000platform3>.

45. *The 2000 Democratic National Platform: Prosperity, Progress, and Peace* (Washington, D.C.: Democratic National Committee, 2000), p. 6.

Chapter 20 / Global Policy / pp. 638–671

1. Nicole Winfield, "Turner Donation Helps U.S. Trim UN Payment," *Chicago Sun-Times*, 23 December 2000 (interactive edition).

2. Barbara Crossette, "U.N. Agrees to Cut Dues Paid by U.S., Easing an Irritant," *New York Times*, 23 December 2000, pp. A1 and A6.

3. Carroll J. Doherty, "Panel's Plan for Paying U.N. Debt May Signal a Breakthrough," *Congressional Quarterly Weekly Report*, 14 June 1997, p. 1383.

4. Christopher S. Wren, "Figuring Dues: From Each According to Its GNP (Back in '46)," *New York Times*, 23 December 2000, p. A6.

5. Dan Smith, *The State of the World Atlas* (London: Penguin Books, 1999), p. 38.

6. "General Assembly Adopts Overhaul of U.N. Finances," *Wall Street Journal Interactive*, 23 December 2000.

7. Miles A. Pomper, "Helms Gives Blunt Message to U.N. Security Council: Don't Tread on U.S.," *Congressional Quarterly Weekly Report*, 22 January 2000, p. 144.

8. Miles A. Pomper, "U.N. Security Council Cool to Debt Payment Proposal Despite Wooing by Helms," *Congressional Quarterly Weekly Report*, 1 April 2000, p. 784.

9. "General Assembly Adopts Overhaul of U.N. Finances," *Wall Street Interactive*, 23 December 2000.

10. *Ibid.*

11. "General Assembly Adopts Overhaul of U.N. Finances," *Wall Street Journal Interactive*, 23 December 2000.

12. Eric Schmitt, "Senator Helms's Journey: From Clenched-Fist U.N. Opponent to Fan," *New York Times*, 23 December 2000, p. A6.

13. "Ted Turner Donates $1 Billion to 'U.N.' Causes," CNN Interactive (19 September 1997) at <www.cnn.com/US/9709/18/turner.gift/index.html>. See also Monica Langley, "How Turner Decided to Give a Fortune to U.N. Programs," *Wall Street Journal Interactive*, 22 September 1997.

14. Lyn Ragsdale, *Vital Statistics on the Presidency* (Washington, D.C.: Congressional Quarterly Press, 1998), p. 297. Ragsdale cites twenty-three treaties having been rejected by the Senate as of 1998. However, the official Senate Web site lists twenty-one having been rejected, including the 1999 nuclear test ban treaty. See <http://www.senate.gov/learning/brief_4.html>.

15. "Pros and Cons Testify at Charter Hearings," *Life*, 30 July 1945, pp. 22–23.

16. *Congressional Quarterly Weekly Report*, 16 October 1999, p. 2477. See also R. W. Apple, "The G.O.P. Torpedo," *New York Times*, 14 October 1999, p. 1.

17. Barbara Crossette, "Around the World, Dismay Over Senate Vote on Treaty," *New York Times*, 15 October 1999, p. A1. The article quotes *The Straits Times of Singapore.*

18. Chuck McCutcheon, "Treaty Vote a 'Wake-Up Call,'" *Congressional Quarterly Weekly Report*, 16 October 1999, p. 2435.

19. *U.S.* v. *Curtiss-Wright Export Corporation*, 299 U.S. 304 (1936); *U.S.* v. *Belmont*, 301 U.S. 324 (1937).

20. Jack C. Plano and Roy Olton, *The International Relations Dictionary* (New York: Holt, Rinehart and Winston, 1969), p. 149.

21. Lyn Ragsdale, *Vital Statistics on the Presidency* (Washington, D.C.: Congressional Quarterly Press, 1998), pp. 317–319. After 1984, government reports eliminated the clear distinction between treaties and executive agreements, making it difficult to determine the ratio.

22. Ragsdale, *Vital Statistics on the Presidency*, p. 298.

23. David E. Sanger, "Economic Engine for Foreign Policy," *New York Times*, 28 December 2000, pp. A1 and A12.

24. These critics included both conservative Republican senator Barry Goldwater of Arizona and liberal Democratic senator Thomas Eagleton of Missouri. The latter's feelings were succinctly summarized in the title of his book *War and Presidential Power: A Chronicle of Congressional Surrender* (New York: Liveright, 1974).

25. R. W. Apple, "A Domestic Sort with Global Worries," *New York Times*, 25 August 1999, p. 1; and Pat Towell, "Congress Set to Provide Money, but No Guidance, for Kosovo Mission," *Congressional Quarterly Weekly Report*, 1 May 1999, pp. 1036–1037.

26. Richard Morris (ed.), *Encyclopedia of American History: Bicentennial Edition* (New York: Harper & Row, 1976), p. 146.

27. Duncan Clarke, "Why State Can't Lead," *Foreign Policy* 66 (Spring 1987), pp. 128–142.

28. <http://www.usnews.com/usnews/issue/970414/14week.html>.

29. Eric Schmitt, "The Powell Doctrine Is Looking Pretty Good Again," *New York Times*, 4 April 1999 (on-line at <http://www.freerepublic.com/forum/a37074e9f5f77.html>).

30. Harry Crosby (pseudonym), "Too at Home Abroad: Swilling Beer, Licking Boots and Ignoring the Natives with One of Jim Baker's Finest," *The Washington Monthly* (September 1991), pp. 16–20.

31. Elaine Sciolino, "Compulsion to Achieve: Condoleezza Rice," *New York Times*, 18 December 2000, p. 1.

32. Loch K. Johnson, "Now That the Cold War Is Over, Do We Need the CIA?" in Charles Kegley and Eugene Wittkopf, eds., *The Future of American Foreign Policy* (New York: St. Martin's Press, 1992), p. 306.

33. Elaine Sciolino, "As Bush Ponders a Leader for the C.I.A., Some Say That No Change Is Needed," *New York Times*, 29 December 2000, p. A17.

34. "Helms: Show Me the Savings," *Congressional Quarterly Weekly Report*, 19 February 2000, p. 342.

35. Dag Ryen, "State Action in a Global Framework," *The Book of the States* (Lexington, Ky.: The Council of State Governments, 1996), pp. 524–536.

36. "X" (George F. Kennan), "The Sources of Soviet Conduct," *Foreign Affairs* 25 (July 1947), p. 575.

37. Richard M. Nixon, *U.S. Foreign Policy for the 1970s: A New Strategy for Peace* (Washington, D.C.: U.S. Government Printing Office, 1970), p. 2.

38. Thomas Halverson, *The Last Great Nuclear Debate: NATO and Short-Range Nuclear Weapons in the 1980s* (New York: St. Martin's Press, 1995).

39. See, for example, Francis Fukayama, *The End of History and the Last Man* (New York: Free Press, 1992).

40. Daniel Deudney and C. John Ikenberry, "Who Won the Cold War?" *Foreign Policy* 87 (Summer 1992), pp. 128–138.

41. See, for example, Paul Kennedy, *Preparing for the Twenty-First Century* (New York: Random House, 1993), especially Chapter 13.

42. Richard H. Ullman, "A Late Recovery," *Foreign Policy* 101 (Winter 1996), 76–79; James M. McCormick, "Assessing Clinton's Foreign Policy at Midterm," *Current History* (November 1995), 370–374; Michael Mandelbaum, "Foreign Policy as Social Work," *Foreign Affairs* (January–February 1996), pp. 16–32.

43. Michael Mastanduno, "Trade Policy," in Robert J. Art and Seyom Brown, eds., *U.S. Foreign Policy: The Search for a New Role* (New York: Macmillan, 1993), p. 142.

44. Statistics derived from Office of Trade and Economic Analysis, International Trade Administration, U.S. Department of Commerce, "GDP & U.S. International Trade in Goods and Services, 1970–1997," available at <http://www.ita.doc.gov/industry/otea/>.

45. "Hills, in Japan, Stirs a Baby-Bottle Dispute," *New York Times*, 14 October 1989, p. 35.

46. Information available as of 1 January 2000 from the World Trade Organization's Web site at <http://www.WTO.org/>.

47. "WTO Rules Against U.S. Dumping Laws," *Wall Street Journal*, 7 June 2000, p. A2.

48. R. C. Longworth, "WTO Deserves Some but Not All of the Criticism It's Getting," *Chicago Tribune*, 2 December 1999, p. 25.

49. John Stremlau, "Clinton's Dollar Diplomacy," *Foreign Policy*, 97 (Winter 1995), pp. 18–35.

50. R. C. Longworth, "A 'Grotesque' Gap," *Chicago Tribune*, 12 July 1999, p. 1.

51. Steven Erlanger, "For U.S. Russia-Watchers, Bipartisan Fear over Future," *New York Times*, 17 June 1996, p. A7.

52. Steven Kull, "What the Public Knows That Washington Doesn't," *Foreign Policy* 101 (Winter 1995–1996), pp. 102–115.

53. Steven Lee Myers, "U.S. Signs Treaty for World Court to Try Atrocities," *New York Times*, 1 January 2001, pp. A1 and A6.

54. Andrew C. Revkin, "U.S. Move Improves Chance for Global Warming Treaty," *New York Times*, 20 November 2000, p. A6.

55. Ray Moseley, "Climate Meeting Extended a Day Amid Controversy," *Chicago Tribune*, 25 November 2000, p. 3.

56. Joseph Kahn and Judith Miller, "Getting Tough on Gangsters, High Tech and Global," *New York Times*, 15 December 2000, p. A7.

57. John E. Rielly, ed., *American Public Opinion and U.S. Foreign Policy, 1999* (Chicago, Ill.: Chicago Council on Foreign Relations, 1999).

58. *Ibid.*, p. 6.

59. *Ibid.*, pp. 10–12.

60. *Ibid.*, pp. 18–21.

61. *Ibid.*, pp. 23–25.

62. *Ibid.*, p. 26.

63. Alvin Richman, "American Support for International Involvement: General and Specific Components of Post–Cold War Changes," *Public Opinion Quarterly*, 60 (Summer 1996), pp. 307–308.

64. Lydia Saad, "Americans Support Active Role for U.S. in World Affairs, but Don't View Ethnic Conflicts as Critical to U.S. Interests," The Gallup Organization, Poll Release, 1 April 1999. Available at <http://www.gallup.com/poll/release/pr990401.asp>.

65. "From the K-Street Corridor," *National Journal*, 9 March 1996, p. 540.

66. Charles Kegley and Eugene Wittkopf, *American Foreign Policy: Pattern and Process*, 4th ed. (New York: St. Martin's Press, 1991), pp. 272–273; Lester Milbrarb, "Interest Groups and Foreign Policy," in James Rosenau, ed., *Domestic Sources of Foreign Policy* (New York: Free Press, 1967), pp. 231–252.

67. Alison Mitchell, "Bush, Invoking 3 Presidents, Casts 'Vote' for China Trade," *New York Times*, 18 May 2000, p. 1.

68. Lori Nitschke, "White House in Full Battle Mode in Final Push for China NTR," *Congressional Quarterly Weekly Report*, 18 March 2000, pp. 606–609.

69. "Voter Preferences Vacillate: Gender Gaps on the Candidates, Guns, China, and Missile Defense," *News Release* (Washington, D.C.: Pew Research Center for the People and the Press), 11 May 2000, p. 37.

70. Helene Cooper, "Eclectic Grass-Roots Campaigns Emerge on China Trade," *Wall Street Journal*, 13 March 2000, p. A48.

71. Steven Greenhouse, "Unions Deny Stand over Trade Policy Is Protectionism," *New York Times*, 24 April 2000, p. 1.

72. Helene Cooper, p. A48.

73. "Voter Preferences Vacillate: Gender Gaps on the Candidates, Guns, China, and Missile Defense," p. 37.

74. Adam Clymer, "House Vote on China Trade: The Politics Was Local," *New York Times*, 27 May 2000, p. A3.